*The Rise of the Anglo-German
Antagonism 1860–1914*

# The Rise of the Anglo-German Antagonism 1860–1914

## PAUL M. KENNEDY

*Reader in History, University of East Anglia*

London
**GEORGE ALLEN & UNWIN**
Boston          Sydney

First published in 1980

GEORGE ALLEN & UNWIN LTD
40 Museum Street, London WC1A 1LU

© Paul M. Kennedy, 1980

**British Library Cataloguing in Publication Data**

Kennedy, Paul Michael
    The rise of the Anglo-German antagonism,
    1860–1914.
    1. Great Britain – Foreign relations – Germany
    2. Germany – Foreign relations – Great Britain
    I. Title
    327.41′043        DA47.2        80-40461

    ISBN 0-04-940060-6

Set in 10 on 11 point Plantin by Western Printing Services Ltd, Bristol and printed and bound in Great Britain by
William Clowes (Beccles) Limited, Beccles and London

# Contents

# Acknowledgement of Copyright

I am pleased to acknowledge the gracious permission of Her Majesty the Queen in permitting me to reproduce extracts from the correspondence of Queen Victoria from the Royal Archives at Windsor. Unpublished Crown Copyright material from the Public Record Office, the India Office and the Ministry of Defence libraries appears by permission of Her Majesty's Stationery Office. I am grateful to the Trustees of the British Library for permission to quote from the A. J. Balfour papers; and, in the same way, to the Scottish Record Office and Lord Balfour in respect of the A. J. Balfour and G. W. Balfour papers; to the Trustees of the Liddell Hart Centre for Military Archives in respect of the Robertson papers; to the Bedford Estate and the National Maritime Museum in respect of the Arnold White papers; to Colonel Terence Maxwell, the trustee, in respect of the Joseph Chamberlain papers; to Lord Rosebery and the Trustees of the National Library of Scotland in respect of the Rosebery papers; to the Clerk of the Records, House of Lords, in respect of the collections held there (but, separately, to the *Spectator* and Mr A. J. P. Taylor in respect of the St Loe Strachey papers); to the Warden and Fellows of New College, Oxford, in respect of the Milner Papers; to the Master and Fellows of Balliol College, Oxford, in respect of the Morier papers; to the Bodleian Library, Oxford, in respect of the Bryce, Grey-Newbolt, Ponsonby, Sandars and Anglo-German Society papers owned by it; to the National Army Museum in respect of the Roberts papers; to the British Library of Political and Economic Science, and Mr R. Morel, in respect of the E. D. Morel papers; and to Times Newspapers in respect of papers held in its archives.

I wish to thank the following individuals for allowing me to quote extracts of unpublished material to which they hold the copyright: the Rt Hon. Julian Amery (L. S. Amery); Lady Arthur (Sir Frank Lascelles and Sir Cecil Spring-Rice); the Earl of Clarendon (the Fourth Earl of Clarendon); the Earl of Derby (the Fifteenth Earl of Derby); Mrs P. Dower (C. P. Trevelyan); Lord Esher (the Second Viscount Esher); Mrs Sheila S. Grant (Grant-Duff); Sir Geoffrey Harmsworth (Viscount Northcliffe); Admiral Sir Ian Hogg (H. A. Gwynne); Colonel Malet (Sir Edward Malet); Major and Mrs Maxse (L. J. Maxse); Lord Mottistone (the First Baron Mottistone); The Dowager Countess of Onslow (the Fourth and Fifth Earls of Onslow); Mrs Mary Z. Pain (George Saunders); Sir Antony Rumbold (Sir Horace Rumbold, Snr); the Earl of Selborne (the Second Earl of Selborne); the Marquess of Salisbury (the Third and Fourth Marquesses of Salisbury); Mrs Patricia Wildblood (J. L. Garvin).

Every effort has been made to trace and to secure permission from owners of all manuscript material under copyright quoted in this book. If I have inadvertently trespassed upon such rights, I offer humble apologies.

## NOTE UPON CURRENCY VALUES

In this period the £1 sterling was approximately equal to 20 German marks and to 5 United States dollars

# Introduction

Why was it that the British and German peoples, who had never fought each other and whose traditions of political co-operation were reinforced by dynastic, cultural, religious and economic ties, drifted steadily apart in the late nineteenth and early twentieth centuries, and went to war against each other in 1914? This was a question which virtually every important historian of modern Europe in the interwar years (Meinecke, Ritter, Rothfels, Schmitt, Fay, Sontag, Langer, Gooch, Taylor, Woodward) felt bound to explore, albeit chiefly on the basis of published documents and diplomatic memoirs. Only in the decades after 1945 has it been possible for historians to gain access to the full array of original sources in official and private archives: yet although in these years many books and articles upon particular aspects (the naval, the cultural, and so on) of Anglo-German relations have been published, there exists no recent full-length study of that relationship as a whole. This is a gap which the present work seeks to fill.

The original intention of this book was simply to produce a political narrative based upon as wide a range of unpublished sources as was currently available. Although that in itself was a physically testing enterprise – involving visits to over sixty public archives and private houses during the past decade – it did not pose unusual methodological problems. In the course of time, however, the intended structure of the book began to be affected by two influences. The first was my own growing interest in comparative history, which made me increasingly ready to ask questions about (say) the military planners or the fate of liberalism or the role of the press in both Britain and Germany. The second was the recognition, now common to political historians, that descriptions of the relations between two states lack real depth – and explanatory power – unless the diplomatic events and actors are placed within their wider context. Recent German historiography in particular has stressed the need to analyse the background social, economic, ideological and domestic-political factors which influence and in some cases dictate the course of foreign policy. In an exaggerated form, this can be developed into the concept of the *Primat der Innenpolitik* ('the primacy of domestic politics'), which is as inflexible and one-sided an approach as the contrary emphasis upon the autonomy or 'primacy' of foreign policy; and it takes no great genius to perceive that in reality internal and external factors interact with each other, the exact degree of influence at any one time depending upon the specific circumstances.

While it is not difficult to acknowledge the necessity of making controlled comparisons and of scrutinising the background developments which influenced the course of Anglo-German relations, it is quite another matter to work out the most suitable structure for this sort of book. Immediately, there arises a clash between the need to tell a story (about the rise of the Anglo-German antagonism), which assumes *movement* and *change*; and the need to undertake a structural analysis of non-diplomatic factors, which assumes a *static* situation in which the various elements can be compared and seen in relation to others. The solution adopted in the present work has been to blend these twin requirements by giving the book an overall chronological format but also providing two 'stopping-places' on the way, where the deeper analyses can be undertaken. The first of these investigations (Part Two of the book) occurs after the political story is already started. It in turn is followed by a fairly extensive narrative of some twenty-five years of Anglo-German relations (Part Three) before the second 'stopping-place' (Part Four) is reached: at this point, the attempt has been made not only to repeat the comparative and structural analyses, but also to show what things have changed in the background context over the preceding two-to-three decades which help to explain the alterations at the diplomatic level. Thus, the overall shape of the book is as follows:

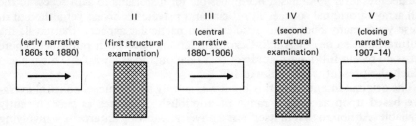

| I | II | III | IV | V |
|---|---|---|---|---|
| (early narrative 1860s to 1880) | (first structural examination) | (central narrative 1880–1906) | (second structural examination) | (closing narrative 1907–14) |

This represents, of course, no claim to a solution of the permanent dilemma which writers face in trying to reconcile narrative history with extensive analysis; it is simply a crude compromise of the competing claims. But I would be interested, to say the least, to have reactions to this approach and to learn how other diplomatic historians have grappled with this problem, if not in the specific case of Anglo-German relations, then in regard (say) to explaining the changes in Sino-Soviet or Franco-Italian relations over a certain period of time.

In researching for and writing this book I have incurred extensive obligations in many fields, but it is only proper to begin by thanking those foundations and institutions whose financial support made the venture possible. I am deeply grateful to the Alexander von Humboldt Foundation (Bonn/Bad Godesberg) for underpinning most of my numerous archival trips in the Federal Republic, the German Democratic Republic and Austria; to the Research Grants Committee of the School of English and American Studies at the University of East Anglia, for additional allocations during a period of several years; to the Twenty-Seven Foundation, for funding a research trip to Germany and a later tour to privately held papers in England and Scotland; to the German Academic Exchange Service (DAAD), for financing a one-month archival tour in Germany; to the British Academy (Small Grants Research Fund in the Humanities), for covering repeated journeys to the Public Record Office in the closing stages of my research; and to the Social Science Research Council, for similar help in order to investigate sources relating to Anglo-German commercial relations. Finally, I should like to acknowledge my great debt to the Institute for Advanced Study, Princeton, and to the Leverhulme Foundation, for making it possible for me to complete the writing of this project under quite idyllic circumstances.

Were I to detail my obligations to the archives I have visited over the past decade, and to their helpful and willing staffs, the list would become enormous;* but I should at least like to thank all concerned for their indispensable assistance. In particular, I should like to acknowledge my gratitude to those individuals, both in Britain and Germany, who permitted me to bother them in their own homes in my pursuit of papers held in family hands.

Having been so long engaged upon this project, I have incurred multitudinous obligations to fellow academics in many parts of the world with whom I have exchanged ideas, before whose seminars I have presented papers, and from whose suggestions and encouragement I have gained greatly. I will not try to list all those accumulated debts, but my scholarly creditors will know how much I owe them. It is only fair, however, to pay tribute to those who read parts of the draft manuscript – David Blackbourn, Lamar Cecil, Roger Chickering, Gordon Craig, Geoff Eley, Gerald Feldman, Eric Homberger, Otto Pflanze, James Sheehan, Iain Smith, Zara Steiner and Joan Taylor; and especially to those long-suffering individuals who went through virtually the entire text – Volker Berghahn, Arno Mayer, Geoffrey Searle, Fritz Stern and Marvin Swartz. Even a fleeting glance at the first draft would reveal how much I benefited from such advice in trying to put my ideas, and the book's structure, into order. The responsibility for the final outcome remains, as ever, the author's own.

I should like to thank my agent, Bruce Hunter, for his continuing support of my activities, and my publisher's editor, Keith Ashfield, for his good humour, forbearance and encouragement. Vera Durrell (Norwich) and Peggy van Sant (Princeton) contributed greatly to the typing of the manuscript.

My greatest debt is to my wife, Cath, who has had the 'Anglo-German Antagonism' as an additional member of our family for over a decade and has sustained me in innumerable significant ways.

The book itself is dedicated to Father Denis Anderson, who diverted me into the study of history at St Cuthbert's Grammar School, Newcastle-upon-Tyne, nearly two decades ago; and to Mrs Joan Taylor, Department of History, University of Newcastle-upon-Tyne, who first aroused my interest in this particular period.

PAUL M. KENNEDY
*The Institute for Advanced Study*
*Princeton*

* A full list of archives used is given below on pp. 550–3.

# List of Abbreviations

| | |
|---|---|
| AA Bonn | *Auswärtiges Amt Archiv*, Bonn |
| AAHP | *Auswärtiges Amt, Handelspolitische Abteilung* |
| Adm. | Admiralty Records, Public Record Office, London |
| BA Koblenz | *Bundesarchiv*, Koblenz |
| BA-MA Freiburg | *Bundesarchiv-Militärarchiv*, Freiburg im Breisgau |
| BD | *British Documents on the Origins of the War*, edited by G. P. Gooch and H. Temperley, 11 vols (London, 1926–38) |
| BLPES | British Library of Political and Economic Science, London |
| BM | British Museum, London |
| BT | Board of Trade Records, Public Record Office, London |
| Cab. | Cabinet Records, Public Record Office, London |
| CID | Committee of Imperial Defence |
| CO | Colonial Office Records, Public Record Office, London |
| DZA Potsdam | *Deutsches Zentralarchiv* I, Potsdam |
| FO | Foreign Office Records, Public Record Office, London |
| GP | *Die Grosse Politik der Europäischen Kabinette*, edited by J. Lepsius *et al.*, 40 vols (Berlin, 1922–7) |
| GSA Berlin-Dahlem | *Geheimes Staatsarchiv* (now part of the *Stiftung Preussischer Kulturbesitz*), Berlin-Dahlem |
| *Hansard* | Parliamentary Debates (with year, volume and column reference) |
| HHSt.A Vienna | *Haus-, Hof- und Staatsarchiv*, Vienna |
| HoLRO | House of Lords Record Office, London |
| NMM Greenwich | National Maritime Museum, Greenwich |
| PRO | Public Record Office, London |
| QVL | *The Letters of Queen Victoria*, 1st series (1837–61), 3 vols (London, 1907); 2nd series (1861–85), 3 vols (London, 1926); 3rd series (1886–1901), 3 vols (London, 1930–2), edited by Viscount Esher, E. C. Benson, and then G. E. Buckle. |
| RA Windsor | Royal Archives, Windsor Castle |
| *Reichstagsverhandlungen* | *Stenographische Berichte über die Verhandlungen des Reichstages* (with legislation-period, session, year, sitting and day reference) |
| RKA | *Reichskanzlei-Akten, Deutsches Zentralarchiv* I, Potsdam |
| RKolA | *Reichskolonialamt, Deutsches Zentralarchiv* I, Potsdam |
| T | Treasury Records, Public Record Office, London |
| WO | War Office Records, Public Record Office, London |

*To*

*DENIS ANDERSON and JOAN TAYLOR*

*who*

*set me on the way*

# PART ONE

## *Anglo-German Political Relations from 1860 until 1880*

# CHAPTER 1

# *Anglo-German Relations in the 1860s*

In view of the sheer variety of the relationships that may develop between two closely situated peoples, any attempt to begin an analysis of those ties at the formal political and diplomatic level alone is bound to appear unsatisfactory. Is it not true, after all, that one country's diplomacy towards another is largely the implementation of policies which can only be explained and understood by reference to those larger historical forces which influence the workings of government? The social structure of that country, and the ideas which justify that structure or seek to have it amended; the state of the national economy, and the claims of interest groups within it; the cultural and religious traditions of a people, and their regard (or lack of regard) for alternative traditions; the constitutional forms of the country, and the tactical calculations of political groups which operate within that system; and the perceptions of the governing classes about their nation's place in the world, and its relations with third powers – are not all these the features to which the historian points when endeavouring to explain, say, United States policy towards Russia during the Cold War or Chinese policy towards the West today? So it must also be with any adequate story of the Anglo-German relationship, and the only justification for saying something about political relations first of all is that official government policy has so often been seen as representing, at least legally and symbolically, the overall attitude of one nation towards another. Yet it remains unsatisfactory; and it will soon be necessary to break off this diplomatic narrative in order to give more attention to the background influences.

Even if the first two chapters of this study essentially deal with the political relations between Britain and Germany, they need to be prefaced with brief remarks about both countries. In the convenient historical shorthand, 'London' and 'Berlin' may be allowed to exist as similar entities, as equal-ranking pieces on the diplomatic chessboard; in actual fact, they were very different from each other in so many spheres of life, and without an appreciation of this it is impossible to understand why the two peoples viewed each other in the 1860s as they did.

The most obvious difference lay in the sphere of national unity. Ever since the English conquest or acquisition of neighbouring Celtic territories in the

3

sixteenth and seventeenth centuries, Britain had been recognised as a single political unit: in her forms of government administration, system of political representation, currency, language and many other modes of social expression, there was uniformity and coherence. Germany, by contrast, was still a 'geographical expression' in 1860, consisting of thirty-nine states: Prussia, strong, militaristic, conservative and agrarian to the east of the Elbe, and more industrialised and 'modern' in its Rhineland regions; Hanover, only one generation away from its connection with the British crown; the Kingdom of Saxony, resentful of being in Prussia's shadow; the various smaller powers of north and central Germany, Mecklenburg, Oldenburg, Weimar, and so on; the important southern states, Baden, Württemberg and Bavaria, different from Prussia in certain cultural, religious and political traditions; the Free City of Frankfurt, and the Hanse cities of Hamburg, Bremen and Lübeck; and a plethora of minor duchies and principalities. A common language, and an impressive intellectual heritage, gave a certain coherence to these assorted states; but there was little else. Even the Germanic Federation, despite its promising name, meant little in terms of future unity, since its boundaries excluded East Prussia and Posen but included possessions of the kings of the Netherlands (Luxembourg) and Denmark (Holstein), and was presided over by an Austrian. In the pre-1871 years, when so many of these German states had their own foreign service of sorts, it is much more accurate to refer to Anglo-Prussian or Anglo-Bavarian relations than to Anglo-German relations.

The second obvious difference was geographical. The German peoples occupied the central plains and mountains of the European continent, a region characterised by few 'natural' borders. Germans represented the greater part of the Swiss and Austrian populations, contested Schleswig-Holstein with the Danes, lived amidst a preponderantly Polish population in the east, and far into Alsace and parts of Lorraine in the west. All this formed ready materials for conflict with the surrounding great powers, which over previous centuries had offered as much opposition to German unification as particularists had from within. On the one hand, this had meant that Germany was a 'power vacuum' in the heart of Europe, the scene of repeated battles, and vulnerable to the military incursions of ambitious neighbours; on the other, it had fostered in many circles a strong national consciousness, less based upon a clear-cut perception of geographical boundaries than upon a belief in the shared culture of *Deutschtum*. The British, in contrast, not only enjoyed the benefits of territorial definition and relative freedom from invasion which flowed from their insular state, but also had built up in the course of the preceding three centuries an overseas empire in various parts of the globe. This particular difference, it should be added, was much more likely to make for Anglo-German friendship than to lead to a conflict; for the British, being more interested in imperial issues and in the occasional naval threat from France or Russia, wished to keep all foreign influence out of Germany and usually encouraged the idea of unification; while the Germans, aware that Britain sought merely stability, prosperity and the preservation of the balance of power within Europe, hoped for London's aid in combating the actions of the Danes, the French and possibly the Russians.

4

Economically, the Britain of 1860 was remarkably different, not merely from the German states, but from all other European countries apart from Belgium. If she was not the 'workshop of the world', she was at least producing about two-thirds of its coal, about half its iron, five-sevenths of its steel, two-fifths of its hardware and about half its commercial cotton cloth; 40 per cent of the world's trade in manufactures came from her factories, and about one-third of the total exports of all other countries went to the British market. In addition to being responsible for a large part of international, or better, transoceanic, commerce, she was also the centre for banking, insurance, investment and commodity-dealing and possessed more registered steamship tonnage than all other countries combined. Already by this stage, the greater part of the British workforce was engaged in manufacturing and the majority of the population lived in urban areas.[1] Few of these comments applied to the German states. There were specific centres of commercial and financial activity such as Frankfurt, Leipzig and the Hanse ports, and there were certain parts of the Rhineland, Saxony and Upper Silesia where industrialisation was making rapid advances; but the economic structure of the rest of Germany was agrarian, indeed feudal, in its prevailing practices and attitudes, and most peasants and large-scale landowners looked with disfavour upon the signs of 'modernisation'. Of course, by 1860 it is possible for the later historian to point to various promising hints – in the adaptation of new industrial techniques, the growth of railway communications, developments in joint-stock banking, concentration within industry, and so on – of the quickening pace of Germany's economic transformation. When compared with, say, Austria-Hungary, Russia or even France, she looks more modern; but when compared with Britain, the gap (despite exceptions in certain fields) was still enormous.[2]

This difference is recognisable not merely in the social structure of the two countries, but also in the concomitant social attitudes. There can be no doubt that landed wealth still played a crucial role in British politics; the influence of the Cecils, Russells, Derbys and Cavendishes was testimony enough to that, as was the unconcealed scramble by businessmen to acquire a country seat. Nevertheless, the old order had compromised with the new and increasingly took account of the country's commercial interests – in which, after all, many an aristocratic family had a stake; and this development was reflected in the fact that in 1865 around 52 per cent of MPs were merchants, industrialists and men of finance (whereas only 8 per cent of the members of the 1871 Reichstag came from such circles).[3] Moreover, while Britain possessed a large and growing proletariat whose needs – such as cheap food and clothing and fuel – had to be catered for by a government anxious to avoid the social disturbances of the 1840s, there was no large-scale force of independent peasantry capable of retarding the processes of socio-political modernisation in order to preserve their own economic position. On the German side, the pre-industrial (and, in some cases, anti-industrial) forces were altogether more substantial: handicraftsmen, peasant-farmers, out-workers in the clothing trades, Prussian Junkers and the royal heads of minor principalities presented a variety of obstacles to the circles pressing for change. Furthermore, these obstacles were not merely economic – as, say, in the resistance to *laissez-faire* practices in tariffs and industry – but also, inevitably, political – in the clinging to particularist privileges, in restricted franchises, in the police apparatus erected to check 'revolutionary' tendencies, in the extensive rights of the hereditary ruler, his government and his army. In the post-1848 era, the possibility that diehard elements might resort to force to resist further social and political change was never far from the surface; on the other hand, the creation of an embryonic industrial proletariat with its own party and trade unions further complicated the political scene, since it forced many among the middle classes and some of the bolder Junkers to consider a compromise between the established orders so as to check this third force. In mid-Victorian Britain, it may be argued, such a compromise already existed; but its ruling groups, having ridden out the social turbulence of the preceding generation and accepted an overall strategy of pragmatic adaptation to change, had achieved both a far greater symbiosis of aristocrats and businessmen and possessed a robust confidence in their ability to handle the lower orders. One of the chief complaints of Palmerston and others about continental regimes, after all, was that by repressive actions they actually stirred up unrest.[4]

The ideological justifications of the respective political structures and habits in Britain and Germany are, in consequence, easy to understand. Not every Briton swallowed the gospel of Mill, and very few in positions of power fully shared Cobden's view of British external policy; but in the cosy circumstances of mid-century, when the country enjoyed relative domestic tranquillity, rising economic standards and a maritime and colonial influence unequalled by any other state, it was not difficult for most politicians and thinkers to arrive at a consensus about their politics. Rumbles of dissatisfaction might come from Carlyle, Marx and other critics, half-concealed fears about the future of society may be pointed to, yet there was an almost unquestioned acceptance of the essentials of the British system: constitutional monarchy, parliamentary controls, civic freedoms, low military budgets, free trade and its concomitant, the avoidance of war with a major power if at all possible.[5] In the German states, predictably enough, this consensus was not yet formed, either in regard to the merits of modernisation and industrialisation, or upon the ideal structure and aims of society, or upon what properly constituted the body politic. Conflicting ideologies and perceptions matched the rivalling between political and social forces; generalisations about the 'German mind' are difficult to make about a country in which Hanseatic free-traders, Rhineland Socialists, rigid East Elbian landowners and Bavarian particularists each believed that they possessed the philosopher's stone. What one can say is that, even in middle-class circles, there was a far greater emphasis upon deference to authority, upon the role of the state in political life, and upon the individual's acknowledgement that he was part of a larger, corporate whole; the cultural traditions of Hegelian idealism and the reiteration of the notion of a *Volksgeist* provided a formidable resistance to the unquestioned importation of 'westernised' assumptions about the natural law, utilitarianism, parliamentary government and the political economy.[6] This, in turn, was to condition German views of peace and war, their place within Europe, the ordering of their internal constitution and politics, and their relations with other peoples.

6

There were other, more specific 'conditioning' factors in the Anglo-German relationship: for example, the connections between the royal families, the many cultural interactions, the shared bonds of religion and race. They will all need to be examined below. Yet it seems fair to claim that the attitudes of each people towards the other essentially flowed from the general economic, geographical and domestic-political circumstances described above. On the German side, because of its splintered political structure, there existed a variety of attitudes: the Catholics in the south had few links with the island state; peasants and handicraftsmen tended to dislike it as the home of industrial capitalism; socialists shared that suspicion yet, with progressive Liberals, also admired it as the fount of constitutional liberty; free-trading merchants sought to emulate its economic system, although other interest groups disliked the competition it offered and sought for protection against British imports; and the landowning classes, although suspicious of the British constitution, favoured that country as the greatest market for their corn, a historic ally against France, and a symbol of social stability and continued aristocratic rule. In addition to all these general points, however, the Germans viewed Britain in the light of their most pressing political problem – the struggle for national unity. In the 1850s and 1860s, it would not be unfair to claim, how the Germans judged a foreign country depended very centrally upon the latter's attitude to the future of Germany: France was assessed on its policy towards the Rhineland and Luxemburg; Denmark on its stance over Schleswig-Holstein; Russia on its treatment of the Polish Question, and its general capacity to interfere in German affairs; and Austria – the only German state which really had interests and lands outside the German world – upon whether it could or should be included within some future *grossdeutsch* state. In just the same way, most Germans would judge Britain. Would she keep objecting to the *Zollverein*, or at last appreciate that its growth was also a political issue? Would she intervene to stop French moves into the Rhineland or simply sit by, proclaiming a pious neutrality? Would she, appealing to anachronistic treaties, object to the 'rounding-off' of a coherent Germanic geographical unit by taking up the cause of certain small neighbouring peoples? On the whole, the German upper and middle classes were favourable towards Britain; but this derived, not merely from the knowledge that London vaguely sympathised with the principle of national self-determination, but from the hope that British help would be forthcoming under certain circumstances. Were this not to be the case, then the German image of Britain would undoubtedly alter.

The British view of Germany was also generally positive, but with an equal number of reservations. Economically, the further industrialisation and creation of a common German market would probably be of benefit to Britain, always provided that the *Zollverein*'s tariffs were not increased. Ideologically, the British enthusiasm for Greek and Italian unification prejudiced them in favour of a united German state, although London ambitiously hoped that this might occur peacefully, without a threat to the European equilibrium and without endangering the rights of weaker neighbours. In power-political terms, British statesmen such as Castlereagh and Palmerston had long advocated the creation of 'an impregnable bulwark between the great States in the

7

East and West of Europe', which would not only check French or Russian endeavours to interfere in the German territories but also deter both those powers from extra-European adventures. An elaborate system of checks and balances, both within Europe and (at least until 1866) within Germany itself, was the best way to ensure 'a general system of tranquillity and pacification' which could only be to the benefit of Britain, 'a Nation whose paths should be, and must more than those of any other power be, the paths of peace . . .'[7] Despite all these encouraging noises, however, the post-Crimean War recoil of the British establishment from interventionist policies meant that the Germans could expect little *active* support in their quest for unity. Moreover, the British were interested not only in the end, but in the means. What would happen if unification came about, not as a consequence of justifiable, progressive pressure from below, but was imposed from above, by means of armed force and external diversions and conquests, leaving certain reactionary, military cliques in charge of the destinies of this enlarged power-political unit? What blows might be dealt to Liberal ideals, to the superior Liberal methods of forestalling unrest and conflict, to the economic prosperity of the age, by violent and irresponsible deeds? In theory, the British liked the idea of German unity, which was less contentious an issue to them than it was among the Germans themselves; but in practice they wished to observe how exactly that goal would be reached.

In the early 1860s, the differences which existed between Britain and Germany seemed confined to the ideological aspect, that is, to the differing perceptions of how domestic politics and external strategies should be arranged. This 'gap' was the more obvious because both countries were affected by (ostensibly) similar pressures for reform. In Britain, Progressive circles were arguing for a further extension of the franchise, improvements in the machinery of government and an abjuration of Palmerstonian diplomacy which, they contended, diverted the nation's attention and resources from more worthwhile objects. In similar fashion, the German Liberals (especially in Prussia) were gearing themselves up to insist upon the introduction of constitutional liberties and parliamentary controls over the executive, demands fiercely resisted by the King of Prussia and most Conservatives. It was among the German reformist circles, however, that there flourished the strongest sentiments for national unity, if possible under the leadership of the Prussian monarch. Whereas the British reformers' programme of internal reconstruction and external peace appeared coherent, therefore, the German Liberals were pressing (in various degrees) for an active policy in both spheres, which in consequence made them vulnerable to the Bismarckian counter-strategy of external expansion and internal stabilisation;[8] to most of the German middle classes, national goals were more important than Liberal ones. With contending groups in each country struggling to have their own particular views upon domestic and foreign policies accepted, it is not surprising that they judged events in the other state in the light of their own preoccupations.

One good illustration of this was the British attitude to the constitutional quarrel between the Prussian king and his Landtag over the military budget in the early 1860s. To those raised in the Whig interpretation of history, the similarity with the 1640s was obvious, as was the line of advice which they felt they should offer the German Liberals. Wilhelm I's assertion in 1861 that he held his crown by divine right was so bitterly attacked in Britain that the queen was driven to beg Palmerston to try to dampen down the press commentary, 'which could not fail to produce the deepest indignation amongst the people of Germany, and by degrees estrange the people of this country from Germany'.[9] Yet the British mood of superiority and dislike could not be erased by missives from Windsor Castle, and it stiffened still further at the news that Wilhelm I had called Bismarck to be his Prime Minister. The latter's domestic-political views were known to be ultra-conservative, but what was just as alarming was his previous diplomatic record of urging a pro-Russian policy for Prussia, thereby supporting Britain's greatest rival in world affairs. As early as 1854, the British ambassador, Lord Bloomfield, had warned his superiors that he could only regard the future accession to power by Bismarck 'as the complete triumph of the *Kreuzzeitung* party and the successful result of Russian intrigues'.[10] That possibility having now occurred, even British germanophiles were bound to be disturbed.

The mixed feelings of the British towards Prussia and German unity had their counterpart in Bismarck's own view of England, which, being part friendly and part hostile, confused both contemporaries and later historians alike.[11] As with other members of the German establishment, Bismarck was a strong admirer of English culture: he spoke the language well, and had read widely in English literature and history; and the life-style of an English gentleman appeared to him to be the most admirable in the world. There is no reason to doubt his claim that 'all my habits and tastes are English';[12] but there is also no reason to assume that he allowed his cultural and political proclivities to go hand in hand, as the German progressives did. German political circumstances, he insisted, did not admit the adoption of English modes:

> We lack that class that makes politics in England, the class of wealthy and therefore conservative gentlemen, independent of material interests, whose entire upbringing is directed towards becoming English statesmen, and whose whole aim is to partake in public affairs . . . Give us all the English things we don't have . . . the entire English land-ownership, English wealth and the English public spirit, and especially an English lower house . . . then I also will say: 'You can rule us by the English methods.'[13]

Whether or not he really believed in this argument – and other facts suggest that it contained more rhetoric than conviction – it formed a suitable starting-point for justifying a set of domestic and foreign policies which did *not* follow the English model. Prussia's policies, as the Realpolitik-historicist school taught, would be guided not by abstract principles but by consideration of her real circumstances: domestically, by that confusion of rivalries between the various states, confessions and classes which suggested, conveniently enough, that the lack of English-style 'stabilising elements' in society required the crown and aristocracy to possess great powers; and externally, by a

9

vulnerability to diplomatic encirclement and possible overland attack which demanded, with equal convenience for the Junkers, a strong army, free from parliamentary controls, and an obedience to the state which the insular British did not need.

Bismarck's foreign policy towards Britain was equally pragmatic, the more so since the English two-party system and the dominance of Parliament seemed to him to ruin the prospect of some form of fixed military alliance between the two powers. Furthermore, in his view that British statesmen 'were much better informed about China and Turkey than about Prussia', he possessed a more accurate idea of England's willingness to intervene in continental affairs than did the optimistic German Liberals. Yet even this did not prevent him from proposing an Anglo-German alliance on a number of later occasions. Neither his prejudice against Gladstonian liberalism on the one hand, nor his admiration for English culture on the other, influenced him into making a dogma of his foreign policy towards Britain – just as he could not allow his conservative political inclinations to dictate a permanent pro-Russian attitude. What was significant for his attitude towards Britain were the general conditions of that particular time:[14] that is, the state of Berlin's relations with third powers, especially France and Russia; the relative strength of liberalism within Germany, and the corresponding need to weaken its standing; and the requirements of domestic politics, especially near election time, when success at the polls might have to be induced by an appeal to nationalist sentiments and by embarking upon an adventurous foreign policy.

The differing criteria with which British statesmen and Bismarck judged political problems was soon to be vividly illustrated in their reactions to the Polish uprising of 1863. Given its earlier enthusiasm for Greek and Italian independence, it was not surprising that British public opinion embraced the cause of the Poles; the House of Commons, Palmerston informed Russell, was 'unanimously Polish' and the Foreign Secretary himself was well prepared to lecture the Russians upon the need to restore civil liberties.[15] Bismarck, on the other hand, not only shared the typical Prussian detestation of the Poles but needed to maintain good relations with St Petersburg if he was to fend off French and Austrian intrigues in German affairs.[16] This amoral policy of supporting Russia through the Alvensleben Convention outraged the British press: 'Whatever may be our hostility to the bear, there is no doubt of our feeling towards the jackal', growled *The Times*.[17] Nevertheless, this affair did not mark a decisive turn in Anglo-Prussian relations, for the greatest animosity was naturally directed towards Russia; and if *The Times* seemed to feel differently, much of its indignation was provoked by the fear that Prussia's action would give the French an excuse to move upon the Rhine![18] A large part of the British government's energies was thus devoted towards preventing France from taking advantage of the situation, and by the end of 1863 the Anglo-French *entente* which had existed since the Crimean War was in ruins, both because of differences over Poland and over related issues of nationality within Europe.

Diplomatically, the estrangement of Russia from the west, and of France from Britain, offered ideal circumstances for Bismarck to begin his long-term scheme to redraw the map of Germany. Nothing could have suited him better at this time, therefore, than the eruption of the Schleswig-Holstein question late in 1863. With Russia still grateful for Berlin's support over the Polish troubles, with Austria persuaded into a joint enterprise with Prussia, and with France too annoyed at the British to agree to a *démarche* or any more extreme measures on behalf of the Duchies, Bismarck felt free enough to move irrespective of Palmerstonian protests.[19] Yet, important though the Danish War was for Anglo-German relations at the diplomatic level, it hardly bears comparison, in terms of historical significance, with the light shown by the incident upon the decision-making processes and domestic-political attitudes in Berlin and London.

By 1863 the internal crisis in Prussia appeared to have reached new heights.[20] There was no lack of arch-conservatives in this situation who urged a *coup d'état* against the recalcitrant Prussian Landtag; but Bismarck was not of their number. In his opinion the reformist movement could be crushed, not by the sabres of the Potsdam troopers, but by a policy of stubborn defiance on constitutional matters combined with successes in international affairs; that is to say, successes in the 'German question', for only here could he hope to attract enough domestic attention and support so as to bolster up the popularity of the monarchy and to confound its critics. In this, of course, he was not only offering an alternative to the progressive-Liberal mixture of internal reforms and external peace, but he was also flouting the Conservatives' desire for legitimism and the *status quo*. It was a very daring strategy, dependent in the last resort upon sufficient military successes by the Prussian army to outweigh the fact that those very forces had been paid for by illegally collected taxes: to this extent, at least, Bismarck was justified in declaring that the great questions of the day would be settled, not by speeches and majority decisions, but by blood and iron.

In Britain of the early 1860s, by contrast, the political constellation was plainly against foreign adventures and in favour of a pacific, reformist path.[21] It is true, of course, that Palmerston in his later years exhibited what seemed to be the 'Bonapartist' tendencies of blocking constitutional change at home and of seeking to rouse public opinion on points of national honour in foreign affairs; and it was also true that there was still a number of newspaper editors who assumed that Britain could act, if not always as the world's policeman, then at least as its schoolmaster. Yet in many ways Palmerston's stance was becoming increasingly outdated. Given the delicate state of party politics, his influence was still formidable enough to neutralise the forces for change; but many of his fellow Whigs were uneasily aware that an accommodation would soon be necessary with the demands of the middle-class reform movements, the trade unionists and skilled artisans, and the Nonconformists; and, out of a mixture of economic self-interest, moral conviction and a sensitivity to Britain's global obligations, they were increasingly accepting the Manchester School's view that peace, if it could be decently preserved, was overwhelmingly in the country's interests. Even at the height of the Polish agitation in the previous year, it had been apparent that warlike actions would have been bitterly attacked from within and without government circles. This was not a situation out of which much political capital could be gained by waving the flag and beating the drum.

There is one further ground for distinguishing Palmerston's policy from that of Bismarck: the former had, after all, an undeniable record of opposition to the forces of reaction in Europe, together with an aversion to the unilateral tearing-up of international treaties. Much of the justification for his and Russell's arguments for intervention in 1864 was, in fact, founded upon the latter point – which, on account of Britain's role in the 'internationalisation' of the Schleswig-Holstein question since 1848, they clearly regarded as of considerable importance. But the British press, although almost united in condemning the German deeds, was divided over the question of doing anything about it; the Conservative Party was similarly split and, under the cautious Derby, was unlikely to be rallied by their leader into a call for intervention; business circles, especially in the north, were aghast at the prospect of war; the queen, exploiting to the fullest extent the undefined but substantial influence of the mid-century monarchy, conducted her own vigorous campaign against the two 'dreadful old men'; and, most important of all, a Cabinet predominantly composed of moderate Whigs and 'Manchester' men repeatedly overruled proposals for action. Gladstone's 1864 budget, for example, which proposed yet further reductions in the military vote, was drafted at the height of the crisis – which gives a fair indication of where his priorities lay. By the early summer of 1864, the message was clear, even to Palmerston and Russell: the country would not tolerate a war on behalf of the Danes.[22]

The reverberations upon British policy from this crisis were far-reaching. If it had confirmed many Englishmen in their dislike of Bismarck's policies, it had also strengthened their aversion to entanglements in continental politics. John Bright's boast that Palmerston's defeat had dealt the death-blow to that 'foul idol', the balance-of-power policy, was hardly correct when one considers that the government was even then still more alarmed about French than Prussian designs.[23] Yet the lesson which subsequent ministries took from this affair came very close to the Bright-Cobdenite view that in future a belligerent policy could only be initiated when the vast majority of the country supported the government. Given the confusion of opinions over foreign affairs, such a precondition was sufficient to rule out the resort to war in all but the most pressing circumstances; and thus confirmed the existing tendency towards national introspection and domestic reforms, leaving it to diplomacy alone to preserve Britain's voice in European issues.

On the German side, the results of the Danish issue also confirmed an earlier pattern, that of the role of foreign affairs in driving a wedge between the varied ranks of liberalism, and also between the Liberal nationalists and England. Palmerston's earlier intervention in 1848 had helped to discredit the position of the Frankfurt Parliament, causing the anglophile Stockmar to lament then that 'Our only natural friend has acted as an enemy bent upon our destruction';[24] now it was the English Prime Minister who had been discredited, but the effects upon the confused groups of German Liberals were the same. Moderate and left-wing leaders in Prussia, such as Twesten, warned that they would not support the Danish War; but other Liberals like Loewe were proclaiming that

'We value freedom at home very highly, but independence abroad above all.'[25] The more such elements preferred national victories to constitutional ones, the more they came to execrate the threatened English intervention over Schleswig-Holstein and, at the same time, to modify their former English-style liberalism. To these and to the following generation of German nationalists, the figure of Palmerston, who had opposed the growth of the *Zollverein*, frustrated the Frankfurt Parliament, and interfered in the process of German unification – and all, despite his references to international law and morality, for the material interests of England – was one to mock:

> Hat der Teufel einen Sohn
> So heisst er sicher Palmerston.[26]

It was an ironic, if understandable, reputation for someone who, politically, had always favoured German unification and, even in his last few weeks of life, had repeated to Russell his conviction that 'Germany ought to be strong in order to resist Russian aggression, and a strong Prussia is essential to German strength', however 'selfish and unprincipled' he felt Berlin's actions towards the Duchies had been.[27]

To the English Liberal admirers of Germany, then, the worst consequence of the Danish War had been the strengthening of agrarian conservatism. The blindly patriotic Prussian Liberals, wrote Bryce in disgust to Freeman, 'have given everything up for this wretched triumph, and allowed Bismarck and the feudalists to regain all that the long constitutional struggle seemed to have won'.[28] That this was Bismarck's aim seems clear from his various actions. He encouraged his Austrian allies with the thought that 'British interference would unite all Germany around its Princes and would rob the German Liberals of many illusions';[29] the government-inspired press was instructed to 'howl' for the Duchies; petitions for annexation by Prussia (rather than by the House of Augustenberg) were secretly encouraged; and the Liberals were castigated for their lack of patriotism. 'You reject the Prussian *Volksgeist . . .*', Bismarck taunted. 'You reject the glorious traditions of the past, for you disavow the position, the great power position, of Prussia acquired through the heavy sacrifices in the people's blood and property.'[30] These charges seemed to be so useful in discrediting the opposition whilst diverting attention from his own unconstitutional actions that other members of the Prussian Cabinet of ministers were now tempted to argue that the time was ripe to dissolve the Landtag and to exploit the military victory on the electoral battlefield.

But the time was not yet suitable, and the practical problems still appeared great to Bismarck as he prepared the diplomatic ground for a showdown with a far greater opponent than the Danes – the Habsburg monarchy. This was a much more hazardous game, since there was still considerable opposition by the middle classes to the illegal collection of taxes, the censorship of the press, the hounding of Liberal judges and civil servants, and the moves against freedom of speech in the lower house. The opposition was highly unlikely to approve of a 'civil war' with Austria for the purposes of the greater glory of the Prussian regime; and its criticisms would be echoed by all supporters of a

*Grossdeutsch* solution, by the Catholic Church, by the Socialists under Bebel and Liebknecht, by businessmen who feared an economic collapse, by most of the non-Prussian states of Germany, by most of the royal family and – last but certainly not least – by traditional Prussian Conservatives, who would regard an attack upon Austria with horror. This was stiff opposition, even for Bismarck, and it is scarcely surprising to learn that reports of his manner just before the outbreak of the 1866 war referred to his 'all or nothing' mood, or that his confidant Bleichröder was required to supply him with a reserve of gold and silver coins as he rode off towards the battlefield.[31]

As risky as his lunge against Austria was the bid Bismarck made in the early summer of 1866 for fresh sources of domestic support within Germany. The proposals he then introduced for a national assembly with powers to harmonise tariffs, transportation and business practices between the German states was clearly aimed at buying over that large body of middle-class interests which was keen to be reconciled; but the truly revolutionary aspect came with his suggestion that the assembly was to be chosen through direct elections by universal manhood suffrage. This accorded with his view that the restricted franchise for the Prussian Landtag permitted that body to be dominated by 'intractable professors and pedants', whereas he suspected that an appeal to the masses would give the king 'nine-tenths' of the vote.[32] The Liberals, thus confounded, would be forced to draw closer to the establishment out of a fear of the enfranchised peasants and workers which they themselves could neither lead nor control. The troubled circumstances of 1866 made this an experiment worth trying, in Germany as a whole if not in Prussia itself. This radical proposal caused confusion abroad, and consternation and incredulity at home; but one party above all was shattered by the news – Austria. Just as the Habsburg monarchy was unable to go as far as Prussia in the tariff struggle to gain economic primacy within Germany, it could not also keep pace in the battle for political ascendancy if demagogic tools were all that were available. Thus Bismarck could strike another blow at his Austrian challenger.

Such considerations suggest that the driving-force behind Bismarck's bold foreign policy in this period cannot be seen *solely* as a wish to avoid the domestic-political crisis. Of course he was going to fight to preserve the peculiar powers of the Prussian monarchy and the privileged status of the aristocracy by whatever means possible, and of course he was willing to pursue the radical course of conquering all Germany to achieve those conservative aims; but it was a moot point in 1866 whether an adventurous foreign policy would strengthen or undermine his purpose. His decision was also affected by a deep-seated wish for Prussian aggrandisement for its own sake: 'Prussia's mission is to extend itself', he declared in 1864, and years before then he had announced, 'All of us want the Prussian eagle to spread his wings, to protect and rule from Memel to the Donnersberg.'[33] When his fellow ministers now pointed to 'the favourable influence which a vigorous appearance in foreign affairs and a war undertaken for the honour of Prussia would exercise in the solution of the domestic conflict', Bismarck's reply was instructive: 'Even if the government found itself at peace with the country [I] would have advised in

14

favour of war . . . Domestic conditions do not make a war necessary, but they are additional reasons for making it seem advantageous.'[34]

What *was* clear, was that if a military victory occurred, Bismarck would wring all possible internal advantages from it. In this sense, once again, the devastating performance of that Prussian army fashioned by the king, Roon and Moltke in defiance of the Landtag was the ultimate source of Bismarck's success in both foreign and domestic aims. The most obvious and immediate consequence was the result of the Prussian elections, which took place on the very day of Königgratz: with 142 seats (in contrast to their previous twenty-eight), the Conservatives' electoral fortunes were greatly restored. At this, the criticism of Bismarck from the Right began to break; and when the government's policy of reconciliation with the Liberal opposition was made plain a few weeks after the war, the 'realistic' Free Conservatives moved to support official policy while the traditionalists exploded in discontent at the steady undermining of their principles. In just the same way, and more predictably, the Liberal camp also split under the impact of Bismarck's successes, with the Progressives left to lick their wounds while the 'National' Liberals gladly accepted a compromise with the state, vainly trusting to reform from within what they had been unable to alter from without.[35]

Yet however significant the year 1866 was in inner-German affairs, and however momentous it was seen to be later in European terms, it had relatively little impact upon German attitudes towards Britain. This is understandable when one recollects how crowded and confused the German mind must then have been with Bismarck's schemes for a national assembly and universal manhood suffrage, the Austro-Prussian War, the seizure of Hanover, Hesse-Kassel, Frankfurt and other territories by Prussia, the moves to end the constitutional conflict, and the divisions within Conservative and Liberal ranks. What time was given to foreign affairs was devoted to a concern with Austria's condition after her defeat and, increasingly, with France's ambitions in the Rhineland. Britain, by comparison, was almost as remote a factor as the United States to most Germans at this time.

The same could not be said about British attitudes towards the German problem in 1866. The intricacies of continental politics were well beyond the average Englishman, but something as serious as an Austro-Prussian war could not be ignored by the 'political' part of the nation, nor by the press. That the two powers should fall out so soon after their combined action against Denmark was difficult to understand, but most commentators laid the blame at Bismarck's door. Austria might be wrong in maintaining her 'unnatural' hold upon Venetia, but she was evidently innocent of provoking war in central Europe – although many British newspapers later expressed admiration at Prussia's swift victories.[36] If the press at first generally criticised the bold, bad Junker, the Liberal government was even more outraged. 'There is but one remedy – one certain way of preserving peace – it is the dismissal of Count Bismarck by the King', wrote Russell.[37] Clarendon, the Foreign Secretary, agreed with this diagnosis: 'two millions of men armed to the teeth by bankrupt governments, preparing to cut each other's throats and set all Europe in flames, for *nothing*, or rather for the gratification of one man – Bismarck – who says he would rather go down to posterity as Atilla than as John Bright.'[38] And the queen, especially distraught at the fate of the small German courts which supported Austria and paid the penalty, had the last word, as usual: 'Prussia seems inclined to behave as atrociously as possible, and as she *always has done*! Odious people the Prussians are, *that I must say*.'[39]

Yet despite this indignation, there was no thought of actual intervention on London's part. The queen, it was true, wanted some action and even tried to plead privately with Wilhelm to avoid the impending war and dismiss the 'one man . . . responsible for all this evil'; but the king's cool reply, together with the news that Bismarck was furious at the intrigues of other members of the Prussian royal family, confirmed Russell and Clarendon in their belief that gratuitous advice would be impolitic.[40] As for military intervention, that was ruled out from the start. 'We are willing to do anything for the maintenance of peace', Clarendon informed Cowley, then ambassador in Paris, 'except committing ourselves to a policy of action.'[41] When, a few weeks later, a Conservative administration took over, with Stanley as Foreign Secretary, the policy of abstention became more marked than ever. 'Ours will be a pacific policy, a policy of observation rather than action', Stanley told the Commons. 'I think there never was a great European war in which the direct national interests of England were less concerned.'[42]

If the reasons for this policy appeared inexplicable to a later generation of Britons, they were all too obvious to statesmen of the late 1860s. In the first place, the consciousness of both parties was ridden with the memory of the Schleswig-Holstein humiliation, Clarendon noting that 'Our experience of two years ago has taught us how little the advice and cautions of England are regarded in Germany'; and Derby, in his first ministerial statement in the Lords, promising that his government's foreign policy was 'above all to endeavour not to interfere needlessly and vexatiously with the internal affairs of any foreign country'.[43]

The second reason for British non-intervention was that of naval and military weakness. In the years following the French naval 'scare' of 1859, the mid-Victorians had relapsed into their usual state of complacency about the navy; and with the main calls upon the Admiralty being anti-slave patrols and 'showing the flag' in the tropics, there was little to spare for operations in European waters.[44] An even more substantial point was that warships alone could hardly influence a conflict in central Europe. Yet the other service, the Victorian army, had never been more than a pigmy compared with its continental equivalents, and this disparity was further increased precisely in this period by the reorganisation of the Prussian army on mass lines. Only if the British had a European ally could they play a significant role on the continent; but no such partner was in sight. Even if they had possessed the military capacity to intervene in Germany, could they afford to become bogged down there while they had so many obligations elsewhere? Apart from the troops in the Crown Colonies, the War Office was still being pressed to keep a large force in New Zealand to quell fresh Maori unrest; problems with the Ashanti and Abyssinians threatened the dispatch of more soldiers to Africa; and, in the aftermath of the Indian mutiny, fully 65,000 men were required to 'stiffen' the now-suspect Indian army. Russia, recovering from the Crimean War, seemed as restless in Asia as she was ambitious in the Balkans. A potentially dangerous Cretan revolt broke out at almost the same time as the Austro-Prussian War, and the problem of Venetia was still complicating Anglo-French discussions about the German question. France's moves over Egypt gave fresh grounds for concern as the construction of the Suez Canal steadily progressed. Above all, there was the latent threat of the United States, and the burden of defending Canada from Fenian raiders, which allowed Clarendon to argue that 'the military and pecuniary resources of England must be husbanded with the utmost care' when he sought to resist the queen's pressure for interference in Germany.[45]

Yet all these arguments were, one suspects, justifications for a policy of non-intervention which ministers preferred in any case. The blunt fact was that British statesmen had not just negative, but sincerely held *positive* reasons for standing aside from the Austro-Prussian War. The first of these, by any reckoning, was economic. There was probably no other period, before or since, when so many members of the British establishment were imbued with the doctrines of political economy; and an intense dislike of the destructive processes of war was, of course, one of the fundamentals of that faith. Whether this derived from an altruistic horror at the slaughters that would inevitably accompany armed conflict, or from a self-interested awareness of the decline of trade, ruination of credit and material losses of war, and of the possible civil unrest which might follow, is hard to assess; for all these elements seemed inseparable parts of a coherent mid-century *Weltanschauung* which was by no means confined to the circle around Cobden and Bright. An experienced Whig such as Clarendon, who wondered what 'in the name of all that is rational, decent, humane' Bismarck's justification for provoking a war with Austria could be, clearly felt unable to relate Prussian political habits with those pertaining in Britain.[46] Stanley, much impressed by the impact upon Lancashire of the American Civil War and quite enjoying his reputation as the favourite of the middle classes, held that 'finances govern the world'.[47] Disraeli, in the debate over the censure-motion upon Russell and Palmerston in 1864, maintained that his party was 'interested in the tranquillity and prosperity of the world, the normal condition of which is peace';[48] and two years later Derby put this somewhat more candidly when stating that since Conservative supporters were men who had 'the largest stake in the country', they automatically also possessed 'the greatest interest in the peace and prosperity of the State'.[49] These were the sentiments of a comfortable, satiated élite, appreciative of the benefits of peace and having little to gain by war; being now forgetful, or ashamed, of their own more adventurous past, it was not surprising that they found Bismarckian policies disturbing and wasteful.

Furthermore, since the death of Palmerston had at last opened the floodgates of reform, both parties preferred to concentrate their activities upon domestic issues, well aware that this was what increasingly determined the rise and fall of governments. Compared with the political manoeuvrings of Disraeli, Gladstone and their respective aristocratic backers, events in Germany naturally took second place.[50] Any attempt at a forward policy in Europe would be bitterly resented by a public opinion so manifestly eager to give its attention to domestic affairs. 'The country would not tolerate any direct interference in a quarrel with which we had no concern', Clarendon explained to the queen, 'and all those Ministers of Your Majesty's Government, who attended the Cabinet on Thursday last, expressed themselves in the strongest terms against it'.[51] In sum, here was a cluster of motives, economic, moral, strategical and domestic, operating in the public consciousness and prompting the British government to favour a foreign policy which was, particularly in regard to European issues, pragmatic, conciliatory and reasonable.

Of course, a more energetic policy might *still* be implemented, but only if the political establishment judged that national interests were so seriously threatened that recourse should be made to armed action. What was clear about 1866, however, was virtually no Briton felt that way about the rise of Prussian dominance within Germany. Although Clarendon personally thought that the destruction of the power balance between Prussia and Austria 'would be a misfortune for the rest of Europe', he was equally certain that 'the case is one in which neither English honour nor English interests are involved'.[52] A few British diplomats on the continent were more apprehensive, Cowley going so far as to write, 'I have no faith in the friendship of Prussia and if ever she becomes a naval power she will give us trouble';[53] but these were isolated voices and did not compare with the general sentiment, which perhaps *The Times* captured when declaring that whether Prussia or Austria were victorious was less important than the fact that Germany would then be 'more capable of preserving peace within its limits and repelling aggression from abroad'.[54] The latter argument was the leitmotiv in Stanley's policy throughout this period:

> while on the one hand [the British government] are not responsible for the steps that Prussia has taken to increase her power at the cost of other States, they have on the other hand no cause to object to such increase of power on her part . . .
> The growing jealousy of Russia, and, I suspect, of France also, against Prussia is natural. We should feel the same in their position. But to us there is no loss, rather a gain, in the interposition of a solid barrier between the two great aggressive powers of the Continent.[55]

The pattern of Anglo-German relations established in 1864–6 was one which lasted up to, and included, the Franco-Prussian War itself – so much so that a detailed investigation of the diplomacy of the late 1860s is not required here. On the one hand, there was the Prussian government, or rather Bismarck, determined to bring all of Germany under Berlin's control but in no way dogmatic about *when* that event should occur; if anything he needed time to consolidate the North German Federation, complete the rout of his Liberal opponents and to disarm the suspicions of the south German states, yet he always kept an eye open to see if French interference would provide the excuse for a military showdown which would establish Prussia in Germany. On the other hand, there was a succession of British governments, eager for all the reasons described above to preserve peace in Europe but usually much more preoccupied with the 1867 Reform Bill, the advent of Gladstone's first ministry and the various distractions of Crete, Canada, Abyssinia and New Zealand. While Bismarck sought to solve some of his domestic problems through external actions, therefore, the British government recoiled from foreign commitments which would – in Gladstone's words – distract 'the mind of the public and of Parliament'.[56]

Two instances in the diplomatic sparring which preceded the Franco-Prussian War are sufficient to illustrate this distinction in national practices. In 1867 Napoleon's attempt to bolster his own domestic position by obtaining compensation in Luxembourg for Prussia's earlier gains ran into a storm of criticism from German nationalists, deftly encouraged by Bismarck since it served the dual functions of breaking down the remaining barriers of German particularism on the one hand and of frustrating French ambitions on the other.[57] To cover his flank, Bismarck sounded out Britain about its attitude towards a Franco-Prussian war over Luxembourg and, by extension, over Belgium; but he found Stanley stressing the 'wide distinction between taking up arms in case of necessity for the protection of Belgium, in fulfilment of promises solemnly and repeatedly given, and joining in a war between France and Germany [that is, over Luxembourg] in which no English interest was involved and in regard to which we stood absolutely free and unpledged'.[58] Luxembourg was in no way a *casus belli* for Britain and the most Stanley would do – very reluctantly – was to arrange a conference of the powers in London which would produce a collective guarantee of the neutrality of the Grand Duchy in return for the withdrawal of its Prussian garrison. Even here, the government felt that it had not assumed any further responsibility, Derby telling the Lords that such a 'collective' guarantee did not bind Britain to action if France or Prussia (who were also signatories) broke that collectivity by overrunning Luxembourg.[59] England's stance, the queen was told by Stanley, was that of a 'rigidly impartial neutrality': 'without leaning (in the event of future disputes) to either side, but endeavouring to hold fairly and impartially the balance between them' – yet as he was not prepared to give any pledge 'to take up arms', this was a very passive sort of balancing-act.[60]

Although Derby's statement in the Lords appeared to make a nonsense of the Luxembourg guarantee, Bismarck could secretly be satisfied with the British stance. If a Franco-Prussian war should occur, London's chief aim would be to localise that conflict, which suited Prussia's purposes. Similarly, the decision by Derby's government in April 1868 to strike out from the annual Mutiny Bill any reference to the army's obligation to maintain the balance of power in Europe intrinsically favoured the state which intended to restructure that equilibrium to its own advantage.[61] The replacement of Stanley by the more suspicious and francophile Clarendon at the end of 1868 did not alter this basic trend, therefore, since Gladstone and his colleagues would never tolerate the interruption of their extensive domestic reform programme by entanglements in Europe, provided Belgium was safe. In addition, the queen would certainly seek to block any policy hostile to the general cause of German unity; and the Foreign Secretary himself was shaken by what appeared to be a French attempt to take over one of Belgium's major railways in 1869.[62]

The second example of the different approaches of London and Berlin to foreign affairs in these years lay in the question of limitation of armaments. If Clarendon could not keep the peace of Europe by threatening to throw Britain's weight against the aggressor, he might achieve it by persuading each side to abandon the spiralling arms race. Here, in his proposal to Bismarck to reduce 'those monster standing armies', lay a quintessential aspiration of the school of political economy, and one which both Liberals and Conservatives had already sought to implement by unilateral reductions in Britain's own military budget.[63] Yet, however much Clarendon and Gladstone talked at this time about the *general* benefits from arms limitations, the British proposals in fact favoured the French for two reasons. The first was that, as Loftus, the British ambassador in Berlin, recognised, 'It is not the actual army, but the Prussian system which is a standing menace to her neighbours.'[64] Roon and Moltke's successful use of reserves to create a mass army of almost a million men was now forcing all other continental powers to follow suit – and the strains upon the French economy were already telling. To limit the size of armies was thus to affect the relative striking power of Prussia, the creator of the new system and virtually the only state able to pay for it. This, of course, would fit in with Clarendon's personal desire to favour the French, his dislike of Prussian militarism, and his wish to 'freeze' the *status quo* – or at least to put off the unification of Germany until some indefinite time in the future.

The second, and closely related, reason why this proposal favoured the French concerns the Prussian side of the question: it would restrict Bismarck's capacity to achieve his political aims by *force majeure*. It is true that he often talked of a peaceful evolution towards German unity as an alternative to another war; and it is true that French policy itself was scarcely all that conciliatory, even before the announcement of the Hohenzollern candidature heightened mutual tensions. Nevertheless, while often carrying out a forward policy in other parts of the world, the French position over the German question was essentially defensive; Bismarck's, by contrast, was offensive and a freezing of the *status quo* would be for him an absolute defeat. By early 1870, moreover, his hopes of tempting the south German states into a union with the north seemed to have failed, and he was evidently considering afresh the possibility of bridging the gulf between north and south 'through a common war against the traditionally aggressive neighbour'.[65] His abortive scheme at this time to have Wilhelm named 'Kaiser' of Germany – something which Clarendon discouraged since it would clearly provoke the French – was a minor bid in the same direction and as such useful until the question of the Spanish succession provided a better pretext.

Finally, the arms reduction proposal might strike at the autonomy of the most important bastion of the autocratic Prussian system of government – the army: hence Bismarck's claim that he did not even dare mention Clarendon's scheme to Wilhelm. The king had not endured for years a domestic-political crisis concerning the size and disposition of his beloved army simply to have it affected now by a foreign trick, and the generals around him would be equally apoplectic at this civilian interference. That which Clarendon and Gladstone regarded as a distasteful excrescence upon the body politic of any nation was held by Prussia's leaders to be the most essential instrument of state and nationhood.[66] It was probably no great coincidence that the Prussian Liberals had been mounting another assault upon the military budget in this period – an assault which Bismarck was fiercely resisting but which Clarendon privately wished 'success to', for 'there is no other way of checking the enormous military expenditure, and restoring one or two hundred thousand men to useful pursuits'.[67] Predictably, the confidential discussions of 1869–70 about reduced armaments were soon dropped by London when Bismarck's objections became clear; but with this failure went a significant chance, perhaps the final chance, to arrest the rising tension between Frenchmen and Germans.

# CHAPTER 2

# From the Franco-Prussian War to the Fall of Disraeli (1870–80)

It is tempting to speculate whether the emphasis placed by historians upon the events of 1870–1 is not to some extent a retrospective exaggeration by later generations conscious of Germany's role in 1914 and 1939. The founding of the Second Reich did, indeed, mark a watershed – the most decisive for centuries in the history of central Europe – and it would be absurd to play down its significance. Yet, from the standpoint of the Anglo-German relationship at least, this occurrence marked a caesura neither in the diplomatic practices and assumptions of the two governments, nor in their assessment of the other country. The Franco-Prussian War was characterised by a continuation of previous trends: with, on the one hand, Bismarck seeing, through the isolation, provocation and defeat of an external enemy, to weld together a German nation under Prussian leadership; and on the other, Gladstone's government deploring the bloodshed but refusing to intervene with anything more than words so long as its own interests were not affected. In that sense, and in many other ways, it was a repetition of the war of 1866, although admittedly on a far larger scale: the defeat of France was an event which caused even the most dogmatic 'little Englanders' to raise their heads, while its effect upon the German population was naturally immense. Even so, it did not lead to a major reassessment of British external policy; and, both within and without Germany, it was to be a number of years before Bismarck's *kleindeutsch* solution was perceived to be permanent enough to vitiate centrifugal tendencies and to make further expansion unlikely.

Even if the war was seen by some observers to be a turning-point in European history, this in no way moved the British government to think of intervention.[1] Such a conflict had been likely for at least a decade, and London's position had not altered throughout that time – except in so far as the growing power of Prussia had made the British less concerned about French aggrandisement in the Rhineland. Only the ruthless invasion of Belgium by one side or the other could have affected this policy of British abstention, and when Granville, Clarendon's successor, secured fresh promises from Prussia and France to respect Belgian neutrality, even that prospect was excluded.[2] This non-interventionist policy was not abandoned during the discussions upon a possible mediation by third parties. Despite all his talk of Britain's 'good offices', even Gladstone saw that she 'must not move alone except when requested to do so by both parties';[3] but since Bismarck had 'bought off' Russia, and Austria-Hungary was paralysed by indecision, London would indeed be 'alone' if it tried to interfere. The transfer of Alsace-Lorraine, and especially its inhabitants, tested Gladstone's self-control rather more. Yet Granville, who privately agreed with him that it was 'a violent laceration', joined other ministers in overruling the Premier's wish for a diplomatic protest. While Gladstone declared that he had 'a great faith . . . in moral forces, and in their growing effect upon European politics', his more cautious Whig colleague was forced to remind him of the cruder realities of life: 'Palmerston wasted the strength derived by England from the great [that is, Napoleonic] war by his brag. I am afraid of our wasting it by laying down general principles when nobody will attend to them, and when in all probability they will be disregarded.'[4] Anxious though the British Cabinet was about the war, its regard for the isolationism of public opinion, awareness of Britain's own powerlessness and continued apprehension about relations with Russia and the United States combined to outweigh twinges of conscience over France's fate.

Because of this, it seems unlikely that Bismarck's attitude to England was much altered by these events. No doubt he, like many other Germans, was disappointed at this policy of neutrality and also resented the growing British sympathy for France; but, unlike his countrymen, he had long expected that the island state would wash its hands of continental affairs provided that Belgium was safeguarded. Naturally, he resented the sale of British arms to each side, and the various appeals to humanity and tolerance, since both, in his opinion, could benefit France more than Germany; and he ordered the press to write of England's 'fraudulent neutrality' and personally complained about the arms shipments.[5] Yet despite this, he did not wish to see a permanent worsening of Anglo-German relations. In the short term, it was vital to keep all neutrals happy and to prevent the war from becoming a general European one: hence his willingness to urge Russia to submit its abrogation of the Black Sea clauses of the Treaty of Paris to a conference when Odo Russell warned him in November 1870 that Britain would go to war on that issue.[6] In the long term, there seemed to Bismarck no real clash of interests with Britain, whereas France would be forever hostile; Austria-Hungary could not be trusted to have forgotten 1866; and Russia's friendliness would last as long as the present Tsar, if that. Although quiescent at the moment, the British lion might rediscover its old spirit later and become a useful partner, especially against France; and in the power-political world he had helped to create, it was a mistake to be too fastidious about whom one might hunt with in a few years' time.

If Anglo-German relations were not greatly impaired at the official level, this could not be said of their respective public opinions. A fuller analysis of public attitudes will be made below, but a brief synopsis may be appropriate here. In Britain there existed a recognisable group of pro-Germans, including the queen; an equally distinctive group of supporters of France; and a much larger body of non-interventionists. In Germany, there were Conservative and

23

National Liberal circles which bitterly attacked the treacherous and hypocritical policy of the British; but there were many Liberals who, while disappointed at English comments and actions, shared at least some of the British reservations about Bismarck's methods. On both sides the volume of criticism grew, as the British watched the despoliation of France and the Germans responded angrily to criticisms and 'un-neutral' acts. Yet all this needs to be set in its context: 'British disillusionment with Germany . . . had only begun and did not match the all-pervading dislike and mistrust of France before 1870';[7] and the roar of anger at Russia's denunciation of the Black Sea clauses showed which country the British still regarded as their chief enemy.[8] Similarly, the contempt for England shown by the German nationalists did not compare with the venom and bitterness directed at the *Erbfeind* of France.

Although it is easy to understand the German belief (held especially by its royal family) that 'England would have had it in her power to prevent this awful war, had she . . . declared she would take arms against the aggressor',[9] the objections to such a course were overwhelming. Whatever the convictions of British germanophiles and German anglophiles, an intimate Anglo-German relationship – let alone the alliance favoured by the Crown Prince – was not so 'obvious' and 'natural' to others. For every English voice sympathetic to the German case in 1870, there was, at least after Napoleon's fall, another favouring France; and every German complaint about Britain's lack of understanding was matched by French expressions of bewilderment that the island state was not intervening to assist its old Liberal ally! Both sides made, in London's opinion, unreasonable demands upon British neutrality. 'How can a neutral be warm?', wondered the queen upon learning that her tactful reference to 'two brave and great nations' had been greeted with dissatisfaction in Germany.[10]

In retrospect, it is more significant to note that this particular test of British neutrality concerned, not a distant conflict, but a fundamental foreign policy problem of how to react to the antagonism between her two nearest great power neighbours. The ideal solution would have been a harmonious threesome, but such are rarely equal and workable. To be sure, the British position of (usually) being wooed by the other two was preferable to the French or German situation; but it was still an immensely difficult one, and not made the less so by the clash of domestic opinions upon this subject. Viewed in long-term perspective, the decision made by the British government as to which side to favour appears to confirm the classical rules of the balance of power. In the eighteenth century, when a strong and ambitious France seemed to menace a weaker Germany, the latter received British support; in the twentieth century, when the relative strengths – and ambitions – of the two peoples was thought to be reversed, the direction of the British intervention was changed accordingly. The events of 1870–1 came, however, in the middle stage of this slow transformation, when the *tertius gaudens* had neither fully abandoned its suspicions of France nor fully appreciated the rising power of Germany.[11] Add to this the global and domestic reasons for non-intervention, and the fact that the Low Countries remained inviolate, and the neutral position of Britain appears much more understandable. But it was also understandable that she had to suffer what Lyons called 'the ordinary fate of neutrals'; and that the choice she made on that occasion in no way solved the longer-term dilemma.

Perhaps the greatest significance of the war for Anglo-German relations lay less in the stimulation of temporary press quarrels than in its long-term effects upon the internal politics of both countries. In the case of Britain, for example, the growth of Prusso-German power and the transformation of the European equilibrium without the British government being able to do anything about it had begun to provoke a rising tide of criticism from those who resented this 'humiliation' and enforced inactivity. The classical Gladstonian recipes of non-intervention, armaments reductions, colonial retrenchments, appeals to 'moral forces' and – to borrow a loaded term from another age – 'appeasement' in foreign affairs had already come under a sporadic but growing fire during the 1869–70 debates upon future links with the self-governing colonies and upon the government's refusal to force Russia to abandon its denunciation of the Black Sea controls.[12] This yearning for a less self-effacing stance may also be seen in the criticisms of the Liberal administration's policy towards France and Prussia. The most persistent of these critics was actually the queen herself, who, although opposing intervention in 1864, was distraught at the complacency of Clarendon and Stanley during the Austro-Prussian War and the later Franco-Prussian quarrels over Luxembourg and Belgium: 'England cannot remain a passive spectator . . . England . . . MUST NOT stand aloof; England must show the world that she is *not* prepared to abdicate her position as a great Power.'[13]

On the whole, the queen's desire for intervention was intended to benefit Prussia – as was the case with other pro-Germans such as Morier, who argued that 'a coalition between Britain and Germany' would have prevented the 1870–1 war;[14] but those favouring France also complained about the British government's passivity. Salisbury, who had disliked the fumbling over Schleswig-Holstein, now called for a more active diplomacy to forestall the transfer of Alsace-Lorraine: 'Is not the crisis worth some risk? . . . we fear that [the government] are yielding a mistaken obedience to the doctrines of a commercial school'. And the positivist Frederic Harrison, an odd bedfellow for the Cecil family in any other regard, yearned for a return to the more glorious days of Elizabeth, Cromwell and Marlborough as he agitated for intervention against the Prussian 'military despotism'.[15] Finally, there were those who, like Disraeli, were neither pro-German nor pro-French, but simply wished to restore England's importance *vis-à-vis* the rest of the world. 'I think myself . . . that we might begin to dictate a little to Europe', he encouraged Stanley in 1867. 'Gladstonism is at a discount.'[16] Yet, despite these sentiments, the facts pointed in the opposite direction to Disraeli's conclusion: Gladstonism was still strong; and the contradictory impulses of those who sought a more active policy cancelled each other out.

Thus, although the effects of this spreading sentiment of unease were far-reaching, it would be unwise to exaggerate their immediate significance. Moreover, even when Disraeli saw that this patriotic mood could be usefully orchestrated for electoral purposes, his advocacy of imperial issues tended if anything to drive Britain into conflicts with Russia and France rather than with

Germany. The point was less that these feelings of discontent pushed the country in an anti-German direction than that they indicated perhaps the first signs of a drift from liberalism, a touchiness about Britain's place in the world, and an apprehension about decline which – *if ever there should be a direct clash of Anglo-German interests in the future* – suggested that the British policy then might be much more vigorous than it had been with regard to the rise of Germany in the 1860s.

The same might be said, although with such equally necessary reservations, about the impact of the war upon Germany. With the victory over France and the creation of the Second German Empire, Bismarck had now squared all the circles. He had sustained conservatism by a compromise with the new economic interests, but he had checked liberalism by military successes and an extended suffrage; he had overcome particularism by provoking, and then defeating foreign foes, but had ensured that the *kleindeutsches* state of 1871 would respect the particular interests of Prussia; he had outwitted the traditionalists by tapping that massive strain of German nationalism, yet he had ensured that the bourgeois patriots were placed within a political framework which made them dependent upon an autocratic élite; he had begun his work by defending the constitutional claims – or pretensions – of the King of Prussia, overcome that crisis by the truly radical device of uniting and conquering the whole of Germany, yet never lost sight of the need to defend the king's claims. Finally, the war itself and its effects had given a further boost to the rapid industrial expansion of Germany without, however, displacing the pre-industrial leaders and attitudes of mind. Both the idealist-historicist philosophy of German nationalism, and the 'cultural pedigree' of the Junkers, had survived the turbulent events of the founding of the German Empire as a great military and industrial power.

The 'gap' between the dominant political traditions of the two countries was now wider than ever, therefore, with Bismarck confirmed in his success within Germany, and Gladstone convinced of the glorious future of reforming liberalism within Britain. The pre-1870 hopes of the Liberals in both countries that Anglo-German friendship was 'natural' was hard to sustain just so long as Bismarck continued in power – as Victoria and many others recognised when pinning their expectations upon the future regime of Crown Prince Frederick.[17] What was more, while the first German Chancellor was flexible enough not to show too much open hostility to England as a nation, this was less likely to be the case with those intellectuals, civil servants, merchants and other members of the middle classes who were now gripped by patriotic fervour. Having approved the attacks of the inspired press upon Britain's 'un-neutral' arms trade during the Franco-Prussian War, they would not forget this so readily; and, as noted above, the more they embraced nationalism and abandoned liberalism, the more scornful they became of England.[18] The calls which they were already making for colonies, for a large navy and for territorial boundaries which embraced all Europeans of Germanic stock might not be Bismarck's aims, but he would not last for ever; and, given the balance of forces within German society, his eventual going was as likely to be followed by 'national' policies as by 'liberal' ones.

But this is looking too far into the future. The decade of the 1870s was not one marked by a fundamental antagonism between Britain and Germany, or even by a steady rise in points of friction; it was characterised instead by the ebb and flow of the various elements which made up the relationship between two closely connected peoples. This could be seen, at a very personal level, in the very mixed attitudes of Gladstone and Disraeli towards Germany. Although the former delivered a powerful speech in 1871 against Chesney's pamphlet *The Battle of Dorking*, which had achieved 'best-seller' status through its lurid and imaginative tale of England being overrun by German troops, and although in 1875 he contributed to the *Kulturkampf* controversy by references to Germany as that land of Luther which 'still retained her primacy in the domain of conscience', it would be erroneous to conclude that Gladstone was pro-German.[19] His political sympathies, like those of most British Liberals, were with the beaten French, especially after the annexation of Alsace-Lorraine; and his distaste for Prussian military and political traditions was well known. Nevertheless, being so involved with domestic issues, Gladstone did not give much time to foreign affairs in these years, and Anglo-German relations were not a great concern of his: a temperate relationship, free of acrimony, was all that he asked.

Disraeli's best-known comment about Germany's rise appears at first sight to be far more hostile: 'The balance of power has been entirely destroyed, and the country which suffers most, and feels the effect of this great change most, is England.'[20] Yet while he pointed to the 'German revolution' of 1870–1 as the best illustration of how Britain had been ignored during great political changes, the Conservative leader did not harbour resentment of Berlin on this account. Bismarck, it was clear, had to be watched carefully, but Disraeli rather admired his formidable German colleague, shared few if any of the English Liberals' ideological suspicions of him, and slowly came to believe the Chancellor's claim that Germany was a 'satiated' power. When, moreover, Disraeli sought to turn British attention and energies towards extra-European regions, especially Asia, he hoped for at least benevolent neutrality from Berlin in the event of Anglo-Russian quarrels; and only a blatantly aggressive attempt by Germany to dominate its western neighbours would cause an alteration in the Conservative government's 'policy of reserve, but proud reserve . . . with respect to Europe'.

In other words, the perceptions of Germany held by these two British statesmen, and many of their followers, were not clear-cut and absolute, but complex and relative, being conditioned by a variety of factors; and precisely the same was true on the German side. The elder Moltke, for example, repeatedly informed Odo Russell that 'the peace of Europe could be secured by a close alliance between England and Germany'; but this Prussian-Conservative vision of two kindred and Protestant powers standing together was being ruined, the Field Marshall felt, by the inexplicable British preference for 'corrupt Catholic France'.[21] Ties of religion, race and culture, together with the more tangible prospect of surrounding the French, attracted Moltke to Britain; but its parliamentary institutions, dislike of militarism and Liberal sympathies towards France caused him to regard the island state with disappointment and disapproval. Any emphasis upon the first-named elements, as occurred during the *Kulturkampf*, always raised his hopes; any reminder of the last-named, such as the criticism in the British press at German 'sabre-rattling' against France, dashed them to the ground.

These mixed feelings towards Britain in the 1870s were shared by Bismarck himself.[22] Although always concerned with the tactical handling of political problems, he was also influenced by emotional and ideological considerations. The high esteem of Britons towards him was valued; racial and cultural ties were significant; and he was visibly gratified, for example, at the encouragement which Lord John Russell and other Protestants gave him during the *Kulturkampf*. But it was precisely because the Chancellor could be affected by non-diplomatic factors that he felt so strongly about developments in British politics in these years: the Liberal obsession with internal reforms, the undermining (as he saw it) of the established orders and privileges, the British government's tolerance of the revolutionary republican movement in Europe, were hardly likely to please a Prussian Junker concerned about the political and social stability of his own country. For the fact was that, however successful Bismarck's policies appeared to be, he was still extremely worried about the long-term threats to the Prusso-German conservative state. In his eyes, the future offered no security, only a constant – and, perhaps, ultimately futile – struggle against the forces of disruption: German particularism, especially in Hanover and the south, the Catholic Church with its international connections, the rapidly growing Social Democracy, and the disaffected Danes and Alsatians as well as the Poles. The importance of liberalism (especially of the Gladstonian variety) in this context was that by its practice of seeking to remove all reasonable grievances, it encouraged such forces; it was to Bismarck not only a pernicious form of politics on its own account, but also because it opened up a Pandora's box of many other movements which threatened the Conservative ascendancy. London's cool reply to his efforts to forge a common alliance against international socialism in 1871, for example, indicated the markedly different attitude of the two governments to the 'red peril'.[23]

These domestic-ideological elements were not separate from, but coincided with, Bismarck's foreign policy assumptions. The post-1871 period witnessed a rapid French recovery, and the concomitant efforts of the Quai d'Orsay to ensure that, when the next war with the Germans came, France would not be isolated. Bismarck's chief task was to make certain that, on the contrary, the French gained no allies; but that was now less easy than before, because of the suspicions to which the Chancellor's policies had given rise in the neighbouring capitals of Vienna and St Petersburg over the past decade. A close Anglo-German understanding would have been doubly welcome to Bismarck, therefore, because not only would it have deterred all French thoughts of revenge but it would also have prompted the Austrians to gravitate towards this London–Berlin axis. Yet the British would never play the leading role envisaged for them by the casting-master in Berlin. In vain did he proclaim that 'He loved England but it will not let itself be loved'; and his feelings were better represented by his testy remark on a later occasion that 'he had lost five years of his political life by the foolish belief that England was still a great power'.[24]

This did not mean that he was openly hostile to Britain in these years, but that he felt that the latter could not occupy a major place in his grand strategy, especially with Gladstone as Prime Minister.

The major thrust of Bismarckian diplomacy in these years was thus concentrated upon the creation of the *Dreikaiserbund*, by which he not only hoped to keep his eastern neighbours from each other's throats and from French embraces but he also bound the three emperors into a common stand against the forces of disruption within and without their respective territorial boundaries.[25] Yet this very emphasis upon a conservative-monarchical coalition marked a further drift away from Gladstonian England and provoked many a Liberal journal in London to refer unflatteringly to the revival of the reactionary Holy Alliance. Even so, this was not a fundamental breach; and some future development – a diplomatic crisis, the return of the monarchy to France, or a change of administration in London or Berlin – could lead to a closer political and diplomatic relationship.

The years 1875–6 furnish a good example of this complex, shifting pattern of Anglo-German relations, involving serious discussions of an alliance only half a year after British alarm at the rumours of a German assault upon France! Indeed, the advent of Disraeli's administration early in 1874 had already led to a change in Bismarck's attitude, which welcomed the Conservatives for both diplomatic and ideological reasons. Such sentiments were reciprocated by the new Foreign Secretary, the 15th Earl of Derby, who felt 'we ought to look to the German Empire as the state with which we have most in common. Germany has no interest hostile to ours in the East. Germany does not threaten Belgium . . . A strong Germany, keeping down at once the ultramontane and the red factions, is what we want in the general interest of Europe. This Bismarck has given us.'[26] As for the new Prime Minister, he declared that Britain and Germany should always go hand in hand because they shared common interests and views, race and religion.[27] This was Disraelian hyperbole, but it no doubt sounded better to German ears than Liberal moralising – to which might be added the not inconsiderable fact that Russian advances upon Merv and the French attitude over Zanzibar and Egypt made the Conservatives naturally incline towards Germany, whose chief contribution to world affairs Derby had always generously envisaged as being the curbing of the extra-European pretensions of St Petersburg and Paris.

There was only one proviso to this vision of Anglo-German harmony: that Bismarck should not provoke 'an aggressive and an unnecessary war' against France.[28] Yet almost as soon as they had entered office, the Conservatives were warned by Odo Russell of Berlin's expectation of another Franco-German conflict. This itself was not news to London: the post-1871 years had abounded with rumours about a German assault upon France, or the annexation of the Netherlands, or the fulfilment of the pan-German dream of taking over Austria; for it was difficult to believe that a state which had expanded so swiftly was now content with the territorial *status quo* in Europe. But by early 1875 a full-blown Franco-German crisis was at hand, intensified (in British eyes) by Bismarck's threatening tone towards Belgium over religious matters. This was enough to cancel at a stroke all those factors which had operated in

Germany's favour within Britain; and, to judge by St Petersburg's reaction, within Russia too.

The details of the combined Anglo-Russian representations to Bismarck are covered in most studies of this period.[29] Although significant, it is worth stressing that the incident did not denote an irremediable deterioration in Anglo-German relations – if only because Bismarck denied all intention of molesting France and blamed the whole affair upon the newspapers. The Chancellor was certainly resentful when he learnt that London had asked other powers to assist by putting pressure upon Berlin, and he angrily noted that 'if England had deployed but one-tenth of its present ardour to stop the French attack in 1870, that bloody war could well have been avoided';[30] but it was the Russian pressure which was the most evident and ominous, and which gave Bismarck more cause for concern and resentment. What the incident *did* indicate, as one scholar points out, is that 'the endangering of the European balance through a hegemonial policy' would be seen by London as a challenge which must be answered politically and, perhaps, militarily.[31] One is compelled to add 'perhaps' to this judgement, since Derby himself felt that all depended upon Russia and, as ever, he was not eager to commit the country to a substantial intervention.[32] Disraeli, on the other hand, was keen to use this opportunity to restore Britain's place among the great powers, and his imperial mistress felt that the 'overbearing, violent, grasping and unprincipled' Bismarck was becoming 'like the first Napoleon whom Europe had to join in *putting* down . . . *no one* will tolerate any Power wishing to dictate to all Europe'.[33]

This mention of 'the first Napoleon' renewed in more intensified form the debate which had occurred in 1871. Within a decade a massive new power had arisen in west-central Europe, often through means regarded as unorthodox by the established states. Was it now going to settle down peacefully; or would it, as Odo Russell believed, strive instead for 'the supremacy of Germany in Europe and of the German race in the world'?[34] Even if the latter was not consciously premeditated, might not further expansion come about as a consequence of tensions and wars which, given the efficiency of its military machine, Germany would most probably win? If this contingency was to be avoided, much would depend upon the way in which the Germans conducted themselves politically and militarily; and, in the early 1870s at least, the signs were not always encouraging. The British, to be sure, were pompously secure in their island refuge; but they did perceive that the actual *manner* of conducting politics was important, especially for a new and expanding state, if it was not to bring unending suspicion upon itself. Derby put this nicely when he observed that Bismarck's scare-mongering was 'fast leading moderate men to doubt whether the German Empire is consistent with repose and security for any other European state. That does not seem to be the impression which it is in his interest to create.'[35] Even if, as Professor Hillgruber suggests, the Chancellor's strategy in 1875 was fundamentally defensive, warding off the potential threats to the new Reich, the offensive tactics employed were bound to alarm the other powers.[36] It was, Morier felt, 'the business of a giant [like Germany] to be good-natured and tractable, above all not to have nervous fits . . . A hysterical giant was a terrible neighbour to a company of pigmies.'[37] Viewed from this longer-term perspective, a stable and conciliatory diplomacy was perhaps a better form of true Realpolitik than a vigorous display of energy and touchiness; but a new nation, like a youthful warrior, is rarely attracted to the path of caution and moderation.

It was a testimony to Bismarck's percipience that he drew the correct lessons from these events and sought to forestall any realisation of his *cauchemar de coalitions* by assuring the great powers that Germany was inherently peaceful. In 1875 he recognised, as one historian has put it, that his past achievements 'could only be jeopardised by pressing for further expansion of German power'.[38] Fortunately for him, his protestations that he sought no war with France were almost immediately followed by a fresh and prolonged crisis in the Eastern Question, which inevitably attracted elsewhere the attention of Russia and Britain. By the time that that crisis was 'stabilised' in the early 1880s, interest would then be switching to colonial and naval rivalries, and it would be another thirty years before the question of Germany's latent capacity to dominate west-central Europe assumed as critical a form as it had in the 'war-in-sight' crisis of 1875. Almost by definition, therefore, the lengthy absence of this issue from diplomatic calculation (apart from tremours during the Boulanger years) ensured that one likely cause for Anglo-German estrangement remained only latent as well.

For a variety of reasons, the crisis over the future of Turkey which dominated European politics between 1875 and 1879 was accompanied by spasmodic consultations between the British and German governments about the possibility of some form of understanding or alliance.[39] The chief advocate of this *rapprochement* was Bismarck himself, for it was clear to him by this time that his efforts to stabilise the European power balance – in Germany's favour, naturally – were becoming increasingly difficult. France would not, and could not, be suppressed; and the *Dreikaiserbund*'s chief function, of keeping Austria-Hungary and Russia in a harmony which was controlled by Berlin, was collapsing. British support for Germany in these circumstances was not only welcome but, with the advent of Disraeli, quite possible; the new Prime Minister's assertiveness during the 'war-in-sight' crisis had just been confirmed by his purchase of the Suez Canal shares, and he was obviously determined to have a say in Turkish affairs. A combined Anglo-German presidency over the dissolution of the Turkish Empire, offering bits of booty to the others (and Egypt to the British), or even an Anglo-German alliance in the event of complications and opposition from another state, would be equally useful alternatives to the Chancellor now that he sensed that his original diplomatic structure was breaking down.

To Disraeli, these approaches from Bismarck in early and mid-1876 were most tempting. Not only was the Prime Minister manifestly eager to be consulted upon matters of European diplomacy, but he could see that an Anglo-German alliance would 'spring' the *Dreikaiserbund*, which had tended to isolate Britain and to reduce her influence. Moreover, such an agreement would check the Russians, certainly at Constantinople, and perhaps further afield also. Thus Disraeli was willing, in October 1876, to contemplate an

Anglo-German alliance, and was openly impatient when Berlin then appeared to be in no hurry about the matter. In this he was vociferously supported by the queen, to whom her late husband's dream of a strong link between London and Berlin at last seemed within grasp.[40] This eagerness, it may be noted, in no way contradicted Disraeli's attitude of the previous year, when he had been willing to enter into an alliance against Germany. In the first place, the whole theory of 'checks and balances' to preserve the European equilibrium presumed a flexible policy on the part of a 'flank' power such as Britain.[41] Furthermore, since his entire political purpose was to restore a Palmerstonian age now shrouded in myth, anything which furthered that aim – and a proposed coalition to frustrate Russian expansionism clearly qualified – was not to be ignored. Beside serving the 'national interests', it nicely fitted in with his whole style of politics, involving gesture and symbolism and striking acts.[42]

Yet the enthusiasm of the Prime Minister was not enough. Derby, predictably, was not keen to respond to Bismarck's approach. A friendly relationship with a fellow-Protestant state, and a willingness to discuss joint measures to preserve the peace of Europe, was one matter; a binding alliance was another. Not only might it provoke strong reactions from the public, for which the Foreign Secretary had an enormous deference, but he doubted whether there could ever be 'a complete understanding between the military despotism of Berlin, and a free and pacific community such as ours'.[43] Furthermore, in his eyes the European balance was an automatically self-regulating mechanism – Russia's actions in 1875 had confirmed that – and there was therefore no need for Britain to carry out an interventionist policy à la Palmerston when others would do this task in any case. Finally, Derby had come to distrust Bismarck more and more: 'I fear his only object just now is to embroil us, or Russia, or Austria, or any other Power, no matter which: so long as a general good understanding is prevented, the result he works for is achieved.'[44]

However formidable his reputation as an opponent of any 'forward' policy, Derby alone would not have frustrated an Anglo-German alliance had all the other indications been favourable. What happened was that Bismarck himself, by his actions in this period, assisted in cooling the ardour of Disraeli and Victoria. In the first place, the Chancellor had been noticeably reticent early in 1876 about what *he* would do in the event of a deterioration in the Eastern Question. Then, the British government's wish to see Turkey preserved ruined the Bismarckian idea that London and Berlin might preside over a diplomatic 'carve-up'; yet it also suggested to his capacious and flexible mind *either* that Britain might support Austria-Hungary in the Balkans, thus relieving Germany of that burden, *or* that an Anglo-Russian conflict (preferably without any other belligerents) might occur, once again permitting Berlin to maintain its freedom of action. Hence, in part, the Chancellor's lengthy retreat to the country during the Bulgarian crisis of September 1876, when Disraeli was so anxious to know the German attitude. Thirdly, Bismarck confirmed Derby's deepest fears by asking in January 1877 whether Britain would be benevolently neutral if the formation of an anti-German coalition between Russia and France were to lead to another war in western Europe. Such a possibility, with the overrunning of France and even the Low Countries as its most likely outcome, always made London more cautious. The bland British answer, that it would always be ready to lend its *moral* support to Germany to preserve peace, was therefore easy to foresee although the Chancellor pretended to receive this message with deep disappointment, declaring that 'one of his fondest political dreams had been an active and intimate alliance with England', but that 'his repeated offers . . . met with so little encouragement'. Now, without the assurance of British *material* support, Germany would have no alternative but to keep France and Russia divided by diplomatic means, which implied giving support to the latter's Balkan policy.[45]

Moreover, despite his avowed support for Turkey and his concern about the threat to British possessions in Asia, Disraeli himself did not totally excude the possibility of an Anglo-Russian understanding in these years. Such a solution, if genuine, was preferable to the arduous policy of seeking to isolate Russia diplomatically or to meet her militarily; and it was bound to receive the support of Derby, who suspected that Germany secretly sought to engineer an Anglo-Russian war. On the other hand, it would cause Bismarck to fear that he was being outmanoeuvred. Thus, to a large extent the Anglo-German diplomatic negotiations in the late 1870s were tending to revolve around Russia. Both powers, fearing her capacity to harm them, wished to stand well with her; but, unable to be assured of this benevolence and fearing a Russian understanding with either France or Austria-Hungary, they also looked to each other for support; yet both were suspicious of being pushed by the other against the Tsarist colossus. Neither Bismarck nor Disraeli, it has been shown, was willing to become the other's tool; but in actual fact neither was fully successful, for London could not improve its relationship with St Petersburg and Berlin could not revive the *Dreikaiserbund* at this time.[46]

When the Eastern Question approached its peak late in 1877, Britain's stance tested Bismarck's diplomacy to the full. As he himself kept remarking, 'We can bear a break between Russia and England better than one between Russia and Austria' – a useful reminder of Britain's place in his scale of diplomatic priorities.[47] Yet, although he felt that a lasting peace in this affair was 'not in Germany's interests',[48] he also feared that an Anglo-Russian war might escalate into a European conflagration with unfavourable consequences for Germany; it was an open question, for example, how long Vienna would stay out of such a war. Thus, the Chancellor felt bound, just as in November 1870, to attempt to mediate between the two 'flank' powers even if such intervention, in the form of calling the Congress of Berlin, meant taking sides. The overall result of the Congress, therefore, was a temporary victory for Disraeli, not so much because of the actual Balkan settlement but because Bismarck had been forced to support the Anglo-Austrian position, which St Petersburg bitterly resented. While acknowledging the tributes to his role as the 'honest broker', the Chancellor was privately aware that Germany's basic diplomatic dilemma remained. Clearly, a new strategy had to be evolved, one which would improve Germany's position, replace London's influence over Vienna by that of Berlin, and bring the increasingly belligerent Russian press to its senses. For all these reasons, Bismarck now came to argue in favour of an Austro-German military alliance, with the possibility of British adhesion.

While Bismarck's change of front here has primarily to be viewed in diplomatic terms, it is not too fanciful to see certain connections with the reorientation of his domestic policies in the late 1870s.[49] At home, the *Kulturkampf* had proved a disaster, and the Chancellor was now willing to contemplate a compromise with Catholicism. At the same time, his parliamentary alliance with the National Liberals had proved unsatisfactory and he was eager to break with them, taking with him that section of the party which would accommodate itself to his whims. The National Liberals would be divided, he calculated, over the anti-socialist legislation which was introduced after the excuse provided by the attempted assassinations upon the Kaiser; by the return of protectionism, which heavy industry and agriculture were now demanding in consequence of the business depression and falling prices; and by the introduction of a social insurance scheme, which would offend *laissez-faire* tenets but could possibly cement the loyalty of the working classes to the state.

These various actions of the German government in the years 1878–9, some of which were regarded by bewildered Liberals as almost revolutionary, were simply the use of new means for an old end: the shoring-up of the Prussian monarchical establishment. Socialism would be crushed by legislation, but the workers seduced by measures of social welfare; a compromise would be made with the Centre Party, while liberalism was driven to the wall; big business would be placated by protectionism, and the Junkers also would see that their economic salvation lay only in the state. The whole accent was one of increased conservatism, consolidation, introspection – combined with suppression of the forces of disruption. There is some connection here, surely, with Bismarck's parallel manoeuvres in foreign policy. Even if it is not possible to show conclusively that his 1879 alliance bid to Vienna contained the intention of creating a central European customs union,[50] it is clear that the ending of the *Kulturkampf* made an Austro-German understanding easier; and it is also apparent that he was hoping to reinforce the Conservative, pro-German circles in Russia and to check the panslavic forces (which he equated with 'revolution'[51]) by the creation of a solid Austro-German bloc, with which it would be necessary to come to terms. Internally and externally, the bulwarks of Prussian conservatism were being strengthened.

Although the Austro-German alliance of 1879 has been seen as instigating the era of binding treaty commitments and the division of Europe into power blocs in peacetime, it was also a short-term Bismarckian device to regain the diplomatic initiative. The prospect of Russian animosity forced him to take precautions but his essential aim was not so much to isolate his eastern neighbour as to 'strengthen his position in relation to Russia in order to bring her to terms – to return to the *Dreikaiserbund* under his leadership and the less erratic policy this implied'.[52] It was not prudent to let the Austrians know of this; nor the British; nor his imperial master, who fought bitterly against what he imagined was 'the parting of the ways' with St Petersburg. Yet, as soon as Russia had indicated that it wished to patch up its differences with Berlin and had no plan to move closer to France, Bismarck was willing to encourage the idea of a *rapprochement*.

It is from this standpoint that his alliance 'bid' to Britain in 1879 must be viewed.[53] When first suggesting it to Disraeli, Bismarck still feared that his relationship with Russia would deteriorate further, in which case an Austro-German-British alliance would fortify Berlin's position; but the very threat of such an accord would also serve his secret aim of bringing the Russians to their senses, which indeed it did. Even before Münster had reported upon the initial British reactions to Bismarck's approach, the government in St Petersburg was holding out the olive branch to Berlin. The change in Russian policy obviously required further exploration, but even these first hints were sufficient to cool Bismarck's ardour for an Anglo-German alliance – news of the signing of which, he felt, would permanently alienate the Russians. Faced with the choice of a revived *Dreikaiserbund* and a disappointed Britain, or an Austro-German-British alliance (from which the last-named might defect in the future) and an enraged Russia, Bismarck would always plump for the former. His aim, as he put it, was to 'dig a ditch' between Austria-Hungary and the west, not between Russia and Germany.

Seen from this viewpoint, the British reactions to Bismarck's soundings had lost their importance even before the Chancellor learned of them. Disraeli, still strongly desirous of breaking up the *Dreikaiserbund*, was certainly willing to contemplate an alliance that would hold Russia in check; with regard to France, he felt, Britain would be able to keep her quiet in the event of a war breaking out among the three eastern monarchies. This was a major concession by a British statesman, although Bismarck later was to declare that it was insufficient. As it was, the mere mention of France was enough to cause the queen, Salisbury and Northcote to hesitate. Victoria feared that an alienated France might be goaded into an alliance with Russia and Italy. Salisbury, as suspicious as his predecessor of Bismarck, found it difficult to believe that Britain would not try to assist Vienna in the event of Russian aggression, in which case a fixed alliance with Berlin was unnecessary and simply provoked the French. On the other hand, the announcement of the Austro-German alliance itself could only be welcomed, since it checked Russia (or seemed to) without putting Britain in the front line or harming Anglo-French relations: little wonder that Salisbury publicly declared its signing to be 'good tidings of great joy'.

Disappointed that Bismarck refused to discuss the matter again after his first soundings, Disraeli also came to accept this line of reasoning. It would have been 'a difficult, and even dangerous affair to have altogether rejected the contemplated alliance', although Britain did not want to be pushed against France, he informed the queen; as things turned out, Anglo-German relations remained cordial but Her Majesty's Government was 'as free as air'.[54] In the short term, it appeared that Britain had again triumphed, in that Germany, and not it, had been pushed into openly siding against Russia; in the longer term, the episode forced the Russians to repair their fences with Germany, tied Vienna firmly to Berlin and away from London, and thus hastened the return of Britain's diplomatic isolation – all of which, needless to say, could be accompanied by expressions of regard for the island state by the German Chancellor.

All this suggests that, in diplomatic affairs at least, the British and German governments occupied a rather similar position in the late 1870s, which was made even more alike by the fact that their political leaders were flexible and undogmatic about the tactics they employed to achieve their respective aims. Both wished for security against a coalition of other powers, and were conscious of the perils to which a too-obvious position of isolation exposed them; both were seeking to direct the course of European diplomacy to ensure that it did not prejudice their own security or weaken their domestic-political prestige; both saw the other as a potentially useful and friendly state since their interests did not directly clash, and wished to gain the other's aid in the event of a grave emergency. Yet neither saw a firm Anglo-German friendship as a political absolute; 'normal' relations were one thing, but a tighter bond would depend upon diplomatic circumstances, that is, upon the role of third parties. Britain did not want an Anglo-German alliance at the expense of France; Germany did not want one at the cost of Russian friendship. It was to be expected, therefore, that they were sometimes manoeuvring in harmony with, and sometimes against, the other's policies.

In looking retrospectively at the whole sweep of Anglo-German relations from 1860 until 1880, it is clear that the most important change lay in the shift in the relative power positions of the two countries. On the German side, the transformation wrought in those two decades upon the former chaotic tangle of greater and lesser states was so momentous that it was bound to dominate the consciousness of all upper and middle-class Germans, whether old Conservatives, fervent nationalists or bitter particularists. Whatever the flaws in the Prusso-German state created in 1871, there were few who felt that progress had *not* been made and many who rejoiced at the realisation of their fondest political dream. 'What happiness it is to be a German in days such as these and to live to see such a great time', exulted one typical commentator.[55] Moreover, if the first decade testified to Germany's military qualities, the following one bore witness to the central diplomatic position achieved by Berlin. Under these circumstances, was it all that surprising for even the Crown Princess to declare that 'Prussian *Wesen*, discipline, habits etc. etc., is now appreciated and . . . its superiority acknowledged' whereas France was finished and so might her dear England be one day if it followed those Gallic habits of 'immoderate frivolity and luxury'; for Treitschke to look forward to Germany's future growth; and for other nationalists to speculate upon the acquisition of colonies and a navy?[56] Despite the considerable domestic problems, a glorious future surely beckoned in international affairs.

The transformation in Britain's external position was less marked in those twenty years, but still attracted speculation. The impression that London had been humiliated in 1864 and ignored by Europe during the following six years provoked a certain amount of unease in those circles which interested themselves in foreign affairs. Yet such fears were not widespread, and there were many who argued that a strong and united Germany had actually been of benefit to Britain's European policy. Even those who sounded the alarm clearly believed that all that was required was the reassertion of a sturdier, more forthright diplomacy. Kinglake, for example, rejoiced at the notoriety gained by Chesney's 'Battle of Dorking' pamphlet, for it had conveyed a 'much-needed warning';[57] Disraeli held that Britain could and should be the diplomatic leader of Europe, throwing its weight into the balance with traditional Palmerstonian dash (an assumption which the events of 1875 and 1878 seemed in some measure to justify); while Gladstone and the progressive Liberals felt that all talk of decline was a ruse, intended to upset the movement for domestic reform and military retrenchment. Even if, at the economic level, the *Annual Register* of 1867 was warning 'that the English . . . may, at no distant time, lose their position through the neglect of ordinary precautions', the fact remained that in 1870 Britain contained 31.8 per cent of the world's manufacturing capacity compared with Germany's 13.2 per cent.[58] In other words, while we may notice a relative British decline in the period 1860–80, identify certain early expressions of concern and see in them the forerunners of that veritable chorus of alarmists around the turn of the century, it would be unwise to exaggerate their significance.

The same warning can be made apropos of the rise of the Anglo-German antagonism – by which is meant here a fundamental clash of interests and a strong distrust exhibited by the decision makers and public in both countries against the other. This, despite mutual criticisms, was not the case in 1870 or 1880. At the political and diplomatic level, the Anglo-German relationship was rather negative in tone; given the circumstances, that was perhaps inevitable. Yet, as Derby remarked,[59] at least Germany knew that Britain would not make war on her, and the reverse was equally true. London occasionally worried about a conflict with Russia, or even with France or the United States. Berlin more frequently worried about a war with France, or with Russia, or even with Austria-Hungary. There was never any thought of an Anglo-German war, and that in itself was a significant fact. Within another twenty years or so, however, the prospect of a direct conflict would emerge. It would be partly due to diplomatic reasons, to an intensification of the inter-state manoeuvrings as each side sought not to be outwitted by the other; but much more due to non-diplomatic factors, to certain *forces profondes* of late-nineteenth-century Britain and Germany. In order to be able later to assess the nature of those forces, and the role they played within the Anglo-German relationship, it is necessary at this point to penetrate beneath the world of chancellories and ambassadors and diplomatic documents which has engaged our attention so far.

# PART TWO

## The Structure of the Anglo-German Relationship in the Age of Bismarck and Gladstone

The function of this section deserves a brief explanation. It is not intended here to present the Anglo-German relationship in its *totality*, for it would be difficult to know where to commence and, even more, where to stop. The following half-dozen chapters have the more modest aim of focusing upon those aspects of the relationship which contemporaries, and later historians, thought were important influences upon the *political* connection. Inevitably, such commentators differed about the weight to be attached to each of these aspects, and it has been difficult in the present work also not to put them in some order of priority and to pass judgement upon their relative significance. Nevertheless, the chief purpose of these chapters has simply been to provide evidence and analyses of, say, the role of the press or of the monarchy in the years when Bismarck and Gladstone were at their zenith; and a more detailed commentary upon the importance to be attached to each of these background factors has been reserved until later in this book, when it will also be possible to measure how far they altered by the first decade of the twentieth century.

A second remark may also be necessary about what follows: the isolation of any one 'strand' from the seamless web of the past obviously produces a historical distortion. It has been done here for the purpose of seeing more clearly the form and the dimensions of each particular strand. Even when this exercise is carried out, it is impossible not to refer to other aspects which relate to that under scrutiny; and it scarcely needs emphasising that, however important the reader holds any one of them to be, it is always necessary to recall its place in the wider context.

# CHAPTER 3

# Anglo-German Economic Ties

Commercial links between the British and German peoples had originated in the mists of time, flourished under the Hanse merchants and continued through the age of Dutch trading supremacy, mercantilist doctrines and the *Kabinettskriege* of the eighteenth century. This trade had been distorted, but never totally blocked by the military occupations and economic warfare of the period 1793–1815, but after Waterloo it resumed at an even more hectic pace then before. To the producers, merchants and customers of both sides, Anglo-German commerce was highly significant. It was also markedly unbalanced. In the early years of the *Zollverein*, for example, the Germans were the best customers for British goods, taking one-third of all exports to Europe – more, indeed, than the exports to France, Russia, Sweden, Denmark, Spain, Portugal and a half-dozen other states together. Restricted by historical and geographical circumstances to a purely European field of action, German merchants were heavily dependent upon the importation of such wares as sugar, spices, coffee, tobacco, silk and cotton, which were mainly produced in the British colonies or, if they were not, at least were traded through London to form the core of that city's entrepôt commerce; they also relied upon certain raw materials produced in Britain itself, such as coal, lead and wool; and they imported in ever-increasing amounts finished woollens, cotton cloth, pewter, wrought iron and pottery. As certain regions of Germany began to industrialise, it was also necessary to import steam engines, textile machines, locomotives, rails and other manufactures – as well as the engineers and workmen to use them. By contrast, there was little that the British needed from Germany in the way of manufactures, and it was not until the abolition of the Corn Laws that German agricultural produce could penetrate the British market. The flow of Anglo-German economic traffic in the century before 1860 was, therefore, very much in the nature of a 'one-way street'.[1]

If British goods predominated in the balance of trade between the two countries, the great German contribution came in terms of the *personnel* engaged in such commerce. The textile revolution in the late eighteenth century had drawn a number of German merchants (including N. M. Rothschild & Sons) to the northern industrial towns, where they purchased cloth to send to their parent-firms and other customers within Germany. A second wave of German merchants and financiers moved into Britain during

41

the Napoleonic War, hoping thereby to keep their international businesses going. By around 1840, in fact, there were eighty-four German merchant houses in Manchester and twenty-five in Bradford; and by that time, too, German firms were supplying about 60 per cent of the capital for British-European trade. In addition, a whole army of German clerks and travelling salesmen were working for British companies, either in the home offices or on the continent. This migration of Germans 'brought valuable reserves of entre-preneurial experience to Britain' and helped to make its industrialisation a *European* process in which they contributed their experience, 'much as British enterprise was contributing to the development of commerce and industry on the Continent and in the newly-developing regions of the world'.[2]

This basic economic structure helps to explain the very varied attitudes which specific groups of people within each country had towards the other, quite irrespective of those political and diplomatic considerations which influ-enced official policy. Many a small German manufacturer, together with the various guilds of craftsmen and the out-workers in the textile trades, agitated strongly against the flooding of the country with cheaper and (usually) superior British goods, against the importation by businessmen of textile machinery, the fresh competition brought by new railway links, and so on; and these essentially selfish protests were clothed with patriotic arguments by intellectu-als such as Friedrich List, advocating a '*National* System of Political Economy' and urging higher tariffs to protect the infant German industries from the competition of their fully grown British equivalents.[3] In List's later years, however, the mid-century boom and the further liberalisation of trade seemed to undermine his arguments, which were by then being vigorously contested by John Prince-Smith and other German advocates of unrestricted free trade.[4] In any case, protectionist arguments could gain little sympathy among all those who acted as middlemen for British imports, the entrepreneurs who wished to buy the new machinery, the merchants and shippers of Hamburg, the bankers of Frankfurt and elsewhere who financed this trade, those engaged in export-ing grain and timber to Britain from the Baltic ports, and – last but not least – the Junkers, who found a fresh market for their superfluous agricultural produce after Peel abandoned the Corn Laws in 1846 and who did not want to pay the tariffs upon either imported agricultural machinery or luxuries. When one adds to all this the Prussian government's repeated trick of reducing the *Zollverein*'s tariffs so as to make it impossible for Austria to join that body, then it is clear to see why protectionism in Germany seemed a dying cause by 1860.

British attitudes towards Germany in the first half of the nineteenth century had also been affected by these commercial trends. The importance of this region as a market for British produce, the mediating role of so many Anglo-German mercantile and banking families, the steady reduction in the *Zoll-verein*'s tariffs, and the absence of any substantial German competition in the British home market, generally made for good relations. Some industrialists, it is true, worried about the future of their trade within Germany or about a nascent German challenge, but these fears were usually confined to what might be termed the 'less advanced' sectors of the economy: for example, while the exporters of textile machines enjoyed increasing sales, the English and Scottish textile industry had sought in vain to prevent the creation of rival factories within Germany. More significant, in political terms, had been the creation of the *Zollverein* itself, for its aim of internal free trade might be accompanied by ever higher tariffs against the goods of foreign states. For this reason, and although proclaiming its wish not to interfere 'with the internal concerns of other nations', the British government had generally tried to encourage the German states and cities to stay out of the *Zollverein*[5] – a policy which, of course, contradicted its political desire to encourage German unity and only confirmed the suspicions of German nationalists that Liberal England's pious claims to be acting for the general good were belied by its official policy. By mid-century, this incipient rivalry had largely died away, although some of the older suspicions lingered on.

The general pattern of this economic relationship prior to 1860, marked by Britain's great superiority and Germany's relative 'retardation', did not appear to be significantly altered in the years following Bismarck's appointment as Prussian Prime Minister. In terms of total population, of course, the Germans had long enjoyed a lead. In 1860 the British population totalled 29 million; in 1870, 31 million; and in 1880, 35 million.[6] In 1860, Prussia's population totalled 18·5 million; but there were also 19·5 million in the other German states, and 31·7 million in the multinational Austrian Empire. By 1871, when the 'German question' had been settled in Prussia's favour, the new Reich totalled 41 million and by 1880 it had increased to 45 million, with numbers still rising fast. For centuries, political divisions had tended to cancel out the fact that the Germans were so populous; now, their sheer size – second only in population in Europe to Russia – was obvious to all. This was, moreoever, an age in which it was first being realised that industrialisation could harness the productivity, and military conscription could utilise the power, which had always been potential in a large population; and it was also an age in which progressivist and Social Darwinist notions were giving to birth-rate trends a significance which they had never previously possessed.

Yet the political and military power implicit in a large population was only a *potential* power. To compare the crude population totals of Britain and Germany does not offer much of an insight into their economic strength or political influence: even the creation and effectiveness of mass armies depended more upon the political assumptions and the technological-administrative efficiency of government than upon sheer numbers. More significant figures are the degree of industrialisation and the productivity of each state. In 1871, for example, the percentage of the markedly smaller British population living in towns was 54·5, whereas in the more populous Germany it was only 36·1; the horse-power employed in British industry was just over 4 million, in Germany it was almost 2·5 million; and the *total* British national income was 50 per cent larger than that of Germany – *per head of population*, of course, it was almost twice as large. All this simply signifies that Britain was still a lot wealthier and produced a lot more than Germany, which is scarcely surprising when it is recalled that the former country then contained no less than 31·8 per cent of the world's manufacturing capacity whereas the latter possessed but 13·2 per cent.

This difference is confirmed by reference to specific industries. In coal, for example, Germany's production of 34 million tons per annum put her clearly in second place in the world league, but it was well behind Britain's total of 112 million tons; her pig iron production of 1·3 million tons was similarly dwarfed by Britain's 6 million tons, which was greater than all the rest of the world's production put together; even in the newer steel industry, the British annual output of 0·7 million tons was more than double Germany's 0·3 million tons; and her annual consumption of raw cotton – a little under 600,000 tons – was almost five times as large as the German total of 116,000 tons.[7] The same proportions were to be seen in foreign trade, Britain's share of world trade in 1870 being 25 per cent and Germany's 9·7 per cent. In absolute terms, this meant that British foreign trade in that year was worth the staggering sum of £547 million (1880: £698 million), and the value of Germany's foreign trade was a very creditable £212 million (1880: £294 million).[8]

Two points need to be made about these crude figures. The first is that, on the whole, they confirm what contemporaries assumed – that Britain was still a 'special case', and that, as the *Annual Register* had claimed, her great influence in the world was due 'not to military successes, but to her commanding position in the arena of industry and commerce'.[9] It thus helps to explain later why the British believed that there was no good reason to alter their commercial practices and fiscal policies even during the Great Depression, whereas the instinctive German reaction was to protect what they had already attained from the competition of commercially stronger rivals. The second point is that, despite the 'gap' that undoubtedly existed between the British and German economies, these rather simple statistics offer little indication of certain *qualitative* differences which were already beginning to occur between the two countries. The British pattern of heavy reliance upon the earnings of a few basic industries remained fairly constant throughout the 1870s, whereas it was in those years that Germany was laying the foundations for important newer industries: chemicals, electricals, optics, advanced machine-tools. It was significant that, of all the comparative statistics given above, the 'gap' was narrowest in steel production, itself a new industry. It was also narrow in regard to total railway mileage: Britain had 24,500 miles compared with Germany's 19,500 in 1870, but within another decade or so the latter country was to forge ahead. This was an indication of its concentration upon the economic development of its secure *domestic* market, and it is noticeable that the comparative statistics for merchant shipping (Britain possessed 5.6 million tons in 1870 to Germany's 0·9 million tons) reveal a far wider margin. Even at the time of the Franco-Prussian War, the massive imbalances in Britain's visible trade were being covered by the earnings from shipping, insurance, banking and especially the receipts from foreign investment;[10] in other words, the real growth areas in her economy were already in the 'service' industries of the City of London (and also in commercial retailing). Germany, by contrast, represented a much 'tighter' economy, less dependent upon world commerce, possessing a far less acute 'gap' in visible trade, still investing heavily in large-scale industries at home rather than in public utilities or government bonds abroad, with more state control over, and intervention in, such important areas as railways, banking and tariffs, and with private industry itself becoming ever more cartelised and concentrated.

Yet this is looking too far ahead. In the period between, say, Bismarck's coming to power and the establishment of the first German colonies, the overall British lead remained substantial. The trade figures themselves, difficult though it is to rely upon them as a genuinely comprehensive guide,[11] give sufficient indication of this basic picture: see Tables 3.1, 3.2 and 3.3. Even a very crude calculation reveals the importance of Anglo-German trade to both peoples. In 1860, probably only the United States (£44·7 million) sent more produce to Britain than Germany's £15·4 million; the registers did record

Table 3.1  *Britain's foreign trade* (£ million)[12]

|  | 1860 | 1865 | 1870 | 1875 | 1880 | 1885 |
|---|---|---|---|---|---|---|
| Net imports | 181 | 218 | 259 | 316 | 348 | 313 |
| Exports | 136 | 166 | 200 | 223 | 223 | 213 |
| Re-exports | 29 | 53 | 44 | 58 | 63 | 58 |

Table 3.2  *Germany's foreign trade* (£ million)[13]

|  | 1860 | 1865 | (1871) | 1875 | 1880 | 1885 |
|---|---|---|---|---|---|---|
| Net imports | 55·6 | 60·4 | 163·1 | 176·5 | 141·7 | 147·2 |
| Exports | 51·2 | 53·1 | 116·0 | 124·7 | 152·3 | 143·0 |

Table 3.3  *Britain's trade with Germany* (£ million)[14]

|  | 1860 | 1865 | 1870 | 1875 | 1880 | 1885 |
|---|---|---|---|---|---|---|
| Imports from Germany | 15·4 | 16·1 | 15·4 | 21·8 | 24·3 | 23·0 |
| Exports to . . . | 13·5 | 17·7 | 20·4 | 23·2 | 16·9 | 16·4 |
| Re-exports to . . . | 5·2 | 7·1 | 7·6 | 10·9 | 12·1 | 10·6 |

slightly higher totals of British imports from France (£17·7 million) and Russia (£16·2 million) in that same year, but against this has to be set the fact that a large proportion of British imports from Belgium and the Netherlands (£12·2 million together) were probably German in origin.[15] Twenty years later, while the massive British imports from the United States (£102·4 million), India (£30·1 million) and Australasia (£25·6 million) were indicative of the increases which had occurred in the global trade in foodstuffs and raw materials, France and Germany were still the major sources of British imports from Europe: the French total in 1880 was at a freakishly high level of £41 million, compared with German imports of £24·3 million plus a large proportion of the £36·1 million of imports which came to Britain from Belgium and the Netherlands.[16] It was as a market, however, that Germany remained of the greatest importance to Britain, taking more of the latter's produce in 1860 than any other country except the United States, and being in addition the largest market for re-exported goods from Britain. By 1880, Germany still took more British produce than any other country apart from the United States and India, and vied with France as the chief market for British re-exports. To sum up: whilst the USA always remained Britain's first trading partner in these decades, Germany jostled with France and India for the second place. Viewed from the German perspective, the trade with Britain was even more important: although the statistics are confused by the separation of Hamburg and the Zollverein until 1888, there seems little doubt that Britain and her Empire constituted Germany's primary trading partner in both imports and exports in this period, with Austria–Hungary occupying second place. Indeed, trade with the British Empire possibly constituted as much as one-fifth of Germany's foreign commerce.[17]

It is only when the annual totals of imports and exports are broken down, however, that the real complementarity in Anglo-German trade – and the different stages of their respective economies – is properly revealed. In 1860, out of the total British imports from Prussia valued at £7·5 million, £3·4 million consisted of wheat and £1·5 million of wood; and all the other listed items were also either foodstuffs or raw materials. The statistics relating to imports from the Hanse towns told a similar story: the five most valuable wares were wool, butter, wheat, bacon and barley, with any 'advanced' manufactures concealed in the general category of 'All Other Articles' at the foot of the list. By contrast, the principal exports of British produce to Prussia in 1860 were cotton yarns, ironware and herrings; and to the Hanse towns, textiles (a staggering £7·2 million worth of the total British exports of £10·3 million), followed by ironware, silks, coal and hardware. To this must be added the prodigious amounts of raw cotton, coffee, palm-oil, indigo, tea and hides which constituted the leading British re-exports to Prussia, the Hanse towns and indeed all the German states.[18] Twenty years later, the nature of this Anglo-German commerce had not greatly altered. Wheat (because of causes described below) was now only fifth in the list of British imports from Germany, its value of £0·9 million having been surpassed by that of unrefined sugar (£4·7 million), potatoes (£1·7 million), barley (£1·3 million) and bacon and hams (£1·1 million). Similarly, British exports to Germany in 1880 remained dominated by cotton goods (£3·2 million), woollens (£2·7 million), ironware (£1·1 million), herrings (£1·1 million), machinery (£1·07 million) and coal (£0·86 million); and these were supplemented by such major re-exports as raw wool (£2·9 million), tobacco (£1·3 million), coffee (£1·2 million) and raw cotton (£1·1 million).[19]

Although we shall need to identify shortly the areas of Anglo-German commercial *rivalry*, it is worth repeating that these figures leave an overwhelming impression of the manner in which the two economies *complemented* each other. As such, this conclusion simply confirms the general structure of their respective trade: in 1870, for example, 88 per cent of Britain's exports consisted of manufactured goods, 8 per cent of raw materials and only 4 per cent of food, drink and tobacco, whereas the German figures were 39·7 per cent, 34·7 per cent and 25·6 per cent respectively.[20] Even as late as the early-to-mid 1880s, Germany's chief function – so far as the British economy was concerned – was to supply vast amounts of foodstuffs and to purchase vast amounts of textiles and other manufactures. British re-exports of colonial wares somewhat redressed the balance by providing Germany in turn with her required food-stuffs and raw materials; but even the latter commodities – for example, raw wool – seem to have been needed for the German domestic market rather than for working-up and subsequent export to Britain. Although it is undoubtedly true that industrialisation and urbanisation in Germany still continued apace during the Great Depression and led to an increasing interest in export opportunities, it is also clear that businessmen were still primarily concentrating upon their domestic customers and had scarcely begun to venture into the competitive British market. When we examine the structure of Anglo-German trade twenty-five years later, this will be the element which has altered most of all.

Several industries and regions were particularly involved in this trade between Britain and Germany. As late as the 1870s, approximately 55 per cent of Hamburg's total imports came from the British Isles, and even in the following decade it averaged 42 per cent.[21] It was precisely this 'cosmopolitan' nature of the city's economy which caused it to be unwilling to join the Zollverein, and continued to make it strongly pro-British and Liberal in its political sympathies. As mentioned earlier, German landowners also had strong commercial ties with Britain, even if they lacked the corresponding ideological sympathies. In the late 1850s, Germany's export of 1,120,240 tons of wheat to Britain had represented 23·5 per cent of the latter's total wheat imports, and in the early 1870s a respectable 902,818 tons of German wheat reached Britain, even if it only represented 8·2 per cent of the total; by 1879, however, it had shrunk to a mere 2·9 per cent.[22] Yet the vast rise in the export of German sugar to Britain more than made up – at least in value – for the decline in wheat exports; and this, too, was predominantly grown in Prussia. In 1872, Germany exported sugar to the value of only £475,000; by 1880 it was worth £5·5 million; by 1890 it was worth £10·8 million – and was in that year the most valuable single export commodity from Germany.[23] Yet, whether this sugar was raw or refined, the fundamental fact was that between two-thirds and three-quarters of it went to the British market, to satiate its sweet-toothed and tea-drinking population.

Quite apart from such large-scale elements in the Anglo-German commercial relationship, there were a host of smaller enterprises which were very dependent upon trade between the two countries: for example, wine-shippers from the Moselle region, such as Deinhardt & Son; exporters of Welsh steam coal, which flowed in ever-growing quantities from Cardiff to Hamburg; the weavers of Krefeld and Elberfeld, who relied upon the import of fine cotton yarns from Lancashire; the jute manufacturers from Dundee; and a large number of general merchants, import-export firms, and shipping companies. Above all, there were the commodity dealers, insurers and bankers, who organised and financed – and immensely profited from – this flourishing Anglo-German trade. The newer German joint-stock banks soon established connections with the London market and co-operated with their British opposite numbers in the floating and financing of international loans. As for certain private banks, like the Rothschilds, Warburgs and Oppenheims, the Anglo-German relationship – financial and, in many instances, quasi-political[24] –

remained a part of their daily lives; other private banks, by contrast, would be much more involved in financing Russo-German trade. Banking, like many other industries, was a specialists' business and generalisations about it are, given the present access to primary sources, dangerous.

What is clear is that financial connections formed an important part of the overall relationship between the two countries, however 'invisible' the nature of this trade was. To a large extent, specific economic interests tied these circles together. When German industrialisation stimulated a vast increase in imports of raw materials from overseas, for example, this trade was primarily financed by London banks, who would pay in sterling for the requisite Australian wool or Peruvian silver on behalf of their German clients, arrange for the shipping, usually by a British line, of such commodities (either via London, or direct to Hamburg), order the necessary insurance at Lloyd's, and at the end of the six month period request the payment, plus charges, from their clients.[25] If, as we shall see, certain British firms and industries were to complain about the increasing German competition, this was *not* the attitude of the London bankers who were making that challenge possible – and were also, of course, earning such large amounts in 'invisibles' as to cover handsomely Britain's increasing deficit in 'visible' trade. More generally, good Anglo-German relations were desired by the financial world because bankers in both countries shared the same sort of assumptions about the international economy and were often part of a cosmopolitan family with branches in each of the major capitals of Europe. All this makes it hardly surprising that, say, the Rothschilds were interested in the preservation of good Anglo-German relations. But it is also not surprising that protectionists and nationalists in both countries were to complain that these liberal-minded, unpatriotic, 'Jewish financiers' frequently failed to see that their own personal interests were not identical with the interests of the state.

The main points of contrast between the British and German economies prior to the 1880s clearly derived from this fact that the two countries were at different stages of industrial development; but it also seems that political and ideological factors had a contributory part to play in those dissimilarities, which were to continue to exist even after that time. When the Great Depression of 1873–96 occurred, for example, the alternative responses of the British and German governments to it were due to a combination of reasons: economic interests and trends, *plus* tactical political considerations by the statesmen concerned, *plus* ideological assumptions about the nature of the national economy and achieving of the common good.

This study can only touch upon the peripheries of the great debate over the meaning of the economic depression in the final quarter of the nineteenth century.[26] It now seems established that an undifferentiated treatment of this phenomenon will no longer do: there were 'mini-booms' during these decades of alleged slump; many industries, or parts of industries, continued to grow steadily; agriculture, even when (as in Britain) completely unprotected from transatlantic imports, diversified and improved itself in many ways; and the fall in commodity prices, freight rates and interest charges led to advantages as well as to disadvantages – the standard of living of *employed* labour rose throughout this period, for example. Nevertheless, reference to the 'myth' of a great depression may tend to obscure the fact that things *were* going wrong in so many areas of the economy of the Western world: lower receipts upon industrial and agricultural produce, falling profits, reduced output and wages, rising unemployment, collapsed banks and ruined companies all contrasted sharply with the earlier expansion. Furthermore, these years of depression generated fears, uncertainties, suspicions and demands for action which, however subjective in inspiration, also possessed a historical reality.

In Germany the change of mood was the more marked, partly because the recession followed so swiftly upon the national unification and the boom years of 1871–3. Psychologically, the slump came at the worst possible moment, knocking off its balance the new nation-state whilst its institutions, political traditions and social coherence were still immature and untested. If, as Keynes later quipped, the second German Empire was built upon coal and iron, then it was scarcely surprising that people feared for the future when, by the late 1870s, the value of the shares of the twenty largest ironworks in the country had slumped to only 21 million marks as opposed to their nominal value of over 178 million marks. In 1876, in fact, 210 of Germany's 435 blast furnaces were standing idle, and even Krupp's great concern had been pledged to a consortium of banks to save it from collapse.[27] Shortly afterwards, this chorus of industrial complainants was being joined by German landowners and peasants, suddenly aware that massive amounts of American and Russian grain were flooding into their traditional domestic and foreign markets and causing a drastic drop in prices.[28]

The most significant consequences of the depression in Germany, however, were not so much economic as political. It is all too easy, of course, to point to the contrasts between British and German reactions at this time and to forget that most European countries adopted policies – involving higher tariffs, state interventionism and a general abandonment of Liberal principles – similar in many respects to those implemented in Berlin.[29] Nevertheless, it is also true that the complete package of new measures carried out inside Germany at the end of the 1870s constituted a fundamental shift in political practices and assumptions. The chief feature was a strong move to the Right in national politics and ideology, complemented by increasing fissures within the Liberal parties and the widespread denigration of Liberal principles. In economic terms, this was indicated by the return to a protectionist tariff system in 1879, a move which was supported not merely by those disenchanted circles among the *Mittelstand*, craftsmen and peasantry, but also by two much more influential pressure groups, heavy industry and the Junkers. Although strange and often quarrelsome bedfellows, Ruhr iron barons and east Elbian landowners were now forced to ally in what one protectionist termed 'the struggle with the international doctrines of the Manchester school'.[30] This conversion to the merits of protectionism was not universal: it was denounced not only by the left-Liberals and the Socialists, but also by the Hanse towns, many commercial houses and even a large number of farmers (including some in Prussia). Even within a specific industry, some parts preferred free trade, whilst others demanded protection. But the blunt fact was that the free-traders did not possess the political 'muscle' of those who now advocated a tariff system.

This rightward shift in the economic and parliamentary arenas was accompanied by strident attacks upon the Liberal parties, and also by anti-socialist measures – ostensibly as a reaction to the attempted assassinations upon the Kaiser, in reality to check the growth in the Labour movement; together with an ugly anti-Semitic outbreak which the authorities did little, if anything, to prevent. As one curious but perfectly logical corollary to the government's assault upon the SPD, a system of 'state socialism' was soon introduced. Another equally logical corollary, this time at parliamentary level, was the re-creation of a pro-government bloc, consisting of Conservatives and right-wing National Liberals with occasional tacit support from the Centre Party – and with the left-Liberals pushed ever more into the cold.[31] Moreover, it was both a cause and a consequence of this move towards protectionism that party politics became ever more a question of *Interessenpolitik*, of bargaining and manoeuvring for solid material advantages for those economic interest groups which supported the various circles of political representatives. In this situation, the Conservatives representing agriculture, the Free Conservatives with their ties to heavy industry, the Centre, and even the SPD, could operate more efficaciously than *laissez-faire* Liberals. An emphasis upon 'deals' rather than principles also increased the political weight of that arch-bargainer, Bismarck, and produced a further obstacle in the way of any progress towards parliamentarism and democracy, which in any case were likely to be casualties in a time of severe depression unless carefully nurtured.

It is also worth suggesting, however, that this virtual revolution in German fiscal and social policies could hardly have been pushed through so easily had it not been for the insecure and superficial hold which the doctrines of liberalism had achieved within the country. The older 'statist' visions of an organic community in which the government was entitled to intervene in social and economic matters to protect the common weal had been regarded as something of a lost cause during the Liberal ascendancy of the 1860s and early 1870s, and its protagonists – the craft guilds, or the Old Conservatives – had often seemed to be voices from the past. In the depression years, however, when Liberal economic theories appeared to be bankrupt, when the 'social question' was gaining ever greater importance, and when the government was eager to mobilise the support of artisans, peasants, Junkers and industrialists behind itself, an emphasis upon paternalistic, protective policies no longer appeared to be so outmoded. What was more, there were now respected, highly persuasive intellectuals arguing that 'free, quite unlimited interest struggle often has as its result the exploitation and the destruction of the weak' and requesting both protection for the worker and for 'vital, but at the same time hard-pressed, national industry against foreign competition'.[32] With this programme of protective tariffs and state socialism, introduced and controlled by a strong conservative regime and buttressed by constant appeals to national solidarity, it was no surprise that the 'Socialists of the Chair' found it useful to revive many of the teachings of List.[33]

Just as the concept of the 'protection of national work' formed a strong element in German economic thought, so, too, did the military and strategical appeals for protectionism awaken the traditional Prussian preoccupation with the requirements of power-politics. No doubt many of those who put forward arguments for the preservation of German industry and agriculture did so because they personally stood to gain by a change in fiscal policy. Maintaining the Junkers by direct measures of support was a very uneconomic way of propping up the army, although it no doubt made a lot of sense to those anxious to preserve that institution as a bastion of social conservatism. Yet the wider argument that only a prosperous industrial and agricultural base, together with the introduction of new indirect taxes, would produce the funds necessary for Germany's defence did appeal to patriots. So, too, did the claim that to allow the country to become heavily dependent upon imported foodstuffs would be most dangerous in time of war. 'If we really came to a position in which we could no longer produce the grain which we must necessarily consume, then in what state would we be if in wartime we had no Russian grain imports and perhaps simultaneously were blockaded along our coasts – in other words, if we had no grain at all?', Bismarck plaintively asked the Reichstag.[34] It was certainly a good argument, in any case, and one which accorded with Prusso-German traditions – as Thorstein Veblen spotted when he suggested that

the country would have been better off, simply in point of material prosperity and in the rate of economic progress, if no such barrier as the Imperial [tariff] frontier had been kept up; but the immediate result would have been such a specialisation of industry and such a web of trade relations as would have left the community dependent for a large and indispensable part of its current consumption on foreign countries; from which it would follow that the Empire would be relatively vulnerable in case of war, at the same time that the community, the people, would be much more reluctant to go to war. Such a policy would, in other words, nowise compart with the strategy of dynastic politics, at least not as seen by statesmen of the school of Frederick the Great.[35]

The final factor was Bismarck himself. The reasons for his turn away from his earlier adherence to Liberal economic tenets were many, and no one of them necessarily excluded the others. There was his well-known resentment at the compromises he felt he had to make with the National Liberals in the Reichstag, and his desire to ruin the prospects for a future 'Gladstone ministry'; his wish to abandon the *Kulturkampf*, and to attract both the Centre and the German-Conservative parties into the government lobby; his own awareness, as a Junker, of the plight of German agriculture and of the socio-political consequences for the Prusso-German establishment; his dislike at the growth of the SPD and his determination to employ all means to throttle it; his wish to improve the financial independence of the Reich government; and his general recognition that the many deleterious effects of the slump, if allowed to continue unchecked, could begin to undermine the social and political foundations of the state. All this, together with his natural willingness to preserve the existing power relationships by any device at hand – be it the abandonment of free trade, or the introduction of anti-Socialist legislation – helps to explain his actions during the late 1870s, when he observed those shifts within the economic interest groups, and within the world of ideas, which now favoured a turn to protectionism and conservatism. With the Chancellor also willing to support these new policies, the fate of *laissez-faire* liberalism was decided.[36]

In Britain the economic consequences of the depression were, on the face of it, similar to those in Germany.[37] There was less of a financial collapse, but British agriculture was devastated in many respects, and industry was also sorely hit. Transatlantic grain threatened all European farmers west of Russia, yet with the exception of tiny Belgium, only Britain resisted the call for agricultural tariffs – and the land suffered as a consequence. Coincidental bad harvests and animal diseases simply made things worse. In many regions it was difficult to subsist on farming incomes, let alone to make a profit. By the end of the century, the amount of land under wheat was only half of the 1872 figure, and the number of male agricultural workers was down by over one-third. In industry, too, prices and profits tumbled remorselessly; the rate of increase in industrial output and national wealth slowed down significantly (although that may already have begun before the mid-1870s); and businessmen grumbled about the poor prospects for trade. If the domestic market was affected by the general fall-off in prosperity, many of Britain's external markets were doubly hit, for the revival of protectionism in almost all advanced countries was bound to affect many of the products of 'the workshop of the world'. The statistics of the values of British exports told a sorry story. Previously, they had been bounding upwards: in the quinquennium 1860–4 the annual average totalled £138 million, in 1865–9 £181 million, in 1870–4 £235 million. Then they fell off, and stabilised: in 1875–9 they averaged only £202 million, in 1880–4 £234 million, in 1885–9 £226 million – and all this time the total British population was still rising rapidly. So too, was the 'visible' trade gap.

Why, then, was there no widespread revulsion against free trade when it became clear that all other countries except Belgium were introducing tariffs which hit British exports? In the first place, one needs to recognise the sheer weight of the economic interests for whom any move towards protectionism would be regarded with the utmost hostility: for example, the textile industries, which still represented around two-thirds of the value of British exported wares in these years, sent over three-quarters of their entire output overseas. Any advance towards domestic protectionism could easily provoke a stampede towards ever-higher tariffs elsewhere and thus threaten their much more lucrative external markets. The same was true, obviously, of the expanding British shipping industry, which was dependent upon the carriage of the *world*'s goods and not simply upon inter-imperial commerce – to which it might well be reduced if a full-scale return to the age of mercantilism occurred. The bankers, insurers, commodity dealers and investors in the City, all cosmopolitan minded and nearly all Liberals politically, were bound to share this view. The blunt fact was that Britain's only *substantial* tariff weapon was a tax upon foreign foodstuffs and raw materials – which would increase the domestic cost of living – whereas the greatest threat to herself came in the form of foreign tariffs upon her manufactures. To fight the latter with the former was, for most Britons, a nonsense; but so, too, were any measures against the (relatively) small amount of imported manufactures if this jeopardised the far larger total of exported goods.[38]

Secondly, even within an industry which appeared to be badly hit by foreign tariffs and competition, there were always to be found many exceptions: armament production flourished whilst pig-iron producers were hit; the export of fine yarns to Europe continued to rise while those of coarser yarns fell; and Welsh steaming-coal, which had no real equivalent on the continent, was in steady demand. Thirdly, many firms switched their exporting efforts from the newly protected markets to those which were opening up inside the empire and Latin America; and even if this transition caused many grumbles about the extra effort involved, it was often the case that the new markets were found to be more profitable than the old.[39] All this meant that the demand for protectionism could never become as widespread in British industrial and commercial circles as it was in the United States, Germany, France or Russia. Finally, it has also to be remembered that, both because of the earlier Agricultural Revolution and because of the diverse economic interests of the great landowners, the farming lobby in Britain was nowhere near as powerful as elsewhere[40] – and what influence it possessed had to be measured against the fact that all other sections of the community were benefiting from the drastic fall in food prices.

Only at this stage is it right to introduce the ideological and political factors which ensured the preservation of free trade. The sheer strength of *laissez-faire* Liberal thinking in the country was certainly enormous. Even if Cobden had long since departed, the Cobden Club, with its speakers, pamphlets and books, kept the memory of his ideals very much alive. The principles of *laissez-faire* should not be departed from, even in extreme cases: Henry Fawcett, for example, dismissed all the cries about the unemployment caused by foreign competition by stating that it 'corresponds to that which is caused to workmen who possess a special manual skill in any handicraft, if the necessity for their labour is superseded by the invention of a machine'.[41] Foreign countries which returned to protectionism were widely regarded as members of a church who had inexplicably apostasied. It was 'hardly rational', Lord Bateman argued, '. . . to say that the French, the Germans, the Austrians, the Americans and all who held Protectionist principles were a pack of fools'; yet when he had attempted to argue against free trade, he protested, *The Times* 'had called me a dodo'![42] *Punch* preferred the term 'old ladies' and the London *Echo* referred to voices 'issuing from the tomb'.[43] Indeed, almost all newspapers and journals denounced the concept of protectionism, and the upper levels of the Civil Service were also staffed by convinced free-traders. When the Cobden Club authorised a book on the subject *Free Trade v. Fair Trade* in 1881, little surprise was occasioned by the fact that it was penned by Lord Farrar, the Permanent Secretary to the Board of Trade. In the prevailing climate of opinion, protectionists found it necessary to take cover beneath the much less offensive banner of 'Fair Trade'.[44]

Protectionism, in other words, could not capture the decisive part of the political nation, and it is significant how coolly the two main political parties regarded the efforts of the 'Fair Trade' movement in the 1880s – in great contrast to the responses to the Anti-Corn Law League four decades earlier. The Liberal Party, as may be supposed, was fiercely pro-free trade: criticism of that policy was, according to Gladstone, a heresy; and it is interesting, to say the least, to read Joseph Chamberlain's passionate attacks upon 'protectionist fallacies' in the parliamentary debates of this period.[45] Even the establishment in 1885 of the famous Royal Commission on the Depression in Trade and Industry was greeted with hostility by Liberals, lest it give prominence to pro-tariff arguments. This only left the Conservatives. Would they dare pluck the forbidden fruit? Disraeli firmly resisted the temptation. It was no use, he told the Lords, quoting 'musty phrases of mine 40 years ago'. He had bitterly opposed Peel then, but the clock could not be reversed. The landed interest, whose greatest admirer he was, would have to suffer and bear it. In any case, he added pragmatically, the only way to hit the foreigner nowadays was to inflict a wound upon the domestic population by putting tariffs on goods which normally were imported freely.[46]

Yet the Conservative Party was clearly the one most susceptible to protectionist arguments, partly because it was ideologically flexible and partly because it was coming to represent more and more of those businessmen and industrial centres which were beginning to abandon liberalism. Its very pragmatism, however, caused the party leaders to avoid a full identification with the Fair Trade movement, even if certain Tory MPs were converted. In 1884 that talented and unorthodox demagogue, Randolph Churchill, seemed to be making a bold bid for a new policy: 'I suspect free imports of the murder of our industries much in the same way as if I found a man standing over a corpse and plunging his knife into it I should suspect that man of homicide', he melodramatically informed a Blackpool audience. The results of the 1885 election soon caused him to rethink. The idea of protecting the manufacturing centres had provoked a revolt in the county seats: yet to protect agriculture in its turn it would be necessary to have a duty on the price of corn – and Churchill felt that 'high prices in the necessaries of life and political instability in a democratic Constitution are . . . practically inseparable'.[47] To increase sharply the cost of living would, he thought, mean political suicide and, possibly, social unrest – an argument which, interestingly enough, was rarely if ever used by the establishment in Germany despite their apprehension about the labouring classes. This realistic approach by the Conservative Party was typified by Salisbury himself. The chorus of complaints about foreign competition drew him to indicate his sympathy with the plight of industry and agriculture; but his fear of electoral defeat, and in particular his need to preserve the parliamentary alliance with the Liberal Unionists after the 1886 Home Rule crisis, made him willing to accept the fiscal *status quo*, much to the relief of the Tory press. The defeat of free trade, after all, could not compare with the Irish question in importance: even that arch-protectionist James Lowther admitted 'I am a Unionist first, and a protectionist afterwards.'[48] In the same pragmatic way, whenever 'slump' conditions appeared to be ending and trade improving, Tory leaders distanced themselves from their more protectionist followers, whose case always rested upon evidence of impending economic catastrophe.

For a variety of reasons, then, the Great Depression had a far more decisive impact, both economically and politically, upon the German scene than upon the British. Yet one consequence of the slump was to be detected in both countries: the increase or, in certain respects, the creation of a commercial rivalry. The first noises here are to be detected in the German camp. One wonders, in fact, if that earlier dislike of British economic supremacy – the 'los von England' mentality – was ever fully eradicated, even in the years when *laissez-faire* doctrines were at their zenith. By the time of the mid-to-late 1870s, when prices and profits were tumbling, the older animosity raised its head again. The Central Association of German Industrialists, for example, besides campaigning for a variety of tariffs to protect their industries against (chiefly) British competition, also demanded 'the elimination of London as the clearing-place of the German foreign trade'.[49] The spinning industry, much affected by English competition since the 1865 reduction in tariffs, was also alarmist: 'the only enemy to be contended against was Great Britain', claimed Johann Dollfuss, a Reichstag deputy whose own business was hit by these foreign imports.[50] She was out 'to strangle the continental industries in their cribs', warned the leader of the South German cotton spinners, Friedrich Stöpel.[51] But the greatest agitation against Britain was probably set up by the iron and steel industry, which at that time had not yet benefited from Thomas's method of making steel from phosphoric ores and claimed to be suffering from large-scale British imports, produced more cheaply by Bessemer's method and 'dumped' on the German market by firms who produced far too much for the depressed British domestic consumption.

In actual fact, it now seems fairly clear that the economic plight of the German iron and steel industry was never as bad as its proponents made out.[52] In many respects it was already technologically and managerially better than its British equivalent; and its exports were rising rapidly – 1879, in fact, saw the first year of an export surplus in raw iron. It was the drop in prices and profits which made *any* competition – and Britain's was still the greatest – seem intolerable. Objective fact, however, wilted before subjective claims and emotions in these crisis years. Even that great believer in closer Anglo-German relations, Odo Russell, felt compelled to report in 1879 that 'There is great commercial hostility against England in Germany just now, I regret to say'[53] – an intriguing admission in the year in which Bismarck was to make his 'alliance bid'.

In Britain the sense of commercial rivalry came somewhat later. It is true that even as early as 1875 the *Saturday Review* and other journals had pointed to the fierce German competition: 'In every part of the globe they are cutting out English traders, and even in England they are seizing on whole branches and even centres of trade as their own';[54] and consular reports were already bemoaning German encroachment upon traditional British markets. Yet these expressions were still few and far between. 'The [small number of] instances of competition which have been given virtually exhaust the evidence yielded up', concluded R. J. S. Hoffman, after his analysis of consular reports prior to 1880.[55] Manifestations of a more widespread dislike of German commercial and industrial rivalry were, however, a characteristic of the following decade.

In part, this arose as a reaction to the return of the protectionist movement in Germany, which *The Times*, in schoolmasterly tones, regarded as 'one of the most unsatisfactory signs of the limited political training of that country'.[56] The Dundee jute producers, for example, who had hoped to persuade the German government not to place duties upon their manufactures, could hardly warm to the blunt, negative answer from Berlin – and even less to the way jute imports to Germany tumbled after the introduction of the 1879 tariff.[57] German imports of British woollen and cotton cloths were also badly affected by the new tariff, the total of the former falling from 23·6 million yards in 1879 to 10·7 million yards in 1883, and that of the latter from 53·4 million yards to 38·5 million yards in the same period. Since the total value of German exports to Britain sharply increased in these four years whereas German imports of British manufactures actually decreased overall, complaints about the unfairness of the 1879 tariff were common.[58]

An equally strong cause for complaint was the sudden inrush of German competition in the British domestic market and in overseas markets. It would be pointless here to repeat many of the extracts from consular and press reports upon the German 'challenge'; it was precisely in the early to mid 1880s that she overtook Britain as the prime exporter of manufactures to such neighbouring markets as the Netherlands, Sweden and Rumania, and began to make significant inroads into many overseas markets as well. With the *Spectator*, among others, claiming that 'had it not been that the new or neutral markets of the world had been violently attacked and almost taken by storm by German competition in the last half dozen years, the depression would ere have passed away', it was scarcely surprising that some Britons came to resent their neighbour's economic expansion.

The focus of British complaints was less upon the superior efficiency of German industry and salesmanship – although there was plenty of evidence of that – than upon the 'unfair' and 'underhand' methods which their Teutonic rivals employed. The first of these concerned the extent to which German diplomatic agents abroad actively supported their own businessmen in concession-hunting and gaining contracts – a perfectly logical endeavour for the representatives of a protectionist state whose government was committed to the idea of supporting industry, but one which advocates of *laissez-faire* economics angrily denounced. 'Touting for orders', bribing local officials and putting pressure upon Oriental regimes were just three of the tricks which, the British press alleged, were used by German diplomats and consuls to further their nation's trade. Yet to counter these German methods by active diplomatic interventions, as some demanded, was regarded with disfavour by others, not least in the foreign service itself.[59]

In addition, there was the complaint about shoddy German produce being shipped via London all over the world with British trade-marks and labels upon them. The outcry over this provoked a diplomatic *démarche* to the German government, which had consistently declined to be a signatory to the international convention on this subject; and it led, in 1887, to the much tighter Merchandise Marks Act – or the 'Made in Germany' measure, since its chief intention was to compel German manufacturers to state the true country of origin upon their wares. To a large extent, however, this move backfired. In the first place, the German goods, now properly marked, were soon recognised by customers as being in many cases both cheaper *and* better, causing a switch in their future orders from British to German producers. Secondly, a too energetic search and control of German *through*-goods by London customs officials provoked numerous complaints against what was alleged to be deliberate obstructionism and also led to demands for countermeasures. Despite this irritant, however, Bismarck decided not to take strong action against the 'dislocation' of German trade in London, but rather to encourage the German press to call attention to these 'vexatious workings of the Mercantile Marks Act' and to suggest 'means and ways whereby Germany's exports to overseas countries can be freed from the English middle-man (*Vermittelung*)'.[60] Already Hamburg and Bremen were developing more and more *direct* connections with the outside world; inept British customs procedures could only further this tendency.

Nevertheless, the evidence about a growing Anglo-German commercial rivalry has to be placed in its context. In the first place, the complementarity in their trading relationship needs to be emphasised once again. As Germany, too, gradually became a major industrialised nation this difference between the two economies had narrowed; but such a trend was countered by the increasing specialisation within industries, so that – as we shall see again when we re-examine the trading pattern around the turn of the century – there remained a healthy exchange of special products inside any one general trade, in addition to the better-known sale of wares which were produced in one country and not in the other. Furthermore, the commercial competition of the 1870s and 1880s was not purely an Anglo-German phenomenon, but one carried out between *all* the industrialised countries. The Anglo-German relationship, it is worth recalling, was generally free from the bitter feelings provoked by that intense rivalry in *agricultural* produce which worsened Germany's relations with many East European states, particularly Russia, in the 1880s.[61] The same point can be made with regard to tariff disputes. German commercial diplomacy was obviously far more engaged in measures against other protectionist states than against free-trading Britain, which tolerated all her wares and remained her best customer; and even the British found more to complain about the tariffs of *third* powers, which were usually far higher than those of Germany. There is no evidence, for example, that the 'Official Mind' singled out the German tariff for special attention in the late 1870s;[62] and if the prolonged Commons debate of 1881 upon the commercial treaty with France demonstrated yet again the strength of free trade sentiments in Parliament, it also revealed a widespread resentment against the massive imbalance in Anglo-French trade in these years.[63]

While it remains true that, as the Royal Commission itself put it, the severity of foreign competition was 'especially notable in the case of Germany',[64] even this did not inevitably lead to feelings of animosity. Free-traders, predictably enough, vigorously criticised the 'Made in Germany' campaign. There may be certain illegal commercial or trade-mark practices which require checking, wrote Lord Farrar; but the real success of the Germans lay in their salesmanship, their linguistic and technical competence, and their overall manufacturing efficiency – all of which Englishmen should imitate, instead of seeking restrictions upon this competition.[65] Like their German counterparts, English Liberals and radicals sought to check the insidious appeals to chauvinism which so frequently lay beneath the surface of protectionist arguments. Nevertheless, the onset of the Great Depression, the quickening pace of competition in old and new markets, and the general questioning of the precepts of liberalism had provoked a greater sense of economic insecurity and jealousy than existed hitherto. Whether justified by the objective economic facts or not, there was more dislike and concern in Britain and Germany about the other country's commercial rivalry in the 1880s than there had been twenty years earlier. The first signs of Anglo-German estrangement seemed to occur in the ideological-political sphere – although this was neither irreversible nor absolute. The second area of discord, that of a real or alleged clash of economic interests, was now opening up – yet, once again, the same caveats against teleological arguments, which might assume the 'inevitability' of some future conflict between the two peoples, need to be made. In the 1870s and 1880s there were still too many economic forces tending towards reasonable (if not warm) Anglo-German relations to permit the historian to argue that an ineluctable process of mutual antagonism was under way.

What one can say is that the causes for irritation and dislike were likely to grow, and not merely because of the commercial competition but also because one response of both sides to the depression was an energetic search for new markets in hitherto uncolonised regions of the globe. This search, almost inevitably, gave another dimension to the economic rivalry, which in turn provoked fresh calls on each side for protection against the foreign competitor. Those who originally emphasised the need to concentrate upon fresh markets had not always desired territorial annexations, and the 'scramble' for colonies, as we shall argue later, was not solely motivated by economic factors; but the logic of protectionism, tariff wars and overproduction on the one hand, and of the calls for Imperial Federation or a 'place in the sun' on the other, drove men to take much more seriously the future disposal of the unexploited lands of the tropics. In other words, the colonial rivalry of the mid-1880s was to a considerable extent to grow out of the economic anxieties of the previous decade; and because a dispute over rival commercial interests in, say, an African territory involved questions of national prestige, it alerted the hyper-patriots, excited newspaper and pamphlet comments, and brought in the diplomats and statesmen – all of which raised the issue to a new level, which could easily become quite distinct from the original commercial arguments. Here was to be one further cause for Anglo-German irritation and dislike – at least, for those circles to whom colonial gains and national prestige mattered a lot.

# CHAPTER 4

# *The Position and Attitude of the Parties*

The first point which needs to be made about the political parties in Britain and Germany is that they occupied a different place in their respective societies. Although their position was somewhat obscured by the lack of a written constitution and constricted by the still considerable prerogatives of the monarchy and the growing powers of the bureaucracy, parties were at the centre of British politics; electoral success and the concomitant control of the House of Commons turned a party's leaders into the government itself, with control over the machinery of state as well as the legislative process. In Germany, such a system did not exist; reformist political groups might be pushing for what they termed 'parliamentarism', and in certain states the legislature had secured important rights, but in general the hereditary ruler still possessed powers which had been ceded by his British equivalent in the previous two centuries. In other words, a flourishing Liberal party in, say, Prussia did not have the same importance as in Britain, for it could still be denied office and the realities of power. Nevertheless, even in Germany the parties appeared to be significant organisations of political and social opinion, and therefore could not be altogether disregarded by governments. In this particular chapter, which will examine the attitude of the parties in both countries to Anglo-German relations, this constitutional difference will not be emphasised; but it is as well to remember it at the outset.

A second general point, so commonplace that it is almost forgotten, is that the followers of a particular party and the name of the associated ideology were by no means the same thing. Liberalism in mid-Victorian Britain, for example, was considerably more diffuse and arguably more important than the Liberal Party: tenets about *laissez-faire*, freedom of speech, parliamentary government, tolerance of opposition, and free trade were the property of a much larger part of the community than those who voted for Russell, Palmerston and Gladstone. The same may be argued about conservatism, or at least about elements of the Conservative ideology, in Bismarckian Germany; it was not simply the Junkers, after all, who revered the strong state, were dubious about allowing political parties to govern the country (as opposed to checking upon the government), believed in the necessity of a large standing army, and were

59

at best lukewarm about free trade. This issue needs to be examined again below, when the 'political cultures' of the two countries are discussed; but for the moment it is sufficient to note that the present chapter is dealing with the more restricted topic of the parties, and not the ideologies.

## THE LIBERALS

The Liberal Party of mid-Victorian Britain was 'not an organisation, but a habit of co-operation . . . a coalition of convenience, not the instrument of a creed'.[1] At its head was a coterie of Whig aristocrats, owners of vast tracts of land and dispensers of enormous political patronage, often interrelated by marriage and made socially cohesive by their common education and philosophical heritage. They were, in most of the ways which mattered, the real rulers of Britain, being now so established that they required ever-decreasing amounts of traditional rhetoric of anti-monarchism or felt no pressing compunction to appeal to a wider 'body politic' than that created by the Reform Act of 1832. Small in numbers, they were strong where it mattered – in every Liberal Cabinet between the 1860s and the 1890s; and they could usually count upon the support of those social groups which made up the middle legions of the Liberal Party, small landowners, businessmen, lawyers, retired officers and others who filled the backbenches of the Commons. Had this been the social and intellectual limits of the Liberal movement, however, it might well have suffered from the lack of popularity which afflicted the Tories in the 1850s and early 1860s; but the Whigs were also in a political alliance, uneasy and sometimes close to breakdown, with an articulate group of Radicals and intellectuals (Bright, Mill, Samuel Morley, Henry Fawcett, and so on) on the 'left' flank of the parliamentary party. These fifty or so MPs made up in rhetoric and intellectual brilliance what they lacked in day-to-day influence upon political decision-making, and could not be fully ignored. Being predominantly Nonconformist themselves, they received the support of that powerful and country-wide religious body, which had no sympathies for the Anglicanism of the Conservative Party yet also suspected that the Whigs were lukewarm in pushing ahead with the reforms which the Nonconformist community now demanded as of right. Having close links with industry, the radical flank could claim to provide the party with control of the burgeoning cities of the midlands and the north, which (even before redistribution) offered an important counterweight to the Tory hold upon the small county-towns in the south; yet this connection was not merely with businessmen *per se*, for reformist liberalism also aspired to bring the skilled artisans and other working-class élites within the party's fold. In addition, the development of a cheap provincial press of an overwhelmingly Liberal hue meant that yet another manifestation of 'public opinion' was intimately associated with the Nonconformist-industrial-intellectual groups within the parliamentary party. All of these larger-scale processes – the steady industrialisation of the country, the rising standard of living and expectations of the skilled artisans, the continued strength of nonconformity, the spread of learning and literacy –

suggested that the party might gain even greater sustenance from such forces in the future. Yet if this meant that the Whigs had to pay deference to radical wishes on certain matters, and if indeed it offered to that unorthodox Whig, Gladstone, fresh sources of legitimacy, it is also clear that Radicals, merchants, trade unionists and Nonconformists were willing to defer to an aristocratic leadership because they believed that the party would foster their own interests. On this tacit compromise, the bargain between the various sub-groups of the Liberal Party was struck; and the party was likely to remain strong just as long as each section felt that the bargain was beneficial to it.

It is only when the conglomerate nature of the party is recalled that it is possible to understand the gap which so often occurred between the Liberal *ideology* upon external affairs and the practical implementation of foreign policy by Liberal Cabinets. All members of the party paid lip-service to its prevailing tenets: free trade; distaste for the reactionary regimes of eastern Europe, and corresponding support for the idea of national self-determination in Greece, Italy, Poland and elsewhere; avoidance of entangling alliances with another European power; lack of enthusiasm for colonial expansion; and a general preference, subject to the need to preserve British maritime supremacy, for arms reductions and the settlement of international quarrels by arbitration and compromise rather than war.[2] Yet despite such sentiments, there was no guarantee that policies concomitant with these ideals would actually be carried out. Often the practical realities of the international scene seemed to preclude the implementation of a truly 'Liberal' foreign policy. Could Britain really assist the Poles in 1863, for example, or prudently abandon Egypt after 1882? It was in this area, above all, that the Whig influence was felt; for the aristocratic hold upon the Foreign Office and diplomatic corps was strong and its membership was more inclined to caution than to enthusiasm, less moved by ideals than by practical considerations, and more conscious of the dangers which might attend a policy of interference and reform. Add to this the Whig position on Ireland (where many possessed estates) and sensitivity to Britain's world position – which made them less inclined to pull out of overseas territories, less sanguine about cuts in the Royal Navy's budget, and less willing to believe that the foreigner held the same enlightened views as the average Englishman – and it is once again not surprising to find that Liberal idealism in foreign affairs was often sacrificed to the exigencies of the moment.[3] On the other hand, the rhetoric of a Liberal external policy was never abandoned, and this disparity between theory and practice infuriated foreign and domestic critics, who could see in it nothing more than 'cant'.

Compared with this influence of the Whigs, that of the 'Manchester men' in foreign affairs remained small. Moreover, Gladstone himself, for all the similarity in moral earnestness, differed fundamentally from the Radicals over various issues, particularly the policy of non-interventionism;[4] and even when he agreed with them, he found himself as Prime Minister too busy with his great schemes of domestic reform to give external affairs the necessary time and concentration. When he did shift his glance to the foreign scene, his immediate impulses were usually stifled by Whig advice and by his own second thoughts. The very fact that both he and the Radicals possessed but incomplete knowledge of the intricacies of some international or colonial crisis strengthened the influence of the 'Official Mind'. Nevertheless, because radical circles were so articulate, and because such leaders as Cobden and Bright (and later Joseph Chamberlain and Sir Charles Dilke) were important in domestic-political terms, then it is easy to understand why their views on foreign policy occupied a considerable share of public opinion in that field. They also knew that, in most cases, they could rely upon the support of religious dissenters, who were now entering the Commons in substantial numbers and were bitterly opposed to the amoral nature of most diplomatic business.[5]

It was probably true, however, that the differences of political opinion which existed within the party were more in evidence over domestic-political than foreign affairs, at least after Palmerston's death. While there were to be disputes between 'interferers' like Gladstone and 'non-interferers' like Granville and the Radicals, the party on the whole was rarely as divided in this arena during the period 1865–80 as it was in either the decades preceding or following. This relative uniformity was probably due less to a real harmonisation of opinions than to a tacit agreement not to quarrel when the actual policy of non-intervention and caution abroad was satisfying to all: for the fact was that the post-Palmerstonian policy of recoil from Europe by his Whig successors fitted in nicely with the well-known desires of the Radicals for peace, retrenchment and reform; and also fitted in with the less idealistic but very sober assessments in Whitehall about Britain's external capabilities.

Consequently, it would have been easy for most Liberals to agree with that encouragement of a united Germany which the British ambassador in Berlin, Loftus, expressed as follows:

> She [Prussia] was the great Protestant state of Continental Europe. She represented the intelligence, the progress and wealth of Germany. We have . . . nothing to fear from her. She will become a Power of great importance in maintaining the peace of Central Europe. She will gradually advance in a constitutional system of government, and she will play the part of a moderator in Europe. We have much in common with her – our race, our religion, our mutual interests are all interwoven with Prussia, and our political interests should be identical.[6]

Here was a nice collection of motives, pragmatic and emotional, which combined to influence the Liberal view of Prussia and, by extension, its leadership within Germany. It fitted in with the notion of an Anglo-German Liberal *entente* which had been preached by the Prince Consort, with the idealists' confidence in the general progress of Western, Protestant civilisation, and with the political calculation that a strong power would be a force for peace, which British interests required.

The flaw here was, of course, the assumption that Prussia-Germany would indeed 'gradually advance in a constitutional form of government', for Berlin gave little sign of following such a path. During the Prussian constitutional crisis of the 1860s, British Liberals were firmly on the side of their German counterparts and thus bitterly disappointed at Bismarck's victory. Yet if this, and the Danish and Austrian wars, suggested that the government in Berlin was in 'the wrong hands', this did not mean that an anti-German feeling was gaining ground in Britain. In the first place, it was a commonplace of progressive ideology to distinguish between a people, which was always good, and a ruling élite, which might be bad although it could not resist the forces of light for ever. Furthermore, many British Liberals still looked to Germany because of their disapproval of the actions of Russia and France. The Tsarist regime, after all, contained features which offended both the Radicals' belief in constitutional democracy and the Whigs' concern for British interests in Asia; and the unpredictable policies of Napoleon III were an obstacle to all those Liberals who cherished the tradition of an Anglo-French *entente*. It was, therefore, quite logical for many British Liberals to disapprove of the manner in which the Austro-Prussian War had been provoked but to admire the result – which fitted in not only with their general approval of German national unification but with their support of what they identified to be the forces of 'progress'. If the pro-German enthusiasm of Goldwin Smith, Dicey and other intellectual Liberals knew no bounds in the summer of 1866, even Gladstone was willing to endorse the Prussian hegemony in Germany. Not only was it a good thing in itself that the great German people should be united, he told the Commons, but that result would eradicate what had formerly been 'a perpetual cause of difficulty and apprehension. The time had been when millions have been added to the Military Estimates of this country, chiefly on account for what might take place in Germany' if foreign powers interfered.[7]

The outbreak and course of the Franco-Prussian War saw the confirmation of this attitude, and then its sudden collapse. Few in Britain doubted that Napoleon III had been the chief cause of that conflict; but his defeat and the proclamation of a republic removed the chief stumbling-block to Liberal sympathies towards France. By contrast, the Prussian despoliation of northern France, the demand for reparations and the annexation of Alsace-Lorraine swung British Liberal opinion steadily against Germany. In this regard at least, Gladstone's attitude was typical of that of much of his party; what distinguished him was his willingness to try to prevent the transfer of territories, whereas the Cobdenites and the Whigs, motivated by divergent principles, would have none of that.

Without doubt, 1870–1 represented a watershed in British Liberal attitudes. It is true that there still remained a number who believed that the dominance of Prussian authoritarianism was only temporary. One source of hope lay in the potential influence of the south German states, and both Acton and Morier thought that the federal constitution would 'foster *Germanism* rather than *Prussianism*'.[8] An alternative source for the possible liberalisation of Germany lay in the Prussian Crown Prince and the prospect of his future rule, an optimism strengthened by Friedrich Wilhelm's frequent assurance that 'the liberal Principle will rule in Germany'.[9] Nevertheless, to the great bulk of British Liberals the new German state symbolised Junker backwardness, militarism, cynical Realpolitik and the suppression of constitutional freedoms, especially in regard to the powers of the elected assembly and the political parties. Bismarck's various policies, from the creation of the *Dreikaiserbund* to his apparent intention to fall upon France in 1875, and from his repeated scare-mongering whenever an army bill needed passage through the Reichstag to his adoption of protectionism in 1879, all confirmed this unfavourable image. At the same time, the Liberal picture of France improved during the 1870s. Even the Whigs, despite their unease at the Commune and their dislike of French imperial policies in the 1880s,[10] manifested this preference for France, in part because of political principle but in the main probably because of their francophile cultural heritage. Moreover, as Flournoy notes, 'France had at all times been a main source of Liberal thought, and with French intellectuals British liberals always found much in common.'[11] The left wing of the Liberal Party reinforced this francophilia with a deep respect for their neighbour's republican and democratic form of government (about which the Whigs were obviously less ecstatic). Labouchere, French by birth and an observer of the Prussian siege of Paris, had 'a constitutional dislike of the German people', and his magazine *Truth* contained frequent disparaging references to the Hohenzollerns.[12] Gladstone himself had argued as early as 1860 that 'the alliance with France is the true basis of peace in Europe',[13] and if this desire for so strong a link was later to be modified, his admiration survived all the diplomatic and colonial clashes of the decades following.

To a large number of British Liberals in the 1870s and 1880s, then, policy towards Berlin was influenced, if not dictated, by attitudes towards Paris. Hence every move in the direction of a German alliance was more or less bound to provoke a domestic-political quarrel, as the queen, Salisbury and Northcote recognised in 1879. The Foreign Secretary's welcoming of the Austro-German alliance in the autumn of that year soon evoked a spate of Liberal reservations, with Hartington declaring that 'the people of this country . . . would not for one moment countenance any alliance which indicated distrust or illwill towards the great Republic of France'.[14] Again, the profound unease which permeated Liberal ranks in the late 1880s lest Salisbury conclude some form of secret alliance with Germany was motivated not simply by an opposition in principle to an entangling military obligation, but also to a suspicion that any such Anglo-German combine would have its natural target in France. 'Our sympathies would be with France' in the event of a Franco-German war, Labouchere warned the Conservative government.[15]

Whatever the specific Liberal complaints about German policy, the chief point to be emphasised was their objection to what they termed 'Bismarckism', a political system completely antithetical to their own assumptions and practices. Indeed, as the century progressed and more countries seemed to be poisoned by the doctrines of Realpolitik, so the British Liberals' opposition to what had originally been regarded as a Prussian phenomenon broadened out into a general denunciation of this new, harsher, illiberal political culture. 'Bismarckism is a terrible word', wrote one Radical MP, 'but no more terrible than that which it is meant to express. A course of political action based on principles antagonistic to the whole tendency of Liberal thought . . . It also excites our fear.'[16] Acton, one of the torchbearers of German culture and education in Britain but also the quintessence of English Liberal idealism, symbolised this anxiety by his repeated attacks upon the glorification of power which Machiavelli had introduced into European thought, and by his emphasis upon the dangers which Treitschke's teachings and Bismarck's habits represented.[17] Even John Morley, that untypical Liberal defender of Germany's higher culture, devoted his Romanes lecture upon Machiavelli to a sustained criticism of 'the Bismarckian gospel of Force and Fraud, which now masters Europe and has some foothold in England'.[18]

Yet, if opposition to 'Bismarckism' was a characteristic of mainstream liberalism, it is worth noting that by the late 1870s not all followers of the Liberal Party felt this way. In those years, it has been argued, a 'fault line' was developing within British liberalism between the adherents of the established creed and that

> considerable section of the higher Liberal intelligentsia [which was] becoming increasingly uncomfortable in the company of Gladstone and developments associated with Gladstone – 'vulgar, impulsive, unreflecting' democracy, threats to property, irresponsible emotionalism in politics, far too much concern for popular liberty and the rights of subjects, far too little appreciation of the nature of political society and the rights of authority.[19]

If it was to take some years – and the catalyst of the Irish issue – to expose this fault line, then its subterranean existence already ensured that those Liberals growing uneasy at Gladstonian enthusiasms and radical social schemes felt less critical of the German political structure. Seeley, for example, openly defended Bismarck's policy towards his constitutional foes in Germany and asked an audience in 1879 to consider whether the blessing of parliamentary government was, 'like most other earthly blessings, relative?'; land-girt countries bordered by jealous neighbours 'needed secrecy, promptitude, justice, and severity in their governments'.[20] In the same way, Matthew Arnold, whose growing concern about liberalism's incapacity to solve Britain's internal and external problems was even more pronounced than Seeley's, rejoiced at being able to have an interview with Bismarck, 'the sagacious mind, going from success to success', who compared most favourably with the dreadful Gladstone, 'the fertile tongue, going from failure to failure'.[21] Another good example was the young Alfred Milner, still eager to gain a Liberal seat in the Commons but admitting to an audience in late 1885 that 'I can't stand the Foreign Policy of the late government', – in general, because it had neglected to preserve Britain's world position, and in particular because it had badly handled relations with Germany, whose colonial bids it ought to have welcomed.[22]

When next the attitude of British Liberals towards Germany is examined, thirty years on, the picture will have been transformed: the radical and Cobdenite groups within the party will be eager to improve relations with their Teutonic neighbours, whereas the imperialist wing (that is, the part which had not defected to the Unionists) will be more suspicious of Germany and antagonistic towards her ambitions. Yet this apparent contradiction is, upon closer study, explained by reference to the latent division within the Liberal movement which was already identifiable in this earlier period. The changes of position towards Germany in both camps were, in fact, perfectly consistent with the Left's policy of opposing 'Bismarckism' wherever it occurred and the Right's advocacy of a realistic and patriotic external policy by an ordered nation-state.

Since much of the historiography of German politics from Bismarck to Hitler has focused upon the failure to develop liberalism along the lines of an assumed west European 'model', it is difficult to begin an analysis of the German Liberal parties without immediately hinting at their incipient weaknesses.[23] The latter, admittedly, could be spotted in at least two areas even before the Bismarckian Reich was founded: in the fact that there was no ready way by which Liberals could gain executive power if the monarch resisted their claims; and, secondly, in the superficial place which the tenets of classical liberalism had within the German public mind. Nevertheless, it is also worth recalling the enormous preponderance of seats held by Liberals in the Prussian Landtag during the 1860s, and the further fact that only in the general election of 1881 did the National Liberal Party lose its position as the largest political group in the Reichstag. Between the Austrian War and the establishment of a united Empire, Liberals had pursued a path of compromise with Bismarck; but most regarded that as a symptom of expediency, not of impending mortality. Their belief in Progress meant that during the 1870s they could still hope, as Twesten had done in 1866, that they would 'sooner or later . . . also become the possessors of political power in our State':[24] already by the early 1870s, so it appeared to outraged Conservatives and Catholics, the National Liberals had entered into an alliance with the Chancellor which (however distinctive from Gladstonian England) suggested the onset of a 'Liberal Era',[25] especially in legislating for further economic liberalisation. Finally, the party was always willing to claim that, unlike its rivals, liberalism could represent all classes and regions in the land.

Yet, despite its impressive parliamentary position, even in the early years of the Reich the movement was never as firmly rooted as its British equivalent;[26] and despite its claims, it was not long able to maintain itself as a truly national party, encompassing all ranks. The great bulk of the Junkers adhered, predictably enough, to the Conservative Party; and, despite the considerable number of landowners in the National Liberal Party, there was no real equivalent to the English Whigs, performing the critical function of introducing reforms from above in conjunction with their middle-class political allies. On the other hand, despite early successes when the SPD was still weak, the German Liberals found it increasingly difficult to keep the working classes in their embrace, because of a social snobbishness which refused full membership of parties and organisations (like the *Nationalverein*) to the proletariat, and then because of a horror at the latter's aims which – at least as articulated by Bebel and Liebknecht – seemed to threaten the social and economic position of so many of liberalism's supporters among the German *Mittelstand*. Finally, the existence of a political party which cut clean across class lines – the Centre Party – further weakened the potential electoral basis for a mass Liberal movement. Having neither the power and prestige of the decision-making élite, nor the will to maintain a mass following with which (if necessary) to oppose that élite, the Liberals were in difficulties from the beginning, as their ambivalent stance towards Bismarck indicated.

What strength and popularity liberalism possessed, in other words, derived from a conjunction of circumstances peculiar to the 1860s and 1870s – the movement for national unity, the impetus of *laissez-faire* industrialisation, the embryonic state of German socialism, the low turn-out at the polls. If this weakness was not so apparent in the early 1870s, it was because the euphoria which unification produced took time to ebb and because the rival political parties were in disarray. Within another decade, however, the Conservatives, Socialists and Catholics had readjusted to the Bismarckian state and were beginning to make their impact upon its electoral geography. In the constituencies east of the Elbe (and in the voting for the Prussian Landtag) the Liberals were opposed by entrenched conservatism, in Berlin and the other cities they were challenged by the Social Democrats, in the Rhineland and much of southern Germany they encountered the growing strength of political Catholicism. The Liberal parties, too, had their own regions of electoral strength, but it is not surprising that many of them disliked that universal manhood suffrage which now made their political ambitions so difficult to realise.

Liberalism's deficiency as an active and united force was evident in its paralysis during the challenges posed by the 'Great Depression', the military budgets, the rise of the SPD and the anti-socialist laws, protectionism and state interventionism.[27] Unable either to lead the workers or to undermine the dominance of the Junkers or to understand the Catholics, Liberals became increasingly conscious of their lack of appeal; and, for electoral reasons as well as their internal divergence over principles, they turned in various directions to find an ally they might compromise with in order to sustain their own position. In Britain, too, sub-groups of the Liberal Party exhibited similar centrifugal tendencies but for several decades Gladstonian leadership offered a universal amalgam which checked any formal splits. Not only was such leadership lacking in Germany, but from early on Bismarck had perceived that by offering Liberals some of their goals and simultaneously blocking others, he could drive repeated wedges into the movement as a whole. As early as 1866, the 'realist' majority had broken away from an oppositionist stance, founded the National Liberal Party, and committed itself to supporting unification from above while bargaining with Bismarck over some – but not all[28] – of their domestic political aims. During the crisis years of 1879–80, not only did the extreme right of the National Liberal Party break away, but a considerable number of the left wing set up their Liberal Union (*Liberale Vereinigung*) and gradually moved closer to the older Progressive Party, which under Eugen Richter had remained critical of Bismarck since the Prussian constitutional crisis. By 1884, these two left-of-centre groupings had reconstituted themselves as the *Deutschfreisinnige Partei* under Richter's leadership but that was by no means the end of their 'splits'. Not all of these fissures were permanent and Liberals of all hues often came together at local levels to combat a perceived common danger; but the divisions were serious enough. Further-more, the electoral results revealed that gains for one of the Liberal parties meant losses for the other: in other words, they shared 'the same reservoir of voters'[29] at a time when liberalism was beginning to lose its overall share of the electorate.

These comments form a necessary preface to any analysis of German Liberal views about Britain, if only because the latter were as varied as – and directly related to – the many divisions within the movement over domestic politics. It is, indeed, a testimony to those divergences that liberalism contained the most anglophobe and the most anglophile elements in the whole of Germany. Just as there was a great and growing difference of opinion between members of the German middle classes who committed themselves wholeheartedly to the conservative Bismarckian state and others whose reservations were still considerable, so, too, was there a parallel split between those who saw Britain as a fundamental obstacle to German interests and those who remained hopeful of an Anglo-German 'liberal' *entente*.

The most glaring example of the 'type' of German Liberal who abandoned his early beliefs in favour of an unrestrained nationalism was Treitschke.[30] It is no exaggeration to say that, as the historian and National Liberal deputy marched ever further to the Right, so also did his earlier enthusiasm for Britain give way to a venomous dislike. In his first article for the *Preussische Jahr-bücher*, in 1858, he had asserted that 'Admiration is the first feeling which the study of English history calls forth in everyone.' By 1876, he had quite a different view of that country's history: 'She was enthusiastic about the wickedness of North American slave traders; she was the screaming, though – thank God! – cowardly counsel behind Denmark's domination of Schleswig-Holstein; she venerated the *Bundestag* and Welf kingdom; she permitted the French attack on united Germany when she could have prevented it, and lengthened the war by selling France arms.'[31] Not all of this can be explained by Treitschke's hyper-patriotism and his genuine disappointment over British policy in 1870. The change of mood also relates, psychologically and politically, to his overall rejection of the Liberal creed of his youth. While on the one hand he showered criticisms upon the Socialists, left-Liberals, Catholics, Jews, Poles and other particularists and 'subverters' of the Reich; and on the other hand praised the Prusso-German state, defended the privileges of its monarch and campaigned in favour of every alteration in Bismarck's tortuous diplomacy: so it becomes clear that Treitschke was making direct connections between domestic politics and foreign affairs. To him, as to most other German conservatives, Britain – especially under Gladstone – served as an example of what dire things might befall Germany if she also conceded full parliamentary government.

In the 1870s and 1880s, it is fair to say, Treitschke was an extreme personification of German patriotism and anglophobia: his function as a tribune of the people was only properly fulfilled in later years, when nationalist circles required a set of concepts to grace their striving for *Weltpolitik*. It is also true that the historian was not a typical National Liberal, to the extent that he broke with the party and voted with the Free Conservatives. Nevertheless, for all that

Treitschke exaggerated the views of right-wing liberalism, it is clear that the essentials of his political beliefs did not markedly differ from those of his parliamentary colleagues. Most National Liberals did, after all, support Bismarck, defend the *status quo*, suspect parliamentary rule, abandon free trade, oppose the claims of the Progressives, Social Democrats and Catholics, and stress the importance of national unity and power. In the same way, they also shared many of Treitschke's views upon foreign policy in general, and upon relations with Britain in particular. During the 1870s, the position was still fluid, for many had not fully thrown in their lot with the Bismarckian system and their enthusiasm for the *Kulturkampf* drew them closer towards their fellow-Protestant state; just as antagonism towards France and the Slavs softened attitudes towards the British, if only for negative reasons. But even in these years National Liberal deputies and newspapers attacked what they considered to be the growing ineptitude of Gladstone's administration, which had abandoned its earlier robustness and common sense in favour of internal demagoguery and external faint-heartedness and cunning. By the late 1870s and early 1880s, the nature of these German complaints was beginning to alter, as commercial and colonial rivalry presented a *direct* cause for criticising Britain in place of *indirect* grounds such as its parliamentary government and social policies.

On the other side of this fault-line lay a cluster of left-wing Liberals, Progressives and Democrats who, although often disagreeing on other matters, shared a common distrust of the Bismarckian system of government and – by no great coincidence – a high esteem of England. These common characteristics were clearly two sides of the same coin since such groups, being the most 'pro-Western' parties within Germany, inevitably disliked the conservative, autocratic and therefore 'pro-Eastern' course which the Reich followed in its domestic and foreign policies.[32] There was no question but that these left-wing, middle-class critics accepted, and even welcomed the founding of the German Empire under Prussian leadership; what they also wished for, however, was a set of constitutional and political changes which would bring their country much closer to the English conditions which they so admired. Like their nominal leader, the Prussian Crown Prince, they lacked the power to effect such changes and may have shown themselves to be lukewarm Liberals in reality, had they ever assumed office;[33] certainly, they disliked Bismarck's damaging assertions that they aspired to form a 'Gladstone ministry'.[34] In respect of Anglo-German relations, however, their views were more firmly put.

Baron Franz von Roggenbach, a leading south German Liberal and critic of Bismarck, was a fair example of this tradition. He was a daily reader of *The Times* and an enthusiastic visitor to England, where, as he informed his friend Stosch, 'there are people in all walks of life with whom one can naturally discuss things, there is freedom of ideas, having and tolerating one's judgement without enraging one's opponent'. Disliking Bismarck's pro-Russian policy, Roggenbach offered praise for the Chancellor only at the announcement of the Austro-German alliance in 1879, since he and his friends hoped that it would rapidly be extended to include Britain. Although gradually realising that the island state would seek to avoid a military commitment to Germany, he continued to defend its policies from the anglophobes, declaring on one occasion that England's possession of Egypt was the best thing possible for mankind, and criticising on another Stosch's belligerent reactions during the Kruger Telegram crisis.[35] Such pro-English views were reinforced by the contacts these circles had with Morier, Sir Joseph Archer Crowe (British consul-general, and father of Eyre Crowe), and of course with the Crown Prince and his wife.

Other German Liberals took their inspiration and information about Britain from less exalted sources. Schulze-Delitzsch, a Bismarck critic on the left of the Progressive Party, had borrowed from English examples when attempting to establish co-operatives in Germany.[36] Max Hirsch, who with his fellow-Progressive Franz Duncker sought to develop democratic but pro-capitalist workers associations, had been influenced by the efforts of John Ludlow and the Christian Socialists to solve the 'social question'.[37] Ludlow was also the inspiration for the famous economist Lujo Brentano, whose advocacy of a modified liberalism and the enhancement of trade union rights was a direct imitation of Britain, which, as he told his students in 1890, was 'a nation many decades ahead of us in social and economic developments'.[38] But the largest number of latent or active anglophiles inside Germany were probably the bankers, merchants and others who had been brought up to regard free trade, individualism and parliamentary restraint upon the executive as the 'natural' attributes of all advanced societies. Such circles, represented politically by the Progressive Party under Richter and by the *Liberale Vereinigung*, had entertained doubts about the military laws, criticised the pro-Russian tone of the government, and also been more troubled than other Liberals about the anti-socialist legislation, much as they disliked the SPD; but the real touchstone of this opposition to Bismarck came only with the return to protectionism and then the beginnings of colonialism. To this extent, it might be fair to say that their leanings towards Britain derived more from their wholehearted commitment to economic *laissez-faire* than to dislike of a hierarchical society.

Nevertheless, the fact remains that these Progressive and left-Liberal circles provided the only pro-British voices outside the SPD during the 1870s and 1880s.[39] Richter attacked the nationalist press for spoiling the Anglo-German friendship, Bamberger expressed the hope that the two countries could stand together, and other *laissez-faire* advocates sought to rebut the arguments which protectionists used against England. In 1886 Bamberger informed his friend Spenser Wilkinson that, although the German 'jingos' were bitterly attacking Gladstone as a free-trader and humanitarian, he personally had the warmest admiration for the Grand Old Man.[40] This did not necessarily mean, however, that they all urged an Anglo-German alliance as keenly as, say, the Crown Princess. Many of them were disappointed by British policy in 1870–1 and later perceived that, whatever its domestic policies, a Gladstone administration was of little use to Germany inside Europe – another reflection of their growing appreciation of the rules of Realpolitik. In fact, many shared Bismarck's wish for a Conservative government in London, expecting that it would carry out a more active European policy in general and provide more support for Austria-Hungary in particular; to have England's 'moral sympathies', Geffcken argued, was not enough.[41]

At the end of the day, one is bound to wonder whether it greatly mattered to the Anglo-German relationship that these Liberal groupings were pro-British when they had no chance of influencing policy and when their own domestic position was slowly worsening. The fact that there was already a scarcity of advocates of close relations was an indication of the overall weakness of progressive forces in the new Reich, however, and this in turn made any future growth in friendly feelings towards the island state unlikely.

## THE CONSERVATIVE PARTIES

The history of German conservatism in Bismarck's time was one of a general change from 'a party of beliefs' to 'a party of interests';[42] in neither case did these characteristics bode well for friendly relations with Britain.

To begin with, the political ideology of the Prussian Conservatives was far removed from that of Liberal, industrialised Britain. Lacking that flexibility in thought and action which Burke and Peel had bequeathed to British conservatism, the Junkers continued to praise the constitutional and social practices of an earlier age. After all, taught ideologues such as Stahl and Ludwig von Gerlach, this was not only a God-ordained state of affairs, but it was also the only way of preserving their privileges and way of life against the encroachments of a centralising, national government on the one hand and of the middle classes and workers on the other. While their patriotism was not in doubt, this feeling was restricted to a love of Prussia (or Bavaria) alone, and not of a united Reich: to advance the greater glory of Prussia and its monarch was axiomatic, but nationalism itself was a 'swindle'.[43] The Bismarckian exploitation of popular nationalism, the use of unscrupulous and 'un-Christian' methods, the war with Austria, the abolition of the monarchies in Hanover and elsewhere, and the adoption of manhood suffrage in the dubious new Empire, were acts which had to be opposed and criticised.

The trouble with this stance of unreconstructed conservatism was that it was being steadily undermined by the forces of liberalism, industrialisation and national unity. Only with Bismarck's coming did there emerge a positive and effective strategy for countering, albeit by questionable methods, the pressures for political and social change. But it was precisely on the issue of Bismarck's methods that the Conservatives, like the Liberals, began to split. To Ludwig von Gerlach, the attack on Austria was 'a fratricidal war', one which destroyed the 'living character' of Germany; yet this charge was promptly answered by the young Wilhelm von Kardorff, who symbolised that new school of Prussian Conservatives who recognised in their Prime Minister's policies the only means of salvation for their class. 'Nothing could be less conservative', Kardorff argued, 'than to fight for forms which in the course of time had lost their importance.'[44] For this group, a steady desertion of traditional principles was not too high a price to pay if Bismarck could guarantee the maintenance of their essential interests; and with people such as Stumm,

Krupp and other industrialists joining Kardorff in the Free Conservative Party, it was not surprising that 'essential interests' now embraced more than the needs of an agricultural society.

Yet this utilitarian approach to politics was also apparent among the traditionalist Junkers when the agricultural depression of the late 1870s threatened economic ruin. The numerical dominance of the Liberals in the Reichstag, the 1872 reform of the administration of the counties (*Kreisordnung*) and many other measures had suggested that the older Conservatives could not hold their own simply by the deployment of political arguments: they also needed an economic power-base, and this became ever more pressing as food prices tumbled and foreign grain competition increased. 'Absolutely nothing can be done here with a conservative program and conservative agitation, but only with the steps in the direction of an agrarian party', one landowner reported.[45] With such a party, the Conservatives could then go, albeit reluctantly, into an alliance with heavy industry in favour of commercial tariffs and domestic reaction; and while this implied coming to terms with the new order, the idea offended fewer and fewer members of *Junkertum*. The electoral results of the late 1870s and early 1880s, when a revamped German Conservative Party gained many seats and (despite the opposition of its own right wing) actually managed to replace the National Liberals as Bismarck's chief supporters, seemed to confirm the correctness of this metamorphosis from a party of ideas to a party of interests.

Quite apart from this electoral recovery of German conservatism, it always needs to be recalled that the Junker influence in German politics could not be measured by Reichstag seats alone. Although the 1871 constitution offended the Old Conservatives with its manhood suffrage, Bismarck had predictably ensured that the reins of power did not leave the hands of the establishment. The particularist privileges of the German states and, above all, of Prussia – which retained its three-class electoral system and thus remained a bastion of conservatism – checked the reformers' hopes for a steady transition to parliamentary democracy. More important still, the Kaiser possessed a whole series of powers and, if anything, Wilhelm I sympathised with the Old Conservative viewpoint rather than with that of the pragmatists. In addition to the entrenched political and social conservatism of the court, the Prussian army offered yet another, enormously powerful support to the *status quo*; and this was reinforced during Bismarck's years of power by the elimination of Liberals from the Prussian bureaucracy and judiciary. Finally, there was the Chancellor himself, who despite – or, rather, because of – his tactical flexibility and unscrupulousness as to the methods he employed, was the most formidable conservative force of all in mid-to-late nineteenth-century Europe.[46]

The massive powers enjoyed by Conservatives obviously had repercussions upon the Anglo-German relationship. After all, if the establishment was basically distrustful of Britain, then the anglophilia of left-Liberals and Social Democrats was of little account; and could, in fact, serve only to confirm the Conservatives in the correctness of their prejudice. Moreover, the division of the Junkers into two basic 'types' did not fundamentally alter their image of

British politics. All that happened was that there were now two differing clusters of criticisms directed against the island state.

The first 'cluster' came from the Old Conservatives and was predictable enough. Britain, in their eyes, was the *fons et origo* of the deadly process of industrialisation, democratisation and *laissez-faire* liberalism which threatened to undermine the conservative order throughout Europe. This point of view was best represented by Stahl, who asserted that to take even the most moderate steps towards an English-style parliament was to gravitate inexorably 'towards a republic'.[47] This dislike was also strong in the sphere of economic liberalisation, for nothing could be more harmful to a stable, hierarchical way of life than the extreme effects of industrialisation. If they were not deplorable enough in themselves, they became even worse in the eyes of patriotic Conservatives because of what the *Kreuzzeitung* called 'the cosmopolitan conspiracy against national goods and interests',[48] that is, the alliance of German bankers and entrepreneurs with foreign countries – of which Britain, as the most advanced industrial state, was the Number One example.

Against all this, it has to be remarked that there also existed a more favourable German-Conservative image of Britain: namely, that of a stable, Christian society controlled by patriotic aristocrats whose twin functions were, domestically, a preservation of the best features of the past and, externally, an interventionist policy to check French aggressions. This was an approach which, above all, Ranke typified but it was shared by other Conservatives. It meant not merely a heavy concentration of attention upon *Aussenpolitik* but also a rather perverse exaggeration of those aspects of British life which best resembled Junker conditions: the House of Lords, the trappings of the English law courts, the liturgical revival in the Anglican church, the social life of the gentry of 'merry old England'.[49] In the post-Palmerstonian decades, however, even the most anglophile German Conservative could not fail to see that this image was crumbling rapidly. 'The turn with the reform bill in England has made such an impression on me that I dreamed about it all night', wrote an anguished Gerlach. 'In old England [even] with a Tory ministry there is no resistance against advancing democracy, that is, against advancing socialism.'[50] As for Gladstone, his 'revolutionary' administrations offered revealing examples of what the fate of Prussian conservatism would be if ever Liberals were allowed to gain the upper hand in Germany. All this inevitably strengthened the conviction of those who had already been preaching that their country's natural allies were the fellow conservative-monarchical states of Austria-Hungary and Russia. In the *Dreikaiserbund*, at least, the principles which should determine the external and internal policies of the state were properly enshrined.

For the Free Conservatives, the Bismarckian party *sans phrase*, this ideological dislike of Britain was perhaps less important than their opposition on the practical grounds that Germany's political and economic interests did not accord with those of her Anglo-Saxon neighbour. 'Advocates of expediency' such as Stolberg-Wernigerode, Wagener and Blanckenburg, who had swallowed their early doubts and now urged their followers to give 'unconditional support for the government in its foreign policy',[51] recognised that Prusso-

German diplomacy would have to be based upon the realities of the international scene and not upon ideology alone. Had the British government offered its full support for German unity in the 1860s, it is more than likely that these nationalist Conservatives would have responded warmly. London's apparent coolness to this aspiration, and especially the pro-French sentiments of the British press and the flow of munitions across the Channel in 1870-1, aroused predictable bitterness in German right-wing circles, which contrasted all this with Russia's assistance. Thus, the Free Conservatives, like many National Liberals, provided a ready audience when Treitschke offered them an historical presentation of perfidious Albion, whose egoistical foreign policy was as offensive as its ruinous domestic-political development. By 1881, indeed, Treitschke was virtually one of their number during Reichstag votes and the *Preussische Jahrbücher* had undergone a similar metamorphosis.

The further blending of 'realist' National Liberal and 'realist' Conservative forces which took place in the late 1870s under the impact of the depression reinforced this feeling against Britain. Many of the Free Conservatives who had argued for a compromise between agriculture and industry were themselves involved in heavy industry and banking; and when the economy faltered they were quick to agitate for a return to protectionism, deploying anti-British arguments in the process. Free trade was *not* a selfless ideal, argued Kardorff in his 1875 brochure 'Against the Current': it was a hypocritical British way of weakening the less advanced among the industrialising nations by flooding them with cheap iron goods and textiles. Only tariffs, hitting those imports, would give Germany the chance to hold its own.[52] Coinciding with this industrial agitation came that drastic change in the condition of German agriculture, which pushed the Junkers towards becoming a party of interest and simultaneously towards seeking their economic future behind high agricultural tariffs. After 1879-80, moreover, their traditional link with Britain as a market for grain faded away, so that economic self-interest no longer restrained the domestic-political grounds for keeping Anglo-German relations at a minimum.

Predictably enough, therefore, Conservative writers and journals showed a clear preference for Russia, were critical of Disraeli's policy in the Eastern Question (which, as they saw it, was intended to embroil Europe in war), expressed a strong dislike for British hypocrisy in taking over Egypt and rejoiced at the news of colonial reverses. 'The English have nicely burnt their fingers in Afghanistan – the "honourable" swine', chuckled Rantzau (Bismarck's son-in-law) in 1880.[53] The majority of German Conservatives were also harshly critical of Gladstonian Britain when it appeared to be frustrating Bismarck's colonial ventures a few years later, although it is also true that the Free Conservatives at least were pragmatic enough to modify this sort of criticism if word came from 'above' that it was necessary to be friendly towards London in order to check Franco-Russian policies.

Finally, it is worth noting that German conservatism was not, even in its outward political form, a movement embracing only landowners, higher officials of state and industrialists. It also consisted of a substantial mass of peasant-farmers, handicraftsmen and other members of the *Mittelstand* who felt that they were suffering as a consequence of industrialisation, who sought to cast off the burdens imposed by the (inevitably, Jewish) moneylenders, and who yearned for the recreation of a stable, older society in which agrarian and craft-based values predominated. The historian of international affairs can refer only briefly to this world of economic resentments, anti-modernism, racial myths and 'cultural despair' which made up the dark side of the Teutonic ideology, and which received such an enormous stimulation because of the anti-Semitic writings of Stöcker, Böckel and Ahlwardt on the one hand and the discomforts of the Great Depression on the other.[54] But the development of pseudo-scientific racialism and the articulation of an 'anti-modern' ideology, the growth of anti-Semitic parties and the arousal of the political consciousness of the German peasantry, craftsmen and clerks *were* to have a long-term impact upon the political scene and, indirectly, upon Anglo-German relations. Even at this stage, it is worth remarking upon such movements, not merely because they have no real equivalent on the British side, but also because this criticism of what Stöcker termed 'modern mammonism'[55] indicated a set of prejudices against liberalism and cosmopolitanism which would make close relations with Britain extremely unattractive. By no means all of these forces were anti-democratic and in many there lingered a strong resentment of the Junkers; but as time went on the populist drive of small farmers and artisans was much more likely to be represented in peasants' leagues or in the German Conservative, Centre and National Liberal parties – all of which were seeking to accommodate this discontent and none of which had much affection for Liberal Britain in any case – than in SPD or Progressive groups. Furthermore, the radicalised anti-Semites, being obsessed about Germany's own 'Manchesterite Jews', found it all too easy to portray Britain as given over to decadence and corruption, despite all the hypocritical efforts to conceal this: the English, claimed Paul Föster, were 'Jews six days a week and Christians on one'. If final proof were needed, argued Glagau, then his readers should consider the ominous fact that Britain was alternately ruled by two Jews, Disraeli and Glattstein, *alias* Gladstone![56] This was not a nation to cherish any affection towards.

Compared with its German equivalent, British conservatism retained a remarkable overall coherence during the second half of the nineteenth century. There were, inevitably, differences of opinion underneath the umbrella of party unity but in general the party managed to contain these disputes and such defections as did occur – Derby in 1880, Randolph Churchill in 1886 – could usually be presented as the actions of the unorthodox. This adamantine strength and growing popularity of conservatism was based neither upon the traditions of party loyalty alone, nor upon any stranglehold which its followers may have had upon the machinery of government, as was the case in Germany; it also derived from an ability to adapt to changing ideas and circumstances whilst seeking to minimise the practical impact of such changes upon their fundamental interests. As Disraeli, the archetypal pragmatist, put it: 'In a progressive country change is constant; and the question is not whether you should resist change which is inevitable, but whether that change should be carried out in deference to the manners, the customs, the laws and the traditions of the people, or whether it should be carried out in deference to abstract principles, and arbitrary and general doctrines.'[57] This was a viewpoint which, although in certain respects close to Bismarck's own, was anathema to the greater number of Junkers; and even if Britain, too, produced its 'diehards', they rarely influenced the Conservative Party into adopting an untenable, dogmatic stance. Even the most traditionalist landowners came to appreciate that the party needed Disraeli if the Liberal monopoly of power was to be broken. All this meant that, although one can point to an *ideology* of British conservatism, the essence of the movement lay elsewhere, in its tactical handling of political problems and in its admiration of a set of prejudices and beliefs which would appeal to many men's inclinations.

It was here, of course, that Disraeli was in his element, bidding for the newly enfranchised working-class vote with his appeal to the idea of 'Tory democracy' yet simultaneously reassuring the middle classes that the party was a safe home for those retreating from Gladstonian 'radicalism' – and capping all this with the assertion that the country required the leadership of its traditional 'aristocratic settlement'. This tactical ingenuity doubtless gave British conservatism a larger potential electoral base than that of its Prussian equivalent but it also involved a constant guidance from above in order to paper over the cracks between the various social groupings which were brought under this Disraelian panoply. Not only did the party leadership have to 'trim' between the landed and the industrial interest, it also had to engage in a similar balancing act between the bourgeoisie and the working classes. If its record upon social reform in the 1870s is any guide, then it is clear that these contradictions were generally resolved by a large amount of rhetoric and a much smaller amount of legislative and executive action.[58]

British conservatism required, of course, more than its leader's flexibility to sustain its continued vitality between the Second and Third Reform Bills, and its growth thereafter. In the first place, the party always insisted that any general extensions of the franchise be accompanied by specific redrawings of electoral boundaries and redistribution of seats in order to preserve their own interests – a good example of surrendering the shadow while retaining the substance.[59] Secondly, as a consequence partly of redistribution, and partly of the expansion of suburbia, the Conservatives were able steadily to expand their hold upon borough seats as well as to retain those in the counties. 'Villa Toryism' was, for a number of reasons, to be a phenomenon which had no proper German equivalent. Moreover, the party itself improved its organisation from the early 1870s onwards, a fact which became ever more obvious when the temporary neglect of this machinery a few years later contributed to the electoral débâcle of 1880.[60]

Nevertheless, despite these advantages, it remains clear that the Conservative Party was – like the Liberal one – an uneasy conglomerate; and it is therefore not surprising that historians have detected in Disraeli's external policy yet another means which he employed in order to preserve party unity and his own position:

Disraeli's purchase of the Suez Canal shares, his belligerent attitude towards Russia in 1878, and his 'forward' policies in Afghanistan and South Africa in 1879, were not just the result of his own interests and prejudices and misapprehensions. They were also, in a sense, an attempt to escape from the internal contradictions of Conservative domestic policy in the 'seventies by a brilliant display abroad.[61]

Although the Conservatives could benefit by picking up the patriotic mantle of Palmerston when his Liberal successors preferred to leave it lying on the ground, this strategem was only effective when it coincided with suitable external events. Sabre-rattling made little impact when the British electorate felt unthreatened, as the mid-1860s had demonstrated. A decade or so later, things were different:

The advance of Russia in central Asia bringing a powerful European military state menacingly near to the frontiers of India, the sudden overthrow of France by the swift use of Prussian strength, the emergence of a united Germany and a united Italy and the avidity with which the European powers hurled themselves into the race for colonies, all disturbed Englishmen and compelled them to think about home defence and their imperial possessions and responsibilities.[62]

In this situation, the Gladstonian recipes of tolerance and non-intervention in response to foreign challenges appeared to be a dreadful blunder; and when this external factor was combined with middle-class concern that the Grand Old Man was increasingly the captive of the Radicals and the Irish, the trickle of businessmen, scholars and clerks into the Conservative Party soon became a flood. To a considerable extent, the Tories were beneficiaries of the failure of their opponents to agree upon a long-term strategy once liberalism had secured its original aims of constitutional and economic freedoms; and of their parallel failure to respond with sufficient energy to the challenges to the British Empire throughout the world.

Although Conservative propaganda increasingly emphasised a 'strong' external policy, the party also avoided a stated commitment to a set of political principles which burdened their opponents' foreign policy. Instead, there was a habit of pragmatic, flexible Realpolitik, well suited to a power needing to preserve its world position and only occasionally disrupted by fits of Disraelian impatience or enthusiasm. With Salisbury's coming to power, even those spasmodic aberrations disappeared and there was a corresponding increase in the awareness that external policy had to be seen in global terms, with developments in one continent impinging upon those in another. In turn, this implied that the British Conservatives' view of Germany was not dictated in advance, but would be moved primarily by their assessment of whether or not the rising new Reich posed a threat to England's own place in the established global order. Such flexibility was again exemplified by Disraeli, who in the 1850s had held that 'a good understanding with France should be the basis of British foreign policy' before Napoleon III's adventures caused the Tory statesman to incline instead towards Germany. This opinion he retained in 1870 but by the 1875 'war-in-sight' crisis, as his biographer relates, 'His former tendency to a political friendship with France was revived.' By 1879, he was again keen to embrace the idea of an Anglo-German alliance, a sentiment quite explicable in the light of his suspicions of Russia at that time.[63]

It was *not* the case, therefore, that the Conservatives' anxiety about the challenges to Britain's world position in the final third of the nineteenth century automatically propelled them into an anti-German stance. There were, admittedly, voices in the party suspicious of a 'Prussianised' Germany from Bismarck's advent to power onwards, chiefly from the belief that the Chancellor's unscrupulous methods, the potential German threat to the Low Countries and the dynastic link between Berlin and St Petersburg made it difficult for Britain to achieve her diplomatic aims in Europe. Hence, for example, the fear of the British Cabinet in 1870–1 that the Tory 'ultras' – by which was meant Salisbury, Peel and the columns of the *Quarterly Review* – would combine in some unholy alliance with the Radicals, Positivists and Republicans on behalf of France and thereby embarrass the official policy of neutrality.[64] This also explains the Conservative dislike of the *Dreikaiserbund* which, so far as Disraeli and his colleagues were concerned, not only rendered Britain diplomatically ineffectual on the continent but indirectly assisted Russia's Asian ambitions by relieving her of problems on her western borders; and it accounts for their reaction during the 1875 crisis, since a second and more thorough German overrunning of France would destroy the European balance completely. Finally, it has to be admitted that the two Conservative Foreign Secretaries of this period, Derby and Salisbury, were far more suspicious of German policy than many of their less involved colleagues.[65]

Yet against all this, it needs to be repeated that, provided the Low Countries were left alone and France was not dismembered, the Tories saw no reason why there should not be a united and powerful Germany in the middle of Europe. This suggests again, of course, both that Berlin's own actions would be decisive, and that there existed, however vaguely, a British sense that there were 'natural' limits to the size of the German Empire in Europe; but since Bismarck seemed opposed to a *grossdeutsch* solution, this question never arose in these years (with the partial exception of 1875). Secondly, the Conservatives' emphasis upon the consolidation – and, under Disraeli and Carnarvon, the occasional extension – of the overseas empire inclined them further towards the two Germanic powers, which appeared to possess no colonial or naval ambitions detrimental to British interests, and whose very existence held in check the extra-European activities of France and Russia. In 1873, for example, the Tory peer Lord Dunsany published his work *Gaul or Teuton?: Considerations as to our Allies of the Future*, in which he plumped strongly for a British coalition with Germany, Austria-Hungary and Italy and derided the fears occasioned by the 'Battle of Dorking' episode; and a year later Derby himself privately welcomed the news of increases in the German fleet as adding 'one more to the many causes which already operate on the Russian mind where Germany is concerned'.[66] This belief in an identity of interests also explains the vigorous reaction of the Indian viceroy, Lord Lytton – preoccupied, like all holders of that office, with the Russian 'danger' – to the 1877 rumour that the Cabinet was contemplating an Anglo-Russian alliance against Germany. In a short space of time, he had circulated a private memorandum which denounced this alleged scheme and, as Derby tartly put it, 'winds up by an appeal to the Queen and to the Protestant feeling of the country to prevent us from accomplishing our work of mischief'![67] Since the rumour in question had little real foundation, this literary effort on Lytton's part was unnecessary but it represented a widely held Conservative viewpoint and one which became ever more widespread as the Eastern crisis reached its zenith in 1878.

By the early 1880s, Conservative anxieties about a German threat to France had weakened as the republic's expansionism in Africa and naval ambitions appeared to pose a challenge almost as great as the Russian one. In these circumstances, Bismarck was not only worth some kindly words but to the Right in Britain his foreign *and* domestic policies contrasted sharply with those of the 'blundering' Mr Gladstone. The party's weekly journal *England*, for example, offered fulsome praise to Bismarck on the occasion of his sixty-ninth birthday in 1884:

> [He is] the greatest man in the world . . . He has formed a great and invincible confederacy in the heart of Europe, which is a bulwark against the restless chauvinism of France and the perfidious aggression of St. Petersburg . . . Under Lord Beaconsfield England shared the happy and secure position of third partner in this splendid union. Alas, that the faction and folly of his successors should have alienated England from the German powers, isolated her in Europe, and caused the deplorable display of blundering and helplessness which has marked the Imperial policy of Mr. Gladstone for the past four years.[68]

Here one finds, predictably enough, the worship of success and praise of 'firm' policies and ordered government which was also becoming the habit of many Liberal Imperialists in this period; and which, taken together with their dislike of Gladstone's domestic policies and apprehension about France and Russia, explains why Conservatives did not at first react in a hostile manner to Bismarck's colonial bids. The party's 'Campaign Notes' for 1885, for example, concentrated their fire upon Liberal mishandling of external policy and in particular singled out Derby for having 'alienated the friendship of Germany'. Analyses of 'Why we lost New Guinea' or '. . . Angra Pequena' emphasised British incompetence, not the German threat.[69]

Nevertheless, it was also true that the creation of a German overseas empire alongside the British would have repercussions upon Conservative opinion in the future if there was seen to be a direct clash of interests. This, however, deserves a later analysis and it would be more convenient to halt the scrutiny of the Tories' perception of Germany here, before the new dimension is added. What emerges overall is the ironic fact that, whereas it was the 'Left' in Germany which was pro-British, in England itself the 'Right' was recognisably the group which, if it had sympathies for foreign states at all, inclined towards Germany and Austria-Hungary. Twenty-five years later this picture had altered – on the British side, remarkably so – and it will be again necessary to look at the interconnections between the changing circumstances and the position of the parties to discover why these perceptions of the other country also alter.

## LABOUR AND ITS ALLIES

Any analysis of working-class attitudes towards external events in mid-century Europe inevitably suffers from the fact that the great masses of labourers, farmworkers and domestic servants hardly possessed a political 'voice' at all and, given their material circumstances, were highly unlikely to take much interest in affairs overseas. What is known is that the internationalist viewpoint of the more articulate trade unionists and Socialists in Britain and Germany was not dissimilar from that of radical Liberals, although the philosophical routes by which this common position had been reached were different. In theory, the identity of interests of the working classes in all countries was an axiom of socialist ideology; in practice, this had never been properly realised, partly because of the defeat of Chartism and the 1848 revolution, partly because of the lack of communications, and partly because of indifference to affairs outside the workers' immediate interests. By the 1860s, however, trade struggles between employers and workers in Britain had provoked many of the skilled labourers to accept that their industrial aims could not be divorced from political activity; and this rise in political consciousness manifested itself not only in the London Trades Council, newspapers such as the *Beehive* and the struggle for a wider franchise, but also in a growing interest in foreign affairs. Part of this concern was, admittedly, self-interested: 'When the [First] International was established, the most important single motive impelling trade unions to affiliate was the desire to prevent strike-breaking through the introduction of European labour.'[70] Yet it is also true that many workers demonstrated an interest in issues such as Italian unity, the American Civil War and the fate of Poland; if they disputed about whether political or economic emancipation at home was the more important, they could at least see foreign controversies in black and white, and this consciousness was also reflected by the large numbers of working men who joined the Volunteers. The illiberal Austrian rule in Italy, the slave-owning landlords of the American South, the brutal internal terrorism of Tsarist Russia, were readily identifiable enemies of the working class.[71]

The interest shown by British labour circles in foreign affairs was strongly reinforced by their connections with two intellectual forces, Marx and the Positivists. Marx's role, especially in regard to the First International, is too well known to require much analysis here: he gave an 'international' thrust to the British labour movement, not merely by his contacts with socialist leaders on the continent but also by the impress of his own views about various foreign powers – especially his animosity towards the Russian regime.[72] Moreover, despite the ambiguities in the great mass of their day-to-day writings and evolving ideas, it is clear that Marx and Engels laid stress upon the cosmopolitan nature of the class struggle. Workers' movements might be national in form, but not in substance, and they had to avoid being thrown against each other by their respective establishments. Modern nationalism, in Marx's words, was 'bourgeois nationalism'.[73] The association of the Positivists with the British working classes had different roots but many similar consequences.[74] The way in which leading Positivists such as Harrison and Beesly agitated for suffrage reform, assisted the trade unions during the strikes of the early 1860s and campaigned against the selfishness of the middle classes as well as the privileges of the aristocracy, established their credentials as genuine and articulate supporters of organised labour. As a consequence, their already well-established views upon external policy – a hostility to the 'follies' of empire, a deep dislike of the forces of reaction and a strong sympathy towards France[75] – influenced British trade unionism, the more especially since the working-class press contained numerous contributions from the pens of the Positivists.

The attitude of the varied ranks of the British 'left' towards the rise of Prussia-Germany under Bismarckian direction was, therefore, almost uniformly hostile despite their belief in national self-determination. Wilhelm I and Bismarck represented all that the Socialists detested and the more so because, from the Polish crisis of 1863 onwards, the Berlin court appeared to be in close touch with its Russian equivalent, the centre of world reaction. The only point of dispute in the 1860s related to France, but by 1867 even Harrison and Beesly had been alienated by Napoleon III's policies and were eager, like Marx, to see a revolution in that country. Believing (like everyone else) that the Franco-Prussian War was France's fault, all these groups were silent during the first stages of that conflict; but Napoleon's fall, the occupation of French soil by Prussian soldiers and the suspicion that Berlin was in liaison with St Petersburg, changed all that. Within a short space of time, the British labour movement had become markedly pro-French and anti-German. Marx, for his part, was merely acting in accordance with his earlier warning that the German working classes should only fight a defensive war, but the Positivists' viewpoint was dictated as much by an emotional fervour for the land of Comte as by any political calculation. Congreve, their leader, presided over the Anglo-French Intervention Committee; and this organisation received massive support from the Land and Labour League and the International Democratic Association, which had also been penetrated by the Positivists. Again, these intellectuals were behind that 'enormous deputation, made up of representatives of more than a hundred Unions, which waited upon Gladstone to demand a strong [that is, pro-French] policy from his government'.[76] Joining them was the radical *Reynolds' News*, which was full of praise from France, and Bradlaugh's *National Reformer*, which called the foundation of the Third Republic 'a beacon to light the nations to liberty'.[77] On the other hand, while there was uniformity among the Left for the recognition of the republic, many British trade unionists dissented from the idea of London's intervention against Germany and Marx, too, found it unrealistic.

When the Commune was proclaimed, further fissures occurred in British working-class circles; many of the more moderate leaders dissociated themselves from support for such revolutionary events, although the news from Paris brought together the Positivists and Marx. The former objected to the socialist attack upon private property but still saw in the French proletariat the main driving-force for the future progress of Western society; whereas Marx, swallowing his doubts about the tactics employed, felt bound to encourage the Communards and to defend their position in his *The Civil War in France*.[78]

While the Paris uprising uncovered certain divisions within the loosely related groupings of the Left, this in no way affected their general attitude towards the new German state. Whatever the opinions about Thiers' government and its treatment of the Communards, the hostility towards its eastern neighbour was virtually unanimous. 'With Prussia, with Bismarck, with military autocracy, a semi-feudal aristocracy, a semi-Russian Government, we can have no such sympathy, no such common policy [as is possible with Liberal France]', claimed Harrison.[79] For the following three decades, this was to be the received view of Imperial Germany in British working-class and progressive circles. To be sure, this was probably less a concern amongst the trade unionists themselves, for after 1871 they were gradually to lose much of their earlier interest in foreign affairs as they concentrated upon domestic reforms; and their opinions upon external policy were, as usual, scarcely to be heard amidst the noise made by their intellectual fellow-travellers, the Positivists, the Republicans, a variety of progressives ranging from Dilke and Labouchere to Bradlaugh, and the early British Socialists under Hyndman. Yet there is no reason to suppose that, even if the workers' voice had been more independent and articulate, it would have offered a picture of Germany very different from the standard image in progressive minds of a country being ruined by its reactionary, militaristic establishment.

The development of an organised labour movement in Germany, although it was to have a different shape and impact, paralleled that in Britain in many respects.[80] The extent of working-class consciousness also differed from region to region, and was economic rather than political in origin and aim; many of the workers involved were Christian and democrat rather than socialist and revolutionary; and labour organisations chiefly concerned skilled artisans, with very few from the unskilled trades, even fewer Catholics and none from the peasantry – which were major deficiencies indeed for a truly popular party. The massive suspicion held by the establishment towards the labour movement, however, provided the stimulus for the creation inside Germany of the largest socialist party in the world. Faced both by the employers' opposition in the workplace and by the hostility of the Prusso-German state, the workers had little alternative but to seek by political means to realise their social and economic aims.

Already in the 1860s there were two political organisations (under Lassalle in the north, and Bebel and Liebknecht in Saxony and the south) towards which individual craftsmen and trade unionists could turn; and this tendency was given a further boost by the introduction of universal manhood suffrage for the North German Parliament and then for the Reichstag itself. A mass political party was worth organising, it was clear, when all adult male workers had the vote. Furthermore, the actual leadership of this movement, which by 1875 had become a united party with nine deputies in the Reichstag, had a much more developed political consciousness than trade union leaders in Britain. The German worker may have thought differently, but for Bebel and Liebknecht their long ties with Marx and their identification (however wavering) with the First International made it certain that it was issues of state politics rather than those of the factory bench which preoccupied their minds. In addition, their commitment to socialism always mingled with a passionate anti-Prussianism – which explains their support for Austria in 1866, their intimate links with south German Liberals and their decision to abstain from approving war credits in July 1870.[81]

The exaggerated fears of the German establishment at this stance by the SPD leaders, and at contemporary events in Paris, are not for scrutiny here;[82] but what is significant were the effects of the party's ideology and formative experiences upon its attitude towards Britain. Here the democratic and left-Liberal influences of south Germany clearly made their mark, as did Liebknecht's fond memory of his years of exile in England: both factors help to explain why there were many more bitter references to Prussian militarism than to the evils of capitalism in the writings of these early Social Democrats. Moreover, the unwillingness of the British government to persecute suspect members of the International, and the reformist trail blazed by Gladstone's first administration, could not but provoke the admiration of many among the German Left; and even Marx, in his final speech as a member of the First International in 1872, suggested that in Britain, the USA and perhaps the Netherlands the workers could 'hope to secure their ends by peaceful means' – which, by implication at least, was a favourable reference to the political cultures of those countries.[83]

All this meant that the SPD image of Britain was, despite occasional reservations about her as the home of capitalism and a distrust of Disraeli's domestic policy, essentially favourable. In contrast, Bebel and Liebknecht had from the earliest times followed Marx's line of hatred towards Tsarist Russia. By the late 1880s, in fact, this bitterness was causing many German Socialists to give tacit support to official foreign policy, especially when the links with Austria-Hungary and Italy were emphasised; but even before then, the SPD had chorused its disapproval of the *Dreikaiserbund*. If the party had any criticism of Gladstone by the late 1870s, it was on account of his apparent toleration of Russian expansionism against Turkey; hence the SPD, like the left-Liberals, tacitly approved of Disraeli's 'check' to Russia in 1878 and of the prospect of an Anglo-German-Austrian alliance in 1879.[84]

It was for these general reasons, as well as on account of their specific dislike of colonialism, that Bebel and Liebknecht criticised German overseas expansion in the 1880s.[85] As the SPD leadership saw it, this not only diverted the nation's attention from internal concerns and from the Russian danger, but it also ran the risk of antagonising Britain. It is interesting to note once again that their chief objection to colonisation was based not so much upon the (as yet undeveloped) theory of capitalist imperialism, but rather upon the older ideas of the Radicals. 'Who talks today of colonies', warned the *Sozialdemokrat* in

1884, 'talks also of colonial wars, of warships, colonial troops and standing army, in a word, of militarism' – a classic Cobdenite objection.[86] All that German colonisation was doing was revealing the reactionary Junker system in yet another form. Hence the otherwise inexplicable distinction which Bebel and Liebknecht made between the British and German overseas empires: the former, being the product of a liberal-democratic society, was essentially good, a veritable 'civilising mission' which benefited the motherland and the colony alike; whereas the latter, being the product of an unfair and reactionary establishment, was – like the Russian empire in Asia – a brutal enterprise, which brought to the native neither culture nor reforms. Although certain 'revisionist' socialists made more favourable references to German colonisation in the mid-1880s, especially over the Steamship Subsidy Bill, the party leadership held to its original line. Needless to say, by doing this they confirmed the 'unpatriotic' image of the Social Democrats in the eyes of the establishment and encouraged right-wing feelings against Liberal England – which, it was argued, must be dangerous if German 'revolutionaries' thought so highly of it.

## THE CENTRE PARTY

The attitude of the German Centre Party towards Britain was similarly conditioned by the two great formative experiences of this era: the creation of the Reich, and then, only a little later, by the impact of industrialisation and depression. The political position of the Centre flowed from the fact that it soon occupied – as its name implied – a pivotal position in the Reichstag, between the conservative, pro-establishment forces on the right and the Progressive and Socialist deputies on the left. By 1874, the party had 91 Reichstag seats; by 1878, 93 seats; and by 1890, 106 seats, becoming the largest of all the parties.[87]

The key function of political Catholicism up until Bismarck's later years pertained less to its role in the Reichstag, however important, than to the way in which it seemed to place a question-mark over the constitutional and political unity of the Empire itself.[88] Despite all the contrary economic and patriotic arguments for national unity, there had been little doubt about the widespread south German hostility to Prussia; most of their governments had taken the Austrian side in 1866, and the defeat still rankled; even in 1870, Bavarian particularists had tried to reduce the funds allocated for the war against France; and, when national unity appeared unavoidable, such circles sought to ensure that the rights and privileges of the individual states were protected.[89] The unleashing of the *Kulturkampf* a few years later simply increased the causes and the regions of Catholic unrest, with the Centre Party in the Rhineland making strides at liberalism's expense as the church mobilised its followers into a political defence of their religion. Not surprisingly, many of the smaller dissatisfied parties gravitated towards this large, oppositional voting bloc – Guelph particularists, Poles, Alsatians, outraged traditionalists like Ludwig von Gerlach, and so on. It was also not surprising that Bismarck felt that he had to lean towards the National Liberals during the

1870s, thus further alienating the Catholics and provoking intensive debates about the future solidarity of the new nation.[90]

All this inevitably determined the Centre Party's attitude towards Britain in the 1870s, although it has to be said that Anglo-German relations were not a great issue. To the average German Catholic, relations with Austria-Hungary (especially for the Bavarians) and with France (especially for the people of Alsace-Lorraine) were obviously much more important; with those two countries there existed cultural, religious, linguistic and commercial connections which far outweighed those with Britain. The latter, in the eyes of many in central Europe, had come to symbolise Godless industrialism, the breakdown of the old social order and *laissez-faire*. Moreover, the emphasis placed by anti-Catholic forces during the *Kulturkampf* upon the common struggle of the northern European peoples against the Ultramontanes inevitably identified Britain as an ally of Prussia, Protestantism and National Liberalism. For the same reason, the *Germania* and other Catholic journals took a close interest in the affairs of Ireland, frequently reminding their readers of the horrifying effects of the Protestant ascendancy since Tudor times. Gladstone, here as elsewhere, provoked mixed feelings: his anti-papal pamphleteering bout of the mid-1870s annoyed German Catholics; his Land Act and disestablishment of the Church of Ireland impressed them.[91] Disraeli, unloved because of the Tory policy on Ireland, was praised when he tried to help Catholic Austria to withstand Russian intrigues in the Balkans in the late 1870s.

The alteration in the position of the Centre Party after 1878, when Bismarck slowly began to abandon the *Kulturkampf*, did not greatly affect the attitude of German Catholics towards Britain. Once the dissensions over religious matters took second place, the party found it possible to agree with the Chancellor on a number of issues, notably the abandonment of free trade and the introduction of social measures. Having suffered for decades the verbal and legislative assaults of the German Liberals, it was a pleasant experience for many a Catholic deputy to assist in passing laws which were burying liberalism. Yet by this stance, and by their gradual if irregular support for Bismarck during the early 1880s, it is evident that the social and political preconceptions of German Catholicism were moving further away from those of Liberal England. It was less necessary now to compare the 'repressions' inside Germany with the 'freedoms' enjoyed by Britons; and as the party became secularised, it increasingly revealed itself as a Conservative force, a sort of Catholic *Interessenpartei* which, in representing the aspirations of small farmers, businessmen and craftsmen, would have even less in common with Britain than before.[92] To repeat: Anglo-German relations were not of great importance to the Centre Party in any case; but should they worsen further, that trend was unlikely to be combatted by the largest party in the Reichstag or by the substantial Catholic population which it represented.

This essentially negative conclusion about the Centre Party also applies to the overall role of the parties in the Anglo-German relationship in these decades. No one imagined that parliamentary parties themselves *made* policies, but they were a significant forum of public opinion to which statesmen, especially on the British side, paid heed. The point was, however, that the messages coming from the parties offered no comprehensive guidance for the day-to-day conduct of diplomacy. British Conservatives on the whole approved of Bismarckian Germany, subject to certain provisos about the maintenance of British interests; Liberals on the whole disapproved, but didn't really wish to quarrel. The German Left admired Britain, the Centre was non-committal, and the Conservatives and National Liberals were critical. Given the fluidity of British and German politics in these years, there were exceptions to all these statements; but the overall impression is that, since the parties were not acutely concerned about Anglo-German relations except during a few periods of crisis, their governments were left with a relatively free hand. This again suggests that the relationship between the two peoples was stable, generally uncontroversial and lacking the aspects which produce a permanent antagonism. Had a deep-seated enmity and a perceived clash of basic interests existed, then it is clear that the parties, as foci and reflectors of political opinion, would have been more actively concerned about relations with the other country – as they were to be twenty-five years later.

# CHAPTER 5

# The Press, Pressure Groups and Public Opinion

One of the key developments of nineteenth-century European politics was the growing awareness of governments that they required a much larger body of support to sustain and 'legitimise' their rule than had been thought necessary hitherto. To many statesmen of the older school, this trend was an alarming one, for it was difficult to see if there was any permanent resting-place between a system of feudal autocracy on the one hand and full-blown democracy on the other. Yet even Bismarck, as we have seen, felt the need to demonstrate that his policies were 'popular'; and one of his strongest complaints against his Liberal opponents was that they did *not* represent the true feelings of the people at large but only the views of a dissatisfied bourgeois minority. This did not make Bismarck a democrat any more so than Napoleon III, but it showed that all but the recalcitrant few wished to justify their rule in terms of something more than God-given rights. Statesmen might disagree about just how widely the 'political nation' extended, and what forms of opinion should be recognised, but most would have agreed with Clarendon that 'Governments no more than individuals can afford nowadays to despise public opinion'.[1]

How precisely one measured that 'public' opinion was, of course, a key problem of politics, simply because every party felt bound to claim that its stance attracted popular support. In the nineteenth century, before the Gallup polls and other forms of measuring opinion were introduced, the chief indicator – apart from the ballot box itself – seemed to be the newspaper. As Disraeli made Coningsby say, 'Opinion is now supreme and Opinion speaks in print. The representation of the Press is far more complete than the representation of Parliament'; or, as Carlyle put it, 'Journalists are now the true Kings and Clergy.'[2]

This deep respect for the influence of the press, however much it may be questioned by later historians, was partly justified by the growing circulation figures of the better-known daily, Sunday and weekly journals. In the main, though, the conviction that the newspaper represented public opinion arose from the widely held belief that its development was yet another manifestation of the new, progressive, liberating forces at work in modern society. As the *Westminster Review* put it:

> The newspapers . . . are the best and surest civilisers of a country. They contain within themselves not only the elements of knowledge but the inducement to learn . . . It is necessary to have seen a people among whom newspapers have not penetrated, to know the mass of mischievous prejudices which these productions instantly and necessarily dissipate.[3]

The advancement of knowledge, the swift dispersal of information, the logical and refined analysis of political problems, the dissipation of falsely based prejudices and the critical scrutiny of untenable claims: in carrying out these functions, it was predictable that the press was often regarded as 'the fountain of intellectual light'.[4]

At the beginning of this period, moreover, it is worth recalling just how relatively new this industry was. Newspapers and journals had existed for many decades beforehand, but it was only in the 1850s and 1860s that the real 'take-off' occurred: the coming of new printing machinery, the building of a railway network and the inland telegraph, the growth in large urban centres, the increase in literacy rates, the expansion of joint-stock companies and the bourses, all offered incentives and opened new possibilities for the establishment of newspapers; and the repeal of stamp duties, the moderation or abandonment of governmental interference and the massive reductions in the price of a daily paper eliminated the political and practical objections which had hitherto stood in the way of a service that could cater for that readership market unattracted by expensive society journals on the one hand and cheap pamphlets on the other. The very fact that the major trend of these years was the rise of the *provincial* press, catering to its substantial local readership although also commenting upon national politics, was generally reckoned to favour the progressive forces in both Britain and Germany. Such papers were, after all, likely to make themselves attractive to their growing readership of merchants and professional men; and, in the German case, to offer opinions quite at variance with – because culturally and geographically remote from – those of the Prussian government in Berlin.

It followed from all this that the flourishing of a free press was generally thought to be of assistance to liberalism: 'The form of government becomes liberal in the exact proportion as the power of public opinion increases', William McKinnon had observed in 1828, and the early-to-mid nineteenth-century struggles between conservative and progressive forces throughout Europe over the freedom of the press had usually confirmed this diagnosis.[5] The sheer number of Liberal papers and the size of their readership also suggested this conclusion. During the Prussian constitutional struggle, for example, 'the conservative press was hopelessly outclassed',[6] and when one adds to this the non-Prussian totals of newspaper circulations, the balance shifted even further away from the Conservatives. Nor could the Reich establishment expect any support from the substantial Catholic and Socialist press when these were also developed in the 1870s. In Britain, the overall situation was the same, even if the balance was less substantially tipped against the Conservatives. London in 1870 was 'journalistically a Liberal capital', and in the provinces this preponderance was even greater. 'There was in 1874 no

Conservative daily paper in Birmingham, Huddersfield, Darlington, Hull or Leicester, and they were outnumbered by three to one in Liverpool and Leeds.' With the inclusion of the weekly press, the national total was 489 Liberal to 294 Conservative papers – and even these figures probably underestimate the Liberal superiority.[7]

Despite these facts, and despite the assumptions of Liberal ideology, there was no inherent reason why the press should remain permanently in the progressive camp: like many other aspects of liberalism, its success in the realm of newspapers was rooted in specific political and economic circumstances favourable to the movement as a whole. If those circumstances were to change, the political balance within the press world would follow suit. Liberal newspaper pronouncements about free trade or national self-determination could be challenged by Conservative appeals to law and order, to national honour and unity and to 'fair trade'; and both the spreading suburbs of the large cities and the rise in the number of white-collar workers were as likely to provide a growing readership for Conservative papers as for those of a Liberal persuasion. The gradual shift to the Right, in overall terms, of the ownership and corresponding editorial tone of the press in both countries was by no means an impossibility.

One reason why the press was so highly regarded was the sheer extent of politicisation. There was, it was true, a large number of trade and specialist journals, and many of the best-selling papers devoted space to crimes or 'human interest' stories; yet, notwithstanding the basic desire to make a profit out of the business, the fact remains that most newspapers did give a great deal of their space to the dispersal of information upon, and solemn editorial pronouncements over, the events of the day. Full-scale reporting of parliamentary and Reichstag debates, column after column of some politicians' address to his constituents and the closely set layout of all these newspapers did not make for light reading. Yet until the last years of the century it was assumed that the contents of a newspaper were chiefly intended for those classes of the community to whom political events were of significance. Papers directed at the working classes in no way differed from this assumption: if anything, the *Beehive* and *Vorwärts* expected more political consciousness from their readers than the *Daily Telegraph* and *Lokal-Anzeiger*, whose pages were at least spiced with items of local interest, scandals, advertisements and the rest. Moreover, if the press gave priority of coverage to the political arena, this regard was amply returned by politicians themselves despite their disparaging remarks about the Fourth Estate. No party felt that it could survive without its own press organs, and great anxiety attended the death or retirement of a friendly proprietor lest the journal concerned fall into the 'wrong' hands. The efforts to influence the press – in the subtler British way (well refined by Palmerston) of having a word in the editor's ear at the club, or in the cruder German fashion of creating a press bureau – indicated how important it was regarded, especially near election times.

The intimacy of the political and newspaper arenas may not only be measured by the efforts of each to influence the other, but also by the tradition of the dual profession: owners, editors and journalists became politicians, and politicians regularly wrote for newspapers.[8] In addition, the monthly and quarterly journals not only published articles composed by politicians but offered a variety of commentaries by other members of the 'political nation'. Morley's *Fortnightly Review*, for example, contained contributions in 1871–2 from Mill, Bagehot, Spencer, Huxley, Freeman, Goldwin Smith, Beesley, Harrison, Leslie Stephen and Justin McCarthy;[9] while the *Preussische Jahrbücher* boasted the services not only of Treitschke and Hans Delbrück, but also Theodor Mommsen, Max Duncker, Theodor von Bernhardi, Wilhelm Wehrenpfennig, Julius Jacoby, Friedrich Thudichum, and many others.[10] The weighty nature of the political weeklies and monthlies – the supreme form of disputation, in so many ways, for a cultured élite – reminds one yet again that their audience was still reckoned to be able to read these various issues at leisure, during the long weekend or the parliamentary recess. Ever more people might be entering the political fold – and steps should be, and were being taken to ensure that they were also properly advised and directed on the affairs of the day – but the circle of those who could personally influence decision-making, even in a little way, remained select and exclusive. Articles in the *Quarterly* or *Saturday* reviews, and leaders in *The Times* and *Kreuz-Zeitung*, were simply another means of communication within what Gladstone liked to call 'the upper ten thousand'.

Of all the newspapers of mid-Victorian Britain, *The Times* was still the most important. It had lost ground compared with the previous two decades and by now a number of London dailies had overtaken its circulation total of around 60,000; yet the influence of the paper remained, for obvious reasons. Its readership was indisputably Gladstone's 'upper ten thousand', plus many others who aspired to that category; and it retained its appeal for that audience not merely out of considerations of snobbery but because of the authoritative nature of its news and commentary – guaranteed, as it were, by its high technology, business acumen and profitability on the one hand, and by its strong editorship and superb army of (especially foreign) correspondents on the other. During Palmerston's later years, Delane had greatly favoured the government – without becoming subservient to it – and its overall stance could in general be termed 'Whiggish'. It approved neither of democracy nor reaction; despised Cobdenite radicals and pacifists as much as Tory 'ultras'; rejoiced in the country's constitutional, economic and cultural progress; defended the tenets of Protestantism and free trade; and had no hesitation in lecturing home and foreign governments if they failed to come up to the standards it demanded of them. Palmerston's death meant no change in its basic politics – which gives us a fair clue to its attitude on foreign affairs in general and to the Gladstone–Disraeli rivalries in particular. Finally, its special position was compounded by the fact that almost every foreign state believed that, if it was not directly a government paper, its comments had official approval or inspiration – a charge which *The Times* loftily shrugged off but which continued to be a source of exasperation to successive British governments.[11]

What the other London dailies lacked in stature, they made up for in sales and, so far as the parties (or party sub-groups) were concerned, in political reliability. The *Daily Telegraph*, the first successful metropolitan daily, was already selling 150,000 copies in the early 1860s and this total had risen to around 240,000 copies by 1880. Describing itself as 'independent Liberal', its price of 1d, popular features and general tone catered for the vastly expanding lower middle classes of the capital city and the Home Counties – all of which, it was reckoned, reinforced the Liberal Party's hold upon those constituencies in the mid-Victorian era. The party's position in the metropolis was also supported by the *Daily News*, with somewhat smaller sales (rising to 150,000 daily copies during its successful reporting of the Franco-Prussian War)[12] but a far more dedicated adherence to Gladstonian liberalism; and the new *London Daily Chronicle*, which grew rapidly to challenge the *Telegraph*'s circulation figures by the 1870s although undoubtedly hurting the *News* in the process. Together, the three of them ensured Liberal domination of newspaper sales in this critical region, and the ½d *Echo* and 2d evening *Pall Mall Gazette* (despite Frederick Greenwood's disapproval of Gladstone) extended this influence socially downwards and upwards.

The chief representative, in sales terms, of metropolitan conservatism was the *Standard*, a 1d morning paper expressing, as its editor William Mudford put it, 'the thought of the villa resident order of Englishmen'.[13] On this firm and growing base its sales figures steadily expanded, so that by the 1880s it had come close to the *Telegraph*. By that time, too, its ideological stance – characterised in its early years by support for the American South and opposition to almost every Gladstonian reform, and leavened by articles from the young Robert Cecil – seemed to accord much more clearly than hitherto with those of many middle-class Englishmen. Higher up the social scale came the *Morning Post*, equalling *The Times* in its high price of 3d but differing from the 'Thunderer' both in its far smaller circulation figures (3,500 in 1871) and in its open efforts to represent the opinions of aristocratic conservatism; its owner, Lord Borthwick, was appropriately rewarded with a knighthood by Disraeli and membership of the peerage by Salisbury.

When one includes the provincial press, the Conservative position in the 1860s and 1870s appears almost hopeless. At this time, when the non-metropolitan journals were in their heyday, freed from stamp duties and benefiting from the inland telegraph but not yet fully affected by rail deliveries of the London dailies, liberalism, too, was at its height – the two factors, as we have seen, being not unconnected. For example, the north-east, 'a stronghold not only of Liberalism but of republicanism and Chartism', boasted of two substantial 1d morning papers, the *Northern Daily Express* and the *Newcastle Daily Chronicle*, but there were also other ½d evening papers and weeklies, and this list was joined in 1870 by the *Northern Echo* under the irrepressible W. T. Stead. A similar pattern could be observed throughout the other regions of England (except the rural south), with Liberal papers outnumbering those of their rivals by about two or three to one; and with certain of these provincial journals – the *Manchester Guardian*, *Birmingham Daily Post*, *Western Times* – enjoying a reputation far outside their localities. 'It was a domination both weighty and qualitative, and gave the Conservatives much to worry about.'[14]

Two further categories of journals need to be mentioned here. The first, the

Sunday newspapers, were among the most popular of all in terms of circulation. Virtually all of them – *Reynolds' Weekly News*, the *Sunday Times*, the *Observer*, the *News of the World*, *Lloyds Weekly News* – were Liberal, not to say radical in their politics; but against this it has to be noted that by the 1870s their contents were far less political (*Reynolds'* excepted) than hitherto and they relied upon sensationalist stories and eye-catching illustrations to capture their audience.[15] Of far more weight than any of these, at least among the political establishment, were the weekly reviews and quarterlies mentioned earlier: affected little by the new technology, and not at all by the rise of the popular press, these expensive journals (some cost 2s 6d and most 6s per issue) offered solemn and considered commentaries upon the political and social trends of the age.[16] Here again, however, the balance was tilted towards liberalism. The Conservative *Quarterly Review* and independent *Saturday Review* might display the brilliant and polemical talents of Sir Henry Maine and Lord Salisbury, and would usually receive support from *Blackwood's Magazine*; but they were opposed by Morley's *Fortnightly* and the less sparkling but quite definitely Liberal *Edinburgh Review* and *Westminster Review* – not to mention the weekly *Spectator*, a firm advocate of Gladstone in these years, and those two further important and rather special weeklies, the *Economist* and *Punch*, neither of which could tolerate the misdeeds of aristocratic conservatism.

This British press tended to reflect – or, in many ways, helped to create – the views of the major political parties towards Germany. Liberal newspapers and journals, for example, were overwhelmingly favourable to the cause of German unity in the 1860s, even if their doubts were growing about the methods Bismarck used to achieve that aim. The Schleswig-Holstein crisis exposed this ambivalence more clearly than ever, as well as showing that the Liberal press was as divided for and against action as the Liberal Cabinet itself.[17] Even in 1866, despite their suspicion that Bismarck had provoked the war with Austria, it was difficult for the Liberal newspapers to be anti-Prussian. Austria was, on account of her Italian policy, a *bête noire* to British Liberals; the German middle classes seemed incapable of uniting their country by themselves, and their *grossdeutsch* pretensions seemed either dangerous or absurd; and France under Napoleon III could now no longer be trusted. The *Fortnightly Review* was thus by no means the only Liberal journal which decided, in the wake of Sadowa, that 'a strong, united, free-trading Protestant Germany was beneficial to England'.[18] The widespread conviction that Napoleon had been responsible for the Franco-Prussian War explains why so many editors and journalists – apart from the Positivists and Irish – denounced France and sympathised with Germany in 1870. The *Economist*, *Spectator*, *Pall Mall Gazette*, *Manchester Guardian* and *Daily News* of 16 July all regarded Napoleon's actions as 'a crime against humanity'.[19] Yet, within two or three months, this Liberal sentiment had vanished. As Arthur Russell informed Morier:

The change in England is very remarkable, the German cause has few friends left and the massacre of French peasants, the increasing cruelty of the Germans, the destruction of French property and capital have com-

92

pletely turned the sympathies of the great majority of Englishmen . . . I still defend the German cause, though somewhat feebly, and I feel the influence of surrounding opinion, waxing daily higher.[20]

With Germany united, the lingering sympathy of the British Liberal press for that country was fast disappearing, to be replaced by a deep dislike of the Junker state and its domestic arrangements – whilst Liberal sympathy was transferred to republican, democratic France, a move which was urged on by all the left-wing of the party, by *Reynolds' News*, by Bradlaugh's *National Reformer*, by the Positivists and Republicans. It is true that this trend was slowed down by Whiggish caution and by liberalism's strong dislike of the ultramontane forces in Europe; but the 'war-in-sight' crisis and the steady rightward drift of German domestic politics in the late 1870s could only provoke criticism from British Liberal newspapers. By the early 1880s – and despite the Whigs' greater fears of French hostility following the occupation of Egypt – the main body of Liberal opinion became convinced that Bismarck was fundamentally hostile to their creed and was seeking to discredit Gladstone in particular. Both the *Daily News* and the *Economist* devoted articles to an exposé of 'Prince Bismarck's Motives'; and the violent and immediate denials by the obviously inspired *Norddeutsche* and the *Kölnische Zeitung* strongly suggest that this interpretation had struck a sensitive spot.[21] So heated became the exchanges between British Liberal papers and German right-wing journals early in 1885, indeed, that Granville expressed the hope to Escott, the editor of the *Fortnightly Review*, that his own contribution on the subject would not be too strong.[22]

If there was one thing which the Conservative press of Britain cared little about, then it was Bismarck's anti-Liberal ideology. A disapproval of his repressive internal *methods*, which it was thought might create further unrest, by no means implied that British Conservatives quarrelled with the Junker's *aims*; what they were more concerned about were the power-political repercussions of his diplomacy, especially when it involved a disregard for British national interests or an insult to national pride. This was why, for example, the *Standard*, the *Quarterly* and *Blackwood*'s all denounced Prussia's war upon Denmark in 1864.[23] Yet this same calculation, taken in conjunction with alarm about the French and Russian policies in the late 1860s, inclined most of the Conservative journals to favour the unification of Germany under Bismarck. Only certain 'ultras' like Salisbury and Peel supported France early in the war of 1870–1, but since they had long ago split with Disraeli and Derby it is difficult to regard their articles in the *Quarterly* as representative of mainstream conservatism. However, with France defeated and a united Germany apparently all-powerful in western Europe, it was not surprising that papers such as the *Standard* then began to deplore the annexation of Alsace-Lorraine and to wonder about the security of the Low Countries – or even of England itself.[24] It was in *Blackwood*'s, after all, that the 'Battle of Dorking' articles first appeared, serving the dual purpose of calling English attention to Germany's alleged striking power *and* of criticising the Liberal government for its neglect of the armed services.

93

Against this has to be set the Tory alarm at the Russian denunciation of the Black Sea clauses of the Treaty of Paris, and their dislike of the distasteful combination of republicanism and chauvinism which appeared to characterise the Third French Republic. Throughout the 1870s and early 1880s, in fact, the Conservative press's suspicion of a German annexation of the Netherlands or disapproval of Berlin's close attachment to St Petersburg was mitigated by the hope of gaining Bismarck's support in the Eastern Question and by a fear of French and Russian expansion in Africa and Asia respectively. Thus, when the 'war-in-sight' crisis was swiftly replaced by the turbulence in the Balkans, the Tory press abandoned its criticisms of German chauvinism and asserted that Russia remained 'English Enemy No. 1'.[25] In the same way, whatever the criticism by Conservative journals of Germany's commercial policies and colonial annexations in these years, anti-German sentiment rarely, if ever, approached that degree of animosity shown to the much more serious challenges of France and Russia. Indeed, by the end of the 1880s, the Tory press was vocal in its praise of the new German Empire, with the *St. James's Gazette* enviously wishing that England possessed men like Bismarck and Wilhelm I to reinvigorate the British Empire and strengthen its defences, if necessary at the cost of Liberal traditions and susceptibilities;[26] and with the *Standard* and the *Morning Post* echoing the opinion of the *Sheffield Telegraph* that 'a union of hands and hearts between Germany, the greatest Military Power, and Britain, the greatest Naval Power, is an alliance in the interests of Peace'.[27]

This wavering but, on the whole, pro-German stance was shared by *The Times*, which deserves special mention at this point, because in this period it was not closely aligned with either political party, and also because of its importance – especially in German eyes. Its pro-Palmerstonian attitude during the 1860s had made it a supporter of German unification under Prussia, even if its leading articles vilified Bismarck's policies during the constitutional conflict and the war with Denmark.[28] If this conclusion seems at odds with Clarendon's observation that '*The Times* articles drive them [the Germans] all mad & everybody is asking what motive a journal supposed to represent the public opinion of England can have in insulting Germany 3 times a week',[29] one needs to compare the schoolmasterly tone adopted by the paper towards its Teutonic cousins with the open suspicion and hostility shown to France. Napoleon III was, Delane informed Palmerston, 'a suspicious friend and a most dangerous enemy';[30] and since the French Emperor represented a much greater threat to Britain's colonial, naval and European interests, he was treated with hostility – and the Germans were accordingly encouraged to hasten their moves towards unification as a counterweight to France's pretensions. When Prussia showed itself supreme in Germany in 1866, *The Times* could only applaud; and its likely attitude in the event of a Franco-German war was a major reason in Bismarck's decision to 'leak' Benedetti's draft scheme to divide Belgium and Luxembourg to the paper.[31]

With the founding of the German Empire, then, *The Times* felt that the 'policy of past generations of English statesmen [for 'a firm barrier erected in Central Europe'] is fulfilled' – although at this point it characteristically warned the new state to be content with the position it had now attained, for any ambition 'to menace the freedom of the Continent' would eventually provoke counter-moves even from the isolationist British.[32] After the 'war-in-sight' crisis and the evidence that Germany was playing a key role in the deteriorating Eastern Question, *The Times* made its position even more plain: 'We have no jealousy of the new Empire. Within its own bounds we wish it every success. But we feel that an enormous power for good or evil has risen up somewhat suddenly in the midst of us, and we watch with interested attention for signs of its character and intentions.'[33] Given this Palmerstonian attitude of keen regard for 'England's eternal interests', the paper's policy towards Germany in the years following was fairly predictable. A continued dislike for Bismarck's domestic policies (especially his return to protectionism), suspicion of his support for Russia and desire to take advantage of the Egyptian embroglio, and vigorous verbal duels with the German nationalist press, were counterbalanced by an ever greater opposition towards Russian expansionism in the Balkans and French annexations in Africa. Whatever the blows given and taken by *The Times* during the Anglo-German colonial quarrels of the mid-to-late 1880s, therefore, the larger perils were always kept in mind; and by the early 1890s it was asserting that if Germany were to endure some future 'hour of trial', then 'there is no country to which she can more confidently look for sympathy and support than to our own'.[34] To cynics, this could easily be seen as a sign of Printing House Square's apprehensions about the pressures upon Britain's world position by the final decade of the nineteenth century.

If one can divide the British political press roughly into two great camps – with certain 'independent' and Irish papers wavering from side to side – in Germany one requires at least five such divisions, each corresponding to the political movement which fostered it. Moreover, even within the Conservative ranks in Germany, there were frequent fissures between the political sub-groups and between their respective papers, as the clash between the slightly 'Whiggish' *Preussische Wochenblatt* and the arch-conservative *Neue Preussische Zeitung* in the 1850s had demonstrated.[35] Neither of these had very large sales; but in the case of the *Neue Preussische Zeitung* this was compensated for by its influential circle of readers, including many at court. The editorial tone of the paper was a constant denunciation of Bismarck's 'betrayals' of Conservative principles and an equally constant emphasis upon agrarian values and interests. This standpoint was echoed by the social journal *Berliner Revue* and also by the *Preussische Volksblatt* (later the *Neue Allgemeine Volksblatt*), but the sales of all these papers were small and they were not greatly reinforced by the isolated Conservative journals outside Berlin. On the other hand, the Free Conservatives, with their more than adequate funds from industrial circles, could rely upon the *Post* and the *Berliner Neueste Nachrichten* to promulgate their views. To this grouping of pro-Bismarck papers one might add the half-official *Nordeutsche Allgemeine Zeitung*, together with the *Hamburger Nachrichten* which, although occupying no official role, came gradually under the influence of the Bismarck family.

If the National Liberal press lacked the prestigious readership of Conservative newspapers and journals, it made up for it in sheer numbers and variety. Its best-known paper, the *Nationalzeitung*, had been started at the time of the

*Nationalverein* and, when the Liberal movement began to break up, the editorship under Friedrich Hammacher generally supported the drift to the Right although never going so far as Treitschke and others would have liked. With this paper, and with the *Berliner Börsenzeitung* and the earlier *Berlinische Nachrichten*, the party covered the capital; with the *Deutsche Allgemeine Zeitung* and the *Leipziger Neueste Nachrichten*, Saxony; with the *Münchener Neueste Nachrichten*, which sometimes inclined towards the Progressives' position, and the *Süddeutsche Nationalliberale Korrespondenz*, the south; and with the *Rheinisch-Westfälische Zeitung*, the west. In this latter region, the party was generally supported by the popular *Kölnische Zeitung* except when it came to criticisms of governmental policy, for the Cologne paper was a frequent mouthpiece of the Foreign Ministry. It is worth emphasising, however, that these were the better-known National Liberal newspapers; and that there were many others which were important in their localities without achieving the 70,000 circulation of the *Münchener Neueste Nachrichten* or the 60,000 of the *Kölnische Zeitung* in these years.[36] Finally, there was the most famous political review of all, the *Preussische Jahrbücher*, which had moved under Treitschke's influence to the extreme right wing of the National Liberal Party. Its political stance, in the view of one critic, could be summed up as follows: 'strict monarchism – struggle against Manchesterism and parliamentary-liberal assumptions – eradication of the Progressive Party, often deploying the instrument of anti-semitism; further – an emphasis upon the religiosity of the people – reform of the educational and judicial systems – care and growth of the military spirit, historically through reference to Prussian legends – and not least, a carrot (social reform) and stick (anti-Socialist law) programme for the working classes.'[37]

The increasingly bitter attacks by some right-wing National Liberal journals upon those middle-class circles who had adhered to the older, progressive ideology – attacks which were returned with interest by the left-Liberals – remind us why German liberalism as a whole was slowly decaying under Bismarck. In terms of newspapers and readership, as we have seen, the National Liberals occupied a much stronger position than the various groups of Conservatives; yet this itself paled in comparison with that of the Progressive parties. This may partly be explained by the quality of the journalism and entrepreneurship within the latters' press; and partly by the fact that, as in England at this time, liberalism was still benefiting from the support of many intellectuals and from the growth of big-city suburbs. The left-Liberals' *Parlamentarische Korrespondent* and Richter's *Reichsfreund* may have had closer connections with their party leadership; but the real journalistic distinction of the left wing of the Liberal movement was represented by such papers as Sonnemann's *Frankfurter Zeitung* and the old-established *Vossische Zeitung*, or by the flourishing mass-circulation newspapers like the *Berliner Tageblatt*, *Berliner Volks-Zeitung* and *Berliner Zeitung*, which (with the *Vossische*) possessed the same position in the Berlin market as the *Telegraph*, *News* and *Chronicle* did in London.

The Catholic press of Germany, too, occupied a strong position. In 1871 it already claimed 126 newspapers with a total print-run of 322,000 copies, and by 1881 this had risen to 221 papers with 626,000 copies.[38] As may be imagined, a large number of these were small regional journals – the *Schlesische Volkszeitung*, the *Fränkische Volksblatt*, and so on – which is not to say that they lacked significance in reinforcing the sectarian consciousness of their readers. Much better known, however, were the *Augsburger Postzeitung*, important in the south, and the *Kölnische Volkszeitung*, which under the Bachem family sought not only to challenge the hold of the *Kölnische Zeitung* in the locality but to become a trans-regional Catholic paper. The famous journal *Historisch-politische Blätter für das katholische Deutschland* continued to offer its sustained anti-Prussian, anti-Protestant commentary, and complemented in many ways the *Germania*, which was founded in 1871 as the Centre Party's official organ, with its base in Berlin.

For the SPD leadership, as for the Catholics, a flourishing press was vital in order to develop the political consciousness of their followers and to offer a sustained critique of Bismarckian policies. The earliest publications were either in the form of circulars or, despite their claim to be an official organ (like the *Sozial-Demokrat* and the *Verbote*), were produced in such low numbers that their impact was slight; but the unification of Germany and of the Socialist parties themselves permitted an impressive growth. At the Gotha Congress of 1875 it was reported that twenty-three party-oriented papers were in existence with sales of nearly 100,000 copies; and at the same time the decision was taken to found a central party organ, *Vorwärts*, which was selling over 12,000 copies by the following year. At the time of the anti-Socialist law, in fact, the party claimed forty-two journals with total sales of around 150,000 – all of which had either to be wound up or to be produced in exile, with copies smuggled from Zurich, London and elsewhere into the fatherland.[39]

To these five political groupings of newspapers and journals should be added one final category: the Bismarck-inspired press. From early in his career, Bismarck was aware of the importance of using newspapers as one of the many weapons in his political armoury: the Prussian government's struggles, on the one hand against Austrian manipulation of the press in the smaller German states, on the other against Liberal criticisms of domestic policy, had both pointed to the necessity for concerted and vigorous action in this arena. When his authoritarian rule in the early 1860s provoked enraged newspaper attacks, he struck back with brutal force. 'In 1862, 74 legal processes against the press were taken in the Berlin City Court. Confiscation-orders were issued against 92 journals in Berlin and 29 in the rest of Prussia . . . In 1864, 175 legal processes against the press, chiefly on grounds of libel, were instituted.'[40] A purely negative policy, however, was not enough for Bismarck; nor did he wish to rely simply upon the dubious support of the arch-Conservative papers – 'one cannot rule according to the views of the *Kreuzzeitung*', he once declared. Instead it would be necessary to win over parts of the press to the government's side, partly through the stick of further fines, threat of closure and other such measures, and partly by inducement. Thus, the old 'Literary Bureau' of the Prussian Council of Ministers was reinvigorated in 1862, placed under the Internal Ministry, and given the task of checking upon the press and favouring friendly journals with information which was denied to others. Only later, during the Franco-Prussian War, was a Press Bureau established in the Foreign Ministry to deal with newspaper treatment of foreign affairs. Such was the strength of this Bismarckian counter-offensive that one of the earliest tasks which the parties in the Reichstag set themselves after 1871 was the formulation of legislation which specified the constitutional position of the press, and permitted legal processes against newspapers to be taken only under certain circumstances – with the Liberal parties in these debates pointing repeatedly to the much more tolerant English situation. Thus, if such progressive circles still felt afterwards that the 'freedom of the press' remained circumscribed in various ways – in particular, by the idiosyncratic interpretation of the new law by the police – this had, at least, been a step forward.[41] But the initiative and balance of influence in the press had now shifted very definitely in Bismarck's direction, compared with a decade earlier.

The most notable aspect of the Chancellor's relationship with the press lay in the positive efforts made to get pro-government articles into print. The earliest examples lay in the development of the *Provinzial-Korrespondenz*, which offered 'healthy political instruction'[42] in the form of a government-edited supplement to the hitherto fairly apolitical district gazettes (*Kreisblätter*). At the national level, the greatest advance came with the acquisition in 1863 of editorial control over the *Norddeutsche Allgemeine Zeitung*, whose proud claim to 'stand above party' and be 'uninfluenced by factional spirit'[43] was belied by the fact that it received a government subsidy (30,000 marks in later years), exclusive news, official advertising, and a standing order for 5,000 copies daily. In return it issued official notices, *dementi* and corrections, waged unceasing war on anti-government journals, and supported Bismarck in all areas: it was, as a consequence, rarely bought by individuals in need of a daily paper, but it was more or less compulsory reading for all who wished to know the government's stance on any topic. Since nobody was fooled into assuming that the *Norddeutsche* had an independent voice of its own, the government resorted to further endeavours to gain support for its views, of which the most common was the 'inspiration' of certain journals and correspondents – the money for this coming chiefly from the interest accrued from the captured fortune of King George V of Hanover. From the 'reptile funds' a propaganda war would be carried out against the 'reptiles' (that is, the Guelphs) by use of the 'reptile press', a habit which could be put to more general application when the problem of Hanoverian particularism had subsided.[44]

The best-known of the government-inspired papers in later years was the *Kölnische Zeitung*, which sent up trial balloons from, or defended the viewpoint of, the *Wilhelmstrasse* by the simple expedient of its Berlin bureau chief calling in to see the Foreign Ministry officials every day. The *Berlinische Nachrichten*, the *Magdeburgische Zeitung* and certain other smaller journals also allowed themselves to receive this sort of 'inspiration'; the Berlin *Post*'s famous 'Is War in Sight?' article of 1875 was drafted by one of the Foreign Ministry staff, Constantin Rössler; Wehrenpfennig was willing to write pro-Russian articles in the *Preussischer Jahrbücher* to suit the government's diplomacy in the mid-1870s; and the close governmental supervision of messages sent and received by the principal German news agency, Wolff's Telegraphic Bureau, enormously enhanced the Foreign Ministry's ability to influence the press's treatment of foreign affairs. Of all the reviews, however, the *Grenzboten* appears to have been the one most frequently used by Bismarck and his officials; and Moritz Busch's account of the close interest shown by the Chancellor in the influencing of the press provides ample illustration of how regularly and exactly this was done.[45]

Because, in the German case, 'strict adherence was enforced, both in news and editorial policy, to the party line',[46] a detailed analysis of the respective comments by all these papers upon Britain is scarcely necessary here. In particular, the Social-Democratic and Catholic newspapers and journals had little to say about the island state at this time, simply because their political leadership was engrossed in much more pressing concerns at home. *Vorwärts* and other Socialist papers, it is true, did make favourable references to Britain's domestic affairs and offered a constant criticism of Bismarck's diplomatic support for Russia; but such comments respectively stemmed more from a desire to illuminate the reactionary nature of the Prusso-German state and from the ancient loathing of Tsarism rather than from any deep love of the English, however fondly Liebknecht himself remembered his days of exile. Disraelian adventurism, and the occasional reports of further British colonial annexations in the 1870s and early 1880s, were likely to attract sarcastic comments from the SPD press. As for the Centre Party newspapers, the British policy in Ireland, the links of Windsor to the Prussian court, and the public displays of support given by Protestant circles in Britain during the *Kulturkampf* dictated that its commentary upon the Anglo-German relationship would be at the least reserved and cool, and sometimes critical. The only occasions when the remarks became friendlier were, significantly enough, when the Catholic press wished to draw attention to the religious freedoms enjoyed in Britain; or when, because of their firm support for Austria-Hungary in its rivalry with Russia, those newspapers applauded Disraeli in the late 1870s for his 'manly abandonment of the Manchester-trader's policy' in standing up to the Panslavic menace.[47]

The only pro-British journals were those in the radical and left-Liberal camps; and even here, one suspects, their anglophile sentiments may have been motivated less by a regard for Britain than by the recognition that anti-English criticisms in the right-wing press were in reality assaults upon themselves – to which appropriate replies had to be made. Defence of free trade, for example, meant a defence of the country which was the source and centre of that doctrine, just as attacks upon the dangers of parliamentarism could only be answered by reference to the superiority of English institutions. Similarly, when the right-wing papers, in the midst of their assaults upon the left-Liberal parties in the wake of the 1881 general election, also turned and attacked the hypocrisy of the Gladstone government's intervention in Egypt, the *Frankfurter Zeitung* felt bound to point out this 'ill-concealed feeling of jealousy and hatred – an ungrateful return for the friendly feelings towards Germany evinced by the English press during the Franco-Prussian War'.[48]

Whether or not it was intended, that historical recollection would be bound to provoke the strongest disagreement in National Liberal papers: to these journals, the stance adopted by the British government and public in 1870–1 – that of hypocritical *Händler*, prattling about peace and selling arms to both sides – was one which could only be deplored. To the *Kölnische Zeitung*, for example, Russia was the only power which deserved German gratitude in 1870, whereas England as usual had put her 'trade interests in the foreground'.[49] These attacks partly died away during the *Kulturkampf* but by the late 1870s – with the right-wing National Liberals in bitter conflict with their former progressive allies, with their business interests favouring protection, and with the first serious stirrings of interest in overseas colonies – it revived anew.[50]

These anglophobe sentiments were echoed by various Conservative papers, particularly during the Eastern crisis of 1876–8, when it was feared that Disraeli's real aim was to set the members of the *Dreikaiserbund* against each other, thus allowing Britain to escape from the Russian pressure upon India. England's interests at Constantinople, observed the *Post*, 'are hostile to those of Europe'. An Anglo-Russian war over India, declared the *Kölnische Zeitung*, would be 'Good – it would be a war between two Asiatic powers', this no doubt enhancing Germany's relative position. Even when Russia's hostility in 1879 began to alarm these nationalistic circles, their overriding concern – like Bismarck's – was to tie Vienna to Berlin, rather than have the Austrians led into a disastrous war by devious London.[51] The return to power of Gladstone, the news of his domestic reform programme and the reports of British reverses and problems in South Africa, Ireland, Egypt and elsewhere, simply provided fresh ammunition for those who saw in Liberalism a hated foe. By 1885, the *Kölnische Zeitung* could scarcely control itself after enduring years of Gladstonian rule. 'English parliamentarism will brand-mark itself before the whole world as the worst of all state institutions' if the Commons did not throw his government out, it declared – an ingenious argument, for if this advice were to be followed, the hated Gladstone would be finished; and if it were rejected, parliamentarism would (it was implied) be sorely discredited.[52]

The greater part of this anti-British-cum-anti-Liberal commentary was undoubtedly genuine: no one needed to suggest to Treitschke in the *Preussische Jahrbücher* or the protectionist circles behind the *Berliner Neueste Nachrichten* how to portray the British political scene. Nevertheless, it is also clear that many of these articles were inspired by Bismarck and his helpers. Busch's recollections of the instructions given to him about influencing the press again make interesting reading: July 1870 – articles prepared upon England's 'fraudulent neutrality'; February 1872 – received directions 'from the Chief' about a long article on Swedish affairs, with references to England's 'hypocritical love of liberty, its calculating policy of peace, and its too successful efforts to tear open the wounds of Poland in order to distract attention from its greed of conquest in India and its oppression of Ireland'; May 1877 – published in the *Grenzboten* the 'Angel of Peace' article, which sarcastically referred to Queen Victoria's appeal to Berlin to prevent a Russo-Turkish war; October 1884 – prepared another *Grenzboten* article on 'the scandalous treatment of Ireland by England'; April 1888 – instructed by Bismarck to give a brief account of England's perfidious policy of playing the European states off against each other during the past two centuries; and so on.[53]

On other occasions, it is true, Bismarck, Busch and the Foreign Ministry Press Bureau prepared articles against France, Russia, Austria and a whole array of external and internal foes; but this does not detract from the significance of the role which the Chancellor himself played in the exciting of German nationalistic animosities against Britain. It is also worth noting that, whereas on occasions the 'inspired' *Norddeutsche Allgemeine Zeitung* and *Kölnische Zeitung* would warn against the excessively violent language which other right-wing papers deployed against the British, this plea for moderation was always actuated by coldly calculated assessments of the immediate political situation. If circumstances demanded it, anti-British articles would be drafted; if those circumstances did not exist, all that happened was that such articles ceased also. There were never any positive and pro-British instructions emanating from the Chancellor and his acolytes. All this makes it difficult to agree with the assertion of the *Manchester Guardian*'s pro-German Berlin correspondent, J. L. Bashford, who argued that a distinction had to be drawn 'between the ignorant criticism of the anti-English and chauvinist-German press and the *real opinion* in high quarters'[54] – for the only feature which seems to have distinguished the two positions was the latter's greater unscrupulousness.

Finally, it is worth recording that these years also witnessed the beginnings of a number of organisations and pressure groups which were to play a considerable future role in orchestrating and reflecting 'public opinion'. In most instances, the function of these pressure groups was the defence of specific economic interests: for example, the Fair Trade League in Britain and the *Centralverband Deutscher Industrieller* in Germany, both campaigning for a return to protection during the 'Great Depression'. On the German side, too, there was the *Verein für Sozialpolitik*, which offered an intellectual centre for the assault upon the ideas of the various free-trade associations.[55] As concern over colonial issues grew in both countries, further pressure groups were founded in order to organise and stimulate this new topic of public interest: the Imperial Federation League and the Primrose League in Britain, the *Verein für Handelsgeographie* . . . and the *Kolonialverein* in Germany, were responses *and* stimulants to the changing circumstances and conditions. In virtually all cases, the organisation and activities were similar: a central committee, graced wherever possible with an aristocratic chairman but chiefly composed of intellectuals, business and professional men; regional branches, with meetings focused around a guest lecture or social event; a series of pamphlets, and a league newspaper, which articulated the aims of the movement and sought thereby to give coherence to it; and a lobbying of political parties and governments to secure legislation and actions which would fulfil those aims.[56]

The existence of this sort of organisation was new neither in Britain nor in Germany. Over the previous half-century, both had witnessed the flourishing of pressure groups, either for economic purposes (the Anti-Corn Law League, the *Deutsche Handels- und Gewerbsverein*) or for political causes (the *Nationalverein*, or the various anti-slavery or constitutional reform associations in Britain).[57] What is worth suggesting is that, whereas the earlier movements had generally been concerned with 'liberalising' certain laws or achieving various freedoms, these newer pressure groups tended to be much more consolidationist, protective and conservative in their assumptions. Organisations calling for colonial annexations and imperial preference, or demanding tariffs and other forms of state assistance for particular economic interests, hardly accorded with *laissez-faire* tenets. Already, an anti-Liberal ethos is detectable in most of these organisations – together with a practice of appealing to 'national' interests and patriotic pride which predictably took little account of the feelings of other nations. If the propaganda put out by the Fair Trade League or the *Kolonialverein* is any guide, then the formation of interest groups in this period can hardly be said to bode well for the tone of Anglo-German public relations in the future.

Whatever significance newspapers and pressure groups claimed for themselves, it would be wrong for the historian to assume that they always were of overwhelming import. Public opinion *was* a political factor in these years, and sometimes one of great influence, but it was rarely the case that politicians became the helpless puppets of the press. In the first place, by being party leaders, they were more or less certain of the support of those newspapers and groups which shared the same inclinations and economic interests as themselves. Abuse by the rival party's press was usually of no concern, therefore, and it was only when one's own party newspapers became critical that a change of course was necessary. Secondly, politicians as masterful as Palmerston and Bismarck were frequently able to exploit 'public' opinion for their own ends, by influencing journalists and by open appeals to what Disraeli once called the 'sublime instincts' of the people. Thirdly, statesmen could often point to the state of public opinion as a reason for carrying out policies which they themselves secretly favoured – for example, Bismarck's pressure for colonial concessions in 1884–5, or British avoidance of an alliance with Germany.

Yet, if politicians could stimulate and, in certain cases, influence opinion, it proved much more difficult to silence public sentiments once they had been aroused: newspaper ownership was too varied, the political parties too much at odds, editors and writers for pressure groups too idiosyncratic and independent to be silenced from above. Herein, above all, lay a danger for future good relations between two peoples – not because public opinion should never have been consulted, but because it was a force which could be and was exploited (especially on the German side) without the statesmen concerned being responsible for what followed or being able to control what they had begun. As the alarmed British *chargé* at Berlin put it to Busch, 'nothing could be more disastrous to friendly relations than the recent appeals to the forum of the general public to pass judgement on differences between the 2 governments which seemed to me quite capable of being settled in the way of confidential diplomacy'.[58] The 'old diplomacy' had its many disadvantages but it was, in the last resort, a controllable process. To combine appeals to public opinion with the traditional methods of regularising inter-state relations was starting to make the whole process altogether more unstable and unpredictable.

# CHAPTER 6

# *Religious and Cultural Connections*

The historian in search of bonds between the British and German peoples in the middle decades of the nineteenth century cannot help being struck by the frequency of references to religious and cultural ties as being a, if not *the* major reason for mutual respect and friendship. Although it would be simpler to exclude such aspects from what is basically a political study, the sheer number of these references – and the fact that many previous scholars of the Anglo-German relationship have focused upon them – suggests that some examination of their place in the overall story is required. Are the appeals to a common religious and cultural heritage merely the rhetoric of politicians, or evidence of the unworldly vision of artists and academics? Did this have any influence at all upon governmental policy and public attitudes? May it not be that, in an age untroubled by colonial quarrels and a naval race between the two countries, those allusions to such a shared heritage loomed correspondingly larger and thus reflected the lack of serious clashes of national interests? Finally, just how uniform and 'common' was the assumption that religion and culture strengthened the bonds between the British and German peoples? Even to the historian concerned with politics and diplomacy, the answers to such questions can be of value.

Religion, it may be conceded, was important at the time because it was all-pervasive. Such questions as civic rights and responsibilities, social *mores*, education, political morality and many others simply could not be separated from a consideration of ethical and theological principles; and, to a European ruling class perturbed at the way traditional assumptions and the conservative social order was being challenged in so many fields, the dissolving certainties of religion boded ill for the future. It was difficult, too, for men to escape from a deeply ingrained historical consciousness which made issues from the time of the Reformation still appear to be of pressing importance, despite the rise in scepticism and tolerance among many intellectuals. Secondly, religious factors were significant because they became inextricably connected with cultural and nationalistic issues in mid-century Europe – as the Irish problem, local Polish-German disputes, or the widespread Bavarian dislike of Prussia and corresponding inclination towards Austria, all indicated. Thus, religious differences appeared both to stimulate, and to be exploited by, cultural antagonisms. Finally, these years saw massive controversies arising in the doctrinal sphere which also had political repercussions: the pronouncement of papal infallibility; the campaign for the disestablishment of national churches; the wrangles over ritualism; the doubts caused by advances in biblical historical scholarship; and the intellectual assaults of the 'Darwinists' and the free-thinkers.[1]

Given the multitude and complexity of these religious issues, it is no easy task to analyse their collective impact upon, and place within, the Anglo-German relationship. Let us take, for example, the commonly proclaimed statement of contemporary politicians and writers that Britain and Germany, being the two chief Protestant powers of Europe, possessed a natural affinity for each other. This proposition was certainly advanced by the great majority of the leading figures in both countries. 'The English nation', Queen Victoria assured the German Emperor, 'as a whole is essentially Protestant, and its sympathies would be entirely with Germany in any difference with France', unless Berlin unreasonably sought to provoke a war. William, equally stout in his support of the traditions of the Reformation, urged that 'both nations are naturally allied to each other by the principles of Protestantism'.[2] Similarly one can read of Gladstone regarding Germany as Europe's leader 'in the domain of conscience' during the protests against papal doctrines; or note above that Derby saw her function as, conjointly with Britain, combatting ultramontane subversives; or that Lytton, alarmed in 1877 at the false rumour of Britain joining an anti-German alliance, appealed to the Protestant feeling in the country to frustrate this. The echoes on the German side to these expressions were equally loud: from Bismarck himself, who, Odo Russell observed 'thirsts after the moral support of England in waging war against the Pope';[3] from Moltke; from certain of the Prussian Conservatives; from historians such as Ranke, Mommsen, Sybel and Pauli; and from virtually every German Liberal.

There is no doubt, then, that the Protestant religion was one of the 'shared assumptions' of the élites in both countries during this whole period, and every sociological investigation simply confirms the fact. In the German foreign service between 1871 and 1914, for example, 82 per cent of the senior staff were Protestants, 17 per cent Catholics and 1 per cent Jews;[4] in the navy, despite its claims to be open-minded and modern, the proportion of Catholics and Jews slipped to 14 per cent and less than 1 per cent respectively;[5] in the Prussian army, which made no such claims, the proportions were far less. In Britain, too, the pattern was similar: the religious restrictions upon entrance into Oxford and Cambridge preserved for many years the Anglican primacy; Catholic aristocrats, such as Norfolk, were a rare phenomenon, and intellectuals, such as Acton, even rarer; Ripon, as a politician of Cabinet minister rank, caused a sensation by converting to Catholicism; and, although the sociological data are less forthcoming, it is clear that the upper branches of the bureaucracy, of Parliament and of 'society' in general were overwhelmingly Protestant, although this was less the case in the diplomatic corps.

It was, of course, the issue of papal infallibility – and the assumption that this would encroach both upon the civic domain and upon the position of Protestantism – which provoked so many declarations of Anglo-German religious solidarity in these years. Perhaps the most remarkable was Gladstone's dispatch to Bismarck of the very first copy of his pamphlet *Vaticanism, an Answer to Replies and Reports* 'as a token of my sincere admiration'; and the Chancellor's letter of reply, expressing his 'deep and hopeful gratification to see the two nations, which in Europe are the champions of liberty and conscience, encountering the same foe, standing henceforth shoulder to shoulder in defending the highest interests of the human race'.[6] Members of the Carlton, Reform and National Clubs in London formed a committee to protest against the 'pretensions' of the Catholic Church, and to express their admiration for Bismarck and William during the *Kulturkampf*; the aged Earl Russell, having quite forgotten the humiliation of Schleswig-Holstein, gave full support to this movement – 'the cause of the German Emperor is the cause of liberty', he wrote – and was thanked for it in a personal letter by the emperor; German parliamentarians, ministers, professors and generals assembled in Berlin to indicate their gratitude for these expressions of British sympathy. Even the press on both sides had kindly words for each other. *The Times* believed its fellow countrymen should sympathise 'with the Germans because they are carrying out in principle the very policy we put into force at the Reformation';[7] and the *Norddeutsche Allgemeine Zeitung* announced that 'Old England, in the spirit of Elizabeth and Cromwell, in full conscience of her true mission, is joining us as an ally against Rome.'[8]

It was not simply during the *Kulturkampf* that religious ties between the two nations flourished. Decades beforehand, Germany had already established itself as the world's centre for advanced study in theology, employing modern methods of biblical criticism, historical investigation, and evidence from geology, biology and other sources. Slowly but surely, these ideas seeped across the Channel. Even in the 1820s and 1830s, individuals such as Julius Charles Hare, Connop Thirlwall and Thomas Arnold had presented translations and interpretations of Schleiermacher and Niebuhr; and their students and friends such as Bunsen, John Sterling, Dean Stanley and F. D. Maurice soon added to this movement. A few years later, the various translations of Strauss's *Leben Jesu* – including one by George Eliot – and the publication of many more books and articles upon German theology and rationalism were received with great interest by Broad Church circles. Jowett, whose contribution to the controversial *Essays and Reviews* (1860) was one of the most significant, was an open admirer of the liberalism of German theologians like Ferdinand Baur of the Tübingen school.[9] For such thinkers, the Christian faith could only be rescued from the steady assault of geological, biological and historical discoveries by a reformulation of theological assumptions; and, just as many of the challenges to belief came from Germany, so, too, did many of the answers. For a Catholic thinker such as Acton, the same was also true: hence his growing friendship with Döllinger.[10]

Yet, for all the above, any attempt to portray the British and German peoples as being united on religious matters cannot withstand closer scrutiny. During the *Kulturkampf*, for example, a careful distinction was made on the British

105

side between support for the principles of Protestantism and approval of Bismarck's methods. Liberal politicians and journalists in particular, although usually the most critical of papal claims, shook their heads at the news of the May Laws and of the many examples of repression which were reported from Germany. As the *Edinburgh Review* put it: 'We are indignant at the exaggerated pretensions of the Ultramontane clergy; but we are much more indignant at the attempt to crush the faith and the independence of any form of religious belief by State persecution and intolerance.'[11] This stance was shared by Derby, who in 1874 had approved of 'a strong Germany, keeping down at once the ultramontane and the red factions', but within months had sensed that the 'harshness and violence' of Prussian administrators was actually strengthening the position of the Ultramontanes.[12] And when the *Kulturkampf* suddenly seemed to threaten Germany's relations with France and Belgium, the British tone cooled considerably. 'Notwithstanding the sympathy felt in the main for the Protestant German Empire', Odo Russell was informed, 'the outrageous justice of picking a quarrel with France because she does not choose to remain disarmed would produce its effect. There would be a great revulsion of feeling.'[13]

Such reservations inevitably cause the historian to wonder what weight can be attached to utterances about religious solidarity between Britain and Germany at this time. There were, no doubt, Lutheran divines in Prussia and extreme Low Churchmen in Ulster or Lancashire for whom this consideration had overriding priority; yet the type of fanatical anti-Papist who alleged that even Gladstone must secretly be a Catholic because of his Irish policies was not of great account in the determination of foreign affairs. That was in the hands of people who, although almost uniformly Protestant in their religious affiliations, nevertheless recognised that other factors came into play. Disraeli and Derby might pay great respect to 'Protestant feeling' when contemplating the passage of religious items through the Houses of Parliament; but any concern for sectarian prejudices was instantly obliterated when it seemed possible that Germany was planning to turn upon France and Belgium: the Prime Minister's idea in 1875 of a 'peace league' with *Orthodox* Russia and the *Catholic* powers of Europe to restrain *Protestant* Germany from aggressions might not have been feasible on diplomatic grounds, but it was unlikely that it would be upset because of religious scruples. In the same way, one is bound to wonder whether Bismarck's repeated praise of Anglo-German solidarity against ultramontanism was anything more than a tactical bid for allies at a time when the *Kulturkampf* was at its height; or whether those National Liberals and Free Conservatives who so warmly welcomed the support rendered by British Protestants in 1873–4 felt impeded by the memory of this during their demands for protection against British imports in 1879 or during their pleas for an active colonial policy in 1884? A common religion may have caused the majority of Britons and Germans, and more especially their establishments, to feel a certain affinity with each other; but this sentiment alone would not suffice to preserve friendships if more pressing clashes of national interests occurred.

As for the theological influences of German scholarship upon Britain, the

106

blunt fact remains that for every English churchman and intellectual who welcomed the new approaches of the Tübingen school and the 'de-literalisation' of the Bible, there were ten who regarded such developments as a threat. It was bad enough to have assumptions about the historical events of the Old Testament or of the life of Jesus criticised by geologists or classical philologists or evolutionists with the biting tongue of a Huxley, without ministers of religion themselves contributing to these tendencies and admitting – at least in part – to their validity. The clearest indication of this widespread feeling against German theological influence can be seen in the reaction to *Essays and Reviews*. Two of the seven contributors to it were suspended from their benefices; and when this action was revoked by the Privy Council, the archbishops of Canterbury and York abstained from its proceedings, at which 137,000 laymen signed a petition of thanks to them. Pusey, although claiming that the essays 'contain nothing with which those acquainted with the writers of unbelievers in Germany have not been familiar these thirty years',[14] organised a protest declaration on the Inspiration of Scripture, which was countersigned by 11,000 clergy. The *Essays and Reviews*, claimed Wilberforce, were 'trains of German doubts', and 'weapons forged in the workshops of German criticism against the faith'.[15] Gladstone, who took church matters very seriously, felt the proceedings against the two essayists a mistake, but feared that the effects of the Privy Council's judgement would be 'hostile to that definite teaching and unfavourable also to the moral tone and truthfulness'.[16] Salisbury, whose religious interests were equally pronounced, had shown great scepticism towards the revised German theology and, even many years later, Lord Arthur Russell noted 'how deeply Lord Salisbury hates Germany which he accuses of having poisoned the Theology of Oxford and misled many young Englishmen'.[17] Yet here, too, it is doubtful whether a theologically based prejudice much affected the actions of state.

The final flaw in the assumption that Protestantism was always to be seen as a binding force in the Anglo-German relationship lies in the rather awkward fact that not all Britons and Germans were Protestants! On the British side, it is true, the Catholic minority was not so numerous; but since it was involved in fierce internal wrangles throughout the years over Irish affairs and papal infallibility, size alone was a guide neither to its significance nor volubility. To a people like the Catholic Irish, acutely conscious of the cultural and nationalistic aspects of politics, the frequent references to Germany as the 'natural ally' of Protestant England naturally were no recommendation. Even before the formal declaration of the Franco-German War, Irish papers were full of support for Paris's standpoint; and the more that London and Ulster journals deplored Napoleon III's conduct, the more it was praised by the Irish Catholics. Many Irishmen refused at first to believe the news of French military defeats and, although appalled at the actions of the Commune, they remained as Francophile as any English radical or positivist.

The debate upon papal infallibility and the coming of the *Kulturkampf* added further complications to the Anglo-Irish relationship. As Derby noted in 1874, a 'religious war' in Germany would not greatly disturb English opinion 'but in Ireland we shall feel the effects of it' – which goes some way towards explaining the British unease at Bismarck's repressive methods.[18] Well before then, however, the impact of developments in Germany were being felt across the English Channel and the Irish Sea. In the first place, the papal claims and the *Kulturkampf* had provoked, as mentioned above, a bitter reaction in British Protestant circles – yet this, in turn, only led to further Catholic and Irish resentment. Gladstone's own pamphleteering efforts against 'Vaticanism' and especially his open dispute with Manning produced a further alteration in the Grand Old Man's complicated attitude towards the Irish problem; and this worsening of relationships allowed the Catholic hierarchy and the Irish press to compare the 'persecutions' against Catholicism in Britain and Germany. Gladstone, claimed Cardinal Cullen, had become 'an imitator of the policy of despotic foreign Statesmen' – a clear reference to Bismarck and no doubt a dreadful insult to anyone with a large Liberal conscience.[19] Manning, who had already criticised the Falk Laws in a letter to *The Times*, bitterly denounced everyone who had attended the pro-German meeting in London in January 1874 as 'an accomplice in these acts of tyranny'.[20] Windhorst and the Centre Party, on the other hand, were the heroes of the hour; and there would always be fair words, too, for the Poles and the Alsatians – fellow-Catholic peoples, oppressed by an overbearing Protestant power. All in all, a pro-German policy on the part of the British government would be bitterly disliked across the Irish Sea – which meant little or nothing to many Tories, presumably, but could serve to reinforce Liberal sensibilities about Berlin's embrace.

Sectarian prejudice also affected German attitudes towards Britain, and in the same double-sided way. In Germany, the position of Catholicism was much more significant politically. In the first place, German Catholics formed 36 per cent of the total population (1871 census) and, given that quite a few of its members came from the upper and middle classes, a united stand by them would have significant effects upon national politics. Moreover, they managed from the start to organise along confessional lines; and their overall sense of identity was heightened by the *Kulturkampf*, which had the ironic effect of ensuring that Catholicism remained a substantial *political* force throughout the years of the Second German Empire. The most obvious manifestation of this was the formation of the Centre Party itself, which, as noted above, was certainly influenced in its attitude towards Britain by the Irish question and the *Kulturkampf*.

Furthermore, just as German Catholics watched Irish affairs with the intention of relating them to their own situation, so, too, did the Prusso-German establishment. If the parallels were not realised by the naïve observer, the *Norddeutsche Allgemeine Zeitung* was willing to make them clear:

if one exchanges the words Poles and Parnellites, the situation in our country is very similar to that beyond the Channel. Polish propaganda against Prussia is exactly the same as that of the Parnellites against England. Both in this country and Ireland the subversives are finding zealous support for their aspirations in certain radical circles and from a number of ultramontanist priests. Our situation is still more dangerous in so far as in Germany the Social Democrats, the Guelph, French and

Danish elements are supporting the Poles with the common aim of destroying the re-established Empire.[21]

Apart from demonstrating once again the 'Official Mind's' fear of subversive forces, this editorial also gives a clue to the German government's own attitude towards Britain and her Irish problem. In the early years of the *Reich*, and especially during his struggle with the Catholic Church, Bismarck clearly felt a certain affinity with Protestant England – and that was connected with the suspicions he entertained about the vulnerability of Germany in certain sensitive border areas. After 1879, when the alliance with Austria-Hungary dissolved his *cauchemar de coalitions* and the propaganda about the struggle with Rome was being quietly abandoned, there was obviously less need to be on good terms with the British. This did not mean that comment upon Irish affairs declined, but simply that the emphasis shifted. References to a joint Anglo-German stand against Rome, Ireland and Poland became less frequent; and applause at the British efforts to suppress unrest in Ireland under Disraeli were replaced after 1880 by concern and criticism at Gladstone's fruitless efforts (as Berlin saw it) to appease recalcitrant Fenians. In other words, the evidence once again suggests that Berlin's frequent allusion to the religious factor in Anglo-German relations during the age of Bismarck was motivated more by tactical political reasons than by theology or spiritual conviction.

The cultural ties which the two peoples had developed with each other were created in two main ways. The first was a virtual extension of the commercial relationships described above. The visits of engineers, traders and bankers across the Channel, and their accounts of life on the other side; the exchange of wares, particularly in the domestic field such as furniture, fashions and wines; and the establishment of more or less permanent 'colonies' of exiles who then intermarried and blended into their new places of abode, were the obvious means by which mutual knowledge of the other country was transmitted.[22] In Hamburg, Bremen, Frankfurt and in the smaller Baltic ports there were large numbers of Englishmen engaged in the grain and timber trade, shipping, banking and other forms of commerce – Prince-Smith, after all, first went to Hamburg to serve on the staff of the *English*-language newspaper there. In London in the 1840s there was estimated to be about 40,000 Germans; in Manchester, far fewer, yet enough to found the Schiller-Anstalt and the Halle Orchestra. Some of these foreign residents were admittedly political *émigrés*, such as Wilhelm Liebknecht, or Marx and Engels, avoiding the German reaction after 1848; and many were Jews, such as Francis Oppenheimer's father, who found it more congenial to make his fortune in London before returning to his native Frankfurt. Clustering around their leading representatives, one of whom was perhaps the honorary Consul-General or Vice-Consul, they formed a 'club', arranged social events, celebrated the national holidays of their former homeland and the birthday of its sovereign, and in general were fervent advocates for good Anglo-German relations – upon which, in the last resort, they depended.

The other form of cultural interaction arose less from economic than from intellectual causes: from the transmission of ideas by scholars, the published accounts and the paintings of the many travellers to each other's lands, the attendance of students at foreign schools and universities, the occasional visits of celebrated writers, artists and musicians – all of which had been stimulated and greatly expanded in the age of the Enlightenment, and resumed with fresh vigour after 1815. In many respects, of course, the cultural impact of this form of Anglo-German 'traffic' merely reproduced that arising from the commercial connection, albeit in a more articulate and stylistic form; but it also added an extra dimension, in that historians, philosophers and other members of the *literati* in general tended to regard, and to portray, a foreign culture – and, by extension, its society and politics – as a whole. To put it another way, when (say) Carlyle wrote of German culture or Ranke of English, they were no longer dealing with specific mannerisms or characteristics in that country, but with totalities; and, in so doing, they offer valuable insights into their conceptions of their own society as well. Yet, precisely because such cultural attitudes merged into the world of politics and ideology, this aspect of the Anglo-German relationship, like the economic aspect, sometimes reinforced and sometimes weakened the links between the two peoples.

The very case of theology noted above provides a good example of the *general* nature of intellectual exchanges between Britain and Germany in this period. Of course, because the new German scholarship upon religious doctrine had touched upon the very central and sensitive problem of the mid-Victorian 'crisis of belief', its impacts reverberated far outside the field of academic theology and this in turn caused it to acquire a certain public notoriety which most other subjects escaped. Yet the *pattern* of the transmission of new ideas and approaches was common to many other disciplines: German scholars were at the centre of the latest development; its university system appeared to encourage further intensive researches; consequently, more and more Britons who wished to engage in serious study of their subject felt that they must attend a German university or, at least, become acquainted with the German language. As early as 1844, Hallam asserted: 'No one Professor at Oxford, a century since, would have thought a knowledge of German requisite for a man of letters; at present no one can dispense with it.'[23] Dean Stanley, Mark Pattison, Archibald Tait, Jowett and many others felt they had to make an academic 'pilgrimage' to Germany to acquire greater knowledge of their field, and the same was true in the neighbouring subjects of philology, languages and the classics.[24]

In such subjects, as in so many others, even a brief description of the interactions and 'influences' runs the danger of becoming a lengthy list of German authorities, making important contributions to the development of their subject, and an almost equally long list of Britons who paid tribute to this superiority, either by attending German universities or at least reading the books which were being published across the Channel. In regard to the performing arts, too, such as music, the English seemed again to be in Germany's debt. Simply to recall the names of the early composers like Bach and Handel, of that brilliant cluster of Haydn, Mozart, Beethoven and Schubert, and of contemporaries such as Brahms and Mendelssohn and

Wagner was both to indicate the 'imbalance' and to explain why the mid-Victorians had so great a respect for German music: the contributions of other countries were of course also important, declared Balfour, but 'if the music of Germany were destroyed, we could not get on'.[25]

Only in literature, one suspects, was the equilibrium restored. Shakespeare's genius had long been widely recognised within Germany on account of the excellent translations that had appeared during the Romantic period; and it was those selfsame arbiters of literary taste, Goethe, Schlegel and their fellows, whose choices had determined the popularity of other British authors. Byron and Scott especially enjoyed a colossal reputation – an indication, one suspects, of their appeal to the restless-romantic and historical-Gothic elements in the German psyche – whereas Wordsworth, Keats and Shelley were scarcely known. By the mid-century, Dickens had captured German minds, not merely because of his characterisation and stories, but because of other features – realism and social concern – which were of relevance to a people just beginning to experience the turbulence of rapid industrialisation. Dickens's novels were swiftly translated and widely reviewed; and in his wake other Victorian novelists, Thackeray, George Eliot, Kingsley, Bulwer-Lytton, Charlotte Brontë, also became known to German readers. The cheap Tauschnitz translated editions spread these works to a much larger audience than hitherto. Even Disraeli benefited from this 'boom', and *Coningsby* was soon sold out of its German edition.

In Britain, too, the mid-century witnessed a rise in public awareness of German literature. Nevertheless, the way had been prepared some time earlier, due to the influence of Coleridge, Carlyle and then Matthew Arnold, who acted in just the same way as Goethe had done in introducing foreign authors to the native readership. The high praise of Carlyle, the spate of good translations and the publication in 1855 of George Lewes's two-volume *Life of Goethe* ensured that the latter was the best known of all German authors in mid-Victorian England – although it was not until 1886 that the English Goethe Society itself was founded. Schiller, too, had many admirers, of whom the most ardent was Bulwer-Lytton, who translated *The Poems and Ballads of Schiller* in the early 1840s; but Heine only achieved real fame in Britain when George Eliot called attention to his work in 1856. Contemporary German authors gained relatively little attention during the mid and late nineteenth century, however, so that the image of German culture firmly established in English minds was that of the Romantic authors and their time.[26]

The arena of literature – like that of other creative fields such as music and art – offers extraordinary difficulties to the historian seeking 'influences' and connections which may have a bearing upon the political world. There were, admittedly, notable examples of where an enthusiasm for another country's culture affected the reader's political inclinations: Carlyle, for instance, could scarcely separate the two spheres; and it is no surprise to discover that George Eliot, translator both of Strauss's *Leben Jesu* and Feuerbach's *Wesen des Christentums*, traveller in Weimar, Heine-enthusiast, neo-Hegelian, and avid reader of historians such as Ranke and Mommsen, could *not* join her Positivist friends in supporting the French cause in 1870. Yet there is also a case for

111

saying that the creative arts, demanding no territorial boundaries for their reception, can often be isolated from political events. Bismarck enjoyed Byron, Shakespeare and Goldsmith, but this seems in no way to have influenced his day-to-day policy towards England; Salisbury wrote regular reports upon German literature for the *Quarterly*, yet was similarly unaffected in his diplomacy; and Treitschke produced essays in praise of Byron and Milton. It may well be, in fact, that famous novels and plays – like a Spitzweg drawing or a Beethoven piano concerto – created idealistic impressions about another country's culture which stood in sharp contrast to its current political actions. Interestingly enough, in this respect, one of the justifications for the founding of the English Goethe Society in 1886 was the need felt by its organisers to keep alive the writer's ideals and spirit 'now when international relations between the leading countries of Europe have become worse than among savages in Africa'.[27] Moreover, one is also bound to wonder whether the 'influence' as indicated by the sales of books and numbers of translations was always favourable. Dickens's novels, for example, furnished evidence to many more German critics of the 'English model' of *laissez-faire* capitalism than could possibly have been reached by Engels' contemporaneous *Lage der arbeitenden Klasse in England*.

In philosophy, the cultural 'gap' which existed between the two countries was probably more pronounced than in any other subject – and had, moreover, obvious connections with the world of ideology and politics. Nothing stood in greater contrast than the dominance of idealist philosophy in Germany and its near-total neglect (despite Coleridge, Carlyle and Arnold) in mid-Victorian Britain, where the traditions of Locke and Hume still ran strong.[28] As late as 1867, Acton himself was bemoaning the way English philosophy had isolated itself for the past century, and arguing that the national tendency to appeal to 'Common Sense' was in no way to be seen as a philosophy but simply as a protest against unusual forms of conceptualisation.[29] Fluency in the ordinary German language was an achievement even amongst educated Britons, and the task of comprehending the specialised terminology of idealist philosophy was a double obstacle. Moreover, the pragmatic approach and individualistic assumptions of Anglo-Saxon thought seemed to serve English society and politics and business very well, so that even when the first serious attempts were made to promulgate Hegel's teachings, they attracted the fierce criticism of, among others, John Stuart Mill – which is scarcely surprising since so many of those who were to turn towards neo-Hegelianism were themselves rebelling against the dominant English thought-system.

Hegel only became known to many British readers with the publication in 1865 of James Stirling's book *The Secret of Hegel*, which stilled much of the native criticism by its claim that the German thinker had actually managed to reconcile philosophy and Christianity, thus offering a 'solution to the Victorian crisis of faith'.[30] Oxford in particular developed as the centre in England for the study – and, more important, the practical application – of Kant and Hegel's philosophy. Jowett, predictably, had sought to spread the message to his colleagues and students but a far greater influence, by all accounts, was T. H. Green – who returned (like so many of his generation) from visits to the continent 'full of German philosophy, politics and the higher poetry'.[31] It is true that Green's impact was to be felt fully from the 1870s onwards rather than earlier. Nevertheless, it was to be a formidable one: it caused not merely the stimulation of further work in philosophy itself, such as that by Bosanquet, F. H. Bradley and others; but it also gave an intellectual boost to the notions of state interventionism and social concern, through his distinction between a 'simple freedom from restriction' and 'freedom in a higher sense', and his claim that the state represented the 'common good'; and, finally, his attempts to reconcile freedom and authority, the individual and the larger community, could also be utilised – although this was not intended by Green – by those who were concerned with the world of power-politics and antagonistic to Cobdenite liberalism, which they felt weakened national loyalty and coherence.

If German idealist thought only gradually established a foothold in Britain as an academic subject, it is doubtful whether the traditions of English empiricism and rationalism made any impact at all in German university departments of philosophy. What was, of course, well known were associated ideas about individualism, if only because they had been borrowed by German Liberals seeking economic and political reforms. To this extent, Ricardo, Adam Smith and Mill had many disciples in mid-century Germany, but they were more likely to be found among businessmen or students of politics than among professors of philosophy. Even in the early nineteenth century, Hegel had inveighed against the English 'shallowness' about principles, and this set the pattern for later generations of Germans: either they simply accepted that the philosophical traditions of the island state were unworthy of serious study and turned their attention elsewhere, or – if for any reason they harboured a grudge against that country – they presented a picture of two opposing thought-systems. The English and German *Weltanschauungen*, according to this view, were polarities: crass materialism versus spirituality; individualism versus the common good; cosmopolitanism versus the power of the nation-state; selfishness and *laissez-faire* versus collective responsibility; atomism versus organic unity. The theme of '*Händler und Helden*' was already being strongly emphasised as the nineteenth century reached its final quarter.[32]

It is, therefore, an ironic commentary upon the blurred and often one-sided nature of cultural 'influences' that, just as T. H. Green was discovering in Kant and Hegel the basis for his philosophical assault against utilitarianism and against 'the dogmatic individualism and insensitivity to suffering of a Herbert Spencer',[33] the German public mind was disparaging *all* English social thought on precisely the same grounds. Mill had once asserted that every Englishman was either a Benthamite or a Coleridgean; but to the Germans, they all seemed Benthamites – so that even the metamorphosis in the later Mill himself was not recognised. The growth of interest in positivism, the beginnings of sociology and the popularity of Darwinistic theories in Britain, rather than influencing German thinkers, offered fresh evidence to the latter of the shallow and purely mechanical character of the British. Darwinism was a common trait of popular literature, and the theory of evolution appealed to those who saw each nation as a historically distinct and organically coherent entity; but to German eyes it seemed a travesty that people such as Spencer, Bagehot and Buckle should represent society as a complex structure with many moving parts *without* considering the larger essence which gave that society its true spirituality and 'reality'.[34] English and French sociology, to put it bluntly, was simply another manifestation of an atomistic and materialistic view of mankind.

The interactions in the field of historical scholarship were much more positive, although no less one-sided. The practical reasons for the British admiration for German writing and research were very clear to contemporaries: in place of the well-written but nevertheless amateurishly researched and opinionated writings of belle-lettrists and 'Whig' historiography, here was a flood of detailed, massive tomes, adorned with footnotes and all other signs of scholarship which seemed to proclaim their objectivity and authority, emerging from the pens of Ranke, Mommsen, Niebuhr, Dahlmann, Pauli, Gneist and other German historians. Even if one wished to concentrate upon British history alone, it was now necessary to take account of German scholarship, so thorough and respectable did it appear. 'As a rule', Seeley noted in 1867, 'good books are in German.'[35] When the *English Historical Review* – the intended counterpart to the *Historische Zeitschrift* – was first published in 1886, it was no accident that it contained an article by Acton on 'German schools of history'. Acton himself may have had a uniquely cosmopolitan upbringing, but there was nothing special about his years of study in Germany: A. W. Ward also received his education in Germany, Bryce went to Heidelberg, Prothero to Bonn, Poole to Leipzig, and the economic historians Cunningham and Ashley to Tübingen and Göttingen respectively.

However, the development of what was termed the 'German school of history' in Britain derived only in part from this recognition of the superiority of German scholarship: its main boost, certainly in the mid-century, came from the proclamation of the island people's 'Teutonic' heritage. Kemble's famous study *The Saxons in England* (1849) – itself the product of someone who had studied under Jakob Grimm at Göttingen – was the first of these, but perhaps an even greater influence at university level was Thomas Arnold, who declared in his *Introductory Lectures . . .* at Oxford that modern history in England

> clearly begins with the coming over of the Saxons; the Britons and Romans had lived in our country, but they are not our fathers; we are connected with them as men indeed, but nationally speaking, the history of Caesar's invasion has no more to do with us, than the natural history of the animals which then inhabited our forests; we, this great English nation, whose race and language are now overrunning the earth from one end to the other – we are born when the white horse of the Saxons had established his dominions from the Tweed to the Thames.[36]

This, in a nutshell, was the message of the Oxford school: Stubbs in his *Constitutional History*, Freeman in his *Norman Conquest*, Green in his bestselling *Short History of the English People*, sought to demonstrate their 'common stock' with fellow Teutons, to prove that the origins of English democracy lay in the Germanic folk-moot and other institutions which the coming of the

Normans had utterly failed to eradicate, and that their country's 'Language, law, custom, and religion preserve their original conformation and colouring. The German element is the paternal element in our system, natural and political.'[37]

From this twin basis, of scholarship and racial identity, it was no great leap for such historians also to be pro-German in their contemporary political attitudes (however much their views upon other issues differed). The most enthusiastic of all was Freeman, who rejoiced at the course of the Franco-Prussian War (which he followed on the maps which covered his walls), fervently defended the German 'recovery' of territories 'stolen' by the Gauls, and climaxed all of this with his attempt to go to Paris in order to witness the triumphal entry of the Prussian troops into that city.[38] Even the more moderate Bryce thought that Napoleon's policy had been an 'atrocious public crime' and that Britain might have warned France 'that if she declared war on such grounds, she would have us also to fight'.[39] Stubbs, too, took a strong pro-German stance in 1870, and Seeley, in his Life and Times of Stein, openly praised 'the character and greatness' of the German wars of 1813, 1866 and 1870.[40]

The German historians' response to this emphasis upon the common heritage of the two peoples was, by 1870 at least, much more muted. In the first place, respect for the other country's scholarship was lacking: as Matthew Arnold noted, 'In general the Germans are very supercilious towards academic books written by modern Englishmen.'[41] There were some exceptions: for example Acton, Bryce and Carlyle received honorary doctorates or decorations for their work. To the great majority of German historians, however, their earlier interest in English history had been provoked by a concern for current German problems. This was why especially the years 1840 to 1870 had seen such a flourishing of essentially favourable German-language publications about the constitutional, political and foreign policy aspects of Britain's past: constitutional reformers such as F. C. Dahlmann, Robert von Mohl, Karl von Welcker, Gervinus and others who 'warmly admired the unwritten English constitution and believed that at least some English institutions of government could be transferred to German soil'; Ranke, cautious, conservative and Protestant, full of praise for England's past role 'as the leader of coalitions for the defence of Europe's liberty'; and Johann Lappenberg, who anticipated the 'Oxford school' by seeking to demonstrate the racial and cultural links which Anglo-Saxon England had with the Teutonic tribes and the essentially superficial impact made by the later Norman Conquest. Admittedly, there had been others whose portrayal of Britain's past had been less rosy: Victor Huber, Stahl and Bucher, who were turning more and more towards an idealisation of the Prussian state; Johann Droysen, much more respected academically than those three but, being a student of Hegel, already critical of the British version of freedom; Marx and Engels, who viewed the island state's past from a quite different but equally critical standpoint; and List, who, much though he admired England, had his own axes to grind. Yet, at the time of their writings, as Professor McClelland reminds us, 'they were all men out of season in some respects, whose voices, as in the wilderness, reached few contemporary ears and changed few minds'.[42]

Already by the late 1860s, the balance of German historical opinion was beginning to change, reflecting to a large degree the coming of the age of Realpolitik, the disappointment of so many German Liberals with the British stance during the wars of unification, and the growing disapproval of the 'leap into the dark' of the Second Reform Act. The 'sea-change' which occurred overall in the political views of the National Liberals in this decade could be detected in the writings of their historians, Rudolf von Gneist, Karl von Noorden and Heinrich von Sybel. Slowly recognising that Prussia-Germany was not going to develop along English lines and laying more stress themselves now upon the need for strong state power with which to combat the jealous rivals of Germany on all sides, these historians came to make a distinction between the historic Britain and the present introspective and bumbling state. Even Pauli, the most anglophile of this school, admitted to the differences between 'Old England', which represented 'parliamentarism, mercantile dominion of the seas, predominance of old [political] forms, ascent', and 'New England', which stood for 'reform, free trade, new forms, and decadence'.[43] The most notable – and extreme – exemplar of this metamorphosis was, of course, Treitschke himself; but he was unusual in that his disappointment was then channelled into a virulent anglophobia. For most of the others who lived through the period of unification, 1871 represented a culmination point which meant that their earlier preoccupation with English conditions was now far less relevant.

In the world of the natural sciences, it was not merely the members of academe itself who took notice of Germany's achievements, for the effects of that very superiority could obviously be detected in the outside world too. The neglect of the sciences – except in the most abstract and antiquarian fashion – by Oxford and Cambridge, and the lack of higher education offered elsewhere in England, stood in sad contrast to the many institutions in Germany where research was undertaken, professors supervised teams of scholars and laboratories and other physical equipment were provided: the laboratory itself was hardly known in *any* university science department in England, and similar neglect was shown in the secondary schools.[44] The small number of students graduating each year in chemistry, in medicine, in biology, was pitiful in comparison with the thousands leaving their German equivalents; and the gap was wider in *technical* subjects, where the British continued to rely upon the inspired, amateur engineer-inventor on the one hand and the basic instruction provided by the mechanics' institutes on the other.

One effect of this disparity was that British scientists and technologists, even more than historians or theologians, felt compelled to study in Germany if they were to gain real knowledge in their field. From the picture which emerges in Professor Haines's detailed researches, in fact, it is difficult to avoid the conclusion that almost *every* notable mid-to-late Victorian scientist had studied in Germany, or at the very least had been greatly influenced by developments first carried out in that country; often the greater part of a science department at a British university by the end of the century would be staffed by people who had obtained their doctorate in Germany; and almost all their textbooks were in German or translated from the German.[45]

The second consequence was to be found in the political rather than in the academic arena: within an astonishingly short space of time statesmen, educationalists and businessmen realised that Britain, hitherto regarded as the world's leader in the fields of science and technology, was now quite backward compared with the advances which had taken place in Germany. For many mid-Victorians, indeed, this Teutonic efficiency and application provided the real explanation for the Prussian military triumphs over Austria and France: as Norman Lockyer, the founder of the scientific journal *Nature*, observed in 1870: 'The same method is necessary to raise, organise, and equip a battalion, as to perform a chemical experiment. It is this great truth that the Germans, above all other nations, if not alone among nations, have thoroughly realised and applied.' What was true of the arts of war was equally valid, it was argued, in the realms of business and commerce – a point which gained credence when the latter were affected by the Great Depression and the stagnation of British industry. As Lord Playfair (who himself had been trained in Liebig's laboratory at Giessen) told the British Association for the Advancement of Science in 1885:

How is it that in our great commercial centres, foreigners – German, Swiss, Dutch and even Greeks – push aside our English youth and take the places of profit . . . How is it that in our colonies . . . German enterprise is pushing aside English capacity? How is it that whole branches of manufactures, when they depend on scientific knowledge, are passing away from this country? . . . The answer to these questions is that our systems of education are still too narrow for the increasing struggle for life . . . Even Oxford and Cambridge . . . are still far behind a second-class German University.[46]

From the late 1860s onwards, therefore, the calls for drastic reforms in the British educational system – especially in regard to technology and the natural sciences – grew ever louder, provoking repeated (though piecemeal) responses from successive governments. In 1868, neatly sandwiched between the battles of Sadowa and Sedan, Matthew Arnold published his *School and Universities on the Continent*, which praised the German educational system but also warned of the coming commercial rivalry. In 1870, W. E. Forster introduced his Elementary Education Bill, urging fellow MPs to consider that 'if we leave our work-folk any longer unskilled . . . they will become overmatched in the competition of the world'. Between 1870 and 1875, the Royal Commission on Scientific Instruction and the Advancement of Science (the so-called Devonshire Commission) took evidence and furnished massive reports about Britain's needs. In the same years, serious efforts were made, from within and without, to reform Oxford and Cambridge universities, particularly in the field of science; and, perhaps more significantly, a cluster of new colleges of science were founded in the large commercial centres of Newcastle, Leeds, Sheffield, Liverpool, Bristol, Birmingham and Nottingham, and further growth occurred in the London colleges and at Owen's College (Manchester). Between 1881 and 1884, following Mundella's prodding, a Royal Commission in Technical

Education was at work, and its message was reinforced by the gloomy reports emanating from the slightly later, and very famous, Royal Commission on the Depression in Trade and Industry. By that time, the pattern of growing national concern about the relative deficiencies within the British educational system, and a corresponding anxiety for the commercial and other consequences of this weakness, was well and truly established.[47]

It would be wrong, of course, to portray all of this concern for the educational system as deriving from the example or 'influence' of Germany alone: the trends at work were far too general for that. Nevertheless, it was also true that the most frequent comparisons and analogies were made between the British and German systems; that, both in the field of natural sciences and in technical instruction, Germany had provided the 'model', the inspiration and, indeed, the personal experiences which fashioned the convictions of the scientists concerned; and, finally, that irrespective of his specific subject virtually every university reformer of the mid-Victorian period had either studied in Germany or been influenced by its overall superiority. Indeed, the favourite cry of the opponents of reform was that people such as Jowett, Mark Pattison, Seeley, Matthew Arnold, Max Müller and T. H. Huxley were trying to 'Prussianise' Oxford and Cambridge – as, of course, they were, at least in the methods of research and instruction.

Given that Germany was seen as (in Pattison's words) 'the model to which we must look in making any alterations of our own', it becomes much clearer why so many British politicians and especially intellectuals supported the German cause in 1866 and 1870. Was she not, by her achievements, satisfying the progressive, 'liberal' criteria by which the Englishmen judged the other nations of the globe: refined scholarship, scientific endeavours, world leaders in so many academic subjects, fine artistic and musical traditions, an unequalled educational system, commercial and technological advances, an adherence to free trade, and so on? Furthermore, there also existed that coterie of British germanophiles who, steeped in the tradition of Coleridge and Arnold, could turn to this continental exemplar because of their own distaste for 'economic man', their apprehensions about the cultural shallowness and deprivation of mass, industrialised life, and their belief that Germany represented a more refined, organic, idealistic society, in which 'good government' was properly given preference over 'representative government'. Add to this the growing emphasis in mid-Victorian England upon their country's essentially Teutonic character, *and* a political code which favoured the 'winners' in history; and it is scarcely surprising to encounter a whole host of enthusiastically pro-German expressions in the 1850s and 1860s. In 1866, as the essayist Richard Congreve put it, 'we clapped hands over Sadowa';[48] and a similar outburst occurred during the early stages of the Franco-Prussian War. 'God save Germany! She is the leading shoot now of European civilisation. The French Empire is reaction and barbarism', wrote Goldwin Smith, the erstwhile leader of the Oxford reformers, to his friend Bryce.[49] George Eliot, too, felt that this was a struggle between two different cultures and that the future 'period of German ascendancy' would be a great improvement; John Morley praised Prussia's 'moral' war aims; and *The Times* assured a readership whose eyes were uneasily opening to

118

a revolution in the continental balance of power that the Germans were 'a people which, by its history, its geographical position, its educational progress, and its domestic character, is of all the continental nations the least dangerous to Europe'.[50] But the most extreme example of this view came, predictably enough, from Carlyle, with his Hegelian attachment to the meaning and importance of *Kultur*. In his public letter of 8 November 1870 he declared: 'That noble, patient, deep, pious, and solid Germany should be at length welded into a nation, and become Queen of the Continent, instead of vapouring, vain-glorious, gesticulating, quarrelsome, restless, and oversensitive France, seems to me the hopefullest public fact that has occurred in my time.'[51]

The only worry to many Liberals, if not to Carlyle, was the distinction they had always made between Germany and Prussia – or, at least, between the 'good', scholarly professors, the bustling, pro-free trade businessmen, and the fine, upstanding peasantry on the one hand, and the 'bad', reactionary, Junker clique which controlled the Prussian government on the other. Thus, the caustic comments made by *The Times* upon the outcome of the Prussian constitutional crisis, the anger expressed by so many Britons over Schleswig-Holstein, and the deep suspicions entertained towards Bismarck personally were in no way incompatible with the germanophile sentiments noted above. The fundamental question which remained, however, was whether Germany would be *prussianised*, or Prussia *germanised*. As Morier, who was perhaps more acutely aware of this distinction than any other Briton, put it in 1870: 'What untold heights of civilisation may not the world attain to with a German Empire preponderant over the destinies of Europe, if only there is as much wisdom in the upper stories of the building as there has been valour and self-sacrifice in the lower.'[52]

To a great number of British intellectuals, then, the events of 1870–1 marked a watershed in their attitude towards Germany: that country had at last realised the desirable aim of national unity, to be sure, but it had been achieved under Prussian military direction, and with no regard for Liberal scruples concerning the annexation of Alsace-Lorraine. The people of Alsace 'are not cattle', wrote the pro-German historian J. R. Green; George Eliot, too, was pained by this German lust for territory, and Meredith thought that his nostrils now detected the 'cognac of victory' which was clouding Germanic minds; Dilke, who only a short while earlier had declared that 'our true alliance is . . . with our brothers in America, and our kinsmen in Germany and Scandanavia', was soon criticising the British government for doing nothing to prevent the loss of French territory; and the greater part of the Liberal press, as we have seen, also swung against Berlin and in favour of Paris.[53] The *Edinburgh Review* typified this trend by asserting in its April 1871 issue: 'we have the greatest distrust of [the new Germany] as long as it is mainly directed by a warlike sovereign, a military aristocracy, and an unprincipled minister'.[54]

Not all Britons changed their minds as swiftly as this, of course. The 'ideological germanophiles'[55] such as Carlyle, Freeman, Blackie and Seeley still asserted that France had received all that she had asked for and that Britain's 'natural ally' remained Germany – an attitude which many Tory imperialists were to share the following two or three decades. Others, such as Granville, Derby, Morier, Max Müller and Grant-Duff, could console themselves with the thought that within a few years the accession of the Crown Prince would ensure that Germany developed along the proper, constitutional, liberal lines. There was little, if any, decline in the reputation Germany had attained for herself in the fields of education, scholarship and science, by which criteria British intellectuals preferred to judge a country's worth. That German culture itself was also being 'prussianised' was perceived by only a few, such as Acton who increasingly warned against the revived doctrine of Machiavellianism; and Bryce, who upon his return to Heidelberg in 1886 was shocked to observe the *trahison des clercs* that had taken place: 'Nothing has struck me more than the intense monarchism and Hohenzollern imperialism of these professors, whose predecessors twenty-five years ago were, so far as political at all, republicans in sentiment.'[56]

Two further points are also worth making about this British admiration for German prowess. The first is whether this may be properly termed german*ophilia* on all occasions. The name which Germany had acquired for herself in regard to efficiency, scientific productivity and erudition might appeal to those British academics who wished to see more thought and resources devoted to their own subjects; but, besides offending all those opposed to reforms or new dogmas, the 'Prussian model' also seemed to produce a respect and deference which were quite different from a heartily felt enthusiasm. *Punch*, with its traditional irreverence for all things foreign and its acute sense of less congenial aspects of German 'culture', nicely caught this mood in its doggerel verse of January 1885:

I haf brought you German culture for the poddy and the mind.
*Die erhabene Kultur* of efery sort and efery kind;
All the pessimistic dogtrines of the Schopenhauer school
And the blessings of a bureaucratish-military rule.
. . .
I do not intend to long-while you mit missionary rant,
But to brighten up your intellects mit Hegel and mit Kant.
Mit our Army-Service system I'll begift you by-and-by,
And mit all the priceless blessings of our *Hohe Polizei*.[57]

Moreover, by the time references were being made to Germany's efficiency in manufacturing and commerce, that respect was also being tinged with some apprehension and fear and – as the 'made in Germany' campaign of the 1880s illustrated – an active dislike of this extremely competent rival.

The second point is that, whereas out-and-out germanophiles like Freeman quite cheerfully contemplated the eclipse of France, this view was not shared by the majority of Britons. Whatever weight one attaches to the cultural 'pull' of Germany has always to be balanced, in the proper degree, by that felt for France: its art, music, literature, philosophy, had also won a firm place in British minds, and it is worth recalling that many more people were acquainted with the French language than with the German. Not many public schools had imitated Thomas Arnold's efforts at Rugby to spread the German language; and even that pronounced expert upon German affairs, his son, was fluent in French but had some difficulties in German![58] Morier, appalled like many others at the condition of France by early 1871, pleaded with his friend Stockmar to recognise the necessity for its survival. 'They can furnish an element which the pure Teuton cannot – lightness, grace, form. Surely a world wholly peopled by Germans and Englishmen would not be so perfect as one in which Frenchmen had a place.'[59] This was also the opinion of the (then pro-German) *Saturday Review*:

> It is very much pleasanter to be in France than in Germany. Life is so much brighter and happier; there is so much more civility and kindness, so much more fun, so much less domineering and hectoring in France. Germany is a great country, and the Germans are a great people; but to get away from Germany into France is like getting from schooltime into holiday.[60]

On the German side, too, it is possible to see the cultural factor operating at various levels. In regard to a liking for, say, English literature or dress or furniture or church hymns, there was little question of direct association with the world of politics and ideology. This was also true of that well-known admiration of the German upper and middle classes for *der englische Lebensstil*, by which, rather selectively, was meant the life-style of an English 'gentleman', a word itself which had no German equivalent even though it evoked such a widespread and positive response. A Gentleman was seen to be not only a person of some standing, but the upholder of a high moral code and an enviable social style. His closeknit world of public school and Oxbridge education, his London clubs, his indulgence in horse-racing, shooting, yachting and other sports of the gentry, his long weekends in the country, his effortless participation (as a member of this chosen élite) in the weighty affairs of empire, were regarded with great approbation by the German establishment. Count Münster, as ambassador in London, invested in a carriage-and-four so as to ride around Hyde Park in the manner of a Regency lord; Herbert Bismarck, freed from his family and official obligations during his stays in England, gloated over his invitations to country houses, or to a grouse-shooting weekend, or to Ascot races; Kaiser Wilhelm II, inculcated from birth into this tradition (which, unfortunately, he never fully understood), simply adored this *Lebensstil*; and, predictably enough, a fair sprinkling of the sons of the German aristocracy and *Grossbourgeousie* were packed off to Oxbridge to complete their education. Somewhat lower down the social hierarchy, the imitation of the English lifestyle, especially in cities such as Hamburg, had been carried even further. 'In many regions the Tudor-style [in houses] spread "like a plague"; one played whist in a drawing-room full of English furniture, on the walls of which hung coloured lithographs of London scenes, or strolled in one's "English-landscape" garden.'[61] When the honorary British Consul at Frankfurt was searching for a successor, Sir Francis Oppenheimer recalled, he 'was impressed by my father's knowledge of British commercial affairs and

. . . attracted by a family life on the English pattern, with lively children, winsome English nurses, English food, and *The Times* and English illustrated papers'.[62]

In an earlier age, this enthusiasm for the English life-style had led some Germans to affect only to read London newspapers or even to anglicise their names – the merchant Wilhelm Oswald becoming William O'Swald and Alfried Krupp, after his stay in England, returning with his Christian name altered to Alfred. That sort of cultural emulation and affectation – rather like the German imitation of things French in the eighteenth century – was already fading away by the 1860s; and the creation of a unified German state, to which the middle classes could transfer their loyalties, marked its full demise. But the admiration for the life-style of an English gentleman, or the purchase of English clothes and furniture, was not politically objectionable and could continue with little or no alteration after 1871, just as the presentation of English drama in Germany, and the sales of Dickens's novels, did not suffer from the proclamation of the new Reich.

However, in such fields as philosophy – especially as between the idealist and empiricist traditions – and history – especially with regard to the investigation of constitutional struggles and forms – there were obvious interconnections between the academic and the political arenas; and here one can see the foundation of the German Empire as representing a watershed. Following this *fait accompli*, there was now no contemporary need for most German historians and constitutionalists to devote so much of their time to an investigation of the English 'model'; instead, they acknowledged that the two societies had different characteristics, justifying this with a Rankean historicism which asserted that all states were 'unique concentrations of moral energy, individual forces operating according to their own unique divinely-implanted logic'.[63] Moreover, while Ranke himself and the other 'moderates' were reasonably content with the idea that Germany was *different*, many others, their minds excited by the events of 1870–1, were to argue that she was also *better*. Here it was all too easy, as Treitschke and his fellow-travellers found, to appeal to the opinions of Hegel, Fichte, Kante, List and other 'founding fathers' of the German public mind in order to emphasise the superiority of their *Kultur* over the shallow, materialistic, atomistic traditions which seemed to predominate in Gladstonian England. In addition, this Hegelian-Rankean sense of a slowly unfolding national destiny, reinforced by the language and notions of Social Darwinism, suggested to some ambitious observers that the age of the 'Pax Britannica' would soon be drawing to a close, to be replaced by one in which the superior Germanic civilisation claimed and achieved its due share.

This does not mean that there was a total rejection of English political traditions in the new Reich. In the first place, those devotees of Bismarck who found it possible to agree with every alteration in his policy, were also aware that, according to the game of Realpolitik, it was ill-advised openly to show one's animosity; and the habit of viewing foreign countries through historicist-racialist spectacles often meant that far greater scorn was displayed to the Gallic and Slavic peoples – and even, on occasion, that the old references to the common interests of the two Germanic-Protestant nations could be made. There also existed many left-wing politicians and writers, like Richter, Roggenbach, Bamberger, Mommsen and Brentano, who did not join in the execration of all things English. Furthermore, there always remained that admiration, which we have noted in Herbert Bismarck, for the life-style of an English gentleman – even to the extent of using such expressions as 'Hang it!' and 'jolly good' in private correspondence. The English influence upon sport – and sporting expressions – was prodigious among the German establishment. Yet it would be idle to suppose that these considerations were going to be as significant in the formation of German attitudes towards Britain as the growing awareness of ideological differences, the rise of commercial and colonial quarrels, and the pragmatic manoeuvring in the realm of power-politics.

Thus, the cultural aspect of the Anglo-German relationship in these years presents a varied and complex picture. Both at the simpler stage, and at the level where one spoke of an admiration or dislike for the totality of the other country's culture, it is clear that this aspect has some significance. It certainly helps, for example, to explain better the attitude of specific individuals and, on occasions, of a whole group of people towards the other nation. Nevertheless, because of the variegated nature of the artistic, literary, scientific and all other forms of cultural interaction between two large and complex societies; because there is the inevitable danger that the views of an articulate intellectual like George Eliot or Max Müller or Pauli appear to outweigh by far those of a merchant, a trade unionist or a Prussian general; and because it seems to have been the case that cultural considerations often influenced but rarely seem to have determined the actions of statesmen such as Derby, Salisbury and Bismarck, it is surely not possible to assert that this aspect was a vital one. Carlyle and Treitschke may have thought that this was the only real way in which to assess foreign nations; their respective Foreign Offices had to take other factors into account.

# CHAPTER 7

# *Monarchs and Governments*

Both Britain and Germany after 1871 were constitutional monarchies; and the fact that historians have regarded the one as being on the way towards parliamentary democracy and the other as tending towards a 'Caesaristic dictatorship'[1] does not detract from the truism that the respective monarchs and their court circles played an important role in the formulation of official relationships between the two governments in these years. Nor does it seem correct to assume that the British monarch, lacking many of the prerogatives of her German cousin, had the lesser influence of the two: for Victoria's personality and great knowledge of German affairs, together with the fact that she remained whilst successive British administrations came and went, considerably enhanced her *actual* – as opposed to her constitutional – position in the formulation of the country's policy towards Germany. Whereas Wilhelm's right to determine external policy was in theory supreme, his passivity and reliance upon Bismarck reduced his effectiveness to those few occasions when his ancient prejudices (for example, the prerogatives of the army, sympathy for the conservative order) still played a considerable part. The real role of the Junker king, in other words, was to indicate the limits of diplomatic and political manoeuvre within which his Chancellor had full freedom to operate, and the only clashes occurred when Bismarck sought to venture beyond such limits. With Victoria, the position was reversed: her ministers, aware of their responsibilities to a wider public, were at hand to prevent the queen from exceeding her prerogatives; but the 'grey area' lying in between what was clearly improper interference and what was justifiable influence on her part, was so extensive that Victoria ensured that she was a central part in the decision-making process.[2]

The queen's conception of British policy went back to the time of her beloved Albert, who earnestly desired a lasting liberal *entente* between the two Teutonic peoples;[3] and while Victoria's attitude was affected by many vicissitudes thereafter, it is more than likely that it remained basically unchanged during the next few decades – perhaps until the death of Frederick III in 1888. Her own German heritage, the influence of Albert and Stockmar, the marriage of her eldest daughter to the Prussian Crown Prince, and the innumerable other connections which she had with Germany, made it impossible for her fully to separate personal and political actions, or to regard that land as being 'foreign', at least until the last decade or so of her life. The royal family, noted Derby in some despair, 'being half German, half English by connection, think of the two countries as inseparably connected, and do not understand how those who are only German or only English fail to see the relations between them in that light'.[4] Whenever proposed changes of policy towards Germany were concerned, Cabinet ministers knew that they must tread more carefully than usual and that the queen was bound to insist upon being consulted in advance. By and large, it must be said, Victoria's views were not only more generous but also more sensible than those of many ministers; and only on a few occasions did her innate sympathy for a close Anglo-German *entente* lead her to underestimate the difficulties involved.

The most striking of Victoria's interventions in foreign policy-making occurred during the Schleswig-Holstein crisis, where she was determined to prevent an Anglo-German rupture. Given the large number of other voices opposed to the forward policy of Russell and Palmerston, it is doubtful whether the queen's influence itself could be termed decisive; acting in combination with the more cautious members of the Cabinet, however, the monarch's role was very significant, and in this instance she did exceed 'the bounds of constitutional propriety'.[5] Two years later, ironically enough, it was to be Russell (aided by Clarendon) who checked Victoria's own impetuous wish to see Britain interfere before Bismarck could fulfil his aim of humiliating Austria. Although the 'system of checks and balances' between the queen, Prime Minister and Foreign Secretary was now working in the opposite direction to that of 1864, it produced the same unadventurous result – a policy which was 'moderate, prudent and safe' and which was therefore 'likely to be approved by the cabinet, by parliament and by the country at large'.[6]

Those two episodes pinpointed the ambivalent nature of the queen's attitude towards Prussia-Germany. Emotional, cultural and dynastic ties made her an unreserved supporter of the idea of German unity under Prussian leadership, whose monarch would soon be (so she hoped) her beloved son-in-law, and also made her a warm advocate of Anglo-German friendship; but the personality of Bismarck, his unscrupulous methods and the way in which, as she saw it, he was perverting the whole course of German politics, appalled her and made her increasingly suspicious of Berlin's actions. Her correspondence abounds with vivid denunciations of the Junker's character: he was 'evil', 'horrible', 'unscrupulous', 'wicked', and so on. Moreover, she found nothing inconsistent in writing, on the one hand, that 'A strong, united, liberal Germany would be a most useful ally to England'; and, on the other, that France 'who stands on a par – or at least next to us – in the advancement of civilisation!' should always remain a first-rate power.[7] It was all a matter of balance and there was nothing in the Liberal view of international politics (which, in many respects, the queen shared at this time) to make a close Anglo-German relationship irreconcilable with a good Anglo-French understanding. The Bismarckian assumption that in any triangular relationship two would combine against one was foreign to her and to many of her countrymen.

The queen's policy towards Germany in the 1870s and for most of the 1880s is, therefore, easily summarised. At the outbreak of the Franco-Prussian War she was shocked at 'the unjustifiable conduct of the French';[8] by early 1871, her emotions were moving in the opposite direction, especially as the German peace terms became known. In 1875, as we have seen, her anger at the 'overbearing, violent, grasping and unprincipled' Bismarck knew no bounds;[9] yet during the Eastern crisis of the following year she was urging Disraeli 'that Germany would be our safest ally in every way, and it might have the double advantage of preventing Bismarck from doing anything else and of going to war with France. It might also draw Austria towards us again.'[10] The trouble was, as many other Britons came only slowly to recognise, that the 'good' Germany and the 'bad' Bismarck were impossible to separate in practice. Hence, once again, the reappearance of Victoria's ambivalent attitude in 1879 when it seemed that Bismarck was making another offer of an Anglo-German alliance. She was, the queen informed her daughter, 'naturally pleased' at the news of the Austro-German alliance and, by implication, the intended check upon Russia; but 'any league against France [that is, either an Austro-German or Anglo-Austro-German one] would never be tolerated by this country'.[11] Under almost all other circumstances than a combination against France, however, Victoria would have favoured close Anglo-German co-operation, and it is therefore not surprising to find her chiding Granville during the colonial quarrels with Bismarck:

> The Queen must call Lord Granville's attention to the Despatch [from Berlin] & would ask him whether it is *really* wise (certainly not quite just) that we should protest against *any* country but *ourselves* having colonies. Germany especially cannot & would not, unless treated with suspicion and opposition, hurt us. And surely our alliances ought to be with her?[12]

By the mid-1880s, indeed, the queen's dilemma remained as acute as it ever had been. Colonial and naval rivalries with the French had by then somewhat weakened her regard for that country, and made her lean towards Berlin; but Bismarck's open actions against the 'English influence' and violent opposition to the Battenberg marriage made her dislike Prussian political traditions more than ever.

Of the attitude of the other members of the British royal family and court towards Germany, little need be noted here. Functioning as an 'extended family',[13] with their private nicknames for each other and their trans-national social life, they represented the dynastic icing on the Anglo-German cake. Personal quarrels occasionally produced political or quasi-political problems, but in general these family relationships both reinforced, and tended to confirm in the eyes of non-royal observers, the special links which existed between the two countries. One is tempted to wonder, however, whether the Anglo-German relationship might not have been more straightforward had such family links *not* existed. The case of Queen Victoria's heir, the future Edward VII, certainly suggests such a conclusion. His marriage to Alexandra, daughter of King Christian IX of Denmark, put him firmly on the 'other side' during the Schleswig-Holstein crisis.[14] This anti-Prussian sentiment increased rather than diminished during the late 1860s, and he not only advocated an

Anglo-French *entente* to check Bismarck in 1866 and was appalled at the annexation of Hanover, but he also strongly disagreed with his elder sister over the events of 1870–1. So strong was the Prince of Wales's francophilia, in fact, that he had to be repeatedly warned – by the queen, by Gladstone and by Granville – against un-neutral actions and utterances. After the Peace of Frankfurt, Albert Edward added Alsace-Lorraine to his list of unjust annexations by Prussia which, he optimistically believed, would all be handed back when his brother-in-law Frederick became German emperor.

Since much of the prince's time was spent in foreign courts and spas, where he made his opinions well known, it was scarcely surprising that these utterances irritated his German relations, who refused to accept that he was 'irresponsible' – in the original sense of that word. Occasionally, therefore, British Foreign Secretaries had to set the record straight, as Derby did to the British Minister at Stuttgart in 1877:

> The Prince of Wales is not diplomatic: he has strong likes and dislikes, and expresses them freely. I hear continually of sayings of his which are commented on at foreign courts. My answer to all enquiry and criticism as to his utterances is always the same: that he is not a responsible official person: that his ideas are personal to himself: that they are not necessarily those of the Queen, and still less of the Cabinet: and that the intentions and feelings of the Government must be gathered from what they say and do, not from the speeches of members of the royal family, over whom we have no control and who in turn have no control over us. [This is] . . . not easily understood abroad.[15]

Quite apart from the differences of political opinion between the Prince of Wales and many of his Prussian relations, the contrast in the 'life-style' of the easy-going Albert Edward and that of the Hohenzollern court was most marked. The raffish company he kept, his fondness for horse-races and gambling, his rumoured *affaires* and the delight he took in visiting 'decadent', 'immoral' Paris attracted continual newspaper criticism in the German popular press and offended the stricter Prussian sensibilities, including those of the Prince of Wales's prim young nephew, Wilhelm.

On the Prussian side, Wilhelm I's basic attitude towards England was straightforward enough, even if his day-to-day utterances oscillated between warm reference to, and then expressions of disgust about, the island state. To the Prussian king, any inconsistency lay with the British. A stable, conservative, Protestant England, willing to take its share in checking the ambitions of 'revolutionary' France and in preserving the European order – an England, in other words, such as Gerlach and Ranke had described in their early works – was obviously to be welcomed. In addition, he had a great respect for his fellow-monarch, Queen Victoria, and this dynastic sentiment was reinforced by his son's marriage to her eldest daughter. On the other hand, an England controlled by demagogues and radicals (that is, Gladstone), curbing the privileges of the Crown and the House of Lords, imposing parliamentary controls over even such sacred areas of government as the army, pressing ahead

127

with a full-scale assault upon other bastions of the established order, and abdicating from its traditional role of checking French pretensions in Europe, was not to Wilhelm's liking at all. He was, moreover, reinforced in this prejudice, negatively, by his own bitter experience of the clash with the Prussian Liberals, who had cited British parliamentary theory in their efforts to attain financial control over his beloved army; and, positively, by the opinions of his close military advisers, who fought strongly against the importation of such British political traditions and ideas. To have the Prussian army run by a 'Parliament-controlled British commander-in-chief' was, indeed, the bogy which the generals had constantly held before Wilhelm's eyes in what was, to him, the greatest crisis of his life.[16]

Two further factors inclined Wilhelm away from Britain, or at least ensured that he was not part of the 'pro-English camp' at the German court. The first was the high regard which he had for Russia and especially for his nephew, Tsar Alexander. No assessment of the role played by dynastic factors in the Anglo-German relationship can ignore the fact that, to the first German Kaiser, the links with St Petersburg outweighed those with Windsor. This regard derived partly from the respect which Wilhelm and the Prussian Junkers paid to Russia as the mainstay of European conservatism; and partly from a genuine feeling of gratitude at Russia's policy of non-interference from Schleswig-Holstein to Sedan, which had contributed more towards the success of German unification than any other *external* factor. In the post-1871 period, this sentiment expressed itself in Wilhelm's very firm commitment to the *Dreikaiserbund*, the existence of which in his eyes was crucial to the European order. The second consideration which drew the Kaiser away from any close attachment to England was Bismarck himself. To what degree he was under the influence of the Chancellor is difficult to measure exactly. One historical image is of a bluff, simple-minded Prussian soldier who, whatever his reservations and counter-arguments, was always going to accept Bismarck's advice in the long run. Another is of a monarch whose political convictions were so unalterable that, while the two men shared the same *ends*, the Chancellor was at times seriously restricted in the *means* he could deploy to achieve them; and thus the king's well-known prejudices made even Bismarck realise that there were certain tactics which even he could not propose. The evidence tends more towards the latter image, but whichever view of Wilhelm I the historian prefers, the result has little significance for the Anglo-German relationship: for if he was indeed putty in Bismarck's hands, then he was bound to follow the Chancellor's own tortuous policy towards the island state; but if he was in certain respects independent, then this expressed itself in a more pro-Russian and anti-Liberal direction, which could scarcely be welcome in London.

Two instances should be sufficient to demonstrate Wilhelm's attitude and role in this respect: namely, his russophile sentiments in the 1870s, and his disgust at Gladstone's administration in the early 1880s. Russia's support in 1870, together with Wilhelm's own horror at the Commune, made the new Kaiser a warm supporter of the *Dreikaiserbund* – the ideological and sentimental grounds for which Bismarck, like Disraeli in his various dealings with Victoria, tended to lay on with a trowel.[17] However, the Chancellor's unscrupulousness often led him to tell his monarch only those facts which the latter would find plausible; and then to be not a little embarrassed when Wilhelm wished to act on the basis of this incomplete knowledge. For example, the semi-official press (under Bismarck's encouragement) tended throughout this period to avoid anti-Russian expressions but to be critical of British policy: with the embarrassing consequence that the Kaiser, from his reading of these journals, was provoked into writing to London to complain at Britain being the main obstacle to German policy in the 1875 war crisis and, a year later, at her seeking an Anglo-Russian war.[18] Furthermore, when Bismarck himself saw that the *Dreikaiserbund* was foundering in the late 1870s and decided instead to attach Vienna to Berlin's side, he discovered that the chief obstacle to this new policy was the Kaiser, who held firm to the traditional Russo-German friendship and would have made even more of a fuss had he known that England was being considered as a possible partner to the Austro-German alliance of 1879.[19]

Wilhelm's pro-Russian stance did not entirely obliterate any regard for England. He was aware of Queen Victoria's sympathies towards Germany, and equally aware of the pro-English sentiments of his own family. Moreover, disappointment with the British government's attitude in 1870–1 did not prevent him from hoping in 1874 that their two countries, being 'naturally allied to each other by the principles of Protestantism', would join with Austria-Hungary and Russia in the preservation of the European peace[20] – as well as the combating of the ultramontane menace. The advent of Gladstone's administration in 1880 naturally dealt a blow to these already sagging hopes, and for the next five years the Kaiser was fed a whole series of diplomatic reports and press clippings which claimed that Britain was now in the hands of a group of radical demagogues and Irish MPs whose ultimate aim was to turn the country into a 'red republic'.[21] No doubt Bismarck had a ready believer of such stories in Wilhelm; but that still did not mean that the latter was totally a dupe or a pliable instrument. In 1884, for example, the Kaiser found the anglophobia of the German press too sweeping and wished a distinction to be made between Gladstone's government and the British people.[22]

If the old Prussian king had many reservations about British policy, his son was almost the opposite. While it may well be the case that Frederick was not the convinced instigator of progressive domestic reforms which his followers had anticipated,[23] there is no doubt about his warm feelings towards England. Quite apart from the powerful influence of his wife, the Crown Prince felt drawn to that country by a respect for his mother-in-law and by a genuine admiration for most things English. All this, together with the aversion towards Russia which he and his circle possessed, made him the natural centre for pro-English feelings inside Germany – and also made him acutely anxious to eradicate any antagonism between the two countries. 'Nothing lies closer to my heart', he informed the ambassador in London, Münster, 'than the closest possible *entente* of these two Empires, which are allotted to each other through so many naturally-developed interests.'[24] Whenever Bismarck's policies shocked London – for example, in the annexation of Alsace-Lorraine or in the 'war-in-sight' crisis – Frederick sought in his letters to distance himself from

129

these habits of Realpolitik and to reiterate his own belief in 'the liberal principle'.[25] During the 1870s and 1880s, Frederick applauded Disraeli's purchase of the Suez Canal shares; worried that England would become too entangled in the Afghan War; continually wished to replace the *Dreikaiserbund* with an Anglo-German-Austrian combination and fervently supported Bismarck's alliance 'feeler' to London in 1879; defended the Irish policy of Gladstone against German criticisms, since he felt that 'People on our side are remarkably inclined to portray events in England in the gloomiest fashion'; and rejoiced (with fellow German nationalists) when Germany acquired overseas colonies, but was deeply grieved (unlike the nationalists) at the way in which these ventures had made the German press more anglophobic than ever.[26] Because of his premature demise, it is impossible for the historian to estimate the effect a long reign by Frederick might have had upon Anglo-German relations. It is, after all, worth recalling that both his early views of Germany's place in Europe and his hopes for a colonial empire inclined more in the *grossdeutsch*-National Liberal direction than did Bismarck's. Yet since Frederick combined these sentiments with a fervent desire for English friendship, a suspicion of Russia and a 'Whiggish' belief in the need for gradual domestic reforms, it may still be reasonable to argue that he represented the last chance to marry German liberal-nationalism with (rather than to have it set *against*) a pro-English foreign policy.

The Crown Prince's disposition towards England and distrust of Bismarck were feelings strongly shared by his mother. A Weimar princess of considerable character, an 'enlightened' Conservative, and a cultured woman with a deep distaste for the coarser habits and reactionary politics of the east Elbian Junkers, the Empress Augusta had a strong record of opposition to the German Chancellor.[27] No doubt a great deal of this may be attributed to an intense dislike of the man who, as she viewed it, exerted so undue an influence over her husband; but they also reflected the views of a person who believed that the course of German history was being perverted by Bismarck. The latter, true to form, returned these feelings with interest, and in 1873 the empress confided to Odo Russell's wife that the Chancellor had 'only twice spoken to her Majesty since the war'.[28] To Bismarck, the knowledge that Augusta was in frequent correspondence with Queen Victoria and with the other royal dames of Weimar, Coburg and Baden – 'the womanly intriguers', as he called them – and that she was also in close contact with such detestable German Liberals as Vincke, Roggenbach, Stosch and even, in her earlier years, with the unspeakable Morier automatically meant that he regarded the empress as one of his greatest foes.

Nevertheless, Augusta could be – and always was – checked. This, however, was less of a certainty in respect of that other feminine opponent, the Crown Princess of Prussia. Her intellectual and moral domination of Frederick, together with the independence of position (and therefore the relative freedom from Prussian court pressure) that came from her being first and foremost an Englishwoman, meant that she posed a greater *potential* counter-influence than ever Augusta could offer; and, once again, Bismarck acted in a predictable fashion, by continually snubbing and neutralising her actions and by unleashing attacks in the press upon the unwelcome 'English intrigues' against German policy. In the 1860s, despite the many differences, this animosity had not been of great significance to Bismarck, who knew that the securing of German unification would nullify most criticisms; and the Crown Princess, in turn, had consoled herself with the thought that 'Bismarck is not eternal'.[29] Throughout the years following, however, the relationship steadily deteriorated and her voluminous correspondence rang with complaints against the man who was both ruining the prospects of a 'liberalisation' of Germany and who seemed to be bent upon blackening the image of England in the minds of his countrymen. Nevertheless, it is hard to avoid the conclusion that the young Victoria had brought much of this upon herself – or, to put it more accurately, she had made herself astonishingly vulnerable to Bismarck's many counter-attacks. The Austro-Hungarian ambassador in Berlin voiced but a common feeling when he reported: 'The future Queen of Prussia and Empress of Germany has remained so completely an Englishwoman in all her feelings, thoughts and strivings that she regards all steps taken here in defence of German interests against English presumptions as an offence personally afflicted upon herself.' In constantly complaining about conditions in Berlin or expressing relief when she was 'going home' to England, the ambassador added, she greatly weakened her own position and seemed to justify Bismarck's claim that she could never act out of consideration for the interests of Germany alone.[30] Ironically, it was probably the case that, despite all her efforts to establish a firm Anglo-German friendship, the overall impact of the Crown Princess was negative rather than positive; and that the political relations between the two countries might have been less frequently unsettled had this dynastic link not existed at all.

The above paragraphs assume, of course, that the personalities and prejudices of the rulers of Britain and Germany did have some effect upon the overall relationship, difficult though it often is to measure the effects precisely. To the student of long-term political and economic trends in both countries, and of the shifts that occurred in the global power-balance during these decades, such an assumption may appear a questionable one. However, the answer to these reservations must always be that both the decision-makers and the public of the time clearly regarded the character of their sovereigns as being of critical importance. Whatever the constitutional theory, the British Prime Minister or Foreign Secretary could not ignore Victoria's views upon their policy towards Germany, which (especially in the 1860s) she herself helped to formulate. With regard to the German side, the case may be put more strongly, not on account of the greater constitutional prerogatives of the monarch-cum-emperor, but rather because of the actions and reactions of his Chancellor. If Bismarck held that the attitude of the Kaiser in certain questions was critical; if Bismarck showed, by all his manoeuvres, how crucial it was to gain the ear of Wilhelm, or how dangerous it would be to the Junker-dominated state if ever Frederick and his wife were able to grasp the reins of power; if, to put it bluntly, the man whose character and role no historian of Germany can disregard, considered this factor to be a significant part of the historical process, then it would be rash for the later student of this period to downgrade it. Above all, it would be unhistorical to forget what the Bismarcks always felt

131

acutely, that a great deal of the early shaping of the Second Reich hung upon the prejudices and sheer longevity of a simple old emperor.

The opinions of the British and German courts, however important we may judge them to have been, were one of various influences which were exerted upon the respective governments; but how significant was this central policy-making and information-gathering machine itself? If, as has recently been argued in the British case, only the 'Official Mind' of government 'registered and balanced all the contingencies',[31] then it is surely worthwhile to examine that institutional system itself, upon which all the influences of monarchs, parties, newspapers and pressure groups converged. While the latter clearly had an impetus of their own which would be felt in almost *any* form of governmental structure, it was also true that the prejudices and personalities of the office-holders concerned, together with the effective power of their offices, was a very real factor – at least so far as the handling of Anglo-German political problems in these decades was concerned.

On the British side, the decisive office-holders were the Foreign Secretaries themselves, simply because they directed the day-to-day course of external policy. All four in this period, Clarendon, Granville, Derby and Salisbury, were experienced and senior politicians, well able to blend the views of their Prime Ministers, the mood of the Commons and the general prejudices of the country at large with their own particular assumptions about foreign policy. They possessed a similarity of style – an essential pragmatism, a habit of understatement and a feigned nonchalance in their private dispatches – which tends to disguise some of the basic differences which did exist in their attitudes to events such as the Eastern Question. With regard to Bismarckian Germany, however, the identity of view among the Foreign Secretaries was very close indeed. Clarendon's acute dislike of all that came out of Berlin by the late 1860s was well known: 'the Prussians', he informed Cowley, 'are the most swaggering robbers who were allowed to despoil their neighbours' – a sentiment which not only explains his wish to help the French secure a disarmament agreement, but also why Victoria sought to prevent his resumption of the Foreign Secretaryship.[32] Granville was milder in manner, but shared the same preference for the French before the Germans, and was well aware of Bismarck's dislike of English liberalism: in 1881, he informed his fellow-Whig Hartington that the Chancellor 'detested us as free-traders, & liberals, belonging to a country whose press was so hostile to his domestic policy'.[33] This did not prevent Granville from frequently offering the hospitality of his house to Herbert Bismarck, or from seeking to eliminate all differences in the Anglo-German relationship – just as the rational Liberal code taught; but it was also clear that his hope for a real and lasting improvement lay in the expected accession of the Crown Prince and in the demise of the Bismarckian system of diplomacy.

Derby's attitude towards Bismarck altered at such a pace that, by the middle of the 1870s, his dislike of the Chancellor was markedly greater than that of either of his two predecessors as Foreign Secretary. In the years 1866–8, as we have seen, the youthful Stanley was quite willing to contemplate – and, indirectly, to assist – the unification of Germany by Prussia as a check to

France and Russia; and even on his return to office in 1874 he thought that the German Empire was 'the state with which we have most in common'.[34] This, however, was altered by the Foreign Secretary's discovery that Bismarck was always warning the Russians about the British, and the British about the Russians; and by Odo Russell's alarming reports from Berlin. The actual 'war-in-sight' crisis strengthened Derby in his suspicions, and from that time onwards he never trusted Bismarck again. 'I read all reports of Bismarck's conversations with extreme distrust', he informed Odo Russell in 1877. 'I may be wrong, but he is not a man in whom anybody can have confidence.'[35] It was on this account, as well as others, that Derby strongly opposed all Bismarck's hints that Britain should involve herself in the Russo-Turkish War; and resigned over this point when Disraeli wished to adopt the contrary policy. In the final clash between Bismarck and Derby, when the latter as Colonial Secretary appeared to be frustrating Germany's imperial annexations in 1884–5, it seems clear that he strongly felt that he was under no obligation to change his normally lethargic ways at the behest of Berlin: his letters of this period refer to how 'cool' and 'sharp' Bismarck's actions were, and in one he argued that 'No conclusion seems possible except that he [Bismarck] wants a quarrel.'[36]

The change in Salisbury's attitude was in the opposite direction, although the evidence suggests that the transition was more apparent than real. In the 1860s, he was well known as a critic of most things German. He disliked its theology and, despite his wide reading in German literature, he regarded the German language as 'intolerable'. He was extremely critical of the Schleswig-Holstein fiasco, and it was at this time that he suggested that Germany *had* to attack Denmark to gain access to the sea which its chauvinists deemed essential for its future expansion.[37] These two points – the ineptitude and weakness of the British government, and the long-term ambitions of the German – he returned to in his articles upon the Franco-Prussian War, where he suggested that the neutral nations 'will be disposed to think that there is more to fear from the intoxication of German triumph, than from distracted and revolutionised France'.[38] In February 1877 he noted that Bismarck's alliance proposals 'have happily not been accepted', and a little later argued that the real danger in the impending Russian assault upon Turkey was that Germany would then fall upon France:

If any dangers threaten England, they are much nearer home, and will come from a far more formidable military power [than Russia] . . . The object most of all desirable is, if possible, to keep Russia out of war for the present. If it can be done for twelve months more, France's preparations will be sufficiently complete to make a *coup de main* from Berlin impossible . . . The crisis is an anxious one, for it is quite conceivable that if things go wrong, we may be fighting for Holland before two years are out.[39]

In view of this sentiment, it is easy to understand why Salisbury, fearing the effect upon Anglo-French relations, strongly opposed Bismarck's renewed alliance bid in 1879; and, when he returned to direct British foreign policy in the late 1880s, was much more suspicious of German aims than most of the Conservatives.

Advice and information upon which the Foreign Secretaries based their German policy came from two bureaucratic sources: the Office itself, and diplomatic representatives overseas. The former does not appear to have had much independence of opinion in these years.[40] Under Palmerston, the officials had well understood that their task was simply to execute his orders without question and to provide swift answers to all his requests for information; and even if such successors as Clarendon, Granville and Derby were less demanding and overbearing, the permanent staff kept a low profile. Under-secretaries such as Hammond (1854–73), Tenterden (1873–82) and Pauncefote (1882–9) certainly ventured opinions upon diplomatic questions of the day but this usually related to their tactical handling and there seems to have been no profound political prejudice. A conservatism in regard to bureaucratic habits in the Office itself, and a generally Whiggish view of foreign affairs was a characteristic of most of the senior staff, which is scarcely surprising given their social background and the means of recruitment.[41] They shared the diplomatic corps' distrust of Bismarck; shook their heads disapprovingly when Germany returned to protectionism, which is not surprising when it is recalled that the only economic book which they were recommended to read before entry into the service was *The Wealth of Nations*; and they resented the brusqueness of German colonial demands in 1884–5. Even in this latter respect, however, it is worth recalling that such a person as Sir Percy Anderson, the African expert at the Foreign Office, had a greater fear of French than of German imperialism.[42] Moreover, that influential Proconsul of Empire, Cromer – who may be said to have shared with Anderson the formulation of Whitehall's African policy in so many respects – provided a further reinforcement to this viewpoint by his frequent reminders to the Foreign Office that good relations with Berlin were necessary for the satisfactory settlement of the Egyptian embroglio.[43]

The role of the 'man on the spot', the ambassador himself, was held to be much more important: although the historian in retrospect may wonder whether a good or bad diplomat made much difference to the overall course of Anglo-German relations, contemporary opinion seemed unanimous that it did. Not only was he the monarch's personal representative to the other court – a consideration which Victoria and her German equivalents took very seriously – but he also possessed the function of helping to co-ordinate policy when the two governments were in agreement, and of trying to assuage the mutual tension (without surrendering national interests) when disputes and unpleasant incidents occurred. In all cases, what really mattered was less the actual ability of the ambassador than the confidence he had acquired both with his own government and with that to which he was accredited. The British ambassador in Berlin during the late 1860s, Lord Augustus Loftus, possessed neither – 'our goosey-gander in Berlin', Disraeli once called him although the fact that Bismarck also distrusted the ambassador temporarily raised the latter in the eyes of his royal mistress. This was, however, a very negative basis for an appointment, and the queen and her daughter constantly railed at the second-rate calibre of the staff sent to the Berlin embassy. 'Lord Augustus – the best-intentioned of men – was not gifted by Heaven with intellect; and in such times as these – and affairs so difficult to understand as our German politics – I should surely think that about the only Englishman who thoroughly understands them must be in the right place', complained the Crown Princess in an attempt to boost the chances of her favourite, Morier.[44] Although the official and semi-official reports by Loftus come over as a perfectly adequate account, and he seems in no way to have been taken in by the Prussian Prime Minister,[45] his general mannerisms, and the way in which his post was rendered somewhat superfluous during the Franco-Prussian War by Odo Russell's attendance upon Bismarck at Versailles, increased the pressure for his removal. By late 1871, the deed had been done and the unfortunate Loftus had moved to St Petersburg.

His successor, Odo Russell (after 1880, Lord Ampthill), was the most brilliantly successful of all ambassadorial appointments to Berlin in these decades.[46] His family ties no doubt gave him a flying start in life; but to these attributes could be added intelligence, tact, a perfect charm of manner and a remarkable fluency in English, French, German and Italian. Whilst irritated beyond measure at most of his other companions during his stay at Versailles in 1870–1, Bismarck enjoyed 'letting go' with Odo Russell for a few hours after dinner almost every evening,[47] and so obvious was the favour shown that the Crown Prince and Princess, the generals and many others pestered Russell for details of what Bismarck was planning to do! Later, during his years at Berlin, he achieved the near-impossible feat of being trusted by Bismarck *and* by most of the latter's enemies. He was a firm favourite at court, and frequently reported home that the emperor and empress, or the Crown Prince and Princess, had called at the embassy for tea or dinner – a privilege rarely if ever extended to the other ambassadors. Only Disraeli, predictably, found fault in him – for being unable to gain access to Bismarck during the early stages of the Eastern crisis, and for deferring too much to the Chancellor thereafter; but no others complained and even the caustic Tenterden held that 'Odo Russell is the right man at Berlin'.[48]

Despite this general approbation of Odo Russell's ambassadorship, however, there were several occasions when his touch was less than perfect. Throughout the early-to-mid 1870s he was convinced that Bismarck intended to achieve the *grossdeutsch* aim of incorporating Austria as well, and his reports to this effect could hardly have improved Germany's image in the minds of Granville or Derby – or Tsar Alexander, to whom Russell freely offered this opinion in 1875.[49] In the later 1870s, by contrast, he had become (like so many ambassadors of the two countries) a firm believer in an Anglo-German alliance, and frequently regretted the British government's hesitation on this score – not seeing, perhaps, that his own argument that 'An unaccountable, ambitious, irresponsible genius with a million of soldiers at his disposal like Bismarck is a friend to cultivate' would hardly appeal to the likes of Lord Derby![50] Finally, and perhaps most significant of all, Russell's concentration upon the opinions of Bismarck and the gossip at court seems to have meant that his references to the more general aspects of the Anglo-German relationship – the strongly anglophobic tone of much of the right-wing press, or the growing commercial rivalry – were only brief and fleeting. It was on this account, no doubt, as well as his failing health, that he played down the growing popular demand in Germany for colonies in the early 1880s in preference to the Chancellor's repeated assurances that he was 'kein Kolonialmensch'. By the time the ambassador had perceived that Bismarck was now responding to such pressure,[51] his own premature death was only weeks away.

Odo Russell's successor was bound to have a hard task. Nevertheless, the British government made an effective choice in Sir Edward Malet, the son of Bismarck's old colleague at Frankfurt, Sir Alexander Malet.[52] His range of contacts in Berlin was nowhere as wide as Odo Russell's – perhaps Malet sensed that it would be imprudent for anyone other than his predecessor to move in the circles of Bismarck's political enemies – and he never had the close rapport with the old emperor. He was, however, on good terms with the Crown Princess and, later, with Wilhelm II. In the handling of official business, Malet had a rough start, assuming his new post just as the Anglo-German colonial quarrels reached their peak; but his general competence, discretion and sense of balance earned him the respect of both governments, and he then enjoyed a decade in Berlin when Anglo-German relations, if not free from periodic disagreements, seemed to be relatively friendly. If Malet appeared socially less convivial and open a character than Odo Russell, he fulfilled his diplomatic functions in a perfectly satisfactory manner – until, that is, his famous final audience with the State Secretary, Marschall, in October 1895, when he bluntly warned that German interference in South Africa would lead to severe consequences, a remark which the outraged Wilhelm regarded as tantamount to an ultimatum.[53]

Apart from the ambassadors to Berlin themselves, there were several other sources of information about German policy open to the British government. The first of these, the ministers attached to the smaller German courts, had been of great value during the confused period of unification itself; but after 1871 they tended more and more to offer merely additional information about German public opinion and regional politics. More important than these were the various categories of *attachés* at Berlin. In a military monarchy, where the opinions and influence of the chief of the Prussian General Staff before the emperor might be as important as those of the Chancellor himself, the British military *attaché* often picked up significant information. Consequently, military *attachés* such as Walker, Swaine and Grierson had an importance quite distinct from their roles as *rapporteurs* of the affairs of the German army.[54] Another important source of information in the early years was the commercial *attaché*, Sir Joseph Archer Crowe. His more-or-less constant sojourns on the continent, his friendships with the Crown Prince and Princess, and the contacts he had established with Stosch, Roggenbach, Treitschke, Freytag and many other German Liberals in the 1860s had made him into probably the best-informed Englishman of all upon the German political scene. Moreover, his connection with Reichstag deputies, business and intellectual circles, and with the smaller German courts (rather than with Bismarck), turned him into a keen observer of the larger processes which were at work in German society, a characteristic which was transmitted to his son, Eyre Crowe.

Finally, mention should be made of two further important commentators upon German politics. The first was Lord Lyons, ambassador in Paris from 1867 to 1887 and often regarded as Britain's 'second Foreign Secretary' on account of his outstanding diplomatic career. His cool aristocratic style and his detached, sceptical assessments of Bismarck's policies suggest that he would have been wryly amused rather than outraged had he known that the Chancellor believed that the British government's intervention during the 'war-in-sight' crisis was engineered by himself for reasons of 'Norfolk [that is, Catholic] house politics'.[55] Lord Lyons's chief function during these years, however, was to cause the British government to be more aware than ever of the *French* dimension to the Anglo-German relationship. The second commentator, Sir Robert Morier, was quite different: brilliant, assertive, vigorous, one of Jowett's *protégés*, he had made German politics the centre of his career and his knowledge of the country matched that of Crowe's in its comprehensiveness. Morier was a fervent supporter of German unity and of an Anglo-German alliance but, having pinned all his hopes upon a Liberal solution, he fell foul of Bismarck's wrath on account of his intimacy with the Crown Princess and the left-Liberals: thus, his aspiration to the Berlin ambassadorship was constantly vetoed by the Bismarck family, who rightly feared his energies. In 1888–9 he was the subject of a scurrilous and inspired newspaper campaign, to which he responded with such vigour that even the Chancellor and his son must have regretted starting it.[56] If Morier was, in his later years, something of an embarrassment to the British government in its Berlin diplomacy, he kept successive Foreign Secretaries aware of an 'alternative' Germany and reinforced their suspicions of Bismarck and his methods.

One final observation is worth making upon the British diplomatic corps at this time: despite its renowned social exclusiveness, its political inclinations were almost without exception Liberal. Odo Russell, for example, declined to accept a peerage after the Congress of Berlin, preferring to receive that honour when Gladstone returned in 1880. He was also willing to stay in London in 1881 in order to give his vote in the House of Lords to the Irish Land Act.[57] Lyons, too, was a Liberal, although he was much more resentful of having to leave Paris every so often to vote in the Lords.[58] In the early 1880s, in fact, Paget complained bitterly in a private letter to Salisbury that he was the only British ambassador who was a Tory and that his professional career had suffered as a consequence.[59] No doubt the vigorous expression of preferences by Palmerston, and the more subtle selections by Clarendon and Granville, had played a role in the composition of the higher ranks of the service; but this ideological colouring was much more the consequence of general factors, of the domination of the Whig aristocracies in the older entries into the diplomatic corps, combined with the newer infusions from the universities in the mid-century. 'The Lights of Liberalism', to use Mill's phrase once again, were also beginning to shine in the foreign service, with Morier being a prime example of a Jowett-coached meritocrat.[60] In the consular service the Liberal tendency was probably even more marked, and someone like Crowe would have regarded it as unthinkable *not* to have supported the tenets of Mill and Cobden, whether in their stronger English or paler Germanic forms. This did not mean that the diplomatic corps favoured every aspect of Liberal foreign policy – indeed, being Whiggish by inclination as well as by breeding, it was often severely critical of Gladstone's 'self-effacement'. Morier writhed with embarrassment in 1870 at 'the entire ruin of our national policy, and the loss of all our European prestige', and even the loyal Odo Russell was moved to write 'Oh! for a Palmerston, a Russell, or a Clarendon'.[61] By the time of the Home Rule crisis, moreover, the pro-Liberal colouring of the service was beginning to fade, along with the domestic Whiggish forces and the 'age of equipoise' which had sustained it. This seems an altogether more interesting factor than the personality of a specific ambassador, and needs to be examined again later in the story.

The British Foreign Secretaries were, of course, only part of the larger decision-making process; and the strategic nerve-centre always remained the Cabinet itself, whose members were all too aware of pressures upon them from the Commons and the constituencies, and of the urgings of interest groups and the quiet conversation with journal editors on the one hand and the interventions of the monarch on the other. Nevertheless, for the greater part of the time 'the Cabinet proved a poor check on the work of the Foreign Office and most ministers stood somewhat in awe of their foreign secretary. Few Cabinet ministers had the time for a detailed study of foreign affairs. They intervened sporadically, save in moments of crisis, and in the day-to-day business of diplomacy the foreign secretary had a free hand.'[62] With regard to Anglo-German relations in particular, there were very few occasions (apart from the issue of Belgian neutrality in 1870) when one can detect signs of a collective Cabinet decision: its members were prodded into one, chiefly by the queen, at the time of the Schleswig-Holstein affair, and twenty years later, they intervened in the Anglo-German colonial disputes of 1884–5 – once again, one suspects, because they felt that it was necessary to extricate the government from an embarrassing and potentially dangerous position. Given the leisurely nature of the Cabinet process (with its mainly aristocratic membership only reluctantly coming in from their country or town houses to attend meetings), it could hardly be otherwise.

What influences were exerted upon British foreign policy-making at the Cabinet level usually came, therefore, from individual interested ministers – either by informal meetings at Westminster or, more usually, by an interchange of views recorded, not in formal Cabinet minutes (for there was no secretariat), but in the private letters sent from one landed seat to another.[63] The 'war-in-sight' crisis was handled by Disraeli, Derby and the queen; Bismarck's alliance 'bid' of 1877 was apparently discussed (briefly) in Cabinet, but that of 1879 was dealt with by Disraeli, Salisbury, Northcote and the queen. Even at the level of individual ministries, there is little evidence of interest in policy towards Germany: the Treasury, for example, had no opinions upon that country, apart from the irrepressible Randolph Churchill, whose brief venture into the field of foreign affairs alarmed both Salisbury and Bismarck before he received his political quietus; the gaze of the India Office was fixed upon Russia; the navy, too, was unconcerned about Germany; and only the army showed some interest. The War Office was obviously interested in the news (conveyed by its *attachés*) of technical and other advances instituted by the Prussian General Staff and some of the Cardwellian reforms had been influenced by Prussia's example, even if the British army regarded itself as having no European role to play in these years. Some observers, like General Brackenbury, could occasionally appreciate that Bismarck's diplomacy aimed to 'see Russia committed further and further to Asiatic wars and conquests', which would inevitably affect Britain's own strategic dispositions[64] – but this does not seem to have led to any political interest in Germany and German politics. It was to be another two or three decades before Germany occupied the centre of the Admiralty and War Office's attention.

For many years, this lack of interest was also true of the Colonial Office, but the German colonial annexations of 1884–5 were soon to alter that – not so much because Derby and his successors as Colonial Secretary had strong personal feelings about whether or not Germany should pursue an imperialist course, but because the self-governing colonies in South Africa and Australasia violently objected to these incursions into territories geographically close to themselves. From 1884 onwards, these 'sub-imperialists' formed a new and distinctive pressure group, and the British government always 'had to attempt to balance the expansionist demands of its self-governing colonies with the need to avoid disturbing its relations with . . . Germany, upon whose diplomatic support in Europe and the Near East it greatly depended'.[65] Under Salisbury, the latter consideration was usually given priority, although such a decision was to be increasingly more difficult to sustain as imperialist sentiment and ideas about federation grew in the public consciousness.

Of all the Cabinet members, then, 'Only the prime minister kept a close watch and the relationship of the premier with his foreign secretary remained one of the most important factors in the changing patterns of British diplomacy.'[66] The consultation between Palmerston and Russell had usually been very close; Stanley had been given a freer hand by Derby, and Gladstone usually deferred to the experience of Clarendon and Granville, although the extent of their private correspondence upon foreign policy was not diminished by this fact; Disraeli, predictably, involved himself repeatedly in what the Foreign Office was doing under Derby and Salisbury; and Salisbury was so interested in the diplomatic world that (apart from Iddesleigh's brief period in 1886) he preferred to combine the Foreign Secretaryship with the Premiership. The impact of all these Prime Ministers upon the Anglo-German relationship emerges in the narrative sections of this study, and does not require much repetition here: the Russell-Palmerston stance in 1864 was a blot upon what was basically a pro-German policy; Derby's benign support for Stanley's non-interventionism was a form of tacit assistance towards German unification; Gladstone, by his very nature, unconsciously emphasised the 'gap' between British and German political developments, even if he in no way desired a worsening of relations; Disraeli combined a tactical inclination towards Berlin with a natural combativeness which often caused him to be manoeuvring against Bismarck; and Salisbury combined a deep suspicion of things German with a realistic acknowledgement of the necessity for an understanding with that country in various parts of the globe. In all cases, it is worth suggesting, the various Prime Ministers added an emphasis to, and placed their personal imprint upon, the conduct of British policy towards Germany without significantly altering a pattern which was being shaped and coloured by many broader developments.

According to the German constitution, the State Secretary's position was in no way equivalent to that of the British Foreign Secretary. It is true that an influential personality such as Bernhard von Bülow made the post appear an important one in the years 1897–1900, but one only has to consider its quick decline under Richthofen thereafter to realise that its significance rose and fell according to the personality of the Chancellor himself; and, under Bismarck, it was all too clear that the State Secretaryship was simply regarded as a *bureaucratic* rather than a *political* position. After Bismarck had dismissed Hermann von Thile in 1872 for taking action without his approval, the office settled down to being little more than a post office for the receipt and dispatch of diplomatic reports: the new State Secretary, Bernhard Ernst von Bülow (Bülow Senior), regarded the *Wilhelmstrasse* not as 'an arena for discussion but rather the instrument for carrying out Bismarck's instructions to the letter'.[67] Under Bülow it was, at least, an efficient post office; under his successor, Hatzfeldt, it became steadily less so, a fact which Bismarck did not greatly notice since, through inclination and poor health, he was by then conducting the country's diplomacy from his retreats at Varzin or Friedrichsruh.

In 1885, when Hatzfeldt replaced Münster in London, Herbert Bismarck achieved his long-expressed ambition of becoming State Secretary; but, given his family ties, it is difficult to regard the latter as an 'independent' factor in the German decision-making process. Nevertheless, because of his period as an *attaché* and his frequent social visits and 'missions' to England in the 1880s, he did offer an important source of information and political commentary upon the island state. His correspondence about his English experiences is extraordinarily contradictory, and offers a superb example of that ambivalence of attitude which so many Prussian Junkers appear to have had towards Britain. As one historian observed, 'The same letters which announced his renewed good fortune in sojourning in the British Isles and recovering from Berlin society amongst Englishmen, contained the harshest judgements about parliamentarism in England.'[68] The glamour and pursuits of the English aristocracy quite enchanted Herbert: splendid banquets at Hatfield, Walmer Castle or Chatsworth, eye-catching and witty English girls, cards and billiards after dinner, racing at Ascot and Epsom, shooting on the estates – and throughout all this the free-and-easy conversations with members of an élite which effortlessly manifested its social and political superiority. So obviously did this 'outsider' make excuses to return to England and then report back home that he was 'feeling so well here . . . sleeping through the night, without wakening',[69] that one is bound to speculate whether he did not secretly yearn to have been born a member of this circle instead of being the son of a famous father who not only overworked him but had crushed his marital plans.

Yet, outside the parkland estates and London clubs, Herbert Bismarck could see newer and less attractive forces at work: imperial disasters in South Africa, blunders in Egypt, and a general neglect of Britain's traditional interest in European affairs; murder and chaos in Ireland; a House of Commons paralysed by the Irish Party; radical demagogues gaining a hearing in the English political system; and – worst of all – these trends not being combated, but rather being encouraged by a Liberal administration which itself was voluntarily extending the franchise, introducing land reforms, tolerating atheists, pontificating about the rights of the Boers and the Afghans, pandering to the demands of the Irish and Indian nationalists, and in general bringing a once great country to its knees and setting a dreadful example to the rest of the world. Reports of all this, it may readily be imagined, simply confirmed to the Chancellor what he had long suspected and was receiving from other sources in any case; but the extent to which Herbert emphasised these trends, and thereby reinforced his father's prejudices, *is* significant – for this was to be the dominant image of England in the German 'Official Mind' throughout the 1880s and, in many respects, beyond.

Certain Counsellors and confidential secretaries also were of importance, providing the Chancellor with technical expertise and with first drafts of dispatches. Lothar Bucher, declared Bismarck, was 'like an organ to me. You only had to note the registration and it would play all the notes and chords by itself.'[70] If Bucher had any political influence upon the Chancellor, then it can scarcely have been to the benefit of Anglo-German relations, for by this time the former Liberal and 'forty-eighter' had become profoundly suspicious of both Britain's domestic and external policies. The transition in his opinions since the 1840s was not dissimilar to that of Treitschke, the only difference being that many of Bucher's writings on the theme 'perfidious Albion' were drafted anonymously (often at Bismarck's request) for insertion in the press. In 1881, he enjoyed great success with the second edition of his anti-parliamentary study *Der Parlamentarismus wie er ist*; and in 1890 he, too, retired to Friedrichsruh to help his master concoct his memoirs.[71] Even closer to the Chancellor was his son-in-law, Count Cuno von Rantzau, who wrote the daily directions to Berlin from Bismarck whenever the latter was on his country estates; and the many remarks by Rantzau in his confidential letters to Herbert Bismarck indicate that he had no love of England, especially under a Gladstonian administration.[72] The same was true of Heinrich von Kusserow, the Foreign Ministry's 'expert' upon colonial affairs, who, in the early 1880s, divided his time between writing lengthy memoranda in favour of German overseas annexations – to frustrate future moves by the ever-acquisitive British – and composing political speeches against parliamentary government as advocated by the 'unrealistic', anglophile Progressives.[73] Kusserow's great role came in 1883–5, when he assisted (and encouraged) Bismarck's colonial bids, and acted as a 'link man' with commercial interest groups.

One other Counsellor, Friedrich von Holstein, was already beginning to acquire some influence in the Foreign Ministry in these years, having earned Bismarck's goodwill by the part he played in Arnim's downfall and consolidated his position by his professional expertise and by his close relationship with Herbert Bismarck. In the 1870s and early 1880s, his view of Britain reflected those of his superiors, and he had fully imbibed the Bismarckian nostrum that London and Paris should always be somewhat at odds over Egypt and other colonial affairs. Holstein's scorn for Liberal England, however, derived less from ideological and domestic-political factors than from a concern for Gladstonian 'weakness' towards France and Russia. With the advent of a Salisbury administration, he warmed towards London in direct proportion to his growing mistrust of Bismarck's deference towards St Petersburg; and this led him on the one hand into his secret manoeuvres to cut the Chancellor's 'wire' to Russia;[74] and on the other, to such a desire to buy British support that in 1888 he actually sent word to Salisbury not to be too conciliatory towards Germany in colonial affairs lest the Prime Minister endanger his political position at home.[75] As the architect of the diplomatic aspects of the 'New Course' after 1890, Holstein was manifestly in the pro-English 'camp' during the early years of Wilhelm II's reign.

The quality of the ambassadors in London during this period was somewhat uneven. The diplomatic career of Albrecht von Bernstorff had already been a long and honourable one, but representing Bismarck to England, and England to Bismarck, in the 1860s was a difficult task for any person, and in this case it was compounded by Bernstorff's increasing age and by the strong hostility shown towards him by Queen Victoria and by her eldest daughter, the Crown Princess, both of whom held him to be a gossip, 'a serious misfortune and a great danger'.[76] Although able to retain his post because of the old king's gratitude for his loyalty, Bernstorff's effectiveness was already in doubt before his death in 1873, and both governments were pleased when Count George Herbert zu Münster arrived as his successor. Having actually been born in London, and married an Englishwoman, the new ambassador was a great success socially: 'He had almost become a British institution', wrote *The Sportsman* sorrowfully on his recall in 1885, 'and his coach and four was as generally expected at the Hyde Park parades as those of our own nobility.'[77] Münster was also a great favourite of the Prussian Crown Prince and Princess, whose political views he shared. All this served him well during his early years, when there were few rifts in the Anglo-German relationship.

However, Münster's deep conviction that an Anglo-German-Austrian alliance was the 'sole correct combination' for German diplomacy was bound to be held against him when the interests of the two countries began to differ;[78] and even if his Whiggish susceptibilities were offended by Gladstone's more radical measures in the 1880s, the ambassador could never share the pro-Russian attitude and detestation of the British political system which many Junkers possessed. Indeed, the way in which he suffered from the political discrepancy between the two countries by that time was well captured by Odo Russell's remark that 'Münster, who prides himself on being a grumbling Tory in London, is thought in Berlin to be an advanced Liberal, suffering from Anglomania.'[79] The real climax of his disagreement with German policy came only with Bismarck's colonial bid, of which the ambassador totally disapproved. Living up to his reputation for insubordination, Münster not only privately denounced this new anti-English course, claiming that Bismarck was only doing it to gain popularity; but he also firmly rebutted, clause by clause, the Chancellor's charges against his alleged negligence – putting this all in a dispatch which was so devastating a critique of Bismarck's tactics in the summer of 1884 that it is scarcely surprising that it was never reproduced in *Die Grosse Politik*.[80] When an enraged Bismark finally transferred the ambassador to Paris late in 1885, Münster made no secret of the fact that this was being done against his will.

His successor in London, Count Paul von Hatzfeldt-Wildenburg, was a different character altogether and, although his activities had scarcely begun in the period covered by this chapter, it is convenient to offer a brief description of him at this point. Described by Bismarck as 'the best horse in my diplomatic stable', Hatzfeldt had first been used by the Chancellor during the peace negotiations in Versailles and then made a further name for himself at Madrid and Constantinople. Although favoured to become Bülow Senior's successor as State Secretary for Foreign Affairs, his temporary tenure of that post proved a personal strain and an official disaster; and he was happy to accept the London post in 1885, holding that his lack of knowledge of the English language was no great impediment. As a diplomat of the old school, Hatzfeldt believed in personal and confidential exchanges with successive British Foreign Secretaries as the best way of arranging Anglo-German relationships – adding to this an almost daily mutual speculation (by telegram) with his friend Holstein about the delicate fluctuations within great-power diplomacy and the nuances of meaning which they contained. The finesse, not to say indirectness of his approaches irritated some of his audience, but his friendship with Salisbury was genuine and he was a competent and useful ambassador during the first ten years of his stay in London. Disliking Russia and believing that Britain must eventually 'come' to Germany for an alliance at almost any price, he usually supported the idea of postponing that event until better times. In his later years, and quite apart from the fact of his failing health, one is bound to wonder whether his attachment to the personal side of diplomacy did not blind him somewhat to the changes which were being wrought upon the Anglo-German relationship by ideological, commercial, colonial and naval considerations[81] – which raises again the question of how vital a role ambassadors played in the overall relationship during an epoch increasingly symbolised by steel production and mass-selling newspapers rather than by absolute monarchs and their courtiers.

The influence of ministries other than the Foreign Ministry to the formulation of German external policy was negligible. This was because, in the first instance, there was no real Cabinet system of government in the German constitution: neither the Prussian Council of Ministers, nor the Bundesrat, represented an equivalent to that group of British ministers, formed out of the majority party in Parliament and constituting the effective political headship of the decision-making process. In the critical areas of war and peace, the control of military affairs and the conduct of foreign policy, the monarch was supreme in Germany – which meant, of course, that except in strictly military affairs Bismarck himself was virtually unchallenged until 1888: 'a congress of roaches presided over by a very big pike',[82] was how Morier once described the

Bundesrat under Bismarck, but that description could apply to all the other higher bodies in the German governmental system. Any additional views – or influences – upon the Anglo-German relationship would have to come from individual ministries, therefore: yet the fact was that, outside the Foreign Ministry, this subject was *not* considered to be of great importance. Moltke, as has been seen, occasionally uttered sentiments about an Anglo-German Protestant union but his mind – and that of the entire army – was concentrated upon France, Russia and Austria-Hungary; and the dislike of Waldersee and his circle for Bismarck's pro-Russian policy in the late 1880s did not entail a corresponding warmth for Britain. Neither the Imperial Treasury, nor the Prussian Ministry for Trade and Industry, had much to do with Britain in these years, since there was no 'naval race' to affect governmental spending and she had no tariff system to hurt German industry. Even the Imperial Navy, the service perhaps most affected by Britain's world policies, cast only a rare glance across the Channel – although when it did, it is worth remarking that this glance was usually favourable. The *Admiralität* disliked the dispatch of German warships for colonial purposes and possible disharmony with the British in the tropics, for example; and Caprivi, in his draft of a war plan against France and Russia in 1887, pointed encouragingly to the assistance which could be rendered by the Royal Navy, especially to Germany's ally, Italy, in time of war.[83] With regard to the other 'layers' of the German constitution, there is no evidence either that the individual states or the Bundesrat's Council on Foreign Relations had any influence upon foreign policy towards Britain; and whatever utterances were made upon external affairs in the controlled circumstances of the Reichstag had only as much impact as Bismarck chose to give them. This did not mean that the political parties and their interest groups had no influence, for the Chancellor needed them – or some of them – as allies in order to achieve his various aims; but the legislative body *per se* was severely circumscribed in its powers, and even those political parties which were strong and friendly to Bismarck tended to leave foreign affairs to him.

In other words, all paths led, sooner or later, back to Bismarck; and this is true whether one regards him as the stalwart national hero, or the 'Caesaristic dictator'. This does not imply a 'Great Man in History' approach to our topic, however, and the Chancellor himself constantly denied that he could change the fundamental course of events: 'Man can neither create nor direct the stream of time. He can only travel upon it with more or less skill and experience; he can suffer shipwreck and go aground and also arrive in safe harbours.'[84] Nevertheless, because of his constitutional position as the 'fulcrum' of the new Reich, and because of his personal expertise in throwing his weight to one side or the other, Bismarck's role *was* decisive for the development of Germany in general and for the course of Anglo-German relations in particular. It was he, after all, who rescued and enhanced those traditions and forces in German society which were most suspicious of the British political system, and who at the same time gave a 'pseudo-constitutionalist' (Weber) façade to the essentially conservative German state of 1871; who undermined what chances there were for progressive liberalism in Germany, by his twin

144

exploitation of foreign 'threats' and of the weaknesses of the domestic opposition; who ensured the 'Prussianisation' of Germany rather than the 'Germanisation' of Prussia; who perpetuated and raised to new heights the practices of Realpolitik and *Machtpolitik*, rending terrible damage to the Cobdenite alternatives in the process; who encouraged and, in many cases, instigated the press campaigns in Germany against England; who agreed to the return to protectionism, and fought to eradicate the doctrines (and disciples) of free trade; who inaugurated the first stages of colonial expansion and readily exploited the differences with, and weaknesses of, Gladstone's administration in the process; and it was he who incessantly opposed, by whatever means at his disposal, the 'English influences' in Germany, whether represented by the Crown Prince and Princess or by the left-Liberal parties.

Finally, it was Bismarck – or, in its larger form, 'Bismarckism' – which by the 1880s had repelled so many Britons from the land whose unification and growing strength they had welcomed two decades ago. 'The heart-breaking part of it', Morier had earlier moaned, was that Prussia's aims 'are so thoroughly legitimate, whilst the means used are so thoroughly damnable';[85] and it was Bismarck – always Bismarck – who chose the means. That other great germanophile, Odo Russell, felt the same sense of despair at the way things had gone wrong when, after pouring out his disappointment at the failure to achieve an Anglo-German alliance, he admitted that the chief reason was

the universal distrust of Bismarck which prevails in England. Nor can I wonder at it. A man who has secretly planned three successful wars, defeated two Great Powers, created an Empire in the centre of Europe and made himself the irresponsible leader of a nation of warriors, is open to suspicion and distrust ever after – as no-one can foretell what he may do with the power he has acquired.[86]

It does not follow from this that the Anglo-German relationship in this period would *inevitably* have been greatly improved had Bismarck not existed. The general forces would still have remained, and other statesmen would have had to steer the Prusso-German ship of state through the same 'stream of time', perhaps foundering on the rocks, perhaps embracing more enthusiastically than Bismarck did the cause of *Grossdeutschland* or a vigorous overseas expansionism. Nor is it intended by the above comments to suggest that attention should be concentrated exclusively or even predominantly upon the German side of this study – for it is obvious that, irrespective of events in Germany, the British political scene had its own momentum and actors who contributed just as fully to the *mutual* interactions which we refer to as the evolving Anglo-German relationship. What the historian can say, is that the Iron Chancellor played a very significant role in the development of that relationship; and that this role, whatever the mitigating factors, was basically – and intentionally – a negative and harmful one.

# CHAPTER 8

# *Discourse – The Weakening of Liberalism?*

The preceding five chapters have sought to describe certain important aspects of the relations between the German and British peoples. Taken together, they constitute only a *partial* cross-section of the total relationship; and, like all cross-sections, the perspective offered is largely static. Even so, by ranging between the 1860s and the mid-1880s, these analyses have necessarily referred to certain changes which took place in the two societies over that period. One of these requires a little further discussion, if only on account of its importance for the overall story of the Anglo-German antagonism: namely, the decline of liberalism. Both in the economic assumptions, and in the moral and philosophical teachings of classical liberalism, stress was always laid upon co-operation, goodwill and free exchange between nations. In consequence of this, the overwhelming proportion of German anglophiles consisted of Liberals, and the same was true of the greater part of the British germanophiles; Conservative admirers of the other state, besides possessing different motives, were far fewer. Thus a weakening of liberalism in both countries, and its replacement by or metamorphosis into the harsher creeds of preclusive imperialism, ethnic nationalism and domestic reaction, obviously meant that there were far fewer people on each side to admire the achievements of the other and to plead the cause of international harmony. In so many ways, the rise of an Anglo-German antipathy was the obverse side, and natural consequence, of this tendency.

To a large degree, the transformation might be explained in economic terms. Liberalism, the creed of the *laissez-faire* bourgeoisie, had flourished politically and ideologically when Europe enjoyed the industrial boom of the 1850s and 1860s; but when the trade cycle produced a slump which was longer and more severe than any in modern times, the economic basis upon which the social self-confidence, belief in constitutional progress and firm adherence to the doctrines of Adam Smith rested, was weakened beyond repair.[1] This explanation may hold good in the German case; there, it was true, liberalism seemed only to be a 'fair weather' movement, easily dispersed by the storm-clouds of the Great Depression. In its place came a rejection of free-trade ideas by both heavy industry and agriculture, a return to the commercial policy of protectionist

146

tariffs and an increasing intervention by the state in social policy. The advocacy of *laissez-faire* doctrines shrank again to 'that small band of intellectuals, theorists and publicists, as was the case before economic liberalism reigned supreme . . . between 1862 and 1875'.[2] By contrast, the economic forces hoping for protection could now rely upon Adolph Wagner, Schmoller and many other notable pens to provide the ammunition for an intellectual assault upon the Manchester school. The writings of List finally came into their own, with Treitschke joyfully calling to his readers' attention how the national economist's arguments had hit the Cobdenite abstractions 'like a thunderbolt'.[3]

The vast mass of German peasants and artisans, and a large number of industrialists and Junkers, did not require such intellectual arguments to propel them towards demands for state assistance. The sheer speed of the industrial revolution in parts of the country, and the critical fact that this (unlike in Britain) had *coincided* with a political transformation and the demand for a social revolution, produced a considerable amount of unease and domestic turbulence, albeit of a usually non-violent character. The Hegelian inheritance of respect for the state and List's message about an organic national economy were no doubt significant; but debt-ridden farmers and anxious ironmasters felt that they needed the help of authority in any case. And the specific nature of the German economic development meant that the social groups agitating for state intervention were larger and more powerful than those who still benefited from the free play of market forces.

To these groups the German government soon responded, in part because of Bismarck's political calculations in the late 1870s but also, perhaps, because in almost all late-industrialising societies the state tended to play a large role, and the traditions of dirigism in Prussia-Germany had remained strong. In turn, this response to the urgings of pressure groups gave a boost to the importance of the latter and caused the founding of a whole coterie of organisations, anxious to achieve for their members the material successes gained by the east Elbian landowners and the *Centralverband deutscher Industrieller*. By the same token, political parties also became organised along lines of 'interest' rather than 'principle' in response to the demands of their supporters. Finally, the protectionist system gave further impetus to the process of cartellisation, especially among the big banks and heavy industry, so that in certain sectors the individual entrepreneur was becoming a thing of the past.

Yet all these changes wrought upon the political economy of Imperial Germany seem to have had few equivalents in Britain during the late 1870s and 1880s. Even if a 'Fair Trade' movement existed, it did not attract the support of many businessmen and it made no real impact upon party politics; in consequence, it also failed to command government sympathy. Thus, the differing response on the British side may also be explained to a large extent on economic grounds, in that the most powerful social groups in the country still benefited from an adherence to free trade or, at the least, feared its abandonment. Yet comparison solely on this level is insufficient: after all, France and the United States also adopted protectionist policies during the depression without those effects upon political liberalism which occurred inside Germany, suggesting that the fiscal policies and economic infrastructure of a society are not always the best way of measuring its degree of liberalism.[4]

If the British political nation rejected protectionism, it nevertheless was true that *laissez-faire* economic tenets were coming under increasing scrutiny in the light of the country's changing internal and external circumstances. Even if it failed, the Fair Trade movement was indicative of discontent with the prevailing order. Equally interesting was the assault being launched by the Positivists, with Frederick Harrison telling a sympathetic Trades Union Congress in 1883 that 'the older school of economists . . . claimed especially to understand the laws of production, and the conditions of labour and capital. Time has proved that it thoroughly mistook them.'[5] This was a criticism soon to be echoed by the Fabian Society, founded in the following year; and, in much more forthright terms, by Hyndman's Social Democratic Federation (1881), with its orthodox-Marxist critique of the prevailing economic and social order. In a somewhat quieter fashion, T. H. Green and others were replacing the older adherence to *laissez-faire* by university men with a belief in the need for sustained state action, as well as their own personal commitment, in order to remedy the social problems of the age; from Green, it has been argued, came 'something close to a practical programme for the left-wing of the Liberal party'.[6] Even professional economists were beginning to shift their ground, with Jevons calling in 1876 for an investigation of 'the limits of the *laissez-faire* principle', and Marshall gradually moving towards his later call, 'Let the State be up and doing'.[7] Herbert Spencer's blast, in his essays *The Man versus the State* (1884), is significant here as a desperate attempt to reassert economic and social doctrines which were steadily losing support in certain Liberal circles.

All this, it may be argued, fits in with that growing appreciation by the late Victorians of arguments about the 'common good' and the need for a higher frame of reference than that derived from the dogma of individualism; it also fits in with the interest social-reform Liberals were to show towards theories of an organic society.[8] Admittedly, none of this produced practical results in Britain until the end of the century, with the emergence of the rival schools of constructive imperialism and the 'new' liberalism; but the ferment of thought which was taking place two decades beforehand was indicative of the way things were going.

This, in turn, suggests two conclusions about British liberalism as it approached its late- or post-Gladstonian phase. The first is that, far from dying, it was undergoing a metamorphosis, readjusting sensibly to the altered circumstances of the age; this, certainly, was how New Liberals and Liberal Imperialists were to justify their abandonment of some of the received assumptions about the movement's aims and methods. The brief electoral revival of 1892, and the impressive victory of 1906, were to offer strong evidence that the Liberals could still attract the support of important social groups throughout the country, even if the various parts making up this conglomerate had somewhat altered since the 1860s.[9] The second conclusion is that what weakening of classical liberalism did occur, was measured more by changes in social thought and politics than in *strictly economic* events. This may seem a curious distinction when fissiparous issues such as the Radicals' agitation for land reform in the early 1880s and the mobilisation of the Irish peasantry behind Parnell were clearly economic in purpose and form. But all it means was that the strains upon British liberalism were not so much the direct consequence of the Great Depression as was the case in Germany. As noted above, calls for protective tariffs tended, if anything, to keep the Liberals together; whereas sub-groups within the party quarrelled repeatedly over the size of the franchise, redistribution, disestablishment and Ireland, as well as over imperial issues. For years, Gladstonian leadership held Radicals and Whigs together, in forced harmony; but his dramatic conversion to Home Rule in late 1885 was in many ways merely the catalyst for a party revolt which had long been possible.

Even if these internal convulsions under Gladstone can charitably be viewed in retrospect as growing pains, they obviously affected the party's short-term electoral prospects. Failure to solve the Irish problem had lost Ireland for liberalism and given the tactical advantage to Parnell; and Gladstone's bid for his support alienated most of the Whigs and many Radicals, although for different reasons. Given the wider franchise, and the elimination of 'corrupt practices' at elections, the defection of the Whigs was not a great blow to the party as a whole. The same might also be said about the rightward drift of intellectuals such as Arnold, Tennyson, Fitzjames Stephen, Seeley, Dicey, St Loe Strachey and others who increasingly disliked the party's implied commitment to satisfy the desires of 'the vast mass of the uneducated and the unintelligent';[10] for if these former 'Lights of Liberalism' now doubted the gesture towards democracy, the Liberal Party itself was soon to boast of a fresh generation of social thinkers able to suggest what the movement might stand for as it approached the twentieth century. The defection of Chamberlain himself, and much of the midlands vote, was more serious but still not a catastrophe. Even the years in the political wilderness following the débâcles of 1886 and 1895 were not a bad thing, if the party could eventually settle its leadership problem and work out its priorities. What was much more ominous was the steady drift of businessmen and of the middle-class inhabitants of suburbia towards the Conservative Party precisely at a time when the Liberals' disarray, and the temporarily enhanced power of the Nonconformist element, prevented the party from making a sustained effort to capture the working-class vote. Perhaps British electoral geography was moving inexorably towards a class basis in any event; but even if that were so, liberalism's political demise between 1886 and 1906 gave a great boost to that development, as it lost supporters to the left and right. The social tendencies which were polarising German politics at great speed were, in the long run, to have an impact in Britain as well; but little of this was detectable in the mid-1880s.

More immediate signs of the reassessment of the validity of Liberal beliefs came, not surprisingly, in the realm of foreign and imperial policies. In the German case, it is true, Bismarck had held the advantage from the outset, frequently using external affairs as a means to consolidate his own political position and to drive wedges into the Liberal movement. Through this tactic, he had long crushed the prospects for what might be termed a 'Liberal' foreign policy; and by the early 1880s the anti-Liberal thrust was more developed than ever before, with Bismarck and the 'inspired' press seeking every opportunity to portray the Progressives and the *Liberale Vereinigung* as dangerous and unpatriotic. Even more significant was the fact that his foreign policy was no longer deplored, as in 1866, by the greater part of the political nation; instead, it was applauded by Conservatives, National Liberals and by what one observer termed the whole '*Schola Theologiae* of Prussian politicians', who supported policies 'only soluble in the last instance by "blood and iron"'.[11] The way in which chauvinistic and expansionist appeals were now finding not merely listeners but a whole host of proselytisers also among the business, professional and academic classes was discomforting to those who recalled that twenty years earlier such sections of the community had constituted the backbone of the Liberal movement.

In Britain, too, one could detect such a groundswell of opinion, occasioned in part by a growing pride in an empire whose significance was only now being explained by Froude, Dilke and Seeley (of whom the two latter were Liberals), and even more by an appreciation of the rising challenges to Britain's world position. If early signs of this were to be seen in the Tory attacks upon the Gladstone administration's relations with the settler colonies and its failure to prevent the Russian denunciation of the Black Sea clauses in 1870, such issues transcended mere party politics; and genuine Liberals such as Morier bemoaned the fact that their leader had gone around at the outbreak of the Franco-Prussian War 'on the steamer of the Cobden Club, collecting opinions from individual members like a monkey asking for ha'pence, asking this one if he really believed England would be ready to go to war, that one whether he considered England's honour engaged in Belgium, etc. etc.'.[12] This was *not* the manner in which a great empire should be ruled! Moreover, the pattern was repeated in Gladstone's second ministry, when the humiliation of Majuba and the blundering into Egypt were followed in 1884–5 by a whole series of reverses: a naval 'scare' generated by that eccentric Liberal W. T. Stead with his *Pall Mall Gazette* articles on 'The Truth about the Navy';[13] the prolonged buffeting by France and Germany during the early stages of the scramble for Africa and the Pacific; the disaster in the Sudan; and a near-war with Russia over the Penjdeh incident. In these circumstances, it was no surprise to find the likes of Lord Wharncliffe lamenting 'the depth to which we are fallen in the eyes of all foreign Powers', or General Wolseley exploding at the 'comatose state into which [the nation] has been lulled by a number of vestrymen, Whigs and Tories alike, who diverted all public attention from all affairs of Empire, to those of paving and lighting'.[14] Significantly enough, the press, too, was shifting its political ground in reaction both to Gladstone's foreign and internal policies – with *The Times*, *Daily Telegraph*, *Spectator*, *Punch* and many other journals adopting an increasingly Conservative tone and the Victorian music halls, in place of their former praise of the 'people's William', now resounding with songs which mocked his foreign policy reverses.[15] In both Germany and Britain, in other words, there seemed to be a growing temper of nationalism and distrust of other peoples and other classes. Demands were being made for substantial navies to protect overseas colonies and trade, in addition to those massive standing armies which burdened the taxpayers of Europe. References to 'the struggle for survival', intolerance of the claims of others, an appeal to the doctrine of 'might is right', were becoming the order of the day; the principle of national self-determination (whether for the Irish, the Poles or the Africans) was increasingly disregarded. Nationalism, which for so long had run in tandem with liberalism, was now in the possession of the Right in many countries.[16] Belief in the ameliorating processes of free trade and international co-operation was depicted as mere 'cant'. Both in its conceptions of external and internal politics, liberalism was now under fire.

While the above implies that the two countries were being influenced by broadly similar trends, it is also important to stress that the actual effects upon each were significantly different. In the 1860s, the political traditions and dominant forces in Britain had been markedly more liberal than those in Germany; and while there had been signs of a rightward shift in both societies during the two decades following, the distance which still separated their respective political cultures remained about the same. If even in the 1880s the greater part of the British political nation – including such eminent non-progressives as Derby, Salisbury, the queen herself and many other members of the establishment – could view with distaste the intolerant, 'immoral' actions of the Prusso-German state; and if all except that small rump of left-Liberals and moderate Socialists in Imperial Germany disliked the parliamentarism and doctrinaire liberalism which (in their view) was ruining the island state,[17] then there seems little reason to doubt that an overall difference still did exist.

Of course, this 'gap' did not strike all observers all of the time. It was, after all, a period in which direct clashes of fundamental interest between Britain and Germany were by and large absent and in which scarcely anyone contemplated a future war between them; and as such, it obviously contrasts with the atmosphere after 1900. It was also a period in which one frequently encountered that rhetoric about the common links between the two peoples – their shared race, religion, culture and dynasties, their past alliances and present interests, their mutually beneficial economic ties, and so on. The preceding chapters have sought to show how much, indeed, of this was mere rhetoric; but in such a situation even knowledgeable observers made the occasional slip of assuming that the two societies were much more similar than they really were. In 1874, for example, even the anglophile, 'Whiggish' Münster was shocked to discover that in Britain 'one did everything possible to avoid general national service, . . . seeing in it merely compulsion', whereas in Germany all parties (including the SPD) accepted conscription.[18] And in 1881 Odo Russell expressed the hope that the Crown Prince's accession 'would compel his Chancellor to submit to the constitution of the Empire and accept the accidents of a parliamentary system based on universal suffrage, which at present Bismarck absolutely refuses to do';[19] yet the truth was that Germany did not really have a 'parliamentary system' and that, as the quotation indicates, the only hope for reform lay in actions taken from above.

The most remarked-upon distinctions between the two countries, it should be noted, did not so much relate to the commitment to full democracy, which so engaged the politics of the twentieth century. The criteria applied by

151

contemporaries were, rather, those pertaining to the period of classical liberal-ism's zenith and referred to practices which went far beyond those of a formal Liberal Party programme: for example, constitutional monarchy, control over the executive by an elected assembly, freedom of speech and conscience and religion, a belief in individual action and responsibility, a sense of 'fair play', an appeal to ethical considerations, a dislike of war, and so on. It is in these respects, rather than in the common concern at incipient socialism or in their mutual annexation of colonies, that the establishments of Britain and Germany appeared so different at this time.

This conclusion would apply even to the opponents of the Liberal Party inside Britain. However much the Tories and disenchanted ex-Liberal intel-lectuals might splutter at the 'ruin' which Gladstone had brought upon the country, the governments of Disraeli, Salisbury and Balfour threw up no equivalent to the Puttkamer measures to quell internal opposition; there were no anti-socialist or anti-Jesuit laws; and there was no brooding, all-powerful presence like Bismarck whose ultimate threat against too great a liberalisation was a *coup d'état* on the part of the army, followed by an even greater restriction upon parliamentary powers and a return to a more selective franchise.[20] Nor, in the wider political spectrum, did there exist a true British equivalent for the east Elbian Junkers, or for the influence they wielded; and no equivalent at all for that antisemitic, anticapitalist discontent among the peasantry, skilled artisans and other members of the lower middle classes which poisoned the German political scene. The sheer venom and blind hatred behind so many of the assaults in Germany upon *Manchestertum* strikes the historian used to reading the ponderous criticisms of *The Times* or the elegant, rapier-like exposés of Balfour upon, say, Gladstone's Irish policy. Only in Ireland itself, significantly enough, does one see in the passion of the nationalists, the dour obduracy and sectarian prejudice of the Ulstermen, the economic distress, the frequent crimes and states of emergency, evidence of 'illiberal' political emotions and practices.

All this emerges, to a greater or lesser degree, from the analysis of the various aspects of the Anglo-German relationship undertaken in the preceding five chapters. Despite the many similarities which such a detailed comparison is bound to produce, the two countries still appear to have been significantly different in their handling of economic problems, especially during the Great Depression, and in their assumptions about the role of the state in the economy; in the balance of their constitutional arrangements, and in the powers possessed by an unrepresentative autocracy; in the toleration accorded to ethnic minorities, especially in the border regions, and to religious dissen-ters, especially at the time of the *Kulturkampf*; in the respect for a free press and the existence of anti-establishment criticism; in the place accorded to military values, and to the army, in society at large; in the intellectual veneration paid to the individual as opposed to the state; and finally, in the general acceptance of the political leaders of their respective countries. The very fact that this age was willing to use such terms as 'Gladstonism' and 'Bismarckism' is an indication that these two statesmen had become, in the eyes of contemporaries, more than mere individuals.

Clearly, exceptions can be found to all the above comparisons: there were Germans like Brentano who adhered to the policies of free trade, toleration and genuine social reform; and Britons like Wolseley who detested the economic and political colouration of Victorian Britain. Yet the fact remains that these exceptions to the general rule were precisely that – voices of despair, lamenting the awful truth that their personal opinions were making little headway and that the dominant forces in the nation preferred a set of constitutional, economic and social arrangements which differed greatly from their own. This 'gap' between Britain and Germany was not such as to drive them into conflict, for nations only do that to defend or enhance much more concrete, material interests. But it does help to explain why, despite the widespread references to the common ties between the two countries, many members on each side would have disliked a closer connection.

# PART THREE

*The Rising Antagonism in Anglo-German Political Relations from 1880 until 1906*

# CHAPTER 9

# Bismarck and the Ideological War against Gladstonism (1880-5)

When we left our narrative of Anglo-German political relations, the two governments had just been exploring the possibility of an alliance. For reasons explained above, neither side really wished to commit itself, yet their very consideration of the matter indicated that official relations were ostensibly rather good. This situation was altered by Disraeli's surprise defeat in the general election of 1880, which caused 'a perfectly ridiculous panic in Berlin', according to Odo Russell, because of 'the terror Mr. Gladstone inspires Bismarck and the German court with'.[1] If true, it suggests once again that the most noticeable aspect of the differences between Britain and Germany in these early years was the ideological – by which we mean the perceptions which the respective governments had of the European order in 1880 and of the domestic-political aims which its member-states should seek to achieve. Disraeli's policies and poses may have obscured that fact to a certain extent; but Gladstone's return, coinciding as it did with Bismarck's rightward shift in domestic policies, now emphasised the differences more clearly than ever before.

This is not to say that political ideology was the only factor of discord in Anglo-German governmental relations at this time. Both powers would have to react to the troubled affairs of, say, Greece or Montenegro irrespective of whether a Liberal ministry had assumed office in London; and, even without this new ideological colouration, it is worth recalling that they each had different foreign policy ambitions. Although both were reassuring the other of their affection and of the need to stand together – 'The good understanding between Germany, Austria and England was the best guarantee [for the peace]', Disraeli informed Münster early in 1880, and Bismarck gave virtually the same message to Odo Russell[2] – London and Berlin differed about how that peace could best be secured. Each wished to retain Austro-Hungarian support and to check Tsarist expansion against their own areas of interest without, however, being involved in an armed struggle with Russia. For Disraeli and Salisbury, this could only be achieved if the *Dreikaiserbund* were permanently broken up, and if Vienna and Berlin joined London in deterring the Russians from any fresh move into the Balkans or against Constantinople – hence their

157

unconcealed joy at the Austro-German alliance of 1879. For Bismarck, this pact with Vienna was only the means to an end: the diplomatic pinning-down of Austria-Hungary and the checking of revolutionary panslavism in Russia, prior to the reconstitution of the *Dreikaiserbund*. At the same time, the German Chancellor was secretly keen to encourage both the French and the Russians into extra-European adventures, a nice diversion of their attention and resources from the borders of Germany and Austria-Hungary but also one which would materially affect the security of Britain's overseas interests.[3] Neither London nor Berlin had fully realised these respective intentions by early 1880, but the differences in overall aims were not unknown to both sides, even if it behoved them to reassure the other of their continued friendship.

Gladstone's advent to power replaced Disraelian interventionism with a strong dose of Liberal idealism – and this despite the more pragmatic influences of Granville, Tenterden and most of the diplomatic corps. The particular form of the new Prime Minister's idealism lay in the resurrection of that noble instrument, the Concert of Europe, which in his eyes restricted the egoistical ambitions of individual powers by requiring international actions to be approved of in advance by all members of the European family of nations and, by extension, by their public opinions.[4] Given the conflicting interests of the various states and the nationalist passions which were engendered by such rivalries, it was no doubt easy for Bismarck to dismiss the notion of conducting diplomacy through the Concert of Europe as an elaborate nonsense. What was more alarming to him were Gladstone's twin beliefs that independent, selfish actions by any one power should be abandoned and that a European public opinion existed which provided the moral justification for all statesmens' actions. Such doctrines, if generally accepted, would quite undermine the Bismarckian conception of diplomacy: it would affect his practice of playing off the other members of the European 'family' so that Berlin remained the fulcrum of diplomatic manoeuvres, and it would throw into question the traditional forms of power-politics, which had usually worked so well for the Prussian state. In the early 1880s, for example, it was the wish of the German government (and of other great powers) to let the Eastern Question stagnate, regardless of local misdeeds; but the British Prime Minister, by reputation a man of peace, was arguing that 'Europe' should not flinch even from military measures to force reforms upon the Turks. Such moral poses, in Bismarck's view, made the task of diplomacy less easy than ever.

Bismarck also had more specific reasons for disliking the return of a Gladstonian administration. In the first place, whereas Disraeli had seemed willing to go to war to check Russian aggrandisement in south-east Europe and had leant towards Vienna and Berlin, Gladstone was, according to Münster, 'more Russian than the Russians themselves, he is slavophile, a bitter enemy of Austria, and he regards Germany as half-lost since it has formed an alliance with Austria. So far as Italy is concerned, he sympathises with the wildest revolutionaries and with *Italia irredenta*.'[5] If this was an exaggerated portrait, which also ignored the restraints which a predominantly Whig Cabinet and his own concern with domestic and Irish affairs placed upon Gladstone's external policy, the fact remains that the Liberal leader had recently castigated

Austro-Hungarian policy; that reports from Russia indicated that Panslav circles hoped for much from this change of British government; that there were rumours current that Italy would turn away from Germany and Austria-Hungary, and join with France and Russia in the hope of extending her north-eastern borders, with Gladstonian encouragement; and that the French revanchist press was jubilant at the news of the 1880 election, assuming automatically that a Liberal administration would be much more sympathetic towards Paris than towards Berlin. If this event gladdened the hearts of so many of the 'revolutionary' and anti-German elements in Europe, therefore, it could hardly be welcome to Bismarck. Thus the fear, not so much of Gladstone himself, but of his impact and influence abroad, became a leitmotiv of German policy in these years.[6]

Gladstone's return was in no way a total disaster in diplomatic terms to the Chancellor, however, for there were certain advantages he could wring from it. In the first place, he consoled himself with the thought that the restoration of the Anglo-French *entente* would actually frustrate any prospects of a French assault upon Germany, since on the one hand the British Liberals would seek to pacify their Gallic neighbour's bellicosity, while on the other Tsarist Russia would be more suspicious of the friendship between its old Crimean War enemies, the more especially that they now both possessed a radical government. Furthermore, the disappearance of Disraeli simply reinforced Bismarck's earlier conviction that, since Britain was too unreliable to be tempted into a firm alliance with the central powers, it was necessary to try to revive the *Dreikaiserbund* as the main diplomatic 'plank' for Germany's security. Such a strategy would normally have foundered upon Vienna's opposition, particularly when the Austrians were still rejoicing at the conclusion of their anti-Russian alliance with Berlin; but Gladstone's public attacks upon Austria's past would make it easier for Bismarck to persuade his southern neighbour to join him in the restoration of a conservative, monarchical combination. At the same time, the Chancellor would please his own imperial master by improving relations with Russia, *and* make Germany's foreign policy conform more with the rightward move in domestic affairs, outraging once again the left-Liberals and the Crown Prince's circle.

Two obstacles remained to be overcome before this aim could be realised. The first concerned Bismarck's fear that the Russian government might be tempted by Gladstone's return to settle its various Asiatic disputes with Britain and to adopt a fully panslavic (and aggressive) policy in the Balkans: this had to be frustrated at all costs. As the Austrians were confidentially told, 'the essential point is always that between Russia and England no agreement or rapprochement exists; I cannot emphasise too strongly how necessary it is to avoid everything that can facilitate this'.[7] Fortunately for Bismarck, the Anglo-Russian differences were too wide to be healed and the Russian government, conscious of its relative economic and military weakness, was willing to improve its relations with Germany and even to compromise with Austria-Hungary in the early 1880s.

The second task was to persuade the government in Vienna to cease looking towards London for help and to turn again in the direction of St Petersburg.

This was by no means easy work, especially while Haymerle remained Austro-Hungarian foreign minister, but Bismarck perceived that it could best be done in stages, under the cloak of the frequent consultations which took place between the great powers to settle the affairs of Montenegro and Greece. While Gladstone enthusiastically saw this collective enterprise as an example of the Concert of Europe at work, the Chancellor was engaged in using it to build bridges between Austria-Hungary and Russia, with the ultimate aim of drawing both away from London's influence. By the middle of 1881 the *Dreikaiserbund* had been restored once again. Within another year Bismarck had brought Italy within his diplomatic orbit, by the signing of the Triple Alliance in May 1882. All this not only ruined the prospects for that genuine concert of the powers which Gladstone had envisaged, but it also meant that Britain and France, the western Liberal states, were alone excluded. If this threw them together in the first instance, the French intervention in Tunis and, even more, the British occupation of Egypt, soon drove them apart. By 1882, the favourable diplomatic position which Britain had appeared to have attained following the Congress of Berlin was a thing of the past. That position of eminence had rested, like many of Disraeli's successes, upon shaky foundations and was liable to collapse for various reasons; but in this case it had been undermined, to a very considerable extent, by the deliberate diplomacy of Bismarck himself.[8]

All this did not mean that Bismarck was *openly* hostile to Britain. Such a stance, as he well knew, would have immediately improved the bargaining position of France and Russia, both of which stood to gain from any Anglo-German disagreements. It would also have caused trouble with his Triple Alliance partners, for both Austria-Hungary and Italy still hoped to win British support for their combination. Given the intricate nature of the Chancellor's diplomacy, which became even more complicated with the secret support of Rumania in 1883, it ill behoved him to come out directly against *any* power in these years. For this reason, he was willing on occasions to use 'Concert language' to Odo Russell or to British visitors to Berlin like Goschen and Dufferin, even if he did not really mean it; and he was also willing to give diplomatic support to the Anglo-French attempts to reform Egyptian finances, although it is true that he sometimes worried about the lengths to which an assertive Gambetta might lead a weak Gladstone.

When London and Paris gradually became estranged following Wolseley's military overrunning of Egypt, moreover, Bismarck inclined to favour the British rather than the French position; he did not partake in the abuse showered by the Conservative and National Liberal press in Germany upon the 'hypocritical' English occupation; and he tended to play down the significance of the German financial stake in the Egyptian debt, although German membership of the six-nation Debt commission was obviously going to allow him to occupy a key role, if that was ever necessary. There was, as ever, a good reason for this Bismarckian benevolence. The restoration of the *Dreikaiserbund* had freed him, temporarily, from the fear of a Franco-Russian alliance and thus he had less need to court Paris; while the growing Anglo-French differences over Egypt would make both the Western powers less effective in Europe, and more dependent upon his diplomatic goodwill. The Chancellor may not actively have encouraged the colonial rivalry between Paris and London, knowing as he did that any sign of this strategy would immediately arouse their suspicions; but the fact was that he did not need to. Germany, he informed Hohenlohe, could quietly stand by and watch 'if the English and French locomotives collided somewhere'.[9]

All this explains why there are few signs at this time in the British diplomatic correspondence of hostility towards Berlin. It was, after all, difficult for them, as for anyone else, to comprehend Bismarck's deeper designs in 1880; and, although the Liberal government did not fully trust the formidable German leader and knew from Odo Russell that he disliked its domestic policies,[10] it was not in its nature to sit down and try to work out what he was up to. It was further encouraged, of course, by the fact that the powers did at first seem to be working conjointly to deal with Greek and Moroccan questions – even if the solutions reached were not all that satisfactory to the British mind. In the same way, Bismarck was clearly not unfriendly in regard to proposals for settling the Egyptian affair, offering repeated confidential assurances of his 'moral support'[11] – a nice, meaningless term which he no doubt remembered from his many earlier attempts to gain British backing inside Europe. More negatively, London looked towards Berlin because it had not been possible, despite Gladstone's hopes, to come to a *modus vivendi* with the Russians, both Granville and the queen being less than willing to trust a power whose forces were continually expanding in central Asia.[12] Finally, the growing estrangement between Britain and France over Egypt after 1882 – and especially the fact that without the support of the Triple Alliance (that is, Bismarck) it would be impossible for the British government to carry out their proposed financial reforms – made the Foreign Office the open supplicant of German advice and diplomatic aid in these years.

At this level, then, the formal Anglo-German relationship was fairly uncontentious, and even rather predictable, suggesting relatively little change from the situation which had existed when Disraeli was in office. What needs to be added to this traditional diplomatic picture, however, are the ideological and domestic-political aspects, which were always present in the Chancellor's mind and were indeed crucial parts of his 'grand strategy' of seeking to preserve Prusso-German interests in the volatile circumstances of the 1880s. Viewed from this broader perspective, the Anglo-German relationship can no longer be portrayed in relatively rosy colours.

During the years in which Gladstone's second administration held office, Bismarck was feeling acutely conscious that his whole domestic 'system' was in danger. The fundamental problem was the great age and increasingly poor health of the emperor, who was 83 years old in 1880; and the associated fact that the Crown Prince was more hostile than ever to the Chancellor, partly because his request to be made regent in 1878 had been brusquely refused, and partly because of his disapproval of that whole cluster of conservative policies inaugurated by Bismarck in 1878–80. There is no sign at all that Bismarck regretted these actions, but he was aware of the risks he ran: 'If Bismarck went on flouting the political principles as well as the vanity and self-respect of the

Crown Prince, it was very possible that Friedrich Wilhelm would dismiss him out of sheer personal hatred, no matter how great the Chancellor's personal prestige or how strong his political position in the Reichstag and the country.'[13] Little wonder that Herbert Bismarck prayed: 'God grant the Kaiser a long life.'[14] Nevertheless, it was also true that the unassertive Crown Prince would hesitate to act against Bismarck if the balance of political forces in the country could be kept decisively titled in an anti-Liberal direction.

This latter strategy implied not merely the establishment of a new right-wing bloc in the Reichstag and the enactment of illiberal legislation, but also the elimination of all those Progressive circles and parties who had opposed Bismarck since the 1860s. Hence the zest with which the Chancellor engaged in his battle with Stosch, forcing the supposed leader of the dreaded future 'Gladstone ministry' to resign as head of the Admiralty in 1883; hence, too, all of Holstein's manoeuvres to discredit the anti-Bismarck advisers surrounding the Crown Prince.[15] Attacks upon individuals were not enough, however, unless they were accompanied by repeated and full-scale assaults upon Liberal ideas and upon the two parties which still adhered to those tenets, the left-Liberals with such leaders as Forckenbeck, Bamberger and Stauffenberg, and the Progressives under Richter. It was in this situation, of course, that the Conservative and National Liberal press, 'inspirers' and polemicists such as Bucher, Busch, Treitschke and others joined in a combined chorus against the 'unpatriotic', 'crypto-republican' enemies of the Reich, the 'Jewish Manchesterites', those 'forerunners of Socialism'.[16] Yet, to the dismay of the Bismarck camp, this tactic did not work for once: the 1881 Reichstag election produced the worst defeat for the government since 1863, with the National Liberals losing fifty-two seats and the Free Conservatives twenty-nine, whereas the left-Liberals and Progressives enjoyed massive increases and the Centre, Socialists and Poles each gained a few places. Although this provoked considerable speculation that the Chancellor was losing both his grip and his popularity – a judgement reinforced by the widespread anxieties as the temporary upturn in the trade cycle fell away again after 1882 – these reverses predictably had no effect upon Bismarck's determination to preserve all his powers. What they did do, was to make him ever more embittered against the Liberal movement, and ever more eager to do it harm.

It is from this standpoint, as well as from his distaste as a Realpolitiker for the idea of the Concert of Europe, that we have to view Bismarck's overall attitude towards Gladstone's second administration. What was happening in contemporary Britain – and was being followed with great interest by all the parties in Germany – represented both a threat and an opportunity. The threat lay in the fact that successes gained either in external or (more especially) in internal affairs by the new British government would boost the credit of liberalism throughout Europe and give heart to German Progressives – and that, perhaps, just as a new, impressionable emperor was stepping into his father's shoes. The opportunity for Bismarck, logically enough, was the obverse of this. If liberalism, especially in its Gladstonian variety, could be discredited; if it could be shown that it was leading to the ruination of Britain as a great power; and was, because of its attachment to false principles and the lack of firm leadership, unleashing the forces of revolution and discontent: then there was a very real prospect that the Chancellor could attract into the Conservative camp both the German middle classes and a number of neighbouring governments. In all this there was a great element of tactical calculation and manoeuvring for political advantage, habits for which Bismarck was famous – but this is in no way to imply that he was not deadly serious in this struggle against his most formidable foe. With the Socialists, he felt 'one could either do a deal or crush them, for they will never be dangerous to the present government'; but victory for the Progressives would gradually bring about a republic.[17]

The most interesting dispatches which were sent from the German embassy in London to the *Wilhelmstrasse* in these years did not, therefore, relate to the affairs of Greece or of Egypt; they were concerned instead with 'The Internal Conditions of England' (as the archival series was termed),[18] and they were interesting because of the use to which they were put when they reached Bismarck himself. Take, for example, the growing crisis in Ireland, which, because of the parallels with Polish conditions, could in no way be regarded by the German establishment as an irrelevant or purely academic matter. In the early reports from Münster, it had been made clear that the new Liberal government, headed by Gladstone but penetrated now by Radicals such as Chamberlain and Dilke, was likely to push ahead with Irish reform measures which the Whigs would find difficult to resist. Yet even the most experienced observer of Anglo-Irish politics could scarcely have predicted the events which were to follow: the alternating pattern of coercion and redress; the growing agricultural distress and evictions, answered by agrarian outrages; the astonishing scenes in the House of Commons, and the dissensions within the Liberal Party itself; the tactical battle between Gladstone and Parnell; and the recurrent tragedies, such as those at Phoenix Park and Maamtrasno.[19]

All this, inevitably, was grist to Bismarck's mill. Did it not prove, more conclusively than ever before, the total inadequacy of Liberal doctrines and practices? The Chancellor, at any rate, had no doubt of it, and he was determined to see that this moral was made clear to everyone. In June 1881, Münster reported that the English Radicals were supporting the Irish Land Act primarily in order 'to bring about a fundamental change in the landowner-relations in the United Kingdom as a whole' – a frightening precedent to the Junker mind, as was the further news that the newly formed Land Court was reducing rents by between 25 and 50 per cent.[20] In the following year, commenting upon Gladstone's latest change of policy in Ireland, the ambassador observed that 'Should the radical party really become strong enough to carry out their plans, then this country stands at the beginning of one of the most dangerous crises which it has experienced since Cromwell's time.'[21] These reports were utilised by Bismarck in a typical fashion. They were laid before the emperor during the regular audiences he had with the Chancellor, so that the old man could be confirmed in his prejudices against liberalism in general and Gladstone in particular; and they were also sent to the Crown Prince in the hope that he would see the errors of which Liberal politicians were usually guilty. Furthermore, copies were usually sent to all the smaller

German courts to convince this fresh circle of readers of the follies of demo-cratic statesmanship. Finally, 'improved' versions were often inserted in the *Norddeutsche Allgemeine Zeitung* and certain other papers, as reports from their 'special correspondent'.

The exploitation of Gladstone's Irish troubles by the German government for propaganda purposes was but one example of Bismarck's strategy. Another lay in his portrayal of the evils of parliamentarism; and, once again, events in Britain such as the Bradlaugh fiasco and the obstructionism of the Irish members offered useful ammunition for this purpose. Thus, the parliamentary chaos early in 1882 was portrayed in loving detail by the *Norddeutsche All-gemeine Zeitung*, although it added sarcastically that 'We do not flatter our-selves with the expectation that these and similar interesting facts, which are almost a daily part of the English parliamentary debates, will be admitted by the Progressive press here.'[22] By the same token, reports from Münster or his assistants about the rising power of the Commons *vis-à-vis* that of the Lords or the monarchy could be utilised – as always, on Bismarck's orders – to suggest that England was slowly but surely turning into a republic.[23] From time to time, the Chancellor would frighten his royal master, too, with this awful prospect: 'if Gladstone stays at the rudder for several more years, then Her Majesty the Queen herself could witness *the statutory abolition of the monarchy in England*, just as the abolition of the Lords does not seem odd to anyone these days. May God continue to preserve our Fatherland from ministers similar to Gladstone.'[24] It would be tedious to repeat the whole host of further instances of Bismarck's attempt to portray Britain as being ruined by the Liberals: the widening of the franchise, the Radicals' attacks against the House of Lords ('just as here, against the *Herrenhaus*', the Chancellor noted),[25] Ripon's reforms in India, and many other aspects of governmental policy, were all utilised for Bismarck's domestic propaganda purposes. The plain fact was that throughout these years the Chancellor was waging ideological warfare against what he considered to be dangerous political opponents, and the most suitable way to do this was to discredit their creed and their proposed policies by a continuous, one-sided assault upon the 'parliamentary model-state' itself. In doing this, he may not have shaken the convictions of such people as Richter, Bamberger or Brentano – although it was undoubtedly true that many other left-Liberals were unhappy about the course of events during Gladstone's administration; but this propaganda campaign could well have influenced uncommitted members of the German middle classes, as well as providing fresh evidence for those Conservative and National Liberal circles who had already developed deep reservations about the political scene in Great Britain.

This ideological offensive against 'Gladstonism' was not separate from, but an integral part of, Bismarck's efforts to create a Conservative alliance bloc in Europe in these years. Genuinely convinced himself that British foreign policy was unreliable, he needed to bring together the three empires of east-central Europe as the only way of ensuring Germany's security and of preventing an Austro-Russian war. Yet this policy, which suited the interests of the Junkers, could only be sustained under certain conditions, for example, the supremacy of the conservative aristocratic faction in Russia, the personal friendship of the three emperors themselves under the banner of 'monarchical solidarity', the 'digging of a ditch' between Britain and Europe (especially when Gladstone was appealing to the notion of a harmonious concert), and the suppression of the forces of nationalist unrest within the continent. Out of a fear that any one of the three partners in the *Dreikaiserbund* might incline towards Britain, it was always necessary to discredit the latter. Hence Bismarck's forwarding to Vienna of copies of many of Münster's reports, and his constant emphasis to the Austrians of his own conviction that 'no one knows what Gladstone finally desires; he doesn't know himself. His conduct is unacceptably antimonarchical, revolutionary, unpeaceful.'[26] Hence the frequent assertions in the 'inspired' German press that, with such 'Manchester men' as Bamberger and Richter in charge, Germany would be led into the camp of the Western powers, thus precipitating a possible war with Russia. To keep the peace, the electors should keep the Chancellor in power, and not vote for any 'Gladstone ministry'.[27] Hence, too, the repeated efforts to convince the Crown Prince, who still hankered for such an English alliance, that this course was impossible given the indiscretion of British ministers and the prospect of swiftly changing governments which could repudiate the obligations of their predecessors.[28] And hence – because he could not trust the Crown Prince and his wife – the constant 'stiffening' of the old emperor's suspicions of his son, which was usually best achieved by sending reports to the palace about how Gladstone and the English Radicals looked forward to the time when Friedrich Wilhelm would begin the liberalisation of Germany: on the receipt of such news, Wilhelm I's reactions were all too predictable.[29]

Hence, above all, Bismarck's repeated attempts to drive a wedge between Britain and Russia by suggesting that Gladstone was unreliable and by appealing yet again to the traditions of Conservative autocracy. By the early-to-mid 1880s, in fact, the Chancellor had come to regret more than ever that it had been necessary to act against Russian interests at the Congress of Berlin, thereby provoking the bitter hostility of the Panslavs. There seems little doubt that he genuinely feared a war with Russia and, without allowing Austria-Hungary to be destroyed as a great power, he was determined to appease the Russians wherever possible. This policy seemed all the more necessary since, by 1883 or so, it was becoming apparent that the revival of the *Dreikaiserbund* had not, after all, eliminated the Austro-Russian rivalry in the Balkans; and no one could foretell how the Russians would respond to their loss of influence in Bulgaria. In addition, the Prussian General Staff was growing increasingly alarmed about Russian troop concentrations along the Polish border areas, and about Germany's prospects in a two-front war. All this was taking place, moreover, against a background of growing Russo-German economic rivalry, which was grist to the mill of the Russian nationalists.[30]

England affected Bismarck's policy towards Russia and the Balkans in three ways. In the first place, as he complained to Wilhelm I, she no longer seemed to possess that 'race of great statesmen of earlier times', who were willing actively to intervene in Europe – presumably, by checking any Russian advances and thereby relieving Germany from that onerous task.[31] Secondly, Gladstone's policies, much as they might disappoint the German and Austro-Hungarian governments, encouraged the Panslavs, because they assumed that he would be at worst unwilling to resist, and at best sympathetic to Russian advances against Turkey-in-Europe. Throughout this period, in fact, Bismarck received frequent reports that the panslavic faction at the Russian court was trying to persuade the new Tsar to throw over the *Dreikaiserbund* and to come to terms with Britain; and, in such an eventuality, it was not difficult to guess what France's response would be. This explains Bismarck's famous dispatch to St Petersburg in February 1884, when he feared that Giers was contemplating a *rapprochement* with London – a dispatch in which not only was doubt cast upon Gladstone's reputation as a russophile, but he was also attacked as an irresponsible and erratic being who would (here Bismarck enjoying recalling Palmerston's comment) die in a madhouse.[32] It also explains Berlin's alarm at the prospect of Shuvalov becoming Russian ambassador in London, for he was reckoned to be clever enough to bring the two countries together, whereas (as Rantzau put it) 'for us it would be better if their relations remained as tense as they are now'.[33]

Thirdly, the news that the Prince of Bulgaria, Alexander of Battenberg, was hoping to marry the daughter of the Prussian Crown Prince and Princess – and that the proposed match was being warmly welcomed by the mother and by the grandmother, Queen Victoria – drove the German Chancellor into paroxysms of fury. Once again, those 'womanly', 'English' influences were seeking to pervert the proper course of German foreign policy and to provoke a clash with the Russian government, which would never believe that the marriage of a Hohenzollern princess to Alexander was not a sign of German support for Bulgaria's recent defiance of St Petersburg's overlordship![34] This tactic had to be crushed (whatever the cries of anguish at Windsor or Potsdam), the Russians had to be reassured that Germany would not oppose their ambitions in the Balkans, and Britain had to be diplomatically isolated and discredited, so that the Tsarist regime would not be tempted into friendship with London.

How far the British government knew of Bismarck's manoeuvres and his personal role in the newspaper commentaries of this time is hard to judge: probably not very much. The point was that Bismarck could operate his overall policy on different (but not totally separate) levels, and that in the circumstances of the early 1880s it quite suited him to be outwardly polite to the British government while secretly combating its hopes for a European concert and conducting a propaganda campaign to discredit its policies in the eyes of others. Nevertheless, if the circumstances altered and advantage could be gained by demonstrating to the world that Germany was at odds with, rather than a friend of Great Britain, it was clear that the Chancellor would not hesitate to enter into such a quarrel – and would, indeed, personally enjoy the prospect of humiliating a Liberal government. Only if this is kept in mind is it possible fully to understand his actions in the summer of 1884 when the situation altered in two important ways: another general election was due, in which it was vital to discover a means of crushing the left-Liberals; and an influential campaign for the creation of a German overseas empire was under way. Together, these provided solid reasons for Bismarck to consider achieving his basic aims by yet another change of tactics.

# CHAPTER 10

# Bismarck's 'Colonial Bid' and its Impact upon Anglo-German Relations (1883–5)

Bismarck's 'colonial bid' of the mid-1880s not only constitutes an important stage in the development of the Anglo-German relationship but it also offers to the historian an excellent example of the multi-dimensional nature of the Chancellor's policies, in which short-term and long-term considerations were inextricably connected. If it is the impact upon the London–Berlin 'axis' which is of primary concern to us, it is worthwhile devoting some space first of all to an analysis of German policy alone, since there now exist so many interpretations of Bismarck's motives that it is becoming difficult to see this event in its entirety.[1]

It is worth noting, as a preliminary comment, that measures taken by the German government to protect the economic interests of its nationals was hardly a revolutionary step in itself; and with the rejection of *laissez-faire* economic policies in 1879, it could be argued that it was but one further logical step in the pattern of state interventionism that the government should now be willing to extend its support to German enterprise overseas, just as it had provided tariffs to rescue industry and agriculture at home.[2] Of course, the difference between establishing a domestic tariff and founding colonies was a very large one; and it was in this case made the more marked by Bismarck's previous repudiations of Germany's need for an overseas empire. Several significant changes had occurred, however, since those earlier days. In the first place, other states seemed to have ceased regarding colonies as political and economic 'millstones', as they undoubtedly had in the 1860s: the Gold Coast, Tunis, Egypt, Cyprus, Senegambia, Indo-China, Fiji and the other Pacific island-groups had all been taken over in recent years, a clear hint that the age of so-called 'anti-imperialism' was coming to a close. Secondly, Bismarck was no longer simply the Prime Minister of Prussia, but also the Chancellor of a fast-industrialising nation whose economic requirements were different from, or at least more than, those of the east Elbian Junker. This nation was, moreover, facing for the first time the problems caused by industrial over-production and, although various pressure groups had hoped that the adoption

167

of protective tariffs in 1879 would counter the alarming trends of unemployment, overcapacity, falling profits and increasing bankruptcies, the blunt fact was that by 1882–3 the German economy was in as bad a way as ever.[3] The domestic market alone, it was increasingly being argued, was no longer adequate for German industry: instead, there must be a search for alternative markets throughout the world, secured if need be by governmental protection. Although in hindsight the historian is aware of the relatively low economic value of the German overseas empire even by 1914,[4] there can be no denying that many contemporaries hoped that it would form a most useful prop to the domestic economy: New Guinea, for example, was at first envisaged as a potential Java, East Africa as a second India.[5]

Furthermore, some German publicists were now beginning to suggest that to these newly opened regions could be sent not merely goods and capital, but also the 'surplus population' of the Reich, whose numbers totalled over 45 million despite the colossal outflow (in 1882: 203,000 emigrants) each year. The creation of settlement-colonies would thus lessen the two great fears which many Germans had about the population and emigration question: it would halt the outward flow of good German stock which at present was 'furnishing knowledge and skill to our national enemies';[6] and the knowledge that the country would have colonies of its own could well tempt many more Germans than otherwise to go out to such regions, thereby relieving the pressures of overcrowding and unemployment at home. Behind this calculation, moreover, lay a deeper anxiety concerning social disorders and industrial unrest. Imperialist writers such as Fabri and Hübbe-Schleiden constantly hammered home the dangers that were arising from the unsolved 'social problem', thereby offering an argument for colonisation which might appeal to those who traditionally had no interest in overseas affairs. Thus, in 1882 the president of the newly founded *Kolonialverein*, Prince Hermann zu Hohenlohe-Langenburg, encouraged his more famous relative, the future Chancellor Prince Chlodwig zu Hohenlohe-Schillingsfürst, with the remark that 'The conviction takes hold in me more and more, that we in Germany can find no more effective counter to Social Democracy than by giving ourselves an outlet overseas, and that as soon as possible.'[7]

This leads on to a second, but closely related factor. Not only were colonies being viewed in general in a much more favourable light by the early 1880s, but there were growing up within German society powerful pressure groups who were articulating the pro-imperialist message and asking the government for assistance. One predictable cluster of pressure groups consisted of various economic circles: certain firms trading out of Hamburg and Bremen to West Africa (Woermann), Zanzibar (O'Swald) and Oceania (Godeffroy); chambers of commerce and individual industries which, in the midst of the depression, were keen to develop new, and secure, markets; the commercial interests behind the *Zentralverein für Handelsgeographie und Förderung deutscher Interessen im Ausland*; and financiers, such as Hansemann and Bleichröder, who for various reasons thought it worth their while to have a finger in the colonial pie.[8] In addition, there also existed a growing number of intellectual advocates of a German colonial empire: the economists around Schmoller and the *Verein für*

*Sozialpolitik*; Fabri, whose well-known tract of 1879, 'Does Germany Need Colonies?', had answered that question with an emphatic 'yes'; Treitschke, of course, who stated 'We want and ought to claim our share in the domination of the earth by the white race';[9] and all the other professors and pundits who joined with the merchants and industrialists under the umbrella organisation of the *Kolonialverein* which was to have over 10,000 members within three years of its founding in December 1882.[10] This is in no way to imply that all of the previous domestic opposition to colonisation had disappeared – for there were still considerable political and commercial circles who disliked the whole idea of overseas annexations – but it does seem that many more individuals than hitherto were now attracted by pro-imperialist arguments.

Two remarks are worth making about these commercial and intellectual advocates of German imperialism. The first is that they cannot always be regarded simply as 'tools' of the imperial government, manipulated by an adroit Bismarck to suit his own purposes and then cast aside when the end had been achieved. They possessed, in contrast, a volition and an impulse of their own and, if they applauded the government when it took the 'right' steps, did not hesitate to criticise also or to press for further actions when such appeared necessary. Karl Peters and the *Gesellschaft für deutsche Kolonisation* (founded early in 1884) made it quite clear, for example, that if they could not persuade the German government to support their East African plans, they would proceed independently[11] – by sending out colonial expeditions on the one hand, and by appealing for support from 'national-minded' opinion throughout Germany on the other. In other words, 'manipulation from above' coexisted with co-operation and pressure from certain interest groups below, at least until 1886, when the Chancellor's disillusionment with colonial affairs led to a gradual breakdown in this political *mariage de convenance*, thus allowing us to see more clearly the two independent elements which had co-operated so closely before then.[12]

Secondly, the advocates of colonialism were known to be very strong within the National Liberal and Free Conservative parties – precisely the political bloc upon which Bismarck relied for support of government policies during Reichstag debates and votes. Since he had felt it necessary to respond to the request of these allies to introduce protectionism in 1879, it is reasonable to suppose that he could not completely turn his back upon their campaign for colonies in 1883–4. In particular, he was seeking to tempt the right-wing National Liberals to remain separated from the left-Liberals and 'jump back into the arena' with the Conservative parties.[13] In other words, he needed their support just as they needed his. They were agitating for colonies well before June 1884 and provided an enthusiastic response when he made his change of policy into a 'national' issue – just as they had always responded to the regular calls for army increases. He utilised their support, inside and outside of the Reichstag, and offered them the *Weltpolitik* they craved for – although he, in turn, never became their tool and he gave their general colonial enthusiasm a specific direction, dictated by his own acute sense of political and diplomatic priorities. When pro-imperialist circles showed some interest in Brazil, Morocco and

Indo-China, for example, they were quickly called to order. The supreme control always remained in the Chancellor's hands.

If it was advisable to consider rendering support to the *reichstreue* elements within German society, it was even more vital that the government's foes be smashed. In this instance the most formidable enemy was not so much the 'red peril' of social democracy but the various circles of left-Liberals and Progressives, which seemed to Bismarck both willing and able to present a 'Gladstonian' alternative to his own policies. This is a quite vital point. The proponents of the theory of 'social imperialism' have tended to assume that the domestic-political dangers which Bismarck had in mind were the Social Democrats; yet, although he had obviously made frequent references to that party during the years of the anti-socialist legislation and the re-forming of the *Dreikaiserbund*, he seems to have uttered few, if any, remarks about the connection between his colonial policy and the SPD 'threat' in the years 1884–5.[14] On the other hand, he and his sons made constant references to the Radicals in this period, the point being that a party led by such people as Bamberger, Rickert, Roggenbach, Stosch, and so on, was reckoned to be *regierungsfähig* under the Crown Prince, whereas the Socialists clearly were not. Once a 'Gladstone ministry' was in power, of course, its lack of resolution and its 'traitorous' encouragement of 'revolutionary' elements such as the Poles, Alsatians, SPD and the like would mean the end of the old Prusso-German autocracy. To this extent, it could be argued that whereas the Radicals provided the immediate and direct threat, the Socialists ('lurking' in the background, as the Right liked to portray them) offered a longer-term and, arguably, more substantial indirect threat.

In the early part of 1884, Bismarck was in a state of almost uncontrolled fury at the 'intrigues' of the left-wing Liberals. In January and February, the *Norddeutsche Allgemeine Zeitung* had launched a fresh campaign against liberalism's dire effects within Germany and Austria-Hungary, this propaganda coinciding with a new 'low' in the relations between the Chancellor and the Crown Prince – with Bismarck refusing to give the latter any information upon state matters since Friedrich Wilhelm's new Hofmarschal was supposed to be passing this on to the left-Liberal opposition.[15] It was in February 1884, too, that the Chancellor vented his bitterness in his attack upon the recently deceased left-Liberal deputy, Lasker, and sent his lengthy dispatch to the St Petersburg embassy, denouncing Gladstone. And, as a further coincidence, the Bismarck camp discovered in the early spring of 1884 that the Crown Princess and Queen Victoria were pushing for the marriage of the young Princess Victoria to the Prince of Bulgaria. Sensing an 'English intrigue' to worsen Russo-German relations, Bismarck immediately launched his counter-attack, mobilising the old Kaiser and the young Prince Wilhelm in support, denying in the *Norddeutsche Allgemeine Zeitung* that the German government would ever consent to such a match, and making repeated threats to resign. Throughout 1884 and 1885, in fact, the notion of the proposed Battenberg marriage appeared as a constant threat to Bismarck's pro-Russian policy and stiffened his dislike of the Crown Prince's party – even though Friedrich Wilhelm himself was no great advocate of his daughter's cause.[16]

Since the emperor had become so ill again by May of 1884 that he was forced to cancel his various engagements, here was a further cause for alarm.

Bismarck was also concerned at the news of the fusion of the left-Liberals and the Progressives into the *Deutschfreisinnige Partei*, just six months before the autumn 1884 election. If this party, now the largest in the Reichstag and led by such known enemies of the Chancellor as Richter and Bamberger, was not halted at the election itself, then it might well pose the most formidable parliamentary threat since Bismarck had faced the massed ranks of the Prussian Liberals in the early 1860s – and this time he might not have his old master Wilhelm to provide the crucial support. This does *not* mean, however, that the Chancellor immediately saw in the colonial issue the 'trump-card' against German liberalism: after all, the government's attempt to introduce the Samoa Subsidy Bill in 1880 had met with formidable opposition, and had permitted Bamberger to claim a great psychological and political victory for the Reichstag.[17] Furthermore, the 1881 election was generally reckoned to have indicated that large numbers of Germans were discontented because of the Bismarckian tariff system, and had shown this by turning away from the right-wing National Liberals towards the free-traders. Only gradually, as the clamour for a colonial policy developed in 1883 and 1884 – and as Bismarck's first moves in that direction won such applause – did the Chancellor see that here was an issue which might bind the National Liberals closer to the government whilst splitting and discrediting the *Freisinnige* groupings, many of whose supporters were more eager than the leadership about colonies and would be acutely embarrassed at the charge that they were acting unpatriotically.

If the above points made a more forceful overseas policy attractive to the government in general, the threat (however unlikely it appears in retrospect) posed by a revival of German liberalism under the Crown Prince also seemed to justify an *anti-British* colonial venture in particular. Some years later, Herbert Bismarck explained this calculation to the ambassador Schweinitz:

> When we entered upon a colonial policy, we had to reckon with a long reign of the Crown Prince. During this reign English influence would have been dominant. To prevent this, we had to embark on a colonial policy, because it was popular and conveniently adapted to bring us into conflict with England at any given moment.[18]

Such a statement, possessing all the characteristic clarity of a retrospective assessment, is far too bald: it disguises the halting, tentative nature of the first stages of the Chancellor's colonial policy, which already had under contemplation some measures of support for German interests overseas before the advent of the 1884 election and before it possessed such a definite anti-British thrust. Nevertheless, as has been shown above, the Bismarck circle was attempting to discredit the 'English influence' within Germany in the early 1880s and – if another opportunity arose to achieve this aim and, simultaneously, to hurt the left-Liberals electorally – no personal scruples existed on the Chancellor's part to restrain him from moving against the British, and their friends within Germany. It was in July 1884, significantly enough, that both the *Norddeutsche Allgemeine Zeitung* and Bismarck himself openly attacked the idea of a 'Gladstone ministry' for Germany, under the aegis of the Crown Prince.[19] Hence the constant emphasis that the historian discovers being laid upon the domestic-political aspect of Bismarck's colonial policy: sometimes put cynically, as when the Chancellor was heard to tell one of his ministerial colleagues that 'All this colonial business is a sham, but we need it for the elections'; and sometimes more anxiously, as when, in the middle of his campaign against the Radical-Clerical majority in the Reichstag which was voting down his various colonial projects but becoming nervous itself about the 'national' agitation, the Chancellor informed Münster that 'for internal reasons, the colonial question . . . is of vital importance for us . . . The smallest peak in New Guinea or West Africa, though it may be quite worthless objectively, is at present more important for our policy than the whole of Egypt and its future.'[20] The more that the pro-governmental press applauded the colonial annexations and responded with approval to the anti-British manner in which it was being done, the greater became the Bismarck family's conviction that they were on an electoral winner. 'Everything is now bubbling over on account of the colonial policy', wrote Herbert Bismarck in August 1884 – so it would 'be wise to hold the elections *soon*' before there was a swing to the Progressives.[21] Here, as Holstein noted, both 'as a means of combating foreign influences' and to check 'the liberals and the democrats', was a very substantial reason for supporting German interests overseas wherever they appealed for help: 'the best card in the government's hand at present is definitely a harsh move against England. One can hardly believe *how* popular it is in the business world.'[22]

Indeed, although no detailed analysis of the 1884 election exists, it seems evident in retrospect that Bismarck's calculation was correct. Weeks before the voting took place, Odo Russell was bemoaning the fact that the Chancellor 'has discovered an unexplored mine of popularity' in awakening the latent anglophobia and desire for colonies among the German people, and the Austro-Hungarian ambassador was reporting that Bismarck had 'indisputably a very lucky hand' since he could go into the electoral struggle with the decisive popularity produced by his colonial programme.[23] Certainly, the gains made by the National Liberals, who (with the Free Conservatives) had been the chief advocates of colonialism, seemed to testify to the popularity of the Chancellor's new measures. On the other hand the SPD, which despite a considerable amount of internal opposition maintained its policy of criticising what Engels termed 'the colonial swindle', doubled the number of its Reichstag seats to twenty-four – indicating that at least its supporters were not swayed by pro-imperialist arguments: indeed, many of its leaders claimed that it was simply a cunning attempt 'to export the social question'.[24] The same may also have been true about the supporters of the German Conservative Party, whose numbers rose from fifty to seventy-eight seats; and those of the Centre Party, which with its ninety-nine seats emerged as the largest party in the Reichstag in 1884. Neither of those two parties were enthusiastic about colonialism, although individual Conservatives were willing to rally to Bismarck's call for national solidarity, and certain Centre Party deputies were interested in the protection of Catholic missions overseas.[25] On the whole, it seems likely that the non-Liberal parties – being much more of *Interessenparteien* – gained or lost seats chiefly as a result of local and economic issues.

The party which was hardest hit by the October 1884 election was, of course, that of the *Freisinnige* coalition. In 1881, its two sub-groups had obtained 105 seats: now it possessed sixty-seven. Here again, one suspects, this result may not be totally attributable to the colonial issue: but the important point was that all observers, recognising in Bismarck's electoral campaign a fresh attempt to crush the free-trade Liberals, automatically assumed that this was the factor which had caused their defeat. Certainly, the colonial 'card' was highly embarrassing to critics such as Richter and Bamberger. Even supporting papers such as the *Frankfurter Zeitung* and the *Volkszeitung* found it difficult to explain or defend the British government's policy in the Angra Pequena affair; and a fair number of the merchants, bankers and professional men who supported the party were less hostile to the creation of a colonial empire than the doctrinaire *laissez-faire* leadership, and had in fact previously been campaigning for governmental support for German overseas interests. Most of them, like the Crown Prince, had simply supposed that Germany would one day expand with England's approval, not against England.

Then there were other members of the *Deutschfreisinnige Partei* who, when they saw how popular the Chancellor's policy was, prudently wished to abandon a politically weak position. Bismarck, conversely, was always seeking to expose their lack of patriotism. When the Reichstag again defeated the Postal Steamship Subsidy Bill at the end of 1884, so many protests and petitions (all published by the government press) were sent to Berlin that the nerve of a number of the Radicals gave way and they voted in favour on the third reading, thus ensuring its success.[26] Finally, in early March 1885 (in the midst of his open quarrels with Granville), Bismarck attacked the opposition parties in the Reichstag, claiming that their obstructionism 'has strengthened still further the English government in its opposition to German colonial enterprises', and warning that he would appeal to the patriotic instincts of the people. This charge of lack of patriotism was immediately denied – a clear sign that the opposition admitted how effective Bismarck's tactic was.[27]

To this complex of domestic considerations which caused Berlin to view colonial policy in a more favourable light, it is necessary to add several external factors. The first, and most famous of these, concerns the argument that Bismarck sought to provoke a series of quarrels overseas with the British government as 'a move in his European policy', an ultra-subtle tactic of creating a Franco-German *rapprochement* – now that Ferry was in power – on the basis of their common enmity towards London's imperial arrogance, thus deflecting the French from their traditional revanchist course.[28] This seems a dubious argument, at least as an explanation of the *original motives* for the Chancellor's decision. The documents suggest that the actual causal sequence was in reverse to that interpretation: that is, that Bismarck sought an accommodation with France, not as an end in itself, but as a means to ensure the success of his colonial ventures when he discovered that he was involved in a prolonged quarrel with the British.[29] The appearance of a common front with the French in all questions relating to tropical Africa was, like the Chancellor's slightly later use of the *baton égyptien*, a powerful diplomatic weapon; but for a number of reasons it is difficult to believe that Bismarck actually thought he could produce a lasting improvement in the Franco-German relationship. Hence the Chancellor's refusal to help the French to compel the British to leave Egypt, which was what Paris really wanted out of a Franco-German *entente*. In any case, Bismarck was less concerned about the danger of a French war of revenge now that he had managed to restore the relationship between the three emperors. What one *can* say about the diplomatic situation, however, is that it was so favourable to Bismarck that it permitted him to press his claims in London, often in the most offensive manner, without the fear that Gladstone's government could respond with effective counter-measures.

What was more, it is difficult not to believe that he personally wished to inflict a defeat upon Gladstone and Granville. In part, this derived from sheer spleen – by the 1880s, the Chancellor's bad temper was almost uncontrollable at times, and certainly affected the *extent* of his reaction to events: in part, his feelings could be explained by the hindrances which the British government, and more especially its officials in the tropics, seemed to be repeatedly putting in the way of legitimate German enterprise; but there was also that element of political calculation mentioned above, the desire to discredit a Liberal government. Herbert Bismarck put this, predictably, at its crudest when he wrote of his hope 'that our policy *will avail itself of this most favourable moment* to squash Gladstone against the wall, so that he can yap no more. He must be driven *ad absurdam* in the general interest, but first he must ride the English deeper into the mire so that his prestige will vanish even among the masses of the stupid English electorate.'[30] Occasionally, Liberal newspapers and politicians in both countries would make the charge that the Chancellor's chief aim was indeed to discredit Gladstone, a point which was always swiftly denied.[31] This answer rarely sounded very convincing: an article in the *Norddeutsche Allgemeine Zeitung* of late December 1884 – probably composed by the Chancellor himself – which argued that no such aim was intended since 'the Gladstone government was the best one conceivable for all countries – with the exception of England' was simply another way of exposing the Liberal administration's incompetence.[32]

The final external aspect is probably the most important of all: namely, the *genuine* fears which existed within Germany, and were very strongly shared by the Chancellor himself, that the nation's overseas commerce was in grave danger of being damaged by the actions of foreign governments. The point to be emphasised yet again is that, however small a percentage of Germany's total foreign trade was involved in these tropical regions, there were considerable expectations that it would increase rapidly in the future, thus bringing the hoped-for economic (and other) benefits to the fatherland: Hamburg's exports to West Africa, after all, had risen six-fold between 1871 and 1883.[33] Moreover, in specific areas the German economic interest was substantial, at least relative to those of other countries.[34] In an age now characterised by discriminatory tariffs and fresh annexations, even the preservation – let alone the expansion – of this overseas commerce called for a radical change in the German government's traditional policy.

It is now known that an Anglo-French agreement of 1882 over West Africa was misinterpreted by the 'colonial expert' of the German Foreign Office, Kusserow, as implying a 'carve-up' of certain territories by the two powers and a mutual immunity from customs duties which they were going to levy upon foreign trade; but even if this alarm was a false one, what mattered was the suspicion it bred within Germany, which could only increase when individual merchants, naval commanders and the Hamburg Chamber of Commerce all called attention to the obstacles which were being put in the way of German traders in West Africa.[35] In the same year, the 'sub-imperialists' of Australia and New Zealand appeared to be planning widespread annexations in the Pacific regardless of the distaste with which such plans were regarded on the other side of the globe by Gladstone, Derby and their colleagues.[36] It is true that powers other than Britain were often equally obstructive – the French and Portuguese local officials in Africa, the Spaniards in the Carolines – but this simply increased the *Torschlusspanik*; and British interests, because of the extent of that country's formal and informal empire, seemed to be in the way wherever German commerce existed or was trying to expand. (When, in February 1885, Granville rather feebly explained to Berlin that Britain's various recent annexations had not been motivated by any anti-German design but simply because those territories had been 'deemed essential to the safety or welfare of some neighbouring British possession', Bismarck's marginal comment was obvious: 'That is the entire world?!'[37])

Even in late 1884, when it had become clear to all that Germany was willing to annex colonies, it is worth remarking that these 'blocking' manoeuvres continued: the Australian governments renewed their claims to New Guinea, as did New Zealand to Samoa; the news of the activities of Rohlfs and Peters in East Africa immediately provoked counter-moves by the British consul-general at Zanzibar, Sir John Kirk; and St Lucia Bay, and Bechuanaland, were prudently annexed to prevent any direct links between Germans and Boers in southern Africa. Although in certain instances the British government had not authorised or even known of this local opposition, it is easy to see why Bismarck could accuse London of a systematic *Deutschfeindlichkeit* – and also easy to understand why, from late 1883 onwards, he was weighing up the various possible counter-measures.

The latter point is also crucial. Bismarck did *not*, at the beginning, have a fixed intention to establish a centralised overseas empire like, say, that of the French: nor, indeed, did many of the Hamburg and Bremen merchants who petitioned for governmental assistance wish for such an empire, for a substantial number of them had remained Liberal free-traders in their political inclinations. What they did want were more signs of Berlin's willingness to protect German foreign commerce: diplomatic action against Portuguese or New Zealand trickery; an increase in the number of warships on overseas stations, and possibly the lease of land for a naval station; and the creation of more full-time consular officials, in Africa and the Pacific. It was in responding to the many requests for this sort of aid – which, after all, were unremarkable, since Germany already had a number of warships and consuls overseas – that Bismarck gradually became ever more involved in the problem of maintaining German interests in the un-annexed parts of the globe; and equally gradual was the process whereby he came to appreciate that, if other nations were actually annexing those regions, the traditional forms of support by Berlin were now inadequate.

What was more, even when he decided to take more vigorous steps, he was clearly attracted by the scheme – put to him by Kusserow and by the various trading interests – to establish overseas possessions which would be run by the companies themselves, under a government charter, along the lines of Britain's former East India Company or the newly established North Borneo Company. All that the German government was required to do, in other words, was to grant *Reichsschutz* (Reich protection), thus avoiding the need to ask the Reichstag for financial support.[38] With all the pressures upon him to act, and the very real prospect existing that German overseas interests – and the government's future electoral position – would be hurt if he did not, it becomes easier to see how this idea of 'colonies on the cheap' could be attractive to him. In June 1884, when Granville expressed his surprise that Bismarck had begun a colonial policy, the Chancellor minuted testily: 'What is colonial policy? We must protect our countrymen.'[39] On the other hand, because this was a pragmatic and reluctant change of policy on his part, he was not obsessed (like Wilhelm II) with the notion of gaining an empire for its own sake and he did not intend to support every German merchant's claim, for many of these were spurious and 'stretched too high': there was considerable hesitation in Berlin, for example, about giving support to Peters' treaties with the East African chiefs. Bismarck's motto, as he put it in one minute, was 'Property and trade must first of all be formed privately, then the flag and protection can come in as well.'[40] Only if the commercial enterprise was genuine and economically viable would it be possible to entrust the administration of a tropical region to it. If this was what colonialism meant, Bismarck was now willing to drop his objections to this idea.

The above considerations, thematically set out, appear from the evidence available to be the arguments which swayed Bismarck into adopting a colonial policy; but it is highly unlikely that all of these motives were present at the same time. Instead, they gradually accumulated, layer upon layer, allowing him to employ a variety of justifications, to the confusion of contemporaries and later historians alike. In the beginning there probably only existed the pleas of the overseas merchants and his own worries about the German economy and the prospect of some future 'Gladstone ministry'. When, by the early summer of 1884, he had begun to offer ever-increasing forms of 'protection' to Luderitz's claims in South-west Africa, additional factors entered into his calculations: the proclamation of a *Reichsschutz* there was warmly applauded within Germany: the Reichstag elections were soon to come; and he was becoming furious at the reports of the repeated obstacles placed in his way by the British and colonial governments. Thereafter, the more that Anglo-German relations deteriorated, the more he was driven to apply the *baton égyptien* and to suggest to the French that they combine to create an anti-British *entente*. By the final months of 1884, moreover, the field of differences had widened, from South-west Africa, West Africa and New Guinea, to East Africa and Samoa, as further petitions for governmental support overseas reached Berlin. By that time, Bismarck knew that he was winning. The electoral results of October 1884 stimulated a further resort to this tactic of brusque demands upon London for colonial concessions, and a continuation of the government-inspired press assault upon British and German liberalism. By March of 1885, with the Reichstag opposition to his colonial policy wilting and with Herbert Bismarck reporting from London upon the British government's acquiescence in most of the outstanding issues, victory was assured.

The number of birds which Bismarck sought to kill with this one stone is truly remarkable, even for him. A successful colonial policy might well increase German exports, assist the economy and help – to a greater or lesser degree – to reduce the prospects for social unrest; more specifically, it would please certain National Liberal and Free Conservative circles, and bind them closer to the government. At the same time, it would hurt the political fortunes of the *Freisinnige* coalition; and it would make it virtually impossible for 'liberal' and 'English' influences to operate with success inside Germany, even if a new emperor came to the throne. Finally, these successes would enhance Bismarck's own position, identifying him yet again in the public's eyes as the great national hero. All this seems very logical, and confirms one's impression of a man who, whatever other explanations he gave of his policies, could always be relied upon to be thinking ultimately of the advantages to himself, to the Prussian establishment and to the German state. Seen in this light, the varieties of tactic which he adopted in 1884–5 – the attempted *rapprochement* with the French, the utilisation of the London Egyptian financial conference and the Berlin West Africa conference, the deliberate concealment of certain of his African plans, the Reichstag denunciations of Granville on the one hand and the frequent visits of Herbert Bismarck to London on the other – are of less significance overall, even if it is necessary to study them in detail in order to appreciate the manner in which his motives and his methods were interwoven.

Because the Chancellor's policies were logical and rational, they were also controllable. The same can be said about bankers like Bleichröder, who dabbled in certain colonial enterprises in the hope of good profits or to demonstrate their patriotism, but who soon abandoned that field in preference for foreign government loans when they learned more about the real economic situation in Germany's colonial empire.[41] It could not be said, however, of the various German merchants engaged in commercial rivalry with their British equivalents in East Africa and the Pacific; and it was even less the case with the 'ideological' imperialists at home, the intellectuals and journalists and others who had yearned for Germany to become a world power and who applauded every time that Bismarck scored off that detestable, hypocritical British government, which preached moral doctrines while secretly preventing Germany's efforts at overseas expansion. Undoubtedly, there was deliberate encouragement from above of newspaper criticisms of Britain and the German anglophiles, just as these 'inspired' journalists were coached to applaud each fresh colonial acquisition; but in many cases, one suspects, it was scarcely necessary for the German Foreign Office to manipulate the press, since certain journals were already strongly anglophobe. 'Germany has for one hundred years sacrificed its civilisation to England', claimed *Hübbe-Schleiden*; and Fabri and Weber also argued that they must not shrink back if 'John Bull' showed annoyance at German actions, for the Anglo-Saxons had to realise that other nations, too, claimed a share of the tropical world.[42] As the British chargé in Berlin observed, 'the rabid anti-English press are still dissatisfied and distrustful of us . . . [It was officially encouraged] chiefly in order to carry the colonial schemes through the Reichstag, but it was excited too far and cannot be so easily allayed.'[43] The same was true of the colonial pressure groups: in late May 1885, when official Anglo-German relations were improving, the president of the *Kolonialverein* was writing about further African expeditions and about the lessons that had been learnt from the recent British obstructionism: namely, 'how much people on the German side must speed up their efforts, so that entry into the negroid parts of the world is not permanently closed to us'.[44] And in the Pacific, agents of the *Deutsche Handels und Plantagen-Gesellschaft* . . . were preparing for another effort to gain control of the Samoan Islands.[45] This combination of anti-British nationalists at home, and continuing local rivalries in the tropics, was soon to cause Bismarck to curse at the way such unplanned and unofficial actions disturbed his diplomatic plans and embarrassed Anglo-German relations; but the fact remains that he himself had played a very significant role in encouraging such forces to regard Britain as their chief colonial opponent.[46]

The creation of a German overseas empire was, by any reckoning, of considerable significance in the history of that country as a great power, in the development of its national consciousness and in the political affairs of its government and parties. It also marks a new stage in the story of the Anglo-German relationship. Yet it was not regarded at the time as especially important by the British government, or even by the greater part of the British press – simply because the attention of both was concentrated elsewhere during those critical years of 1884–5. Gladstone and Granville, it seems fair to say, were innocent of any design to prevent Germany from becoming a colonial power; but it is also true that they appeared to be obstructing or at least delaying that development because, ironically enough, it took them quite some time to understand that Bismarck seriously intended to annex overseas territories. Even the extraordinarily energetic Gladstone could hardly have managed to devote much of his attention to Germany's policies during a period in which the Egyptian-Sudanese débâcle, the Irish crisis and the extension of the franchise were dominating the British Cabinet's agenda.[47] In part, it may also reflect their lack of interest, and unwillingness to anticipate, in the realm of international diplomacy; and, arguably, to that British tradition of regarding the Germans as a *quantité négligeable* in the extra-European world, where only France, Russia and the United States were worthy of much consideration. In part, too, it was probably due to their own lack of interest in regions such as Africa and the Pacific: being disinclined to permit further additions to the British Empire in those places, the Liberal government was unlikely to guess that Germany should suddenly manifest a desire to annex parts of them.

Furthermore, this belief was confirmed by the assurances which the British Foreign Office received from Münster in London and Ampthill in Berlin. Admittedly, both ambassadors did indicate by early 1884 that Bismarck was taking an increasing interest in the plight of German traders overseas.[48] Even this information gave no clear hint that Bismarck favoured colonies, however, and neither the British government nor its ambassador in Berlin were aware that the Chancellor – now quite alarmed at reports of contemplated action by the Cape government in South-west Africa and British consuls in West Africa, and at last reconciled to the idea of proclaiming a *Reichsschutz* over those areas – had secretly embarked upon an imperialist course. Only with the news of the various flag-hoistings and with Herbert Bismarck's visit to London in June 1884 was this made fully clear, and British ministers then fell over backwards to placate Berlin. Granville was genuinely embarrassed at the misunderstanding over South-west Africa; and the Home Secretary, Harcourt, asserted: 'Good God, I had no idea of this, you may have the whole of Fidji [*sic*] if you like.'[49]

Despite such protestations of British goodwill, two obstacles lay in the way of a reconciliation at this stage – assuming, that is, that Bismarck himself would have been willing to bury the hatchet. The first was that, however cavalierly Harcourt wished to give away Fiji, South-west Africa and indeed all of that continent, such feelings were not shared by colonial politicians or British traders in the tropics. At the Cape Colony, for example, the parliament decided in mid-July 1884 to annex the entire south-west coast up to the Portuguese border, and was bitterly annoyed at Germany's pre-emptive moves: as one of its politicians declared, 'we are told that the Germans are good neighbours, but we prefer to have no neighbours at all'.[50] Similarly, although the metropolitan government had a long aversion to further colonisation in West Africa, the cries of British merchants in the Niger region for counter-measures against French and German annexations could not be totally ignored. On the East African side, moreover, the Foreign Office took some pride in the informal paramountcy which Sir John Kirk exercised from Zanzibar, and their concern at the scramble was shared by the India Office, where Kimberley declared: 'From an Indian point of view I regard it as of very serious importance that no Foreign Power should oust us from that coastline.'[51] Finally, in the Pacific the self-governing colonies of Australia and New Zealand were enraged at the incursion of a German as well as a French 'threat', and prepared to take counter-measures themselves if the London government would not. At first this stance had been ridiculed by the lethargic Derby as a 'Monroe Doctrine' for the Pacific, but by the summer of 1884 even he had been forced to alter his purely negative stance – and his officials were nervously writing that 'the idea of allowing any of these islands to fall into the hands of European Powers . . . might almost drive the Australasian Colonies into revolt'.[52] All of these pressures automatically conflicted with the ambitions of German traders in the tropics and caused Bismarck – who firmly refused to recognise the self-governing colonies as being anything other than subservient to London – to explode at what he sensed was deliberate obstructionism.

Quite apart from this 'sub-imperialist' agitation, certain members of the

Cabinet also came to argue for more decisive steps overseas. By late 1884 even Derby thought it prudent to respond to some of the demands of the self-governing colonies; Kimberley was anxious to preserve British paramountcy in the Indian Ocean; right-wing Whigs like Hartington, Northbrook and Selborne, pressing Gladstone to take action in the Sudan, wished the government to stand firm south of the Sahara as well; Dilke, as author of *Greater Britain*, could hardly be unresponsive to the agitations at Cape Town and Wellington. In many cases, one suspects, such motivations were mingled with the much simpler drives of anger at being pushed around by foreign powers, irritation at a whole series of domestic and external problems, and concern lest foreign policy reverses be exploited by the Conservative opposition. Chamberlain, who five months earlier had informed Herbert Bismarck that 'there was no power to whom we would render favours more than to Germany', was by December 1884 writing: 'I don't give a damn about New Guinea and I am not afraid of German colonisation, but I don't like being cheeked by Bismarck or anyone else' – and his fellow-Radical, Dilke, was saying the same.[53] Ironically enough, Gladstone himself – who was always denounced so strongly by the German government and press – was the most conciliatory of all ministers towards the German colonial bids, welcoming them in public speeches and, with the assistance of Harcourt and Trevelyan, combating the annexationist instincts of the Whigs, the Chamberlain–Dilke duo, and the sub-imperialists in private. The latter combination was a strong one, however, and often forced him forward against his better judgement.

Although these two considerations disposed the British government to stand firm against Bismarck's threats, it was all to no avail; for the crude fact, which he never ceased rubbing in, was that while his diplomatic position was incredibly strong, its was unprecedently weak. In June 1884, just as the Angra Pequena issue was coming to the boil, the powers were meeting in London to discuss the British proposals for balancing the Egyptian budget and allowing a withdrawal from that country – a matter which was convulsing the Cabinet throughout this period. Because Bismarck's earlier veiled hints at the need for British concessions – in Africa, possibly also over Heligoland – had been toned down by Münster and thus not fully appreciated in London, the German support for the French position now caused great confusion and forced Granville to close the conference. The *baton égyptien* was being wielded with a vengeance, and the British government, try as it might, was unable to escape the blows. The Anglo-Portuguese treaty over the Congo was abandoned, only a short while after Britain had recognised the German claim to Angra Pequena; an international conference on West Africa, to be presided over by Bismarck himself, was agreed to; the German demand for the whole South-west African coast was met; their claims in the Cameroons and Togoland also had to be conceded. By that time, of course, Bismarck had discovered how popular an anti-British colonial policy was and, although he kept a careful eye upon his French 'allies' throughout the months of his *entente* with Paris, he was confident that, whenever he pressed hard enough, the British government would give way.

The crux of the matter, as Gladstone informed Derby in December 1884, was that Germany could do 'extraordinary mischief to us at our one really vulnerable point, Egypt'.[54] Thus, although the Cabinet's resentment of Bismarck's 'blackmail' and the colonial pressure for counter-measures were reaching their high point at the turn of the year, those factors could not outweigh the Liberal administration's desperate need to buy Berlin's goodwill. Already split from top to bottom over Egypt, Ireland and domestic affairs, Gladstone and his colleagues shrank from a prolonged quarrel with a Bismarck who held most of the trump cards. Within a few months, moreover, the Chancellor's hand was strengthened still further. On 5 February, the fall of Khartoum and the death of Gordon was made known; and in the outcry and confusion that followed Gladstone was obviously telling the truth when he admitted to the Commons 'that the difficulties of the case have passed entirely beyond the limits of such political and military difficulties as I have known in the course of an experience of half a century'.[55] Yet there was worse to come. On 21 February, Russian troops established themselves at the head of the Zulficar Pass, threatening not only Afghanistan but also the security of India. The Anglo-Russian war, which Europe had expected for over two decades, was in sight and it appeared to be a virtual certainty when London received news on 8 April of an Afghan defeat by the Russians at Penjdeh.[56]

Hard pressed, as it seemed, all over the globe, the Liberal government could no longer sustain the objections of the various parts of the British Empire to Bismarck's imperial claims: the stiffening tendency of the turn of the year soon was replaced by alarm at the greater predicaments. When the Chancellor's son arrived in London in early March to emphasise 'how unpleasant we could make ourselves',[57] the surrender was virtually complete. 'It is really impossible to exaggerate the importance of getting out of the way the bar to the Egyptian settlement', Gladstone urged, '. . . as, if we cannot wind up at once these small colonial controversies, we shall, before we are many weeks older, find to our cost.'[58] On the same day, Australian wishes about the New Guinea border were overruled in favour of Germany, and New Zealand's aspirations in the Pacific were soon checked with the explanation of the need to acknowledge 'the good claims of a great friendly power'.[59] The Fiji land claims, too, were settled in Germany's favour; and the alarm of the Sultan of Zanzibar, and local British interests, at the announcement of a German East African protectorate during that month did not cause Whitehall to alter its priorities. Its gaze in these days was not upon Kilimanjaro or Apia, but upon Kabul and Khartoum, and still more upon St Petersburg, Berlin and Toulon.

'If Germany is to become a colonizing power, all I say is "God speed her!" She becomes our ally and partner in the execution of the great purposes of Providence for the advantage of mankind.'[60] Although Gladstone uttered these words to the Commons only a few days after Herbert Bismarck had been repeating his father's threats, it is probable that the Prime Minister meant what he said. For virtually all other members of the British government, however, the widespread German annexations were agreed to reluctantly, for *negative* rather than positive motives. Few if any of them felt that Germany should have no colonies at all, and some ministers thought that this would be a good thing in principle, for Berlin would then be more dependent upon the friendship of the

181

greatest seapower, whilst the self-governing colonies (wary of this new neigh-bour) might well be more deferential towards London. Against this, however, there was the British Cabinet's wish to placate their own merchants and the self-governing colonies; their suspicion that Bismarck was seeking to discredit a Liberal government; and their dislike, and hurt pride, at being blackmailed and humiliated. Yet such sentiments also need to be measured against their belief that they required German support to counter the far more serious threats posed by France and Russia.

It was France, after all, which was leading the opposition to Britain's Egyptian policy, and counter-attacking in many other parts of the globe; whose anglophobia and sensitivity to overseas disputes was causing even the cool-headed Lyons to fear that a collision somewhere might escalate into war;[61] and whose fast-expanding fleet had produced a naval scare in Britain, forcing the government by December 1884 to ask for a further £5½ million for new warship construction. Even this threat was not as alarming as the crisis with Russia over Penjdeh in the following spring: the panic on the stock market, the vote of extraordinary credits, the occupation of Port Hamilton and other preparations for war, could not but remind the British Cabinet of how small scale, by comparison, Bismarck's demands were. Germany was a nuisance, but Russia was the traditional enemy, and France a possible foe: no one in Whitehall yet thought of the possibility of an Anglo-German war. The same was true, incidentally, at the *Wilhelmstrasse*; in the autumn of 1884, Bismarck had talked to the French ambassador about a maritime combination against Britain, a sort of up-dated League of Armed Neutrality – but such an invention was simply intended as a bluff to increase the pressure upon London. There was no real chance of any conflict, the Chancellor admitted: the English would be compelled to bargain because of their diplomatic weakness in Egypt.[62]

The British government's attitude towards German colonisation was shared, by and large, by the press and public opinion. At times, the newspaper 'war' had seemed to indicate that relations between the two peoples had seriously deteriorated. Ampthill's last private letter to Granville captures his personal anxiety about this trend:

> The 'Times' lectures Bismarck for his 'passing fit of ill-humour' – the 'Norddeutsche Allgemeine' replies that the 'passing fit may become eternal as regards England' – the 'National Zeitung' thinks Germany strong enough to disregard English annexations and take what she pleases in Africa – whilst the 'Standard' proposes 'to return blow for blow'![63]

Much of this abuse on the British side occurred, however, when it appeared likely that Bismarck was teaming up with the French to undermine their countrymen's trade in the Niger and Congo basins; and when the Berlin conference secured the first region for Britain and ensured that free trade was to prevail in the second, the tone of the newspapers modified. For the British press, as for the Cabinet, it was difficult to spend too much time abusing the Germans when other powers posed a greater danger. *The Pall Mall Gazette*, just then beginning its series of alarmist articles on 'The Truth about the

Navy', found it necessary in August 1884 to warn the Foreign Office for its dilatory handling of Germany's requests and to refer to 'the good relations which have existed, which now exist, and which always must exist between the German Empire and the British Empire'. The *Standard*, concerned about rumours of a continental combine against Britain, was also conciliatory towards Germany.[64] All this is not to say that British newspapers kept quiet when reports arrived of fresh German gains in Africa and the Pacific, or of the anglophobic utterances in the German press. Yet the dissonance was, as always, relative. Radical, pro-free trade journals had no real wish to prolong a verbal feud with the German press, and Conservative papers, while sympathising with the cries of the self-governing colonies, preferred to lay most of the blame for these setbacks at Gladstone's door.

In commercial circles, too, the founding of a German overseas empire was not badly received. The Chambers of Commerce, which had taken little real interest in Africa, China and the Pacific as markets in the 1860s and 1870s, had been forced by the trade depression and by the coming of protectionist tariffs in Europe and the USA to give much more attention to those regions by the early 1880s. Consequently, the colonial scramble – with the prospect of these newly annexed territories also being surrounded by discriminatory tariffs – caused the Chambers to campaign loudly for Foreign Office assistance. The fact that, at the Berlin West Africa conference, Germany (in contrast to France and Portugal) showed a preference for free trade in all colonial territories came as a great relief; and, as one scholar has noted, it accounts for 'the relative indifference of the principal British Chambers of Commerce towards German colonialism'.[65] As Granville himself put it, 'We would certainly be happy [about German colonisation], but it is quite different with the French, for wherever they colonise they introduce high tariffs, up to 50%, and thereby damage our trade.'[66]

The one notable exception to this general British acceptance of German colonisation lay in the tropics: there the rough-handed methods used to extend Germany's influence in, say, East Africa or Samoa were heartily disliked by British missionaries, by certain British trading interests and by 'sub-imperialists' in Zanzibar, the Cape and New Zealand.[67] In due course, these agitations were going to become more important, especially when taken up by British politicians and newspapers which favoured the cause of Imperial Federation. In later years also, it was going to be remembered how Bismarck had ungenerously taken advantage of Britain's many other difficulties to get his own way during the colonial quarrels of 1884–5. At this time, however, the attention of imperialist circles within Britain was chiefly concentrated upon the threat to the Mediterranean route, the defence of India and the strength of the navy. Germany, by contrast, could be regarded as a nation which, although brusque in its diplomatic methods and less congenial than Britain in its internal and social arrangements, was well worth cultivating as a counterpoise to the really 'hungry' powers of the world.

# CHAPTER 11

# Bismarck, Salisbury and the Problem of an Anglo-German Alliance (1885–9)

The final, and most serious of the foreign policy crises which Gladstone's second administration had had to face was the Russian defeat of the Afghans at Penjdeh. During the period of acute Anglo-Russian tension which followed, most observers thought that war was unavoidable. Only in September, three months after Salisbury had taken over as Prime Minister and Foreign Secretary, was an agreement respecting the Afghan-Russian border signed, bringing the two great Asian powers away – for the time being, at least – from the brink of war.[1] With regard to Anglo-German relations, as we have seen, the crisis simply re-emphasised the diplomatic weakness of the British government and the necessity of subordinating its interests in Africa and the Pacific to the securing of German goodwill. It also offered Gladstone's Cabinet an excuse to withdraw from the Sudan, although it remained impossible to do the same in Egypt: indeed, by agreeing to the Franco-German proposals of March 1885 to maintain that country's finances under the international *Caisse de la Dette*, on which each of the great powers had a vote, the London government had virtually institutionalised the hold which the Triple Alliance (that is, Bismarck) had over Britain in this critical matter.[2] For two pressing reasons, therefore, the British government was looking for support from a man whom they knew detested their political ideals. Yet it was one further indication of London's foreign policy priorities that, despite Gladstone's private complaints in these months about being 'tortured' by Bismarck over Egypt,[3] the German Kaiser was approached to be the arbitrator in the Afghan boundary settlement.

Although the British government was leaning towards Berlin, the German Chancellor was not as eager to reciprocate. To him, there was a vital difference between supporting Britain against France, and doing the same against Russia. The first came naturally to Bismarck and was only suspended when he believed that he could gain tactical advantages from a temporary Franco-German *entente*: thus, by the early summer of 1885, he was already taking the first steps to distance himself from Paris and to improve his relationship with London, which had given way on all the remaining colonial questions. This

184

about-turn was caused partly by the French themselves, for Ferry had now been replaced by Freycinet, who seemed to be less eager about Bismarck's embraces, more quarrelsome over Franco-German disputes in West Africa, more willing to reach an arrangement with Britain over Egypt, and patently disturbed lest an Anglo-Russian war leave Germany dominant on the continent. Furthermore, the Chancellor might have feared (as Holstein suspected) that the probable death of the Kaiser in the near future would make it necessary to improve Anglo-German relations if he wished to stay in office.[4]

The prospect of assisting the British against Russia over the Afghan dispute was quite another matter to Bismarck. On ideological and personal grounds alone, he had no wish to favour Gladstone and rebuff the Tsar. An even more compelling calculation, however, was the military one. As the Chancellor could clearly perceive, the *Dreikaiserbund* – with its mutually agreed abstention from unilateral action in the Balkans – would not long satisfy expansionist circles in Russia unless their energies could be diverted into another channel; and nothing was more suitable for this purpose than an Anglo-Russian entanglement in central Asia. 'If the Russian army has nothing to do in Asia, it will make itself busy on its western borders', Bismarck reminded the Kaiser.[5] Bernhard von Bülow, at this time attached to the St Petersburg embassy, was actually hopeful of an Anglo-Russian conflict; Holstein thought it 'a great misfortune for Germany' that war had been avoided; Prince Wilhelm of Prussia wrote a number of inflammatory letters to the Tsar, urging him forward and even giving details of British military dispositions; and some right-wing German newspapers openly encouraged Russia to take what she wanted in Asia.[6]

Bismarck's own thoughts on the question of war were more complex. At the very least, a state of Anglo-Russian tension in Asia was always desirable, for that enhanced Germany's diplomatic position in general and eased her eastern border defence problem in particular. By extension, an actual war over Afghanistan could be reckoned to weaken both powers, but perhaps especially Russia, whose financial resources were not large. Yet this also contained two possible disadvantages. The first was that the British, unable to answer the Russian challenge effectively in the mountain passes of Afghanistan, would riposte with a naval thrust into the Black Sea – in other words, with a return to their Crimean War strategy, which not only implied a defiance of the neutrality of the Straits but might also have repercussions in the Balkans or at Vienna. Fearful of convulsions in eastern Europe, Bismarck had no hesitation in agreeing to the Russian request of April 1885 that pressure be put upon the sultan to resist by force any British attempt to enter the Black Sea.[7] In so doing, the Chancellor was openly confirming that the maintenance of the *Dreikaiserbund* had clear priority over any regard for British feelings.

Bismarck's second fear related to the reverse possibility: that, instead of a dangerous escalation of an Anglo-Russian war, the two rivals would sit down and come to a far-reaching colonial *entente*. Unlike his clumsier successors, who were blithely to assume that an alliance between 'the bear and the whale' was out of the question, the Chancellor was always sensitive to this possibility. The fact that the Russian ambassador in London, Staal, was engaged in intensive negotiations with the British government throughout May for a settlement of the boundary dispute was thus a matter of some concern to Bismarck:

> the idea of an Anglo-Russian alliance [suggested by certain voices] is entertained by the Pan-Slavist party, whose policy includes war with Austria and later on with Germany. This alliance also forms part of Gladstone's programme, as declared in the House of Commons. Should it be realised, with its pretended Christian and anti-Turkish, but in reality pan-Slavic and radical tendencies, the possibility would be open that this alliance could if necessary be strengthened at any time by the addition of France, should the Anglo-Russian policy meet with German resistance. It would constitute the basis for a coalition against us, of which nothing could be more dangerous to Germany.[8]

If, therefore, these two rivals were anxious to avoid an open conflict, probably nothing would strengthen that tendency more than the knowledge that Berlin was gleefully anticipating a war between them. This meant that, with the exception of his diplomatic intervention at Constantinople, Bismarck was determined to sit still. Germany could neither press Russia forward, nor hint that she should compromise with England, Bismarck warned Wilhelm, for Russia would be suspicious in either case.[9]

The fall of Gladstone's government in June 1885 did not lead to any immediate change in Anglo-German relations. In Berlin's assessment, the Tories were less likely to negotiate a Russian *entente*, but more inclined to consider forcing the Straits: which made it all the more necessary for the German government to retain its sphinx-like pose. Hence the various approaches from London during that summer and autumn for actions which could be interpreted as anti-Russian – and these ranged from the request for Bismarck's mediation over Penjdeh, through the notion of a joint Anglo-German guarantee of Persia's integrity, to Sir Philip Currie's mention of 'an alliance in the fullest sense of the term' – were all either ignored or politely declined by the Chancellor.[10] However welcome a Salisbury administration might personally be, and especially one which seemed so manifestly willing to buy Germany's goodwill by colonial concessions, this could never be as important to Bismarck as the preservation of good Russo-German relations. Furthermore, the minority status of the Conservative government in the House of Commons meant that it could be turned out of office at any time, so that it would have been foolish for Bismarck to place any great hopes upon a close Anglo-German friendship. What *was* permissible was German diplomatic support for the British in Egypt – at the usual price, of course, and with the further calculation in Bismarck's mind that it would keep the two Western powers divided.

This position of diplomatic impregnability, which Bismarck had secured and anxiously maintained since the restoration of the *Dreikaiserbund* and which had given him such a strong hand during the Anglo-German colonial quarrels, began to crumble after September 1885, when the Eastern Question broke out anew with the unification of Eastern Roumelia to Bulgaria. Whereas the Russians expressed their fury at the ingratitude of Prince Alexander, the Austrians were delighted with this new check to panslavic ambitions, and even the British, who at first disapproved of the union, soon came to see that a 'big Bulgaria' would suit their own interests.[11] If murmurs of support for Alexander were uttered in Vienna and London, the sounds emanating from Friedrichsruh were of anger and disgust. Bulgaria, so far as Bismarck was concerned, was a Russian sphere of influence – for which reason he had fought so bitterly against the proposed marriage of Prince Alexander to the Kaiser's granddaughter. Now, just as that danger had been temporarily suspended, an even greater one was occurring because of the Austro-Hungarian wish to exploit Russia's discomfort and because the Serbs, Greeks and other Balkan peoples would all be seeking compensation, thus spreading the original crisis. Even at the Skierniwice meeting of the three emperors in 1884, it had been clear that the fundamental Austro-Russian antagonism could not be erased by Bismarckian appeals to monarchical solidarity, and it was going to be extraordinarily difficult to hold back Vienna if the Russians marched into Bulgaria. Yet an Austro-Russian war would not last long before Germany was dragged in, however reluctantly, to save her southern neighbour.

To the Chancellor, a war with Russia was the height of folly. 'We can gain nothing which we need from a war with Russia', he told Wilhelm I, 'and against that, the sacrifices which we would have to make even for a victorious conflict are incalculable, quite apart from the Polish question which it would bring to life again.'[12] It was, therefore, absolutely vital to warn the Austrians that Germany would not lift a finger to assist the Bulgarians in their resistance to Russia. If anyone had to bear the brunt of Russian hostility, it must be the British, who should be encouraged to reassume Disraeli's forward policy and warned that, if they didn't, the central powers would not prevent Russia from taking even Constantinople. England had to take her own chestnuts out of the fire, and the fact that Salisbury (under pressure from Queen Victoria) was now making noises on behalf of Prince Alexander was all to the good. If forceful diplomacy by London served to keep the latter in Bulgaria, then he would be, Bismarck thought, 'an apple of discord between England and Russia'; and that in turn would frustrate any prospects of an Anglo-Russian agreement, 'which is for us at any time a danger and would be an even greater one with the adhesion of France, if she became a monarchy again'.[13] This encouragement of an Anglo-Russian quarrel might, of course, lead to a war between those two powers; but as the Baden minister in Berlin discovered when he visited the *Auswärtiges Amt*, 'of all the possible complications that would be considered the least evil'.[14]

For the first year or more of the Bulgarian crisis, Bismarck's policy looked as if it was succeeding. In August 1886, however, the intrigues of Russian agents finally forced Alexander's deposition and provoked loud protests in both London and Vienna. By November of that year, Russo-Bulgarian relations seemed strained to breaking point, and influential Hungarians like Tisza and Andrassy were declaring that Russian action against Bulgaria 'would not be admissible'.[15] This, in turn, infuriated not merely the Panslav circles in Russia but also the Tsar. To make matters worse, in the latter half of 1886 certain circles in France appeared to be affected by a revanchist passion; and, just as the French chauvinists looked with hope towards Russia, so the Panslavs were urging upon the Tsar the rejection of Giers' pro-German foreign policy and the conclusion of a Franco-Russian alliance. A war on two fronts, from which Germany could gain nothing, was now a distinct possibility.

By the beginning of 1887, in other words, the Bismarckian diplomatic system was under question – and not merely from without, but from within. The greater part of the German press, including those nationalistic papers which usually supported his foreign policy, were responding to the Panslav attacks upon Germany and voicing their disagreement with the Chancellor's pro-Russian stance. The General Staff, too, was highly alarmed at what it believed were the worsening military prospects: if early in the year it was concentrating its attention chiefly upon the French threat, then by that autumn it was actually pressing for a pre-emptive strike with Austria-Hungary against Russia. Moreover, it was being supported in this by Prince Wilhelm, who had freed himself from his former Bismarckian tutelage and gravitated into the 'war' camp of Waldersee; and it was being further encouraged (although secretly) by Holstein at the *Auswärtiges Amt*, who was urging the Austrians to take a firm stand against Russia.[16] Finally – and of quite substantial importance – the Russo-German political relationship was now very seriously affected by their growing tariff war and by the economic rivalries consequent upon the German exploitation of Russia's relative 'underdevelopment'.[17]

Under such circumstances, Bismarck's achievements in 1887 were altogether remarkable, especially in view of his own deteriorating health. He did not succumb to the pressures to go to war. Instead, the French 'threat' was utilised in traditional style, being presented as the chief justification for a new military bill which he laid before the Reichstag; and when that body, with its Catholic-Progressive-Particularist majority which he so detested, threw out the measure, he was able to mount an electoral propaganda campaign which ruined the left-Liberals for ever.[18] Externally, too, he gained benefit from adversity. On the one hand, he used the dangers in western and eastern Europe to prolong and reshape the Triple Alliance to the satisfaction of the Italians; and he manoeuvred behind the scenes to bring about the Mediterranean *ententes* between Britain, Italy and Austria-Hungary. On the other hand, whilst privately calculating that these blocs would deter both Paris and St Petersburg from aggressive action, he hastened to forestall Russia's resentment and to keep her out of the embraces of France by signing the secret 're-insurance treaty' with the Tsarist government. By pushing others forward in Germany's place, by seeking to divide and divert the attention of political enemies and by creating a complicated system of open and secret alliances which neutralised each other, Bismarck sought to remain the master of Europe's destinies.[19] If at all possible, a great European war had to be avoided; if that was impossible, Germany would certainly not fight alone.

In this elaborate strategy, Great Britain now occupied an increasingly important role. After nearly six years of trying to keep the island state diplomatically isolated from the continental powers, the Chancellor was forced to alter his policy and to get her ever more committed, first of all to Germany's allies, and then ultimately to Germany herself. However, the pace of this conversion was both slow and erratic: on many occasions over the next four years, Bismarck was to express his disgust at Britain's hesitant and unreliable stance; at other times, he himself wished to play down the Anglo-German relationship out of a fear of upsetting Russia. In the first fifteen months following the revolution in Eastern Roumelia, Bismarck's aim was limited to pushing Britain forward as the chief defender of Bulgarian independence, thereby acting as a lightning-conductor for Russian resentment; yet this was much harder to achieve than it had been in the late 1870s, which was partly a reflection of the general post-Disraelian attitude towards Balkan affairs in Britain, but chiefly a consequence of the weakness of successive administrations during the Home Rule crisis.[20]

By early in 1887, the prospects of tempting the British into a more definite commitment were increasing. The patriotic revival in France appeared to be directed as much against London as against Berlin and, in addition to the Egyptian sore, Anglo-French relations were strained by disagreements over the New Hebrides, Morocco and Newfoundland. Moreover, reports from London and Rome suggested that Salisbury would not be averse to some form of arrangement with Italy to preserve the *status quo* in the Mediterranean. This news was only a small step forward to Bismarck, but well worth encouraging. It would satisfy Italian anxieties concerning its defencelessness against French naval assaults: even a sober assessment (by General Caprivi, later in 1887) forecast the overwhelming of the Italian and Austro-Hungarian navies – without Germany being able to do anything about it – unless the British Mediterranean fleet entered the fray.[21] It would also assist Bismarck, then seeking to renew the Triple Alliance, in his own efforts to persuade the Austrians to look somewhat less suspiciously upon their Italian allies. An Anglo-Italian arrangement would not only cause the French to think twice about going to war, but it might also prove the first step in drawing Britain into a firm policy of maintaining the *status quo* in the Balkans, thus easing Austro-Hungarian anxieties on the one hand and deterring the Russians on the other. Furthermore, although Bismarck did not mention it to Vienna or London, Germany could then avoid being thrust directly against Russia; and could, indeed, assure the Tsar that Berlin would not lift a finger if it was thought necessary to take either Bulgaria or Constantinople.

As the year 1887 unfolded, therefore, the British connection became of ever-greater importance to Bismarck, and perhaps the more so *after* he had made his secret treaty with Russia in June. For the fact was that the Chancellor, despite his determination to maintain the 'wire' to St Petersburg, was in no way as russophile as critics like Waldersee and Holstein imagined and he was privately anxious to keep all panslavic ambitions in check; hence, within a short while of pledging Germany's support to the Tsar, he was encouraging the Italians and Austrians to come to a further and much firmer agreement to defend the integrity of Turkey; and then, predictably, employing all his diplomatic skills in tempting the British government to become the third guarantor. When, following this encouragement, the so-called Second Mediterranean Agreement was accepted by the British Cabinet in December 1887, Bismarck could be content with the reflection that it was 'more nearly an alliance with a group of Great Powers than any Great Britain had ever made in time of peace'.[22] This having been achieved, the Chancellor could scuttle back to the Russians, assuring them once again that he would not oppose their annexation of Bulgaria. With one hand, he waved the Russians forward; but with his other hand, he secretly ensured that there would be sufficient opposition to make them hesitate about moving at all.[23]

There was one further reason why, by the late 1880s, the German Chancellor looked towards London. His entire strategy was postulated upon the assumption that by creating a complex system of checks and balances he could maintain the peace – on Germany's terms, as ever. But the alternative possibility also had to be faced, and a contingency plan formulated lest Germany actually was attacked by France and Russia. In late 1888 and early 1889, this could no longer be regarded as outside the bounds of reality. Boulanger, dismissed from the army, had now diverted all his energies into mobilising a nationalist revival which threatened not only to overthrow the French government but to vent itself against Germany and Italy. To a certain extent, this demagoguery would cool the Franco-Russian relationship, but there were substantial pressures in the other direction. The panslavic press was keeping up its assault upon Germany, which it correctly recognised to be the chief obstacle to the realisation of Russia's aims. The economic antagonism between the two countries had gone from bad to worse, and the ban placed by the German government upon the acceptance of Russian securities – the so-called *Lombardverbot* of November 1887 – was causing the Russian government to turn instead to the Paris market.[24]

Neither this, nor (had the Germans known of it) the secret Russian orders at this time for the new French rifle, constituted a Franco-Russian alliance *per se*; and, although the new Kaiser, Wilhelm II, and the General Staff expected some aggressive act soon on the part of Russia, St Petersburg was still behaving cautiously. The real source of alarm concerned what Russia would do if – as seemed much more likely – France and Germany were engaged in a war, arising perhaps from an Italo-French conflict. In the lengthy negotiations surrounding the Re-insurance Treaty in 1887, Alexander III had persistently declined to promise that Russia would abandon France, just in the same way as Bismarck refused to abandon Austria-Hungary. Thus, it seemed quite possible that, however a war in the West began, the Russian government could not tolerate the crushing of France as it had in 1870–1. This was, moreover, increasingly the assumption of the German General Staff, in part because it feared that it would be difficult to achieve a swift victory against France's formidable border defences and therefore preferred to turn eastwards first and try to knock Russia out of the war. Although Bismarck always claimed that Germany's role was to sit still during a Balkan war and to concentrate instead upon her French foe, the indications were that a two-front war was perhaps unavoidable.[25] In such altered circumstances, he thought it prudent by early in 1889 to make the last of his famous 'alliance offers' to Britain. The Chancellor had come a long way since his assertions, three or four years earlier, that the British were a *quantité négligeable* in European politics.

Bismarck's proposal for an open Anglo-German alliance, to last for a fixed number of years and to be directed ostensibly against France, was turned down, politely but firmly, by the British Prime Minister. To understand the reasons for this it is necessary to examine the evolution of the British government's policy towards Germany since the formation of the first Salisbury administration in 1885. From the beginning, two themes above all others dominated the minds of the Prime Minister and the small group of colleagues with whom he consulted about external policy. The first was the chronic strategical weakness of the British Empire in the face of widespread challenges during the late 1880s. Quarrels with the United States in the Western hemisphere, over such disparate matters as the Bering Sea seal fisheries and the Sackville West affair, suggested that Anglo-American relations were still cool – and might, indeed, worsen.[26] The steady increase in French animosity towards Britain, something which the Conservative government had not had to face in the years 1874–80, meant that, unless they were prepared to abandon Egypt, little could be done to improve the Anglo-French relationship. Moreover, being the second imperial power, France could make herself unpleasant across the globe. Colonial disputes, however, paled into insignificance compared with the threat France posed in the Channel and Mediterranean, primarily because of widespread British unease about the weakness of the Royal Navy; could its obsolescent ships hold the Mediterranean route, protect British maritime commerce from the fast French raiders and, above all else, ensure that there was no possibility of a cross-Channel invasion? By 1888, indeed, both the press and prominent politicians were anxiously discussing the chance of a 'bolt from the blue'. France, conceded Salisbury, 'is, and always must remain Britain's greatest danger', simply because it was the only foreign power which could threaten the homeland.[27]

To many other Britons, especially those concerned with the defence of India, the Russian threat was equally great. The occupation of Merv and Penjdeh in 1884–5 was the culmination of a long phase of Tsarist expansionism through Turkestan, and the expectation both in London and Simla was that the very borderlands of India itself would soon be penetrated from the north; and while it would be difficult to defend that vast region in any case, the greatest fear (as General Roberts put it) was that 'the first disaster would raise throughout Hindustan a storm, compared with which the troubles of 1857 would be insignificant'.[28] Worse still, the traditional riposte of sending British forces into the Black Sea seemed, after 1885 at least, no longer feasible. Instead, there was a growing possibility that Russia herself would be able to gain control of Constantinople soon, thereby not only becoming invulnerable to British attack but also posing a threat to the vital system of imperial communications which ran through the Mediterranean. Moreover, Russia was now constructing a very sizeable fleet which, if ever joined with the French navy, could well force the British to withdraw altogether from that sea. In the words of the Director of Military Intelligence of April 1887, 'The countries with which we are most liable to go to war are France and Russia, and the worst combination which we have any reason to dread is an alliance of France and Russia against us.'[29]

Since these threats were increasing, rather than diminishing, throughout the 1880s, it was to be expected that the British government would incline towards the Triple Alliance, hoping to find in it the much-needed counterpoise. Nevertheless, the forces which pushed Salisbury *against* too close a commitment to the central powers were also very strong. The first was the sheer insecurity of the government's tenure in office, with the crumbling of the two-party system that seemed to be taking place by the mid-1880s: uncertain of whether he might be Prime Minister on the day following, Salisbury could hardly indulge in a recasting of British foreign policy. This, together with Britain's military weakness and diplomatic isolation, put a premium upon caution and non-commitment. When, in August 1886, the queen urged swift British action to counter the Russian-inspired *coup* against Prince Alexander, Salisbury could only reply by listing the disadvantages under which Great Britain laboured. The Cabinet, he concluded, was 'making bricks without straw. Without money, without any strong land force, with an insecure tenure of power, and with an ineffective agency, they have to counterwork the efforts of three Empires, who labour under none of these disadvantages.'[30] Five months later, his pessimism remained:

> The prospect is very gloomy abroad, but England cannot brighten it. Torn in two by a controversy which almost threatens her existence, she cannot in the present state of public opinion interfere with any decisive action abroad. The highest interests would be risked here at home, while nothing effective could be done by us to keep the peace on the Continent.[31]

Here was evidence, indeed, of the influences of domestic affairs upon foreign policy; yet Salisbury's reaction was not that one could overcome such problems by appeals to nationalist sentiment *à la* Bismarck, but that Britain's external policy would have to be more reticent than ever.

In actual fact, this advocacy of caution was expressed just as Salisbury was about to take the first tentative – but non-committal and secret – step towards the Triple Alliance, in the form of the Mediterranean Agreement with Italy of February 1887. Nevertheless, throughout this period he remained acutely aware that the Conservative Party was in a minority in the House of Commons, and depended upon the goodwill of the Liberal-Unionists to survive. Whereas this uneasy coalition was relatively unanimous in its opposition to Gladstone's Irish policy, and could agree upon such things as the Naval Defence Act, it was likely to come apart if there was any move towards a fixed military commitment on the continent. The older Liberal traditions of sympathy for the French Republic, dislike of Austria-Hungary and of 'Bismarckism', and, above all, non-entanglement in the European alliance system were still strong.

Faced with these external problems, there were one or two voices advocating a complete break with the traditional assumptions about what constituted Britain's 'vital interests'. Randolph Churchill, for example, urged throughout these years that a deal should be done with Russia, whereby the Indian empire would be protected in exchange for a British abandonment of Constantinople; at the same time, Egypt would be firmly held, and France offered no concessions; and Germany and Austria-Hungary would be invited to protect the Balkans themselves, if they so wished.[32] From the St Petersburg embassy, another controversial figure, Morier, repeatedly pushed for an Anglo-Russian *entente*, with its twin attractions of preserving India and of depriving his great personal enemy Bismarck of his role as 'omniscient and omnipotent arbitrator'.[33] Not surprisingly, the Bismarck circle detested and feared Churchill and Morier: both were highly intelligent, ambitious and always willing to countenance an unorthodox policy to achieve their ends, just like the Chancellor himself. They had, therefore, to be combated;[34] although in actual fact Bismarck need not have worried. Whereas Salisbury himself was increasingly doubtful about Britain's ability to resist Russia in the Balkans or at the Straits, he opposed the idea of cutting loose from Austria-Hungary and of abandoning the traditional policy of keeping Constantinople in Turkish hands, since the Russian government could not be trusted.[35] Only the changed global circumstances of the post-Salisburian era could permit the creation of an Anglo-Russian *entente* such as Morier envisaged.

The final factor which inclined the British government against a close understanding with Germany was actually Salisbury himself. His deep and long-lasting distrust of Bismarck has been noted above; and this basic attitude remained unaltered in the Prime Minister's later years despite the tactical necessity of leaning towards Berlin on many occasions. It was not difficult for him to deduce that Bismarck's only answer to the Bulgarian crisis was to push other powers forward to check Russia and to bear the brunt of her resentment – a prospect which did not attract Salisbury at all. Moreover, behind his apprehension that the German government would encourage Russia to move against Constantinople and Bulgaria lay a far deeper fear: that, having succeeded in embroiling his powerful eastern neighbour in a war against an Anglo-Austrian-Italian-Turkish combination, Bismarck would then seize his chance to unleash the German armies upon France. Again and again in Salisbury's private correspondence of this period, such an apprehension is expressed: together with his parallel amazement at the many occasions that the French, instead of realising their danger, appeared to be provoking Britain into a conflict which, in his opinion, would tempt Germany to join with the aim of crushing its Gallic neighbour for ever. An Anglo-French war was, for both personal and political reasons, anathema to Salisbury, but of almost equal gravity would be a further Franco-German war, with its likely outcome of a Germanic domination of west-central Europe.[36]

Salisbury's European policy was, therefore, a complicated one. He had to devise a course which both avoided the isolationism of the Radicals and of 'eccentric' imperialists like Morier, *and* evaded being pushed forward by Bismarck into a conflict with Russia or France unless the latter truly became unavoidable. He had never to admit – and never did admit – that Anglo-French or Anglo-Russian relations had worsened beyond repair; yet he also needed to lean towards Berlin in order to gain diplomatic assistance in the Egyptian question, and to secure a greater measure of support for Austria-Hungary and Italy than he felt Britain alone could give. These were almost impossible requirements and yet, slowly and patiently, Salisbury was to achieve them all.

The main threads of this policy could be seen even in his short-lived first administration, where he sent friendly messages to Berlin and encouraged Currie to repeat those reassurances personally at Friedrichsruh, yet remained on guard against being 'hoodwinked' by the Chancellor; and where he offered assistance to Germany in Zanzibar and the Caroline Islands in the hope of receiving Berlin's support nearer home.[37] During the first six months of his second administration he resumed this stance, offering Germany support in extra-European affairs and requesting the continuance of Bismarck's assistance in the Egyptian question. Salisbury did much less during the Bulgarian crisis of late 1886, however, because a section of the Cabinet did not want Britain to oppose Russia, and because he personally feared what Bismarck would get up to if Britain did. The first Mediterranean Agreement, on the other hand, *was* worth making. It did not, in the Prime Minister's opinion, commit the country to anything; it reassured Italy and Austria-Hungary that Britain was deeply concerned to maintain the *status quo*, made her appear less isolated and gained the approbation of Berlin; yet it excluded any promise of British support in an aggressive war against France – which, Salisbury by April 1887 was beginning to perceive, was probably only being held back by Russian disapproval.[38] Ironically, therefore, the Tsarist colossus which threatened Britain's interests in so many places had to be deterred from a Balkan war for the additional reason that France would not be 'crushed'[39] by Bismarck. Preventing the latter might not seem so important to many Britons, but it obviously was to Salisbury. This was probably in his mind when he declined to make any statement, even to his ambassador in Brussels, about the speculation caused by the 'Diplomaticus' letter in the *Standard* of 4 February 1887, which asserted that Britain would not feel bound to oppose a German military push through Belgium for the purpose of defeating France: for Salisbury then to have made known his own personal views would not only have caused immense diplomatic reverberations but it might have provoked criticism from the Conservative Right, which now strongly disliked French imperial pretensions.[40]

The Egyptian negotiations of 1887 – that is, Drummond Wolff's prolonged efforts at Constantinople to arrange a British withdrawal from Egypt, under certain guarantees – nicely illuminate Salisbury's attitude once again. At first, he favoured such a withdrawal, one of his major motives being that, by restoring Anglo-French relations, it would lessen considerably Britain's reliance upon Berlin and her vulnerability to German 'blackmail' in colonial matters. The bitter resistance of France (assisted by Russia) to the Drummond Wolff mission, together with a whole series of fresh Anglo-French quarrels that summer, inevitably drove Salisbury towards the Triple Alliance again and caused him to muse about 'a silver lining even to the great black cloud of a Franco-German war?'[41] While this setback did not deter the Prime Minister from his patient efforts to settle the affairs of the New Hebrides and the Suez Canal with France late in 1887, his main attention was given to the negotiations leading up to the second Mediterranean Agreement – a more extensive involvement than the first, however much he himself argued that it was in accord with the British traditions of non-commitment.[42] Here, too, Salisbury and his Cabinet were at first deeply suspicious of an agreement to which Bismarck would not adhere formally – and might secretly exploit, to his own advantage – yet they also feared that all further efforts to sustain Turkey's independence from Russia would be futile if Britain did not indicate her willingness to help at this stage. Once again, the connection between the Eastern Question and the Franco-German antagonism weighed heavily in Salisbury's mind:

> I think . . . we are merely rescuing Bismarck's somewhat endangered chestnuts . . . If he can get up a nice little fight between Russia and the three Powers [Britain, Italy, Austria-Hungary], he will have leisure to make France a harmless neighbour for some time to come. It goes against me to be one of the Powers in that unscrupulous game. But a thorough understanding with Austria and Italy is so important to us that I do not like the idea of breaking it up on account of risks which *may* turn out to be imaginery.[43]

Other events in 1888 served only to increase Salisbury's conviction that, however much the French and Russian threats made it necessary for Britain to associate herself with the Triple Alliance, it would be unwise to rely absolutely upon the benevolence of Germany. The first and most important factor was that the death of Wilhelm I and the seriousness of his son's cancer made the accession of the young Prince Wilhelm of Prussia only a matter of months away; and the latter's allegedly pro-Russian stance in the mid-1880s greatly worried the British Cabinet, one of the major causes of its hesitation before entering into the second Mediterranean Agreement being its apprehension of Wilhelm's 'lively, Russian sympathies'.[44] Although the alteration in the young Kaiser's attitude towards Russia by 1888 came as some relief in London, it also suggested an instability of character. This impression was furthered by a blazing row which Wilhelm had over the Prince of Wales's visit to Vienna in October 1888 – an incident which caused Salisbury to suspect, not for the last time, 'that the Emperor Wilhelm must be a little off his head'.[45] If such events made the British see in Bismarck a stabilising influence – a sentiment nicely captured by Tenniel's *Punch* cartoon showing the aged Daedelus warning the impulsive Icarus against his flight into the sun[46] – the actions of the Chancellor himself did not inspire a great deal more confidence. In the spring of 1888, he had waged open political war against the dying Emperor Friedrich Wilhelm and especially against the empress over the long-running score of the 'Battenberg marriage', threatening immediate resignation and encouraging the right-wing press into further polemics against the 'English influence' – actions which infuriated Queen Victoria and caused Salisbury to reflect 'that friendship with Germany is a more uncertain staff to lean upon than friendship with France'.[47] Furthermore, near the end of 1888, the Bismarck-inspired press launched its famous attack upon Morier's alleged conduct during the Franco-

Prussian War and the resultant verbal duel with that most combative personality could only confirm the British government's dislike of German political methods – as well as provoking expressions of support for Morier in many British newspapers.[48] With all these considerations in mind, it is scarcely surprising that, when Hatzfeldt conveyed Bismarck's alliance offer in January 1889, Salisbury did not display any great enthusiasm although he immediately recognised the importance of the news.

What the Chancellor's real aim was in making this alliance 'bid' Salisbury could not tell, and it has continued to puzzle later historians. A large number of them have argued that Bismarck, knowing full well that constitutional and domestic-political difficulties would prevent Britain from entering into a formal military alliance, simply wished to use the expected negative reply in order to justify his own pro-Russian policy and to cool the ardour of the Waldersee circle for a conflict with Paris and St Petersburg. To other scholars, however, the Chancellor's approach to London was seriously meant, arising as it did from his growing conviction that he could neither appease panslavic ambitions nor persuade Russia to stand aside in a Franco-German war: in which case it behoved him to bring Britain into his alliance system, even if the public announcement of such a treaty would impel St Petersburg to draw even closer towards Paris. Both interpretations, and the variations upon them, can point to supporting evidence.[49] Yet since Bismarck throughout his political career had preferred to keep his options open when seeking to achieve some great aim, it is worth suggesting that on this occasion, too, his tactical position was flexible. If Britain did agree to a public alliance against France for a fixed term of years, it would almost certainly deter even Boulanger from any rash action – which was particularly important at a time when both Germany's small-arms and Britain's battleships were thought to be obsolescent. However, if a war in the West came, and Russia also entered it, Germany would have the odds on her side. If, on the other hand, Britain turned down this confidential German approach, Bismarck would at least know more closely what London's attitude to a continental commitment was, and would act accordingly – by remaining on civil terms with St Petersburg if at all possible, and by seeking once again to divert the energies of France and Russia into the extra-European arena. Since the British refusal was not a public one, however, it was still worthwhile to maintain an appearance of Anglo-German friendship, in colonial and dynastic affairs, for that would keep both the French and Russian governments uncertain and therefore unwilling to provoke Berlin. This explains why he did not react with anger when Salisbury regretfully declared that the alliance offer would have to be left 'on the table, without saying yes or no'.[50]

The Prime Minister's calculations in this affair are somewhat easier to understand than Bismarck's. Given his suspicion of the Chancellor's motives and of German political methods, together with his apprehensions about the 'enormous potency' of Wilhelm's erratic impulses,[51] Salisbury's reaction to the alliance offer was bound to be circumspect. More particularly, the fact that the proposed arrangement was directed ostensibly against France only served to confirm his long-standing feeling that Germany was out to crush that country, an enterprise in which he believed Britain should take no part. The Chancellor (perhaps hoping to get British support in his clash with the United States over Samoa) had also referred to the threat posed by Washington – but that hardly helped his cause, since London was even less keen upon fighting Americans than Frenchmen; and it could hardly fail to notice that Bismarck made no mention of opposing Russia. Holstein, perhaps, was the more realistic in wondering whether Germany would have to offer to guarantee India, but there is no sign that the Chancellor ever thought in such terms.[52] Furthermore, Salisbury foresaw that such an alliance would produce a domestic-political row of the first order: the queen was, to say the least, going to be cool to the idea; and the Liberal-Unionist members of the coalition would also be disinclined – Hartington, for example, held that a German alliance was at the moment 'inopportune', which effectively killed the idea.[53]

In addition to these traditional British motives for avoiding a German alliance, there was also the short-term disquiet felt in London at Crispi's belligerent attitude towards France in 1888–9. Bismarck, similarly worried that the Franco-Italian antagonism should explode into open war, was obviously eager to ensure British support for the Italians (and for the entire Triple Alliance, should that conflict escalate); but it was precisely this prospect of being dragged into a war against France on behalf of Crispi's ambitions which reinforced the British desire to keep on friendly *but uncommitted* terms with Rome and Berlin. Rather than deter France and Russia by committing Britain into a fixed-alliance bloc and then being bound willy-nilly to the incalculable actions of its members, therefore, the British government elected instead to increase the Royal Navy. In March 1889, just as the German alliance offer was being left 'on the table', the Naval Defence Act (which was planned to give the Royal Navy maritime superiority over the combined Franco-Russian fleets) was announced. In the same month, the reluctant queen was finally persuaded by Salisbury to invite the overjoyed Kaiser to visit England that summer. Both the naval increases, and the royal visit, had been urged upon the Prime Minister by Berlin and could now be represented by him as pro-German gestures; but what they really indicated was that, whilst cherishing good outward relations with Germany, the British government preferred to maintain a free hand.

Nothing more was to be heard of an Anglo-German alliance while Bismarck remained Chancellor, and this tacit agreement to lean towards each other without formalising their relationship probably suited both him and Salisbury: they gained, so it seemed, the respect which Paris and St Petersburg paid them out of a fear for an accord *à quatre*, without suffering the domestic-political and diplomatic disadvantages which might result from a formally proclaimed alliance. Moreover, by April 1889 the Boulangist movement had collapsed and, although Crispi's actions were still regarded with concern, it did appear as if the prospect of a European war had temporarily receded. In the Bulgarian issue, too, no fresh developments occurred, which kept German-Russian relations in fair outward shape. This was not, of course, the attitude of those critics inside Germany who were still pressing for a tougher line against St Petersburg; but it was the internal dispute over the politics of the *Kartell* and

197

the Socialist law which occupied most of Bismarck's formidable energies in the latter part of 1889 and into 1890.[54] Apart from a slight diplomatic skirmish in June 1889 over whether Britain or Germany should take the first step in ensuring that Austria-Hungary did not succumb to Russian pressure in the Balkans, little else of note occurred relating to the *European* aspects of this five-year-old 'diplomatic duel' between Bismarck and Salisbury.[55]

The extra-European aspect of the Anglo-German relationship, however, had *not* died away in the late 1880s; in contrast, it became, in the eyes of the British public, more significant than before. Since it was inextricably connected with the way in which Bismarck and Salisbury conducted their continental diplomacy, the colonial policies of the two powers were also affected by this larger political 'duel' which those two statesmen were fighting. The notion advanced by certain historians that Bismarck abandoned his colonial policy some time in 1885 – after the fall of Ferry, or upon the news of the revolution in Eastern Roumelia – would have come as a great surprise to the Sultan of Zanzibar and King Malietoa of Samoa, to the sub-imperialists of Wellington and McKinnon's Imperial British East Africa Company and, last but not least, to the British Foreign Office itself, whose correspondence upon Anglo-German colonial relations continued to grow throughout the latter part of the 1880s. For the fact was that the rivalry between British and German overseas interests formed a very important – although to Bismarck and Salisbury, still secondary – aspect of the overall relationship between the two countries. Since, in addition, it offers fresh material for the debate upon the motives behind the Chancellor's colonial policy in particular and upon imperialism in general, it deserves some scrutiny here.

The high point of the colonial quarrel between London and Berlin was over, admittedly, by the spring of 1885: Germany had secured a colonial empire, Britain had given way on most points, and the issues which remained were being consigned to joint commissions. Such investigations, as viewed from the chancellories of Europe, may have appeared as tidying-up operations; but it was not how they were viewed by those two other elements in the interacting process of imperialism: the local interests, whether they consisted of native chieftains, small trading firms or Australasian and Cape politicians; and the colonial enthusiasts in the metropolis, whether they represented economic interests or were intellectual advocates of a Greater Britain and a Greater Germany. The blunt fact was that imperial expansionism, like the nationalistic movements with which it had so much in common, was not simply a force which could be switched on and off by statesmen at the turn of a tap. Neither Bismarck nor Salisbury, it may safely be surmised, were personally enthusiastic about the ownership of various Pacific islands or the lands to the west of Kilimanjaro; but if other, politically important groups were, then it behoved them also to take an interest in such affairs.

In East Africa, for example, the *Gesellschaft für deutsche Kolonisation* was pressing ahead with its aim of carving out an extensive empire on the mainland opposite Zanzibar; and the Dänhardt brothers, having secured a protectorate over Witu, were also contemplating further expansion towards the Great

Lakes. This twin-pronged drive, especially when executed by such forceful individuals as Peters, led to frequent clashes: with British commercial interests, which were however relatively insignificant until McKinnon's Imperial British East Africa Company received its charter in 1888; with a multitude of local chiefs, who attempted to resist German expansionism; and, most important of all, with the Sultan of Zanzibar.[56] An equally dangerous and even more complex situation existed in Samoa, where the *Deutsche Handels und Plantagen-Gesellschaft* was endeavouring to gain the necessary 'security' for its plantations, and was being opposed both by the Malietoans, British traders and New Zealand adventurers, and by a succession of excitable American consuls.[57]

To Bismarck, the policy which Germany had to adopt was clear. The German firms operating in East Africa and Samoa were not all that powerful, but their economic claims, at least as detailed in the information which was laid before him, could not be disputed; and their activities were being followed by imperialist circles at home, including members of the National Liberal and Free Conservative parties. Consequently, the *Auswärtiges Amt* files for this period are full of requests to a reluctant Admiralty to send cruiser squadrons to overawe the Zanzibari, East African and Samoan opposition, and of instructions to the German consular officials to use their political influence to ensure that German commerce could proceed unhindered. Yet it was also necessary to gain British support for this policy, if only because it was assumed that London's influence over Sultan Barghash and King Malietoa, and over Sir John Kirk and the New Zealand government, would decisively affect the ease with which German aims were secured. It would not, of course, please the British government to have to work for Germany, but that was of little weight: the fact was that, if London desired Berlin's assistance in the critical Egyptian issue, it would have to pay for it by compliance elsewhere. The Bismarckian motto of *Du Ut Des* was never put to more systematic account than in the hints, and sometimes open threats, relayed to the British government in these years about the penalty for resisting Germany's colonial claims.[58]

For the years 1885 to 1888, this Bismarckian assessment of Britain's need to secure Berlin's diplomatic friendship was quite correct. Given the prospect of a possible war with Russia, and the pressing requirement to settle the Egyptian imbroglio, it was absolutely vital to the British government that Germany was also not ranged against them. With his global sense of British external priorities, Salisbury was hardly going to oppose Bismarck on account of the unrewarding coastline of East Africa or the limited economic and strategical prospects of the Samoan Islands. Within months of forming his second administration, he told Malet that British policy was to go along with Germany 'in all matters of secondary importance – indeed in all matters where we have not an imperative interest to the contrary'. As for Samoa and Zanzibar, he informed Randolph Churchill, 'We have no interests in either of those two places – and Germany may do her worst – except so far as we are bound by previous engagements.' Consequently, British consuls in those trouble-spots were warned not to oppose German activities; and the Colonial Office, pressing the claims of New Zealand, was firmly 'sat upon' in the interests of the Prime Minister's *grosse Politik*.[59]

Although Salisbury appeared to be openly dancing to Bismarck's tune, there were certain limits to this policy of diplomatic obeisance. The Prime Minister did not intend, for example, to allow a German annexation of Zanzibar itself, for its loss would be too great a blow to British interests in the Indian Ocean; similarly, he warned off the Germans from the Tongan Islands, for they possessed fine harbours and were too close to Fiji to tolerate another power taking them over. Moreover, even where he gave way – in the East African hinterlands and in Samoa – he assumed that if the Germans allowed a policy of ˌgenuine free trade, then British merchants would be able to profit from it and perhaps even regain their former commercial predominance. What *was* annoying was the incompetence and unscrupulousness of the Germans on the spot: by unfair commercial practices and, more significantly, by provoking widespread indigenous resistance, they 'ruined everybody else's trade at Samoa and Zanzibar'.[60] Even more infuriating was the Bismarckian habit of demanding that pressure be put upon British officials to comply with German aims. The Holmwood case, in particular, where Bismarck threatened to torpedo the Drummond Wolff mission of 1887 unless the consul in question was removed, severely tested Salisbury's patience;[61] and in his private letters he expressed his anger at 'the monstrousness of the demand or the danger we shall incur if we remain exposed to sallies of temper of this kind'.[62] The Bismarckian habit of *chantage*, as Salisbury termed it, was simply one more reason for the Prime Minister's dislike of Berlin. If, therefore, the German government drew the conclusion in these years that Britain's various and unenviable external problems forced her to offer a constant payment of colonial tribute, Salisbury's increasing view was that this dependency relationship made it ever more important to achieve a *modus vivendi* with Russia in Asia and with France in Africa.

In the period 1887–8, this British need to demonstrate support for Germany's colonial enterprises diminished, at first slowly, and then with increasing speed. One reason for this, ironically enough, was the failure of the Drummond Wolff negotiations: now that an agreement upon British withdrawal from Egypt had proved to be impossible, the Prime Minister resolved to stay there to see its finances set in order under Cromer's long-term plan, which was already beginning to bear fruit. Although Britain still faced French opposition to the occupation and also still required the consent of a majority of the powers to introduce new financial measures, there was nevertheless far less urgency to secure Berlin's constant support. Furthermore, the British government was now forced to give much more attention to the protection of the entire Nile valley – which was under threat not merely from the French or King Leopold to the west and south-west, but also from those German expeditions which were pressing towards the Great Lakes. Certain Foreign Office officials had never at any time welcomed the prospect of unchecked German expansionism in East Africa, but now Salisbury and his colleagues were also becoming less receptive to the idea.[63] Yet this stiffening in the Official Mind's reaction to German colonialism might not have counted for much had it not been for that other factor: the growing threat to Germany of a two-front war in Europe, and the crumbling of Bismarck's diplomatic hegemony, which made him wish to draw Britain closer to Berlin. Even during the period when the Chancellor was in a much stronger diplomatic position, he had recognised that there were limits beyond which British tolerance should not be pushed – a perception which his son Herbert and others at the *Auswärtiges Amt* did not have. He had constantly refused to annex Samoa, for example, as distinct from taking stern measures to maintain German interests there; and when the virtual protectorate of the Sultanate of Zanzibar was proposed late in 1886, he had promptly vetoed it with the remark that this was demanding too much from England, whose interests there 'are more important than ours'.[64]

Furthermore, the repeated reverses which German colonial enterprises suffered in the late 1880s caused the Chancellor to become aware of the fragility of his policy and to hope for British assistance; with the USA apparently threatening to take military action over Samoa, it was prudent for Berlin to try to get Britain on to its side; and when a large-scale revolt broke out along the East African coast in 1888, the presence of a British as well as a German naval squadron was a useful way of covering up the original German responsibility for having provoked that unrest. By this stage, it is interesting to note, Salisbury was much more the master of the diplomatic situation, declining to be involved against the United States on the one hand, and actually insisting upon British participation in the East African naval blockade (to frustrate unilateral German actions) on the other.[65] Yet, if Bismarck was keen to secure Britain's friendship – referring to the island state as 'our old and traditional ally' in his Reichstag speech of January 1889, and minuting slightly later that 'At present we need England, if peace is to be maintained'[66] – this was even more the case with those who opposed the Chancellor's 'pro-Russian' policy. In October 1888, in fact, Holstein was writing: 'Our colonial crises lie upon us like a nightmare, and we need England in all places. Our relations with the English government are being most carefully cultivated' – to which efforts he added his own, by seeing Malet three times in one week to emphasise that Salisbury should not 'go too far' to satisfy Germany's colonial wishes if thereby he made himself unpopular with the British public and ran the risk of endangering his position.[67]

This introduces the final factor in the steady tilting of the diplomatic balance from the German to the British side in the late 1880s: namely, the rise of an imperialist sentiment in Britain and in the self-governing colonies which Salisbury had to take into account. If its origins are to be traced to the widespread public unease at the growing threats to Britain's global position, its outward appearance consisted of a demand for a 'forward' policy, for positive government actions to protect what parts of the world were left.[68] Obviously, the greatest alarm was caused by the French and Russian challenges, but certain circles were also agitating against German expansionism as well. The New Zealand press continued to protest about the roughshod German methods in Samoa and, when the first Colonial Conference was held in London to coincide with the queen's jubilee in 1887, Salisbury was very bluntly told of what antipodean opinion thought of his appeasement of France and Germany in the Pacific.[69] In East Africa, moreover, the German moves were regarded with anxiety by a whole variety of pressure groups: by the missionaries in Uganda, and around Lake Nyasa, who campaigned for British protection: by the Imperial British East Africa Company, with such influential friends as Lord Aberdare, Baron Rothschild and Jacob Bright: by empire-builders like Stanley and Harry Johnston, who returned to Britain to expiate upon the untold economic opportunities which beckoned in Africa, and – in Stanley's case – to warn against craven politicians who surrendered such potential El Dorados: and to many (chiefly Tory) newspaper editors, who reported all these facts with relish.[70] Herbert Bismarck, arriving in London in March 1889 to discuss his father's alliance offer and the Kaiser's proposed visit to England, was astonished to find the conversation being constantly turned to East Africa:

> Consistently I met with anxiety lest East African affairs might take a turn likely to excite public opinion here and threaten the existence of the Government. The other questions, some of them far more important, were made less of, but I was obliged to discuss Zanzibar in detail with Chamberlain, Goschen, Rosebery and Lord Salisbury's two Under-Secretaries of State, each for a good hour.[71]

Although Salisbury publicly ridiculed Stanley's speeches, it is also clear that he was far less willing than before to disregard this jingo sentiment; and, when it came to bargaining with the Portuguese or the Germans, it was very convenient for him to refer to the impossibility of making concessions which would offend the national temper. Just how seriously that unruffled, sceptical mind regarded this factor is difficult to judge, but the important thing is that the Germans believed that he was under heavy domestic pressure to stand firm on colonial issues – and the prospect of another Gladstone ministry precisely at the time of the great European crisis of the late 1880s caused shivers at the *Wilhelmstrasse*. During the joint naval blockade along the East African coast, for example, the news that Salisbury's agreement to British participation was 'extremely unpopular in England' made Bismarck uneasy.[72] The Chancellor, the *Auswärtiges Amt* was informed, declares repeatedly 'that a good understanding with England means much more to him than the whole of East Africa; but until now he had assumed that the blockade agreement could not seriously endanger Salisbury's position'.[73] Even a year later, when Boulanger was no more, Bismarck's assessment of the situation was unchanged. 'With regard to the Witu question', Holstein reported, 'His Highness has said that we should conciliate the English where they have, *or think they have*, claims. Salisbury's preservation in office is more important than the possession of Witu.'[74] Consequently, all proposals put forward by Krauel on behalf of the DOAG were immediately rejected by Bismarck on the grounds that they might prejudice 'our good relations with England'.[75]

It was *not* the case, of course, that Germany lacked its equivalent to these British imperialist circles. Karl Peters, in particular, was seeking to play upon the German national consciousness in the same way as Stanley did upon the British; and the attempts by German firms to dominate Samoa or to push inwards from the East African coast in the late 1880s were warmly applauded

202

by many German newspapers and Reichstag deputies. Two things, however, now told against them. In the first place, Bismarck was bitterly disappointed at the trouble which this new German colonial empire had caused him. If he had not expected that these territories would overnight produce a rich economic harvest, he had certainly believed in 1884-5 that they contained a commercial potential which German firms were already beginning to tap. Yet his scheme to run this empire through chartered companies had plainly foundered; the high-handed actions of these interest groups and of the German consuls and administrators had provoked a fierce native resistance, in New Guinea, in South-west Africa, in East Africa, in Samoa and elsewhere, necessitating frequent calls for help from the Admiralty, whose commanders, when they reported upon the causes of such unrest, were usually scathing in their denunciations of these local agents and tended to get on better with the British consuls.[76] What was more, this *furor consularis* threatened to disturb diplomatic relations with other powers; with the equilibrium in Europe altering to Germany's disadvantage by the late 1880s, it was foolhardy to push ahead in Samoa and East Africa if there was a risk, respectively, of an open conflict with the United States, and of provoking British public opinion to turn against Salisbury's pro-German foreign policy.

Because of these two factors, it was Bismarck rather than the British Prime Minister who 'sat upon' imperial enthusiasts now: the German Consul-General to Zanzibar was plainly told 'Listen, Herr Michahelles, I am sick and tired of colonies'; and the agitation of the *Kolonialgesellschaft* for expansion in East Africa was brutally rejected. The Hanse cities were urged by Bismarck to administer the protectorates since the Chancellor was determined that the *Auswärtiges Amt* should no longer have to bother itself with colonial problems – 'The Foreign Office can either get rid of colonies, or get rid of me', he declared. Hamburg's polite refusal to accept these millstones, and the general fact that the big banks and industry had displayed little interest in the German colonies, further infuriated the Chancellor: 'if commerce has no interest in keeping the colonies, then neither have I', he minuted.[77] All this caused great gloom in German colonial circles, which were arguing that, despite the setback encountered overseas, further expansion was still necessary. Instead, here was their great national leader deriding their earlier efforts and actually ordering the German navy to co-operate with the British in preventing Peters from landing in East Africa.

This is all the more striking – at least, if one accepts that the main motive behind Bismarck's imperialism had been to secure electoral support for the government so as to prop up the conservative *status quo*[78] – for the German imperialists whom the Chancellor was now bitterly disappointing consisted predominantly of National Liberals and Free Conservatives, precisely those groups whose loyalty it should have been his overriding aim to preserve; and, in fact, one of the reasons for the disintegration of the *Kartell* in 1889-90 was this disagreement between the Chancellor and the National Liberals (the largest of the parties supporting him after the 1887 election) about the need to defer to British sensibilities in Africa. If, however, one holds that the main determinants in Bismarck's adoption of a colonial policy were the desire to protect what he thought were promising economic interests, the wish to defeat liberalism within Germany and his resentment against 'English influences', it becomes easy to see why he found little reason to be enthusiastic about further acquisitions in the changed circumstances of 1889–90.

Although Samoan affairs were patched up at the Berlin conference of June 1889, the more significant set of problems which had arisen between British and German interests in East-Central Africa was not settled until after the Chancellor's fall and can only be properly understood in the context of the 'New Course' itself. The main tendencies, however, were already clear before then: a certain retreat by the German government in the light of its European problems and despite the protests of its own imperialists; and a certain advance by the British government, in response to public pressures. Although the year 1890 marks a watershed in so many other respects, therefore, it is difficult to argue that any revolutionary alteration occurred in the attitude of the German and British governments in colonial affairs as a consequence of Bismarck's fall.

The Chancellor's demise was, Salisbury confidentially wrote, 'an enormous calamity of which the effects will be felt in every part of Europe'.[79] In making this statement, the Prime Minister was in no way indicating any personal commitment towards the retired Chancellor but simply his apprehension at the course German policy might take when directed by Wilhelm II and his military cronies. Although Bismarck, with his irritability and inclination to blackmail those powers which needed his support, was regarded as untrustworthy, it was also thought unlikely that he would rush willingly into a European war: what the young Kaiser would rush into, it was difficult to say. Moreover, the unruly elements of Europe – from Crispi to the Panslavs – might be tempted into an adventurous policy now that Bismarck no longer controlled German policy. For this reason, and this only, people such as Queen Victoria, Salisbury and certain of his Cabinet colleagues preferred to see the Chancellor remain in power.

Nevertheless, Bismarck's overall impact upon the Anglo-German relationship can only be described in negative terms. What 'Bismarckism' had done was to make every British government from the 1860s to the 1880s, whether Liberal or Conservative, so distrustful of Berlin's real motives in its external policy, and, in many respects, so disapproving of its domestic-political arrangements, that a firm, public and binding Anglo-German alliance was out of the question.[80] Although many individual Britons (especially imperialists) came to admire Bismarck's achievements, the 'Official Mind' only really leant towards Germany in these years for negative reasons, that is, out of concern for the more immediate threats posed to the British Empire by France and Russia. A pro-German policy on the part of the British government in the age of Bismarck took place, in other words, *despite* the Chancellor rather than because of him: which is hardly a resounding accolade for someone who was widely regarded as the greatest statesman Germany had ever produced.

# CHAPTER 12

# The 'New Course' and Colonial Rivalries (1890–6)

In June 1890 the high point of the so-called Anglo-German 'colonial marriage' was reached, when the two governments came to a wide-ranging agreement whereby Germany received Heligoland in exchange for substantial concessions in East Africa and Zanzibar.[1] It was the nearest equivalent, in both its range and its purpose, to the Anglo-French colonial settlement of 1904: yet, whereas the latter marked the beginning of an *entente* which was to grow ever firmer as the years progressed, the Heligoland-Zanzibar treaty was to be followed within a short space of time by mutual disillusionment and distrust. The very fact that, despite the wishes of the German government and of many British Conservatives, an Anglo-German alliance could not be effected in this, arguably the most favourable period for such a step, indicates once again the strength of the forces which kept the two countries apart.

Recent researches have elaborated upon, but not greatly altered our knowledge of the motives and tactics of both sides during the 1890 negotiations. The German government's calculations, in particular, are easily understandable. In the first place, the men of the 'New Course' – Caprivi the Chancellor, Marschall the Foreign Minister, and Holstein – were patently anxious to convince observers inside and outside Germany that the political direction was in secure hands following Bismarck's fall.[2] A successful understanding with Britain would be, Malet observed, 'a feather in the cap of the new Government, while failure would be ascribed to the absence of the master directing mind of Prince Bismarck';[3] and the fact that Salisbury had offered them the island of Heligoland would furnish the necessary evidence that Germany had not lost out in the bargain. This latter judgement was, of course, a subjective one but no less important for being that: Wilhelm, for example, was already keen to obtain Heligoland in the summer of 1889 and had pressed for 'a quicker tempo' in instituting negotiations until Herbert Bismarck and his father advised against such a course at that time;[4] and Caprivi confidentially admitted to the Bundesrat that he had long writhed at the fact that a place so close to the German coast was in foreign hands.[5] He and the Kaiser also believed that the German acquisition of Heligoland would prevent the French from instituting a blockade of the coastline and the new Kiel Canal in a future war. Holding, therefore, that Heligoland was 'the most valuable object' in the negotiations, it was not surprising that Bismarck's successors believed that both their country, and they themselves, would benefit from the arrangement with Britain.

Furthermore, the Kaiser and his entourage were genuinely concerned about the threatening European situation and the need to draw Britain closer to the Triple Alliance: to Holstein and others in the *Auswärtiges Amt*, this was the chief motive and one which fitted in with their earlier criticisms of Bismarck's policy of leaning towards Russia. Although initially not averse to maintaining the Reinsurance Treaty, Wilhelm had already shown himself more willing than Bismarck to accept the inevitability of a future Russo-German conflict; Waldersee and the General Staff concurred; and Holstein, now very much the *spiritus rector* in foreign affairs, therefore had no difficulty in convincing the new leaders of Germany of the danger of maintaining Bismarck's 'criss-cross of commitments . . . [like] the tangle of lines at a big railway station'.[6] Thus, the Anglo-German negotiations over East Africa and Heligoland ran in parallel with the repeated German refusals to renew in any form whatsoever the secret treaty of 1887 with Russia, lest it compromise their standing with Vienna, Rome, Bucharest and especially London; and Caprivi's own account to the Bundesrat of the 'deal' with Britain, on 18 June 1890, was actually the day on which the Reinsurance Treaty lapsed. Only a little earlier, observers such as Münster were reporting upon a rising anti-German sentiment in Britain and a corresponding inclination amid some circles there to come to an agreement with Russia. All this inevitably made the new German leaders eager to reach a colonial settlement with London, so as not to fall between two stools; but they compounded this diplomatic vulnerability by actually letting Salisbury know in confidence of the total reorientation of their foreign policy.[7]

The repeated – and genuine – emphasis of Caprivi, Marschall and Holstein about the overriding importance of the general European aspect of their foreign policy was complemented by a disregard for German colonial enterprises. All that the latter represented, in Holstein's personal opinion, was a hindrance to good Anglo-German relations; and, in Caprivi's view, 'millstones' which required constant visitation by warships urgently needed in European waters. The second consequence of this emphasis upon the continental balance was the high regard paid by the German government to Salisbury's retention in office, an attitude already in evidence under Bismarck but now elevated to become almost the leitmotiv in his successors' handling of Anglo-German relations. 'The position of the English government was not an easy one in view of the excited public opinion', noted Caprivi. 'Germany had to keep in mind the need to lighten Lord Salisbury's task and to make possible his retention in office.'[8] Wilhelm himself had been fervently anglophile since his English visit of 1889 and his 'giddy' joy at being made an Admiral of the Fleet; and it was quite in character, therefore, for him to inform Malet that 'He had said to General Caprivi that it was of the highest importance that Your Lordship's position in Parliament should not be weakened, and had asked him (Caprivi) to bear this in mind as a first condition in the negotiations. Africa, His Majesty said, was not worth a quarrel between England and Germany.'[9] Obviously enough, Salisbury's bargaining position was again strengthened, and consequently any indication by him that he could not give way on a certain point usually produced compliance in Berlin. Even when the main details of the Anglo-German arrangement were being ventilated in the press, the *Wilhelmstrasse* felt that it could not produce a full argument of the advantages Germany would derive, lest this be seized upon by Salisbury's critics in order to discredit the Prime Minister. Here was a curious, and quite remarkable example of German ministers and their advisers preferring, at least in the early stages, to take criticism upon themselves rather than see it directed at No. 10 Downing Street.[10]

British policy in 1890 was affected by different considerations. Of course, Salisbury's Cabinet was also concerned about the European situation and about the weakness of the Royal Navy; but perhaps neither of these were as threatening as in 1887-8. In the first place, all the signs from Berlin were that the new regime would be much more willing to support Austria-Hungary in the Balkans than ever Bismarck had been, and this took an immense burden from Salisbury's shoulders. Secondly, although the Anglo-French relationship remained poor on account of colonial differences, the French government appeared to have recognised the danger of quarrelling with all its neighbours at once and in April 1890 it engaged in amicable talks with Salisbury about the conversion of the Egyptian debt – the tacit agreement upon which not only eased London's position, but also caused concern in Berlin, the more especially since the Italians might be forced to compose their own differences with the French.[11] Yet if the European scene was now more favourable to Britain, the situation in East Africa was not: the treaty-signing activities of Peters, the news that Emin Pasha had been recruited by Wissmann to take an expedition in the direction of the Upper Nile, the general unrest caused by the indigenous revolt and the naval blockades, and the renewed German pressure upon the Sultan of Zanzibar, all suggested that the next cable from that region might bring uncomfortable or even disastrous news, which in turn could affect the impulsive Kaiser. If a local Anglo-German clash occurred, Salisbury would be in a far stronger diplomatic position than he was in 1885 to maintain British interests; but the overall circumstances, and his own natural inclination, prompted him to search for a permanent settlement to all these problems – the more especially that he had now come to see the need to gain control over the entire watershed of the Nile. Given these considerations, the idea of ceding Heligoland (which he had strongly opposed in the previous year) seemed to offer the only means whereby he could obtain substantial German concessions in Africa.[12]

The second and arguably the most critical determinant of Salisbury's policy in 1890 was the strength of domestic opinion pressing him to maintain British claims in Africa.[13] Although he admittedly exploited this mounting public sentiment in order to gain fresh points in the diplomatic negotiations, there seems no doubt that the 'Official Mind' felt itself to be under some pressure. This alone explains the *differentiation* in Salisbury's treatment of the various interest groups: the more extreme demands of Mackinnon's Imperial British East Africa Company could be resisted, but it was politically impossible to override the claims of the Scottish missionaries for the fabled 'Stevenson

Road'. What was more, this public agitation occurred at a time when the Salisbury Cabinet's standing in the country was weak.[14] Within the coalition Cabinet itself, there was no consensus upon African policy, and Salisbury encountered many colleagues who showed hostility to German claims, who opposed his scheme to cede Heligoland and who even supported the 'hard line' taken by Stanley and Mackinnon.[15] Ironically, however, all this worked to Britain's ultimate advantage because of the German government's concern for Salisbury's position.

There were, predictably enough, a number of critics who remained dissatisfied even after Salisbury had secured last-minute concessions from Berlin. The queen was most loth to part with Heligoland until the Prime Minister exerted his great powers of persuasion.[16] Imperialists who dreamed of a Cape-to-Cairo route complained that this objective had now been ruined; radicals and humanitarians tried to insist upon a plebiscite in Heligoland and deplored the 'carving-up' of Africa; francophiles wondered about the effect of the treaty upon Anglo-French relations. But most of these reactions were mixed rather than clear-cut, occasioned by the many-sided nature of the treaty: Gladstone, for example, welcomed the settling of African differences but deplored the surrender of Heligoland without consulting its inhabitants; Rosebery, speaking in the Lords, listed a variety of specific weaknesses in the agreement but, true to his belief in 'continuity' in foreign policy, refused to oppose the measure as a whole; and the Liberal leadership eventually decided to abstain, leaving only 61 (mainly radical) MPs to vote against the measure.[17] The British press, too, was generally in favour of the deal, although Liberal journals echoed the party's various reservations. Many Conservative papers, like the *Morning Post* and *Standard*, praised Salisbury for preserving good relations with Britain's 'natural ally' and for having regard to the general European situation; but what was perhaps the most remarkable aspect was the assertion made by some papers that their country's share was just 'adequate', with the *Pall Mall Gazette* and *Daily Chronicle* actually claiming it to be a surrender and a 'humiliation'.[18] One wonders how much more critical the British press would have been had Salisbury obtained a less satisfactory treaty.

On the German side, the reaction was not so favourable, although it is fair to say that the notion that Britain had inflicted a great and symbolic defeat over an inexperienced German diplomacy was to take some time to develop. The news that Germany had at last acquired Heligoland was received with great acclaim, and for a few days it overshadowed everything else; but then the colonial pressure groups struck back, with National Liberal journals especially mounting a bitter attack upon the sacrifices which had been made in Africa. Although the influence of these colonial enthusiasts was not large, it was able to merge with general nationalist sentiment at this time because of two factors. The first was the acclaim with which the non-governmental parties greeted the news of the treaty: the Centre, disapproving of colonial expansion, agreed with Caprivi's declared motives; Bamberger, who had praised all the indications in 1889 and 1890 of an Anglo-German *entente*, was obviously in favour; Richter in the Reichstag and many of the left-Liberal newspapers openly rejoiced at the blow which had been dealt to the 'colonial fanatics' and to German imperialism.[19] As this open applause by the *Reichsfeinde* annoyed many Conservatives and National Liberals, causing them to look afresh at the terms of the treaty, the second factor – the government's diplomatic need to avoid proclaiming all the arguments in its favour – came into play. Instead of being able to expiate upon the strategical importance of Heligoland or upon its hope of driving a further wedge between Britain and France, both of which would have had some weight in patriotic circles, the government could only refer in the most general terms to the need to preserve good Anglo-German relations – a far less satisfying argument, and one which immediately caused the *Kreuzzeitung* and other arch-conservative circles to abandon their first support for the treaty. By early July, it was the turn of the men of the 'New Course' to feel under some pressure.

What was significant about all this was not so much the actual African settlement – it is doubtful whether one German (or Briton) in ten knew where Witu was – but the growth of an imperialistic sentiment quite independent of government manipulation. 'Radical nationalism', as it has been termed,[20] was not perhaps a new force in Germany, but it was in the 1890s that it acquired its chief characteristics: a hard-edged chauvinism, a proclamation of a cultural mission, an unwillingness to listen to arguments about diplomatic and political exigency, an open assault upon Liberal cosmopolitanism and Socialist 'revolution', and a systematic sniping at the establishment itself. It was during the press debate upon the Heligoland–Zanzibar treaty that the *Kölnische Zeitung* published the first advertised summons – under the title '*Deutschland wach auf!*' – for the formation of a new patriotic body which in time was to become the Pan-German League.[21] Furthermore, in the background lurked more eminent figures, seeking to utilise and direct this sentiment: the Bismarck clan, which (after hinting in the early summer of 1890 that they could more easily reach an understanding with Britain than Caprivi) let it be known that they would never have surrendered Zanzibar; Treitschke, more than ever the tribune of German nationalism, whose early welcome for Wilhelm II had given way to a disillusionment that he had become too pro-English;[22] National Liberal leaders, sensitive to the stirrings in their ranks and eager to find a good rallying-point for the party; and – some distance away yet but already flexing their muscles – the Prussian Conservatives, who were endeavouring to mobilise the peasantry into a solid agricultural bloc which, in both its material aims and in its socio-political composition, would have little in common with England.[23] All these tendencies were to take some time to manifest themselves; but in the debate upon, and reverberations following the 1890 treaty, one can perceive early signs of a reviving German imperialism which would make impossible any future policy of concessions to British colonial interests. At the end of that year, Kayser, the head of the Colonial Division, noted the significance of this agitation for the future:

No government, no *Reichstag*, would be in the position of giving up colonies without humiliating itself before Germany and Europe. Nowadays a colonial policy has supporters in all parts of the nation and no political party, apart from the socialists, [could ignore this feeling].[24]

Perhaps these developments might have been less significant had the Anglo-German diplomatic link become ever closer, as Caprivi and Marschall hoped. Instead, the German government felt that it was being repeatedly disappointed by London in the early 1890s. To a large extent, this may simply be seen as the steady deflating of Berlin's unrealistically optimistic assumptions, and as a sign of the increasing nervousness of the men of the 'New Course' as they encountered ever greater domestic and external problems; but in their eyes the prime fault lay with Britain, which was increasingly showing both a blindness to the realities of European diplomacy and a selfishness in colonial matters. The British treatment of Portugese claims in Central Africa in 1890–1 was a good example of this. The vigorous expansionism of Rhodes and his supporters perturbed Berlin and increased the desire to establish a Portuguese 'buffer' between German East Africa and the regions claimed by the British South Africa Company; but the main motive of the German government was the earnest wish to preserve the monarchy in Portugal, which might well collapse if it took the unpopular step of giving way to Britain in Africa. Thus, time and time again, Hatzfeldt was instructed to urge a compromise upon Salisbury; but the latter always refused to give way, insisting that Portugal 'should abstain from exasperating South African opinion'.[25] This was not, in Berlin's opinion, a very statesmanlike attitude to assume, and both Hatzfeldt and Holstein soon came to believe that Salisbury would not mind the collapse of Portugal since this would give Britain the chance to seize her colonies.[26]

There was a similar feeling of disappointment at the Prime Minister's refusal to engage himself more fully in a variety of Mediterranean issues in which Germany, conscious of its relative weakness in that area, was very eager to secure British support. Italy, which threatened to defect towards France or Russia or both, incessantly pressed Berlin for assurances about Tunis, about the safety of its coastline in the event of a French attack and about possible gains in Europe or Africa; and the only way Germany – now unable to call Crispi's bluff because it had lost the Russian 'wire' – could respond was by urging Britain to reassure the Italians.[27] On some occasions Salisbury reluctantly complied, but his responses never reached the degree of certainty for which Berlin had hoped and he was strongly opposed to offering Crispi concessions in the Nile valley. London's attitude was virtually the same towards Turkey, another potential member of that Mediterranean bloc which the German government sought, by blandishment and insinuation, to fashion into a solid counterweight to France and Russia. Yet if a firm Anglo-Turkish alliance made good sense from the German perspective, it was less attractive to Salisbury, for a variety of reasons: distrust of the Turk, fear of domestic criticism and unwillingness to make concessions to the Porte over Egypt. Moreover, since the German pressure upon the Prime Minister to take forward steps was accompanied by statements of Berlin's unwillingness to become involved itself – as when, for example, it declined to protest against armed Russian ships passing the Straits since it did not wish to antagonise St Petersburg[28] – Salisbury was bound to be reminded of Bismarck's own attempts to use Britain as a lightning-conductor for Russian resentment.

More important still, London's policy of reserve indicated that the quadruple alliance which the Germans hoped for was not materialising. This might have been less of a disappointment at any other time, but it was a cause for grave concern in the early 1890s when France and Russia were moving, slowly but surely, towards a formal understanding: the increasing financial connections, the enthusiastic reception of the French fleet at Kronstadt, the Tsar's visit to Paris, were all intimations of a friendship which received formal expression in the Franco-Russian military convention of August 1892 – the date, according to one authority, when 'the system by which Germany directed the affairs of Europe came to an end'.[29] From the viewpoint of the two signatories, this was a *mariage de convenance*, a defensive measure forced upon them out of the fear of being defeated in isolation; in Berlin's eyes, however, it was an ominous development and one which, by 'encircling' Germany, provoked the call for yet another increase in the size of the army. German prospects of victory in a two-front war would not be greatly helped by Britain's military commitment to the Triple Alliance, but such a step would be warmly welcomed by Italy and Austria-Hungary, whose demands for increasing support sometimes caused Berlin to fear that, if not complied with, a defection might take place. Salisbury's obvious coolness towards all Berlin's hints that he try to satisfy the desires of the Italians, Austrians and Turks was, in such circumstances, highly disappointing. As Hatzfeldt reported, 'I have to struggle against weakness, fear and indecisiveness here, as well as dislike and mistrust of Crispi.'[30]

Nevertheless, the picture of German disappointment in Britain should not be exaggerated. That country was still regarded as friendly, a mainstay of peace and, in the eyes of the *Wilhelmstrasse*, a potential ally. For all his hesitations, the Conservative Prime Minister was seen as the chief obstacle to a British policy of selfish isolationism – which is why Hatzfeldt described the elections of July 1892 as being 'of the greatest importance for the development of the foreign policy of the whole of Europe'.[31] Thus, assurances of German goodwill, tributes of respect and many other signs of approval flowed from Berlin to London in these years, even if they were intermingled with requests for British action and support which Salisbury often found difficult to accept. Furthermore, this anglophile tendency fitted in nicely with the personal proclivities of Wilhelm himself, who was greatly enjoying his annual visits to Cowes and expressing his desire for Britain's welfare by sending his own 'expert' observations upon the manner in which the Royal Navy's deficiencies could be remedied. A pro-English policy also accorded with the sentiments of the left-Liberals and Socialists and, because it involved support for Austria-Hungary, of the Centre; and if such leanings were opposed by Conservative papers, colonial enthusiasts and the Bismarck *Fronde,* their criticism was at this time sufficient to stiffen Wilhelm's conviction in the righteousness of his cause. German diplomacy in the early 1890s might be described as clumsy and, occasionally, offensive; anti-English it was not.

On the British side, many Conservative politicians and newspapers continued to refer to Germany as their 'natural ally', and *The Times* on the occasion of Wilhelm's visit of July 1891 claimed, 'Germany does not excite in any class among us the slightest feeling of distrust or antipathy';[32] but the government itself, and its leader in particular, were more reticent. Too close an association with the Triple Alliance provoked hostile attacks from Radicals in the Commons and caused unease among the Liberal-Unionists, and Salisbury had enough problems to face in domestic and Irish affairs without gratuitously adding to his burdens: in August 1890, he openly warned Hatzfeldt that the government had 'plenty of opponents who are anxious to raise the cry that the German Emperor has too much influence over us'.[33] Moreover, because the Prime Minister regarded the colonial settlement of 1890 as a way of 'wiping the slate clean', he was more inclined to treat such later questions as Portugal's colonial claims, Crispi's fears about Tunis and a possible arrangement with Turkey over Egypt, solely on their merits; and, on that basis, he could hardly be enthusiastic about the various suggestions emanating from the *Wilhelm-strasse*. Caprivi and Marschall 'are much pleasanter and easier to deal with' than Bismarck, Salisbury confided to Dufferin, but they lacked 'the extraordinary penetration of the old man', feared that Italy was 'slipping through their fingers', and consequently were excessively sensitive about Britain's European policy.[34] Finally, Salisbury's mistrust of Wilhelm's instable character deepened rather than evaporated in these years. Lord George Hamilton's wartime recollection that the Prime Minister described the Kaiser in 1891 as 'the most dangerous enemy we ever had in Europe' may have been exaggerated in retrospect; but Salisbury is also supposed at this time to have referred to him as 'the dark cloud', to have wondered whether he was 'all there', and to have repeatedly asked the queen to speak with him and calm him down – a task which quite appalled the aged grandmother.[35]

These considerations did not make Salisbury an isolationist in the same way that Derby had been, and many Liberals and Radicals were; but it did cause him to seek, like Clarendon before him, to keep his hands free. A firm and public commitment to the Triple Alliance, in addition to causing a political *furore* at home and making Britain dependent upon such unstable characters as Wilhelm and Crispi, would also render impossible Salisbury's hope of settling Anglo-French and Anglo-Russian differences. This latter calculation never left him: when the French fleet sailed out of Kronstadt after its sensational visit, Salisbury invited it to call in at Portsmouth, in the hope – as he told the queen – of persuading the French 'that England has no antipathy to France, or any partisanship against her'; and throughout these years he had also patiently sought to negotiate an arrangement over the hinterlands of India with Russia.[36] Neither Paris nor St Petersburg was ready for such a *rapprochement* on Salisbury's terms, and to check their ambitions he fell back, as always, upon other means: increases in the Royal Navy, attempts to strengthen Persia and, finally, the policy of leaning towards the Triple Alliance without, however, belonging to it. As one writer puts it, he 'wanted the advantages of friendship without the encumbering engagements of an alliance'.[37]

While German hopes of attracting Britain into a quadruple alliance gradually sank during the two years following the African accord, they were weakened still more by the news that a Gladstone administration had been returned in the general election of July 1892: as in 1880–5, Berlin disliked a

Liberal government both on account of its domestic politics, and because its existence increased Britain's isolationism, gave hope to France and Russia, and weakened the resolve of Italy and Austria-Hungary. Some comfort was gained from the fact that Rosebery, who was more anti-French than any of his predecessors in this period, had assumed the Foreign Secretaryship on virtually his own terms; but it was an open question as to whether he would be able to maintain his principle of 'continuity' in British foreign policy in the face of the predominant radical and isolationist opinion in the Liberal Party itself.[38] As it was, neither wing of the Cabinet fully got its way; but the dissensions over Ireland, House of Lords, Uganda, naval increases and domestic reforms were such that Rosebery was eager not to do anything in European politics. Consequently, his foreign policy towards the Triple Alliance was little more than a watered-down version of Salisbury's, with a similar flow of assurances about 'identity of interests' being complemented by an even greater reluctance to make any positive moves. Yet since Rosebery was, in Hatzfeldt's words, 'the sole element in the present cabinet whom it is in our interest to maintain and support', an impatient Berlin was compelled to agree with the ambassador's further argument that they should not embarrass the Foreign Secretary by forcing the pace in Mediterranean matters.[39]

After allowing a 'probationary' period of six to nine months, however, the *Wilhelmstrasse*'s impatience with London grew, intensified by the conviction that the British had to be jolted into the defence of their own interests instead of hoping that others would do that job for them. The clinching evidence for these suspicions was provided by Britain's shifting policy during the Siam confrontation with France, which varied from Rosebery's anxious pleas for the Kaiser's aid when war seemed likely, to an attitude of reserve towards the Triple Alliance when it was all revealed as a false alarm. Given Britain's global and domestic circumstances, this willingness to compromise with France was both sensible and understandable; but it appalled the German government, which had accepted that it was ultimately bound to prevent the collapse of British power; and it caused Berlin to feel that the previous policy of importunings in London should be replaced by one of cold reserve, making it clear that in the future no German assistance would be offered unless and until the British abandoned their habit of getting others to pull their chestnuts out of the fire. 'For us the best opening of the next great war is for the first shot to be fired from a British ship', minuted Caprivi. 'Then we can be certain of expanding the triple into a quadruple alliance.'[40] Until the moment that Gladstone himself had signed such an alliance, Britain had to be treated according to the strict Bismarckian rules of *Du Ut Des*, according to which she ought to be constantly showing her gratitude to Germany, whose mere existence restricted French and Russian adventures. As Holstein put it plaintively,

If you consider 'How are we of use to England, and how is England of use to us?', then we assist England every day – even by sitting still – simply by being there. England, or at least Gladstonian England, assists us damned little up to now. Even in little matters, let alone greater things, it is always: *non possumus*.[41]

213

The period of Berlin's open striving for an English alliance had come to an end, to be replaced by a policy of virtually hoping for embarrassments and setbacks to occur, in order to drive the British towards the Triple Alliance; and even of hinting that Berlin might have to abandon the Balkans and Constantinople to Russia if Britain would not stand firm in all the pending Mediterranean questions. The two countries stood before a crossroads, wrote Holstein in December 1893; and a few weeks later Vienna was discouraged from accepting anything less than London's firm commitment to act first in the defence of the *status quo*.[42]

If the consequence of these diplomatic manoeuvrings was to make both governments irritable and suspicious, it hardly compared in importance with a second factor: namely, the revival of colonial clashes and sentiments in a much more heightened form than had occurred in the 1880s. The actual causes of the quarrels were not very important, but the way in which they escalated was quite remarkable. Marschall, irritated by London's general policy, read into a number of minor matters (the refusal to allow Singapore coolies to be recruited for the German New Guinea Company's plantations; opposition to an Asia Minor railway concession; moves into the Cameroons hinterland) a deliberate series of British snubs to which he responded by ceding to France early in 1894 a place on the Upper Niger – only a few months after an Anglo-German agreement over that region, through which London had hoped to block a French advance to the Nile. Although this German concession to France had been provoked by resentment at British dealings in their sphere, the Foreign Office did not realise this and considered that Berlin had 'double-crossed' them. The British in turn arranged a new treaty, this time with the King of the Belgians, aimed chiefly at keeping the French from the Upper Nile once again; but since the famous 'corridor' clause of this Anglo-Belgian treaty of 12 April 1894 ignored German reversionary rights to the eastern part of the Free State, it provoked an explosion of annoyance in Berlin – whose temper was already frayed by reports that New Zealand was again seeking to take control of Samoa. Linking up with Paris in a manner reminiscent of Bismarck's *rapprochement* with Ferry, Berlin mounted such an assault upon the Anglo-Belgian treaty in the summer of 1894 that it was withdrawn by both signatories.[43]

It is doubtful whether the Foreign Offices in London and Berlin cared all that much about the Upper Niger, or the Samoan Islands, or even the Congolese border; but the significant thing was that other circles obviously did, and that the statesmen felt that they had to respond. In Germany, the colonial enthusiasts had recovered from their nadir of the early 1890s and were pressing for a forward policy; the Pan-German League was particularly active, but its general outbursts of anglophobia and chauvinism were echoed by a large variety of National Liberal and Conservative newspapers, as well as by the Bismarck press; and the German Colonial Society was urging the *Wilhelmstrasse* to exploit Britain's difficulties with France and Russia in order to gain concessions in Africa and the Pacific.[44] This might not have been so serious had it not been that the Kaiser himself now emerged as an enthusiastic advocate of German expansionism, both naval and colonial. This, of course, fitted in with

214

his earlier aim of making a great name for himself, and of leading the German Empire towards a future more glorious than ever Bismarck had achieved, the virtual 'peaceful' Napoleonic supremacy of continental Europe and the establishment of a *Weltreich*.[45] If these ambitions could not be secured by going hand-in-hand with Britain, then they would have to be attained by other means. But perhaps even more important – if only because Wilhelm could at least be guided back on to a pro-English course – was the rightward shift which was now definitely taking place in Germany by the mid-1890s, as Caprivi's policies of cautious liberalisation collapsed in discredit. In the country at large the agrarians, instead of slowly atrophying, had organised the powerful *Bund der Landwirte* and prepared to stand out in open defiance of the government's commercial policies: German conservatism no longer implied an unquestioned obedience to the monarch, but represented instead an independent and awkward pressure group, constantly demanding measures of support.

As this agrarian Right grew in strength, the commercial classes became restive. In the background the SPD continued to expand, and a renewed economic recession dispelled earlier business optimism and allowed the Bismarck press to insinuate that the depression and the 'New Course' went together. Other Germans feared that the increasing fissures between Prussia and the southern states could lead to a disintegration of the Reich itself. The paralysis in the Reichstag over the School law, the trade treaties and other issues caused some reactionaries to urge a *coup d'état* from above and the restriction of the franchise.[46] All this made Bismarck's successors extremely sensitive to criticism, especially when their patriotism was cast in doubt and unfavourable comparisons made with German diplomatic successes under the first Chancellor: in April 1894, just as the Anglo-German quarrel was coming to the boil, the German Colonial Society reminded the country that it was the tenth anniversary of the founding of an overseas empire and pointedly sent Bismarck a telegram expressing the hope that his spirit 'will live long in the German people'. Only when the historian bears these circumstances in mind, is it possible to understand why Marschall could put into his diary a remark such as 'The Samoan Question worries me. The reputation of the New Course depends upon it.'[47] Malet, observing the public excitement over the Congo treaty, felt bound to report that the Kaiser was not so much leading the colonial enthusiasts, as 'following, almost from necessity, an unmistakeable ebullition of feeling'; but it was Holstein who drew the inevitable, ominous conclusion that, unlike June 1890, the German government dare not now offend patriotic circles, even if it meant a worsening in Anglo-German relations. 'English dislike of the Kaiser is a lot less serious than German', he cabled to Hatzfeldt.[48]

If this caused Berlin to resent British policies in West Africa and the Congo, and to seek to take over Samoa, such sentiments had their equivalents in London, even under a Liberal administration: indeed, it appears probable that Rosebery and Kimberley, aware of the traditional charge that Liberal governments failed to protect British interests overseas, felt bound to demonstrate to the country that they would stand firm – with the additional calculation that, having secured a diplomatic success, the new Prime Minister's position would then be strengthened against his many critics within the party who did not

215

share his belief that liberalism and imperialism should go hand-in-hand. Moreover, Rosebery was anxious not to disappoint the sub-imperialists at Wellington and the Cape. 'Our foreign policy has become a colonial policy', he claimed, 'and it is in reality dictated much more from the extremities of the Empire than from London itself.'[49] As it was, the Anglo-Belgian treaty, far from enhancing Rosebery's status, provided Harcourt and other ministers with good grounds to intervene and force a change in the country's foreign policy: under assault from within and without, the Prime Minister and Foreign Secretary were compelled to back down, but it is doubtful if they ever forgave Berlin on the one hand or Harcourt on the other.[50] Nevertheless, they only gave up the treaty with Belgium reluctantly and adamantly resisted all German requests to discuss Samoa. Thus, while Marschall sought to gain the islands by diplomacy so as to achieve 'a political triumph at home', the British government felt itself under a contrary pressure. 'There would be the devil's own row in Australia & New Zealand if we [surrendered Samoa]', Sidney Buxton informed the Foreign Office; 'and the power & position of the growing party of secessionists there would be enormously strengthened. It would be suicidal.'[51]

Equally significant in the long term were the conclusions which the British and German governments drew from these colonial quarrels. Rosebery, who had found the tone of the German messages 'thoroughly insufferable', became convinced that Berlin's motives, as in 1880-5, were primarily ideological: as he put it to Cromer, 'Germany hates Liberal Governments in England.'[52] Continuing to believe that 'Great Britain, if her policy be properly guided, holds the key of the situation', he countered the German colonial pressure by issuing threats to Vienna and Rome that London would offer no help to the Triple Alliance in the Mediterranean.[53] Kimberley, for his part, suspected German intrigues everywhere: they 'thwart us whenever they can all over the world', he informed Rosebery; and, on a slightly later dispatch from Berlin, he minuted: 'We must oppose in every way the attempts of Germany to interfere in the Transvaal. It would have a most disastrous effect in South Africa if she were to get a footing there . . . We must be prepared for Germany doing us all the mischief she can in Africa (if not elsewhere).'[54] For this reason, both he and Rosebery were anxious to come to an arrangement with Russia in Asia – in November 1894 an Anglo-Russian agreement was reached over the Pamirs – and they interpreted German unease at these talks as a sign that Berlin did not welcome improved relations between London and St Petersburg.

To the German government, the flare-up over the Congo had seemed to demonstrate that the British would only give way if they were subjected to diplomatic pressure, at Egypt and elsewhere, and made to see the perils of isolation: to this extent, it can be argued that Marschall and Holstein were still hoping for an ultimate *rapprochement* between Britain and the Triple Alliance and did not view the break with London as irrevocable – although such a future understanding would have to be bought by British, not German concessions. Yet even Holstein had begun to appreciate that, for diplomatic purposes, it behoved Germany to improve her own relations with Russia; and there were many others inside the establishment who bitterly regretted that the decisions of 1890 had caused Paris and St Petersburg to come together, and who hoped for the re-creation of the traditional Russo-German friendship. Such a policy was also beginning to attract Wilhelm himself and it was being urged by the Conservative *Fronde*, which appeared to have enhanced its position further when it helped to engineer Caprivi's dismissal in October of the same year. This change in diplomacy was more difficult to effect in practice, owing to Russo-German commercial rivalries and to St Petersburg's unwillingness to abandon its useful connection with the French; but these were all signs, as one historian has observed, of a return to Bismarckian attitudes, which obviously would imply a coolness in Berlin's relations with Liberal England.[55] In addition to this attempted shift in European policy, there was also an enhanced awareness among German decision-makers of the importance of colonial issues, and a corresponding suspicion of London's policies in Africa and the Pacific. In the hurricane season of late 1894, for example, both the German and British Foreign Offices wished to keep warships in Samoan waters despite the protests of their respective admiralties; in West Africa, the negotiations upon the delimitation of the northern reaches of the Gold Coast–Togoland and Nigeria–Cameroons boundaries were bogged down by claim and counter-claim; and in southern Africa the Anglo-German rivalry over Rhodes's drive to the north, the future of the Portuguese colonies and German assistance to the Boers, all contributed to produce a further series of disagreements.[56] In December 1894, Hatzfeldt and Kimberley had a blazing row over these issues, in the course of which the ambassador warned that Germany would 'not permit' a change in the *status quo* of the Transvaal and the Foreign Secretary retorted that Britain, with her larger navy, would 'speak the strongest word' and would not even 'recoil from the spectre of war' to preserve her supremacy in southern Africa.[57]

During the first half of 1895, before Salisbury's return to office in June, these trends intensified. Viewed in global terms, it was an altogether curious situation. The consolidation of the Franco-Russian alliance appeared to threaten both Britain and Germany, the former in its maritime supremacy and in the Mediterranean, the latter within Europe itself. Yet if, on occasions, both Rosebery and Marschall privately acknowledged this identity of interests, neither was eager to admit it openly, fearing that to do so would worsen their diplomatic position and hoping that they could each get on better terms with St Petersburg. This German calculation was most clearly shown in the *Wilhelm-strasse's* policy during the Sino-Japanese War of 1894–5, when it deliberately associated itself for a while with Russia. The British equivalent was Rosebery's effort to come to an understanding with Paris and St Petersburg over the Armenian crisis, an event which not only possessed most of the domestic ingredients of Gladstone's 'Bulgarian Horrors' campaign two decades earlier but also re-emphasised that traditional Liberal aspiration of combining with Russia in a political campaign against the unspeakable Turk. Meanwhile, imperialist newspapers and pressure groups in the two countries watched the other's moves in Africa, the Far East and the Pacific with suspicion and loudly demanded respect for their own 'national interests' as the price for not with-drawing their support in Europe. Not surprisingly in this atmosphere, the Mediterranean agreements of 1887 and 1888 were almost the first casualty and had fallen into desuetude by the time Rosebery left office. All of this was a very remarkable change from the early 1890s. As one historian has expressed it, 'The years 1892–95 therefore seem to mark a very important watershed, if not in British foreign policy itself, at least in the attitudes and assumptions upon which foreign policy was based';[58] and exactly the same can be said about the alteration in German policy, too.

What was more, this cooling in the Anglo-German relationship cannot simply be ascribed to the tactlessness of their leaders or to the existence of a Liberal administration in Britain. Wilhelm and his advisers were certainly very relieved when Salisbury returned to power, but the differences between the two countries were more fundamental than those which could be settled by expressions of mutual personal esteem, or even – and this *was* a significant change – by the relative narrowing of the ideological 'gap' between London and Berlin, as had happened when Conservative governments took office in 1874 and 1885. The sweeping gains by the Unionist coalition in July 1895 brought into power politicians whose own convictions and whose business, social and intellectual supporters in the establishment were keen to preserve, and in many cases to enhance Britain's world interests. The popularity and influence of Joseph Chamberlain, now regarded by many as virtual 'co-premier' to Salisbury, together with the public exuberance to be shown over such matters as the Diamond Jubilee and Imperial Federation, and the continued concern about the maintenance of Britain's naval supremacy and access to overseas markets, all suggested that, as Chamberlain himself put it, 'nothing could be more unpopular than an uncompensated concession' to Germany in colonial matters, for that would offend patriotic pride.[59] It was, moreover, precisely at this time that the British press (especially the new mass-selling and 'jingo' papers) were beginning to focus their attention upon the increasing trade rivalry with Germany. These developments will be examined in detail in a later section; suffice that it be noted here that they were forming very significant aspects of British politics during Salisbury's final administration. By the same token, such trends were also beginning to affect Wilhelmine Germany to a very substantial degree by the latter half of the 1890s, as the rightward shift in politics and national ideology continued, as the country emerged from the final phase of the Great Depression and was exhorted by various interest groups to follow the path of a world policy, and as the crisis provoked by Wilhelm's 'personal rule' deepened, with the Kaiser now actively seeking to get rid of the men and the institutions which stood in the way of his schemes for grandiose naval and imperial expansion. In this situation, neither the British nor the German governments were willing or able to make concessions; slights, whether real or imagined, were deeply resented; and each was hyper-sensitive to rumours of apprehended gains, whether territorial or economic, by the other.

Furthermore, the Conservative electoral victory saw the return of a leader who, whatever his global perspective and cool balance, remained basically distrustful of the exuberant Wilhelm – partly because of the latter's personality, but even more because of the detailed reports which the Prime Minister received of the internal crises in Germany and of the intrigues and political prejudices of the court camarilla. For his part, Wilhelm's earlier feelings towards Salisbury soon evaporated, especially after the mutual misunderstandings concerning the 'Cowes interview' of August 1895.[60] The two governments were also at odds in the field of foreign affairs. They had taken separate paths over the Far Eastern crisis, and were even further apart over the Armenian affair and the future of Turkey. At the *Wilhelmstrasse*, Salisbury's policy in the Eastern Question was interpreted as a cunning way of producing a European crisis and possibly a war, from which Britain herself would keep aloof in order to further her colonial aims; and this tactic had to be answered by reserve towards London, and by endeavouring to improve relations with St Petersburg so as, in Bülow's words, to achieve a 'free hand' in all respects.[61] In turn, the results of the Armenian crisis convinced Salisbury that the traditional policy of willingness to fight for Constantinople was now both a military and a political anachronism and must be abandoned, albeit without a public proclamation of such a change.[62] If on the one hand this implied a firmer British hold upon the Nile and an intensification of the struggle with France – and even this was not a certainty in Salisbury's mind in these months, as he sought to achieve a colonial *détente* with Paris – on the other it meant that the Prime Minister saw ever less reason for the Mediterranean commitments he had made in 1887–8.[63]

Nevertheless, these European bonds were only slowly dissolving and it was to be some time before contemporary observers could detect what has been termed 'the new course in British foreign policy';[64] although mutually suspicious and reticent, London and Berlin were not averse to occasional co-operation over European affairs, the more particularly since it enhanced their bargaining position *vis-à-vis* France and Russia. Such co-operation also fitted in with the Kaiser's highly erratic policy in these months: within a few weeks of his anger at Salisbury over the Cowes interview and some hostile *Standard* articles, for example, Wilhelm was seriously perturbed at the thought that the Franco-Russian combine might turn upon a weak Britain, with whom Germany had so many racial, religious and other ties; and only a few days later he angrily noted, 'The Russians have an entente with France, and are arming against *us*.'[65] The real running sore in the Anglo-German relationship by late 1895 lay elsewhere, in the colonial arena and especially in their growing antagonism in southern Africa. In his final conversation with Marschall before retiring as ambassador in Berlin in October of that year, Malet had openly warned that South Africa was the 'black point' in Anglo-German relations and that German encouragement of the Boers would lead to 'serious complications' – an opinion which provoked the excitable Wilhelm into claiming that Britain had threatened 'war': 'We are not Venezuelans', he protested.[66]

To Salisbury, who apart from reading reports upon the Malet 'incident' and upon the Kaiser's criticisms of Britain's 'incomprehensible' Armenian policy, had also been perusing an analysis of Eulenburg's 'mesmeric' hold over Wilhelm and the way the latter's mind was 'subject to hallucinations',[67] German policy was both puzzling and malevolent. Lascelles, Malet's successor, reported the Prime Minister as saying:

The conduct of the German Emperor is very mysterious and difficult to explain. There is a danger of his going completely off his head . . . In commercial and colonial matters Germany was most disagreeable. Her demand for the left bank of the Volta was outrageous, so much so that Lord Salisbury thought it must have been the idea of the Emperor himself as no responsible statesman could have put it forward. The rudeness of German communications, much increased since Bismarck's time, was perhaps due to the wish of smaller men to keep up the traditions of the great Chancellor . . . In the Far East, the Germans are up to every sort of intrigue, asking for concessions & privileges of all sorts, with a view to cutting us out. The only way of meeting them is by counter-mining, & we are in a position to do so.[68]

It was in such an atmosphere of mutual distrust that news arrived in Europe on 31 December 1895 of the Jameson Raid, which provoked in rapid succession the notorious 'Kruger Telegram', British counter-measures like the formation of a Flying Squadron, and a vitriolic press war. The details of that confrontation are well known, and recent archival researches have not offered any substantial reinterpretation of what was without doubt the most serious moment in the Anglo-German political relationship since the Schleswig-Holstein crisis.[69] Two points of great significance for the development of that relationship stand out. The first was that, as distinct from earlier quarrels, this was an issue which one of the protagonists held to be a vital national interest. In 1894–5, Kimberley had repeatedly attempted to warn Berlin that southern Africa was 'perhaps the most vital interest of Great Britain because by the possession of it communication with India was assured . . . [it was] of even greater importance to England than Malta or Gibraltar';[70] but the German government had either failed to understand or chose to ignore this. Touching upon such a delicate nerve was bound to provoke a reaction from that whole coterie of British nationalists whose concern at the growing challenges to the empire manifested itself in calls for an assertive, and even bellicose, diplomacy. This change could best be measured in the British press, whose outpourings of rage in January 1896 took the German government by surprise and stood in sharp contrast to its much milder tone over the Congo quarrel eighteen months earlier.[71] Hatzfeldt himself nervously reported 'an entirely changed situation . . . a deep-seated bitterness of feeling among the public, which has shown itself in every way . . . I myself received many insulting and threatening letters . . . if the Government had lost its head or had wished for war for any reason, it would have had the whole of public opinion behind it'.[72] British imperialists would henceforth consider carefully whether the German challenge to that vital interest of the Cape was of a greater or lesser nature than the Russian and French threats to Britain's other vital interests. In the event, a rather embarrassed German government was to indicate within a year or so that it was willing to wash its hands of the Boers in exchange for concessions elsewhere; but the whole episode had indicated how sensitive the British were to external threats. A German challenge to their hold over Egypt or India, or to their maritime supremacy, should ever one occur, was inevitably going to provoke a similar response.

The second point to be noted lay on the German side, where a whole host of nationalist intellectuals and Pan-Germans were now calling for an expansionist *Weltpolitik*, if possible with England, if necessary – and this seemed much more likely – against her.[73] But it was no longer merely the National Liberal expansionists who chanted such slogans: they were also now believed by the leaders of the German navy itself, in sharp contrast to the attitude of that service towards Britain when Caprivi was its head. Admiral Müller's lengthy and well-known memorandum of 1896, asserting that German opinion was determined to break 'England's world domination so as to lay free the neces-sary colonial possessions for the central European states who need to expand', was symptomatic of this feeling; and if he personally thought that there was just a possibility that the two powers 'could co-exist peaceably', other German admirals did not. Stosch, once the potential head of a 'Gladstone ministry', now began to work out in his retirement how to 'wage a successful war against England' and supplied these ideas to his *protegé*, Tirpitz; and Admiral Senden, who had encouraged the Kaiser throughout the 'Kruger Telegram' crisis, was known to be a bitter anglophobe.[74] More symptomatic still, this quarrel caused the official planners in the High Command to consider for the first time whether an Anglo-German war was now a possibility, and in March 1896 steps were taken to prepare an operations plan against Britain.[75] The details of this scheme are not especially significant, but the fact that it was drawn up at all *was* very important, for it marks the first time that part of the German 'Official Mind' began to see the British as potential enemies, rather than as uncertain friends or devious neutrals, as was still the view at the *Auswärtiges Amt*.

Furthermore, throughout his quarrels with Britain over South Africa – from the Malet incident to the Kruger Telegram itself – the Kaiser was eagerly pressing for an enormous Naval Bill to be laid before the Reichstag whilst the current anglophobia raged, and was threatening a *coup d'état* if that body declined to pass the measure. If both these proposed actions had to be post-poned for political reasons, the event itself formed a notable precedent. Henceforth, proposed naval increases and a propaganda campaign against Britain would always go hand in hand, for if the political parties and press were still dubious about fleet expansion, there seemed no doubt about their resent-ment of the British. This development was, in Salisbury's eyes, 'a more serious phenomenon: for their temper does not go up and down with the ease and rapidity which marks the movements of their master'.[76] The Austro-Hungarian ambassador in Berlin, for his part, feared that the German govern-ment would not be able to control this domestic anglophobia in the future:

The rivalry for world markets, opposing interests in their colonial policy, and the traditions of the Bismarckian political school, according to which England was portrayed as totally untrustworthy and often as perfidious, have prepared the terrain for the hostile feeling towards England which has manifested itself here with unusual unanimity. In my opinion, it will be no easy task to convince influential circles that, in their own well-known interests, they must keep within limits in their stance against England.[77]

221

Anglo-German relations during the rest of 1896 and into early 1897 were never as critical as in these days: both sides were not eager to push things too far and, reckoning that they had given the other a lesson, pulled back.[78] The Germans were perturbed that they had not been able to persuade the French to join them, as in 1894 – although the very fact that the *Wilhelmstrasse* itself had been unwilling to challenge the British hold upon Egypt was a clear indication that all its threats about a continental league against London had really been a bluff to bring Britain back into line with the Triple Alliance. Wilhelm himself, as erratic as ever, was soon indicating that he did not wish to be on bad terms with Britain since, *inter alia*, it prevented him from racing at Cowes; but, in any case, the German government had to devote the greater part of its attention to the internal crisis which convulsed it throughout 1896 and the first half of 1897. There was disagreement, as ever, over the handling of the final phases of the Armenian affair, and Berlin also suspected London of trying to raise the Eastern Question in another form when the Cretan revolt broke out in 1896; in China, as in southern Africa, the two governments were watching each other's moves carefully; there was a quarrel in August 1896 over the way the German consulate and warships had offered asylum to the leader of the revolution in Zanzibar to keep him out of Britain's clutches; and a temporary fear – on Wilhelm's part – that British agitators were behind the Hamburg dock strike; but, by and large, none of these events appeared to the German government to involve such a direct and massive conflict of interests as to merit a reorientation of their policy of cool reserve towards Britain, the more especially since it also regarded French and Russian actions with suspicion.

As for the British, they had to surmount a critical phase in Anglo-American relations following Cleveland's Venezuela message; and they had also decided to begin the reconquest of the Sudan, which would automatically cause a worsening of relations with France. For this reason, and because it might afford indirect relief to the Italians after their defeat at Adowa, the *Wilhelmstrasse* approved the operation; and Salisbury in turn sent encouraging noises to Berlin about wishing 'to be good friends with Germany' and 'to lean to the Triple Alliance'.[79] The fundamental processes mentioned above – the rise in nationalist suspicions and colonial ambitions, the German naval plans, the press debate about the Kaiser's *Weltpolitik* and the growing commercial rivalry, the gradual weakening of Britain's links with Vienna, Rome and Constantinople, the rightward swing in German domestic politics – were not concealed by such temporary improvements in the Anglo-German relationship, and the historian of this period can observe both the negative and the positive elements coexisting together. But to the two governments, at least, it was a time when it seemed best to pretend that all was well.

# CHAPTER 13

# *Weltpolitik and Alliance Talks (1897–1902)*

By the late 1890s, the world was emerging from the 'Great Depression' with many features altered since the crash of 1873, and yet it was not clear which of the newer trends were to be the most decisive. Inside Europe, the Bismarckian system had manifestly dissolved, leaving in its place a number of smaller blocs, the Triple Alliance, the Dual Alliance and Britain, moving towards and away from each other in a curious sort of three-sided minuet. Even within these alliances there were tensions, and the whole picture was further complicated by the way in which extra-European events gave rise to unexpected (although usually temporary) combinations and interpenetrations between the blocs. In Germany itself, the 'New Course' had failed but it was impossible to return to pure Bismarckism. In Britain, Salisbury symbolised policies of cautious and pragmatic conservatism, yet many in his party doubted whether the older assumptions about British foreign policy were any longer valid now that the empire was under challenge in all four corners of the globe. By 1902, it will be argued below, some of this dust had settled and shapes emerged which became ever firmer in the years following. Yet even in 1897, despite the confused political scene which confronted contemporaries, it is possible for the historian – aided quite unashamedly by the benefit of hindsight – to detect the most significant pointers to the future.

In the German case especially, the year 1897 has been very properly regarded by recent historians as a significant date, one which witnessed the appointment of new men to implement more efficaciously than before the Kaiser's 'personal rule', which saw the inauguration of a full-scale *Weltpolitik* and the beginnings of the battlefleet, and which also recorded a fresh attempt at stabilisation in domestic politics.[1] The person supervising these changes was Wilhelm himself, aided and abetted by his friend Eulenburg. Yet, however conscious these two were of the vague but grandiose ends towards which they steered the German ship of state, it is unlikely that they fully understood the new means which were to be employed, or anticipated how swiftly and deleteriously such means would affect the Anglo-German relationship.

The appointment of Tirpitz to be State Secretary of the *Reichsmarineamt* provides a good illustration of this point. For some years previously, various groups of German nationalists had been campaigning for a bigger fleet;

Hanseatic merchants, shippers and chambers of commerce – possessing little in common with the Pan-Germans in other respects – had also called for increased naval protection for German commercial interests in Latin America, China and elsewhere; the shipbuilding, and iron and steel industries were obviously keen for naval orders; and, most important of all, Wilhelm himself had become almost obsessed with the notion of possessing a large navy. Despite these various forms of support, Admiral Hollmann had never managed to persuade the Reichstag to grant the necessary finance; Tirpitz, much superior in presenting the navy's case, was to be astonishingly successful in securing repeated increases of funds from that body. The greatest difference of all, however, lay in the fact that from the very beginning he planned for a powerful battlefleet, and one which was to be directed against Britain. At his first audience with the Kaiser in June 1897, Tirpitz already had his 'plan' ready:

For Germany the most dangerous enemy at the present time is England. It is also the enemy against which we most urgently require a certain measure of naval force as a political power factor . . . our fleet must be so constructed that it can unfold its greatest military potential between Heligoland and the Thames . . . The military situation against England demands battleships in as great a number as possible.[2]

There were, as Tirpitz's defenders have pointed out, various technical and strategical arguments in favour of building battleships rather than cruisers at this time.[3] Yet the blunt fact remains that Tirpitz's overriding motivation was not technical, but political: to create, as he himself put it, a 'political power factor' against England. This itself stemmed from his fundamental conviction that an Anglo-German conflict was, in the long term, unavoidable. This was an assumption which Wilhelm occasionally seems to have accepted; but at many other times, because of his mixed feelings as a 'half-Englishman', he gave indications that nothing would suit him better than for the British and German navies to rule the seas together. And, as a middle position between war and alliance, he most clearly felt that possession of a large navy by Germany would gain him the respect and *Ebenbürtigkeit* which the proud yet practical British only paid to powerful states. In this aim, of course, Tirpitz's new strategy appeared ideal. As Wilhelm explained to the Württemberg minister in Berlin, Germany needed a strong battlefleet, based on Heligoland,

which at any moment could leave this base for the Channel and threaten English coastal towns, while British sea power was busy in the Mediterranean against France or perhaps simultaneously against Russia in Far Eastern waters – a circumstance whose possibility people in England could not fail to perceive and for which a sufficient reserve to control the Channel and cover their own coasts was prevented by the lack of trained crews, whose procurement under the voluntary enlistment system was already causing great difficulties. Only when we can hold out our mailed fist against his face, will the British lion draw back, as he did recently before America's threats.[4]

For a short while, this aspect was to remain concealed under a massive propaganda campaign about the need to protect the growing overseas trade of the Reich: indeed, people within the government like Holstein and Hatzfeldt did not at first understand its implications; but when it became fully appreciated on both sides of the Channel, the effect upon Anglo-German relations was disastrous – and irremediable.

Another 'quantum leap' in the development of that relationship had been taken in the appointment of Bülow as State Secretary at the *Auswärtiges Amt*. Most experienced observers in Berlin could guess that he would fit in much more enthusiastically than the reluctant Marschall with the Kaiser's demand for striking successes in foreign policy and for the acquisition of a larger colonial empire. Whereas the Badener's diary is full of notes about the impossibility of preventing Wilhelm's interventions in foreign affairs, Bülow's private correspondence in the 1890s possesses a totally different tone: praise for the Kaiser's noble personality (doubtless in the confident assumption that Eulenburg would report this to the highest quarters); declarations that the monarch must be given *his* men to carry out *his* policies; confidence in the growing power of Germany as witnessed in its industrial and commercial expansion, together with the belief that this power had to be controlled and directed from above; and the repeated assertion that the best way to gain popularity for this caesaristic rule – as well as to cover over the rightward shift in domestic politics – was to emphasise 'the national idea', a task which (as a devoted reader of Treitschke) he found easy to undertake.[5] Rather than be pushed reluctantly into imperialist ventures, Bülow intended to get at the head of such a movement in order to gain political capital from it, just as had happened in 1884–5. 'Bülow will be my Bismarck', declared Wilhelm happily.

But even this was not the most significant aspect: given the domestic discontent with the Kaiser and the pressures for expansionism by the late 1890s, it was more than likely that any German politician who succeeded Caprivi and Marschall would go towards *Weltpolitik* with a greater alacrity than they had done. Bülow's unique contribution to the worsening of Ango-German relations and, be it said, to the ultimate ruination of Germany's external policy, lay in two other areas. The first was that, from the time of his audience with the Kaiser in August 1897, he recognised that the chief task of the *Auswärtiges Amt* in the years to come would be to provide diplomatic cover whilst Tirpitz's fleet-building programme was brought through the 'danger zone' to a strength where it really would be a power-political instrument. 'The task which was given to me in summer 1897 was: development of our commerce, transition to Weltpolitik and especially the creation of a German fleet without a collision *with England, whom we were in no way a match for*', he noted. As he himself confessed, in this period German foreign policy had to be subordinated to armaments policy.[6] Quite apart from other considerations, the naval programme alone made a 'free hand' policy necessary: 'In our development as a sea power we could reach our desired aim neither as England's satellite nor as her antagonist.'[7]

Bülow's second contribution neatly complemented the first. Already confident of his own diplomatic skill, he could contemplate with equanimity the task of keeping Germany at arm's length from Britain because he had never at any time shown enthusiasm for an alliance with that country. This was a major shift in German foreign policy assumptions, for even when his predecessors had quarrelled with London they had ultimately hoped, either through the use of a carrot or a stick, to secure British adherence to the Triple Alliance. To Bülow, such notions were anachronistic – and dangerous; but in this period it was scarcely necessary to spell out his opposition to an English alliance. Even Holstein and Marschall had become so suspicious of Britain by 1894–6 that they were adopting, perforce, a sort of 'free hand' policy – as the Far Eastern triplice demonstrated; and they had also come to believe that London should pay a colonial 'entrance fee' to the Triple Alliance in order to pacify the German nationalists. Since Bülow was to place heavy emphasis upon both these factors over the next few years, there seemed to be little real break in Germany's policy towards Britain – a conclusion suggested also by Hohen-lohe's continuation in office as a 'caretaker' Chancellor, and of course by Wilhelm's own enthusiasms, which oscillated between contemplating war against the British and welcoming an alliance with them.

To Bülow, the following considerations were paramount. In the first place, he not only believed that an Anglo-Russian war in Asia was inevitable but also held that it should be secretly encouraged: this was a notion which, as a youthful member of the *schola theologiae*, he had picked up at St Petersburg at the time of the Penjdeh crisis, and the calculation never left him thereafter. His efforts, he reported to Herbert Bismarck in 1886, were to set 'Russia and France away from each other, Russia and England *against* each other, Russia and Austria with each other'; and nine years later he confidentially told Eulenburg, 'I consider an Anglo-Russian collision not as a tragedy but as "an aim to be most fervently desired".'[8] From these and certain other private statements, it might appear that Bülow regarded Britain and Russia equally; yet there is also a great deal of evidence that he usually inclined, out of a mixture of fear and respect, towards the Russian side. In part, this derived from his belief in the military strength and strategical near-invulnerability of the Tsarist colossus which he had gained during his period at St Petersburg. In part, it derived from Bülow's acute awareness that – as will be discussed below – an alliance with Britain would provoke strong criticism from those circles whom it was hoped to tempt into the government camp. Thirdly, it seemed incontrovertible to him that a Germany searching for new colonies and what Wilhelm termed 'maritime fulcra' would be involved in more disagreements with Britain, which wished to prop up the 'dying' empires of China, Portugal, Persia, and so on, than with Russia. Finally, the knowledge Bülow possessed about German fleet aims made it highly unlikely that he could regard Britain as anything more than a country with whom it was necessary to preserve formally good relations for a specific period of time: he himself told the Kaiser and Tirpitz in 1897 that 'a really honest and trustworthy Anglo-German alliance' was irreconcilable with the intended naval expansion and 'more or less means the renunciation' of it.[9] What his overall vision of Germany's future was, it is still difficult to pinpoint exactly – given the fluctuations in world politics, and the likelihood of dissent from people such as Holstein, it is not surprising that he did not commit a 'plan' to paper. But the evidence suggests that he anticipated a future Anglo-Russian war (with possibly France joining in) which would greatly weaken the British Empire and agreeably set back the Russians as well; and that this event, together with the natural growth of Germany's economic strength and Tirpitz's battlefleet, would then permit Berlin to come to the centre of the world's stage. If colonial quarrels and British suspicion led to an open conflict with London before then, it would probably be necessary to fall back upon some form of alliance with St Petersburg. Overall, Bülow believed, he had to eliminate Britain's global predominance in order to secure Germany's 'place in the sun', just as Bismarck had brought Russian hegemony in Europe to an end thirty years earlier.[10]

Connected with, and indeed an integral part of Bülow's assumptions were the domestic-political calculations which he and especially Eulenburg fashioned in the mid-1890s. If Germany's future as a world power looked rosy and inevitable, the domestic scene was far less satisfying. The Socialist movement continued to grow inexorably, and provoked a rising number of voices calling for a *Staatsstreich*. Particularism, especially in the south, had actually been encouraged by Caprivi's well-meant efforts to improve the constitutional relations between Prussia and the other states. These problems were accentuated by the knowledge that the government could only secure a majority in the Reichstag with the assent of the Centre Party; and the paralysis of the main legislature, together with the social and economic trends attending this age of swift industrialisation and protectionism, was an important reason why so many Germans were seeking to achieve their aims by joining the many extra-parliamentary *Verbände*. Here were matters which would have tested the wisest and most judicious statesmen; but they were made much worse by the awful fact that the Kaiser – the personal as well as the constitutional epicentre of virtually all the reverberations and crises in German high politics at this time – was so temperamental, erratic and prejudiced. Some observers, like Holstein, despaired of Wilhelm's ever becoming wiser with age; but Eulenburg and Bülow believed that he could be controlled, *if* he had the right advisers and *if* they could develop policies which emphasised the 'national idea'. Throughout their correspondence of the 1890s, this latter point was repeated again and again. Bülow, Eulenburg and Miquel were frequently assuring each other that 'Only a successful foreign policy can help to reconcile, pacify, rally, unite'; and this thought was also present in the mind of Tirpitz, as a political weapon 'against educated and less educated Social Democrats'.[11] The cynical Count Adolf von Monts, reporting from Munich upon the deep-rooted anti-Prussian sentiments there, frequently urged that 'only the Kaiser-idea, a successful external policy and stability internally, can gradually hit at the roots of particularism and local prejudice'.[12] Even Holstein, deeply worried about Germany's internal and external problems, conceded that 'Kaiser Wilhelm's government needs some tangible success abroad which will then have a beneficial effect at home. Such a success can be expected either as a result of a European war, a risky policy on a world wide scale, or as a result of territorial acquisitions outside Europe', although this was in his eyes an argument for improving

227

relations with Britain and he was soon protesting against 'people, who have the plan "to deflect outside" the internal difficulties'.[13]

If this emphasis upon Germany's world mission would gain the support of intellectual patriots, members of the *Kolonialverein* and the Pan-German League, and perhaps other segments of the middle classes, it was not of course sufficient to win over the harder-nosed members of the hoped-for governmental majority, or *Sammlung*. That would come about, it was calculated, partly by giving a more right-wing flavour to ministerial appointments (as did indeed happen in 1897), partly by appeals to all members of the established classes to combine against the socialist 'menace', and partly by offering solid economic favours to the agrarians and to heavy industry. Nevertheless, it was probably also true that an anti-English policy by the government would gain the support of many industrialists (because of their rivalry with British firms, and interest in shipbuilding) and Junkers (because of their dislike of 'Liberal' England).[14]

So much for the theory of the 're-re-shaping' of the Reich in 1897, a date which in recent historiography has come to be regarded as equally important as 1879, if not 1871. Yet the flaws in this grand design were many and, especially on the domestic side, not difficult to spot. In the first place, if this scheme possessed a 'totality' in the minds of Bülow, Eulenburg and the Kaiser, their intended collaborators only perceived, or accepted, parts of the whole. The commercial classes would welcome colonial and maritime expansion, but how would they like the bargaining over higher tariffs which would take place between heavy industry and agriculture? The leaders of the Centre Party might commit themselves – at a price – to co-operation with the government over 'national' issues, but could they do this without losing the support of many of their particularist, peasant-farmer supporters? And how would the National Liberals react to being displaced by the Centre – and the Pan-Germans to co-operation with the Catholics? The Prussian agrarians were keen on internal stabilisation, but would they swallow their bitter detestation of naval expansionism?; and did they know that Bülow's intention was that a *Staatsstreich* should be avoided and the 'revisionism' which was taking place among the Social Democrats encouraged by cautious domestic politics?[15]

In the external aspects, too, the scheme contained several substantial flaws. Even if, which was doubtful, the country could be persuaded to rally behind the Kaiser in pursuit of the 'national idea', for how long could fleet expansionism and an inspired propaganda campaign with a necessarily anti-English tone be carried out without arousing attention in London? Further, how could Bülow satisfy the urgings of Wilhelm, the Pan-Germans and many others for quick successes and colonial acquisitions whilst preserving ostensibly friendly relations with Britain during the 'danger zone'? And what would happen if an Anglo-Russian or Anglo-French war did not occur, but instead those powers composed their differences because of their suspicion of Germany's intentions? Finally, would the considerable mistrust which domestic and foreign politicians nursed towards Wilhelm be allayed even if – an unlikely event – he managed to control his well-known impulses?

The British political scene in these years appeared to be far less fissured in its domestic aspects, where the Conservative–Unionist alliance offering social stability and a few, piecemeal reforms, had re-emerged as the 'party of government' whilst the Liberals retired into opposition to continue their lengthy internal review of their policy priorities. The external scene, however, was much more worrying. Naval expenditure spiralled, and yet the former unchallenged maritime supremacy was never regained. The British economic growth-rate was persistently less than that of her greatest challengers, and there was a renewed concern about industry's ability to match foreign competition; in some quarters, at least, Cobdenite assumptions were beginning to be seriously questioned. In all parts of the world, the British Empire – both formal and informal – appeared to be endangered by foreign encroachments. To most foreign observers, and to many internal critics like Harcourt, it was no doubt rather cool for the British government to deplore the naval and colonial expansion of others when it remained the Number One power in both spheres; yet the blunt fact was that here, as in the realm of commerce, Britain was *relatively* declining and consequently anxious about the future: if any of the great powers (other than Austria-Hungary) would have wanted the territorial and power-political *status quo* to be 'frozen', then it would have been her. Moreover, being a country which had so much to lose and so little to gain from a great war or a redivision of the globe, Britain was forced to consider very carefully the circumstances under which she would actually run the risk of a conflict which might hurt her worldwide commerce. Rosebery put this attitude very well in 1895 when arguing that Britain could not embroil herself in Far Eastern quarrels unless her interests 'imperatively' demanded it:

> Imperatively, I say, because our commerce is so universal and so penetrating that scarcely any question can arise in any part of the world without involving British interests. This consideration instead of widening rather circumscribes the field of our actions. For did we not strictly limit the principle of intervention we should always be simultaneously engaged in some forty wars.[16]

For a while, Tory imperialists suggested that most of the empire's troubles had been caused by Liberal weakness and neglect; Salisbury, for one, frequently protested at Kimberley's 'disastrous inheritances'. Yet even this argument dried up when it was observed that each year of the new administration witnessed further crises in Britain's external policy. It was, after all, Joseph Chamberlain himself who, after wrestling with these problems for some time, described Britain as 'the weary Titan, staggering under the too-vast orb of his fate'; and Salisbury's intimate subordinate at the Foreign Office, Sir Thomas Sanderson, who used the less flattering image of the 'huge giant sprawling over the globe, with gouty fingers and toes stretched in every direction, which cannot be approached without eliciting a scream'.[17] What was more, whereas almost everyone could spot symptoms of the country's relative decline, and some could soberly admit that she had now lost her massive mid-century leads in economic, naval and colonial strength, no one had a ready and agreeable solution. Certain pundits called for a return to protectionism;

others talked of Imperial Federation, or urged a campaign of 'national efficiency'; some voices were heard pleading for a total reconstruction of governmental defence policy, including perhaps conscription; navalists suggested that a 'three-power' standard should be set; there were even voices questioning the principles of party government.

All these were drastic and, in most cases, financially or politically impossible solutions; and however many Cassandra-like voices the historian of the late 1890s can discover, it is important to recollect that the majority within the political establishment still believed that Britain's external problems would be eased by a policy of cautious readjustment and pragmatic, short-term responses. Only in the aftermath of the Boer War reverses, when Chamberlain gambled upon his Tariff Reform campaign, was any attempt at a full-scale alteration in policy made – and defeated. In the period beforehand, however, there appeared to be only two feasible solutions. The first was to seek, by all reasonable means possible, to come to an agreement with the powers whose expansion seemed most likely to threaten British interests, viz. France in Africa and Russia in Asia. A surrender of those interests (whatever the arch-patriots charged) was not intended; but this policy was based instead upon the belief that with a little 'give-and-take' such colonial rivalries could be amicably settled. This, certainly, was Salisbury's stance: he had long wished to settle Anglo-Russian differences over Turkey and Persia, and in 1898 he was to make an attempt to do so over China. Similarly, he had been eager in 1895 to reach a colonial settlement with Paris.[18] Even when disappointed by signs that Paris and St Petersburg preferred expansion to compromise, the Prime Minister never fully abandoned his hope of a future *détente*. It was a position also occupied by most of the Liberal leaders (especially the Liberal-imperialists) in the post-1895 years – a fact which was later to be of great importance, especially since they shared Salisbury's dislike of diplomatic dependence upon Berlin. It was enhanced, at least in the long term, by the fact that in 1897 Britain's secret links to the Triple Alliance were finally abandoned by the non-renewal of the Mediterranean Agreements, whereas Russia and Austria-Hungary actually managed for a time to put their Balkan disputes 'on ice':[19] for if this initially gave the Russians greater freedom to expand in Asia and caused the British to regard the defence of the Nile from French incursions as more vital than before, it also meant that the so-called Eastern Question was no longer one on which Anglo-Russian aims were fundamentally opposed and it removed one of the basic reasons why London had looked for the support of the central powers in the 1880s.

The alternative view of British foreign policy was, in the short term, of even more significance for our story. It argued that the time had now arrived for Britain to re-examine her traditional policy of isolation from the European alliance blocs. In concrete terms, this always meant a British commitment to Germany or to the Triple Alliance as a whole, for those who pressed for this solution fervently believed that the French and Russian challenges were too fundamental to be settled by some territorial compromise. In the years when the Anglo-French struggle for the Nile reached its climax at Fashoda, when Russia appeared to be threatening the entire China market, and when fears of a

French invasion at the height of the Boer War alarmed many Britons, it was obviously not an idle assumption. Currie, for example, looking over the notes he had made of his conversations with Bismarck fifteen years earlier, wrote to Salisbury in 1900 that 'they have to a certain extent revived my belief in the advantages of a close understanding with Germany'; Sanderson felt in 1898 that 'France is pushing us more and more towards a German alliance'; Spenser Wilkinson, in his book *The Nation's Awakening* (1896) and in private correspondence, urged a firm commitment to Berlin, even to the extent of defending Alsace-Lorraine; Hamilton, preoccupied with the Russian advance upon the Himalayas, informed Curzon that such an alliance 'would very greatly strengthen your position in India', and certain members of the military staff in Whitehall agreed;[20] Selborne, grappling with the equally uncongenial problem of retaining British supremacy at sea, thought the 'one possible alternative' to the spiralling naval budget was 'a formal alliance with Germany'. Even Goschen was less disinclined to this course than he had been ten years earlier, and other powerful Cabinet ministers such as Balfour, Devonshire and Lansdowne were willing to explore the idea in a positive spirit. Above all, Chamberlain himself pressed for – and repeatedly sought to bring about – a German alliance as the only realistic way of solving Britain's global defence problems.[21] Even *The Times* wavered over the idea, and many other imperialist papers (including the *Daily Mail*, *Pall Mall Gazette* and *Morning Post*) pushed it on certain occasions.

These circles, it is clear, had no apprehension as yet about the meaning of the naval and colonial policies currently being inaugurated by Tirpitz and Bülow. What is perhaps more surprising – and says much for the difficulty of generalising about the role of economic factors in this story – is that the Britons pursuing a German alliance also appear to have paid little attention at this stage to the commercial rivalry between the two countries which was being featured so prominently in their respective newspapers. The cause of this debate, which requires further analysis below,[22] was the enormous German economic advance, and the faltering British response, as the world re-emerged from the Great Depression. Early signs of commentary upon this trade rivalry were noted in the press polemics which followed the Kruger Telegram; but they greatly increased when, in July 1897, the British government gave one year's notice of the termination of its commercial treaties with Belgium of 1862 and with the *Zollverein* (which Germany inherited) of 1865. Only those two treaties, signed at the zenith of the free trade movement, had gone so far as to grant to the signatories the same commercial rights with the British colonies *as the motherland itself* and they therefore constituted (as the British note put it) 'a barrier against the internal fiscal arrangements of the British Empire'.[23]

Although the British government, in denouncing these treaties, expressed itself willing to sign a new one without the offending clause, the German reaction was cool: Wilhelm privately regarded it as heralding 'the commencement of war to the knife against our state', and called excitedly for 'a large and speedy increase in the building of new ships'; and many nationalist newspapers claimed that German industry was in danger of being excluded from its greatest export market, the British Empire. Others talked of the need for an economic *Mitteleuropa*, to withstand the coming commercial pressures of the Anglo-Saxon powers.[24] Under considerable domestic pressure, the German government felt unable to negotiate a new treaty with Britain without securing guarantees for equal treatment in the rest of the empire, and since precisely this was the reason for the British denunciation in the first place, it was adamantly refused by Chamberlain and the Colonial Office, flushed by the success of the queen's diamond jubilee celebrations with their emphasis upon closer imperial ties. Eventually, and to forestall Anglo-German trade coming to a near stand-still when the year's notice ran out, the *Wilhelmstrasse* granted most-favoured-nation status to British and empire goods during a 'Provisorium' of a further year (a grant which was to be repeatedly renewed); but this whole affair led to an animated discussion in the press and to much talk of an Anglo-German struggle for commercial survival. Yet despite this, imperialists like Chamberlain and his followers were evidently hoping at the same time that they could enter into an alliance *with* Germany, one of the chief motives of which was to protect British trade in China and elsewhere. Only in 1903, with the Tariff Reform campaign under way and these pro-German aspirations forgotten, was this curious contradiction finally resolved.

If this wing of British imperialism was full of optimism about the future of Anglo-German relations, it is interesting to note that the meaning of the 1897 changes in the German government was not lost upon certain British observers. Cecil Spring-Rice, then Second Secretary at the Berlin Embassy, wrote a variety of letters analysing the tensions between the agrarian and the industrial faces of the Second Reich, and the way in which they could at least unite in opposing England, in a manner astonishingly close to the later researches of Eckart Kehr:

> Between these two elements the Government is in a terrible condition. They are irreconcilable, and without one Germany can't fight and without the other she can't live . . . while the commercial classes in Germany are bound to be our rivals and at the same time to look to Russia for support – the aristocracy whose personal influence is now on the increase have precisely the same inclination for different reasons. Hating one another in every respect they agree in hating England. And as just at this moment the government is trying to conciliate both at once – they will be only too glad to find *this* point at any rate.[25]

Meanwhile, George Saunders, Chirol's successor as *The Times* correspondent in Berlin, was already beginning to study the navalist agitation and its meaning:

> the scheme is most important. To my mind it means that for years to come the agitation against England here will be conducted in an intensified form . . . it would give the nation a 'cause' to spout about and since 1870 & more especially since 1888 the Government cannot get on without excitement and *fanfaronnades*. Else the electors would begin to propose reforms, to tinker with the constitution, assail and privileges of the Army

and other classes. . . . [I believe] that we shall have to reckon with this people long before anything like a decisive reckoning with Russia comes; and further that a *modus vivendi* with Russia is more easily attainable than with Germany both now and in the future.[26]

To Salisbury, who only a little earlier had been wondering about possible German 'control over Holland' and its maritime population, the reports from Berlin were disturbing; but he consoled himself with the thought that the Franco-Russian alliance 'makes for us – and for peace. It is a decided check to the Emperor William, who, if he had elbow-room, would certainly be nasty for us. Family quarrels have made him really bitter against this country, and I am always glad to see him "hobbled".'[27] At this stage, however, the Prime Minister's suspicions of Germany were evidently not shared by the majority of his Cabinet colleagues.

To sum up: the years 1897 to 1901 are characterised, so far as Anglo-German political relations are concerned, by two contradictory trends: on the one hand, by the inauguration of German external and fleet-building policies which, in direct consequence of the motives and means put forward by Bülow and Tirpitz, would soon lead to a worsening in those relations; and on the other, by the attempts of a group of British politicians and by certain German officials – none of whom fully appreciated the implications of the turn to *Weltpolitik* – to explore the possibility of an Anglo-German alliance. In retrospect, the historian cannot fail to agree with Bülow's statement that these two tendencies were contradictory. Even if there had not been that change in personnel at Berlin in 1897, the traditional obstacles to an alliance such as Salisbury's distrust of German policy, the German insistence upon an open military commitment ratified by Parliament, the disagreement over whether Russia or France was the main enemy, were formidable enough: but under these new circumstances, there really were no prospect at all. By 1902, at the latest, this had become clear to both sides.

At first, events proved relatively easy for Bülow to regulate. Nevertheless, Wilhelm's 'pathological activity and restlessness' as Holstein called it, soon gave this world policy its first baptism of fire. For some years the German navy had had its eye upon obtaining a port on the Chinese coast and in November 1897, at the urgings of the Kaiser, steps were taken to secure Kiaochow – despite the worries of the *Auswärtiges Amt* and the temporary disapproval of Tirpitz himself. When the Russian government took offence at this step, Berlin turned anxiously to London for some support, although Holstein bitterly remarked that 'the only really valuable trump against Russia, namely the possibility of entering into closer relations with England, had been taken out of our hands by the navy with its continuous agitation against England'.[28] In fact the crisis blew over within a few weeks; unable to accept the humiliation of a retreat, Berlin stood firm over its possession of Kiaochow. Domestically, the effect was excellent: 'The affair is useful for the Kaiser', noted Hohenlohe. 'He has gained popularity.' The German nation has been given 'new aims', noted the Baden minister in Berlin, and the newly formed government has been strengthened.[29] These events confirmed, however, that it would be a trying job to placate the Russians, but they also led to no reassessment of Anglo-German relations. Indeed, Salisbury's refusal to give assistance deepened the *Wilhelmstrasse*'s suspicion of England and furthered its determination to create a 'free hand' between London and St Petersburg.

On the British side, this crisis, far from driving the two countries openly apart, was actually the occasion for the first of Chamberlain's attempts to create an Anglo-German alliance. The seizure of Kiaochow, followed by Russia's move upon Port Arthur, presaged the possible carving-up of the Chinese Empire; the blow to British pride, and to British trade, which this implied led to an outcry in the press and in commercial circles, with the greater part of this criticism being directed at what *The Times* openly termed the 'weakness' of Salisbury's diplomacy. An arrangement with Russia, such as the Prime Minister had been angling for at the turn of the year, turned out to be impossible; the 'cartographic consolation' of annexing Wei-hai-wei was no real answer, and contradicted the government's declared policy of maintaining the Open Door. Right-wing backbenchers like Howard Vincent openly showed their dissatisfaction, and warned of political repercussions:

> It is now or never. Delay is absolutely fatal. The God of Battles is no lover of tomorrow. Failure to act . . . is today the theme of every Radical canvasser in East Berks, as it was in Stepney and Maidstone. It will, if persisted in, dissipate a majority of 150 . . . there is grave and unmistakeable unrest . . . The time for action – vigorous, unmistakable action, that of a united nation – has come.[30]

It was out of his own apprehension that 'grave trouble is impending upon the Government if we do not adopt a more decided attitude in regard to China', that Chamberlain ventured into his series of discussions about a possible alliance. Since this matter has probably been the subject of more historical investigations of the Anglo-German relationship than any other, the details need not be repeated here.[31] The chief points to note are: Salisbury's discouraging attitude, based upon his traditional distrust of Wilhelm and unwillingness to pay Germany's price – 'You ask too much for your friendship', he told Hatzfeldt;[32] Chamberlain's willingness to meet the German demand for a treaty underwritten by Parliament, and to offer to clear up all their colonial disputes (Samoa, Neutral Zone, Cape-to-Cairo railway, and so on)[33] as well; and, finally, the Colonial Secretary's remark that 'if his idea of a natural alliance with Germany must be renounced, it would be no impossibility for England to arrive at an understanding with Russia or with France'.[34] Although Chamberlain was no great diplomat, it was at least clear that he was searching for a radical and final solution to Britain's global dilemma, and was therefore more likely than Salisbury to swing violently from one course to another.

Berlin's reaction to these British approaches indicates how much things had changed since the early 1890s, when the *Wilhelmstrasse* was panting after an English alliance. Although encouraging noises were made for a time, merely to discover how far Britain needed Germany's support, Bülow soon outlined why he would never agree to such a step. While emphasising the possibility of a later Parliament refusing to recognise the treaty, the German leaders also genuinely feared that Russia would turn hostile, just as they were hoping to distract her in Asian adventures. Germany's aim, Bülow felt, was to straddle and exploit the Anglo-Russian antagonism: 'We must hold ourselves independent between the two', he minuted, 'and be the tongue on the balance, not the pendulum oscillating to and fro.'[35] Wilhelm was therefore encouraged to pick his way delicately between the two rival powers, since an inclination in any direction would be dangerous: at the same time, the British were to be persuaded to be conciliatory in specific colonial arrangements and thereby to smooth the way to a more permanent *rapprochement*. In this respect, and despite the Colonial Secretary's warning to Hatzfeldt, German hopes clearly lay with Chamberlain, for Salisbury was always recognised to be less amenable to such suggestions and was particularly disliked because of his known attempts to reach an understanding with France and Russia, which would nullify Germany's bargaining position. Berlin was extremely annoyed, for example, when the Prime Minister's approach to Russia in the spring of 1898 was revealed by the Tsar.[36]

In theory, all that Germany needed to do was to sit quietly until the British, in sheer desperation, made further approaches. In practice, such a passive policy could never be sustained for long: the world situation, with China near to collapse, with the British poised to expand in southern Africa, and with Spain's overseas empire being disposed of following her defeat by the United States, tempted the Germans to act quickly in order to gain a share. In April 1898 the *Deutsche Zeitung* was one of many papers which was arguing that Germany had too few colonies: she should acquire, the paper asserted, the Neutral Zone in West Africa, Liberia, the Spanish and Portuguese islands off the Cameroons, Walfish Bay, Zanzibar, Delagoa Bay and Mozambique, half of the Congo Free State, Samoa, a fleet base on the North African coast, another in the Dutch East Indies, and a third in the Danish West Indies. Just how German diplomacy was to secure these territories, the author did not say; but it was indicative of the pressure which was being put upon the government. In naval circles, too, as the Baden minister in Berlin reported, there 'prevails a forward urge, which will very much complicate calm direction in foreign policy'. Some admirals favoured gaining the Danish West Indies, others a base in the Philippines; the Kaiser sought to acquire Samoa, the Carolines, Borneo and one of the Philippine Islands, although the latter aim served only to arouse American anger.[37]

It was with this hope of extracting concessions, and thereby satisfying domestic demands for expansion, that the German government burst in upon the Anglo-Portuguese discussions of the early summer of 1898: and the list of compensations for allowing Britain to offer a loan to Lisbon upon the security of Portugal's African customs receipts (and implicitly upon the colonies themselves) revealed just how enormous Berlin's colonial demands had become.[38] It was, predictably enough, just this feature of German policy which Salisbury detested; and equally predictable that the Prime Minister's stubbornness to assist Berlin's *Weltpolitik* would provoke Wilhelm's fury.[39] Nevertheless, Bülow was able to persuade Wilhelm that breaking off the talks would make

Germany more dependent upon France and Russia and thus reduce Berlin's freedom of action. Yet it was only to be a few weeks later, if may be noted, that the State Secretary had to rescue his imperial master from getting too interested in Lascelles's remark that Britain and Germany might agree to combine if either were attacked by two or more other powers. Ignoring the positive aspects of such a plan, Bülow strove to underline the disadvantages and to congratulate the Kaiser for indicating that 'Your Majesty will never pull English chestnuts out of the Russian fire *pour les beaux yeux de John Bull;* and that the English could give no practical help to Your Majesty in case of war with Russia'. An Anglo-Russian war, on the other hand, was an elemental necessity and even now Wilhelm could regard himself as *arbiter mundi*.[40] After a year in office, one suspects, Bülow could already see that his chief task in diplomacy was to keep the Kaiser from being either too pro-British or too anti-British.

Fortunately for the State Secretary, these twin dangers were again avoided. Wilhelm himself let the Tsar know of these British 'approaches' in the hope of winning Russia's favour; and, in the negotiations over the future of the Portuguese colonies, Salisbury went on holiday and abandoned the direction of these talks to Balfour. As a result, an agreement was rushed through and signed on 30 August 1898. Although the deputy Foreign Secretary hoped that by it he had not only excluded Germany from any further interference in southern Africa but also increased the prospects of more general Anglo-German co-operation, this secret treaty could hardly be said to have boded well for that relationship. On the one hand, Salisbury regarded German policy with greater distaste than ever, and after his return he did all within his power to ensure that the arrangements regarding the future disposal of the Portuguese colonies never came into effect. Even Chamberlain, it is worth noting, had felt reluctant to make special concessions to the Germans in this affair.[41] On the other hand, Berlin did not consider the treaty as being unduly favourable to it and also suffered some embarrassment, since the clauses were not to be revealed to the public which suspected another 'sell-out' to the British.[42] Bülow was also worried lest it affect his relations with the Russians and even before the treaty was signed arrangements were made to impress upon St Petersburg the fact that this was confined purely to Africa and should not be interpreted as an anti-Russian move.

In the other international events of 1898, Berlin's policy was again very typical. During the Spanish-American War, Wilhelm had privately expostulated against the 'Yankee' plunderers of monarchical Spain; but Bülow had held him back from any open criticism, and also sought to smooth over the German–American press war which had arisen out of the Dewey-Diederichs 'incident' in Manila Bay.[43] Despite his attacks upon American annexations, the Kaiser was not averse to securing for Germany – in return for a money payment – some of Spain's Pacific possessions. It was also characteristic of Bülow to send an open message to the Kaiser at the acquisition of the Carolines, stating that 'This gain will stimulate people and navy to follow Your Majesty further along the path which leads to world power, greatness and eternal glory' – whereas the German navy, more realistically, thought that the group was worthless.[44] Equally symptomatic was Berlin's attitude during the Fashoda crisis. Wilhelm certainly believed that the Anglo-French confrontation over the Nile valley would lead to a war, during which Germany's position would be strengthened. To ensure that this took place, he indulged in some of that private diplomacy which so alarmed Holstein. On the one hand he told the Russians that he would stay neutral if the continent went to war with England, on the other he assured Lascelles that the British could easily beat the French but that Germany would intervene should London be opposed by Russia also. Doubtless his wish was to see France weakened militarily, while perhaps picking up compensations later from London for his neutrality.[45] The settlement of the Fashoda question without a war bitterly disappointed him and he let these feelings be known when criticising the Russian Foreign Minister, Muraviev, for advising Paris to give way.[46]

In London the Kaiser's actions were regarded with deep suspicion. 'The one object of the German Emperor since he has been on the throne has been to get us into a war with France', Salisbury had told Balfour earlier in the year, and Victoria was also incensed at the 'systematic and hardly concealed attempts' of the Kaiser to set Britain against the Dual Alliance. Sanderson, upon learning that Wilhelm had claimed that 'he was like a man with a pail of water, trying to damp down the explosives which were lying about', aptly retorted that he appeared more like someone 'running about with a lucifer match and scratching it against powder barrels'.[47]

To Wilhelm, who claimed that the French 'had not read their Mahan', the affair demonstrated once again that Germany must possess a large fleet if she were to avoid a similar humiliation in the future. Bülow's directive to the German press at this time again indicates how it was hoped to gain advantage from the misfortunes of others:

In the discussion of the present world situation, His Majesty desires that over-careless and damaging attacks against Russia or against England and America be avoided, but on the other hand the following points be placed in the foreground:
1. How necessary the increase of the fleet has been. No successful overseas policy without a strong fleet. The role of the fleet in the Spanish-American war and during the Fashoda quarrel. Why does Spain lie on the floor? Why does France retreat before England?
2. So long as we possess insufficient naval forces, their deficiency must be made up by a unanimous consolidation of the Parties, the Reichstag and the nation in all great matters of foreign policy. Never would there be more cause to direct the gaze from petty party disputes and subordinate internal affairs on to the world-shaking and decisive problems of foreign policy.[48]

In the following year, too, the Kaiser's blueprint for a greater Germany was faithfully carried out and could be seen at its clearest in the heated disputes with Britain over the partition of the Samoan Islands, and in the preparations for the second Navy Law. The island group was again plagued by native discontents, a weak king and quarrelling consuls, all of which hurt its trade prospects; but this made no difference to those colonial enthusiasts who continually pressed for a German annexation, basing this claim upon their long involvement in the group. During the interventions of an Anglo-American naval force against the German-backed candidate in the kingship succession dispute of March and April 1899, the German newspapers went wild with rage: 'Anyone ignorant of geography', Professor Hale has noted, 'would have assumed from the racket made by the German press that a continent was at stake rather than a small island.'[49] This factor dictated Bülow's attitude from the outbreak of the native civil war until the eventual partition of the group in November 1899. Since it was precisely those Reichstag parties who favoured colonial expansion which the government sought to enlist in its conservative domestic policy, he was forced to be most careful in handling this affair and at the end of March admitted that 'the Samoan question stands now as before in the forefront of my interest'.[50] Unlike Bismarck, who had only been concerned to protect Germany's commercial interests in Samoa, he was willing to admit that 'the entire Samoan question has absolutely no material, but an ideal and patriotic interest for us'.[51] So crucial had minor colonial disputes such as this become that Bülow was forced to refuse Chamberlain's extremely generous offers of territorial compensation elsewhere for withdrawal and to insist upon control of the main island of Upolu. In fact, the matter became so serious that Hatzfeldt was forced to warn Salisbury that, unless it was settled in a manner satisfactory to the Kaiser, there would be 'un changement complet de notre politique generale' and he would be withdrawn.[52] When, at last, Salisbury did agree to give way, the German government's relief was immense: yet it is worth noting that everyone in the Foreign Ministry realised that the treaty was unfavourable to Germany from the material point of view, one expert in colonial affairs bluntly admitting to a friend that Samoa had been 'simply a prestige victory'.[53]

Bülow's task of satisfying public opinion whilst maintaining friendly though distant relations with Britain was most severely tested by the Samoan quarrel, which revealed the true meaning of his 'free hand' policy. As in the Portuguese Colonies affair, Chamberlain (whom the Germans hoped to play off against Salisbury) was to be encouraged to prepare for an alliance by offering Samoa – but even if he did this, of course, no such general political agreement would be concluded. 'If England shows herself prepared for a fair settlement of the Samoan affairs', Bülow minuted, 'we will be able to pursue our present independent policy du juste milieu'; if she did not, Germany would be forced 'to draw closer to Russia and even to France'.[54] But this latter course also had its dangers. Hence his anxiety that Wilhelm's angry exchanges with Victoria and Salisbury in the summer of 1899 would derange his 'free hand' policy and force Germany into a hostile position before the fleet was ready:

A so heated personal relationship, which has existed for four months between His Majesty on the one side and the English royal family and Lord Salisbury on the other, cannot last very long without causing serious complications for us and in any case hurting the freedom of action of our policy . . . in view of our naval inferiority, we must operate so carefully, like the caterpillar before it has grown into a butterfly.[55]

Operating carefully was difficult enough for the Kaiser's government at any time, however, and the more so following the outbreak of the Boer War in October 1899, which placed a severe strain upon this complicated German diplomacy. While on the one hand the conflict excited the nationalists into calling for a complete break with Britain, on the other it frequently aroused in Wilhelm the wish to assist his English cousins; while it offered superb propaganda material for the government's campaign to expand the navy, the public anglophobia threatened to arouse London's attention just as Tirpitz's fleet was entering the 'danger zone'; while it offered Berlin the opportunity to indulge in a little colonial 'blackmail' at Britain's expense, these demands had not to be pushed so far that London was alienated and switched its attention from the Franco-Russian challenge to the German one. In seeking to satisfy these contradictory demands, Bülow's diplomacy became in reality little better than Wilhelm's own zigzag course in the years 1895–6.

The first few months of the South African War witnessed many examples of this oscillation in policy. In October 1899, fearing that the British might take temporary control of Delagoa Bay (to cut the supply route to the Boers) and that this would provoke roars of protest in German colonial circles, the government made secret plans to seize Tiger Bay in Angola as 'compensation':[56] what that event, had it occurred, would have done to Anglo-German relations just as Salisbury was signing his secret treaty to protect Portugal's possessions, is not difficult to imagine! A few weeks later, after applying pressure in London, Bülow achieved a settlement of the Samoan question – of which the most significant aspect, apart from the satisfaction of imperialist sentiment, was that the treaty could be announced just a few hours before the Tsar arrived in Potsdam on a courtesy visit; this was the 'free hand' policy with a vengeance, although feverishly hard work.[57] The Samoan settlement also permitted Wilhelm to fulfil his wish to visit Windsor, and it was while he accompanied his imperial master on this trip that Bülow took the opportunity to assure Chamberlain and other British politicians that Germany's intentions were friendly; yet as soon as he returned into the anglophobic atmosphere of Berlin, Bülow made pains to distance himself from the Colonial Secretary's famous Leicester speech of late November 1899, calling for an Anglo-German-American alliance.[58]

Bülow's cold public reply to Chamberlain's speech was necessary because it was precisely at this time that German opinion was being prepared for a virtual doubling of the battlefleet, only two years after the first Navy Law. On the other hand, it remained of crucial importance not to be pushed into a war against Britain while the fleet was still weak. 'In 20 years' time, when it [the fleet] is ready, I shall speak another language', Wilhelm told the French ambassador; until then, though, Germany must maintain the 'strongest neutrality'.[59] It was therefore most important to control the anglophobic utterances in the German newspapers in case this was noticed by Britain, which might adjust her policy accordingly. Wilhelm thus ordered 'Double watchfulness in the press and every insolent article against England to be cut off at the head', while Bülow sent instructions that

A cool and calm language is recommended for our press towards the English defeat at Ladysmith. A too clearly prominent *Schadenfreude* and open jubiliation would only turn the bitterness of the English against us, whom we are not yet strong enough to meet at sea, and simultaneously nourish the hopes of the French and the Russians that we would be ready to let ourselves be directed alone against England.[60]

This was a particularly difficult policy to carry out since Bülow and Tirpitz had at the same time to utilise the domestic anglophobia in order to persuade the public and the Reichstag to accept the necessity for further fleet increases. Even the Bavarians were losing their suspicions about the Navy Law, Monts reported, and the clerical-particularists feared that the German government could gain electoral advantages by taking up the cries of the Pan-Germans: 'Yet the chief agency in this is the hatred of England and the desire to get at her. The many official quenchings of this anglophobia are therefore well advised, only the greatest care will be necessary in order not to subdue too much the enthusiasm for the fleet.'[61] Thus, Bülow's first act, upon learning of the seizure of the German steamers at the turn of the year, was to cable to the Press Bureau:

His Majesty desires that the taking of the *Bundesrath* should be utilised (without impolitic bitterness or heat against England but factually) with vigour and persistence for the fleet measure. My latest speech for the fleet (no-one can know today what consequences the war in South Africa would have, etc.) can also be alluded to.[62]

To add to the complications, Wilhelm's enthusiasm for the doubling of the German battlefleet – which Tirpitz had aroused by his audience on 28 September, when he outlined a vision of Germany as one of the four world powers[63] – threatened to produce a return to the constitutional crises of the mid-1890s, since the Kaiser vowed to dissolve the Reichstag if it would not accept the second Navy Law. Reference to Britain would have to be made to convince the Reichstag to pass this new measure, but its offensive aspects would be cloaked to avoid forewarning the British. As Tirpitz admitted to the Saxon military representative, 'One could not say directly that the fleet increase is in the first line against England, with whom we must doubtless come into conflict in the next century in some part of the earth, be it out of economic rivalry or as a consequence of colonial disputes.'[64] Britain, as Bülow confidentially told the Budget Committee of the Reichstag in March 1900, had now become their most dangerous foe, 'the one power which could attack us without special risk to itself': today a conflict with her 'is not outside the bounds of possibility'.[65]

This anti-English direction in German foreign policy stood in such remarkable contrast to that of a decade earlier that, at exactly this time, the shrewd and experienced Austro-Hungarian ambassador in Berlin, Szögyeny, thought it worth while to send a long memorandum upon Germany's future aims to his political masters in Vienna:

> The leading German statesmen, and above all Kaiser Wilhelm, have looked into the distant future and are striving to make Germany's already swiftly-growing position as a world power into a dominating one, reckoning hereby upon becoming the genial successor to England in this respect. People in Berlin are however well aware that Germany would not be in the position today or for a long time to assume this succession, and for this reason a speedy collapse of English world power is not desired since it is fully recognised that Germany's far-reaching plans are at present only castles in the air. Notwithstanding this, Germany is already preparing with speed and vigour for her self-appointed future mission. In this connection I may permit myself to refer to the constant concern for the growth of German naval forces . . . England is now regarded as the most dangerous enemy which, at least as long as Germany is not sufficiently armed at sea, must be treated with consideration in all ways . . . but because of the universally dominant anglophobia, it is not easy [to convince public opinion of this].[66]

Interestingly enough, Szögyeny also drew the conclusion that a Germany which possessed an enormous fleet as well as the most powerful army in the world would 'scarcely be satisfying' to the Russians; and he forecast that, when Berlin encountered complications with other powers outside Europe, she would come to rely more and more upon Austria-Hungary inside, thus increasing Vienna's own bargaining power. This was a different prospect to that which exercised Bülow's mind, but in retrospect it seems remarkably prescient.

Despite the evidence about German intentions which was available even to outside observers, British policy towards that country still showed the same ambivalence throughout 1899 and 1900. Salisbury himself had put up a tenacious resistance to making any undue concessions to Berlin in the Samoan affair, which to him had simply illustrated once again the unreasonableness of German colonial demands and the impulsiveness of the Kaiser. The other Cabinet ministers, however, were alarmed at this tension and tried to ease it; and it was Chamberlain who, although asserting that 'the policy of the German Empire since Bismarck has always been one of undisguised blackmail!', came up with the proposals for a satisfactory final solution of the Samoan tangle. To this extent, Wilhelm was not far wrong when he complained to the British military *attaché* of the 'two-headed' government in London.[67] The main concern of the Colonial Minister, and of such colleagues as Balfour, Goschen, Devonshire and Brodrick, was not of course an undiluted love of Berlin; but when the crisis in South Africa loomed they were anxious to show the world that Anglo-German relations were on a good footing, just in case the rumours of a continental coalition against Britain had some foundation – whereas Salisbury, being more sceptical about the formation of such a league, was not

241

eager to pay a high insurance premium against a remote risk. The greater part of the patriotic press was, however, motivated by the wish to show that Britain still had friends in the world: when Wilhelm and Bülow visited Windsor in November 1899, the *Daily Mail* welcomed them with the words 'A Friend in Need is a Friend Indeed'; the *Saturday Review*, better known for its *'Germaniam esse delendam'* article two years earlier, suggested that Britain 'would do better work with her than against her'; and Chirol, now foreign editor of *The Times*, resisted the assertions of his Berlin and Vienna correspondents that the German government's intentions towards Britain were malevolent.[68] Even Chamberlain's clumsy appeal at Leicester for an Anglo-German-American alliance was not unwelcome to some of these papers, and others questioned the manner rather than the intention of the speech.

What alternative, such statesmen and editors argued, was feasible for Britain at this time? The Boer War was turning out to be a prolonged and difficult struggle which not only exposed the inadequacies of the late-Victorian army but also tied it down in South Africa for the next three years, caused a sharp rise in taxes and a severe fall in the government's credit, and revealed just how unpopular 'John Bull' was in the eyes of the rest of the world. Reforms in British defence policy, now demanded by Conservatives and Liberals alike, would take years to carry out; and in the meantime Russian troops were massing on the Afghan border; French forces moved into parts of the disputed border region between Algeria and Morocco; Spain, antagonised by the British stance during the Spanish-American War, threatened Gibraltar; rumours still abounded that a continental coalition was being formed against Britain; and in the spring and early summer of 1900 there was a further scare about a French invasion. 'The Empire', warned W. T. Stead melodramatically, 'stripped of its armour, has its hands tied behind its back and its bare throat exposed to the keen knife of its bitterest enemies.'[69] When, to add to all this gloom, the news arrived of the Boxer rebellion and fears arose of the impending partition of China which might follow the operations of the multinational force dispatched to suppress that uprising, it was scarcely surprising that many Britons turned again to Berlin. This, certainly, was the reaction of the majority in the Cabinet, which by late August of 1900 was desperate to accept what seemed to be a German offer of an arrangement to preserve the *status quo* in China. Here was the final chance to salvage Britain's interests in that part of the world by getting Germany to (in Chamberlain's words) 'throw herself across the path of Russia'; and Salisbury's objections to this scheme had to be overruled. Faced by the unanimous stand of virtually all his senior colleagues, he gave in and signed the so-called Yangtse Treaty in mid-October 1900.[70] Within a month, he had also retired from the Foreign Office, with Lansdowne assuming that heavy responsibility.

Yet, for all his apparent weaknesses, Salisbury was correct in one thing: his assessment of Germany policy. The Boxer uprising and its subsequent defeat was almost as unwelcome to Bülow as it was to the British Cabinet. China was an area, like the Middle East, where Germany anticipated a very large expansion of its own commercial and political interests within the next decade. If, therefore, the powers actually 'carved up' China after they had suppressed the

Boxers, Germany's share would not be as large as she desired; here, as with the fleet, she needed to buy time. One obstacle to this waiting policy was Wilhelm himself, who enthusiastically embraced the cause of crushing the 'Yellow Peril', sent his bemused *Weltmarschall* Waldersee to lead the allied forces, urged his troops as they left Bremerhaven to act 'as the Huns' did before them, and even dispatched a squadron of battleships to the Far East – a blatant contradiction of Tirpitz's North Sea strategy, which the State Secretary of the *Reichsmarineamt* only acquiesced in when he was assured by Bülow that no difficulties were expected with 'the greatest sea-power in the near future'.[71] It had, however, the consolation for Wilhelm that the Chinese question appeared to be boosting the name of 'our so-often derided military system', and to be turning public attention away from domestic problems: 'All eyes gaze at Peking, which is very annoying for Richter, Bebel [the Left] and Kanitz and consorts [agrarian Right]; for no-one has time for their nonsense!'[72]

The second danger to Germany's China policy came not, as London believed, from the Russians but from the British themselves: for the latter's alarm at the prospect of losing the 'China market' was such that many Britons were beginning to advocate that a division into spheres of influence was necessary *now*, with the Yangtse basin (where their main trade was concentrated) falling to them. Since it was precisely Berlin's intention to expand its own commercial activities in that lucrative region – and not to be bottled up in Shantung province – it was vital to stop such a carve-up from occurring: hence the otherwise unusual occurrence of Germany approaching Britain for an agreement to maintain the *status quo*.[73] London's main aim, manifestly, was to check Russia through this display of Anglo-German solidarity; Berlin's aim, as Richthofen told the Bavarian minister, 'had simply been the binding of England'.[74] As for Chamberlain's hope that Germany would throw herself across Russia's path in Asia, such an idea was doomed from the start for it contradicted one of the basic rules of German policy since 1895; thus, the vague reference in the treaty to upholding freedom of trade for all China 'as far as they can exercise influence' was privately interpreted by Berlin to mean that they would not contest Russia's claims in Manchuria. In the words of the sharpsighted and anglophile US Secretary of State, John Hay, the Yangtse agreement was 'a horrible practical joke on England'.[75]

Before the dénouement of Germany's China policy occurred, the Kaiser unwittingly tested the 'free hand' policy once again. In mid-January 1901 Wilhelm informed his Chancellor (as Bülow had then become) that he was setting off immediately for Windsor, where his grandmother was slowly dying. This was a highly unpopular gesture at the height of the Boer War anglophobia, and Eulenburg informed Bülow that 'the feeling in Germany against our dear master is quite alarming', for this visit occurred only a month after the German government (fearing a British backlash) had decided not to receive Kruger in Berlin, and had then been castigated by all the nationalist newspapers and pressure groups.[76] What upset Bülow almost as much as Wilhelm's prolonged stay were the reports that Chamberlain and Devonshire favoured another effort to attach Britain to the Triple Alliance. For two weeks, the Chancellor worried lest his impressionable master compromise Germany's relations with Russia by concluding some deal with the 'perfidious' British statesmen and with that 'sly old hen, Uncle Eddy'; and despite all the efforts of the *Auswärtiges Amt*'s attendant, Metternich, the Kaiser did tell his audience at a farewell meal that 'We ought to form an Anglo-German alliance, you to keep the seas while we would be responsible for the land'. This message was, predictably, suffocated by Wilhelm's courtiers, and Bülow himself took great pains to fend off agrarian and Pan-German questioning when the Kaiser eventually returned to Berlin: the visit had no political meaning, the Chancellor assured the Reichstag; Anglo-German relations remained the same, with Germany ready to live in peace with the British 'on the basis of mutual regard and absolute parity'. The more that the cheering British crowds, and even *The Times*, praised the Kaiser's devotion to his grandmother, the more Bülow had to deny its importance inside Germany.[77]

The British hopes of German support were to be very short-lived indeed. At almost the same time as the visit, news arrived that Russia was manoeuvring for an exclusive concession at Tientsin. Japan was ready to resist this, but wanted Anglo-German help: would Berlin, standing on the basis of the Yangtse Treaty, join London in giving in? The German answer, thoughtfully communicated by Bülow to St Petersburg as well, was frank: German interests were not directly involved, and she could only adopt a policy of the 'strictest and most correct neutrality' if Japan and Britain opposed Russia. As Bülow assured the Reichstag, Manchuria's fate was of 'absolute indifference' to Germany and was *not* covered by the agreement with Britain. This was just as Salisbury and the permanent staff of the Foreign Office, with their daily knowledge of German diplomacy, had anticipated; but to the other Cabinet ministers, Berlin's answer came as a bitter disappointment. 'It was from this moment', Monger notes, 'that the pro-German sentiment of the Cabinet, which had been so strong in the winter of 1900-1, began to decline.'[78]

It was at this moment, too, ironically enough, that Baron von Eckardstein of the London Embassy made his last, desperate bid to arrange an alliance by the simple device of confidentially assuring both sides that the other was eager for one. The full story of this 'comedy of errors', recounted and scrutinised in innumerable studies, does not bear a further telling. Two facts, however, stand out very clearly. The first was that British Cabinet ministers, suitably chastened by their experience over the Yangtse Treaty, were in general much more cautious than hitherto about the idea of an alliance with Germany and even more so with its two partners. Salisbury's classic memorandum of May 1901, defending the virtues of isolationism and stressing that such an alliance 'would excite bitter murmurs in every rank of German society', has been regarded by many historians as the decisive contribution; but Lansdowne himself admitted that it was 'a big fence . . . to ride at'; and it is likely that by this time Chamberlain had already abandoned his pursuit of a German alliance and was turning to France – as he had always warned he would. The fact that the two governments were quarrelling just then about Chinese indemnity payments and about a joint policy towards France in Morocco simply increased the tendency of the Cabinet to regard all German suggestions with distrust by the summer of 1901.[79]

The second, and very important point to be made about these confused Anglo-German alliance negotiations is that the permanent staff of the *Auswärtiges Amt* were not averse to the idea in principle and were willing to explore it in practice. Despite the frustration and irritation which Hatzfeldt and Holstein, and also other foreign policy advisers such as Klehmet, Rosen and Lichnowsky had felt about (as they saw it) Britain's selfish policy over the past decade, their more positive attitude was not altogether surprising. Few if any of them yet recognised the true meaning of Tirpitz's fleet policy; most of them, certainly Holstein, still clung to the idea of the early 1890s that the creation of a quadruple alliance was desirable, always provided the terms were right; and certain events over the past two years may have reawakened their ancient suspicion of Russian intentions. In mid-1899, for example, Berlin had also become involved in a nasty dispute with Russia, which appeared determined to prevent the German economic penetration of Asia Minor, and which had gone on to hint that not only might St Petersburg ally with London to keep Germany out of the Near East but that it would also not allow the Germans to take over Austria-Hungary if that state should collapse. Furthermore, during these negotiations, and in the secret exchange of views about a league against Britain during the Boer War, Berlin had requested a permanent mutual guarantee of the existing boundaries of the continental powers; and each time the Russians had drawn back, indicating thereby that they would never put pressure upon France to abandon the hope of regaining Alsace-Lorraine. By the beginning of the new century, too, many observers held that Austria-Hungary was close to collapse (including Salisbury, which is another reason why he disliked any commitment to the Triple Alliance); and Italy was drifting away, into a private agreement with the French over North Africa. One wonders whether the *Auswärtiges Amt* staff also felt, as Wilhelm did, that there was a danger of falling between two stools and that the 'free hand' policy could not go on for ever without incurring failure.[80] Ironically, therefore, part of the German 'Official Mind' was warming to the prospect of an alliance just as the British themselves were becoming less enthusiastic.

The decisive role in Berlin – and the one which reveals yet again that he was determined to pursue his own conception of German foreign policy – was Bülow's.[81] In February 1901 he had queried or rejected a number of the points which Lichnowsky (the official responsible for English affairs) had suggested inserting in the press as suitable arguments for better relations with Britain; and in March, he brushed aside a memorandum by Klehmet which both warned of the dangers of German isolation and suggested that, following the China débâcle, public opinion was now less insistent upon colonial concessions. Between March and May, Bülow was sent on five occasions a copy of Bismarck's famous letter to Salisbury of 22 November 1887, together with Holstein's draft of a covering letter to London, hinting that now as before Berlin required a firm treaty of alliance from Britain; but Bülow always postponed a decision to have these documents dispatched to the London embassy. Finally, the Chancellor struck upon a demand which was virtually guaranteed to bog down the negotiations: Britain must promise to defend not only Germany, but also Austria-Hungary and Italy. Perhaps Lansdowne could first direct his approaches to Vienna, he suggested ingeniously. It was precisely this which the British Foreign Secretary termed 'a big fence', and his dismay would have increased had he known that Bülow had also vetoed his permanent advisers' draft clause that Germany would engage to fight not merely to defend the British Isles but also the empire. 'One had the impression', Holstein later reflected, 'that Bülow clung to all the obstacles which stood in the way of the alliance.'[82] It is not surprising to learn that the Chancellor kept his tactics secret from his imperial master, who at his meeting with Edward VII in August 1901 indicated to the somewhat bemused British that he was 'dissatisfied that the negotiations . . . had not led to a definite result'. When the danger of further talks was fully removed after the exchange between Lansdowne and Metternich (now Hatzfeldt's successor in London) in November, Bülow could revert to his habit of assuring the British government of his private hopes for an eventual alliance at some indefinite time in the future; but his real feelings were perhaps best expressed when he cynically pencilled upon the *Auswärtiges Amt*'s final memorandum on the subject: 'R.I.P.'[83]

So far, Bülow had been very successful in his 'free hand' policy towards England; and yet, within months, the diplomatic foundations of that position began to crumble. The basic reason for this change was the growing British suspicion of German policy, particularly in the Conservative press and in various imperialist circles: in other words, among those forces which for the previous few years (and in some cases even longer) had looked to Germany as a 'natural' ally in the common struggle against French and Russian expansionism. Now that they were beginning to perceive that Germany could be a potential threat to, rather than a supporter of British interests, the same calculations made them join hands with those who – like *The Times* Berlin correspondent, and some members of the Foreign Office and diplomatic corps – had always been suspicious of German policy since the inauguration of *Weltpolitik*.

Apart from the failure of the alliance negotiations and the growing dislike of Bülow's devious diplomacy, two factors were of critical importance in this alteration in British imperialist thinking. The first was the rampant and uncontrollable anglophobia in Germany during the Boer War, of which enough details are known to spare much repetition here. What is clear is that its impact upon British opinion was immense. English visitors to Germany were quite staggered by the abuse: the young Evelyn Wrench, for example, witnessed pro-Boer demonstrations and found himself in 'tremendous arguments' with his hosts during the months he spent on a German tour.[84] Rosebery, virtually the only pro-German among the Liberal-imperialists, sent his sons to Germany to complete their education; but, as he complained to both Herbert Bismarck and to Mensdorff, they had reacted against the attacks upon their country and now become 'rabid anti-Germans'.[85] Other visitors sent back to England examples of the offensive and obscene postcards of the German gutter press. The Athenaeum Club actually displayed on its walls a large collection of anti-British cartoons and articles by the continental press, and (as Chirol informed Holstein) 'both in volume and in virulence the German section is *facile princeps*'. Chamberlain received details of the organisation and agitations of the Pan-German League from Heinrich Angst, the British Consul-General in Zurich.[86]

Most Britons learnt of this hostility from reading their daily papers and other magazines, however, and it may have been precisely because the 'serious' press illustrated this anglophobia so fully that observers in London such as Metternich, Eckardstein and Mensdorff were struck by the change of moods towards Germany in the socially select circles with which they came into contact. Saunders, as is well known, conceived it to be his duty to report every manifestation of anti-British feeling, so that the influential readership of *The Times* would take notice of this new challenge: not for nothing did Bülow describe him and Chirol as being among 'the most dangerous Englishmen for us', since they knew 'from personal observation how sharp and deep is the German dislike of England'.[87] But, with few exceptions, readers of the other British papers were given a similar impression: by April 1900, the *Spectator* had abandoned its earlier warmth for Germany and was publishing articles with such titles as 'England's Real Enemy'; and the Liberal Imperialist *Daily Chronicle* doubtless made British breakfast-times uncomfortable by its full descriptions of the anglophobic cartoons in German dailies and weeklies:

In front of a scorched and blackened background, a huge cauldron is placed over a blazing fire. Two demons, naked, painted scarlet, are engaged at the cauldron, with horns, tails and vampires' wings. One of these is Mr. Chamberlain and the other Lord Kitchener. Mr. Chamberlain is stirring up the cauldron, out of which two childish arms are stretched. Lord Kitchener, who is represented with a particularly Satanic visage, is collecting children, and his arms are full of them. In the clouds of smoke arising from the boiling cauldron are the phantom forms of children, represented as winged cherubs. Above this horrible drawing are the words 'Twelve Thousand Boer children'. Below it the words, 'How the devils are filling heaven'.[88]

Judging from other reports, the anti-Boer-War literature in France, Russia and the Netherlands was almost as bad; but most of the British newspapers asserted that they had expected such treatment from their traditional rivals, and trusted that they would have secured more understanding from their 'natural' friend, Germany – thus, the disappointment was correspondingly greater.

The second, related factor was the growing concern in the British press about the real aims of German naval expansion. A study of the British press around the turn of the century demonstrates the falseness of the claim that it was not until the naval scare' of 1904 that the German fleet played a significant role in the public estrangement between the two countries. Suspicious observers like Saunders at Berlin believed this expansionism was directed from the very beginning against Britain, and by 1900 Chirol had also been converted to this view. 'Germany is, in my opinion, more fundamentally hostile than either France or Russia, but she is not ready yet', he told Leo Amery. 'She looks upon us as upon an artichoke to be pulled to pieces leaf by leaf.'[89] Even as early as

January 1896, when the two countries were quarrelling over the Kruger Telegram, some British navalist writers like H. W. Wilson and Arnold White took alarm at Germany's naval ambitions and from that moment on, that is, even *before* Tirpitz took office, never let this consideration escape their minds. In January 1898 the arch-imperialist *National Review* asserted: 'We clearly cannot afford to allow the German Emperor to hold the balance of sea power in Europe in the early years of the twentieth century'; but it was really the passing of the second Naval Law which caused many British journals to announce that the German threat was directly aimed at displacing Great Britain as the mistress of the seas. Once the Kaiser's visit to the queen's deathbed was over, these articles resumed. Certain writers, including Calchas (J. L. Garvin) in his famous *Fortnightly Review* article of January 1901, 'Will England Last the Century?', pointed to the German naval 'menace' and called for the construction of a new naval base on Britain's North Sea coast. Other writers, with even livelier imaginations, were beginning to speculate upon the possibility of a surprise German invasion of England.[90]

If these suspicions were not shared by the majority of the British Cabinet during 1900–1, then it was due to differing perceptions of Germany in imperialist circles, and to disagreements about the relative seriousness of the threats to the British Empire. Most of the anti-Germans were already arguing that it would be better, as H. W. Wilson put it, 'to *rapproche* with Russia rather than with Germany. I used to be all the other way, but the more I see of Germans, the more I distrust them.'[91] The Cabinet, with the exception of Salisbury, had still not reached that position by the summer of 1901; most members were paralysed by the prospect of Russia's continual expansion in Asia; and others were aghast at the spiralling defence costs, which had compelled the Admiralty to abandon the strict Two Power Standard in favour of the less abstract criterion of 'the reasonable certainty of success in a war with France and Russia'.[92] The German refusal to denounce Russian actions in Manchuria and the failure of the alliance talks had undermined the argument that Britain's world interests would be best preserved by close co-operation with Berlin; but this did not turn the majority in the Cabinet into anti-Germans overnight. Nevertheless, these Conservative-Unionist politicians could not fail to be affected in some degree by the fact that almost all the newspapers which supported their party were agitating about the coming German danger.

By the turn of the year 1901–2, however, it is possible to point to two further developments which significantly worsened the Anglo-German relationship and, by extension, the assumptions upon which the Kaiser's *Weltpolitik* had been based. The first of these was that series of public and bitter arguments between Chamberlain and Bülow, and between their respective supporters in the patriotic press, over the conduct of British forces in South Africa in 1899–1901 as compared with that of the German troops in 1870–1.[93] Chamberlain, as Britain's Colonial Secretary and leading imperialist, was bound to be sensitive about criticisms of the South African situation; he was smarting over the German refusal to help in China, and still resenting Bülow's unfriendly response to his Leicester speech of November 1899. Thus, the public quarrel with Bülow served only to encourage his growing suspicion that Germany had been unfriendly all along, and to increase his wish for a *rapprochement* with the Dual Alliance. Bülow's action was also symptomatic because it once again revealed that, faced with the choice of either offending the domestic anglo-phobes or annoying the British, he would always plump for the latter. From this time onwards, the bulk of British politicians and press came to regard Bülow with such dislike and suspicion (sometimes contrasting this with Wilhelm's erratic but evident regard for things English) that his continuance in office alone may be said to have constituted a stumbling-block to improved Anglo-German relations in the future. The Chancellor's firm determination to make a strong speech in the Reichstag against Chamberlain and thereby to secure popularity among the agrarians and Pan-Germans was regarded with dismay by Metternich in London and by Holstein, Hammann and other members of the *Auswärtiges Amt*, who sought in vain to dissuade him from this action. Although Bülow gained his domestic-political aim, his 'granite speech' had driven a further nail into the coffin of Anglo-German friendship. It was, one Berlin observer felt, 'Bülow's first great mistake'.[94]

Precisely at the time of these exchanges, the British government was moving towards its alliance with Japan, the actual treaty being signed on 30 January 1902. The initial German reaction to this news was favourable, for the *Wilhelm-strasse* was pleased that the two signatories were taking a firmer stand against Russia and that an Anglo-Russian understanding over China was made more difficult than ever before. Nimbly avoiding a request from St Petersburg that she join a Franco-Russian counter-declaration, Germany declined to get involved on either side, convinced that the great *Krach* (which would enhance her own position) had come a little closer.[95] In the longer term, however, this alliance was to work to Germany's detriment. In the first place, by giving a measure of security to the British position in the Orient, it removed the chief reason why Chamberlain and many others had sought a German alliance in these years. The Anglo-Japanese alliance may have ended 'splendid isolation' – if it was possible to define what that state was[96] – but in fact it actually accentuated Britain's isolation from Europe by strengthening its naval position and weakening its need to purchase German support. It was for this reason, no doubt, that Salisbury found its terms less offensive than a German alliance, and that Foreign Office members like Bertie and newspapers like *The Times* applauded its conclusion. If the Opposition expressed greater unease, this was chiefly because Liberal Imperialists feared that an alliance with Japan would render an eventual British *rapprochement* with Russia impossible. Only Balfour, perhaps with the philosopher's love of the logical antithesis, argued now for a European alliance and suggested that Britain *had* an interest in fighting for the independence of Italy, Austria-Hungary and Germany. But he did not press his case, which by the end of 1901 was clearly a most unpopular and impracticable standpoint.[97] If co-operation with Germany was to continue, therefore, it would have to be in the form of smaller-scale agreements – and even this seemed to have been made unlikely by Metternich's statement that it should either be 'the whole or none'.[98]

The second, longer-term consequence of the Anglo-Japanese alliance was its impact upon the Dual Alliance or, more properly, upon France. Initially, Paris felt bound to support St Petersburg in issuing the counter-declaration of March 1902; but the French Foreign Minister Delcassé was no more eager to fight over China than the Russians had been for French interests on the Nile three years earlier. Moreover, the specific terms of both the Franco-Russian and the Anglo-Japanese alliances – that each signatory would fight if its partner was opposed by two or more foes, but remain benevolently neutral if only one enemy was involved – meant that it was going to be in France's interests to ensure that Britain remained aloof from a Russo-Japanese conflict in the Far East. Since, *pari passu*, it was also in Britain's interests to remain a 'second' in such a war, the circumstances were created for Paris and London to consider co-operation – if only to avoid fighting each other when they had no direct motive for doing so. All this was, admittedly, some way in the future; but it is nevertheless fair to argue that the Anglo-Japanese alliance, by lessening Britain's links with Germany and by strengthening the Japanese in their determination to stand up to Russia, was to provide one of the causes for the creation of the Anglo-French *entente*. The likelihood of one event leading to the other was increased, moreover, by the fact that the French always watched Berlin's actions with the greatest care. At the time of the Fashoda crisis, Delcassé had been aware that Wilhelm II was gloating at the prospect of a French defeat by Britain; later in 1899, he became so concerned that Germany would be the heir to the crumbling Austro-Hungarian Empire and gain a port on the Adriatic that he had renegotiated the terms of the Dual Alliance to frustrate such an event; and during the Boer War he had reacted with anger to Berlin's message that German participation in a continental league against Britain could only be purchased by France's full and open recognition of the permanent loss of Alsace-Lorraine. Delcassé's conclusion from all this was not only the Franco-German interests were irreconcilable, but also that the Kaiser and Bülow were not to be trusted. If, therefore, the *Wilhelmstrasse* was now sanguine about a future war in the Far East, then it was the plain duty of French diplomacy to prevent such a conflict or to ensure that at least it remained localised. In Paris, as in London, certain elements in the 'Official Mind' and imperialist circles had become profoundly suspicious of Bülow's 'free hand' policy and were already wondering whether it might not be possible to arrange an Anglo-French and even an Anglo-Russian understanding in order to check German ambitions.[99] Although it is far too early to refer to an 'encirclement' policy in 1902, the basis for such a possibility – as Eckardstein (for all his other faults) recognised – was being fashioned.

# CHAPTER 14

# The Flowering of the Antagonism (1902–1906)

The years 1901–2 mark a watershed in British attitudes towards Germany which may be compared in both scope and importance with the alteration in the German view of England that had occurred in 1896–7. From the time of the Boer War onwards, it is possible to detect a growing British conviction that there existed a 'German threat' or 'German challenge' which had to be countered. Furthermore, this was a view which was held not merely by certain right-wing journalists, but also by influential figures in the navy, the army and the Foreign Office; by the Crown; by significant members of the Liberal Party; and, last but not least, by a part of the Cabinet, although not by the new Prime Minister, Balfour, nor by Lansdowne. Although the latter attempted a conciliatory policy towards Berlin, they neither felt willing nor able fully to counter this fast-growing germanophobic sentiment.

Even at the time of the Reichstag debates upon the first two German Naval Laws, the British Admiralty had shown concern, both because those measures might give a further impetus to the arms race and because of a specific dislike at the idea that Germany could soon hold the balance of naval power between the British and Franco-Russian fleets.[1] Two further general points about the Admiralty's strategy are also worth making. The first was its repeated insistence that, even when urgent calls came for reinforcements to Far Eastern and Mediterranean waters, naval predominance in home waters should not be impaired: in 1900–1, for example, the First Sea Lord, Sir Walter Kerr, repeatedly refused to accede to Admiral Fisher's demands for further vessels to be sent to the Mediterranean if this involved a weakening of the Home Fleet.[2] The second was the abstract, yet flexible manner in which the two-power standard operated against *any* new threat: thus, in December 1900, the Director of Naval Intelligence, Custance, argued that since the German navy would be larger than the Russian after 1906, the strength of the British fleet would have to be calculated against 'the navies of France and Germany' as the next two maritime powers. 'As the German Navy will be at that date a much greater danger to this country than the fleet of Russia', Custance wrote a little later, it will be necessary '. . . to maintain a force in the North Sea sufficient to mask the German Fleet.'[3] In other words, Tirpitz's calculations that Germany could

251

develop a formidable naval force in home waters without the British either noticing it or being able to respond to it was flawed from the start.

Because of the financial strains placed upon the British Empire by the Boer War, Selborne, the First Lord, at first thought it necessary only to anticipate the case of a war against the Franco-Russian fleets; but by early 1902 he was sufficiently concerned by the evidence of German anglophobia to query both Lascelles and the British naval attaché in Berlin about Germany's fleet aims. The reply that 'the German Navy is professedly aimed at that of the greatest sea power – us', and the repeated pressure by the Director of Naval Intelligence for counter-measures to neutralise German designs, spurred Selborne into action.[4] In April of 1902 he, Balfour, Lansdowne and Chamberlain had 'a conference on certain naval matters', and as a consequence accepted an Admiralty proposal that an attempt be made secretly to purchase the land necessary for a North Sea naval base, a decision which could be publicly justified later 'from a dockyard and berthing point of view'. The size of the battlefleet to be stationed there, however, was to 'be practically determined by the power of the German Navy'.[5] When in August 1902 the parliamentary secretary Arnold-Foster returned from a visit to Kiel and Wilhelmshaven with an alarming account of German naval expansion (and an implied criticism of the Admiralty's neglect of this factor), both Kerr and Custance replied tartly that 'those responsible for these matters have not allowed the growth of the German Navy to escape their notice'. 'We shall have to fight for command of the North Sea', Custance minuted, 'as we did in the Dutch wars of the 17th century'.[6] Their political chief, Selborne, originally an advocate of an Anglo-German alliance, was by now convinced of Berlin's hostility: thus, he agreed to stay on as First Lord on condition that the Treasury would not be allowed to veto his demand for an adequate 'margin' of battleships above the two-power standard 'in view of the rapid expansion of the German Navy'; he urged a Cabinet sub-committee to recommend that a governmental subsidy be given to the Cunard Line, so that the Admiralty could have the use of the firm's new Atlantic liners in wartime to counter the possible German use of the *Hamburg-Amerika* and *Norddeutsche Lloyd*'s vessels as auxiliary cruisers; and when Erskine Childers's novel *The Riddle of the Sands* received great publicity with its fictional account of a German plan to invade England, Selborne insisted that the Naval Intelligence Department consider the feasibility of such a scheme.[7]

At almost the same time the army, too, was taking a fresh look at Germany, a power which had never previously figured in its operational planning simply because of the War Office's almost exclusive concern with the Franco-Russian challenge outside Europe.[8] This may be seen in part as a search by certain ambitious staff officers for a new or at least rediscovered role for the service following the disasters of the Boer War; but it was also prompted by an awareness that there had been considerable discussion in German newspapers about the feasibility of a surprise invasion of England. At the end of 1902, the Assistant Quarter-Master-General, Colonel Robertson, drafted a memorandum which not only argued against an alliance with Germany on the grounds that its government and people were intent upon 'superseding us in the commercial and naval supremacy', but also went on to advocate a *rapprochement* with Russia and France. Even more remarkable was Robertson's argument that Britain should remember her ancient strategical principle of maintaining the European balance of power, which might well be upset in the future by an expanding Germany, 'our most persistent, deliberate, and formidable rival'.[9] No other serving officer appears to have gone so far, but there were signs that many were at least giving thought to the possibility of a German invasion: early in 1903 the War Office re-examined the state of its home defences to see if they were strong enough to withstand 'a [German] dash at our Eastern coast . . . at a time when we were at war with France and Russia'; and the Royal Commission on the Militia and Volunteers also investigated how far those forces could meet an invasion army either of French or German troops.[10]

By far the most persistent dislike of Germany in these years was held by certain members of the Foreign Office staff and the diplomatic corps. Spring-Rice, as we have seen, never lost his suspicion of German designs after his period of duty in Berlin, and his correspondence in these years is full of complaints about Germany's *chantage* and about the need to come 'to some defensive understanding with other nations, equally threatened by the new German chauvinism'.[11] Rumbold, an ancient critic of Prusso-German expansionism since 1870, had carefully studied German anglophobia during the Boer War from the vantage-point of the Vienna embassy and, shortly after his retirement, published an attack upon German ambitions in the *National Review* – upon which he received the congratulations of Drummond Wolff and the approbation of Cromer.[12] Curzon, too, was suspicious of Germany, constantly opposing the Baghdad Railway project and privately criticising Chamberlain for 'slobbering' about an Anglo-German alliance in his Leicester speech.[13] Charles Hardinge, already rising fast through the ranks of the diplomatic corps, was equally critical of the Yangtse agreement and argued instead for a *rapprochement* with Russia.[14] In the Foreign Office itself, the forceful Francis Bertie, who showed dislike of Berlin's diplomacy during the Portuguese Colonies and China negotiations, had become so mistrustful by 1902–3 that he was arguing for a policy of checking any German attempts to obtain colonies and of encouraging Franco-German quarrels;[15] and his views here were shared by other members of the office such as Louis Mallett, Tyrrell, Eyre Crowe and Tilley.[16]

It would *not* be true, of course, to suggest that all of the permanent staff of these influential ministries held such antagonistic views towards Germany. Sanderson, very much the bureaucratic reflection of his previous political masters Derby and Salisbury, disliked Berlin's diplomatic methods and had been very doubtful about the feasibility of the Anglo-German alliance talks; but he also disapproved of the extremeness of the swing away from Germany, 'for there are a good many questions in which it is important for both countries that we should work cordially together'.[17] Lascelles, the recipient of this letter, could not agree more with the sentiments expressed therein; and the ambassador in Berlin was a constant advocate of good Anglo-German relations, incurring the enmity of the anti-Germans as a consequence. Moreover, most members of the 'Official Mind' who had to grapple with the acute problem of checking Russian expansionism in Asia at this time were bound to be less enthusiastic about a cooling in Anglo-German relations, if only for this negative reason. Even Eyre Crowe, later to be regarded as the 'evil spirit' of the Foreign Office germanophobes,[18] warned against the facile assumption that an Anglo-Russian agreement could be reached 'by the exercise of a little goodwill and a modicum of common sense', and argued the case for internal reforms and reorganisation of the armed forces rather than running after *any* power.[19] This apprehension about the more pressing threats to the British Empire posed by Russia and France predominated in the service ministries. When Robertson presented his memorandum on 'The Military Resources of Germany . . .' early in 1903, the other Assistant Quarter-Master-General, Colonel Altham, not only offered a strategical counter-view but concluded with the further observation that 'an understanding with that Power on questions as to which we have common or conflicting interests would greatly strengthen our general position'.[20] Given that both the army and the newly founded Committee of Imperial Defence were concentrating the greater part of their attention upon India's vulnerability to a future Russian assault, this sentiment is easy to understand. Even at the Admiralty, the First Sea Lord, Kerr, declared that he was less convinced than the Director of Naval Intelligence and the naval attaché in Berlin that the German fleet was directed against Britain; and, just as he had previously resisted the appeal to devote all attention to the Mediterranean, so now he declined to concentrate exclusively upon the North Sea – 'the German element' was *one* of several considerations to be borne in mind.[21]

What one can say is that the notion of a fundamental clash of interests between Britain and Germany had entered several sections of the 'Official Mind', and usually among the younger element – or, at least, among those circles who chafed at the traditional ways and desired a drastic 'shake-up' in the practices and assumptions of British external policy. A similar division of views, it may be argued, also existed at the Cabinet level. Salisbury's going in 1902 had symbolised the end of an era, and there were many voices among the middle-to-higher ranks of the Unionist Party who pressed for a radical reconstruction of defence and foreign policy, if necessary in an anti-German direction. Selborne was now deeply concerned about Germany's designs; so, too, was Arnold-Foster, who took over the War Office in the following year: but the best example of all was Joseph Chamberlain himself, who was not only in the process of recasting his economic and imperial policies but also much more willing to achieve a reconciliation with France and Russia.[22] Furthermore, through the intercession of Leo Maxse, the belligerent right-wing editor of the *National Review*, Chamberlain had been introduced to Saunders (then on leave from Berlin) and instructed not only in the day-to-day tactics of Bülow's diplomacy but also in the ideology of a German world mission as preached by Housten Stewart Chamberlain and others.[23] In this growing mistrust of German aims, the Colonial Secretary was supported by his son, Austen, now in the Cabinet as Postmaster General and even more suspicious of German intentions.

Nevertheless, there were still many Cabinet ministers who clung to the historic assumptions and would have openly disapproved of an anti-German policy, just as they were to disapprove of Chamberlain's radical break with

Britain's traditional fiscal policy in 1903: Devonshire, Cranborne and Brodrick might be included in this category. Above all, the Prime Minister and the Foreign Secretary still hoped for good relations with Germany, even if an alliance had proved impossible. Lansdowne, with his cool Whig mentality, was not inclined to take the popular germanophobia very seriously, and certainly believed that it would eventually die away. Balfour, as was seen at the time of the signing of the Anglo-Japanese alliance, genuinely believed that there was a basic identity of interests between Britain and the Triple Alliance; and when he was appraised of Selborne's fears about the meaning of German naval expansion, he was somewhat sceptical.[24] Furthermore, as several historians have demonstrated, Balfour's mind was exercised in these years with the problem of Indian defence. Although this made him desperately keen to achieve an Anglo-Russian understanding on Asian questions, he was also much more pessimistic about St Petersburg keeping its word – and correspondingly anxious at least to give the impression that Anglo-German relations were normal.

Balfour and Lansdowne were not only more tolerant of German policy than many of their Cabinet colleagues and advisers, but also less hostile than their monarch. Edward VII still harboured that dislike of Prussian manners and political ambitions which had been aroused in him during the 1860s; he found it difficult to remain on good terms with his pushy, tactless nephew; he had been disgusted at the anglophobia of the German press during the Boer War; he was so outraged at Bülow's 'granite' speech that he resolved to cancel the planned visit of the Prince of Wales to Berlin, which in turn provoked Wilhelm to threaten the recall of ambassadors until Lansdowne stepped in and smoothed things over;[25] and he was another advocate of an Anglo-French *rapprochement*. However, his intentions were far more sporadic – and, to that extent, less influential – than those of the ministers and officials engaged in the day-to-day processes of managing Britain's external policy. And, at Whitehall and Westminster, as recounted above, attitudes towards Germany were finely divided.

What *did* affect this balance of official opinion in the period after 1902 was the pressure of nationalist sentiment, especially as manifested in the political press. The Liberal newspapers were, by and large, too concerned with party fissures, the Boer War and education to devote much attention to foreign affairs but when they did, they were not markedly anti-German. By this time, however, the greater part of the Conservative press had been galvanised by the Boer War into a fit of patriotic excess on the one hand, and into repeatedly calling for a drastic reconstruction of defence and imperial affairs on the other. More particularly, the great majority of these journals now firmly believed that German hatred of Britain was irreversible and that the German fleet was aimed at wresting maritime supremacy from the Royal Navy: all efforts by the government to hold out the olive branch to Berlin were therefore regarded with deep mistrust, and heavily criticised. Here *The Times* led the way, shooting off (in Sanderson's words) like an old-fashioned war rocket;[26] but its line was echoed by the *Morning Post*, the *Spectator*, *Fortnightly Review*, the *Observer* and the *Mail*. Perhaps the most vigorous anti-German line of all was taken by the *National Review* under Maxse, who worked with a number of writers to expose, as he saw it, Germany's devilish designs: from October 1901 onwards, his journal mounted a sustained attack upon Berlin, coupled with repeated urgings that the British government compose its differences with France and Russia so as to be able to present a solid front to German expansionism. These editors and journalists frequently urged each other on in their endeavours; and they had many points of contact with Cabinet ministers, with Opposition statesmen, and with the staff of the Foreign Office and the service ministries, exchanging ideas with, but also occasionally coming out in open opposition to the policies pursued in Whitehall. A powerful campaign by the press, acting in combination with those members of the political and bureaucratic establishment who shared their wish for change and their suspicions of Germany, was quite likely to tilt the balance against those who strove to work in harmony with Berlin.

The two classic examples of this nationalist outcry against co-operation with Germany concern the Venezuela blockade and the Baghdad Railway negotiations. The attitude of the British Right to the joint blockade of Venezuela in 1902–3 was, of all these matters, the most predictable; for, however much they disagreed over the nature of London's relations with Berlin, Paris and St Petersburg, they were virtually unanimous in their advocacy of a firm Anglo-American friendship, and the likelihood of this joint action against Venezuela leading to a cooling in London's relations with Washington drove them wild with anger and resentment. The Foreign Secretary himself was less moved by these considerations: in the first place, to refuse to co-operate with Germany at *any* time would severely hamstring his diplomatic freedom of action, and that at a time when relations with Russia were still bad, and with France uncertain; and secondly, the situation in Venezuela itself had so deteriorated that, by the normal standards of Victorian 'gunboat diplomacy', some form of physical pressure and retribution was called for.[27] It was just at this time, moreover, that he had moved strongly against the ex-ambassador, Rumbold, for writing in the *National Review* an attack openly critical of German policy. Obviously, the Foreign Secretary's chief cause for anger there was the unwelcome precedent of former members of the diplomatic corps being involved in press polemics and revelations, but it seems also clear that Lansdowne was eager to maintain reasonable relations with Berlin.[28]

To the Germans, the Foreign Secretary's attitude was most welcome. The rising crescendo of anti-German press articles, all of which were passed on by Metternich, Eckardstein and Coerper (the naval attaché) from the London embassy, caused great concern at the *Wilhelmstrasse*: the articles in the *National Review* especially, Saunders reported gleefully, 'almost struck their powder magazine' and caused an immense stir in Berlin.[29] Even if Bülow did not believe that Britain could be reconciled with the Franco-Russian alliance, the attacks in the English newspapers had to be taken seriously, for they heralded the beginning of the 'danger zone'. As he put it to Wilhelm, 'they make difficult Your Majesty's hitherto so successful efforts carefully to cultivate our relations to England and to allow no mistrust to arise there during the growth of our fleet'.[30] It may also have been the case that, as Holstein noted, the repeated English emphasis upon the distinction between the Kaiser, who was not thought to be fundamentally hostile to Britain, and Bülow, who could not be trusted, was beginning to weaken the Chancellor's position in his master's eyes.[31]

The attempts made by Berlin to defuse the Anglo-German newspaper war were certainly remarkable. There were the usual efforts by the Press Bureau to prevent criticism of Britain: 'all further attacks of the German press on Chamberlain can only strengthen his position', Bülow instructed, adding that there should also be no insults of the dying Cecil Rhodes – 'That would only be grist to the mill of English imperialism.'[32] Others, too, were pressed into the great task: Waldersee, who was to be feted by Roberts and other British officers at a dinner in London, was encouraged to make a speech praising the British army and the cause of Anglo-German friendship; and the government-inspired press in Germany was then told to report this event in a welcoming manner. It was also warned against any display of *Schadenfreude* at the news of Edward VII's illness and the postponement of his coronation.[33] Similarly, the Hamburg Senate was asked to hinder any efforts by the Pan-German League to welcome Boers due to arrive at the port – just as, a few months later, Wilhelm declined to receive the Boer generals in Berlin, fearing that the enraged British public would force its government to break off relations 'and my fleet is not ready'.[34] Sometimes, of course, these efforts backfired: all pressure upon *The Times* to recall Saunders strengthened his position; and an interview which Wilhelm granted to the popular journalist, Arnold White, simply confirmed the latter's germanophobia and convinced him that the Kaiser was 'a neurotic, with a diseased taste for relieving the Most High of his natural functions of running the universe'.[35] On the other hand, Bülow did manage to persuade the *Daily Telegraph* to keep its pro-German correspondent, Bashford, in Berlin; Lucien Wolf was encouraged to write some friendly articles in the *Daily Graphic*; and the newly founded *Empire Review* was secretly subsidised to the extent of a standing order of 1,000 copies for each issue when it was learned that it would seek to counter the attacks of the *National Review*.[36]

At the *Reichsmarineamt*, a similar concern was shown about the British press coverage of the German navy. 'They demonstrate once again', the naval attaché warned, 'that a certain caution is very advisable in the publications which justify the need for a strong German fleet' – so that, when the *Morning Post* noticed the *Deutsche Revue* article by the retired Admiral Livonius advocating a navy as big as the British, Tirpitz immediately ordered his News Bureau to produce 'Something against the foolish article of Livonius'.[37] Nothing appeared to be able to eradicate the British mistrust, however, and when Wilhelm paid a visit to Sandringham in November 1902 he was shocked at the hostility shown towards the German government – though not, he flattered himself, towards himself – and cabled urgently that the German press must be kept in check and no risky measures taken which could lead to a quarrel with London. 'Therefore, careful! They have 35 battleships in service here, and we only 8!!'[38] When Prince Henry visited England slightly later he informed Tirpitz that 'the cat is out of the bag', and regretfully added that 'we

257

would have been much further than we are now, had we understood the art of keeping quiet!!'[39]

The actions of the two chief architects of German *Weltpolitik*, Bülow and Tirpitz, indicate that they especially were shaken by this turn in British opinion. 'I do not yet believe that the English are intentionally and consciously working for a war with us', Bülow wrote, 'but it is quite certain that they would like to prepare a "Fashoda" for us.' The Chancellor was therefore delighted at the news of a fresh Anglo-Russian quarrel over Afghanistan, for the failure of those powers to achieve an Asian agreement was 'more than ever of the greatest importance'.[40] As for Tirpitz, he was busy cooking up probably the most bizarre example of what one scholar has termed his various 'concealment manoeuvres'[41] to defuse the Anglo-German antagonism. In October 1902 he asked Captain Hollweg to have prepared 'a sort of Battle of Dorking', a futuristic account of an Anglo-German conflict occurring in the year 1906. Its purpose was 'to make clear to the German people that it underestimates the danger of war with England', although Tirpitz could not resist adding that this could also be made into an 'Indirect appeal for the expansion of the German fleet'. Nevertheless, the 'scenario' that was envisaged in this publication was to show that not only Germany, but also England was severely weakened by the war, while third powers gained at their expense – a delightful fictional presentation of the risk theory. It was hoped by this, Tirpitz told the *Auswärtiges Amt*, to sober up the wilder press on both sides of the Channel; but both Bülow and Richthofen advised against its publication since they feared that it would simply be interpreted as a new means of propaganda for an increased German fleet. Officially, this bright idea was abandoned there and then; but a little later a Leipzig publisher brought out a futuristic war novel entitled *Seestern 1906* which had exactly the same plot as that drafted by Tirpitz and Hollweg![42]

Given all these fears, then, it was not surprising that Berlin welcomed the idea of co-operation with Britain over the Venezuelan issue: it would demonstrate to the world that the two countries could work together, and thus strike a blow at the forces urging an Anglo-French or Anglo-Russian *rapprochement*; a joint blockade offered a greater likelihood of the Venezuelans agreeing to meet the demands of the powers; and it avoided the possibility of Germany being isolated by the two Anglo-Saxon countries, as had happened in Samoa and to a lesser extent in the Philippines. Action against Venezuela had been deferred earlier in 1902, lest it prejudice Prince Henry's visit to the United States; now that was over, and the British would act in conjunction, circumstances could not be more favourable. There were, inevitably, still some complications arising from the basic contradictions of Berlin's *Weltpolitik*: for example, early in 1903 it was feared that Bülow would be asked in the Reichstag whether he recognised the Monroe doctrine. As the *Auswärtiges Amt* put it,

> If the Chancellor then follows the example of English ministers in more or less expressly recognising the Monroe Doctrine, this will cut across the many hopes of a future German possession in South or Central America and the imperial government will have to reckon with fresh opposition internally – I refer in this connection to the exaggerated article on 'The

Recognition of the Monroe Doctrine' in the *Alldeutsche Blätter* of the third of this month.

If, in contrast, the Chancellor avoids expressing any recognition of that doctrine, then in view of the present unfriendly American sentiments a break with the United States would be the certain result.[43]

Even before this conundrum could be resolved, however, Berlin's hopes of a joint stand with London were collapsing. To the imperialist press, Britain's actions were totally wrong. 'It is obvious', screeched the *Daily Mail*, 'that she has placed herself in a ridiculous position by allowing herself to become in South America the faithful henchman of a power with which she has, and can have, no sympathy, because that power is aiming at her fall'. Germany was deliberately seeking to undermine the Anglo-American friendship, asserted *The Times*; and precisely on this account even normally moderate Liberal newspapers such as the *Manchester Guardian* and *Westminster Gazette* castigated the government's action. Campbell-Bannerman and Grey both spoke openly against the Foreign Office, and the latter privately opined that 'Germany is our worst enemy and our greatest danger . . . Close relations with Germany mean for us worse relations with the rest of the world, especially with the U.S., France and Russia.'[44] Sir Charles Beresford, Canon MacColl, Sir Robert Giffen and many other notables weighed into the assault, which had reached its literary high point when *The Times* published the poem 'The Rowers' by Kipling – very much the poetic mouthpiece of the alarmed imperialists – which denounced this unholy co-operation with 'an open foe' and 'the shameless Hun'. Under this sort of pressure, those within the government who were already distrustful of Germany felt desperately anxious to escape from the entanglement: Arnold-Foster wanted a question put in the Commons so that the Admiralty could, in its answer, differentiate between the actions of the British and German squadrons; Hamilton and, more predictably, Bertie, opposed the whole operation; and Onslow, parliamentary secretary at the Colonial Office, informed Chamberlain that 'it will be a good thing when we are well quit of it'. Lansdowne and Balfour, and even Austen Chamberlain, protested against the clamour, argued that the British demands upon Venezuela were just and urged the press not to become over emotional about Germany;[45] but it was all to no avail. Caught between the violent disaffection of the government's traditional supporters, and an increasingly aroused American opinion, London was compelled to inform Berlin that it would be necessary to cease further naval actions and to agree to take the issue to arbitration.

These developments were, to say the least, embarrassing to the *Wilhelmstrasse*. It was the British government, after all, which had instigated this joint action and Germany which had agreed to go 'hand in hand' with Lansdowne. Instead of reducing the popular germanophobia in Britain, this had raised it to fresh heights: indeed, by February 1903, Metternich was warning that the unrest amongst Conservative backbenchers was such that it could lead to the fall of the Foreign Secretary, perhaps of the entire government, with its successor all too aware that co-operation with Germany was anathema. There was also the possibility that London might unilaterally withdraw its warships, thus leaving Germany exposed to American anger. To abandon the action against Venezuela was distasteful in Berlin, especially since the Kaiser had made too much noise about the operation, but this time the external requirements overrode consideration for nationalist sentiment at home. Even the fact that the British themselves had originally suggested the joint blockade was kept out of the German press, which in general maintained a very cautious and factual coverage of the affair. Although 'seriously frightened' (in Lascelles's opinion) by the British press reaction, Bülow shared Metternich's view that Lansdowne was a 'man of honour', who had honestly tried to co-operate and who could be trusted in the future.[46] And the Foreign Secretary himself maintained even years later that 'the Germans, upon the whole, ran straight as far as we were concerned'.[47] The formal relations between the two governments were not, therefore, affected by the Venezuelan affair, yet the incident remained remarkable. As Maximilian Harden pointed out in the *Zukunft*, 'English ministers had to invent a thousand excuses and stammer daily apologies because they had dared to go in alliance with Germany, although it had been limited to a single question.'[48]

Fresh from what they considered to be their 'victory', the anti-German forces returned to an old theme: the rise of the German fleet, and the need to counter it by the construction of a new North Sea base. 'There is a menace growing up in the east which cannot be ignored', the *Morning Post* informed its readers, 'and which means that an adequate squadron must be at some strategical point in home waters.' To increase the effectiveness of this campaign, a public meeting was held in London in February 1903. If the leaders of this agitation were already well known for their views – Maxse, Strachey of the *Spectator*, Spenser Wilkinson of the *Morning Post*, Repington and Saunders of *The Times*, Garvin, H. W. Wilson, and leaders of the Navy League, but also Dilke and Haldane! – the demonstration indicated their growing confidence and cohesiveness.[49] The North Sea base was, as noted above, something which the Admiralty had been pressing for, and the Cabinet had agreed to, quite some time before this newspaper campaign; but that the decision was only announced in the spring of 1903 gave the impression that the government was responding to public clamour

Scarcely had this agitation died away than it became known that the government was contemplating British support for the Baghdad Railway. From both sides, this appeared to be a sensible arrangement. The German banks themselves could not raise the enormous capital necessary for this enterprise and, in the manner common to the profession, sought to persuade British and French firms to share the investment: soon, Revelstoke, Cassell and Clinton Dawkins were hammering out the details with Gwinner of the *Deutsche Bank*. In this they were strongly supported by Lansdowne, who reasoned that since it would be impossible for the British government to follow Curzon's advice of insisting upon a 'hands off' policy to all other powers in the Persian Gulf, the best solution would be to internationalise both the railway and the port at its terminus. Moreover, since the traditional threat to British predominance in the Gulf had always been seen as Russia, a number of writers had been arguing for years that the best means of checking Tsarist expansionism was to introduce German influence into the Middle East. This line of reasoning, however, clearly ignored the growing desire among British imperialist circles to check Germany and to settle with Russia. The *National Review*, predictably, led the assault in its issue of April 1903:

> There is every reason to believe that so far from having learnt from the Venezuelan mess the necessity of keeping this country free from all entanglements with Germany, that deplorable episode has had a similar effect upon our Mandarins as dram-drinking in other classes: the victim simply craves for more. The ordinary onlooker innocently imagined that 'Shanghai' and 'Venezuela' must have sickened the British Government of any desire for further 'cooperation' with the Government in Berlin . . . etc.

Immediately, Maxse's allies took up the call. The *Spectator* was the next to fire off, then the *Morning Post, Daily Chronicle* and *Daily Mail. The Times*, quite forgetting that in 1899 it had encouraged Anglo-German co-operation over the railway, also joined the attack.[50] From the private correspondence of these editors and writers, it is clear that they encouraged each other: 'The *Spectator* is magnificent on the Bagdad Railway', Maxse told Strachey; *The Times* today is 'very good', wrote Bernard Mallet; and from Berlin Saunders urged that the pressure be kept up.[51] At first Lansdowne, loyally supported by Balfour, dismissed the pressure of this 'anti-German fever from which the country is suffering'; but the British right-wing journals were joined not only by Conservative backbenchers but also by Joseph Chamberlain, who threw his immense political weight against Lansdowne's scheme. Under assault from within and without, the government felt that it had little option but to withdraw from participation in the project. Lansdowne was clearly deeply hurt by this opposition, and by the government's abrupt about-turn because of this germanophobia – 'it is ridiculous and to my mind humiliating'. Even Selborne, no great friend of Berlin, deplored the agitation and wondered whether it helped the country's diplomatic bargaining position when Maxse, Strachey and others openly pressed for an *entente* with Russia at all costs. As for the German government, which had stood on the sidelines during all this, the message was clear: even when leading British statesmen were convinced that co-operation with Berlin was useful, there was now no guarantee that this could be carried through.[52]

In retrospect, it appears to have been no great coincidence that Chamberlain launched his attack against Anglo-German economic co-operation in the Baghdad Railway project precisely in those weeks when he was drafting his famous speech of 15 May 1903, in which he rejected the traditional commercial policy of free trade in favour of the creation of an imperial *Zollverein*, with tariffs being imposed upon imports (including foodstuffs) from foreign countries. Anglo-German trade relations had been in an unsettled state ever since the denunciation of the 1865 treaty by the British government in July 1897; but the fact that Berlin had found it prudent and, indeed, necessary, to keep prolonging from one year to the next the 'most favoured nation' status for British and imperial goods had caused this issue to recede a little into the background. After the turn of the century, however, the general trade recession, together with the poor performance of the army in the Boer War and the staggering costs of that conflict, provoked a further anxious debate upon Britain's ability to preserve her economic supremacy. More particularly, the recession prompted German firms to export their produce at what appeared to be ludicrously low prices, and this not only renewed the British charges about German 'dumping' but provoked a great deal of discussion about the growing imbalance in Anglo-German trade. It was argued, furthermore, that the German competition was doubly 'unfair' because her industries sheltered behind high tariff walls, which hindered the export of British goods to that market. This was likely to worsen in the future, for it became clear that the German government was going to accede to the demands of agriculture and heavy industry for large increases in the general tariff. Consequently, the British government was placed under considerable pressure by a whole variety of industries and chambers of commerce to forestall this expected blow, and the agitation so increased that the Board of Trade Intelligence Committee was instructed to make its own assessment of the various trades which would be hit by the German tariff proposals.[53]

The specifically anti-German nature of this commercial agitation was heightened by the tariff war which had been waged between Canada and Germany since 1897. Economically, this commercial war did not affect much of British industry, although it is true that its exports to Canada rose while those of Germany fell in these years. Politically, however, the quarrel was of the utmost importance, being regarded as a test case by all imperially minded Britons. What Germany was trying to do, it was argued, was to prevent the hoped-for federation of the motherland with the self-governing colonies by punishing any of the latter which dared to grant commercial privileges to Britain. When, in late April 1903 – just as the Cabinet was extricating itself from the Baghdad Railway project – Richthofen warned that any further self-governing colonies which followed Canada's example would incur a similar German response, and added that even British goods might have their 'most favoured nation' status withdrawn, the reaction in London was extremely hostile. Lansdowne immediately replied that 'the outcry in England would be so great that His Majesty's Government would be forced, however unwillingly, to take retaliatory measures'; and Chamberlain's response was even more emotional. The Foreign Office was requested to instruct Lascelles to take a much stiffer tone and to let Berlin know that 'the people of the United Kingdom will strongly resent any further attempt by a foreign country to dictate arrangements within the Empire, and to prevent our children and fellow-subjects from giving advantages to the mother country or to any other part of the British Empire'.[54] It is not without interest that Lansdowne, perhaps eager now to show that he did not bow before German demands, instructed that the stiff British reply be drafted so as to be 'fit for publication at the proper moment'.[55]

Within a few weeks of sending off this warning, Chamberlain had come out openly for Tariff Reform, and had soon resigned his ministry in order to campaign the more wholeheartedly for the measure. The varied response to this decision by the economic interest groups, and by the political parties, in both Britain and Germany is examined in more detail below;[56] what is important at this stage is to understand how this debate upon British economic policy related to contemporary hopes and fears about the future of the empire, and in particular to the public animosity existing between nationalist circles in Britain and Germany. From the outset, tariff reform and germanophobia went hand in hand. British politicians, eager to attract support for the proposal to abandon free trade, found it all too easy to stir up anti-German sentiments: Chamberlain had struck this note from the beginning, and even the more cautious Balfour spoke of the 'huge injustice' of the German threats against Canada.[57] If it was true that this resentment was genuinely felt, it was also the case – as the opponents of protection were swift to point out – that an appeal to chauvinism seemed tactically very opportune. Goschen, one of the leading Free Trade Unionists, felt that arguments in favour of 'retaliation' would gain much support, for 'the keen will to forge a weapon by which to defeat those d––d Germans is very strong'; and Seeley, who left the party altogether over this issue, admitted that if retaliation were to be implemented, 'nine out of ten would say: "We had better begin on Germany"'.[58]

To the pro-Tariff Reform press in Britain, the glorious opportunity beckoned of both undermining the hated free trade policies *and* of hurting the Germans. The *Daily Express*, whose owner (C. Arthur Pearson) was a fervent protectionist, claimed that Germany was so alarmed that Chamberlain's policies would frustrate its long-term plan to expand at the expense of 'industrially and financially decaying' Britain that it was now cunningly supporting the Cobden Club and other free traders. 'Will the electors of Great Britain play into foreign hands?', the *Express* asked; and again, 'Who doesn't vote for Chamberlain, votes for the national enemy.' The *Mail*, too, asserted that Berlin was seeking to frustrate Chamberlain by secret propaganda within Britain. Even the *Pall Mall Gazette*, although itself uncertain at first about the Colonial Secretary's scheme, rejoiced that it was 'obviously giving serious alarm to England's greatest and most vigilant enemy', which 'has evidently the strongest motives for preventing, if possible, the fiscal consolidation of the British Empire'.[59] It is worth noting, however, that many traditional germanophobes, such as Strachey of the *Spectator*, could hardly make use of these arguments when they themselves adhered to free trade doctrines; and that the split in the Unionist ranks, and more particularly the crudity of this chauvinistic appeal, permitted the Liberals to reunite and then counterattack.

If British free traders claimed not to be alarmed by the protectionists' appeal to the germanophobic instinct, the German government was deeply concerned. Once again, Bülow and his colleagues found themselves in somewhat of a cleft stick. In the first place, Canada's actions and the prospects of the entire British Empire going over to tariffs one day had drawn forth a predictable response from German nationalists: the agrarians immediately demanded strong counter-measures to satisfy the country's interests and pride, and (conveniently for themselves) proposed an even higher set of German tariffs; the Pan-Germans urged a European economic union, naturally under German leadership; the navalists argued that a larger fleet was needed in order to compel the British – exactly how, it was never made clear – to keep open their markets.[60] Normally, Bülow tended to defer to this nationalist-Conservative pressure, but this time it was quite impossible: not only was the call for a full-scale trade war attacked by progressive and SPD politicians, but it was also deprecated by the Centre Party and – most important of all – by a very large number of trading centres, chambers of commerce and individual industries, all of which feared they would suffer in such a conflict. The blunt fact was that since virtually a quarter of all their country's exported produce went to Britain and her empire, it was vital to avoid an open quarrel.[61]

Quite apart from this pragmatic economic calculation, Berlin was anxious to reduce the germanophobia in Britain and especially eager to avoid that sentiment being exploited by Chamberlain. The latter had always been regarded as an energetic, if tactless, politician: increasingly now he was seen as a dangerous, unscrupulous and demagogic leader who would use any device to further the cause of British imperialism – one of the *Gewaltmenschen*, to use Schmoller's term, who were again taking control of the empire now that the Cobdenite interlude was drawing to a close. It was very difficult, however, openly to counter the Colonial Secretary without running the risk of strengthening his position. As Metternich reported,

> *The more Mr. Chamberlain can strike a chauvinistic note, the more ground he gains.* Nothing will assist the striking of this note more, however, than attacks from foreigners – and, in the present state of public opinion in England, especially from the German side. (Bülow: 'quite correct'). A tariff war with us would enjoy a certain popularity everywhere that Britons live, and be suitable for firmly uniting the colonies with each other *and with the motherland*. (Bülow: 'quite correct').[62]

Bernstorff, whose task it was to work upon the British press, reported that all Chamberlain's opponents complained that nothing had so assisted the Colonial Secretary's plans than the proposed new German tariff: 'If Germany subscribed to free-trading views, then this [British] imperialism would be defeated', for it was only the impending loss of the German market which caused British industrialists to follow Chamberlain's plea for increased trade with the colonies.[63] An open repudiation of protectionism was, of course, impossible for the German government but it was certainly willing to avoid any further escalation of the quarrel. Consequently, no further measures were taken against Canada, the 'most favoured nation' status was prolonged for Britain and the rest of the empire, and statistics were assembled to show that the new German tariff would not really be that damaging to British exporters. One final, and extremely ironic conclusion which the German government drew from all this was that a Liberal administration in Britain – traditionally a *bête noire* because of its ideology, domestic programme and dislike of the conservative regimes of Europe – was now better for Germany's interests: as Metternich put it, 'Quite apart from the trade aspect, it would be most useful for us if the English Government was free from the influence of the turbulent and unpredictable personality of Mr Chamberlain (Wilhelm: 'Yes'), which is only possible through the election of a Liberal government.'[64]

The role of Chamberlain's decision for tariff reform has been considered at some length here because, first, this aspect has usually been omitted from the predominantly diplomatic accounts of the rising Anglo-German antagonism;[65] and secondly, because it usefully confirms – and helps us to see more clearly – the pattern which was being set in the years after 1902. The period 1895–1901 had been marked by Britain's global embarrassment at the advances which the other powers (inter alia, Germany) were making in colonial, naval and economic terms; and by the German government's confident hope that the 'free hand' policy and naval expansionism were already laying the foundation for the country's drive towards an increasingly successful Weltpolitik. The nadir of British weakness and isolationism was reached in the early stages of the Boer War. Following the defeats of 'Black Week', in fact, the Prussian General Staff concluded that Britain would find it impossible to defend India against a Russian assault and that, without a total reorganisation of its military system, the empire itself would be dissolved within two decades.[66] Thereafter, and despite the tremors of alarm and discontent in British right-wing circles, a gradual improvement got under way. There was no continental coalition. The situation in the Far East had been stabilised, at least for some time, by the alliance with Japan. The prospect of a conflict with the United States was virtually removed after the signing of the Hay-Pauncefote treaty of 1901 and the Alaskan boundary settlement of 1903. The French challenge on the Nile had been held, and Paris was sending out hints of the possibility of a colonial agreement. By late 1902/early 1903, too, the British government had at last fully admitted to itself that 'the maintenance of the "status quo" as regards Constantinople is not one of the primary naval or military interests of this country', thus escaping from an obligation which had weighed so heavily upon Salisbury a generation earlier.[67] The army was being thoroughly shaken up, and the naval budgets repeatedly increased: between 1900 and 1903, as one of Tirpitz's assistants noted gloomily, the British had built or were building ten battleships and eighteen armoured cruisers.[68] A new mood, both of defiance and of a willingness to adopt radical solutions to problems, was in the air.

All this was taking place at the same time as Anglo-German relations were worsening, and the effect upon Bülow's calculations can easily be imagined. Britain appeared far more resilient than before and, should Chamberlain ever come to power, potentially very dangerous. She was clearly looking very carefully at the expansion of the German fleet, which, due to the agitation of the National Review, Spectator, The Times and other journals, had entered the 'danger zone' much earlier than Tirpitz had suggested was likely. Her public opinion was exceedingly touchy about dealings with Germany, and her government manifestly unwilling to incur unpopularity on that account. Up until his 'granite' speech, Bülow had clearly thought that assuaging German nationalist sentiment was more important than showing respect for English feelings; since then, and realising (although never publicly admitting) that he had gone too far, he had reversed course. Anglophobic and navalist agitations in the German press had been suffocated wherever possible; no formal or open complaints had been made when Britain insisted upon abandoning the Venezuela blockade; a policy of apparent calm, and injured innocence, had been the response to the British newspaper agitation for a North Sea naval base; the Baghdad Railway débâcle was also officially ignored, it being described as a private business matter. In the same way, and despite certain domestic and commercial pressures for a strong response, the German leaders pretended not to be affected by Chamberlain's tariff reform movement, which in secret greatly frightened them. Overall, the strategy was the same: as Bernstorff put it, 'If we betray no touchiness, demand nothing, show ourselves accommodating in outward form, and discreetly cultivate public opinion here, people in England will then think less and less about a conflict with us.'[69]

Berlin's apprehensions would have been far greater, of course, had it believed that it was also possible for Britain to bury its differences with France and Russia; but it was a fundamental assumption of German policy that colonial quarrels in Africa and Asia made such a *rapprochement* unthinkable. It was, however, precisely their awareness that the German government relied upon continuing tensions between Britain and the Dual Alliance which made the Bertie–Hardinge clique in the Foreign Office and the anti-Germans in the Unionist press so keen to settle differences with Paris and St Petersburg. While it is important not to lose sight of these groups, it must also be stressed that the growing friendship with France which occurred in 1903–4 had the support of a much wider circle of people, many of whom could in no way be described as anti-German. Business interests, for example, were very keen to see Anglo-French relations improved, and their feelings were manifested in the activities of Sir Thomas Barclay and his friends in Paris and by the warm support given by British Chambers of Commerce to Cambon's speeches in England.[70] The same was true of the great majority of Liberals and Radicals, to whom the traditional *entente* with the French republic remained a priority in foreign policy; and when the colonial settlement was eventually announced in April 1904, the Liberal press chorused its approval. 'Every Englishman rejoices, and particularly every Gladstonian Englishman', asserted the *Speaker*; and the *Daily News*'s sole regret that it was not concluded by a Liberal government was 'alleviated by the knowledge that it is after all only the flower of the historic policy of Liberalism'.[71]

Within the 'Official Mind', too, a distinction must be drawn between those who saw in an *entente* with France an ideal means for checking Germany, and those whose intention was simply to reduce the pressures upon Britain's global position. In the former camp, as already has been seen, could be counted Bertie, Spring-Rice, Hardinge, Mallet and their associates. The growth of the German fleet obviously influenced British naval circles in this direction: Fisher argued that 'it's our vital necessity to establish a French alliance'; and Arnold-Foster doubtless had the North Sea situation in mind when he wrote of the strategical 'advantage of coming to a peaceable agreement with a great Nation'; but it is also worth noting that the army opposed until the end the idea of permitting French predominance in Morocco.[72] It is also likely that Chamberlain, in his private calculations about the items which might be included in a colonial settlement with France,[73] was not free from the thought that this would pay back Bülow for his misdeeds. On the other hand, the Prime Minister's energies were now chiefly devoted towards preserving unity in the party over tariff reform; and although he certainly did not neglect foreign affairs, his eyes were still focused upon the Russian threat to Persia, Afghanistan, Tibet and especially the Far East. This made him, like Lansdowne, eager to come to a settlement with France for that 'would not improbably be the precursor of a better understanding with Russia',[74] but neither statesmen referred much to Germany.

This motivation, of easing Britain's global difficulties, was repeatedly stressed by Cromer in addition to the latter's arguments that the much-needed financial reforms in Egypt depended upon an arrangement with France; and it was the consul-general, too, who increasingly referred to the possibility that the colonial *entente* could lead to unpleasantries with Germany – which, however, Cromer himself was willing to face.[75] Only by the turn of the year 1903–4 did Lansdowne begin to anticipate that Berlin might make difficulties. Nevertheless, this clearly referred to a possible German demand for 'compensations', a traditional feature of Anglo-German diplomacy, and there is no reference at all to any general strategy of checking the Kaiser's *Weltpolitik*. Even the news that Bernstorff at the London embassy had been seeking to persuade Lucien Wolf ('Diplomaticus') to write an article attacking any Anglo-French deal over Morocco does not seem to have affected the Foreign Secretary, however much it angered his permanent officials.[76] Concern about the worsening situation in the Far East, and recognition of the local as well as the global benefits which would flow from a settlement of the many colonial disputes with France, were Lansdowne's uppermost thoughts; and Lascelles's report that Holstein, at least, wished to 'keep the door open' for better Anglo-German relations even if an Anglo-French *entente* was announced, immediately drew a friendly message for Berlin from Lansdowne.[77] In the light of the anxious Cabinet debate at this time over going to war against Russia, this is scarcely surprising; but it is worth emphasising the point, in view of later assertions that the British government was consciously attempting an 'encirclement' of the Reich.

In theory, an Anglo-French accord would be fatal to Germany's diplomatic position, since it would create a bloc strong enough to check the hoped for colonial and naval expansionism. Delcassé was known, of course, to be seeking to create an anti-German coalition; and from London Eckardstein sent repeated warnings that many Britons favoured such a scheme.[78] Yet the German government still assumed that the chief result of any Anglo-French *entente* would be the breaking up of the Dual Alliance; indeed, Bülow thought that this was the chief purpose of Edward VII's visit to Paris.[79] Although this was unlikely to succeed, it would be no disaster for Berlin if it did, for Russia was then likely to gravitate towards Germany and even Austria–Hungary, thus allowing the reconstitution of the *Dreikaiserbund*. This belief, remarkably optimistic in view of the commercial and nationalistic rivalries between the three empires of eastern Europe, rested upon the German Chancellor's fond assumption that he had really secured the friendship of Russia; and the obvious differences between Paris and St Petersburg over the Macedonian crisis of

1903 increased Berlin's confidence. The Russian hints that the Tsar desired German 'backing' (in the form of loan, and the neutralisation of the Baltic) in the event of a Far Eastern war were also encouraging, although Berlin was not eager to be openly associated with St Petersburg.[80]

Yet, however much Bülow enjoyed the idea that Germany really had become the *tertius gaudens* in world politics, the blunt fact was that there was no alternative to the policy of non-commitment and reserve. The germanophobia of the British public meant that it would be most unwise to take Russia's side in Asian affairs, or even to show alarm at the Anglo-French colonial negotiations: in the latter case, there was nothing that Berlin could do, except carefully observe events in London and Paris. Germany's 'present position as the tongue on the scales', as Holstein fancifully described it, was not an indication of her freedom of movement but of the reverse: she could neither step to the Russian side, nor away from it. In these circumstances, it was not surprising that the *Wilhelmstrasse* saw in the growing Far Eastern crisis, not a dark cloud, but a silver lining. A war there would cause the Russians to be even more reliant upon German goodwill, and this could be used to extract acceptance of Berlin's terms in the trade negotiations. It would sharpen still further the Anglo-Russian antagonism in Asia (if only because a Russian defeat of Japan and expansion in China was expected), turn British attention from the North Sea and render impossible Delcassé's efforts to create a Triple Alliance. It could also fulfil the age-old strategy of diverting German domestic attention outwards; as Bülow noted to Holstein, 'from the point of view of our internal policies and to counteract the general dissatisfaction in Germany, it would of course be a good thing if "somewhere far away" the nations came to blows'.[81] As a consequence, Berlin indulged in what can only be described as the cynical and unscrupulous tactic of encouraging both Russia and Japan into a conflict – usually by sending messages that the other side was only bluffing – while ostensibly remaining aloof and declaring its disinterest in Far Eastern affairs. On learning that Delcassé was striving to mediate in the dispute, Bülow at once informed Holstein that 'I leave it to your sagacity to decide whether and how – without uncovering ourselves and provoking suspicion in any way that we were encouraging a war! – we can hinder the mediation which Delcassé, in his effort to prevent the outbreak of war in the Orient, seems earnestly to want.'[82]

Yet, ironically, it was to be the Russo-Japanese War above all else which undermined Germany's 'free hand' policy and, directly or indirectly, led to the creation of that Triple Alliance which Bülow was so dismissive about in his writings and utterances of 1903. In the first place, the crisis in the Far East helped to accelerate the conclusion of the Anglo-French colonial negotiations. It is true that the tenacity with which both governments treated the proposed exchange of territories in question clearly shows that the *entente* cannot solely be regarded as a move in European diplomacy; but whenever the pace of negotiations flagged, there were always advocates – Cromer, the king, the Foreign Office staff – of a fresh attempt at a settlement. When it was finally announced, in April 1904, it was impossible to conceal the fact that this was a great blow to German diplomacy. Even if the treaty was to be viewed (as Lansdowne saw it) merely as the elimination of various long-standing overseas quarrels, that in itself meant that the Bismarckian device of taking advantage of the tension between London and Paris had been rendered obsolete; if, on the other hand, the *entente* was to be the basis for the furthering of an Anglo-French political friendship, then Germany's more general diplomatic position would also be affected. In line with the *Wilhelmstrasse*'s general policy of maintaining a low profile there was little open reaction to the news of the Anglo-French treaty; and Bülow even went so far as to welcome it publicly as a contribution to world peace.

To the German patriotic press and to the official adherents of Realpolitik, however, the development was a serious one.[83] It was in April 1904, too, that Italy's defection from the Triple Alliance was most obviously symbolised by the welcome given in Rome to President Loubet; and the fact that the two great Mediterranean naval powers had announced a colonial understanding was a virtual guarantee that Italy would not dare to enter a general European war on the side of Germany and Austria–Hungary.[84] In that same month, news arrived of the uprising in South-west Africa which was soon to cast a pall over German colonial policy for the next few years. It was the Anglo-French understanding which constituted the largest defeat, however, and led Holstein (who, with the Kaiser, had been more apprehensive about this possibility than Bülow) to write privately of his discontent, to castigate the Chancellor's previous unwillingness to oppose the domestic anglophobia, and to point out the obvious consequences for Germany's *Weltpolitik*: 'No overseas policy is possible against England and France.' Elsewhere in the *Auswärtiges Amt*, too, there prevailed deep unrest at 'one of the worst defeats for German policy since the creation of the Dual Alliance'; and Lichnowsky argued for 'a success in foreign policy' in order to counter the public unrest.[85]

In order to extricate Germany from this position of humiliation, therefore, the *Wilhelmstrasse* resolved upon an approach to London for 'compensation' for the proposed changes in Egypt's administration. Although a predictable response, it turned out to be an unfortunate one, partly because Berlin demanded the settlement of all other outstanding differences, and partly because Lansdowne was looking upon Germany's willingness to accept the Egyptian changes as a 'test case' of her goodwill. When Berlin hinted that it would turn to Russia if these demands were not met, even the Foreign Secretary exploded into anger – while the more anti-German elements in the 'Official Mind' had their suspicions confirmed. The fact that all the other powers with Egyptian interests settled easily the terms of their withdrawal identified Germany as the chief obstacle in the British view; the fact that Whitehall appeared willing to 'buy off' the others, but not Germany, suggested to Berlin that a deliberate policy of snubbing the Reich was being attempted. This rather squalid bargaining lasted until June and was only resolved by reluctant compromises on both sides in time to allow the king's visit to Kiel to take place. Its significance lay less on the German than on the British side, where it caused even Balfour to refer repeatedly to this 'blackmail' and to the tactical need to 'isolate' Berlin's opposition to the Egyptian reforms.[86]

The second blow administered to German foreign policy calculations was that the war in the Far East did not totally distract British attention from the

North Sea. It is also true that the war caused a temporary division among anti-German circles. Some, such as Spring-Rice, regarded Russia as so malevolent and unpredictable that they began to wonder whether it might not, after all, be better to seek a *modus vivendi* with Berlin; and Chirol's policy at *The Times* was to attack Russian policy repeatedly and to hope that Japan would break its power in the Far East. Others, such as the Mallet brothers and Hardinge, deplored the conflict as an obstacle to a better understanding with Russia, criticised *The Times* for its articles, and repeatedly stressed that 'the real danger in the future comes from Germany'.[87] At the Cabinet level, too, this ambivalence towards Russia and Germany was evident. Despite the Egyptian quarrel, Balfour and Lansdowne were still so alarmed about the Russian threat in Asia that they endeavoured to keep up the appearance of good relations with Berlin, an enterprise in which Bülow had at least as strong an interest. On the other hand Selborne was growing more and more alarmed about the size of the German battlefleet, the relative importance of which had been enormously enhanced by the easing of the age-old Mediterranean naval problem and by the sinking of the Russian ships in Port Arthur. The Admiralty repeated its view that:

> If the Russian navy does emerge from the present war materially weakened, the result will be that the two power standard must hereafter be calculated with reference to the navies of France and Germany, instead of those of France and Russia . . . The fact is that the German navy has, in point of numbers, been steadily overhauling the Russian, till at the outbreak of the present war it was practically equal, while in point of quality it is greatly superior to the Russian . . . The more the composition of the new German fleet is examined, the clearer it becomes that it is designed for a possible conflict with the British fleet.[88]

This, of course, was what the British navalist press had been saying all along; and the courtesy visit of a powerful and well-trained German squadron to Plymouth gave further propaganda to the alarmists. Yet, whereas Selborne's unease deepened after he accompanied the king to the Kiel regatta in June 1904 and witnessed the full strength of the German fleet, both Balfour and Lansdowne had hoped that the visit would lead to improved Anglo-German relations – so much so that Mallet and others feared that Britain's friendship with both France and Japan would be compromised by Bülow's cunning diplomacy.[89] Perhaps the most significant feature of the British commentaries upon the Kiel festivities was the strong emphasis by Conservative newspapers that the king's visit had no political significance and would not be permitted to affect the *entente cordiale* – an interesting echo of the German press's insistence that Wilhelm's visits to England during the Boer War were 'family' matters which did not disturb Berlin's relations with St Petersburg. To the monarchs in question, however, this personal diplomacy was significant and both returned from their respective visits believing that they had done something to improve the Anglo-German relationship.[90]

Although Balfour and Lansdowne were also encouraged by the Kiel visit, the British government's suspicion of Germany increased sharply thereafter. In the first place, Whitehall was struck by the calmness with which the Germans took the news of the seizure of the merchant vessel *Prinz Heinrich* by the Russian navy and the way in which its official press concentrated upon Russian acts against the British ship *Malacca* instead. It was, reported the secretary of the Committee of Imperial Defence, Sir George Clarke, to Balfour, 'a little suspicious. Nothing could suit Germany better than to see us embroiled with France, which would at once place her [that is, Germany] in a commanding position.'[91] These private suspicions, which were strengthened by reports that the Russians were treating the captured German merchantmen with great care and that a confidential agreement permitted the transfer of Russian troops from the Polish border to the Far East, gained far greater publicity when, in mid-September 1904, *The Times* announced that Russia and Germany had signed a secret treaty of co-operation.

To a large extent, these British suspicions of German diplomacy were justified – except that Berlin was probably less eager to see Russia weakened than Balfour imagined. This indulgence towards St Petersburg derived partly from the *Wilhelmstrasse*'s (but not the General Staff's) belief that Russia was no longer hostile to Germany; and partly from Wilhelm's own impulsive attachment to his fellow-monarch, who was fighting for Christendom against the 'Yellow Peril'. It was also motivated, predictably enough, by domestic-political considerations: given that the Socialists and many Progressives were critical of this pro-Russian policy, it was important that neither the Romanov dynasty – nor, by association, the Hohenzollern – suffered too severe a blow to its prestige because of defeats in the East. Finally, there remained the powerful argument, which Tirpitz and Richthofen deployed on occasions, that 'through the weakening of Russia was lost a heavy counterweight to England'.[92] At first, all that was necessary was to encourage the Russians to pursue the war more actively against Japan, and to hope that she would also quarrel with Britain: thus the Anglo-Russian argument over the seizure of the *Malacca* was greeted with secret relief, especially since it eclipsed the seizure of the *Prinz Heinrich*; and Wilhelm privately wrote that the more the British annoyed the Russians, the better.[93]

These calculations were thrown into total confusion by the Dogger Bank crisis of late October 1904. At first, the *Wilhelmstrasse* was rather pleased at the news, even though Bülow immediately ordered the German press not to gloat about the clash between Britain and Russia: in secret, as the Austro-Hungarian ambassador learned, 'people here are rubbing their hands with satisfaction and are delighted that the Russian stroke was carried out against an English and not – as could easily have happened – against a German fishing flotilla!'[94] Within days, however, this glee had changed to alarm as the British press began to assert that Germany was behind the Russian action. Moreover, Berlin felt further compromised by the fact that the Hamburg–Amerika Line was acting as collier to Rozhdestvensky's fleet; which made the prospect of Germany being involved in a war with Japan and possibly also with Britain now much greater. As a consequence, Wilhelm, Bülow and Holstein felt it necessary to abandon the 'free hand' policy and to approach Russia for an alliance, an idea which the nervous Tsar was eager to accept. Here was a diplomatic revolution with a vengeance.[95]

These German manoeuvres, which the British could guess at although the exact details remained a secret, only made London more suspicious. Even before the Dogger Bank episode, the First Sea Lord, Kerr, and more especially the Director of Naval Intelligence, Battenberg, kept reminding Selborne of the growing size of the German battlefleet, the danger to Britain's North Sea interests which would be posed by a combined Russo-German force, and the need to bring some battleships home from the China station.[96] When Fisher took over from Kerr on 21 October – the day before the Dogger Bank shooting – the Admiralty's attitude became even more pronounced and the new First Sea Lord was not alone in his belief that 'It's really the Germans behind it all . . .' Chirol at *The Times* was as well informed as usual when he reported to Spring-Rice and Lascelles that during the crisis 'an eye was kept on Kiel' as much as on the Russian and French fleets, for it was only a few weeks later that the Admiralty announced a redistribution of the Royal Navy's main squadrons, which strengthened the Channel [that is, Home] Fleet at the expense of the Mediterranean Fleet.[97] If these were intended by the British government as precautionary measures, ultra-chauvinistic journalists such as Arnold White and the leader writers of *Vanity Fair* and the *Army and Navy Gazette* had no reservations about calling for the Germany navy to be 'Copenhagen-ed'. The story of the fear which spread throughout Germany of such a surprise attack has been recounted many times, and need not be detailed here.[98] The point was that, from this moment on, the British were to make it clear that they regarded the ever-growing German fleet as the most serious obstacle to good relations between their two peoples and that, unless a change in Germany's naval policy occurred, counter-measures would be taken which would keep Tirpitz's creation permanently in the 'danger zone'. Even Lascelles felt impelled to inform his counterpart, Metternich, that 'if the German fleet had not been built', the Royal Navy's moves would hardly have been necessary; and Selborne, although very willing to denounce the 'outrageous' call of the *Army and Navy Gazette*, explained at length to the Kaiser's friend, Admiral Eisendecher, why the average Briton was bound to regard the diversion of funds from the German army to its navy as being a measure directed against England.[99] Without a modification of *Flottenpolitik*, there could be no lasting friendship with Britain.

German documents relating to the 'war scare' of 1904–5 also reveal two further (and interrelated) flaws in the foreign policy assumptions of the Kaiser's government. The first was that the earlier hopes of witnessing an Anglo-Russian war, with France also drawn in, or at least of splitting the Dual Alliance were proven false. If ever there had been a cause, since the Penjdeh crisis of 1885, for Britain and Russia to have gone to war, then it would have been over the shooting of the fishing boats. In the event, unless St Petersburg was willing to see the total destruction of its Baltic fleet, it had to give way to British demands for an inquiry and the punishment of those responsible. Furthermore, Delcassé, fearing the collapse of his grand design, strove feverishly to mediate between London and St Petersburg, impressing upon the latter the need to assuage the British wrath – for which activities, of course, his credit with Balfour's administration rose even higher. 'Our relations with France are now on a better footing than ever', reported Clarke.[100] In Britain, the desires of Balfour and Lansdowne for better relations with Russia (although not, of course, at any cost) coincided with the fears of the anti-Germans in the Foreign Office, Admiralty and CID that a war with Russia would simply play into Berlin's hands. Ironically, therefore, it was precisely the self-proclaimed German policy of the 'free hand' which caused other powers to be cautious and not to commit themselves into war lest Berlin exploit its neutral position to their disadvantage.

An equally great blow was dealt to Bülow's diplomacy when the Russians, after at first seeming to favour the German approach for an alliance, insisted upon consulting France before any such treaty was signed. Although the *Wilhelmstrasse* dared not openly show its anger, it became increasingly clear from this – and from the inadequate Russian response to the German demand for guarantees of aid should Britain or Japan attack Ballin's coaling vessels which were accompanying the Baltic fleet – that St Petersburg was reluctant to be tied to Berlin. The French alliance offered the Tsar's government a steady flow of funds, the possibility of effecting a compromise with Britain, and the assurance that Russia remained an independent great power. A German alliance might not only lead to the defection of France, but it could provoke the British into war; and, in any case, a Russia allied solely to Germany would never be free from the old Bismarckian blackmail, as could be seen in the way Berlin pushed for tariff concessions when Russia's position in the Far East crumbled.[101]

However, the real clue to the collapse of Germany's diplomatic position in this period is to be found less in the correspondence with its ambassadors abroad than in the deliberations of its military and naval staffs: here, more than anywhere else, can be encountered what one scholar has described as the confusion of purpose which frequently lay behind the imposing façade of the Second Reich.[102] The redeployment of the Royal Navy, and the acute hostility of parts of the British press, certainly frightened many in Berlin. Even Holstein wrote that he now believed 'in the possibility of war with England, in which the attack would come from England', and Metternich was hurriedly summoned to a meeting at the *Wilhelmstrasse* to be questioned about British intentions.[103] In the offices of the German navy, where an Anglo-German war had been under consideration for almost a decade, the alarm was even greater, for the sheer weight of maritime power which the British were assembling in the North Sea was making the 'risk theory' look less viable than ever before. The crisis also stimulated the *Admiralstab* to intensify preparations for its operations plan against Britain, which since 1899 had involved a defensive strategy in the North Sea together with the overrunning of Denmark and even southern Sweden by the German army in order to make the Baltic a *mare clausam*. At first the Kaiser agreed to this scheme, and in mid-November 1904 Schlieffen was ordered to have two corps in readiness near the Danish border. Soon, however, the plan came under a heavy counter-attack. Bülow, eager to remain on good terms with Russia even if an alliance with that power presented

273

difficulties, increasingly feared that St Petersburg would react with anger to the news that Germany was in control of the Baltic entrances.

More important and revealing still was the attitude of the Prussian General Staff. Ever since 1899 it had been quarrelling with the *Admiralstab* over this Danish operation, which it could not regard as anything other than a diversion of the troops so desperately needed for the successful implementation of Schlieffen's great scheme to overrun France by an assault through the Low Countries. In vain, the naval planners had argued that the days when Germany had simply to take into account a war against the Dual Alliance were over; in vain, they had hinted that a German overrunning of Belgium and the Netherlands would give the British the excuse they needed to seize the colonies of those two countries and to extend the Royal Navy's blockade to their home ports; in vain, they had pointed to the danger of allowing British naval squadrons into the Baltic. To Schlieffen, the priority given to the strike against France was unalterable. Before 1904, the General Staff had shown little interest in war planning against Britain and had refused to lend the troops for the early and rather fantastic naval plans for an invasion of England; after 1904, or at least after the conclusion of the *entente cordiale*, Schlieffen argued that since Germany could not directly hurt Britain, its proper course in any war with that country was to hurl itself upon Britain's friend, France. Although momentarily appearing to agree to the navy's request for troops for the overrunning of Denmark at the height of the 'war scare', the General Staff soon reversed its position and insisted upon having full freedom of action to attack France: the violation of Belgium's neutrality, rather than Denmark's, was at the forefront of Schlieffen's mind.[104]

Not only was Schlieffen's stance a blow to the *Admiralstab* (which had totally to recast its operation plan against Britain in the course of 1905), but it also complicated the diplomatic bid which was being made for a Russian alliance. If Wilhelm and Bülow still placed great weight upon Russo-German relations in case a war with Britain broke out, it would be absurd to permit the General Staff's first action in that conflict to be the overrunning of France, which St Petersburg was clearly opposed to. Yet, in all the hastily assembled conferences of Germany's military and political leaders which took place in late 1904/early 1905, this dilemma was never resolved. Finally, to add to the confusion, both Tirpitz and the *Admiralstab* strongly opposed the signing of an alliance with Russia, fearing that it might provoke the British into a preventative strike. This was becoming an absurd circular argument: Wilhelm and the *Auswärtiges Amt* favoured a Russian alliance because they were scared that the Royal Navy would throttle Germany's sea power before it grew any larger; and the German admirals opposed a Russian alliance for exactly the same reason, that it might hasten the event which they all wished so desperately to avoid. The confidential documents of this time refer repeatedly to Germany's helplessness, to the seizure of her colonies, the ruination of her foreign trade, the disastrous effects of a blockade upon the economy: Tirpitz's *Risikoflotte* had only increased the risks, and the German 'Official Mind' had no unified response (let alone, a solution) to the problem.

Seen in this light, the so-called 'Copenhagen Complex' acquires an added

274

irony. That anxiety was motivated not only by the recognition of German Realpolitiker that 'from their standpoint the English would be quite right to present us with an ultimatum to reduce our naval armaments'.[105] Nor was the complex caused solely by the Germans' fear of being 'punished for the audacity of their aspirations' – for their drive to gain equality with, or possibly the destruction of, the British Empire.[106] These general sentiments and vague aspirations were there alright, and had indeed existed for some years; and the actions of the British newspapers and navy after the Dogger Bank shooting gave them a much more concrete form. But, at a time when the Reich leadership was earnestly discussing such contingencies as the invasion of Denmark, or of France and Belgium, was it not also the case that *the Germans feared that Britain would do to them what they were thinking of doing to their own neighbours*?

By the spring of 1905, this uncoordinated German leadership had fastened upon a quite different issue with which to salvage some of its diplomatic prestige – Morocco. The general circumstances for this attempt were certainly better than they had been a few months earlier. In the first place, the threat of a British pre-emptive strike upon the German fleet had receded: from London Metternich insisted that there had been a reaction against the germanophobia of the right-wing press, and, although the report of Arthur Lee's speech in February about the Royal Navy getting 'its blow in first' before a declaration of war had caused Wilhelm to be alarmed, more senior British ministers indicated that they did not seek a collision with Germany. In the Far East, Russia's position was swiftly crumbling but if she was not to be relied upon as a potential ally of Germany, then the news of her defeats was not a total disaster from Berlin's point of view. Although the overall weakening of the Tsarist colussus strengthened Britain's world position, it also enhanced Germany's relative power in Europe. Above all, German action over Morocco allowed the Kaiser and his advisers to seek to achieve two important aims: first, to satisfy the general dissatisfaction in nationalist circles that the Reich's interests were being disregarded and her world position undermined without the leadership doing anything to 'stop the rot'; and secondly, to outwit and humiliate once and for all the arch-foe Delcassé, whose diplomacy had hitherto checked all German efforts to benefit from the course of the Russo-Japanese War.

In the specifically Moroccan aspects of the German diplomatic offensive of 1905, Berlin's case was a strong one. Her share of Morocco's foreign trade was much less than that of Britain and France, but it was guaranteed full commercial freedom by the Madrid international agreement of 1880. Certain traders and travellers, as well as the Pan-Germans, had earlier urged the imperial government to increase German influence in that country, but although Bülow believed that Germany should have a share of the Moroccan coastline in any partition he felt it wisest then to adopt a policy of reserve. A three-way split between Britain, France and Germany sounded fine in theory but would be difficult to achieve in practice, and the informal soundings with Salisbury and Chamberlain in 1899 suggested that in an Anglo-German deal Germany's share would not be as large as desired. It therefore made good sense for the *Wilhelmstrasse* to act, as Bülow put it, 'as a sphinx', not allowing the other powers to

275

know the German attitude, and content that Berlin's position would be more effective in the future, when the German fleet was bigger and the Anglo-French rivalry for Morocco sharper.[107] The news of the *entente* of April 1904 came, then, as an unpleasant surprise, but the German government still believed that its position was a strong one: it had committed no action itself in Morocco such as to prejudice international opinion against the German case; it could stand upon its treaty rights, and claim that it had interests there to protect; and it could argue with some justification that Delcassé was discriminating against Germany by totally ignoring her Moroccan rights whilst being willing to 'buy off' the British, the Spanish and the Italians.

When, therefore, the French mission arrived in Fez in January 1905 to negotiate with the Sultan, Berlin recognised that if action was not taken soon Germany would publicly appear as a *quantité négligeable*. The weakening of Russia in the Far East clearly influenced Germany's tougher policy, but in any event France was not to be permitted to turn Morocco into 'a second Tunisia'.[108] Moreover, the unleashing of this German challenge seemed less risky than hitherto precisely because of the *Wilhelmstrasse*'s assumption that those powers which had already been 'bought off' by France would have no further interest in a Franco-German quarrel. As Richthofen blithely stated: 'England is now out of it, for it no longer has any interest in how Germany deals with France over Morocco' following Berlin's compromise with London over the surrender of German rights in Egypt. And, after all, Germany could claim to be defending the 'Open Door' in Morocco, an argument which would appeal to many Britons and Americans.[109]

The assumption that Morocco could be treated solely as a Franco-German colonial dispute was, of course, quite illusory. Just as the *Wilhelmstrasse*'s mind operated at the two levels, that of the local issue and that of the general balance of power, so also did the other powers. Indeed, they were more or less bound to, since the German press openly emphasised that the French must be given a lesson and that the *entente* with Britain should be shown up as totally ineffectual in protecting France from Germany's wrath. Whether Berlin seriously contemplated war upon France in the summer of 1905 remains, as ever it was, unclear. Although eager to use the tension for purposes of naval propaganda, Wilhelm himself was not keen for a showdown and had been a reluctant adherent to the 'hard line' policy ever since the *Wilhelmstrasse* had virtually forced him to make his landing at Tangier. It may also be assumed that Tirpitz was still opposed to a war which would be characterised by a display of the army's efficiency on the one hand and by the powerlessness of the High Seas Fleet to protect the nation's overseas trade and colonies on the other. Precisely for this reason, it seems that Schlieffen and the rest of the military leadership were not reluctant to let it come to a conflict under the existing favourable conditions. The War Minister, Von Einem, declared repeatedly that a break could not be avoided; General Bernhardi called for the 'cutting of the Gordian Knot'; and Schlieffen himself told Count Schulenburg, the military attaché in London, that it was vital 'either to exploit the favourable military situation or to carry through a complete understanding with France over Alsace-Lorraine', the latter being an improbable alternative indeed.[110] In between these two schools of thought was Holstein, who (rather than Bülow) was 'the driving force' in German Moroccan policy and who would not have shrunk from war, but hoped to gain all that was desired by means of this diplomatic bluff.[111]

The crucial factor, however, was not so much what the German government really intended as what others *believed it intended*; and Berlin's conduct forced many observers to conclude that it was anxious to provoke a showdown. This was certainly the attitude of Rouvier's government, which, fearing the worst, had jettisoned Delcassé only to find that Germany still adamantly refused a private settlement with France. What other conclusion seemed plausible when German officials declared that 'Morocco lay on *our* western frontier', and when Wilhelm himself, prodded from behind to assume a belligerent pose, told Battenberg: 'we know the road to Paris, and we will get there again if needs be. They should remember no fleet can defend Paris.'[112]

Berlin's forward policy once again exposed the fissures within the British establishment. In the early part of 1905, many were eager to improve Anglo-German relations. Clarke urged that 'a war with Germany would be peculiarly idiotic'; Sanderson criticised 'the lunatics here who denounce Germany'; and at Cabinet level, too, there was a broad feeling of tolerance towards Berlin. Austen Chamberlain, very much his father's voice, had severely attacked both Bülow's diplomacy and the British ambassador, Lascelles, for not taking a stronger line towards it; but Lansdowne defended the latter's mild language and then developed this into a general apologia for Germany's previous policy. Balfour, too, was still willing to view German faults in a detached manner.[113] Despite the increasing evidence of Russia's military and domestic collapse, both men continued to fear that India was threatened – and, indeed, that this threat might actually increase if Russian expansionism, blunted in the Orient, turned again to central Asia. For this reason, the British government was now striving to renegotiate the Anglo-Japanese alliance so that it would in future give protection to India. Furthermore, the slow but steady progress of the Baltic Fleet eastwards raised the fear that, as it called at some French port *en route*, it would be attacked by the Japanese, thereby dragging France and Britain into the conflict: the very thought of this complication agitated British minds until the news of the Tsushima battle, but it also meant that Balfour and Lansdowne had little time to spare for Morocco. Consequently, the Foreign Secretary took the Kaiser's Tangier escapade without resentment, although suggesting in schoolmasterly fashion that 'a judicious spanking' might do Wilhelm some good. Even when he wrote of the emperor's efforts to 'put spokes in our wheels' and to 'discredit the Entente', Lansdowne's tone hardly altered; and while he feared that France might under pressure give Germany a Moroccan port, which the Royal Navy bitterly opposed, he was still uncertain in late April whether the French should be encouraged to resist that pressure.[114] The Cabinet's position was probably best summed up in Gerald Balfour's letter to Spring-Rice: 'France may or may not think it worthwhile to buy off this troublesome blackmailer. If she refuses, she will have our moral support; but I think you may dismiss from your mind any idea that we are engaged to more than this, or that we are in any way encouraging her to a provocative policy.'[115]

At exactly this time, in fact, the Cabinet was discussing the possibility of renewing negotiations with Berlin over the Baghdad Railway and it was only the anti-German state of public opinion – which Austen Chamberlain was keen to emphasise – which caused the matter to be shelved once again.[116] Admittedly, Lansdowne grew more worried about German policy after Delcassé had been forced to resign, but one lesson which was drawn from that episode was that the French were too weak to be relied upon absolutely. The refusal of the British government in these months to accede to French requests to persuade Japan to be more lenient in its peace terms is a further indication of Whitehall's priorities. Even Lansdowne's warning to Metternich in June 1905, that if Germany attacked France 'it could not be foreseen how far public opinion in England would drive the government to support France',[117] suggests that the Foreign Secretary could scarcely contemplate the Cabinet entering a Franco-German war on its own volition: it would have to be pushed. If Lansdowne was eager to improve relations with any power in this period, then it was with Russia – for imperial defence considerations – and not with France, which (however useful a colonial partner) threatened to drag Britain willy-nilly into continental power-politics. For this reason, his most critical comments upon the Kaiser's diplomacy occurred when the rumours reached London of the German-Russian accord at Björkö in July 1905, for he could appreciate that if the Tsar fell under Wilhelm's influence there was little chance of settling Anglo-Russian differences in Asia.[118]

By contrast, it was precisely the breakdown of the European equilibrium following Russia's defeat, and the fear that France might be compelled by diplomatic or even military pressure into dependence upon an all-powerful Germany, which so alarmed the anti-German circles in Britain. This very apprehension itself, it may be noted, represented an additional and very massive element in the Anglo-German antagonism. Hitherto, Germany had been disliked by British imperialists because (as it seemed to them) of her policy of *chantage* and greed in colonial matters, or because she sought to keep all the other powers quarrelling among themselves, or because so many of these imperialists were still 'Liberal' enough to detest Hohenzollern authoritarianism, or finally because Germany was seeking to gain naval supremacy in the North Sea. It is true that the *National Review*, *The Times*, *Spectator* and other such journals had frequently featured Pan-German ambitions upon the Netherlands, or Austria, or elsewhere; and in 1902, in a prescient article, the *Morning Post* had discussed the need for Britain to rediscover its traditional balance-of-power strategy in the face of the growing power of Imperial Germany.[119] At a time when the Dual Alliance and the Triple Alliance were in equilibrium, however, few shared this concern; once that equilibrium went, the danger appeared obvious. The Kaiser is in 'something like the position of a Dictator of Europe', wrote Clinton Dawkins to Maxse. 'We are face to face with the same state of things which existed in Europe under Charles V, Louis XIV and Napoleon. The only issue is either submission to the dictator or a defensive war', claimed Spring-Rice.[120] Unlike Lansdowne and Balfour, the anti-Germans were also willing to accept the logical military consequences of their arguments. The British army should be reorganised so as to be able to operate with the French in the Low Countries or Schleswig, urged Saunders; 'Nothing short of conscription and a businesslike devotion to war on land will enable us to maintain our position', felt Satow, although himself fearing and disliking this development.[121] Finally, it may be noted that behind all of this apparent concern for France lay a much deeper apprehension for *Britain*'s own future, should Germany dominate the continent.[122]

Given the state of international politics at the time of Delcassé's fall, it is hardly surprising that the professional military advisers to the British government were also beginning to formulate a strategy in the event of a Franco-German war. The Admiralty, under Fisher's hectic driving, was preparing the fleet for some possible future action in the North Sea by introducing a whole variety of reforms; and, although it has been pointed out that the pace of this reorganisation of British naval policy from an anti-Dual Alliance to an anti-German posture should not be exaggerated,[123] there can be no doubt that by the early summer of 1905 the Royal Navy no longer saw much of a threat in the French or Russian fleets. Moreover, the 'diplomatic revolution' and the Japanese naval victories had combined to give Britain a battleship superiority over the next largest fleets which she had not enjoyed for many a decade; and the fighting power of her vessels would soon be enormously enhanced by the launching of the *Dreadnought*. Apart from urging the cautious Lansdowne to consider this 'golden opportunity for fighting the Germans in alliance with the French', Fisher was also in touch with the French naval attaché to see what help could be given.

This enthusiasm for the *entente* was marred, however, by the admiral's confident assumption that his beloved ships constituted the main defence not only of the British Isles, but also of France. This was not how the French or German General Staffs – or, indeed, an increasing number of Britons – saw it: of what use to France would British maritime operations be when German troops were pouring into Paris? The probable German strategy, so far as Rouvier's worried government knew of it, had been outlined in a semi-official article by Professor Schiemann in the *Kreuz-Zeitung* of 14 June 1905: whatever losses Germany suffered in the naval and colonial fields would be compensated for by the overrunning of France, the 'hostage'. While Fisher wanted to fight Germany, the problem was that he wanted to do it in a fashion which offered little help to France.[124]

To the British army, by contrast, the need to consider ways of aiding the French came as a blessed relief after the defeats of the Boer War.[125] Under the newly established General Staff, it at last had an effective planning centre; but its chief problem was that it lacked a viable strategic *raison d'être* since it was precisely in these years 1903–5 that Balfour led the CID towards the conclusion that a large army was not needed for purposes of home defence, and the protection of overseas colonies was not a pressing task by 1905. Although the Indian army itself and the viceroy never ceased to point to the vulnerability of the British position there, the reinforcements demanded by them were so large that the General Staff and CID hoped that India, too, might be protected by diplomacy. Besides, to professional soldiers such as Generals Nicholson and Grierson, Colonel Robertson, and (later) General Wilson, planning for a

European commitment not only offered a greater challenge but it gave the service a strategical justification and purpose which, many of them felt, had hitherto been lacking – and consequently raised their status *vis-à-vis* that of the navy.[126]

The sheer pace of this strategic reorientation was remarkable. At the beginning of 1905 the War Secretary, Arnold-Forster, was still pressing Balfour for a definite statement on 'what the Army was for, and what ought to be its true dimension', although the General Staff, acting on its own accord, was just then studying a war game postulated upon an Anglo-French combined operation to check a German sweep into Belgium. While Clarke thought this to be 'among the least likely of many contingencies', the generals were so enthusiastic that in March Grierson and Robertson were to be found personally touring the Franco-Belgian border and dropping broad hints to the French about the prospect of British military assistance.[127] By July and August, when a CID sub-committee was considering an Admiralty proposal to plan for amphibious raids on the German coast, Clarke was beginning to be swayed by the army's alternative strategy – the dispatch of troops across the Channel. In the words of the General Staff's critique of Fisher's Baltic schemes, 'An efficient army of 120,000 British troops might just have the effect of preventing any important German successes on the Franco-German frontier'. In January 1906, as a final irony, Clarke wrote to Kitchener, wondering about the employment of Indian troops in Europe.[128]

Whatever the disagreements between the Admiralty and the War Office, both agreed by the summer of 1905 that 'a second overthrow of France by Germany . . . would end in the aggrandisement of Germany to an extent which would be prejudicial to the whole of Europe, and it might therefore be necessary for Great Britain in her own interests to lend France her active support should war of this nature break out'.[129] Not since 1875, and then only temporarily, had the European balance of power been an issue in the Anglo-German relationship. From now on, it would be a fundamental obstacle to good relations even when other points of discord died away; and, given the German capacity to defeat France, it would be impossible to remove it unless and until the government in Berlin managed to persuade Britain that it would never undertake that westward strike. This is not to say that there were no Germans who would have genuinely given that undertaking; or that every Briton accepted the argument that Germany posed a threat to France's independence which was so great that in the event of war British military intervention on the continent was called for. But there were to be sufficient influential people within the British and German establishments (especially the latter) to ensure that their country's potential ability and will to fight if need be in France and the Low Countries was never abandoned. Furthermore, although political leaders in London were repeatedly to declare that these were merely contingency plans which did not commit the country to fight for France, their very existence – as shall be seen – created a *moral* bond from which it would be difficult to escape.

Whilst the British 'Official Mind' was thus pondering over the means by which it might counter the German pressure upon France, the Kaiser and his advisers were making a further bid to break out of Germany's impending isolation. Although the fall of Delcassé and the manifest efforts of Rouvier to stand well with Berlin were regarded with great satisfaction in the *Wilhelm-strasse*, this feeling mingled with unease at the possibility of an Anglo-French-Russian alliance being negotiated in the near future. Delcassé's supporters were assumed to be urging such a grouping; Lamsdorff and Witte were suspected of having sympathies for it; King Edward VII, at this time bitterly critical of his nephew's policies, was already enjoying a reputation in Berlin as the arch-protagonist of the encirclement of Germany; and confirmation that this plot was in British minds was provided by reports that papers such as *The Times, Daily Express, Spectator* and *National Review* were urging the need for a *rapprochement* with Russia in order to preserve the European equilibrium.[130] When, therefore, the Kaiser cabled from the Bay of Björkö in July 1905 that he was on the verge of signing an alliance with the Tsar, Bülow's first reaction was one of relief. The subsequent weeks and months illustrated yet again, however, the dilemmas facing the German statesmen. The treaty itself was clearly anti-British in origin, being motivated by Wilhelm's genuine fear of an Anglo-German conflict; and for this reason he personally was not only keen to win Russia's friendship but was also willing to be conciliatory to France. Yet even the prospect of a Berlin–St Petersburg axis was insufficient to tempt Wilhelm into a *global* pact lest this complicate Germany's relations with Japan: hence the restriction of the Björkö treaty's effectiveness to Europe itself, a wording which provoked Bülow into offering his resignation since it would also exclude any Russian commitment to put pressure upon India in the event of a Russo-German war against Britain. Furthermore, the Kaiser's efforts to be friendly to France directly contradicted Holstein's strategy of compelling the French to recognise that they could not act without Germany's consent and goodwill.

With Bülow oscillating between these two positions, it was perhaps not surprising that French diplomacy made significant advances in the pre-Moroccan Conference negotiations during the autumn of 1905. Paris's gains were partly the consequence, too, of the German wish to please Russia, since the more Berlin laid store upon a Russian alliance, the more it felt obliged to heed the Tsar's requests to be conciliatory over Morocco. This ought to have alerted Berlin to the futility of hoping to split the Dual Alliance; but the disappointment in Berlin was considerable when, in October, the Tsar suggested postponing the signing of the Björkö treaty 'until we know how France will look upon it'. If this in turn was to lead to further internal dissensions (including Holstein's attempted resignation) just before the Moroccan Conference opened, its chief meaning was that Germany had failed to break out of her isolation. As the Kaiser dramatically and bitterly put it: 'The coalition is *de facto* there! King Edward VII has cleverly wangled it!'[131]

By the end of 1905, the chief grounds for hope of escaping isolation appeared to lie in the fact that Balfour's administration had at last collapsed and had been replaced by the Liberals under Campbell-Bannerman. As early as 1903, as was noted above, Berlin had tended to regard the latter in a new light. Gladstone's successors were now seen as a potentially attractive alternative to a Unionist government which had ominously recalled its overseas fleets to the North Sea, which was working with Delcassé to frustrate Germany's *Weltpolitik* and may indeed have offered to assist France militarily on the continent, and which threatened to deal a devastating blow to German export industries by adopting protectionism. If this was an unfair view of a Cabinet whose foreign policy was chiefly in the hands of Lansdowne and Balfour, the *Wilhelmstrasse* felt that it had to take account of the decidedly germanophobic tone of the Unionist press and was also perturbed at the prospect that Chamberlain would become party leader after the next general election. As Metternich repeatedly pointed out, the Liberals 'will be less aggressive and capable of action in foreign affairs, and despite all their friendships [with France and Russia] less inclined than a Conservative government to intervene on behalf of their friends'.[132] Encouraged by Asquith's remark to Metternich that 'an English government which promised armed assistance to France against Germany would be thrown out of office within a week', Berlin greeted the advent of Campbell-Bannerman's administration with pleasure – even if it needed to conceal this sentiment until the January 1906 general elections.[133] On the commercial front, too, the coming of the Liberals could only be welcome to German industry and to the State Secretary for the Interior, Count Posadowsky, who had become so alarmed at the Tariff Reform campaign that he had drafted various anonymous articles in praise of free trade – an ironic position for a Prussian minister to adopt – which were then discreetly inserted in British journals in order to assist the Liberals' election propaganda![134] With Cobdenite commercial policies now reasserted, it was not surprising that Berlin also expected a Cobdenite foreign policy. As Holstein put it, 'The place where German policy should dig is in England, not France . . . We should use the next few years, when Russia will be occupied with her own affairs, to prevent England from afterwards joining the Dual Alliance. Without England, even the Dual Alliance will think twice before making war on us.'[135]

In the realms of domestic and commercial policy, the Liberal landslide of 1906 may indeed be viewed as a significant turning-point. With regard to the diplomatic and naval/military fields, however, there was no real improvement in the Anglo-German relationship. Indeed, it can fairly be argued that, despite certain superficial signs of better relations, the two countries were further away from each other by the middle of 1906 than they had been at the beginning of that year.

In the first place, the German government misjudged the way in which Liberal foreign policy towards France would develop, since the heated campaign against tariff reform and other Unionist policies had concealed from outside observers the division of opinion over foreign affairs which existed between the Liberal Imperialists on the one hand and the vast mass of the party on the other. In particular, Grey, the new Foreign Secretary, had long regarded Germany with suspicion and pleaded for a close understanding with France. He had, in fact, encouraged the *National Review*'s attacks of 1901–2 upon Germany's diplomatic record, although admitting that a government minister might publicly have to repudiate such strongly expressed views.[136] In the years following, he had been constantly critical of German policy and expressed his dislike whenever Balfour's administration had appeared to be working too closely with Berlin or whenever it was thought 'that a Liberal Government would unsettle the understanding with France in order to make up to Germany'.[137] Moreover, Grey – in contrast to Lansdowne – was to be primarily concerned with the European balance of power and was to be less interested in imperial issues *per se*. When, therefore, he entered office to find the Moroccan crisis near its peak, he had no hesitation in approving the informal talks which were taking place to consider ways whereby Britain could send military aid to France and Belgium in the event of a German strike westwards. Furthermore, on 3 January and 19 February Grey repeated to Metternich – in a much more extended form – Lansdowne's warning of the previous June that public opinion would make it 'impossible for England to remain neutral' if such an assault took place; and he took a further step on 10 January by stating the same to Cambon, the French ambassador, which was something Lansdowne had never done.[138] Whatever one may say about these Anglo-French military talks (for instance, that they did not legally commit the government, but were merely contingency measures) or about Grey's warnings (for example, that he stressed they were only his personal opinion), historians have rightly seen in such actions a *qualitative* difference in British policy towards Germany as compared with that carried out by Lansdowne and Balfour.[139] While it is important not to suggest that from this time onwards Britain would inevitably join France in a war against Germany, it nevertheless remains true that any future German pressure upon its western neighbour was going to provoke that small but influential part of the British Cabinet to become ever more convinced of the need to uphold the Anglo-French *entente*, if necessary by force.

Grey's policy of regarding British interests as virtually identical with the French was demonstrated during the Algeciras Conference itself. Reinforced by the urgings of Louis Mallet (now Grey's private secretary) that 'We must go to Algeciras, determined to back up the French and see them through', the Foreign Secretary saw every German effort to put pressure upon France as a threat to the *entente* itself – although he was willing to permit the Germans to obtain a Moroccan port if this was agreeable to Paris.[140] Early in 1906, he was in frequent touch with Clarke, with Tweedmouth (the new First Lord of the Admiralty) and even with Repington (*The Times* military correspondent, and one of the instigators of the Anglo-French staff talks) about British preparations in the event of a conflict. During the months of the conference itself, Grey was willing to suggest occasional compromises to the French; but whenever the latter stood firm, he felt bound to give his full support. Although unwilling, because of domestic constraints as well as his own preference for loose arrangements, to push for a full military alliance with France, the Foreign Secretary did seem to regard Britain as being diplomatically linked to, and even dependent upon, its Gallic neighbour. His attitude was repeatedly shown in the following year, when he remained sceptical of all the efforts to improve Anglo-German relations if these could lead to any slighting of France: in 1907, in fact, he was virtually threatening resignation if the band of the Coldstream Guards visited Germany.[141] A high regard for French susceptibilities, and a deep suspicion that Berlin was always manoeuvring to break the *entente cordiale*, had been the hallmarks of the anti-German circles in the Foreign Office staff and Unionist press for some years. That the British Foreign Secretary should share such beliefs was a very significant development.

Of perhaps even greater importance than this Anglo-French amity was the British desire for better relations with Russia. Even when Balfour's government was in the middle of its renegotiations of the Anglo-Japanese alliance, Clarke had been urging the advantages which Britain might gain from an agreement with St Petersburg over central Asia, Persia, the opening of the Straits, and a Russian branch line to the main Baghdad Railway. While this idea fitted in with the Balfour/Lansdowne strategy of easing Britain's imperial obligations by diplomatic *rapprochements*, and while Clarke repeatedly insisted that if this proposed agreement had an obvious anti-German flavour it would scare off the Russians, others such as Austen Chamberlain were attracted to the scheme precisely because it would block Germany's ambitions.[142] On the other hand, a strong body of Conservative opinion had always regarded Russia with suspicion, whereas it had been a tradition of liberalism since Gladstone's day to hope and work for an improvement in Anglo-Russian relations. As early as December 1895 Grey had written that 'a bold and skilful Foreign Secretary might detach Russia from the number of our active enemies without sacrificing any very material British interests',[143] and for the next ten years the Liberal Imperialists in particular were to urge this policy, which explains why they so disliked Chamberlain's turn-of-the-century bids for a German alliance and why – in contrast to the Unionists – they remained cool to the Anglo-Japanese alliance. By the time Grey entered the Foreign Office, moreover, friendship with Russia also had European implications: as he himself put it at the height of the Algeciras crisis, 'An *entente* between Russia, France and ourselves would be absolutely secure. If it is necessary to check Germany it could then be done.'[144]

All this is not to imply that the historian can detect a straight line of cause and consequence between the Liberal accession to power and the signing of the Anglo-Russian agreement in August 1907. In the first place, there was little certainty that Russia itself would welcome a compromise with its traditional foe. Moreover, all of the previous British hints for an understanding carried with them the assumption that finite limits were to be placed upon Russian expansionism in Asia, and this few if any statesmen at St Petersburg wished to accept. On the other hand, although the Tsar himself still inclined towards Wilhelm, Lamsdorff and Witte could hardly forget the way Berlin had taken advantage of the Far Eastern conflict to wring more favourable terms in the Russo-German commercial negotiations and had urged Russia forward into its disastrous struggle with Japan, whilst the German press rejoiced that this was leading to the steady weakening of Russian power in Europe.[145] Furthermore, St Petersburg's refusal to sign the Björkö treaty showed that any pro-German policy had definite limits and that the Tsarist government was bound by financial and treaty terms to France, which was anxious to improve Anglo-Russian relations. In all probability, Russia at this time wanted neither to be closely allied with Germany, nor to be pushed against her.

One further complication in the Anglo-German bid for Russia's friendship lay in the impact of the 1905 revolution. As Spring-Rice put it, 'If there is a real movement in favour of reform we shall become more popular with the new Government. On the other hand the Autocracy, if frightened, will look to its monarchical friends for help and that means a closer union with Germany.'[146] This, certainly, was how the Kaiser and his Chancellor viewed these events. 'In my opinion, the question is thus', wrote Bülow: 'Either we feel certain of Russia in the future, and must therefore wish for the preservation of the Russian Empire and especially the dynasty; or we assume that Russia will not let herself be prevented from joining England, and then we have no interest in peace and order being restored.'[147] As the revolution in Russia developed, Wilhelm could not contain his rage at how this helped the British: 'Just as Albion used Japan in order to break Russia's land and sea power, so it will exploit the revolution in order to throw out him [Nicholas II] and to create a "liberal" Russia, which with "liberal" England and France will turn upon "reactionary" Germany!' The 'old Russia' had gone, and the new Russia would be *bündnisfähig*, so Wilhelm feared, to the Western powers.[148] The Tsar's withdrawal from the Björkö agreement simply confirmed the way things were going; and the open glee of the increasingly powerful German Socialists at the events in Russia brought the dangers nearer home and helps to explain Wilhelm's hysterical instructions to Bülow that Germany should not run the risk of war over Morocco until the internal foe was crushed, 'if necessary with a blood bath'.[149]

The thought that France was encouraging a democratised Russia because the latter was bound to be 'more anti-German and more bellicose than the Russia of the absolute Tsar' caused Holstein to urge a firm line at the Algeciras Conference;[150] yet the results of that policy turned out to be quite different from his expectations. Not only did the Liberal, 'isolationist', British government support the French, but so, too, did the Russians. This in turn provoked the German government to forbid its banks to participate in the joint loan of April 1906 to Russia, so that St Petersburg was driven further away from Berlin and towards not only Paris, but also London.[151] Despite the Russian wish to avoid a complete break with Berlin, and the ideological mistrust between Liberal England and Tsarist Russia, therefore, it was clear that the myth of Russo-German monarchical solidarity had been broken for ever, and the even stronger myth about the inability of Britain and Russia to settle their colonial differences was now very questionable. The keystone in the diplomatic assumptions behind Bülow's *Weltpolitik* had crumbled, and the sense of failure and isolation was increasing. In March 1906 Tschirschky privately listed a gloomy catalogue of defeats: instead of restoring German prestige, the Moroccan policy had been a diplomatic disaster; Russia had turned to France, France in her turn had abandoned Rouvier and resumed Delcassé's pro-British line; Italy was unreliable, and Spain was drifting away.[152] In the extra-European world, Japan was Britain's ally and the earlier German hopes in Roosevelt had been misplaced. By April, Holstein himself had finally resigned. And the Chancellor's own speeches of this time referred ever more to the necessity of Germany being prepared to fight against foes on all sides.

The third and final sign that Anglo-German relations were unlikely to improve with the coming of the Liberal administration in Britain lay in the naval sphere. As early as 1903, in fact, Tirpitz's staff had been studying the possibility of a further increase in the battlefleet programme – perhaps to give a total battleship strength of fifty-seven – but the worsening of the Reich's finances and of the government's position in the Reichstag following the 1903 elections caused the decision to be postponed. When the matter was seriously discussed again, in 1904–5, it was complicated both by external and internal developments. The results of the Russo-Japanese War, the 'navy scare' of December 1904, the growing diplomatic isolation of Germany, all appeared to justify further measures to increase the country's defences: at least, Wilhelm thought this was so, and both he and Bülow used such incidents as the 'Copenhagen' call of the *Army and Navy Gazette*, Arthur Lee's reported speech and Delcassé's revelations in the *Matin* as propaganda for increases in the fleet.[153] This also was the attitude of the German Navy League, which contained a strong and vocal section of 'radical nationalists' who criticised Tirpitz for his moderation.[154] On the other hand, it was precisely the rising danger from the massive British battlefleet assembling in the North Sea which caused the State Secretary to hesitate: just as he had opposed a formal Russo-German alliance in November 1904, lest this provoke the British into war, so now he resisted the pressures from the Kaiser and the nationalists for an enormous increase in the German battleship-building programme. Tirpitz's problems were compounded, moreover, by the rumours that the Royal Navy had ordered a battleship which would be much larger and more powerful than anything afloat. Given the inner logic of the 'Tirpitz-Plan', he felt bound to follow suit; but this strengthened still more his conviction that he dared not press both for a *quantitative* and a *qualitative* increase in the battlefleet. The Reichstag would hardly accept it; and the British reaction would be terrible. If we bowed to the Navy League's proposal for fifty-seven battleships, which was actually more than the Royal Navy itself possessed, Tirpitz argued, then it 'implied such a shift in *real power factors* that even a calm and rational English government *must* come to the decision to crush such an opponent before he had reached the military strength so dangerous for England's world position'.[155] As one scholar has tartly remarked, 'Tirpitz was a "moderate" only because he had to be'.[156] All that had happened was that the State Secretary preferred a somewhat slower pace of fleet expansion than the navalist agitators; but he never wavered from his long-term aim. Moreover, even the 1906 supplementary law was not a minor matter. As a slightly later memorandum put it,

If one summarises the achievements of the 1906 amendment:
    6 new cruisers of the *Invincible* type
    Changeover to Dreadnought-building
    Prolongation of the 3-large-vessels-per-annum tempo for another 7 years
    Doubling of the annual torpedo-boat production
    A considerable increase in personnel
    Money grant for U-boats

then one must concede that the bill of 1906 was in no way as insignificant as the fleet-agitators then suggested; in contrast, the demands were measured as high as ever they could have been with the prospect of being carried through.[157]

To this total should also be added the complementary bill for funds to widen the Kiel Canal, which had become necessary with the decision to build Dreadnought-class battleships although this measure was justified by reference to Germany's growing seaborne commerce. What these various increases meant overall was that Germany had taken up the challenge to build a new class of super-battleships, and that the Anglo-German naval race had moved to a higher and much more expensive level.

The final indication that the Anglo-German antagonism had now become a permanent feature in international politics was given, ironically enough, by the various unofficial attempts at this time by well-meaning circles in both countries to improve public relations. Sir Thomas Barclay, fresh from his efforts to better Anglo-French friendship, decided to devote himself to doing the same for Anglo-German relations and in February 1905 he visited Berlin, where he gave two speeches to businessmen. By May of that year, an 'Anglo-German Union Club', with many distinguished political, military and financial members, had been founded in London for the purposes of promoting cultural and sporting activities between the two nations. In September, the British delegates to the International Peace Conference at Lucerne had met privately with their German colleagues and resolved to form an 'Anglo-German Conciliation Committee'; and by 1 December sufficient progress had been made for a public meeting to be held at Caxton Hall, attended by 2,000 people and presided over by Lord Avebury. Hard on its heels followed a speech at the Lyceum Club by Metternich, in favour of Anglo-German co-operation. By early 1906 the Caxton Hall meeting had turned itself into the 'Anglo-German Friendship Committee' and was producing its own weekly newspaper. This in turn led to responses on the German side: the Kaiser replied in warm words to Avebury's cabled greetings; a meeting at the Berlin Stock Exchange of over 2,000 people called for an improvement in Anglo-German relations; Chambers of Commerce at Cologne, Wiesbaden, Berlin and elsewhere added their voices to this movement. In 1906 and 1907, visits of groups of burgomasters and mayors, and then of editors and journalists from one country to the other were taking place.[158]

What was significant about these various activities was not so much that there existed numerous groups with rather diverse backgrounds – Quakers, businessmen, intellectuals, landed aristocrats and radical journalists – who favoured an improvement in Anglo-German relations, but that the antagonism between the two countries had become so marked a feature of public life that it was now felt to be necessary to take positive actions against it. All the references to 'conciliation' and 'friendship' were, therefore, a recognition of and a reaction against what was felt to be *the prevailing rivalry and enmity*; had a true friendship existed, such unofficial and spontaneous manifestations would have been superfluous. The Wiesbaden Chamber of Commerce, in its approach to the Association of British Chambers of Commerce, 'observed with much regret the growing estrangement during the last years between England and Germany';[159] businessmen referred to their fears of an Anglo-German tariff war; Progressive and pacifist circles pointed to the dangers of the escalating naval race; others referred to the systematic campaign of hatred which the chauvinistic press in each country had carried out. The second noticeable feature was the reaction which this movement produced elsewhere: nationalists in both countries deprecated the 'woolly-minded idealism' of its members; Foreign Office personnel disliked such attempts at amateur diplomacy; many Britons feared the effects of these demonstrations upon their *entente* with France; many Germans, attracted to the idea of improved relations with Britain, still insisted that France would remain the *Erbfeind*; military circles, and especially the Kaiser, warmly rejected the accompanying notions of arms reductions and international arbitration; protectionists discovered in the movement a devious free trade plot.

Yet all these expressions of criticism and suspicion simply confirmed the original point: namely, that there had arisen over the previous decades an enmity and a clash of interests between Britain and Germany which could not easily, if at all, be eradicated. In 1906, as in 1880, a Liberal administration had just taken power, and this was bound to mean that there would be distinct ideological differences between the two governments, if not the two establishments as a whole. By the latter date, however, a large number of further and very substantial points of difference had arisen, as compared with the *relatively* untroubled state of Anglo-German relations in 1880. The commercial rivalry, then only embryonic, had become much more serious; the two countries had quarrelled repeatedly over colonial issues, and each held the other to be a threat to its overseas interests; an escalating arms race in the North Sea, unthinkable twenty-five years earlier, worsened relations year by year; the latent German threat to France, and the reawakened British concern with the balance of power in Europe, was another potentially explosive topic of discord; a powerful nationalistic press in both countries articulated these differences and stimulated mutual fears; more conciliatory and tolerant forces on both sides appeared to be less effective than earlier; the dynastic ties were much less warm, and the cultural and religious connections now seemed to be of little import.

Most of these changes have been discussed, or at least referred to, in the present chapter: indeed, it is impossible to write a narrative survey of the altering Anglo-German relationship between 1880 and 1906 without constant allusion to such developments. Nevertheless, the allusions have often been brief and without accompanying analysis. Now that it has been argued that an 'antagonism' had been well and truly established, it is necessary to undertake a further structural and comparative examination of these various background factors in order to comprehend more clearly the role each of them played in the general story of that changing relationship.

# PART FOUR

*The Structure of the Anglo-German Relationship in the Age of Bülow and Chamberlain*

# CHAPTER 15

# *Economic Transformation and Anglo-German Trade Relations*

The analysis of Anglo-German economic relations earlier in this book termi-nated in the year 1885, when the world was still in the middle of the 'Great Depression'. It was to remain so until around 1896, when a general revival of manufacturing productivity and commercial interchange began which lasted until the outbreak of the First World War. Even within those two broad periods there were cyclical booms (around 1890, in the last five years of the century, in the five years after 1902, and in the period after 1909) interspersed by recessions (especially in 1893–4, 1902 and 1907–9), and it is important to keep the dates of the various phases of the trade cycle in mind since this related to protectionist agitations in both Britain and Germany. However, each burst of expansion raised world trade to new heights, and each subsequent recession never fell to the level of the preceding one, so the overall trend was firmly upwards.

This long-term growth is reflected in the detailed statistics of the trade of the two countries (even if some of the cyclical variations are concealed): see Tables 15.1 and 15.2. Although both nations were sharing in the general expansion of

Table 15.1  *Britain's foreign trade*[1] (£ million)

|  | 1890 | 1895 | 1900 | 1905 | 1910 | 1913 |
|---|---|---|---|---|---|---|
| Net imports | 356 | 357 | 459 | 487 | 574 | 659 |
| Exports | 264 | 226 | 291 | 330 | 430 | 525 |
| Re-exports | 65 | 60 | 63 | 78 | 104 | 110 |

Table 15.2  *Germany's foreign trade*[2] (£ million)
('Special' Trade)

|  | 1890 | 1895 | 1900 | 1905 | 1910 | 1913 |
|---|---|---|---|---|---|---|
| Imports | 208 | 206 | 283 | 350 | 439 | 537 |
| Exports | 166 | 165 | 226 | 281 | 367 | 505 |

world productivity and commerce, Germany's rate of growth (especially in exports) was far swifter than Britain's. Since other countries, and in particular the United States, were also expanding at a faster rate than Britain, the overall trend – when measured in *relative* rather than *absolute* terms – was that the former 'workshop of the world' was being ousted from that position. By 1906–10, Britain's relative share of the world's manufacturing capacity was down to 14·7 per cent, while Germany held 15·9 per cent and the United States 35·3 per cent.[3] Moreover, the absolute rate of expansion of British exports continued to decline in the last years of the nineteenth century[4] and although the decade before 1914 saw a strong revival in the British export trade, that of her chief rivals increased even faster. Consequently, even in prosperous times her share of world trade shrank (see Table 15.3). In the export field, moreover, the British lead had been reduced to an even narrower margin: in 1913, whereas she exported 14 per cent of the world's goods, Germany exported 13 per cent.[6]

Table 15.3    *Percentages of world trade*[5]

|         | 1880 | 1900 | 1913 |
|---------|------|------|------|
| Britain | 23   | 20   | 17   |
| Germany | 10   | 13   | 13   |
| France  | 11   | 9    | 8    |
| USA     | 10   | 11   | 11   |

The fact that Germany was catching up would come as no surprise to the expert in 'the stages of economic growth'; having previously been the more backward of the two nations economically, Germany was able, by utilising steam, electrical and rail power, to achieve growth rates which were higher than those of a 'mature economy' like Britain's. The Reich's population, to begin with, was considerably greater: the 49 million Germans in 1890 increased to 56 million (1900) and then to 65 million (1910), whereas the 38 million Britons (1891) rose less swiftly to 41 million (1901) and then to 45 million (1911). Not only was the German birthrate higher – 35 per 1,000 compared with Britain's 29 per 1,000 – but the fact that this coincided with the rapid industrialisation and urbanisation of Germany meant that there was a proportionately higher number of future 'operatives' being born to provide the labour force for the new factories. Urbanisation had also continued apace in Britain, so that by 1911 73·4 per cent of the population was living in towns compared with 60·7 per cent in 1881; in Germany, however, the speed of change had been such as to alter the country, at least in a statistical sense, from being mainly rural to mainly urban in population – 41.4 per cent of all Germans lived in towns in 1880, but by 1910 that had risen to 60 per cent.[7] By that later date, the Germans had constructed a much more extensive railway complex: 61,000 miles of track to Britain's 38,000 miles. Her coal production, virtually only half of Britain's in 1890, had almost caught up – 279,000 tons was mined in 1913 compared with the British total of 292,000 tons. Given the basic similarity of environmental conditions and aptitude of the population in the two countries, it was more than likely that Germany's greater land size and workforce would give her the edge in all these areas of the economy.[8] Were a comparison made with United States economic development in these years, then it would be seen that, *pari passu*, its even greater population and natural advantages had led to quite spectacular growth rates.

A more significant point is that Germany's industrial expansion was, in many respects, in the more advanced and qualitatively superior sectors of the economy. A brief glance at the pattern of her export trade over this period well captures the nature and speed of this transformation. In the early 1890s, beet sugar was still the most valuable German export in most years, although woollen goods were pressing it close. By 1913, the country's leading produce sent abroad had been transformed: chemicals (£52 million), machinery (£34 million), ironware (£32·5 million), coal (£25·8 million), cotton cloths (£22·3 million), woollen cloths (£13·5 million) and only then beet sugar (£13·2 million). Among the less valuable categories of exports, it is possible to detect very swift increases in such items as smelted iron, wire, electrical equipment and motor cars.[9] These were all indicators of a highly modernised economy, confirming in their way what economic historians tell us about the features of this industrial growth in the Wilhelmine era – advanced technology, high rates of investment in new plant, ready utilisation of scientific advances, high level of managerial training, aggressive entrepreneurship and salesmanship, amalgamations of smaller firms into large, powerful combines, and so on.[10]

It is these features, rather than any natural advantages, which explain why Germany was able to overtake Britain in the production and export of what would be considered more modern wares. In 1890, British pig-iron production (8 million tons) had been twice that of Germany's (4·1 million); by 1914, her total production of 11 million tons had been comfortably passed by the German output of 14·7 million. In steel, the shift in the economic balance was more remarkable: Britain's 1890 total of 3·6 million tons had risen to 6·5 million by 1914, but Germany's had jumped spectacularly from 2·3 million to 14 million in the same period. The export figures told a similar story. By 1910, the value of German chemical exports was almost twice that of Britain's and she was handsomely ahead in exports of machinery and had a narrow lead in the export of metals and metal wares; but in the more traditional areas of textiles and coal, the British retained their lead.[11]

These larger trends were reflected in Anglo-German trade. It, too, had shared in the overall growth in world commerce, as shown in Table 15·4. Quite

Table 15.4   *Anglo-German trade* (£ million)[12]

|  | 1890 | 1895 | 1900 | 1905 | 1910 | 1913 |
|---|---|---|---|---|---|---|
| British imports from Germany | 26·0 | 26·9 | 31·1 | 53·8 | 61·8 | 80·4 |
| British exports to Germany | 19·2 | 20·5 | 27·9 | 29·7 | 37·0 | 40·6 |
| British re-exports to Germany | 11·2 | 12·1 | 10·5 | 13·0 | 17·8 | 19·8 |

apart from the possibility that the figures of British imports from Germany do not include the considerable commerce which went through the Low Countries,[13] it is clear even from these crude statistics that the visible trade balance between the two powers was altering steadily in Germany's favour. In the decades before 1914, Britain was becoming an increasingly important market for German *manufactures*, which greatly exceeded in value Britain's own rising exports to Germany of traditional staple goods (textiles, ironware, but also raw materials such as coal, herrings and wool), and this gap remained considerable even when the valuable re-export trade in colonial raw materials (rubber, skins raw wool, coffee) is included in the British total. However, this deficit was reduced by the fact that Germany's booming industry was directly importing ever more raw materials both from the British Empire and certain parts of the 'informal' British economic empire; and these latter regions took increasing amounts of the manufactures of Lancashire and the midlands which (because of tariffs and domestic competition) could no longer penetrate European markets. The deficit was probably eliminated altogether by the 'invisible' earnings which the City of London acquired in arranging this multilateral trade. By 1913, it is also worth pointing out, a full £56 million of Germany's £80·4 million exports to Britain consisted of manufactures, whereas foodstuffs (£16·4 million) and raw materials (£7·1 million) were much less important[14] – a sharp contrast to Bismarck's time, when Germany's chief economic function had been to supply the British market with vast amounts of foodstuffs.

If, therefore, Britain and Germany remained important trading partners, the nature of the commercial flow had altered. Britain, it has been remarked, escaped from the Great Depression 'not by modernising her economy, but by exploiting the remaining possibilities of her traditional position': that is, by exporting more of her staple goods to her relatively secure imperial markets and by utilising her role as the world's leading banker, commodity-dealer, shipper, insurer and investor.[15] Germany (together with the United States) was overtaking Britain as a manufacturing nation, but as a further consequence was needing to import more and more raw materials and foodstuffs. So great had become the import of German goods into Britain that the 1913 total of £80·4 million was second only in value to imports from the United States (£141 million), and well ahead of imports from India (£48 million) and France (£46 million). As a market for British exports, Germany with her 1913 total of £40·6 million was in second position, well behind India (£70·2 million) but some way ahead of Australia (£34 million) and the United States (£29·2 million); and she was also in clear second place as a market for British re-exports, her total of £19·8 million comparing with the United States' £30·1 million and France's £11·9 million.[16]

Viewed from the German perspective, however, the alteration in the trading relationship becomes much clearer. Because of Germany's enormous demand for raw materials and foodstuffs, the United States and Russia had become the chief suppliers of German imports by the eve of the First World War, and Britain's share had slowly declined, from 15 per cent (1890) to 8·1 per cent (1913); but, by the same process, Germany's imports of raw materials and foodstuffs from the British overseas possessions had also been steadily rising, to a total of 12 per cent by 1913, with India's share alone being 5 per cent. A full fifth of German imports still came from the total British Empire, therefore, but the United Kingdom's own share was down to one-sixteenth. By contrast, Britain had remained the leading market for German exports throughout this entire period, and in 1913 took 14·2 per cent – whereas the rest of the empire imported only 4·4 per cent of Germany's exports.[17] Perhaps nothing illustrates the multilateral trading relationship better than the fact that in 1913 Germany had a *visible* trade surplus with Britain of around £20 million, whereas Britain had a surplus of £30 million with India and Australia, and those two latter countries had a surplus of slightly over £20 million with Germany!

It is impossible to obtain specific figures of the *invisible* trade balances between Britain and Germany at this time, but it is known that British earnings from services such as shipping, banking and insurance, together with the returns upon overseas investment, were rising at such a spectacular rate (the annual average surplus on 'invisibles' was £186 million in the years 1891–5, and £346 million in the years 1911–13) that the deficit in visible trade was effortlessly covered.[18] Since less than 10 per cent of British foreign investments were in Europe by the decade before the First World War, it is highly unlikely that the flow from Germany to Britain of monies from dividends and interest could have matched the imbalance in visible trade between the two countries. On the other hand, the multilateral nature of the trade relations between Germany and the British Empire as a whole allowed the service industries of the City of London to accumulate substantial earnings each year. Despite the impressive growth of the German mercantile marine, the greater part of direct Anglo-German trade and a very considerable proportion of Germany's trade with third countries was carried in British vessels. In addition, the greater part of the German mercantile marine (including *Hamburg-Amerika* and *Norddeutsche Lloyd* ships) was insured by Lloyds of London, whose own profits were therefore boosted by the rise of the Reich to a great commercial power. The same was true of the London banks, and one prominent banker in 1911 asserted that Germany 'is, in fact, our principal debtor'.[19] The accumulation of fees charged to German industry by their British shippers, insurers, bankers and commodity-dealers went a long way, it may safely be reckoned, to render illusory the apparent imbalance in Anglo-German trade.

Only when the overall and complex nature of the economic relations between the two countries is kept in mind is it possible to understand the Anglo-German 'trade rivalry'. Rivalry there certainly was, but it occurred at specific times and in specific industries; and this in turn helps to explain both the fragmented nature of the commercial antagonism, and the contradictory opinions about its role in the general estrangement between the two peoples. What cannot be denied, however, is that a long list of particular industries and firms felt themselves to be engaged in a struggle with their German – or British – equivalents and much resented this rivalry, often hinting that the competitors were using unfair methods or possessed unjustifiable advantages. The greater number of complainants was to be found upon the British side and they concentrated their criticism upon Germany's tariff system – which, it was well known, had been scientifically designed to block the importation of manufactured goods but allowed in free of charge the raw materials required by German industry. With the large domestic market secured and prices kept high by cartel arrangements, German firms had been willing (especially in bad years) to export their produce at extremely low prices, which were reduced even further by governmental subsidies in the form of reduced rail charges. Against this form of *state*-assisted competition, many British firms felt that they could offer little or no answer. As one iron and steel manufacturer put it, 'Nothing less than the removal of German tariffs would enable us to compete against that country either in England, Germany, or any other part of the world. In our opinion it is because Germany by her tariff is able to secure her home market that she is able to attack us elsewhere.' The two-sided nature of the 'unfair' German challenge was also described by the British Tube Trade Association (centred in the Birmingham and south Staffordshire area), which reported that its exports of tubes to Germany had dropped steadily from 4,706 tons in 1874 to 442 tons in 1902; and that their German rivals, safe behind their tariff walls, was now exporting 46,000 tons of tubes each year to the rest of Europe. The only solution, the Association felt, was for British tariffs and colonial preference.[20] The Tariff Commission – admittedly no objective body – summarised the following instances of loss in the engineering export trades to Germany:[21]

| | |
|---|---|
| Agricultural machinery | Duties gradually closed the market. |
| Chaff cutters | Until 1880 good trade, and then cut off by the tariff. |
| Cranes | Change in the tariff classification complained of. |
| Fixed engines | Trade has almost entirely gone. |
| Food-preparing machinery | Duty has almost annihilated the English trade. |
| Hydraulic machinery | Duties prohibitive, trade almost gone. Hamburg free importation. |
| Locomotives | Can never export except under very special circumstances. |
| Mining tools | Trade has been lost since tariff was raised. |
| Portable engines | Duty has driven us out. |
| Scythes | Since rise in tariff trade has entirely ceased. |
| Structural machinery | Trade lost through tariff. |
| Ventilating machinery | Until 1878 a large staff employed making ventilators, especially for the German market. Bismarck tariff stopped it suddenly. |

The British textile industry had a similar list of complaints. In 1897 the Dundee Chamber of Commerce informed the Foreign Office that its exports to Germany of linen and jute had tumbled in value from £1,497,000 to £520,000 in the twenty years 1875–95; and that the drop in the value of jute-cloth exports was much steeper, from £447,000 to £17,000 because the German tariff placed higher charges upon *manufactured* goods.[22] The woollen and worsted trades felt even more bitter: 'Germany is our most formidable competitor. We meet her everywhere', representatives of the industry told the Board of Trade. Furthermore, while the number of employees in British mills had declined from 258,000 to 236,000 in the years 1891–1901 because of the blows dealt by foreign tariffs, the German total had been rising, from 197,000 to 262,000 in the period 1875–95.[23]

The reports around the turn of the century that the German government was planning a further set of tariff increases provoked widespread protests in British industrial circles. Sheffield, Swansea and Wolverhampton agitated about the proposed increases on steel, South Wales expressed alarm at the higher duties upon tinplate, the south of Scotland was concerned at the new duties upon imported textiles, and the Engineering Employers' Federation, having inspected the draft German tariff of 1902, called it 'a most disastrous blow', for it contemplated higher charges upon locomotives, electrical machinery and fittings, steam and gas engines, traction-engines, road rollers, portable steam-engines and threshing machinery.[24] So great was the reaction, reported Lord Avebury, the pro-free trade Chairman of the Association of Chambers of Commerce, that many businessmen were arguing for a special retaliatory tariff against Germany if the new rates came into effect; and the Huddersfield Chamber of Commerce, whose members sent nearly half of all British woollen exports to Germany, specifically demanded higher duties upon German wines in order to deter these attempts 'to exclude English manufacturers from their markets'.[25] It was in such an atmosphere, it is worth recalling, that Chamberlain announced the beginning of his Tariff Reform campaign.

Nevertheless, complaints and fears were not restricted to the British side alone. The German wine industry reacted with alarm in 1899, for example, at the news that the Chancellor of the Exchequer, Hicks Beach, was planning to increase the duty upon wine imports, especially since it was also reported that imperialist circles were pleading for supplies from the British colonies to be exempted from the increase; and the German embassy in London was instructed to argue against such discrimination.[26] The Society of South German Cotton Associates – chiefly spinners – had been protectionist since the 1870s and, as soon as the Anglo-German trade treaty was denounced in 1897, once again pressed for higher tariffs upon British imports.[27] The German Cloth and Woollen Manufacturers, in their turn, inveighed against 'the deplorable preference shown in certain circles of society for English cloth' – this appeal for a patriotic taste in clothing being motivated by its concern at the great rise in such imports in the period 1910–13.[28] But the most formidable interest group of all was the sugar-beet industry, which was far and away the most valuable commodity exported by *agrarian* circles and which sent most of its produce to the British market. The rumours that a tax on beet sugar (but not cane sugar from the colonies) was being considered by the British government as one of the measures to pay for the costs of the Boer War caused great concern in the *Wilhelmstrasse*, and it seems that Bülow would have probably allowed it to come to an Anglo-German trade war rather than lose the support of the Conservatives.[29] Just as the Foreign Ministry was drafting articles arguing against the discrimination which it hoped to insert secretly into *British* newspapers, word arrived that the Cabinet had decided against a sugar tariff.[30]

If the agrarians' discontent was stilled on that occasion, it nevertheless remains the case that its party leaders and its newspapers were the most anti-British of all in the debate upon trade relations. By comparison with the *Deutsche Zeitung* and *Deutsche Tageszeitung*, heavy industry papers such as the *Berliner Neueste Nachrichten* and the *Post* were quite moderate in their comments. The agrarians' line of argument, if it may be graced with that description, was not especially sophisticated. From 1897 (that is, from the British denunciation of the existing trade treaty) onwards, Reichstag deputies such as Paasche, Hahn, Kanitz, Reventlow and others argued as follows: the adoption of protectionism by Britain was a virtual certainty, since only the most purblind Cobdenites could still cling to the fallacies of free trade nowadays; the granting of preferences by Canada (and, later, several other British colonies) to imports from the motherland marked, therefore, the beginning of this trend, the chief intention of which was to cripple the economy of Britain's most formidable rival, Germany, and the *Wilhelmstrasse* should cease using the methods of appeasement and instead adopt stronger, more 'national' measures to check the movement. 'In the entire commercial stance of the English I can recognise . . . the clear intention to exclude Germany from the English colonies', claimed Hahn. When it became clear that the government feared to provoke an all-out trade war which would only benefit Chamberlain and his followers, the agrarians once again exploded in discontent. One can achieve nothing by showing sweet reasonableness to Mr Chamberlain, insisted the *Deutsche Tageszeitung*, but one might by 'a swift move against Canada'.[31]

Since what the agrarians meant when they talked of 'strong measures' and 'swift moves' was the introduction of higher tariffs, it is plain that their traditional dislike of Britain's socio-political arrangements internally was now being strongly reinforced by their own crude attempts to gain economic advantage from this commercial rivalry; and such arguments, predictably enough, encountered strong opposition from all those circles within Germany which disliked the agrarians' influence. Nevertheless, the swift progress of the Tariff Reform movement caused concern in circles other than the east Elbian landowners. 'Further blows [like Canada's] would lead to a catastrophe for the German textile industry', the *Auswärtiges Amt* was warned, 'for without the exports to England and her colonies this industry cannot flourish.' As *Die Zukunft* put it, 'undiminished shipments to Great Britain are almost a necessary condition for our economic existence'.[32] An impressive number of Chambers of Commerce urged the German government not to let it come to a trade war; and even the vigorous Union of Hamburg Shipowners (with Ballin as President) warned Bülow against any escalation:

It is true that a tariff war with Great Britain, and the differential treatment of British ships in German ports might perhaps confer some temporary advantages upon German shipping; but this in any event somewhat uncertain advantage would be of no account in comparison with the incalculable harm which such a tariff war would cause to the economical interests of both countries.[33]

Hamburg was as aware as ever that its own prosperity still depended a great deal upon trade with Britain, even if it had developed many more direct links with the outside world since Bismarck's time.

Such fears, however, indicate the stake which many industries and regions had in *good* Anglo-German relations and undermine the impression, which Tirpitz and Reventlow and certain of the British Right tried to convey, that there existed an all-out struggle between two rivalling species of mankind. The more one examines the economic structure in detail, the less easy is it to accept the argument – put forward, say, by Hewins and the Tariff Commission[34] – that such rivalry was inevitable because Germany's industrialisation was leading her to produce exactly the same type of goods as in Britain. That there were many more areas of industrial and commercial competition than thirty years earlier is clear from the general statistics given above and represents one of the chief alterations in the Anglo-German relationship between the age of Bismarck and Gladstone and that of Bülow and Chamberlain; yet there still remained many complementary elements in the trading pattern between Britain and Germany, and many interests benefited greatly from the steadily rising commerce and thus had a strong incentive to prevent a trade war.

The most obvious of such interests were those engaged in what was a 'one-way trade': German wine firms, the manufacturers of German toys and clocks, the producers of dyestuffs and of various electrical devices in Germany, and the British firms which specialised in textile machinery or fine yarns. One might add to this all those engaged in the massive trade in imported herrings (for salting) and in coal (both the unique Welsh steaming-coals for ships, and the supplies from Yorkshire and the north-east for domestic purposes); for although these competed respectively with German fishermen and Westphalian coal producers, the Reich's growing demand for both goods outstripped the home supply. The second point to be made is that, even within a particular industry, specialisations existed which make it difficult to generalise about the 'threat' posed by its German or British equivalents. In 1907, for example, Britain exported £1,518,000 worth of partly manufactured and £1,557,000 of fully manufactured iron and steel to Germany, which in turn exported £2,410,000 worth of partly manufactured and £2,532,000 of fully manufactured iron and steel to Britain! A similar complexity existed in the trade in machinery, and in cotton.[35] In the cotton trade, for example, it was impossible for German spinners to produce the very fine yarns for which Lancashire was climatically so suited; and it was also true that British weavers encountered far less competition in the more expensive types of cloth – whereas the export of coarse yarns and cloth to Germany had been wiped out by tariffs and domestic competition years earlier.

Moreover, some manufacturers were so specialised, and protected, that they encountered no opposition at all from foreign rivals, the best example here being the shipyards and other firms which received orders from the British and

German navies. According to one calculation, the Admiralty had given out £150 million for shipbuilding, repairs and maintenance, £30 million for naval armaments and £15 million in works and building at home and abroad, in the ten years between 1899–1900 and 1908–9; and since it insisted upon only British articles, various manufacturers of boilers, auxiliary machinery, anchors, refrigerating equipment, and so on, admitted that they were freed from all foreign competition. On the other hand, certain leading shipbuilders – Sir Andrew Noble, Sir Charles Parsons, John Thorneycroft – claimed that the industry was so superior to all rivals that it had no apprehension of foreign competitors in any case.[36] This is not to say, however, that the shipbuilding firms and their suppliers did not play an *indirect* role in the sharpening of Anglo-German feelings, for the agitations of Krupp, Mulliner and the like for further orders was often to result in a further escalation of the naval race.[37]

A third, and related point is that the various stages within a certain industry could blunt any clear-cut demand for tariffs against a foreign rival. When the south German cotton-spinners asked for more protection from imported English yarns, for example, the weaving interests of Aachen, Bielefeld, Hagen and elsewhere immediately opposed the idea, as it would raise their costs; yet whenever the weavers in turn opposed the growing importation of fine English cloth, the tailors of Berlin and other big cities warned against any increase in the duty upon such imports. In the years around the 1902 reshaping of the German general tariff, one can find evidence of German importers begging their British producers to agitate in Whitehall against the proposed increases, lest a mutually profitable trade be ruined![38] The fact that one man's rival product was another man's raw material is probably the single clearest conclusion which could be drawn from the investigations of the Chamberlain-backed Tariff Commission. Witness after witness testified to the fierce competition which 'dumped' German goods posed to their own products in home and foreign markets, but many frequently admitted that they themselves imported materials from Germany because they undercut comparable British products.[39] Whereas some industrialists concluded that it would be better, for the industry as a whole and for British prosperity, if tariffs were introduced at *all* stages of production, this was vehemently opposed by many others. Possibly the greatest beneficiary was the British shipbuilding industry, whose representatives admitted to importing more and more 'dumped' German sheet steel; but justified this by showing that it enabled them to construct vessels at a much cheaper price than their German equivalents, who had to rely upon high-priced steel from domestic producers; and that, as a further consequence, British yards continued to receive orders from German shipping lines. Thus, German steel-producers, British shipyards and German shipowners gained, but British steel-producers and German shipbuilders felt aggrieved at it.[40]

The trade cycle and geography also played a part in blunting the rivalry. To begin with, the revival of the 'Made in Germany' debate and the allegations of British *Handelsneid* were much more a characteristic of the years 1896–1905 than of the decade before or after. In the 'climacteric of the 1890s',[41] Britain's economic performance was very sluggish when compared with her nearest rivals; and it was in that decade, too, that the *visible* trade gap (the only one contemporaries could measure adequately) was at its largest, averaging £160·6 million p.a. in 1896–1900 and £174·5 million p.a. in 1901–5 before falling off in later years. Since it was exactly in this decade that British commercial outlets, in China and other markets, were felt to be at risk and that the strategical pressures upon the empire – Fashoda, Far East, defence of India, the Franco-Russian naval challenge – were the greatest, it is not difficult to understand why there was gloom in certain British commercial circles about the economic future and demands for action against foreign competitors. Yet the Chamberlainite solution of Tariff Reform was not only a response to these specific circumstances but also, in its turn, intensified the debate over Anglo-German trade relations. Only in 1906 was this commercial uncertainty and agitation subdued. If there were later rumblings in the press about the German commercial 'menace' or about Britain's deliberate obstructionism, it is difficult to discover a prolonged period in time when *business* circles were as agitated as they had been immediately before and after the turn of the century.

These general remarks can be substantiated by details from specific industries. In the recession around 1902, German manufacturers (especially in the iron and steel industries) sent a large amount of their produce at rock-bottom prices to the British market.[42] It was not surprising, therefore, that British producers of iron and steel, and of machinery, should be among the most prominent supporters of protectionism; that their names are to be spotted in the list of subscribers to the Tariff Commission;[43] and that Chamberlain (Birmingham) and Vincent (Sheffield) were extremely popular in their own constituencies for their defence of local interests. But it is also unsurprising that, when trade revived generally after 1903, the logic of abandoning free trade was weakened in the public eye: in the election year of 1906, the total of British exports (£460 million) was £100 million more than it had been when Chamberlain declared for Tariff Reform three years earlier. As Winston Churchill chortled, 'It is one of Nature's revenges upon those who seek to violate economic harmonies, that the very period which had been predicted for our downfall and disaster should have witnessed the most surprising manifestation of our industrial productivity.'[44] The same fate attended the Unionist Party's pro-tariff propaganda in the 1910 elections: it was difficult to respond to the argument 'Vote for what the foreign "Dumper" dreads . . .', when exports (and, indeed, total trade) had just reached a new record.[45]

Moreover, the trends noted earlier, of an expansion in British exports to the non-industrial world *and* of a growing German trade imbalance with British colonies and with such countries as Argentina, Brazil and Chile, suggest that the manufacturers of Lancashire and the Midlands were finding new buyers for those standard goods which could no longer compete inside Europe. In a booming country such as Argentina, where British investment rose from £20·3 million in 1880 to a staggering £357·7 million by 1913, and where 80 per cent of the railways were British-owned, it was not surprising that exports from Britain had a distinct advantage: traditional commercial connections, the sophistication of the credit system and, in many cases, the patriotism of British managers overseas, 'tied' the orders to British factories without any more formal obligations being necessary. Was it so important that German imports to Argentina rose from £2·3 million in 1902 to £11·7 million in 1912, when British imports rose in the same period from £7·8 million to £21·3 million?[46] Or was it, to take another example, really all that alarming that Germany's trade with China was steadily increasing when, even as late as 1912, it was only one-fourth the size of Britain's? In the 'formal' British Empire, the hold of the mother country upon the import trade was even firmer: in 1913, Australia and Canada each imported ten times as much British goods as they did German, and India fifteen times as much.[47]

It was, finally, the unique nature of the changes which were occurring in the late Victorian/Edwardian economy (the rise in overseas investment, the strength of the service industries, the relatively poor performance of such industries as steel, machine tools, electricals and chemicals but the 'Indian summer' for textiles and coal) which explains why so many of the most influential economic interest groups opposed Tariff Reform in 1906 – and thereby, in consequence if not in original intention, prevented the outbreak of an Anglo-German trade war. The greater part of the cotton industry, for example, remained hostile to protectionism: it was impossible to move the employers to change their attitude whilst trade was so good, the Conservative Party managers admitted ruefully, and when Hewins gave a lecture upon 'Fiscal Reform in Relation to Cotton' in Manchester itself he met with considerable heckling from his audience of 'cotton-spinners, manufacturers, merchants, shippers and agents'.[48] The latter feared, with some justification, that tariffs would raise the price of machinery, the cost of raw materials and the general level of wages, and thus undermine their price advantage. The protectionists' agitation about the *relatively* greater expansion of foreign cotton industries meant nothing so long as the British industry was increasing *absolutely*. If some Manchester businessmen voted Unionist by 1910, it was out of a fear of Lloyd George, not a love of Joseph Chamberlain.[49] The same calculations swayed the shipping industry. It was true that the German merchant marine had become the second largest in the world, and was offering strong competition on the prestigious North Atlantic passenger route; that the irrepressible Ballin annoyed British shipping lines in many ways, from trying to push into the Persian Gulf trade, to seeking to corner a monopoly of carrying East European emigrants to the New World; and that the German practice of giving rail rebates upon exports carried in German vessels provoked frequent protests from British shipping firms, especially those plying the Hamburg–South African routes.[50] Nevertheless, the shipping trade as a whole was intent upon preserving its position as carrier *for the entire world* and rightly feared the effects of a tariff war: shipping, in Grey's words, was 'one of the keystones of the arch, which Protection will pull down'.[51] The industry was one of *the* great earners of foreign currency; and even if the size of rival merchant navies increased rapidly, it was easily holding its own. Between 1901 and 1913 the German merchant marine rose from 1,941,000 to 3,153,000 net tons, the British from 9,608,000 to 12,119,000 net tons.[52]

Perhaps the most persistent economic lobby for good Anglo-German relations were the financial circles in the City of London and their equivalents in Frankfurt, Berlin and Hamburg. Since the reasons for their attitude have been mentioned before, it is not necessary to repeat them:[53] suffice it to emphasise that those who had probably profited most from the vast increase in world trade during the thirty years after 1880 were the people who had financed and insured that expansion. Furthermore, since most still adhered to the classical rules of political economy, they were already perturbed by two events in this period which were upsetting the money market's capacity to finance a continued world boom. The first of these was the Boer War, which – whatever it may have done for those holding gold-mining shares – had quite definitely diverted capital from productive into unproductive fields, had forced the British government not only to raise taxes but also to float enormous loans which had siphoned off funds, and had caused a rise in interest rates. The decline in the government's credit, the rise in the National Debt by 25 per cent and the dearness of borrowed money was being constantly alluded to by Unionist Chancellors of the Exchequer when they sought to control public expenditure after 1900; and it is not surprising to learn that most City men, already alarmed at Chamberlain's Tariff Reform campaign, were happy to see a Liberal government returned in the 1906 election.[54] The second sin against 'sound finance' was being committed on the German side, where the political difficulties of paying for rising public expenditure (especially Tirpitz's navy) by direct taxation had led to a large increase in government borrowing, a steep rise in the National Debt and higher interest rates; so poor was the German government's credit that it could only borrow at much higher rates of interest than those usually available to the French and British governments, and the increases in national indebtedness which followed the 1906 and 1908 Navy Bills were such that some observers began to suspect that the only solution contemplated by the establishment to solve this financial and domestic-political crisis was war.[55] Yet however attractive this may or may not have been to the Kaiser's military entourage, it was regarded with horror by financiers, whose delicate network of international exchanges and credit would be swept away altogether. By 1907, merely on the rumour that Edward VII was taking further steps to 'encircle' Germany, the Berlin bourse fell dramatically; but even that upset could not match the financial convulsions which took place after the second Moroccan crisis.[56]

Nor, it must be said, was this anxiety confined to the German side. When, from 1906 onwards, the CID began discreetly to inquire what impact upon the British economy a war with Germany could have, it found to its alarm that (i) the gold reserves were minimal, and would probably need to be supplemented by drawing upon the Bank of France, as had happened in the 1857, 1866 and 1890 financial crises as well as in the Boer War – this suggesting, in Clarke's words, that 'the entente cordiale is almost a financial necessity';[57] (ii) that Lloyds of London insured not only the British mercantile marine but also a great part of the German, and was so reluctant to lose these earnings that it wished to maintain its promise to pay compensation for war losses, even when inflicted by the Royal Navy!; and (iii) that since German industry paid for much of its overseas raw materials by drawing upon its London bankers, the onset of an Anglo-German war – which would leave massive debts outstanding – would probably be marked by the collapse of certain very large clearinghouses in the City.[58] Yet if the members of the CID went away from these inquiries considerably shaken about the country's economic vulnerability in wartime, the representatives of the City departed in a much more depressed mood at the very idea of an Anglo-German conflict; and the latter's attitude was to be very apparent in 1914 itself, when the international crisis provoked a commercial collapse even *before* the outbreak of war and caused many City men to urge a policy of conciliation upon Lloyd George and the rest of the Liberal government – so much so that Crowe felt obliged to weigh in with a fierce counter-attack upon their 'pusillanimous counsels' which, he claimed, were really the work of Anglo-German financial houses trying to prevent Britain from intervening in the European conflict.[59]

Despite Crowe's charges, and despite the frequent allegations of right-wing journalists in both countries, there is no indication that banking circles were lacking in patriotism. They advised their respective governments in the prewar period about the economic preparations necessary for a great conflict; they financed loans to foreign states at the request of their Foreign Offices, and supported projects (Baghdad Railway, railway-building and shipping ventures) which would enhance their country's prestige and position abroad; and, especially in the German case, they were inextricably connected with heavy industry and armaments firms. British bankers were often to be found calling for unchallenged naval superiority, arguing that if it were ever lost the government's long-term credit would suffer; and in 1908, when the German government launched a loan at such a low price and such a high interest rate that the City of London suspected that it was in effect a 'war loan', individuals who were tempted to take it up were warned that they 'might be boycotted in consequence'.[60] Nevertheless, if the bankers did not work against the national interest, it is true that they wished it to be harmonised with their own personal interests, which favoured international prosperity and an absence of political uncertainty and tensions. It is also true that, being eminently pragmatic individuals, financiers were always willing to co-operate with colleagues *across* international boundaries when the prospects seemed attractive enough.[61]

Economic motives, personal and family connections, and their own subscription to *laissez-faire* conceptions of the world order, all thrust financiers towards efforts to improve Anglo-German relations. They ranged from Alfred Rothschild's attempts around the turn of the century to produce an alliance by the simple expedient of inviting Chamberlain and Hatzfeldt (or Eckardstein) to dinner, to Max Waechter's urgings that the British government have translated into German a reasoned defence of why it went to war in 1899, so as to counter all the pro-Boer slanders.[62] But it was the first Moroccan crisis and the naval race which, by making the Anglo-German antagonism plain to all, stimulated financial circles to their greatest efforts. When the 'Anglo-German Union Club' was founded in 1905, its committee members predictably included Baron Percy de Worms, Baron Bruno Schröder, Alfred Beit and Edgar Speyer; as the reconciliation movement under Avebury (himself a City banker) got under way, the *Deutsche Bank* informed Bülow that it also wished to give support; Beit financed the *Anglo-German Courier*, which was the newspaper of the movement, and Cassell paid for various cultural and charitable activities; and Schröder in Hamburg helped to entertain the party of visiting British journalists, smothering his dislike for that profession with the thought that 'a war [with England] would ruin German trade'.[63] Obviously, a banker like Schwabach, who was also the British consul-general in Berlin, felt bound to aid these efforts; but so, too, did many who helped to finance Germany's imperial expansion. George Siemens, director of the *Deutsche Bank*'s foreign investments, supported colonial and naval growth around the turn of the century, but also favoured Anglo-German co-operation; Warburgs might be 'a bank house in *Weltpolitik*', but with Hamburg's close links to London it realised the need to cool the tension between the two countries – as did, of course, Max Warburg's friends Ballin and Cassell, who played their part in the inauguration of the Haldane mission.[64]

To sum up: any analysis of the role which direct economic factors played in the rise of the Anglo-German antagonism is bound to arrive at a mixed result. The economies of the two countries were so complex, the interest groups so diverse, the question of co-operation or rivalry so dependent upon regional and chronological factors, that it could not be otherwise. What one can say is that in the years between 1880 and 1910 Germany had become a much more formidable rival to Britain in many areas of economic production, and that this – together with the German tariff system – had caused resentment in various British industrial circles; and further, that the proposed counter-measures, especially Tariff Reform, provoked great alarm within Germany. Anglophobes and germanophobes are not missing here: it surely *is* significant that neither Prussian agrarians nor Birmingham machine-makers joined the various Anglo-German friendship committees, whereas Lancashire mill-owners and Hamburg bankers did. It is also significant that those interest groups which agitated about rivalry with the other country were associated with the political parties – Conservative and National Liberal in Germany, Conservative and Liberal Unionist in Britain – which most readily articulated these feelings of dislike and anxiety. In just the same way, left-of-centre parties put forward arguments in favour of international co-operation and lower tariffs which were also advocated by the social groups which supported them.

It is at this point, however, that the economic arguments developed by each side begin to merge with those relating to politics and strategy, and this suggests that it would be both artificial and restrictive to measure the significance of the Anglo-German trade rivalry only in terms of direct commercial competition. In everyday life, economic developments 'spill over' to affect – and be affected by – social relationships, political actions and ideological argument. When viewed from this broader perspective, of the *indirect* consequences and impulses which came from these economic changes, the historian begins to see much more clearly their role in the worsening of Anglo-German relations.

## CHAPTER 16

# Rising and Declining Empires: Power-Political Interpretations of Global Economic Trends

In December 1903, during a furious debate between the Left and the Right in the Reichstag over Anglo-German trade relations, Eduard Bernstein rounded upon Graf Reventlow and demanded:

> The entire question is this: do we consider the position of one land to another in the manner of jealous, acquisitive tribes, where if one robs, the other is robbed – or do we consider it from the standpoint of a peaceful exchange between nations?[1]

In posing that question, Bernstein summarised the two alternative views of the international system which were most widely held in the nineteenth and early twentieth centuries: the free-trading, harmonious vision of an expanding world economy as propagated by Cobden and his disciples; and, on the other hand, the protectionist-mercantilist idea,[2] which regarded competition and conflict as an inevitable fact of life, given that all nations strove to acquire a larger share of Earth's limited land and wealth.

Such opposing viewpoints can be analysed in an abstract form, as ideal conceptions of how the world was or should be ordered; but it is also clear that they were articulated not simply as intellectual constructs but by specific individuals and interest groups to whom the one philosophy or the other made a lot of sense. Few generals and admirals of this period, so far as is known, went around advocating international co-operation and disarmament; few bankers or shipowners anticipated with relish a great power conflict; few politicians, playing for the patriotic vote, resisted the temptation to appeal for national solidarity against the eternal threat; few Socialists felt inclined to rush into a 'capitalists' war'. What is even more important is that these views of world politics should be understood in relation to, and in reaction to, the economic trends described earlier: for it was upon those trends that the various advocates rested their case, and it was from their interpretation of the evidence that they received a confirmation of their own standpoint.

Objectively viewed, the indices of manufacturing output, inter-state commerce and national wealth in the years between the Franco-Prussian War and the First World War revealed two major trends. The first was the *absolute*, if somewhat uneven rise in global production, trade and prosperity. The second was the *relative* decline of Britain as the leading industrial and commercial nation, and the corresponding rise of Germany (and certain other states). The evidence for both developments was overwhelming, even to contemporaries, and few attempted to dispute them once the passing of the Great Depression had removed the question-mark over the first conclusion. Yet the significant, if unsurprising, fact was that the advocates of Cobdenite internationalism concentrated almost exclusively upon the first trend, whereas the protectionists and nationalists always emphasised the significance of the second. The debate upon the meaning of these global economic changes was conducted on the basis of selective evidence, therefore, although none the less interesting for being done so.

To the British Right, the loss of economic supremacy and, with it, of national *power*, was frightening: no other event preyed upon their minds or galvanised them into action more than this. The basic point was, as Garvin put it, that 'Power is a purely relative conception.'[3] Even if the national wealth was now much greater, and the working man better fed and clothed than was the case under Pitt or Palmerston, it was no consolation at all: indeed, it was not only irrelevant but also a dangerous obfuscation of what was the fundamental tendency of global politics in the late nineteenth century – the collapse of Britain's position as the *Number One world power*. With the application of technology to the massive but hitherto unexploited resources of continent-wide states, and with the industrialisation of the United States, Russia and Germany, the relatively insignificant material bases of British power were made clear for the first time; as Mackinder explained in a prescient article, there would now be 'a correlation between the larger geographical and the larger historical generalisations', that is, numbers and size would be more accurately reflected in the sphere of international developments.[4] The consequences for a small island state were obvious: as Selborne suggested to Curzon, 'in the years to come the United Kingdom by itself will not be strong enough to hold its proper place alongside of the U.S., or Russia, and probably not Germany. We shall be thrust aside by sheer weight.'[5] 'The day of the small nations is gone past', declared a Conservative Party *Campaign Guide*; 'the tendency of the time is to throw all power into the hands of the greater empires', insisted Chamberlain.[6] Amery, seeking to tempt the voters of Wolverhampton East to send him to Parliament, painted an even more lurid picture:

Every year the competition for power among the great world states is getting keener, and unless we can continue to hold our own, unless we can keep our invincible Navy, and unless we can defend the Empire at every one of its frontiers, our Empire and our trade will be taken away from us by others and we shall be starved out, invaded, trampled under foot and utterly ruined.

But how can these little islands hold their own in the long run against such great and rich Empires as the United States and Germany are rapidly becoming, or even such as Russia will be when it recovers from its present [1905] disasters?

How can we with our forty millions of people compete against states nearly double our size?[7]

A Social Darwinistic tone, much commented upon by later historians,[8] permeates virtually all the writings of these imperialist politicians and intellectuals; and the sheer tempo of economic developments, and the constant upsets and clashes in world politics, suggested continuous movement, of empires rising and falling. 'If there is one thing certain in this world it is that nothing can stand still', Robertson taught the British staff officers.[9] But, in contrast to the self-confident expansionism of the age of Palmerston and even Disraeli, many Britons around the turn of the century were less certain that the future was on their side. As if the growing challenges to the imperial frontiers, the frequent navy and invasion 'scares' and the intense debate about the country's industrial weaknesses were not enough, the Boer War defeats sent reverberations through the whole imperialist camp. 'Our disasters are so unbroken, our generals so uniformly incompetent, our inability to make any headway so consistent as to engender serious suspicions that our system must be rotten at the core', moaned Curzon.[10] 'Oh, but it makes me sick!', fumed Kipling, 'not because it's [General] Buller but because it's *us* – England. Our own face in a foul mirror but our own face!' Would this generation, he asked in one of his poems, be the first to lose the thousand-year heritage bequeathed by their forefathers?[11] 'Will the Empire which is celebrating one centenary of Trafalgar survive for the next?', wondered Garvin in 1905.[12] It was increasingly difficult to answer that question with a positive 'yes'. 'If only we had the mark of the nations which prevail', complained Milner, wondering 'whether we shall succeed in saving the British Empire'.[13] And Chirol wrote sadly: 'Every day I realise more and more the truth of my Chinese friend's remark that "there is a wonderful similarity between England and China".'[14]

This deep-seated *Angst* among British imperialists is to be most clearly detected in their private correspondence and diaries; in public speeches and writings, there was a tendency to put a brave face upon it and to suggest various means of salvation. But it is worth emphasising the essentially pessimistic outlook of most of them, and their conviction that their stance was in origin a *defensive* one, the preservation of the existing position of the Empire – if only because of the suggestion by later historians that 'If any nation had upset the world's balance of power, it was Great Britain.'[15] Had the establishments within the various great powers been asked at the turn of the century how they would react to the 'freezing' of the existing power-political *status quo*, then it is a fair surmise that the British (and, one suspects, the Austro-Hungarian) reply would have been positive. Even more predictable would have been the sharp reply from the rising powers of Germany, Russia, the United States and Japan, all of which took comfort from the economic and geopolitical trends and looked forward to occupying a more prominent position as the twentieth century unfolded.

Being passionately concerned about these shifts in the global balance and arguing that there soon would be no further 'vacuum' into which the rising powers could expand, British imperialists assumed that a clash between their nation and Germany was virtually unavoidable. German resentment of Britain was quite understandable, thought Spring-Rice: 'We stand in their way everywhere – we have the most to take – and we are personally objectionable.'[16] 'They mean, if they can, to have from us something which we have got and which their spokesmen in the Press in effect tell us we mis-use', explained Strachey. 'Their attitude in fact is very much that which our Elizabethan people adopted towards the Empire of Spain'.[17] To the lessons of history could be added the discoveries of Darwin:

the strong and hungry will eat the weak, fat & defenceless whenever they can get a chance . . . No matter what the sentiments of the sheep are, mutton to wolves will continue to be an agreeable form of diet . . . We have all we want and now only wish to be left alone; but that desire is not shared by the great military nations on the Continent. If we want to keep what we have got, we must defend it.[18]

By the same thought-processes, of course, the British imperialists had feared the expansion of the Russian Empire in Asia and regarded a clash with it as inevitable; but that apprehension was the hallmark of the older Tories and, although many among the 'new' Right had followed Chamberlain's assumption of the late 1890s that the natural counterpoise was an alliance with Germany, they had soon become disillusioned with Berlin and suspicious of its intentions. Well before 1905, when the myth of Russian military invincibility was being shattered by the Japanese, Germany was viewed as a much more formidable rival *precisely because* she was technologically advanced and industrially competitive. What was more, German expansion beyond its present frontiers would bring this great challenger uncomfortably close to Britain. Time and again, connections were drawn between economic strength and territorial aggrandisement: as Grey put it, Germany 'has reached that dangerous point of strength which makes her itch to dominate'.[19] Time and again, there is that clear assumption about the *inevitability* of events which most catches the attention of the later historian: *The Times* correspondents in Europe, like Lavino (Paris) and Steed (Vienna), were convinced that 'German intrigue would destroy the House of Hapsburg, cripple Italy, and place a German fleet within striking distance of Malta, Egypt and the Suez Canal';[20] others, pointing both to Pan-German literature and to the economic penetration of the Low Countries, forecast the absorption of the Netherlands or Switzerland or argued that the solution to Germany's internal problems would be sought at the hands of France.[21]

Lest it be thought that these were simply the phobias of an unofficial, alarmist 'fringe' of British political society, it should be remarked that such assumptions did not greatly differ from those of the government planners. The General Staff's case for a 'continental commitment' during the years 1906–14 rested upon the belief that France alone would be unable to hold off a Germany booming both in population and industry; Eyre Crowe's famous memorandum of January 1907 focused above all else upon the political consequences of the colossal expansion of German industry and energies; and Esher, who was intimately concerned with military planning, felt that

> there is no doubt that within measurable distance there looms a titanic struggle between Germany and Europe for mastery. The years 1793–1815 will be repeated, only Germany, not France, will be trying for European domination. She has 70,000,000 of people and is determined to have commercial pre-eminence. To do this *England* has got to be crippled and the Low Countries added to the German Empire.[22]

And when the British Admiralty made its first war plans (in 1907) it assumed that 'further expansion [by Germany] is felt to be necessary', either towards the Low Countries, or Austria-Hungary, or Latin America:

> It is now a question which has gone beyond the personal ambition of one or two men. The country has been launched on a road which has led to this enormous increase of material prosperity, and whether the authors of the policy would like to draw back now or not, they cannot do so. The expansion must go on until it meets a force stronger than itself, or until the policy directing the [German] State ceases to be of a sufficiently virile nature to stimulate growth and encourage prosperity.[23]

These were deterministic views indeed and, as we shall see, they were by no means universally held by Britons. Nevertheless, it is also true that people such as Crowe, Spring-Rice, Chirol, Garvin, Amery and Steed were scarcely writing and speaking in ignorance of German conditions, for most of them were fluent in that language and attentive students of the politics and ideology of the Reich. The plain fact was that there *did* exist an abundance of evidence to confirm all their worst suspicions, precisely because large numbers of German politicians and intellectuals were drawing the same conclusions from, and spoke in the same deterministic manner about, the long-term economic trends. The post-1896 commercial expansion in particular gave solid grounds for the belief that Germany was one of the new, rising world powers. 'The German race brings it', exulted Naumann. 'It brings army, navy, money and power . . . Modern, gigantic instruments of power are possible only when an entire people feels the spring-time juices in its organs.'[24] 'The German', predicted Adolph Wagner, 'is again emerging as the major people. If anyone is to be first among equals, then it will be he and not the Frenchman or the Briton.'[25] The massive increases in population alone made it impossible for German society to stand still. 'We need land, land, land', claimed the Pan-German *Heimdall*; we are 'forced by our geographical situation, by poor soil . . . by the amazing increase in our population . . . to spread and to gain space for us and for our sons', Schiemann argued.[26] Industrialisation was absorbing the masses which were leaving the land and reaching adulthood, but this in turn necessitated an ever-greater dependence upon selling in the markets of the world and an enormous increase in the importation of foodstuffs and raw materials. Once the process had begun, it could not be halted: even old Hohenlohe, commiserating with a friend about the ruinous consequences of modernisation, regarded it as inevitable.[27]

What was more, it is clear that Hohenlohe's conviction was held – much more positively, of course – by the architects of German *Weltpolitik*: Szögyeny had been absolutely correct in his characterisation of Wilhelm and his leading statesmen as people who were anticipating a glorious future for their country as it continued to expand.[28] This does not imply that the German leaders had no other motives (for instance, domestic-political) in mind, but simply that they genuinely believed that commercial and industrial growth made some sort of 'world policy' inevitable. 'The question is not, whether we want to colonise or not', Bülow insisted, 'but that we *must* colonise, whether we want it or not.' To say that Germany should cease her *Weltpolitik* was like a father telling his son: 'If only you would not grow, you troublesome youth, then I would not need to buy you longer trousers! We can't do anything other than carry out *Weltpolitik*.'[29] Tirpitz, a convinced Social Darwinist, was even more dogmatic. It was not only in retrospect that he argued 'We had global commerce (*Weltwirtschaft*), which compelled us to *Weltmacht*.' In his Rominten audience with the Kaiser of September 1899, he tried to show that Germany's industrialisation and overseas expansion was 'as irresistible as a natural law'.[30] As for Wilhelm, all his private utterances and public speeches from at least 1896 onwards indicated that he had become imbued with a sense of Germany's mission. She also, he told Szögyeny, 'had great tasks to accomplish outside the narrow boundaries of old Europe'; her future lay 'less in Europe than in the entire world'.[31]

But, accepting that her massive economic growth pushed her to a greater role in world affairs, what could Germany do when so much of the globe was already divided into the formal or informal empires of the established powers? On this point, the German establishment was virtually unanimous: the teachings of Treitschke, the Hegelian and Darwinistic concepts of national development and fulfilment, the Bismarckian tradition of Realpolitik, made the answer inevitable.

> For German strength and German tongue
> There must be *room* still on this earth!

was the doggerel verse of the *Flottenverein*;[32] and Bülow rendered this into a less poetic form when he told the Reichstag, 'We cannot allow any foreign power, any foreign Jupiter to tell us: "What can be done? The world is already partitioned . . . ".' Germany would be the hammer or the anvil.[33] 'He who is strong enough to demand something has not come too late after all!' insisted Max Lenz. Senden, for his part, referred to the *re*-division of the globe in the coming century. Claims to the title of any particular piece of land were legal irrelevancies compared with the fundamental laws of growth and decline. 'The decisive fact', taught Adolf Wagner, 'is the principle of power, of force, the right of power, the right of conquest, and this must continue to be decisive.'[34]

It was for this reason, explained the National Liberal Party's Handbook, that Germany could not contemplate any idea of armaments limitation: having developed later than the others into a world power, she still 'had to catch up with what other nations had already gained centuries ago'.[35]

If, however, Germany's unavoidable expansion would cause her to challenge the established world order, than it was easy to recognise which power's interests would be most affected. There were, obviously, many Germans who were deeply engaged in the struggle against the Poles in the East, or looked forward to crushing the French *Erbfeind*; but if the talk was about world policy and colonies, then an altogether larger opponent came into view. Which power, after all, had continually sought to frustrate Germany's overseas expansion – in Angra Pequena and New Guinea and East Africa and China and Mesopotamia? 'From Zanzibar to Samoa! An unbroken line of disappointments!', screeched the *Schlesische Zeitung* as it reviewed the 1890s: 'The German people is gradually coming to recognise that England is Germany's worst enemy'.[36] Had not their mentor, Treitschke, always insisted that 'the final reckoning' would be with England? And was it not clear that the real motive behind the British hostility was economic, the jealousy of the *Krämervolk* at Germany's commercial success? Hence, of course, the 'Made in Germany' agitation and the ominous suggestion of the *Saturday Review* – which Tirpitz lovingly recalled each time he acquired some evidence – about *Germania esse delendam*. Having been repeatedly warned about the difference between their own 'idealism' and the hardheaded ruthlessness of the English, German imperialists deployed reductionist and deterministic arguments which surpassed those of any vulgar Marxist. 'The fury of the English against us', Stosch informed Tirpitz, 'has its real explanation in Germany's competition on the world market . . . Since the foreign policy of England is determined exclusively by commercial interests, we must henceforth reckon with the opposition of that island people.' His protegé agreed: 'The older and stronger firm inevitably seeks to strangle the new and rising one before it is too late.'[37] Not surprisingly, this viewpoint permeated the Kaiser's new navy, so that virtually every memorandum upon operations plans against Britain or Anglo-German relations in general contained, as a political prologue and apologia, references to the fact that 'England sees in us its most dangerous rival as a trading power.'[38]

What had happened, then, to that portrayal by the Bismarckian press of a Britain being led into decadence, internal disarray and external powerlessness by the actions of Gladstone and the lessons of Cobden? That period, explained German historians, had only been a temporary one, caused by economic trends: having crushed all her commercial rivals in the wars of the seventeenth and eighteenth centuries, England had (as List showed) cunningly abandoned mercantilism for free trade in order to undercut the infant industries of the continent. This plan had been frustrated by the readoption of protectionism in Germany and elsewhere in the 1870s and 1880s, so that British industry was now feeling effective competition for the first time in a hundred years; and thus her actions in the present 'neo-mercantilist' era would be similar to those employed by Cromwell and Pitt. Fashoda and the Boer War were writings on the wall. The Gladstones and Campbell-Bannermans in British politics were anachronisms; the 'up-and-coming' man was Joseph Chamberlain, the 'Cromwell' of the twentieth century.[39] Mr Chamberlain's speeches, thought Admiral Diederichs, 'gave us a tip about where the English wish to go, and in Copenhagen, as in Toulon under Hood, England showed that it recognised no moral scruples when it came to crippling a likely future opponent'. Britain's present opposition to Germany, Tirpitz informed Bülow, had 'similar causes to those which had led to the crushing of, first Spain, then Holland and finally France. It was always the "City of London" which in the final analysis decided to begin those wars.'[40] Karl Peters, recoiling at the German humiliation during the second Moroccan crisis, came to the same conclusion:

The City of London is the great devouring beast, through which foreign peoples are plundered; and Downing Street is in the service of Throgmorton Street. The rivalry of a healthy, hard-working nationality like the German does not suit such forces. Germany is for the normal John Bull what Spain was in the sixteenth century, France in the nineteenth, and Russia in the twentieth. [Kaiser: 'Correct.'] The Germans must understand this deepest conflict of interests with Great Britain.[41]

The increasingly nervous tone of the German references to Britain after the turn of the century stands in contrast to the confident assumptions of earlier years, but is easily explicable. In the mid-1890s, Britain must have appeared to almost all observers of world politics as the 'weary Titan', under pressure from so many directions. During the early stages of the Boer War especially, German commentators – like their English equivalents – had placed a question-mark over the future of the British Empire and references were made to the coming 'War of English Succession'. Within a few years of reaching that nadir, however, Britain had effected a remarkable recovery: its naval strength had been expanded and overhauled, its army was being reformed and its diplomacy had managed to reach understandings with France and the United States while its ally, Japan, crushed Russian power for a decade. Given their beliefs about the fundamental struggle between the great powers for the world's wealth and territory, it was difficult for German nationalists to accept that these would be anything other than uneasy *rapprochements* between London on the one hand, and Washington, Tokyo and St Petersburg on the other; but, for the next decade at least, such conflicts might temporarily be stilled and this meant that only Germany appeared to be challenging Britain's commercial and power-political position. Yet, whether the island state was seen as (in Bülow's choice phrase) a bull which had become too fat to defend itself, or as one which had 'aroused itself to become the fighting-steer once again',[42] the basic situation remained the same: another animal wished to graze on the British bull's patch.

The theory of the 'danger zone' which Tirpitz and Bülow felt Germany *must* go through was also a reflection of their assumptions about the future. The apprehensions which they expressed on occasions about a possible British attack derived from the present imbalance of naval power but, provided a war was avoided, the scales would soon begin to tilt in Germany's direction: hence the language of organic growth which permeates their writings. During the Samoan crisis in the spring of 1899, Tirpitz informed a considerable number of people that England, cherishing a deep resentment of Germany as a commercial rival, 'wishes to ruin us before our fleet has emerged *from the egg-shell*'; and Bülow, for his part, wrote of the need to 'operate so carefully, *like the caterpillar before it has grown into the butterfly*'.[43] According to the detailed calculations of the *Admiralstab* around the turn of the century, Britain would find it difficult to maintain its present superiority in battleship numbers over Germany in the long term; and even when, after 1908, he was under pressure to slow down the naval race, Tirpitz always insisted that the British would soon be feeling the financial strain and thus be willing to give up her attempt to retain a monopoly of sea power.

It is only when the importance which nationalist circles placed upon *economic* strength and *commercial* rivalry is recognised, that one can fully understand why Chamberlain's Tariff Reform movement became entangled in the general debate about Anglo-German relations. Of course the German export trade and many middlemen had legitimate grounds to fear that, if an imperial tariff were introduced, German economic interests would find it much more difficult to gain access to their largest overseas market; but the interesting point to notice is that such apprehensions pale in comparison to the anger expressed by patriotic intellectuals and pressure groups that Chamberlain's movement was a deliberate blow, aimed at checking Germany's expanding power. This was why a widely publicised article on 'The Denunciation of the English Commercial Treaty, and its Danger for Germany in the Future' could declare:

> The ultimate result is this – that the fight for supremacy in the world must inevitably lead Germany into a conflict of interests with Greater Britain and to an extent which cannot occur with any other European Power. The vital struggle will be for the markets remaining open to the Germans; and the best of these markets are the Colonies.[44]

Yet, whenever the *National Zeitung* or other papers demanded that Bülow take energetic steps to warn London against adopting protection, the alarm bells sounded in British imperialist circles. To many (but, as we shall see, not to all) of the British Right, the creation of a tightly knit imperial customs union was the *only* means left to preserve their country's position in world affairs. 'There perhaps lies the promise of salvation for us', thought Chirol. 'We want rejuvenating, and the colonies will undertake to do it.' Had not Seeley in *The Expansion of England* taught that only when Britain and the white dominions were fused into one was there a chance of remaining 'in the first rank'.[45] Now, just as Chamberlain was seeking to convert the nation to the wisdom of this step, the Germans were trying to undermine it, so as to keep Britain weak. As one rabid patriot asserted:

> Germany's ambition now is, first to ruin our oversea trade, by any means,

314

fair or foul, and then – having impoverished us until we can no longer afford to compete in warlike preparations – to attack us by force of arms upon the first suitable opportunity. The provocation we give is that we stand in the way of her declared ambitions.[46]

As Philip Kerr (the later Lord Lothian) put it, in a letter ridden with Social Darwinistic fears about a disintegrating empire, Germany's long-term aim in building a massive battlefleet was to be able to say 'No. I will not allow Imperial Preference.'[47]

What all this suggests (and it is no novel conclusion) is that the arch-nationalists in each country saw economic strength and military strength as two sides of the same coin. This was why Northcliffe, after a prolonged motoring tour of Germany, could assert: 'Every one of these new factory chimneys is a gun pointed at England, and in many cases a very powerful one.'[48] What was more, because the patriotic intellectuals and journalists thought in *totalities*, because they conceptualised about the *national* good, they were often more concerned about economic developments than businessmen themselves. To Schmoller and the *Kathedersozialisten*, or to a fellow-mercantilist like Professor Hewins, purely economic considerations were not enough: as Hewins put it,

Suppose an industry which is threatened [by foreign competition] is one which lies at the very root of your system of National defence, where are you then? You could not get on without an iron industry, a great Engineering trade, because in modern warfare you would not have the means of producing, and maintaining in a state of efficiency, your fleets and armies. Therefore, you see, you have to look at these things not only from a strictly economic point of view, but from another. It is conceivable that under conditions of strict and ruthless international competition the great industries of England would be reduced to a very few. Why should not we all become financiers of one kind and another, because we can do financially better than other people? But you cannot make a nation or an empire out of financiers.[49]

Such views are very close to Adolf Wagner's assertion that *Kriegsmacht* is 'the first and most important of all national, and I may add, of all economic necessities'.[50]

Nevertheless, if it would be easy to give many further instances of this belligerently mercantilist *Weltanschauung*, it would be wrong to suggest that it was universally shared by the British and German élites. Indeed, part of the near-hysteria that is evident in the speeches and writings of the extreme Right derived from the fact that they detected weakness, uncertainty and a readiness to compromise with 'essentials' in their own Conservative leadership. Salisbury, much criticised by the imperialist wing of the party in his later years, had typified this approach. He had never respected the alarmism of the military experts and once wrote that 'Admiral Fisher is subject to some of these hallucinations of which Admirals are the victims';[51] he was always more confident that Britain and British merchants would be able to hold their own in the world – this was especially true in Africa[52] – and, when many of his colleagues feared an impending collapse of the British position in Asia, the Prime Minister sarcastically noted that he 'rather liked' the notion of Russia first conquering China and then using China to overrun India.[53] Despite his distrust of German diplomacy, Salisbury also refused to be upset by stories of her commercial rivalry: 'All that we hear, I think, of the Germans and their rivalry, which is supposed to be driving us so far, must take its origin more from the fertile and inventive writers who have to produce adequate copy than from any real foundation in fact.'[54] In much the same way, Balfour and his political friends, although more alarmed than Salisbury about the future of the British Empire in the twentieth century, wished to proceed cautiously in any reform of the system. Perhaps this mentality was best captured by the comment of Salisbury's son upon Chamberlain's scheme for Tariff Reform, which was so appealing to the new, activist elements in the party:

> The more I think of the matter, the more impressed I am with apprehension at the violent nature of the changes proposed. The whole of my Conservative training revolts against the catastrophical theory of politics. Chamberlain and Milner and Ashley, all in their several ways adhere to that theory . . . My conception of tariff reform is to go a step – and that only a short step – at a time.[55]

Thus, although the party leadership moved gradually (and under heavy pressure from the Chamberlain-ites) towards the idea of Tariff Reform, many Conservatives refused to abandon free trade; and even when Balfour and Lansdowne themselves did so, it is clear that they still did not view the world through the mercantilist and Social Darwinistic spectacles which characterised the extreme nationalists of this period. As a result, they never subscribed to the argument that commercial rivalry was at the root of the Anglo-German antagonism: that idea, argued Balfour, was 'a complete delusion', and Lansdowne also thought it preposterous that anyone could maintain that it was in Britain's interest to provoke a quarrel or a war with Germany.[56] These same comments would apply, but even more strongly, to the Liberal Imperialists, for they all remained true to a commercial doctrine which preached that the exchange of goods between nations led to interdependence, peace and harmony: in his first letter to Berlin after assuming office, Grey specifically denied that commercial rivalry played any role in Britain's suspicion of Germany.[57] This meant that the new Foreign Secretary, like his predecessor, was willing to explore the possibility of an understanding with Berlin over the Baghdad Railway; and held, moreover, that such commercial and colonial arrangements could provide a useful way of 'de-fusing' the tense Anglo-German relationship. It did *not* mean that he believed a conflict of interests between the two countries was impossible; but rather that it would come at the political and strategical level. Would Germany be content solely to expand economically, thus contributing greatly to the general level of Europe's prosperity; or would her rulers seek to translate this industrial strength into political advantage, by forcing her neighbours to become satellite states, by constructing an enormous battlefleet for possible future use, and by demanding colonial concessions under the threat of taking military action in Europe? It was impossible for Britain's leaders to *know* the answer to these questions – even Crowe's 1907 memorandum postulated a policy of general, non-violent growth for Germany as an alternative to 'aiming at general political hegemony and maritime ascendancy'[58] – and it was therefore necessary for London both to keep a watchful eye upon Berlin and to be willing to explore all occasions which might safely lead to the improvement of relations. Not surprisingly, such explorations brought accusations of weakness, or even treachery, from those who held that a conflict was unavoidable: Maxse, for example, never visited the Foreign Office again after the Haldane mission, holding that the institution was infected with what he termed 'Potsdamism', that is, subservience to the behests of the Kaiser.

Echoes of this more moderate standpoint are also to be heard on the German side. In certain cases, it derived from a traditional view of the Reich as essentially a European power, sandwiched between France and Russia and having no fundamental conflict of interests with Britain. This 'Caprivi-ite' position was held by Holstein even after the Chancellor's fall, and if the *Geheimrat* had a greater appreciation than Caprivi of the regime's need to satisfy pro-colonial circles, he still felt that this could be done in co-operation with Britain and that Germany should not demand the lion's share.[59] The evidence of an economic jealousy of Germany disturbed him around 1902, but he seems soon to have dismissed this and to have sought to improve relations; at his attempted resignation from office in January 1906 he was still bitterly complaining about Bülow's programme: 'Always with Russia, never with England, and everything with the Centre Party!'[60]

If it is somewhat artificial to place leading members of the Prussian General Staff in the same category – for their 'moderation' towards Britain was frequently based upon the negative reason of wishing to prepare single-mindedly for an assault upon France, which might well provoke British intervention – it was shared by various officials at the *Wilhelmstrasse* and in the diplomatic corps. The commercial department was always at pains, for example, to point out how much Germany benefited from harmonious trade relations with the British Empire; and this viewpoint was strongly reinforced by both Metternich and Bernstorff at the London embassy, who insisted – *contra* Tirpitz – that the British government was not motivated by economic jealousy. By 1906 they seem to have convinced even Bülow that Britain's losses in the Boer War and its annual trade with Germany of 3 milliard marks were guarantees of peace.[61] In the years before 1914, moreover, other Germans sought to bring the two countries together in the commercial and colonial fields: the talks between Lulu Harcourt, the British Colonial Minister, and his German equivalent Solf, who argued that the Reich should be willing to be the 'junior partner' in certain areas, is a case in point.[62] This notion of compromise, in one scholar's view, reflected a 'modern', industrial conception of German overseas colonisation and economic investment – like Ballin and Gwinner and Helfferich, it was able to 'do a deal' with the British even if it also believed in the need for German

317

expansion.[63] It thus stood in contrast to the more ideologically charged *Blut und Boden* theories of colonial emigration, which the anti-modern (and anti-British) agrarian propagandists were developing. This interpretation would help to explain the curious alignments which occurred in the pre-1914 debate over a naval limitations treaty with the British; on the one hand, certain industrial and financial circles, which were used to co-operation at international level and did not believe that Britain would go to war for trade reasons, were willing to support a compromise in the naval race – and shared this view with Bethmann Hollweg and the General Staff; whereas it was criticised by Tirpitz, who, although ostensibly 'modern', was being supported not only by the Pan-Germans and the Navy League but also by various anti-modern ideologues. For the rest of his life, it is worth noting, Tirpitz bitterly described Bethmann's supporters in terms which one more commonly associates with the anti-industrial advocates of 'the politics of cultural despair', for example, for their cosmopolitanism and materialism, their traitorous yearnings for 'western' culture, their failure to see 'that what matters is to succeed with German *Kultur* and the German *Wesen*'.[64]

The assumption that commercial competition must lead to an Anglo-German conflict was most stridently opposed by virtually all the 'left-of-centre' political groups in the two countries: that is to say, by both the traditional *laissez-faire* Liberals and those 'social reform' or 'new' Liberals who were anti-imperialist, and by the Socialists. It is noticeable that very few members of these circles addressed themselves to the shifting balances of global and European *power* consequent upon Britain's relative economic decline and Germany's rise. One contributor to the *Contemporary Review* was an exception to this rule, but after arguing that Germany and the United States would each achieve economic and naval equality in the long run and that 'the British Empire exists at all only on the sufferance of other nations', he concluded that 'we should act towards other nations as one gentleman does to another'[65] – an interpretation which no doubt confirmed all the dark suspicions which Arnold White, Maxse and their fellows harboured about liberalism's 'weakness'. On the whole, however, the Left concentrated upon attacking the protectionists' assumption that one country's gain in exports was another's loss. 'No free trader', sniffed the *Daily News* (25/7/1896) in its comment upon Williams's book *Made in Germany*, 'can seriously contend that the importation of German goods into this country is a misfortune. If it were so, all foreign commerce would be in itself an evil.' This argument was helped by the flaws which economists had pointed out in Chamberlain's tariff scheme by 1905, and thereafter by the general rise in world trade: what did it matter if Germany was making economic advances when Britain also was growing wealthier and they had such flourishing trade links with each other? How could you protect a failing industry (for instance, steel) without hurting a flourishing one (for instance, shipbuilding)? Moreover, 'Why single out Germany?', as Avebury demanded of Bonar Law. Why not criticise a country which had far higher discriminatory tariffs against British goods?[66] There was no Anglo-German trade rivalry, claimed Hobson in a pamphlet called *The German Panic*: it was simply 'some private English firms competing with some private German and

American firms'. The whole thing was got up by capitalists 'to divert the force of popular demands for drastic social reforms'.[67]

Similar arguments could be found among the pro-English circles in Germany. First reactions to the Tariff Reform campaign were to play it down. 'The world is big enough in any case to offer enough room for this competition', was the *Hamburgische Börsenhalle*'s comment upon Williams's book – a typical free-trader's retort. The whole Imperial Federation idea was to be explained in terms of Dominion patriotism, claimed another writer: it would have little practical effect upon Germany's trade. The British remain 'economically our best friends and customers', reminded a third.[68] Eagerly they claimed that Chamberlain's schemes would fail and that the problems of a change to protection were too great, all this being intended to calm any unease inside Germany. At other times, they proffered advice across the Channel, with Richter's *Freisinnige Zeitung* warning the British to note the evils which had befallen Germany since Bismarck's adoption of tariffs, and with Bernstein writing an article on 'Protection and Labour in Germany' for the new British free trade journal *The Independent Review*, in which he painted a bleak picture of social conditions inside Germany.[69]

More often than not, however, the Liberal and other left-wing elements inside Germany had to go on to the offensive, not only to ward off the prospects of an Anglo-German estrangement and right-wing attacks upon them for being unpatriotic, but also to warn the electorate of what was behind their enemies' campaign. The real anglophobes, claimed M. Brauer (anticipating parts of Eckhart Kehr's analysis by about twenty-five years), were the agrarians, and their stand 'was a demonstration against the hated industrial course of the government since industrial Germany naturally turns towards England and agrarian Germany towards Russia'.[70] Others went further, placing all the blame for the British tariff campaign upon Germany's own action of 1879. 'Since when', Bebel asked the Reichstag,

> did this movement for a closer link between motherland and colonies exist? Since when did the movement in Canada to concede different conditions to the home country than to others exist? Only since the time that we went over to the system of high import tariffs and especially since we introduced the taxes on agricultural produce.[71]

But the really ominous fact, as Brentano argued, was that history showed that a mercantilist policy inevitably led to war. Cobden and Bright had recognised this and tried to convert the world to a peaceful system of free trade; but the return to protectionism by certain states, especially Germany, had provoked a similar movement in Britain and darkened the future of Europe.[72] As the Progressive deputy, Barth, put it to his old English friend, James Bryce: 'What now matters for all friends of good relations between Germany and England in our two countries is to prevent the outbreak of a tariff war . . . Never has the close connection between *free trade and good will among nations* been more conscious to me than at present.'[73] Even if the Unionist electoral defeat of 1906 removed the immediate danger of a tariff war, it remained necessary for the pro-free trade forces in both countries to keep a watchful eye open for all efforts by their internal foes to draw false and alarmist conclusions from economic trends and statistics – just as it was vital to oppose proposals for massive naval increases and to counter any manifestations of zenophobia.

This returns us to Bernstein's comment at the beginning of this section. The question of Anglo-German economic rivalry was not one which affected business interests alone: it also impinged upon the furious internal debate which was taking place in both countries between the advocates of global peace and co-operation, and those who saw the world as a harsh, competitive jungle in which each people had to adjust in order to survive. In the eyes of the Pan-Germans, or Chamberlain's followers, the cold economic facts told one story; in the eyes of their Liberal and Socialist critics, they told another. 'Objective' statistics mingled with subjective assumptions; economic developments were related to national strategy and internal politics; ideas about power were intertwined with those about profit. This is why it is impossible to treat the rise of the Anglo-German antagonism simply at the diplomatic (or even the power-political) level and to relegate the economic aspects to the historical antechamber.

# CHAPTER 17

# The 'Social Question', Armaments and Finance: The Response of the Parties

The previous section sought to show how various political groupings in Britain and Germany reacted to the power-political consequences of the global economic trends around the turn of the century: it did *not* imply that the changing Anglo-German relationship has to be seen solely from the Rankean perspective of 'the primacy of foreign policy'. This present section will seek to explore the reactions of those same political groupings to the other chief consequence of the economic trends: the urbanisation, 'massification' and growing class consciousness of the workforce in pre-1914 Europe. In turn, it does *not* imply that the Anglo-German relationship will be viewed from the contrary assumption about 'the primacy of domestic politics', which sees the foreign policy of a state (as one scholar has put it) as a 'branch of internal policy'.[1] What this present study suggests is the overwhelming interconnectedness of, and constant interactions between, external affairs and domestic politics. The blunt fact is that those political circles whose differing conceptions of the international order were analysed above were themselves constantly relating that to the domestic-political scene, and did not 'compartmentalise' their politics according to the constructs of later scholars. An ideal imperial programme, in the view of Milner or Tirpitz, possessed both internal and external aspects – and the Left felt just the same about a comprehensive and genuinely 'progressive' programme. All perceived that the galvanising motor of economic change was having significant impacts upon their own society as well as upon relations with foreign societies; and recognised that they would have to grapple with both if they were to maintain, or to establish, the political structure which they deemed best for themselves and their fellow-countrymen.

The 'social question', as it was euphemistically termed, had always been there, whether in Elizabethan England or *Vormärz* Germany; and an undue emphasis upon its novelty in the decades before 1914 would rightly surprise historians of an earlier age. Nevertheless, it is fair to maintain that 'the scale of the cumulative demands for economic, social and political reform arising

321

within this period was of a size sufficient to distinguish the period qualitatively from previous eras of reformist agitation, such as the 1840s or the 1860s'.[2] Arthur Balfour, whom the historian rarely thinks of as being deeply concerned with the British 'social condition', was one of many who now felt that it occupied the forefront of political debate, shouldering aside the 'ancient controversies' about the proper constitution for the nation. There was, overall, an increased sensitiveness to 'poverty and want', which led not only to many proposals for their alleviation but also to an 'impatience with existing social arrangements'. This was an age, he concluded, in which 'discussions on the distributions of power are slowly being replaced by discussions on the distributions of wealth'.[3]

At the root of this concern was that growth in the overall population and urbanisation of Britain and Germany described earlier. In the German case, where industrialisation was so swift, some 30 to 40 per cent of the entire population in 1914 consisted of industrial workers and their families, many of whom were working in large factories and almost all of whom lived in urban slums. The first consequence of this, not surprisingly, was the creation of trade unions which could improve wages through collective bargaining. Here, the socialist or 'free' unions were numerically dominant, with over 2,548,000 members in 1913; but anti-socialist political groups had attempted to organise the working man, and by that date there also existed 107,000 workers belonging to the Hirsch-Dunker (or progressive) unions, 342,000 to the Christian (i.e. Catholic) unions, and around 280,000 in employer-sponsored (and usually pro-National Liberal) unions.[4] In Britain, the rise in trade union membership was even more spectacular: the 1·5 million members in 1892 had swollen to 2·5 million by 1909 and to 4 million by 1913. The sheer strength of the unions, whether in the elite trades or in 'new' unions like the gas and dock workers, seemed to be amply demonstrated by some of the more spectacular strikes of this period, such as the 1889 dockers' strike, the 1893 miners' dispute and the great wave of unrest in 1911–12.[5]

The creation of formal political parties to ensure the implementation of the aims of the working classes was an outgrowth of the above. In Germany, the SPD had already been regarded as a formidable political force in Bismarck's time, despite his various efforts to destroy it; and after 1890, when the party was again made legal, it expanded further. By 1912 it was the largest party in the Reichstag with 110 seats – and only the disparity in the size of urban and rural constituencies prevented the total from being considerably higher. In Britain, the growth of a parliamentary Labour party came much later: the Labour Representation Committee, formed in 1900, already had thirty seats by 1906 (or fifty-three, if one counted the miners' representatives, 'Lib-Labs' and others not strictly affiliated to the LRC); and by December 1910, forty-two seats. Although the 'social reform' wing of the Liberal Party was striving, in many cases successfully, to arrest the trend, and although the Tories still obviously garnered an amount of the working-class 'deference' vote, it could be argued that in Britain, too, the political balance was beginning to reflect the social balance as between classes.

While the working classes of Britain and Germany were taking steps to organise themselves, their social superiors were becoming increasingly aware of the dreadful living conditions and poor health which afflicted so many of their fellow countrymen. Here again, such 'revelations' had a long ancestry, but in the late nineteenth century, there appeared a fresh spate of reports on poverty – by Booth and Rowntree, for example; there were the various efforts to counter urban conditions, by the Salvation Army, Stoecker's Christian-Social movement and Toynbee Hall; there was the sheer rapidity of German industrialisation after 1890 on the one hand; and, on the other, the shocks caused by the number of volunteers turned away as unfit for service during the Boer War. Little wonder, then, that it was more than the workers who concerned themselves with social policy. It was not a 'new' Liberal, but an ex-proconsul of Empire who attacked the 'squalor and degradation of the slums of our big cities'.[6] And it was not merely Socialists but also the leader of the *Kathedersozialisten*, who presented grim portrayals of the plight of the worker under the capitalist system.[7]

On the German side, moreover, the social question and the related fear of socialism was complicated by one further factor: an agrarian backlash. The landed estates to the east of the Elbe, and the millions of peasant holdings in Bavaria and elsewhere were not untouched by industrialisation; but their owners were strongly resistant to its processes, which they rightly perceived would affect their own way of life and (in the case of the Junkers) would undermine their privileged position in society and politics. There is probably no stronger contrast between Britain and Germany in the nineteenth century than the way in which the landed interest reacted to modernisation. The British aristocracy was no paragon of democratic virtue, to be sure, but it generally preferred to take advantage of (rather than to oppose) industrialisation and to make certain concessions to demands for constitutional reform in the hope of blunting their full effects. Their Prussian equivalents were 'last-ditchers' – to use the language of 1910 – throughout the entire century. 'The masses will make their weight felt and rob us, the aristocrats, of our influence', declared Heydebrand, but, he grimly added, 'we will not voluntarily sacrifice our position.'[8] The aids to this policy of obstructionism were, moreover, immense: the sheer influence of the landowners at the Hohenzollern court, and in the army and bureaucracy; the 'rigged' nature of the constitution, which permitted a preponderance of influence to Prussia, whose electoral arrangements ensured that it remained a bastion of conservatism; and their ability to call upon a mass pressure group, the *Bund der Landwirte*, which unhesitatingly threw its influence against any candidate for the Reichstag who ignored the needs of agriculture. The economic boom of the two decades before 1914 not only intensified the debate over the rising 'threat' from the SPD, therefore, but it also sharpened the cleavage between 'industrialisers and agrarians'.[9] Max Weber, Schmoller and, slightly later, Thorstein Veblen, might regard these anti-modernist forces as a social and political anachronism; but they were still formidable and combative. As their intransigent opposition to Caprivi had shown, they were bound to complicate, and would possibly ruin, any efforts to solve the 'social question' – for they were, in fact, another equally formidable social question themselves.

323

Despite the dissimilarity in their membership and aims, both the industrial trade unions and the *Bund der Landwirte* had in common the recognition that individuals with similar economic interests needed to organise themselves more effectively if they wished to protect or to enhance those interests. That such interest groups should arise, and then establish contacts with or even create political parties to assist the implementation of their aims, may not seem unusual; but the extent to which this was done in Wilhelmine Germany was rather remarkable. Commerce (as opposed to heavy industry), shopkeepers, craftsmen, clerks and others formed their own organisations, maintained their own publicity and sought to secure the favours of candidates for, or holders of, political office.[10] In Britain, this was much less formalised, although it was broadly recognised that each of the main parties received support from certain economic and social interests: the Unionists from the landowners, brewers, and many industrialists and white-collar workers; the Liberals from interests associated with free trade, regions where nonconformity was strong, and many of the working classes. This is not to imply that there was always agreement between, say, the 'free' trade unions and the SPD leadership, or between Lancashire cotton men and the Liberal Party, or that one can regard a party simply as the political manifestation of a single class rather than a 'community of beliefs'. Nevertheless, if we are to examine the variety of reactions to the social question, it is important to bear in mind that the way a particular party responded was often – in the German case, almost always – due to the influence of the interest groups which were associated with it.

At the same time as the political parties in both countries were reacting to this growing concern about social problems, they were also having to grapple with the interrelated question of central government finance. That question was acute because the decade or so before 1914 saw the breakdown of the budgetary assumptions and practices to which the political élites in both nations had traditionally adhered, in part because of the debate upon a redistribution of wealth by means of taxation, but in the main because of very swift rises in expenditure upon the armed forces. The budgetary assumptions which hitherto had prevailed in Britain were those laid down in Mill's *Principles of Political Economy*.[11] Central government expenditure, jealously controlled both by the Treasury and the House of Commons, should concern itself with those areas in public life in which the individual was recognisably ineffective. This meant, above all, national defence: in the decade 1890–9, for example, 40 per cent of government expenditure (£36·4 million annual average) went to the armed forces, and 26 per cent (£23·6 million annual average) went to pay National Debt charges, which were themselves the result of past wars. Civil government and postal administration took a mere 22 per cent (£20·2 million) and education 10 per cent (£14·9 million), although both were higher proportionately than they had been in mid-century.[12] On the revenue side, 'the great pillars', as *The Times* termed customs and excise,[13] still brought in 49 per cent of all central government income in the 1890s (averaging £51·5 million p.a.) and the so-called 'taxes on transactions' (for example, stamps, post office charges) a further 22 per cent, or £23·1 million yearly average. In theory, any other taxes – especially a direct tax – should be proportionate upon the classes involved and not be graduated, and both Liberal and Conservative Chancellors of the Exchequer had tended to follow Mill's argument that taxation should *not* be used to redress inequalities of wealth. This principle had not been strictly adhered to, and the 1890s as a whole produced some 17 per cent of revenue (£17·9 million p.a. average) from land, property and income tax, and a further 12 per cent (£12 million p.a. average) from death duties. Generally, however, it was still held that direct income tax was the great 'reserve-engine' of revenue, to be increased substantially from its 1890 rate of sixpence in the pound (2·5 per cent) only in wartime. The other key assumption of this time was that the budget should always be balanced, for a government which went to the market for loans was not only siphoning from productive investment but lowering its own credit – which would once again affect its ability to obtain funds in wartime. 'Its Credit and its Navy', Selborne informed the Cabinet, 'seem to me to be the two main pillars on which the strength of this country rests and each is essential to the other.'[14]

In Germany there was a similar tradition of reliance upon indirect taxes.[15] Since only the individual states levied direct taxes, the Reich government had to rely upon income from such sources as duties upon sugar, brandy and beer, stamp and money-exchange taxes and receipts from the posts and railways; any additional funds had to come from the states themselves, which jealously guarded their rights. Even when Germany returned to protectionism in 1879, the Reich government was unable to secure all of the increased customs receipts but was forced to hand over a considerable amount to the states. In theory, this dual system of revenue collection could be justified by the division in the forms of expenditure incurred by the two layers of government: the Reich needed to pay for the central administration and, above all, the armed forces, which in the period 1891–5 took on average each year £44 million (or 93·9 per cent) of the total expenditure of £47 million; the states would pay for such civil costs as education; while the much-vaunted Bismarckian social insurance and pensions schemes were in the main paid for by the workers and their employers, although the authorities added a bonus to it. In practice, the central government discovered that it could rarely match expenditure with revenue, so that it was constantly having recourse to the money market; the imperial (that is, non-state) public debt, which was as low as £92,000 in 1873, had risen to over £61 million by 1890 and to over £119 million by 1900. Not only was the principle of a balanced budget disregarded, therefore, but the steady rise in national indebtedness through these decades before 1914 contrasted sharply with the general trend of reductions in the British National Debt. A natural consequence of this was an intensification of the scarcity of capital, and the weakening of the Reich's credit – a problem which was both reflected, and temporarily countered, by offering high interest rates which then attracted an inflow of private funds from London and especially Paris, although this also made for instability since large amounts were hurriedly withdrawn during the two Moroccan crises. In general, as historians have pointed out, the German leadership was shifting the burdens of military and naval expenditure on to the shoulders of two groups: the future generations, which were saddled with an ever-increasing national indebtedness; and the poorer classes, because the indirect taxes upon sugar, beer and other consumables fell equally upon them as upon the rich. This latter tendency was reinforced in two further ways: by direct repayments to the producers of brandy and beet-sugar, and the exporters of agricultural produce (that is, to the agrarians, who had demanded this as a sort of budgetary *Danegeld*); and by ever higher tariffs, which protected the profits of domestic producers but sharply increased the general cost of living.

It was the 'new imperialism', and even more the 'new navalism' which destroyed any possibility of either the British or the German governments living within the financial constraints of the age of Gladstone and Bismarck. The Boer War of 1899-1902, which it was at first thought would cost approximately £20 million, eventually led to the additional expenditure of over *ten* times that figure – with all the consequences of higher taxes, extraordinary loans, rise in National Debt and reduced governmental credit mentioned earlier.[16] On the German side, the China expedition of 1900 and the Southwest African revolt four years later, which cost £10 million and over £30 million respectively, caused almost as much embarrassment to the Reich Treasury, for the immediate recourse to loans to pay for these military operations depressed the government's credit further and weakened national finances.[17] Yet these were the extraordinary, if not totally unpredictable, consequences of empire-building. The really ominous long-term danger to what bankers liked to call 'sound finance' lay in the ever-increasing expenditure upon the armed forces – and in particular (apart from the colonial wars noted above) upon the navies. In consequence of the 'scares' and 'races' of this period and of the technological revolution in naval architecture and gunnery, both British and German naval expenditure as a whole were more than doubling every decade, which was quite an unprecedented event in peacetime. Unless the governments concerned could agree to some form of naval limitations agreement, the long-term consequences were ominous: either there would have to be a 'financial revolution', with all its possible social and political consequences, or one power might have to suffer the humiliation of pulling out of the race to avoid bankruptcy, or it might seek to settle matters by force.

Thus, the situation confronting the governments, the political parties and the various interest groups in Britain and Germany in the decade or so before the First World War was not one in which the different aspects of policy could be dealt with separately. The arms race impinged upon government finance, and that upon taxation, and that upon social policy and the domestic-political constellation; the 'rise of labour', in its turn, could also affect government spending and taxation, and have impacts upon external policy; the furious debates in both countries about tariffs in particular, or about direct versus indirect taxation in general, were immediately related by the parties concerned to the naval race, social reforms, the *entente cordiale*, the 'threat' to capital, and so on. Armaments policy and foreign policy and taxation policy and social policy all hung together. It makes little sense, therefore, to argue about the 'primacy' of one political aspect over the other.

## SOCIALISTS AND LABOUR

One further, and very significant area in which the economic and social trends had been making their impact felt was upon the political parties: the sheer size of the electorate was, despite the many restrictions remaining, much larger in 1910 than it had been in 1880; demographic shift, urbanisation and – just as important – the growth of suburbs, the very swift rise in the numbers of clerks and other 'white-collar' workers, all affected electoral geography; the simple fact that three parties might be campaigning in a constituency where two or only one did before, could profoundly alter the outcome of elections in, say, the London and Berlin constituencies; the intervention of economic pressure groups, such as the campaign by the *Bund der Landwirte* against certain National Liberal candidates in Hessen or the miners' transfer of their loyalties from the Liberal to the Labour Party in Britain, had a similar significance. Parties had to be much better organised than ever before; their leaders felt, and probably were, under much greater pressure from the economic and social circles which supported them than was the case earlier; all showed a new concern about publicity, and sought to cobble together a programme which satisfied the various elements within the party as well as attracting new voters to it. Mass politics was undermining that mid-century Liberal dream, according to which strong-minded and moral leaders appealed to an enlightened electorate to support their proposed policies on rational (but not selfish) grounds; it had never actually been practised in mid-century, but now it was further away than ever.

On the German side, the SPD was not simply the catalyst for change, but in many ways the model. There was a central organisation, financed by an increasing flow of funds from local branches; a heavy reliance upon modern mass communications, such as the telephone and the cheap newspaper, of which ninety different ones were being sold each day by 1914; the establishment of workers' libraries, educational societies, clubs, athletic groups and youth organisations, all of which helped to give the industrial worker a sense of identity and solidarity; an ever-growing trade union membership, which made up around 70 per cent of the party's total rank and file by 1913;[18] and, in many constituencies, a well-organised system for identifying the SPD electorate and persuading all concerned to cast their ballots on polling day. If the physical and economic and demographic circumstances were ripe for a large-scale increase in the public's support for the SPD, it is also true that the movement utilised its opportunities in a systematic fashion.

Given the enormous powers of the Prusso-German state to contain physical unrest, and the immediate environmental and economic needs of the majority of the SPD's supporters, especially as articulated by trade union leaders such as Legien, the party leaders preferred to focus attention upon social conditions rather than to appeal for revolutionary mass action as suggested by the intellectual Socialists.[19] Thus, the crisis in governmental finance was both tactically the most suitable and in reality probably the most immediate concern of the SPD, simply because decisions over taxes, tariffs and naval bills affected the standard of living of their followers. Their assault upon the first two Naval Laws provides a good example of the interconnectedness of these different aspects of politics. The whole *Flottenschwindel* – to use Liebknecht's term – was simply the work of an irresponsible monarch, heavy industrialists who sought to boost their profits, and agrarians consumed with dislike of England. The arguments about the protection and furtherance of German commerce were a nonsense for various reasons, said Bebel, but most of all because the hypocritical supporters of the Tirpitz Plan would soon be voting for increased tariffs designed to restrict international trade. The cry about 'our future lies on the water', Liebknecht felt, was a clumsy attempt to divert the people's attention away from the need for drastic constitutional and social reforms; there was also a danger that Tirpitz might free the navy from the Reichstag's financial control, which meant that that body lost what little muscle it possessed to bargain for constitutional reforms. The crowning blow of all, however, was that the forces favouring naval expansion were determined not to pay for it themselves, but to foist the cost upon the general public and upon future generations of Germans.[20] All this was nicely summed up by Parvus' brochure on 'Naval Demands, Colonial Policy, and the Workers' Interests': 'No costly armoured-ships! No heaping burdens upon the people! Away with this yearning for sea-power! No colonial adventures! No war provocations! Maintenance of the peace! Alliance with England! Trade treaty with North America!'[21]

When, after 1902, Germany's financial and diplomatic position steadily worsened, the Socialists could feel justified in their earlier criticisms. The higher agricultural tariffs, demanded by the Conservatives as the price of their reluctant acquiescence in the second Navy Law, caused widespread discontent. Moreover, the trade slump after 1901 had undermined Tirpitz's over-optimistic contention that the rise in naval costs would be met by the increased receipts from Germany's continued economic expansion; instead, the budgetary gap was widening, and even if fresh loans were floated it was also imperative to raise new taxes. All this, predictably, was grist to Bebel's mill. The entire fleet policy was a disaster, he claimed, and was leading to a financial catastrophe. Instead of pointing to the 'English threat' (as the Navy League did), a pro-English policy should be adopted; instead of talking about a trade war, the protectionists should recognise Britain's generosity in allowing the free importation of German goods whereas the Reich deliberately sought to exclude British wares; instead of building battleships, the government should build 1,000 hospitals. That was what the workers wanted! If, however, the German establishment wished to maintain its costly armaments expenditure, it should pay for this itself: only £4 million estate duty was raised from 60 million Germans each year, whereas £19 million in estate duty was raised from a British population of 40 million, taunted Bebel.[22] Finally, although there was little chance of the Reichstag being allowed to levy direct taxes on incomes, estates and inheritances, the SPD leaders could console themselves with the knowledge – which troubled successive Chancellors – that every steep rise in indirect taxation brought many more voters to its side (as in 1903 and 1912).

The SPD's attitude towards England was naturally a part of this overall stance towards Reich politics. While this does not mean that the average party member gave much thought to the Anglo-German relationship, the leadership certainly did. During the Reichstag debates upon Bismarck's 1896 'revelations' about the non-renewal of the Reinsurance Treaty with Russia, for example, Liebknecht claimed that 'if England stood on Germany's side, then all these [strategic] difficulties would be removed: England has the same interests as Austria and Germany as against a coalition of Russia and France. There prevails a full harmony of interests between us and England; the little colonial policy counts for nothing.'[23] Even during the Boer War, when to adopt an openly anglophile position was to run the risk of great unpopularity, Bebel pleaded for Britain and Germany to come together. The plundering of the Transvaal was despicable, he admitted, but Chamberlain did not represent the 'true England'; the common sense of the English people would reject his imperialism, and his protectionism. Instead of building a fleet against her, Germany should go hand in hand with Britain, especially in China.[24] As late as 1908, when the Anglo-German antagonism was clear to all, Bebel was referring to the 'colossal moral and material gains for Germany' which would have been the fruit of an alliance with Britain.[25] The logic of this argument, the way it dove-tailed into the social and financial policies of the SPD, is obvious; but it was also true that the deep personal attachment of Bebel and the elder Liebknecht played a great role. 'It is a great debt of gratitude which I owe to your country', the latter assured William Morris; 'The twelve years of exile I spent there gave me my political education. And your working classes have been my teachers.'[26] One cannot avoid the suspicion, however, that it was more the democratic and reformist impulses within left-Liberalism, and the ethical approach to politics of Gladstone and Bright, which appeared attractive to these German admirers – and which helps to explain Bebel's otherwise curious preference for secret contacts with Asquithian liberalism rather than with MacDonald in the years before 1914.[27]

In the first decade of the twentieth century two developments, one external, the other internal, began to undermine this position. The first was the formation of the Anglo-French and Anglo-Russian *ententes*, which destroyed at one blow Bebel's concept of a pro-English-but-anti-Russian stance. Admittedly, the secret military calculations of the Schlieffen Plan play a vital part here, because in consequence of them a defensive war on the Eastern front, which the SPD seemed increasingly willing to support, would spill over into the Low Countries and very probably lead to British intervention. As the Reich leadership itself saw, socialist support for a struggle against the Triple Entente could best be achieved by emphasising the 'Russian danger' alone.[28] The second development was one of the most famous in the history of socialism – the growth of 'revisionist' ideas and forces within the SPD from the late 1890s onwards.[29] It was not necessarily the case that a person who was a 'revisionist' over the SPD's domestic strategy should also be a 'social-imperialist' supporter of German *Weltpolitik*; indeed, the most famous of the revisionists, Eduard Bernstein, was as anglophile as Bebel himself and justified his apostasy by reference to his own years of exile in England, which had confirmed his suspicion that there was an alternative route to socialism from that of revolution. In his book *The English Peril and the German People* and in other writings,

329

Bernstein praised the British adherence to free trade, denied that there was any 'encirclement' of Germany, and ascribed the growing antagonism between the two countries to the imperial government's reckless and unnecessary colonial and naval policies.[30] Nevertheless, a considerable number of other 'revisionist' SPD members argued, especially after the 1907 electoral setback and the second Moroccan crisis, that Britain must be opposed because it was seeking to frustrate Germany's natural growth: 'The English bourgeoisie . . . are seeking just as vainly through the idea of disarmament to sentence the other capitalist states, and especially the strong, young, and lusty German capitalist empire, to perpetual inferiority upon the seas and thereby preserve England's hegemony over the waves forever.'[31] Tirpitz himself could hardly have put it better. It was also logical, although somewhat ironic, that the extreme left wing of the SPD had little pro-British feeling and saw the growing antagonism as a quarrel between two greedy capitalist states. If the centre of the party under Bebel remained anglophile, it is nevertheless clear that Kehr's description of the movement as being 'outspoken in demanding an alliance with England' requires ever more modification the closer one comes to 1914 itself.[32]

The smaller and politically less significant parliamentary Labour Party in Britain adopted virtually the same viewpoints as the SPD towards social reform, financial policy and foreign affairs – although, here again, one would admit that the latter field was not a central preoccupation of the working man or of most of their Members of Parliament. Moreover, as many observers have pointed out, much of the British labour movement was pragmatic and to a large extent ignorant of any historical conception of socialism as developed by Marx.[33] However, the Labour leaders themselves were much more definite in their recognition of the relationship between domestic and foreign politics – partly because of their own developed political consciousness, partly because of their association with the Fabians or the Social Democratic Federation, and partly because of their earlier co-operation with the 'left' wing of the Liberal Party during the Boer War and Tariff Reform campaign. Thus, their attitude to current financial and social questions was fairly predictable: Labour was certainly not against high governmental spending but, as Philip Snowden told the Commons, it wanted this to be directed towards social reforms and not towards the armed services (as favoured by the nationalists) or paying off the National Debt (as favoured by *laissez-faire* economists).[34] The stance which probably gained the Labour leaders most support in this area was their bitter opposition to conscription. As one member of the party's 1910 campaign against armaments put it,

> [This meeting] affirms that militarism, whilst profitable to certain finan-
> ciers and speculators, imposes a blood-tax on Labour, and threatens to
> impose on Great Britain the evils of compulsory military service and the
> barbarities of war . . . The working men of England . . . were not afraid
> of the German invasion; they were much more afraid of the capitalists who
> were sweating them (Applause).[35]

This Marxist rhetoric was, moreover, blended into the more traditional

Radical-pacifist thought of the British left, and together they ensured that the movement as a whole remained critical of the *ententes* (especially with Russia), demanded an end to the naval race, sought to control Grey's diplomacy and sent frequent messages of goodwill to their German opposite-numbers. To MacDonald, who took a great interest in the 1910–11 campaign on disarmament, and to Keir Hardie, who went more frequently than others to meetings of the Socialist International, the stance which the labour movement should adopt towards external affairs was both obvious and important.[36] In the country as a whole, however, Labour attitudes were much more fissured. Many working men did not share the internationalism and pacificism of their parliamentary spokesmen and were willing recruits to the Volunteers or Territorials. In much the same pragmatic way as had characterised their German equivalents, British trade unionists and MPs such as Henderson also rejected the idea of a general strike as an anti-war weapon: the 'great labour unrest' of 1911–14 certainly caused the government's planners to wonder how any future mobilisation for war and the maintenance of food supplies could be affected in the face of union non-co-operation, but the aims of the strikers in this period were more industrial than political.[37] Moreover, there were the 'eccentric Socialists' represented by Hyndman's SDF or by the popular author Robert Blatchford, whose views upon foreign policy were the exact opposite of those put forward by MacDonald and Hardie. Hyndman, who in many respects was much more of an orthodox Marxist than his British colleagues, followed Bebel's reasoning that Germany as the *Junkerstaat* should be opposed by all possible means – including the introduction of conscription so as to create a 'citizens' army' to throw back the German invader: this he found in no way inconsistent with his bitter criticism of the capitalist system.[38] Blatchford, an ex-soldier with a superabundance of patriotism, insisted that his socialism and his advocacy of national service, an enormous fleet, a self-sufficient empire and energetic opposition to German expansionism all went together: 'The masses must be better educated, better governed, better trained and better treated, or the Empire will go to pieces', he insisted.[39] Although the executive of the Labour Party condemned his anti-German writings of 1909–10 as 'an absurd and wicked outburst', the obvious conclusion must be that the movement was not unified in its attitude to foreign affairs, however much it chorused in one voice for social reforms. Finally, just as the German Socialists found it difficult to oppose appeals for national unity against the 'Russian danger', so the British Labour leaders and trade unionists would probably find it difficult to hold out against such calls as 'naval supremacy in danger' or 'poor little Belgium'.

## LIBERAL VIEWPOINTS

In all this, the Labour Party held views which were not remarkably different from those of the left flank of the Liberals. The latter was a powerful influence group, for not only did they form a considerable body in the House of Commons but they were represented in Campbell-Bannerman's, and in Asquith's Cabinet; they could, in such matters as criticising high naval armaments or the Foreign Office's 'secret diplomacy', secure the support of a large number of other Liberal MPs of the more traditional Cobdenite and Non-conformist sort; and they had access to an articulate and widely read press and, at least after Brunner took the presidency, had control of the National Liberal Federation.[40] Most important of all, the party to which they cast their loyalty was in office after 1906 and had at least the opportunity to push through all or parts of their programme. No doubt liberalism's victory in that election depended in part upon certain tactical factors, such as the 'pact' with Labour, the Catholic vote and the support from pro-free trade circles, which might not recur in the future; that it garnered support, in Wales and elsewhere, on issues which had little to do with the slogans 'imperialism' and 'social reform'; and that its electoral strength may well have been enhanced by the fact that there still existed a *restricted* franchise.[41] To observers at the time, however, it was not the fragility or artificiality of liberalism's dominance which was apparent, but rather – and hence the alarm on the Right – its strength and appeal.

This confidence of the 'new' Liberals was enhanced by their claim to represent a promising blend of several key features of left-of-centre politics. On the one hand, they could pose as the spiritual heirs of Gladstone, Bright and earlier notables since they opposed continental entanglements, disliked colonial wars and wished to see the military and naval budget kept to a minimum. They were also convinced free-traders, combating Chamberlain's campaign with the dual argument that Tariff Reform would damage certain key industries and also hit the working man. Nevertheless, what really distinguished people such as Hobson, C. P. Trevelyan, Masterman and their like from John Morley, F. W. Hirst and typical *laissez-faire* Liberals was the former group's redefinition of their movement's aim so as to favour economic and social 'freedoms' as well as constitutional liberty, to permit the social or collective good to override the claims of an individual, and to justify progressive taxation for redistributive purposes so that the poor man's lot would in future be eased by an active state-interventionist policy.[42] Resolved upon alterations in British society by means of 'peoples' budgets', the social-reform Liberals opposed the anti-German trend in politics and the press for *two* reasons: the first was that an escalating naval race, a continental commitment and possible war were immoral and desperately risky policies for which the nation's manhood might have to pay a large price one day; but the second – and here the 'new' liberalism differed from the 'old' – was that the funds spent upon the armed services diverted monies which could go towards social reform.

Agreeing with the Chamberlainites only in believing that the day of the 'night watchman' state had passed, the new Liberals offered criticism on all other counts – and in particular, on the policy to be adopted towards Germany. The balance of power, a term so beloved by the school of Realpolitik, dangerously divided Europe into two camps instead of that radical-ethical ideal of 'a unity of Christendom, a family of nations, a concert of Europe'.[43] The naval race was not Germany's fault; it was the British Admiralty which had been the pacemaker in armaments increases, especially with the Dreadnought class of battleships. Above all, the constant attempts to check Germany's natural growth should be abandoned. There should be instead 'a frank recognition of the legitimate needs of a great nation, yearly advancing in population, in industrial progress, in every form of beneficent human activity'. Of course, the British Radicals partly justified their favourable view of Germany by comparing her with Tsarist Russia, which they detested;[44] but their overwhelming motive was that an anti-German policy, and even more an Anglo-German war, would undermine all their hopes for a progressive and peaceful harmony between the European states, which would then permit each of them to devote their energies and resources to remedying social evils.

It was in the field of foreign policy that the 'new' Liberals could merge with the central mass of the party in desiring an end to the armaments race, colonial wars, and the like;[45] in regard to social reforms and financial policy, however, a wide gap opened up. The centre of the party, under Campbell-Bannerman, believed that it had been elected into office to return the country to those good habits of 'peace, retrenchment and reform' – with the emphasis being very much upon the middle item.[46] Mainly because of Fisher's reforms in the navy, and the relative security which the *ententes* provided, central government expenditure did fall after 1906; and even the introduction of old age pensions in Asquith's last budget, although a landmark in many ways, did not immediately excite a great debate. When the trade depression, the 1908–9 naval scare and the need to pay for the growing pensions bill prompted Lloyd George to devise his 'People's Budget', the traditionalists within the party became increasingly disturbed. To combat the House of Lords, or to defeat the Tariff Reformers, was one thing; but to introduce a whole new series of direct taxes, and to talk of using those proceeds for the purposes of wealth redistribution and social reform was another. Thus, although the bitter debate between Tories and Liberals in the feud of 1909–10 has rightly occupied the centre of historical attention, it is the fissures within liberalism itself which are of interest here. F. W. Hirst, the Gladstonian-Liberal editor of the *Economist*, had hailed the electoral victory of 1906 but now grew gloomy at the 'unsound' finance and 'extravagance'; and in 1914 some forty Liberal backbenchers intervened to influence the Cabinet to modify Lloyd George's proposals for a further large rise in direct taxation.[47] It is therefore not surprising to find that certain of the party's earlier supporters were slipping away by 1910. The Lancashire cotton bosses were still predominantly free-traders, but that was no longer sufficient a motivation for them to vote for a party which was abandoning *laissez-faire* on the domestic front.[48] As for the City, the 'socialism' of the 1909 budget proposals caused a decisive alteration in loyalties; and Garvin gleefully reported that people like 'Sir Walter Gilbey who spent thousands of pounds to put [the Liberals] in, says he would spend six times as much to put them out'.[49] But perhaps the final word from this quarter should be left to that quintessence of Gladstonian tradition, John Morley, who became ever more concerned at the fact that 'Socialism' was now 'the catchword of the hour' and the 'key to our politics'. Old Age Pensions, for example, was to him a profound challenge to Liberal individualism, and yet its ramifications were not being properly discussed. This leftward slide in the party would lose it the support of the middle classes and ruin the movement.[50]

One further remark deserves to be made about this more traditional or 'retrenchment' liberalism; while it always assumed that the annual vote of monies to the armed services was too high and could have been reduced, it nevertheless also accepted the principle of British naval superiority.[51] If the Liberal Cabinet itself defended the annual naval budget, it was very difficult for most of their followers in the Commons to stand out in opposition to it. In November 1907, 136 Liberal MPs petitioned Campbell-Bannerman to cut armaments expenditure; and in February 1908, 82 members 'of the centre section of the Liberal party' urged him to resist pressure from the Liberal Imperialists for 'a great new naval programme'; yet, after the government had introduced an increased allocation and defended it in the Commons, only 73 votes (including many from Labour and Irish MPs) were cast against it.[52] The same pattern is to be seen in later years; when Churchill made his ingenious suggestion in 1912 about a 'naval holiday', papers such as the *Manchester Guardian* and all but the most rigid proponents of disarmament applauded the idea; and when the Cabinet accepted Churchill's further argument that Germany's refusal to agree forced Britain to build further, only a small number of Radicals had the heart to oppose the vote on the naval budgets. Unless and until Lloyd George and others actually walked out of the Cabinet – and, despite all the noise and threats, that never happened – there would be no backbench revolt on the naval issue.[53]

The third 'force' within British liberalism, the 'imperialist' right-wing, was chiefly responsible for the external policy which the government adopted in the years 1906–14. Although the respectable total of fifty-nine adherents of the Liberal League was returned to the Commons in 1906, their great influence derived not from any regional or economic base but from the Cabinet offices which Asquith, Haldane and Grey occupied. The last-named's role was obviously a vital one, and has always been the focus of historians' attention:[54] a combination of his adherence to the Whig perception of Britain's role in the world, the memory of his period at the Foreign Office in the 1890s, and the conclusion he drew from external events during the Liberal Party's decade out of office, all made Grey deeply suspicious of German intentions. Haldane was more optimistic about the possibility of reaching an accord with Germany, but he never opposed his colleague and spent a great deal of his energies in seeking to make the army efficient for a possible continental role.[55] Asquith, acting as Prime Minister as 'honest broker' to the various factions within the party, kept a low profile on issues of foreign affairs; yet there can be no doubt that he supported the Liberal-imperialist position, as the events of August 1914 were to show.[56] After 1911, this group was to be reinforced by the defection of Churchill from the radical wing, and by Lloyd George's support during the Agadir and Belgian crises. Here, then, was a powerful hindrance to the party ever being able to carry out what both the 'social reform' and the traditionalist sections regarded as a truly Liberal foreign policy.

Nevertheless, these differences were not usually reflected in the sphere of domestic politics, where the Liberal-imperialists tended to support the social reforms and financial innovations which so concerned traditionalists such as Morley. It was not, of course, that Grey and Haldane ever seriously contemplated 'government by the people', but they certainly favoured 'government for the people' – partly because they had subsumed the ethical traditions of liberalism which the teachings of T. H. Green and the example of Toynbee in the 1880s had reinforced, partly because of their close connections with the Fabians and others interested in social reform and 'efficient' government, and partly because they recognised that a great power policy needed to rest upon a contented domestic base.[57] Although in many respects overlapping with the social imperialists in the Unionist Party, they strongly opposed tariff reform – which, as Asquith put it, would 'tend to make the Empire odious to the working classes'[58] – and they were also critical of the campaign for national service. It was Haldane, moreover, who in 1908 urged Asquith to see the problem of old age pensions, the poor law and financial reform as one: 'We should boldly take our stand on the facts and proclaim a policy of taking, mainly by direct taxation, such toll from the increase and growth of this wealth as will enable us to provide for (1) the increasing cost of social reform (2) national defence (3) a margin in aid of the sinking fund.'[59]

In Grey's case, his sensitivity to domestic interference in his foreign policy was not matched by a self-exclusion from internal affairs.

> He took an active part in the House of Lords reform; he conducted the negotiations with the miners in February 1912; he supported the decision in favour of the payment of members and, in sharp distinction to some of his more radical colleagues, took up the cause of the female suffragettes. He strongly advocated the passage of the National Insurance Bill and formed an alliance with Lloyd George from the summer of 1911 until the spring of 1912.[60]

Given his favourable credentials in the vital matters of internal policy, did it make sense for the radical Liberals – even if they had the strength and the willpower – to force out the imperialist wing, and thus allow the execrable Tories to gain power? As the *Nation* put it, 'When the average Liberal member goes reluctantly into the Government lobby to sanction the present conduct of the Foreign Office, he is voting not at all on the partition of Persia or the handling of Anglo-German relations, or the increase of our armaments. He is voting for Free Trade, and Home Rule and Social Reform.'[61]

Whatever its internal disagreements, the Liberal Party of pre-1914 Britain – as opposed to the classical doctrines and practices of liberalism itself – did not appear to be suffering any 'strange death'.[62] The contrast with German liberalism could hardly have been greater, for the movement remained fissured and was never able to recover its former vitality and electoral predominance. The National Liberals managed to hold on to a more or less settled core of fifty seats in the Reichstag – in the 1907 'Hottentot' election it rose to fifty-five but in 1912 it was down to forty-five; and the left-Liberals' total, after being virtually halved from 1890 (sixty-seven seats) to 1893 (thirty-five), then settled at around forty. Yet the latter was not a coherent group, for the *Freisinnige Partei* broke in two over the 1893 military budget, when the 'moderates' marched out to form the *Freisinnige Vereinigung* while the rest reconstituted themselves as the *Freisinnige Volkspartei* under Richter's tight leadership. Only in 1910 did the two wings manage to come together again as the *Fortschrittliche Volkspartei*, which brought within its umbrella for the first time the small Württemberg-based *Volkspartei* as well – although even this tentative step towards unity had led to the secession of Theodor Barth and his supporters. Yet even when so combined, the left-Liberals could only secure forty-two seats in the 1912 Reichstag elections. Of the 12·25 million votes cast, the left-Liberals obtained 1·5 million, and the National Liberals 1·7 million: taken together, the total was still eclipsed by the 4·25 million who favoured the SPD.[63]

Viewed psephologically and demographically, the German Liberals were arguably the chief victims of that economic 'modernisation' to which they had looked forward so confidently in the 1860s. The cities and industrial regions had attracted an ever-greater share of the total population, but they had also generally become strongholds of the SPD. By contrast, the flow of labourers from the eastern farmlands tended, if anything, to strengthen the hold of the Conservative Party upon the sparsely populated constituencies of Prussia, for without a redrawing of the electoral boundaries many Junkers were sent to the Reichstag from a constituency which had only one-quarter (and some only one-tenth!) the population of an urban voting area. Moreover, as noted earlier, German liberalism possessed one further historical characteristic: it was unmistakably Protestant. This meant that, although the Centre Party had some success in acquiring non-Catholic voters, it was unusual for Catholics to vote Liberal (although many did turn to the SPD or even to the Conservatives). When the twenty or so districts of the various small particularist parties (Alsatians, Danes, Poles) are also taken into account, it is easy to see why the Liberal parties commanded only eighty or ninety Reichstag seats: electoral victory in two-thirds or perhaps even three-quarters of the constituencies appeared, on economic, religious and ethnic grounds, unattainable.

Yet to leave the analysis of liberalism's failure here is to ignore the question of the individual will and initiative of the movement's leaders. Why was it not possible to attempt a genuine reconciliation with Catholicism, as Gladstone did for so many earnest years? Why not make a bid for the peasants' vote, as Chamberlain and Jesse Collings had tried to do with their 'three acres and a cow' campaign? Why not seek, as Bright and later (and much more effectively) Lloyd George sought, to offer leadership to the working man? Why not redefine liberalism, as Hobson and Hobhouse and the other 'new' Liberals in Britain were doing, as a movement which encompassed the demand for social and economic freedoms, as well as constitutional liberty? Was it because the Germany Liberals had never really had to fight for the advances which occurred in the 1860s and 1870s? Or because of their narrower definition of liberty, the so-called 'German idea of freedom'?[64] Or because they, and their increasingly nervous *Mittelstand* supporters, did not favour an alliance with the common man? Or was it simply because Bismarck's repeated counter-assaults had 'knocked the stuffing' out of the movement already by 1890, leaving its leaders pessimistic and negative?: for there certainly were a large number of Liberals at the beginning of Wilhelm II's reign whose thoughts echoed Bamberger's: 'German parliamentarism was only an episode . . . never mind.'[65]

Whatever the long-term causes of its weakness, liberalism's break-up into

several subdivisions could only perpetuate this condition. It not only intensified the personal antagonisms between the leaders of each faction, but also
encouraged the inclination to seek for alliances with other parties, at state level
and in the Reichstag. Right-wing Liberals headed into Miquel's *Sammlung*,
those to the left discussed an enormous anti-Conservative coalition to include
everyone 'from Bassermann to Bebel', and the Liberals in Baden found
themselves sometimes allying with the SPD and sometimes with the Centre![66]
Of course, given the lack of an overall majority in the Reichstag, all parties
needed to negotiate the terms on which they might co-operate in a pro- or
anti-government *bloc*, and all suffered from internal differences between those
who favoured a tactical coalition with others and those who wished to preserve
the party's ideological purity and political identity; but whereas the agrarians,
the Centre and the SPD each had a strong electoral base – a cluster of safe seats
which they could hold under virtually any circumstances – the Liberals did
not. By 1912, only four Liberal deputies were elected to the Reichstag on a first
ballot victory; all the others gained their place after 'a tangled and often
contradictory set of alliances with the other political parties'.[67]

From this, it follows that for present purposes it would be superfluous to
provide more than a brief résumé of the attitudes of German Liberals to the
pressing questions of social reform, constitutional change, taxation and armaments: for not only did immense differences between the various factions exist,
but standpoints altered over time, partly for tactical reasons and partly because
of a change of leaders (for example, Richter's death). The confusion which
existed in the ranks of German liberalism over the issue of social reform was
symptomatic of the movement's paralysis. Richter, by far the most outspoken
critic of imperial politics outside the SPD itself, had no sympathy with the
socialist movement and refused any alliance with it. *Laissez-faire* was to remain
untouchable, property rights to be preserved, collectivism in any form to be
opposed; a socialist government could turn Germany into a 'great national
penitentiary'.[68] Other left-Liberals were much more sympathetic: many were
involved in, or had encouraged, the Hirsch-Dunker unions which, even if
aimed at helping the working class 'on the basis of the existing social order', did
proclaim the need for social justice and political freedom. Theodor Barth, the
German politician who probably came closest to being a British style 'new'
Liberal, joined Theodor Mommsen in advocating an alliance with the SPD on
an agreed platform of social reforms, and later argued that it was only by
gaining influence with the workers and their leaders that liberalism could
survive as an effective force.[69] Brentano, deeply impressed by developments in
British trade unionism and a bitter critic of *Junkertum* in Germany, was even
more convinced that the enlightened bourgeoisie should put itself at the head
of a national campaign for social reforms.[70]

As a third category, there were those 'reformist' Liberals who wanted state
interventionist policies and 'modernisation' in order to equip Germany for her
twentieth-century role as a great power. To people such as Max Weber,
Naumann and Paul Rohrbach, the starting-point was the rapid industrialisation which was both turning Germany into a *Weltmacht* and creating a dissatisfied proletariat which threatened national stability and strength: as Naumann

put it, 'The new era comes imperialist and proletarian . . . It is impossible at present to separate these two elements.'[71] Since the workers, like every other class of German, were becoming ever more dependent upon foreign trade and markets for their prosperity, then they too must be persuaded to see that the country needed a great fleet and decisive leadership. On the other hand, the German Liberal Imperialists (and *Kathedersozialisten* such as Schmoller) accepted that unless the lot of the common man was bettered – by limited constitutional changes in Prussia, freedom for trade unions, improvement of conditions in factories and slums, adult education and progressive taxation – the worker had no reason to support a national foreign policy. Thus, although these men insisted that there was a 'primacy of foreign policy', that *Machtpolitik* necessitated *Sozialpolitik*, it is clear that in practice they regarded both as being inseparable.[72]

The last, but by no means the least group were the industrialists and traders and bankers who supported the various Liberal parties but in turn expected consideration to be paid to their economic interests. Admittedly, many German businessmen, like their British equivalents, were slipping rightwards in response to the rise of Labour: many leaders of heavy industry found their political and social requirements best fulfilled by membership of the Free Conservatives.[73] Nevertheless, the connections between the Liberal parties and the business/financial world were substantial, and thus the right wing of the National Liberal Party in particular reacted sharply both to the growth of trade unions and the SPD, and to the various proposals to buy industrial peace through concessions and social reform. Such heavy industry circles often joined with the agrarians and military in urging a *coup d'état* as the best means of solving the 'social question'. Many had been strong supporters of the laws to restrict strikes and picketing in the 1890s; and when, around 1910–11, there were proposals for the creation of corporatist 'chambers of Labour' and for sickness insurance, both were rejected – the first because trade union representatives would be included, the second because it would cost the employers money. Even the business supporters of the left-Liberals backed away from proposals which would involve further costs or too great an expansion in trade union powers. Not surprisingly, heavy industrialists and others roundly denounced the *Kathedersozialisten* for 'stirring up' the workers. Little thanks came from these quarters for the efforts of Naumann and Schmoller to achieve social stability at home and to further the cause of Germany's greatness abroad.[74]

What occurred in the realm of social policy was repeated in other fields. In the turn-of-the-century discussions about a new tariff, for example, heavy industry and the National Liberals plumped for higher industrial duties and were willing to haggle with the agrarians about increased protection for agriculture, especially since many of their own deputies were under local pressure from the *Bund der Landwirte*; whereas most of the left-Liberals, and a large number of their supporters in export trades, finance and light industry bitterly opposed this sort of deal and campaigned instead for a more liberal tariff system. Virtually all Liberals favoured giving increased taxation powers to the Reich, for this implied national unity over (chiefly Centrist and agrarian) particularism; but the left-Liberals disliked the constant agrarian pressure for taxes upon bank and stock transactions, and they also opposed proposals for indirect taxes either in the form of increased customs tariffs or in, say, duties upon sugar and beer since that would cause discontent among the working classes. To the National Liberals, this latter concern was not so strong but as the party was committed to all armaments increases and under some internal pressure from its own left wing, it also agreed to consider such schemes as an inheritance tax; when it did so in 1908, however, it simply caused the Conservatives to gravitate towards an alliance with the Centre Party, thereby breaking up the *Sammlung*. [75] On the equally touchy question of reforming the selective three-class franchises of Prussia and the other states, the Liberals found themselves even more divided. Those on the left, recognising that any identification with that system would blacken them for ever in the eyes of the workers, pressed for some changes and they were joined in this by Naumann, Weber and others eager to see the political structures reflect the 'modern', 'efficient', industrial state. Yet the right wing, increasingly afraid of the SPD's rise, bitterly fought these ideas, warning Bassermann repeatedly against making concessions on this issue.

By the same token, then, it would be impossible to discover uniformity in the foreign policy assumptions of the German Liberals, simply because these were related to that sheer variety of attitudes upon domestic politics. [76] To Richter, as to Bebel and Liebknecht, the whole colonial and fleet policy was a 'swindle'; Germany's overseas possessions were worthless, and the pursuit of more simply worsened relations with the other powers; it was also a waste of the taxpayers' money. The fleet bills were especially pernicious, first because it was yet another strategy of the reactionaries to develop a militarism that was freed from the Reichstag's financial control, and secondly because Tirpitz's strategy was aimed directly at England. [77] In the years around the turn of the century, Richter's dogmatic stand against *any* naval increases and overseas expansion increased his isolation from the other left-wing Liberal parties with the exception of the Württemberg People's Party. Apart from the negative calculation of not wishing to be regarded as 'unpatriotic', people such as Barth, Brentano, Siemens and their friends welcomed the growth of Germany as a world *commercial* power because it would further undermine the country's agrarian backwardness, and because the interest groups allied to the left-Liberals (Hanseatic merchants, international finance, shipping, export-oriented industries) were eager for fresh markets and also eager to obtain naval protection in overseas waters. Nevertheless, this stance did *not* imply that they were anti-British. If the Boer War embarrassed such Liberals (as it had done the SPD leadership), they were quick to argue that there was a difference between the jingoism of Chamberlain and the essentially peaceful, free-trading British people; and by the later stages of the war Barth, Brentano and Mommsen were taking steps to counter the press warfare which had blown up between the nationalists in each country, and to destroy the arguments of the protectionists. In the same manner, left-Liberal circles were by far the most prominent supporters of all the post-1905 efforts at Anglo-German reconciliation; quite a few of them were members of the pacifist movement; and they were also advocates of a naval limitations agreement. It is true that they continued to support a German colonial policy, especially after one of their number, Dernburg, became Colonial Director; but this was because they expected, not conquests, but a more active commercial development of existing colonies, going hand in hand with British enterprise and capital. Yet if these circles were not anglophobes, they always lacked the power and – as patriotic intensity mounted in the decade before 1914 – the will to frustrate anti-British policies and to stand out openly against fleet increases.[78]

The attitude of the 'social-imperialist' Liberals to Britain was, therefore, a bone of contention in their otherwise close relationship with the left-Liberals. Perhaps the best example here is the quarrel between the anglophile Brentano and his associate Naumann, who by 1900 was writing of the 'certainty' of a war with Britain. To the intellectual advocates of the primacy of *Machtpolitik*, a clash between the rising power and the established one was inevitable; it arose (as their arguments in the previous section show) from fundamental economic processes. Germany, Weber argued, must recognise 'one fundamental fact: the unchangeable eternal struggle of men with men on the earth as it actually occurs' – and, in this case, against the power which stood in Germany's way. The firmness of their intent was perhaps best shown by Naumann's reply to the vexed question of *how* a great colonial empire could be acquired: 'by peace treaties after successful naval wars'. On occasions, the language was modified: all that Germany sought, the *Kathedersozialisten* and neo-Rankean historians intimated, was a restoration in the global equilibrium – yet the meaning behind such political euphemisms remained the same: Britain had to be displaced from her maritime 'monopoly'. In the immediate pre-1914 period, however, a realist such as Weber could appreciate the need to carry out *Weltpolitik* in co-operation with Britain rather than to follow the prescriptions of the Navy League.[79]

The party which most persistently pressed for an energetic colonial and naval policy against 'English arrogance' was the National Liberals. Tirpitz could always reckon upon them to respond enthusiastically to every announcement of a further naval increase; Bülow and Bethmann Hollweg could play for the National Liberal vote by appeals to the 'Bismarckian tradition' and national honour; and the *Weltanschauung* of the Pan-Germans and the Navy League was most regularly articulated by the party in the Reichstag. In part, this no doubt derived – as Kehr suggested – from industrial interest groups close to the party, which were to benefit from naval orders and/or were engaged in competition with British rivals in domestic and foreign markets; but as was seen above, the attitude of the German business world towards Britain was a mixed one.[80] The driving force behind the anglophobic stance of many National Liberals who had no direct links with industry was psychological and political, rather than strictly economic. As a party which did not possess a uniform socio-economic or doctrinal base and which threatened to be rent asunder over issues such as social and constitutional reform, its leaders found in patriotic appeals the necessary emotional 'cement' to preserve unity among their diverse and wandering flock; their constant rhetoric about national solidarity and attacks upon 'sectional interests' are, therefore, to be seen as a conscious effort to mobilise the Protestant *Mittelstand* electorally by appealing to the one issue which was not contentious and on which, indeed, that electorate was already demanding action and leadership. As one scholar has acutely remarked, 'The principle of national interest above party interest – *Das Vaterland über die Parteien* – offered welcome refuge from the material struggle.'[81] Psychologically, the individuals who constituted the party's following seem to have responded to this sort of appeal – as at least the election results of 1893 and 1907 suggest – whereas many of them had become 'non-political' on other issues. There were, in other words, good reasons for the National Liberal Party to identify itself as a supporter of a 'strong' national party towards Britain – and towards many other states, for that matter.

## CONSERVATIVE RESPONSES

The closest equivalents on the British side to the National Liberals, and to the Liberal-imperialists of the Weber/Naumann sort, were actually to be located within a certain sub-group of the Unionist Party. This does not imply, however, that the British Conservatives as a whole were in a similar position to the German Liberal groups. In the first place, the former had gained (just like Bismarck's *Kartell*) from divisions in their opponents' ranks: Gladstone's concentration upon Home Rule, the inner feuds for the Liberal leadership and over a new Liberal policy in the 1890s, and the tactical adherence of both the Whigs under Devonshire and the 'industrial' radicals under Chamberlain had enhanced the electoral strength of the Conservatives, even if the British Right became a less coherent group of bedfellows than hitherto. Yet even when Tariff Reform brought these fissures into the open, and mistakes in policy (the 1902 Education Act, 'Chinese labour') alienated groups of supporters, the movement as a whole was not suffering from long-term social and demographic trends. Redistribution, and the nature of rural society, kept the county seats in Tory hands; the increase in white-collar workers, and the growth of suburbia, allowed the party a large share in the city and 'commuter' constituencies; working-class deference, and regional anti-Catholicism, together with the appeal and organisation of Chamberlain, kept many parts of the midlands and Lancashire in Unionist hands; and, apart from the 1906 election, the Conservatives always held more than half of the London county seats.[82]

If the electoral position generally gave comfort to the Conservatives, why did the party begin to exhibit the fissures and in-fighting which had seemed such a Liberal monopoly after 1886? The first, and still the most valid reason, is *external* pressure. By the 1890s, that long-term trend of Britain's relative decline as a great power had become so obvious to many in the party, and it could no longer be ascribed – as was the usual habit in 1868–74 and 1880–5 – to Gladstonian incompetence. Salisbury's unruffled, slow-moving approach to diplomatic problems provoked rising criticism from within and outside the party; and it was not stilled by the advent of Balfour, whose ability to see at least two sides to every case was regarded as a weakness, not a strength. As shown above, the Unionist government's handling of the China crisis, the Boer War, the Baghdad Railway negotiations and the Venezuelan affair of 1902–3 was strongly criticised by arch-imperialists demanding a more decisive and a more 'national' stance. Although such internal criticism is understandable by itself, the composition of this *Fronde* also merits investigation. A considerable number of them had originally been middle-class Liberals or at least come from a Liberal background: Chamberlain is the leading example here, but it was true of Milner and Arnold White (who stood as Liberal candidates in 1885 and 1886 respectively), and of Strachey, Spenser Wilkinson, Ashley, Spring-Rice, Saunders at Berlin, F. S. Oliver (author of *Ordeal by Battle*) and many others. But it was also perhaps a 'generational' phenomenon, since there were younger Tory peers as well as activists such as Garvin, Maxse, Page Croft, Gwynne and Amery in this movement against the 'mandarins' and the 'fuddy-duddies'. 'All these past-60 politicians, bar Joe [Chamberlain] . . . must go', thought Milner. After all, argued Maxse's *National Review*, 'An assemblage of sexagenarians . . . who are bound by the shibboleths of a bygone era . . . is not the kind of body to reorganise the nation.'[83]

The differences between the two 'ideal-types' was nicely characterised at the turn of the year 1894–5, when Salisbury penned those famous lines about the state of British politics which seem to typify his fatalistic, resigned attitude:

Governments can do so little and prevent so little nowadays. Power has passed from the hands of Statesmen, but I should be very much puzzled to say into whose hands it has passed. It is all pure drifting. As we go down stream, we can occasionally fend off a collision; but where are we going?[84]

Yet at virtually the same time the key figure of the *other* sort of right-winger, Joseph Chamberlain, was privately complaining that neither Salisbury, nor Devonshire, nor Balfour had made 'one single creative or suggestive idea from beginning to end' in all their speeches that session; 'there is not the slightest intimation of a practical consistent policy of their own'. He, on the other hand, had been doing all in his power 'to define and popularise a [social] Programme, which may be at the same time perfectly safe yet popular'.[85] With these words 'creative', 'practical' and 'popular', Chamberlain had summed up much of the distinction between himself and the more traditional Conservatives, whose politics, he felt, had none of those attributes. And the retort of the traditionalists was nicely captured by the fourth Marquis of Salisbury's pained disapproval, as noted above,[86] of the 'catastrophical' theory of politics: the argument that only radical changes would ward off the impending disasters was not attractive to the true Conservative.

Thus, whereas the 'old' Right preferred pragmatic adjustments in foreign policy and rather minimal changes internally, the 'new' Right was willing to consider drastic changes in foreign policy (as witness the attempts for a German alliance in 1898–1901, and the later pressure for a full commitment to France prior to 1914) *and* to be much more active in domestic politics.

Preserving the *status quo*, or what Chamberlain called 'obstructive' conservatism, was no longer possible: 'you cannot do with any party or any policy which is not essentially progressive'.[87] To him and to his followers, the relative decline of British power was obviously economic in origin, but any campaign to alter that trend could not content itself with industrial measures alone – even if this was a major feature of Tariff Reform propaganda. It was also necessary to grapple with the social condition of the nation, less out of any philanthropic concern than out of the recognition that a healthy and contented populace was the soundest basis for an effective great power policy. The Boer War revelations about the poor health of the country's manhood sent a shock-wave through the establishment. An interdepartmental committee was set up to inquire into the 'physical deterioration' of the nation. The interest in eugenics increased. *Kulturpessimisten* like Arnold White and H. W. Wilson wrote about 'racial decay', the 'putrifying' degeneracy of the city-dwellers, the poor food and housing conditions of the masses, and so on.[88] 'Unemployment', Lyttelton Gell informed Milner, 'is only the first warning of the terrible, long-drawn slow decadence involved in starving down the Population and Capital of the Imperial Headquarters [i.e. Britain] to the Insular level. Yet we cannot produce leaders. We are paralysed by the dead hand of Social Conservatism, which has no faith, foresight, or policy.'[89] Alarmed by this situation, the 'new' Right grappled with the issue of social reform, sometimes joining with the Left on common ground (for example, the 1906 Bill to permit the feeding of poor schoolchildren to be charged to the local rates), but usually preferring to link a programme of old age pensions, national insurance and health improvements to the Tariff Reform campaign. The intimate link between external and internal events was also urged upon the party by a figure such as Roberts, who wrote in his *Address to the Nation* that

> [Unionists must have a constructive policy] above all as to the two problems that are the most pressing and the most vital – Social Reform and National Defence . . . The conditions amid which millions of our people are living appear to me to make it natural that they should not care a straw under what rule they may be called upon to dwell, and I can quite understand their want of patriotic feeling . . . Social Reform is a preliminary to any thorough system of National Defence.[90]

Of course, it was not simply the external challenge which motivated this platform of 'imperialism and social reform'. After 1906, if not earlier, Unionists could see that it would be necessary to hit at the alternative strategies being offered to the British public by the Liberals and by the Labour Party itself. For quite some time, the chief target was the free-trading, 'Little England' liberalism of the Campbell-Bannerman sort, the 'purblind cosmopolitans' who reduced the strength of the armed forces and were friends of the Irish, the alien immigrant and the German 'dumper'. However, with the Labour Party established as a voting block in Parliament, and with the details released of Lloyd George's budget, the main enemy became 'socialism' – which the Right used not with scientific precision, but as a term of abuse:

## BRITONS, CHOOSE BETWEEN EMPIRE AND SOCIALISM

Are we to stand under the *Union Jack*, like our Fathers before us, for the
Power, Glory and Welfare of Great Britain and her Empire,
or
Are we to hoist the *Red Flag* of Socialism, civil war, and national ruin at
the bidding of Mr. Lloyd George?[91]

Liberalism was 'dying', noted one of the key 'ideas-men' of the new Right;
socialism was the 'only active coherent creed in the field'; and the alternative to
set against it was '*constructive* Imperialism'. It was vital to provide 'the working
man with a permanent alternative to a Labour Party committed to Socialism,
little Englandism and a variety of other theories with which he has no real
sympathy'.[92] Nevertheless, if an upset in the social order was to be resisted for
its own sake, it was even more detestable because of the effect it would have on
Britain's 'proper' external policy. As Milner, in the midst of the crisis over the
People's Budget and House of Lords, privately put it, 'National Defence is
more important than any of the things we are fighting about, and my principal
reason for wishing to get the Liberals out is that they are even more apathetic
about it than the Unionists'.[93]

This was why Chamberlain's idea of Tariff Reform acted as a catalyst – and
appeared as the ideal solution – to these new Conservatives searching for an
answer to Britain's external *and* internal problems. As Amery put it,

> on a stationary economic basis all attempts to deal with imperial and social
> problems resolved themselves in a vicious circle. In imperial matters you
> are either ruined by taxation or else driven into war and deprived of your
> empire. In social matters you have to face distress and possible revolution
> on the individualist plan; or on the socialist plan, relieve the sufferings of
> one class by piling the burden on the others.[94]

Protection, on the other hand, strengthened industries, cut unemployment,
reduced the appeal of socialism, dealt a death-blow to *laissez-faire* liberalism
and ensured that the state had both the industrial sinews and the finances to
pay for its defence budget and social reforms. State intervention was thus far
less abhorrent to this circle than to traditional free-traders and the businessmen who had abandoned the Liberal Party. Indeed, while the latter trend
strengthened conservatism's electoral base in many English constituencies, it
was often deprecated by the imperialist intellectuals. 'The Unionist party',
Garvin complained to Maxse, 'has suffered extremely in the last twenty years
by absorbing the middle classes, and it is much less vital and daring in that
sphere of social reform than it was when it passed the Factory Acts, when
Randolph Churchill's Tory Democratic campaign was at its height, and when
Mr. Chamberlain's Unionist radicalism was fresh.'[95] And a few years later, in
another private letter, Garvin gave an eye-opening explanation of what he
meant:

In the last three weeks I have seen the Socialists face to face for the first time in many years. I am amazed. It is not a new party. It is a new religion. It is getting all the young men who will be coming on the voters' register in a year or two. Nothing but a much greater constructive programme than we started with three years ago will save us now; and we want men of vision and thought and sincerity and fearless power, understanding the people, believing in the people, rejoicing more to be with the people than to be among fashionable audiences, and able to talk to the people about the conditions of their lives. A new light has broken in upon me and I see that unless there is a complete reformation soon in our methods and spirit the vast social movements of the future will sweep right past us.[96]

It is not necessary to belabour this point further. It is clear that the 'new' Right detested traditional liberalism, and also came to detest – and to fear – what it termed 'Lib-Lab socialism'; but it did not fear the working classes or contact with them or a bargain with their leaders. Labour militancy, Chamberlain had thought in 1893, 'can easily be overcome by a political leader with a genuine sympathy with the working class and a practical programme'; and in 1906 he wrote, 'I see no reason why the Labour Party should be more hostile to us than to the Radicals.'[97] When this hope was dashed, Amery and others sought to create a Trade Union Tariff Reform League or even a 'Unionist Labour Party', which would 'send a certain number of representatives to Parliament to counteract the claim continually made by the present Labour Party that they are the only true representatives of the working man's special point of view'. But these ideas, noted Amery sourly, 'never secured from Conservative head-quarters the attention or support they deserved'.[98] In the same way, he, Maxse, Roberts and others had favoured a reform of the House of Lords – involving the 'swamping' of the influence of the hereditary peers – since the time of the Boer War, and did not have the same views as either the cautious Balfour–Lansdowne group or the 'backwoodsmen' during the 1910 crisis. The diehard peers were not all, in fact, simple reactionaries who only attended the House of Lords to block Liberal reform legislation: many were politically active and intelligent, concerned about external developments, willing to work out internal reforms, and somewhat embarrassed at being forced to fight on this issue. Milner, for example, had been contemplating a break with the Conservative Party in 1907 because of its 'anti-Socialism' and 'middle-class timidity, lethargy and narrow mindedness', but felt forced back into the fold by Lloyd George's clever counter-attack; and, after the House of Lords crisis was over, he urged the younger Radicals to withhold their attacks upon the party leadership until the Unionists were back in power – and could then move forward on 'Ireland, Second Chamber, Plural voting, redistribution, – all'.[99]

Traditionalists among the party not only disliked this growing move towards state interventionism, but also joined with the ex-Liberal businessmen to form the Liberty and Property Defence League.[100] Many right-wingers bitterly attacked the Liberal government's spending priorities, arguing that battle-ships came before old age pensions; and they were joined in this by arch-imperialists and navalists like H. W. Wilson, White and Maxse, who were much more lukewarm on social policy than Garvin, Amery and Milner.[101] The willingness of both the New Liberals and the Tariff Reformers to contemplate large increases in public spending was especially disliked by the financially orthodox such as Cromer, Strachey and Bernard Mallet, who consequently found themselves crushed between a radicalised liberalism and a radicalised toryism; and, whereas Chamberlain argued that Tariff Reform was the only constructive 'alternative . . . to socialism', the free-trade Unionists felt that their rivals' eagerness for imperialist collectivism was a major step *towards* socialism.[102] Moreover, like many traditional Liberals, the Cromer group held that financial retrenchment actually enhanced Britain's military strength by preserving her fiscal reserves instead of diverting capital to such 'unproductive' fields as old age pensions and mass armies (the navy, as a national 'insurance' force, was always excepted).[103] Other traditionalists shrank back from what the fourth Marquess of Salisbury termed 'Milnerism: that is to say, a complete change of method in our government from the English system to the German system', especially to compulsory military service, which 'In England might produce a revolution'.[104] It was ironic, to say the least, that the circles most obsessed with the need for drastic changes to meet the German challenge were so frequently pointing to Germany as a model.

In the years before 1914 it is possible to detect a rise in the influence of these newer Tories, obscured though it often was by the general increase of right-wing intransigence to 'Lib-Lab' policies. Balfour's succession to the premiership had already provoked rumblings about the 'Hotel Cecil', but it was not until the Tariff Reform campaign was under way that the discontent became obvious. The nationwide organisation set up by Chamberlain to agitate for protection was regarded by the Conservative Party leadership as 'a wholly mischievous institution' which was in fact rivalling the official party bodies in the constituencies; the tariff reformers were also in control of the Liberal Unionist organisation; and the greater part of the Unionist press followed Chamberlain rather than Balfour.[105] Furthermore, the sweeping Liberal victory of 1906 did not affect the Chamberlainites so badly, and they secured around eighty seats whereas the 'free-fooders' had about thirty and the Balfourite 'middle party' about fifty.[106] Chamberlain's stroke then deprived this group of leadership but the activists felt in no way constrained by loyalty to the party chiefs whom they no longer trusted. 'Tariff Reformers should be continually showing their teeth and making themselves thoroughly disagreeable to the powers-that-be', Maxse told Amery. 'No movement has ever been promoted by mere amiability.' The Chief Whip nervously reported that there was a growing preference in the party for 'an obstinate, hard-hitting and brutal pugilist rather than a courteous, gentlemanly fencer' as their leader, and soon the 'confederates' had launched a campaign to expel the free trade Unionists from the party.[107] Even in foreign affairs, it is worth noting, a certain distance separated the radicals from the traditionalists. The party leadership was generally unwilling to assault Grey's foreign policy; and, fearing electoral unpopularity, they did not embrace the cause of the National Service League, which so attracted Milner, Roberts, Amery, Maxse and the other hyper-nationalists. The great feuds at this time over naval policy and leadership, involving not only the Fisher-Beresford quarrel but also the defection from the Navy League of discontented right-wingers who then formed the more extreme Imperial Maritime League, once again produced differences within the Conservative movement.

If these disputes were temporarily stilled by the constitutional crisis of 1910, they arose again in reaction to defeat, and by the following year Maxse and his companions were at last successful in their 'Balfour Must Go' campaign. Yet although Bonar Law was regarded as 'their man' by the newer Tories, he himself recognised that it was vital to preserve party unity – an aim made considerably easier by the revival of the Irish question – and he refused either to expel the free-traders or to tie the party to the single issue of Tariff Reform. United in their dislike of the Liberals, *and* in their general mistrust of Germany, the Conservatives remained to the end divided on many points of domestic policy.[108]

While British conservatism was not keen to abandon its Disraelian claim to represent the working masses, German conservatism had taken an entirely different route. Measured simply in parliamentary terms, the story of the two German parties is one of steady, unrelenting decline.[109] The Free Conservatives (*Reichspartei*) had already been losing ground to the more 'orthodox' agrarian party since the late 1870s, apart from their short-lived success in the 1887 Reichstag election; by 1912, they had been reduced to only twelve seats. The German Conservative Party shared a similar fate; in 1912 it only possessed forty-three seats, compared with the eighty it controlled in 1887. Even taken together, the Conservatives had fewer voting supporters by 1912 than either the National Liberals or the Centre, and one-third as many as the SPD. Yet the reaction of the agrarians to this trend was one which both fascinated and amazed contemporaries, whose anticipations of what would happen were based upon precedents set in Britain and elsewhere in the Western world; instead of compromising with the up-and-coming orders, the Junkers resolved to oppose them. In many respects, their methods were very modern, for they were quite willing to change their 'political style' in order to achieve their desired ends. Instead of regarding themselves as unquestioned supporters of the Prussian king and his ministers, they pulled out of that pro-government tradition. 'We must refuse all honorary offices', one of their new leaders asserted. 'We must pursue a policy solely dictated by our own interest.'[110] Consequently, the agrarians proceeded to organise the most vociferous and persistent pressure group of all in Wilhelmine Germany, the *Bund der Landwirte*. By seeking to mobilise all those whose livelihoods depended upon the land, by threatening to deploy the voting power of this body against any Reichstag candidate opposing their aims, and by being willing to embrace every demagogic art – from exploiting the anti-Semitism among the peasantry and handicraftsmen, to reforming their own ideology so as to make it less obviously Prussian and much more national *völkisch* – they gave to German conservatism a hard, radical, anti-modernist edge which had no equivalent in Britain. What was more, the German Conservative leaders felt this distinct pressure from below and knew that, to maintain their own position and the

347

party's coherence, they would have to go with this 'radicalisation'. It was Heydebrand's achievement to absorb these impulses into the party; but the price was a marked rise in resistance to compromise with other social groups inside Germany and the increasing habit of acting – at least in the Reichstag – as an opposition party to the German government.

Given this basic stance, the attitude of the Conservatives to the political problems of the day was easy to predict. The mere mention of constitutional reform, for example, was sufficient to stiffen their backs, for the very simple reason that it was only in Prussia and other states with a restricted franchise (usually of a three-class sort) that they retained control of the legislatures. It was therefore vital to block any moves to change the Prussian franchise system; to fight all notions of a redistribution of seats to take account of the far larger number of voters in urban constituencies; and to become the most fervent defenders of the fiscal and legislative autonomy of the individual German states, and of the powers of the Bundesrat (where Prussia predominated) over the Reichstag (where anti-agrarians predominated). This intense concern with preserving the *status quo* – and, on occasions, calling for the abolition of the empire's 'too-liberal' suffrage – explains why the agrarians defended a monarch whose passion for modernisation, technology, a big fleet and a grandiose foreign policy they bitterly detested. When, for example, the *Daily Telegraph* crisis erupted, the Conservatives could not allow their own criticism of the Kaiser to extend to support for the Reichstag's claim to enhance itself at the expense of the Crown. For better or worse, they were tied to the Hohenzollern dynasty – but they were never subordinate to it and expected it to support all their pretensions in return.

In the matter of revenue collection and budgetary allocations, the Conservatives were equally hard-nosed. From 1879 onwards, the greater part of them (although certainly not all farmers) had seen in high agricultural tariffs the only means for economic salvation: Caprivi's fate was a warning to all who would ignore this pressure, and only with the coming of the 'Bülow tariff' did they rest content. On the other hand, the Conservatives resisted all suggestions of direct taxation by the Reichstag, partly because the most obvious taxes would be upon income, property and inheritance. As one Prussian minister remarked, it was impossible to place 'the tax screw' in the hands of the Reichstag without enraging 'the loyal and monarchically inclined population'.[111] The most notorious example of this Conservative unwillingness to pay came in 1908, when the Reich's budgetary deficit was so large that the Treasury demanded the raising of an extra 500 million marks (£25 million), of which one-fifth would come from a direct inheritance tax: at this, the agrarians preferred to break up the Bülow bloc and force the Chancellor's resignation rather than concede the crucial principle.

It goes almost without saying that the German Conservatives had no developed policy of social reforms. This is not to imply that they totally ignored the matter, but that they identified the 'social problem' as yet one further consequence of untrammelled industrial capitalism, which was also responsible – as one Bavarian farmers' journal put it – for 'sending thousands with open arms towards Social Democracy'.[112] These sentiments were repeatedly articulated by such Conservative 'social' theorists as Adolf Wagner and Karl Oldenberg, who referred with Carlylean gloom to 'the economic and social contrasts between property and labour, employer and worker, rich and poor'.[113] To most anti-modernist ideologues and agrarian circles, however, their society could only return to its organic, 'wholesome' state if it abandoned the foolhardy pursuit of modernisation; and if the de-industrialisation of Germany itself was impossible, then the government should at least take steps – by higher tariffs, better credit, subsidies, anti-*laissez-faire* legislation, and so on – to preserve such 'healthy' parts of the nation as the landowners, the declining crafts and the peasantry. The debate upon the 'social problem' in the cities was thus neatly turned into one about support for agriculture. Any suggestion of solving the social question by direct taxation and a redistribution of income, as the 'new' Liberals were proposing in Britain, was anathema: it offended virtually every canon in the Junkers' political code.

The consequence of all this was that the agrarians' attitude towards Britain, and towards a possible clash with that country, was rather complex. One can leave out of the reckoning for the moment those *grand seigneurs* – often Silesian, sometimes south German – who adhered to a more traditional aristocratic stance, who were cosmopolitan enough to appreciate English culture, and who collectively were (in one scholar's phrase) 'more a magnates' club than an instrument of political resolution'.[114] It is the hard core of the politically radicalised and poorer Junkers, and the peasant leagues, which are of concern here. To all these, virtually without exception, England was regarded with dislike and, in some cases, with venomous hatred. Measured in *direct* economic terms, this made little sense: the export of sugar and other agricultural produce to Britain was still very considerable, and the import of tea, coal and certain types of cloth and farm machinery from there offered no rivalry to German agrarian interests. The real reason for the animosity was that England still remained a symbol of all that might happen to German society if the hated course of industrialisation and parliamentarisation continued unchecked. The agrarian position was thus the exact opposite of those who, like Bernstein or Richter or Brentano, looked for varied reasons to England as a 'model'. This also meant that the debate upon Anglo-German relations could not be separated from – and, to most protagonists, sprang directly from – the quarrel over German modernisation.[115] After the turn away from Caprivi's 'liberal' course in the mid-1890s, this became very clear indeed: in the Reichstag debates over the *Hamburger Nachrichten*'s 'revelations', for example, Liebknecht, Richter and Haussmann urged good relations with Britain, whereas Manteuffel and Kardorff openly stated their dislike of any intimacy with a parliamentary state, with the hypocritical *Händler*, and demanded instead closer contact with agrarian and monarchical Russia.[116]

It was around the turn of the century, however, that the Conservatives' open dislike of Britain probably reached its peak, being occasioned by two events: the Boer War, and then the interaction between the Tariff Reform campaign and the parallel quarrels in Germany over the proposed Bülow tariff. The identity claimed by the agrarians between themselves and the Boers has been noticed by many historians, and needs little repetition here: as the president of the *Bund der Landwirte* claimed in 1901, 'we feel deeply that the struggle which is being fought out there is only another form of the struggle we are carrying on . . . The results [are] the same, ruined peasant farms, ruined peasants.'[117] However far-fetched a comparison, there is no doubt that it was widely held, and that it lay at the root of that bitter criticism of the Kaiser's 'pro-English' policies which so alarmed Bülow at this time. It also allowed the anglophobia of the Conservative élites to merge into the tensions and resentments of the lower agrarian orders: thus, at frequent meetings of the *Bauernbund* in Bavaria, mass resolutions were passed against 'Jewish capitalism' and egoistical *Manchestertum* for trampling upon the healthiest part of the South African peoples, the Boer farmer. As for the rabid anti-Semites, they mounted a frenzied attack upon that 'thorough Jew', Cecil Rhodes, for crushing their 'race-related' brothers. It was the anti-Semites who were chiefly responsible for organising the visit of Boer generals to Berlin in October 1902, and it was the faction's leader in the Reichstag, Liebermann, who shocked even the other anti-British parties by openly describing Chamberlain as 'the most infamous rogue who ever profaned God's earth'.[118] To one worried observer of this trend, the strength of the anglophobe agitation was not less than that of the 'Bulgarian Horrors' movement of 1876 in Britain; in both cases, an outside event had catalysed deep-rooted internal impulses.[119]

It was from this standpoint that the agrarians approached the reports of attempts to create imperial preference. Such a development, especially when advocated by their *bête noire*, Joseph Chamberlain, could be instantly used for propaganda purposes. It proved that even the free-trading British were admitting that the era of Cobden was over; on the other hand, it also signalled an intensification between the great powers in their economic struggle for supremacy, and reinforced the agrarians' argument that Germany should be made self-sufficient in foodstuffs – which could only happen, of course, when the nation's tariffs were raised to adequate levels. Finally, since the British government's denunciation of the 1865 trade treaty, and the extra duties levied upon German goods by Canada, were both a blow to German pride and to the German economy, Berlin should forthwith take all sorts of strong countermeasures, ignoring the cries of the cosmopolitan and 'un-national' traders who were pleading for a compromise.[120]

When it came to a question of the Conservatives' support of an anti- British colonial and foreign policy, however, there was much less unanimity. The Free Conservatives, with their many close links to heavy industry and their identification since Bismarck's time as *regierungstreu*, were strongly in favour: indeed, the danger with them was that their mouthpieces (such as the *Berliner Neueste Nachrichten* and the *Post*) would be pushing for fleet increases at a time when it was politically or diplomatically unsuitable. On the other hand, there were Junkers who echoed the sentiments of those Bavarian peasants who had declared themselves to be against Jewish-Liberal England *and* against German navalism! The fleet issue, however much it attracted the support of the middle classes, was most unsuitable 'cement' for Miquel's *Sammlungspolitik*, symbolising as it did the modern, industrialised, outward-looking face of Germany. Time and again, therefore, spokesmen for the agrarian interest in the

Reichstag referred to the 'detestable fleet' and insisted that the country's real strength lay on the land, not at sea. Nevertheless, outright opposition to an issue which the Kaiser was so bent upon was not possible for the party as a whole, especially when it was so prone to emphasise its own 'national' character and to denigrate the patriotism of others. To some agrarians, this was a heaven-sent opportunity to demand a *quid pro quo* in the form of higher tariffs, and their contributions to the Reichstag debates on the Fleet Laws (especially in 1900) were chiefly descriptions of the plight of agriculture: only the most solemn promises of the government on the future tariff increases were sufficient to cause many Conservatives to swallow their dislike of the fleet. Yet there also existed Adolph Wagner and other preachers of *Machtpolitik* who wished – without upsetting the balance between agriculture and industry – to see Germany have a large fleet and settler-colonies overseas, if need be by standing up to British arrogance. 'Power policy with a feudal accent', as Kehr termed it, made up in emotion what it lacked in logic.[121]

After the higher tariffs were established, many Conservatives forgot the earlier *quid pro quo* arrangement, and their coolness turned to resentment once it was seen how much the 1906 and 1908 naval supplements were deranging the country's already unbalanced budget. In December 1907 Tirpitz noted that the agrarians regarded the navy 'with a completely cold heart'; and nine months later he deduced from an article in the *Kreuz-Zeitung* that 'influential forces are at work to limit the development of the fleet'.[122] In actual fact, this opposition would have been much more substantial had it received any encouragement from the army, which the agrarians revered as the true bulwark of Prusso-German might; but during the first ten or twelve years of *Weltpolitik* the army had been content, for technical and domestic-political reasons, to keep a low profile and not to challenge the massive expansion of this rival service. With the growing 'encirclement' of Germany and the inability of the Reich leadership to achieve recognition as a world power by 1911, a reaction set in: a European war, whether offensively or defensively begun, seemed much more likely than before, and the army required large increases in men and materials if Schlieffen's plan was to stand a chance of success. When, to popularise this trend, the *Wehrverein* was founded, it was noticeable how much more enthusiastically the diehard agrarians greeted it than they had done the heavy industry-financed *Flottenverein*. Britain was no friend of Germany, to be sure, but only the extreme nationalist and Pan-German elements among the Conservatives looked with relish to a clash of rival fleets in the North Sea.[123]

## THE CENTRE PARTY

The steady decline in the number of Reichstag seats held by all the Conservative and Liberal parties (from a total of 201 in 1890 to 144 in 1912), and the corresponding growth in the SPD's hold (from 35 to 110), enhanced the importance of the Centre Party, which straddled these two blocs and appeared to possess adamantine electoral strength. It survived the assaults of 1907

351

intact, for example, and even when Catholic workers turned to the SPD in the 1912 election it still retained 91 seats. In part, its strength was maintained by the built-in bias towards the sparsely populated rural constituencies; but the chief reason probably lay in the ability of its leaders to readjust to the changing circumstances of the post-Bismarckian era. Recognising – not through any particular intuition but simply because of pressure from below – that the new age was one centred upon mass politics and interest groups, the party responded not only by articulating the demands of their various groups of supporters, but also by creating organisations which would give them a sense of identity. By 1914, there existed almost 450 pro-Centre newspapers; for the Catholic industrial worker, there were the Christian trade unions; for the peasants, the Catholic farmers' leagues; for the Catholic youth, a youth movement. In addition, there was the more general *Volksverein für das katholische Deutschland*, which claimed 800,000 members by the eve of war. Moreover, these bodies were usually effective where it mattered, in the localities.[124] On this substantial base, could not the Centre become the power-brokers of Imperial Germany, compelling the government to pay attention to more than simply the Junkers and heavy industrialists?

In actual fact, while the Centre *did* play a decisive role in the politics of the Reichstag from about 1895 onwards, it was largely a negative one: it tended to prevent things from happening or, at the most, to modify and delay the impact of various measures. Personality had something to do with this; the Centre Party never threw up another Windhorst, nor did it produce a leader with the unbending dislike of the *persönliches Regiment* which characterised Richter or Bebel. Moreover, in their search to make the party less confessional and more national, Centre politicians such as Lieber, Hertling and Peter Spahn were often anxious to pose as responsible statesmen who weighed up the 'common good': in effect, this meant that they almost always sought a compromise with the imperial government.[125] The second, and no doubt the most important reason for the Centre's role as a political trimmer was its own diffuse membership. Bismarck's claim that the party portrayed 'all the colours of the political rainbow from the most extreme right to the radical left',[126] actually became less true as time went on: the clerical and aristocratic elements in the party declined; representatives from heavy industry and *Grosskapital*, who had been very few in any case, found little appeal in a movement which attacked their business activities; and, most important of all, the Catholic industrial working classes became increasingly disenchanted with a party which paid but lip-service to social reforms and concentrated instead upon appeasing the demands of the peasant-farmers, small merchants and shopkeepers who made up the bulk of the Centre's supporters. By the eve of the First World War, it was overwhelmingly a party of the Catholic *Mittelstand*, with around three-quarters of its deputies coming from constituencies where agriculture and small business predominated.[127] Nevertheless – and this was the important point – the Centre's leaders remained keen to demonstrate that they represented virtually all classes in the nation.

The interlocking issues of social reform, constitutional change, taxation and state interventionism illustrate the shiftiness of the party superbly. Ostensibly, the Centre's record on social issues was a creditable one. Yet, since their voting strength really was in the countryside, the leadership could never think of coming forward with a full programme of social reforms: besides provoking a break with its pro-government allies in the Reichstag, it would arouse the fury of the independent farmers, retailers and the like. The party's political priorities were made clear during the debate upon the Bülow tariff. Having been thoroughly frightened by the way the *Bund der Landwirte* and the Bavarian *Bauernbund* were attracting the Catholic peasantry, the Centre felt that it simply had to outbid those organisations in demonstrating its advocacy of higher food tariffs, regardless of how this might hit the standard of living of the urban workers; yet, seeking to be all things to all men, it then asked for part (actually, about one-eighth) of the increased revenues to be devoted to a widows' and orphans' insurance scheme.[128]

In the heated issue of the suffrage, the Centre was once again ambivalent. It was strongly opposed to Stumm's notion of restricting eligibility to vote in Reichstag elections, but it paid only lip-service to the idea of reforming the three-class Prussian franchise and was content to await a move from the government, aware no doubt that such a step was hardly likely to be forthcoming. Taxation, however, exercised them much more. Lieber and other leaders did refer to the need for an inheritance tax, but were also aware that the particularist traditions in the party were still strong. The Centre therefore joined the Conservatives in favouring indirect taxation at Reich level – either through tariffs or by fees upon stock market dealings or other movements of capital – yet it also protested against the extreme demands of the *Bund der Landwirte* and thus nimbly avoided incurring the onus for the 1902 tariff increases which were so unpopular among the public. Sensing this mood, the party leaders then judiciously joined with the Left in opposing taxes which would hit 'the ordinary man' – thereby frustrating Bülow's tax reform scheme of 1905. By 1908, however, the Centre was keen both to re-enter the government bloc and to pay back Bülow; and on the latter's proposal for an extension of the inheritance tax it found the ideal issue for opposition. In the quite exceptional financial circumstances of 1912–13, the Centre again reversed its policy and joined with the other parties – with the Conservatives bitterly opposing – in approving a direct Reich property tax to help pay for the military increases.[129]

In view of the above, it was scarcely feasible that the Centre could have a unified approach to *Weltpolitik* in general, or to relations with Britain in particular. During the early 1890s, the party leadership and chief newspapers tended to favour good Anglo-German relations: the Irish question had died down somewhat; there was little direct enthusiasm for colonialism, apart from the matter of protecting Catholic missionaries; Caprivi's pro-British policy (for example, over the Heligoland-Zanzibar treaty) was approved of; and the Centre's far greater concern for Austria-Hungary and dislike of Russia made it welcome the apparent intimacy between London, Berlin and Vienna. During the rest of the 1890s, however, the two main tendencies within the party which were mentioned above – the radicalisation of the Catholic *Mittelstand*, and the attempts of the party leaders to pose as responsible 'national' politicians –

353

began to make their impact in this field too. Since these tendencies were to a large extent contradictory, they made the Centre's attitude towards Britain ever more confused.

Lieber and his colleagues moved only slowly towards a pro-government stance on questions of external policy. Following the Kruger Telegram, for example, their Reichstag speakers were anxious to hear Marschall's soothing words about Anglo-German relations, and also pressed for an assurance that no enormous fleet plans would be laid before them. Yet by the next year, Lieber was already in consultation with the government about terms for the party's support of Tirpitz's first measure;[130] two years later, the Centre was on the whole willing to support the much larger second Navy Law; and it also voted for the additions of 1906 and for later fleet and army increases. If there was some fear that a rejection of the fleet increases would provoke the excitable Wilhelm into ordering a *coup d'état*, this was probably less strong a motive than the desire both to demonstrate that Catholics were 'good Germans', and to enhance their bargaining posture. Moreover, they not only found Bülow and Tirpitz willing to bargain with them but also were impressed by their 'moderation': in 1904-5, they approved of Tirpitz's resistance to the extreme demands of Keim and the Navy League. One feature which does not seem prominent, however, is that of anglophobia, at least in the early years. Centre leaders often deprecated the chauvinistic attacks of the Pan-German League; they welcomed the 1900 Yangtse Treaty, as demonstrating that Britain and Germany could go hand in hand in developing the commerce of China; and, when nationalist circles pressed for higher tariffs upon British goods following the denunciation of the 1865 trade treaty, the Centre pointed out the importance of the economic ties between the two countries.[131] When the Naval Bills were debated, the Centre's speakers tended to concentrate upon the financial aspect, although occasionally they expressed the conviction that it was futile and dangerous to engage in a naval race with Britain. Germany's wars, insisted the *Kölnische Volkszeitung* and *Germania*, would be fought on land. In this respect, the Centre remained very traditional. Erzberger, of course, hardly fits that description, but his own utterances upon England were both confused and second-hand: mingled in with speeches in favour of *Weltpolitik* and criticism of the British for seeking to block this, were private remarks about an 'alliance with England'.[132]

One reason why the party leadership never expressed open enthusiasm for the fleet – and the most compelling reason why they always fastened upon the financial aspects – was their awareness that large segments of the movement opposed *Weltpolitik*. Early in 1898, for example, local party leaders in the Rhineland warned Lieber directly that they would lose working-class members to the SPD if the first Navy Law resulted in higher taxes for the average family. More important still, however, was the bitter opposition of the Bavarian agrarians and others who felt they were losing out as a consequence of Germany's industrialisation: like the *Bund der Landwirte*, these groups hated all efforts by the government to 'modernise' the economy and saw in the *Reichsmarineamt*'s constant references to Germany's growing industry and overseas trade a confirmation of their deepest suspicions.[133] When the first

Navy Law received its second reading, fifty-five Centre deputies voted for it, twenty-six (mainly Bavarians) against, and fifteen had absented themselves; in June 1900, thirty-five deputies voted for the second Navy Law and only nine against, but fifty-six found an excuse to absent themselves. If it was too impolitic to vote against the measure, especially when Bülow was already dangling promises of higher tariffs, the party as a whole showed little enthusiasm for the Kaiser's grand design.

Ironically enough, it was the agrarian, 'anti-modern' element in the Centre which probably possessed the most deeply felt dislike of Britain as the home of *Manchestertum* and all the other evils of rampant capitalism which were now seeping into Germany: to them, as to the *Bund der Landwirte*, the island state was not a direct commercial or military enemy so much as a symbol of unhealthy economic and social trends. Catholic peasant meetings, and their local newspapers, seem to have had as many references to 'overpowering capitalism', 'Jewish finance' and the 'greed of the City of London' as their Protestant equivalents; and, during the Boer War especially, they joined in the general denunciation of British actions. Curiously, then, it was the party leadership, in seeking to be 'national', which supported measures that were going to lead to a worsening in Anglo-German relations, even though few if any of them were outright anglophobes; and it was the economically 'backward' sections of the party which opposed *Weltpolitik*, even if they possessed a greater animosity towards Britain. This would alter somewhat as 1914 approached, as shall be seen: the Centre's leaders, and many of their supporters, were not unaffected by the rising nationalist fervour; votes for a bigger army did not cause so much unrest in the party, even though the peasantry disliked the disturbances caused by conscription; and the sheer expansion of the SPD, and their own *Mittelstand* supporters' detestation of the Socialists, pressed them ever more into the pro-government camp. Indirectly, rather than directly, therefore, the Centre would find itself supporting policies that tended to lead to a clash with Britain; and, given the party's internal dynamics, it was never likely to stand out for some drastic gesture to improve relations. At an individual level, Centre supporters did not flock to join the Pan-German or Navy Leagues or even (except Arenberg) the Colonial Society; but nor were they prominent in the Anglo-German Friendship societies and other private attempts made by the left-Liberals to defuse relations with Britain. In sum, the Centre's 'moderation' meant very little, especially when they generally conceded the *substance* of imperialist and right-wing policies whilst striving to preserve the *appearance* of being much more reasonable. If anyone looked to the Centre to 'Gladstonise' Germany,[134] either in its external or internal aspects, they looked in vain.

## THE BALANCE-SHEET

Is it possible to extricate conclusions from the above comparative analysis which will also remain valid for the increasingly tense international scene and the rising domestic tensions in both countries after, say, 1910? It would be a mistake, certainly, to base one's final conclusion upon a period when the second Moroccan crisis, the SPD electoral gains of 1912 and the impasse over Ulster have not yet been fully discussed. Nevertheless, some main points should already be clear.

The first is the impossibility of simple generalisations about the political characteristics of either nation, for each contained party groupings which favoured imperialism, or social reform, or both, or neither. Given the complexity of the picture, one is compelled to abandon a descriptive assessment and to concentrate instead upon what was achieved in each. When this is done, it will become even clearer that the significant factor is not whether Germany contained certain social reformers or whether Britain possessed reactionaries but rather, what the overall balance of forces was which could combine to pursue one set of policies or another. Even this may be an artificial measuring rod if one takes into account only the political parties, and neglects to assess the influence of the state apparatus as well.[135] But for the purposes of this section, it will suffice to draw conclusions from the party political balance alone.

On this basis, it is impossible to argue that in Britain both imperialist (meaning here: big navy, concern for the balance of power in Europe) and social reform policies were being implemented in the years before 1914. If this was an obvious consequence of a conglomerate Liberal movement being in power, then it was true that the increasingly powerful Chamberlainite wing of the Unionist Party also favoured a strong external policy, and (albeit by means of a tariff system) a 'reformist' social policy. On the German side, the balance was different. A big navy and a big army policy was pursued, and a world mission proclaimed, with either the enthusiastic or the tacit consent of the majority of political parties; but a programme of social reforms, as advocated by the SPD and to a lesser extent by certain left-Liberal and Liberal-imperialist circles, could not win acceptance against the combined opposition of the Conservative, National Liberal and Centre parties. (The Bismarckian scheme of insurance and pensions does not seem to have been welcomed with gratitude, partly because it involved compulsory contributions and partly because it was accompanied by an unrelenting stream of abuse, discrimination and legal actions against the SPD.) In addition, a similar combination of forces had prevented the Reichstag from agreeing to support constitutional reforms.

The best way of measuring these differences, and the similarities, between the British and German responses to the general external and internal trends is to return again to a consideration of the respective budgets – for finance, it is not unfair to say, was the measure of all things. In the British case, central government expenditure rose in every area. By the eve of war, just under £200 million p.a. was being spent, of which a quarter went upon the navy alone (£51 million), whereas army expenditure took a more modest £28·8 million. The remarkable fact, however, was that civil expenditure (of which the most important items now were education, old age pensions and national health insurance) had maintained its slight edge over the navy, and the 1914–15 estimates allowed for a total of £57·0 million in that field. Central government expenditure on the Social Services proper had risen by 630 per cent between 1888 and 1913, admittedly from a very low base.[136] Perhaps the most interesting fact of all was that this expenditure was being more than matched by taxation, rather than increased loans. Indeed, the size of the National Debt had been dropping steadily since the Boer War years, and the £24·5 million voted for 1914–15 for debt services (that is, about 12 per cent of the central government expenditure) contrasted sharply with the 40–50 per cent in the mid-century decades. The government was balancing the budget, then, not by going to the money markets, but by increasing indirect and especially direct taxation. In the year ended March 1914, customs and excise revenue yielded £75 million, but this was not significantly greater than the receipts ten or fifteen years earlier. However, death duties, which brought the Exchequer £6.8 million in 1889–90, produced £27·3 million in 1913–14 – a fourfold increase; and income tax rose at almost the same pace, from £12·7 million to £47·2 million (by the later date, including super-tax). One-quarter of the revenue had come from these two sources in the earlier period; now close to 40 per cent did; and 58 per cent of total revenue came from direct taxes. In addition, liability for income tax only began when a man earned £160 p.a. – in Prussia it began at £45 p.a., Saxony at £20 p.a. – so that few British working men paid this tax at all. To later generations, this might all seem unremarkable. To contemporaries it was an object, variously, of self-congratulation, astonishment or perturbation. The colossal rises in governmental expenditure; the 'unlimited confidence in the efficacy of public action and public money in dealing with social problems'; the newer 'conception of the objects for which taxation may legitimately be imposed'; and the increasingly accepted principles of redistribution of wealth and graduated taxation, were all – according to one of the budgetary experts of this period – 'without a parallel in the fiscal history of great civilised states'.[137]

Whether or not the British pattern really was so unique would require an extensive investigation; only the comparison with Imperial Germany can be pursued here, and that in a very cursory manner, given the fiscal division between the Reich and the individual states. The chief item of expenditure of its central government remained, as ever, the armed forces: in 1913, as in 1900, about 80 per cent of expenditure went to that end. The allocations to the German navy continued to rise, from a yearly average of £10·5 million in 1900–5, to almost £21 million (1909), to £24 million (1913): this still seemed much less than the British Admiralty's budget but – something German navalists did not touch upon, and British radicals scarcely understood – the amount spent upon construction by both navies was much closer, since the voluntary British system demanded much more in wages than German conscripts received. The really startling change, however, came with the alteration in the army's allocation after the second Moroccan crisis: the slow rise in military expenditure – from £33·6 million in 1900 to £40·8 million in 1910 – jumped sharply upwards, and the 1914 army estimates totalled a massive £88·4 million.[138]

The mainstay of central government revenues still remained customs and excise, which provided around £64 million in 1913; other (mainly indirect) taxes and fees brought in £29 million, and loans a mere £7 million. To this total of £100 million was added the £18 million from the individual states, which

357

were bound to 'close the gap' with the Reich's expenditure of £118 million. In earlier years, it is worth noting, the habit of covering the budgetary deficit by recourse to the money market had been much more common: in 1905, over £17 million (nearly 21 per cent) of the Reich's income had come from loans, and in 1909 a full £34 million (28 per cent). On both those occasions, when it was clear that this was having serious economic effects, the government had summoned the courage to introduce new taxes; but this always provoked a bitter political row and, in the latter case, Bülow's fall. The adamant stance of Wermuth, the secretary of the Treasury, against uncovered governmental spending reduced the *pace* of indebtedness after 1910; and the great army increases were paid for in the main by a special, non-recurrent 'defence contribution' of around £40 million, although the additional recurrent expenditure from that measure had to be raised by an unprecedented (and bitterly contested) direct Reich tax on the increase in the value of inherited wealth. The overall trend, however, was unchanged: the central government debt steadily grew, from its 1900 total of £119 million to £260 million by 1913–14. Because of the row made by the Conservatives about direct taxation, armaments continued to be chiefly paid for by the consumer, in indirect taxes, and by future generations, through the growing debt charges. In Britain, by contrast, the panoply of income, super-, estate- and death-duty taxes which obtained by 1914 virtually paid for defence expenditure.

When the total expenditure of the Reich, the states and the localities (*Gemeinde*) are brought together – and then compared with the totals of British central *and* local government spending, the pattern looks much more similar. In Germany, the central government spent only one-third of the total funds in 1913 (£118 million out of £358 million); whereas in Britain the central authorities spent over half (£169 out of £305 million). Inevitably, the proportion allocated to the armed services shrinks, to 25 per cent in Germany and 29 per cent in Britain, the actual sum in each case being £91 million; and the proportion given to the 'social services' and education rises correspondingly, to around 28 per cent (£103 million) in Germany and 33 per cent (£100·8 million) in Britain. In other words, the most noticeable differences between the two countries lay less in their *allocation* of funds than in the way in which *taxes were raised*; and, secondly, in the German practice of floating loans to cover expenditures. In Edwardian Britain, there had been complaints that while the National Debt was falling, the indebtedness of local authorities was climbing rapidly, from £380 million in 1900–1 to £629 million in 1910–11. In Germany, it was not merely the Reich government which preferred to borrow rather than to levy taxes: the indebtedness of the states by 1913–14 was £842 million, and of the *Gemeinde* a further £540 million. The total indebtedness of the German authorities by the eve of war was astronomical to many observers – a cool £1,642 million.[139]

Although some historians have found in the Reichstag's passing of a direct inheritance tax in 1913 a sign of 'reformism', with the possibility of the Conservatives being subjected to similar assaults on their pockets by a combination of the other parties in future years also, it is difficult to see the grounds for such optimism. Far from retreating, the Junkers seemed to be mobilising for a counter-attack, assisted by the nationalist pressure groups; Bethmann Hollweg himself was apprehensive about a further contest, and talking of resigning; and heavy industry, and many in the National Liberal and Centre parties were more afraid of the steady rise of the SPD than of the intractibility of the agrarians. The financial crisis, the domestic-political trends and the armaments increases were combining to cause a paralysis in government – or, more properly, in legislation, for the Chancellor could still carry on provided he laid no controversial measures before the Reichstag.[140]

One or two further observations upon the interaction of domestic (social and financial) factors and external events arise from the above study. The first is the manner in which Grey's much-criticised 'middle of the road' diplomacy – neither joining France in a full alliance, nor agreeing to abandon her – fits in with the compromises which were being made within the Liberal Party at a time when the Cabinet was at least as likely to be grappling with House of Lords reform or National Insurance as with *entente* policy. A majority of the party would not, in the pre-1914 period, have accepted a fixed alliance with France: on that, 'new' and 'old' Liberals could combine. But they would also agree, despite misgivings, to British naval increases; and they would not dare run the risk – with the Tories waiting in the wings – of forcing the Liberal Imperialists out of the party by demanding that Grey's pro-French diplomacy be abandoned altogether. This preservation of party unity ensured, further-more, that neither protection nor conscription became official policies in Britain. On a slightly different point, one can appreciate more clearly than before G. L. Monger's observation that the *entente cordiale* paid for old age pensions;[141] for if, in the post-1904 years, the British had needed to be arming against *another* great power as well as Germany, it is difficult to see how this could be financially carried out in 'splendid isolation' without cutting social expenditure or introducing much higher rates of taxation. The argument of economy was also to the fore in the Cabinet's acceptance of the 1907 Asian *entente* with Russia; and in 1912 in the decision for the Mediterranean agree-ment with France, rather than spending another £20 million on battleships.[142]

Finally, it seems worth looking again at the current use by German his-torians of the term 'social imperialism' – that appeal to, and pursuit of imperialist objectives in an effort to divert attention from the domestic socio-political scene, thereby stabilising the *status quo*. What the above has tried to show is that politicians in all parties were making connections between domes-tic affairs and external policy; but it is quite a jump to argue that there was always a *primacy* of domestic politics. There were politicians, of a left-Liberal or Socialist hue, who could see that a jingoistic foreign policy and a spiralling arms race would endanger hoped-for social reform – just as they could also argue that a correct (that is, pacific, free-trading) external policy would benefi-cially affect the domestic scene. There were also frightened members of the establishment, especially among the Junkers and the Pan-Germans, who before 1914 were arguing for an 'active' policy against Germany's foreign foes as a solution to the domestic crisis; and they were joined by certain industrial-ists, although few among the latter – however much they feared the SPD – were eager for a world war. By contrast, those groups which most emphasised the interconnectedness of imperialism and social reform – Naumann, Weber, the Chamberlainites – argued that for a country to exist as a powerful and healthy *Machtstaat* it was necessary to look after its population. No doubt the historical argument as to which aspect really had 'primacy' will continue; but the more the facts are analysed in detail, the less likely is it that the historian can plump wholeheartedly for one side or the other.

In the final analysis, then, the motives of successive British and German governments over their armaments, taxation and social reform policies will probably seem less significant than the actual results and the constellation of political forces in each country which produced those results. By this criterion, many of the nuances between and within the political parties (however necessary it is to describe them) assume only secondary importance compared with the overall balance in each country, which may be summed up as follows: first, that a considerable distinction existed between the British and German establishments in regard to their willingness to achieve social peace by a political compromise with the working classes and by measures of increased direct taxation; and secondly, that despite tactical differences there was a broad agreement within each 'political nation' about the fundamentals of its external position. Most influential Germans believed that their country should secure a larger place in the world order; most influential Britons held that a forcible violation of the *status quo* should be resisted. Given this constellation of opinions it is not difficult to forecast what the respective national responses would be to certain eventualities in international politics.

# CHAPTER 18

# *The Impulse and Orchestration of Patriotism*

In one of the most famous commentaries upon the state of mind of prewar Europe, Colonel House reported to his political chief, Woodrow Wilson: 'The situation is extraordinary. It is militarism run stark mad.'[1] The daily press, and a host of books and pamphlets in every language, abused their country's rivals, glorified the art of war, referred ominously to the need to defend their 'national interests', and bitterly criticised their own statesmen if they flinched from 'resolute' and 'strong' action. The arms race, both on land and at sea, was becoming ever more hectic, and was cheered on by the nationalists in each country. Patriotic pressure groups, often with hundreds of thousands of members, urged their various causes by means of journals, deputations and mass assemblies. The older, Cobdenite vision of a harmonious world community appeared to have been overwhelmed by this excess of chauvinism. But it was not merely an outside observer like House who was perturbed by the change of mood: traditional Liberals and pacifists were appalled at popular sentiment in Britain during the Boer War; Salisbury and Hicks Beach felt themselves facing 'a Jingo hurricane'; and Roggenbach, Hohenlohe and other German 'moderates' shook their heads at the excesses of the Pan-Germans and other nationalist agitators.[2] The frequency of the remarks made by contemporaries, and the attention which later historians have paid to the role of pressure groups and the prewar press in Europe, necessitates at least a brief analysis of the way popular nationalism manifested itself, of the interests and motivations behind it and of its relationship with governmental authorities.

The expansion of the circulation figures of most newspapers in pre-1914 Europe was the consequence of trends noted earlier: rising population, increased standard of living, the expansion of primary education and the steady growth in literacy. But the whole process only achieved *political* significance because this all coincided with a great increase in the number of voters. Neither Britain nor Germany could be said to possess a democratic franchise at this time, but by 1910 or so some 6 million Britons and 11 million Germans were participating in general elections; appealing to and attempting to direct the sentiments of this vast audience became the business of all politicians, and of any group which wished to claim that it had 'public opinion' behind it. What

361

the press offered was the means of doing this, on a daily basis if necessary. The second significant point is that it was not the Morleys and the Hobsons but the Harmsworths and the Pearsons who first tapped that new layer of lower middle class and skilled artisan readers who would subscribe to a daily newspaper provided it was cheap enough – ½d rather than a full 1d, or the 3d demanded by *The Times*; and it was this new generation of press entrepreneurs who gradually transferred to the *Daily Mail* and *Daily Express* the attributes of the weekly *Titbits* and of Sunday papers such as the *News of the World* – gossip, police reports, short stories and (slightly later) eye-catching headlines and then photographs, all of which appealed much more than the columns of parliamentary reports in the 'serious' papers. As Kennedy Jones, the *Mail*'s editor, openly confessed, their motto was: 'Don't forget you are writing for the meanest intelligence.'[3] The average man, Conservative Party officials suspected a little later, did not purchase a newspaper to get a daily confirmation of his political beliefs: 'So long as it gives them full details on sport, war, crime, etc., they don't trouble about the politics of the paper, but read its political articles, and gradually, often involuntarily, fall under their influence.'[4] Yet while this sensationalism might easily have been blended with radical 'influence', it was instead associated with the cause of imperialism. The average Briton, Harmsworth argued, 'liked a good hate'; now he could have one every day.

The Boer War appeared to furnish the clinching evidence of the effect of 'jingo' newspapers upon the public mind. 'You would be astonished', Bryce reported to his old friend Goldwin Smith, 'remembering the England of forty years ago, to see the England of today, intoxicated with militarism, blinded by arrogance, indifferent to truth and justice . . . We have had a formidable lesson of the power which the press and financial groups can exert.'[5] Ironically, one of the persons who now protested most loudly against this trend was W. T. Stead, whose use of American techniques and whose earlier sensationalism in the *Pall Mall Gazette* were being imitated by the mass-selling dailies. In a famous article of 1886, Stead had proudly declared that 'In a democratic age . . . no position is comparable for . . . the influence and far-reaching power to that of an editor [who], better than any other man, is able to generate . . . public opinion, excite interest, . . . provoke public impatience.'[6] By the early twentieth century, with people dressed up in Prussian military uniform and paraded along Oxford Street in order to advertise the *Daily Mail*'s serialisation of an 'invasion scare' novel, it had become questionable whether liberalism would benefit from these developments.

It is worth recalling, however, that the political colouration of the British press had been moving against liberalism for other, unconnected reasons. Gladstone's external policy, together with his adoption of Home Rule, caused many newspapers and journals to drift rightwards; and the rise of suburbia and the white-collar workforce in the London region provided a readership which reinforced the shifting balance within the political press and conservatism's strength in the south-east of England. Moreover, the rise in capital costs and the reduction in the selling price of many papers from 1d to ½d meant that revenue increasingly needed to come from advertisers – another factor which, it has been argued, was likely to reinforce the press's deference to middle-class, Conservative values. A good example of the disadvantages, both external and self-inflicted, under which liberalism suffered can be seen in the history of the *Tribune*, which had strong initial financial backing and commanded the services of a brilliant array of radical journalists; but, with Nonconformist rectitude, refused to cover sports, publish racing results or consider advertisements for a variety of items; and, to compound its problems, adhered to the older, mid-Victorian layout of the news and spurned the Harmsworth technique.[7] Finally, the improvement in rail communications now allowed the London dailies to reach most of the provinces by overnight train, thus posing a new challenge to the real areas of Liberal strength – the regional dailies.

It would be unwise, however, to paint the scene completely black. Given the general social and political trends, it is worth arguing that the role of the *Mail* and the *Express* was to offer confirmation to the values and prejudices of an expanding middle class which was drifting towards the Conservative Party in any case. Calculations of the *actual* readership of the press are notoriously difficult, but it appears that a large part of the nation (including many on the electoral registers) was still not reading a daily paper. Furthermore, the 'appeal' of the new journalism to London clerks would damn it in the Welsh valleys and other strongholds of Nonconformity. If the focus is switched from the possible influences of newspapers upon the public to their role in providing ideas and criticism for the political élites, then the balance is much less one-sided. In many ways, this was another 'golden age' of intellectual Liberal journalism, with the luminaries being C. P. Scott (*Manchester Guardian*), J. A. Spender (*Westminster Gazette*), A. G. Gardiner (*Daily News*), H. W. Massingham (*Nation*) and F. W. Hirst (*Economist*).[8] All of these, by their frequent contacts with Liberal and radical politicians, had an influence – like Garvin, Maxse, Strachey and Gwynne on the 'other side' – which cannot be measured by circulation figures. Finally, as many observers have pointed out, the bland assumption about the power of an increasingly Conservative national press which the election results of 1895 and 1900 appeared to confirm, was thrown into question by the Liberal landslide of 1906.

The German press, as noticed earlier, differed from the British in a number of ways. It did not possess any national newspapers like *The Times*, and it was much more tightly tied to the various political parties. Furthermore, although the sales of better-known papers like the *Berliner Tageblatt* and *Kölnische Zeitung* grew steadily, the most noticeable innovation in the German press world – the *General-Anzeiger*, which provided local news, advertisements and entertainment, and achieved sales of hundreds of thousands of copies – passed the political press by and thus forced it to rely much more upon the financial support of a central committee or a local benefactor.[9] All this makes it difficult to measure a rightward shift in the ownership and political tone of the German press as was done above with the British *national* newspapers: only a state-by-state, city-by-city analysis could produce the necessary evidence. On the other hand, since the role of the German political papers was to confirm and articulate the beliefs of the party faithful, it may be an artificial exercise to measure their influence upon the 'public' at large or to see them as something distinct from the parties themselves. Northcliffe, after all, was in the business to sell newspapers to as many people as possible, and when he perceived that food taxes and conscription were both unpopular, he tended to have those items played down in the *Daily Mail*. No such calculations would alter the editorial policy of the agrarian *Deutsche Tageszeitung* or the heavy industry-supported *Berliner Neueste Nachrichten*.

Although this makes an analysis of the general 'influence' of the German press much more hazardous, some tentative conclusions are possible. The first is that a party's reliance upon small-circulation, local newspapers is not necessarily a sign of weakness. In the case of, say, the Centre Party, which was intent upon stressing 'parish-pump' politics, the support of over 400 regional papers was another way of retaining the loyalty of the peasant-farmers, shopkeepers and other members of the Catholic *Mittelstand* which voted it into power. The *Germania* and *Kölnische Volkszeitung* might have the editorial resources to comment upon foreign affairs at length and to maintain a London correspondent; but the great mass of local Catholic newspapers concentrated on the things which interested their readership – regional news, agricultural prices, attacks upon the SPD or the 'Prussian' government. The chief contribution of the party press to the Anglo-German relationship was, therefore, indirect: it helped to maintain the power-base of a party which, as noted earlier, was preventing any decisive alteration in Wilhelmine politics at the Reichstag level.

The socialist press's role was, similarly, to stiffen party consciousness and to create for the worker a greater sense of identity within the movement. These papers not only offered the opportunity for a sustained criticism of existing society and politics which the Reichstag – even when it contained over a hundred SPD deputies – patently lacked; but they were also a means of informing the party faithful in the localities and of reaching out for new members among the fast-growing proletariat. Given the particularism of so many of the German states, the lack of cheap national newspapers and police restrictions upon political mass meetings, the socialist press was a major instrument of proselytisation and information among the working classes.[10] The bitter attacks by the government-inspired press, and the frequent legal battles and police visits, were in their way tributes to the effectiveness of this propaganda; but by the same token it is obvious that SPD editorials could have no influence upon official policy towards Britain.

For the purposes of a brief analysis of the rise of nationalist sentiment in the German newspapers, and of the related issue of government–press relations, it is probably easiest to focus attention upon that cluster of Conservative, National Liberal and (to a lesser extent) left-Liberal journals which offered a running commentary upon foreign states and upon the Reich government's policy towards them. By scanning these newspapers it was possible for Bülow to get a good sense of, say, how the various Liberal parties were responding to the seizure of Kiaochow, or how fierce the agrarians' opposition to the fleet bills was likely to be. For this reason, the editorial commentaries were carefully monitored – the proportion of the surviving records of the *Auswärtiges Amt* and *Reichsmarineamt* which consists of newspaper clippings is quite remarkable – and this literary seismograph of 'public' opinion was frequently laid before the

Kaiser and his Chancellor. The impact made upon this distinguished reader-ship, as measured by their marginal comments or subsequent instructions, naturally depended upon the circumstances: in many cases, a newspaper clipping was the starting-point for some governmental counteraction in order to influence the public.

Any comparative study of government–press relations in Britain and Ger-many needs to recall how much more organised the newspaper-influencing apparatus was in the latter country, and how much more purposefully the German government sought to manipulate public opinion. Although there was a far broader tolerance of political criticism in Britain, the more illiberal German government showed a much greater concern to *appear* popular: this was particularly obvious following the 1897 decision to go for a glorious foreign policy. Hence the frequent occasions when open telegrams of congratulation were sent at the acquisition of colonial territory (Kiaochow, Samoa, the Carolines), when references were made to the incalculable 'prestige' or 'idealis-tic' element in, say, the German interest in Samoa, and when ostensible diplomatic victories (the resignation of Delcassé) were awarded with decora-tions and promotions. Hence, above all, the constant concern about the impact upon internal politics, and about strengthening the Kaiser's position by direct-ing public attention 'onto the world-shaking and decisive problems of foreign policy'.[11] To Bülow in particular, this was an *essential* aspect of his political operations. Almost every day when in Berlin he consulted with Hammann, the head of the *Auswärtiges Amt* press bureau; and when out of the city he wrote brief directives, suggesting what line should be taken in the 'inspired' press, asking the Prussian minister at another German court to intervene with the editor or owner of a regional paper, or demanding that a certain journalist be reprimanded for his 'tactless' (that is, politically or diplomatically embarras-sing) articles. Some newspapers, such as the *Kölnische Zeitung*, adhered so faithfully to this direction that their editorial pronouncements upon foreign affairs reflected more or less exactly the week-by-week tactical shifts in Bülow's diplomacy.[12] Efforts were also made, usually by offering subventions, to influence the press in Austria-Hungary, Portugal, the USA, Britain and elsewhere – not only to be able then to point to the pro-German tone of this doctored 'public' opinion, but also to be able to begin a rumour or a report *outside* Germany itself, as a diplomatic tactic. And while the nearby *Reichs-marineamt* did not carry out such tricks abroad, Tirpitz was acutely aware of the need to influence the German press, and his 'News Bureau' orchestrated an enormous campaign to win public favour for the various fleet bills, to promote (with the help of academics and journalists) the idea of German naval power, and to direct the occasionally over-enthusiastic efforts of the Navy League.[13]

In Britain, such blatant press-influencing simply did not exist. Nevertheless, the older habit of private consultation between politicians and the news-papers continued, although this was often understood to be 'without commit-ment' by either side: Buckle of *The Times* regularly saw Balfour, J. A. Spender consulted with the Liberal-imperialists, C. P. Scott maintained close links with Lloyd George, Maxse with the Chamberlains (for a while), Strachey with Cromer and other Free Trade Unionists. The partners concerned, it is clear, shared the same political beliefs and they were much more likely to meet in their London club, or at a country house at weekends, than in any governmental bureau. The relationship between the two professions was subtle, and the future historian of this fascinating topic will require extremely sensitive antennae. Only occasionally does one discover written evidence of attempted manipulation of public opinion, as when Garvin and Gwynne urged the Tory leaders to seize upon the issue of Britain's naval weaknesses in 1907–9 to 'put the other side in a fix' and 'strike the national imagination'.[14] Or when that most active practitioner, Fisher, encouraged his journalistic contacts to agitate about naval weaknesses in order to 'stiffen up' public opinion 'against that brute Hicks Beach and that cursed Treasury obstruction'[15] – a habit which rebounded in his face when an equally unscrupulous admiral, Beresford, later proceeded to leak all sorts of details about the Admiralty's failings during their great confrontation of 1907–8.[16] Government–press relations in Britain were usually managed in a 'gentlemanly' fashion, which deplored the cruder tactics either of Fisher or of the press bureaus of continental regimes.

That such attempts to influence opinion took place, whether in the British or the German system, is unremarkable. The most interesting phenomenon lies elsewhere, in the fact that both establishments steadily lost whatever control they had of the arch-patriotic press. This development was rarely understood by foreign observers or indeed by domestic critics, who explained the chauvinistic excesses by reference to the wire-pulling of governments or 'big business'. That was, however, too simple an explanation of the reverberations occurring within right-wing politics in Edwardian Britain and Wilhelmine Germany. In the German case, a radical-nationalist *Fronde* had emerged in the early 1890s, consisting of Pan-Germans, disgruntled Bismarckites, the *Bund der Landwirte* and various other groups which opposed Caprivi's efforts to liberalise the country's commercial, social and foreign policies, and which saw in the *Wilhelmstrasse*'s pro-English course a further sign of failure to perceive 'true German' interests: Marschall's claim to Chirol that the government 'has for the last five years struggled constantly against the tide' of anglophobia was a fair summary.[17] These agitations were paralleled by the much more important campaign against the 'anti-national' (and pro-British) SPD, but the most significant fact of all about the barrage of criticism from the *Post, Berliner Neueste Nachrichten, Deutsche Tageszeitung, Hamburger Nachrichten* and other such papers was that the forces behind them claimed to be the natural supporters of the Hohenzollern Crown. This was, therefore, a much more unnerving attack than any socialist or progressive or Centre criticisms – unless, of course, Wilhelm decided to repudiate the monarchy's traditional supporters.

These criticisms rose to new heights during the Boer War, when the government was endeavouring to 'manage' German patriotism so that it would be anglophobic enough to agree to the second Navy Law but not so outspoken as to catch the attention of the British. While the first aim was achieved, the second patently was not. To the Pan-German press, or the Bismarckian newspapers, or the agrarian and anti-Semitic pamphleteers, the *Wilhelmstrasse*'s regard for London's feelings was deplorable: why on earth did the Kaiser rush across to England so often, or refuse to receive the Boer generals?

'*Los von England!*' Even when the government privately hinted that this deferential diplomacy was only motivated by the need to get through the 'danger zone', many right-wing journals kept up their assaults – and had the sympathy of the Crown Prince, many at court, and other forces of reaction.[18] Since all this was duly reported back to Britain, Bülow fell between two stools: he was suspected both by the British *and* by the radical nationalists.

In truth, the German government's stance towards public opinion was always ambivalent. Holstein once wrote, 'Cries in the street have no influence upon German policy', yet a few paragraphs later he admitted, 'But even the most powerful monarch and his government have to take a certain account of popular feelings'.[19] With the Boer War ended, and the government urgently warning its Conservative and National Liberal contacts of the danger of a British reaction, this tumult subsided. It flared up again over the proposed naval increases in 1905, but both sides suppressed their differences in the run-up to the 1907 election. The *Daily Telegraph* affair opened the fissures forever. Thereafter, the radical nationalists never trusted either Wilhelm or his Chancellors, and a further intensification of this trend occurred during the second Moroccan crisis, to which the chauvinist newspapers responded with the now-traditional double assault: upon Britain, for obstructing Germany's *Weltpolitik*, and upon its own government, for its cowardice. 'Oh!, would that we had been spared this moment of unspeakable shame, of deep ignominy, far deeper than that of Olmütz!', the *Post* declared. 'What has happened to the Hohenzollerns . . . ?'[20] Such attacks – from such circles – shook the regime to its roots: being unable to contemplate a repetition, Bethmann Hollweg began to move further to the right while still denouncing the extremists; and the same was true of Liberal papers such as the *Vossische Zeitung* and *Berliner Tageblatt*, whose editorials defending the Chancellor's 'moderate' policy actually represented a shift by them from the left into the political centre.

In Britain the chief target of press abuse, the Liberal government and its 'traitorous' allies, fulfilled the same role as the SPD did in Germany by compelling Conservative forces to draw together at a time of crisis (over the 1909 budget, or Ulster). Yet this easily predictable pattern should not obscure what was arguably the more interesting trend: the increasing frustration of the activists at a Conservative leadership which was failing to grapple with Britain's external and internal foes. A great empire was decaying, and yet it was still being run casually by 'mandarins' and (until 1905) supervised by a philosopher – 'arid, aloof, incurious, unthinking, unthanking, gelt' was Kipling's devastating description (so it is assumed) of Balfour in his poem 'The Islanders', published by *The Times* in 1902.[21] This pressure, detectable already in the agitations over the Far Eastern and Fashoda crises of 1898, came fully into the open as a consequence of the Boer War reverses: the attacks upon the army leadership, the campaign for a North Sea naval base, and the open revolt by *The Times, Spectator, National Review, Morning Post* and other right-wing papers at co-operation with Germany over Venezuela and the Baghdad Railway, all reveal the strains within unionism at this time, with Chamberlain's withdrawal from the government giving the discontented forces their natural leader. In the 1906 election, for example, only the *Daily Telegraph* properly supported Balfour. These convulsions continued in the years following. The struggle to make Tariff Reform the obligatory policy of the Unionist Party, the taking of sides in the Fisher–Beresford dispute, the internal disagreements over the House of Lords crisis, were all mirrored in the right-wing press: the *National Review* called *The Times* 'a snake in the grass', H. W. Wilson, Spenser Wilkinson, Gwynne and Maxse assaulted Fisher's naval policies, and Balfour often found himself as much under attack from Conservative newspapers as from Liberal ones.

Were it not for the frequent assertions in historical literature about the 'wire-pulling' of newspapers by governments, party leaders and press lords, it would scarcely be necessary to argue that such attempts were not always successful. A fanatical nationalist such as Friedrich Lange, founder of the racialist *Deutschbund für ein reines Deutschtum*, collaborator with the Pan-German League, advocate of German supremacy in the world and editor of the *Deutsche Zeitung*, was bound to find the 'moderate' diplomacy of Bülow and Bethmann Hollweg unsatisfactory. Graf Ernst von Reventlow, defender of the Junker interest but equally fervent in pushing for an enormous fleet, a rabid anglophobe (as his wartime book *The Vampire of the Continent* well shows), a leading Pan-German, and the foreign editor of the agrarian *Deutsche Tages-zeitung*, could hardly be nobbled by surreptitious governmental appeals: when consulted during the second Moroccan crisis, he warned the *Auswärtiges Amt* that accepting inadequate compensation from France would be attacked.[22] On the British side, the same was also true: Maxse of the *National Review* was his own master; so was Strachey of the *Spectator*; Spenser Wilkinson, H. W. Wilson and Arnold White were assertive, independent-minded critics who would resent dictation or 'influence'; Garvin broke with his chief, Northcliffe, over imperial preference in 1911. These remarks would also apply to Liberal editors such as Scott, Labouchere, Spender and Massingham – the last-named resigning from the *Daily Chronicle* in 1899 rather than abandon his 'pro-Boer' line.

Even *The Times*, which foreigners still regarded as a government organ, was independent of 'wire-pulling' from above in this age of the Anglo-German estrangement. In 1902, the Rothschilds sought to get its strongly anti-German tone modified but were rebuffed; and early in 1903 the king himself apparently requested the paper to desist and was told that, while it would generally respect his wishes, in this matter it would not change its policy.[23] Yet that policy, as detailed above, was essentially the product of two men. The first was Chirol, the foreign editor, whose knowledge of international affairs (sustained by a remarkable private correspondence and numerous trips to various parts of the world) was probably greater than anyone's outside the Foreign Office. He frequently exchanged information with the Office; but, as Sanderson noted, 'he is always looking out for anything which he considers weak or over-conciliatory – and is prepared to have his knife into us immediately'.[24] A strong nationalist although not a fervent Tory, Chirol had at first looked to Germany as an ally, but German policy during the Boer War (especially Bülow's false promises before the 'granite speech') finally caused a change. Moreover, Chirol was converted to believe in a German threat by the unceasing efforts of his own Berlin correspondent. To Saunders, Germany was 'a new, crude, ambitious, radically *unsound* power', and the dominant circles within it were, despite Bülow's attempts at concealment, set upon an anti-British course: this fact must be made known in Britain. At times, the correspondent's sense of mission was positively Buchan-esque: 'I feel like a scout who has got through the enemy's lines with the result of his observations. It does not matter if a last long shot hits him, if he only gets his message to headquarters.'[25] Despite constant German hostility, and the quite valid observations of English critics that he never reported anything good about Germany, Saunders was manifestly successful. Chirol and Moberley Bell at *The Times* became convinced he was right; Strachey at the *Spectator* was influenced by him; Maxse's *National Review* campaign against Germany was done in close consultation with him; and Rosebery, Grey and Chamberlain were brought into contact with him. He was, Maxse asserted, '*the* sound man on Germany'.[26]

The impulses within the newspaper world which led to patriotic outbursts well in excess of what governments could find useful is merely one area where radical nationalism is to be observed. An even better guide was the creation, and the agitations, of the patriotic leagues – a phenomenon which hardly featured in the politics of Gladstone and Bismarck's time. It would be impossible here to analyse in detail what one scholar has nicely described as 'the proliferation of bodies devoted to the eradication of surmised national weaknesses'[27] in turn-of-the-century Britain and Germany, for there was scarcely an area of social activity which was not affected. These included a whole variety of moral and cultural bodies such as the National Social Purity Crusade, the Empire Day movement, the Society for Germandom Abroad and the various book leagues, all of which tended to encourage an identity with the nation and its prevailing social mores. This was even more the case with the *Reichsverband gegen die Sozialdemokratie* (1904) and the Anti-Socialist Union (1908), for by their assault upon the 'disruptive' elements in society the contrary values were obviously emphasised.

Seven well-known organisations which were exclusively concerned with the articulation of nationalist aims deserve more attention: the German Colonial Society; the two navy leagues, and the breakaway Imperial Maritime League; the National Service League and the *Wehrverein* (Defence League); and the Pan-German League. Apart from the first-named, these were all creations of the post-Bismarckian era; and the German Colonial Society remained to the end a 'respectable' body, usually in close contact with officialdom and possessing leading members from the political and social establishment. On occasions, the society did try to put pressure upon the government: the fear of a further 'surrender' akin to the Heligoland-Zanzibar treaty, which it had bitterly opposed, was always prominent and in 1898, for example, it attacked the rumoured Anglo-German deal over southern Africa, fearing another 'sell-out'.[28] Usually, however, it was a pro-government body, welcoming Bülow's *Weltpolitik* and providing lots of supporting propaganda for Tirpitz's first two Naval Bills. By the same token, its criticisms of Britain did not reach extremes: Rhodes' activities in Africa were feared, and the Boer War aroused indignation, especially among the Pan-German elements within the society. But it did not push for aggressive action in Morocco, the Near East or South America, and tended to concentrate upon the economic development of the existing empire; even after 1911 it usually identified with Solf at the Colonial Ministry, who favoured an amicable arrangement over imperial territories with Britain, rather than with the radical nationalists.

Tensions between government policy and the patriotic leagues were much greater in the area of navalist agitation. The British Navy League, founded after the great 1893–4 quarrel over the estimates, was the first to get off the ground. By 1901 it had only 14,000 members, but the Anglo-German naval race worked wonders for its recruitment figures and by 1914 the league claimed 100,000 members. This body bore all the hallmarks of an imperialist pressure group. Its presiding committee was a mixture of aristocrats, bishops, retired admirals and other notables, together with the ubiquitous hyper-patriotic intellectuals and political activists such as Spenser Wilkinson, Arnold-Foster, Dilke and Kipling. It produced its own magazine, printed masses of leaflets and brochures, had talks given at branch meetings, proselytised in the public schools, and was guaranteed to produce a fanfare of alarmist cries at the time of the annual naval estimates. It had no official connection with the Admiralty, which disapproved of its frequent erroneous claims and in particular of Spenser Wilkinson's agitation for a 'naval Moltke'; but the authorities privately welcomed the raising of public consciousness about the fleet since it increased the chances of getting their claims passed by the Treasury and the Commons.[29]

The German equivalent, founded in Berlin in 1898 by the heavy-industrialist lobby, was more closely in touch with officialdom and usually worked hand-in-hand with Tirpitz's 'News Bureau'. Its membership rose at a truly remarkable rate (which suggests that the idea touched some deep psychological chord), and by 1914 it claimed 331,000 individual members and another 776,000 who had been affiliated in groups. Its agitational activities were similar to, but in sheer momentum quite surpassed, those of its British counterpart.[30] Both bodies fed off, and contributed to, the tensions generated by the Anglo-German naval rivalry: they added notably to the already existing press tumult about the 'German threat' and the fears of another 'Copenhagen'. Both also suffered from internal rows and divisions, on the German side in 1899, 1905 and again in 1908, on the British side from 1907 onwards – out of which grew the Imperial Maritime League, the so-called 'navier league', which however never managed to achieve the numbers or the respectability of the parent body.

Before examining those disputes further, it is probably convenient to cover the other three organisations. The creation of the Wehrverein in 1912 occurs late in this story and is not directly connected with the rise of the Anglo-German antagonism. It is interesting nonetheless because its founding symbolised that general turn in nationalist sentiment after 1911 from Weltpolitik to anticipations of a continental war, which by that stage was also likely to provoke British involvement; because this fast-growing body (with 78,000 individual and another 200,000 corporately affiliated members by May 1913) was less concerned to respect official policy, denounced the massive army increases as being inadequate and was heavily penetrated by the Pan-Germans – all characteristics of the later stages of radical nationalism; and because it acquired an immensely strong public position as compared with its British equivalent.[31]

The National Service League was founded in 1902 as one of the many reactions to the poor showing of the regular army in the Boer War; its original text was George F. Shee's *The Briton's First Duty* (1901), with its appeal for a one-year term of military training by 'every able-bodied white man in the Empire'. Its early membership figures were derisory – only 2,000 by 1905; but in that year Roberts finally broke with the CID and then accepted the presidency of the League. The greatest boost came with the naval and invasion scares of the next few years, so that by the eve of war it claimed around 100,000 full members and another 120,000 associates – a fair reward for the league's untiring efforts to convince their countrymen that they could no longer sleep safely in their beds at night. Apart from Roberts, the organisation attracted the usual coterie of imperial enthusiasts – Kipling, Wolseley, Beresford, Clarke, Milner, Curzon, Amery, Moberley Bell, Repington, Lord Meath, (later) Strachey, and so on. To give this unpopular cause a lower profile, its speakers, pamphlets and house journal (*The Nation in Arms*) alluded to the Swiss model of military training rather than to the hated Prussian 'barrack-ground' image, and laid stress upon the physical and spiritual rewards which came from such personal commitment.[32]

The last of these leagues was the most notorious radical-nationalist body in pre-1914 Europe: the Pan-German League. Its membership was relatively small – about 22,000 at the height of the Boer War, and 17,000 in 1912 – but it made up for this in vociferousness and private influence, particularly within the worlds of education and business and within right-wing political parties, and it established connections with many of the other nationalist organisations of Wilhelmine Germany. Proclaiming that the Reich of 1871 was only a temporary halting-place in the development of a Greater Germany, the Pan-Germans were to be found agitating about everything from colonies in the Pacific and Brazil to the problems of *Deutschtum* in the Netherlands. Ideologically, the league's generalist function was reflected in its satisfyingly 'total' conception of a healthy, ordered power-state, which may explain why it attracted so many university and school teachers to its ranks.[33]

The second major characteristic of the Pan-German League was that it was part of the 'national opposition' from its inception, when it was protesting against Caprivi's concessions to the British, Poles and Catholics. No Prince Henry of Prussia gave it his royal 'protection', and no office of state intimated the limits of its agitational activity, as was the case with the Navy League. Of course, the Pan-Germans and the imperial government were frequently united in their purpose; but it is important to note that this tactical co-operation occurred *when the government moved closer to the league's position* – as in the Kruger Telegram, the post-1897 campaigns for a larger fleet and more colonies, the 1906–7 assault upon the Centre Party, and the post-1911 agitation for army increases.[34] Whenever the government appeared to be falling below

371

the high standards of 'truly national' policies as advocated by the league, its denunciations were bitter, persistent and uncontrollable: witness the open disgust expressed at the Kaiser's visits to England during the Boer War, the attacks upon the *Wilhelmstrasse*'s denials that Germany had any ambitions in Latin America, the criticisms of the 'moderate' nature of the 1906 fleet increases, the dissatisfaction expressed at the two Moroccan reverses, and the outrage at Wilhelm's revelations in the *Daily Telegraph* interview. The more radical section of the movement under Class (who became president in 1908) was especially critical. If the government wished to eradicate such attacks, then it would have to satisfy these critics.

The first and perhaps most essential feature of all of these hyper-patriots was their belief that the country's policies were not being handled properly. Externally, one can see how this connects to the apprehensions on the British side about relative economic decline, the growing challenges to the empire and the alarm expressed at the possibility of losing the 'heritage' of Pitt and Palmerston. On the German side, patriots sensed that their country had lost influence and the respect of others since Bismarck's fall (which is why veneration of the first Chancellor became a general symbolic gesture of disapproval of the Wilhelmine regime); and even the post-1897 *braggadacio* about Germany's glorious future was frequently mixed with fears about failure – a 'foreign Jupiter' blocking their path, or misguided actions by the government. During the series of diplomatic reverses which occurred after 1902, these misgivings broke to the surface again and produced the chorus of criticism not only against rival nations but also against the frivolous, inept, cowardly Reich leadership. Such apprehensions related to – and in many cases stemmed from – pessimism about the particularist fissures within the Reich, dislike of the Poles, Jewish immigrants and other 'aliens' (paralleled to some extent by British portrayals of the Irish, and the debate upon the Aliens Bill), and the bitter quarrels over the necessity and effects of rapid industrialisation. Politically, the nationalists' fears focused upon the evil influence of *laissez-faire* liberalism and then, with ever-increasing impact, upon the rise of socialism, which was seen as both a cause and an effect of internal weakness.

All these disturbing trends were to be countered, in the view of the patriotic leagues, by appeals to the opposite values: discipline, unity, healthy activities, the supremacy of the nation over individual or class interests, heroic endeavour, and civic instruction. (It is ironic, to say the least, to see how many of the German propagandists bemoaned the fact that these virtues existed in Britain but had no place in their own country – whereas British patriots urged their countrymen to follow the superior German example!) In many cases, the arguments and aims came close to a form of spiritual revivalism: 'We must as a nation wake up and face seriously the need for preparation, and preparation in the very widest sense. We have got to prepare not merely new Dreadnoughts but a new and more serious type of men and women or we shall go under.'[35] Given this sort of political fundamentalism, it was scarcely surprising that the arch-patriots in Britain disliked both the Liberal *and* the Conservative leadership, and sought to work outside either party; or that Class in 1903 scornfully derided the unstable, unserious, bombastic style of Wilhelm and Bülow as follows: 'Pageants and festivals, parades and unveilings of monuments, as well as an influencing of the press as has never been conducted on such a scale heretofore, corrupts the picture of our public life, but cannot deceive intelligent persons as to the fact that we have in reality no government.'[36]

By far the most suspect claim of these bodies, as many historians have pointed out, was that they were non-party organisations. Again and again, one encounters this assertion. In 1903, the National Service League appealed for support from 'Conservatives, Liberals, Radicals, Democrats, Socialists, Employers, Working Men, Clergymen, Members of the Peace Society and Haters of Jingoism, Physicians, Philanthropists, Taxpayers and (lastly) Women';[37] Baron von Würtzburg of the German navy apparently hoped for the time when *every* German would be a member; and the Pan-German leader, Adolph Lehr, wrote: 'We do not ask: "Are you conservative? Are you liberal?" We do not ask: "Are you a Protestant or a Catholic?" We ask only: *"Are you German?"*'[38] Yet this ostensible non-party stance was belied in two ways. The first was that the parliamentary supporters of the leagues were overwhelmingly in the right-wing parties. By the eve of war, the National Service League claimed, variously, between 105 and 177 MPs as members – but only three were Liberals. Similarly, of the Pan-German League members who were also Reichstag deputies, 47 per cent belonged to the National Liberal Party, 29 per cent to the two Conservative parties, and the rest to the smaller anti-Semitic groups.[39] The two navy leagues were more successful in recruiting from outside the Right – it was not difficult for a 'moderate' Liberal deputy or businessman to agree to the arguments in favour of a strong fleet – but this certainly was not the case with the Imperial Maritime League. As all could see, the Pan-German League's definition of what was properly German and national would involve a left-Liberal capitulating in a whole variety of beliefs, and made it virtually impossible for a Centre Party or SPD supporter to join; just as the acceptance of conscription in Britain implied a drastic recasting of traditional Liberal (and Labour) conceptions of society.

The second questionable aspect concerned the word 'non-political'. To the traditionalists, this seems to have implied 'non-controversial', that no action would be taken which would offend the established parties. On the British side, this accorded nicely with the theory (much contested by the Radicals, admittedly) of 'continuity' in British foreign policy and with the social coherence of the decision-making élite. From this perspective, there was little wrong in Liberal politicians and journalists (Dilke, W. T. Stead) joining with the Conservatives in the Navy League; and this was similar to Tirpitz's hope of attracting as many parties as possible to support his naval programme, and to Würtzburg's belief that the German Navy League could 'raise matters of national defence above the bustle of the parties'.[40] Yet there were other, more radical groups to whom 'non-political' meant *anti*-party. Perhaps the supreme example here was Milner, the 'political Ishmaelite', who thought party government 'almost universally bad'; and this strain of belief, sometimes involving the demotion of parliament, is also detectable in certain other adherents of 'national efficiency' government.[41] On the German side, it is interesting to note that early leaders of the Pan-German League such as von der Heydt and van

Eycken contemplated turning it into a new 'National Party' until the more regular party-affiliated members (Hasse, Lehr, Hugenberg) crushed the idea; and that a recrudescence of these populist, *völkisch*, anti-establishment pressures occurred within the Navy League and Pan-German League in the period before 1908.[42]

The consequence of this was that, while Bülow and Tirpitz and 'moderate' leaders of the Navy League were seeking to tempt the left-Liberal and Centre parties into the establishment fold, the more rabid Pan-Germans were bitterly attacking these 'un-national' forces. Similarly, the radical element within the British Navy League found it intolerable by 1907 to withhold their criticisms of the Liberal government, and of the 'traitorous' Sir John Fisher who had agreed to the reductions in the navy estimates. When breaking away to found the Imperial Maritime League in January 1908, they openly assaulted the Liberal-Radicals and Socialists as being 'poisonous to the life of Britain' and 'advance agents of a Foreign Power'. 'Subject to these limitations', they added, 'the League will have no "party" prepossessions'; but this new organisation's 'definite and comprehensive endeavour . . . to lift National Defence out of the domain of party politics' meant, in effect, obeisance by all the political parties to the programme as set out by the league's leaders.[43] Even in the Navy League itself, there were individuals who felt by 1912 'that our business is to get this [Liberal] Government out, to secure the largest possible majority to enable us to restore 2nd Chamber, reverse Home Rule, reduce Irish Representation, start our Land Policy, etc.'[44] – none of which had anything to do with the formally proclaimed aims of the organisation.

Given this emphasis upon their non-partisan character, it was predictable that the leagues would appeal to 'the common man'. Not only would this correspond with their alleged national role, but evidence of strong public support legitimised their action in putting pressure upon governments to take certain measures. Above all, of course, it was hoped that a successful recruitment of the masses would counter the internal weaknesses, confound the agitators on the Left, preserve social and political stability by taking certain matters out of the party arena, and strengthen the nation in its dealings with other stages. It is nonetheless remarkable what an amount of hope and propaganda was directed by the leagues towards the working classes: 'It is because the [British] Navy League trusts the people, because it believes that you are honest and patriotic, when you know the truth, that it appeals to you.' Not content with the distribution of pamphlets, the league urged members to arrange small meetings with working men 'and put the facts before their audience. When they cannot hold meetings, let them attack the working-man in the train or on the omnibus.'[45] The league's German equivalent also felt that 'the enlightenment of the workers' was its special task, and that it had to get across the message 'that each individual shares the responsibility for the fate of the German people far into the distant future'.[46] Both naval leagues employed the argument that the workers and their families would suffer greatly if supplies of foodstuffs and raw materials were ever blockaded; both army leagues, in their turn, offered the lurid scenario of their country being overwhelmed and plundered by foreign hordes unless all able-bodied men gave their support.

The other main area to which such propaganda was directed was the country's youth. In Britain especially, the two decades before the First World War witnessed a whole variety of attempts to proselytise among the youth. The Boy Scouts, the most famous of all these creations, became so popular that it eventually transcended the aims and circumstances of its founding – and needs to be treated with corresponding care; but there also seems little doubt that Baden-Powell established the movement specifically in reaction to the post-Boer War alarm about 'physical deterioration', and that scouting was to secure the twin aims of a healthy, stable society and a nation of patriots. As the youthful readers of *Scouting for Boys* were told,

> don't be disgraced like the young Romans who lost the Empire of their forefathers by being wishy-washy slackers without any go or patriotism in them. Play-up! Each man in his place, and play the game . . . Remember, whether rich or poor, from castle or from slum, you are all Britons in the first place, and you've got to keep Britain up against outside enemies, you have to stand shoulder to shoulder to do it. If you are divided among yourselves you are doing harm to your country. You must sink your differences.[47]

Given the large numbers, and fairly rapid turnover among the scouting population (over 150,000 current members in 1913), this was a message which – if correctly imbibed – was reaching out to an extensive audience. And alongside the scouts, there existed a host of other organisations – the Boys Brigade, the Church Lads Brigade, the British Girls Patriotic League, the Lads Drill Association – whose activities (even if not originally so intended) seemed to many observers to be increasingly concerned with military preparedness for its own sake.

Perceiving this scene, the patriotic leagues themselves very quickly moved in. The Navy League sent Beresford and other speakers into the public schools to lecture on life in the service, with pamphlets in large numbers being circulated to this juvenile audience, and with headmasters being persuaded to have Trafalgar Day celebrations or even to become vice-presidents of the League. Lantern-slide shows were given, and sea-training offered. The Junior Branch of the Imperial Maritime League produced simplified biographies of Rodney and Nelson, and urged its readers to follow these examples of patriotism and valour. The National Service League, once under way, engaged in similar activities. Meath's Lads Drill Association was soon incorporated into the league; a campaign was begun for rifle-shooting in the schools; Roberts and other notables came along to give prizes, and to preach the doctrines of physical fitness, discipline and loyalty to country. By 1910, over 150 schools and some twenty universities and colleges had their own Officer Training Corps. As Esher put it, when returning the fifty-eight essays on Boer War subjects submitted by Eton boys for a competition, 'rational thinking men who watch the trend of events, not only in Europe but all over the world, begin to see that the use of arms is also an essential part of a sound educational curriculum'.[48] Boy-scouting, and drill, were not just 'games'; patriotic history, and exhortations to imitate former (Nelson, Wolfe) and recent (Gordon, Roberts) heroes, had an earnest purpose. 'If you avail yourself of the opportunity . . .', Roberts encouraged Spenser Wilkinson upon the latter's appointment to the newly created Professorship of Military History at Oxford, 'your tenure of the Chair may prove as important to Great Britain as Fichte's work after Jena proved to Prussia.'[49]

Such activities are hard to separate from the general overtones of patriotism and duty which were inculcated in Victorian and Edwardian society. Quite apart from the prejudices emanating from school history textbooks,[50] popular literature also emphasised imperial themes: schoolboys reading Henty could travel with Wolfe to Quebec and with Roberts to Kandahar; Austin, Newbolt, Kipling and earlier Tennyson wrote poems on the navy and the empire; the novels of Stephenson, Rider Haggard and Buchan were great successes. The market for futuristic war stories was booming. The ever-flexible pen of William Le Queux, whose 1894 novel on *The Great War in England in 1897* had envisaged an Anglo-German alliance against France and Russia, was encouraged by Northcliffe in 1905-6 to write the best-selling work *The Invasion of 1910*, which now portrayed a German attack upon England – in its way, a neat reflection of the change of national enemies in the imperialist mind. Of course, some of these pieces were either pure (that is, non-political) adventure stories for a juvenile audience or, like the works of Conrad and in certain respects Kipling, serious and creative efforts to explore eternal themes by using an imperialist context.[51] But others were blatantly propagandistic. In one gorgeous novelette for children – dedicated appropriately enough to Lord Meath – the local schoolboy hero confronts the socialistic 'agitator' on the village green:

> 'Look here', Denys [the hero] said, 'we don't know who you are, or where you come from, but we would have you understand we will have none of your treasonable talk here. We're all for the King and the Empire, and the sooner you leave our village the better. We are not going to stand it!'
> The little man laughed, but it was not a pleasant laugh . . .[52]

Although the popular literature in Germany was a mirror image of all this – with some of the British invasion 'scare stories' being translated and then refashioned to suit a German audience – the main patriotic organisations themselves appear to have paid less attention to youth. Active proselytisation in the schools would have aroused protests from the Centre Party and others, and transgressed the laws against the politicisation of youth. But the chief reason was probably that the orchestration of patriotism was effectively being carried out by other agencies, *including government ministries*. In Prussia, for example, the Ministry for Education and Religious Affairs ordered the schools to place greater emphasis upon the lives of the Prussian monarchs and their deep concern for social welfare; they also had to expose 'the perniciousness of Social Democracy'. School history books were to have a definite pedagogical purpose: as the ministry's edict explained, 'It would be a sin against the coming generation if we were to delay familiarising it with the blessings which accrue to it by virtue of its connection with the Prussian state. It would be an equally great injustice to the state itself if an unpatriotic generation were reared.'[53]

The patriotic flavour of these works may not have been that much different from many a British textbook – one praised Frederick the Great, the other the Elder Pitt – but in the German case the state itself played an active role. The distinction is a critical one, therefore, as soon as the focus is shifted from private initiatives to governmental activities. As the British patriots always claimed, they could receive no assistance from officialdom; yet in 1903 the Prussian Ministry was itself distributing posters about Germany's *Flottenpolitik* to the schools. Similarly, whereas the *Reichsverband gegen die Sozialdemokratie* worked in close co-operation with state officials, especially at the time of the 1907 election, the Anti-Socialist Union had to work on its own in Britain.[54] Also very active in Germany was the Christian Journal Society (*Christlicher Zeitschriftenverein*), which was heavily subsidised by the government and assisted by local magistrates and officials in its efforts to distribute pro-establishment newspapers, morally uplifting novels and patriotic calenders; with more than 12,000 agents, this organisation bombarded hospitals, barracks, factories, railway stations and local libraries with 'suitable' matter.[55]

Another active force in this field was the army. It is worth making the obvious remark here that the chief purpose of the National Service League in Britain was quite superfluous in a country like Germany, which regarded conscription as axiomatic; but this brought further problems for the conservative Reich leadership in an age when recruits were as likely to be SPD sympathisers as more docile farmworkers. In consequence, the army took seriously its self-appointed task as 'the educator of the nation' and followed the Elder Moltke's recommendation 'to train the rising generation in order, punctuality, cleanliness, obedience, and loyalty'.[56] Even when the period of active duty was completed, the propaganda continued. The veterans' associations, which by 1913 had almost 3 million members in nearly 32,000 branches, were quickly seen by the army and the civilian government as further instruments for patriotic and anti-socialist propaganda, despite their 'non-political' status; and they were subjected not only to a special barrage of leaflets and newspapers but to constant pressure for political conformity – upon the threat of expulsion, loss of certain financial benefits, and other penalties.[57] By the eve of war, the army was considering extending the period of indoctrination backwards, to the time *before* teenagers did their military service, by requiring every able-bodied youth between the ages of 13 and 20 to undertake a course of physical and ideological training.[58] Needless to say, such activities were hardly thought necessary for the business and professional classes, where the possession of a reserve-officer's commission and uniform was highly treasured, since it involved considerable social prestige. Flaunting of the uniform, and the corresponding stress upon military rather than civilian values, had been boosted by the habit of Bismarck and his successors as Chancellor so dressing for important Reichstag events. Yet the very idea of Gladstone, Campbell-Bannerman or Asquith in uniform appears absurd; Salisbury, who had little respect for the military, would have snorted in derision; and Balfour would simply have felt uncomfortable.

Before leaving this issue of patriotic indoctrination, one further point is worth discussion: the role of the activist. Amery, who upon being asked during his first class at Harrow (aged 13) what had been the most important political event of the summer, had precociously replied 'The Nizam of Hyderabad's offer to the Queen to supply money and troops in case of trouble with Russia'[59] – and appropriately followed this early interest with his varied careers at *The Times*, as a stalwart Tariff Reformer, as Lord Roberts's 'ideas-man' in the National Service League, as a member of the Coefficients and of the Compatriots, and then as a Tory MP with little respect for the two front benches. Lord Meath was another who devoted his energies (and lots of his capital) to this sort of work: founder of the Empire Day movement and the Lads Drill Association, a leading light in the Navy League, the National Service League and the League of Frontiersmen, and also active in the Boy Scouts, League of the Empire, British Girls Patriotic League, and so on.[60] Lieutenant-General August Keim was a similar sort of activist: as one of the leaders of the radical wing of the German Navy League, he broke with the organisation in 1908 because its policies were not 'national' enough and it deferred to governmental influence; he then turned to running bodies such as the Patriotic Book League and German Youth League, as well as an anti-Ultramontane organisation; but finally returned to greater prominence when, with Pan-German backing, he became head of the *Wehrverein* in 1912.[61] Dietrich Schäfer, a student admirer of Treitschke and himself professor at Berlin University, propagandist for the German fleet and in close contact with Tirpitz, was just as ubiquitous: he was a member of the Pan-German League from its inception, a leader in the Navy League, a member of the Society for the Eastern Marches, and in 1912 one of the initiators of the *Wehrverein*, drafting its first two public appeals.[62] It would not be difficult to name twenty or perhaps fifty such individuals in each country – without whom the leagues would scarcely have functioned – and a 'collective biography' would be enormously interesting.

What even a preliminary analysis of these people suggests, however, is the need for a closer definition of patriotic 'manipulation' in this period. That there took place a deliberate and cynical orchestration of public sentiment, especially by the German government and with financial support from heavy industry, is undoubted: yet while their actions and aims ran in parallel with those of the arch-patriots, they never fully merged with the latter. To the nationalists, it is not unfair to suggest, the impulse to their activities derived from a firm belief in the idea of the strong, ordered nation-state, and considerations about party political advantage or preserving the 'face' of the establishment came a poor second. Hence the frictions within the Right when, say, the German government sought to conciliate the Centre Party, or when Balfour declined to commit himself openly to the unpopular policies of Tariff Reform and conscription. In this post-Bismarckian age, there seems to have been at least as much pressure from the activists below as there was wire-pulling from above.

To stop the story at this point would be to leave a completely one-sided impression. Although it has been argued that the manifestations of nationalism in British and German society in these years were far in excess of anything which occurred under Bismarck and Gladstone, it is also true that this development had its critics. Indeed, the various campaigns against militarism, the attempts by individuals and organisations to improve Anglo-German relations, and the growth of the peace movements (even if some had earlier origins) were *reflections* of concern at this chauvinism. The SPD's campaign in this respect was probably the most widespread of all, for not only did its leadership attack *Weltpolitik* and 'Prussian militarism' in their extensive press and in Reichstag debates, but they created various organisational counter-measures such as socialist youth movements, sports clubs and cultural associa-tions; instructed those about to undertake military service of their legal rights; and produced newspapers and leaflets for a youthful readership. All this inevitably led to a further series of clashes with the authorities, the seizure of materials, and innumerable court cases, the most famous being the trial of Karl Liebknecht for his pamphlet *Militarismus und Antimilitarismus . . .*[63] This was paralleled on the British side, with the ILP organising around 200 meetings against militarism and conscription in November/December 1913 alone. They were joined by a phalanx of Liberal-Radicals and Cobdenite traditionalists, who applied a constant counter-pressure upon the government to those urging 'national' policies. Hobson critically analysed the foe in his work *The Psychol-ogy of Jingoism*. Liberal papers like the *Daily News, Speaker, Reynolds' News*, the *Morning Leader* and the *Tribune* campaigned for 'pacific' foreign policy, while Scott's *Manchester Guardian* greeted Labour's campaign against arma-ments with enthusiasm and claimed that it put many Liberals to shame. The frequent speeches of Ponsonby, Trevelyan, E. D. Morel and other Radicals produced a shoal of congratulatory letters from Nonconformist circles, trade unionists and all who regarded the growing militarism with distrust; and they were assisted by the remarkable publicity which attached to Norman Angell's *The Great Illusion*.[64]

In addition to this *political* opposition, there was the work of the various peace societies in Britain and Germany. Although British pacifists had been saddened by opinion during the Boer War and public support for armaments, other signs were promising: the Nobel Peace Prize was established in 1897; the two Hague conferences upon disarmament gave sustained publicity to the pacifist case; and the various international conferences – such as the Inter-Parliamentary Union one in 1906, and that of the Peace Congress in 1908, both being held in London – secured the warm praise of Campbell-Bannerman and Lloyd George. Their work was also encouraged by thousands of churchmen.[65]

A particular characteristic of these anti-militaristic campaigners was that they could work with similar groups in the other country: British and Germany nationalists, by contrast, could only glare at each other in mutual suspicion. Barth, having contacted Bryce and Mommsen in order to ease Anglo-German tensions after the Boer War, later co-operated with the *Manchester Guardian*'s German correspondent; and, after talking with Spender, Massingham and Hirst in London in 1908, recorded their friendly assurances towards Germany in a *Berliner Tageblatt* article.[66] The *Sozialistische Monatshefte* published articles by Ramsay MacDonald, and C. P. Trevelyan wrote pieces for the *Deutsche*

*Revue*, furiously attacking *The Times*, the National Service League and other 'agitators' but assuring Germans that all was well while a Liberal government remained in power in London.[67] The Anglo-German Friendship Society naturally encouraged all sorts of mutual visits, by journalists, burgomasters, trade unionists and churchmen. If there were many Britons and Germans who came to regard the other country with suspicion, therefore, it is clear that other individuals, journals and organisations opposed this trend.

On balance, however, the old cause of 'peace, retrenchment and reform' lost ground in this period. This was due, in the German case especially, to the sheer strength of the social forces favouring patriotic policies. One scholar puts it nicely:

As they approached political parties, churches, schools, newspapers, and other sectors of German society that they identified as important in shaping popular attitudes about international politics, the pacifists discovered that these agencies rejected not only the specific international reforms the peace movement advocated but the pacifists' most basic assumptions about the reality of an international community.[68]

The society was bitterly attacked as 'traitorous' by the arch-patriots, which undoubtedly deterred a number of the middle classes from joining, and it actually had to make its base in liberal Württemberg rather than in hostile Berlin. Moreover, whereas the SPD made no attempt to co-operate with the pacifists – seeing the latter both as unrealistic and as committed to rescuing capitalist society from the perils of an all-out war – its own campaign against militarism damned the cause in the eyes of all 'respectable' members of the community.

In the British case, the advocacy of international co-operation and arms reductions was more socially acceptable – British pacifists were even welcomed to Windsor Castle by Edward VII in 1908 – but the *specific circumstances* of the Anglo-German rivalry undermined the peace movement. The Liberal government was always in a strong tactical position in declaring that it was willing to reduce the naval building programme if Germany would do the same. Yet, whenever the Anglo-German Friendship Society wished to see this explored further, or agitated for the creation of an Anglo-German-French *entente*, it encountered hostility in Berlin.[69]

Despite this, many radicals and pacifists continued to present the German government in very favourable terms: Bishop Boyd Carpenter, for example, proclaimed Wilhelm II to be 'a lover of peace, earnestly desirous of promoting the welfare of mankind'.[70] The blunt fact was that, in general, the British 'peacemakers' had no real knowledge of German politics: perceiving their shared religion, race and industrial circumstance, they superimposed the assumptions of British political culture upon a society which was different in so many respects. When, in an interesting flurry of letters in the *Daily News*, one Liberal pointed to the promising friendship shown to Britain by the visiting burgomasters, Arnold White retorted that the latter 'have as little to do with their country's decision to make war as the Bank Holiday crowd on Hampstead

Heath' – an acerbic, but reasonably accurate view of the German constitutional position.[71] Over other questions – Morel on the Congo, Professor Browne on Persia – the Radicals' knowledge was extensive, unsettling the Foreign Office in the process; over Germany, their ignorance was immense. They shared the common ideological dislike of Hohenzollern autocracy, but failed to measure its powers – ironically, one suspects, because their German contacts were almost all left-Liberals and Socialists. This may not have been such a disadvantage in their quarrels with the arch-patriots, for too many of the latter suffered from the *opposite* misperception, that Germany was about to fall upon Britain. But it did weaken the case which the Radicals made to the British government, for Asquith and Grey could hardly reconcile such optimistic portrayals of Germany with either the secret information from Bebel or, say, the detailed and often brilliant analyses of German society and economy provided by the commercial attaché, Sir Francis Oppenheimer.[72]

What were the effects, then, of all this patriotic propaganda? It is worth making the point that the 'influence' was meant to flow in *two* directions: upon the public at large, and upon specific parties and governments. The first area is the most difficult to analyse. Sweeping contemporary claims by the patriots, for example, that the working classes were on 'their side', need to be heavily discounted. A regular SPD member, and many a German trade unionist, could hardly fail to be influenced by party literature, or by the establishment's attacks upon socialist leaders and union activities. Politically conscious Labour men in Britain were unlikely to enthuse about conscription, especially when advocated by people who had been involved in the Boer War and 'Chinese slavery'. Moreover, the average man's point of entry into a patriotic league could only occur at *branch* level, where both the social composition of the local committee and the manner of meeting – formal agenda, points-of-order, a learned talk on 'German settlements in Rio Grande do Sul and Brazil',[73] possibly the embarrassment of a collection afterwards – were distinctly middle-class. Only 26 out of the 9,000 committee members in the German Navy League in 1912 were working-men.[74] The county organisers of the National Service League were almost all retired army officers, a type whose previous experience of 'the common man' was somewhat limited. The impact of patriotic indoctrination was also slight among certain other social groupings. Adherents of the Centre Party were not only being abused by the nationalists, but they had their own nexus of local organisations and events: how could the quarterly branch meetings of the Navy League compare in importance with the day-to-day *material* role of the Catholic peasant associations? In Britain, the leagues made very little impact in Wales; Anglican churchmen generally approved of their work, but most Nonconformists were cool; the south and east were areas of recruiting strength, much of the north of weakness.

The bodies most successful with the working classes were, not surprisingly, those which accorded with their interests and local traditions: where working-class unionism had a hold, as in Lancashire, Birmingham and of course Ulster, the National Service League did well. Rifle-shooting was a popular sport for its own sake; the Volunteers offered this activity, and a great deal of *cameraderie*, and consequently had an overwhelmingly working-class membership. Moreover, although Milner and his circle associated conscription with the need to preserve the European equilibrium, local propaganda wisely concentrated upon the anticipated expulsion of a foreign invader; it also avoided too open an attack upon the voluntary principle, for large numbers of the National Service League's members were enthusiastic Volunteers or Territorials.[75]

The attitude of the trade unions was also rational and pragmatic: radical and socialist MPs in shipbuilding constituencies and naval ports (where the Navy League did well) hesitated to risk the disaffection of the local trades by opposing the fleet estimates;[76] and it was the union leaders, as noted above, who cold-shouldered the idea of a general strike to paralyse mobilisation for war. The 'man in the street' was quite capable of distinguishing between a justified and unjustified act of war, and if the government appealed to him to resist a Russian invasion of the fatherland, or to protect Belgium from 'the Hun', his response was likely to be favourable. It would take a remarkably independent mind to resist the popular enthusiasm which an ostensibly *defensive* conflict would trigger off. On the German side especially, one is left wondering how many SPD members, who had been subjected to years of abuse and social pressure by the Kaiser, the churches and other authorities, were not psychologically relieved to be accepted by society in the days of August 1914. In the words of one of them:

The conflict of two souls in one breast was probably easy for none of us. [It had lasted] until suddenly – I shall never forget the day and hour – the terrible tension was resolved; until one dared to be what one was; until – despite all principles and wooden theories – one could, for the first time in almost a quarter century, join with a full heart, a clean conscience and without a sense of treason in the sweeping, stormy song: *'Deutschland, Deutschland über Alles'*.[77]

However tentative the conclusions about the incidence of nationalism among the working classes must remain, the propaganda was much more likely to impress those higher up the social scale. The middle classes were arguably the most natural audience for popular adventure stories, 'invasion scare' novels and other pieces of literary ephemera on both sides of the North Sea; the social composition of the Boy Scout movement was overwhelmingly middle-class, a fact attributable in part to the cost of the uniform; and the patriotic leagues, as is clear from the details given above, were rooted in this social stratum, with only a few exceptions. If the nationalistic message was of influence, then it must be here that it made the greatest impression. This remark applies, *pari passu*, to the official influences in Imperial Germany which deliberately encouraged 'love of the Fatherland'. All that is known about those institutes of higher education which were more or less exclusively middle or upper class – the public schools, the grammar schools and *gymnasia*, the universities – supports such a conclusion: the flourishing of the Officers' Training Corps, the emphasis upon 'muscular patriotism' and other military virtues, the debates in the students' unions in favour of a bigger fleet, the unruly but definitely right-wing *Burschenschaften*, the activities of the hundreds of *Flottenprofessoren* and thousands of Pan-German schoolteachers in Germany, and – finally – the casualty rate among the newly-recruited junior officers in the early part of the war, all seem to point in one direction.[78]

On the German side, moreover, it is possible that this stimulation of nationalism coincided with certain reverberations within the *Mittelstand* which ostensibly had little to do with Anglo-German relations or militarism: namely, the creation of national organisations for those various occupations which now found it necessary to imitate the trade unions and agrarian leagues. Certain of these groupings, like the artisans and the shopkeepers, were on the economic defensive but others, such as the shop assistants and commercial employees, were growing in numbers. They had little in common with the Reich establishment, or with the pushing intellectual advocates of *Weltpolitik*, and in other parts of Europe these groups were fertile breeding-grounds for radicalism. In Germany, it is true, parts of the *Mittelstand* associated with left-of-centre parties; but the majority of these interest groups became stalwart monarchists and supporters of a large fleet and army. The German-National Commercial Assistants Association joyfully anticipated war in 1913 with its call:

> Break out, you storm, with fearful weather,
> We stand Hohenzollern-true forever.[79]

The fact that the association's leader, Wilhelm Schack, was connected with the Pan-Germans and *Bund der Landwirte* only partly explains this phenomenon. A more significant reason was that most of these groupings had cause for complaints against 'big capital', and that this resentment had been channelled into a strong anti-Semitism, against the Jewish moneylender, the Jewish-owned department store, and so on. On the other hand, they were usually very caste-conscious and feared being dragged down into the proletariat, whose political leaders seemed in any case 'cosmopolitan-Jewish' and who (just like Richter and many *laissez-faire* Liberals) were unwilling to promise legislative protection. What these organisations had in common with the specifically patriotic leagues, therefore, was an anti-liberal rhetoric, which preached about 'protection of national work', about support for the 'small man' and other 'healthy' elements in society, against the twin evils of internationalism and socialism, and in favour of the monarchical system. Thus, the innate social conservatism of the German *Mittelstand* was transmuted into support for parties (the anti-Semites, the Conservatives, the National Liberals) which were avowedly royalist and nationalist. Their image of England – the home of unrestrained capitalism – was not a favourable one; but their more important, if indirect effect upon Anglo-German relations was that they reinforced, especially in the *Kartell der schaffenden Stände*, an already illiberal society.[80]

The impact of this increasing nationalism upon the political parties before 1914 is, to a large extent, a consequence of these broader trends: perceiving the changing sentiment among their followers, the party leaders were obliged to review their own positions. In Germany, the establishment's success in the 1907 election signified the utility of a strongly national campaign; and even those parties which were not enthusiastic supporters of *Weltpolitik* could not afford to have the adjective 'unpatriotic' applied to them. After 1907 the Centre Party was moving back towards the government bloc, both in response to the rightward trend among its supporters and out of a desire to regain political respectability and influence; and its press, party leaders and bishops alike emphasised that 'we Catholics are not second-class but first-class patriots'.[81] The same thing happened among the left-Liberals, especially after Richter's death: many Progressives disliked the spiralling arms race and yearned for a good understanding with Britain – but to have openly opposed the naval increases requested by the government would have been too dangerous and politically embarrassing. Even among the SPD and related trade unions there arose that strong nationalist segment – the original 'social imperialists' – which increasingly supported the Reich's foreign policy, and the 1913 Army Bill provided further evidence of this rightward shift. It would be interesting to know how often even Bebel felt obliged to declare that the SPD was not unpatriotic, that it would support the Fatherland in peril, and that it did not disapprove of conscription but merely wished it to be in the form of a citizens' militia.[82]

Within the German Conservative Party, too, one can detect a steady change of tone, and their leaders' statements in the Reichstag became far less 'Prussian-particularist' and more 'national-imperialist'. As for the National Liberal Party, recent research has shown how much it benefited from the active support of the patriotic leagues at election time – which meant that in turn it became ever more a mouthpiece for the *Flottenverein* and Pan-German League.[83] During the Boer War, the Pan-Germans had been denounced as 'beer-bench politicians' by Bülow; by 1912 or so, and especially with the formation of the *Wehrverein* and the *Kartell der schaffenden Stände*, the radical nationalists were no longer voices in the wilderness and their ideas were common currency among most of the anti-socialist forces. To a considerable degree, the patriotic pressure groups had assumed the same role as the economic/occupational interest groups which, if not becoming rivals or alternatives to the formal parliamentary parties, had forced the latter to pay deference to their interests. On the other hand, if Wilhelm and many of his entourage could greet this rise in patriotism and the shift in party attitudes with satisfaction, it made the execution of any moderate diplomacy very difficult; and the excessive hopes and demands of the chauvinists threatened, when disappointed by diplomatic failures, to rebound in anger at the very sorcerer's apprentices which had helped to instigate these feelings in the first place.

How did this compare with the political impact in Britain of a rising nationalism? Whatever the similarity in the aims and actions of the arch-patriots in the two countries, it is clear that German society was much more amenable to their message: not only was the massive government-instigated propaganda missing in Britain, but it was the advocates of military preparedness who found themselves in a minority. In the post-1906 parliaments, the vast majority of the governing party was critical of the 'jingo' press and leagues, and so were the Labour and Irish parties: as one scholar has remarked, the greatest pressures upon Grey to change his foreign policy came from the Left, not from the Right.[84] As against all this, however, it needs to be said that the charge of lack of patriotism had its effect in British politics also: this applied especially in regard to the navy, and it was a brave candidate for parliamentary election who did not say 'yes' to the Navy League's standard question of whether he was for the maritime supremacy of Great Britain. In the naval race with Germany, all that the Radicals could do was to question the Admiralty's figures, not its *aims*; and on that issue, they were abandoned by Dilke, W. T. Stead and others who, whatever their 'progressive' views on the domestic front, advocated two-keels-to-one as the proper naval ratio with Germany.

Even in the far less popular matter of conscription, it is possible to see this idea make headway in the ranks of conservatism at least, with three MPs supporting the National Service League in 1905 and over a hundred by 1914 – a development which reflects the growing influence of the Tariff Reformers, and also perhaps the stiffening of attitudes over Home Rule. It is therefore interesting to note a corresponding rise in the leadership's acceptance of conscription: although still insisting that the issue should not be settled by one party alone, the concept itself was regarded favourably by Curzon, Lansdowne, Wyndham, F. E. Smith, Arthur Lee and Bonar Law by 1911 – a sign that Milner's earlier idea that conscriptionists should penetrate the party in order to (as he put it) 'force the pace'[85] had had considerable success, somewhat resembling the Pan-Germans' penetration of their establishment. Yet this trend, in turn, had its impact upon the power balance within the Liberal Party, for it compelled the Radicals to modify their assault upon the Liberal-imperialists. The conscriptionists' attack upon Haldane's Territorial scheme, for example, made it necessary for those in the party who normally regarded the War Minister with distrust to spring to his defence: the War Office was better in his hands than in Milner's![86] By the same token, as noted earlier, all Liberal disputes over Grey's foreign policy could only take place under the proviso that it did not lead to a party split and a Conservative government. Such a cramping of a 'truly Liberal' external policy was to be of immense significance in 1914.

# CHAPTER 19

# *Religious, Racial, Cultural and Dynastic Connections – and their Relevance*

If the rise in chauvinism was tending to drive the British and German peoples apart, could not this be countered by an appeal to those factors which bound them together? This, certainly, was the line taken by the Anglo-German Friendship Committee:

> We know of no possible ground of serious quarrel between the two countries. On the contrary, we find in their history, their common faith and long friendship, their mutual indebtedness in literature, science and art, the strongest reasons for the maintenance of cordial and friendly relations.[1]

Could not also the common bonds of race and religion, so emphasised by earlier generations, dampen down the animosities in public opinion? Did not the dynastic links between Windsor and Potsdam, and the frequent visits of the respective monarchs to each other's country, demonstrate how closely the two powers remained connected at this, the highest level? Was no 'cement' to be found in their shared cultural traditions which, as the historian Erich Marcks claimed in 1900, made England more like Germany than any other country in the world?[2]

The blunt answer must be that, with one exception (that is, the peculiar role of Wilhelm II), the religious, racial, cultural and dynastic ties which, so many people felt, bound Britain and Germany together were of little or no weight in the changing relationship. Religious controversies themselves were, in all respects, much less important than in the 1860s and 1870s. In part, this was due to the general 'secularisation of the European mind';[3] and, more specifically, to the rise in scepticism and in socialism – churchmen had now much more in common with each other, as against these new challenges. In Germany, for example, the Centre Party's steady move towards the Reich government was paralleled by the Catholic bishops' approbation of the Kaiser's stand against 'atheism and revolution'. Of course, in specific regions – in

386

Wales, because of the issues of education and disestablishment, in Poland, and in the Irish question – religion *was* politically significant; elsewhere, it was much less so. Within the Anglican Church, theologians in the 1890s had managed to blend the newer German scholarship into the accepted doctrines without any of the rows which had convulsed the previous generation.[4] All this did not mean that the popular manifestations of religious differences, or the pamphlets produced by fanatical Protestants against ultramontanism and 'papal plots', suddenly ceased; but that it was only on odd occasions – such as the question of Edward VII calling upon the Pope during his 1903 Rome visit[5] – that the factor of religious prejudice affected governments and élites.

But the chief argument against allocating any weight to the Anglo-German religious tie must be that, among those affected by deep sectarian prejudice were many of the arch-patriots! It was the Radicals within the German Navy League, for example, who not only pressed for a much larger fleet against Britain but also were opponents of the Centre Party; it was the Pan-Germans who, when taking time off from combating the Catholic Poles and Alsatians, were the bitterest anglophobes – and they had their apt counterpart in someone like Arnold White, who strove with equal devotion to expose the intrigues of Germans, aliens, Jews, Socialists and papists.[6] Similarly, the most stalwart English defenders of Protestant privilege in Ulster were those nationalists who were alarmed about the 'German peril' – Milner, Roberts, Garvin, Kipling, Amery, and so on. If there were undertones of anti-Catholicism, and a desire to use the Ulster crisis as a further means of assaulting the Liberal government, it is clear that the chief motivation behind these people was nationalism. The *Observer*, Garvin insisted to Strachey, would not fight from the 'narrower Ulster point of view and . . . identify it with mere class interests and sectarian rancour. The question of imperial integrity and power is and always has been decisive for me.'[7] And Kipling felt so committed to the cause that he gave £30,000 – a colossal sum in those days – to the Ulster Defence fund.[8] The enthusiasts for outright British ascendancy in South Africa in 1899–1902 now reassembled for, as they saw it, a similar struggle over Ireland after 1910. The sectarian argument being in no way as important as the national one, it was no paradox for them to be simultaneously opposed to Irish Catholics and Protestant Germany. Religious ties, as one scholar has remarked,[9] could *reinforce* a political alliance but they could never overcome the hostility which derived from a clash of national interests; and the clearest example of this is that in 1914 'Protestant' Germany and 'Catholic' Austria-Hungary engaged in war with 'Protestant' Britain, 'Catholic' France and 'Orthodox' Russia!

Against the logic of power-politics, the activities of well-meaning clerics in prewar Europe counted for little. In parallel with, and in many cases overlapping the efforts of the Anglo-German Friendship Society, churchmen in the two countries made strenuous efforts after 1905–6 to improve relations between their peoples: the creation of national organisations (with thousands of clerical members), exchange visits and the dispatch of mutual expressions of goodwill were their chief activities. On the British side, the predominant roles were played by Quakers and Methodists, with the Anglican Church less involved, although the Archbishop of Canterbury and other leading bishops did encourage the movement; in Germany, many Lutheran pastors responded eagerly. Catholics were generally not part of it, which is hardly surprising when one notices the frequent references to the common links between the descendants of Luther and those of Wycliffe and Wesley.[10] Like the pacifists and Liberal-internationalists with whom they so often intermingled, these churchmen proclaimed the everlasting friendship of Britain and Germany, but had no means of turning that aim into state policy. Moreover, it also needs to be recalled that many an Anglican vicar encouraged the National Service League;[11] and that among the most rabid Pan-German utterances of Wilhelmine Germany were those of the *Allgemeine Evangelisch-Lutheranische Kirchen-Zeitung* and the *Reichsbote* (which was financed by church funds). Large numbers of 'militarised' clerics argued that Christ never really spoke of 'eternal peace between the peoples'; international differences, they preached, were like those between individuals, 'God-willed' and unalterable on this earth, and thus very likely to lead to clashes.[12]

In just the same way, allusions to the common racial stock of Britons and Germans litter pre-1914 speeches and press articles – yet counted for little in actual political terms. The Kaiser's frequent reference to this racial connection, usually in contrast to his less favourable remarks about the Slavs and the Latins, was notorious. Our two countries, he informed Edward VII,

> are of the same blood and they have the same creed and they belong to the great Teutonic race which Heaven has entrusted with the culture of the world; for – apart from the Eastern races, there is no other Race left for God to work his will in and upon the world except ours; that I think is grounds enough to keep Peace and to foster mutual recognition and reciprocity in all what [sic] draws us together and to sink everything which could part us![13]

If a large amount of this was tactically induced rhetoric, there are too many other utterances by Wilhelm to allow one to assume that race was a negligible factor with him: he simply did think and speak in racial terms, and was encouraged in this by luminaries such as Houston Stewart Chamberlain, by all the Pan-Germanic ideas of the time, and by advisers such as the younger Moltke. Yet, being the common currency of the period, it could be used in various conflicting ways: when, in early December 1912, Berlin was warned that Britain would intervene in a continental war to uphold the balance of power, Wilhelm angrily accused the 'nation of shopkeepers' of racial treachery, joining 'the Slavs against its own race in the struggle of the Teutons against the Slav flood'; but his friend Eisendecher used the opposing argument that, since 'Western Europe, Latins and Teutons, will have to make a stand against the Slavs, the United States and later perhaps against the yellow races', Berlin should seek an Anglo-German-French alliance.[14]

Perhaps the best example of the irrelevance of the racial connection lies on the British side, in the turn-of-the-century efforts of the arch-imperialists to secure solidarity between their country, Germany and the USA. Chamberlain, in his controversial Leicester speech of 1899, openly referred to his hopes for 'a new Triple Alliance between the Teutonic race and the two great branches of the Anglo-Saxon race';[15] and Rhodes made his contribution to this idea by financing a number of German Rhodes scholarships in addition to those for the Empire and the USA.[16] Such gestures obviously accorded with the Oxford School's teaching about the 'teutonic' origins of the British race, and with the current atmosphere of Social Darwinism; but they related even more directly to the British imperialists' search for an ally in an increasingly hostile world. Within a few years of this, however, the Chamberlainites had quite altered their attitude and perceived in Germany their greatest foe, against which they urged an alliance with Gauls, Slavs and Japanese. In specific colonial contexts, a sub-current of this notion of the racial identity of the healthy, industrious Teutons – especially as contrasted with the 'decadent', 'immoral' French and Portuguese colonists – was to continue until 1914 itself. However, most British and German nationalists appear to have adopted a rather neat reinterpretation which encompassed both a recognition of their enmity *and* of their racial similarity: namely, that the qualities of the other people, being similar to their own, made it into a formidable and worthwhile opponent. The 'final reckoning', which the Pan-Germans (in allusion to Treitschke) anticipated, would have an epic quality about it. This was also the message of Homer Lea's *The Day of the Saxon* and F. S. Oliver's *Ordeal by Battle*, although neither went to the lengths of Professor Cramb, whose book *Germany and England* (June 1914) was much influenced by Treitschke and Nietzsche, and envisaged a Teutonic war-god looking down 'upon his favourite children, the English and the Germans, locked in death-struggle, smiling upon the heroism of that struggle'.[17]

The same tendency can be observed in the Anglo-German cultural relationship, although that is obviously so broad a field that it allows for numerous variations. It needs to be noted straight away, for example, that all of those 'non-political' interactions covered earlier in this study[18] continued unabated. The English Goethe Society widened the appreciation of Germany's literary heritage upon its side of the North Sea, and the Shakespeare societies in Germany carried out a similar task on the other. Hegelianism gradually became an accepted part of the philosophy curriculum and, under Bosanquet, Bradley and their colleagues, received further modification into English forms of thought. Oxford (1907) and Cambridge (1911) at last received chairs in German language and literature. Admiration for German music in Britain remained unaltered, while Germans – now confronting the problems of an industrial society – followed with keen interest the designs and ideas of William Morris, and the creation of 'garden cities'. The art of Burne-Jones and Beardsley also produced many German admirers. Further up the social scale, aristocrats and their architects imitated the style of *das englische Landhaus* – especially after Muthesius' book of the same title – and flocked into the newly created yacht clubs, social clubs and other social institutions of the 'gentleman'. A grand seigneur such as Lichnowsky would only order his suits from a London tailor. In the world of higher education, a stream of British students continued to flow to German universities for research purposes, although it is interesting to note that the numbers of natural scientists and mathematicians fell in the decade before 1914, when further expansion occurred in those subjects in Britain.[19]

Indications, which some historians point to,[20] that the turn of the century witnessed a revival of British interest in the Celtic and Gallic (as opposed to the Teutonic) elements in the national heritage should not be taken to imply that the purely cultural 'pull' of German scholarship was diminishing. Where a transformation took place was in the decline of that mid-Victorian tendency of *political* germanophilia, deriving from cultural admiration: in the era of Wilhelm II, as may be imagined, an unqualified pro-German stance was difficult to sustain, especially among the newer generation. It was no longer possible to believe, as Max Müller had once done, that 'With two such ambassadors as Shakespeare and Goethe, we should soon have a true alliance between Germany and England, an alliance quite independent of changing cabinets for it is based upon mutual respect and inclination.'[21] Instead, the admirers of German culture in England, such as Maitland, were now content if the mutual abuse and false presentations of the other country were abandoned, and there was instead 'an amendment of manners on both sides of the sea'.[22]

In many areas of life, traditional assumptions about the other people did linger on, despite changes in global politics and newspaper opinion. There was a regular scramble by members of the *haute bourgeoisie* to fill any vacant (and unpaid) British honorary consular office in Germany, for this still brought with it social prestige and, possibly, a coveted British decoration.[23] Even more interesting was the continued appeal of an Oxbridge education. In the years before 1914, for example, there were enough Germans in Oxford (many of them Rhodes scholars) to form a society which met for debates and social events. Its membership appears to have been overwhelmingly aristocratic, including Baron Marschall von Bieberstein, Count Felix von Schwerin, Baron von Plessen, Baron von Richthofen, Prince Heinrich XLI Reuss;* so, too, were its political proclivities, for the votes at the end of their various debates were strongly against 'the principles of Liberalism', in favour of the 1913 German military increases, and so on – yet they also voted 'that, from every consideration of national temperament, culture and politics, Germany and England ought to be ABSOLUTE ALLIES in the strictest sense of the phrase'.[24] The general belief that the German aristocracy was anglophobic because of an ideological dislike of the British socio-political system hardly accords with this sentiment, which was shared by the families of the students concerned: to the great magnates of Silesia and south Germany, unlike the poorer Junkers or the fervent Pan-Germans, there was still much to admire about British society and culture. It is both a dreadful irony, and a comment upon the political efficacy of such social affections, that Bethmann Hollweg's son (a Rhodes scholar) and Asquith's son were educated at Balliol and then fell on the western front within a year of each other.[25]

The traditionalism inherent in the fondness of certain German aristocrats for Oxford college life prompts the historian to wonder to what extent references to the common cultural ties were characteristic of an earlier generation and its

* In all cases, younger relations of the statesmen and diplomats of the same surname.

received assumptions. The Duke of Argyll (born in 1845), influenced by Anglo-German dynastic ties, was not a person to change his political convictions late in life; thus, he willingly joined Avebury (b. 1843), Sir Herbert Maxwell (b. 1845), Sir John Kenneway (b. 1837), Lord Stanmore (b. 1829) and other elderly notables as honorary presidents or vice-presidents of the Anglo-German Friendship Society in 1905. The society, as one scholar has shown, 'was to a large extent a league of pensioners, who were born in mid-century and had already withdrawn from active service in business, the military or government. Their average age lay between 60 and 70.'[26] This 'generational' aspect obtains some reinforcement from a glance at the prominent anglophiles in Wilhelmine Germany, such as Richter, Bebel, Wilhelm Liebknecht, Bamberger, Roggenbach and Theodor Mommsen; and if this age factor is not universally applicable, then the appeal also made by, say, Bernstein, Morel, C. P. Trevelyan and Brentano to the common cultural heritage of Britain and Germany as being a reason for their friendship harked back to a cosier world in which navy leagues and Pan-German pamphlets had simply not existed.

On the British side, interest in things German greatly increased around the turn of the century, although it would be difficult to describe this trend as being necessarily germanophile in tone and purpose: it derived rather from the concern at Britain's relative economic and strategical decline, and from the belief that the German state offered a 'model' capable of adaptation to British circumstances. It was the Boer War reverses, or the lessons of Williams's *Made in Germany* (1896), which provided the stimulus for this increased study of German practices, and not a revival of any Arnoldian reverence for *Kultur* itself. The attention of British university reformers, for example, was now much less upon the ideal of a 'rounded' education than upon the technological and industrial benefits which, it was reckoned, would flow from the establishment of British equivalents to Charlottenburg: the development of Imperial College and the University of Birmingham, and the interest shown in this field by 'national efficiency' enthusiasts such as Chamberlain, Rosebery and Haldane, indicated the purpose behind such a trend. Similarly, Britons were not so much interested in imbibing Hegelian conceptions of the state as in studying specific features of government action, especially in the realm of social policy. Even in the 1880s, acute politicians such as Chamberlain had watched the new German insurance legislation with great interest, and this had been heightened by Dawson's book *Bismarck and State Socialism* (1890), which asked in its preface: 'Who will give to the British working-man the blessing which Prince Bismarck has conferred on his German brother?'[27] This was a matter on which both Liberal and Unionist politicians, without checking whether the German worker showed appreciation for these Bismarckian devices, were keen to acquire credit with the electorate. Lloyd George's famous visit to Germany in 1908 to study the social insurance system was only one of the many trips made by Britons in these years, and there is little doubt that, with Dawson acting as one of Lloyd George's advisers, the German practice was indeed held up as a 'model' to emulate. As Churchill put it to Asquith, it was intended 'to thrust a big slice of Bismarckianism over the whole underside of our industrial system'.[28] In Dawson's own case, it is clear that his respect for German efficiency mingled with admiration for that country as a whole; but it is difficult to believe that Lloyd George and Churchill felt the same way.

The same remark can be made, with even more emphasis, about other areas in which Germany functioned as exemplar to those seeking to correct perceived British weaknesses. Ever since Sedan, certain military reformers such as Sir John Maurice had pointed to the superior organisation of the Prussian army, especially with its fabled General Staff, although the War Office took little account of such suggestions for change. In the harsher world of the 1890s, and with the publication of Spenser Wilkinson's *The Brain of an Army*, opinion began to shift; and the Boer War, predictably, served to justify the claims of those who saw the military system as being typical of the traits of casualness and *laissez-faire* neglect which were the cause of the nation's decline. However, it was not until Haldane moved into the War Office to create his 'Hegelian army' that the German influence was fully visible, although the formation of the Committee of Imperial Defence in 1902 and the Esher Committee's recommendation of the establishment of an army General Staff in 1904 bore obvious signs of deference to the alleged Teutonic habits of planning and efficiency.[29] In much the same way, many who agitated about Britain's comparative industrial retardation pointed to the German 'model' – and not simply to the need for better technical education but also for an improvement in management techniques, a greater emphasis upon professional salesmanship, investment in new plant, and so on. By this emphasis upon 'efficiency', of course, Liberals such as Rosebery and Haldane hoped to take the wind out of the sails of the British protectionists; yet the latter also found it useful to point to German precedents, in the form of a carefully calculated tariff system and a variety of other means of state support for industry. The Tariff Reform League even paid for visits by British workers to Germany – to allow them to witness industrial and social conditions there, and to counter the free-traders' argument that their German equivalents lived only on black bread – which forms a neat contrast to the mid-century years, when the *Nationalverein* had sent German workers to Britain, to convince them of the merits of imitating the 'workshop of the world'.[30] Emulation of a rival, in order to *counter* his competition, certainly led to an increased interest in the other country; but it would be stretching the meaning of the word to extremes to describe these various groups of reformers as pro-German.

Given the obvious motivations behind such movements, it is also not surprising to discover their opponents showing a dislike of this German model, or 'Prussianism' as they termed it; opposed to a radical extension of the activities of the state, traditionalists argued that Teutonic practices were unsuitable for 'free-born Englishmen'. Salisbury, Campbell-Bannerman, the Duke of Cambridge and War Office bureaucrats were unmoved by Spenser Wilkinson's agitations for a 'Moltke' figure to direct British grand strategy. Bismarckian social insurance schemes produced shudders among the defenders of *laissez-faire*, who maintained that state interventionism had encouraged rather than defeated socialism. Free-traders felt it necessary to counter protectionist arguments by pointing to the impact of tariffs upon the German workers' standard of living. Even the radical Liberals, although pressing for social reforms, were usually unhappy with German precedents since this emphasised cold-blooded, scientific state management alone rather than *ethical* renewal and a concern for the quality of life.[31] Haldane's praise of Hegelian efficiency-cum-statism therefore drew attacks not only from germanophobes like Maxse but also from Radicals like Stead and Hobhouse; and the *Speaker* scored an important point when it claimed that the illegal flogging of Chinese labour in the Transvaal occurred because an 'essentially German mind' like Milner's directed British policy.[32] In much the same way, although denouncing the germanophobe 'invasion scares' and pleading for Anglo-German harmony, Radicals always found it useful to counter the National Service League's propaganda by deprecating references to the 'Prussian barrack-room' system. It all depended, in other words, upon *which characteristic* of the other country it was momentarily expedient to fasten upon for the purposes of the argument.

On the German side, too, there was no strict correlation between the cultural world and the political. The German Crown Prince had his new residence near Potsdam, the Cecilienhof, built along the lines of *das englische Landhaus* just before the First World War, but the historian would be rash to deduce that its owner was an anglophile! Many German naval officers in this period respected the Royal Navy for its advanced technology, the *corps d'esprit* of the deck officers, and so on, yet this hardly implied a promise of eternal goodwill. Even Tirpitz, who became steadily more bitter against Britain as his great 'plan' was neutralised, shared much of the traditional German admiration for the way of life and self-assurance of the 'English gentleman': his daughter attended Cheltenham Ladies College, the family governess was an Englishwoman, and that language was often spoken at home – but none of this was a guide to his political views.[33]

By the same token, it would be equally erroneous to assume that, because a Briton had studied in a German university, his intellectual debt ensured that he would be germanophile: G. P. Gooch and W. H. Dawson (both of whom had a German wife) remained so, despite the fact that the former had attended Treitschke's lectures;[34] but many more Britons were offended by the rampant anglophobia. Cramb, Wickham Steed and Austen Chamberlain heard Treitschke's denunciations of the 'pepper-jobbers' of London, and drew an obvious conclusion from the applause which greeted the old man's outbursts.[35] An excellent example of knowledge leading to *suspicion* is provided by Garvin, who wrote in 1912 that his study was full of German works, including:

> my edition of Kant, which once belonged to the historian Buckle; my Clausewitz, whom I should like to name as the greatest analyst not only of military operations but of all human dealings; my Ranke in its entirety; the complete edition of Treitschke and of Sybel, and similarly of Mommsen, Curtius and later authors; Bismarck's speeches, letters and memoranda; most of Moltke's publications, social-economists of all schools and – it is probably superfluous to say – the poets from Goethe downwards. Nothing will break the bonds between me and these old friends, and they testify that on my part there is no lack of an initial good

will. But, of course, next to these stand all the volumes of 'Nauticus' and of the 'Marine-Rundschau', which remind me *daily* that the second-largest fleet in the world has been created in scarcely ten years and so far no limit has been placed upon its expansion.

Being then engaged in reading Bernhardi's *Deutschland und der nächste Krieg*, and in re-reading the section in Treitschke's *Deutsche Kämpfe* about 'the final reckoning' with England, Garvin concluded that admiration for German culture could not outweigh Britain's need for 'security'.[36] As he and Northcliffe (who also regularly read German books and journals) agreed, it was because the Germans and their culture and their technical achievements were so impressive 'that the danger is great: they have every qualification for taking our place, and are bound to aspire to it more and more ardently as time goes on and their trade and wealth and fleet expand together'.[37]

Men in official positions felt the same way as journalists and intellectuals. Crowe and Tyrrell, both brought up in Germany for some years, mingled respect for German prowess with suspicion of that country's long-term aims. Haldane for years openly preached the merits of Germany's achievements – and paid the penalty for this during the war itself; but despite the arch-patriots' suspicions of him, his political view of the *Kaiserreich* was different from that of the Radicals. Even during his various endeavours to improve Anglo-German relations (so frowned upon by the Foreign Office staff), he repeatedly warned the German government that Britain would defend France against aggression, and his army reforms were designed to that end. In Berlin, too, officialdom made a distinction between culture and politics. Early in 1901, Lichnowsky had suggested that the German press might be encouraged to dwell upon the 'identity of religion, race and culture' between the two peoples, but Bülow minuted: 'This argument does not weigh with us . . .'[38] By 1912, as ambassador in London, Lichnowsky had learnt his lesson. Such considerations as Britain's great indebtedness to German philosophers, poets and musicians were, he wrote, 'useful at after-dinner speeches and other occasions, but break down in the face of harsh reality and prove themselves to be powerless when the vital requirements of a people and the laws of human advancement come into question'.[39] Even the Kaiser, whose own taste for the theatrical was probably the real reason for his enthusiastic support of the visits of the English Theatre and the *Deutsches Theater* to each other's country, can hardly have been serious in his assertion that 'Drama is a mediator between nations' – and that remark became even less plausible when a Berlin theatre produced du Maurier's 'An Englishman's Home' in 1909 and provoked a riot among an audience unwilling to accept their army being portrayed as marauding Huns![40]

This leads to one further and very obvious point about the role of cultural and intellectual figures in this period: namely, their portrayal of the *differences* between the two countries and, more generally, the reinforcement they gave to the notion of the particular merits of their own nation. The great danger in any such investigation always lies in taking certain expressions out of their proper literary context, so that observations upon England in (say) Fontane's *Der Stechlin* or upon Germany in Ford Madox Ford's *The Desirable Alien* are given a political significance which they do not really deserve. Similarly, to lump Nietzsche in an undifferentiated way along with Treitschke and Bernhardi as a sort of *spiritus rector* of German expansionism, as many Britons did during the war years, is to compound that sin of misinterpretation.[41] Nevertheless, various other writers do have a significance in the story of the changing Anglo-German relationship, either because they deliberately sought to comment upon that development or because their writings can be seen to have had a measurable impact upon contemporary politics and thought.

Analysis of the first category, the overtly political, is obviously the easier task. Whatever their artistic merit and literary motivation, many of Kipling's works were direct contributions to the debate upon contemporary issues. His 1902 poem 'The Islanders', with its assault upon 'the flannelled fools at the wicket', had been suggested to him by Roberts, and fellow imperialists rejoiced at the impact which it made: these 'stinging phrases', Maxse informed Amery, 'may do what all that criticism and exhortation has failed to do by rousing the British out of that dangerous self-complacency and laziness which must inevitably bring us to grief as a great Power.'[42] The political symbolism in a short story such as 'The Mother Hive' (1908), featuring the decay of a once-healthy breed after an 'alien' wax-moth is permitted entry and the subsequent salvation of a determined core of bees which break out of the hive to found another 'colony', was earnestly debated in the private correspondence of the imperial federationists. In other words, Kipling functioned – and *willingly* functioned – as the Poet Laureate of the Chamberlainites, articulating their message in a specific artistic fashion. If Germany produced no equivalent to him, then it certainly did not lack in 'ideas-men' who gave expression to nationalistic stirrings. It is scarcely possible, for example, to go through the memoirs of the Wilhelmine Right without encountering some reference to the impact which Treitschke had made upon their formative thoughts: Bülow, Tirpitz, Monts, Waldersee and Kardorff paid tribute to his noble message, university professors and publicists such as Lamprecht, Schäfer, Schiemann and Meinecke testified their indebtedness to his patriotic ideas, and advocates of Germany's world mission such as Peters, Rohrbach and Houston Stewart Chamberlain all insisted that – in the words of the Pan-German leader Heinrich Class – 'Treitschke was my master, who determined my life'.[43] To the Pan-Germans in particular, and to National Liberal politicians seeking to cover up party fissures by an appeal to the 'national idea', Treitschke offered not merely a cluster of suitable ideas but an intellectual respectability to match them.

This, too, was the dual function of that host of professorial advocates of a large fleet, or a *Mitteleuropa*, or a greater colonial empire, mentioned in the previous section. It was not simply that people such as Schmoller and Schäfer and Lamprecht lent the considerable prestige of an *Ordinarius* to imperialist propaganda campaigns and partook in the patriotic indoctrination of youth. It was also that they provided, to statesmen and public alike, an original interpretation of what was happening in the rapidly changing circumstances of the post-Bismarckian era. It was Schmoller, and after him Schulze-Gaevernitz, who explained to contemporaries the changing stages of the British political economy, from the earlier aggressive mercantilism, through the superficially peaceful age of Cobden, to the recent revival of the older piratical traditions by Disraeli and Chamberlain. It was Weber (*The Protestant Ethic* . . . ), Erich Marcks, O. E. Meyer, Schäfer and Schulze who undermined the older idea of a common religious bond by pointing to the differences between the egoistical English 'Puritanism' and the more ordered and idealistic German 'Lutheranism'. Many of the same writers, and Wilhelm Busch, also argued now (like Tout in Britain) against the earlier view that the basic forms of English political life had been inherited from the Teutonic folk-moot: things German were thus different from things Anglo-Saxon. It was also these historians who shifted the focus of attention from Britain's slow internal evolution towards parliamentarism, to her unscrupulous empire-building through the centuries (just as German opinion was shifting from internal reforms to external greatness); and who no longer alluded to the Anglo-Prussian unity in the wars against France, but rather to the benefits which England alone had secured in 1763 and 1815 from German sacrifices. In the same way, economics professors offered arguments and evidence about German trade and population as a justification for colonial and naval expansion; geopoliticians pointed to the secular trends of rising and falling empires; and 'neo-Rankians' refashioned the theory of the balance of power to suit a global rather than a European framework, thus justifying Germany's expansion with the idea that Britain's excessive and unhealthy predominance in the world equilibrium demanded a shifting of the weights.[44]

If such academic pundits willingly joined the government's attempts to evolve a national ideology, then, it is important to recognise that a *two-way* process of influencing was at work, since Wilhelmine intellectuals offered ideas which often captured the minds of the politicians – in just the same way, of course, as Seeley's book *The Expansion of England* and Mahan's *The Influence of Seapower upon History* had affected certain British decision-makers. While Wilhelm himself was notoriously susceptible to some startling or fashionable concept – as in his instantaneous response to Houston Stewart Chamberlain for singing 'the High Song of the German' and summoning the people 'to take up the task of being God's instrument for the spreading of his *Kultur*'[45] – then it is interesting to see how even a sceptical observer such as Baroness Spitzemberg was affected by reading the *Grundlagen des 19. Jahrhunderts*, or how the outwardly cynical Bülow privately enthused about the teachings of Treitschke well before he assumed high office.[46]

Inevitably, the messages which the establishment liked were those which preached a special German mission in the world and urged the people to coalesce behind the Kaiser in fulfilment of that goal. Nevertheless, there were also significant literary tracts which, although ostensibly critical of the prevailing social mores and objecting to the modernising tendencies which were turning Germany into a world power, indirectly reinforced the anti-Liberal and anti-British tone of the German public mind. Intellectual exemplars of 'the politics of cultural despair', it has been argued,[47] have less to offer the historian seeking to understand the Wilhelmine Right than either the thrusting personalities within the patriotic leagues or the broad-based reverberations within the *Mittelstand* which took place during this period of rapid industrialisation. Yet it was just because a book such as Langbehn's *Rembrandt als Erzieher* touched upon important cords within the German consciousness that it became such a best-seller – and is relevant to a study of the radical Right. The revolt against reason and the emphasis upon inner emotions, the appeal to a mystical *Volk*-idea, the preference for the countryside over the corrupting city, the criticisms of the superficiality and luxuriousness of the established orders, the attacks upon an atomistic society and the corroding influence of the Jews, *were* significant precisely because they articulated prejudices shared by a broad mass of people who felt trapped between an advancing proletariat on the one hand and the shallow and unsatisfying practices of 'official' Wilhelmine society on the other. Such sentiments obviously did not offer direct support to the *Flottenkaiser* or act in any way as a substitute for the material activities of agrarian leagues and shopkeepers' organisations; but they did contribute towards the evolution of a 'Germanic ideology' which defined itself, as it were negatively, by its dislike of a Liberal, free-trading, parliamentary democracy as symbolised by Britain; and they did reflect broadly held feelings of frustration, insecurity and yearnings for some psychic release – which goes a considerable way towards explaining the enthusiasm with which war was greeted by so many individuals in 1914.[48] Even the anti-establishment youth movement (which was overwhelmingly bourgeois in composition) 'channelled its wild exuberance directly into the war', as the casualty rate among their leadership well shows.[49] These cultural manifestations of the 'Revolt against the West' did, in other words, reflect profound reverberations within German society, especially among those groups capable of being mobilised to support the right-wing parties.

The images of England suggested both by some of the most respected Berlin professors and by obscure pamphleteers of *Blut und Boden* policies were, in consequence, highly unfavourable: a land of hypocritical tricksters, covering their misdeeds with appeals to morality; steeped in an egoistical, profit-and-loss mentality, unlike the German *Helden*; jealous of Germany's expansion and determined to check it, either by commercial counter-measures or by invoking the old cry about the European balance of power; weakened by the forces of liberalism and the blight of party politics, but nonetheless still a considerable foe because of its accumulated resources and ability to find diplomatic allies. Left-Liberal and SPD deputies in the Reichstag contested this picture, anglophiles such as Brentano strove to show the pleasanter aspects of British society, and 'moderate' imperialists and industrialists were willing to attempt co-operation between Berlin and London: yet the image remained among a broad mass of the German people.

Despite its many other social fissures, Edwardian Britain simply did not have this widespread anti-modernism and political anti-Semitism which would blend so easily with intellectual portrayals of a devious and dangerous foreign power to produce a stereotyped *Feindbild* (picture of the enemy). Nevertheless, a popular image of Germany was perpetuated by many sources, from *Punch* magazine to the 'invasion scare' literature, and from National Service League speeches to anti-militarist tracts. It was the picture already known during the 1860s in Britain (and in the south German states): namely, of Hohenzollern autocracy, of jackboots and mailed fists and preventive wars, of distaste for civilian and pacifist values, of internal obsequiousness to authority and a Prussian lust of conquest. In its way, it was as sweeping a dismissal of German political society as the portrayal of a 'nation of shopkeepers' was of Britain; but both were effective because it was what many people wanted to believe and also because certain incidents (the Boer War, the two Moroccan crises) lent some credence to this image.

What the rise of the Anglo-German antagonism did was to blur, but not totally obscure, the ideological 'gap' which Britons had detected between the two countries from the early or mid-Victorian period onwards. British Radicals in particular had always preferred France to Germany, which was why it took them a little while to get their bearings after the formation of the *entente cordiale*. In early 1906 Repington reported with amusement that he had told some Liberal MPs 'how indispensable it was to support France in order to preserve the liberties of Europe and the immortal principles of the French Revolution. This puts the extreme Rads in a fearful quandary'.[50] Certain older Liberals (such as Morley) and newer ones (such as Angell) did praise Germany's impressive cultural developments, but many more found it impossible to revise their traditional image of 'Prussian militarism'. Instead, they concentrated upon the dangers of 'Prussianisation' in Britain; or compared Germany with the even more reactionary Russia; or grew steadily more critical of the chauvinist revival in France, some going so far as to argue that it was the expectation of British support which had caused 'the monstrous recrudescence of the Revanche theory since 1905'.[51] Finally, Liberals fell back upon a very common argument, that a distinction should be made between the ruling clique in Imperial Germany, who were reactionary and bad; and the greater part of the German people, who were peace-loving and good and gaining in influence. This theory of the 'two Germanies', encouraged as it was by Bebel and to a certain extent (in his fight with Tirpitz) by Bethmann Hollweg, slowly permeated the thinking of Grey, Haldane and many others in official positions.

The majority of the British Right happily accepted this distinction. While it is true that many of them admired such features of German society as the educational system, compulsory military service, protective tariffs, and so on, only Milner and Cramb appear to have been fully committed to Prussian-Hegelian values. At times, the British germanophobes were willing to imitate what they considered to be their foe's unscrupulous methods: in 1901 Saunders argued that London should forget Liberal scruples about Russia's domestic politics and, following the traditions of Bismarckian Realpolitik, seek an alliance with her; in 1909 Gwynne warned Conan Doyle against taking the Congo atrocities campaign too far, lest it drive Belgium into Germany's arms;[52] and in 1911 Steed urged 'from the point of view of practical politics' against any moral denunciations of Italy's seizure of Tripoli in order to detach her further from the Triple Alliance.[53] This was blatant power-politics; yet they all insisted that this was justified 'since the success of the German plans would mean the predominance of the most reactionary and autocratic sovereign and of the most cynically arbitrary government in Europe'.[54] The toleration of Italian aggression was a venial sin, the turning of a blind eye to the fate of the Congolese natives a lesser evil, to those convinced of 'the determination of the

Prussian Junker class to force on, if possible, some foreign complication in order to prevent the destruction of Junker privileges by internal reform'.[55] As Strachey put it, 'I am [always careful] in the "Spectator" to distinguish between the ruling caste in Germany and the German people, for whom I have a most genuine love and respect. Unfortunately, however, the real German people, I mean the democracy, count almost for nothing.'[56]

It was the perpetuation and, indeed, the elaboration of this concept of a Junker-dominated autocracy which provides one of the two main reasons for the otherwise inexplicable distinction which the British Right made between the rising nation of Germany, which they disliked, and the rising nation of the United States, which almost uniformly they warmly admired. The latter feeling, which constantly puzzled Wilhelm, involved a disregard of many aspects of American politics which were not favourable to Britain; and it has been described by one scholar as the 'myth' of the Anglo-American special relationship, a cosy vision belied not only by the considerable Irish-American and German-American elements in the USA but also by the elemental growth of that country to become the world's greatest economic and naval power. If it was a myth, it was certainly widely held, by Liberals such as Harcourt and Churchill and Grey, Unionists such as Balfour and Chamberlain, navalists such as Fisher and Beresford, editors such as Garvin, Chirol, Strachey and many more – although much less so by the ageing Salisbury or by certain Eurocentric members of the Foreign Office.[57] What gave credence to the idea of a special relationship was not only the abstract bonds of a common language, high culture and set of legal assumptions, but also the various friendships between the élites of the two countries. With the 'WASP' element apparently friendly to Britain, the anglophobe rumblings of other ethnic groups was less alarming – in contrast to the image of Germany, where the élite was regarded as dangerous, but the people as peace-loving. This similarity in the political outlook of Washington and London permitted Selborne to argue in 1905 that the defence of Canada was assured simply because of the 'innate justice' of the Americans – a reasoning never applied to Germany when, say, the question of the defence of Belgium was being discussed. In one of the most remarked-upon articles of the time upon the 'Anglo-German Rivalry', Philip Kerr articulated the essential distinction in the British imperialists' views of Germany and the USA:

> During the years of her supremacy has [England] lifted a finger against the United States, which have now a population twice her own and resources immeasurably greater? No, for the ideals of the United States, like her own, are essentially unaggressive and threaten their neighbours no harm. But Germanism, in its want of liberalism, its pride, its aggressive nationalism, is dangerous, and she feels instinctively that if it is allowed to become all powerful it will destroy her freedom, and with it the foundation of liberty on which the Empire rests.[58]

To sum up: the cultural factor, especially when related to national policy, was always a two-edged weapon, useful both for justifying friendships *and* for explaining antagonisms. It was never the artistic and philosophical and organisational features of a society *per se* which were important; but rather the interpretations which different groups placed upon them.

If an analysis of the dynastic factor causes the gaze to shift from the world of general ideas and symbols to the role of specific individuals, the task facing the historian of the Anglo-German relationship remains the same: how to fit this particular aspect of the story into the overall framework. In certain biographical studies, the personality of Kaiser Wilhelm II looms larger than life, dominating the tone and direction of post-1890 German politics: yet in more recent, 'structural' accounts, he almost disappears altogether or assumes the position of a mere figurehead.[59] And, if some studies of Edward VII's reign are to be believed, he was personally responsible for the reshaping of British world policy and the 'encirclement' of Germany – whereas he receives little or no mention in the broader analyses of this period.[60]

No investigation of dynastic influences can begin without returning to the obvious point that the constitutional position of the two monarchs were very different: this was blurred earlier, as we have seen,[61] by the great personal influence of Queen Victoria over her ministers, as compared with Wilhelm I's deference to Bismarck, but the distinction became more marked after 1890. By the final decade of her life, moreover, the queen was obviously not as capable as before of interfering in the day-to-day processes of diplomacy; and, trusting in Salisbury's judgement, she felt much less need to exercise what vague constitutional prerogatives she still possessed. Nevertheless, the Prime Minister consulted her frequently and, although his letters employed the deferential language of subject to monarch, they give the impression that it was her qualities of moderation and good sense – rather than her position as Queen-Empress – which evoked his respect, and the consequent wish to consult her often, as with some senior Cabinet colleague. In the specific field of Anglo-German relations, these qualities emerge consistently. She disapproved of 'Willy's' antics, rebuked him firmly in her letters when he overstepped the bounds of decorum, and deplored the rise of reactionary and chauvinistic forces in Germany; yet she also strove, within the natural limitations of her own prejudices, to be 'fair minded' to her grandson. Furthermore, she appreciated the benefits which Britain derived from seeking to be on good terms with Germany *and* France, and therefore agreed both to Salisbury's policy of not being pushed against the latter, and to accept the necessity of inviting the Kaiser to England every so often, despite the personal strain. In the aftermath of the Kruger Telegram, she and the Prime Minister felt that it would be wise neither to 'cut' Wilhelm for his impetuous action, nor to inquire too much into his motives.[62] Thus, although Salisbury and the Kaiser never got on well together, both regarded the queen as having an ameliorating effect upon the other: 'Your Majesty's personal influence over the Emperor William is a powerful defence against danger in that direction', Salisbury assured her in 1899.[63]

On Wilhelm's part, and despite oscillations of feeling, there was nothing insincere about his admiration for the old lady, as was most dramatically illustrated by his visit to her deathbed. At the outbreak of war in 1914, he still clung to this image of her: 'To think that George and Nicky should have played me false! If my grandmother had been alive, she would never have allowed it.'[64] Yet it is also necessary to recall that, however much the Windsor–Potsdam connection favourably affected the Kaiser's view of England, it also threatened to divide him from the forces of German nationalism, which had no such sentimental attachment and indeed claimed on numerous occasions (the 1890 Heligoland-Zanzibar treaty, the 1896 'revelations' by Bismarck, the Kaiser's visits to England during the Boer War and the *Daily Telegraph* affair) that the 'English influence' deranged a truly German foreign policy. It was also resented by Bülow, who could perceive in it a potential source of influence which – unlike most other rivals for Wilhelm's ear – could not easily be shut off. When, in 1898, the Empress Frederick revived her husband's old notion of an Anglo-German alliance and '*Weltherrschaft* by two', Bülow had to employ all his diplomatic dexterity to draw the Kaiser away from that tempting idea.[65]

If the queen generally had a good influence upon Anglo-German political relations, then her successors manifestly did not. Nevertheless, it is necessary to distinguish between the *intention* and the *effect*, and to relieve Edward VII from the accusation – or the proud claim – that he 'reshaped' Europe and played a major role in the encirclement of Germany. What is indisputable is that he rarely, and only temporarily, was on good terms with his pushful nephew – 'the most brilliant failure in history', as he acidly described him. This personal dislike was of long standing, originating in the Prince of Wales's criticism of Prussian manners and policies, in the German treatment of the Empress Frederick and in Wilhelm's disapproval of Edward's social habits and raffish friends.[66] In 1898, Deym found the Prince of Wales raging at his nephew and claiming that an alliance would not come off because Germany would ask too much; in 1905, Lansdowne reported that 'the King talks and writes about his Royal Brother in terms which make one's flesh creep'; and Lascelles was so uncomfortable in the middle of this mutual abuse that he sought repeatedly to resign.[67] After Edward's death, his great confidant Esher drafted an article for the *Deutsche Review* which was intended to assure its readers that the late king had possessed no resentment of Germany's rise; but Knollys, the Royal Secretary, informed Esher that he felt uncertain 'that you do not impute a kinder feeling towards [Germany] on the part of King Edward than was really the case. From numerous conversations I had with him, I should have said that he felt towards Germany as 999 Englishmen out of 1000 do; very considerable distrust.'[68]

However, the chief point about Edward's dislike of Germany was that it was chiefly rooted in personal factors, in the up-and-down relationship with his nephew. On several occasions, the quarrels between the two monarchs were easily settled by a personal meeting – which is not remarkable since they usually involved points of honour, family jealousies and misunderstandings or false gossip about the opinions of the other, rather than substantial political matters; and after these meetings the two men went away, declaring themselves well pleased with the other. Edward's influence was, therefore, both inconsistent and lacking in direction. Nor is it possible to argue that the latter was provided by friends and protegés who had a more recognisable anti-German bias: for while it was true that he patronised people such as Hardinge, Bertie, Fisher and the Portuguese minister in London, Soveral, he also had close friendships with 'pro-Germans' such as Cassell, 'Natty' Rothschild, Sir Felix Semon and the Austro-Hungarian ambassador Mensdorff.

Least of all can it be argued that Edward was the purposeful 'encircler' of Germany, as the Kaiser claimed in that spectacular outburst on the eve of war:

> So the celebrated *encirclement* of Germany has finally become an accomplished fact, in spite of all the efforts of our politicians to prevent it. The net has suddenly been closed over our head, and the purely *anti-German policy* which England has been scornfully pursuing all over the world has won the most spectacular victory . . . Even after his death Edward VII is stronger than I, although I am still alive![69]*

In actual fact, Edward's personalised form of diplomacy worked as much against the conclusion of the French and Russian *ententes* as for them. Even the famous 1903 trip to Paris (which he loved to visit in any case) was less of a deliberate counter-move to the rising German 'menace' than was imagined, although it is true that the king was out of humour with Wilhelm at that time, was eager to improve Anglo-French relations and did have a spectacular success with the Paris crowds. All of Edward's felicitous speeches were drafted by Hardinge, 'and he [the king] never changed a single word';[70] and Mensdorff, who was frequently with Edward, shrewdly wrote that the monarch did not expect the visit to have such consequences but was now willing to bask in the general praise.[71] If he played this contributory role, however, it was the exigencies of the Russo-Japanese War and the growing concern of the French and British Cabinets about German intentions, which fashioned the *entente cordiale*. By the summer of 1904, moreover, Edward had re-established relations with Wilhelm, and therefore assumed that Anglo-German tensions were over; and his initial reaction to the Dogger Bank shootings suggests that he – unlike the real anti-German groups in Britain – had not considered that an Anglo-Russian war would allow Berlin to become the *tertius gaudens*. Many years later, Balfour wrote to Lansdowne that he was puzzled to read a history book which 'quite confidently attributes the policy of the *entente* to Edward VII', whereas the fact 'during the years which you and I were his Ministers, he never made an important suggestion of any sort on the larger questions of policy'.[72]

Far from the king being the clever director of British foreign policy, he was often puzzled by the course it was taking. One of the most ironic discoveries about this period must surely be that Eyre Crowe's famous 1907 'Memorandum on the Present State of British Relations with France and Germany' – generally regarded as the classic statement of London's prewar policy of moving against Germany in order to preserve the balance of power – was originally asked for by Edward who 'had repeatedly expressed himself per-

---

* That this 'myth' still enjoys a considerable vogue can be seen in the current television series on Edward, who, as I write this section, is alleged (*New York Times*, 18/1/1979, advertisement on p. A21) to have 'singlehandedly forged a new Anglo-French alliance that changed the world'.

turbed by what he thought was our persistent unfriendly attitude towards Germany contrasted with our own eagerness to run after France & do anything the French asked'![73] Although the king 'expressed satisfaction' at Crowe's explanation, he frequently clashed with Grey and the Foreign Office over measures to improve Anglo-German relations in 1906–7, and one observer reported in May 1907 that he 'was now frightened and said Grey was too anti-German for his tastes'.[74] In the following two years, predictably enough, the 'Tweedmouth' and *Daily Telegraph* affairs and the escalating naval race inclined Edward much more in an anti-German direction; but it is doubtful whether the many visits he paid to fellow-monarchs in this period were by themselves successful – or even designed – as a counter to Berlin's policies. In a neat comment upon the diplomatic rumours which attended the royal visit to Stockholm in 1908, Onslow noted:

> To hear our courtiers talk one would think that the King's visits to the various courts of Europe had revolutionised our foreign policy. They do not seem to comprehend, what one would have imagined would be obvious to the most fatuous flatterer, that relations between two countries are friendly so long as the interests of both are served, & all the Kings in the world won't bring about rapprochements unless they are.[75]

Whatever the interpretation placed upon Edward's actions by 'courtiers' and foreigners – which has, of course, a significance even if it misinterprets the king's intentions – it is surely correct to argue that he 'never showed understanding of the larger, impersonal forces bearing upon the relations between states' and had 'no real influence upon the formation of policy'.[76]

If Salisbury complained that it was sometimes hard to persuade his royal mistress to agree to a particular action (especially if it involved a change in her residential schedule), and if Lansdowne and Grey on occasions had great difficulty in insisting that Edward VII's personal predilections must yield to the requirements of state policy, their task was a bed of roses compared with the problems faced by a German Chancellor in handling Kaiser Wilhelm II.

The greatest point of contrast was not so much in the unique personality of the last German emperor but in the fact that, constitutionally, he was a crucial political figure. Wilhelm may have claimed to have been above parties, but he was also at the centre of the governmental decision-making process, and all chains of authority terminated in him. He, and not the Reichstag, was the only body which could select and dismiss the Chancellor. Ministers were *his* men, and not senior politicians from the party or parties which had acquired the largest number of seats in the Reichstag; indeed, ministers could not be members of that institution. The entire conduct of foreign policy was in the hands of the Kaiser, and by delegation in those of the Chancellor and the *Auswärtiges Amt*: in August 1914, it is worth recalling, the Reichstag was informed after the event that Germany was at war, whereas the British government's decision still awaited the response which the Commons would give to Grey's speech on the 3rd. An even more important exclusion from the purview of *all* civilians was the military realm: appointments, structure, war-planning and other related issues were the business of the generals and their imperial Commander-in-Chief, and not of the Chancellor or a Cabinet committee or opinionated backbenchers. Even the Reichstag's financial powers were limited by the fact that so large a part of the budget was military expenditure, and that was allocated for seven or five years in advance. In other aspects of politics, especially where new legislation or additional monies were requested, Chancellors recognised that it was better to haggle with the parties than to risk a repetition of the constitutional conflict of the 1860s, and the party leaders were even more willing to compromise – but it still meant that the balance of power remained heavily tilted against the popular assembly. It was even difficult to envisage how a change in the system could be begun, for the Reichstag could not initiate any legislation, and it could be overridden by the Prussian-dominated senior house, the Bundesrat. To sum up, the legislature could not control the executive and, after 1890, the executive was conscious of the fact that it could only influence, but not control, the Kaiser. Wilhelm's powers were closer to, and probably greater than, those of George III than of Edward VII.

A related complication was that the Chancellor was by no means the only person who tendered Wilhelm advice. Quite apart from private individuals such as Stumm and Ballin who could 'sell an idea' to him, or an ambassador *en suite* such as Eulenburg whose confidential opinions extended to cover the dismissal and selection of Chancellors, the military authorities had unrestricted access to him, and so had the head of his own Civil Secretariat (*Civilkabinett*); the *Kabinett* heads, the Chiefs of Staff and the courtiers and *aides-de-camp* saw the monarch much more often than the Chancellor – with the exception of the assiduous Bülow. But the chaos of the German governmental system – rarely perceived by foreigners whose attention was focused upon the Reich's military and industrial achievements – went further than that. For example, within the navy, not only the heads of the *Reichsmarineamt*, the *Admiralstab* and the *Marinekabinett* but also of the Baltic and North Sea stations, the overseas cruiser squadron and even individual naval attachés could directly communicate with Wilhelm: just as there was no civilian Cabinet with collective responsibility for overall governmental policy, so also there existed no Board of Admiralty to direct naval policy. Nor, in the specific field of external affairs, was there anything like the Committee of Imperial Defence, which at least offered some form of institutionalised co-operation between the various ministries. Under the dominating personality of Bismarck, most of these threads of government had been gathered together and given a respectable degree of coherence: his dismissal in 1890 signified that the new Kaiser would not tolerate such a concentration of executive influence outside the monarchy. Now all the threads of government, whether official or semi-official, could only be woven together by Wilhelm himself. Although this system placed immense burdens upon the monarch, it could in theory be made to work if he possessed the required qualities of diligence, perspicacity, tolerance and sheer political maturity. Wilhelm, alas, had none of these.

It is impossible within a short space properly to portray that complex, effervescent individual, possessing knowledge and energy but without wisdom, impatient to add to his dynasty's glories, bored by the routine affairs of state and requiring continual attention and entertainment, expansive and cheery one day, moody and irritable the next, sensitive to suspected slights, erratic in so many of his policies, constantly active and interfering in all manner of topics to the exhaustion and despair of his advisers. 'The Kaiser is like a balloon', Bismarck observed. 'If you do not hold fast to the string, you never know where he will be off to.' His successors agreed. Caprivi, very regular and orthodox in his habits, found it increasingly impossible to deal with Wilhelm and his dismissal was only delayed because it would otherwise come too soon after Bismarck's. Hohenlohe, a more phlegmatic character, consoled himself with the thought that 'The purpose of my existence is after all simply to prevent overhasty decisions' – a task at which he was usually successful.[77] This was too negative an approach to endure for long, however, so that Eulenburg and Bülow resolved that the only solution was to go with the Kaiser, securing his long-term objects but steering him away from many potential disasters and never taking his day-to-day utterances as a 'lasting Principle'.[78] Here, too, only a temporary tranquillisation in German governmental policy occurred – at the cost of Eulenburg's health, and with occasional catastrophes which shook the system and (in the case of the *Daily Telegraph* affair) contributed to Bülow's fall. Even the widespread outcry against Wilhelm's erratic rule following upon that incident did not enable Bethmann Hollweg to gather up the threads of government in Bismarckian fashion; and this state of confusion and instability at the top continued until 1914, and after.

Even to the historian primarily concerned with long-term, structural changes, Kaiser Wilhelm II provides a classic example of the importance of the individual in politics. Of course, had his position been akin to that of, say, Ludwig of Bavaria, then the character failings, the intrigues of the camarilla, the personal crises and all the rest would have been of little import. Yet the crucial fact was that Wilhelm was not merely the epicentre of the many explosions at court but also the mainspring of a governmental system superimposed upon the most powerful and fastest-growing state in western Europe, and one which – as we have seen – was experiencing considerable social and political turmoil as a consequence of rapid industrial change. It was the interaction between these two fields of instability – the monarchical and the socio-political – which made the task of government in Wilhelmine Germany so difficult. The inner contradictions of German politics and society at the end of the nineteenth century are well known to historians; but in some curiously appropriate way, Wilhelm's personality symbolised many of those paradoxes. He was, Eulenburg noted, both modern and mediaeval[79] – enthusiastic about technology, new industries, a great navy and Germany's future mission in the world, yet also a stalwart defender of traditional Prussian-monarchical privileges, a convinced believer in the Divine Right of kings and prone to be carried away by feudal and mystical conceptions of politics. The critical 'management' problem of the leaders of the second Reich – how to preserve the old order in the face of the unstoppable processes of industrialisation and the 'massification' of politics – were to a large degree incorporated within

Wilhelm. It would not be fair to say that post-Bismarckian Germany got the leader it deserved; but simply to focus upon his personal eccentricities is to ignore the way in which the Kaiser both reflected and intermeshed with the country's broader problems. By the same token, Wilhelm's relationships with his five Chancellors, or with people such as Marschall, Tirpitz, Holstein, Miquel – and the crises, resignations and dismissals which were part of those relationships – revolved less around issues of political 'style' than around concrete political matters: how to deal with the SPD, how to preserve the *Sammlung*, how to forward the fleet policy, how to manage Anglo-German relations, and so on.

Only the last-named issue, of Wilhelm's impact upon relations with Britain, can be dealt with here. It is in itself difficult to unravel, partly because the Kaiser was, as Holstein observed, 'half an Englishman',[80] and possessed love-hate feelings towards his Anglo-Saxon cousins; and partly because the Anglo-German relationship in these years was so central to the external policy of both governments that it required continual care. A blow-by-blow account of Wilhelm's attitude from the fall of Bismarck to the outbreak of war in 1914 is not likely to contribute to an understanding of his overall role, if only because he *was* so changeable and so liable to make spectacular gestures or indulge in 'unofficial' diplomacy in a quite unpredictable fashion. 'He is continually interfering in foreign affairs', Marschall noted angrily in his diary: 'A monarch must speak the final word, but His Majesty always wants to have the first word, and that is a cardinal failure.'[81] A year later, in November 1896, Holstein complained to Eulenburg:

> On August 30th the Kaiser, utilising the confidential utterances of Lobanov to you, warned the English about the Russians.
> On 25th October the Kaiser telegraphed to the Chancellor that it was necessary to bind ourselves to Russia and France, as a security for our colonies against a threatening English attack.
> On 12th November the Kaiser telegraphed to the Chancellor that he had warned Grand-Duke Vladimir about England.
> On 21st November he told the English ambassador that he would always hold fast to England and that, to pave the way for a better understanding, he was ready to exchange the greater part of the German colonies for a coaling-station.
> How will this end?[82]

Admittedly, these were the complaints of people keen to restrict Wilhelm's interventions overall in politics; but even when their negative stance towards the Kaiser was replaced by the more subtle management techniques of Bülow, there was no guarantee that their imperial master would stay constant to the agreed lines of foreign policy towards Britain: a friendly visit to Windsor could influence Wilhelm one way, a critical article in *The Times* could produce the opposite effect. The amazing 'ups and downs' in his mood during the crises of early December 1912 and late July 1914 when his confident belief that Britain would stay neutral changed abruptly to furious disappointment, suggests that to the end he failed to understand his relations with the island state.[83]

Ultimately, Wilhelm's volatile behaviour towards England mattered much less than the long-term policies of the Reich which he either instigated or encouraged, and the general impact of his actions upon British observers. Without ascribing to him too great a share of responsibility – for he was a child of his times, influenced by other people's ideas and aware that the pro-royalists had to be placated – it is fair to argue that he threw all the weight of his office in favour of the illiberal, anti-parliamentary and anti-SPD forces of the establishment, at least once he had recoiled from his brief flirtation with Caprivi's 'liberalisation' policies in the early 1890s. Even Chancellors with impeccably conservative tendencies, such as Hohenlohe, Bülow and Bethmann Hollweg, saw that from time to time certain small-scale reforms (for example, on military courts-martial) were necessary if only because the existing practices were indefensible; but Wilhelm was frequently not to be moved in issues touching his royal prerogatives, and he certainly gave heart to the arch-conservative elements who shared his view that the SPD and the Reichstag should be dealt with much more firmly than successive Chancellors preferred. It is impossible to tell how German history would have turned out had its third Kaiser been a progressive, enlightened leader, bent upon reforms; arguably, since the illiberal system had been created 'from above', it could only be properly changed from the same source. By so fortifying the German Right, incidentally, Wilhelm not only helped to delay 'democratisation' but also enhanced the position of socio-economic groups which were much more hostile to Britain than he originally had been. The swing against Caprivi was also a swing against London, and a return to a pro-English diplomacy could only come about at the cost of disenchanting important groups of governmental supporters, as indeed occurred (to Bülow's distress) during the Boer War. Unable to see the logic of this, Wilhelm himself continued to oscillate between favouring an Anglo-German agreement and reacting in disappointment when London showed itself unwilling to accept his terms; yet, whatever his own complex motivations, he can hardly escape the charge that he allied himself with those forces least inclined to favour warm Anglo-German relations.

Quite apart from this general contribution, Wilhelm's role in the furtherance of German sea power – with all its consequences for relations with Britain – was decisive. However much one may point to the appeals of overseas commercial interests for increased protection, the sharp eye for a profit of the iron-and-steel firms and the growth of public interest in imperialism and navalism, the blunt fact remains that during the critical decade of the 1890s the decision-making élite was being pushed into a naval policy not from outside, but from *within* – by Wilhelm himself; even during the anglophobia which attended the Kruger Telegram crisis, it is worth recalling that the main parties were not to be won over to large naval increases. The 1897 changes in personnel, and especially the appointment of Bülow and Tirpitz, meant above all else that Wilhelm at last had the men who would give him 'his ships'. At this point, it is true, his new servants took over: they knew how to apply 'spiritual massage' (in Bülow's awful phrase) to Reichstag deputies, how to orchestrate public opinion, how to draft a Naval Bill which appeared much more reasonable than the preceding ones yet was both politically and militarily far more effective. In addition, it was Tirpitz who fashioned the Kaiser's general wish for more warships into a specific shape, producing a North Sea battlefleet deliberately aimed at one potential opponent above all others; who beat off every suggested alternative strategy, or alternative warship types (including Wilhelm's own designs for fast armoured cruisers); and who fought so tenaciously to maintain his 'plan', stage after stage.[84] Yet it was also true – as Tirpitz recognised – that had he failed to keep the Kaiser's favour, he would have been lost immediately. Within another decade, the Hanseatic merchants could see that their overseas interests were threatened, not protected, by this battlefleet-building; 'moderate' Liberals were regretting their support for the Naval Bills; even Liberal Imperialists like Weber had come to see how disastrous the naval race was for Germany's world policy; Bülow tentatively, and Bethmann Hollweg more determinedly, were exploring the possibility of buying British goodwill by agreeing to limit naval expansion; and army circles were arguing that funds for the fleet should be channelled to better purposes. No doubt the arch-patriots would join Tirpitz in claiming that the unrestricted development of the battlefleet was a 'matter of honour', but there were now substantial forces in favour of settling with London over the issue which more than anything else had alienated the British public from Germany. Yet Tirpitz's grand design was never fundamentally altered, because the admiral retained Wilhelm's support. From the beginning to the end of the *Flottenpolitik*, the Kaiser played a critical and fatal role.

Finally, it is worth arguing that Wilhelm contributed to the worsening of the general image, and increasing distrust of German policy, in Britain. An ideological 'gap' already existed, as we have seen above; but the Kaiser helped to widen it further. His bombastic phrases about 'the trident in our hands' and 'Admiral of the Atlantic', his public proclamation of Germany's world mission, dramatic diplomatic gestures such as the Kruger Telegram and the 1905 landing at Tangiers, the rumours about the crises at court, the constant appearance in military uniform and the restless travelling, all combined to create an impression of instability, unreliability and uncontrollable ambitions. Lascelles, one of Wilhelm's apologists, admitted that this 'impulsiveness' and the 'exaggerations' had produced two erroneous effects: the first was that foreigners believed that 'the Emperor is directly responsible' for German policies, whereas they were often the products of his advisers; secondly, they believed that Germany 'constitutes a danger for the peace of Europe', whereas Lascelles personally felt that the Kaiser wanted peace.[85]

These disastrous impacts were not, of course, confined to Britain: Wilhelm's bombast and escapades had a similar effect upon long-suffering allies, increased the suspicions of the French and the Russians – a tendency unlikely to have been countered by the Kaiser's effusive letters to the Tsar[86] – and worried the Belgians, Dutch and Danes. In the specific British context, he greatly hampered the efforts of those who argued for Anglo-German cooperation, and he came to symbolise for many a personification of 'Prussian militarism'. Such impressions, moreover, pervaded the highest levels. As we have seen, Salisbury's traditional suspicion of German policy was sharply reawakened by the dismissal of Bismarck, and he felt unable to trust Wilhelm, 'the dark cloud' on the skyline of Europe; Lansdowne, initially much more favourable to Berlin, was writing by 1905 that 'the Kaiser's language and demeanour fills me with disquiet. What may not a man in such a frame of mind do next?'[87] and Grey, who after his first meeting with Wilhelm thought him 'not quite sane' (the Foreign Secretary had been harangued about the Jews), was a little later comparing him to a battleship going at full speed with its rudder stuck. Kiderlen's private nickname was 'Wilhelm the Sudden'; the Foreign Office in London preferred to call him 'His Impulsive Majesty'; but the end result was the same.[88] The Kaiser, by no means always anti-British in thought and action, nevertheless made a personal and substantial contribution to the worsening of Anglo-German relations.

# CHAPTER 20

# Colonies, Navies and the
# Balance of Power

The decisive elements in the Anglo-German relationship, and the causes of the rising antagonism, are to be found not among such nebulous elements as race, religion and culture but in the cold world of *Machtpolitik*, in the perception of clashes of interest between the two nations. This does not mean that the growing rivalry can be understood only at the level of international politics. As has been seen, the press and patriotic pressure groups offered interpretations of these clashes of interest which often gave the rivalry an added dimension; and domestic-political exigencies caused politicians to react to, and utilise, a colonial quarrel or the 'naval race' in various ways. Above all, the considerations of so-called *Machtpolitik* were in themselves intimately connected with, because they arose out of, economic changes. The colonial quarrels, naval rivalry and disagreement over the European balance of power which drove Britain and Germany apart, were in effect the strategical and geopolitical manifestations of the relative shift in the economic power of these two countries between 1860 and 1914.

The Anglo-German colonial rivalry was the longest-lasting but, ultimately, the least important of these three manifestations: it played a significant role in fostering the mutual animosity but the issues at stake were – to all except the diehard nationalists – much more capable of resolution than the other two. In stating that, it is of course important to differentiate between the various phases of the rivalry: in 1895–6 and 1904–5 overseas disputes – had they escalated further – might have caused the two powers to stumble into an armed conflict: in 1890 and 1898 and 1913, the circumstances seemed much less threatening. What is common to almost all of the colonial disputes throughout this period is that they were the consequences – unintended, perhaps, yet inevitable – of *economic* expansionism. The same long-term processes which were causing many British merchants and investors to shift their gaze from Europe to the 'underdeveloped' world were also responsible for German penetration of those same regions. After all, the Germans originally sought to dominate Samoa not, as the New Zealanders claimed, to threaten Australasian security but to gain protection for their plantations; they jostled with Britons and Frenchmen in West Africa and around Zanzibar because of the local trade prospects; they took an interest in British–Transvaal relations because they

had investments – and economic ambitions – in southern Africa; they instigated the Baghdad Railway-building not, as Curzon and others feared, to
undermine the Indian Empire but because this was a potentially lucrative
undertaking; they became involved in Far Eastern politics because their trade
with China was rising fast; they carried out the bombardment of Venezuela,
and developed relations with Brazil and Argentina which were disapproved of
by Washington, because South America was an important, swiftly growing
market; even in Morocco, German trade was certainly one factor in the
arguments and the calculations of the *Wilhelmstrasse*. Were the economic
element removed: or, more specifically, had Germany not developed into a
great commercial nation with global interests, then it is difficult to see why
London and Berlin would have quarrelled and consulted so frequently about
colonial issues.

This does not mean that such matters *remained* purely economic, for in an
age of strong domestic nationalism and preclusive imperialism, commercial
influence seemed inexorably to lead to political control. The German territorial
claim to South-west Africa, the British assertion of special influence in the
Yangtse valley, the quarrels over East Africa, were all based upon the evidence
of plantations, trading posts, commercial treaties with the natives, the pattern
of the trade figures, the creation of a railway line, and so on. Furthermore,
colonial quarrels which arose out of commercial rivalry also became 'politi-
cised' because of that other critical factor – the role of domestic opinion and the
element of prestige: as Paul Kayser put it, 'Colonial policy has already become
an important factor in governmental policy [and] forms the criterion for the
strength of the government externally and for its position internally.'[1] Thus,
domestic-political calculations, and a desire for prestige, were behind the
*Wilhelmstrasse*'s acquisition of the Caroline Islands and other 'maritime fulcra';
and a concern to maintain the 'cold rules of national safety handed on from
Pitt, Palmerston and Disraeli'[2] affected British decision-makers in certain
parts of the globe, particularly the approaches to India.

Nevertheless, because many of the colonial disputes had their origins in
commercial activities – and were to that extent concrete and quantifiable; and
because they concerned so much of the world – and only megalomaniacs could
insist that *every* region was indispensable for British security or Germany's
growing trade requirements – a *modus vivendi* was possible. The Australians
may not have liked the German presence in New Guinea, the French resented
their exclusion from the Nile valley, the Germans disliked the 'liquidation' of
the Boer republics, the British felt that they had the worst of the bargain over
the Alaska boundary and Isthmian canal agreements; but each recognised that
it did not serve its national interests to fight for such territories. Colonial
bargains, often conducted with both sides protesting that they had made the
greatest concessions, were common enough events. Quarrels *and* compromise
were thus a feature of Anglo-German rivalry in overseas regions. In Salisbury's
words, these difficulties

depended on the fact that the two were rival colonial powers. Such a
condition was not inconsistent with pacific and friendly relations, but it

would always tend to encourage the occurrence of contested questions, which would make the relations of the two countries more liable to disturbance than would be the case in regard to countries which had no colonial competition between them.[3]

Admittedly, the effects of Anglo-German colonial rivalry were serious enough. It was the British obstructionism (intended or otherwise) towards Bismarck's 'first bid for colonies' in 1884–5, the extensive acquisitions insisted upon by Salisbury in the Heligoland-Zanzibar treaty, and the evident desire to forestall German wishes in Samoa, the Portuguese colonies, China and elsewhere around the turn of the century which appeared to justify the assertions of the Pan-Germans and other anglophobes that Britain was bent upon keeping Germany within Europe, and which caused even pro-British circles such as Marschall, Holstein and Hatzfeldt to argue that Berlin needed to apply 'pressure', or diplomatic 'blackmail', in order to get her demands met. It was also true that this image of the 'foreign Jupiter' malevolently checking German *Weltpolitik* gave the greatest possible boost to the naval propaganda campaign; and Tirpitz was genuinely concerned – indeed, obsessed with the notion – that Germany required 'a certain measure of naval force as a political power factor' against England.[4] On the other hand, it was the 'pin-prick' diplomacy of the *Wilhelmstrasse* which increased Salisbury's dislike of that country, led to growing resentment among the 'new men' in the Foreign Office, and angered many right-wing editors and journalists; Grey, it will be recalled, claimed that it was 'the abrupt and rough peremptoriness' of the Germans in the mid-1890s which first caused him to feel that Berlin's policy 'was not that of a friend'.[5]

Yet, if these legacies were weighty enough, even a brief survey of the Anglo-German colonial relationship from 1890 to 1914 would reveal that there had frequently been a predisposition for 'give and take', either by one of the governments, or by both. Such a sentiment had clearly existed in the early 1890s on the German side, because of the concern felt by Caprivi and Holstein for the European situation. The years 1894–6 were much more tense because, while the British imperial drive was still continuing, the German government was responding to nationalist and business pressures to play a greater role in the outside world. The following period, characterised by Berlin relinquishing any claim to interfere in southern Africa and transferring its energies to other parts of the globe, was somewhat less strained. Bülow, entrusted to guide Germany through the 'danger zone', repeatedly sent messages to London that 'Germany and England do not at all need to be rivals in colonial matters. The world is big enough for both of us';[6] and the British, aware of the *much more serious* colonial challenges of the French and the Russians, generally recognised the need to remain on good terms with Berlin – and often advocated German expansion into Asia Minor or China. The colonial 'deals' over Samoa, the Portuguese colonies and the Yangtse valley were hard-fought, but settlements were reached. After 1901–2, when the British Right came to see in Germany an actual danger, co-operation again became difficult and whenever it was attempted (Venezuela, Baghdad Railway) it ended in bitterness and confusion. By contrast, German policy outwardly appeared much more reasonable, although this was chiefly because Bülow and Tirpitz were now very anxious to reduce British mistrust. Finally, the years after 1906 produced another new set of circumstances, which allowed both governments to consider again the possibility of colonial arrangements.

One of the major reasons for this change was, obviously, the advent of the Liberal administration in Britain. To Berlin, it meant the defeat of that alarming rise of Chamberlainite imperialism with its strong anti-German flavour; and in particular, it destroyed the prospect of an enclosed imperial *Zollverein*. Of course, this did not prevent the arch-patriots from maintaining that such a blow had only been postponed; but the pro-English forces in Germany could now more convincingly claim that the thesis of British 'trade jealousy' and impending protectionism was a myth. On the British side, a majority of the governing party felt that gestures should be made in the colonial field to convince Berlin that London did not oppose *all* German expansionism. Grey himself wrote that he was willing 'to study the map of Africa with . . . a pro-German spirit',[7] and was often under considerable backbench pressure to make up to Germany. Furthermore, although Britain had technically 'settled' her imperial disputes with France and Russia, she still had a traditional dislike of their colonial methods of rule and, in the case of Persia, there were frequent disputes about the activities of Russian agents.[8] Germany at least was not the only sinner in British eyes, and some felt that (despite the savage repression of the Herero and Maji-Maji uprisings) her colonial record was a relatively good one.

In Germany the 'colonial scandals' of 1906–7 took much of the turn-of-the-century enthusiasm for tropical territories. It was now a time for the consolidation and economic development of existing possessions; and here German businessmen found British partners who were willing to share in such enterprises. British traders actually secured a very considerable share of the commerce of the German colonies[9] – which was largely attributed to the lack of discriminatory tariffs, unlike the colonial empires of the other powers – and British appreciation of this fact was more than matched by German industry's own reliance upon imported raw materials from British Empire territories. Moreover, the post-1900 phase of German overseas expansion was chiefly characterised by her *penetration pacifique* – in Turkey and the Euphrates valley, in Latin America, in the Dutch East Indies, and in the Belgian and Portuguese colonies in Africa, all of which appeared to offer greater economic rewards than the formal German colonial empire itself.[10] If, as some circles obviously hoped, this economic influence could one day be turned into political control, then it was impossible to do so without British support unless Berlin was willing to risk a full-scale war. Given also the post-1908 return to the older European antagonism between an Austro-German bloc on the one side and the Dual Alliance on the other, it was predictable that 'moderate' imperialists and businessmen would argue that colonial arrangements with the British were not only more practicable than 'going it alone' but also offered the tempting prospect of a general diplomatic *détente* between Berlin and London.[11]

It hardly needs emphasising that there were significant limits upon what could be arranged between the two governments by this stage. In the first place, London's concern about imperial security meant that concessions to Germany were a *non possumus* in certain key zones like South Africa, Egypt and the approaches to India: the Baghdad Railway issue was only settled, for example, when Britain gained her point about controls at the southern end. A surrender of any British-owned territory was also highly unlikely in view of the prevailing nationalist sentiment before 1914; a Liberal administration would not risk retiring in Germany's favour from, say, Zanzibar or Sierra Leone without compensations. Furthermore, not only Whitehall's (or Simla's) viewpoint had to be considered but also the attitude of the 'sub-imperialists' in the Dominions. In 1908, Grey encountered resistance from the South African government when he proposed to let the Germans in South-west Africa have an outlet through Walfish Bay: although feeling that a 'churlish' policy of obstructionism would justify the Germans 'in saying that we were really unfriendly, & that their efforts to build a fleet against us must be increased', he gave up this idea in the face of Dominion opposition.[12] In addition, the British government would not make colonial deals at the expense of France, nor permit German pressure upon France since events such as the two Moroccan crises were viewed not simply as a colonial squabble but as a possible challenge to the European balance of power. Finally, it is worth remarking that the British government was not alone in establishing the parameters for German expansion: the Americans would not tolerate an infringement of the Monroe Doctrine; and it was not easy to see how Germany could unilaterally acquire territory in the Far East after 1906 without provoking the resistance of several powers, above all Japan.

Thus, if the possibility existed after 1906 of Anglo-German colonial understandings, the chief difficulty always was to find areas suitable for negotiation. As Karl Peters angrily put it, in the aftermath of the second Moroccan crisis:

> if Germany carefully keeps away from British spheres of interest, Britain will be pleased to live in peace with her. But what are British spheres of interest on this planet these days? Or rather, what is not a British sphere of interest? [Wilhelm: 'good'] . . . I am first waiting until when and where London will find a German attempt at expansion 'justifiable'. [Wilhelm: 'good']¹³

Moreover, there were substantial forces in Britain which would bitterly attack any 'deals' with the arch-enemy, arguing instead that this would unsettle the French and that the past history of German policy scarcely entitled her to forbearance and appeasement. The suspicion with which the Unionist press regarded the Haldane mission, and the unconcealed dislike with which the Foreign Office staff observed the Harcourt–Solf talks in the period following, were characteristic of this sentiment.[14]

In both countries, in other words, a rather similar debate was taking place over the merits of Anglo-German co-operation in the colonial field. Such an idea was welcome to all the left-of-centre parties, as contributing to an improved international atmosphere and dealing a blow at the chauvinists who claimed that a war was inevitable. This latter group, the radical nationalists, were equally predictable in their stance: to them, all arrangements were suspect, in that their 'weak' governments would fail to pursue a truly national policy. Between these two groupings, there manoeuvred the pragmatic imperialists, Grey and Haldane, Crewe and Harcourt, Ballin and Gwinner and Rathenau and Solf and Dernburg, Lichnowsky and Kühlmann at the London Embassy, and Bethmann Hollweg himself, who were alarmed by the second Moroccan crisis and willing to explore ways in which a colonial agreement could be reached. All of these, it is fair to claim, accepted the argument that Germany's bursting population, industrial productivity and overseas trade entitled her to a larger share of the world's surface, but they hoped that such a readjustment might take place peacefully: it was to be 'World Policy and No War!', in the words of a well-known pamphlet of that time.[15]

The colonial understandings negotiated between London and Berlin in the years 1912–14 did not, however, achieve much. The secret agreement about a redivision of the Portuguese colonies was put into cold storage in 1913 because of the problem of publishing the earlier treaties, and this weakened the claims of the pro-English party in Berlin that they could secure substantial territorial benefits by working with London. More success was achieved in the talks over the Baghdad Railway, and the convention which was hammered out in the summer of 1914 showed a businesslike approach by the two sides. Conceivably, its formal signing and publication could have led to a further easing of tension; but the developing crisis in the Balkans swept it away, and with it the hopes of all who had sought to arrange an Anglo-German *détente* by redrawing their respective spheres of interest in the few 'safe' regions left at the close of the age of the imperialist scramble. Any more substantial redivision of the globe to Germany's benefit was only likely to come about – in Naumann's ominous words – by a peace treaty after a successful war.

In conclusion, one remains struck by the difficulty which existed of hammering out *any* arrangement satisfying the 'national interests' of the two sides, and of the *insignificance* of the issues agreed upon (or nearly agreed upon) by 1914 in comparison to the more fundamental causes of disharmony. To put it bluntly, the British and German governments were able to negotiate upon such matters as the Portuguese colonies and the Baghdad Railway because both saw that the compromises they were required to make were not vital. If a concession of fundamental German aspirations or existing British interests had been necessary, such agreements would have been out of the question.

The real reasons for the British estrangement from Germany in the years before 1914 lay in the North Sea and along the river Meuse, not in Central Africa and the Euphrates valley. This was made plain in repeated messages from the German embassy in London, some going so far as to claim that even British Conservative papers would be glad to see Germany make extensive colonial gains if only she would reduce her shipbuilding tempo. Yet, although these messages provoked a flood of abusive marginal comments from Wilhelm about the 'blindness' of his diplomatic corps,[16] it was a correct judgement. As Grey pointed out in the midst of the negotiations about the Baghdad Railway, naval expenditure was '*the* test of whether an understanding is worth anything'; and, further, that Britain 'cannot sacrifice the friendship of Russia or of France', and must remain free to give support to them in the event of German aggression.[17] By comparison, colonial settlements were far less significant.

So far as contemporary opinion was concerned, it was the naval question above everything else which exacerbated Anglo-German relations. The history of British policy towards maritime affairs over the preceding three centuries revealed how much the preservation of naval supremacy had been ingrained into the national consciousness. As Selborne argued, 'our stakes are out of all proportion to those of any other Power. To us defeat in a maritime war would mean a disaster of almost unparalleled magnitude in history. It might mean the destruction of our mercantile marine, the stoppage of our manufactures, scarcity of food, invasion, disruption of Empire. No other country runs the same risks in a war with us.'[18] In consequence, as the editor of the *Globe* warned Bernstorff, 'Germany's most ambitious naval projects form a spectre in the eyes of Englishmen which it is impossible to ignore. [England] cannot forget that "supremacy at sea" is the very life-blood of her existence and any power which challenges that supremacy offers her a menace which she cannot ignore.'[19] This was the one issue over which British statesmen, who so often were (or posed as being) flexible, cool and full of aristocratic disdain for dogmatism, were always adamant. 'The Navy is our one and only means of defence and our life depends upon it and on it alone', Grey insisted in 1913.[20] If Germany wished to have British friendship, she must not tamper with that maritime hegemony.

From the German side, predictably enough, the issue was viewed differently. In the first place, there was the very widespread and respectable argument that the rapid growth of the country's overseas commerce and merchant marine entitled her to greater naval protection than that provided by the meagre fleet of the mid-1890s. This increased force might not be as large as the Royal Navy but would be of a size commensurate with German overseas interests. Few Britons at the time would have found it possible to deny the reasonableness of this argument, the more particularly since the 'age of navalism' saw virtually every country increasing the size of its fleet. In addition, nationalist enthusiasts, including the Kaiser, wanted more ships as a manifestation of Germany's *Seegeltung*, of her general power and influence in world affairs. Heavy industry and the shipbuilding yards had the most obvious of motives. And there is no doubt that there was a domestic-political component in Tirpitz's calculations: 'already in 1899', recalled Admiral Hollweg, he 'explained to me in lengthy discussions that, in view of the Marxism and the political radicalisation of the masses, he saw Germany's industrialisation in no way as fortunate'[21] – but he also accepted that the only feasible solution to the 'social problem' was an overall expansion of industry, foreign trade, colonies and the navy. All this undoubtedly propelled Germany towards a bigger fleet.

However, the essence of the naval factor in the deteriorating Anglo-German relationship lay not so much in the abstract fact of an increase in German sea power but in the particular form that expansion was to take, in the sheer size of the fleet and in the political atmosphere of anglophobia in which it was developed. As detailed above, the pro-English stance of the German navy under Caprivi's direction changed within a very short space of time. By early in 1896, German officers were working upon the first operations plans against Britain; and Tirpitz and his mentor Stosch were exchanging letters upon how best to undermine British naval supremacy. Within another year and a half, Tirpitz had taken over at the *Reichsmarineamt* and was laying the foundations of that plan. It is, furthermore, not difficult to see why the circumstances of the late 1890s made anglophobia and the *Flottenpolitik* almost inseparable. Had not the British response to the Kruger Telegram been the creation of a special 'Flying Squadron', designed to overawe potential foes? Had not the Anglo-American naval forces used their superiority to interfere against the German-backed candidate in the Samoan civil war of 1898–9? Was it not the British government which, on learning that Germany intended to send an imposing squadron to Lisbon in May 1899, directed a far larger fleet to arrive there earlier and occupy all the nearest anchorage berths?[22] Was it not the Royal Navy's blockade ships which, in seizing the *Bundesrath* and other German steamers on suspicion of carrying contraband to the Boers, had irritated almost the entire nation? To be sure, these incidents – some of which were accidents or genuine misunderstandings on the part of British naval officers – were exploited by clever politicians in Berlin with other aims in mind; but it still remains easy to understand why there should have been widespread resentment in Germany at these frequent demonstrations of British maritime supremacy.

To the historian of Anglo-German relations, however, these varied reasonings are ultimately less important than the fact that Tirpitz sought to create an effective power-political instrument which would cause the British to lose 'every inclination to attack us and as a result concede to Your Majesty such a measure of naval influence and enable Your Majesty to carry out a great overseas policy'.[23] Just how this instrument would work *strategically* has been explained so many times that it requires no great elaboration here. Rejecting as unsuitable the *guerre de course* theories, Tirpitz concentrated upon building a North Sea battlefleet which, once it had emerged from the 'danger zone', would be so powerful that the British would hesitate to attack without risking their overall maritime superiority – a calculation reinforced by the dispersal of the Royal Navy's squadrons in many parts of the globe. Thus, presuming Tirpitz's calculations were correct, the British would soon see that they could no longer oppose Germany's expansion, and concede to her a 'world-political freedom'. Or, in the actual event of an Anglo-German war, the Royal Navy would receive a decisive defeat shortly after it had instituted a close blockade in the Heligoland Bight; a defeat which the hasty recall of squadrons from the Far East and Mediterranean would probably not recoup; a defeat which could possibly lead to peace talks and which would certainly compensate for the temporary loss of any German colonies.[24]

Yet, almost as soon as this strategy had been adopted, it was shown to be based upon a whole series of political and strategical miscalculations. British suspicions were aroused almost immediately, and by 1902 the Admiralty was considering counter-measures. An enormously expensive naval race was under way, straining Tirpitz's delicate financial calculations and prejudicing the earlier domestic consensus; while the 'Dreadnought-leap' threw doubt upon his hopes of achieving technical superiority over the Royal Navy. On the diplomatic front, Germany lost her place as *tertius gaudens*, while Britain steadily improved relations with the USA, Japan, France and even Russia; by 1907, Germany did seem encircled. The British brought home more and more battleships, and Tirpitz could no longer cling to the assumption that only part of the Royal Navy would be available in the North Sea. Finally, the developments in constructing mines, torpedoes and submarines strengthened existing doubts about close blockade and caused the British to elect to seal off the North Sea entrances and wait for the High Seas Fleet to emerge to fight. If it did, it would be on unfavourable terms; if it did not, then Tirpitz's entire *Flottenpolitik*, so far as it concerned relations with Britain, would have been in vain.

Well before the actual outbreak of war, it had become clear that, far from achieving British respect and securing concessions, the naval expansion was creating a lasting enmity. Yet the only way the naval race could be halted, short of open conflict or the admission of economic strain by one of the rivals, was by a mutual agreement to restrict their shipbuilding programmes. This would not immediately eradicate the antagonism and clash of interests which caused the feverish armaments construction in the first place; but it would at least lessen the public tension and, by eliminating the prospect of sudden naval increases, create a basis on which the two governments might be able to build understandings in other spheres. Why could not, then, such an argument be reached? Why, in particular, did the German government dislike London's various schemes for fixed ratios between their battlefleets or a 'naval holiday' in construction plans?

Some of the reasons given at the time cannot bear sustained scrutiny: the argument that the fleet law was unalterable was a legal nonsense; the objection to a mutual visit by naval attachés to the shipyards to monitor the building schedule, on grounds that this prejudiced security, had never been invoked to prevent such visits before the naval race became a political issue. Even the point that a bilateral limitations agreement disregarded the warship construction of third powers was, as Grey remarked, probably not an insuperable objection given the wish of other states to reduce the proportion of their defence budgets spent upon a navy.[25] The fatal flaws in an Anglo-German understanding were political. The first was that, even those German circles willing to agree to a fleet limitations treaty demanded a *quid pro quo* in the form of a British promise of neutrality during a continental war – and this, as will be shown, London felt unable to give. The second obstacle was that any such naval understanding was in effect a statement about the validity of the existing maritime equilibrium. And, while the British desired the preservation of the *status quo*, the Germans (or, at least, Wilhelm, Tirpitz and the other navalists) believed that it should be altered. At the root of the naval race lay two conflicting assertions about the contemporary strategic balance and the world order.

To the German navalists, for example, Britain's disapproval did not justify the surrender of their aims. Germany was a vigorous young nation, entitled as all her predecessors had been to claim an ever greater share in the world's wealth and territories commensurate with her own growing power and population. In Wilhelm's words, 'The Greeks and Romans each had their time; the Spaniards had theirs and the French also.' Now it was the turn of the rising powers.[26] No one had asked that the Spanish fleets under Phillip II, or Cromwell's 'new model navy', be restricted to a certain size; why should Germany have to do so now? It was, in any case, a limitation upon the absolute sovereignty of the state – an objection which, given the mingled traditions of Hegel and Treitschke, had great weight in German politics.[27] More significant still, however, was the practical fact that Germany would be admitting that she could not alter the global equilibrium in her favour in the way her professors had advocated a decade earlier and Tirpitz himself had outlined in his September 1899 memorandum. After all the strains which the *Flottenpolitik* had placed upon the country's finances and diplomacy, Germany would be no nearer achieving that 'world-political freedom': yet to abandon this great aim, as Tirpitz constantly warned Wilhelm, would mean a severe blow to the prestige of the monarchy, with alarming internal repercussions. While this motivation was rarely publicised, German navalists could always fall back upon the old argument that their seaborne commerce required adequate protection, which would only exist when the naval balance moved in their favour. As one German officer put it, in 1908:

The thought that there is a Power on earth always in a position to annihilate any other navy, and therefore to cut off the country in question from the sea, is a cause for anxiety . . . only when our fleet is so far developed that it can successfully prevent any blockade can we breathe freely and say that our sea-power is equal to our needs.[28]

It hardly needs stressing that not all Germans were so fundamentalist. Tirpitz's 'logic' could be answered by counter-arguments. As Richthofen had noted, an alliance with Britain would *ensure* the preservation of Germany's colonies and overseas trade.[29] By contrast, the naval propaganda campaign and the North Sea battlefleet simply worsened Germany's position and consequently was disliked by all who believed that, not Britain, but Russia and France were their country's real foes. What Tirpitz was doing – so claimed people such as Ballin, Metternich, Bethmann Hollweg, the younger Moltke and Holstein – was driving the British further into the camp of those foes. Surely the fleet was large enough, by 1907 or so, for all purposes other than the foolish policy of trying to take on the Royal Navy? Furthermore, the strategical experts in the Admiralty staff were already pointing out Tirpitz's erroneous assumptions, well before the First World War confirmed these doubts: that it was highly unlikely for Germany to get through the 'danger zone' without detection; that it was rash to assume that the Royal Navy could not concentrate its battlefleets in home waters; and that it was by no means certain that those fleets would, at the beginning of a conflict, rush into the Heligoland Bight.[30] As the years developed, each of these criticisms was proven correct; yet Tirpitz, with the ear of the Kaiser, refused to acknowledge these arguments. The race would go on regardless.

Some features of the British reaction, it needs to be said, also had little strategical or political logic to them: the whole 'invasion scare' campaign, which began to influence even Haldane and Balfour, appears to have been conducted without any regard for the probable attitude of the Prussian General Staff. Naturally, the National Service League agitators could not possibly have known that in 1897–8 Schlieffen had disliked the German navy's early operations plan, which did involve an invasion of England,[31] but the tension between the European alliance blocs by 1908, the building of strategic railway lines in border zones, and the general tenor of the manoeuvres and equipment favoured by the General Staff, hardly suggested that it was either willing or able to indulge in large-scale amphibious operations across the North Sea.

Nevertheless, the overall British response to Tirpitz's creation of a 'power-political instrument' was exceedingly logical, deriving from the classical strategical axioms about the maintenance of sea power. As seen above,[32] the Admiralty always felt that the two-power standard should operate against the next two strongest navies, *whichever* they were; and it was also determined to preserve its maritime supremacy in what Mahan termed 'the vital centre of English commerce', that is, 'the waters surrounding the British islands'.[33] 'It is', the Sea Lords insisted, 'a fundamental principle of Admiralty policy that sufficient force shall at all times be maintained in home waters to ensure command of these seas.'[34] The steady strengthening of the home squadrons was thus only a matter of time. As a *Fortnightly Review* article of 1905 – possibly inspired by Fisher – claimed, the North Sea 'frontier of the British Empire has been threatened by the growth of the German Navy, and it is as natural that Great Britain should safeguard her interests in this direction as that France, Russia and Germany should patrol their land frontiers with troops'.[35] This was, indeed, similar to Selborne's comment to the Kaiser's confidant, Eisendecher: 'What would the German War Office say if there were suddenly created on the German land frontier a new Army, first class in quality, which bore the same proportionate strength to the German Army as the German Navy does to the British Navy?'[36]

Thus, the more the German fleet expanded, the more the Royal Navy was concentrated to contain it; and if this redeployment was assisted by the fortuitous solution of differences with the USA, France and Japan before the naval race began in earnest, it is hard to believe that the Admiralty would have accepted Tirpitz's rigid logic that 'on account of her foreign policy commitments [England] can only utilise a very small part of [her] ships in the North Sea'.[37] By 1906, apprehensions about the German fleet increases were such that vessels were being pulled back from 'imperial police' duties in tropical waters even when the Foreign and Colonial Offices wanted them kept overseas for political reasons. 'Our only probably enemy is Germany', Fisher explained to the Prince of Wales. 'Germany keeps her whole fleet always concentrated within a few hours of England. We must therefore keep a fleet twice as powerful as that of Germany always concentrated within a few hours of Germany.' She was much more dangerous than Russia, it was asserted, because 'she threatens not an outlying possession but our vitals'.[38]

To a considerable degree, geography was a major cause in the Anglo-German antagonism: the sheer proximity of Wilhelmshaven to the English coast made inevitable this sort of response by the Admirality. On occasions, Wilhelm and Tirpitz complained that the British never seemed to get as excited about the growth of the United States, Brazilian or Japanese navies – a remark which once provoked the sarcastic Foreign Office reply that 'If the British press pays more attention to the increase of Germany's naval power than to a similar movement in Brazil – which the Emperor appears to think unfair – this is due no doubt to the proximity of the German coasts and the remoteness of Brazil.'[39]

Yet, if the German threat appeared intolerable to the British, the latter's response was equally intolerable to the German navalists. Here again, geography played a role, if only because the Reich's booming overseas trade was more or less totally dependent upon British goodwill as its merchant ships steamed up and down the Channel. The British simply did not need to institute a close blockade of the German ports, a fact which made the decision to assume the strategical defensive that much easier.[40] As Mahan had pointed out in a well-known article:

> The dilemma of Great Britain is that she cannot help commanding the approaches to Germany by the mere possession of the very means essential to her own existence as a state of the first order . . . Sea defence for Germany [cannot] be considered complete unless extended through the Channel and as far as Great Britain will have to project hers into the Atlantic. This is Germany's initial disadvantage of position, to be over-come only by adequate superiority of numbers.[41]

This made a nonsense, therefore, of all the claims that while the German navy was not aiming to be as large as the British, it must at least be in a position to defend German seaborne commerce. As the *Admiralstab* admitted, 'In the final analysis, we are fighting for access to the ocean, whose entrances on that side of the North Sea are in England's hands. However the war may be fought, we are therefore basically the attacker, who is disputing the enemy's possession.'[42] The strategical implication was that Germany needed what Mahan had termed 'adequate superiority of numbers'; and the very fact that she refused all attempts to limit her naval expansion, yet persisted with such explanations as 'being entitled to build to her own requirements regardless of others' and 'needing to protect German seabound commerce', filled the British with disquiet. As Crowe, a close student of Mahan, put it:

> it is quite ridiculous to believe that we are taken in by the pretence of the necessities of 'defending German commerce' etc. as the reason for a bigger fleet. Commerce is defended in one way and one way only: namely the destruction of the opponent's naval force. There is in reality no difference. . . . We are entitled to form our own conclusion as to the object for which the German navy is built up and we have and will claim every right to act accordingly.[43]

Here was a race which, at first sight, the Germans could not win. Yet Tirpitz was by no means an unintelligent person: on the contrary, he was an astute politician, flexible in his tactics, with a sense of timing and realism far in excess of most contemporaries. It is worth posing the question, therefore, why he persisted in his 'plan' after 1906 when it was not only driving the British into ever more energetic counter-measures but also splitting the German establishment. No doubt one motive was domestic-political: it would be too great a blow to the prestige of the monarchy openly to admit defeat. It would also be a great personal blow. Moreover, as a bureaucratic empire-builder,[44] Tirpitz recognised that only by insisting upon full control of the 'plan' would he preserve his own position, although the Grand-Admiral's active involvement in radical-Right politics after his dismissal in 1916 suggests that there was much more to him than the archetypal ambitious bureaucrat. Yet one further possibility remains: that he still hoped that Germany would achieve her 'political independence'[45] from England, due to an alteration in world affairs or in British internal politics which would cause the island state to give up its claim to maritime dominance.

Tirpitz's own utterances about his *final* goal were always clouded in vagueness: 'If one wishes to achieve a great aim, one is not always in the position to reveal one's final thoughts'; 'the building of a fleet is the work of a generation'; one cannot cut up 'the bear skin [England] before the bear has been killed', and so on. Even Admiral Capelle, Tirpitz's closest aide in the *Reichsmarineamt*, confessed that his chief 'held back from him his final plans for the national policy and fleet-laws of the future'; 'no-one among us', claimed Hollweg, another close aide, 'knew the final aims of the fleet-building master'.[46] At times, Tirpitz hinted that even the colossal programme of sixty large warships, replaceable at the rate of three each year, was the necessary *minimum*.[47] Just after the onset of war, moreover, he informed a colleague – in part of a letter which he later 'censored' from his memoirs – that 'a fleet of equal strength to England's' was their 'natural and single aim [which] could not be admitted in the past two decades but could only be kept in mind if Germany's trade and industry and colonies expanded further'.[48] If *this* was his hope – and, it is fair to add, it was scarcely as preposterous as some writers have suggested given the German lead over Britain in population, in steel, iron, chemical, electrical and other industries, and in total national wealth by 1914 – then many of the strategical inconsistencies of the 'Tirpitz Plan' become much more explicable. This would also explain his devastating critique upon Bethmann Hollweg and the generals for prematurely provoking war over the Sarajevo deed – comments which, once again, had to be censored to protect Germany's 'good name'.[49] Of course, one might finally add that, if this was Tirpitz's long-term aim, then it also makes the British reaction and political 'encirclement' of Germany somewhat more defensible than Grey's critics asserted.

Whatever the admiral's own design – which after all required the permanent relegation of the Prussian army into second place – the overwhelming impression left upon one after a study of the documents of both sides is the *absolute incompatibility* of British and German naval aims. What the Germans supporting Tirpitz desired, whether the vaguer 'world political freedom' or the more specific security for German commerce in the event of war, they could not have without affecting Britain's existing naval supremacy. What the latter in turn wished to preserve, command of those waters vital for her own safety as a maritime nation, would be impossible if Germany's goal was reached. What one power wanted, the other would never voluntarily concede; security for one meant danger to the other. As E. D. Morel noted, each side claimed that it should possess 'manifest strength, showing all likely enemies that war is unprofitable for them owing to the difficulty which your enemy has in defending himself'.[50] In mutually striving for that 'manifest strength', the Germans and British each contributed to the arms spiral, with Germany never improving its strategic position but so alarming her rival that many Britons increasingly identified the new Reich as their most formidable and single foe.

It was, therefore, a blatant misinterpretation of past events for Tirpitz, writing in 1924, to claim that the naval race had played no part in the causes of the First World War. As Bülow privately pointed out to him, even if Germany was 'dragged into the war through our clumsy handling of a Balkan problem . . . there is the question whether France and particularly Russia would have let it come to war had public opinion in England not been so greatly enraged precisely at the construction of our great ships'.[51] The public animosities engendered by the naval race on occasions became so heated that the French sometimes feared they would be dragged into a conflict with the British!; and it was surely true that both Paris and St Petersburg could reckon that, unless an Anglo-German naval limitations treaty was signed, Britain would never dare to return to her former policy of isolation. It may also be true – though it remains only a hypothesis – that the constant emphasis by the press and novels upon Britain's vulnerability in the North Sea and the prospects of a 'bolt from the blue' induced people to side with any country likely to be injured by Germany.[52] Those who, like Blatchford, lay awake at night wondering where Tirpitz's armada might strike were unlikely to assume an attitude of benevolent neutrality should Germany be involved in a struggle with third powers.

Despite the popular British animus against Germany, it had nevertheless seemed astonishing to many contemporaries that London should be willing to involve itself if necessary in continental politics, even to the extent of committing itself *militarily* to the anti-German side. Here was a complete revolution in British policy, which quite deranged the traditional strategy. Had not Salisbury remarked 'we are fish'? Provided that the Royal Navy's strength remained unquestioned, there was surely no need to get entangled in Europe. This gradual abandonment of the 'British way in warfare' in favour of a 'continental commitment' disturbed not only traditionalist Liberals and Radicals, who constantly pressed Asquith and Grey to specify what promises may have been made to France; but it also appalled navalists such as Fisher and Esher, the latter protesting in 1913 that 'For the first time since the final overthrow of Napoleon in 1815, Great Britain appears to stand committed to military adventure oversea under circumstances not of her own choosing, and in a cause that may have no immediate or direct bearing upon purely British interests'.[53]

As described earlier, the British concern that the continental equilibrium was in danger, and the concommitant decision at least to consider the possibility of intervening militarily to restore that balance was of very recent origin.[54] It was the unexpected collapse of Russia and the forced resignation of Delcassé in 1905 which confronted London with the problem which had been dormant since 1887, or even 1875: namely, the latent capacity of the new Reich to overrun France and, if need be, the Low Countries. Furthermore, by comparison with those earlier crises, three new factors had to be taken into account. The first was that, in regard to the Moroccan question itself, the British were diplomatically bound to support French aims and, having disposed of these colonial issues which had clouded the Anglo-French relationship in the preceding decades, were all the more inclined to do so. Secondly, Germany was much more powerful, *vis-à-vis* her neighbours, than hitherto. Thirdly, as compared with the Bismarckian era, she also appeared to be much more hostile towards Britain.

Since the argument of those favouring a 'continental commitment' was that an entirely new situation existed – which neither the older-fashioned navalists nor the Liberal Radicals seemed to grasp; and since this was the line of reasoning which gradually gained influence, it merits a brief examination. Once again, the historian is confronted with the phenomenon of Germany's rapid industrial and population growth as being the starting-point of the rationale. For a decade or more prior to 1905, the British had been measuring the indices of their wealth and productivity with those of Germany – and becoming perturbed at the results. When they also examined the French position *vis-à-vis* Germany, the disparity was staggering: by 1910, for example, Germany led France in total population by 65 million to 39 million, in coal production by 222 to 38·4 million tons, in steel production by 13·8 to 3·4 million tons.[55] In one recent attempt to measure the relative *power* of the great European states – admittedly by the rather crude conflation of manufacturing production and population – Germany is allocated 37·2 per cent and France a mere 10·6 per cent by 1910: even an Anglo-French combination could only raise the total to 27·5 per cent.[56] The German navy was superior to France's, and the gap was growing every year. More important still, the German army had always been regarded as vastly superior, although only spending a little more than France: yet between 1910 and 1914 the German army budget jumped from £40·8 million to £88·4 million, whereas the French budget rose only from £37·6 million to £39·4 million; and despite this large-scale increase, Germany still devoted a smaller percentage of her national income to armaments than did France.[57] The message was plain to all: even when France strained to keep up, she was being easily outdistanced by Germany in the great power stakes.

Hitherto, this French weakness had been compensated by her alliance with Russia. In 1905, this assumption was blown to the winds; and the German diplomatic victory in the Bosnian crisis of 1908 simply confirmed that Russia was still out of the reckoning as a great power. In these altered circumstances, it was scarcely surprising that a host of official and unofficial commentators on the British side referred to the old historical problem of how to prevent one continental power from becoming too strong, and that their writings are full of allusions to Philip II, Louis XIV and Napoleon. Wilhelm, Bethmann Hollweg and later apologists for the German position always found these references to the 'balance of power' irritating and mistaken: they seemed to them to ignore the fact that Russia's vast manpower reserves and rapid industrialisation put even greater pressure upon Germany and her Austro-Hungarian ally; and even those deeply critical of Berlin's pre-1914 policies have pointed to the deep-seated *Angst* about the Tsarist colossus.[58] Was it not the case, as Morley, MacDonald and many others among the British 'Left' argued, that London's growing adhesion to the Dual Alliance was likely to end in the Tsarist domination of central Europe in the event of a broad-scale war? Why did Grey, his Foreign Office advisers, the General Staff, the Unionist Party and newspapers so one-sidedly point to the German danger to the European equilibrium?

In analysing the 'continental commitment' school, the following points seem the most important. In the first place, their formative experiences with this problem were indeed the years 1905–11 when the balance was most deranged; being impatient, like Grey, to see Russia 're-established as a factor in European politics',[59] it was going to be difficult for them to perceive the time when the balance was tilting against Germany. Furthermore, for obvious geopolitical reasons, their attention was concentrated much more upon western Europe than upon the eastern frontiers: it was the German threat to Belgium and northern France, not the Russian threat to east Prussia, which held their attention. Finally, it seems worth arguing – despite that superficially impressive revival of Russia after 1906 which so worried the German leaders – that Germany *was* actually getting relatively stronger year by year. Many of the crude statistics certainly point to A. J. P. Taylor's claim that, had peace continued after 1914, the Reich would soon have achieved 'the mastery of Europe' in any case;[60] and those other unquantifiable characteristics of Germany which so impressed foreigners – efficiency, planning, discipline, advanced technology, good communications – were not so marked in the French and Russian case. With the wisdom of hindsight, those who feared German power were probably right. As one sober commentator later remarked,

> for the four and half years of the First World War, Germany, with no considerable assistance from her allies, had held the rest of the world at bay, had beaten Russia, had driven France, the military colossus of Europe for more than two centuries, to the end of her tether, and, in 1917, had come within an ace of starving Britain into surrender.[61]

The greatest misperception of those willing to offer military aid to France in the event of German aggression lay not in their judgement of Germany's power, therefore, but in their naïve belief that only a limited amount of support was necessary. To assert that the German government posed the greatest threat to Europe since Napoleon yet could be checked by the dispatch of a few British divisions appears as questionable as the opposing contention which denied that Germany was such a threat yet insisted that a military commitment to aid France would be limitless. It is true that British politicians and generals, like many others in prewar Europe, believed that a future war between the great powers would not last very long; but there did exist some contrary evidence, and voices, to say that it would be a mighty affair.

As it was, the British leaders slipped into the first stages of their 'continental commitment' for what seemed to them two practical reasons. The first was that the Royal Navy under Fisher offered no convincing strategy which would materially aid the French in the event of a massive German drive westwards: whatever his abilities as an organiser and propagandist, Fisher's strategic thoughts were not impressive. His withdrawal from co-operation with the French naval authorities, and his successor, A. K. Wilson's, inept perfor- mance at the CID meeting of 23 August 1911, did not help the Admiralty's case in the eyes of civilian ministers: yet it probably also was true that, in an era of swift mobilisations and the deployment of vast armies, there actually was *no* naval counter-measure to prevent the German overrunning of France.[62] By contrast, the General Staff's arguments appeared most persuasive: calculating that Germany would have a manpower superiority of around 200,000 on its western front, the British military planners found it easy to suggest that the dispatch of an expeditionary force would nicely 'close the gap' and thus save France from eclipse. To the few Liberal ministers in the know, with little personal experience of military affairs, this logic was appealing, and it was made the more so by the fact that this was what the French themselves desired. Furth- ermore, Grey and his colleagues consoled themselves with the thought that, while contingency staff talks were being held between the military experts, this did not compromise the British government's freedom of action: there was no binding pledge, no signed treaty. Strategical logic pushed the Liberal- imperialist ministers in one direction, yet the knowledge that they were a minority in the party inclined them in the other. London could plan to help the French, but not promise that it would: it warned the Germans against aggres- sive action, but denied that it was pledged to oppose such a move. Just how free they actually were was to be seen in 1914 itself, but there seems little doubt that the conviction that they had not bound the country was very important in persuading the Liberal-imperialist ministers to support the staff talks.

That the Conservative Party, and especially the Realpolitik advocates among the Chamberlainites should uphold the principle of the balance of power was scarcely surprising, although it took their more cautious leaders a little longer. In 1903 Balfour did not think a German occupation of Holland 'fatal to this country'; but by 1909 the party's *Campaign Guide* was praising the way the Anglo-French *entente* was 'to a certain extent restoring the balance of power' and by 1911 the leadership felt it could not 'allow a friendly nation like France to be crushed or despoiled by another Power'.[63] Grey's own conversion was also a gradual one. While much more anti-German than Balfour or Landsdowne before he took office, he felt at that time that 'we ought to be able to pursue a European policy without keeping up a great army. The friendship of the Power with the biggest Navy in the world ought to be worth enough';[64] yet by January 1906 he was so impressed by the German threat to France that he was encouraging the informal military conversations. Even then, one suspects that his perception of military matters was not great: in talking with

Clemenceau in 1908, he stressed German *naval* expenditure and thought Russia a counterpoise to Germany on land, whereas the Frenchman insisted that Russian forces were still weak and that Britain must intervene against a power which sought a Napoleonic 'position of dominance'. Even during the early stages of the second Moroccan crisis, Henry Wilson recorded that Grey

advanced the theory that Russia was a governing factor, which I shattered rather rudely by telling him that Russia in 28 days could only produce 36 divisions in Poland, which Germany could oppose by 27 and Austria by 36, and I said that Russian interference could scarcely relieve pressure from Paris, the Germans being able (in spite of Russia) to put 96 divisions against the French 66.[65]

It was not surprising, therefore, that at the critical CID meeting a few weeks later Grey was to be heard opining that 'the combined operations outlined [by the Admiralty] were not essential to naval success, and the struggle on land would be the decisive one . . . our military support would be of great moral value to the French'.[66]

Yet the essence of the interventionist argument has still not been plumbed. The logic of offering the French the 'moral support' of a few divisions and simultaneously filling the numerical 'gap' between the French and German armies was reasonable enough; but it was open to counter-arguments, not only on traditional Cobdenite and moral grounds but also on practical-strategical ones: as C. P. Trevelyan pointed out, an army in France reduced British flexibility, tied the navy to home waters, was too small to be really decisive, would consequently increase the pressure for conscription and was 'a risk not worth running for the uncertain chance of saving the French from disaster, which is the best to be hoped'.[67] Yet such arguments still missed the point: *that it was not a disaster to France which petrified the 'interventionists', but the consequent isolation and defeat of Britain.*

The whole point, wrote Grant-Duff in his diary, 'is what we must do to keep the French from selling themselves body and soul to Germany without a serious struggle or to prevent them being beaten in case of war'.[68] If this was not done, Spring-Rice feared, we shall be 'quite alone in Europe and find it out too late'. 'We ought to be thankful that Germany annexed Alsace and Lorraine as that act has made a combination between Germany and France against us impossible', Bertie pointed out. Grey, emphasising the importance of not making the French 'nervous', agreed with all this: 'we shall run the risk of returning to our position of isolation in Europe and of losing much of the strong position which our recent policy has won for us'. Britain had to be willing to take its share 'of the hard knocks of war', wrote the Director of Military Operations, since 'A regrouping of the European powers leading to our isolation in the next few years would constitute a serious danger to the British Empire and such a change in condition is not altogether improbable should our value as allies be held to be of little worth.'[69] After reading the arguments of all those who urged the necessity of staying close to France, or of the smaller circle around Nicolson who were even more concerned to

427

preserve the fragile Russian *entente*,[70] the historian is entitled to wonder whether the turn-of-the century popular alarmism about the perils of isolation and the 'War of English Succession' had not been more deeply ingrained in the political consciousness of the establishment than is generally imagined. Having reached the comparatively safe haven offered by the *ententes*, the interventionists – but not, of course, the navalists or traditional Liberals – were unwilling to sail out into the turbulent waters of isolationism.

Yet this deep-seated *Angst* only made sense when a further logical step was taken, and it is recalled that Germany not only appeared to be capable of overrunning western Europe but was also disputing British naval hegemony. The development most feared, in other words, was what the Germans would do *after* they had achieved the military or political domination of the continent. With France defeated, and Germany holding 'Antwerp and Rotterdam, with an Empire extending from the North Sea to the Adriatic, . . . she would become, navally as strong as Great Britain and militarily 10 times as strong', wrote Milner. 'Invasion would then no longer be a remote danger, but a very imminent one'.[71] If France was 'bullied' into accepting German hegemony because she had been deserted by Britain, the problem remained the same: were the government to accept Bethmann Hollweg's 1909 request for a 'neutrality' declaration, Hardinge pointed out,

> the duration of the agreement would be strenuously employed by Germany to consolidate her supremacy in Europe, while England would remain a spectator with her hands tied. At the termination of the whole agreement, Germany would be free to devote her whole strength to reducing the only remaining independent factor in Europe.[72]

'Then the German position from the point of view of [naval] competition with England will be enormously strengthened, so much so that it will be entirely beyond our capacity to meet', Amery urged. 'If we wish to prevent the consummation of those conditions and to preserve our supremacy on the sea, it is on the land that we must meet her [Germany]. That is the real justification for and meaning of the entente. The entente is not a mere convenience, it is a matter of existence.'[73] This is clearly what Churchill – an unexpected but enthusiastic convert to this reasoning – meant when he argued that the 'looting' of France by 'Prussian junkers' would be 'swiftly fatal to our country'; why Grey minuted, 'if we sacrifice the other Powers to Germany we shall eventually be attacked';[74] and why Blatchford, in his famous tract of 1910, *Germany and England*, felt that a Germany dominant in Europe 'would wipe us out'.[75]

In a curiously convoluted way, therefore, the real reason why Tories and Liberal-imperialists advocated a 'continental commitment' was *naval*. The person who expressed this most clearly, on repeated occasions, was Grey himself: as he explained to Dominions representatives,

> if a European conflict, not of our making, arose, in which it was quite clear that the struggle was one for supremacy in Europe, in fact, that you got back to a situation something like that in the old Napoleonic days, then

. . . our concern in seeing that there did not arise a supremacy in Europe which entailed a combination that would deprive us of the command of the sea would be such that we might have to take part in that European war. That is why the naval position underlies our European policy.[76]

More than ever, then, it is necessary to qualify the protestations of Tirpitz and his followers that it was the inflexible operations plan of the Prussian General Staff, and not the naval race, which caused British participation in the First World War – for the 'interventionist lobby' in British government and politics would never believe that the German government, once dominant in Europe, would not resume its fleet expansion with greater devotion and resources than before. On the other hand, it was also true that although successive chiefs of the Prussian General Staff criticised the anti-English direction of the naval expansion, encouraged German Chancellors to 'buy off' British hostility by restricting the fleet, and even wrote of a possible Anglo-German alliance,[77] what they ultimately desired from London was tacit assent to their plan to overrun France and Belgium in the event of certain contingencies occurring in Europe. It is doubtful whether the British government would have willingly agreed to that request at any time, although in earlier decades (1870, 1887) it was manifestly eager to avoid fighting on this issue; but in an age in which Germany had become the second naval power in the world, its General Staff's attitude was unrealistic. It *might* have been possible to forestall British intervention had the German fleet been cut back to the size and role it occupied under Caprivi; and it *might* also have been possible if the army itself had returned to the Older Moltke's strategy of a defensive stand in the west and an eastward offensive. Best of all would have been a combination of those two conditions, for very few Britons would have accepted the argument that it was necessary to declare war upon a country which was not a naval threat and was engaged in fighting along some distant and obscure borders in eastern Europe. No one actually posed these conditions at the time – no doubt because it was perceived that they, too, were utterly unrealistic in the age of Bülow and Tirpitz. Politically, militarily, economically, it was impossible to put back the clock; but that meant that the British and German governments, despite attempts at reconciliation on the diplomatic level, possessed contrary national aims which were reflected in their respective contingency war plans.

This also means that the rival strategies put forward by the military and naval authorities in *both* countries were more closely connected than appears at first sight. Grey, the permanent officials in Whitehall and the Chamberlainites believed that, in checking German domination on land, they were preserving their own hegemony at sea: ironically, then, it was the repeated efforts of Bethmann Hollweg (encouraged by Moltke) to buy British neutrality which raised London's suspicions more than anything else. In addition, the Schlieffen Plan and the 'Tirpitz Plan' were also bound to be inextricably linked in the British mind, simply because a military victory in the west would enhance Germany's capacity to mount a future naval offensive. Retrospectively, the German generals could blame the *Reichsmarineamt* for creating an additional enemy which (arguably) prevented the defeat of France, and the admirals could blame the General Staff for an operations plan which caused war with Britain before the fleet was ready; but a more balanced assessment might be that the actions of each service had mutually contributed towards arousing the distrust of the island state.

All this, inevitably, appears to be placing the onus upon the German side alone: yet in strategical and political terms, this was precisely the situation. Given its satisfying status as *the* established power, Britain would benefit if there was no fresh naval challenge and no potential threat to the balance of power. For Germany, conversely, the permanent freezing of the *status quo* was intolerable – or it was, at least, to an establishment convinced that their country was entitled to claim a greater relative share of the world. Whether or not the post-Bismarckian leadership envisaged eventual German predominance of Europe is far from clear. Wilhelm and Eulenburg certainly debated the issue in the 1890s, usually when they wished to put pressure upon the British in colonial disputes or to counter the American economic challenge by rumours of a German-led 'continental league'; yet this was always far more difficult, and less appealing, than the idea of overseas expansion, and it was only in the changed circumstances of the post-Agadir crisis that the notion was more broadly discussed. The key fact, however, was that even the traditionalist General Staff, which had little enthusiasm at all for *Weltpolitik*, had settled upon a plan which – given the balance of forces, technology and industrial power in western Europe – was almost certain to lead to German dominance of that region in the event of war and thus to jeopardise Britain's 'guiding principle' of 'the maintenance of the balance of power in Europe'.[78] On the naval side, the alteration in the existing situation consequent upon Germany's post-1897 policy was even more apparent. As Delbrück readily conceded, 'The emergence of a German sea power changes the basic condition of English existence. That is the fact that we as well as the English must coolly and firmly keep in mind.'[79] If the English kept that fact in mind, no German practitioner of Realpolitik had cause for complaint. After all, was not London's attitude by, say, 1907, remarkably similar to that described by Queen Victoria a full four decades earlier?

> If we keep up an enormous force of volunteers, if we incur a frightful expense to create an Iron-clad Navy, to fortify our coasts and forts, to organise an Army of Reserve etc. etc., it is caused by fear of the possible designs of France. With *Prussia* we have no clashing interests – no possible point of collision. On the contrary, assuming France to be the Power, as she is, which can alone threaten the peace or security of England or Germany, our respective countries have an immense power of giving each other reciprocal support and assistance for defensive purposes.[80]

All that it is necessary to do is to substitute the Germany of 1907 for the France of 1867 – in line with the altered capacity of those two countries to carry out 'a Napoleonic policy' – and the British reaction seems logical and predictable. No established power, one might cynically add, greets the pushful and ambitious policies of others with warmth.

Mention of French policies in the late 1860s leads to one final observation about the British perception of the European balance of power throughout this whole period: namely, that it was *not merely* an automatically self-regulating instrument. While it took into account the shifts in industrial, population and military strength, it was also fundamentally concerned with the mannerisms and sometimes with the ideology of the countries concerned. Britain had accepted Bismarck's political domination of Europe, a fact which caused Grey to admit that she

> has not in theory been adverse to the predominance of a strong group in Europe when it seemed to make for stability and peace. To support such a combination has generally been her first choice; it is only when the dominant Power becomes aggressive and she feels her own interests to be threatened that she, by an instinct of self-defence, if not by deliberate policy, gravitates to anything that can fairly be described as a Balance of Power.[81]

It is, therefore, equally important to notice that all of the adjectives the British had used about France and Russia in earlier years – 'the hungry powers', 'unpredictable', 'restless', 'a threat to the peace', and so on – were now applied to Germany. The Kaiser's own instability and outward aggressiveness, the chaotic decision-making system and lack of coherent planning between governmental ministries, and the blatantly chauvinistic claims of the Pan-Germans and other groups of 'public' opinion, all contributed to this unfavourable image. So, too, did the sheer vagueness of the German arguments: the *Gleichberechtigung* (equal entitlement) demanded by Wilhelm could mean anything, but it clearly implied that at present such a state of affairs did not exist, and that an adjustment should be made in Germany's favour; and the *Seegeltung* (naval influence) which Tirpitz promised the German nation was equally abstract but posed the question of how far such *Geltung* was possible before it affected British naval supremacy. As Spring-Rice complained: 'Germany is a mystery. Does she simply want the destruction of England, pure and simple, as is advocated in her press and by the university teachers, from Treitschke downwards – or does she want definite things which England can help her to get?'[82] Such vagueness of aim was, of course, a typical characteristic of a new power conscious that it is expanding, but unwilling or unable to specify the future limits of that expansion – 'leaving it to an uncertain future to decide', as Crowe described it.[83] If this was a perfectly natural position for Germany to occupy, it was also natural for the British, who were even less able to estimate the extent of those aspirations, to be uneasy about it, to take precautions and, ultimately, to be willing to respond with force if Germany herself moved forcibly.

431

# CHAPTER 21

# Discourse: The Role of the 'Official Mind', and the Questions of Balance and Comparison

Since the preceding chapter dealt with issues such as the future of the Portuguese colonies and the implications of the Schlieffen Plan, whose details were obviously known to only a few people, it may be appropriate here to examine once again the concept of the 'Official Mind'. The latter, it has been suggested, can be viewed as a force having an existence and impetus of its own, able to 'assemble and weigh all the factors' in a deliberate and calculated fashion, 'partly insulated from pressures at home, and remote from reality in overseas situations', and 'consciously above and outside' the political and economic processes. There is a certain amount of truth in this picture: permanent officials, conscious of their 'expertise' and knowledge of confidential information, regarded the outbursts of public sentiment, the probings of parliamentary deputies and the inflated language of pamphleteers and leader-writers with a mixture of disdain and apprehension;[1] government ministers did sit down together on occasions – either at the Cabinet and the Prussian Council of Ministers, or in a smaller forum – and seek to arrive at a common policy, which would then be implemented by the executive; the particular functions of a department (for example, the Treasury and the *Reichschatzamt*'s known position on increased spending) were important, as was the constitutional status of other bodies (for instance, the CID being merely a consultative assembly, the Prussian army being free from civilian control). By extension, the characteristics and prejudices of individuals who held office, be it the optimism of Lascelles, the Social Darwinism of Tirpitz or the suspiciousness of Holstein, did play a part in the overall historical process.

Yet this emphasis upon the 'Official Mind' and the decision-making system *per se* also has its dangers. In particular, it may lead to an exaggeration of two features: first, the aloofness – almost the autonomy – of the government; and secondly, the unity of conviction and direction in the policies pursued. What emerges from the present study is much less the isolation of officialdom than the permeation of ideas, consultations, influences and shared prejudices *across* the borderline between it and the 'outside world'. Henry Wilson might have

432

been on one side of the line in his official capacity, but in his secret dealings with the Ulstermen, his encouragement of the National Service League and his close co-operation with Maxse and others to mobilise the Conservative leadership during the 1914 crisis he was no advertisement for the impartiality of the executive. Conversely, Chirol was not technically part of the 'Official Mind', but by his frequent exchanges of information with Sanderson and his more occasional, lengthy talks with Lansdowne, his intimate correspondence with Lascelles and Spring-Rice and his long stays with Cromer and Curzon there is little doubt that he made a contribution to the thought-processes of the government and its assessment of German policy. And how much of Eyre Crowe's famous memorandum of January 1907, one wonders, derived from the frequent and intimate conversations with his brother-in-law, Spenser Wilkinson?[2] By the same token, it is impossible to understand Tirpitz's role solely within the confines of governmental processes: his success in resisting the post-1908 efforts to restrict naval expansion, for example, lay not simply in the support of Wilhelm or in his own bureaucratic expertise and tenacity (although both were important), but in the fact that he could activate his allies in the political, economic and press world – and since the struggle against Tirpitz also meant a fight against Krupps, the shipyards, the Navy League, Pan-German journalists and the greater part of the National Liberal and Free Conservative parties, it is not surprising that Bethmann Hollweg had to move cautiously, and to look around for his own allies. No doubt there did exist higher civil servants *pur et simple* in both countries; but an undue emphasis upon their isolation from outside processes hardly accords with reality.

The second reservation follows from the first: that, while it is possible to point to certain decisions being hammered out by ministers and their advisers and thus becoming official policy (for example, the German government's despatch of the Kruger Telegram, the British government's decision to withdraw from the Baghdad Railway project in 1903), what emerges from the present study more than anything else was the existence of *conflicting* schools of thought within the governmental machine. The shared assumptions, the ingrained prejudices of a homogeneous élite, the 'high calling to mediate between jarring and selfish interests'[3] which have been detected in the late-Victorians' approach to the partition of Africa, are not notably in evidence in the British and German assessments of the other country. Rather than spotting that unified entity termed the 'Official Mind', the historian of this topic is more likely to encounter a series of rival perceptions about national priorities and the world order. There was much more cohesion in the 'collective mind' formed by Tirpitz, his junior staff, Reventlow, Schäfer, Bassermann, and the Pan-Germans – formed, that is, by people *in* and *out* of government – than there was in the perceptions of all those within that legally recognisable but politically mythical boundary which divided officialdom from everyone else. This was also true with regard to, say, the relative homogeneity of the foreign policy assumptions of Cabinet ministers such as Loreburn, Burns, Morley and Harcourt, senior civil servants at the Board of Trade and Treasury, certain City financiers and Nonconformist businessmen, backbenchers in the Liberal Party, and a cluster of radical Liberal journalists.

The dynamics of British and German politics at this time point to frequent struggles between sub-groups within what one might loosely term the establishment, each sub-group striving to have its viewpoint accepted as the national policy, and each containing members who had a variety of *functions*, in politics, in the press, and in the bureaucracy. The strategic details might be known to only a few, but the debate in Germany upon fleet limitations or in Britain upon the idea of a 'continental commitment' was carried out inside and outside of government, inside and outside of Parliament, in leader columns and party resolutions and pressure-group pamphlets as well as in country houses and sub-committees. In several critical instances, moreover, the balance of forces was such that no unified national policy emerged: instead, there was a 'hung' decision and the different sub-groups went their different ways. If the uncoordinated system of Imperial Germany was the more noticeable in this respect – according to the wits, the Foreign Ministry saw France as the enemy, the army Russia, and the navy England – then it is also true that Asquith's government 'decided not to decide' over the issue of whether Britain should support France in a European war. Hoping that such a contingency would not arise, Radicals and Liberal-imperialists agreed not to press a matter which could split the party and the country in peacetime.

In consequence, it does not appear useful to the purposes of this study to devote a significant amount of space to the Foreign Offices of the two countries, their ambassadors at each other's court and the role of other ministries in the era of Bülow and Chamberlain – as was done for the earlier period.[4] At a time when Anglo-German relations were not so vital or sensitive, when few if any pressure groups sought to exert influence in connection with that relationship, and when election platforms did not refer to the naval race or the invasion threat, there had existed a far greater freedom of action, and potential role, for an individual. By 1906 or so, the growing Anglo-German antagonism was so clearly affected by long-term and fundamental factors that it is difficult to see how a change of individual at a certain post would have made much difference. For example, both Lascelles and Metternich were increasingly criticised by circles within their own governments for not properly representing the 'national' interest;[5] yet while a detailed character-analysis of both ambassadors would show that they had certain failings, the significant fact was that no ambassador by that time could have markedly influenced the level of animosity between the two peoples. Since their unenviable and at times unhappy careers were chiefly affected by larger processes, it is to the latter that attention should be focused. By the same token, of course, it is possible to recognise the particular characteristics of a Fisher or an Eyre Crowe or a Kiderlen or a Younger Moltke while suspecting that their government's policies would not have been substantially different had they not existed. The 'stream of time', to use Bismarck's phrase, possessed currents affecting the Anglo-German relationship which few if any individuals could steer against.

The picture of the so-called 'Official Mind' is, then, similar to portrayals of the economic situation, or of the party-political scene, or of the world of ideas presented in earlier chapters: namely, a variegated pattern, with differing groups and conflicting shades of opinion and alternative policies. This may appear to take the historical art of 'splitting' too far, exaggerating what were mere nuances and complicating the overall story. But there is another way of looking at this fuzzy pattern. The argument has not simply been that, say, some British firms feared German commercial rivalry while others did not; or that certain Germans favoured an English alliance while others disapproved of it; or that many Britons suspected Berlin's intentions but others were more trusting. The 'splitting' and the nuances were only the first stage in the process, and made necessary by the fact that both contemporaries and later historians indulged in sweeping generalisations and comparisons: 'all Germans favoured a big navy', or 'the British also had a yellow press and patriotic leagues', or 'the military planners were out of control in both countries'. The second, and quite critical stage is to return again to the 'lumping' process, or at least to understand what the overall balance of forces in the two countries was which led to the implementation of certain policies and which would mean that, under certain eventualities, the course which the government would take was reasonably predictable. At the end of the day, it is perfectly proper to argue that although pro-English forces existed in Germany, they were in a minority and unable to effect measures which would eliminate the antagonism. Similarly, although the political balance in Britain was less lop-sided, the forces striving to improve Anglo-German relations – either by positive measures or, negatively, by seeking to prevent British participation in a European war under virtually all circumstances – were not strong enough to prevail. Well before the actual events of 1914, therefore, it is clear that the balance of forces in both countries about perceived 'national interests' was such that, if those interests clashed, the Anglo-German antagonism would become an Anglo-German war.

Finally, it is worth returning to the methodological problems raised by this comparative analysis of the two societies. The first stage in the process is the relatively simple one of identifying similarities of ideology and institution and political action in Britain and Germany – say, in the mutual manifestations of a 'new navalism', in the growth of a working-class movement, in the agitations of economic pressure groups and in the articulation of Social Darwinist ideas. The second stage is the process of differentiation, the measurement of how significant these various phenomena were in each of the two societies. After such an exercise it is possible to perceive, for example, how weak was the position of pro-conscription forces in Britain as compared with Germany; or how much more decisive was majority control of the House of Commons as compared with such predominance in the Reichstag; or how significantly different were the taxation patterns which emerged after 1900 in each country.

Yet even this second and more discriminating stage runs the risk of being merely a table of *dissimilarities*, which is a useful counterpoint to the list of *similarities* but not in itself an explanation of why those differences existed. At the end of a cluster of chapters which have been heavily engaged in measuring contrasts and comparisons, a restatement of certain basic background determinants which distinguished the two countries in the age of Bülow and

Chamberlain seems in order. Although the actual number can be added to, the following points at the very least need to be reiterated:

(i) the disparity in the pace of economic development. The much more gradual alterations in the British economy not only explain why its *internal* structure was so much less affected by the possible turbulences emanating from economic expansion, but the relatively slower growth rates also provided the cause for the anxious debates upon the loss of the country's *external* influence. The much faster industrial and commercial expansion of Germany made its existing social and political rivalries that much more intense; and the specific features of that expansion – the emphasis upon heavy industry, the continuing compensation and protection given to agriculture – had their own consequences upon the political culture. 'The fact is that the social base for powerful reactionary or counter-revolutionary mass movements was built into the very structures of Imperial Germany; in Britain, by contrast, it was almost wholly lacking.'[6] In turn, both the fissured domestic-political scene and the rapid pace of post-1895 economic growth offered good cause for the argument that Germany simply *had* to expand.

(ii) the powers of the state apparatus, and of the traditional élites (monarchy and Junkers) who supervised and influenced that apparatus, were altogether more substantial in Germany than in Britain. Whatever the area selected – controls by the representative over the executive, prerogatives of the monarch, role of the army, management of the economy, freedom of the press, supervision of the educational system – the German position was more authoritarian and state-directed. Without a recollection of this fact, all comparisons of the party strengths and moods in the House of Commons and the Reichstag – and, conversely, of the potential influence of such non-parliamentary forces as the patriotic leagues or the agrarian 'lobby' – are likely to be flawed.

(iii) this, in turn, makes the political prejudices of those who held the reins of power of extreme importance. The general willingness of the British élites to contemplate *ad hoc* adjustments to the political order, and the obvious endeavours of such statesmen as Disraeli, Gladstone, Chamberlain and Lloyd George to pacify the working classes and thus head off their rejection of the prevailing system, contrasted sharply with the German establishment's treatment of the SPD and the trade unions. This relative 'liberalism' of the British ruling class is not simply to be understood as an *ideological* trait (for example, a tolerance of other opinions), but was also reflected in a constitutional system which permitted political participation, at least to those willing to adhere to the parliamentary rules. The tactic of offering partial concessions to those outside the political Pale had achieved such a success rate in nineteenth-century Britain that it is not surprising that both Liberal and Conservative politicians felt that they could ride out social unrest without recourse to acts of suppression; but the German élites, facing their own '1832' crisis two-thirds of a century later, were altogether less willing to risk such a tactic. Put crudely, the 'liberal' approach to preserving social stability by abandoning intolerable privileges and outmoded practices was much more efficacious than a policy of reaction. On the other hand, it is fair to remark that

(iv) Wilhelmine Germany possessed two specific political features which the leaders of late-Victorian/Edwardian Britain (or late-Georgian Britain, for that matter) did not have to contend with: namely, a numerically powerful workers' party which contested the legitimacy of the existing order; and an almost equally strong Catholic Centre, which held the balance between Left and Right although at the cost of generally paralysing the parliamentary system and thus preserving the *status quo*. (The exceptional conditions of 1885–6 in Britain, when Parnell held the balance, were the *normal* circumstances in the Reichstag which Bismarck and his successors had to treat with.) Of course, it could well be argued that neither of these 'non-establishment' parties would have been so strong had it not been for the stimulus of the *Kulturkampf* and the anti-socialist measures of the German state in the first place; but it still remains true that Wilhelm II and his Chancellors had to contend with forces which had no real equivalent in Britain, and that this structured the general nature of German politics and helped to keep it more 'illiberal'.

(v) Finally, all the above elements interacted with the fact that, whereas Britain was a well-established *national* state even before the advent of industrialisation, the German Empire was a recent foundation whose exact place in Europe – let alone in world politics – was ambiguous and uncertain. This latter condition not only induced an exaggerated emphasis upon the power and unity of the Reich, which to the middle classes in particular assumed an enormous psychological potency, but it also helped to validate the Prusso-German establishment's appeal for unquestioned solidarity behind the monarch – and, indeed, created both the internal *and* external circumstances which tempted parts of that establishment to repeat the traditional habit of diverting outwards its domestic conflicts. In Edwardian Britain, by contrast, the national boundaries were obviously that much more secure, the internal problems were never as severe, and its leaders reasoned that the country probably had more to lose by embarking upon foreign adventures (especially after the setbacks of 1899–1902) instead of settling international disputes by compromise and with a minimum of fuss. Even a Conservative Party leader under considerable right-wing pressure could assure the king that 'The interest of this country is now and always – Peace';[7] a confession which few if any German Chancellors made to their Kaiser. On the other hand, neither of the two main political parties in Britain was willing to surrender its freedom to act militarily in the event of the continental or maritime *status quo* being forcibly altered to the country's detriment. While this implied that the British, too, would go to war under certain circumstances, the motivation for such a decision was likely to be different from that obtaining in Berlin.

PART FIVE

*From Antagonism to War:*
*Anglo-German Relations, 1907–1914*

# CHAPTER 22

# From Antagonism to War (1907–1914)[1]

The chief events in European diplomacy during the year 1907 confirmed that the advent of a Liberal administration would mean no reversal of the growing Anglo-German antagonism. The first of these was the signing of the *entente* between Britain and Russia in August of that year. This agreement had, as many scholars have shown, specific Asian dimensions which made its conclusion desirable in any case. For decades the British had yearned for the removal of that 'sword of Damocles'[2] which threatened their greatest imperial possession and which, in the light of Kitchener's demands for reinforcements, could only be combated by the deployment of prodigious amounts of men and money: their desire to reach an amicable accord with St Petersburg was thus very genuine. Russia's enthusiasm had traditionally been much less in evidence; but her economic and military weaknesses after the war with Japan, together with the awareness that India was now covered by the terms of the renegotiated Anglo-Japanese alliance, made the exertion of military pressure upon the Indian 'buffer' states a foolhardy proposition. It was far better to call a truce in the 'great game' in Asia and to explore instead the possibilities of a British concession over the Straits and the floating of loans on the London money market.

What is equally clear is that this *entente* also had a European dimension. The Russian government, acutely aware of its weakness *vis-à-vis* Germany and Austria-Hungary, sought to assure Berlin that this new accord contained no anti-German bias, and there were still many within the Russian establishment who did not want to be bound to an Anglo-French bloc; yet the German ban upon loans,[3] and the growing strength of popular panslavism, pushed the government in the other direction. On the British side, apart from certain traditional imperialists and the Radicals, the anti-German calculation was more in evidence: it was not merely Grey, the Foreign Office and the General Staff but also many politicians and editors outside the government who felt, as Chirol did, that 'the restoration of the balance of power in Europe . . . is the *crux*'.[4] Moreover, whatever the intentions of the signatory powers, the *results* were bound to work to Germany's detriment. An Anglo-Russian war, which had been one of the central expectations of European politics for decades and

441

had so enhanced Bismarck's position, now appeared a remote possibility and Bülow's mythical 'free hand' had gone for ever. As Szögyeny had forecast in 1900, the German pursuit of *Weltpolitik* would lead her into rivalry with the 'world' powers, and that in turn would make her more dependent upon Austria-Hungary in Europe. This now was a very serious consequence, for although Russia's 'men-on-the-spot' were often to test London's patience over the Persian accord, St Petersburg was in effect turning from the post-1897 Asian phase of its policy to a renewed involvement in the Balkans – and that just at a time when the area was witnessing another spasm of political instability and when the 'new men' in Vienna (Conrad and Aehrenthal) were resolved upon firm action. In much the same way, the 1907 *entente* had removed the last of Britain's possible imperial challengers and thus allowed her to concentrate upon European affairs: more particularly, Haldane and his planners could prepare the expeditionary force for possible dispatch across the North Sea instead of to the North-west Frontier. Above all, the Asian settlement permitted the French to escape from their earlier dilemma and to be encouraged more than ever in their hopes of creating a triple alliance against Germany.

The second notable event of 1907 was the failure of the attempts at a general naval limitations agreement, followed by an intensification of the Anglo-German naval race. With the knowledge of the difficulties which confronted so many other ventures to limit armaments in the course of this century, the historian can hardly be surprised at the story of the collapse of the second Hague Conference. To many British Liberals, and rather fewer of their German equivalents, this was a disastrous occurrence. The years 1906–early 1907 had been full, as we have seen,[5] of various attempts to improve Anglo-German relations despite the cynicism of right-wing newspapers about 'the artificial creation of social amenities' and the Foreign Office's disapproval of that 'confraternity of international busibodies' whose appeal for an end to the arms race was convincing the Germans 'that England is exhausted'.[6] Given the momentum of such events as the journalists' exchange visits, the conference of the Inter-Parliamentary Union, and the meetings of Edward VII and Wilhelm, Liberals were looking forward to a further harmonisation of relations by means of a naval treaty, which would then permit further reductions in British defence expenditures. The paranoiac response of the nationalists, aware that Campbell-Bannerman fully supported the pacifist stance, suggests that they felt very much on the defensive at this time: 'If seriously carried out, [the defence cuts] would in two years wreck all our alliances and understandings, and leave England in a hopeless position of isolation, weak at sea, defenceless on land, the China of Europe, a nation without patriotism and without the higher form of public spirit.'[7]

As it was, the British arch-patriots need not have worried. Throughout this period Wilhelm had attacked each and every suggestion about naval disarmament, and in a Reichstag speech of April 1907 Bülow openly declared the government's opposition to such an 'impractical' notion as disarmament.[8] To the greater part of the German press, London's explanation that it was 'anxious to make it clear that we were not forcing the pace' was pure hypocrisy. Britain always favoured army reductions, it was pointed out, because it was not a great military power; and it was now offering to slow down its warship production when, with the creation of the first few Dreadnoughts, it had a unique advantage over every other country. The sarcasm heaped upon disarmament schemes by the German delegation to the Hague Conference once again identified that country as a bastion of militarism. To those Britons who had never doubted that fact, the result was not a disaster: 'Bülow has now come into the open, and we know where we are', Grey informed Nicolson.[9] To pacifist and 'reductionist' circles, the event was so disappointing that they began to suspect that the real grave-diggers of their hopes were located in Whitehall, especially when the Admiralty had insisted upon its traditional policy of 'capture at sea'.[10]

Alas for the Liberals, worse was to come. The chief reason why Tirpitz and his assistants had frowned upon either a naval limitations agreement at the Hague or any of the bilateral arrangements subsequently suggested by Grey was that they were secretly planning for a further acceleration in their own building tempo. This could not be done during the Moroccan crisis, Capelle noted, 'for the matter was *too dangerous* as a consequence of the tension with England'; now, the favourable circumstances offered by the existence of a Liberal government should be utilised.[11] In addition, the 1907 election had provided Bülow with a 'national' majority, and there was a temporary budget surplus. Despite Holstein's criticism that the Kaiser and the Navy League were merely consolidating 'an overwhelming naval superiority against us',[12] the time seemed right both to increase the building costs to provide for the much more expensive battleships and to lay these down at the rate of four per annum for the next few years. While formidable enough in themselves, the exact timing of the announcement of the new increases produced a further jolt in Britain – coming as it did a week after Fisher had told his audience at a Lord Mayor's banquet that they could 'sleep quiet in their beds' and a day after Wilhelm concluded his state visit at Windsor (18 November 1907). The 'race' was on again, with a vengeance; and it became even more critical an issue because of the internal politicisation, with the Radicals in the German Navy Leage criticising Tirpitz for his moderation while the Cabinet, Parliament and press in Britain was bitterly divided between those alarmed at German intentions and those decrying this 'scare-mongering'. Fisher's critics were now able to deploy the argument that the move to Dreadnought construction had eliminated the country's previous happy lead in pre-Dreadnought vessels. The Kaiser's impulsive letter to Tweedmouth, 'scooped' by Repington in *The Times* just when (March 1908) the Unionist press was attacking the estimates as inadequate and the radical papers were deploring such 'bloated armaments', brought the Anglo-German relationship to the forefront of politics. With the Imperial Maritime League being formed out of the 'ultras' within the old Navy League, with Fisher and Beresford dividing the service, with another CID sub-committee's examination of the invasion danger failing to satisfy the alarmists, and with Grey, Haldane and other ministers believing that German spies were crawling all over the English coast, the naval issue was the catalyst for all sorts of quarrels.[13]

By the autumn of 1908, the atmosphere was, if anything, even more tense.

Lloyd George and Churchill, now a powerful combination within the Cabinet, were leading the 'Social Reform' wing of the Liberal Party so successfully in opposing increased naval expenditure that Grey was close to resignation. At Edward VII's visit to Cronberg in August, Wilhelm excitedly told Hardinge that Germany would not even discuss naval limitations with a foreign government but would rather 'go to war'.[14] Reports from the British naval and military attachés in Berlin about the 'widespread hatred' of England were markedly gloomier than earlier in the year; and this notion of mass anglophobia was confirmed in the Kaiser's *Daily Telegraph* letter (published 28 October) which – while profoundly affecting the standing of the Crown within Germany – provoked a fresh agitation among navalist circles in Britain. Even more alarming to the Foreign Office was the Franco-German crisis over the Casablanca incident and Berlin's demand for an apology: by early November, Grey was asking McKenna at the Admiralty to have the fleet in readiness, and Esher noted in his diary that 'it looked like war', with the Liberal-imperialist ministers resolved to assist France without even being asked to.[15]

When, therefore, the question of German naval acceleration became acute early in 1909, this accumulated nervousness erupted into a full-scale crisis which divided the Cabinet until Asquith's ingenious formula of '4 battleships now, 4 later if need be' was accepted. The Radicals' fears of the intransigence, opportunism and violent language of the post-Salisburian Right, the phobias of many in the established orders about the 'socialists' and 'little-Englanders' who were seeking to disrupt society and the empire, and the popular alarm about German spies and 'a bolt from the blue', sharply increased the domestic-political feuding. The issue also led to a hardening of positions *between* the two governments: Tirpitz proclaimed himself insulted and hurt at the British refusal to accept his assurances, subjecting the British naval attaché to some unpleasant encounters, and Wilhelm called Grey's suggestion about an exchange of information an 'offence and comparable to the request of Benedetti's in 1870!'[16] On the British side, it was asserted with equal vigour that the German refusal to allow mutual inspection proved that they had something to hide; and that, unable any longer to trust the Navy Law schedule as a guide to when ships' contracts would be placed, London could only rely upon the German building capacity – which, to the alarm of the Admiralty, was almost equal to the British. Subsequently, the debate upon whether the Germans actually hoped to 'steal a march' has led to a historical controversy almost as heated.[17] This seems less significant than the undoubted fact that Anglo-German relations, public and governmental, had now reached a very low ebb.

With the benefit of hindsight, this excitement is bound to appear excessive. Very early in the crisis, Berlin was firmly told that 'the standard and proportion of the British navy to those of the European countries which has been upheld by successive British governments must be maintained'[18] – and so it was; in turn, the Germans insisted that they were accountable to no foreign government for the size of their fleet, and would go on building regardless – which they did. Each side resented the other's actions and arguments, but the mutual resolve to build further warships was typical of a 'cold' war, not a 'hot' one. The profits of the shipyards, and the recruitment figures of the naval leagues, would be nicely boosted; but neither side was at all likely to commence hostilities without some remarkable further provocation. The Casablanca incident, although far less publicised, had brought Asquith, Grey and Haldane much closer to a consideration of naval action.

Even more significant for the future was the contemporaneous Bosnian crisis. By this time, many a German newspaper was referring to the country's 'encirclement'; exaggerating the political importance of Edward VII's visit to Reval in June 1908, they claimed that an Anglo-French-Russian military alliance had been formed to overawe 'peace-loving' Germany and its irresolute government. It was necessary, so went the argument, to stand by Austria-Hungary, their only remaining ally, and to show resolution in any future crisis.[19] In line with these sentiments, Bülow and Holstein offered unqualified support to Vienna in its quarrel with the Serbs – something Bismarck had never done. After years of mutual neglect, the two army staffs began to consult upon their respective war plans: although *Weltpolitik* was not given up, Germany was binding herself more closely to the volatile political affairs of south-eastern Europe. Nothing made this more obvious than when the Russians were bluntly informed by Berlin in March 1909 that they must reply 'yes or no' to the demand for their recognition of the Austrian annexations. This was sabre-rattling with a vengeance and if the German nationalists exulted at the diplomatic victory over Russia, which had been forced to retreat because of its own weaknesses and the unreliability of its *entente* partners, the British government drew a different conclusion. Not everyone was as alarmist as Nicolson, who feared that France and Russia would be 'gravitating rapidly towards the Central Powers', that the German aim was 'to obtain the preponderance on the continent of Europe' and thereafter 'she will enter on a contest with us for maritime supremacy';[20] but the coincidence of this affair with the naval and Casablanca crises, the violence of the Kaiser's language and the tone of the German press, shook many in London.

They would have been much more shaken, however, had they known that in January 1909 Moltke had informed the Austro-Hungarian Chief of Staff, Conrad, that if war with Russia arose from an Austro-Serb conflict, the bulk of the German army would be thrown upon France. We have seen that, even when considering a war with Britain in 1904, this was Schlieffen's sole answer to the problem;[21] but the British, had they known of it then, might at least have consoled themselves with the thought that the inflexible German military plans would have gratuitously brought France on to their side in a war that was already under way. They would have been distraught to know now that an obscure Balkan squabble would, so far as Berlin was concerned, automatically transfer the fighting to that sensitive area of western Europe which many Britons felt bound, morally or strategically, to defend. It was in July 1909, by awful coincidence, that the first serious attempt by the CID to examine the conflicting strategies of the navy and the army had resulted in a tentative statement of support for the General Staff's 'valuable' plan to intervene militarily in the event of a German assault upon France.[22] Although this could still be overridden by the Cabinet as a whole, such an eventuality was increasingly remote; and, on the German side, it is remarkable to observe that the plan to strike westwards whatever the *casus belli* had been acknowledged without protest by Hohenlohe, Bülow and Holstein and was not questioned by the incoming Bethmann Hollweg. The immediate Bosnian crisis was soon to subside; but the legacies, in the Balkans, Russia and ultimately in the plains of Belgium, were to return to haunt the statesmen of Europe within a short while.

For the remainder of 1909 and much of 1910, political attention in Britain and Germany focused upon domestic issues; yet as shown earlier these were not separate from foreign policy but intimately related to it.[23] The armaments race in particular stimulated the mutual financial crises of 1909, and to the political Right and Left weakness or bellicosity in external affairs was respectively seen as the obverse side of 'revolution' or 'reaction' in domestic matters. On both sides of the North Sea a widespread *Angst*, especially among the socio-political establishment, was detectable: 'It is altogether [a] fearfully anxious time – danger within and without',[24] observed one 'moderate' Conservative who had hitherto not believed in the German peril.

Although the public's gaze was upon these internal controversies, there also took place at this time highly significant diplomatic exchanges between Berlin and London, the overall result of which was to demonstrate that, even when both governments were eager to improve relations, the limitations upon their freedom of manoeuvre would prevent any important breakthrough. Grey, now under considerable pressure from Liberal newspapers, MPs and Cabinet colleagues such as Loreburn, was eager to show that Britain did not seek the isolation of Germany. Bethmann Hollweg, more inclined than Bülow to be pro-British and definitely more distrustful of Tirpitz's naval policy, was anxious to reduce the number of Germany's potential enemies: it is worth noting that this period also saw German efforts to achieve a *détente* with Russia and even with France,[25] but British neutrality was clearly the new Chancellor's chief hope. Whether it was because he sensibly and simply sought to rescue Germany from a difficult military-diplomatic position, or because he was clearing the ground for some later German attempt to achieve hegemony in Europe, is still debatable but – from the perspective of Anglo-German relations – irrelevant. Whether German intentions were offensive or defensive, Bethmann was still bound to the General Staff's aggressive operations plan, and the British were still determined not to wash their hands of Europe.

The 'vicious circle'[26] of the Anglo-German negotiations of 1909–11 neatly indicates, therefore, from what differing standpoints the two sides approached the question of a *détente*. Given the strength of the radical nationalist sentiment towards the German navy by 1909, it is difficult to believe that Bethmann Hollweg could hope to do anything more than reduce the *pace* of the fleet increases (although even this might be grasped at by the Liberal government in London); but to make, as he himself put it, this 'substantial sacrifice by acknowledging the actually existing British supremacy at sea', he required the crucial compensation of a pledge of British neutrality in the event of a European war. Grey's offer that Britain would not join in any unprovoked assault upon Germany was insufficient, therefore, since it not only left the freedom of defining that assault in London's hands – a point Tirpitz and the Pan-Germans would be sure to attack – but it would also not cover the exigencies of the Schlieffen Plan.

It was precisely this demand for absolute neutrality which caused shivers to run through the Foreign Office. Was this not merely another German ploy to 'split' the *entente*? Did not the German refusal to accept Britain's offer to remain out of an aggressive war against her imply that she herself contemplated offensive action under certain conditions? How would France and Russia react to the news of an Anglo-German understanding? Again and again, the British correspondence referred to the prospect of isolation: in Grey's words, 'We cannot enter into a political understanding with Germany which would separate us from Russia and France, and leave us isolated while the rest of Europe would be obliged to look to Germany.'[27] It was just at this time that London learned of the Franco-German accord upon Morocco which, even if it mainly concerned business agreements, also showed that there were influential circles in France keen for a reconciliation with Germany. Whether those financial interests would gain the upper hand over the French nationalists, or whether the German pressure to detach Paris – which went to the extent of the chargé, Wangenheim's, warning that France would not be allowed to remain neutral in a European war[28] – would succeed, the apprehended result would be similar. It is difficult to say how realistic were these *frissons* of alarm in Whitehall whenever it seemed possible that either France or Russia would be 'lost' to Germany; but what they clearly reveal is a quite different estimation of European politics than had existed in, say, the mind of Salisbury. Equally, a German refusal to give up the naval race in order to detach Britain from the Dual Alliance would have been out of place in the assumptions of Bismarck or Caprivi. The curious diplomatic minuet of these years was not simply a question of chronology – with Berlin wanting a pledge of British neutrality as a precondition for naval limitations, and London wanting a halt to German fleet expansion before it would consider a political settlement – but an indication that in neither field was compromise possible. Even a Cabinet sub-committee of January 1911, with its radical members eager for a settlement, agreed that Britain could make no concession in either respect in order to break the deadlock: specific colonial understandings, but not a general political *entente*, were quite in order yet they must be accompanied by talks upon naval expenditure.[29]

It was while these diplomatic exchanges were running into the sand that the Agadir crisis erupted. While the details may be left unrecounted,[30] the grave consequences cannot. The first was that the veritable explosion of disgust within the German Right at the 'cowardice' of the government in not insisting upon better terms from the French, together with the identification of Britain as the chief obstacle to German aims, meant that Bethmann Hollweg's freedom of manoeuvre was more circumscribed than ever before. Perhaps the most significant element of all was that this discontent was now shared by traditional Conservative ranks as well as by the more predictable Pan-German and heavy-industry circles: the bitter assault upon the government by the party leader, Heydebrand (applauded from the gallery by the Crown Prince) for not taking up Lloyd George's 'threat . . . a challenge . . . a humiliating challenge' indicated an intransigence which the SPD's victories in the impending Reichstag election would only intensify. This yearning for action, the desire to be avenged, was also rife within the officer corps, many of whom asserted that Wilhelm was too weak and claimed (like Moltke) that they loathed the idea that 'once again we crawl out of this affair with our tail between our legs'.[31] Forty years earlier, Salisbury had observed that the German professors who preached *grossdeutsch* aims were harmless, because they lacked the means to achieve such goals; and the Prussian army, however competent, was also no great danger so long as its Junker generals preserved their traditional foreign policy prejudices; but a blending of expansionist ideology and military efficiency would be fatal to the European balance. By 1912, a year in which the two political 'best-sellers' in Germany were General Bernhardi's *Deutschland und der nächste Krieg* and the Pan-German leader, Class's *Wenn ich der Kaiser wär* (If I was Emperor), this combination of elements was more plausible than ever and was pressing the government to go with it.

This the government did. For all his genuine dislike of the chauvinists and sober appreciation of the dangers Germany faced in executing a 'national' policy, it is fair to say that Bethmann's freedom of manoeuvre was now reduced to giving encouragement to military increases in the hope of curbing further naval expansion. Yet his warm support of the massive army increment of 1913 – which for the first time made the Schlieffen Plan numerically feasible – offered no solution of the Anglo-German antagonism to a British government whose 'radical' Chancellor of the Exchequer had just indicated its interest in supporting France. Furthermore, although many historians have correctly pointed to the reorientation of German interest from *Weltpolitik* to *Kontinentalpolitik* in the post-1911 period, the excitement over the Moroccan crisis also gave Tirpitz the chance to press for a further naval increase: the Agadir affair was 'very useful to naval propaganda' and, he informed the Chancellor, a 'major navy bill' would alleviate 'the growing irritation at home' at the blow to Germany's prestige.[32] It would also avoid the severe drop in the annual capital-ship building from four to two after 1911 and, if three such ships were laid down every year between 1912 and 1918, it would close the 'gap' in his long-term plan to achieve a minimum force of sixty large vessels (battleships and battlecruisers): indeed, the total would then be sixty-four. Agadir may have been an exercise in 'gunboat' diplomacy, but its impact extended to far larger naval units in the cold North Sea.

The reverberations upon the British side were equally great. Agadir was the most spectacular case hitherto of where certain Cabinet ministers and officials no longer felt capable of treating a colonial quarrel from the standpoint of purely local interests – which, though debatable, were not large – but immediately transferred the matter to a higher plane. It is, wrote Crowe, 'a trial of strength, if anything. Concession means not loss of interests or loss of prestige. It means defeat, with all its inevitable consequences.'[33] Germany would be convinced that 'bullying' paid; France, by doing a deal with Berlin, would show either that she felt too weak to resist or that she was indifferent to British interests and actually favoured such a *rapprochement*. In view of this latter worry, it is not surprising that historians have wondered whether Lloyd

George's speech was not aimed more at Caillaux than at Kiderlen:[34] certainly, the bluster about Britain being treated 'as if she were of no account in the Cabinet of Nations' only partly concealed the ancient fears about isolation. It says much for the atmosphere of the time that Grey, who had firmly told C. P. Scott that he would resign if they did not give France 'such support as would prevent her from falling under the virtual control of Germany and estrangement from us', was warning the Admiralty that 'the Fleet might be attacked at any moment'.[35] Yet his demeanour was soon to appear moderate compared with the belligerency of Lloyd George and Churchill.

This leads to the second consequence of the Agadir crisis: the shift in the power balance within the Cabinet. Churchill, who for years had denounced the idea that Germany was a threat, was now enthusiastically involved in urging counter-measures against the 'Prussian Junkers' and pestering Henry Wilson for details about army strengths and mobilisation timetables. While it may be argued that the minister's volatility was such that his change of conviction was not a profound blow to the radical camp, it was none the less important and the more so when he assumed control at the Admiralty.[36] More significant still, however, was Lloyd George's defection, already hinted at in his confidential Criccieth memorandum of 1910 and prefiguring his position in 1914. Although a few years after Agadir he seemed once more to be leading the 'reductionist' wing of the party in the battle against the naval estimates, he could never again be regarded as in the pro-German camp.[37] This in effect meant that, although strong in numbers, the Cabinet ministers opposed to a commitment to France were leaderless: Morley, Harcourt and Loreburn were each in their varied ways unsuitable to assume that role.

The third impact came at the level of strategic planning. When a (very select) group of ministers attended the CID meeting of 23 August 1911 to listen to the two services expound their rival strategies in the event of British involvement in a European war, the Admiralty's unreadiness during the recent crisis was already a matter of concern; and Admiral Wilson's thoughts upon defeating Germany, which Asquith later described as 'puerile', simply enhanced his namesake, Henry Wilson's lucid exposition of how, literally, the six or seven divisions of the British Expeditionary Force would balance out the German army's expected numerical preponderance in north-west Europe. In the words of Hankey, the Secretary to the CID, 'from that time onward there was never any doubt what would be the Grand Strategy in the event of our being drawn into a continental war in support of France. Unquestionably the Expeditionary Force, or the greater part of it, would have been sent to France as it was in 1914.'[38] The replacement of McKenna by the enthusiastic Churchill provided both the symbol and the assurance that the Admiralty had fallen into line. Despite the foamings of Fisher and Loreburn, and the slightly more restrained opposition of Esher, Hankey and McKenna, the strategy of a 'continental commitment' was never reversed.

This did not mean, however, that the political decision to commit British forces had been made: the War Office–Admiralty quarrel was always about *how* to support the French, not *whether* to support them. Nevertheless, warships on the high seas were always freer agents than troops committed to a neighbour's territory and the fact that, unbeknown to most of the Cabinet, confidential staff talks had been taking place since early 1906 caused an explosion of resentment within the Liberal government. From September 1911 until early in the following year, the Liberal-imperialists came under a deluge of criticism from their party colleagues. At the Cabinet meetings of 1 and 15 November there were 'prolonged and animated' discussions, which were concluded with a resolution reasserting that body's ultimate authority to 'commit' Britain and restraining new staff talks without permission. Radical backbenchers, forming a Liberal Foreign Affairs Committee, began a 'Grey Must Go' campaign which focused not only upon Morocco but also upon Persia, armaments and the baneful influences of the Foreign Office staff. Asquith and Grey were repeatedly pressed to make statements in the Commons, assuring their audience that they had entered into no secret commitments which bound the country – which were readily given and did indeed represent the strictly legal position, although many historians have observed they made no mention of the equally important aspects of 'moral' commitments and of arousing French expectations by staff talks.[39] Without doubt, British adhesion to the *entente* came under its severest strain from domestic critics in these months, and it was little consolation that Conservative papers like the *Spectator* praised Grey's diplomacy.

Nevertheless, all this did not affect the essentials of the Liberal-imperialist position. The restriction upon staff talks with the French applied to any fresh round, but not to the existing conversations. The Admiralty did not regain its strategic superiority. Many of the more moderate Liberals were pacified by the public statements of Asquith and Grey. The Prime Minister in particular played a crucial role, seeking to delay decisions and debates until tempers cooled, privately assuring the critics that he, too, disliked the idea of sending troops across the Channel yet always seeing to it that the links with Paris were not broken off. Moreover, the Foreign Secretary, unlike his staff, was not unwilling to explore the possibility of a colonial understanding with the Germans, nor did he yearn to convert the *ententes* into fixed alliances. The Radicals, in their turn, could or would not force through a denunciation of these links, even though the Moroccan crisis had produced a revanchist government in France under Poincaré. The central issue, in other words, had been 'fudged' rather than settled and it was tacitly left to the specific circumstances of the future to decide how the Cabinet would react if a Franco-German war appeared imminent: virtually everybody concerned prayed that such an event would never occur.

Above all, the Liberal-imperialists were assisted by the Germans. Rumours about Tirpitz's plan to introduce another naval increase galvanised the forces on either side who were eager to bring this orgy of battleship-building to a conclusion. The political situation in the two countries was, therefore, rather similar. Those who by now assumed that an Anglo-German conflict was inevitable, from Nicolson to Tirpitz, were sceptical about a lasting agreement and simultaneously fearful lest any partial solution be reached. Those anxious to create an Anglo-German *détente*, from the British Radicals to the more pragmatic Bethmann to the more anxious Ballin, tended to assume that a rational discussion of the issues would produce an accord. Both governments had a massive secular interest in at least exploring the possibility of a naval arrangement; at the same time, both were acutely aware of the restrictions upon their freedom of manoeuvre.

This was the background to the Haldane mission, and at the same time the explanation of its eventual failure. The enterprise got off to a bad start with the publication of the 1912 additional Naval Bill on the day before the minister arrived in Berlin; and since those proposals represented a compromise between Tirpitz and Bethmann after a bitterly fought struggle,[40] it was highly unlikely that they could be further amended. To the British Admiralty, the new law seemed a formidable measure: not only were three additional German capital ships to be laid down, but the number of vessels in the *active* fleet was to be raised substantially, from seventeen battleships and four battlecruisers to twenty-five battleships and eight battlecruisers. Consequently, Haldane and Grey insisted that the German government must make further concessions on this critical issue of the naval race: so far, all that had been mentioned was a reduction in the rate of increase. Yet when Bethmann, after threatening to resign, was allowed by Wilhelm to negotiate a compromise on the naval issue, he predictably demanded the political *quid pro quo* – a treaty pledging 'benevolent neutrality . . . if either of the high contracting parties becomes entangled in a war with one or more other Powers'.[41] With equal predictability, the British government refused to be committed. In Asquith's words, 'Nothing, I believe, will meet her purpose which falls short of a promise on our part of neutrality: a promise we cannot give.'[42] Moreover, despite some protests from Harcourt, the Cabinet as a whole agreed that Britain should not pledge herself to inaction. By late April 1912, therefore, London still insisted that 'although we cannot bind ourselves under all circumstances to go to war with France against Germany, we shall also certainly not bind ourselves to Germany not to assist France'.[43] Knowing that the implementation of the Schlieffen Plan would almost certainly be interpreted by the British as an aggressive act, the Germans in their turn declared as quite inadequate Grey's revived formula that Britain would join no unprovoked attack upon Germany. Despite the fears of the French and Foreign Office staff, London and Berlin were as far away as ever.

The German *Novelle* of 1912 gave a further twist to this spiral, not on account of the three additional battleships (which the British could easily meet), but because the vast increase in German warships on active service compelled the Admiralty to consider pulling its remaining large vessels out of the Mediterranean. This, in turn, provoked a furious row throughout the rest of the year over whether Britain was still an 'imperial' power or merely a North Sea one. The details involved a considerable blurring of the lines (since anti-Germans such as Crowe and Nicolson, and the Conservative opposition, still pointed to the dangers of a Mediterranean withdrawal even if they recognised the High Seas Fleet to represent the greatest danger), and can be followed elsewhere.[44] The most important consequence was that even after Churchill had been compelled, nominally if not in actual practice, to preserve a 'one-power standard' in the Mediterranean, Britain's vulnerability there in the face of the Austro-Hungarian and Italian decisions to build Dreadnoughts was apparent to all; and this inevitably conditioned the Cabinet's response when the French, sensing the moment was ripe, urged that there should be an arrangement about naval distribution *and* about consultation in the event of a threat to either party. Although London indulged in repeated drafting exercises in order to pare down the extent of its commitment, there was no ministerial revolt against what appeared to be the logic of events. It was the whole Cabinet, and not a select Liberal-imperialist clique, which agreed to the Grey–Cambon exchange of notes of November 1912; in them, the staff talks were acknowledged and automatic consultation in times of crisis was agreed upon, although the inevitable references were made to the non-binding character of such arrangements. A fixed alliance was still eluded, yet the moral tie and the expectation that Britain would stand on France's side was increased. It was going to be difficult, to say the least, to be coldly neutral to a country which would claim that it expected Britain to protect its northern coastline since its own fleets were looking after *entente* interests in the Mediterranean.

The next two years form virtually a diplomatic epilogue to this story: the 'gap' between British and German perceptions of their national interests remained as wide as ever. After the failure of the Haldane mission, no fresh attempt was made to discuss a neutrality treaty. Churchill, unwilling to leave things alone and aware of radical pressure for naval economies, floated his notion of a mutual 'holiday' in shipbuilding; yet, as a student of that issue has shown, there was in reality 'no common ground' between the two sides.[45] Even the discussions over the future of the Portuguese colonies and the Baghdad Railway – the first grinding to an *impasse*, the second successful – have seemed in retrospect more to signify the narrow limits within which London and Berlin could agree than to be indications that a real *détente* was under way.[46] The British and French staffs continued to work upon a synchronisation of their operations plans, which now included their navies and extended to the China Sea as well as the Mediterranean and the Channel. By the early summer of 1914, the British Cabinet cautiously agreed to naval conversations with the Russians, which certainly had a political significance although it is difficult to follow the argument that it played a critical role in Berlin's decision for war a few weeks later.[47] On the German side, the last remnant of strategical flexibility – the older war plan to strike eastwards in the first instance – was formally abandoned in 1913, perhaps (no one really knows why) because the personnel increases made the planned sweep through Belgium more feasible than hitherto.

To the uninformed observer, it is true, the Anglo-German relationship now seemed less tense. Newspaper discussions of the naval race or a 'bolt from the blue' were more subdued; no further colonial crisis occurred like the Moroccan one. The relationship between George V and Wilhelm was less subject to temperamental outbursts than was the case with Edward VII and his nephew. And, whatever the outcome of the confidential discussions over the Portuguese colonies, the fact that they did take place was encouraging to politicians on both sides. Bethmann Hollweg continued to hope that Britain's links with her *entente* partners might slowly dissolve. Liberal ministers in London were eager to see an all-round improvement in the political atmosphere, possibly leading to armaments reductions, and they certainly hoped that they might never be faced with circumstances which would call for a decision to intervene militarily on France's side. In addition, the mutual 'brinkmanship' during the Moroccan crisis alarmed many, not merely among the Left, but also in business circles. This was especially true of financial leaders in the City who, called in to provide evidence to a CID sub-committee, testified how 'calamitous' and 'ruinous' an Anglo-German war would be.[48] Economic arguments in favour of peace were promulgated in Angell's world-famous *The Great Illusion*, which influenced many in the British establishment. Esher, for example, was greatly impressed by the book, although still wondering whether the emotional and 'warrior' qualities in man would not reject such rational and businesslike arguments for compromise.[49] On the whole, however, a certain optimism had returned to Anglo-German relations.

What ominous developments did exist lay in the areas of domestic politics, and in the growing Balkan crisis. In Germany, the stunning victory of the SPD in 1912 frightened all the forces of the establishment. The Pan-German call for a *coup d'état* from above was now given a more sympathetic hearing in court and army circles; moves against the Reichstag's (limited) powers were mooted by agrarian and heavy industry leaders who had lost their seats to that assembly. The *Kartell der schaffenden Stände*, cobbled together in 1913, was designed to give institutional and occupational solidarity to all the 'anti-revolutionary' forces. This did not mean that German politics was now split down the middle, with a wide gap between the SPD and the rest. On the contrary, the political scene looked extraordinarily fragmented. As is well known, the SPD itself was divided into various factions; the *Mittelstand* in general was heading towards the Right, but there were exceptions; 'reformist' Liberals and 'moderate' imperialists (the stance probably closest to Bethmann's) were attempting to evolve a middle party or a coalition of parties; and hyper-patriots among the National Liberals were still willing to break with the Conservatives over the question of taxation for the 1913 army increases. The overall picture *at party and Reichstag level* was one of paralysis rather than polarisation: no bloc, whether of the Right, the middle or Left, was strong enough to provide stable support for the hapless Chancellor; uneasy coalitions would form over the Zabern affair, or to push through the 1913 tax on the increases in land values, but they dissolved into their constituent parts immediately afterwards.[50] It was scarcely surprising that Bethmann now sought to bypass the Reichstag wherever possible.

This abstention had its own significance. There is no doubt that, in dealing with party leaders (who themselves were responding to pressures from below), the German Chancellors maintained a reasonably close touch with the realities of political life. This was less likely if there was a concentration upon executive government, 'keeping the machine going' rather than seeking to improve it by evolving compromises with the parties, whose claim to participate was, constitutionally, rather weak. Thrown back upon the bureaucracy and the court, however, the Chancellor was always likely to be pulled to the Right. As one scholar puts it, 'there can be no doubt that his policy of standing above the parties led to an increase in the kind of authoritarianism that the Emperor believed in, while at the same time making his own position more vulnerable to the influence that the military and the bureaucracy and the various private camarillas exercised upon the monarch'.[51]

Yet it was precisely in these circles that the fear of domestic revolution was greatest and whence the calls for a *coup d'état* emanated;[52] and if the Chancellor himself regarded this as too dangerous a solution, it seems clear that he *was* influenced by the other phobia of the Prussian social and military establishment – the feeling that a war against Germany's external enemies was virtually inevitable and that, if the opportunity arose, it should be exploited in view of her relatively good military position. The arguments put forward by the generals, the *Wehrverein*, heavy-industrialist and Lutheran newspapers, Pan-German agitators and others were, inevitably, various. Some saw an all-out war as a 'cleansing' of internal ills, others wanted a small-scale victory which would nicely boost the monarchy's prestige; pessimists pointed to the revival of Russian might and urged a quick blow, optimists argued that Germany's own booming population and industrial production justified expansion across the territorial boundaries, and yet others noted with alarm the post-1913 decline in economic prospects.[53] To reduce this cacophony of voices to one single aim or strategy would be unhistorical; Wilhelmine Germany, both in its public opinion and in its hybrid constitutionalism whereby rival ministries and other 'influences' sought the ear of the Kaiser, never enjoyed the luxury of a coherent strategy. Nevertheless, the historian familiar with the political balance by 1914 and aware of the peculiar strength of the executive and the monarchy, cannot fail to be shaken by the extent of the calls for 'decisive' action, for 'settling accounts' and for standing *nibelungentreu* to the country's perceived commitments. Politically, there was no prospect of Germany backing down from an international crisis as had happened in 1911; yet although that crisis could arise anywhere from Alsace-Lorraine to Constantinople, the military response to it was now reduced to the implementation of one strategy alone. This was where domestic-political tensions, a flawed decision-making structure, undue deference to the military and excessive nationalism blended together into a fatal combination.

On the British side, domestic-political tensions affected consideration of external policy, but in a somewhat different manner. The country was, to be sure, unusually turbulent in the years 1911–14; the constitutional crisis, the industrial unrest and, most dangerous of all, the Ulster question were producing bitterness, intransigence and a willingness to contemplate the use of violence which had rarely been seen in Britain for seventy or eighty years.[54] There is no doubt that this affected many in the political establishment and in the higher ranks of officialdom, including people who claimed to detect links between internal 'dissidents' and external foes: the German exploitation of a civil war over Ulster, for example, was a favourite phobia of the radical Right. Nevertheless, there were significant differences between the British and German situations prior to 1914. The first – which cannot be stressed too frequently – was that the forces of 'reaction' were on the outside and the 'reformers' (however lukewarm their radicalism when judged by later standards) were in the citadels of power. The second was that, although deeply worried by the periodic outbursts of industrial unrest, the Liberal government did not draw the conclusion that an external crisis would nicely distract energies elsewhere, thus preserving the socio-political *status quo*: on the contrary, it is clear from their private assessments of likely working-class attitudes and the power of strikes that they feared a war would *increase* domestic unrest, especially if there was a collapse of credit, shipping difficulties and shortages of food. In 1914, 'Ministers took their resolution in both hands and agreed to go to war *despite* their fears of the repercussions it might produce at home'.[55] The third difference was that the Ulster crisis, besides absorbing all British attention until late in July 1914, was a further reason for caution rather than overseas adventure. The Unionists, some of whom appear the nearest equivalent to those forces in German society pressing for war to cure domestic ills, were hopeful of defeating the government's policy on this issue and felt tricked when the European crisis led to a stalemate over Ireland. The argument about 'domestic causes' of the war might be, of course, that it was the Liberal government which utilised these unexpected events in Europe in order to escape from an untenable position over Ulster; but if that were the case it is remarkable that no evidence of it remains from those intensively researched few days, and it would contradict all the previous attitudes of those ministers when handling internal crises simultaneously with foreign affairs.[56]

What is much more plausible is that the belligerency of the Conservatives, whether over Ulster and the House of Lords issues or in their constant agitation for larger armed forces and a firmer commitment to France, provided the external 'cement' to keep this oddly assorted Liberal Cabinet together. In 1885, and again in 1895, many Liberal ministers had been relieved to give up office and hand over to the Tories. By 1911 or so, it was hard to guess what internal or foreign convulsions might follow if the Opposition gained control;* and this calculation, as shown above, immensely strengthened the hand of the Liberal-imperialist wing in their insistence upon maintaining a certain external policy. A Liberal 'split' could well mean a Unionist government, perhaps supported by the dissident Liberal-imperialists in the fashion of 1886.

The second area of concern in the immediate pre-1914 years lay in the Balkans.[57] That region always possessed sufficient combustible materials of its own, especially after the Bosnian crisis, but it had also been affected by reverberations from the Moroccan quarrel of 1911: the French victory there galvanised the Italians into moving into Tripolitania and into the war with Turkey, which in turn encouraged the Russian-backed Balkan League to assault the Turks as well. In all the complex details of the Balkan Wars, the main factors are clear enough. Although Russia and Austria-Hungary found it difficult (and sometimes impossible) to control their excitable *protegés*, they themselves also insisted that they could not afford to wash their hands of events or tolerate any blows to their prestige; nor would they hesitate to appeal to their allies for aid if the conflicts escalated. Given the ramifications of the alliance system, and the plans of the various General Staffs, even a local war possessed

---

* Although the historian, equipped with hindsight, may suspect that Bonar Law was less of a 'hard man' than contemporaries believed, it is the impression of him in Liberal ranks which is important here.

the potential to spread across Europe. These were not abstract considerations, suddenly made 'real' in July 1914: during the Balkan Wars, the great powers came close to open conflict on a number of occasions, and even the more distant of them were liberal in their allocation of 'blank cheques'. The French under Poincaré informed St Petersburg that they would leave the decision with Russia, and march when she marched; the Germans assured Austria-Hungary that they would not let the Dual monarchy be attacked by Russia. In early December 1912, Haldane warned Berlin – where Bethmann had publicly spoken of supporting Vienna – that Britain would not remain a silent spectator if France was attacked or the existing balance of power set aside. Just a few weeks before then, the Russians had narrowly decided against a mobilisation which, in the view of one expert, would have seen the First World War begin in November 1912 rather than August 1914.[58] On a number of other occasions, the Austro-Hungarian government held back its generals from forcibly intervening in the Balkans; and it partially mobilised in order to get the Serbs out of Albania. In the aftermath of Haldane's warning, the infuriated Wilhelm declared that Germany should at once make preparations for war against France and Russia. During the Liman von Sanders affair, Russo-German relations plummeted to a new low. None of these incidents provided the spark to set Europe alight, and to outside observers (and certain participating diplomats) the most impressive spectacle was the way in which the ambassadors of the powers worked with Grey in London to keep the peace; here was reason, incidentally, for Liberals to hope that the sacred Concert of Europe had been revived, and for Grey to assume that this tactic of co-operation, especially with Berlin, could be repeated in July 1914.[59]

Yet in retrospect it appears that what prevented war then was not respect for any Gladstonian concert but the fact that on each occasion the power wavering on the brink of action felt that the time was not quite ripe or was influenced by its ally's plea for temporary restraint. This in turn meant that, although resisting mobilisation and war over that particular incident, preparations for the future were hastened. A good example here is the now notorious 'War Council' of Wilhelm and his military and naval chiefs on 8 December 1912: one does not have to accept that this meeting implied a *fixed* resolve to go to war in *exactly one-and-a-half years' time*, to be impressed with all the subsequent preparations to be ready for battle on a later occasion.[60] Similarly, the evidence that Moltke was urging Wilhelm and Jagow (the State Secretary) to find a pretext for war need not necessarily mean that the political leadership of the Reich was determined to satisfy the Chief of General Staff regardless of the international circumstances; but it certainly suggests how prepared they were, psychologically, to let a conflict begin if the right cause cropped up.[61]

The heated debate about the immediate origins of the First World War, and in particular about the role and intentions of the German government in July 1914,[62] is in many of its aspects tangential to our investigation of the Anglo-German antagonism. It would be perfectly reasonable to argue, for example, that whatever Wilhelm and his advisers were up to at that time, they possessed no direct anti-British aim akin, say, to the 1897 decision upon naval expansion. On the contrary, it is manifestly clear that the German leadership would have been delighted had their efforts at *détente* paid off and the British elected to remain neutral in 1914. This result the ubiquitous Ballin was still seeking to achieve at the end of July, as was, of course, Bethmann himself – although his clumsy bid for that neutrality was virtually certain to increase British suspicions.[63] To Tirpitz and his staff, a war at that point was a disaster the German navy could well do without;[64] and even the General Staff, to whom in military terms the six British divisions meant little, would have been happy to see London stay neutral if only because the Prussian generals had never given serious thought to an Anglo-German war in the first place. During the July crisis, many Germans suspected that Britain would intervene, and of course after 4 August many more were to claim that they had known that all along; yet it is equally true that her abstention, however surprising, would have come as a great relief.

The question of German intentions towards Britain in 1914 is, therefore, of much less significance than *the impact of German actions*. This comment is not meant as a deliberate evasion of those controversies about whether Berlin has to assume the main or even sole responsibility for the war, whether its intentions were blatantly aggressive or essentially defensive and pessimistic in tone, and whether domestic-political factors were pushing the Reich leadership towards a conflict. To this writer, it seems perfectly reasonable to accept the points made by critics of the 'Fischer school' that the tensions in the Balkans had a dynamic all of their own, that Vienna's fatalistic resolve to settle the South Slav question or 'go under' was of critical importance in transferring those tensions to the great power level, and that France and Russia certainly contained forces who were keen to enter into a trial of strength. It is also true that, within the German decision-making establishment, there is as much evidence of confusion and pessimism about the future as there is of a desire for expansion and conquest; Bethmann's own uncertainty is well captured in his secretary's diary reports.[65] Nevertheless – and this is why the old argument that 'all the powers were equally guilty' is in reality an historical evasion – it is also difficult to avoid the conclusion that, at the end of the day, virtually all the tangled wires of causality led back to Berlin. Austria-Hungary would not have dared to take action without Germany's full support, which was now proferred in a manner that would have amazed Bismarck. It was the unstable Wilhelmine leadership which, by actions such as cutting the 'wire' to St Petersburg, tariff wars, the Kruger Telegram, the *Flottenpolitik*, the Tangier landing, the Bosnian ultimatum and the *Panther*'s 'spring' in 1911 – what, in other words, Crowe called 'the generally restless, explosive, and disconcerting activity of Germany in relation to other states' and Bethmann Hollweg described as 'a strident, pushing, elbowing, overbearing spirit' – had built up in the minds of its neighbours a cumulative impression of Germany's ambitious aims and irresponsible power such that older antagonisms with other powers had to be suppressed in order to meet this newer danger: such that they had to stay together even if the immediate *casus foederis* was not an ideal one. It is also true that Germany's massive economic growth, when combined with contemporary notions of a national 'mission' and the alarm about domestic-political problems, had been (and still was) driving that country forward to claim a greater place in world affairs, which would inevitably involve an alteration of the *status quo* in her favour. The setbacks to some of those claims, and the assemblage of forces pitted against her by 1911, suggest at first sight that by then Germany was reacting, defensively as it were, to the steady encroachment of hostile states upon the central powers; but the long-term secular trend, taken back if need be to 1866 and forward to 1942, is of a steady accumulation of power in central Europe which, unless the ancient habits of *Machtpolitik* were suddenly abandoned, was bound to involve a disturbance of the existing territorial framework. The USA's parallel accumulation of power took place, not in a 'vacuum', but at least in a region where no great adversaries were committed to halting the shift in the political balance; geographically, the Germans were not so fortunate. However loudly they proclaimed that the global balance of power was inequitably weighted and should be 'righted', her neighbours were always more concerned about the de-stabilisation of the European equilibrium.

Finally, the historian's gaze turns to Berlin because not only was its operations plan unique in making no distinction between mobilisation and war, but also because it was responsible for extending the zone of battle from eastern to western Europe.[66] To scholars grappling with the question of responsibility for the First World War, this is an important issue; to those examining the Anglo-German relationship, it is absolutely crucial. As this study has argued, the antagonism between the two countries had emerged well before the Schlieffen Plan was made the only German military strategy; but it took the sublime genius of the Prussian General Staff to *provide the occasion* for turning that antagonism into war.

The first and most obvious point to make about British reactions to the July crisis is, therefore, that whereas Berlin had not centrally been making a decision about war against Britain, the London government and the forces influencing it were exclusively concerned with the question of whether or not to declare war on Germany.[67] The second obvious point is that, given the politico-constitutional structure and the plurality of social groups and opinions in the country, the critical issue once again was the *balance of forces*: no single person or small group of people alone called the tune. To this extent, it might be said that the decision was still an open one, and this was reinforced by the fact that there was no binding alliance treaty or national consensus upon Britain's obligations – at least until the German invasion of Belgium, and even then the nature of Britain's commitment was still disputed by some. In another sense, however, it is precisely this point about the balance of forces which suggests that the ultimate decision made was *not* such an open one, but was predictable in advance, even without the Belgian issue being utilised as political camouflage.

The best way to demonstrate this is to analyse the opposing forces *before* 2 and 3 August, that is, when the debate centred around Britain's obligations to France or, to put it in a more abstract form, to the preservation of the balance of power. Here one sees very clearly the same two coalitions of social groups which, in regard to policy towards Germany, had existed since 1906 and possibly earlier. A great segment of the parliamentary Liberal Party, traditional Cobdenites and 'moderates' as well as the more persistent critics of Grey, were not eager to fight for France. The Foreign Affairs Committee under Ponsonby sought to bring pressure to bear, was checked for a time by Asquith, Grey and Churchill's plea to remain silent while London tried to localise the conflict, and then resumed their agitations. Committed pacifists, too, were crippled by the circumstances but certainly opposed Britain's joining a great power war. The eighty Irish Nationalist MPs were, predictably, on the side of those opposing intervention. The Labour Party strongly attacked any idea of fighting for 'Russian despotism', and held a large protest meeting in Trafalgar Square on 2 August.[68] The Kaiser would have been cheered to learn that Norman Angell and his friends in the hastily formed Neutrality League described Germany in their manifesto as 'wedged in between hostile States, highly civilised, with a culture that has contributed greatly in the past to western civilisation, racially allied to ourselves and with moral ideals largely resembling our own'.[69] British non-participation was also urged by financial circles in the City and by the governor of the Bank of England; the Rothschilds, nicely belying later claims that this was a capitalists' war, pressed *The Times* to cease its campaign for intervention – a stance by the banking world which was utterly predictable given the collapse of the London stock market and the foreign exchanges.[70] So far as one can judge, business circles in general were aghast at the thought of war. All of these opinions were represented in print by the radical-Liberal journalists. Scott at the *Manchester Guardian*, perceiving earlier than most the way things were going, kept up a sustained attack upon all balance-of-power arguments, warned that war would kill liberalism, and roundly declared that Manchester cared as much for Belgrade as Belgrade did for Manchester. Gardiner in the *Daily News* argued 'Why We Must Not Fight'; Massingham in the *Nation* said the same; and so did the *Labour Leader*. (The *Daily Chronicle* and *Westminster Gazette*, much closer to the Liberal-imperialists, wobbled or preached calm.) These forces, and their arguments, were represented at Cabinet level, firmly by Morley, Burns, Harcourt, Simon and Beauchamp, and more moderately by another six or eight ministers.

And in the opposite camp? There were assembled all those who had been suspicious of German policy for the past decade or more, and who had put forward the strategical argument that Britain should defend France for reasons of her *own* security. This was *The Times*'s reply to the Rothschilds' pressure: 'We dare not stand aside . . . our strongest interest is the law of self-preservation.'[71] Is it surprising to learn that this was also the argument of the *Observer, Spectator, Daily Mail, National Review* and *Morning Post*? At any time after 1905 and perhaps before then, the pens of Garvin, Strachey, H. W. Wilson, Maxse, Spenser Wilkinson, Repington and Steed would have been ready to assert that Britain should be prepared to check German expansionism. The same was true for the anti-German element in the Foreign Office, although it is a comment upon the allegedly great power of those permanent officials that neither Crowe's criticisms of the 'German' influences of the City nor Nicolson's emotional appeals to Grey counted for all that much.[72] Henry Wilson, similarly dedicated to France and similarly distraught to learn that the staff talks were still regarded (at least ostensibly) as 'non-committal', had a better antidote to this Liberal neutralism: stir up the Conservatives.[73] Here, his own secret agitations coincided with those of the Tory 'activists', who played a highly significant role despite attracting little attention from later scholars.

At the beginning of July, the Conservative Party was less than solid in its stance; even some weeks later, Bonar Law told Grey that he was not certain of unanimity. The traditionalists, for example, still harked back to the days of the old friendship with Austria-Hungary, and journals such as the *Standard* and *Daily Telegraph* denounced the Serbian 'plot' at Sarajevo. Opinion began to swing when Vienna's ultimatum was known and speculation arose about Germany policy and the threat to the balance of power; yet the party leadership was still taking a leisurely view of things and the 'push' came from the radical Right, as it had over Tariff Reform, conscription and associated issues. Chamberlain, who had just died in early July, would have been proud of his 'men': Maxse, Amery, Gwynne, Steed and George Lloyd were in their element, making the pace of the anti-war groups seem lifeless by comparison. Tipped off by Crowe and Henry Wilson and Cambon about the thinking in Downing Street, the activists went to work, forming what Maxse termed 'an informal Pogrom' and arousing their more casual leaders. Lansdowne was called back from his country house, Amery set off to find Austin Chamberlain, and Lloyd ('famished but triumphant') brought Bonar Law up to town late on the Saturday evening of 1 August. The result was that well-known letter to Asquith of the following day, declaring that 'it would be fatal to the honour and security of the United Kingdom to hesitate in supporting France and Russia' and offering 'unhesitating support to the Government in any measures they may consider necessary for that object'.[74]

This division between the anti-war and pro-war factions of the British body politic placed enormous power in the hands of the Liberal-imperialist ministers. Since 1905, the fulcrum of deciding external policy had lain with them; now it was to be more obvious than ever, even before Belgium became the centre of debate. Nor was there any doubt about how they would decide. Grey was adamant in his conviction that France must be supported against a German attack; Haldane, for all his reputation as a pro-German, was similarly convinced; Asquith, though keeping a low profile, admitted that 'if Grey went I should go'; Churchill's 'profile' as an interventionist was, by contrast, as high as his natural pugnaciousness; and perhaps Crewe, McKenna and Birrell might adhere, but without adding much to the already sufficient weight of those four. What distinguished Grey and Asquith from people such as Churchill, Nicolson and Henry Wilson was not their resolution, but that they were much more politic, capable of waiting upon events and keen to draw as many to their side as possible; by following this strategy of cunctation, they were able to witness and to encourage the steady shift of opinion among Cabinet ministers. (Did that arch-political animal, Lloyd George, who was curiously reserved during the crisis, sense that this was likely to happen?) Days of discussion upon the meaning of the *ententes*, the military conversations, and the November 1912 arrangement and the subsequent fleet distributions in the Channel and Mediterranean began to affect the 'wavering' middle group. Gradually they began to admit (what they may have always suspected secretly) that they were somehow committed, morally, politically, to the defence of France. Tactfully, Asquith postponed the whole issue of the dispatch of the BEF until later, no doubt aware that naval warfare would seem less shocking to his colleagues than continental operations.

Sunday, 2 August, was the decisive day in two respects. Having forbidden Churchill to proceed with a full mobilisation of the navy on the preceding day, the Cabinet now agreed that they would protect the French northern coastline and French shipping if the German fleet came down the Channel – at which Burns, declaring that this was a breach of neutrality, offered his resignation. It was also at this Sunday lunchtime meeting that the pledge of Conservative support was made known, and thereafter (according to accounts of other Cabinet ministers) the Liberal-imperialists increased their pressure. Grey was now openly stating that he would resign if France was not supported. Asquith, while informing the waverers that he would 'stand by Grey in any event', increasingly referred to the possibility of a coalition – of Liberal-imperialists and Conservatives – which frightened some of his audience whilst offering others the perfect excuse to 'stand together' and 'see things through' as a united Cabinet: Samuel, Pease, Masterman and Runciman all explained to confidants that it was better to go into war united than to hand over 'policy and control to the Tories', and Asquith himself obviously preferred this solution either to a coalition or a complete Liberal withdrawal from power.[75] The motives of virtually all the ministers (except Churchill on the one side, and Burns and Morley on the other) were a tangled web of calculations and emotions, to which the Belgian strand was almost immediately added; but if there is a 'domestic cause' for the British entry into war, it would seem to lie here – not in reactionary forces seeking a *Flucht nach vorn*, but in the 'moderates' persuading themselves that, if intervention was increasingly difficult to avoid, it would be better to stay in office so as to carry out both a war policy and the parallel domestic policies by *liberal* methods. Such optimistic perceptions about the 'limited' nature of war were soon to be rudely exposed to reality.

At the second Cabinet meeting that day, it was resolved that 'a substantial violation' of Belgian neutrality would 'compel us to take action'; on the following day, in accordance with the Schlieffen Plan, the Germans obligingly crossed the Belgian frontier. Yet the Cabinet struggle over intervention had already been essentially won in the debates about supporting France and concern about keeping out the Tories. Grey's famous speech on the Monday afternoon, carefully planned and extraordinarily effective, was at least honest enough to focus more upon the 'informal', 'moral' obligations to France and the need to preserve the balance of power than upon poor little Belgium. What the Belgian factor did was to give the Cabinet waverers and their backbench supporters a recognisably Liberal justification for entry into the conflict, to cover up their slow drift towards Grey's position, to allow Lloyd George (whose low profile was still baffling observers, although Esher seems to have guessed his reaction accurately[76]) to break his reserve and announce himself for war, to reduce the number of ministerial irreconcilables to Morley and Burns, and to undercut the agitations of the radicals and pacifists outside the Cabinet.

461

That, to be sure, is an impressively weighty catalogue; yet it is hardly enough to sustain the argument that the German invasion of Belgium was the decisive element. In actual fact, it appears that by 2 August the majority of the Cabinet felt committed to joining the war even if Belgium ranged herself *on the side of the Germans*;[77] but 'Albert the Good's' appeal for aid on the following day avoided such a nasty embarrassment. Belgium was crucial, no doubt, in keeping the Liberal Party so united; but much less so in causing British intervention.

By 6 August, after certain hesitations,[78] the Cabinet agreed to the dispatch of the greater part of the BEF to France. On the 23rd of the month, some 30,000 British soldiers engaged in battle with about 80,000 Germans in the vicinity of Mons. Well before that date, the Royal Navy had imposed its blockade; a German warship had laid mines in the Thames estuary; British squadrons overseas had chased the *Goeben* and *Breslau* through the Mediterranean, and were hunting for Spee's fleet in the Pacific; and Indian and colonial forces were assembling for their assaults upon the German colonies. Although the conduct of war was still chivalrous and restrained compared with later years, Britons and Germans were now beginning to kill each other in large numbers.

Once the two countries had entered into combat, the older, more favourable images of each other were completely eclipsed by the unfavourable stereotypes. On the German side, this change was instantaneous. Those like Ballin, Brentano, the German financial world, the left-Liberal and SPD leaders, some churchmen and others who had hoped for British neutrality and understanding of their fight against 'Slavdom', were shocked by London's declaration of war and unable to explain it. Others were not so reticent: to the radical nationalists, this was the final confirmation that perfidious Albion had never changed, and as the war developed Britain rather than France or Russia became the *Erbfeind*. Tirpitz's long-suppressed fury now broke through: 'England, with brutal egoism, recognises only Englishmen. Niggers and Germans are on the same level to them. Never has the world been so terrorised as by this pirate-people on their island. Only force can help against them.'[79] Here, in the intensified form presented by Reventlow's *Das Vampir des Festlandes* and Sombart's *Händler und Helden*, was the old image – of the greedy, unscrupulous nation of shopkeepers, tainted by egoism and utilitarianism, jealous of Germany's progress and determined to frustrate it by encirclement and brutal force. Even more moderate voices made this distinction: Thomas Mann, invoking 'German spiritual superiority against foreign influence', Meinecke, rejoicing to witness the contest of German idealism against the lower qualities of the Anglo-Saxon, Troeltsch, explaining the difference between 'German freedom' and the superficial Western individualism, were all able to offer intellectual justifications of Germany's mission and to explain the inevitability of the clash with England.[80]

In Britain, much the same thing occurred. Well before 1914, and during the July crisis itself, Grey and his colleagues had believed that there was a struggle for power in Berlin between a 'peace party' (Bethmann, Ballin *et al.*) and a 'war party' (the Prussian General Staff, the Crown Prince, the Pan-Germans and, erroneously, Tirpitz).[81] The course of events showed that 'Junker militarism' had won; the invasion of Belgium, the reprisals against suspected *francs-tireurs*, the artillery bombardment of ancient cities, allowed the Allied propagandists to recall Wilhelm's own maladroit appellation of 'the Huns'. The Kaiser himself was portrayed as an evil Satanic figure, leading the slaughter of Belgian women and children in the name of *Kultur*. Pundits explained how the spirit of Treitschke and Bernhardi had conquered the German mind; and *Punch* summed it up in a doggerel verse:

> Once the land of poets, seers and sages,
> Who enchant us with their deathless pages,
> . . .
> Now the Prussian *Junker*, blind with fury,
> Claims to be God's counsel, judge and jury.[82]

So bitter and widespread was this popular germanophobia that all who had tried to improve Anglo-German relations earlier were suspect. Haldane especially came in for assaults from the jingo press for his praise of Germany; the brilliant and efficient Battenberg was quietly eased out of his post as First Sea Lord; even Eyre Crowe was later to be denounced for his German connections; and the royal family discreetly changed its name from Coburg to Windsor. The mid-Victorian heritage, of shared dynasties and mutually admired cultures, was dissolving fast. Instead, the two sides settled down to a cold, hard fight to the finish.

# *Conclusion*

Why was it that the British and German peoples, who had never fought each other and whose traditions of political co-operation were reinforced by dynastic, cultural, religious and economic ties, drifted steadily apart in the late nineteenth and early twentieth centuries, and went to war against each other in 1914? This was the question put in the first sentence of the Introduction and all that followed it has sought, directly or indirectly, to provide an explanation. Since the topic covered is a complex one, and made the more so by not being presented as a straightforward narrative; and since the investigation has covered a period of fifty-five years, it is only proper to distill the conclusions which occur to this author.

The most profound cause, surely, was *economic*. This does not necessarily mean that the direct commercial rivalry itself was so crucial; as demonstrated above, there were many economic bonds which held the two countries together even in 1914, although there had been a detectable increase in Anglo-German trade rivalry since Bismarck's time as the latter country steadily became more competitive. Nevertheless, historians grappling with the overall alteration in Anglo-German relations have before anything else to confront the fact that whereas Britain produced over twice as much steel as Germany at the beginning of this period, it produced less than half at the end of it. Of course, steel output is a very selective criterion but not a totally unreasonable one in an age of Dreadnoughts, field-cannon and locomotives; and it is worth asking whether the relative productive forces – and, by extension, the relative national power – of any two neighbouring states before or since had altered in such a remarkable way in the course of one man's lifetime as occurred here between Britain and Germany. Lord Welby (b. 1832) could properly claim to be speaking for his own generation when he informed the Royal Statistical Society in June 1914 that:

> The Germany they remembered in the 'fifties was a cluster of insignificant States under insignificant princelings, headed by the so-called hegemony of Prussia and Austria intriguing against each other, with the result that Germany was really of no account in the world either as a power or as a nation. He asked them to compare that . . . with the marvellous progress which was marked in almost every branch of German industry. They must feel that Bismarck had added a great and new industrial force to the productive power of the world.[1]

464

The point was, that this enormous shift in relative economic strength had results far beyond the concerns of businessmen and bankers alone. Without industrial power and advanced technology Prussia-Germany would have remained an 'insignificant' country; instead, it became the strongest and most efficient military state in Europe, capable of taking on at least any *two* of its great power neighbours, and indeed likely to overrun western Europe if ever it came to a general conflict. Moreover, this economic expansionism meant that Germany was not only growing out of its European 'skin' but was also acquiring the early attributes of a world power – booming overseas trade, political influence abroad, colonial acquisitions and an expanding fleet. All this necessarily implied a *relative diminution* in Britain's own commercial/colonial/maritime position unless it in turn was able to export more, colonise more and build more ships, so as to preserve the original relationship. It is worth adding that it was not merely the British but all of her neighbours (Frenchmen, Danes, Austrians, Russians) who were compelled to readjust to this basic fact that the rapid exploitation of Germany's natural economic potential was having its inevitable effects upon the power-political balance as well.

Of course, the British might not have reacted to such a 'spill-over' of German power had it not been for two further factors. The first was geographical. It seems clear that there would have been far less agitation in Britain about German expansionism had this new, bustling, militarily efficient Reich been located at some safe distance away – say, in the Far East (like Japan) or the Western hemisphere (like the USA). Even if the German spill-over had been concentrated into a *Drang nach Osten*, it is unlikely that it would have provoked such an immediate British response; both the generation before *and* after that in power in Whitehall in 1914 held that on the whole the fate of eastern Europe was no great concern of theirs.[2] But geographical proximity caused Germany's maritime expansion – into the North Sea – and her probable military conquests – into western Europe, in accordance with the Schlieffen Plan – to become a substantial infringement of what was held to be British national security.

The second additional factor was ideological. As is argued above, a certain gap in political sympathies and practices existed between 'Liberal' England and 'reactionary' Prussia even at the beginning of this story, and it was never significantly closed thereafter. But it is exceedingly unlikely that ideological antipathy alone could have led to an open conflict, if only because the last thing which British Radicals or east Elbian Junkers desired was an Armageddon in the North Sea. What was significant about these hostile perceptions of the other country was that they gradually became part of the mental furniture of the extreme nationalists in both (as witnessed in their frequent references to 'Prussian militarism', or to the *Händler*) and thus assumed a genuine explanatory power which would justify, on the one hand, British intervention to maintain the 'liberties of Europe' from the Junkers; and on the other, German measures to break the efforts of the *Krämervolk* to preserve their unwarranted global hegemony and the artificially frozen European equilibrium.

But the consequences of the economic changes which occurred in this period were not limited to the power-political arena alone. What also emerges from the analysis in the preceding chapters is that fundamental social trends, especially the growth of an industrial working class, made significant contributions to the changing Anglo-German relationship. The most obvious consequence was that it tempted beleaguered élites in Germany to seek a solution in overseas expansion and, when later frustrated by their failures to gain 'a place in the sun', to repeat the Bismarckian tactic of solving domestic questions by a foreign war: which, given the operational efficiency planning of the army, meant a westward military drive and a probable clash with the British. The intensification of the 'social problem' also had indirect consequences, in that it contributed to the rightward shift of a considerable part of the German *Mittelstand*, which then supported the establishment provided its policies were national enough – and 'national' in this context was more or less equal to a rejection of the existing international *status quo*. In Britain, the effects of the rise of labour were more complex; but it seems fair to argue that this domestic trend, coinciding as it did with gloomy external developments, produced a ferment of discontent with the Unionist Party which gradually pulled it further to the right and thereby not only intensified the party's anti-German stance but also enhanced the tactical position of the imperialist and 'interventionist' wing of the Liberal Party. The harsher, more nervous political tone of Edwardian Britain also meant that the appearance of an external challenger would be greeted with more suspicion than in an earlier, self-confident age.

The other elements covered in this analysis, such as the newspapers and pressure groups, played a contributory role; they were often effective instruments for the articulation and intensification of feelings against foreign 'foes', but did not usually possess a motive force of their own. By the same token, such aspects of the Anglo-German relationship as the cultural or religious or dynastic ties do not take us far in explaining the growing antagonism; in many ways, they often managed to exist *independent* of the clashes of national interest over the European balance and the naval race.

To sum up: the Anglo-German antagonism basically arose from the fact that in the half-century under scrutiny Germany grew out of its position as 'a cluster of insignificant States under insignificant princelings'; and from the further facts that this growth gradually threatened to infringe perceived 'British interests', that these economic shifts increased the nervousness of British decision-makers already concerned about 'saving the Empire', and that they were accompanied by ideas about a German mission which could be adopted by political forces grappling with severe domestic problems.

This summary allows the disposal of a 'red herring' which frequently emerged in earlier debates and studies about the Anglo-German antagonism. It relates to the question: 'Was the clash between the two countries inevitable?' Since this was virtually always asked by circles – either at the time, or after 1919 – who regretted the estrangement, it has an unhistorical quality; it generally rests upon the suspect argument that things might have gone differently had, say, the British been more sympathetic at the time of the *Reichsgründung*, or had Frederick III lived longer, or had Tirpitz not built his battlefleet, or had Salisbury and Holstein not been so suspicious of alliance negotiations. The only response which can be given to this sort of claim is that the forces and personalities which determined events moved, consciously or unconsciously, in a certain direction which the historian obviously wishes to study and understand better; but that it is idle to speculate upon the alternatives which were *not* chosen.

Finally, is it possible – and profitable – to grasp the nettle of allocating 'responsibility' for the growth of the Anglo-German estrangement and the fact that they eventually fought each other? Not to do so, after devoting so much detail to this subject, seems an evasion. Repeating the cosy interwar consensus that the 'guilt' was to be shared by all (and therefore by none) is equally flaccid. Yet sitting in judgement upon past events and actors has its own dangers.

There is one quick answer to this question about responsibility, and then a more complicated one. The immediate reply would be that it chiefly rests upon the German side. Had her leaders not been so determined to alter the maritime balance of power after 1897, and to unleash a westward strike in the aftermath of Sarajevo which with even more certainty would alter the military balance, then an Anglo-German conflict might well have been avoided.

That is, of course, the sort of judgement which the historians and philosophers of Wilhelmine Germany would have felt inappropriate in the arena of power-politics. Had not the British themselves conquered a disproportionate share of the globe? Did not Harold Nicolson concede that 'Our own predatory period – and it was disgraceful enough – dated from 1500 to 1900 . . . Before we blame Germany, we must first blame our own Elizabethans'?[3] Did not Churchill, even in the midst of the 1913–14 quarrels over the naval estimates, willingly admit: 'We have got all we want in territory, and our claim to be left in unmolested enjoyment of vast and splendid possessions, mainly acquired by violence, largely maintained by force, often seems less reasonable to others than to us.'[4] These are arguments which are still detectable today. 'Was Tirpitz all that much worse than Sir John Fisher?', a recent British reviewer asked.[5] Is it not the case that the Fischer school has refused 'to deal seriously with whether the ambitions [of Imperial Germany] were justified by objective circumstances, by the same general standard of international morality that animated the other powers? . . . Was it "wrong" for Germany to want to be a world power like Britain?'[6] Isn't the chorus of denunciations of German policy from Bismarck to Hitler merely a reflection of the disappointment of pro-Western intellectuals, whose 'liberal image' reveals unhistorical wishful thinking?[7]

It is possible, to be sure, to give an Actonian retort to such arguments: namely, that the German desire (and attempt) to grow at the expense of its neighbours cannot be excused by reference to the earlier misdeeds of others, and that it is impossible for the person who knows the post-1914 course of German history not to take an ethical stand. Yet even if one dislikes issuing moral judgements upon the past, there remains the question of whether it was prudent for the German leaders – intent upon improving their country's position – to appeal so often to the code of naked *Machtpolitik*, to revel in their superior 'realism' and to deprecate the hypocritical Liberal concern about means and ends. Whatever the thoughts of Delcassé, Salisbury, Balfour, Grey or Nicholas II, they were not usually to be heard publicly praising 'blood and

467

iron' policies or 'mailed fists'. In one of his perceptive remarks upon Bismarckian statesmen, Gladstone wrote that they gave 'greater consideration to physical than to moral powers'.[8] Finding it inexpedient or difficult to measure the
morality of political issues, successive German leaders rudely attacked that
very criterion.

Yet this was, to say the least, unwise of them. In the first place, it is possible
to argue that third powers (for example, the USA, Scandinavia, or Britain
when still in 'isolation') *were* influenced by questions of right or wrong. The
improvement in global communications and the spread of Enlightenment and
Evangelical and Progressive ideas in the nineteenth century had led to the
partial creation of what Gladstone would have termed a 'world opinion', which
had not existed to complicate the earlier age of mercantilism but was now
becoming a factor in its own right. This opinion was still very selective and
one-sided. It scarcely ever criticised colonial wars and gunboat diplomacy; but
it did become aroused over the Boers (being white), the Bulgarians (being
Christian) and the Poles; and it would react again to further German expansion
*within* Europe, especially against Belgium and France. German leaders never
seem to have taken cognisance of this fact. Yet, as Dehio points out, it was
impossible for Berlin to appeal to the necessity for 'world' freedom and the
breaking of the British maritime monopoly when its own military was simultaneously eliminating (or threatening to eliminate) the 'national' freedom of its
European neighbours. Without a transcending international 'ideology', Germany actually crippled itself in power-political terms as well.[9] Britain, by
contrast, had indeed carved out a colossal world empire; but by emphasising
the rights of European peoples, converting to free trade and allowing open
access to its colonies since the mid-century, it had managed, as Crowe pointed
out, 'to harmonize [its national policy] with the general desires and ideals
common to all mankind'.[10] Just *how* a country appeared to its fellow-states was
important politically. It was partly a matter of 'ideals', and partly of prudence.

If, however, one judges the actions of the two sides purely by the criterion of
Realpolitik – as the defenders of German policy prefer – then it remains equally
hard to approve Berlin's decisions. If friendship with Britain accorded with
Germany's true interests – however that expression was defined – then the
leadership had clearly failed. If German interests dictated a policy of de-
tachment from, or even opposition to Britain, it nevertheless remains true that
the *Wilhelmstrasse*'s inept diplomacy and the failure to control the domestic
anglophobia it had earlier encouraged was to cost Germany dear in the future.
It was also unwise for the younger state to challenge the established power at
the same time as refusing to settle with France over Alsace-Lorraine and
arousing Russian apprehensions over the expansion of German interests in the
Balkans and Middle East. Again, these are not questions of morality, but of
practicality.

By and large, the British élites managed their problems better. Faced with a
decline of relative power which was literally worldwide in its manifestations
and effects, Salisbury and his successors explored in pragmatic fashion the
various solutions open to them, and scrutinised which of their external obligations could be discarded and which had to be defended at all costs. In the cold

logic of power-politics, the preservation of local maritime supremacy and of the European equilibrium was bound to be of more concern than the fate of British interests in the Far East, Africa or the Western hemisphere – and the more especially when the challenge to those prior obligations was being mounted by a power which, ideologically, was increasingly antipathetic to Britain. It is scarcely the case, of course, that the British themselves can be given a clean sheet in their handling of Germany. There was far too much criticism of German conditions, far too much disdain at the failure to imitate British practices, especially in the early decades. There was, in the debates upon commercial rivalry, far too much stress upon 'underhand' or 'unfair' German practices, rather than an open recognition of superior quality and efficiency. There was an all too evident niggardliness in the treatment of German colonial claims, from the first 'bids' of 1884–5, to the late-1890s haggling over Angola, Samoa and elsewhere, to the post-1907 efforts to achieve a *détente* over imperial issues. There was, on occasions, an excessive suspicion of Germany's aggressive intentions, whether it be of Bismarck's desire to fall upon France or of Wilhelm II's eagerness to fall upon England; and, with rare exceptions (for example, Balfour) a lack of comprehension of German *fears* for its own security. Many Britons admitted that it was not in the national interest to be on bad terms with this powerful new state, or to check its overseas growth, 'encircle' it and thus enhance the internal argument that it could only achieve its proper place with the sword. Yet few seem to have possessed the generosity or the perspicacity to seek a large-scale improvement in Anglo-German relations.

These were the accumulated criticisms of contemporary Germans, and also of many of Grey's fellow-Liberals; and they are not, even with the passage of time, totally invalid. The style, the tone, which the British adopted towards Germany as it changed from being an 'insignificant' group of states to a great power was defective in many respects. Yet, at the end of the day, the historian aware of the pressures for expansion in Imperial Germany is bound to wonder whether a change of tone on Britain's part, a greater generosity over this or that colonial boundary, would really have had a significant difference. They might have papered over the cracks in the Anglo-German relationship for a few more years, but it is difficult to see how such gestures would have altered the elemental German push to change the existing distribution of power – which, unless the British were willing to accept a substantial diminution in national influence and safety, was bound to provoke a reaction on their part.

This incompatibility of position (however contested by the Liberals) hardly seems strange when viewed in the long term. If, even at the present time, the 'German question' is suspended rather than solved, with virtually all the responsible leaders within and without the two halves of Germany preferring not to contemplate what the effects would be of some distant reunification, then it is scarcely surprising that this issue was so contentious in the age of imperialism. Even if there had not existed those domestic tensions which pushed the German establishment towards external adventures before 1914 and simultaneously increased the fears of influential Britons about national decline, the problem of Germany's 'proper' place in Europe and the world would have been an immensely troublesome one, simply because its industrial growth would have brought with it a quasi-political influence over its smaller neighbours. In the heightened atmosphere of early twentieth-century Europe, with its navy leagues and press agitations and Pan-German slogans and internal discords, a peaceful solution was much less likely. Unless the Germans surrendered their desire – and their inherent capacity – to alter the existing order in Europe and overseas; or unless the British were prepared voluntarily to accept a great change in that order, then their vital interests remained diametrically opposed. As the above analysis has sought to show, in neither country was the majority of the politically effective population prepared to make such a concession, and thus the antagonism could never be eliminated. An assassination in the Balkans may have provided the 'spark' for war, and the conflagration which followed drew in many countries, for varying reasons. Yet, so far as the British and German governments were concerned, the 1914–18 conflict was essentially entered into because the former power wished to preserve the existing *status quo* whereas the latter, for a mixture of offensive and defensive motives, was taking steps to alter it. In that sense, the wartime struggle between London and Berlin was but a continuation of what had been going on for at least fifteen or twenty years before the July crisis itself.

# APPENDIX

# *Statistics Relating to Anglo-German Trade*

Throughout this book, and especially in Chapters 3 and 15, a variety of figures have been produced to illustrate the nature and volume of the 'visible' trade between Britain and Germany. Such statistics are necessary for a fuller understanding of the economic aspect of the Anglo-German relationship, and also of the very real interconnections which existed between economics, politics and ideology. It is also useful as a means of checking the statistics produced by the various protagonists when they debated the pros and cons of protectionism, or argued about the extent to which Britain's commerce and industry was being overtaken by that of Germany.

The blunt fact remains, however, that it is impossible to provide accurate statistics on Anglo-German trade in this period: neither the official British nor the German customs returns, nor any independent attempts to calculate the exact value and extent of this commerce, are without flaws and inaccuracies. All that the figures can be used for is to give *general indications* of, for example, the differences in the value of the trade in textiles as opposed to that in toys; or of changes as between one year (or decade) and another. Even this assumes that one will be using the same set of statistical returns (and not switching from the British to the German, and back again), and it further assumes that the same criteria and methods of assessment were employed throughout the period in question – which is a dangerous assumption to make, for reasons given below.

Use of the German statistics in the early part of our story is hazardous in the extreme. In the first place, the figures are not those of Germany proper but only of the *Zollverein*; and since the commerce of the Hanse cities was reckoned separately until after 1888, the returns are as likely to sow confusion as to produce enlightenment. The statistics in Table A.1, showing the exports of the *Zollverein* to Britain, the USA *and* to the Hanse cities, give a rough indication of how much of the commerce that was really being exported to the former two countries before 1889 was credited as exports to the third-named.[1] The fact that Hamburg did not produce its own export totals for many years is a minor irritant by comparison, for – with a small allowance for its own consumption and production – the greater part of its exports would be included in those of the *Zollverein* itself; but it is an enormous obstacle to understanding the pattern both of Germany's exports and imports prior to 1888 that the Hanse cities are reckoned as a 'foreign country' and that the final destination of most of the goods which passed through the ports was not indicated. There is a further, but much smaller 'hiccup' in the German figures after March 1906, when the trade totals of the remaining free-port regions were finally incorporated into those of the Reich.[2]

Table A.1    *Zollverein exports* (in million marks)

|       | Exports to: | | |
|-------|-------------|-----|---------|
|       | *Hanse cities* | *USA* | *Britain* |
| 1887  | 537 | 143 | 460 |
| 1888  | 518 | 153 | 495 |
|       | (change in method of calculations) | | |
| 1889  | 50 | 317 | 665 |

Quite apart from this major problem, the early statistics of the *Zollverein*'s trade 'suffer', as the East German historian Bondi puts it, 'from the following main deficiencies':[3] listing of volumes, not values; non-inclusion of all wares crossing the border; extremely crude classification of items, chiefly according to specifications of the customs tariff; no information about the original place of production/final destination of items, simply the border crossing-point; and, finally, from the fact that the area of the *Zollverein* itself was frequently altering. The situation improved rapidly in later years, the more particularly when the return to protectionism brought many refinements in tariff specifications and a far greater official concern about the nature of Germany's imports and exports. Pitfalls, however, remain. There were, for example, two sets of statistics: 'special trade', which consisted of all imported goods for home consumption only and all exports of the produce of the *Zollverein* only; and 'general' or 'total' trade (*Gesamthandel*), which also included goods imported for improvement for a foreign customer – for example, herrings imported from England, treated and then re-exported – and all goods leaving the borders of the *Zollverein*, including those in transit and those brought out of bonded warehouses and the free-port districts. Neither category quite corresponds to the British methods of measuring imports and exports, although to a large extent these 'improvement' goods and transit wares may be compared with Britain's re-export trade. The historian in search of exact details of total *national* German trade is rather at a loss when the statistics in Table A.2 alone are returned.[4] Given that the 'general' trade totals will include large amounts of transit trade – say, Swiss exports to Britain – I have tended *not* to reproduce them in this book, although that does mean that the extent of Germany's 'improvement' trade is thereby ignored.

The blemishes on the British side are at least equal to those on the German, and often seem much worse during the later decades when the German customs procedures were tightened up. In the first place, the records of British imports (but less so for the exports) failed to identify the enormous amount of

Anglo-German trade which passed through Belgium and the Netherlands: being a free-trade country, Britain was much less concerned to demand certificates of origin than a protectionist state. Even in regard to exports, there was no real supervision of statements concerning the final destination; and when one considers that, in addition to the transit trade through the Low Countries, large amounts of Austrian, Swiss and even Russian goods were transported through Germany, the complexity of this commerce becomes apparent – and even more so before the Hanse cities' figures were incorporated with those of the *Zollverein*! Perhaps it was for this reason that the Statistical Department of the Board of Trade did not venture to produce any figures of British trade with Switzerland, and it is reassuring for a political historian to discover that contemporary experts on commercial statistics – Sir Robert Giffen, for example, or William Gastrell, the commercial *attaché* for Germany[5] – frankly admit to the impossibility of separating out the various *national* strands within this intermeshed traffic.

Table A.2    *German foreign trade in 1880*
(in £ million)

| Zollverein | |
| --- | --- |
| General imports | 219 |
| Special imports | 141 |
| General exports | 218 |
| Special exports | 152 |
| | |
| *Hamburg* | |
| General imports | 68 |
| (no export figures) | |

One further complication on the British side was the increasing habit of some exporters of including in their estimates of the value of goods the *insurance and freight charges as well*: that is, their export returns were on a c.i.f. (cost, insurance, freight) basis rather than on the required basis of f.o.b. (free on board) value. Since the freight and insurance charges were also reckoned in Britain's 'invisible' earnings, it was not uncommon for them to be valued *twice* and for the total export figures to be correspondingly swollen.[6] Since, in the British case, the onus of stating the value of any commodity was placed solely upon the merchant concerned, one is bound to wonder how accurate *any* of the valuations of wares really were – apart from those few items such as tea, tobacco and alcohol which attracted duty. Ellinger, who attempted several 'spot-checks' upon the declared value of certain imports and the price they later realised at sale, found errors of between 25 per cent and 100 per cent.[7]

So difficult was it for contemporaries to compare British and German trade statistics that Ellinger found it necessary to explain to an audience of statisticians in 1904 that:

British figures of exports to Germany would appear greater than the corresponding German figures for 4 separate reasons; *but* appear smaller than those corresponding German figures for 2 separate reasons; *and* that British figures of imports from Germany would appear greater than the corresponding German figures for 4 separate reasons; *but* smaller than those corresponding German figures for 1 separate reason.

On the whole, it may seem better to rely upon the German statistics for the later part of this story: being an efficient, protectionist country, its classification of goods was much more specific (for example, its tariff had nineteen classifications of cotton yarn compared with the two on the British customs list) and it was more concerned to discover what were the countries of origin and final destination of goods – after the turn of the century, for example, it listed Australian produce which came *via* London as Australian exports rather than British re-exports.

There was, however, one final flaw in the trade returns of Germany and many of her continental neighbours: namely, a chronic overvaluation of both imports and exports. However vague a British merchant may have been in estimating the value of certain goods, he was generally aware of the market prices – which, of course, had in most cases slumped considerably during the overproduction crisis of the Great Depression. On the continent, the valuation of imports and exports appears to have been more the responsibility of the customs officials themselves; and while the latter took great care in listing the number and size and weight of commodities in order to determine the tariff charges (since the tariff on, say, imported iron bars was so much *per ton*), the notional value of these commodities was only infrequently altered – and thus regarded by British experts as 'notoriously excessive'. The German statistics show the value of their exports to Britain for 1902 as being £50.2 million, whereas the British figure of German imports was only £33.6 million. Even after allowance is made for German goods being transported *via* the Low Countries and for all the other reasons why the German statistics should be larger than those of the British, the 'gap' is still too wide; and the only possible explanation, Ellinger felt, lay in the continental habit of overvaluation of goods.[8]

It is for this final reason that I have normally used British trade statistics, although frequent cross-checkings have been made with their German equivalents. It is worth repeating, however, that there is no guarantee that *any* of the detailed figures given here actually represent objective historical fact. As mentioned above, all that the statistics can be used for is to give general indications of the structure of, and changes within, the Anglo-German trade pattern in the half-century under examination.

# Notes

## CHAPTER 1

1 For general surveys, see P. Mathias, *The First Industrial Nation* (London, 1969); E. Hobsbawm, *Industry and Empire* (Harmondsworth, Middlesex, 1969); J. D. Chambers, *The Workshop of the World*, 2nd edn (Oxford, 1968); C. J. Bartlett (ed.), *Britain Pre-eminent. Studies of British World Influence in the Nineteenth Century* (London, 1969); A. H. Imlah, *Economic Elements in the Pax Britannica* (Cambridge, Mass., 1958).

2 See the excellent essay by C. P. Kindleberger, 'Germany's overtaking of England, 1806 to 1914', pp. 185–236, in his *Economic Response. Comparative Studies in Trade, Finance, and Growth* (Cambridge, Mass., 1978). I have also used: T. S. Hamerow, *The Social Foundations of German Unification 1858–1871*, 2 vols (Princeton, 1969–72); T. Veblen, *Imperial Germany and the Industrial Revolution* (New York, 1966 edn); H. Böhme, *Deutschlands Weg zur Grossmacht* (Cologne/Berlin, 1966); W. O. Henderson, *The Rise of German Industrial Power 1834–1914* (London, 1975); M. Kitchen, *The Political Economy of Germany 1815–1914* (London, 1978).

3 Kindleberger, op. cit., p. 201. For a useful comparative analysis of the two societies, see G. Schmidt, 'Politischer Liberalismus, 'landed interests', and Organisierte Arbeiterschaft 1850–1880: ein deutsch-englischer Vergleich', in H.-U. Wehler (ed.), *Sozialgeschichte Heute* (Göttingen, 1974), pp. 266–88.

4 See the superb comment by Palmerston upon Metternich's failure to 'separate the moderate from the exaggerated' elements in society, quoted in W. D. Gruner, 'Europäische Friede als nationales Interesse. Die Rolle des deutschen Bundes in der britischen Politik 1814–1832', *Bohemia*, vol. 18 (1977), pp. 120–1. Also very important is the analysis of the structure of British society as it affected external policy in Professor M. Swartz's forthcoming book, *The Politics of British Foreign Policy 1865–1885*.

5 ibid.; and see also W. L. Burn, *The Age of Equipoise* (London, 1964); R. T. Shannon, *The Crisis of Imperialism 1865–1915* (London, 1976 edn), pt 1; S. G. Checkland, 'Growth and progress: the nineteenth-century view in Britain', *Economic History Review*, 2nd series, vol. XII (1959), pp. 49–62.

6 Hamerow's two volumes provide the best survey of the plurality of opinions in mid-century Germany. For the 'German mind', see L. Krieger, *The German Idea of Freedom* (Boston, 1957); and H. Kohn, *The Mind of Germany* (New York, 1960).

7 These quotations are from W. E. Mosse, *The European Powers and the German Question 1848–1871* (Cambridge, 1958), p. 15; and Gruner, 'Europäische Friede als nationales Interesse', pp. 99 (fn. 7), 108, 125–8. Apart from the classic general study by R. J. Sontag, *Germany and England. Background of Conflict 1848–1894* (New York, 1964 edn), see two important articles by K. Hildebrand, 'Von der Reichseinigung zur "Krieg-in-Sicht"-Krise. Preussen-Deutschland als Faktor der britischen Aussenpolitik 1865–1875', in M. Stürmer (ed.), *Das kaiserliche Deutschland* (Düsseldorf, 1970), pp. 205–34; and 'Die deutsche Reichsgründung im Urteil der britischen Politik', *Francia*, vol. 5 (1977), pp. 401–24.

8 Hildebrand, loc. cit., discusses these two alternative strategies.

9 QVL, 1st series, III, pp. 587–8; and Sir H. Maxwell, *The Life and Letters of . . . the Fourth Earl of Clarendon*, 2 vols (London, 1913), II, pp. 246–7.

10 V. Valentin, 'Bismarck and England in the earlier period of his career', *Transactions of the Royal Historical Society*, 4th series, vol. XX (1937), p. 19. See also idem, *Bismarcks Reichsgründung im Urteil englischer Diplomaten* (Amsterdam, 1937); and QVL, 2nd series, I, p. 31. (The *Kreuzzeitung* was the paper of the Prussian arch-conservatives.)

11 There is an enormous older literature upon Bismarck and England, of mixed value. A succinct

analysis is in O. Pflanze, *Bismarck and the Development of Germany*, Vol. 1 (Princeton, 1971 edn); and see also L. Gall, 'Bismarck und England', in P. Kluke and P. Alter (eds), *Aspekte der deutsch-britischen Beziehungen im Laufe der Jahrhunderte* (Stuttgart, 1978), pp. 46–59, which tends to play down England's place in Bismarck's thinking.

12 M. von Hagen, *Bismarck und England* (Stuttgart/Berlin, 1941), p. 36.

13 ibid., pp. 36–7.

14 On Bismarck's flexibility in tactics and lack of dogma in handling both domestic and foreign affairs, see O. Pflanze, 'Bismarck's Realpolitik', *Review of Politics*, vol. 20 (1958), pp. 492–514.

15 Cited in Mosse, *The European Powers and the German Question*, p. 117; and see also K. S. Pasieka, 'The British press and the Polish insurrection of 1863', *Slavonic and East European Review*, vol. 42 (1963–4), pp. 15–37; R. W. Seton-Watson, *Britain in Europe 1789–1914* (Cambridge, 1937), pp. 432–8.

16 Pflanze, *Bismarck and the Development of Germany*, pp. 185 ff.; A. Hillgruber, *Bismarcks Aussenpolitik* (Freiburg, 1972), pp. 47 ff.; H. Wendt, *Bismarck und die polnische Frage* (Halle, 1922); R. H. Lord, 'Bismarck and Russia in 1863', *American Historical Review*, vol. XXIX (1923), pp. 24–48.

17 Cited in Pasieka, op. eit., pp. 17–18.

18 See the queen's remark that 'we should have a French Army on the Rhine before we could turn round', in QVL, 2nd series, I, pp. 66–7.

19 Bismarck's policy over Schleswig–Holstein is well covered by Pflanze, *Bismarck and the Development of Germany*, pp. 233 ff.; Mosse, *The European Powers and the German Question*, pp. 146 ff.; L. D. Steefel, *The Schleswig-Holstein Question* (Cambridge, Mass., 1932), pp. 48 ff.

20 See the detailed coverage in E. N. Anderson, *Social and Political Conflict in Prussia 1858–1864* (Lincoln, Neb., 1954).

21 Shannon, op. cit., pp. 19 ff.; M. Cowling, *1867: Disraeli, Gladstone and Revolution* (Cambridge, 1967); F. B. Smith, *The Making of the Second Reform Bill* (Cambridge, 1966); P. Adelman, *Gladstone, Disraeli and Later Victorian Politics* (London, 1970); H. J. Hanham, *Elections and Party Management. Politics in the Time of Disraeli and Gladstone* (London, 1959).

22 K. A. P. Sandiford, *Great Britain and the Schleswig-Holstein Question 1848–1864* (Toronto, 1975), *passim*. For the important role of the queen in this crisis, see W. E. Mosse, 'Queen Victoria and her ministers in the Schleswig-Holstein crisis 1863–1864', *English Historical Review*, vol. 78 (1963), pp. 263–83; and E. Fitzmaurice, *Life of Lord Granville*, 2 vols (London, 1905), I, pp. 453–77.

23 Mosse, *The European Powers and the German Question*, pp. 152–3.

24 Cited in Sontag, op. cit., p. 35.

25 Pflanze, *Bismarck and the Development of Germany*, pp. 262–3.

26 PRO, FO 881/8983 (print), 'General Report on Germany for the Year 1906', p. 7, where the rhyme is recalled by Lascelles.

27 Mosse, *The European Powers and the German Question*, pp. 221–2. For Palmerston's earlier views, see G. Gillessen, *Lord Palmerston und die Einigung Deutschlands* (Lübeck/Hamburg, 1961), esp. pp. 149–55.

28 Bodleian Library, Oxford, Bryce MSS., 9, Bryce to Freeman, 16/9/1864.

29 Otto von Bismarck, *Die gesammelten Werke*, edited by H. von Petersdorff *et al.*, 15 vols (Berlin, 1923–33), IV, pp. 462 ff.

30 Pflanze, *Bismarck and the Development of Germany*, p. 266.

31 Hillgruber, *Bismarcks Aussenpolitik*, p. 70; A. Loftus, *Diplomatic Reminiscences*, 2nd series, 2 vols (London, 1894), I, p. 60; F. Stern, *Gold and Iron: Bismarck, Bleichröder and the Building of the German Empire* (London, 1977), p. 88.

32 Hamerow, op. cit., I, pp. 379 ff.; II, pp. 185 ff.; Pflanze, *Bismarck and the Development of Germany*, pp. 298 ff.

33 ibid., pp. 76, 237; and G. Franz, *Bismarcks Nationalgefühl* (Leipzig, 1926). This patriotism was no less genuine because it was for the Prussian state rather than the German cultural community: see O. Pflanze, 'Bismarck and German nationalism', *American Historical Review*, vol. LX (1955), esp. pp. 559–63.

34 Cited in Hamerow, op. cit., II, pp. 239–40.

35 G. R. Mork, 'Bismarck and the "capitulation" of German liberalism', *Journal of Modern History*, vol. 43 (1971), pp. 59 ff.; J. L. Snell and H. Schmitt, *The Democratic Movement in Germany 1789–1914* (Chapel Hill, NC, 1976), pp. 162 ff.; Kohn, *The Mind of Germany*, pp. 157–61; Pflanze, *Bismarck and the Development of Germany*, pp. 326 ff. On the significance of 1866 in Germany's overall development, see F. Kahlenberg, 'Das Epochenjahr 1866 in der deutschen Geschichte', in M. Stürmer (ed.), *Das kaiserliche Deutschland*, pp. 51–74; and K. G. Faber, 'Realpolitik als Ideologie: Die Bedeutung des Jahres 1866 für das politische Denken in Deutschland', *Historische Zeitschrift*, 203 (1966), pp. 1–45.

36 E. W. Ellsworth, 'The Austro-Prussian War and the British Press', *The Historian*, vol. xx (1958), pp. 179–200.

37 Cited in R. Millman, *British Foreign Policy and the Coming of the Franco-Prussian War* (Oxford, 1965), p. 13.

38 Maxwell, *Clarendon*, ii, p. 315.

39 QVL, 2nd series, i, p. 271.

40 W. E. Mosse, 'The Crown and foreign policy: Queen Victoria and the Austro-Prussian conflict, March–May 1866', *Cambridge Historical Journal*, vol. x (1951), p. 217; and R. Fulford (ed.), *Your Dear Letter. Private Correspondence of Queen Victoria and the Crown Princess of Prussia 1865–1871* (London, 1971), pp. 58 ff.

41 Cited in Millman, op. cit., p. 20, fn. 8.

42 *Hansard*, 3rd series, clxxxiv, 1253–7

43 Millman, op. cit., p. 9; K. Bourne, *The Foreign Policy of Victorian England 1830–1902* (Oxford, 1970), p. 388.

44 C. J. Bartlett, 'The mid-Victorian reappraisal of naval policy', in K. Bourne and D. C. Watt (eds), *Studies in International History* (London, 1967), pp. 189–208; P. M. Kennedy, *The Rise and Fall of British Naval Mastery* (London/New York, 1976), pp. 177–81; Millman, op. cit., pp. 148–58.

45 QVL, 2nd series, i, pp. 314–15. Hildebrand, 'Die deutsche Reichsgründung im Urteil der britischen Politik', pp. 403 ff., details the British concern with the non-European world; and P. Scherer, 'The Benedetti draft treaty and British neutrality in the Franco-Prussian War', *International Review of History and Political Science*, vol. 9, no. 1 (1972), pp. 95–108, shows the British fear of France in the late 1860s.

46 Cited in Bourne, op. cit., p. 384.

47 Cited in Millman, op. cit., p. 227.

48 *Hansard*, 3rd series, clxxvi, 744–6.

49 Cited in Bourne, op. cit., p. 388.

50 See the references in note 21 above; and Gladstone's complaint that a Commons debate on foreign policy in June 1866 required 'five hours of time which ought to have been given to the Reform Bill', in Millman, op. cit., p. 223.

51 QVL, 2nd series, i, p. 315.

52 ibid.; Loftus, *Diplomatic Reminiscences*, 2nd series, i, pp. 43–5.

53 F. Wellesley, *The Paris Embassy during the Second Empire: From the Papers of Earl Cowley* (London, 1928), p. 314.

54 Cited in Millman, op. cit., p. 36.

55 Quoted in Mosse, *The European Powers and the German Question*, pp. 245–6, 249.

56 Millman, op. cit., p. 62. As Morley's biography shows, constitutional reform had by this time become Gladstone's main concern: J. Morley, *Life of Gladstone*, 3 vols (London, 1903), ii, pp. 198–236.

57 Pflanze, *Bismarck and the Development of Germany*, p. 380; E. M. Carroll, *Germany and the Great Powers 1866–1914* (New York, 1938), pp. 30 ff.

58 Mosse, *The European Powers and the German Question*, p. 264; Millman, op. cit., chs iii–iv; M. R. D. Foot, 'Great Britain and Luxembourg 1867', *English Historical Review*, vol. 67 (1952), pp. 352–79.

59 Bourne, op. cit., pp. 392–5; and see the interesting discussion in C. Howard, *Britain and the Casus Belli* (London, 1974), pp. 64–85.

60 Millman, op. cit., pp. 82, 103; Mosse, *The European Powers and the German Question*, p. 276.

61 G. A. Craig, 'Great Britain and the Belgian railways dispute of 1869', *American Historical Review*, vol. 50 (1945), p. 741.

62 ibid., *passim*; Millman, op. cit., ch. VII; Mosse, *The European Powers and the German Question*, pp. 297–8; Lord Newton, *Lord Lyons*, 2 vols (London, 1913), pp. 211–21.

63 Bodleian Library, Oxford, Clarendon MSS., dep. c 744, Clarendon to Loftus (copies), 3/2/1869 and 2/2/1870; Newton, *Lyons*, I, pp. 246 ff.; J. L. Herkless, 'Lord Clarendon's attempt at Franco-Prussian disarmament, January to March 1870', *Historical Journal*, vol. XV (1972), pp. 455–70.

64 Bodleian Library, Oxford, Clarendon MSS., dep. c 478, Loftus to Clarendon, 11/1/1870.

65 Pflanze, *Bismarck and the Development of Germany*, pp. 366, 433 ff.; and see the discussion in J. Becker, 'Der Krieg mit Frankreich als Problem der kleindeutschen Einigungspolitik Bismarcks 1866–1870', in Stürmer (ed.), *Das kaiserliche Deutschland*, pp. 84 ff.

66 On this important topic, see G. A. Craig, *The Politics of the Prussian Army 1640–1945* (New York, 1975 reprint), pp. 136 ff.; G. Ritter, *The Sword and the Sceptre: The Problem of Militarism in Germany*, 4 vols (London, 1972–3), I, pp. 187 ff.; M. Kitchen, *A Military History of Germany* (London, 1975), pp. 88 ff.; M. Messerschmidt, *Militär und Politik in der Bismarckzeit und im Wilhelminischen Deutschland* (Darmstadt, 1975), *passim*; E. Kessel, 'Bismarck und die "Halbgötter"' *Historische Zeitschrift*, 181 (1956), pp. 249–86.

67 Bodleian Library, Oxford, Clarendon MSS., dep. c 474, Clarendon to Loftus (copy), 2/6/1869.

CHAPTER 2

1 Millman, op. cit., pp. 192–3; D. N. Raymond, *British Policy and Opinion during the Franco-Prussian War* (New York, 1967 reprint), pp. 71 ff.; Morley, *Gladstone*, III, pp. 316–58; Fitzmaurice, *Granville*, II, pp. 30–80.

2 Millman, op. cit., pp. 203–7; Howard, *Britain and the Casus Belli*, pp. 86–90, 98; QVL, 2nd series, II, pp. 53–4.

3 P. Knaplund, *Gladstone's Foreign Policy* (London, 1970 edn), p. 53.

4 Cited in Fitzmaurice, *Granville*, II, p. 63. See also Mosse, *European Powers and the German Question*, pp. 338–40; and especially, D. Schreuder, 'Gladstone as "troublemaker": Liberal foreign policy and the German annexation of Alsace-Lorraine, 1870–71', *Journal of British Studies*, vol. XVII (1978), pp. 106–38.

5 See especially his frank exchanges with Odo Russell (British representative at the Prussian headquarters in France in 1870–1), in PRO 30/29/92 (Granville Papers); Carroll, op. cit., p. 80; and Valentin, *Bismarcks Reichsgründung* . . . , pp. 429–32.

6 Mosse, *European Powers and the German Question*, pp. 348–9. Gladstone's later disavowal of Odo Russell's threat does not alter the fact that Bismarck believed (and was reinforced in this by Bernstorff's reports from London) that Britain *would* fight.

7 Millman, op. cit., p. 217.

8 W. E. Mosse, 'Public opinion and foreign policy: the British public and the war scare of November 1870', *Historical Journal*, vol. VI (1963), pp. 38–58.

9 QVL, 2nd series, II, p. 48; and R. Wemyss, *Memoirs and Letters of the Right Hon. Sir Robert Morier from 1826 to 1876*, 2 vols (London, 1911), II, pp. 156 ff.

10 Fulford (ed.), *Your Dear Letter*, p. 320.

11 See Stanley's interesting remark in 1867 that 'The combatants are very equally matched', in QVL, 2nd series, I, p. 458.

12 C. C. Eldridge, *England's Mission: The Imperial Idea in the Age of Gladstone and Disraeli* (London, 1973), chs 4–5; Mosse, 'Public opinion and foreign policy', *passim*.

13 Millman, op. cit., p. 33; Mosse, 'The Crown and foreign policy', *passim*; QVL, 2nd series, I, pp. 364–5, 419–20.

14 Wemyss, *Morier*, II, pp. 153–4.

15 G. Cecil, *Life of Robert . . . Marquis of Salisbury*, 4 vols (London, 1921–32), I, pp. 301 ff.; II, pp. 33–6; F. Harrison, *Autobiographical Memoirs*, 2 vols (London, 1911), I, pp. 295–8; II, pp. 3–17.

16 Millman, op. cit., p. 77. Disraeli's own attitude during the Franco-Prussian War – that of urging a 'strict' but 'armed' neutrality – is covered in W. F. Moneypenny and G. E. Buckle, *The Life of Benjamin Disraeli*, 6 vols (London, 1910–20), V, pp. 125–36. Raymond, op. cit., *passim*, provides a whole host of similar expressions of dissatisfaction at Britain's passive role.

17 QVL, 2nd series, II, pp. 93–4, 122, 154–5.
18 Sontag, op. cit., pp. 88–90; Carroll, op. cit., pp. 79–80; and see Morier's letter of 7/10/1871 to Odo Russell on the German press response to the pamphlet he had written and published anonymously at Granville's request to counter the falsehoods in continental newspapers about British arms sales – in PRO 30/29/92 (Granville Papers).
19 I. F. Clarke, 'The Battle of Dorking, 1871–1914', *Victorian Studies*, vol. VIII (1965), p. 322; Morley, *Gladstone*, II, pp. 507 ff.; K. Meine, *England und Deutschland in der Zeit des Uebergangs vom Manchestertum zum Imperialismus 1871 bis 1876* (Vaduz, 1965 reprint).
20 Cited in Moneypenny and Buckle, op. cit., V, pp. 133–4. For what follows, see ibid., pp. 191–6; Meine, op. cit., pp. 95–9; and W. N. Medlicott, 'Bismarck and Beaconsfield', in O. A. Sarkissian (ed.), *Studies in Diplomatic History* (London, 1961), pp. 225–50. See also the additional details in the thesis by Medlicott's student, M. D. Zier, *Anglo-German Relations 1871–1878* (M.Sc.Econ. thesis, London, 1966).
21 PRO 30/29/93 (Granville Papers), O. Russell to Granville, 2/3/1873; Fitzmaurice, *Granville*, II, p. 113.
22 For what follows, see Hillgruber, *Bismarcks Aussenpolitik*, pp. 129 ff.; Böhme, *Deutschlands Weg zur Grossmacht*, pp. 303 ff.; J. Doerr, 'Domestic influences on Bismarck's foreign policy', in D. K. Buse (ed.), *Aspects of Imperial Germany* (vol. 5, no. 3 of *Laurentian University Review*, 1973), pp. 35–48; I. Geiss, *German Foreign Policy 1871–1914* (London, 1976), pp. 6–16, 25–30; M. Stürmer, *Regierung und Reichstag im Bismarckstaat 1871–1880: Cäsarismus oder Parlamentarismus?* (Düsseldorf, 1974), pp. 29–113; M. B. Winckler, *Bismarcks Bündnispolitik und die europäische Gleichgewicht* (Stuttgart, 1964); and the interesting reports in W. Taffs, *Ambassador to Bismarck: Lord Odo Russell* (London, 1938), ch. II.
23 L. Herbst, *Die erste Internationale als Problem der deutschen Politik in der Reichsgründungszeit* (Göttingen, 1975), pp. 93–107.
24 Hagen, *Bismarck und England*, p. 13; Wemyss, *Morier*, II, p. 330.
25 Meine, op. cit., pp. 74–7; H. Rothfels, *Bismarcks englische Bündnispolitik* (Stuttgart, 1924), pp. 13–14; R. Wittram, 'Bismarcks Russlandpolitik nach der Reichsgründung', *Historische Zeitschrift*, 186 (1958), pp. 261–84; H. Müller-Link, *Industrialisierung und Aussenpolitik: Preussen-Deutschland und das Zarenreich von 1860 bis 1890* (Göttingen, 1977), pp. 106 ff.
26 Liverpool Record Office, Derby Papers 17/1/6, Derby to O. Russell (copies), 3/3/1874 and 7/4/1874.
27 W. Taffs, 'The war scare of 1875', *Slavonic Review*, vol. IX (December 1930), pp. 335–49, and (March 1931), pp. 632–49, who quotes on p. 341 from a dispatch to Bismarck from Münster of 28/2/1875.
28 Liverpool Record Office, Derby Papers 17/1/6, Derby to O. Russell (copy), 3/3/1874.
29 For the 'war-in-sight' crisis, I have used the official British account in PRO, FO 881/6419 (print), and the private memorandum of 1887 by A. Russell in PRO, FO 918/80 (Ampthill Papers), as well as Taffs's article; A. Hillgruber, 'Die "Krieg-in-Sicht"-Krise 1875', in E. Schulin (ed.), *Gedenkschrift Martin Göhring, Studien zur europäischen Geschichte* (Wiesbaden, 1968), pp. 239–53; W. L. Langer, *European Alliances and Alignments 1871–1890* (New York, 1964 edn), pp. 40–55.
30 GP, I, p. 280; Moneypenny and Buckle, *Disraeli*, V, pp. 424–5; Zier, *Anglo-German Relations 1871–1878*, pp. 90–2.
31 Hildebrand, 'Von der Reichseinigung . . .', p. 227.
32 Liverpool Record Office, Derby Papers 17/1/6, Derby to O. Russell (copies), 3/5/1875 and 1/6/1875. (The first of these two letters is reproduced in Newton, *Lyons*, II, p. 75.)
33 Liverpool Record Office, Derby Papers 16/2/1, Disraeli to Derby, 18/5/1875; Moneypenny and Buckle, *Disraeli*, V, pp. 420–6; QVL, 2nd series, II, pp. 391, 405.
34 Newton, *Lyons*, II, pp. 41–2.
35 Liverpool Record Office, Derby Papers 17/1/6, Derby to O. Russell (copy), 12/4/1875.
36 Hillgruber, *Bismarcks Aussenpolitik*, p. 144.
37 Wemyss, *Morier*, II, pp. 337, 346; and see the argument that German diplomacy was the main cause of tension in Europe after 1871 in Winckler, *Bismarcks Bündnispolitik . . .*, passim.
38 Geiss, op. cit., p. 13. Hillgruber, 'Die "Krieg-in-Sicht"-Krise 1875', pp. 251–2, suggests that Bismarck realised that the only way left to preserve Germany's 'half-hegemonial' position in Europe was to divert the other powers' attentions to the periphery.

39 For what follows, see Langer, op. cit., pp. 76 ff.; Taffs, *Ambassador to Bismarck*, pp. 118 ff.; Medlicott, 'Bismarck and Beaconsfield', pp. 228 ff.; D. Harris, 'Bismarck's advance to England, 1876', *Journal of Modern History*, vol. III (1931), pp. 441–56.
40 Medlicott, *passim*; Moneypenny and Buckle, *Disraeli*, VI, pp. 20 ff.; QVL, 2nd series, II, pp. 443–4, 489–94.
41 L. Dehio, *The Precarious Balance* (London, 1963).
42 Shannon, *The Crisis of Imperialism*, p. 104; and R. Blake, *Disraeli* (London, 1966), pp. 529 ff.
43 Liverpool Record Office, Derby Papers 17/1/6, Derby to MacDonell (chargé, Berlin) (copy), 1/9/1875.
44 ibid., 17/1/7, Derby to O. Russell (copy), 8/11/1876. Derby's letters to Odo Russell throughout 1875 and 1876 reveal his suspicion of Bismarck – as do his letters to General Ponsonby, in QVL, 2nd series, II, pp. 383–4, 407–8.
45 Liverpool Record Office, Derby Papers 16/1/6, O. Russell to Derby, 27/1/1877 and 3/3/1877; ibid., 17/1/7, Derby to O. Russell (copy), 30/1/1877; Langer, op. cit., pp. 109–12; Taffs, *Ambassador to Bismarck*, pp. 177–9.
46 Medlicott, 'Bismarck and Beaconsfield', pp. 237 ff.
47 Niedersächsiches Hauptstaatsarchiv, Hanover, *Nachlass* Münster, vol. IV, Bismarck to Münster, 6/7/1876; GP II, p. 108; W. Bussmann (ed.), *Staatssekretär Graf Herbert von Bismarck. Aus seiner politischen Privatkorrespondenz* (Göttingen, 1964), p. 88.
48 Winckler, *Bismarcks Bündnispolitik . . .* , p. 23.
49 Böhme, *Deutschlands Weg zur Grossmacht*, pp. 493 ff.; Stürmer, *Regierung und Reichstag*, pp. 216 ff.; H. Rosenberg, *Grosse Depression und Bismarckzeit* (Berlin, 1967), *passim*; Müller-Link, *Industrialisierung und Aussenpolitik*, pp. 164 ff.; B. Waller, *Bismarck at the Crossroads: The Reorientation of German Foreign Policy after the Congress of Berlin 1878–1880* (London, 1974), pp. 175 ff.
50 Compare Waller, op. cit., pp. 196–7, with Böhme, op. cit., pp. 525–9, 587 ff. See also W. O. Henderson, 'Mitteleuropäische Zollvereinspläne 1840–1940', in *Zeitschrift für das gesamte Staatswissenschaft*, vol. LXXII (1966), pp. 148–54.
51 Geiss, op. cit., p. 38; Herbst, *Die erste Internationale . . .* , pp. 202 ff.; M. L. Brown, 'The monarchical principle in Bismarckian diplomacy after 1870', *The Historian*, vol. 15 (1952), pp. 45–7.
52 Waller, op. cit., p. 195.
53 ibid., pp. 200–2, 251; Cecil, *Salisbury*, II, pp. 364–74; Moneypenny and Buckle, *Disraeli*, VI, pp. 486–94; W. N. Medlicott, *The Congress of Berlin and After* (London, 1938), pp. 385–9; Langer, op. cit., pp. 185 ff.; Rothfels, op. cit., pp. 44–52.
54 Cited in Moneypenny and Buckle, *Disraeli*, VI, pp. 493–4. See also QVL, 2nd series, III, p. 53; Howard, *Britain and the Casus Belli*, p. 106.
55 Cited in Hamerow, op. cit., II, pp. 390–1; and see in general K. H. Höfele, 'Sendungsglaube und Epochenbewusstsein in Deutschland 1870/71', *Zeitschrift für Religions- und Geistesgeschichte*, 15 (1963), pp. 265–76.
56 QVL, 2nd series, II, pp. 60–1; A. Dorpalen, *Heinreich von Treitschke* (New Haven, 1957), pp.161–72, 234; Carroll, op. cit., pp. 69–71, 87.
57 Clarke, 'The Battle of Dorking', p. 320.
58 Cited in Burn, *The Age of Equipoise*, p. 299; and see pp. 43–7 below for an economic comparison. For expressions of British self-confidence in this period, see Hildebrand, 'Die deutsche Reichsgründung im Urteil der britischen Politik', pp. 418 ff.
59 Liverpool Record Office, Derby Papers 17/1/7, Derby to O. Russell (copy), 31/10/1876.

CHAPTER 3

1 K. W. Hardach, 'Anglomanie und Anglophobie während der industriellen Revolution in Deutschland', *Schmollers Jahrbuch*, 91 (1971), pp. 153–81 (the 'one-way street' is from p. 154). See also the details of Anglo-German trade relations in J. B. Williams, *British Commercial Policy and Trade Expansion 1750–1850* (Oxford, 1972); W. O. Henderson, *Britain and Industrial Europe 1750–1870*, 2nd edn (Leicester, 1965), esp. pp. 139–66; and Kindleberger, 'Germany's overtaking of England'.

2 For these activities, see the excellent article by S. D. Chapman, 'The international houses: the continental contribution to British commerce, 1800–1860', *Journal of European Economic History*, vol. 6 (1977), pp 5–48.

3 Apart from the works cited in note 1 above, see also R. H. Tilly, 'Los von England: Probleme des Nationalismus in der deutschen Wirtschaftsgeschichte', *Zeitschrift für das gesamte Staatswissenschaft*, vol. 124 (1968), pp. 179–96.

4 See Henderson's article, 'Prince Smith and free trade in Germany', in his *Britain and Industrial Europe*, pp. 167–78.

5 Williams, *British Commercial Policy . . .* , p. 44; Gruner, 'Europäische Friede als nationales Interesse', pp. 109–15; Kindleberger, op. cit., pp. 195 ff.

6 Unless otherwise indicated, the statistics in the next few paragraphs are taken from A. J. P. Taylor, *The Struggle for Mastery in Europe 1848–1918* (Oxford, 1952), pp. xxv–xxx; and M. L. Balfour, *The Kaiser and his Times* (New York, 1972 edn), Appendix I.

7 J. H. Clapham, *The Economic Development of France and Germany 1815–1914* (Cambridge, 1968 edn), p. 296.

8 R. C. K. Ensor, *England 1870–1914* (Oxford, 1936), p. 104. (The difference between these totals and those based upon notes 12 and 13 below is presumably accounted for by the inclusion of gold and specie.)

9 Burn, *The Age of Equipoise*, p. 299.

10 See the breakdown of visible and invisible trade figures in Mathias, *First Industrial Nation*, p. 305; and Imlah, *Economic Elements*, pp. 70–5.

11 See Appendix A below.

12 *British and Foreign Trade and Industrial Conditions*, Cd 1761 (London, 1903), pp. 403–4.

13 G. Bondi, *Deutschlands Aussenhandel 1815–1870* (Berlin, 1958), p. 145 for 1860 and 1865; then *Statistical Abstract for the Principal and other Foreign Countries in each Year from 1871 to 1880/81*, in *Accounts and Papers* (1892), LXXIII, pp. 492–3; *Ditto . . . from 1880 to 1890*, in *Accounts and Papers* (1892), LXXXVII, pp. 44–5. These are not very satisfactory figures, since they exclude the trade of Hamburg and have many other defects; see Bondi, op. cit., pp. 147–53.

14 *Annual Statement of the Trade of the United Kingdom, 1863*, in *Accounts and Papers* (1864), LVII, pp. 2–13; *Ditto . . . 1873*, in *Accounts and Papers* (1874), LXIV, pp. 9–17; *Ditto . . . 1883*, in *Accounts and Papers* (1884), LXXVII, pp. 10–17.

15 *Ditto . . . 1863*, in *Accounts and Papers* (1864), LVII, p. 2.

16 *Ditto . . . 1883*, in *Accounts and Papers* (1884), LXXVII, pp. 10–11.

17 See *Statistical Abstract for the Principal and other Foreign Countries in Each Year from 1880 to 1890*, in *Accounts and Papers* (1892), LXXXVII, pp. 140–1; B. R. Mitchell, *European Historical Statistics 1750–1970* (London, 1975), p. 526; M. G. Mulhall, *The Dictionary of Statistics* (London, 1903 edn), p. 137.

18 *Annual Statement of the Trade of the United Kingdom, 1863*, in *Accounts and Papers* (1864), LVII, pp. 219–26.

19 *Ditto . . . 1883*, in *Accounts and Papers* (1884), LXXVII, p. 186–9.

20 Lord Farrar, *Free Trade versus Fair Trade*, re-edited by C. H. Chomley (London, 1904), pp. 435, 439. The book was originally published in 1881.

21 E. Böhm, *Ueberseehandel und Flottenbau* (Düsseldorf, 1972), p. 66. See also the statistics in *Accounts and Papers* (1872), LVIII, pp. 696–7, on British trade with Hamburg; and P. E. Schramm, *Hamburg, Deutschland und die Welt* (Munich, 1943).

22 I. Lambi, *Free Trade and Protection in Germany 1868–1879* (Wiesbaden, 1963), pp. 20, 133.

23 *Statistical Abstract for the Principal and other Foreign Countries in Each Year from 1871 to 1880/81*, in *Accounts and Papers* (1882), LXXIII, pp. 522–3; *Ditto . . . from 1880 to 1890*, in *Accounts and Papers* (1892), LXXXVII, pp. 82–3.

24 See again Stern, *Gold and Iron, passim*; and more generally Chapman, 'The international houses', *passim*; J. Viner, 'International finance and balance of power diplomacy 1880–1914', in idem, *International Economics* (Glencoe, Ill., 1951), pp. 49–85; E. Rosenbaum and J. Sherman, *Das Bankhaus M. M. Warburg & Co. 1798–1938* (Hamburg, 1976), esp. ch. v; S. G. Checkland, 'The mind of the City 1870–1914', *Oxford Economic Papers*, 9 (1957), pp. 262–4.

25 PRO, Cab. 16/18A, 'Trading with the Enemy' (CID Sub-Committee); Tilly, 'Los von

England', pp 190–5; W. T. C. King, *History of the London Discount Market* (London, 1936), pp. 264–82.
26 The best brief guide to the literature on the British side is S. B. Saul, *The Myth of the Great Depression 1873–1896* (London, 1969). The seminal work on the German side is H. Rosenberg's *Grosse Depression und Bismarckzeit*, but there is also a massive coverage in H.-U. Wehler, *Bismarck und der Imperialismus* (Cologne/Berlin, 1969), pp. 39 ff., and Böhme, op. cit., pp. 341 ff. For an East German account, see L. Rathmann, 'Bismarck und der Uebergang Deutschlands zur Schutzzollpolitik', *Zeitschrift für Geschichtswissenschaft*, vol. 4 (1956), pp. 899–949.
27 Böhme, op. cit., p. 357; Henderson, *The Rise of German Industrial Power*, p. 170; Clapham, op. cit., p. 284.
28 Lambi, op. cit., pp. 132 ff.; K. D. Hardach, *Die Bedeutung wirtschaftlicher Faktoren bei der Wiedereinführung der Eisen- und Getreidezölle in Deutschland 1879* (Berlin, 1967), pp. 73 ff.
29 H. Rosenberg, 'Political and social consequences of the Great Depression of 1873–1896 in Central Europe', *Economic History Review*, vol. 13 (1943), pp. 58–73; P. A. Gourevitch, 'International trade, domestic coalitions, and liberty: comparative responses to the crisis of 1873–1896', *Journal of Interdisciplinary History*, vol. VIII (1977), pp. 281–313.
30 Lambi, op. cit., p. 139; idem, 'The agrarian-industrial front in Bismarckian politics, 1873–1879', *Journal of Central European Affairs*, vol. XX (1961), pp. 378–96; A. Gerschrenkon, *Bread and Democracy in Germany* (New York, 1966 edn), pp. 42 ff.; and the reports in PRO, FO 64 (Prussia and Germany)/vols 939–40.
31 On the party-political aspects, see again Stürmer, *Regierung und Reichstag*, pp. 183 ff.; W. Pack, *Das parlamentarische Ringen um das Sozialistengesetz Bismarcks 1879–1890* (Düsseldorf, 1961), pp. 17–129; L. Maenner, 'Deutschlands Wirtschaft und Liberalismus in der Krise von 1879', *Archiv für Politik und Geschichte*, vol. 9 (1927), pp. 347–82, 456–88.
32 Lambi, op. cit., p. 91; P. Gottfried, 'Adam Smith and German social thought', *Modern Age*, 21 (1977), pp. 146–53. On the earlier traditions against free trade, see again Tilly, 'Los von England . . .'.
33 On the 'Socialists of the Chair', see Schmoller's own *Zwanzig Jahre deutscher Politik 1897–1917* (Munich/Leipzig, 1920); F. Boese, *Geschichte des Vereins für Sozialpolitik 1879–1932* (Berlin, 1939); J. J. Sheehan, *The Career of Lujo Brentano* (Chicago, 1966) chs 2–3.
34 M. G. Plachetka, *Die Getreide-Autarkiepolitik Bismarcks und seiner Nachfolger im Reichskanzleramt* (Bonn, 1969), esp. pp. 108–14. This is a fair point, although the strategical argument was not as important as Plachetka suggests.
35 Veblen, *Imperial Germany and the Industrial Revolution*, pp. 178–9, 214. It can still be argued, of course, that the peasantry at least was acting in accordance with its best interests by supporting protectionism: see J. C. Hunt, 'Peasants, grain tariffs and meat quotas: imperial German protectionism re-examined', *Central European History*, vol. 7 (1974), pp. 311–31.
36 Bismarck's role in bringing together the many arguments in favour of tariffs is covered in H. Böhme, 'Big-business pressure groups and Bismarck's turn to protectionism, 1873–79', *Historical Journal*, vol. X (1967), pp. 218–36. See also O. Strecker, 'Der Kampf um die Agrarzölle in Grossbritannien (Anti-Corn-Law-League) und Deutschland (1871–1902)', *Berichte über Landwirtschaft. Zeitschrift für Agrarpolitik und Landwirtschaft*, neue Folge, vol. XXXVI (1958), pp. 867–904; and G. S. Graham, 'Cobden's influence on Bismarck', *Queen's Quarterly*, vol. XXXVIII (1931), pp. 433–43.
37 For details, see Ensor, op. cit., pp. 111 ff.; Mathias, *First Industrial Nation*, pp. 395 ff.; A. E. Musson, 'The Great Depression in Britain 1873–1896: a reappraisal', *Journal of Economic History*, vol. XIX (1959), pp. 199–228. For a useful comparison of German and British reactions, see again Gourevitch, 'International trade, domestic coalitions, and liberty . . .', passim.
38 This Gladstone argued in 1881 when he asked if they should risk the £30 to £40 millions of British manufactures exported to the USA for the sake of taxing the £3 millions of American manufactures imported into Britain: see N. McCord, *Free Trade. Theory and Practice from Adam Smith to Keynes* (Newton Abbott, 1970), p. 132.
39 For the changing pattern of British exports, see W. Schlote, *British Overseas Trade from 1700*

*to the 1930s* (Oxford, 1952), pp. 88 ff.; S. B. Saul, *Studies in British Overseas Trade 1870–1914* (Liverpool, 1960), *passim*.

40 F. M. L. Thompson, *English Landed Society in the Nineteenth Century* (London, 1963); Schmidt, 'Politischer Liberalismus, "Landed Interests" und Organisierte Arbeiterschaft, 1850–1880', pp. 273, 281.

41 H. Fawcett, *Free Trade and Protection* (London, 1878).

42 *Hansard*, 3rd series, CCXLV (1879), 1356.

43 B. H. Brown, *The Tariff Reform Movement in Great Britain 1881–1895* (New York, 1943), p. 9.

44 See S. H. Zebel, 'Fair trade: an English reaction to the breakdown of the Cobden treaty system', *Journal of Modern History*, vol. 12 (1940), p. 184.

45 See, for example, *Hansard*, 3rd series, CCLXIV (1881), 1728–1816.

46 ibid., CCXLV (1879), 1388–96.

47 W. S. Churchill, *Randolph Churchill*, 2 vols (London, 1906), I, pp. 291–2; II, pp. 327 ff.

48 Quoted in Brown, op. cit., p. 148.

49 Böhme, 'Big-business pressure groups . . . ', p. 230.

50 PRO, FO 881/3951 (print), J. A. Crowe to Salisbury, no. 24 Commercial of 5/7/1879; Böhme, *Deutschlands Weg zur Grossmacht*, p. 357.

51 Lambi, op. cit., p. 94.

52 For what follows, see Hardach, *Die Bedeutung wirtschaftlicher Faktoren . . .* , pp. 19–22, 36 ff.

53 Hatfield House Archives, Salisbury Papers A9/36, O. Russell to Salisbury, 2/3/1879; and see also his reports 32 and 58 Commercial of 6/3/1879 and 2/5/1879 in PRO, FO 64/940.

54 Quoted in Meine, *England und Deutschland*, p. 83.

55 R. J. S. Hoffman, *Great Britain and the German Trade Rivalry 1875–1914* (New York, 1964 reprint), p. 20. For other studies of the Anglo-German 'trade rivalry', see P. Bastin, *La Rivalité commerciale anglo-allemande et les origines de la première guerre mondiale 1871–1914* (dissertation, Brussels, 1959); W. Duden, *Die Wurzeln des deutsch-englischen Gegensatzes* (phil. diss., Hamburg, 1933), pp. 14–37; B. W. Franke, 'Handelsneid und Grosse Politik in den englisch-deutschen Beziehungen 1871–1914', *Zeitschrift für Politik*, vol. XXIX (1939), pp. 455–75; A. Banze, *Die deutsch-englische Wirtschaftsrivalität* (Berlin, 1935). It is interesting to note that the three German works deny that commercial jealousy was the chief reason for Britain's growing dislike of Germany before 1914.

56 *The Times*, 1/12/1877.

57 PRO, FO 881/3951 (print), J. Walsham to Salisbury, no. 102 Commercial of 5/7/1879; and see Saul, *Studies in British Overseas Trade*, pp. 159–60, for the jute exports.

58 The change in the amounts of woollen, cotton and general British exports to Germany can be traced in *Annual Statement of the Trade of the United Kingdom, 1883*, in *Accounts and Papers* (1884), LXXVII, pp. 10, 14, 188; see also Saul, op. cit., pp. 149, 154–5.

59 D. C. M. Platt, *Finance, Trade and Politics in British Foreign Policy 1815–1914* (Oxford, 1968), pp. xx–xl, 98–126 and Appendix V; see also the requests for Foreign Office support in the Guildhall Library, London, Executive Committee of the Association of British Chambers of Commerce, minutes, vol. 4, 3/3/1886.

60 DZA, RKA 394, Rottenburg to H. Bismarck, 12/7/1888.

61 H.-U. Wehler, 'Bismarcks Imperialismus und späte Russlandpolitik unter dem Primat der Innenpolitik', in Stürmer (ed.), *Das kaiserliche Deutschland*, pp. 235–64; Müller-Link, *Industrialisierung und Aussenpolitik*, esp. pp. 268 ff.; R. Ibbeken, *Das aussenpolitische Problem, Staat und Wirtschaft in der deutschen Reichspolitik 1880–1914* (Schleswig, 1923), ch. II.

62 PRO, FO 881/3834 (print), 'Memorandum on the Commercial Policy of the European States and British Trade', by C. M. Kennedy, 29/1/1879.

63 *Hansard*, 3rd series, CCLXIV (1881), 1728–1816.

64 Quoted in Hoffman, op. cit., p. 73.

65 Farrar, *Free Trade versus Fair Trade*, pp. 18–20.

## CHAPTER 4

1 J. Vincent, *The Formation of the Liberal Party 1857–1868* (London, 1966), pp. 257–8; and see also Adelman, *Gladstone, Disraeli and Later Victorian Politics*, ch. 1.

2 On which, see generally F. R. Flournoy, 'British Liberal theories of international relations, 1848–1898', *Journal of the History of Ideas*, vol. 7 (1946), pp. 195–217.
3 For the role of the Whigs, see D. Southgate, *The Passing of the Whigs 1832–1886* (London, 1962); for the intellectuals, see C. Harvie, *The Lights of Liberalism* (London, 1976), and J. Roach, 'Liberalism and the Victorian intelligentsia', *Cambridge Historical Journal*, vol. XIII (1957), pp. 58–81.
4 A. J. P. Taylor, *The Troublemakers* (London, 1969 edn), pp. 63 ff.
5 N. W. Summerton, 'Dissenting attitudes to foreign relations, peace and war 1840–1890', *Journal of Ecclesiastical History*, vol. 28 (1977), pp. 151–78.
6 Loftus, *Diplomatic Reminiscences*, 2nd series, I, p. 99.
7 *Hansard*, 3rd series, CLXXXIV, 1247–8; and see again, Ellsworth, 'The Austro-Prussian War and the British press'.
8 PRO, FO 918 (Ampthill Papers)/55, Morier to O. Russell, 13/3/1871; Acton, 'The war of 1870', lecture of April 1871, reproduced in *Historical Essays and Studies* (London, 1926), pp. 226–72.
9 QVL, 2nd series, II, p. 104.
10 See Malet Papers (private hands), Dilke to Malet, 15/9/1884, where Dilke exaggerates by claiming that 'the old dislike for the Germans among English Liberals has been replaced by such a much livelier detestation of the French'.
11 Flournoy, op. cit., p. 207.
12 A. Thorold, *The Life of Henry Labouchere* (London, 1913), p. 47.
13 Morley, *Gladstone*, II, pp. 14–15.
14 AA Bonn, *England 69*, vol. 3, copy of *The Times* of 23/3/1880.
15 PRO, FO 800/28 (Fergusson Papers), copy of *The Times* of 11/7/1891, report on a Commons debate; and Howard, *Britain and the Casus Belli*, pp. 121–5. More generally, see R. H. Gross, *Factors and Variations in Liberal and Radical Opinions on Foreign Policy, 1885–1899* (D.Phil thesis, Oxford, 1950).
16 Cited in Meine, *England und Deutschland*, p. 72.
17 G. E. Fasnacht, *Acton's Political Philosophy. An Analysis* (London, 1952), pp. 132–9.
18 D. A. Hamer, *John Morley* (Oxford, 1968), pp. 54, 360 ff.
19 R. T. Shannon, *Gladstone and the Bulgarian Agitation 1876*, 2nd edn (London, 1975), p. 216; Roach, 'Liberalism and the Victorian intelligentsia', *passim*.
20 AA Bonn, *England 69*, vol. 1, copy of *Daily Chronicle* report of 14/1/1879.
21 National Library of Scotland, Edinburgh, Rosebery Papers, 10085, Arnold to Rosebery, 3/1/1886. Rosebery had arranged the interview, no doubt through his friend Herbert Bismarck.
22 Army Museums Ogilby Trust, Whitehall, Spenser Wilkinson Papers, 18, copy of Milner's address, 'Liberalism and Foreign Policy', 16/10/1885.
23 The literature upon the failure of liberalism in nineteenth-century Germany is immense. I have used: J. J. Sheehan, *German Liberalism in the Nineteenth Century* (Chicago/London, 1978); Snell and Schmitt, *The Democratic Movement in Germany 1789–1914*, *passim*; Mork, 'Bismarck and the "capitulation" of German liberalism', *passim*; D. S. White, *The Splintered Party. National Liberalism in Hessen and the Reich 1867–1918* (Cambridge, Mass., 1976); G. Seeber, *Zwischen Bebel und Bismarck. Zur Geschichte des Linksliberalismus in Deutschland 1871–1893* (East Berlin, 1965); W. Bussmann, 'Zur Geschichte des deutschen Liberalismus im 19. Jahrhundert', *Historische Zeitschrift*, vol. 186 (1958), pp. 527–57; F.-C. Sell, *Die Tragödie des deutschen Liberalismus* (Stuttgart, 1953); J. Heyderhoff and P. Wentzcke (eds), *Deutscher Liberalismus im Zeitalter Bismarcks*, 2 vols (Bonn/Leipzig, 1924–5); E. Schraepler, 'Die politische Haltung des liberalen Bürgertums im Bismarckreich', *Geschichte in Wissenschaft und Unterricht*, vol. 5 (1954), pp. 529–44; the various articles in *Geschichte und Gesellschaft*, vol. 4, issue 1 (1978); and the descriptions of the Liberal and Progressive parties in D. Fricke (ed.), *Die bürgerlichen Parteien in Deutschland*, 2 vols (Leipzig, 1968–70).
24 White, *The Splintered Party*, p. 4.
25 The title of Part IV (1866–1877) of Sheehan's study.
26 See again the comparisons in Schmidt, 'Politischer Liberalismus, "landed interests", und Organisierte Arbeiterschaft . . . '; and also L. O'Boyle, 'Liberal political leadership in Germany 1867–84', *Journal of Modern History*, vol. 28 (1956), pp. 338–52.

27 See again Stürmer, *Regierung und Reichstag*; Rosenberg, *Grosse Depression und Bismarckzeit*; and especially, Maenner, 'Deutschlands Wirtschaft und Liberalismus in der Krise von 1879', *passim*.

28 Mork, 'Bismarck and the "capitulation" of German liberalism'; Sheehan, *German Liberalism*, ch. 9; J. F. Harris, 'Eduard Lasker and compromise liberalism', *Journal of Modern History*, vol. 42 (1970), pp. 342–60.

29 E. R. Huber, *Deutsche Verfassungsgeschichte seit 1789*, Vol. IV (Stuttgart, 1969), p. 80.

30 What follows is based upon W. Bussmann, *Treitschke, sein Welt- und Geschichtsbild* (Göttingen, 1952); Dorpalen, *Heinrich von Treitschke*, *passim*; C. E. McClelland, *The German Historians and England* (Cambridge, 1971), pp. 168–90; H. D. Schmidt, *The Characteristics of British Policy and Imperial History as Conceived by the German Historians of the Nineteenth Century, 1848–1902* (B.Litt. thesis, Oxford, 1953), pp. 175–7, 189–98.

31 Both cited in McClelland, op. cit., pp. 168, 182.

32 See Bamberger's remark that 'The task of us liberals was to overcome the spirit of the east with the spirit of the west', cited in S. Zucker, *Ludwig Bamberger* (Pittsburg/London, 1975), p. 225.

33 A. Dorpalen, 'Emperor Frederick III and the German Liberal movement', *American Historical Review*, vol. 54 (1948), pp. 1–31.

34 F. B. M. Hollyday, *Bismarck's Rival. A Political Biography of General and Admiral Albrecht von Stosch* (Durham, NC, 1960); idem, 'Bismarck and the legend of the Gladstone ministry', in L. P. Wallace and W. C. Askew (eds), *Power, Public Opinion and Diplomacy* (Durham, NC, 1959), pp. 92–109.

35 J. Heyderhoff (ed.), *Im Ring der Gegner Bismarcks* (Leipzig, 1943), pp. 149, 166–7, 195, 199, 217, 269–70, 325, 387–8, 429 ff.

36 E. Hasselmann, 'The impact of Owen's ideas on German social and cooperative thought during the nineteenth century', in S. Pollard and J. Salt (eds), *Robert Owen* (London, 1971), pp. 285–305.

37 N. C. Masterman, *John Malcolm Ludlow* (Cambridge, 1963), p. 213.

38 Sheehan, *The Career of Lujo Brentano*, p. 119.

39 For what follows, see especially C.-C. Schweitzer, *Die Kritik der westlich-liberalen Oppositionsgruppen an der Aussenpolitik Bismarcks von 1863 bis 1890* (phil. Diss, Freiburg, 1950).

40 Army Museums Ogilby Trust, Whitehall, Spenser Wilkinson Papers, 4, Bamberger to Spenser Wilkinson, 16/5/1886.

41 Schweitzer, op. cit., pp. 199–200.

42 R. M. Berdahl, 'Conservative politics and aristocratic landowners in Bismarckian Germany', *Journal of Modern History*, vol. 44 (1972), pp. 1–20.

43 idem, 'New thoughts on German nationalism', *American Historical Review*, vol. 77 (1972), p. 69; Pflanze, *Bismarck and the Development of Germany*, pp. 29–32, 300 ff.; A. Dorpalen, 'The German Conservatives and the parliamentarization of imperial Germany', *Journal of Central European Affairs*, vol. 11 (1951), pp. 184–5.

44 S. von Kardorff, *Wilhelm von Kardorff* (Berlin, 1929), pp. 25–6; Hamerow, *Social Foundations*, II, pp. 286–90; Fricke (ed.), *Die bürgerlichen Parteien . . .*, I, pp. 673 ff., and II, pp. 560 ff.; Huber, *Deutsche Verfassungsgeschichte*, IV, pp. 24–49; H. Booms, *Die Deutschkonservative Partei* (Düsseldorf, 1954), *passim*; O.-E. Schüddekopf, *Die Deutsche Innenpolitik im letzten Jahrhundert und der konservative Gedanke* (Braunschweig, 1951), pp. 52–72. For Gerlach, see M. P. Fleischer, 'Die AntiBismarckbroschüren Ludwig von Gerlachs als tagespolitischer Niederschlag einer Geschichtsphilosophie', *Historische Zeitschrift*, vol. 225 (1977), pp. 297–346.

45 Cited in Berdahl, 'Conservative politics . . . ', p. 18.

46 For summaries of the conservative nature of the Prusso-German state, see H.-U. Wehler, *Das deutsche Kaiserreich 1871–1918* (Göttingen, 1973); G. A. Craig, *Germany 1866–1945* (Oxford, 1978), ch. II; and ch. IX, 'Obstacles to democracy', in Snell and Schmitt, *The Democratic Movement in Germany*.

47 Cited in McClelland, *The German Historians and England*, p. 112; and, more generally, see A. von Martin, 'Weltanschauliche Motive im altkonservativen Denken', in G. A. Ritter (ed.), *Deutsche Parteien vor 1918* (Cologne, 1973), pp. 142–64; and H. Christern, 'Einfluss und

Abwehr englischer politischer Ideologie in Deutschland vom 18. bis ins 20. Jahrhundert', in C. A. Weber (ed.), *Die englische Kulturideologie* (Stuttgart/Berlin, 1943), pp. 283 ff.

48 Hamerow, op. cit., II, p. 77.

49 Fleischer, op. cit., pp. 330–1; McClelland, op. cit., pp. 96–102.

50 Cited in Hamerow, op. cit., II, p. 43.

51 ibid., p. 275; and Fricke (ed.), *Die bürgerlichen Parteien . . .* , I, pp. 673–701.

52 Kardorff, *Wilhelm von Kardorff*, pp. 121–2; and see above, pp. 49–50, 55.

53 Friedrichruh Archives, *Nachlass* Bismarck, F 1, Rantzau to H. Bismarck, 1/8/1880.

54 R. S. Levy, *The Downfall of the Anti-Semitic Political Parties in Imperial Germany* (New Haven, 1975); G. L. Mosse, *The Crisis of German Ideology* (New York, 1964); P. Pulzer, *The Rise of Political Anti-Semitism in Germany and Austria* (London, 1964); P. W. Massing, *Rehearsal for Destruction. A Study of Political Anti-Semitism in Imperial Germany* (New York, 1949); S. Volkov, *The Rise of Popular Antimodernism in Germany* (Princeton, 1978); Stern, *Gold and Iron*, pp. 494 ff.

55 R. H. Bowen, *German Theories of the Corporative State* (New York, 1947), p. 141.

56 Levy, op. cit., pp. 18, 211.

57 Moneypenny and Buckle, *Disraeli*, IV, p. 557; and see generally, R. Blake, *The Conservative Party from Peel to Churchill* (London, 1972 edn).

58 See P. Smith, *Disraelian Conservatism and Social Reform* (London, 1967).

59 Cowling, *1867*, and A. Jones, *The Politics of Reform 1884* (Cambridge, 1972), both demonstrate the significance the Tories attached to redistribution.

60 J. Cornford, 'The transformation of conservatism in the late 19th century', *Victorian Studies*, vol. VII (1963), pp. 35–66; Hanham, *Elections and Party Management*, *passim*; E. J. Feuchtwanger, *Disraeli, Democracy and the Tory Party* (Oxford, 1968); Adelman, *Gladstone, Disraeli and Later Victorian Politics*, chs 2 and 5.

61 ibid., p. 19; and see the forthcoming study by M. Swartz, *The Politics of British Foreign Policy 1865–1885*, for a detailed analysis.

62 R. B. McDowell, *British Conservatism 1832–1914* (London, 1959), p. 95.

63 Moneypenny and Buckle, *Disraeli*, V, pp. 126, 132, 421; VI, pp. 486 ff.

64 RA Windsor, I 68/29 and 43, Ponsonby to the Queen, 12/1/1871 and 18/1/1871.

65 See below, pp. 132–4.

66 Liverpool Record Office, Derby Papers 17/1/6, Derby to Adams (chargé, Berlin) (copy), 7/10/1874. For Dunsany's tract, see G. Hollenberg, *Englisches Interesse am Kaiserreich* (Wiesbaden, 1974), pp. 24–5.

67 RA Windsor, N 34/21, Lytton to the queen, 6/8/1877; and N 34/42, Salisbury to the queen, 26/9/1877; Liverpool Record Office, Derby Papers 17/2/3, Derby to Disraeli (draft), 9/10/1877; S. Gopal, *British Policy in India 1858–1905* (Cambridge, 1965), pp. 81–2.

68 AA Bonn, *England 69*, vol. 22, copy of *England* magazine 5/4/1884. The article went on to praise Bismarck's 'brilliant' domestic policy, which had checked the Liberals and the Socialists.

69 Conservative Research Office, London, Campaign Notes, 1885.

70 H. Collins, 'The international and the British labour movement', *Society for the Study of Labour History*, Bulletin no. 9 (Autumn 1964), p. 28. See also, idem, 'The English branches of the First International', in A. Briggs and J. Saville (eds), *Essays in Labour History* (London, 1960), pp. 242–75; R. Harrison, *Before the Socialists: Studies in Labour and Politics* (London, 1965), chs I–III; G. Lichtheim, *A Short History of Socialism* (London, 1970), pp. 157 ff.; K. E. Miller, *Socialism and Foreign Policy* (The Hague, 1967), ch. I.

71 H. Collins and C. Abramsky, *Karl Marx and the British Labour Movement* (London, 1965), pp. 18–19; H. Cunningham, *The Volunteers* (Hamden, Conn., 1975), esp. pp. 106–7.

72 K. Marx and F. Engels, *The Russian Menace to Europe*, ed. P. W. Blackstock and B. F. Hoselitz (London, 1953).

73 J. Petrus, 'Marx and Engels on the national question', *Journal of Politics*, vol. 33 (1971), pp. 797–824, which seeks to refute S. F. Bloom, *The World of Nations* (New York, 1941).

74 W. M. Simon, *European Positivism in the Nineteenth Century* (Ithaca, NY, 1963), ch. VIII; Harrison, *Before the Socialists*, pp. 251 ff.; idem, 'E. S. Beesley and Karl Marx', *International Review of Social History*, vol. IV (1959), pp. 22–58, 208–38; Lichtheim, op. cit., pp. 173–81.

75 Taylor, *The Troublemakers*, p. 62.

76 Harrison, 'Beesley and Marx', p. 54.
77 R. Postgate and A. Vallance, *Those Foreigners. The English People's Opinion on Foreign Affairs as Reflected in their Newspapers since Waterloo* (London, 1937), pp. 129–30.
78 Collins, 'The English branches . . . ', pp. 248 ff.; R. Harrison, *Before the Socialists*, p. 234.
79 F. Harrison, *Autobiographical Memoirs*, II, pp. 3–17, esp. p 11.
80 For what follows, see generally D. Geary, 'The German labour movement 1848–1919', *European Studies Review*, vol. 6 (1976), pp. 297–330; R. W. Reichard, *Crippled from Birth: German Social Democracy 1844–1870* (Ames, Iowa, 1969); W. Conze and D. Groh, *Die Arbeiterbewegung in der Nationalbewegung* (Stuttgart, 1966); H.-U. Wehler, *Sozialdemokratie und Nationalstaat* (Würzburg, 1962); H. Grebing, *A History of the German Labour Movement* (London, 1969); G. Roth, *The Social Democrats in Imperial Germany* (Totowa, NJ, 1963).
81 E. Engelberg, 'Die Rolle von Marx und Engels bei der Herausbildung einer selbststständigen deutschen Arbeiterpartei (1864–1869)', *Zeitschrift für Geschichtswissenschaft*, vol. 2 (1954), pp. 509–37, 637–65; R. Morgan, *The German Social Democrats and the First International 1864–1872* (Cambridge, 1965); W. H. Maehl, 'Bebel and the revolutionary solution of the German problem 1866–1871', *Internationale wissenschaftliche Korrespondenz zur Geschichte der deutschen Arbeiterbewegung*, Jg. 10 (1974), pp. 431–74; S. W. Armstrong, 'The Social Democrats and the unification of Germany 1863–1871', *Journal of Modern History*, vol. 12 (1940), pp. 485–509.
82 Herbst, *Die erste Internationale . . .* , *passim*; H.-J. Steinberg, 'Sozialismus, Internationalismus und Reichsgründung', in T. Scheider and E. Deuerlein (eds), *Reichsgründung 1870–71* (Stuttgart, 1970), pp. 319–44; C. Witzig, 'Bismarck et la Commune', *International Review of Social History*, vol. 17 (1972), pp. 191–221; S. Bernstein, 'The First International and the great powers', *Science and Society*, vol. XVI (1952), pp. 247–72.
83 Collins and Abramsky, op. cit., p. 265.
84 W. H. Maehl, 'August Bebel and the development of a responsible German Socialist foreign policy 1878–96', *Journal of European Studies*, vol. VI (1976), pp. 17–46; idem, 'German socialist opposition to Russian imperialism, 1848–1891', *The New Review. A Journal of East European History*, vol. 12 (1972), pp. 3–24; M. Victor, 'Die Stellung der deutschen Sozialdemokratie zu den Fragen der auswärtigen Politik (1869–1914)', *Archiv für Sozialwissenschaft und Sozialpolitik*, vol. 60 (1928), pp. 147–79; S. W. Armstrong, 'The internationalism of the early Social Democrats in Germany', *American Historical Review*, vol. XLVII (1942), pp. 245–58; H. Wolter, *Alternative zu Bismarck: Die deutsche Sozialdemokratie und die Aussenpolitik des preussisch-deutschen Reichs 1878–1890* (East Berlin, 1970).
85 H.-C. Schröder, *Sozialismus und Imperialismus* (Hanover, 1968), pp. 137 ff.; G. Weinberger, 'Die deutsche Sozialdemokratie und die Kolonialpolitik', *Zeitschrift für Geschichtswissenschaft*, vol. 15 (1967), pp. 402–23; H. Gemkov, 'Dokumente des Kampfes der deutschen Sozialdemokratie gegen Bismarcks Kolonialpolitik und gegen den Rechtsopportunismus in den Jahren 1884/85', *Beiträge zur Geschichte der deutschen Arbeiterbewegung*, vol. 1 (1959), pp. 350–68.
86 Cited in Weinberger, op. cit., p. 406.
87 Huber, *Deutsche Verfassungsgeschichte*, IV, pp. 49–63, 645–831; Fricke (ed.), *Die bürgerlichen Parteien . . .* , II, pp. 879–902; G. G. Windell, *The Catholics and German Unity* (Minneapolis, 1954); R. J. Ross, *Beleaguered Tower: The Dilemma of Political Catholicism in Wilhelmine Germany* (Notre Dame, Ind. 1976), ch. I; R. Lill, 'Die deutschen Katholiken und Bismarcks Reichsgründung', in Schieder and Deuerlein (eds), *Reichsgründung 1870–71*, pp. 345–65; J. K. Zeender, *The German Center Party 1890–1906* (Transactions of the American Philosophical Society, vol. 66, pt 1, Philadelphia, 1976), pp. 1–19; D. Blackbourn, 'The political alignment of the Centre Party in Wilhelmine Germany: a study of the party's emergence in nineteenth century Württemberg', *Historical Journal*, vol. 18 (1975), pp. 821–50.
88 G. G. Windell, 'The Bismarckian empire as a federal state 1866–1880: a chronicle of failure', *Central European History*, vol. II (1969), pp. 291–311; H. Bornkamm, 'Die Staatsidee im Kulturkampf', *Historische Zeitschrift*, vol. 170 (1950), pp. 41–72, 273–306; Sontag, *Germany and England*, pp. 138 ff.
89 Apart from the works by Lill and Windell, see K. Bosl, 'Die Verhandlungen über den Eintritt der süddeutschen Staaten in den Norddeutschen Bund und die Entstehung der Reichsverfassung', in Schieder and Deuerlein (eds), *Reichsgründung 1870–71*, pp. 148–63; and W. D.

Gruner, 'Bayern, Preussen und die süddeutschen Staaten 1866–1870', *Zeitschrift für bayerische Landesgeschichte*, vol. 37 (1974), pp. 799–827, with superb anti-Prussian cartoons of the *Münchener Punch*.

90 Windell, 'The Bismarckian empire as a federal state', *passim*; Doerr, 'Domestic influences on Bismarck's foreign policy', in Buse (ed.), *Aspects of Imperial Germany*, pp. 35–48.

91 F. Prill, *Ireland, Britain and Germany 1870–1914* (Dublin, 1975), pp. 28 ff.

92 Blackbourn, 'The political alignment of the Centre Party . . . ', *passim*.


## CHAPTER 5

1 Bodleian Library, Oxford, Clarendon MSS., dep. c 747, Clarendon to Loftus (copy), 10/2/1869.

2 H. R. Fox Bourne, *English Newspapers. Chapters in the History of Journalism*, 2 vols (New York, 1966 reprint), II, p. 389.

3 Quoted in A. J. Lee, *The Origins of the Popular Press 1855–1914* (London, 1976), p. 21.

4 ibid., p. 21, quoting from the *Edinburgh Review*.

5 ibid., p. 22.

6 Pflanze, *Bismarck and the Development of Germany*, p. 202; K. Koszyk, *Deutsche Presse im 19. Jahrhundert* (Berlin, 1966), ch. XI.

7 Lee, op. cit., p. 134; Fox Bourne, op. cit., II, pp. 276 ff.

8 In 1885, for example, there were twenty-two newspaper proprietors and nineteen journalists in the House of Commons: Lee, op. cit., tables 32 and 34.

9 Ensor, op. cit., p. 145; and E. M. Everett, *The Party of Humanity: The Fortnightly Review and its Contributors 1865–1874* (Chapel Hill, NC, 1939).

10 H. Schleier, 'Treitschke, Delbrück und die "Preussische Jahrbücher" in den 80er Jahren des 19. Jahrhunderts', *Jahrbuch für Geschichte*, vol. 1 (1967), pp. 134–79.

11 Anon., *The History of The Times*, 5 vols (London, 1935–52), II–III, *passim*.

12 L. Brown, 'The treatment of the news in mid-Victorian newspapers', *Transactions of the Royal Historical Society*, 5th series, vol. 27 (1977), pp. 30–1; Fox Bourne, op. cit., II, pp. 280–3.

13 L. Brown, op. cit., p. 25.

14 Lee, op. cit., p. 146 and *passim*. See also A. P. Wadsworth, 'Newspaper circulations, 1800–1954', *Transactions of the Manchester Statistical Society* (1954–5), pp. 18–23.

15 R. D. Attick, *The English Common Reader* (Chicago, 1957), chs 14–15.

16 A. Ellegård, 'The readership of the periodical press in mid-Victorian Britain', *Göteborgs Universitets Årsskrift*, vol. LXIII (1957), pt 3.

17 Sandiford, *Great Britain and the Schleswig-Holstein Question*, *passim*.

18 Ellsworth, 'The Austro-Prussian War and the British press', p. 190.

19 Raymond, *British Policy and Opinion during the Franco-Prussian War*, pp. 74–5.

20 Balliol College, Oxford, Morier Papers, A. Russell to Morier (copy), 12/1/1871. For Max Müller's similar embarrassment, see N. C. Chaudhuri, *Scholar Extraordinary* (London/New York, 1974), pp. 244 ff.

21 DZA Potsdam, RKA 1, copy of *Norddeutsche Allgemeine Zeitung*, 29/12/1884, 9/1/1885 and 5/2/1885; *Kölnische Zeitung*, 2/1/1885; *Economist*, late January(?) 1885.

22 B.M. Add. MSS. 58784 (Escott Papers), Granville to Escott, 10/2/1885.

23 Sandiford, op. cit., pp. 81, 121, 138.

24 Raymond, op. cit., pp. 251–2, 271, 322–3.

25 Postgate and Vallance, *Those Foreigners*, p. 163.

26 RA Windsor, I, 56/25, copy of *St. James's Gazette*, 12/3/1888, articles on 'A Lesson from Berlin'.

27 AA Bonn, *Preussen 1 nr. 1 nr. 40 secr.*, vol. 2, copy of *Standard*, 31/7/1889, and *Sheffield Telegraph*, 3/8/1889; vol. 3, copy of *Morning Post*, 16/8/1889; Postgate and Vallance, *Those Foreigners*, pp. 172–3, 182–3.

28 Sandiford, op, cit., *passim*; *History of The Times*, II, pp. 276–7, 339 ff.

29 Cited in ibid., II, p. 339, fn. 5.

30 A. A. W. Ramsay, *Idealism and Foreign Policy . . . 1860–1878* (London, 1925), pp. 48–9. On

Delane's editorship, see A. I. Dasent, *John Thadeus Delane*, 2 vols (London, 1908); and E. Cook, *Delane of The Times* (London, 1916).

31 *History of The Times*, II, pp. 424–8; Ramsay, op. cit., pp. 73–4.

32 Cited in Meine, *England und Deutschland* . . . , pp. 37–8.

33 Ibid., p. 205.

34 Carroll, op. cit., pp. 312–13.

35 Koszyk, op, cit., pp. 133–5. On the German press in general, see also O. Groth, *Die Zeitung*, 4 vols (Mannheim, 1928–30); O. J. Hale, *Publicity and Diplomacy with Special Reference to England and Germany 1890–1914* (Gloucester, Mass., 1964 reprint), ch. III.

36 Koszyk, op. cit., pp. 139–53. E. G. Friehe, *Geschichte der "National-Zeitung" 1848 bis 1878* (Leipzig, 1933), covers the paper's rightward transition in this era.

37 Schleier, op. cit., p. 145; see also R. H. Keyserlingk, *Bismarck and the Press: The Example of the National Liberals 1871–84* (Ph.D. thesis, London, 1965), ch. VI.

38 Koszyk, op. cit., p. 174; and Windell, *The Catholics and German Unity*, pp. 41 ff.

39 Koszyk, op. cit., pp. 184–209; E. Engelberg, *Revolutionäre Politik und Rote Feldpost 1878–1890* (Berlin, 1960), *passim*.

40 Koszyk, op. cit., pp. 231–2.

41 E. Naujoks, *Die parlamentarische Entstehung des Reichspressegesetzes in der Bismarckzeit (1848–74)* (Düsseldorf, 1975), esp. pp. 200–1. On Bismarck's press policy, see idem, 'Bismarck und die Organisation der Regierungspresse', *Historische Zeitschrift*, vol. 205 (1967), pp. 46–80; idem, *Bismarcks auswärtige Pressepolitik und die Reichsgründung (1865–1871)* (Wiesbaden, 1968), *passim*; idem, 'Bismarck und das Wolffsche Telegraphenbüro', *Geschichte in Wissenschaft und Unterricht*, vol. 14 (1963), pp. 605–16; R. Morsey, 'Zur Pressepolitik Bismarcks. Die Vorgeschichte des Pressedezernats im Auswärtigen Amt (1870)', *Publizistik*, vol. 1 (1956), pp. 177–81; W. Vogel, 'Die Organisation der amtlichen Presse und Propagandapolitik des Deutschen Reiches von den Anfängen unter Bismarck bis zum Beginn des Jahres 1933', *Zeitungswissenschaft*, vol. XVI (1941), ch. 1; I. Fischer-Frauendienst, *Bismarcks Pressepolitik* (Münster, 1963), *passim*, but esp. pp. 27–71.

42 Koszyk, op. cit., p. 234.

43 Cited in Hale, op. cit., p. 59.

44 R. Nöll von der Nahmer, *Bismarcks Reptilienfonds* (Mainz, 1968), *passim*; H. Philippi, 'Zur Geschichte des Welfenfonds', *Niedersächsisches Jahrbuch für Landesgeschichte*, vol. 31 (1959), pp. 189–254.

45 M. Busch, *Bismarck, Some Secret Pages of his History*, 3 vols (London, 1898); and E. Naujoks, 'Rudolf Lindau und die Neuorientierung der auswärtigen Pressepolitik Bismarcks', *Historische Zeitschrift*, vol. 215 (1972), pp. 299–344.

46 Hale, op. cit., p. 50.

47 D. Albers, *Reichstag und Aussenpolitik 1871–79* (Berlin, 1927), pp. 141 ff.

48 RA Windsor, O 16/87, Mr Jocelyn (Darmstadt) to Granville, no. 88 (copy), 21/9/1882; and Carroll, *Germany and the Great Powers*, p. 185.

49 PRO, FO 918 (Ampthill Papers)/55, Morier to O. Russell, 19/9/1870, with enclosure.

50 See the *Grenzboten* attack, cited in H. A. Winckler, 'Vom linken zum rechten Nationalismus', *Geschichte und Gesellschaft*, vol. 4, issue 1 (1978), p. 19.

51 Carroll, op. cit., pp. 136, 144 ff.; Friehe, *"National-Zeitung"*, pp. 184–6.

52 DZA Potsdam, RKA 1, copy of *Kölnische Zeitung* article, 'Deutschland und England nach dem Sturze Gladstones', 21/2/1885.

53 Busch, op. cit., I, p. 54; II, pp. 157, 299, 431; III, pp. 45, 115, 123, 178 ff. For further examples of this anti-Liberal and anti-English press influencing, see E. Naujoks, 'Bismarck in den Wahlkampagnen von 1879 und 1881: Der Zusammenhang von innerer und auswärtiger Pressepolitik', in H. Fenske, W. Reinhard and E. Schulin (eds), *Historia Integra* (Berlin/Munich, 1978), pp. 265–81.

54 Army Museums Ogilby Trust, Whitehall, London, Spenser Wilkinson Papers, 4, Bashford to Spenser Wilkinson, 28/4/1885.

55 On the latter, see W. H. Haller, 'Regional and national free-trade associations in Germany 1859–79', *European Studies Review*, vol. 6 (1976), pp. 275–96.

56 On the German side, see generally H. J. Varain, *Interessenverbände in Deutschland* (Cologne, 1973), esp. pp. 139–86; T. Nipperdey, 'Interessenverbände und Parteien in Deutschland vor

dem ersten Weltkrieg', in H.-U. Wehler (ed.), *Moderne deutsche Sozialgeschichte* (Cologne/ Berlin, 1966), pp. 369–88.
57 See P. Hollis (ed.), *Pressure from Without in Early Victorian England* (London, 1974).
58 B.M. Add. MSS. 52298 (Sir Charles Scott Papers), Scott to Sanderson (draft), 6/3/1885.


CHAPTER 6

1 D. Bowen, *The Idea of the Victorian Church* (Montreal, 1968), esp. ch. IV; M. A. Crowther, *Church Embattled: Religious Controversy in Mid-Victorian England* (Newton Abbot , 1970); B. M. G. Reardon, *From Coleridge to Gore. A Century of Religious Thought in Britain* (London, 1971); S. C. Carpenter, *Church and People, 1789–1889* (London, 1933), pp. 463 ff.; G. I. T. Machin, *Politics and the Churches in Great Britain 1832 to 1868* (Oxford, 1977), esp. pp. 252 ff.; and G. F. A. Best, 'Popular Protestantism in Victorian England', in R. Robson (ed.), *Ideas and Institutions of Victorian Britain* (London, 1967), pp. 115–42.
   On the German side, see J. P. Moody (ed.), *Church and Society: Catholic Social and Political Thought and Movements 1789–1950* (New York, 1953), esp. the article on Germany and Austria, pp. 325–583; K. S. Latourette, *Christianity in a Revolutionary Age*, Vol. II, *The Nineteenth Century in Europe: The Protestant and Eastern Churches* (New York, 1959), chs II–IX; K. Buchheim, *Ultramontanismus und Demokratie* (Munich, 1963); A. Drue, *The Church in the Nineteenth Century: Germany 1800–1918* (London, 1963); K. H. Grenner, *Wirtschaftsliberalismus und katholisches Denken* (Cologne, 1967).
2 QVL, 2nd series, II, pp. 313, 327.
3 PRO, 30/29 (Granville Papers)/93, O. Russell to Granville, Christmas 1873.
4 L. Cecil, *The German Diplomatic Service 1871–1914* (Princeton, 1976), p. 97.
5 H. H. Herwig, *The German Naval Officer Corps. A Social and Political History 1890–1918* (Oxford, 1973), p. 42.
6 Prill, *Ireland, Britain and Germany 1870–1914*, pp. 13–14; and for the background generally, see J. L. Altholz, 'Gladstone and the Vatican decrees', *The Historian*, vol. XXV (1963), pp. 312–24.
7 Cited in Meine, *England und Deutschland . . .* , pp. 118 ff.
8 Prill, op. cit., p. 18; and see the articles on British and German views of ultramontanism in *St. James's Magazine*, January and February 1874.
9 Bowen, op. cit., p. 166; Crowther, op. cit., p. 75; Reardon, op. cit., pp. 332–40; K. Dockhorn, *Der deutsche Historismus in England* (Göttingen, 1950), ch. 4.
10 On Acton and Döllinger, see the references in G. Himmelfarb, *Lord Acton. A Study in Conscience and Politics* (London, 1952); D. Matthew, *Lord Acton and his Times* (London, 1968); L. Kettenacker, *Lord Acton and Ignatius von Döllinger* (B.Litt. thesis, Oxford, 1971); and the edited correspondence, V. Conzemius (ed.), *Johann Joseph Ignaz von Döllinger: Briefwechsel mit Lord Acton*, 3 vols (Munich, 1963–71).
11 Quoted in Meine, op. cit., pp. 121–9.
12 Liverpool Record Office, Derby Papers 17/1/6, Derby to O. Russell (copies), 7/4/1874 and 29/12/1874.
13 PRO, FO 881/6419 (print), Memorandum respecting the Steps taken in 1875 by Great Britain and Russia in Furtherance of the Preservation of Peace between France and Germany, p. 4; see also L. P. Wallace, *The Papacy and European Diplomacy 1869–1878* (Chapel Hill, NC, 1948), ch. VII.
14 Quoted in Bowen, op. cit., p. 182.
15 Crowther, op. cit., pp. 64–5; and, in general, P. E. Schramm, 'Englands Verhältnis zur deutschen Kultur zwischen der Reichsgründung und der Jahrhundertwende', in W. Conze (ed.), *Deutschland und Europa* (Düsseldorf, 1951), pp. 149 ff.
16 Morley, *Gladstone*, II, pp. 164–5; and see his hostile references to Strauss, in Schramm, op. cit., p. 152.
17 Balliol College, Oxford, Morier Papers, Lord Arthur Russell to Morier (copy), 4/10/1877. See also Cecil, *Salisbury*, I, pp. 319–35; and M. Pinto-Duschinsky, *The Political Thought of Lord Salisbury 1854–1868* (London, 1967), p. 71.

18 Liverpool Record Office, Derby Papers 17/1/6, Derby to Adams (chargé, Berlin) (copy), 28/7/1874.
19 E. R. Norman, *Anti-Catholicism in Victorian England* (London, 1968), pp. 88, 103.
20 Prill, op. cit., pp. 15–16.
21 Prill, op. cit., p. 49.
22 See again, Chapman, 'The international houses', *passim*.
23 J. S. G. Simmons, 'Slavonic studies at Oxford: the proposed Slavonic Chair at the Taylor Institution in 1844', *Oxford Slavonic Papers*, III (1952), p. 139.
24 Dockhorn, *Der deutsche Historismus in England*, esp. pp. 205–16.
25 Cited in Schramm, 'England Verhältnis zur deutschen Kultur . . .', p. 142.
26 L. M. Price, *The Reception of English Literature in Germany* (Berkeley, 1932); W. F. Schirmer, *Der Einfluss der deutschen Literatur auf die Englische im 19. Jahrhundert* (Halle, 1947), *passim*; H. Oppel, *Englisch-deutsche Literaturbeziehungen*, 2 vols (West Berlin, 1971); G. Hollenberg, 'Die English Goethe Society und die deutsch-englischen kulturellen Beziehungen im 19. Jahrhundert', *Zeitschrift für Religions- und Geistesgeschichte*, vol. XXX (1978), pp. 36–45.
27 Hollenberg, 'Die English Goethe Society . . .', pp. 41, 45.
28 Harvie, *The Lights of Liberalism*, ch. 2; H. Stuart Hughes, *Consciousness and Society: The Reorientation of European Social Thought 1890–1930* (London, 1974 edn), esp. ch. I; K. Dockhorn, *Deutscher Geist und angelsächsische Geistesgeschichte* (Göttingen, 1954), *passim*; F. Meinecke, *Historism: The Rise of a New Historical Outlook* (London, 1972 trans.); G. G. Iggers, *The German Conception of History* (Middletown, Conn., 1968).
29 Schramm, 'Englands Verhältnis zur deutschen Kultur . . .', p. 162.
30 G. Hollenberg, 'Zur Genesis des Anglo-Hegelianismus. Die Entdeckung Hegels als Ausweg aus der viktorianische Glaubenskrise', *Zeitschrift für Religions- und Geistesgeschichte*, vol. XXVI (1974), pp. 50–9.
31 M. Richter, *The Politics of Conscience: T. H. Green and his Age* (London, 1964), p. 90.
32 See Dockhorn, *Deutscher Geist und angelsächsische Geistesgeschichte*, p. 8.
33 Richter, op. cit., pp. 165–73, 222. See also, D. Nicholls, 'Positive liberty 1880–1914', *American Political Science Review*, vol. 56 (1962), pp. 114–28.
34 P. E. Schramm, 'Deutschlands Verhältnis zur englischen Kultur nach der Begründung des Neuen Reiches', in W. Hubatsch (ed.), *Schicksalwege deutscher Vergangenheit* (Düsseldorf, 1950), pp. 298–319.
35 H. A. L. Fisher, 'Sir John Seeley', *Fortnightly Review* (August 1896), p. 191.
36 T. Arnold, *Introductory Lectures on Modern History* (London, 1871), p. 23.
37 Dockhorn, *Der Deutsche Historismus in England*, p. 149, quoting from Stubbs's *Constitutional History of England*. See also, Hollenberg, *Englisches Interesse am Kaiserreich*, p. 115 ff.; and especially, M. Messerschmidt, *Deutschland in englischer Sicht* (Düsseldorf, 1955), pp. 26–67.
38 Bodleian Library, Oxford, Bryce MSS., 5, Freeman to Bryce, 22/7/1870, 23/10/1870 and 20/2/1871; Messerschmidt, op. cit., pp. 30–4; W. R. W. Stephens, *The Life and Letters of Edward A. Freeman*, 2 vols (London, 1895), II, pp. 2 ff.
39 Bodleian Library, Oxford, Bryce MSS., 9, Bryce to Freeman, 13/7/1870.
40 J. R. Seeley, *The Life and Times of Stein*, 3 vols (Cambridge, 1878), II, p. 99; Fisher, 'Sir John Seeley', pp. 192–3.
41 Schramm, 'Deutschlands Verhältnis zur englischen Kultur . . .', pp. 303–4.
42 McClelland, *The German Historians and England*, pp. 71, 97, 103, 108 ff.; and see also the useful coverage in Schmidt, *The Characteristics of British Policy . . .* , pp. 53 ff.
43 McClelland, op. cit., pp. 155–6.
44 George Haines IV, 'German influence upon scientific education in England, 1867–1887', *Victorian Studies*, vol. I (1958), p. 230.
45 Apart from Haines's article, see also his two books, *German Influence upon English Education and Science 1800–1866* (New London, Conn., 1957); and *Essays on German Influence upon English Education and Science 1850–1919* (Hamden, Conn., 1969). See also J. J. McGlashan, *German Influence on Aspects of English Educational and Social Reform, 1867–1908* (Ph.D. thesis, Hull, 1973), chs 1–5.
46 Citations from this paragraph from Haines, 'German influence . . .', pp. 217, 221, 243.
47 ibid.; and see also Hollenberg, *Englisches Interesse am Kaiserreich*, pp. 160 ff.; W. H. G. Armytage, *The German Influence on English Education* (London, 1969), pp. 26–72; S. D.

Stirk, *German Universities – Through English Eyes* (London, 1946), ch. 1; C. Barnett, *The Collapse of British Power* (London/New York, 1972), pp. 96–106; J. M. Sanderson, *The Universities and British Industry 1850–1970* (London, 1972), chs 1–4.

48 Ellsworth, 'The Austro-Prussian War and the British press', p. 188.

49 Bodleian Library, Oxford, Bryce MSS., 6, Goldwin Smith to Bryce, 16/7/1870.

50 Ramsay, *Idealism and Foreign Policy*, p. 42.

51 ibid.

52 Weymss, *Morier*, II, p. 165.

53 Raymond, *British Policy and Opinion during the Franco-Prussian War*, pp. 94, 145, 296, and *passim*; S. Gwynn and G. M. Tuckwell, *The Life of the Right Hon. Sir Charles Dilke*, 2 vols (London, 1917), I, pp. 104, 133.

54 Cited in Meine, *England und Deutschland . . .* , p. 43.

55 The term used by Hollenberg, *Englisches Interesse am Kaiserreich*, p. 22.

56 National Library of Scotland, Edinburgh, Rosebery Papers, 10086, Bryce to Rosebery, 16/8/1886.

57 Cited in Armytage, *German Influence on English Education*, p. 65.

58 W. Fischer, 'Matthew Arnold und Deutschland', *Germanisch-Romanische Monatsschrift*, vol. 35 (1947), pp. 119–35.

59 Weymss, *Morier*, II, p. 177.

60 Cited in Meine, op. cit., p. 108; and see also Schramm, 'Englands Verhältnis zur deutschen Kultur . . .', pp. 137–41.

61 Hardach, 'Anglomanie und Anglophobie . . .', p. 163, fn. 49.

62 F. Oppenheimer, *Stranger Within* (London, 1960), p. 24.

63 J. A. Moses, *The Politics of Illusion* (London, 1975), pp. 13 ff.

## CHAPTER 7

1 Stürmer, *Regierung und Reichstag, passim*; and the commentaries in A. Mitchell, 'Bonapartism as a model for Bismarckian politics', *Journal of Modern History*, vol. 49 (1977), pp. 181–209.

2 F. Hardie, *The Political Influence of Queen Victoria 1861–1901* (London, 1965 edn), ch. V, provides a useful summary. There is no good study of Wilhelm I (one by E. Marcks was published in 1900) and the picture which usually emerges is that derived from the various biographies of Bismarck.

3 For Albert, see R. Pound, *Albert: A Biography of the Prince Consort* (London, 1973), esp. ch. 11; K. Jagow (ed.), *Letters of the Prince Consort 1831–1861* (London, 1938), esp. pt III. There exist a number of older specialised studies upon Victoria's attitude towards Germany – e.g. R. Kutsch, *Queen Victoria und die deutsche Einigung* (phil. Diss., Berlin, 1938) – but they derive mainly from the standard source, the 9 volumes of *The Letters of Queen Victoria*, which remains irreplaceable.

4 Liverpool Record Office, Derby Papers 17/1/7, Derby to O. Russell (copy), 31/10/1876.

5 Mosse, 'Queen Victoria and her ministers in the Schleswig-Holstein crisis', pp. 281–3.

6 idem., 'The Crown and foreign policy', p. 223.

7 Fulford, *Your Dear Letter*, p. 130 and *passim*; QVL, 2nd series, I, p. 364.

8 ibid., II, p. 44.

9 ibid., p. 405.

10 ibid., p. 490.

11 ibid., III, p. 53.

12 RA Windsor, O 43/279, Victoria to Granville, 27/10/1884.

13 See the 'Royal family tree' (pp. viii–ix) and 'Familiar names used in the correspondence' (pp. 8–11), in R. Fulford (ed.), *Darling Child: Private Correspondence of Queen Victoria and the Crown Princess of Prussia 1871–1878* (London, 1976).

14 S. Lee, *King Edward VII*, 2 vols (London, 1925), I, p. 250; and G. Brook-Shepherd, *Uncle of Europe* (London, 1975), pp. 79 ff.

15 Liverpool Record Office, Derby Papers 17/1/8, Derby to Mr Jenningham (copy), 17/5/1877.

16 M. Howard, 'William I and the reform of the Prussian army', in M. Gilbert (ed.), *A Century of*

*Conflict 1850–1950* (London, 1966), p. 92; Ritter, *The Sword and the Sceptre*, I, p. 176; Craig, *The Politics of the Prussian Army*, ch. IV.

17 Brown, 'The monarchical principle in Bismarckian diplomacy', *passim*; Herbst, *Die erste Internationale als Problem der deutschen Politik, passim*; Wittram, 'Bismarcks Russlandpolitik nach der Reichsgründung', pp. 261–3.

18 QVL, 2nd series, II, pp. 402 ff., 472; Liverpool Record Office, Derby Papers 16/1/6, O. Russell to Derby, 10/7/1876; Niedersächsisches Hauptstaatsarchiv, Hanover, *Nachlass* Münster, Bd. IV, Bismarck to Münster, 6/7/1876.

19 Waller, *Bismarck at the Crossroads*, p. 193; Brown, 'The monarchical principle in Bismarckian diplomacy', p. 45–7.

20 QVL, 2nd series, II, p. 327.

21 See below, pp. 163–5.

22 AA Bonn, *England 78*, vol. 1, Busch to Bismarck, 6/9/1884.

23 Dorpalen, 'Emperor Frederick III and the German Liberal movement', *passim*.

24 Niedersächsisches Hauptstaatsarchiv, Hanover, *Nachlass* Münster, Bd. III, Frederick to Münster, 3/12/1875.

25 QVL, 2nd series, II, p. 104.

26 The chief sources for these remarks, apart from QVL and the Fulford-edited correspondence of the Crown Princess and her mother, are the letters of Frederick in the Münster *Nachlass* in Hanover; and the frequent references to the Crown Prince in Odo Russell's private reports to Granville (PRO 30/29), Derby (Liverpool Record Office) and Salisbury (Hatfield House). I have also benefited from reading several unpublished papers by Professor F. B. M. Hollyday, who is preparing a study of Frederick's brief reign.

27 For this, see Heyderhoff (ed.), *Im Ring der Gegner Bismarcks, passim*; and the letters from, and references to the Empress Augusta in QVL.

28 QVL, 2nd series, II, p. 247.

29 ibid., p. 122. This paragraph is based upon QVL and the Fulford-edited volumes; F. Ponsonby, *Letters of the Empress Frederick* (London, 1928); Balfour, *The Kaiser and his Times*, pp. 64–71; Schweitzer, *Die Kritik der westlich-liberalen Oppositionsgruppen* . . .

30 HHSt.A Vienna, PA III/126, Szechenyi to Kalnoky, no. 6 A-F Geheim, 17/1/1885.

31 R. Robinson and J. A. Gallagher, *Africa and the Victorians* (London, 1961), p. 19.

32 Wellesley, *Cowley*, p. 314; Maxwell, *Clarendon*, II, p. 353; Mosse, 'The Crown and foreign policy', pp. 212–14.

33 PRO, 30/29 (Granville Papers)/206, Granville to Ampthill (copy), 16/11/1881. On Granville generally, see Fitzmaurice, *Granville*, esp. Vol. 2; Millman, *British Policy and the Coming of the Franco-Prussian War*, p. 208, fn. 1; and E. Daniels, 'Die englischen Liberalen und Fürst Bismarck', *Preussische Jahrbücher*, 123 (1906), pp. 220–60.

34 See above, p. 29.

35 Liverpool Record Office, Derby Papers 17/1/7, Derby to O. Russell (copy), 6/7/1877.

36 PRO, 30/29 (Granville Papers)/120, Derby to Granville, 20/8/1884 and 30/1/1885.

37 These articles are in the *Quarterly Review*, 115 (1864), pp. 236–87 and 481–529. See also, A. Mendelssohn-Bartholdy, 'Bismarck und Salisbury', *Europäische Gespräche*, vol. 1 (1923), pp. 89–102; Hildebrand, 'Die Reichsgründung im Urteil der britischen Politik', p. 415.

38 Cecil, *Salisbury*, II, p. 74.

39 ibid., pp. 126–9. Even when Salisbury reassured Odo Russell that 'on the sound rule that you love those most whom you compete with least, Germany is clearly cut out to be our ally', he could not resist referring also to 'a party at the German court which seriously looks forward to the possession of Holland': see ibid., p. 373.

40 There is no up-to-date work on the Foreign Office and diplomatic service to cover the gap between C. R. Middleton, *The Administration of British Foreign Policy 1782–1846* (Durham, NC, 1977), and Z. S. Steiner, *The Foreign Office and Foreign Policy 1895–1914* (Cambridge, 1969). The remarks made in this paragraph come simply from impression, gained by perusing various private papers.

41 R. T. Nightingale, 'The personnel of the British Foreign Office and Diplomatic Service 1851–1929', *American Political Science Review*, vol. 24 (1930), pp. 310–31.

42 W. R. Louis, 'Sir Percy Anderson's Grand African Strategy, 1883–1893', *English Historical Review*, vol. LXXVII (1966), pp. 292–314.

43 PRO, FO 633 (Cromer Papers)/6, Cromer to Rosebery (print), 9/2/1886, is but one example of his basic message in these years that Berlin 'is the real centre of gravity of Egyptian affairs'.

44 Fulford, *Your Dear Letter*, pp. 56, 198–9; QVL, 2nd series, I, p. 463; ibid., II, pp. 366–8; and see also Loftus, *Diplomatic Reminiscences, passim*.

45 See in particular his letter to Clarendon of 20/3/1869 (Bodleian Library, Oxford, Clarendon MSS., dep. c 478), a cool appraisal of Anglo-French-Prussian relations.

46 On him, see again Taffs, *Ambassador to Bismarck, passim*; P. Knaplund (ed.), *Letters from the Berlin Embassy, 1871–74, 1880–85*, in *Annual Report of the American Historical Association for the Year 1942* (Washington, 1944).

47 Odo Russell's reports of these conversations are in the Granville Papers (PRO, 30/29), with copies in RA Windsor.

48 Moneypenny and Buckle, *Disraeli*, VI, pp. 81, 178; Knaplund (ed.), *Letters from the Berlin Embassy*, p. 18.

49 Liverpool Record Office, Derby Papers 16/1/15, O. Russell to Derby, 15/5/1875.

50 ibid., 16/1/16, same to same, 8/1/1876. For Odo Russell's later complaints that the British government had failed to respond to Bismarck's offer of an alliance, see Hatfield House Archives, Salisbury Papers A9/58 and A9/61, O. Russell to Salisbury of 27/12/1879 and 4/1/1880 respectively; and RA Windsor, B 63/16, Disraeli to Victoria, 20/1/1880.

51 Taffs, *Ambassador to Bismarck*, pp. 368–83; PRO, 30/29 (Granville Papers)/178, Ampthill to Granville, 13/4/1884.

52 There is no study of Malet's ambassadorship. For his father's relationship to Bismarck, see Valentin, *Bismarcks Reichsgründung . . .*, pp. 72 ff.

53 See below, pp. 219–21.

54 On their role in general, see L. Hilbert, *The Role of Military and Naval Attachés in the British and German Service with Particular Reference to those in Berlin and London and their Effect on Anglo-German Relations 1871–1914* (Ph.D. thesis, Cambridge, 1954).

55 Taffs, 'War scare of 1875', p. 647. (Lyons was brother-in-law to the Duke of Norfolk.) On Lyons generally, see Newton's biography.

56 Weymss, *Morier*, 2 vols, covers Morier's career until 1876; A. Ramm, *Sir Robert Morier, Envoy and Ambassador in the Age of Imperialism 1876–1893* (Oxford, 1973), thereafter. For the 1888–9 newspaper campaign, see F. B. M. Hollyday, '"Love Your Enemies! Otherwise Bite Them!": Bismarck, Herbert, and the Morier affair, 1888–1889', *Central European History*, vol. 1 (1968), pp. 56–79.

57 PRO, 30/29 (Granville Papers)/177, Ampthill to Granville, 18/7/1881.

58 Newton, *Lyons*, I, pp. 224–6; II, pp. 9–12.

59 See Paget's correspondence with Salisbury in B.M. Add. MSS. 51228 (Paget Papers), and especially the ambassador's letter of 28/1/1886, expressing his dismay at the Conservatives' defeat.

60 Harvie, *The Lights of Liberalism, passim*; Wemyss, *Morier*, esp. vol. I.

61 ibid., II, p. 138 and *passim*; PRO, FO 918 (Ampthill Papers)/84, O. Russell to A. Russell (copy), 13/4/1872.

62 Steiner, op. cit., pp. 2–3. See also the important thesis by N. E. Johnson, *The Role of the Cabinet in the Making of Foreign Policy, 1885–1895 . . .* (D.Phil. thesis, Oxford, 1970), which shows how Salisbury gained his colleagues' trust (and, therefore, a greater freedom of action) by being scrupulously fair in consulting them, whereas Rosebery and Kimberley, who initially had much more freedom, aroused the suspicions of their more radical colleagues.

63 A good example of this can be seen in A. Ramm (ed.), *The Political Correspondence of Mr. Gladstone and Lord Granville 1868–1876*, 2 vols (Camden Society, vols LXXXI–LXXXII, London, 1952); idem, *. . . 1876–1886*, 2 vols (Oxford, 1962).

64 See Brackenbury's memo, 'General Sketch of the Situation Abroad and At Home from a Military Standpoint', 3/8/1886, copy in PRO, FO 364 (White Papers)/3.

65 P. M. Kennedy, *The Samoan Tangle: A Study in Anglo-German-American Relations 1878–1900* (Dublin/New York, 1974), p. 38; M. C. Jacobs, 'The Colonial Office and New Guinea', *Historical Studies: Australia and New Zealand*, vol. 5 (1952), pp. 106–18.

66 Steiner, op. cit., p. 3.

67 Cecil, *German Diplomatic Service*, p. 229.

68 W. Bussmann, 'Monarchie und Republik: Das zweite Ministerium Gladstones im Spiegel der

Privatkorrespondenz Herbert Bismarcks', in W. Berges and C. Hinricks (eds), *Zur Geschichte und Problematik der Demokratie* (Berlin, 1958), p. 288; idem, *Staatssekretär Graf Herbert von Bismarck*, *passim*.

69 ibid., *Staatssekretär...*, p. 442; see also K. Eberhard, *Herbert von Bismarcks Sondermissionen in England 1882–1889* (phil. Diss., Erlangen, 1949), *passim*.

70 Cecil, *German Diplomatic Service*, p. 226. There is a brief review of Bismarck's assistants, and his main ambassadors, in Waller, *Bismarck at the Crossroads*, pp. 12–16.

71 McClelland, *The German Historians and England*, pp. 115–17; Busch, *Bismarck*, II, pp. 13–22.

72 Friedrichsruh Archives, *Nachlass* Bismarck, series F, contains many examples (such as his letter to Herbert Bismarck of 9/7/1882, in F 1).

73 DZA Potsdam, RKolA 2927, Kusserow memo on Samoa, 31/12/1880; DZA Potsdam, *Nachlass* Kusserow, Bd. 26, memos on 'Parlamentarische Regierung', 1881.

74 H. Krausnick, *Holsteins Geheimpolitik in der Aera Bismarck 1886–1890* (Hamburg, 1942).

75 PRO, FO 343 (Malet Papers)/10, Malet to Salisbury, 10/11/1888. On Holstein's role in general, see N. Rich, *Friedrich von Holstein*, 2 vols (Cambridge, 1965), and N. Rich and M. H. Fisher (eds), *The Holstein Papers*, 4 vols (Cambridge, 1955–63); H. Krausnick, 'Holstein und das deutsch-englische Verhältnis von 1890 bis 1901', *Internationales Jahrbuch für Geschichtsunterricht*, vol. 1 (1951), pp. 141–58.

76 K. Ringhoffer (ed.), *The Bernstorff Papers*, 2 vols (London, 1908), *passim*, is the standard biography. The quotation is from Fulford (ed.), *Your Dear Letter*, p. 307.

77 Copy in Niedersächsisches Hauptstaatsarchiv, Hanover, *Nachlass* Münster, Bd. 40.

78 AA Bonn, *Nachlass* Richthofen 1/1, no. 14, Münster to the Crown Prince, 15/1/1879.

79 PRO, 30/29 (Granville Papers)/178, Ampthill to Granville, 18/11/1882.

80 The dispatch is in AA Bonn, London Embassy *Geheim-Akten*, packet 393/3, Münster to Bismarck, no. 83 of 6/6/1884, replying to GP, IV, no. 743. See also his private complaints, in Niedersächsisches Hauptstaatsarchiv, Hanover, *Nachlass* Münster, Bd. XII, Münster to Werthern, 12/3/1885, and Bd. XIII, Münster to Eckert, 8/3/1885. On Münster generally, see H. Nostitz, *Bismarcks unbotmässiger Botschafter, Fürst Münster von Derneburg* (Göttingen, 1968); and W. Suehlo, *Georg Herbert Graf zu Münster...* (Hildesheim, 1968), esp. pp. 115–32.

81 The best guide to Hatzfeldt's career is now the excellent edition by G. Ebel (ed.), *Botschafter Paul Graf von Hatzfeldt Nachgelassene Papiere 1838–1901*, 2 vols (Boppard, 1976); but see also H. Krausnick, 'Botschafter Graf Hatzfeldt und die Aussenpolitik Bismarcks', *Historische Zeitschrift*, 167 (1943), pp. 566–83; and M.-L. Wolff, *Botschafter Graf Hatzfeldt, Seine Tätigkeit in London 1885–1901* (phil. Diss., Munich, 1935).

82 Wemyss, *Morier*, II, pp. 120–1.

83 Caprivi's war plan, dated 15/11/1887, is in GSA Berlin-Dahlem, Rep. 92, *Nachlass* Albedyll, no. 4. He constantly objected to extensive operations in East Africa which might upset the British (see BA-MA Freiburg, F 5070, *Akta betr. Zanzibar*, Bd. 1, Caprivi memo of 25/11/1885), and the commander of the cruiser-squadron, Admiral von Knorr, tended to sympathise with the British consul Holmwood rather than with the pretensions of the German consul Arendt and the German East Africa Company – an attitude which enfuriated Herbert Bismarck: see his letter of 26/1/1887, in BA-MA Freiburg, RMi/PG 65085, *Die Entsendung von Kriegsschiffen nach Ostafrika*, Bd. 3.

84 Cited in Pflanze, *Bismarck and the Development of Germany*, p. 17.

85 Wemyss, *Morier*, II, p. 67.

86 Hatfield House Archives, Salisbury Papers A9/61, O. Russell to Salisbury 4/1/1880.

## CHAPTER 8

1 On this section generally, see W. E. Mosse, *Liberal Europe: The Age of Bourgeois Realism 1848–1875* (London, 1974).

2 Haller, 'Free-trade associations in Germany', p. 289.

3 H. von Treitschke, *Deutsche Geschichte im neunzehnten Jahrhundert*, vol. 5 (Leipzig, 1894), pp. 440 ff. And see again, Gottfried, 'Adam Smith and German social thought', *passim*; Bleugels, 'Die Kritik am wirtschaftlichen Liberalismus...', *passim*; and A. Ascher, 'Professors as

propagandists: the politics of the *Kathedersozialisten'*, in *Journal of Central European Affairs*, 23 (1963), *passim*.

4 See again, Gourevitch, 'International trade, domestic coalitions and liberty'.

5 Cited in P. Adelman, 'Frederick Harrison and the 'positivist' attack on orthodox political economy', *History of Political Economy*, vol. 3 (1971), p. 187.

6 Richter, *The Politics of Conscience*, p. 13; and see again, Nicholls, 'Positive liberty 1880–1914', *passim*.

7 T. W. Hutchison, 'Economists and economic policy in Britain after 1870', *History of Political Economy*, vol. 1 (1969), pp. 236, 246.

8 M. Freeden, *The New Liberalism* (Oxford, 1978).

9 On the post-1886 development of the Liberal Party and Liberal thought, see Freeden, op. cit.; Adelman, *Disraeli, Gladstone and later Victorian politics*, pp. 50 ff.; D. A. Hamer, *Liberal Politics in the Age of Gladstone and Rosebery* (Oxford, 1972); P. Stansky, *Ambitions and Strategies: The Struggle for the Leadership of the Liberal Party in the 1890s* (Oxford, 1964); H. V. Emy, *Liberals, Radicals and Social Politics 1892–1914* (Cambridge, 1973).

10 Shannon, *The Crisis of Imperialism*, p. 187.

11 Wemyss, *Morier*, p. 356.

12 ibid., p. 207. On the rise of imperialist sentiment in Britain, see A. P. Thornton, *The Imperial Idea and its Enemies* (London, 1966), ch. 1; R. Hyam, *Britain's Imperial Century, 1815–1914* (London, 1976), ch. 3; B. Porter, *The Lion's Share. A Short History of British Imperialism 1850–1970* (London, 1975), pp. 82 ff.

13 J. O. Baylen, 'The "new journalism" in late Victorian England', *Australian Journal of Politics and History*, vol. 18 (1972), esp. pp. 376–80; A. J. Marder, *The Anatomy of British Sea Power: A History of British Naval Policy in the Pre-Dreadnought Era 1880–1905* (Camden, Conn., 1964 reprint), pp. 121 ff.

14 Malet Papers (private hands), Wharncliffe to E. Malet, 17/9/1884; Churchill College Archives, Cambridge, Esher Papers 19/5, Wolseley to Esher (typescript), 10/3/1885. More generally, see Roach, 'Liberalism and the Victorian intelligentsia', *passim*; Harvie, *The Lights of Liberalism*, ch. 9; P. Marshall 'The imperial factor in the Liberal decline, 1880–1885', in J. E. Flint and G. Williams (eds), *Perspectives of Empire* (London, 1973), pp. 130–47; B. E. Lippincott, *Victorian Critics of Democracy* (New York, 1964 edn), pp. 93 ff.

15 Lee, *Popular Press*, *passim*; Fox Bourne, *English Newspapers*, II, p. 357; L. Senelich, 'Politics as entertainment: Victorian music-hall songs', *Victorian Studies*, vol. XIX (1975), p. 62.

16 See again, Winckler, 'Vom linken zum rechten Liberalismus', *passim*.

17 See R. Lamer, *Der englische Parlamentarismus in der deutschen politischen Theorien im Zeitalter Bismarcks (1857–1890)* (Lübeck/Hamburg, 1963), pp. 85–98, on the consensus in German political thought that something had 'gone wrong' with Britain by the 1880s.

18 GSA Berlin-Dahlem, Abt. III, 968, copy of Münster to Bismarck, 23/12/1874. On the German attitudes in general, see again Messerschmidt, *Militär und Politik . . .* , and the various contributions, and fine bibliography, in V. R. Berghahn (ed.), *Militarismus* (Cologne, 1975).

19 PRO, 30/29 (Granville Papers)/117, Ampthill to Granville, private, 19/1/1881.

20 E. Zechlin, *Staatsstreichpläne Bismarcks und Wilhelms II., 1890–1894* (Stuttgart, 1929); J. C. G. Röhl, 'staatsstreichplan oder Staatsstreichbereitschaft? Bismarcks Politik in der Entlassungskrise', *Historische Zeitschrift*, vol. 203 (1966), pp. 610–24; M. Stürmer, 'Staatsstreichgedanken im Bismarckreich', *Historische Zeitschrift*, vol. 209 (1969), pp. 566–619. On Puttkamer, see E. Kehr's piece, 'The social system of reaction in Prussia under the Puttkamer ministry', in idem, *Economic Interest, Militarism, and Foreign Policy. Essays on German History*, ed. G. A. Craig (Berkeley/Los Angeles/London, 1977), pp. 109–31.

CHAPTER 9

1 PRO, FO 363 (Tenterden Papers)/3, O. Russell to Tenterden, 10/4/1880.

2 AA Bonn, *England 69*, vol. 2, Münster to Bismarck, no. 3 of 20/1/1880; Hatfield House Archives, Salisbury Papers A9/70, O. Russell to Salisbury, 30/3/1880.

3 See above, pp. 31–6; and also the acute analysis by Lyons of Bismarck's strategy of diverting Germany's rivals into extra-European adventures, in Newton, *Lyons*, II, p. 264.

4 On this point, see W. N. Medlicott, *Bismarck, Gladstone and the Concert of Europe* (London, 1956), which is also very useful for much of the rest of this chapter.

5 AA Bonn, *England 69*, vol. 4, Münster to Bismarck, no. 39 of 31/3/1880.

6 Friedrichsruh Archives, *Nachlass* Bismarck, B 93, Reuss (Vienna) to Bismarck, 24/1/1880; AA Bonn, *England 69*, vol. 2, Bismarck to Hohenlohe, no. 164 of 8/2/1880 (copy); ibid., vol. 3, Bismarck to Münster, no. 162 of 23/3/1880; more generally, see S. A. Kaehler, 'Bemerkungen zu einen Marginal Bismarcks von 1887', *Historische Zeitschrift*, vol. 167 (1943), pp. 98–115.

7 Quoted in Medlicott, *Bismarck, Gladstone* . . . , p. 171; and see the fears about an Anglo-Russian combine against Turkey expressed by Bismarck in GP, IV, no. 719.

8 For the above, see Medlicott, op. cit., *passim*; Taylor, *The Struggle for Mastery in Europe*, pp. 266 ff.; Langer, *European Alliances and Alignments*, pp. 171 ff.; W. Windelband, *Bismarck und die europäischen Grossmächte 1879–1885* (Essen, 1940).

9 Cited in Hohenlohe, *Denkwürdigkeiten*, 2 vols, ed. F. Curtius (Stuttgart/Leipzig, 1907), II, p. 328.

10 PRO, 30/29 (Granville Papers)/177, Ampthill to Granville, 17/9/1881 and 19/11/1881.

11 Langer, op. cit., p. 278; Rich, *Holstein*, I, pp. 124 ff.

12 Ramm (ed.), *Political Correspondence of Mr. Gladstone and Lord Granville*, 2nd series, I, pp. 125–7; II, *passim*; QVL, 2nd series, III, p. 94.

13 Rich, *Holstein*, I, p. 133.

14 BA Koblenz, *Nachlass* Bülow, vol. 65, H. Bismarck to Bülow, 14/2/1885.

15 Rich, *Holstein*, I, pp. 133 ff.

16 Naujoks, 'Bismarck in den Wahlkampagnen von 1879 und 1881', *passim*; Wehler, *Bismarck und der Imperialismus*, pp. 466 ff.; Busch, *Bismarck*, III, p. 58; Lamer, *Der englische Parlamentarismus in der deutschen Theorie im Zeitalter Bismarcks (1857–1890)*, pp. 85–98.

17 Bussmann (ed.), *Staatssekretär Graf Herbert von Bismarck*, p. 108.

18 See again the series AA Bonn, *England 69*, entitled 'Die innere Verhältnisse Englands'. The volumes covering the 1880s should be read in conjunction with Herbert Bismarck's own sarcastic letters about British domestic politics in Bussmann (ed.), op. cit., pp. 110 ff.; and idem, 'Monarchie und Republik . . .', *passim*.

19 Ensor, *England 1870–1914*, pp. 71 ff.; Morley, *Gladstone*, III, pp. 47 ff.; T. W. Heyck, *The Dimensions of British Radicalism: The Case of Ireland 1874–95* (London, 1974), ch. 3; A. O'Day, *The English Face of Irish Nationalism* (Dublin, 1977).

20 AA Bonn, *England 69*, vol. 11, Münster to Bismarck, no. 98 of 11/6/1881; ibid., vol. 13, same to same, no. 175 of 27/11/1881.

21 ibid., vol. 16, same to same, no. 60 of 5/5/1882.

22 See Münster's reports and the *NAZ* articles in ibid., vols. 15–16.

23 ibid., vol. 21, Münster to Bismarck, no. 23 of 20/1/1884; and Rantzau to *Auswärtiges Amt*, 23/1/1884, in ibid., asking for this report to be inserted in the German press but not (interestingly enough) in the *NAZ*.

24 Friedrichsruh Archives, *Nachlass* Bismarck, B 128, Bismarck to Kaiser Wilhelm I, 22/10/1883; Busch, *Bismarck*, III, p. 115.

25 Geheimes Staatsarchiv, Munich, MA 78170, marginal note on Münster report no. 338 of 18/7/1884 (copy).

26 Cited in Windelband, op. cit., p. 184; and for Bismarck's approaches to Austria-Hungary, see pp. 146 ff.

27 Naujoks, 'Bismarck in den Wahlkampagnen . . .', pp. 277–8.

28 Friedrichsruh Archives, *Nachlass* Bismarck, B 44, Bismarck to the Crown Prince (draft), September 1882 (part of which is reproduced in GP, IV, no. 727). See also Bismarck's bitter comments on 'the occasionally astounding policy of succeeding English Cabinets', in PRO, 30/29 (Granville Papers)/22A/9, Ampthill to Granville, 12/9/1882.

29 See DZA Potsdam, RKA 1, with Wilhelm's angry letter to Bismarck of 7/10/1884, on how 'displeasing' he finds the report (conveniently written by Herbert Bismarck) of Gladstone's praise of the Crown Prince and Princess, and how necessary it is to uphold the monarchical system against the forces of democracy and republicanism; also, Busch, *Bismarck*, III, pp. 132 ff.

30 Müller-Link, *Industrialisierung und Aussenpolitik*, pp. 191 ff.; Langer, op. cit., ch. x; Windelband, op. cit., pp. 361 ff.

31 Friedrichsruh Archives, *Nachlass* Bismarck, B 128, Bismarck to Kaiser Wilhelm I, 22/10/1883.
32 The full text is given in Medlicott, *Bismarck, Gladstone* . . . , pp. 341–3.
33 Friedrichsruh Archives, *Nachlass* Bismarck, F 2, Rantzau to H. Bismarck, 20/2/1884.
34 Rich, *Holstein*, I, pp. 150 ff., provides a good recent account.

## CHAPTER 10

1 Wehler, *Bismarck und der Imperialismus*, is the most detailed recent analysis of the problem; but even that impressive study – both because of its ambitious nature, and because of its attempt at a general overview – has provoked a spate of further contributions. Some of these question his overall argumentation, e.g. G. W. F. Hallgarten, 'War Bismarck ein Imperialist?', *Geschichte in Wissenschaft und Unterricht*, vol. XXII (1971), pp. 257–65; and P. M. Kennedy, 'German colonial expansion: has the "manipulated Social Imperialism" been ante-dated?', *Past and Present*, 54 (1972), pp. 134–41. Some are concerned to amend the story in particular areas, e.g. P. M. Kennedy, 'Bismarck's imperialism: the case of Samoa 1880–1890', *Historical Journal*, vol. XV (1972), pp. 261–83; M. Reuss and G. W. Hartwig, 'Bismarck's imperialism and the Rohlfs mission', *South Atlantic Quarterly*, vol. 74 (1975), pp. 74–85; and H. P. Meritt, 'Bismarck and the German interest in East Africa 1884–1885', *Historical Journal*, vol. XXI (1978), pp. 97–116.
2 This argument of 'natural growth' is best put by M. E. Townsend, *Origins of Modern German Colonialism 1871–1885* (New York, 1974 reprint), which tends in consequence to overlook the other aspects of Bismarck's decision: see the remarks in W. O. Aydelotte, 'Wollte Bismarck Kolonien?', in W. Conze (ed.), *Deutschland und Europa* (Düsseldorf, 1951), pp. 41–68.
3 For full details, see Wehler, op. cit., pp. 39–111.
4 See L. H. Gann and P. Duignan, *The Rulers of German Africa 1884–1914* (Stanford, Calif., 1977), esp. Appendix E.
5 S. G. Firth, 'The New Guinea Company, 1885–1899: a case of unprofitable imperialism', *Historical Studies*, vol. 15 (1972), pp. 361–77; idem, 'German firms in the Pacific Islands, 1857–1914', in J. Moses and P. M. Kennedy (eds), *Germany in the Pacific and Far East, 1870–1914* (St Lucia, Queensland, 1977), pp. 3–25; F. F. Müller, *Deutschland–Zanzibar–Ostafrika 1884–1890* (East Berlin, 1959); K. Büttner, *Die Anfänge der deutschen Kolonialpolitik in Ostafrika* (East Berlin, 1959); Meritt, op. cit., *passim*; Wehler, op. cit., pp. 333 ff.
6 Townsend, op. cit., p. 92. See also, Wehler, op. cit., pp. 155–7; M. Walker, *Germany and the Emigration 1816–85* (Cambridge, Mass., 1964), *passim*; K. J. Bade, *Friedrich Fabri und der Imperialismus in der Bismarckzeit* (Freiburg, 1975), pp. 354 ff.; W. D. Smith, 'The ideology of German colonialism, 1840–1906', *Journal of Modern History*, vol. 46 (1974), pp. 645–52.
7 Cited in Wehler, op. cit., p. 163.
8 Apart from Townsend and Wehler's books, see M. Nussbaum, *Vom "Kolonialenthusiasmus" zur Kolonialpolitik der Monopole* (East Berlin, 1962); Böhm, *Ueberseehandel und Flottenbau*, pp. 31 ff.
9 Cited in Dorpalen, *Treitschke*, pp. 236, 253.
10 See, in general, R. V. Pierard, *The German Colonial Society 1882–1914* (Ph.D. thesis, Iowa State University, 1964); Wehler, op. cit., pp. 162 ff.
11 Meritt, op. cit., *passim*; Büttner, op. cit., pp. 34 ff.
12 The co-operation, and the breakdown, is well shown in H. Pogge von Strandmann, 'Domestic origins of Germany's colonial expansion under Bismarck', *Past and Present*, 42 (1969), pp. 140–59.
13 ibid., p. 145.
14 It is worth noting that Professor Wehler himself (perhaps aware of this distinction, if his followers are not) admits that Bismarck personally felt that he could deal easily with the SPD, as compared with the *Freisinnige* circles: see, *Bismarck und der Imperialismus*, pp. 190–1.
15 HHSt.A Vienna, PA III/125, Szechenyi to Kalnoky, no. 6 A. E. Geheim, 19/1/1884, and no. 13 of 6/2/1884. See also the references to the Crown Prince's circle in early 1884 in the *Holstein Papers*, vol. II.

16 HHSt.A Vienna, PA III/126, Szechenyi to Kalnoky (private), 24/5/1885; BA Koblenz, *Nachlass* Bülow, vol. 65, H. Bismarck to Bülow, 9/1/1885; Württembergisches Hauptstaatsarchiv, Stuttgart, Berlin *Gesandtschaftsakten* 12b, Bauer to Mittnacht, 5/2/1885. See also the references in Bussmann (ed.), *Staatssekretär Graf Herbert von Bismarck* . . . , and Rich, *Holstein*, I, pp. 150 ff.

17 Zucker, *Bamberger*, pp. 183–6; Townsend, op. cit., pp. 113 ff.; Wehler, op. cit., pp. 215 ff.; Kennedy, *The Samoan Tangle*, pp. 22–3; W. D. Smith, *The German Colonial Empire* (Chapel Hill, NC, 1978), pp. 31–2.

18 E. Eyck, *Bismarck and the German Empire* (London, 1950), pp. 274–6.

19 See Hollyday, 'Bismarck and the legend of the Gladstone ministry', pp. 101 ff.

20 GP, IV, no. 758; Rich, *Holstein*, I, p. 146.

21 *Holstein Papers*, III, p. 128.

22 ibid., II, p. 155; and Friedrichsruh Archives, *Nachlass* Bismarck, B 58, Holstein to H. Bismarck, August 1884.

23 PRO, 30/29 (Granville Papers)/178, Ampthill to Granville, 2/8/1884; HHSt.A Vienna, PA III/125, Szechenyi to Kalnoky, no. 65 B, 19/7/1884.

24 Schröder, *Sozialismus und Imperialismus*, vol. 1, *passim*; Wehler, op. cit., pp. 175–6; Weinberger, 'Die deutsche Sozialdemokratie und die Kolonialpolitik', *passim*; Gemkov, 'Dokumente des Kampfes der deutschen Sozialdemokratie gegen Bismarcks Kolonialpolitik'.

25 On the Conservatives, see Booms, *Die deutsch-konservative Partei*, p. 125; on Windhorst and the Centre, see Townsend, op. cit., pp. 124–5, 175–8; and Carroll, *Germany and the Great Powers*, p. 208. Wehler's analysis, in *Bismarck und der Imperialismus*, pp. 169–71, is a little disingenuous here, for although his aim is to show that there were members of these two parties who joined the national 'consensus' over colonies, there is no coverage of the strong *objections* which were raised by many other members, on which see H. Spellmeyer, *Deutsche Kolonialpolitik im Reichstag* (Stuttgart, 1931), pp. 16–41.

26 ibid., pp. 14, 21; Zucker, *Bamberger*, pp. 192–4; Townsend, op. cit., pp. 118 ff.; Friedrichsruh Archives, *Nachlass* Bismarck, F 2, Rantzau to H. Bismarck, 24/6/1884.

27 Spellmeyer, op. cit., p. 21, citing Bismarck's speeches of 2/3/1885 and 13/3/1885.

28 A. J. P. Taylor, *Germany's First Bid for Colonies 1884–1885: A Move in Bismarck's European Policy* (London, 1938), *passim*.

29 This is cleverly demonstrated in H. A. Turner, 'Bismarck's imperialist venture: anti-British in origin?', in P. Gifford and W. R. Louis (eds), *Britain and Germany in Africa* (New Haven, Conn., 1967), pp. 47–82.

30 *Holstein Papers*, III, p. 131; and see also, ibid., p. 138.

31 See above, pp. 93.

32 Geheimes Staatsarchiv, Munich, Berlin *Gesandtschaftsakten*, 1054, chargé (Berlin) to Staatsministerium, no. 529 of 31/12/1884, reporting on the *NAZ* article of 29/12/1884.

33 J. D. Hargreaves, *Prelude to the Partition of West Africa* (London, 1963), p. 317.

34 Firth, 'German firms in the Pacific islands'; Kennedy, *The Samoan Tangle*, pp. 28–30; R. Coupland, *The Exploitation of East Africa 1856–1890*, 2nd edn (London, 1968), p. 322.

35 Turner, 'Bismarck's imperialist venture', pp. 53–62; H.-P. Jaeck, 'Die deutsche Annexion', in H. Stoecker (ed.), *Kamerun unter deutscher Kolonialherrschaft*, 2 vols (East Berlin, 1960–8), I, pp. 53 ff.; H. R. Rudin, *Germans in the Cameroons 1884–1914* (Hamden, Conn., 1968 reprint), pp. 32 ff.

36 Kennedy, *The Samoan Tangle*, pp. 28–36.

37 AA Bonn, *England 78*, vol. 3, marginal comment upon Granville to Malet, 7/2/1885.

38 Turner, op. cit., pp. 68 ff.; W. O. Henderson, *Studies in German Colonial History* (London, 1962), ch. II.

39 GP, IV, p. 744; and see Bismarck's Reichstag defence of this view in P. E. Schramm, *Deutschland und Uebersee* (Brunswick, 1950), pp. 434–5.

40 For these minutes, see Kennedy, *The Samoan Tangle*, p. 57. On Bismarck's reaction to Peters' schemes, see Meritt, op. cit., *passim*; Reuss and Hartwig, op. cit., *passim*; and especially Wehler, op. cit., pp. 340 ff.

41 Stern, *Gold and Iron*, pp. 409 ff.

42 Townsend, op. cit., p. 83; Schramm, *Deutschland und Uebersee*, pp. 427 ff.

43 B.M. Add. MSS. 52298 (Sir Charles Scott Papers), Scott to Sanderson, 15/3/1885.

44 DZA Potsdam, *Nachlass* Kusserow, vol. 4, Hohenlohe-Langenburg to Kusserow, late May 1885.
45 Kennedy, *The Samoan Tangle*, pp. 54 ff.
46 It follows from this that, although I have differed at places from Professor Wehler's interpretation of Bismarck's imperialism, I cannot accept the recent criticism of Wehler's analysis of a 'manipulated England-hatred' by the Chancellor for domestic-political purposes, in L. Gall, 'Bismarck und England', *passim*.
47 It is significant how little reference there is to Germany in Morley, *Gladstone*, vol. III; and even in the more detailed Gladstone–Granville correspondence, edited by A. Ramm, op. cit., 2nd series, vol. II, the references only become frequent near the end of 1884.
48 PRO, 30/29 (Granville Papers)/178, Ampthill to Granville, 9/5/1883, 15/3/1884 and 13/4/1884.
49 GP, IV, nos. 745–7.
50 Langer, op. cit., p. 296; Schramm, *Deutschland und Uebersee*, pp. 44 ff.; and, in more detail, W. O. Aydelotte, *Bismarck and British Colonial Policy: The Problem of South West Africa 1883–1885* (Westport, Conn., 1970 reprint), pp. 35 ff.; R. I. Lovell, *The Struggle for South Africa 1875–1899* (New York, 1934), pp. 81 ff.
51 For British policy in West and East Africa in the mid-1880s, see Robinson and Gallagher, op. cit., pp. 163–98; Coupland, op. cit., pp. 359 ff.; Hargreaves, *Prelude to the Partition of West Africa*, pp. 301 ff.; idem, *West Africa Partitioned* (London, 1974); G. N. Sanderson, *England, Europe and the Upper Nile 1882–1899* (Edinburgh, 1965), pp. 23 ff.; G. N. Uzoigwe, *Britain and the Conquest of Africa* (Ann Arbor, Michigan, 1974), pts II and III; J. S. Galbraith, *Mackinnon and East Africa 1878–1895* (Cambridge, 1972); J. E. Flint, 'Britain and the partition of West Africa', in Flint and Williams (eds), *Perspectives of Empire*, pp. 93 ff.; M. E. Chamberlain, 'Clement Hill's memoranda and the British interest in East Africa', *English Historical Review*, vol. LXXXVII (1972), pp. 533–47.
52 Cited in Kennedy, *The Samoan Tangle*, p. 41. See also Jacobs, 'The Colonial Office and New Guinea', *passim*; A. Ross, *New Zealand Aspirations in the Pacific in the Nineteenth Century* (Oxford, 1964), *passim*; W. P. Morrell, *Britain in the Pacific Islands* (Oxford, 1960), pp. 205 ff.; M. P. Knight, 'Britain, Germany and the Pacific, 1880–87', in Moses and Kennedy (eds), *Germany in the Pacific and Far East 1870–1914*, pp. 61–88; Knaplund, *Gladstone's Foreign Policy*, pp. 99 ff.
53 J. L. Garvin and J. Amery, *Life of Joseph Chamberlain*, 6 vols (London, 1932–69), I, p. 497. For Dilke, see Gwynn and Tuckwell, *Dilke*, II, pp. 80–107; and, more generally, Robinson and Gallagher, op. cit., ch. VI; W. R. Louis, *Great Britain and Germany's Lost Colonies 1914–1919* (Oxford, 1967), pp. 17–20.
54 Cited in Aydelotte, *Bismarck and British Colonial Policy*, p. 166.
55 *Hansard*, 3rd series, vol. CCXCIV, 1079–1100.
56 Langer, op. cit., pp. 309 ff.; Fitzmaurice, *Granville*, II, pp. 422 ff.; C. J. Lowe, *The Reluctant Imperialists: British Foreign Policy 1878–1902*, 2 vols (London, 1967), I, pp. 87 ff.
57 GP, IV, no. 766.
58 Ramm (ed.), op. cit., II, p. 343.
59 Kennedy, *The Samoan Tangle*, p. 46.
60 Cited in Langer, op. cit., p. 308.
61 Newton, *Lyons*, II, pp. 331–2.
62 Langer, op. cit., p. 302; S. E. Crowe, *The Berlin West African Conference 1884–1885* (Westport, Conn., 1970 reprint), Appendix XI.
63 PRO, 30/29 (Granville Papers)/178, Ampthill to Granville, 16/8/1884.
64 Carroll, op. cit., p. 202; Schramm, *Deutschland und Uebersee*, pp. 438, 445.
65 W. G. Hynes, 'British mercantile attitudes towards imperial expansion', *Historical Journal*, vol. XIX (1976), p. 973. For changes in mercantile attitudes, see also Uzoigwe, chs II and III; Brown, *Tariff Reform Movement*, pp. 80 ff.; Hoffman, *Great Britain and the German Trade Rivalry*, *passim*; D. C. M. Platt, 'Economic factors in British policy during the "New Imperialism"', *Past and Present*, 39 (1968), pp. 120–38.
66 GP, IV, no. 745; and see also the convincing article by C. W. Newbury, 'The tariff factor in Anglo-French West African partition', in P. Gifford and W. R. Louis (eds), *France and Britain in Africa* (New Haven, Conn., 1971), pp. 221–60.

67 K. Mackenzie, 'Some British reactions to German colonial methods, 1885–1907', *Historical Journal*, vol. XVII (1974), pp. 165–75, offers useful data on this point; but it needs to be stressed that this criticism came from certain interested circles, not from British public opinion as a whole.

## CHAPTER 11

1 R. L. Greaves, *Persia and the Defence of India 1884–1892* (London, 1959), ch. V.

2 Robinson and Gallagher, *Africa and the Victorians*, pp. 141–51; G. N. Sanderson, *England, Europe and the Upper Nile*, pp. 19–21.

3 Ramm (ed.), op. cit., II, p. 380 and *passim*.

4 *Holstein Papers*, II, pp. 200–1; Langer, op. cit., p. 316; Württembergisches Haupstaatsarchiv, Stuttgart, Berlin *Gesandtschaftsakten*, 12b, Bauer to Mittnacht, 2/6/1885.

5 GP, IV, no. 777; and H. Stoecker, 'Zur Politik Bismarcks in der englisch-russischen Krise von 1885', *Zeitschrift für Geschichtswissenschaft*, vol. IV (1956), pp. 1187–1202.

6 For Bülow's attitude, see his letters to Herbert Bismarck, Friedrichsruh Archives, *Nachlass Bismarck*; and Bundesarchiv, Koblenz, *Nachlass* Bülow; for Holstein, see *Holstein Papers*, II, p. 193; for Wilhelm, see Lee, *Edward VII*, I, pp. 485–6, 510–11, and Bussmann (ed.), *Staatssekretär Graf Herbert von Bismarck*, pp. 276–9; for the press, Carroll, op. cit., p. 211.

7 GP, IV, nos. 764 ff.

8 ibid., no. 777; and see again Kaehler, 'Bemerkungen zu einen Marginal Bismarcks . . .', pp. 108 ff.

9 See the comments by diplomats in Berlin on his attitude: PRO, FO 343 (Malet Papers)/6, Malet to Granville (copies), 2/5/1885 and 9/5/1885; B.M. Add. MSS. 52295 (Sir Charles Scott Papers), Scott to Granville, 4/4/1885; HHSt.A Vienna, PA III/126, Szechenyi to Kalnoky, no. 34A-D, 25/4/1885; Württembergisches Hauptstaatsarchiv, Stuttgart, Berlin *Gesandtschaftsakten*, 12b, Bauer to Mittnacht, 14/4/1885.

10 Friedrichsruh Archives, *Nachlass* Bismarck, F 2, Rantzau to H. Bismarck, 30/9/1885; Greaves, op. cit., ch. VI and appendix II.

11 Langer, op. cit., ch. X; F. R. Bridge, *From Sadowa to Sarajevo: The Foreign Policy of Austria-Hungary, 1866–1914* (London, 1972), pp. 154 ff.

12 Friedrichsruh Archives, *Nachlass* Bismarck, B 128, Bismarck to Kaiser Wilhelm I, 10/11/1885; cf. Ebel (ed.), *Hatzfeldt Papiere*, I, p. 459.

13 ibid.; and Friedrichsruh Archives, *Nachlass* Bismarck, F 2, Rantzau to H. Bismarck, 25/10/1885.

14 Badisches Generallandesarchiv, Karlsruhe, Abt. 233, Fasz. 34796, Marschall to Turban, no. 46 of 1/11/1885.

15 Langer, op. cit., p. 369; Bridge, op. cit., pp. 161–2.

16 Craig, *Politics of the Prussian Army*, pp. 266–71; Rich, *Holstein*, I, pp. 174 ff.; and see the interesting report, no. 570 of 13/3/1887, of the Bavarian military plenipotentiary in Berlin on the activities of Waldersee, Prince Wilhelm and the General Staff, in: Bayerisches Kriegsarchiv, Munich, M. Kr. 43.

17 Hallgarten, *Imperialismus vor 1914*, I, pp. 279 ff.; Wehler, 'Bismarck's Imperialismus und späte Russlandpolitik . . .', *passim*; Müller-Link, *Industrialisierung und Aussenpolitik*, pp. 276 ff.; Stern, *Gold and Iron*, pp. 439 ff.

18 See the important correspondence of Bismarck with the War Minister Bronsart, in DZA Potsdam, RKA 1 and 1246; and, more generally, Carroll, op. cit., pp. 238 ff.; and Müller-Link, op. cit., pp. 303 ff.

19 There is an excellent coverage of Bismarck's policies in 1887, in Rich, *Holstein*, chs XVII–XIX.

20 See Hatzfeldt's comments on these years in Ebel (ed.), *Hatzfeldt Papiere*, I, *passim*; and Bismarck's own comments upon the breakdown of the traditional two-party system in Britain in early 1886, in Busch, *Bismarck*, III, p. 152.

21 Caprivi memo, 'Bericht über die Aussichten der Kriegführung zur See zwischen Deutschland, Oesterreich und Italien einerseits und Frankreich und Russland andererseits', 15/11/1887: copy in GSA Berlin-Dahlem, Rep. 92, *Nachlass* Albedyll, no. 4.

22 Taylor, *Struggle for Mastery in Europe*, p. 321.

23 This two-faced policy is nicely dissected by Holstein, in *Holstein Papers*, II, pp. 330–3; and by Malet, in his letter of 4/9/1886 to Iddesleigh in PRO, FO 343 (Malet Papers)/4.
24 Hallgarten, op. cit., I, pp. 263 ff.; Müller-Link, op. cit., pp. 319 ff.
25 ibid., pp. 340 ff.; Hillgruber, *Bismarck's Aussenpolitik*, pp. 186–8; Craig, op. cit., pp. 274–6; Ritter, *The Sword and the Sceptre*, I, pp. 230 ff. I am indebted to Professor I. Lambi (Saskatchewan) for further details upon the Prussian General Staff's plans in the late 1880s.
26 J. A. S. Grenville and G. B. Young, *Politics, Strategy and American Diplomacy: Studies in Foreign Policy 1873–1917* (London/New Haven, 1966), pp. 39–73; H. C. Allen, *Great Britain and the United States . . . 1783–1952* (London, 1954), pp. 527 ff.; C. S. Campbell, *From Revolution to Rapprochement: The United States and Great Britain 1783–1900* (New York, 1974), pp. 149 ff.
27 Cecil, *Salisbury* IV, pp. 185 ff.; QVL, 3rd series, I, pp. 409 ff.; Marder, *Anatomy of British Sea Power*, pp. 71–3, 86–7, 107–9, 124 ff.; C. J. Lowe, *Salisbury and the Mediterranean 1886–1896* (London, 1965), pp. 41 ff.; H. R. Moon, *The Invasion of the United Kingdom: Public Controversy and Official Planning 1888–1918*, 2 vols (Ph.D. thesis, London, 1968), I, pp. 19 ff., and see also the memoranda on 'A French Invasion' considered by the Cabinet, in PRO, Cab. 37/21/14–15, 17–19, and Cab. 37/22/32, 37, 40.
28 Greaves, *Persia and the Defence of India*, p. 197 and *passim*; D. R. Gillard, 'Salisbury and the Indian defence problem, 1885–1902', in Bourne and Watt (eds), *Studies in International History*, pp. 236–48. See also the gloomy assessment by General Brackenbury, 'General Sketch of the Situation Abroad and at Home from a Military Standpoint', 3/8/1886, copy in PRO, FO 364 (White Papers)/3.
29 Quoted in Greaves, op. cit., pp. 1–2.
30 QVL, 3rd series, I, pp. 193 ff.
31 ibid., p. 263.
32 R. Rhodes James, *Lord Randolph Churchill* (London, 1959), pp. 270 ff.; Cecil, *Salisbury*, III, pp. 319–22; Churchill College Archives, Cambridge, Randolph Churchill papers, 1/15 no. 1809, R. Churchill to Salisbury, 19/9/1886.
33 Ramm, *Morier*, p. 235 and *passim*; and see also Weymss, *Morier*, II, pp. 356 ff.
34 See Friedrichsruh Archives, *Nachlass* Bismarck, F 3, Rantzau to Bismarck, 2/8/1885; AA Bonn, London Embassy *Geheim-Akten*, 393/no. 4, H. Bismarck to Hatzfeldt, 9/12/1885; PRO, FO 343 (Malet Papers)/2, Malet to Salisbury, 24/12/1887; GP, IV, nos. 784, 789, 804, 865–74.
35 Ramm, *Morier*, ch. 7; and see the evidence in ch. 10, ibid., of the queen's strong opposition to Morier's pro-Russian policy.
36 There is an excellent brief coverage of Salisbury's suspicions of Bismarck during the 1880s in Sontag, *Germany and England*, ch. VIII: and see also Cecil, *Salisbury*, IV, pp. 6, 8–9, 29–30, 50–1.
37 ibid., III, pp. 223–4, 253; GP, IV, nos 779 ff.; HHSt.A Vienna, PA VIII/101, Karolyi to Kalnoky, no. 38 of 3/7/1886.
38 For Salisbury's almost uncanny sense of the state of Russo-German talks over France at this time (that is, during the secret Reinsurance Treaty negotiations), see Cecil, *Salisbury*, III, p. 26; and QVL, 3rd series, I, pp. 268 ff.
39 ibid., p. 294.
40 Cecil, *Salisbury*, IV, pp. 55–62; Howard, *Britain and the Casus Belli*, pp. 157–9; H. Lademacher, *Die belgische Neutralität als Problem der europäischen Politick 1830–1914* (Bonn, 1971), pp. 264–73.
41 Newton, *Lyons*, II, p. 409 (see also, p. 386). On the Drummond Wolff negotiations, see Robinson and Gallagher, *Africa and the Victorians*, pp. 257–66; and M. P. Hornik, 'The mission of Sir Henry Drummond Wolff to Constantinople, 1885–7', *English Historical Review*, vol. LV (1940), pp. 598–623.
42 On which, see Lowe, *Salisbury and the Mediterranean*, ch. I, *passim*; Howard, *Britain and the Casus Belli*, pp. 14–15; W. N. Medlicott, 'The Mediterranean Agreements of 1887', *Slavonic Review*, vol. V (1926), pp. 66–8; C. L. Smith, *The Embassy of Sir William White at Constantinople 1886–1891* (Oxford, 1957), chs III–IV.
43 Cecil, *Salisbury*, IV, p. 71; Johnson, *The Role of the Cabinet . . .*, pp. 144 ff.

44 Hatfield House Archives, Salisbury Papers, A61/48 and 52, especially the latter (a memo of 20/11/1887 by Colonel Swaine on Wilhelm's character); Cecil, *Salisbury*, IV, pp. 72–3, 101–2.

45 ibid., p. 113; QVL, 3rd series, I, pp. 438 ff.; Lee, *Edward VII*, I, pp. 649 ff.; and the further correspondence on this incident in B.M. Add. MSS. 51229 (Paget Papers).

46 *Punch*, 6/10/1888.

47 The 'Chancellor Crisis' of 1888, and its impact upon Anglo-German relations is best followed in: Hatfield House Archives, Salisbury Papers, A61/77, Malet to Salisbury, 7/4/1888; Cecil, *Salisbury*, IV, pp. 97–100; QVL, 3rd series, I, p. 429. For the German scene, see: Badisches Generallandesarchiv, Karlsruhe, Abt. 233, Fasz. 34798, Marschall to Turban, no. 16 of 9/4/1888; DZA Potsdam, RKA 2301; Hallgarten, op. cit., I, pp. 270 ff.; Busch, *Bismarck*, III, pp. 171 ff., and especially the lengthy unpublished paper by Professor F. B. M. Hollyday, 'Bismarck and Kaiser Friedrich III: The "Chancellor Crisis" of 1888', a copy of which I was privileged to see.

48 QVL, 3rd series, I, pp. 457 ff.; Ramm, *Morier*, pp. 288 ff.; Hollyday, 'Love Your Enemies . . .', *passim*.

49 There is a succinct review of the literature in W. Steglich, 'Bismarcks Englische Bündnisson-dierungen und Bündnisvorschläge 1887–1889', in Fenske, Reinhard and Schulin (eds), *Historia Integra*, pp. 283–6.

50 GP, IV, no. 945.

51 Cecil, *Salisbury*, IV, p. 101.

52 For Holstein's references to India, see Ebel (ed.), *Hatzfeldt Papiere*, II, pp. 716–22, 793. For the American-Samoan aspect of Bismarck's calculations, see Kennedy, *The Samoan Tangle*, pp. 76–84. Steglich's recent article, 'Bismarcks Englische Bündnissondierungen . . .', *passim*, demonstrates very clearly how frequently the Chancellor had hinted to London in the years 1886–1889 that Germany could take care of France; but does not emphasise that it was precisely this reassurance which gave Salisbury the great cause for doubt.

53 Lowe, *Salisbury and the Mediterranean*, pp. 52–3. See also W. H. Smith's deprecating reference to a German alliance, in Ramm, *Morier*, pp. 303–4. Also useful is D. R. Gillard, *Lord Salisbury's Foreign Policy 1888–1892, with Special Reference to Anglo-German Relations* (Ph.D. thesis, London, 1952), ch. 2.

54 On the politics of Bismarck's fall, see especially Rich, *Holstein*, ch. XXII; J. C. G. Röhl, *Germany without Bismarck: The Crisis of Government in the Second Reich, 1890–1900* (London, 1967), pp. 27–55; idem (ed.), *Philipp Eulenburgs Politische Korrespondenz*, vol. 1 (Boppard a.R., 1976), pp. 340 ff.; M. Reuss, 'Bismarck's dismissal and the Holstein circle', *European Studies Review*, vol. 5 (1975), pp. 31–46; G. Seeber (ed.), *Bismarcks Sturz* (Berlin, 1977), *passim*.

55 GP, VI, no. 1357; P. Kluke, 'Bismarck und Salisbury: ein diplomatisches Duell', *Historische Zeitschrift*, 175 (1953), pp. 285–306; and see the clever review article, precisely on these lines, by F. H. Hinsley, 'Bismarck, Salisbury and the Mediterranean Agreements of 1887', *Historical Journal*, vol. I (1958), pp. 76–81.

56 The East African story may be followed in Müller, *Deutschland–Zanzibar–Ostafrika . . .*, *passim*; Coupland, op. cit., pp. 407 ff.; Uzoigwe, *Britain and the Conquest of Africa*, pp. 148 ff.; Galbraith, *Mackinnon and East Africa*, *passim*; G. Jantzen, *Ostafrika in der deutsch-englischen Politik 1884–1890* (Hamburg, 1934), *passim*.

57 Kennedy, *The Samoan Tangle*, pp. 51 ff.

58 See, for example, GP, IV, no. 810 ff., and the furious marginal comments of Bismarck in this period on the reports of British 'obstructionism' at Zanzibar, in DZA Potsdam, RKolA, vols 598–9. For earlier examples, see Ebel (ed.), *Hatzfeldt Papiere*, I, pp. 491 ff., 535 ff.

59 Hatfield House Archives, Salisbury Papers, A44/17, Salisbury to Malet, 13/6/1886; Cecil, *Salisbury*, IV, p. 36; Kennedy, *The Samoan Tangle*, pp. 56–60.

60 Cecil, *Salisbury*, IV, p. 126; and see Uzoigwe, op. cit., *passim*, on Salisbury's hopes for African trade.

61 GP, IV, nos 809–816; E. de Groot, 'Great Britain and Germany in Zanzibar: Consul Holm-wood's papers 1886–7', *Journal of Modern History*, vol. XXV (1953), pp. 120–38.

62 Cecil, *Salisbury*, IV, pp. 40–6. That Rosebery had felt a similar resentment during his brief period as Foreign Secretary is clear from his private letters to Malet, in PRO, FO 343 (Malet Papers)/6.

63 Robinson and Gallagher, *Africa and the Victorians*, pp. 190–202, 254 ff.; Coupland, *Exploitation of East Africa*, p. 433; Sanderson, *England, Europe and the Upper Nile*, pp. 33 ff.
64 Friedrichsruh Archives, *Nachlass* Bismarck, F 2, Rantzau to H. Bismarck, 12/10/1886; DZA Potsdam, RKolA 601, Krauel memorandum of 19/8/1886, with Bismarck's marginal comments thereon; and Müller, *Deutschland–Zanzibar–Ostafrika*, pp. 203, 217, 260, covers his early attitude in East Africa; Kennedy, *The Samoan Tangle*, pp. 57, 71–2, covers the Samoan policy.
65 Cecil, *Salisbury*, IV, pp. 234–5, 246–7; QVL, 3rd series, I, pp. 444, 460; L. W. Hollingsworth, *Zanzibar under the Foreign Office 1890–1913* (London, 1953), pp. 28 ff.
66 PRO, FO 58/245, Malet to Salisbury, no. 37 of 28/1/1889; GP, IV, no. 952.
67 Ebel (ed.), *Hatzfeldt Papiere* . . . , II, p. 697; PRO, FO 343 (Malet Papers)/10, Malet to Salisbury, 10/11/1888.
68 On this change in general, see again Uzoigwe, op. cit., esp. chs I–II; Platt, 'Economic factors in British policy . . .', *passim*; Hynes, 'British mercantile attitudes . . .', pp. 972 ff.; Marder, *Anatomy of British Sea Power*, pp. 44 ff., 119 ff.
69 Ross, *New Zealand Aspirations in the Pacific*, chs XI–XII; Mackenzie, 'Some British reactions to German colonial methods . . .', *passim*; J. A. La Nauze, *Alfred Deakin*, 2 vols (Melbourne, 1965), I, pp. 90 ff.; E. A. Benians, J. R. M. Butler and C. E. Carrington (eds), *Cambridge History of the British Empire*, Vol. III (Cambridge, 1959), pp. 178–9, 237–9, 406 ff.
70 Uzoigwe, op. cit., pp. 191 ff.; Sanderson, op. cit., pp. 49 ff.; Robinson and Gallagher, op. cit., pp. 228–9; R. O. Collins, 'Origins of the Nile struggle: Anglo-German negotiations and the Mackinnon agreement of 1890', in Gifford and Louis (eds), *Britain and Germany in Africa*, pp. 130 ff.; Hale, *Publicity and Diplomacy*, pp. 82 ff.
71 Lowe, *The Reluctant Imperialists*, I, p. 128.
72 S. Miers, 'The Brussels Conference of 1889–1890: the place of the slave trade in the policies of Great Britain and Germany', in Gifford and Louis (eds), *Britain and Germany in Africa*, p. 96; Mackenzie, 'Some British reactions to German colonial methods . . .', pp. 166–7.
73 Friedrichsruh Archives, *Nachlass* Bismarck, B 99, Rottenburg to H. Bismarck, 17/12/1888.
74 ibid., B 58, Holstein to H. Bismarck, 29–30/10/1889 (my italics).
75 DZA Potsdam, RKolA 1132, H. Bismarck memo (drafted by Krauel) of 8/1/1889, with Bismarck's comments upon – for example, 'That would be virtually a hostile act against England!'; and see also the Chancellor's comments on a further memo by H. Bismarck (Krauel) of 5/10/1889, and A.A. to Hatzfeldt, no. 881 of 17/10/1889, in ibid.
76 There is plenty of evidence for this in the official German records in Potsdam and Freiburg: e.g. DZA Potsdam, RKolA. 600, Hoffmann (S.M.S. *Möwe*) to Admiralty, 5/8/1886, referring to the DOAG house in Zanzibar as 'the centre of the dissatisfied elements'; and BA-MA Freiburg, F 7591 (unpublished memoirs of Admiral E. Knorr), vol. 3 with its comments on the DOAG and German consul Arendt at Zanzibar. See generally, A. Harding Ganz, 'Colonial policy and the Imperial German Navy', *Militärgeschichtliche Mitteilungen*, 1/1977, pp. 35–52. For the German-American clash over Samoa, see A. Vagts, *Deutschland und die Vereinigten Staaten in der Weltpolitik*, 2 vols (New York, 1935), I, pp. 640 ff.; H. H. Herwig, *Politics of Frustration: The United States in German Naval Planning 1889–1941* (Boston, Mass., 1976), pp. 14 ff.
77 See Bundesarchiv, Koblenz, *Nachlass* Boetticher, vol. 48, Bismarck to Boetticher, 26/8/1889, and the reply of 9/7/1889 (draft), for the approach to Hamburg; and, more generally, Wehler, *Bismarck und der Imperialismus*, pp. 408–11; Bade, *Fabri* . . . , pp. 338–50; and especially, Pogge von Strandmann, 'Domestic origins . . .', pp. 152–9.
78 See again, Wehler, op. cit., *passim*; and Kennedy, 'German colonial expansion . . .', *passim*.
79 Hatfield House Archives, Salisbury Papers A64/62, Salisbury to Malet, tel. of 19/3/1889, 'Not for Print'; and see the acute report upon Salisbury's apprehension in HHSt.A Vienna, PA VIII/110, Deym to Kalnoky, 21B, very confidential, 27/3/1890.
80 See Sontag's acute comments on Bismarck's role in 'encouraging German belief in English perfidy, and English belief in German brutality': *Germany and England*, p. 262.

CHAPTER 12

1 Apart from the unpublished sources cited below, I have used GP, VIII, nos. 1672 ff.; W. L. Langer, *The Diplomacy of Imperialism 1890–1902*, 2nd edn (New York, 1951), chs I and IV; Cecil, *Salisbury*, IV, ch. X; Sanderson, *England, Europe and the Upper Nile*, ch. III; D. R. Gillard, 'Salisbury's African policy and the Heligoland offer of 1890', *English Historical Review*, vol. 75 (1960), pp. 631–53.

2 See the entries in the Marschall Diary (Schloss Neuershausen) for May and June 1890; and, more generally, Röhl, *Germany without Bismarck*, pp. 56 ff.; and J. A. Nichols, *Germany after Bismarck: The Caprivi Era 1890–1894* (New York, 1968 edn), chs I–II.

3 PRO, FO 343 (Malet Papers)/11, Malet to Salisbury, 19/4/1890.

4 Friedrichsruh Archives, *Nachlass* Bismarck, Berchem to H. Bismarck, 20/6/1889; GP, IV, nos 946, 950–4, and cf. GP, VIII, no. 1681, and Ebel (ed.), *Hatzfeldt Papiere*, II, pp. 775–8.

5 Geheimes Staatsarchiv Munich, MA 95364, Lerchenfeld report no. 297 of 18/6/1890, recounting Caprivi's speech to the *Bundesrat*.

6 *Holstein Papers*, II, p. 332; Rich, *Holstein*, I, ch. XXIV; GP, VII, *passim*.

7 See AA Bonn, London Embassy *Geheim Akten*, packet 394/1, Marschall to Hatzfeldt, no. 428 secret of 29/5/1890, with instructions to let Salisbury know of the altered policy, and with a copy of Caprivi's final refusal [GP, VII, no. 1380] to renew the Reinsurance Treaty. For Münster's report, see *Holstein Papers*, III, pp. 340–2.

8 Geheimes Staatsarchiv, Munich, MA 95364, Lerchenfeld report no. 297 of 18/6/1890.

9 PRO, FO 343 (Malet Papers)/11, Malet to Salisbury, *private & secret*, 31/5/1890.

10 See Lerchenfeld's interesting remark that 'the more unpopular the agreement seems to be in Germany, the more certain it is that it will be favourably regarded by the English parliament', in Geheimes Staatsarchiv, Munich, MA 95364, Lerchenfeld to Crailsheim, no. 338 of 28/6/1890.

11 D. R. Gillard, 'Salisbury's Heligoland offer: the case against the "Witu Thesis"', *English Historical Review*, vol. 80 (1965), pp. 539, 549.

12 G. N. Sanderson, 'The Anglo-German agreement of 1890 and the upper Nile', *English Historical Review*, vol. 78 (1963), pp. 49–72; idem, *England, Europe and the Upper Nile*, pp. 49 ff.

13 ibid.; Robinson and Gallagher, *Africa and the Victorians*, ch. X; R. O. Collins, 'Origins of the Nile struggle: Anglo-German negotiations and the Mackinnon Agreement of 1890'; in Gifford and Louis (eds), *Britain and Germany in Africa*, pp. 119–51.

14 Sanderson, *England, Europe and the Upper Nile*, p. 49; and see also AA Bonn, London Embassy *Geheim Akten*, packet 394/1, Hatzfeldt to Caprivi, no. 295 of 22/5/1890.

15 Johnson, *The Role of the Cabinet in the Making of Foreign Policy* . . . , pp. 233 ff.

16 QVL, 3rd series, I, pp. 610–15; and Ebel (ed.), *Hatzfeldt Papiere*, II, pp. 790–1.

17 Robinson and Gallagher, *Africa and the Victorians*, pp. 248–300; Hollingsworth, *Zanzibar under the Foreign Office*, pp. 46–51; Gross, *Factors and Variations in Liberal and Radical Opinion*, pp. 154–65; Gillard, *Lord Salisbury's Foreign Policy 1888–1892* . . . , pp. 13 ff.

18 Postgate and Vallance, *Those Foreigners*, p. 183; Carroll, *Germany and the Great Powers*, pp. 296–7; Gwynn and Tuckwell, *Dilke*, II, pp. 478–82.

19 The fullest coverage is in M. Sell, *Das deutsch-englische Abkommen von 1890 im Lichte der deutschen Presse* (Berlin, 1926), but see also Carroll, op. cit., pp. 293–9; and Schweitzer, *Die Kritik der westlichliberalen Oppositionsgruppen* . . . , pp. 160 ff.

20 K. Schilling, *Beiträge zu einer Geschichte des radikalen Nationalismus in der Wilhelminischen Aera 1890–1909* (phil. Diss., Cologne, 1968), pp. 20 ff. See also P. R. Anderson, *The Background of Anti-English Feeling in Germany, 1890–1902* (New York, 1969 reprint), pp. 177–210.

21 M. S. Wertheimer, *The Pan-German League 1890–1914* (New York, 1924), pp. 25–38.

22 Dorpalen, *Treitschke*, pp. 272–3; Sontag, *Germany and England*, pp. 326 ff. Bismarck's own criticisms of the pro-English policy of the 'New Course' are now extensively covered in M. Hank, *Kanzler ohne Amt* (Munich, 1977); W. Stribny, *Bismarck und die deutsche Politik nach seiner Entlassung (1890–1898)* (Paderborn, 1977); I. Buisson, 'Aussenpolitische Vorstellungen Bismarcks nach seiner Entlassung', in A. Fischer, G. Moltmann and K. Schwabe (eds), *Russland–Deutschland–Amerika* (Wiesbaden, 1978), pp. 105–16.

23 On German politics and the revival of the right in the early 1890s, see Schilling, op. cit., ch. I; Rich, *Holstein*, I, pp. 375 ff.; Röhl, *Germany without Bismarck*, pp. 85 ff.; Nicholls, *Germany after Bismarck, passim*; H.-J. Puhle, *Agrarischer Interessenpolitik und preussischer Konservatismus in Wilhelminischen Reich (1893–1914)* (Hanover, 1968).
24 DZA Potsdam, *Nachlass* Kayser, vol. 37, Kayser draft of newspaper article, end of 1890.
25 Cecil, *Salisbury*, IV, pp. 272–3; PRO, FO 343 (Malet Papers)/3, Salisbury to Malet (copy), 31/3/1891; Marschall diary entries (Schloss Neuershausen) 20/3/1891 and 24/3/1891; AA Bonn, London Embassy *Geheim Akten*, packet 395/4, Hatzfeldt to *Auswärtiges Amt*, tel. no. 56 of 18/3/1891, and Marschall to Hatzfeldt, tel. no. 59 of 22/3/1891.
26 Ebel (ed.), *Hatzfeldt Papiere*, II, pp. 803 ff.; *Holstein Papers*, III, pp. 365 ff.
27 On the European aspects of Anglo-German relations in the early 1890s, see Lowe, *Salisbury and the Mediterranean*, pp. 54 ff.; T. A. Bayer, *England und der neue Kurs 1890–1895* (Tübingen, 1955), *passim*; W. Herrmann, *Dreibund, Zweibund, England 1890–1895* (Stuttgart, 1929), *passim*; GP, vols. VIII–IX; G. N. Sanderson, 'England, Italy, the Nile valley and the European balance, 1890–91', *Historical Journal*, vol. VII (1964), pp. 94–119; Rich, *Holstein*, I, pp. 328 ff.
28 On this, see again the relevant chapters in GP, vols. VIII and IX; the further correspondence in AA Bonn, London Embassy *Geheim Akten*, packets 396 and 397; and *Holstein Papers*, III, p. 379.
29 Taylor, *Struggle for Mastery in Europe*, p. 339: and, more generally, W. L. Langer, *The Franco-Russian Alliance 1890–1894* (Cambridge, Mass., 1929).
30 AA Bonn, London Embassy *Geheim Akten*, packet 395/1, Hatzfeldt to Holstein, 19/7/1890.
31 Rich, *Holstein*, I, pp. 338, 345.
32 Carroll, *Germany and the Great Powers*, p. 312.
33 Cecil, *Salisbury*, IV, p. 302; and see A. G. Gardiner, *Life of Sir William Harcourt*, 2 vols (London, 1923), II, pp. 124 ff.; and Gross, *Factors and Variations in Liberal and Radical Opinion*, pp. 153–4, on the radical probings about a secret 'deal' with Italy, or the Triple Alliance as a whole.
34 Cecil, *Salisbury*, IV, pp. 374–5, 383–4; Sanderson, 'England, Italy, the Nile valley and the European balance', p. 112 ff.
35 Cecil, *Salisbury*, IV, pp. 367, 371; Balfour, *The Kaiser and his Times*, pp. 122–3; Lord George Hamilton, *Parliamentary Reminiscences and Reflections 1886–1906* (London, 1922), p. 137.
36 QVL, 3rd series, II, p. 65; Graves, *Persia and the Defence of India, passim*.
37 Gillard, *Lord Salisbury's Foreign Policy 1888–92*, p. 246.
38 See the important memo by Raschdau on the advent of the Liberal government, in GP, VIII, no. 1733. For the Gladstone–Rosebery administration, and the internal quarrels on foreign affairs, see: Johnson, *The Role of the Cabinet in the Making of Foreign Policy, passim*; R. Rhodes James, *Rosebery, A Biography* (London, 1963), pp. 253 ff.; Gardiner, *Harcourt*, II, pp. 166 ff.; Stansky, *Ambitions and Strategies, passim*.
39 Rich, *Holstein*, I, pp. 347 ff.; Ebel (ed.), *Hatzfeldt Papiere*, II, pp. 896 ff.; GP, VIII, nos. 1744 ff.
40 GP, VIII, nos. 1753 and 1756; Ebel (ed.), *Hatzfeldt Papiere*, II, pp. 927 ff.; and see also the Marschall diary entries (Schloss Neuershausen) about the Siam episode, 28 July–2 August 1893; Langer, *Diplomacy of Imperialism*, pp. 43 ff.; A. Vagts, 'Wilhelm II and the Siam episode', *American Historical Review*, vol. LXV (1940), pp. 834–41.
41 Ebel (ed.), *Hatzfeldt Papiere*, II, p. 938.
42 ibid., pp. 951, 956; Rich, *Holstein*, II, pp. 354–66; National Library of Scotland, Edinburgh, Rosebery Papers, 10135, Rosebery memos of 1/2/1894 and 14/2/1894; Bridge, *From Sadowa to Sarajevo*, p. 196; Langer, *Diplomacy of Imperialism*, pp. 52–6.
43 The best study of these quarrels is by G. N. Sanderson, 'The African factor in Anglo-German relations, 1892–95' (private paper delivered to the Commonwealth and Overseas Seminar, Cambridge University); but see also M. P. Hornik, 'The Anglo-Belgian agreement of 12 May 1894', *English Historical Review*, vol. 57 (1942), pp. 227–43; and Kennedy, *The Samoan Tangle*, pp. 115–19.
44 Staatsbibliothek, Hamburg, *Nachlass* Kayser, file 16, Hohenlohe-Langenburg to Kayser, 8/9/1893; Schilling, *Radikaler Nationalismus*, pp. 41 ff.
45 J. C. G. Röhl, 'A document of 1892 on Germany, Prussia and Poland', *Historical Journal*,

vol. VII (1964), p. 144; and see Kennedy, *The Samoan Tangle*, p. 112, for Wilhelm's eagerness to obtain Samoa in January 1893.

46 Röhl, *Germany without Bismarck*, ch. 3; Nicholls, *Germany after Bismarck*, chs V–VIII; E. Eyck, *Das persönliches Regiment Wilhelm II . . . 1890 bis 1914* (Erlenbach-Zurich, 1948), chs 2 and 3.

47 Schloss Neuershausen, Marschall diary entry, 30/4/1894; and see his remark in GP, vol. VIII, no. 2024, that Samoa had 'a political importance far beyond its own intrinsic worth'.

48 PRO, FO 343 (Malet Papers)/13, Malet to Kimberley, 16/6/1894; QVL, 3rd series, II, p. 406; and, for Holstein's telegrams, see Ebel (ed.), *Hatzfeldt Papiere*, II, p. 992, fn. 3.

49 Sontag, *Germany and England*, p. 308.

50 Rhodes James, *Rosebery*, pp. 347–52; Gardiner, *Harcourt*, II, pp. 313–23; Johnson, *The Role of the Cabinet in the Making of Foreign Policy*, pp. 261 ff.; Stansky, *Ambitions and Strategies*, pp. 109 ff.

51 Kennedy, *The Samoan Tangle*, pp. 116–19. (Buxton was at that time parliamentary undersecretary at the Colonial Office.)

52 PRO, FO 633 (Cromer Papers)/7, Rosebery to Cromer (print), 22/4/1895.

53 PRO, FO 343 (Malet Papers)/3, Rosebery to Malet, 6/1/1895; and for the threats to Rome and Vienna, see Hornik, 'The Anglo-Belgian agreement . . .', pp. 239–40; Lowe, *Salisbury and the Mediterranean*, pp. 93 ff.; H. Temperley and L. M. Penson, *Foundations of British Foreign Policy from Pitt to Salisbury* (Cambridge, 1938), pp. 491 ff.

54 Quotations from Kennedy, *The Samoan Tangle*, pp. 119–20.

55 Nicholls, *Germany after Bismarck*, p. 375.

56 Kennedy, *The Samoan Tangle*, p. 121; G. W. F. Hallgarten, *Imperialismus vor 1914* 2 vols (Munich, 1951), I, pp. 367 ff.; J. Butler, 'The German factor in Anglo-Transvaal relations', in Gifford and Louis (eds), *Britain and Germany in Africa*, pp. 193 ff.; L. Wolf, *Life of the First Marquess of Ripon*, 2 vols (London, 1921), II, pp. 231 ff.; for West Africa, see BD, I, pp. 322, 327; and B. I. Obichere, *West African States and European Expansion* (New Haven, 1971), pp. 37–41, 174 ff.

57 PRO, FO 343 (Malet Papers)/3, Kimberley to Malet, 5/12/1894; PRO, FO 800/1 (Sanderson Papers), Kimberley to Sanderson, 20/10/1894, demanding that a warship be sent to Delagoa Bay as 'a demonstration of force in the face of the arrogant attitude of Germany'. On the German side, see AA Bonn, London Embassy *Geheim Akten*, packet 398/3, Hatzfeldt to Hohenlohe, no. 271 of 20/11/1894; and Marschall's diary entry (Schloss Neuershausen) for 1/2/1895 on his 'lively' exchange with Malet over South Africa.

58 Sanderson, 'The African factor in Anglo-German relations', p. 1.

59 PRO, CO 225/51, Chamberlain minute on paper 3263, F.O. to C.O., 12/2/1896; and, more generally, Garvin, *Chamberlain*, III, *passim*.

60 Langer, *Diplomacy of Imperialism*, pp. 197 ff.; GP, X, nos. 2372 ff. R. Sontag, 'The Cowes interview and the Kruger Telegram', *Political Science Quarterly*, vol. XL (1925), pp. 217–47; F. Meinecke, *Geschichte des deutsch-englischen Bündnisproblems 1890–1901* (Munich/Berlin, 1927), ch. 3; H. Preller, *Salisbury und die Turkische Frage im Jahre 1895* (Stuttgart, 1930), *passim*.

61 BA Koblenz, *Nachlass* Eulenburg, Bülow to Eulenburg, 25/8/1895; and see also GP, vol. X, nos. 2396 ff.; Rich, *Holstein*, II, pp. 452 ff.; Ebel (ed.), *Hatzfeldt Papiere*, II, pp. 1048 ff.; P. Winzen, *Die Englandpolitik Friedrich von Holsteins 1895–1901* (phil. Diss., Cologne, 1975), pp. 70 ff.

62 J. A. S. Grenville, *Lord Salisbury and Foreign Policy* (London, 1964), pp. 24 ff.

63 J. D. Hargreaves, '*Entente manquée*: Anglo-French relations 1895–1896'; *Cambridge Historical Journal*, vol. XI (1953), pp. 65–92, esp. p. 69; J. A. S. Grenville, 'Goluchowski, Salisbury, and the Mediterranean Agreements, 1895–1897', *Slavonic and East European Review*, vol. XXXVI (1958), pp. 340–69; M. M. Jeffries, 'Lord Salisbury and the Eastern Question 1890–1898', *Slavonic and East European Review*, vol. XXXIX (1960), pp. 44–60; Bridge, *From Sadowa to Sarajevo*, pp. 211–31; Lowe, *Salisbury and the Mediterranean*, ch. V.

64 L. M. Penson, 'The New Course in British foreign policy, 1892–1902', *Transactions of the Royal Historical Society*, 4th series, vol. XXV (1943), pp. 121–38.

65 BA Koblenz, *Nachlass* Bülow, vol. 75, Eulenburg memo of 24/9/1895; GP vol. IX, nos. 2319 ff.

66 Marschall diary entries (Schloss Neuershausen), 14–15/10/1895 and 28/10/1895; PRO, FO 343 (Malet Papers)/3, Gosselin report of 4/11/1895, and Malet to Salisbury (draft), 7/11/1895; Churchill College Archives, Cambridge, Spring-Rice Papers 1/14, Chirol to Lascelles, *very private*, 9/11/1895; Butler, 'The German factor in Anglo-Transvaal relations', pp. 201–2; GP, XI, nos. 2578–84.

67 GP, x, no. 2572; Grenville, *Lord Salisbury and Foreign Policy*, p. 43; and, on Eulenburg's hold over the Kaiser, Hatfield House Archives, Salisbury Papers A120/18, Gosselin (attaché, Berlin) to Salisbury, 29/11/1895; and Röhl (ed.), *Eulenburg Papiere*, introduction.

68 PRO, FO 800/17 (Lascelles Papers), Lascelles's memo on 'Conversation with Lord Salisbury, December 4, 1895'; and see also, QVL, 3rd series, II, p. 583.

69 F. Thimme, 'Die Krüger-Depesche: Genesis und historische Bedeutung', *Europäische Gespräche*, Jg. 2 (1924), pp. 201–44; C. D. Penner, 'Germany and the Transvaal before 1896', *Journal of Modern History*, vol. XII (1940), pp. 31–59; H. Hallmann, *Krügerdepesche und Flottenfrage* (Stuttgart, 1927); Langer, *Diplomacy of Imperialism*, ch. VIII; Lovell, *The Struggle for South Africa*, ch. IX; Rich, *Holstein*, II, pp. 466 ff.; GP, XI, nos 2587 ff.

70 Butler, 'The German factor in Anglo-Transvaal relations', p. 197; Robinson and Gallagher, *Africa and the Victorians*, pp. 419–20.

71 Carroll, *Germany and the Great Powers*, pp. 364 ff.; Hale, *Publicity and Diplomacy*, ch. V; Anon., *History of the Times*, III, pp. 150–3, 257–71; V. Chirol, *Fifty Years in a Changing World* (London, 1927), pp. 278 ff.; Langer, *Diplomacy of Imperialism*, pp. 240 ff.

72 GP, XI, no. 2636.

73 Geiss, *German Foreign Policy*, pp. 80 ff.; Carroll, *Germany and the Great Powers*, pp. 348 ff.

74 W. Görlitz (ed.), *Der Kaiser* . . . (Göttingen, 1965), pp. 37–41; Hollyday, *Bismarck's Rival*, pp. 258, 273; J. Steinberg, *Yesterday's Deterrent* (London, 1965), pp. 82–96; V. R. Berghahn, *Der Tirpitz-Plan* (Düsseldorf, 1971), pp. 82 ff., 173 ff. A. von Tirpitz, *My Memoirs*, 2 vols (London, 1919), I, pp. 62–3.

75 For details of the plan, see P. M. Kennedy, 'The development of German naval operations plans against England, 1896–1914', *English Historical Review*, vol. LXXXIX (1974), pp. 48 ff.; and I. Lambi, 'Die Operationspläne der Kaiserlichen Marine bis zur Auf lösung des Oberkommandos in europäischen Gewässern im Jahr 1899', in J. Hütter, R. Meyers and D. Papenfuss (eds), *Tradition und Neubeginn* (Cologne, 1975), pp. 42 ff.

76 Hatfield House Archives, Salisbury Papers A122/5, Salisbury to Lascelles, 22/1/1896.

77 HHSt.A Vienna, PA III/147, Szögyeny to Goluchowski, IB Vertr., 4/1/1896.

78 For Anglo-German relations in 1896–early 1897, see Rich, *Holstein*, II, pp. 472 ff.; Ebel (ed.), *Hatzfeldt Papiere*, II, pp. 1076 ff.; GP, vols XI–XIII.

79 Hatfield House Archives, Salisbury Papers A122/6, Salisbury to Lascelles, 10/3/1896; PRO, FO 633 (Cromer Papers)/6, Cromer to Salisbury (print), 27/3/1896; Sanderson, *England, Europe and the Upper Nile*, pp. 224–50; GP, XI, nos. 2277 ff.; Rich, *Holstein*, II, pp. 474–6.

## CHAPTER 13

1 See especially here Röhl, *Germany without Bismarck*, pp. 241 ff.; Berghahn, *Der Tirpitz-Plan*, pp. 11 ff.; idem, *Germany and the Approach of War in 1914* (London, 1973), chs 1–2; D. Stegmann, *Die Erben Bismarcks* (Cologne/Berlin, 1970), pp. 63 ff.; Taylor, *Struggle for Mastery in Europe*, ch. XVII; P. M. Kennedy, 'German world policy and the alliance negotiations with England, 1897–1900', *Journal of Modern History*, vol. 45 (1973), pp. 605–25. For valuable reflections upon this 'orthodoxy', see the various articles by G. Eley, including 'Defining social imperialism: use and abuse of an idea', *Social History*, no. 3 (1976), pp. 265–90, and those in note 15 below.

2 This memo is reproduced in full in Steinberg, op. cit., pp. 208–21; and see the analysis in H. Hallmann, *Der Weg zum deutschen Schlachtflottenbau* (Stuttgart, 1933), pp. 238–64; Berghahn, *Der Tirpitz-Plan*, pp. 109 ff.

3 J. Rohwer, 'Kriegsschiffbau und Flottengesetze um die Jahrhundertwende', in H. Schottelius and W. Deist (eds), *Marine und Marinepolitik im kaiserlichen Deutschland 1871–1914* (Düsseldorf, 1972), pp. 211–35; W. Hubatsch, *Die Aera Tirpitz* (Göttingen, 1955), pp. 65 ff.; idem, *Kaiserliche Marine* (private print?, 1975), pt I.

4 Württembergisches Hauptstaatsarchiv, Stuttgart, *Gesandtschaftsakten* (Berlin) 123, Varnbüler to Mittnacht, 5/11/1897.

5 P. Winzen, 'Prince Bülow's *Weltmachtpolitik*', *Australian Journal of Politics and History*, vol. XXII (1976), pp. 227–8 and *passim*.

6 BA Koblenz, *Nachlass* Bülow, vol. 151 (Merkbuch D/168); V. R. Berghahn, 'Zu den Zielen des deutschen Flottenbaues unter Wilhelm II.', *Historische Zeitschrift*, 201 (1970), p. 85.

7 B. von Bülow, *Deutsche Politik* (Berlin, 1916), p. 30.

8 BA Koblenz, *Nachlass* Eulenburg, 39, Bülow to Eulenburg, 27/12/1895; Friedrichsruh Archives, *Nachlass* Bismarck, B 26, Bülow to Herbert Bismarck, 1/9/1886 (and see also the earlier letter of 9/12/1884, in ibid.).

9 B. von Bülow, *Denkwürdigkeiten*, 4 vols (Berlin, 1930), I, p. 116.

10 BA Koblenz, *Nachlass* Bülow, vol. 154, notes of 1900; and, more generally, P. Winzen, *Bülow's Weltmachtkonzept* (Boppard a.R., 1977), and B. Vogel, *Deutsche Russlandpolitik 1900–1906* (Düsseldorf, 1973).

11 Röhl, *Germany without Bismarck*, pp. 251–8; Berghahn, *Der Tirpitz-Plan, passim*; W. Deist, *Flottenpolitik und Flottenpropaganda* (Stuttgart, 1976); and see also the useful dissertation by J. Meyer, *Die Propaganda der deutschen Flottenbewegung, 1897–1900* (phil. Diss., Berne, 1967).

12 BA Koblenz, *Nachlass* Bülow, vol. 106, Monts to Bülow, 20/6/1895.

13 Holstein's remark about the Kaiser's government needing 'a tangible success' is now frequently quoted out of context (e.g. Wehler, 'Bismarck's imperialism', p. 152). The complete letter, to Kiderlen, of 30/4/1897 can be seen in BA Koblenz, *Nachlass* Bülow, vol. 92 (copy), and has to be read in connection with Holstein's fears that Britain would soon take over the Transvaal without regard for German feelings, thereby provoking the Kaiser into the dispatch of troops or some other reckless action which might easily lead to an Anglo-German war, in the course of which France might seize her opportunity for the *revanche*: see ibid., vol. 90, Holstein to Bülow, 31/3/1897 and 5/4/1897; and GP, XIII, no. 3404. For Holstein's later worries about diverting internal problems outwards, see BA Koblenz, *Nachlass* Bülow, vol. 90, Holstein to Bülow, 9/6/1897; *Holstein Papers*, IV, pp. 46–7; H. Rogge (ed.), *Friedrich von Holstein Lebensbekenntnis* (Berlin, 1932), p. 185.

14 The classic argument along these lines is by Eckart Kehr. See especially the now-translated articles in *Economic Interest, Militarism, and Foreign Policy*, chs I–II.

15 G. Eley, 'Sammlungspolitik, social imperialism and the Navy Law of 1898', *Militärgeschichtliche Mitteilungen*, 1/1974, pp. 29–63; idem, 'Reshaping the Right: radical nationalism and the German Navy League, 1898–1908', *Historical Journal*, vol. XXI (1978), pp. 327–54.

16 National Library of Scotland, Edinburgh, MS. 10243 (Rosebery–Kimberley Correspondence), Rosebery to Kimberley, 28/4/1895. For general surveys of Britain's world position at the end of the nineteenth century, see Grenville, op. cit., *passim*; Porter, *The Lion's Share*, chs IV–V; Kennedy, *British Naval Mastery*, chs 7–8; M. Howard, *The Continental Commitment* (Harmondsworth, Middlesex, 1974), ch. I; M. Beloff, *Imperial Sunset*, vol. 1, *Britain's Liberal Empire 1897–1921* (London, 1969), chs II–III.

17 Amery, *Chamberlain*, IV, p. 421; B.D., III, p. 430.

18 Hargreaves, '*Entente Manquée . . .*', p. 69; and see also A. W. Palmer, 'Lord Salisbury's approach to Russia, 1898', *Oxford Slavonic Papers*, 6 (1955), pp. 102–14.

19 Taylor, *Struggle for Mastery in Europe*, pp. 370 ff.; Bridge, *Sadowa to Sarajevo*, pp. 231 ff.

20 For Spenser Wilkinson, see Howard, *Britain and the Casus Belli*, pp. 135–9, and Hollenberg, *Englisches Interesse am Kaiserreich*, pp. 33–7. For Currie, Sanderson and Hamilton, see Greaves, *Persia and the Defence of India*, pp. 220–2.

21 For Cabinet members' views of a German alliance, see the books by Grenville, Monger and Winzen, and also J. M. Goudswaard, *Some Aspects of the End of Britain's 'Splendid Isolation', 1898–1904* (Rotterdam, 1952).

22 See below, pp. 291 ff.

23 Quoted from the British notice of denunciation, 30/7/1897, copy in DZA Potsdam, AAHP, 9340.

24 Wilhelm's comments are in GP, XIII, nos. 3413–14. For the general background, see Anderson, *Anti-English Feeling in Germany*, pp. 272–4. PRO, FO 64/1435, Gough to Salisbury, no. 188 Commercial of 4/8/1897, contains a survey of W. S. H. Gastrell (Commercial Attaché) of German press reactions to the denunciation.

25 Churchill College Archives, Cambridge, Spring-Rice Papers 1/18, Spring-Rice to Chirol, 17/7/1897; and see also PRO, FO 800/170 (Bertie Papers), Spring-Rice to Bertie, 17/7/1897, and S. Gwynn, *The Letters and Friendships of Sir Cecil Spring-Rice*, 2 vols (London, 1929), I, pp. 235–44.

26 *The Times* Archives, London, Saunders Papers, Saunders to Mackenzie Wallace, 8/3/1897; and see also his letter of 21/11/1897 to Chirol, in ibid., on the purpose of the second Navy Law being 'ultimately to get a "staatserhaltend" majority for reactionary legislation'.

27 Salisbury to Goschen, 6/9/1897, quoted in the unpublished vol. 5 of Cecil's *Salisbury*, p. 239. There is a copy of Spring-Rice's letter to Bertie (see note 25 above) in the Salisbury Papers, A120/100. For the Prime Minister's fears about a German acquisition of Holland, see Lord Newton, *Lord Landsdowne* (London, 1929), pp. 145–6.

28 *Holstein Papers*, IV, p. 50. See also Langer, *Diplomacy of Imperialism*, pp. 448–51; Steinberg, *Yesterday's Deterrent*, pp. 154–5; A. Harding Ganz, *The Role of the Imperial German Navy in Colonial Affairs* (Ph.D. thesis, Ohio State University, 1972), pp. 76–134; idem, 'The German navy in the Far East and Pacific: the seizure of Kiautschou and after', in Moses and Kennedy (eds), *Germany in the Pacific and Far East*, pp. 115–36.

29 Niedersächsisches Hauptstaatsarchiv, Hanover, *Nachlass* Münster, vol. IX, Hohenlohe to Münster, 9/12/1897; Badisches Generallandesarchiv, Karlsruhe, Abt. 233, Fasz. 34803, Jagemann to Brauer, no. 193 of 29/11/1897; Röhl, *Germany without Bismarck*, p. 252.

30 Letter to *The Times*, 30/3/1898; and, more generally, L. K. Young, *British Policy in China 1895–1902* (Oxford, 1970), pp. 65 ff.; Grenville, op. cit., pp. 143 ff.; Langer, *Diplomacy of Imperialism*, ch. XIV.

31 ibid., ch. XV; Grenville, op. cit., pp. 148–76; Garvin, *Chamberlain*, III, pp. 251 ff.; Meinecke, *Geschichte des deutsch-englischen Bündnisproblems*, pp. 85–114; H. W. Koch, 'The Anglo-German alliance negotiations: missed opportunity or myth?, *History*, vol. LIV (1969), pp. 378–92.

32 AA Bonn, *Deutschland 148 Geheim*, vol. 1, Hatzfeldt to Hohenlohe, no. 394 of 12/5/1898; GP, XIV, pt I, p. 230.

33 See the various clauses of Chamberlain's rough 'Notes for Agreement' (June 1898?), in Birmingham University Library, JC 7/2/2A/25.

34 Garvin, *Chamberlain*, III, pp. 274–5; GP, XIV, pt I, no. 3793. See also Chamberlain's later threat, in ibid., XVII, no. 4979.

35 ibid., no. 3790. For another good expression of Bülow's 'free hand' theory, see his closing remarks in ibid., pt II, no. 3920.

36 ibid., pt I, nos 3803–904; Rich, *Holstein*, II, pp. 582–5.

37 *Deutsche Zeitung*, 8/4/1898; Badisches Generallandesarchiv, Karlsruhe, Abt. 233, Fasz. 34804, Jagenow to Brauer, nos. 55 of 28/4/1898 and 84 of 17/6/1898; AA Bonn, *Deutschland 167*, memos on the Spanish, Portuguese and Danish colonies; Kennedy, *The Samoan Tangle*, pp. 138–9; Herwig, *Politics of Frustration*, pp. 24 ff.; Ganz, 'Colonial policy and the Imperial German Navy', pp. 44–6.

38 GP, XIV, pt I, no. 1; no. 3806 and enclosure; and Ebel (ed.), *Hatzfeldt Papiere*, II, pp. 1167–8. For the Anglo-German negotiations over Portuguese Africa as a whole, see Grenville, op. cit., ch. VIII; Langer, *Diplomacy of Imperialism*, pp. 520–9; Rich, *Holstein*, II, pp. 586–7.

39 See AA Bonn, *England 78 nr. 1 Secr.*, vol. 4, Kaiser's minute on Richthofen to Eulenburg, no. 22 of 20/7/1898 (and compare with GP, XIV, pt I, no. 3835).

40 BD, I, nos. 122–5; GP, XIV, pt I, nos. 3865–7; Grenville, op. cit., pp. 173–6; Koch, op. cit., pp. 305–6.

41 Grenville, op. cit., pp. 197–8, 260–2; BD, I, nos. 99–100; *Holstein Papers*, IV, p. 141; P. R. Warhurst, *Anglo-Portuguese Relations in South-Central Africa 1890–1900* (London, 1962), pp. 144–5. For Chamberlain's views, see especially Ebel (ed.), *Hatzfeldt Papiere*, II, p. 1183.

42 BA Koblenz, *Nachlass* Richthofen, vol. 5, Bülow to Richthofen, 4/10/1898; AA Bonn, *England 78 nr. 1 Secr.*, vol. 9, Kaiser's comment on Tattenbach (Lisbon) to Hohenlohe, no. 99 of 24/9/1898; ibid., vol. 10, *Deutsche Kolonial-Gesellschaft* to Hohenlohe, 3/10/1898.

43 Herwig, *Politics of Frustration*, pp. 28–33; Vagts, *Deutschland und die Vereinigten Staaten*, II, ch. XII; Carroll, *Germany and the Great Powers*, pp. 411–18.

44 Kennedy, *The Samoan Tangle*, p. 125.
45 ibid., p. 157.
46 GP, XIV, pt II, marginal comment on no. 3938; W. Goetz (ed.), *Briefe Wilhelms II. an den Zaren 1894–1914* (Berlin, 1920), pp. 63–8.
47 B.M. Add. MSS 49611 (Balfour Papers), Salisbury to Balfour, 9/4/1898; Hatfield House Archives, Salisbury Papers, Class F, Victoria to Salisbury, 21/1/1899 and 1/2/1899; QVL, 3rd series, III, pp. 340–1; PRO, FO 64/1469, Lascelles to Salisbury, no. 13, secret, of 20/1/1899; PRO, FO 800/9 (Lascelles Papers), Sanderson to Lascelles, 25/1/1899.
48 AA Bonn, *Deutschland 137 Secr.*, vol. 2, Bülow to A.A., no. 201 of 22/11/1898.
49 Hale, *Publicity and Diplomacy*, p. 192; and generally, Kennedy, *The Samoan Tangle*.
50 AA Bonn, *Südsee-Inseln 5*, vol. 2, Bülow to A.A., tel. no. 1 of 29/3/1899.
51 ibid., vol. 6, A.A. to Mumm (Washington), tel. no. 167 of 5/11/1899.
52 Hatfield House Archives, Salisbury Papers A122/70, Hatzfeldt to Salisbury, private and confidential, 14/9/1899.
53 Heinrich-Schnee-Archiv (located in the GSA, Berlin-Dahlem), no. 52–60, Schmidt-Dargitz to Schnee, 12/11/1899. (I am grateful to Dr S. Firth for this reference.)
54 *Holstein Papers*, IV, p. 118, fn. 3.
55 BA Koblenz, *Nachlass* Richthofen, vol. 5, Bülow to Richthofen, secret, 26/7/1899.
56 AA Bonn, *England 78 nr. 1 Secr.*, vol. 13, Bülow to Richthofen, no. 104, top secret, of 11/9/1899; BA-MA Freiburg, F 5174a, III.1.15., vol. 1, *Admiralstab* memos of 12/9/1899 and 14/9/1899; Winzen, *Bülows Weltmachtkonzept*, pp. 282 ff.
57 Kennedy, *The Samoan Tangle*, pp. 228–38.
58 This is best analysed in Winzen, op. cit., pp. 220–30.
59 GP, XV, no. 4394.
60 AA Bonn, *England 78*, vol. 12, Wilhelm's minute on Tschirschky to A.A., no. 195 of 27/10/1899; GP, XV, Bülow footnote on pp. 414–15.
61 Foreign Office Library, London, Holstein Papers, vol. 60, Monts to Holstein, 3/11/1899 and 14/12/1899.
62 AA Bonn, *Deutschland 138*, vol. 12, Bülow to Hammann and Esternaux, 31/12/1899.
63 P. M. Kennedy, 'Tirpitz, England and the second Navy Law of 1900: a strategical critique', *Militärgeschichtliche Mitteilungen*, 2/1970, pp. 34, 39–40; Meyer, *Die Propaganda der deutschen Flottenbewegung*, pp. 140 ff.
64 Berghahn, 'Zu den Zielen . . .', pp. 67–8.
65 BA Koblenz, *Nachlass* Bülow, vol. 24, draft of speeches to the Reichstag Budget Commission, 27/4/1900 and 28/3/1900. (These references to the possibility of war were omitted from Bülow's published version: see *Denkwürdigkeiten*, I, pp. 414–15.)
66 HHSt.A Vienna, PA III/153, Szögyeny to Goluchowski, nos. 6 A-B and 7 of 5/2/1900 and 14/2/1900 respectively.
67 Kennedy, *The Samoan Tangle*, p. 235 and ch. 5, *passim*.
68 Hale, *Publicity and Diplomacy*, p. 210, fn. 52; Carroll, *Germany and the Great Powers*, p. 444; *The Times* Archives, London, Foreign Letter Book, 4, Chirol to Lavino (copy), 3/11/1899, and Chirol to Saunders (copies) of 27/10/1899 and 24/11/1899.
69 Marder, *Anatomy of British Sea Power*, p. 377; and see more generally, I. F. Clarke, *Voices Prophesying War 1763–1984* (London, 1970 edn), pp. 137 ff.
70 G. L. Monger, *The End of Isolation* (London, 1963), pp. 15–20; Grenville, op. cit., pp. 310–18; Young, *British Policy in China*, pp. 100 ff.; J. D. Hargreaves, 'Lord Salisbury, British isolation and the Yangtse valley, June–September 1900', *Bulletin of the Institute of Historical Research*, vol. 30 (1957), pp. 62–75.
71 BA-MA Freiburg, *Nachlass* Tirpitz, N 253/20, Tirpitz to Prince Heinrich, 14/7/1900; and see also Eulenburg's report to Bülow of 1/10/1900 on Tirpitz's fear of England in Bülow, *Denkwürdigkeiten*, I, p. 461.
72 Württembergisches Hauptstaatsarchiv, Stuttgart, *Gesandtschaftsakten* (Berlin) 12e, Varnbüler to Soden, no. 1308 of 17/11/1900; GSA Berlin-Dahlem, Hohenzollern *Hausarchiv*, Rep. 53, no. a63, Wilhelm to Eulenburg, 17/8/1900.
73 Germany's China policy (and its ambitions in the Yangtse) can be detected in AA Bonn, *China 20 nr. 1 Secr.*, vol. 59, Bülow to Heyking, no. 14 of 28/2/1899; ibid., Wilhelm's comments on Lichnowsky's private letter (from Shanghai), 24/1/1899; and Metternich's letter of 19/8/1900,

reproduced in Bülow, *Denkwürdigkeiten*, I, p. 367. See generally, K. Kawai, 'Anglo-German rivalry in the Yangtze region, 1895–1902', *Pacific Historical Review*, vol. 8 (1939), pp. 413–34.

74 Geheimes Staatsarchiv, Munich, *Gesandtschaftsakten* 1072, Lerchenfeld to Crailsheim, no. 499 of 2/11/1900.

75 Langer, *Diplomacy of Imperialism*, pp. 702–3.

76 BA Koblenz, *Nachlass* Eulenburg, vol. 57, Eulenburg to Bülow, 16/2/1901.

77 The best discussion of Bülow's attitude is in Winzen, op. cit., pp. 296 ff. For the pro-Boer demonstrations of this time, see AA Bonn, *Afrika Gen. 13 nr. 2d;* HHSt.A Vienna, PA III/154, Szögyeny to Goluchowski, no. 58 F of 4/12/1900; U. Kröll, *Die internationale Buren-Agitation 1899–1902* (Münster, 1973), *passim;* Hale, *Publicity and Diplomacy*, pp. 193 ff.; Schilling, *Radikaler Nationalismus*, pp. 116 ff.

78 Monger, *The End of Isolation*, p. 29; Young, *British Policy in China*, pp. 193 ff.; BD, II, nos. 32–8; Taylor, *Struggle for Mastery in Europe*, pp. 392–5; I. H. Nish, *The Anglo-Japanese Alliance* (London, 1966), ch. V.

79 Monger, op. cit., pp. 30 ff.

80 HHSt.A Vienna, PA III/155, Szögyeny to Goluchowski, no. 10, very conf., 6/3/1901; Rich, *Holstein*, II, pp. 626–77; Winzen, *Holsteins Englandpolitik*, pp. 371–88; Grenville, op. cit., p. 335.

81 For what follows, see especially Winzen, *Bülows Weltmachtkonzept*, pp. 293 ff.

82 *Holstein Papers*, I, p. 183. Holstein's hope for a future alliance with England – despite Salisbury's obstructionism – can also be clearly seen in Ebel (ed.), *Hatzfeldt Papiere*, II, pp. 1308 ff.

83 Winzen, *Bülows Weltmachtkonzept*, p. 350.

84 B.M. Add. MSS 59554 (E. Wrench Papers), diary entries for 27/2/1900, 4/3/1900 and 9/6/1900.

85 Friedrichsruh Archives, *Nachlass* Bismarck, B 97, Rosebery to H. Bismarck, 24/2/1901 (the reply to which is in Bussmann (ed.), *Staatssekretär Herbert von Bismarck*, p. 583); HHSt.A Vienna, PA VIII/126, Mensdorff to Goluchowski, 12/11/1901; GP, XVII, P. 151 fn.

86 Birmingham University Library, Joseph Chamberlain Papers JC 11/2/1–5. On the Athenaeum's display, see *Holstein Papers*, IV, p. 243.

87 GP, XV, no. 4398; *History of the Times*, III, pp. 305–8; Hale, *Publicity and Diplomacy*, pp. 205–10; and see the anonymous criticism of Hale (probably by Morison, the author of *The Times* history?), entitled 'Saunders' Berlin Despatches, October to December, 1899', n.d., in *The Times* Archives, London, Saunders Papers.

88 *Daily Chronicle*, 4/1/1902, as enclosed in AA Bonn, London Embassy records, packet 216/2, vol. 4, Eckardstein to Bülow, no. 8 of 7/1/1902. For the *Spectator* quotation, see its issue of 1/4/1900; Hale, op. cit., ch. IX.

89 L. S. Amery Papers (private hands), C 18, Chirol to Amery, 19/1/1900.

90 AA Bonn, *England 69*, vol. 35, Eckardstein to Bülow, no. 16 of 8/1/1901, enclosing Calchas's article – with Wilhelm's minute thereon; Langer, *Diplomacy of Imperialism*, pp. 426, 726, 753; Marder, *Anatomy of British Sea Power*, pp. 288–301, 456–64; Carroll, *Germany and the Great Powers*, p. 430.

91 West Sussex Record Office, Chichester, Maxse Papers, 447, H. W. Wilson to Maxse, 4/3/1900.

92 Monger, op. cit., p. 11.

93 Amery, *Chamberlain*, IV, pp. 162–76; C. D. Penner, 'The Bülow-Chamberlain recriminations of 1900–1901', *The Historian*, vol. 5 (1943), pp. 97–109; F. Thimme, 'Der Ausklang der deutsch-englischen Bündnisverhandlungen 1901', *Berliner Monatshefte*, vol. 16 (1938), pp. 540–56.

94 Cited in Winzen, *Bülows Weltmachtkonzept*, pp. 376–86.

95 Geheimes Staatsarchiv, Munich, Berliner *Gesandtschaftsakten* 1074, Lerchenfeld to Crailsheim (draft), no. 153 of 21/3/1902; AA Bonn, *England 94 nr. 1*, vol. 1, Bülow to *Auswärtiges Amt*, 14/2/1902; ibid., *China 29 secr.*, vol. 1, Kaiser's marginalia on Radolin's report no. 204 of 21/3/1902.

96 For this debate, see C. Howard, 'The policy of isolation', *Historical Journal*, vol. X (1967), pp. 77–88; idem, *Splendid Isolation* (London, 1967); Taylor, *Struggle for Mastery in Europe*, p. 400; Lowe, *Reluctant Imperialists*, I, pp. 248–51.

97 For general reactions to the treaty, see Nish, *The Anglo-Japanese Alliance*, pp. 224–6; Langer, *Diplomacy of Imperialism*, pp. 779–84. For the Liberal Imperialists, see H. C. G. Matthew, *The Liberal Imperialists* (Oxford, 1973), p. 208. For the Admiralty, see Z. S. Steiner, 'Great Britain and the creation of the Anglo-Japanese alliance', *Journal of Modern History*, vol. XXXI (1959), pp. 29–31. For Balfour's comments, see Monger, op. cit., pp. 63–5.

98 BD, II, no. 94; Thimme, 'Der Ausklang . . .', p. 556; Winzen, *Bülows Weltmachtkonzept*, pp. 347–8, esp. fn. 213; F.-C. Stahl, *Botschafter Graf Wolff Metternich und die deutsch-englischen Beziehungen* (phil. Diss., Hamburg, 1951), pp. 85–8, and A 139–44.

99 C. Andrew, *Théophile Delcassé and the Making of the Entente Cordiale* (London, 1968), pp. 93–179.

## CHAPTER 14

1 Marder, *Anatomy of British Sea Power*, pp. 296–301, 463 ff.

2 Bodleian Library, Oxford, Selborne Papers, 143, Kerr to Selborne, 7/5/1901; PRO, Adm. 116/900 B, Confidential Memorandum on the Strategic Conditions governing the Coast Defences of the United Kingdom in War as affected by Naval Considerations, March 1902. For a general consideration of this point, see Kennedy, 'Maritime Strategieprobleme der deutsch-englischen Flottenrivalität', in Schottelius and Deist (eds), *Marine und Marinepolitik im kaiserlichen Deutschland*, pp. 178–210; R. F. Mackay, *Fisher of Kilverstone* (Oxford, 1973), pp. 237–8.

3 Bodleian Library, Oxford, Selborne Papers, 158, Custance memo, 19/12/1900; ibid., Kerr to Selborne, 24/9/1901, enclosing Custance memo of the same date.

4 Monger, *The End of Isolation*, pp. 11, 69–70, 82–3; Bodleian Library, Oxford, Selborne Papers, 158, Custance to Selborne, 2/4/1902, enclosing 'A further statement relative to the German Battle Ships'.

5 ibid., Sandars Papers, MSS. Eng. Hist. c 735, Selborne to Sandars, 16/4/1902; ibid., Selborne Papers, 31, Kerr to Selborne, 11/3/1902, 6/4/1902 and 28/4/1902; ibid., 158, Kerr to Selborne, 28/5/1902, encl. 'Memorandum on the Strategic Position in the North Sea', by Custance.

6 B.M. Add. MSS. 50287 (Arnold-Foster Papers), 'Notes on a Visit to Kiel and Wilhelmshaven, August 1902', and remarks on it by Kerr, Watts (Director of Naval Ordnance) and Custance; Bodleian Library, Oxford, Selborne Papers, 31, Kerr to Selborne, 3/10/1902; Marder, *Anatomy of British Sea Power*, pp. 463–4.

7 Bodleian Library, Oxford, Sandars Papers, MSS. Eng. Hist. c 736, Selborne to Balfour, 12/7/1902; Birmingham University Library, Austen Chamberlain Papers AC 16/6/3, Appendix B (by Selborne) to the printed Cabinet report on 'The Morgan Shipping Combination', 6/8/1902; Bodleian Library, Oxford, Selborne Papers, 44, Selborne to Battenberg, 27/4/1904.

8 For what follows, see J. Gooch, *The Plans of War. The General Staff and British Military Strategy, c.1900–1916* (London/New York, 1974), chs 6 and 9; S. R. Williamson, *The Politics of Grand Strategy: Britain and France Prepare for War, 1904–1914* (Cambridge, Mass., 1969), pp. 21 ff.; Howard, *The Continental Commitment*, chs 1–2; N. W. Summerton, *The Development of British Military Planning for a War against Germany, 1904–1914* (Ph.D. thesis, London, 1970), *passim*.

9 PRO, WO 106/46, memo by Lawrence of 18/1/1902, with Robertson's notes attached; W. R. Robertson, *Soldiers and Statesmen 1914–1918*, 2 vols (London/New York, 1926), I, pp. 20–3.

10 PRO, WO 106/44, 'Provision of Land Forces for the Defence of the United Kingdom', secret, 14/2/1903; PRO 30/40 (Ardagh Papers)/3, H. W. W. McAnally to Ardagh, 21/5/1903; Ritter, *The Sword and the Sceptre*, II, pp. 61–2, and, in general, J. McDermott, 'The revolution in British military thinking from the Boer War to the Moroccan crisis', *Canadian Journal of History*, vol. IX (1974), pp. 159–77.

11 Cambridge University Library, Hardinge MSS., 3, Spring-Rice to Hardinge, 7/3/1900; Churchill College Archives, Cambridge, Spring-Rice Papers 1/19, Spring-Rice to Chirol, 20/1/1902; and, more generally, Gwynn (ed.), *Spring-Rice*, I, pp. 345–6, 350–1.

12 Horace Rumbold, Sen. Papers (private hands), Rumbold to the Empress Frederick (copy), 8/10/1900, and Drummond Wolff to Rumbold, 1/11/1902; M. Gilbert, *Sir Horace Rumbold* (London, 1973), pp. 35–6, 45–6.

13 B.M. Add. MSS. 50073 (Curzon-Brodrick Correspondence), Curzon to Brodrick, 8/1/1900.
14 West Sussex Record Office, Chichester, Maxse Papers, 448, Hardinge to Maxse, very private, 16/10/1901.
15 For examples of Bertie's mistrust, see PRO, FO 800/170 (Bertie Papers), Bertie memo of 5/9/1900; Churchill College Archives, Cambridge, Spring-Rice Papers 1/2, Bertie to Spring-Rice, 26/12/1902; Hatfield House Archives, Cranborne (4th Marquess of Salisbury) Papers, 52/164, Bertie to Cranborne, 30/6/1903.
16 On this important development as a whole, see Monger, *End of Isolation*, pp. 19, 65, 99–103; but especially Steiner, *The Foreign Office and Foreign Policy 1898–1914*, pp. 61 ff.
17 Quoted in Steiner, op. cit., p. 67.
18 H. Lutz, *Eyre Crowe, der Böse Geist des Foreign Office* (Stuttgart, 1931).
19 West Sussex Record Office, Chichester, Maxse Papers, 450, Crowe to Maxse, 15/10/1902.
20 WO 106/46, 'Memorandum of the Military Policy to be adopted in a War with Germany', by Altham, 10/2/1903.
21 Bodleian Library, Oxford, Selborne Papers, 31, Kerr to Selborne, 28/4/1902; Marder, *Anatomy of British Sea Power*, p. 463.
22 See, for example, Churchill College Archives, Cambridge, Spring-Rice Papers 1/19, Spring-Rice to Chirol, 13/12/1902; Amery, *Chamberlain*, IV, pp. 179 ff.
23 This emerges from the Spring-Rice Papers 1/14, Chirol to Lascelles, 18/4/1902; and West Sussex Record Office, Maxse Papers, 450, J. Chamberlain to Maxse, 16/4/1902, with pencil note on reverse.
24 Bodleian Library, Oxford, Selborne Papers, 30, Balfour to Selborne, 5/4/1902; and for Lansdowne, see PRO, FO 800/11 (Lascelles Papers), Lansdowne to Lascelles, 22/4/1902.
25 HHSt.A Vienna, PA VIII/128, Deym to Goluchowski, no. 7 of 31/1/1902; ibid., PA III/157, Szögyeny to Goluchowski, private, 29/1/1902; Monger, op. cit., pp. 67–8; Lee, *Edward VII*, II, pp. 116–54.
26 PRO, FO 800/9 (Lascelles Papers), Sanderson to Lascelles, 5/12/1896.
27 Newton, *Lansdowne*, pp. 255–61; BD, II, pp. 153 ff.
28 On the Rumbold 'affair', see: West Sussex Record Office, Chichester, Maxse Papers, various Rumbold letters to Maxse of November and December 1902; Rumbold Papers (private hands), Rumbold to his son, 12/12/1902 and 4/1/1903; B.M. Add. MSS. 49727 (Balfour Papers), H. Verney to Sandars, 8/11/1902, reporting Lansdowne's intended measures against the ex-ambassador.
29 West Sussex Record Office, Chichester, Maxse Papers, 450, Saunders to Maxse, 4/11/1902; and see also HoLRO, Strachey Papers S/10/5/15, B. Mallet to Strachey, 11/11/1902, on the Germans being 'thoroughly alarmed'.
30 AA Bonn, *England 78 Secr.*, vol. 5, Bülow to Wilhelm, 30/10/1901, encl. Metternich's report no. 453 of 29/10/1901; GP, XVII, nos. 5343–6.
31 *Holstein Papers*, IV, pp. 269–70.
32 DZA Potsdam, *Nachlass* Hammann, vol. 7, Bülow to Hammann, late March 1902.
33 ibid., Bülow to Hammann, 23/6/1902 and 24/6/1902; GP, XVII, nos. 5084–6.
34 Staatsarchiv, Hamburg, *Gesandtschaftsakten* A IVc 6, vol. IX (1902), Klugmann to Burchard, no. 208 of 1/8/1902; GP, XVII, no. 5101 (minute on).
35 National Maritime Museum, Greenwich, Arnold White Papers, 8, typed extract from White's letter to F.A.W., 5/6/1902; for Saunders, see again *History of The Times*, vol. 3, pp. 363 ff.; *The Times* Archives, London, Chirol Papers, Box II, Chirol to Moberley Bell, 18/6/1902.
36 AA Bonn, London Embassy *Geheim-Akten*, packet 406/3, Bülow to Metternich, tel. no. 296 of 26/12/1902; DZA Potsdam, *Nachlass* Hammann, vol. 3, Bernstorff to Hammann, 15/12/1903.
37 BA-MA Freiburg, F 7223, PG 69122, Coerper to R.M.A., no. 574 of 31/10/1901; ibid., F 7182, PG 68917, same to same, no. 96 of 3/2/1902, with Tirpitz's minute thereon.
38 GP, XVII, no. 5031; and see AA Bonn, *England 78 Secr.*, vol. 6, for the original draft of Bülow's reply, which specifically referred to this question of Germany's naval weakness, but was omitted from the final version of GP, XVII, no. 5032.
39 BA-MA Freiburg, *Nachlass* Tirpitz, N 253/16, Prince Heinrich to Tirpitz, 5/10/1903.
40 BA Koblenz, *Nachlass* Bülow, vol. 22, Bülow to Richthofen, 24/9/1902; AA Bonn, London Embassy *Geheim-Akten*, packet 406/3, Metternich to Bülow, no. 313, secret, of 11/7/1902, and Muhlberg's reply (for Bülow), no. 655, secret, of 17/7/1902.

41 Berghahn, 'Zu den Zielen . . .', p. 68.
42 BA-MA Freiburg, F 7590 (*Nachlass* Hollweg), vol. 5, Tirpitz instruction of 14/10/1902, and typescript draft of *Der Krieg mit England 19* . . .; AA Bonn, *England 78 Secr.*, vol. 6, Tirpitz to Richthofen, top secret, 30/1/1903, and reply of 17/2/1903. There are further details about this curious manoeuvre in BA-MA Freiburg, F 2244, PG 94040 (for which reference I am grateful to Dr G. Eley); and Deist, *Flottenpolitik und Flottenpropaganda*, pp. 170–1.
43 BA-MA Freiburg, F 2044, PG 66075, A.A. to R.M.A., secret, 9/1/1903; and see generally, H. H. Herwig and J. L. Helguera, *Alemania y el bloqueo internacional de Venezuela 1902/03* (Caracas, 1977), and E. B. Parsons, 'The German-American crisis of 1902–1903', *The Historian*, vol. 33 (1971), pp. 436–52.
44 Bodleian Library, Oxford, MS. Eng. lett. d 316, Grey to Newbolt, 5/1/1903; *Daily Mail*, 6/2/1903; *The Times*, 6/2/1903; Hale, *Publicity and Diplomacy*, pp. 258–9.
45 B.M. Add. MSS. 50294 (Arnold-Foster Papers), Arnold-Foster to Cranborne (copy), 12/12/1903 (but obviously 1902); Churchill College Archives, Cambridge, Spring-Rice Papers 1/2, Bertie to Spring-Rice, 26/12/1902; Guildford Record Office, Onslow Papers 173/9/7, Onslow to Joseph Chamberlain (copy), 31/1/1903.
46 GP, XVII, no. 5149; PRO, FO 800/18 (Lascelles Papers), Lascelles to Sanderson (copy), 27/12/1902; HHSt.A Vienna, PA III/159, Szögyeny to Goluchowski, nos. 3 and 7 of 27/1/1903 and 25/2/1903; Bülow, *Denkwürdigkeiten*, I, p. 558.
47 Newton, *Lansdowne*, p. 260; Monger, op. cit., p. 106.
48 Quoted in Carroll, *Germany and the Great Powers*, p. 474.
49 *Morning Post*, 20/2/1903; *The Times*, 21/2/1903; Marder, *Anatomy of British Sea Power*, pp. 466–7.
50 GP, vol. XVII, nos. 5257–8; Hale, *Publicity and Diplomacy*, pp. 261–2; E. M. Earle, *Turkey, the Great Powers and the Bagdad Railway* (New York, 1923), pp. 180 ff.; M. K. Chapman, *Great Britain and the Bagdad Railway, 1870–1914* (Northampton, Mass., 1948), pp. 45–70; J. B. Wolff, *The Diplomatic History of the Bagdad Railway* (Missouri, 1936); B. C. Busch, *Britain and the Persian Gulf, 1894–1914* (Berkeley, Calif., 1967), pp. 189 ff.; J. B. Plass, *England zwischen Russland und Deutschland: Der Persische Gulf in der britischen Vorkriegspolitik, 1899–1907* (Hamburg, 1966), pp. 99–106.
51 HoLRO, Strachey Papers S/10/9/6, Maxse to Strachey, 21/4/1903, and ibid., S/10/5/17, B. Mallet to Strachey, 22/4/1903; West Sussex Record Office, Chichester, Maxse Papers, 450, Saunders to Maxse, 15/9/1902, and ibid., 451, same to same, 26/4/1903.
52 GP, XVII, no. 5262 and *passim*; Monger, op. cit., pp. 120–3; and see also the useful article by R. M. Francis, 'The British withdrawal from the Bagdad Railway project in April 1903', *Historical Journal*, vol. XVI (1973), pp. 168–78, which makes the good point about the Cabinet's unease of the specific terms of the British participation, although it probably underplays the extent to which Chamberlain and people such as Maxse were in contact with each other at this time.
53 See below, pp. 296–7.
54 PRO, FO 881/8241 (print), Lascelles to Lansdowne, nos. 83 and 92 Commercial of 18/4/1903 and 23/4/1903; ibid., C.O. to F.O., 27/4/1903 and 2/5/1903.
55 PRO, FO 64/1642, Lansdowne minute on the original of C.O. to F.O., 2/5/1903. The reply, after much redrafting, actually went to the Cabinet for approval, and was finally published as Cd no. 5 (1903).
56 See Chapters 15 and 16 below.
57 Hoffmann, *Great Britain and the German Trade Rivalry*, pp. 286–7; for Balfour's speech, see *The Times* report of 14/11/1903.
58 HoLRO, Strachey Papers, S/7/4/3, Goschen to Strachey, 18/6/1903; Nuffield College, Oxford, Mottistone Papers, Box 7, typescript of speech 'Major Seeley at Shanklin: Why he is a Free Trader', 20/11/1903.
59 See DZA Potsdam, AAHP 9270, Metternich to Bülow, no. 398 of 17/6/1903, encl. *Pall Mall Gazette* of same date; ibid., 9094, same to same, no. 910 of 26/12/1903, encl. *Daily Mail* of same date; ibid., 9349, *Berliner Tageblatt* of 1/9/1903, reporting on *Daily Express* article.
60 For examples of this, see *Kreuz-Zeitung*, 15/8/1902; *Deutsche Tageszeitung*, 13/5/1900 and 27/5/1903; *Deutsche Zeitung*, 6/12/1903; *National-Zeitung*, 9/9/1904; and, even earlier, the

literature cited in Meyer, *Die Propaganda der deutschen Flottenbewegung*, pp. 110–16; Anderson, *Background to Anti-English Feeling*, pp. 280–4.

61 See the two reports by the German consul-general in London, Lindenfels, arguing the case for conciliation, in DZA Potsdam, AAHP 9271, Lindenfels to Bülow, nos. 10917 and 13919 of 5/8/1903 and 12/10/1903; and Bülow's important summary of the arguments, to the Kaiser, of 20/5/1903, in DZA Potsdam, RKA 305/1.

62 DZA Potsdam, AAHP 9350, Metternich to Bülow, no. 819 of 24/11/1903 (copy), with Bülow's marginalia and underlinings.

63 ibid., 9270, Bernstorff to Bülow, no. 322 of 20/5/1903.

64 AA Bonn, *England 69*, vol. 36, Metternich to Bülow, no. 832 of 26/11/1903 (copy), with Kaiser's minutes thereon.

65 There is virtually no coverage of the subject in either the *Grosse Politik* or *British Documents on the Origins of the War*, for example; nor does it receive any treatment in such works as Monger, *The End of Isolation;* Taylor, *The Struggle for Mastery in Europe;* or C. J. Lowe and M. L. Dockrill, *The Mirage of Power: British Foreign Policy 1902–1922*, 3 vols (London, 1972), vol. 1.

66 Ebel (ed.), *Hatzfeldt Papiere*, II, p. 1310.

67 Taylor, op. cit., pp. 382, 409; Monger, op. cit., pp. 84–7.

68 BA-MA Freiburg, Fasz. 2037, PG 66046, Dähnhardt memo of July 1903.

69 DZA Potsdam, AAHP 9093, Bernstorff to Bülow, no. 649 of 7/10/1903.

70 T. Barclay, *Thirty Years Anglo-French Reminiscences* (London, 1914), pp. 175 ff.; HHSt.A Vienna, PA VIII/129, Deym to Goluchowski, no. 14 D of 13/3/1903.

71 *Daily News*, 9/4/1904; A. J. A. Morris, *Radicalism Against War 1906–1914* (London, 1972), pp. 11–12.

72 National Maritime Museum, Greenwich, Thursfield Papers THU/1, Fisher to Thursfield, 29/1/1901 and 6/3/1903; B.M. Add. MSS. 50335 (Arnold-Foster Papers), diary entry, 20/11/1903. For the army's views, see Monger, op. cit., pp. 130, 133.

73 B.M. Add. MSS. 49774 (Balfour Papers), J. Chamberlain memo, July (?) 1903; Amery, *Chamberlain*, IV, pp. 179–206.

74 Monger, op. cit., pp. 128–44.

75 PRO, FO 663 (Cromer Papers)/6, contains print copies of Cromer's repeated urgings to Lansdowne and others in this period; see also, BD, II ch. XV; and Monger, op. cit., pp. 129 ff.

76 B.M. Add. MSS. 49747 (Balfour Papers), copy of Wolf to Bernstorff, 20/1/1904, followed by L. Mallet to Sandars, 24/2/1904; ibid., 49728, Barrington to Lansdowne, 19/2/1904; PRO, FO 800/183 (Bertie Papers), Hardinge to Bertie, 26/2/1904.

77 See PRO, FO 800/12 (Lascelles Papers), Lansdowne to Lascelles, 23/2/1904 – in reply to FO 800/18, Lascelles to Lansdowne (copy), 19/3/1904; and Monger, op. cit., chs 6–7.

78 Andrew, *Delcassé*, pp. 210 ff.; GP, XVII, nos. 5369–76; H. von Eckardstein, *Lebenserinnerungen und Politische Denkwürdigkeiten*, 3 vols (Leipzig, 1919–21), II, pp. 422 ff.

79 Geheimes Staatsarchiv, Munich, *Gesandtschaftsakten* (Berlin) 1075, Lerchenfeld to Crailsheim, no. 203 of 1/5/1903 (draft).

80 Vogel, *Deutsche Russlandpolitik*, pp. 118–23; Rich, *Holstein*, II, pp. 678 ff.; GP, XIX, pt I, chs CXXVIII–CXXIX.

81 *Holstein Papers*, IV, p. 277.

82 BA Koblenz, *Nachlass* Bülow, vol. 91, Bülow to Holstein, 21/1/1904; and, with further details, Vogel, *Deutsche Russlandpolitik*, pp. 154–61.

83 See F. Fischer, *War of Illusions* (London, 1975), pp. 52–3; O. J. Hale, *Germany and the Diplomatic Revolution . . . 1904–1906* (Philadelphia, 1931), pp. 79–80; Carroll, *Germany and the Great Powers*, pp. 494–5.

84 There is a succinct account of Italy's relations with the great powers at this time in D. E. Lee, *Europe's Crucial Years. The Diplomatic Background of World War I* (Hanover, NH, 1974), ch. 2.

85 Rogge, *Holsteins Lebensbekenntnis*, p. 231; GP, XX, pt I, no. 6516; R. Vierhaus (ed.), *Das Tagebuch der Baronin Spitzemberg* (Göttingen, 1960), p. 439.

86 Lansdowne's attitude may be gleaned from Newton, *Lansdowne*, pp. 329–30; and Monger, op. cit., pp. 161–3; and Balfour's from his letters to the king, copies in Bodleian Library,

NOTES FOR CHAPTER 14

Sandars Papers, MSS. Eng. Hist. c 716. More generally, see Rich, *Holstein*, II, pp. 682 ff.; GP, XX, pt I, nos. 6443–80; BD, III, nos. 16 ff.
87 HoLRO, St Loe Strachey MSS. S/10/5/25, Bernard Mallet to Strachey, 18/1/1904; ibid., S/13/14/7, Spring-Rice to Strachey, 3/3/1904; Churchill College Archives, Cambridge, Spring-Rice Papers 1/49, Louis Mallet to Spring-Rice, 29/2/1904 and 30/3/1904, and Bernard Mallet to Spring-Rice 31/5/1904 (from where the quotation in the text comes); Cambridge University Library, Hardinge Papers, 6, Hardinge to Chirol (copy), 3/6/1904; Steiner, *Foreign Office and Foreign Policy*, pp. 74–5.
88 PRO, Cab. 37/69/32, memorandum by Selborne, 26/2/1904; and see also B.M. Add. MSS. 49707 (Balfour Papers), Selborne to Balfour, 12/5/1904.
89 ibid., 49747, Mallet to Sandars, 1/6/1904 and 22/7/1904.
90 Metternich's report on the king's satisfaction at the Kiel visit – see GP, XIX, pt I, no. 6042 – is confirmed by Lee, *Edward VII*, II, pp. 292–7.
91 B.M. Add. MSS. 49700 (Balfour Papers), Clarke to Balfour, 19/7/1904 and 7/9/1904; Churchill College Archives, Cambridge, Esher Papers 10/34, Clarke to Esher, 6/9/1904.
92 Geheimes Staatsarchiv, Munich, *Gesandtschaftsakten* (Berlin) 1076, Lerchenfeld to the Minister-President (draft), nos. 236 and 335 of 12/2/1904 and 21/6/1904. For Wilhelm's attitude to this war against the 'heathen' Japanese, see his long minute on GP, XIX, pt I, no. 6047.
93 HHSt.A Vienna, PA III/160, Szögyeny to Goluchowski, private, 27/7/1904; BA-MA Freiburg, Fasz. 5569, II.-.R.11b, vol. 2, Kaiser's minute on Alvensleben to A.A., telegram (copy), 26/8/1904.
94 HHSt.A Vienna, PA III/160, Szögyeny to Goluchowski, private, 27/10/1904. For Bülow's orders to the press, see DZA Potsdam, *Nachlass* Hammann, vol. 9, Bülow to Hammann, 24/10/1904.
95 German diplomacy in 1904–5 is now covered by a host of studies: Rich, *Holstein*, II, pp. 688 ff.; Vogel, *Deutsche Russlandpolitik*, chs V–VI; H. Raulff, *Zwischen Machtpolitik und Imperialismus: Die deutsche Frankreichpolitik 1904–5* (Düsseldorf, 1976), *passim*; J. Steinberg, 'Germany and the Russo-Japanese War', *American Historical Review*, vol. LXXV (1970), pp. 1965–86. Three older works are still important: Hale, *Germany and the Diplomatic Revolution*; E. N. Anderson, *The First Moroccan Crisis 1904–1906* (Chicago, 1930); and R. J. Sontag, 'German foreign policy, 1904–1906', *American Historical Review*, vol. XXXIII (1928), pp. 278–301.
96 Bodleian Library, Oxford, Selborne Papers, 41, Kerr to Selborne, 11/10/1904; ibid., 44, Battenberg to Selborne, 16/10/1904.
97 Marder, *Anatomy of British Sea Power*, pp. 496–545; Mackay, *Fisher of Kilverstone*, pp. 315 ff. For Chirol's reports, see Churchill College Archives, Spring-Rice Papers 1/10, Chirol to Spring-Rice, 1/11/1904; and PRO, FO 800/12 (Lascelles Papers), Chirol to Lascelles, 2/11/1904.
98 See the brilliant analysis by J. Steinberg, 'The Copenhagen Complex', *Journal of Contemporary History*, vol. 1, pt 3 (1966), pp. 23–46; Berghahn, *Der Tirpitz-Plan*, pp. 410 ff.; P. Padfield, *The Great Naval Race* (London, 1974), pp. 119–30; GP., XIX, pt I, ch. CXXXVI; *Holstein Papers*, IV, pp. 311–25; I. Metz, *Die deutsche Flotte in der englischen Presse. Der Navy Scare vom Winter 1904/5* (Berlin, 1936). On the role of the German coaling-ships, see L. Cecil, 'Coal for the fleet that had to die', *American Historical Review*, vol. LXIX (1964), pp. 990–1005.
99 PRO, FO 800/18 (Lascelles Papers), Lansdowne to Lascelles (copy), 23/12/1904; Bodleian Library, Oxford, Selborne Papers, Selborne to Eisendecher (draft), 17/2/1905.
100 Churchill College Archives, Esher Papers 10/34, Clarke to Esher, 29/10/1904. For the French role, see Andrew, *Delcassé*, pp. 247–52.
101 Vogel, *Deutsche Russlandpolitik*, pp. 174 ff., 201 ff.
102 Steinberg, 'Germany and the Russo-Japanese War', esp. pp. 1966, 1985–6.
103 Rich, *Holstein*, II, pp. 689–90; GP, XIX, pt II, nos. 6149 ff.; HHSt.A Vienna, PA III/160, Szögyeny to Goluchowski (private), 30/12/1904.
104 Kennedy, 'German naval operations plans against England', pp. 57–61; Berghahn, *Der Tirpitz-Plan*, pp. 387–9; Steinberg, 'Copenhagen Complex', pp. 35–7; G. Ritter, *The Schlieffen Plan* (New York, 1956), esp. pp. 69–72, 96–128; L. C. F. Turner, 'The significance of the Schlieffen Plan', *Australian Journal of Politics and History*, vol. XIII (1967), pp. 47–59.

105 GSA Berlin-Dahlem, Rep. 92, *Nachlass* Schiemann, vol. 40, Berchem to Schiemann, 25/5/1904. See also Schlieffen's opinion that, were he Edward VII, he would have 'Copenhagen-ed' the German fleet in 1904, in Moritz, op. cit., p. 217.
106 Steinberg, 'Copenhagen Complex', p. 45.
107 GP, XVII, no. 5159; the most exhaustive survey of Germany's Moroccan policy is P. Guillen, *L'Allemagne et le Maroc de 1870 à 1905* (Paris, 1967), but see also Winzen, *Bülows Weltmachtkonzept*, pp. 231–64; and Anderson, *First Moroccan Crisis*, pp. 181 ff.
108 Badisches Generallandesarchiv, Karlsruhe, Abt. 233, Fasz. 34810, Berckheim report no. 28 of 15/4/1905.
109 Geheimes Staatsarchiv, Munich, *Gesandtschaftsakten* (Berlin) 1076, Lerchenfeld (draft) report no. 356 of 2/7/1904.
110 BA-MA Freiburg, *Nachlass* Schulenburg-Tressow, vol. 1, 'Erlebnisse', p. 18. For an exhaustive (but apologetic) analysis of the 'war party', see A. Mortiz, *Das Problem des Präventivkrieges in der deutschen Politik während der ersten Marokkokrise* (Frankfurt a.M., 1974), pp. 29–32, 213–26; and, more critically, P. Rassow, 'Schlieffen und Holstein', *Historische Zeitschrift*, vol. 173 (1952), pp. 297–313; Craig, *Politics of the Prussian Army*, pp. 277–86; idem, *Germany 1866–1945*, pp. 314–20; Ritter, *The Sword and the Sceptre*, pp. 193–216; Turner, 'Significance of the Schlieffen Plan', pp. 55–9; Raulff, *Zwischen Machtpolitik und Imperialismus*, pp. 89–144.
111 HHSt.A Vienna, PA III/162, Szögyeny to Goluchowski, no. 19B of 31/5/1905; and see Rich, *Holstein*, II, pp. 696–713; and Moritz, op. cit., pp. 154–88.
112 Imperial War Museum, London, Battenberg Papers, DS/MISC/20/no. 33, 'Notes of a conversation with H.M. the German Emperor on board H.M.S. Drake', Gibraltar, 1/4/1905; Andrew, *Delcassé*, pp. 289 ff.; Anderson, *First Moroccan Crisis*, pp. 234 ff.; Raulff, *Zwischen Machtpolitik und Imperialismus*, pp. 118 ff.
113 Churchill College Archives, Cambridge, Esher Papers 10/34, Clarke to Esher, 24/12/1904; Monger, op. cit., pp. 177–9.
114 Hatfield House Archives, 4th Marquess of Salisbury Papers, 56/32, Lansdowne to Salisbury, 11/4/1905; PRO, FO 800/12 (Lascelles Papers), Lansdowne to Lascelles, 9/4/1905; Monger, op.cit., pp. 186 ff.
115 Churchill College Archives, Cambridge, Spring-Rice Papers 1/2, G. W. Balfour to Spring-Rice, 2/5/1905.
116 Monger, op. cit., pp. 222–3.
117 GP, XX, pt II, no. 6860.
118 HHSt.A Vienna, PA VIII/135, Mensdorff to Goluchowski, no. 44 A-G of 11/8/1905; Monger, op.cit., p. 215; Newton, *Lansdowne*, pp. 337–8.
119 See the *Morning Post* article of 6/11/1902, calling for Britain to 'readjust her policy to the new conditions': copy in AA Bonn, *England 78*, vol. 18, Metternich to Bülow, no. 475 of 6/11/1902.
120 West Sussex Record Office, Chichester, Maxse Papers, 453, Dawkins to Maxse, 20/6/1905; B.M. Add. MSS. 46391 (Spender Papers), Spring-Rice to Spender, 11/8/1905.
121 West Sussex Record Office, Chichester, Maxse Papers, 453, Saunders to Maxse, 2/10/1905; Christ Church College, Oxford, Geoffrey Drage Papers, Box 3, Satow to Drage, 16/6/1905.
122 See the discussion below, pp. 427–9.
123 R. F. Mackay, 'The Admiralty, the German navy, and the redistribution of the British fleet, 1904–1905', *Mariner's Mirror*, vol. 56 (1970), pp. 341–6.
124 A. J. Marder, *From the Dreadnought to Scapa Flow*, vol. 1, *The Road to War, 1904–1914* (London, 1961), I, pp. 114–19; idem, *Anatomy of British Sea Power*, pp. 501–8; Monger, op. cit., pp. 206–11; Kennedy, *British Naval Mastery*, pp. 229–35; P. Haggie, 'The Royal Navy and war planning in the Fisher era', *Journal of Contemporary History*, vol. 8, no. 3 (1973), pp. 113–32.
125 For what follows, see the references in notes 8 and 10 above. Also, N. D'Ombrain, *War Machinery and High Politics* (Oxford, 1973), *passim*.
126 McDermott, 'The revolution in British military thinking . . .', *passim*; and more generally, J. Gooch, 'Sir George Clarke's career at the Committee of Imperial Defence, 1904–1907', *Historical Journal*, vol. XVIII (1975), pp. 555–69; Mackay, *Fisher of Kilverstone*, pp. 350–6; Summerton, *Development of British Military Planning*, pp. 26 ff.

127 B.M. Add. MSS. 49723 (Balfour Papers), Arnold-Foster to Balfour, 13/1/1905, and reply of 21/1/1905; PRO, WO 33/364, Records of a Strategic War Game, ordered on 24/1/1905; B.M. Add. MSS. 49701 (Balfour Papers), Clarke to Balfour, 12/1/1905; Andrew, *Delcassé*, pp. 284–5; Monger, op. cit., pp. 229–31, 236 ff.

128 B.M. Add. MSS. 49701 (Balfour Papers), Clarke to Balfour, 17/6/1905 and 1/7/1905; ibid., 59702, same to same, 17/8/1905; Churchill College Archives, Cambridge, Esher Papers 10/36, Clarke to Esher, 7/6/1905; Williamson, *Politics of Grand Strategy*, pp. 44–52; McDermott, 'The revolution in British military thinking . . .', pp. 172–6; Gooch, *Plans of War*, ch. 9; Clarke's letter to Kitchener, of 26/1/1906, can be found in PRO, 30/57 (Kitchener Papers)/34.

129 B.M. Add. MSS. 49711 (Balfour Papers), f. 64, 'Formation of a Permanent Sub-Committee . . .', 1905, p. 4.

130 BA-MA Freiburg, F 7185, PG 68927, Coerper to Tirpitz, no. 539 of 20/7/1905. See also, HHSt.A Vienna, PA VIII/135, Schönburg (attaché) to Goluchowski, report nos. 50E and 50F of 21/9/1905, and no. 51B of 26/9/1905.

131 GP, XIX, pt II, no. 6255; and more generally, Rich, *Holstein*, II, pp. 714–33; Vogel, *Deutsche Russlandpolitik*, pp. 216 ff.

132 AA Bonn, *England 69*, vol. 37, Metternich to Bülow, no. 331 of 11/4/1904 and no. 759 of 17/8/1904.

133 AA Bonn, *England 78 Secr.*, vol. 8, Metternich to Bülow (copy), private, 13/11/1905 (on his talk with Asquith); HHSt.A Vienna, PA III/161, Szögyeny to Goluchowski, private, 12/12/1905; Geheimes Staatsarchiv, Munich, *Gesandtschaftsakten* (Berlin) MA 2684, Lerchenfeld to Podewils, 2/1/1906.

134 For evidence of Posadowsky's concern, and anonymous literary endeavours, see DZA Potsdam, AAHP 9273, Hammann memo of 7/2/1904; ibid., 9098, Posadowsky to A.A., 6/3/1905; ibid., 9352, same to same, 24/4/1905. Perhaps the most astonishing sign of his concern can be seen in his anonymous article 'A general merchant's views on protection: British trade with Germany reviewed', in the December 1906 issue of the *Empire Review* (see the correspondence about placing this piece in DZA Potsdam, AAHP 5408).

135 Rich, *Holstein*, II, pp. 730–1.

136 West Sussex Record Office, Chichester, Maxse Papers, 448, Grey to Maxse, 9/10/1901, 22/10/1901 and especially 24/11/1901.

137 B.M. Add. MSS. (Spender Papers), Grey to Spender, 19/10/1905; and see also Churchill College Archives, Cambridge, Spring-Rice Papers 1/49, L. Mallet to Spring-Rice, 17/10/1905, for Mallet's delight at Grey's 'excellent speech' on this matter. More generally, K. Robbins, *Sir Edward Grey* (London, 1971), pp. 131 ff.; G. M. Trevelyan, *Grey of Falloden* (London, 1937), pp. 94–104; Lord Grey, *Twenty-Five Years*, 2 vols (London, 1925), pp. 36–55; Z. S. Steiner, *Britain and the Origins of the First World War* (London, 1977), pp. 40–1.

138 Monger, op. cit., pp. 269–73, and BD, III, ch. XX, have the details of Grey's diplomatic conversations: and see Williamson, *Politics of Grand Strategy*, pp. 72–87; B.M. Add. MSS. 52277 (Marker Papers), Repington to Marker, 2/1/1906; and Ministry of Defence (Navy), London, Tweedmouth Papers, Grey to Tweedmouth, 16/1/1906, for the Foreign Secretary's concern for military preparations.

139 Monger, op. cit., pp. 254–6, 267 ff.; Taylor, *Struggle for Mastery in Europe*, pp. 437–8.

140 HoLRO, Strachey Papers S/15/4/8, L. Mallet to Strachey, 24/11/1905; Monger, op. cit., pp. 266–7, 274 ff.; S. L. Mayer, 'Anglo-German rivalry at the Algeciras Conference', in Gifford and Louis (eds), *Britain and Germany in Africa*, pp. 215–44.

141 Monger, op. cit., pp. 328–9 and *passim*.

142 ibid., pp. 217–20; but see also Churchill College Archives, Esher Papers 10/36, Clarke to Esher, 19/6/1905; ibid., 10/37, same to same, 1/9/1905 and 7/10/1905; B.M. Add. MSS. 59702 (Balfour Papers), Clarke to Balfour, 7/10/1905, 14/10/1905 and 20/10/1905; BD, IV, pp. 204 ff.

143 T. Boyle, *The Liberal Party and Foreign Affairs, 1895–1905* (M.Phil. thesis, London, 1969), pp. 328–9, quoting Grey to Buxton, 31/12/1895, and *passim*.

144 BD, III, no. 299.

145 HHSt.A Vienna, PA III/162, Szögyeny to Goluchowski, no. 6 A-H of 14/3/1905, reporting a conversation with Osten-Sacken. See also, BD, IV, no. 69 on Witte's hostile remarks about Germany in May 1905.

146 Churchill College Archives, Cambridge, Spring-Rice Papers 4/1, Spring-Rice to Mallet, copy, 27/9/1905.
147 AA Bonn, *Deutschland 131 nr. 4 Secr.*, vol. 4, Bülow to Holstein, tel. no. 28 of 27/7/1905; GP, XIX, pt II, pp. 415 ff.; *Holstein Papers*, IV, p. 357.
148 AA Bonn, *England 78 Secr.*, vol. 8, Kaiser's minute on Metternich to A.A., tel. no. 288 of 1/11/1905; Württembergisches Haupstaatsarchiv, Stuttgart, *Berliner Gesandschaftsakten* 12c, Varnbüler to Soden, no. 9 of 5/11/1905.
149 Bülow, *Denkwürdigkeiten*, II, pp. 197 ff.; and see C. E. Schorske, *German Social Democracy 1905–1917* (New York, 1970 reprint), ch. II.
150 Rich, *Holstein*, II, p. 730.
151 B. F. Oppel, 'The waning of a traditional alliance: Russia and Germany after the Portsmouth peace conference', *Central European History*, vol. 5 (1972), pp. 318–29.
152 Geheimes Staatsarchiv, Munich, MA 2684, Lerchenfeld to Staatsministerium, no. 141 of 12/3/1906; and for Holstein's resignation, see Rich, *Holstein*, II, pp. 746–53. The German press's disappointment is covered in Carroll, *Germany and the Great Powers*, pp. 548–53.
153 DZA Potsdam, *Nachlass* Hammann, vol. 9, Bülow to Hammann, 18/11/1904; HHSt.A Vienna, PA III/162, Szögyeny to Goluchowski, no. 2C of 7/2/1905; BA-MA Freiburg, F 3193, RMA ix. 3. 1. -. 15b, Wilhelm to Tirpitz, tel. of 9/10/1905; Berghahn, *Der Tirpitz-Plan*, p. 444.
154 ibid., pp. 483 ff.; Deist, *Flottenpolitik und Flottenpropaganda*, pp. 171–94; Schilling, *Radikaler Nationalismus*, pp. 217–87.
155 Berghahn, *Der Tirpitz-Plan*, p. 494 and *passim*. For the financial side, see P.-C. Witt, 'Reichsfinanzen und Rüstungspolitik 1898–1914', in Schottelius and Deist (eds), *Marine und Marinepolitik*, pp. 146–77.
156 P. Kelly, *The Naval Policy of Imperial Germany 1900–1914* (Ph.D. thesis, Georgetown University, 1970), p. 217.
157 BA-MA Freiburg, F 7590 (*Nachlass* Hollweg), vol. 1, p. 55.
158 Details of most of these activities can be found in Hollenberg, *Englisches Interesse am Kaiserreich*, pp. 60 ff. For the Anglo-German Union Club (which he does not cover), see PRO, FO 800/12, G. Bennett (Hon. General-Secretary) to Lascelles, 6/5/1905.
159 Guildhall Library, London, Association of British Chambers of Commerce, Executive Committee, vol. 5, report of 13/2/1906.

CHAPTER 15

1 *Statistical Abstract for the United Kingdom, for the years 1885–1899*, no. 47 Cd 306 (London, 1900), p. 49; ibid., *for the years 1900–1914*, no. 62, Cd 8128 (London, 1915), p. 71.
2 *Statistical Abstract for the Principal and other Foreign Countries in each Year from 1888 to 1897–98*, no. 27, Cd 69 (London, 1900), pp. 88–91; ibid., *from 1899 to 1909–10*, no. 32, Cd 6099 (London, 1911), pp. 128–35; ibid., *from 1901 to 1912*, no. 39, Cd 7525 (London, 1914), pp. 128–35; Mitchell, *European Historical Statistics, 1750–1970*, pp. 490, 494.
3 Platt, 'Economic factors in British policy during the "New Imperialism"', p. 137.
4 See the figures in Mathias, *First Industrial Nation*, pp. 399–400.
5 W. Woodruff, *Impact of Western Man. A Study of Europe's Role in the World Economy 1750–1960* (London/New York, 1966), p. 313.
6 ibid., pp. 317, 323; and see also the comments in D. H. Aldcroft (ed.), *The Development of British Industry and Foreign Competition 1875–1914* (London, 1968), pp. 17–24.
7 Balfour, *The Kaiser and his Times*, p. 437 (but see ibid., p. 438, where he notes 'British and German definitions of town do not exactly correspond'). There is a useful comparative article by E. Crammond, 'The economic relations of the British and German empires', *Journal of the Royal Statistical Society*, vol. LXXVII (July 1914), pp. 772–824.
8 Balfour, *op. cit.*, pp. 437–9.
9 *Statistisches Jahrbuch für das deutsche Reich*, vol. 22 (1901), pp. 134–5; ibid., vol. 35 (1914), p. 252. The 1913 figure for German chemical exports is taken from W. G. Hoffmann, *Das Wachstum der deutschen Wirtschaft seit der Mitte des 19. Jahrhunderts* (Berlin, 1965), p. 522.
10 For general surveys of the Wilhelmine economy, see again Kitchen, *The Political Economy of*

*Germany*, chs 9–11; Henderson, *Rise of German Industrial Power*, section III; D. Calleo, *The German Problem Reconsidered* (Cambridge, 1978), ch. 4; H. Aubin and W. Zorn (eds), *Handbuch der deutschen Wirtschafts- und Sozialgeschichte*, vol. 2 (Stuttgart, 1976), chs 11–14; P. Mathias and M. M. Postan (eds), *Cambridge Economic History of Europe*, vol. VII, pt I (Cambridge, 1978), pp. 555 ff.

11 Taylor, *The Struggle for Mastery in Europe*, p. xxx; Balfour, op. cit., p. 439.

12 *Statistical Abstract for the United Kingdom for the years 1885–1899*, pp. 50–1, 94–5, 116–17; ibid., *for the years 1900–1914*, pp. 72–3, 80–1, 84–5.

13 See again, Appendix A.

14 *Statistical Abstract for the United Kingdom, for the years 1900–1914*, p. 103.

15 Hobsbawm, *Industry and Empire*, p. 151.

16 *Statistical Abstract for the United Kingdom, for the years 1900–1914*, pp. 73, 81–5.

17 *Statistisches Jahrbuch für des deutsche Reich*, vol. 35 (1914), pp. 257–8.

18 P. Deane and W. A. Cole, *British Economic Growth 1688–1959. Trends and Structures* (Cambridge, 1967), p. 36.

19 PRO, WO 106/45, copy of CID Standing Sub-Committee 'Enquiry regarding trading with the Enemy', no. 7, minutes of 26/11/1911, testimony of Right Hon. F. Huth Jackson. This contradicts the contemporary German view – as in J. Riesser, *The German Great Banks and their Concentration in connection with the Economic Development of Germany* (Washington, DC, 1911), p. 538 – that German industrialists had dispensed with the use of English bankers. It is true that German banks, such as the *Deutsche Bank*, had established branches in London in order to share in this business; but that no doubt made them even more aware of the need for good Anglo-German relations.

20 These statements emerge from *Report of the Tariff Commission*, vol. 1, *The Iron and Steel Trades* (London, 1904), esp. paras 11, 58–61, and testimony of witnesses 11–13.

21 ibid., vol. 4, *The Engineering Industries* (London, 1909), section III, witnesses 245 and 249, and Summary, para. 35.

22 PRO, FO 881/7038 (print), Dundee C. of C. to F.O., 6/11/1897.

23 Guildford Record Office, Onslow Papers 173/8/34, Board of Trade *very confidential* 'Reports on Certain Branches of British Trade and Industry: Woollen and Worsted Goods', n.d., probably 1903.

24 PRO, FO 881/7937 (print), letters to the Foreign Office from the Swansea Chamber of Commerce (22/1/1901), Sheffield Chamber of Commerce (7/2/1901), Board of Trade (12/2/1901 and 17/5/1901), and Welsh Plate and Steel Manufacturers' Association (1/3/1901); FO 881/8132 (print), Engineering Employers' Federation to F.O., 16/6/1902.

25 PRO, FO 881/7937 (print), Association of Chambers of Commerce to F.O., 24/9/1901; ibid., Huddersfield Chamber of Commerce to F.O., 30/10/1901. See also FO 881/8132 (print), p. 9, report of the Commercial Intelligence Committee, 28/4/1902.

26 DZA Potsdam, AAHP 9085, Hatzfeldt to Hohenlohe, no. 313 of 23/4/1899, and the correspondence following.

27 DZA Potsdam, RKA 305/1, Verein Süddeutscher Baumwoll-Industrieller to Hohenlohe, copy, 20/12/1897; PRO, FO 881/7125 (print), Lascelles to Salisbury, no. 115 Commercial, of 18/3/1898.

28 PRO, FO 368/987/8337, R. Turner (Leipzig) to Grey, no. 4 of 19/2/1914.

29 DZA Potsdam, AAHP 9346, A.A. to Hatzfeldt, tel. no. 51 of 23/1/1900, and Bülow to Hatzfeldt, tel. no. 57 of 27/1/1900; memoranda by Johannes of 26/1/1900 and 29/1/1900 (the latter with Bülow's corrections on the draft).

30 ibid., Johannes' draft of newspaper article, 1/2/1900; Hatzfeldt to A.A., tel. no. 79 of 31/1/1900.

31 Hahn's speech can be found in *Reichstagsverhandlungen*, 10. Legislatureperiode, I. Session, 95. Sitzung (17/6/1899); see also *Deutsche Tageszeitung*, 27/5/1903.

32 DZA Potsdam, AAHP 9349, A. Munch to A.A., 25/8/1903; *Die Zukunft*, 15/4/1905.

33 PRO, FO 881/8241 (print), Ward (Hamburg) to Lansdowne, no. 26 Commercial, 17/7/1903.

34 See, for example, Hewins lecture of 31/3/1906 on 'The New German Commercial Treaties and their Probable Effect on British Industries', in BLPES, London, Tariff Commission Papers TC 8/2/9/887.

35 BLPES, London, Tariff Commission Papers, TC 1: 8/2, 'The Export Trade in Manufactures of the United Kingdom, Germany and the United States', 16/9/1909.
36 *Report of the Tariff Commission*, vol. 4, *The Engineering Industries*, section III, testimony of witnesses 250, 252–5; and Summary, paras 87–96.
37 Marder, *Anatomy of British Sea Power*, ch. III; Deist, *Flottenpolitik und Flottenpropaganda*, pp. 110–18; but cf. C. Trebilcock, *The Vickers Brothers, Armaments and Enterprise 1854–1914* (London, 1977); idem, 'Legends of the British armaments industry, 1890–1914: a revision', *Journal of Contemporary History*, vol. 5, no. 4 (1970), pp. 3–20.
38 PRO, BT 11/3, Minutes of the Commercial Intelligence Committee, 6th meeting, 19/12/1901.
39 See, for example, *Report of the Tariff Commission*, vol. 1, *The Iron and Steel Trades*, section XVI, answers by firms nos. 348, 752, 808, 916 and 1,279, and testimony of witness 16.
40 ibid., vol. 4, *The Engineering Industries*, section III, testimony of witnesses 254 (Thorneycroft) and 255 (Richardson, Westgarth & Co.); S. Pollard, 'British and world shipbuilding 1890–1914', *Journal of Economic History*, vol. XVII (1957), pp. 439–40; S. Pollard and P. Robertson, *The British Shipbuilding Industry 1870–1914* (Cambridge, Mass., 1979), *passim*.
41 See E. H. Phelps Brown and S. J. Handfield Jones, 'The climacteric of the 1890s', *Oxford Economic Papers*, new series, vol. 4 (1952); and the literature in Saul, *The Myth of the Great Depression, passim; Cambridge Economic History of Europe*, VII, pt I, pp. 201–11. A good contemporary analysis (by the British commercial attaché in Berlin) is W. S. H. Gastrell, *Our Trade in the World in Relation to Foreign Competition 1885–1895* (London, 1897), esp. ch. 5.
42 *Annual Statement of the Trade of United Kingdom with Foreign Countries and British Possessions, 1903*, vol. II, Cd 2081 (London, 1904), p. 204.
43 BLPES, Tariff Commission Papers, Box 240, 'Subscribers'.
44 W. S. Churchill, printed address 'To the Electors of North-West Manchester', 11/4/1908; the 1903 and 1906 export totals are taken from *Statistical Abstract for the United Kingdom, for the years 1900–1914*, no. 62, Cd 8128 (London, 1915), p. 71.
45 Conservative Research Office, London, Party Leaflets, no. 1051, 'Tariff Reform: What the Foreigner Dreads', late 1909; cf. *Daily News Year Book*, 1911 (London, 1911), p. 44.
46 Hoffmann, *Great Britain and the German Trade Rivalry*, p. 196; and see especially D. C. M. Platt, *Latin America and British Trade 1806–1914* (New York, 1972), *passim*, which is full of valuable details on this point.
47 Hoffmann, op. cit., p. 201.
48 B.M., Northcliffe Papers, dep. 4890/I, Sandars to Northcliffe, 13/12/1909 and 8/11/1910; BLEPS, London, Tariff Commission Papers TC 8/2/5/B44, Hewins lecture 'Fiscal Reform in Relation to Cotton', 20/7/1909; W. A. S. Hewins, *The Apologia of an Imperialist*, 2 vols (London, 1929), I, pp. 237, 284; and, generally, R. E. Tyson, 'The cotton industry', in Aldcroft (ed.), *British Industry and Foreign Competition*, pp. 100–27.
49 C. W. Marcara et al., *Why Tariff 'Reform' must be Repelled. The Case for the Cotton Industry* (pamphlet, Manchester, 1910); but see also P. F. Clarke, 'The end of laissez faire and the politics of cotton', *Historical Journal*, vol. XV (1972), pp. 493–512, which shows that between 1906 and 1910 many Lancashire businessmen moved towards the Conservatives because of the Liberal government's social and taxation policies.
50 PRO, FO 881/7638 (print), South African Merchants' Committee to F.O., 15/11/1900; FO 881/7125 (print), Union Steamship Co. to F.O., 31/5/1898; FO 881/9311 (print), Powell (Philadelphia) to Grey, no. 11 Commercial, 'Report on the Activity of the Hamburg-American Packet Co.', October 1908; corresp. in FO 368/984–5; Aldcroft (ed.), *British Industry and Foreign Competition*, pp. 326–63; S. G. Sturmey, *British Shipping and World Competition* (London, 1962), ch. II.
51 Newcastle University Library, Runciman Papers WR 300, Grey to Runciman, 22/1/1904.
52 *Statistical Abstract for the United Kingdom, for the years 1900–1914*, no. 62, Cd 8128 (London, 1915), p. 300; *Statistiches Jahrbuch für des Deutsche Reich*, vol. 35 (1914), p. 46*.
53 See above, pp. 47–8.
54 This is a crude summary of a complex situation; but for further details, see PRO, Cab. 17/81, 'Paper on the Finance of War', by E. Crammond (read before the Institute of Bankers, 20/4/1910); Bodleian Library, Oxford, Selborne Papers, 46, A. Chamberlain to Selborne, 8/2/1905; P. H. von Schwabach, *Aus meinen Akten* (Berlin, 1927), pp. 34 ff.; H. V. Emy, 'The impact of financial policy on English politics before 1914', *Historical Journal*, vol. XV (1972),

pp. 112–15; J. M. Winter (ed.), *War and Economic Development* (Cambridge, 1975), pp. 142–3.

55 See the excellent Board of Trade memorandum by P. Ashley, 'The Financial Position of the German Empire', attached to a circular-note by Winston Churchill of 3/11/1909 – copy in Newcastle University Library, Runciman Papers WR 32; Bodleian Library, Oxford, Gwynne Papers, Box 15, Gwynne to Borden (copy), 10/7/1908; Witt, 'Reichsfinanzen und Rüstungspolitik', in Schottelius and Deist (eds), *Marine und Marinepolitik im Kaiserlichen Deutschland*, pp. 156–77.

56 BD, VI, no. 15; Fischer, *War of Illusions*, p. 87; and see especially the report by Oppenheimer, 'War Finance in Germany', 1912, in PRO, Cab. 17/75; and BD, VIII, pp. 796 ff.

57 PRO, Cab. 17/81 (Finance of War), Clarke to Asquith, 7/11/1906.

58 This emerges most clearly from PRO, Cab. 16/18A, CID sub-committee report and minutes on 'Trading with the Enemy' (established in 1911); but see also PRO, Adm. 116/940B, Crowe to Greene, 21/11/1911; Churchill College Archives, Cambridge, Esher Papers 21/16, Esher lecture on 'Modern War and Peace', Cambridge, 1912, esp. pp. 14–16; and BLPES, London, Giffen papers, IV/44, Clarke to Giffen, 7/2/1907, and enclosure.

59 Crowe's protest is reproduced in BD, XI, no. 369. For the financial side of the 1914 crisis, see PRO, T172/163, memo by W. R. Fraser, 'The Emergency Financial Measures of 1914'; R. S. Sayers, *The Bank of England 1891–1944*, 3 vols (Cambridge, 1976), III, Appendix 3; M. de Cecco, *Money and Empire. The International Gold Standard 1890–1914* (London, 1974), ch. 7.

60 Bodleian Library, Gwynne Papers, Box 15, Gwynne to Borden (copy), 10/7/1908. For the more general remarks, see again Crammond's 'Paper on the Finance of War', in PRO, Cab. 17/81; D. McLean, 'Finance and "informal empire" before the First World War', *Economic History Review*, 2nd series, vol. XXIX (1976), pp. 291–305; W. J. Mommsen, 'Europäischer Finanzimperialismus vor 1914', *Historische Zeitschrift*, vol. 224 (1977), pp. 17–81.

61 ibid., pp. 40 ff.; Viner, 'International finance and balance of power diplomacy 1880–1914', *passim*; R. Poidevin, *Les Relations économiques et financières entre la France et l'Allemagne de 1898 à 1914* (Paris, 1969), *passim*.

62 Bodleian Library, Monk Bretton Papers, 88, Max Waechter to Monk Bretton, 3/2/1902.

63 PRO, FO 800/12 (Lascelles Papers), G. Bennett to Lascelles, 6/5/1905, enclosing a list of the committee members of the Anglo-German Union Club; DZA Potsdam, RKA 14, Loebell to Bülow, 12/12/1905 (on a conversation with Steinthal of the *Deutsche Bank*); Hollenberg, *Englisches Interesse am Kaiserreich*, pp. 67, 75; All Souls College, Oxford, Malcolm Papers, Onslow to Malcolm, 27/6/1907, reporting a conversation with Schröder.

64 Schwabach, *Aus meinen Akten*, *passim*; Anderson, *Anti-English Feeling in Germany*, pp. 102 ff.; E. Rosenbaum, 'M. M. Warburg and Co., merchant bankers of Hamburg', *Leo Baeck Institute*, bk VII (London, 1962), pp. 140 ff.; M. M. Warburg, *Aus meinen Aufzeichnungen* (Glückstadt, 1952), pp. 23 ff.; A. Vagts, 'M. M. Warburg und Co. Ein Bankhaus in der deutschen Weltpolitik 1905–1933', *Vierteljahrschrift für Sozial- und Wirtschaftsgeschichte*, vol. 45 (1958), pp. 289–388; Rosenbaum and Sherman, *M. M. Warburg & Co.*, *passim*; L. Cecil, *Albert Ballin* (Princeton, 1967), pp. 143–213; J. Steinberg, 'Diplomatie als Wille und Vorstellung: Die Berliner Mission Lord Haldanes in Februar 1912', in Schottelius and Deist (eds), *Marine und Marinepolitik im Kaiserlichen Deutschland*, pp. 263 ff.

## CHAPTER 16

1 *Reichstagsverhandlungen*, 11. Legislaturperiode, I. Session (1903/4), 6th Sitting of 12/2/1903.

2 I take this description from Brentano, as he used it in his letter of 20/10/1915 to Naumann, in DZA Potsdam, *Nachlass* Naumann, vol. 133.

3 J. L. Garvin, 'The maintenance of empire: a study in the economics of power', in C. S. Goldman (ed.), *The Empire and the Century* (London, 1905), p. 79.

4 H. J. Mackinder, 'The geographical pivot of history', *Geographical Journal*, vol. XXIII (1904), pp. 421–44; and, for an analysis of these ideas, see P. M. Kennedy, 'Mahan versus Mackinder: two interpretations of British sea power', *Militärgeschichtliche Mitteilungen*, 2/1974, pp. 39–66.

5 India Office Library, Curzon Papers EUR F. 111/229, Selborne to Curzon, 21/10/1903.

6 *The Campaign Guide: A Handbook for Unionist Speakers* (London, 1909); Fischer, *War of Illusions*, p. 35.
7 L. S. Amery Papers (private hands), Box 36, 'The Case for Tariff Reform', July 1905.
8 Langer, *Diplomacy of Imperialism*, pp. 86 ff.; H. W. Koch, 'Social Darwinism as a factor in the "New Imperialism"', in Koch (ed.), *The Origins of the First World War* (London, 1972), pp. 329–54.
9 King's College, London, Robertson Papers I/3/I, lecture on 'Persia' of 25/1/1912.
10 B.M. Add. MSS. 50073 (Brodrick Papers), Curzon to Brodrick, 8/1/1900.
11 HoLRO, Strachey Papers 33/1/22, Kipling to Strachey, 17/10/1901; poem, 'The Heritage', in Goldman (ed.), *The Empire and the Century*, pp. 1–2.
12 ibid., p. 69. This is also quoted in G. R. Searle, *The Quest for National Efficiency 1899–1914* (Oxford, 1971), p. 5, which has a wealth of further details about the impact of the Boer War.
13 Bodleian Library, Oxford, Milner Papers, vol. 44, Milner to Lyttelton (copy), 30/11/1904; A. M. Gollin, *Proconsul in Politics* (London, 1964), pp. 46, 102.
14 L. S. Amery Papers (private hands), C 18, Chirol to Amery, 9/3/1900.
15 The quotation is from J. Remak, '1914 – the Third Balkan War: origins reconsidered', *Journal of Modern History*, vol. 43 (1971), p. 356; but it was a common enough refrain in German apologist literature of the interwar years and in the writings which criticise the 'Fischer' thesis on the origins of the First World War.
16 Gwynn (ed.), *Spring-Rice*, I, p. 243.
17 HoLRO, Strachey MSS., Box 41, Strachey to 'Uncle George', 23/6/1908.
18 N.M.M. Greenwich, Arnold White Papers, 145, typescript of address to a National Service League meeting on 7/7/1910.
19 BD, VI, no. 135.
20 *The Times* Archives, London, Steed Papers, Steed to Chirol, 10/12/1906; HoLRO, Strachey Papers 5/15/5/3, Lavino to Strachey, 12/9/1906; O. Eltzbacher, 'The anti-British movement in Germany', *Nineteenth Century and After* (August 1902), pp. 190–200.
21 L. S. Amery Papers (private hands), Box 52, 9 pp. memo by Amery (undated, but probably late 1912).
22 M. V. Brett and O. Esher, *The Journals and Letters of Reginald Viscount Esher*, 4 vols (London, 1934–8); II; p. 180; see also, King's College, London, Robertson Papers I/3/I, on the 'great, healthy, vigorous nation' which lay 'across the North Sea'.
23 P. Kemp (ed.), *The Fisher Papers*, Vol. II (Navy Records Society, Vol. CVI, London, 1964), p. 347.
24 Quoted in Steinberg, 'The Copenhagen Complex', p. 26.
25 Ascher, 'Professors as propagandists', p. 297.
26 *Heimdall*, November 1899 issue, copy in AA Bonn, *Deutschland 126 nr. 2*, vol. 6; Schiemann, as quoted in Fischer, *War of Illusions*, p. 39.
27 Hohenlohe, *Memoirs*, II, pp. 472–3, 479.
28 See above, p. 241.
29 BA Koblenz, *Nachlass* Bülow, vol. 29, draft speeches on 'Kolonialpolitik'; ibid., draft of speech on 'Flotte und Weltpolitik'; and see again Winzen, *Bülows Weltmachtkonzept, passim*.
30 BA-MA Freiburg, F7580 (*Nachlass* Hollweg), vol. 5, comments of Tirpitz on Thimme's letter of 20/11/1921; Tirpitz, *My Memoirs*, I, p. 162.
31 HHSt.A Vienna, PA III/151, Szögyeny to Goluchowski, private, 26/5/1898; ibid., PA III/152, same to same, no. 47B of 22/11/1899.
32 *Den Flottenfreunden zur Jahrhundertwende* (*Flottenverein* brochure, Berlin, 1900), p. 1.
33 *Reichstagsverhandlungen*, 10. Legislaturperiode, I. Session (1898–1900), vol. IV, 119th Sitting of 11/12/1899, pp. 3292–4.
34 Quoted in Ascher, 'Professors as propagandists', p. 296.
35 *Politisches Handbuch der Nationalliberalen Partei* (Berlin, 1907), p. 5.
36 *Schlesische Zeitung*, 1/10/1899.
37 Both cited in Steinberg, 'The Copenhagen Complex', pp. 25–7.
38 See, for example, BA-MA Freiburg, F 2024, PG 65990, Oberkommando *Immediat-Vortag*, 9/4/1897.
39 G. von Schmoller, 'Die englische Handelspolitik des 17. und 18. Jahrhunderts', *Jahrbuch für*

*Gesetzgebung, Verwaltung und Volkswirtschaft*, vol. XXII, no. 4 (1899); W. Michael, 'Englands Flottenpolitik unter der Republik und der Untergang Hollands', in *Beiträge zur Beleuchtung der Flottenfrage* (Munich, 1900); *Kreuz-Zeitung*, 12/8/1904; Freiherr von der Goltz, 'Seemacht und Landkrieg', *Deutsche Rundschau*, Heft 6 (March 1900, Berlin); and see the examples provided by the so-called *Flottenprofessoren* in W. Marienfeld, *Wissenschaft und Schlachtflottenbau in Deutschland 1897–1906* (Frankfurt, 1957), pp. 67–8.

40  BA-MA Freiburg, *Nachlass* Senden N160/7, Diederichs to Senden, 18/5/1898; Tirpitz to Bülow, 20/4/1907, in GP, XXIII, pt II, no. 8006, *Anlage*.

41  Peter's article is from *Der Tag*, 13/12/1911; Wilhelm's marginal comments can be found in the copy in DZA Potsdam, RKA 14.

42  BA Koblenz, *Nachlass* Eulenburg, vol. 38, Bülow to Eulenburg, 5/10/1895.

43  For Tirpitz's remarks, see BA Koblenz, *Nachlass* Bülow, vol. 154, 'Zettelnotiz'; Bülow, *Denkwürdigkeiten*, I, p. 283; Staatsarchiv Hamburg, *Senatskommission für Auswärtige Angelegenheiten* A14, report of the Hamburg plenipotentiary (Berlin), 16/4/1899; for Bülow, see his letter to Richthofen of 26/7/1899, in BA Koblenz, *Nachlass* Richthofen, vol. 5.

44  PRO, FO 64/1435, Gough (chargé, Berlin) to Salisbury, no. 249 Commercial of 25/11/1897, enclosing a synopsis by Gastrell, the commercial attaché, of Professor Karl Rathgen's pamphlet, which had originally appeared in *Schmoller's Jahrbuch*; see also the articles upon this work in *Kölnische Zeitung* (22/11/1897) and *Berliner Neuste Nachrichten* (12/10/1897).

45  Churchill College Archives, Cambridge, Spring-Rice Papers 1/9, Chirol to Spring-Rice, 10/3/1900; Kennedy, *British Naval Mastery*, p. 191.

46  West Sussex Record Office, Chichester, Maxse Papers, 453, C. C. P. Fitzgerald (retired Admiral) to Maxse, 18/11/1905.

47  B.M. Add. MSS. 49797 (Balfour Papers), Kerr memorandum, enclosed in his letter to Balfour of 3/5/1909.

48  B.M. Dept. 4890 (Northcliffe Papers), vol. 49, Northcliffe to H. W. Wilson (copy), 19/5/1909.

49  BLPES, London, Tariff Commission Papers TC 8/2/9/B86, report of a lecture by W. A. S. Hewins . . . , 28/3/1904.

50  Cited in E. A. Clark, 'Adolf Wagner: from National Economist to National Socialist', *Political Science Quarterly*, vol. 55 (1940), p. 380.

51  Bodleian Library, Oxford, Selborne Papers, 26, Salisbury to Selborne, 27/2/1901.

52  See again, Uzoigwe, *Britain and the Conquest of Africa*, pp. 15 ff.

53  PRO, 30/67 (Midleton Papers)/4, Salisbury to Brodrick, 23/8/1899.

54  Salisbury's speech of 13/3/1901 to the Association of Chambers of Commerce of the UK, as reported in anon., 'The Defence of the Empire. An Open Letter to Lord Salisbury', *Contemporary Review* (April 1901), pp. 457–71, which is a strong attack on such complacent attitudes.

55  Bodleian Library, Oxford, Selborne Papers, 5, Salisbury (4th Marquess) to Selborne, 10/8/1904.

56  B.M. Add. MSS. 49747 (Balfour Papers), Balfour to Lascelles, typescript copy, January 1905; PRO, FO 800/12 (Lascelles Papers), Lansdowne to Lascelles, 27/12/1904 and 5/1/1905.

57  PRO, FO 800/61 (Grey Papers), Grey to Lascelles, 1/1/1906 (copy).

58  BD, III, p. 417.

59  BA Koblenz, *Nachlass* Bülow, vol. 90, Holstein to Bülow, 6/5/1897.

60  Holstein's concern about economic differences can be seen in his letter to Metternich of 12/9/1901, cited in Stahl, *Botschafter Graf Wolff Metternich*, pp. A 129–30; and his telegram to Bülow, no. 62 of 3/8/1902 in AA Bonn, *England 69*, vol. 36. His outburst against Bülow is recorded in GSA Berlin-Dahlem, Rep. 92, *Nachlass* Schiemann, vol. 153, diary note of 1/1/1906.

61  See, for example, DZA Potsdam, AAHP 9271, Metternich to Bülow, no. 2799 of 5/8/1903, enclosing Consul-General Lindenfeld's report no. 10917; Geheimes Staatsarchiv, Munich, MA 2684, Lerchenfeld to Podewils, 2/1/1906, reporting upon a conversation with Bülow; and the Metternich-Tirpitz dispute in GP, XXVIII, ch. CCXX.

62  P. H. S. Hatton, 'Harcourt and Solf: the search for an Anglo-German understanding through Africa 1912–1914', *European Studies Review*, vol. 1 (1971), pp. 123–47.

63  Woodruff D. Smith, 'The ideology of German colonialism', pp. 653–7. For examples of this,

see Cecil, *Ballin*, pp. 165–6; J. G. Williamson, *Karl Helfferich 1872–1924* (Princeton, 1971), esp. ch. III.

64 Niedersächsisches Staatsarchiv, Bückeburg, *Nachlass* Trotha, A 362, no. 20, Tirpitz to Hindenburg (copy), 16/7/1916; and, more generally, his letters in the two volumes of his *Politische Dokumente* (Stuttgart/Berlin, 1924–6).

65 H. S. Jevons, 'The Two Power Standard', *Contemporary Review*, XCV (February 1909), pp. 129–35.

66 B.M. Add. MSS. 49668 (Avebury Papers), Avebury to Bonar Law, 16/12/1905.

67 Quoted in B. Semmel, *Imperialism and Social Reform*, (Cambridge, Mass., 1960), p. 137.

68 *Hamburgische Börsenhalle*, 10–14/8/1896; P. Arendt, 'Die Handelsbeziehungen Deutschlands zu England und den englischen Kolonien', *Mitteilungen des Vereins zur Förderung der Handelsfreiheit*, no. 1 (Berlin, 1900), copy in DZA Potsdam, AAHP 9087; ibid., AAHP 9346, F. Laeisz to Koerner (AA Commercial Division), 23/1/1900.

69 *Freisinnige Zeitung*, 20/9/1903; DZA Potsdam, AAHP 9093, Metternich to Bülow, no. 741 of 2/11/1903, enclosing Bernstein's article.

70 M. Brauer, *Die Anti-Englische Krankheit. Eine Streitschrift gegen den Strom* (Berlin, 1900), copy in AA Bonn, *England 78*, vol. 18. For Kehr's essay on 'Anglophobia and Weltpolitik', see pp. 22–49 of the essays, *Economic Interest, Militarism, and Foreign Policy*.

71 *Reichstagsverhandlungen*, 11. Legislaturperiode, II. Session (1905–6), 9th Sitting of 11/12/1905, p. 222.

72 See note 2 above; and Sheehan, *Brentano*, pp. 126 ff., 182 ff.

73 Bodleian Library, Oxford, Bryce Papers, UB 60, Barth to Bryce, 4/10/1903 and 17/2/1905 (the underlined phrase in English in the original).

## CHAPTER 17

1 Vogel, *Deutsche Russlandpolitik*, p. 7; and see the criticism of this in M. Trachtenberg, 'The social interpretation of foreign policy', *Review of Politics*, vol. 40 (1978), pp. 328–50.

2 Emy, 'The impact of financial policy on English party politics before 1914', p. 104.

3 Scottish Record Office, Edinburgh, A. J. Balfour Papers, 78, proofs of Balfour article on 'Land, Land Reformers and the Nation', n.d.

4 There is a good brief description of 'The growth of Social Democracy 1890–1914' in Snell and Schmitt, *The Democratic Movement in Germany 1789–1914*, pp. 249–80; but see also the works by Schorske, Roth, Gay, Conze, Geary and Groh cited below.

5 G. D. H. Cole, *A Short History of the British Working-Class Movement 1789–1947* (London, 1948), pp. 233 ff.; H. Pelling, *The Origins of the Labour Party 1880–1900* (London, 1954); H. A. Clegg, A. Fox and A. F. Thompson, *A History of British Trade Unions, since 1899*, Vol. 1 (Oxford, 1964).

6 Milner, as quoted in Semmel, *Imperialism and Social Reform*, pp. 183–4.

7 See Ascher, 'Professors as propagandists', p. 287, quoting from Schmoller's article on 'Die Arbeiterfrage'.

8 Cited in Snell and Schmitt, *The Democratic Movement in Germany*, p. 230.

9 H. Lebovics, '"Agrarians" versus "industrialisers": social conservative resistance to industrialism and capitalism in late 19th century Germany', *International Review of Social History*, vol. 12 (1967), pp. 31–65; A. Mendel, 'The debate between Prussian Junkerdom and the forces of urban industry, 1897–1902', *Jahrbuch des Instituts für Deutsche Geschichte* (Israel), 4 (1975), pp. 301–38; K. D. Barkin, *The Controversy over German Industrialisation 1890–1902* (Chicago, 1970), *passim*; idem., 'Conflict and concord in Wilhelmian social thought', *Central European History*, vol. 5 (1972), pp. 55–71.

10 A good introduction to this development is K. E. Born, 'Structural changes in German social and economic development at the end of the nineteenth century', in J. J. Sheehan (ed.), *Imperial Germany* (New York/London, 1976), esp. pp. 30 ff.; see also, H.-J. Puhle, 'Parlament, Parteien und Interessenverbände 1890–1914', in Stürmer (ed.), *Das kaiserliche Deutschland*, pp. 340–77.

11 Emy's article on 'The impact of financial policy on English party politics before 1914' is an excellent introduction to this subject; but see also the running commentary in B. Mallet,

*British Budgets 1887–1913* (London, 1913), and some interesting remarks in B. B. Gilbert, 'David Lloyd George: land, the budget, and social reform', *American Historical Review*, vol. 81 (1976), pp. 1058–66.

12 Details are in Mitchell and Deane, *Abstract of British Historical Statistics*; and Mallett, op. cit.

13 *The Times* article, 'Twenty Years' Finance: The Growth of Revenue', 16/2/1899.

14 Quoted in Lowe, *Reluctant Imperialists*, I, p. 5.

15 For what follows, see P.-C. Witt, *Die Finanzpolitik des deutschen Reiches von 1903 bis 1913* (Lübeck/Hamburg, 1970), *passim*. I have also used the statistics available in the two series, *Statistisches Jahrbuch des deutschen Reiches* and *Statistical Abstract for the Principal and other Foreign Countries* . . .

16 See above, p. 242.

17 Witt, op. cit., esp. pp. 88–9.

18 The calculation is in Snell and Schmitt, op. cit., p. 257, which also has a good brief survey of the SPD's organisational activities. See also the references in A. Hall's useful essay 'Youth in rebellion: the beginnings of the Socialist Youth Movement 1904–1914', in R. J. Evans (ed.), *Society and Politics in Wilhelmine Germany* (London/New York, 1978), pp. 241–66; G. A. Ritter, *Die Arbeiterbewegung im Wilhelminischen Reich* (Berlin–Dahlem, 1959).

19 J. P. Nettl, 'The Social Democratic Party 1890–1914 as a political model', *Past and Present*, 30 (1965), pp. 65–95.

20 This is based upon the speeches of the SPD leaders in the Reichstag on the first two naval laws: see especially the *Reichstagsverhandlungen* for 11–14 December 1899, 7/6/1900 and 12/6/1900; Steinberg, *Yesterday's Deterrent*, pp. 194–5; E. Kehr, *Battleship Building and Party Politics in Germany, 1894–1901* (Chicago/London, 1973), pp. 290 ff., 347 ff.; and W. H. Maehl, 'Bebel's fight against the *Schlachtflotte*, nemesis to the primacy of foreign policy', *Proceedings of the American Philosophical Society*, vol. 121 (1977), pp. 209–26.

21 Parvus, *Marineforderungen, Kolonialpolitik und Arbeiterinteressen* (Dresden, 1898); and, more generally, A. Lothholz, *Die Haltung der Sozialdemokratie in den Heeres-, Flotten- und Weltmachtfragen (1890–1914)* (phil. Diss., Freiburg, 1954).

22 See his brilliant, lengthy speech in response to Tirpitz's explanation of the need for the 1906 fleet measure: *Reichstagsverhandlungen*, 11. Legislaturperiode, II. Session (1905/6), 7th Sitting of 7/12/1905.

23 *Reichstagsverhandlungen*, 9. Legislaturperiode, IV. Session (1895–7), 125th Sitting of 16/11/1896, p. 3279.

24 ibid., 10. Legislaturperiode, I. Session (1898–1900), vol. IV, 120th Sitting of 12/12/1899, pp. 3321–2 (Bebel); ibid., vol. VII, 204th Sitting of 6/6/1900 and 209th Sitting of 12/6/1900, speeches of Liebknecht and Bebel.

25 Maehl, 'Bebel's fight against the *Schlachtflotte* . . .', p. 218; idem, 'August Bebel and the development of a responsible German socialist foreign policy', pp. 28 ff.

26 B.M. Add. MSS. 45345 (William Morris Papers), Liebknecht to Morris, 27/3/1896.

27 On which see especially, H. Bley, *Bebel und die Strategie der Kriegsverhütung 1904–1913* (Göttingen, 1975), *passim*; and R. J. Crampton, 'August Bebel and the British Foreign Office', *History*, vol. 58 (1973), pp. 218–32.

28 See again, Maehl, 'Bebel's fight against the *Schlachtflotte* . . . '; and idem, 'German socialist opposition to Russian imperialism, 1848–1891', *passim*; Fischer, *War of Illusions*, pp. 370 ff.; K. Wernecke, *Der Wille zur Weltgeltung* (Düsseldorf, 1970), esp. pp. 244 ff.

29 The literature on this development is now enormous. Schorske, *German Social Democracy 1905–17*, provides a good introduction in English; H.-J. Steinberg, *Sozialismus und deutsche Sozialdemokratie* (Hanover, 1967), a more theoretical analysis. See also P. Domann, *Sozialdemokratie und Kaisertum unter Wilhelm II* (Wiesbaden, 1974), especially the comments on the English constitutional 'model' for the SPD. Geary, 'German labour movement . . .', *passim*, gives a brisk and useful survey of the current state of research, and suggests new lines.

30 P. Gay, *The Dilemma of Democratic Socialism: Eduard Bernstein's Challenge to Marx* (New York, 1952), esp. pp. 54 ff., 271 ff.; and R. Fletcher, 'An English advocate in Germany: Eduard Bernstein's analysis of Anglo-German relations, 1900–1914', *Canadian Journal of History*, vol. XIII (1978), pp. 209–35.

31 Cited in W. Maehl, 'The triumph of nationalism in the German Socialist Party on the eve of the First World War', *Journal of Modern History*, vol. 24 (1952), p. 33. See also, Schröder,

*Sozialismus und Imperialismus*, pp. 183 ff.; D. Groh, 'The "unpatriotic" Socialists and the state', *Journal of Contemporary History*, vol. 1, no. 4 (1966), pp. 151–77; idem, *Negative Integration und revolutionäre Attentismus* (Frankfurt a.M., 1973); and, more generally, J. Joll, *The Second International 1889–1914* (London, 1955), chs IV–VII.

32 Kehr, 'Anglophobia and Weltpolitik', in Craig (ed.), *Economic Interest, Militarism and Foreign Policy*, pp. 30–1.

33 H. Pelling, *Popular Politics and Society in Late Victorian Britain* (London, 1968), chs 1 and 5; R. Price, *An Imperial War and the British Working Class* (London, 1972), *passim*; B. Porter, *Critics of Empire: British Radical Attitudes to Colonialism in Africa 1895–1914* (London, 1968), *passim*; Miller, *Socialism and Foreign Policy*, pp. 23–39.

34 Mallet, *British Budgets 1887–1913*, pp. 318, 339–40, 463.

35 As reported in the *Liverpool Daily Post and Mercury*, 21/10/1910 – copy in PRO 30/69/5/85 (MacDonald Papers), which has further details on the Labour Party's campaign against armaments.

36 D. Marquand, *Ramsay MacDonald* (London, 1977), pp. 164–7; K. O. Morgan, *Keir Hardie* (London, 1975), chs XI and XII; Miller, *Socialism and Foreign Policy*, pp. 40–7.

37 Compare S. Meacham, 'The sense of an impending clash: English working-class unrest before the First World War', *American Historical Review*, vol. 77 (1972), pp. 1343–64, with G. A. Philipps, 'The Triple Economic Alliance in 1914', *Economic History Review*, 2nd series, vol. 24 (1971), pp. 55–67. On the government's reaction, see the forthcoming London Ph.D. thesis by David French on British economic preparations for war.

38 C. Tsuzuki, *H. M. Hyndman and British Socialism* (London, 1961), *passim*. See also his letter of 8/2/1908 to Maxse (!), in West Sussex Record Office, Chichester, Maxse Papers, 458.

39 Semmel, *Imperialism and Social Reform*, pp. 222–33, has a good brief survey of Blatchford; and Hale, *Publicity and Diplomacy*, pp. 373–9, covers his 1909 articles upon Germany. More generally, see L. V. Thompson, *Robert Blatchford* (London, 1951).

40 Morris, *Radicalism against War 1906–1914*, is the best general guide; but see also Taylor, *The Trouble Makers*, ch. IV; and S. E. Koss, *Sir John Brunner: Radical Plutocrat* (Cambridge, 1970), esp. pp. 214–73, 293–5.

41 H. C. G. Matthew, R. I. McKibbin and J. A. Kay, 'The franchise factor in the rise of the Labour Party', *English Historical Review*, vol. 91 (1976), pp. 723–52; N. Blewett, 'The franchise in the United Kingdom, 1885–1918', *Past and Present*, 32 (1965), pp. 27–56.

42 Emy, 'The impact of financial policy . . .', and J. R. Hay, *The Origins of the Liberal Welfare Reforms 1906–1914* (London, 1975) are good brief guides; but see also, Stansky, *Ambitions and Strategies*; Emy, *Liberals, Radicals and Social Politics*; P. Thompson, *Socialists, Liberals and Labour: The Struggle for London 1885–1914* (London, 1967); P. F. Clarke, *Lancashire and the New Liberalism* (Cambridge, 1971); idem, *Liberals and Social Democrats* (Cambrige, 1978); Hamer, *Liberal Politics in the Age of Gladstone and Rosebery*, pp. 208 ff.; Freeden, *The New Liberalism*; C. J. Wrigley, *David Lloyd George and the British Labour Movement* (New York, 1976), esp. chs II–III.

43 Quoted in Morris, *Radicalism Against War*, p. 280; see also H. Weinroth, 'The British Radicals and the balance of power 1902–14', *Historical Journal*, vol. XIII (1970), pp. 653–82.

44 F. M. Leventhal, 'H. N. Brailsford and Russia', *Albion*, vol. 3 (1973), pp. 81–7; Taylor, *The Trouble Makers*, pp. 103–5.

45 See the analysis by J. W. Auld 'The pro-Boers', *Journal of British Studies*, vol. XIV (1975), esp. pp. 96–8; and S. E. Koss (ed.), *The Pro-Boers* (London, 1973).

46 See Pelling, *Popular Politics*, p. 9; and for Campbell-Bannerman's own views, J. A. Spender, *The Life of the Right Hon. Sir Henry Campbell-Bannerman*, 2 vols (London, 1923); J. Harris and C. Hazelhurst, 'Campbell-Bannerman as Prime Minister', *History*, vol. LV (1970), pp. 360–83; J. Wilson, *C-B: A Life of Sir Henry Campbell-Bannerman* (London, 1973).

47 Emy, 'The impact of financial policy . . .', pp. 115, 124, 130.

48 See again, Clarke, 'Laissez faire and the politics of cotton', p. 508.

49 B.M. Dept. 3890 (Northcliffe Papers), vol. 84, Garvin to Northcliffe, 10/5/1909.

50 Hamer, *John Morley*, pp. 354–5.

51 G. H. S. Jordan, 'Pensions not Dreadnoughts: the Radicals and naval retrenchment', in A. J. A. Morris (ed.), *Edwardian Radicalism 1900–1914* (London, 1974), pp. 162–79; and H.

Weinroth, 'Left-wing opposition to naval armaments in Britain before 1914', *Journal of Contemporary History*, vol. 6, no. 4 (1971), pp. 93–120.

52 Morris, *Radicalism against War*, pp. 125–31.

53 ibid., pp. 324 ff.; Marder, *Dreadnought to Scapa Flow*, I, pp. 311 ff.; R. S. Churchill, *Winston Churchill*, Vol. 2 (London, 1967), ch. 17; R. Langhorne, 'The naval question in Anglo-German relations 1912–1914', *Historical Journal*, vol. XIV (1971), pp. 359–70; F. W. Wiemann, 'Lloyd George and the struggle for the navy estimates of 1914', in A. J. P. Taylor (ed.), *Lloyd George: Twelve Essays* (London, 1971), pp. 71–91.

54 Apart from Grey's own *Twenty-Five Years*, see also the contributions in F. H. Hinsley (ed.), *The Foreign Policy of Sir Edward Grey* (Cambridge, 1977), and the excellent commentaries in Steiner, *Britain and the Origins of the First World War, passim*; Robbins, *Grey, passim*; and Trevelyan, *Grey of Falloden, passim*.

55 A. J. A. Morris, 'Haldane's army reforms 1906–8: the deception of the Radicals', *History*, vol. 56 (1971), pp. 17–34.

56 C. Hazlehurst, 'Asquith as Prime Minister, 1908–1916', *English Historical Review*, vol. LXXXV (1970), pp. 502–31; R. Jenkins, *Asquith* (London, 1964), *passim*. For Asquith's role in 1914, see Hazlehurst, *Politicians at War*, Vol. 1 (London, 1971), pt 1.

57 See Semmel, *Imperialism and Social Reform*, pp. 57–64; R. J. Scally, *The Origins of the Lloyd George Coalition. The Politics of Social-Imperialism, 1900–1918* (Princeton, 1975), chs I–II; Hamer, *Liberal Politics . . .* , pp. 233 ff.; Matthew, *The Liberal Imperialists*, ch. VII.

58 Semmel, op. cit., p. 62.

59 Cited in Emy, 'The impact of financial policy . . .', p. 121; and see also Searle, *The Quest for National Efficiency*, p. 245, on Haldane and social reform.

60 Steiner, *Britain and the Origins of the First World War*, pp. 149–50. And see also Robbins, *Grey*, pp. 207–8, 247–50, 279.

61 Cited in Morris, *Radicalism against War*, p. 331.

62 The literature mentioned in note 42 above substantially modifies G. Dangerfield's seminal work *The Strange Death of Liberal England* (New York, 1935). The turn to statistical evidence is a further stage in the debate: e.g., P. F. Clarke, 'The electoral position of the Liberal and Labour parties 1910–1914', *English Historical Review*, vol. 90 (1975), pp. 828–36; C. Cook, 'Labour and the downfall of the Liberal Party, 1906–1914', in A. Sked and C. Cook (eds), *Crisis and Controversy* (London, 1976), pp. 38–65; R. Douglas, 'Labour in decline, 1910–14', in K. D. Brown (ed.), *Essays in Anti-Labour History* (London, 1974), pp. 105–25.

63 Snell and Schmitt, *The Democratic Movement in Germany*, and Sheehan, *German Liberalism in the Nineteenth Century*, both provide excellent analyses of the Liberal parties; but see also L. Elm, *Zwischen Fortschritt und Reaktion. Geschichte der Parteien der liberalen Bourgeoisie in Deutschland 1893–1918* (Berlin, 1968); F. Rachfahl, 'Eugen Richter und der Linksliberalismus in neuen Reich', *Zeitschrift für Politik*, V (1912), pp. 261–374. On the *Volkspartei*, see J. C. Hunt, *The People's Party in Württemberg and Southern Germany 1890–1914* (Stuttgart, 1975). Hunt has also produced a useful bibliographical article, 'The bourgeois middle in German politics, 1871–1933: recent literature', *Central European History*, vol. XI (1978), pp. 83–106.

64 See again, L. Krieger's book of the same title.

65 Cited in Sheehan, *German Liberalism*, p. 218, along with similar expressions by other Liberals.

66 Stegmann, *Die Erben Bismarcks*, and B. Heckart, *From Bassermann to Bebel. The Grand Bloc's Quest for Reform in the Kaiserreich, 1900–1914* (New Haven/London, 1974), have full details.

67 Sheehan, *German Liberalism*, p. 246.

68 Cited in Snell and Schmitt, op. cit., p. 311; and see also Rachfahl, op. cit., *passim*.

69 K. Wegner, *Theodor Barth und die Freisinnige Vereinigung* (Tübingen, 1968), esp. ch. VII; Sheehan, *Brentano*, ch. VIII.

70 ibid.

71 Naumann, *Demokratie und Kaisertum*, as cited in Barkin, 'Wilhelmian social thought', p. 70.

72 The literature upon Naumann is now enormous. Apart from Barkin, 'Wilhelmian social thought', see D. Düding, *Der Nationalsozialen Verein 1896–1903* (Munich/Vienna, 1972); T. Heuss, *Friedrich Naumann* (Stuttgart, 1949); W. Conze, 'Friedrich Naumann. Grundlagen und Ansatz seiner Politik in der nationalsozialen Zeit (1895 bis 1903)', in Hubatsch (ed.),

*Schicksalwege deutscher Vergangenheit*; R. Nürnberger, 'Imperialismus, Sozialismus und Christentum bei Friedrich Naumann', *Historische Zeitschrift*, CLXX (1950), pp. 525–48; J. Shanahan, 'Liberalism and foreign affairs: Naumann and the prewar German view', *Review of Politics*, vol. 21 (1959), pp. 188–223. The best analysis of Weber is in W. J. Mommsen, *Max Weber und die deutsche Politik 1890–1920* (Tübingen, 1959).

73 Snell and Schmitt, op. cit., p. 308; and H. Jaeger, *Unternehmer in der deutschen Politik (1890–1918)* (Bonn, 1967), pp. 112–23.

74 See Stegmann, *Die Erben Bismarcks*, and especially K. Saul, *Staat, Industrie Arbeiterbewegung im Kaiserreich* (Düsseldorf, 1973).

75 Witt, *Finanzpolitik* . . . , pp. 199 ff.

76 A conclusion also reached by K. Holl, 'Krieg und Frieden und die liberalen Parteien', in K. Holl and G. List (eds), *Liberalismus und imperialistischer Staat* (Göttingen, 1975), pp. 72–88.

77 See Richter's interventions during the first two Navy Laws; and the comments on him by Steinberg, *Yesterday's Deterrent*, pp. 168, 194; and Kehr, *Battleship Building and Party Politics*, pp. 306–14. See also Richter's brochure, *Flotte und Flottengesetz* (Berlin, 1898).

78 The best coverage of these attitudes is in Wegner, *Barth*, pp. 67 ff.; but see also Sheehan, *Brentano*, ch. IX; T. Heuss, *Theodor Mommsen und das 19. Jahrhundert* (Kiel, 1956), pp. 193–220; Anderson, *Anti-English Feeling in Germany*, pp. 98–106; Kehr, *Battleship Building and Party Politics*, pp. 321–2; W. J. Mommsen, 'Wandlungen der liberalen Idee im Zeitalter des Imperialismus', in Holl and List (eds), *Liberalismus und imperialistischer Staat*, esp. pp. 125 ff. Also useful is the unpublished dissertation by G. Deckart, *Deutsch-englische Verständigung: Eine Darstellung der nichtoffiziellen Bemühungen um eine Wiederannäherung der beiden Länder zwischen 1905 und 1914* (phil. Diss., Munich, 1967).

79 Barkin, 'Wilhelmian social thought', pp. 66–70; L. Dehio, *Germany and World Politics in the Twentieth Century* (New York, 1959), esp. pp. 38–108; Fischer, *War of Illusions*, passim; but see also Hunt, *The People's Party*, pp. 153, 175, for examples of other left-Liberals who could hardly be described as supporters of German *Machtpolitik*; and Mommsen, *Weber*, pp. 156 ff., on Weber's attitude towards England.

80 See above, pp. 298–300; Kehr, 'Anglophobia and Weltpolitik', in Craig (ed.), *Economic Interest, Militarism, and Foreign Policy*, passim. For later analyses, see Jaeger, *Unternehmer* . . . , pp. 242–7; H. Kaelble, *Industrielle Interessenpolitik in der Wilheminischen Gesellschaft* (Berlin, 1967), pp. 147 ff.; S. Mielke, *Der Hansa-Bund für Gewerbe, Handel und Industrie 1909–1914* (Göttingen, 1976), passim. The specific case covered by H. Pogge von Strandmann, *Unternehmenspolitik und Unternehmensführung. Der Dialog zwischen Aufsichtsrat und Vorstand bei Mannesmann 1900 bis 1919* (Düsseldorf, 1978), esp. chs 8–9, shows how difficult it is to generalise about industry's attitude towards social reform and *Weltpolitik*.

81 White, *The Splintered Party*, p. 157; and see also the comments in Sheehan, *German Liberalism*, pp. 275–8. Also valuable on the mobilisation of the *Mittelstand*, is G. Eley, 'The Wilhelmine Right: how it changed', in Evans (ed.), *Society and Politics in Wilhelmine Germany* pp. 112–35.

82 Blake, *Conservative Party*, chs V–VI; Adelman, *Gladstone, Disraeli and Late Victorian Politics*, pp. 65–74. P. Fraser, 'The Liberal Unionist alliance: Chamberlain, Hartington and the Conservatives, 1886–1904', *English Historical Review*, vol. 77 (1962), pp. 53–78. D. Butler and J. Freeman, *British Political Facts 1900–1968* (London, 1969), p. 145, has the regional breakdown of general election results.

83 Both cited in Searle, *National Efficiency*, p. 53; and see Taylor, *The Trouble Makers*, p. 83, on imperialism being an outgrowth of liberalism.

84 Salisbury to Cranbrook, in A. E. Gathorne-Hardy (ed.), *Gathorne-Hardy, First Earl of Cranbrook* . . . , 2 vols (London, 1910), II, p. 345. Salisbury's comment has also been discussed – although with a different emphasis – in G. Schmidt, 'Parlamentarisierung oder "Präventive Konterrevolution"?', in G. A. Ritter (ed.), *Gesellschaft, Parlament und Regierung* (Düsseldorf, 1974), pp. 249–78.

85 HoLRO, Strachey MSS. 5/4/6/5, Chamberlain to Strachey, 18/12/1894; and Fraser, 'The Liberal Unionist alliance', pp. 64 ff. See also the comments in P. F. Thiede, *Chamberlain, Irland und das Weltreich 1880–95* (Frankfurt a.M., 1977), pp. 217 ff.

86 See above, p. 316.

87 HoLRO, Wargrave Papers A/3/6/1, copy of J. Chamberlain speech at Bristol, 21/12/1905.

88 See Cd 2175, *Report of the Inter-Departmental Committee on Physical Deterioration*, 1904; and Cd 2779, Minutes of Evidence . . . , 1904; N.M.M. Greenwich, Arnold White Papers, 43 ['Deterioration'], esp. a pamphlet by White on 'The Physical Condition of the Nation', given 8/6/1904. For background literature, see Searle, *National Efficiency*, pp. 1–106; B. B. Gilbert, 'Health and politics: the British Physical Deterioration Report of 1904', *Bulletin of the History of Medicine*, vol. 34 (1965); Hay, *The Origin of the Liberal Welfare Reforms 1906–1914*, esp. pp. 30–3. The eugenics movement has now been analysed in G. R. Searle, *Eugenics and Politics in Britain 1900–1914* (Leyden, 1976).
89 Bodleian Library, Oxford, Milner Papers, 194, P. Lyttelton Gell to Milner, 11/1/1911.
90 *Lord Roberts' Message to the Nation* (London, 1912) – copy in the Amery Papers (private hands), 52.
91 Conservative Research Department, London: National Union party leaflet no. 859, 'UNDER WHICH FLAG?', 1909.
92 Amery Papers (private hands), Box 36, notes on 'Tariff Reform and Constructive Policy', n.d., by J. W. Hills and L. S. Amery; and an undated (probably 1911 or 1912) memorandum on the Trade Union Tariff Reform League, by Amery; see also, Semmel, *Imperialism and Social Reform*, ch. v.
93 National Army Museum, Chelsea, Roberts Papers, Milner to Roberts, 24/11/1909.
94 Amery papers (private hands), diary entry, 29/11/1906; and see also his letter to Milner, 27/11/1906, in ibid., Box C 25 – part of which is reproduced in Amery's *My Political Life*, 3 vols (London, 1953), I, pp. 255–6.
95 West Sussex Record Office, Chichester, Maxse Papers, 455, Garvin to Maxse, 4/4/1906.
96 HoLRO, Wargrave Papers A/3/6/2, Garvin to Goulding, 5/12/1909 (?); and see also B.M. Dept. 4890 (Northcliffe Papers), vol. 23, Maxse to Northcliffe, 24/12/1909.
97 Chamberlain to Dilke, cited in P. Thane (ed.), *The Origins of British Social Policy* (London, 1978), p. 90; HoLRO, Wargrave Papers A/3/2, Chamberlain to Goulding, 23/1/1906.
98 B.M. Dept. 4890 (Northcliffe Papers), vol. 5, Amery to Northcliffe, 19/12/1911; Amery, *My Political Life*, I, pp. 298, 336; and see the article by K. D. Brown, 'The Trade Union Tariff Reform Association, 1903–1913', in the *Journal of British Studies*, vol. IX (1970).
99 G. D. Philipps, *The Diehards* (Cambridge, Mass., 1978), *passim*. See also Amery Papers (private hands), Box 18, Amery to Chirol, 3/4/1900, for the scheme to refashion the House of Lords; ibid., Box 25, Milner to Amery, 12/4/1914, urging restraint; B.M. Dept. 4890 (Northcliffe Papers), vol. 3, Roberts to Northcliffe, 4/8/1911, and vol. 23, Milner to Northcliffe, 22/7/1911, urging reform of the Lords; and Gollin, *Proconsul in Politics*, pp. 153 ff.
100 N. Blewett, 'Free fooders, Balfourites, whole hoggers. Factionalism within the Unionist Party, 1906–10', *Historical Journal*, vol. XI (1968), gives an excellent delineation of the different groupings in the party. The essays by N. Soldon on the Liberty and Property Defence League, and by K. D. Brown on the Anti-Socialist Union, in K. D. Brown (ed.), *Essays in Anti-Labour History* (London, 1974), pp. 208–33 and 234–61, illustrate the differences between the totally negative and the somewhat more positive responses to the rise of socialism – but even the Anti-Socialist Union would probably have appeared too cautious and obstructionist to the likes of Milner, Garvin and Amery.
101 H. W. Wilson, 'The sacrifice of sea power to "economy"', *National Review* (1906), pp. 714–25; idem, 'Is the two-power standard abandoned?', ibid. (1908), pp. 902–14; 'Navalis', 'Treason in high places', ibid. (1909), pp. 389–402.
102 Compare West Sussex Record Office, Chichester, Maxse Papers, 453, J. Chamberlain to Maxse, 28/12/1905, with PRO, FO 633 (Cromer Papers)/18, 'The Position of the Unionist Free Traders', December 1908.
103 ibid., FO 633/22, B. Mallet to Cromer, 27/11/1913.
104 Bodleian Library, Oxford, Selborne Papers, 5, Salisbury to Selborne, 20/5/1908.
105 Churchill College Archives, Cambridge, Esher Papers 10/32, Sandars to Esher, 28/4/1905; P. Fraser, 'Unionism and Tariff Reform: the crisis of 1906', *Historical Journal*, vol. v (1962), pp. 149–66; Blewett, 'Free fooders . . .', *passim*.
106 Blewett, ibid., p. 96; A. K. Russell, *Liberal Landslide: The General Election of 1906* (Newton Abbot, 1973).
107 Amery Papers (private hands), undated file H-L, Maxse to Amery, 15/2/1907; Bodleian Library, Oxford, Sandars Papers, MSS. Eng. Hist. c 754, Akers-Douglas to Sandars,

9/11/1907; A. Sykes, 'The Confederacy and the purge of the Unionist Free Traders, 1906–1910', *Historical Journal*, vol. XVIII (1975), pp. 349–66.

108 P. Fraser, 'The Unionist debacle of 1911 and Balfour's retirement', *Journal of Modern History*, vol. XXXV (1963), pp. 354–66. Balfour's continual problem with the Tariff Reformers from 1903 until 1913 is covered in A. M. Gollin, *Balfour's Burden* (London, 1965), *passim*; D. Judd, *Balfour and the British Empire* (London, 1968), pt 2; S. H. Zebel, *Balfour* (Cambridge, 1973), pp. 128 ff. Bonar Law's accession has been analysed by R. Blake, *The Unknown Prime Minister* (London, 1955), ch. 4; and A. J. P. Taylor, *Beaverbrook* (London, 1972), pp. 69 ff.

109 Snell and Schmitt, *The Democratic Movement in Germany*, pp. 228–36; and, for more detailed treatment, see again Booms, *Die deutschkonservative Partei*; Dorpalen, 'The German Conservatives and the parliamentarisation of Germany', *passim*; Fricke (ed.), *Die bürgerlichen Parteien*, I, pp. 673–701; K. Westarp, *Konservative Politik im letzten Jahrzehnt des Kaiserreiches*, 2 vols (Berlin, 1935–6), *passim*; Schüddekopf, *Die deutsche Innenpolitik*, pp. 86 ff.; Otto zu Stolberg-Wernigerode, *Die unentschiedene Generation* (Munich, 1968), *passim*.

110 Cited in Dorpalen, 'The German Conservatives . . .', p. 188. For the change in their 'political style', see Puhle, *Agrarische Interessenpolitik*, pp. 274 ff.; and F. B. Tipton, 'Farm labor and power politics: Germany 1850–1914', *Journal of Economic History*, vol. XXXIV (1974), pp. 964 ff.

111 Cited in Craig, *Germany 1866–1945*, p. 923; Booms, op. cit., pp. 69 ff.

112 *Der Bayerische Landbote*, 11/3/1887. (I am grateful to I. Farr for this quotation.)

113 Cited in Barkin, 'Conflict and concord in Wilhelmian social thought', p. 64.

114 Puhle, op. cit., p. 274; and see below, pp. 389–90.

115 Barkin, *The Controversy over German industrialisation*, p. 277; Kehr, 'Anglophobia and Weltpolitik', *passim*.

116 See the debate in *Reichstagsverhandlungen*, 9. Legislaturperiode, IV. Session (1895/7), 125th Sitting of 16/11/1896; and the reports upon this sent to Queen Victoria, in RA Windsor, I 60/nos. 157a, 159 and 160; more generally, E.-T. Wilke, 'Clipping the wings of the Hohenlohe ministry', *Studies in Modern European Culture and History*, vol. 2 (1976), pp. 211–34.

117 Cited in Anderson, *Anti-English Feeling in Germany*, p. 142.

118 For details of the *Bauernbund* and other peasant meetings on the Boer War, I am grateful to my colleague, Ian Farr; for the anti-Semites and the war, see again Levy, *The Downfall of the Anti-Semitic Political Parties in Imperial Germany*, pp. 211–16.

119 Bodleian Library, Oxford, MSS. Monk Bretton, 88, Max Waechter to Monk Bretton, 3/2/1902.

120 See above, p. 298.

121 Kehr, *Battleship Building and Party Politics*, p. 433. The contradictions in Wagner's position are detailed in Clark, 'Adolf Wagner', pp. 402–7. The tendency to see Tirpitz's scheme as central to the *Sammlungspolitik* has been queried by Eley, '*Sammlungspolitik*, social imperialism and the Navy Law of 1898', *passim*, who rightly points out what a bone of contention the naval expansion was. Booms op. cit., pp. 125–7, also covers the Junkers' dislike of *Weltpolitik*.

122 Cited in Berghahn, *Germany and the Approach of War in 1914*, p. 79.

123 ibid., *passim*; Fischer, *War of Illusions*, pp. 116 ff.; H. Pogge von Strandmann, 'Nationale Verbände zwischen Weltpolitik und Kontinentalpolitik', in Schottelius and Deist (eds), *Marine und Marinepolitik*, pp. 296–317; B.-F. Schulte, *Die deutsche Armee 1900–1914. Zwischen Beharren und Verändern* (Düsseldorf, 1977), *passim*; M. Kitchen, *The German Officer Corps 1890–1914* (Oxford, 1968).

124 Blackbourn, 'The political alignment of the Centre Party in Wilhelmine Germany . . .', p. 849.

125 On this trend, see Ross, *Beleaguered Tower*, *passim*; Zeender, *The German Center Party 1890–1906*, *passim*; and R. Morsey, 'Die deutschen Katholiken und der Nationalstaat zwischen Kulturkampf und dem ersten Weltkrieg', *Historisches Jahrbuch*, 90 (1970), pp. 31–64.

126 Cited in Zeender, op. cit., p. 3.

127 This has been cleverly demonstrated in two further articles by Dr Blackbourn: see 'Class and politics in Wilhelmine Germany: the Center Party and the Social Democrats in Württem-

berg', *Central European History*, vol. IX (1976), pp. 220–49; and 'The problem of democratisation: German Catholics and the role of the Centre Party', in Evans (ed.), *Society and Politics in Wilhelmine Germany*, pp. 160–85.

128 Blackbourn, 'Class and politics in Wilhelmine Germany', p. 248.

129 There is no full-scale study of the Centre's attitude upon taxation policy. These comments are drawn from the sources cited in the immediately preceding notes; from Witt, *Die Finanzpolitik des deutschen Reiches, passim*; and from K. Epstein, *Matthias Erzberger and the Dilemma of German Democracy* (Princeton, 1959), pp. 78 ff.

130 H. Gottwald, 'Der Umfall des Zentrums. Die Stellung der Zentrumspartei zur Flotten-Vorlage von 1897', in F. Klein (ed.), *Studien zum deutschen Imperialismus vor 1914* (Berlin, 1976), pp. 184 ff.

131 Anderson, *Anti-English Feeling in Germany*, pp. 86 ff.; Zeender, *The German Center Party*, pp. 63–74, 81 ff.; Morsey, 'Die Deutschen Katholiken . . .', pp. 48 ff.; Lieber's contacts with the *Reichsmarineamt* are also covered in Kelly, *The Naval Policy of Imperial Germany*, pp. 118–22.

132 Berghahn, *Germany and the Approach of War*, p. 111; Epstein, *Erzberger*, p. 75; Fischer, *War of Illusions*, p. 79, 242.

133 Gottwald, op. cit., *passim*; Kehr, *Battleship Building and Party Politics*, pp. 136 ff.

134 The phrase used by Blackbourn in 'The political alignment of the Centre Party in Imperial Germany', p. 821; and 'Class and politics in Wilhelmine Germany', p. 221.

135 This is a possible weakness in the otherwise excellent, and very suggestive, approach of G. Schmidt, 'Parlamentarisierung oder 'Präventive Konterrevolution'?', *passim*; and 'Innenpolitische Blockbildungen in Deutschland am Vorabend des Ersten Weltkrieges', in *Aus Politik und Zeitgeschichte (Beilage* to *Das Parlament)*, B20/72, 13 May 1972, pp. 3–32. The point about the *political* balance and the decision-making-cum-executive balance is pursued in M. R. Gordon, 'Domestic conflict and the origins of the First World War: the British and German cases', *Journal of Modern History*, vol. 46 (1974), esp. pp. 213 ff.

136 Mallet, *British Budgets 1887–1913*, pp. vii–x. In private, Mallet (with his orthodox financial views) was much more apprehensive about this trend: see PRO, FO 633 (Cromer Papers)/22, Mallet to Cromer (copies) 15/1/1913 and 18/1/1913. The statistics for this paragraph are based upon Mallet, *passim*, but especially Tables I–XXII at the end; *Statesman's Year-Book*, 1914; and PRO, T 171/2, 'Budget Statement 1912: Liberal Finance'.

137 Mallet, op. cit., pt III.

138 Taylor, *Struggle for Mastery in Europe*, p. xxvii; *Statesman's Year-Book*, various years; Witt, *Finanzpolitik* . . . , esp. tables at the rear of the book.

139 It is also worth remarking that the greater part of the (smaller) British official indebtedness derived from the Napoleonic War! For the above paragraphs, see Mallet, Witt and the *Statesman's Year-Book* 1914; and A. T. Peacock and J. Wiseman, *The Growth of Public Expenditure in the United Kingdom*, 2nd edn (London, 1967), esp. pp. 183–201. I have also used a further set of statistics about German governmental income and expenditure, prepared by Professor Witt for a conference on Imperial Germany, at Mannheim in December 1977.

140 Witt, op. cit., pp. 376–7. For further details, see Berghahn, *Germany and the Approach of War*, ch. 8 ff.; Fischer, *War of Illusions*, pp. 177 ff.; and W. J. Mommsen, 'Die latente Krise des Deutschen Reiches 1909–1914', in L. Just (ed.), *Handbuch der Deutschen Geschichte*, Vol. IV, pt I (Frankfurt a.M., 1973 edn); and compare with Schmidt, 'Innenpolitische Blockbildungen . . .', *passim*, and M. Rauh, *Die Parlamentarisierung des Deutschen Reiches* (Düsseldorf, 1977).

141 Monger, *The End of Isolation*, p. 313; and see Pelling's remark, in *Popular Politics* . . . , p. 11, about Admiral Togo being 'the architect of the British Welfare State'.

142 Kennedy, *British Naval Mastery*, pp. 223 ff., with the relevant literature.

## CHAPTER 18

1 C. Seymour, *The Intimate Papers of Colonel House*, 4 vols (Boston, 1926–8), I, p. 249.

2 See the correspondence in Koss, *The Pro-Boers*; Salisbury to Hicks Beach, in Monger, *End of Isolation*, p. 9; Hohenlohe's tart comments upon the Pan-Germans in his memorandum of 2/8/1892 in BA Koblenz, *Nachlass* Hohenlohe Rep. 100 XXI F6.

3 Kennedy Jones, *Fleet Street and Downing Street* (London, 1920), pp. 145–6.
4 Bodleian Library, Oxford, Sandars Papers, MSS. Eng. Hist. c 751, 'Some Thoughts upon the Present Discontent', memo of February 1906.
5 Bodleian Library, Oxford, Bryce MSS., 17, f. 185, Bryce to Goldwin Smith (copy), 23/1/1900.
6 Baylen, 'The "new journalism" in late Victorian Britain', p. 384; also the comments in Lee, *Origins of the Popular Press*, pp. 117 ff.
7 ibid., *passim*; and see especially Lee's article, 'Franlin Thomasson and "The Tribune"', *Historical Journal*, vol. XVI (1973), pp. 341–60. Wadsworth, 'Newspaper circulations, 1800–1954', pp. 24 ff, covers Northcliffe's innovations and the impact upon rival papers.
8 A. J. Lee, 'The radical press', in Morris (ed.), *Edwardian Radicalism 1900–1914*, pp. 47–61, is a brief guide; but see also S. E. Koss, *Fleet Street Radical: A. G. Gardiner and the Daily News* (London, 1973); J. L. Hammond, *C. P. Scott of the Manchester Guardian* (London, 1934); F. Whyte, *The Life of W. T. Stead*, 2 vols (London, 1925), esp. Vol. II; A. F. Havighurst, *Radical Journalist: H. W. Massingham 1860–1924* (Cambridge, 1974).
9 Apart from Koszyck's general survey, there is also the useful I. Rieger, *Die Wilhelminische Presse im Ueberblick 1888–1918* (Munich, 1957), *passim*; and the references in Hale, *Publicity and Diplomacy*, ch. III; E. L. Turk, 'The press of Imperial Germany: a new role for a traditional resource', *Central European History*, vol. 10 (1977), pp. 329–37; and Wernecke, *Der Wille zur Weltgeltung*, ch. 1.
10 A. Hall, *Scandal, Sensation and Social Democracy: The SPD Press and Wilhelmine Germany 1890–1914* (Cambridge, 1977), *passim*.
11 Kennedy, 'German world policy . . . ', p. 616.
12 The *Auswärtiges Amt* Archiv (Bonn), the Bülow Papers (Koblenz) and Hammann Papers (Potsdam) are the chief sources for these comments. See also J. Lehmann, *Die Aussenpolitik und die "Kölnische Zeitung" während der Bülow-Zeit (1897–1900)* (phil. Diss., Leipzig, 1937); Schilling, *Radikaler Nationalismus*, pp. 412 ff.
13 Deist, *Flottenpolitik und Flottenpropaganda*, is now the authoritative work; but see BA Koblenz, *Nachlass* Julius Alter (Sontag), vol. 6, and *Nachlass* Ludwig Boas, vol. 1, for the reminiscences of journalists who co-operated with the 'News Bureau' in producing patriotic propaganda.
14 Bodleian Library, Oxford, Sandars Papers, MSS. Eng. Hist. c 753, Gwynne to Sandars, 25/6/1907; B.M. Add. MSS. 49795 (Balfour Papers), Garvin to Sandars, 20/12/1909.
15 Kilverstone Hall, Norfolk, Fisher Papers, Fisher to A. White, 8/1/1901; and see the various letters to White and Thursfield in A. J. Marder (ed.), *Fear God and Dread Nought: The Correspondence of Admiral of the Fleet Lord Fisher of Kilverstone*, 3 vols (London, 1952–9), I, *passim*; and to Garvin, in A. M. Gollin, *The Observer and J. L. Garvin* (London, 1960).
16 Bodleian Library, Oxford, Gwynne Papers, Box 16, contains Beresford's 'leaks' about naval weaknesses.
17 Churchill College, Cambridge, Spring-Rice Papers, 1/14, Chirol to Lascelles, *very private*, 9/11/1895.
18 Apart from Winzen, *Bülow's Weltmachtkonzept*, and Schilling, *Radikaler Nationalismus*, see also Vierhaus (ed.), *Spitzemberg*, pp. 390 ff.; DZA Potsdam, *Alldeutscher Verbands-Akten*, 15, letters of Hasse to the members of the executive committee; HHSt.A Vienna, PA III/154, Szögyeny to Goluchowski, private, 10/12/1900; and Kröll, *Die internationale Buren-Agitation 1899–1902*, *passim*.
19 BA Koblenz, *Nachlass* Bülow, vol. 91, Holstein memorandum of 26/1/1902.
20 Carroll, *Germany and the Great Powers*, pp. 676 ff.; Wernecke, *Der Wille zur Weltgeltung*, pp. 71 ff.
21 A. Wilson, *The Strange Ride of Rudyard Kipling* (London/New York, 1977), p. 239.
22 Wernecke, *Der Wille zur Weltgeltung*, pp. 45–6.
23 AA Bonn, *England 78 Secr.*, vol. 6, Kaiser Wilhelm to Bülow, tel. no. 8, 30/3/1903; *History of the Times*, III, pp. 365 ff.
24 PRO, FO 800/9 (Lascelles Papers), Sanderson to Lascelles, 28/3/1900.
25 *History of The Times*, III, p. 369; and Churchill College Archives, Cambridge, Saunders

Papers, GS/1/141, Saunders to his father, 14/1/1900, on his 'imperative duty to expose certain German ambitions'.

26 HoLRO, Strachey Papers S/10/9/8, Maxse to Strachey, 15/1/1907.

27 M. J. Allison, *The National Service Issue 1899–1914* (Ph.D. thesis, London, 1975), p. 27.

28 Pogge von Strandmann, 'Nationale Verbände . . . ', *passim*; Fricke *et al.* (eds), *Die Bürgerlichen Parteien in Deutschland*, I, pp. 390–407; Pierard, *The German Colonial Society 1882–1914*, *passim*. Evidence of the Colonial Society's pressure can be seen in the Paul Kayser Papers (Hamburg State and University Library) and Kusserow Papers (Potsdam).

29 Marder, *Anatomy of British Sea Power*, pp. 48–61; W. M. Hamilton, *The Nation and the Navy: Methods and Organisation of British Navalist Propaganda 1889–1914* (Ph.D. thesis, London, 1977), *passim*.

30 Deist, *Flottenpolitik und Flottenpropaganda*, *passim*; Eley, 'Defining social imperialism', pp. 269 ff.; idem, 'Reshaping the Right . . . ', pp. 330 ff; *Die Bürgerlichen Parteien in Deutschland*, I, pp. 432–49; Schilling, *Radikaler Nationalismus*, pp. 179 ff.

31 *Die Bürgerlichen Parteien in Deutschland*, I, pp. 574–81; Fischer, *War of Illusions*, pp. 105 ff.; R. Chickering, 'Der "Deutsche Wehrverein" und die Reform der deutschen Armee 1912–1914', *Militärgeschichtliche Mitteilungen*, 1/1979.

32 Allison, *The National Service Issue*, *passim*; D. James, *Lord Roberts* (London, 1954), ch. XIV. D. Hayes, *Conscription Conflict* (London, 1949), pp. 36 ff.; C. E. Playne, *The Pre-War Mind in Britain* (London, 1928), ch. III. See also the excellent article by A. Summers, 'Militarism in Britain before the Great War', *History Workshop Journal*, issue 2 (autumn 1976), pp. 104–23. The Amery, Milner and Roberts papers all contain further useful information about the league's activities.

33 Wertheimer, *The Pan-German League 1890–1914*, *passim*, and Schilling, *Radikaler Nationalismus*, are best upon the league. There are also details in Anderson, *Anti-English Feeling*, pp. 194–210; A. Kruck, *Geschichte des Alldeutschen Verbandes 1890–1939* (Wiesbaden, 1954), pt 1; E. Hartwig, *Zur Politik und Entwicklung des Alldeutschen Verbandes . . . 1891–1914* (phil. Diss., Jena, 1966), *passim*; *Die Bürgerlichen Parteien in Deutschland*, I, pp. 1–26. See also the ADV's own publication, *Zwanzig Jahre alldeutscher Arbeit und Kämpfe* (Leipzig, 1910).

34 Kruck, Schilling and Wertheimer also argue in this light. A. J. O'Donnell, *National Liberalism and the Mass Politics of the German Right, 1890–1907* (Ph.D. thesis, Princeton, 1973), pp. 312–24, tends to stress the co-operation between the league and the government.

35 National Army Museum, Chelsea, Roberts Papers, Strachey to Roberts (cyclostyled letter), 1/6/1909, enclosing his new book *A New Way of Life*.

36 Wertheimer, op. cit., p. 167.

37 Summers, 'Militarism in Britain . . . ', p. 114.

38 Eley, 'Reshaping the Right . . . ', p. 333; Wertheimer, op. cit., p. 110.

39 ibid., p. 133; Schilling, *Radikaler Nationalismus*, p. 524, has somewhat different figures. Summers, 'Militarism in Britain . . . ', p. 113, and Allison, *National Service Issue*, pp. 144–5, have the numbers of MPs in the NSL.

40 Eley, 'Reshaping the Right . . . ', p. 333.

41 Bodleian Library, Oxford, Milner Papers, vol. 44, Milner to Sir Lewis Michell, 13/5/1904; Gollin, *Proconsul in Politics*, *passim*; and, more generally, Searle, *National Efficiency*, and Scally, *The Origins of the Lloyd-George Coalition*.

42 O'Donnell, *National Liberalism and Mass Politics*, p. 314; Schilling, *Radikaler Nationalismus*, pt G; Eley, 'Reshaping the Right . . . ', pp. 352–3.

43 The quotations are from 'The Passing of the Great Fleet' (Imperial Maritime League Pamphlet, 1908); and 'The Imperial Maritime League and Provision for National Defence' (1909), p. 5. Most of the league's papers can be found in the National Maritime Museum, Greenwich, L. Horton-Smith Papers (joint founder, with H. F. Wyatt).

44 HoLRO, Hannon Papers, Box 2, Yerburgh (President, Navy League) to Hannon, 22/12/1912.

45 Summers, op. cit., p. 121; Marder, *Anatomy of British Sea Power*, p. 52.

46 Eley, 'Reshaping the Right . . . ', p. 343.

47 J. Springhall, *Youth, Empire and Society. British Youth Movements, 1883–1940* (London, 1977), pp. 58–9. P. Wilkinson, 'English youth movements, 1908–30', *Journal of*

*Contemporary History*, vol. 4, no. 2 (1969), pp. 7–14, shows how the 'social-imperialist' message could be blended with the anti-militarist appeal of woodcraft lore and the open air.

48 Churchill College, Cambridge, Esher Papers 16/12, Esher to R. de Havilland (copy), 23/7/1909. More generally, see Steiner, *Britain and the Origins of the First World War*, pp. 157–61; G. Best, 'Militarism and the Victorian public schools', in B. Simon and I. Bradley (eds), *The Victorian Public School* (London, 1975).

49 Army Museums Ogilby Trust, London, Spenser Wilkinson Papers, 14, Roberts to Spenser Wilkinson, 20/10/1909.

50 F. J. Glendenning, 'Attitudes to colonialism and race in British and French history schoolbooks', *History of Education*, 3 (1974), pp. 57–72; V. E. Chancellor, *History for their Masters* (Bath, 1970).

51 Clarke, *Voices Prophesying War*, pp. 144–9; A. Sandison, *The Wheel of Empire* (London, 1967), *passim*; Wilson, *The Strange Ride of Rudyard Kipling*, chs 4–5; Langer, *The Diplomacy of Imperialism*, ch. 3; D. French, 'Spy fever in Britain, 1900–1915', *Historical Journal*, vol. XXI (1978), pp. 355–64; H.-J. Müllenbrock, *Literature und Zeitgeschichte in England zwischen dem Ende des 19. Jahrhunderts und dem Ausbruch des Ersten Weltkrieges* (Hamburg, 1967), *passim*.

52 Amy Le Feuvre, *Us, and Our Empire* (London, 1911), pp. 176–7.

53 W. C. Langsam, 'Nationalism and History in the Prussian elementary schools under Wilhelm II', in E. E. Earle (ed.), *Nationalism and Internationalism* (New York, 1950), p. 243.

54 A. Hall, 'The war of words: anti-socialist offensives and counter-propaganda in Wilhelmine Germany 1890–1914', *Journal of Contemporary History*, vol. 11 (1976), pp. 30 ff.; D. Fricke, 'Der Reichsverband gegen die Sozialdemokratie von seiner Gründung bis zu den Reichstagswahlen von 1907', *Zeitschrift für Geschichtswissenschaft*, 7 (1959), pp. 237–80.

55 Hall, 'The war of words . . . ', pp. 23 ff.

56 Snell and Schmitt, *The Democratic Movement in Germany*, pp. 245–7; Kitchen, *The German Officer Corps 1890–1914*, *passim*; Messerschmitt, *Militär und Politik* . . . , pp. 68 ff.; R. Höhn, *Sozialismus und Heer*, Vol. 3, *Der Kampf des Heeres gegen die Sozialdemokratie* (Bad Harzburg, 1969); Craig, *Politics of the Prussian Army*, pp. 232–8.

57 K. Saul, 'Der "Deutsche Kriegerbund": Zur innenpolitischen Funktion eines "nationalen" Verbands im Kaiserlichen Deutschland', *Militärgeschichtliche Mitteilungen*, 2/1969, pp. 95–160.

58 idem., 'Der Kampf um die Jugend zwischen Volksschule und Kaserne', *Militärgeschichliche Mitteilungen*, 1/1971, pp. 97–143.

59 Amery, *My Political Life*, I, p. 35.

60 J. Springhall, 'Lord Meath, Youth, and Empire', *Journal of Contemporary History*, vol. 5, no. 4 (1970), pp. 98–111.

61 Deist, *Flottenpolitik und Flottenpropaganda*, pp. 194 ff.; Schilling, *Radikaler Nationalismus*, pp. 326 ff. Keim's own story is: *Erlebtes und Erstrebtes, Lebenserinnerungen* (Hanover, 1925).

62 Apart from Schäfer's *Mein Leben* (Berlin/Leipzig, 1926), see also G. Pretsch, 'Dietrich Schäfer—der Alldeutsche', *Wissenschaftliche Zeitschrift der Karl-Marx-Universität Leipzig*, 9 Jg. (1959/60), pp. 729–35.

63 Hall, *Scandal, Sensation and Democracy*, pp. 116 ff.; and 'The war of words', are best here. See also, Saul, 'Der Kampf um die Jugend . . . ', *passim*.

64 Morris, *Radicalism against War*; Morris (ed.), *Edwardian Radicalism*; Taylor, *The Trouble Makers*, ch. IV; and Miller, *Socialism and Foreign Policy*, have general details. See also the *Manchester Guardian* leader of 22/10/1910.

65 K. Robbins, *The Abolition of War. The 'Peace Movement' in Britain, 1914—1919* (Cardiff, 1976), ch. 1; R. Chickering, *Imperial Germany and a World without War: The Peace Movement and German Society, 1892–1914* (Princeton, 1975).

66 Bodleian Library, Oxford, Bryce Papers, UB 60, Barth to Bryce, 4/10/1903 and 19/8/1908.

67 Newcastle University Library, C. P. Trevelyan Papers, 32, Correspondence with Bernstein; ibid., 210, Trevelyan article, 'Das Verhältnis Englands zu Deutschland', *Deutsche Revue*, May 1908.

68 R. Chickering, 'Problems of a German peace movement, 1890–1914', p. 51, in S. Wank (ed.), *Doves and Diplomats* (London, 1978).

69 See, for example, GSA Berlin-Dahlem, *Nachlass* Schiemann, vol. 153, note of conversation with Mr Fox (Anglo-German Friendship Society), 20/1/1906; B.M. Add. MSS. 49670

(Avebury Papers), Metternich to Avebury, 1/11/1907, and Avebury's (draft) reply of 1/11/1907.

70 Robbins, *The Abolition of War*, p. 18.

71 *Daily News*, 2/6/1909. There are copies of these letters in N.M.M. Greenwich, Arnold White Papers, 153 (Pacifists).

72 Bley, *Bebel und die Strategie der Kriegsverhütung*, *passim*. *British Documents on the Origins of the War* contain a number of Oppenheimer's reports; there are many more in PRO, FO 368 and FO 371, and some in the CID and Board of Trade files. See also his autobiography, *Stranger Within*, and the forthcoming work by J. McDermott (Winnipeg).

73 Such was the title of one given at the Leipzig branch in 1900: see Wertheimer, op. cit., p. 113.

74 Eley, 'Defining social imperialism', p. 274.

75 Cunningham, *The Volunteer Force*, *passim*; and see also the many interesting comments in Summers, 'Militarism in Britain . . .'.

76 Weinroth, 'Left-wing opposition to naval armaments . . .', *passim*.

77 Cited in Schorske, *German Social Democracy*, p. 290.

78 Mosse, *Crisis of German Ideology*, pp. 149 ff.; Marienfeld, *Wissenschaft und Schlachtflottenbau*, *passim*; Dehio, *Germany and World Politics in the Twentieth Century*, pp. 38–108; C. E. McClelland, 'Berlin historians and German politics', *Journal of Contemporary History*, vol. 8, no. 3 (1973), pp. 12–21; H.-H. Krill, *Die Ranke-Renaissance* (Berlin, 1962), pp. 174 ff.; Best, 'Militarism and the Victorian public schools', *passim*.

79 Cited in *Die Bürgerlichen Parteien in Deutschland*, I, p. 705. See also I. Hamel, *Völkischer Verband und Nationale Gewerkschaft. Der Deutschnationale Handlungsgehilfen-Verband 1893–1933* (Frankfurt a.M., 1967).

80 R. Gellately, *The Politics of Economic Despair: Shopkeepers and German Politics 1890–1914* (London, 1974), esp. ch. 6; Volkov, *Popular Antimodernism in Germany*, pp. 266 ff.; H. A. Winckler, 'From social protectionism to National Socialism: German small business movement in comparative perspective', *Journal of Modern History*, vol. 48 (1976), pp. 1–18; Massing, *Rehearsal for Destruction*, pp. 136 ff.; Eley, 'The Wilhelmine Right: how it changed', in Evans (ed.), *Society and Politics in Wilhelmine Germany*, esp. pp. 118 ff.; A. Lees, 'Critics of urban society in Germany', *Journal of the History of Ideas*, vol. XL (1979), pp. 61–84. See also the more general observations in A. J. Mayer, 'The lower middle class as historical problem', *Journal of Modern History*, vol. 47 (1975), pp. 409–36: as a 'critical swing group' (ibid., p. 418), it is clear in which direction the greater part of it was swinging.

81 Cited in Snell and Schmitt, op. cit., p. 239; and see again Morsey, 'Die Deutschen Katholiken und der Nationalstaat', pp. 62–4.

82 Groh, 'The "unpatriotic" Socialists and the state', has a good, brief commentary on this point.

83 O'Donnell, *National Liberalism and the Mass Politics of the German Right*, pp. 309 ff.

84 J. Joll, 'War guilt 1914: a continuing controversy', in Kluke and Alter (eds), *Aspekte der deutsch-britischen Beziehungen im Laufe der Jahrhunderte*, p. 73.

85 Allison, *The National Service Issue*, pp. 151, 217.

86 Morris, *Radicalism against War*, pp. 92–6.

## CHAPTER 19

1 'Address of the Committee', n.d., printed copy in GSA Berlin-Dahlem, *Nachlass* Schiemann, no. 1.

2 Cited in Dockhorn, *Deutsche Geist und angelsächsische Geistesgeschichte*, p. 2.

3 See the book of that title, by O. Chadwick (Cambridge, 1975).

4 L. E. Elliott-Binns, *English Thought 1860–1900. The Theological Aspect* (London, 1956), pp. 26, 339; Reardon, *From Coleridge to Gore*, pp. 346 ff.; Schramm, 'Englands Verhältnis zu deutschen Kultur . . .', pp. 153 ff.

5 Lee, *Edward VII*, II, pp. 231 ff.; Brook-Shepherd, *Uncle of Europe*, pp. 182 ff.

6 See the various files on these topics in the White Papers, N.M.M. Greenwich.

7 HoLRO, Strachey Papers, S/7/1/1, Garvin to Strachey, February 1909?

8 Wilson, *The Strange Ride of Rudyard Kipling*, p. 258.

9 Valentin, *Bismarcks Reichsgründung . . .*, p. 467.

10 Hollenberg, *Englisches Interesse am Kaiserreich*, p. 125, fn. 68.
11 See the quotation in Summers, 'Militarism in Britain . . .', p. 120.
12 See the contribution of D. Rogge (former chaplain of the *1. Garde-Infanterie Division*) in *Die Friedensbewegung und ihre Gefahren für das deutsche Volk* (brochure no. 10 of the *Wehrverein*, Berlin, 1914); and the frequent extracts from Protestant journals in Fischer, *War of Illusions*.
13 Cited in Balfour, *The Kaiser and his Times*, p. 234.
14 Fischer, *War of Illusions*, pp. 160–7.
15 Garvin, *Chamberlain*, III, p. 508.
16 Hollenberg, *Englisches Interesse am Kaiserreich*, pp. 126 ff.
17 P. E. Schramm, 'Deutschland in englischer Auffassung am Vorabend des ersten Weltkrieges', in *Tymbos für Wilhelm Ahlmann* (Berlin, 1951), pp. 272–87.
18 See above, pp. 109–22.
19 Apart from Schramm's three articles, see also Hollenberg, *Englisches Interesse am Kaiserreich*, *passim*; idem, 'Zur Genesis des Anglo-Hegelianismus', *passim*; idem, 'Die English Goethe Society . . .', *passim*; B. A. Rowley, 'Die Entwicklung der Germanistik in Grossbritannien und Irland anhand britischer Antrittsvorlesungen', *Akten des V. Internationalen Germanisten-Kongresses Cambridge 1975* (Berne, 1976), pp. 342–51; H. Muthesius, *Das englische Haus*, 3 vols (Berlin, 1904–5); S. Muthesius, *Das englische Vorbild* (Munich, 1974).
20 Schramm, 'Englands Verhältnis zur deutschen Kultur . . .', pp. 146 ff.
21 Cited in ibid., p. 172.
22 Messerschmidt, *Deutschland in englischer Sicht*, pp. 52–3.
23 J. McDermott, 'The British Foreign Office and its German consuls before 1914', *Journal of Modern History* (On-Demand Supplement), Abstract in vol. 50, no. 1 (1978).
24 Bodleian Library, Oxford, MSS. Top. Oxon. d 239, Minute Book of the Oxford Anglo-German Society 1912–1914, 1 vol. See also the list of German names, and biographical details, in *Rhodes Scholarships: Record of Past Scholars elected between 1903 and 1927 Inclusive* (Oxford, 1931).
25 J. M. Winter, 'Balliol's "lost generation"', *Balliol College Record* (1975), p. 22.
26 Hollenberg, *Englisches Interesse am Kaiserreich*, p. 96.
27 McGlashan, *German Influence on Aspects of English Educational and Social Reform 1867–1908*, p. 253; and, in general, chs 6–8.
28 ibid., p. 395. Also important here are Searle, *The Quest for National Efficiency*; Hollenberg, *Englisches Interesse am Kaiserreich*; and Haines, *Essays on German influence . . .*
29 Searle, op. cit., pp. 76–7, 216 ff.; Gooch, *The Plans of War*, ch. 1.
30 Schramm, 'Deutschlands Verhältnis zur englischen Kultur . . .', p. 302.
31 Searle, op. cit., pp. 102–4.
32 Gollin, *Proconsul in Politics*, p. 80.
33 U. von Hassell, 'Tirpitz' aussenpolitische Gedankenwelt', *Berliner Monatshefte*, 17 Jg. (1939), p. 325; Steinberg, *Yesterday's Deterrent*, pp. 163, 202–3.
34 Birmingham University Library, W. H. Dawson Papers, 269, Gooch to Dawson, 24/3/1915?; and see the coverage of both men in Messerschmidt, *Deutschland in englischer Sicht*.
35 See the references to Treitschke in Cramb, *England and Germany*; Steed's *Through Thirty Years, 1892–1922*, 2 vols (London, 1924); and C. Petrie, *The Life and Letters of the Right Hon. Sir Austen Chamberlain*, 2 vols (London, 1939), I, pp. 27–9.
36 *Nord und Süd*, vol. 142 (July 1912), 'Deutsch-Englische Verständigungsnummer', pp. 64–9.
37 B.M. Dept. 4890 (Northcliffe Papers), vol. 85, Garvin to Northcliffe, 20/8/1909; and see Northcliffe's letter to Garvin (copy), 26/5/1909 in vol. 84.
38 AA Bonn, *Deutschland 148 Geheim*, vol. 2, Lichnowsky memo, 9/2/1901, with Bülow's minutes thereon.
39 *Nord und Süd*, vol. 142 (July 1912), pp. 15–19.
40 See the references in the magazine *Era* of 2/2/1907, 9/2/1907 and 17/4/1909; and also C. Derwent, *The Derwent Story* (New York, 1953), ch. 8. (I am grateful to my colleague, Michael Sanderson, for drawing my attention to these sources.)
41 J. Joll, 'The English, Friedrich Nietzsche and the First World War', in I. Geiss and B.-J. Wendt (eds), *Deutschland in der Weltpolitik des 19. und 20. Jahrhunderts* (Düsseldorf, 1974); and M. E. Humble, 'The breakdown of a consensus: British writers and Anglo-German relations 1900–1920', *Journal of European Studies*, vol. VII (1977), pp. 46–8.

42 Amery Papers (private hands), Box 20, Maxse to Amery, 31/1/1902; Allison, *The National Service Issue*, p. 4.
43 Kruck, *Geschichte des alldeutschen Verbandes*, p. 19.
44 McClelland, *The German Historians and England*, ch. 10; Schmidt, *The Characteristics of British Policy* . . . , pp. 200–19; Marienfeld, *Wissenschaft und Schlachtflottenbau*; Dehio, *Germany and World Politics*, pp. 38 ff; W. Schenk, *Die deutsch-englische Rivalität vor dem Ersten Weltkrieg in der Sicht deutscher Historiker* (Aarau, 1967); and Krill, *Die Ranke-Renaissance*, all offer extensive details.
45 H. W. Steed, 'From Frederick the Great to Hitler: the consistency of German aims', *International Affairs*, vol. XVII (1938), p. 668, quoting the Kaiser's letter.
46 Vierhaus (ed.), *Spitzemberg*, p. 403; Winzen, *Bülows Weltmachtkonzept*, pp. 25–35.
47 By Eley, 'The Wilhelmine Right: how it changed', esp. pp. 113–17. The reference is, of course, to Fritz Stern's book *The Politics of Cultural Despair*.
48 See, *inter alia*, K. Schröter, 'Chauvinism and its tradition: German writers and the outbreak of the First World War', *The Germanic Review*, 43 (1968), pp. 120–35; R. N. Stromberg, 'The intellectuals and the coming of war in 1914', *Journal of European Studies*, vol. 3 (1973), pp. 109–22. It is difficult to imagine who the readers of Langbehn, or of the many other anti-Semitic and anti-modernist tracts of the 1880s and 1890s would be other than various groups within the *Mittelstand*, especially (one suspects) the Pan-German schoolteachers.
49 Stromberg, op. cit., p. 110 – a statement confirmed by J. Müller, *Die Jugendbewegung als deutsche Hauptrichtung neukonservativer Reform* (Zurich, 1971), esp. pp. 168 ff.
50 B.M. Add. MSS. 52277 (Marker Papers), Repington to Marker, 1/3/1906.
51 Bodleian Library, Oxford, Ponsonby Papers, MSS. Eng. Hist. c 660, V. Paget to Ponsonby, 15/7/1914; Morris, *Radicalism against War*, passim.
52 West Sussex Record Office, Chichester, Maxse Papers, 448, Saunders to Maxse, 14/10/1901, with enclosed notes; Bodleian Library, Oxford, Gwynne Papers, Box 18, Gwynne to Conan Doyle (copy), 4/10/1909.
53 B.M. Dept. 4890 (Northcliffe Papers), vol. 99, Steed to Northcliffe, 11/11/1911.
54 West Sussex Record Office, Chichester, Maxse Papers, 450, Saunders to Maxse, 10/11/1902.
55 See note 53 above.
56 HoLRO, Strachey Papers, S/17/2/22, Strachey to Collier (copy), 12/12/1911.
57 M. Beloff, 'The special relationship: an Anglo-American myth', in M. Gilbert (ed.), *A Century of Conflict 1850–1950* (London, 1966). See also Lowe and Dockrill, *The Mirage of Power*, I, pp. 96–102.
58 Anon., 'Foreign affairs: Anglo-German rivalry', *The Round Table*, vol. 1 (1910), pp. 26–7. This is the article which begins: 'The central fact in the international situation to-day is the antagonism between England and Germany'. See B. E. Schmitt, *England and Germany, 1740–1914* (Princeton, 1916), p. 1. The authorship, which puzzled many contemporaries, is revealed in J. R. M. Butler, *Lord Lothian* (London, 1960).
59 Compare the handling of Wilhelm's importance in such books as Eyck, *Das persönliche Regiment* . . . – not to mention all the older treatments like J. D. Chamier, *Fabulous Monster* (London, 1934) – with Wehler, *Das deutsche Kaiserreich*, passim.
60 Again, compare Brook-Shepherd's portrayal of the king in *Uncle of Europe* with the scant attention given to Edward in Beloff, *Imperial Sunset*; Lowe and Dockrill, *The Mirage of Power*; Steiner, *Britain and the Origins of the First World War*; and with the strong argument against the 'myth' of his importance in Monger, *End of Isolation*, pp. 261–4, and Steiner, *Foreign Office and Foreign Policy*, pp. 202–8.
61 See above, pp. 124–6.
62 QVL, 3rd series, III, pp. 20–2, 312, 350, 531.
63 Cited in Steiner, *Foreign Office and Foreign Policy*, p. 201.
64 Cited in Balfour, *The Kaiser and his Times*, p. 355.
65 Ebel (ed.), *Hatzfeldt Papiere*, II, pp. 1163–4.
66 Lee, *Edward VII*, vol. I, is best here.
67 HHSt.A Vienna, PA VIII/120, Deym to Goluchowski, 8/12/1898; ibid., PA III/162, Szögyeny to Goluchowski, no. 23C, very confidential, 1/8/1905; Newton, *Lansdowne*, pp. 330–6; Monger, *End of Isolation*, pp. 224–5.
68 Churchill College Archives, Cambridge, Esher Papers, 4/3, Knollys to Esher, 17/9/1910.

69 Fully quoted in Balfour, *The Kaiser and his Times*, pp. 350–2.
70 B.M. Add. MSS. 52302 (Sir Charles Scott Papers), Hardinge to Scott, 20/5/1903. Andrew, *Delcassé*, pp. 209–10, has an acute remark upon how both the influence of *The Times* and of the king 'were greatly exaggerated on the continent'.
71 HHSt.A Vienna, PA VIII/132, Mensdorff to Goluchowski, no. 16D, 11/3/1904.
72 Newton, *Lansdowne*, p. 293. See also the reflections in Lee, *Edward VII*, II, pp. 725–35, which is much more balanced than Brook-Shepherd, *Uncle of Europe, passim*.
73 PRO, FO 371/2993/file 64992, Crowe minute on a parliamentary question, reply to which was given on 28/3/1917. Crowe recalled the king's request as being in 'November or December 1905', and further minuted that 'H. M. expressed satisfaction' at the memorandum. Crowe had insisted that the king's question could not be answered in a few pages, and went off to work on his lengthy essay – now in BD, III, pp. 397 ff.
74 Monger, *End of Isolation*, pp. 326 ff.
75 All Souls College, Oxford, Onslow-Malcolm Papers, Onslow to Malcolm, 5/5/1908; and see also Grey, *Twenty-Five Years*, I, pp. 195–8.
76 Monger, *End of Isolation*, pp. 262–3.
77 Cited in Rich, *Holstein*, II, p. 509; and see also J. D. Fraley, 'Government by procrastination: Chancellor Hohenlohe and Kaiser Wilhelm II, 1894–1900', *Central European History*, vol. VII (1974), pp. 159–83.
78 This is Holstein's phrase – in BA Koblenz, *Nachlass* Eulenburg, vol. 38, Holstein to Eulenburg, 26/11/1895 – but the practice was much better developed by Bülow and Eulenburg, who disagreed with the *Geheimrat*'s constant criticisms of Wilhelm.
79 BA Koblenz, *Nachlass* Bülow, vol. 76, Eulenburg to Bülow, 8/6/1896.
80 ibid., vol. 90(?), Holstein to Bülow, 10/6/1896.
81 Marschall Diaries (private hands), entry for 25/12/1895.
82 BA Koblenz, *Nachlass* Eulenburg, vol. 44, Holstein to Eulenburg, 24/11/1896.
83 Fischer, *War of Illusions*, pp. 160 ff., 494 ff.
84 Berghahn, *Der Tirpitz-Plan, passim*.
85 BD, III, pp. 434 ff.
86 See again the collection of letters, edited by W. Goertz.
87 Newton, *Lansdowne*, p. 383.
88 Churchill College Archives, Cambridge, Spring-Rice Papers, 1/68, Villiers to Spring-Rice, 28/11/1899; Balfour, *The Kaiser and his Times*, esp. ch. VI; Cecil, *The German Diplomatic Service*, pp. 210 ff. See also Rich, *Holstein*, II, p. 847, which very properly calls for a reassessment of 'the crucial part played by Wilhelm in German politics'.

CHAPTER 20

1 Staat- und Universitätsbibliothek, Hamburg, *Nachlass* Paul Kayser, 44, Kayser letter to (?), 26/9/1895.
2 Robinson and Gallagher, *Africa and the Victorians*, p. 463.
3 PRO, FO 64/1468, Salisbury to Lascelles, no. 131A of 19/7/1899.
4 As quoted in Steinberg, *Yesterday's Deterrent*, p. 209.
5 Grey, *Twenty-Five Years*, I, pp. 9–11; and see his 1910 letter to Goschen in BD, VI, no. 407.
6 BA Koblenz, *Nachlass* Richthofen, vol. 5, Bülow to Richthofen, 3/8/1899; AA Bonn, London Embassy *Geheim-Akten*, packet 403/3, Bülow to Hatzfeldt, no. 140 of 8/5/1898.
7 Cited by Louis in Gifford and Louis (eds), *Britain and Germany in Africa*, p. 32.
8 See especially, F. Kazemzadeh, *Russia and Britain in Persia, 1864–1914* (New Haven, Conn., 1968), chs 7–9; O. Hauser, *Deutschland und der englisch-russische Gegensatz 1900–1914* (Göttingen, 1958), *passim*; and E. Hölzle, *Die Selbstentmachtung Europas* (Göttingen, 1975), ch. 2, which however rather exaggerates this fact.
9 W. O. Henderson, 'British economic activity in the German colonies 1884–1914', in idem, *Studies in German Colonial History*, pp. 58–73; S. E. Katzenellenbogen, 'British businessmen and German Africa, 1885–1919', pp. 237–62, in B. M. Ratcliffe (ed.), *Great Britain and her World 1750–1914* (Manchester, 1975).
10 Fischer, *War of Illusions*, esp. chs 12 and 14; J. Willequet, *Le Congo Belge et la Weltpolitik*

*1894–1914* (Brussels/Paris, 1962); idem, 'Anglo-German rivalry in Belgian and Portuguese Africa?', in Gifford and Louis (eds), op. cit.; Henderson, 'German economic penetration in the Middle East, 1870–1914, in idem, *Studies in German Colonial History*, pp. 74–86; G. Meyer, 'German interests and policy in the Netherlands East Indies and Malaya, 1870–1914', in Moses and Kennedy (eds), *Germany in the Pacific and Far East*, pp. 40–58; I. L. D. Forbes, 'German informal imperialism in South America before 1914', *Economic History Review*, 2nd series, vol. XXXI (1978), pp. 384–98; H. Mejcher, 'Die Bagdadbahn als Instrument deutscher wirtschaftlichen Einflusses in Osmanischen Reich', *Geschichte und Gesellschaft*, 1 Jg. (1975), pp. 447–81.

11 Fischer, op. cit., *passim*; Cecil, *Ballin*, pp. 159 ff.; W. Schiefel, *Bernhard Dernburg* (Zurich, 1976), pp. 121 ff.

12 Cambridge University Library, Crewe Papers, c/17, Grey to Crewe, 17/6/1908 and 23/6/1908.

13 *Der Tag*, 13/12/1911, a copy of which (with the Kaiser's marginalia) is in DZA Potsdam, RKA 14.

14 Hale, *Publicity and Diplomacy*, pp. 432–4; Hatton, 'Harcourt and Solf', esp. pp. 133 ff.; R. Langhorne, 'Anglo-German negotiations concerning the future of the Portuguese colonies, 1911–1914', *Historical Journal*, vol. XVI (1973), pp. 361–87.

15 Fischer, *War of Illusions*, pp. 267, 319. Bethmann Hollweg's own position is covered in K. Jarausch, *The Enigmatic Chancellor* (New Haven/London, 1973), ch. 5; H. Henning, *Deutschlands Verhältnis zu England in Bethmann Hollwegs Aussenpolitik 1909–1914* (phil. Diss., Cologne, 1962).

16 GP, XXI, nos. 11345–6.

17 BD, VI, no. 361.

18 PRO, Cab. 37/59/118, Selborne memorandum, 16/11/1901.

19 George E. Armstrong to Bernstorff, 11/12/1905, enclosed in DZA Potsdam, *Nachlass Hammann*, vol. 3, Bernstorff to Hammann, 23/12/1905.

20 Cited in Marder, *Dreadnought to Scapa Flow*, I, p. 272.

21 BA-MA Freiburg, F 7590, *Nachlass Hollweg*, vol. 3, draft of article, 'Tirpitz und die Flottenpolitik . . .', p. 5; Berghahn, *Der Tirpitz-Plan*, *passim*.

22 BA-MA Freiburg, F 3402, *Akta betr. S. M. Schiffen*, vol. 14, Vice-Admiral Thomsen to Wilhelm, no. 5223 of 31/5/1899; Hatfield House Archives, Salisbury Papers, Class E, Goschen to Salisbury, 7/5/1899; *Ueberall* (1899), p. 95.

23 Cited in Berghahn, *Germany and the Approach of War in 1914*, p. 40.

24 ibid., *passim*; Steinberg, *Yesterday's Deterrent*, *passim*; Ritter, *The Sword and the Sceptre*, II, ch. 8; Padfield, *The Great Naval Race*, *passim*; Kennedy, 'Tirpitz, England and the second Navy Law of 1900'; idem, 'Maritime Strategieprobleme . . .', *passim*; R. Stadelmann, 'Die Epoche der deutsch-englischen Flottenrivalität', in idem, *Deutschland und Westeuropa* (Schloss Laupheim, 1948); G. Michalik, *Probleme des deutschen Flottenbaues* (Breslau, 1931).

25 PRO, FO 800/61 (Grey Papers), Grey to Goschen, copy, 26/10/1910.

26 BD, VI, no. 446. In this conversation with the British ambassador, Wilhelm was considerate enough to include Britain with Germany as a rising power; in his remarks and marginal comments elsewhere at this time, the similarity of position disappears.

27 See, for example, Bassermann's insistence on this in DZA Potsdam, *Nachlass Bassermann*, vol. 11, typescript draft, 'England und Deutschland', n.d.

28 PRO, Adm. 116/940B, 'Some Reflections on the Necessary Strength of the German Fleet . . .', F.O. print of article translated from the *Deutsche Revue*, November 1908.

29 Richthofen memorandum of 3/2/1901, reproduced in Bülow, *Denkwürdigkeiten*, I, p. 510.

30 These contemporary criticisms (usually in private memoranda) are assembled in Kennedy, 'Maritime Strategieprobleme . . .', *passim*.

31 idem, 'German naval operations plans against England', pp. 52–4.

32 See above, p. 251.

33 Cited in Kennedy, 'Maritime Strategieprobleme . . .', p. 190.

34 ibid., p. 191.

35 Reproduced in Kemp (ed.), *The Fisher Papers*, II, pp. 301 ff.; the proofs of this article can be found in: Kilverstone Hall, Norfolk, Fisher Papers, packet 36.

36 AA Bonn, *Nachlass* Eisendecher, 4/10, Selborne to Eisendecher, 17/2/1905.

37 BA-MA Freiburg, *Nachlass* Büchsel, vol. 11, Tirpitz to Büchsel, 29/7/1899.

38 PRO, Adm. 116/942, Fisher to the Prince of Wales, 23/10/1906; and CO 537/348, Paper 5520, Admirality to C.O., 11/2/1907. The quotation about Britain's 'vitals' is from Spring-Rice to Strachey, 3/3/1904, in HoLRO, Strachey Papers, S/13/14/7.
39 BD, VI, nos. 84–5. (After consultation with Lascelles, this comment was later allowed to drop.)
40 The notion that Berlin assumed that the British would allow Germany to trade via the Dutch and Belgian ports is unconvincing, in view of German naval officers' own expectations that a blockade would also be imposed on those countries: see Ritter, *The Sword and the Sceptre*, II, pp. 151–3; Kennedy, 'Maritime Strategieprobleme . . .', pp. 199–204; *Nauticus* (1899), p. 34. In any case, if neither the British nor the German merchant fleets were available to Germany in wartime, neutral vessels (which normally carried only about one-fifth of her seaborne trade) could never make up the gap.
41 A. T. Mahan, 'Considerations governing the dispositions of navies', reproduced in idem, *Retrospect and Prospect* (London, 1902), pp. 165–6. See also Marder, *Dreadnought to Scapa Flow*, I, p. 431.
42 Kennedy, 'German naval operations plans against England', p. 66; and see also *Nauticus* (1899), p. 33, where it is publicly stated that defence of the German coastline is not enough.
43 Guildford Record Office, Surrey, Onslow Papers, 173/24/51, Crowe to Cranley, 11/2/1908.
44 See again, Kelly, *The Naval Policy of Imperial Germany*, passim. (I have also benefited from reading Professor Kelly's unpublished paper, 'Tirpitz as bureaucratic thinker: episodes of the interactions among politics, technology and bureaucracy', 1975.)
45 Tirpitz, *Politische Dokumente*, I, p. 222.
46 BA-MA Freiburg, F 7590, *Nachlass* Hollweg, vol. 3, 'Underlagen zu einem Nekrolog fur den Admiral v. Capelle', 29/4/1930; ibid., vol. 4? (n.n.), Hollweg to General Wetzell, 27/3/1929.
47 BA-MA Freiburg, F 2045, PG 66079, Tirpitz to Koebell, 16/11/1905, and enclosed memorandum.
48 BA-MA Freiburg, *Nachlass* Tirpitz, N 253/100, Tirpitz to Lans, 31/8/1914 (and compare with the altered version in Tirpitz, *Politische Dokumente*, II, pp. 81–3). Lans mentioned this omission to Delbrück: see BA Koblenz, *Nachlass* Delbrück, vol. 55 (Parlamentarische Untersuchungsausschuss, vol. 4, Delbrück note, n.d.).
49 Niedersächsisches Staatarchiv, Bückeburg, *Nachlass* Trotha, A 362/44, Tirpitz promemoria of 20/5/1919 on the 'Kriegsschuldfrage'; and see BA-MA Freiburg, *Nachlass* Tirpitz, for his correspondence with Hollweg and Dietrich Schäfer about the presentation of the July 1914 crisis in his memoirs.
50 BLPES, London, E. D. Morel Papers, Additions M 1219, notes by Morel on 'Germany', n.d. but c.1912?
51 Cited in Kennedy, 'Tirpitz, England and the second Navy Law of 1900', p. 51.
52 See the remark in B. Bergonzi, 'Before 1914: writers and the threat of war', *Critical Quarterly*, vol. 6 (1964), p. 131.
53 Churchill College Archives, Cambridge, Esher Papers, 21/17, *The Naval and Military Situation of the British Isles*, By an Islander [Esher] (London, 1913), p. 37; and see generally, P. Fraser, *Lord Esher* (London, 1973), pp. 252 ff.
54 See above, pp. 278 ff.
55 Taylor, *The Struggle for Mastery in Europe*, pp. xxv–xxxi.
56 L. L. Farrar, 'Importance of omnipotence: the paralysis of the European great power system, 1871–1914', *International Review of History and Political Science*, vol. IX, no. 1 (1972), esp. p. 23.
57 Taylor, op. cit., pp. xxviii–xxix.
58 Fischer, *War of Illusions*, passim.
59 Monger, *The End of Isolation*, p. 281.
60 Taylor, op. cit., p. 528; and Farrar, 'Importance of omnipotence', passim. By 1914 the assessment of some (but not all) British officers had altered: see P. Towle, 'The European balance of power in 1914', *Army Quarterly and Defence Journal*, 104 (1974), pp. 333–42.
61 F. S. Northedge, *The Troubled Giant: Britain among the Great Powers 1916–1939* (London, 1966), p. 623.
62 Kennedy, *British Naval Mastery*, pp. 229 ff.; Haggie, 'The Royal Navy and war planning in the Fisher era', passim; Summerton, *British Military Planning for a War against Germany*,

*passim*; and see also the perceptive comments upon the *political* aspect of the rival war plans in K. Wilson, 'To the western front; British war plans and the "military entente" with France before the First World War', *British Journal of International Studies*, vol. 3 (1977), pp. 151–68.

63 Bodleian Library, Oxford, Selborne Papers 34/53, Balfour to Selbourne, 29/12/1903; *The Campaign Guide: A Handbook for Unionist Speakers* (London, 1909), p. 21; HoLRO, London, Bonar Law Papers, 24/3/72, Lansdowne to Law, 22/11/1911.

64 West Sussex Record Office, Chichester, Maxse Papers, 452, Grey to Maxse, 21/6/1904.

65 PRO, FO 800/170 (Bertie Papers), Grey to Bertie (copy), private, 1/5/1908, encl. memorandum of 28/4/1908; C. E. Callwell, *Field-Marshall Sir Henry Wilson. His Life and Diaries*, 2 vols (New York, 1927), I, pp. 98–9.

66 PRO, Cab. 2/2/114, minutes of the meeting of 23/8/1911.

67 Newcastle University Library, C. P. Trevelyan Papers, 30, 'Representations to Members of Cabinet', March 1912.

68 Imperial War Museum, London, Grant-Duff Diaries, entry of 17/8/1911.

69 B.M. Add. MSS. 46391 (Spender Papers), Spring-Rice to Spender 11/8/1905; PRO, FO 800/171 (Bertie Papers), Bertie to Nicolson (copy), personal, 15/3/1911; ibid., FO 800/13 (Lascelles Papers), Grey to Lascelles, private, 18/9/1907, in BD, VI, no. 48; WO 106/45, 'The Value to a Foreign Power of an Alliance with the British Empire', by Director of Military Operations, 8/3/1909.

70 Steiner, *The Foreign Office and Foreign Policy*, pp. 131 ff. The significance of Nicolson's fears of Russia is exaggerated in Hölzle, *Die Selbstentmachtung Europas*, pp. 218 ff.: Taylor, *Struggle for Mastery in Europe*, p. 525, has it more accurately gauged when he refers to Crowe's fears of a German conquest of France as being 'more representative'.

71 Bodleian Library, Oxford, Milner Papers, 44, Milner to Roberts, 13/8/1906.

72 BD, VI, p. 312.

73 Amery Papers (private hands), Box 52, undated 9 pp. memo (late 1912?).

74 Grey minute on p. 261 of BD, VI. Churchill's letter, to Lloyd-George, of 31/8/1911, in R. S. Churchill, *Winston S. Churchill*, Companion Vol. II, pt 2 (London, 1969), pp. 1118–19.

75 R. Blatchford, *Germany and England* (London, 1910), pp. 22–3.

76 PRO, Cab. 2/2/118, CID meeting of 11/7/1912; and see also his earlier speech, reproduced in BD, VI, Appendix V.

77 GSA Berlin-Dahlem, Rep. 92, *Nachlass* Schiemann, vol. 155, diary note of 13/1/1894 (on Waldersee's intention to offer an alliance with England if he became Chancellor); Kehr, *Battleship Building and Party Politics*, p. 368; Ritter, *The Sword and the Sceptre*, II, p. 158.

78 Defined as such by Hardinge in August 1909: see BD, VI, p. 286. Holstein's tart comments upon Eulenburg's 'impractical ideas of a continental alliance directed against England', although made at a later date, are a fair reflection of how he and many others would have regarded the scheme earlier: *Holstein Papers*, IV, p. 415.

79 Cited in Kehr, op. cit., p. 403, fn. 1; and see the penetrating criticisms, along similar lines, in Schmitt, *England and Germany, 1740–1914*, pp. 198 ff.

80 QVL, 2nd series, I, pp. 452–3.

81 Grey, *Twenty-Five Years*, pp. 5, 8.

82 HoLRO, London, Strachey Papers, S/13/14/7, Spring-Rice to Strachey, 3/3/1904.

83 BD, III, p. 417.

## CHAPTER 21

1 See, for example, Steiner, *Britain and the Approach of War in 1914*, pp. 172 ff. The preceding (and admittedly simplified) synopsis of the idea of the 'Official Mind' is taken from Robinson and Gallagher, *Africa and the Victorians*, esp. pp. 18–26.

2 See H. S. Wilkinson, *Thirty-Five Years, 1874–1909* (London, 1933), p. 221 and Appendix.

3 Robinson and Gallagher, op. cit., p. 20.

4 See above, pp. 131 ff. But the story can be traced in Steiner, *The Foreign Office and Foreign Policy*, *passim*; Rich, *Holstein*, esp. vol. 2; P. G. Lauren, *Diplomats and Bureaucrats* (Stanford, 1976); Cecil, *The German Diplomatic Service*, *passim*.

5 Metternich's thankless task is best traced through the volumes of *Die Grosse Politik*, but there

is also Stahl, *Botschafter Graf Wolff Metternich . . .* , with many useful documents. For the problems his successor in London faced, see H. F. Young, *Prince Lichnowsky and the Great War* (Athens, Ga, 1977). By 1902, Chirol was warning Lascelles of the Foreign Office's suspicion that he was the Kaiser's ambassador and not the king's: see Churchill College Archives, Spring-Rice Papers 1/14, letter of 4/2/1902; and this disapproval of Lascelles intensified in later years.
6 Gordon, 'Domestic conflict and the origins of the First World War', p. 200.
7 B.M. Add. MSS. 49683 (Balfour Papers), Balfour to Edward VII, 28/12/1903.

## CHAPTER 22

1 Given the purpose of this book – to explore the rise of the antagonism between Britain and Germany – I have not attempted to cover the years 1907–14 in such great detail as the earlier sections. My own researches into private and governmental papers for the post-1907 period suggest that little has been left unexplored in the realm of foreign and military/naval policies (although a great deal still needs doing in British financial policy, in the history of the British and German Right, and in the political role of business interests and international bankers). Because of the lasting interest in the origins of the First World War, the secondary literature in this area is enormous; but the following would give the general reader a reasonably up-to-date picture of current scholarship: Hinsley (ed.), *British Foreign Policy under Sir Edward Grey*; Steiner, *Britain and the Origins of the First World War*; Berghahn, *Germany and the Approach of War in 1914*; Geiss, *German Foreign Policy 1871–1914*; Fischer, *War of Illusions*; Hölzle, *Die Selbstentmachtung Europas*; and Lee, *Europe's Crucial Years*. L. Albertini, *The Origins of the War of 1914*, 3 vols (Oxford, 1952–7), remains the most detailed single work, although now out of date in certain respects. See also the wide-ranging literature report of K. Hildebrand, 'Imperialismus, Wettrüsten und Kriegsausbruch 1914', *Neue Politische Literatur*, Jg. xx (1975), issue 2, pp. 160–94, and issue 3, pp. 339–64.
2 The term used by Hardinge: see B. J. Williams, 'The strategic background to the Anglo-Russian entente of August 1907', *Historical Journal*, vol. IX (1966), p. 364. Apart from Monger, *The End of Isolation*, ch. 11, and Steiner, op. cit., ch. 4, see also Kazemzadeh, *Russia and Britain in Persia*, ch. 7; Hauser, *Deutschland und der englisch-russische Gegensatz*, ch. 2; and H. Jaeckel, *Die Nordwestgrenze in der Verteidigung Indiens 1900–1908 . . .* (Cologne, 1968).
3 See above, p. 285.
4 Churchill College Archives, Cambridge, Spring-Rice Papers 1/12, Chirol to Spring-Rice, 18/2/1907.
5 See above, pp. 287–8.
6 HoLRO, London, Strachey Papers, S/13/16/8, Strachey to W. T. Stead (copy), 26/3/1907; PRO, FO 800/243 (Crowe Papers), Crowe to Dilke (copy), 15/10/1907.
7 H. W. Wilson, 'Germany's hunger for Moroccan coaling stations', *National Review* (1906), pp. 276–85.
8 E. L. Woodward, *Great Britain and the German Navy* (London, 1935), ch. VI; Marder, *Dreadnought to Scapa Flow*, I, pp. 130 ff.; GP, XXIII–IV.
9 BD, VIII, no. 195.
10 Morris, *Radicalism against War*, pp. 116 ff.
11 BA-MA Freiburg, F 2045, PG 66080, Capelle memorandum (on a conversation with Stengel, September 1907?); and see also Berghahn, *Der Tirpitz-Plan*, pp. 505 ff.; Kelly, *The Naval Policy of Imperial Germany*, ch. V; J. Steinberg, 'The Novelle of 1908: necessities and choices in the Anglo-German arms race', *Transactions of the Royal Historical Society*, 5th series, vol. 21 (1971), pp. 25–43.
12 *Holstein Papers*, IV, p. 488.
13 French, 'Spy fever in Britain', pp. 356–8; Hale, *Publicity and Diplomacy*, ch. XII; Moon, *The Invasion of the United Kingdom*, pp. 307–78; Marder, op. cit., pp. 135 ff.
14 BD, VI, no. 117.
15 Marder, op. cit., pp. 144–50; PRO, FO 800/87 (Grey Papers), Grey to McKenna (copy), 5/11/1908.
16 Cited in Marder, op. cit., p. 168. The reports of the British naval attachés to Berlin for the

years 1903–13 are in Admiralty Library, Earls Court, London; some are reproduced in BD, vol. VI.

17 See Kelly, op. cit., ch. VI; Woodward, op. cit., chs X and XII; and Padfield, *The Great Naval Race*, as well as Marder's own coverage. Balfour, *The Kaiser and his Times*, p. 298, sums it up: 'The expert view now is that Tirpitz was telling the truth when he denied that any acceleration had occurred – though what would have happened had the British remained unsuspicious is another matter.'

18 Cited in Carroll, *Germany and the Great Powers*, p. 568.

19 ibid., ch. XI; and, more generally, Bridge, *From Sadowa to Sarajevo*, pp. 310 ff.; Lee, *Europe's Crucial Years*, ch. 7; B. E. Schmitt, *The Annexation of Bosnia 1908–1909* (Cambridge, Mass., 1937).

20 BD, V, no. 764; and see also D. W. Sweet, 'The Bosnian crisis', in Hinsley (ed.), op. cit., pp. 178–92.

21 See above, pp. 273–4. For Moltke's message to Vienna, see Craig, *The Politics of the Prussian Army*, pp. 288–91; Ritter, *The Sword and the Sceptre*, II, pp. 240 ff.; and N. Stone, 'Moltke-Conrad: relations between the Austro-Hungarian and German General Staffs, 1909–14', *Historical Journal*, vol. XI (1966), pp. 202–7.

22 Williamson, *The Politics of Grand Strategy*, pp. 108 ff.

23 See above, pp. 321 ff.

24 Churchill College Archives, Cambridge, Spring-Rice Papers 1/2, G. W. Balfour to Spring-Rice, 5/12/1909.

25 Taylor, *The Struggle for Mastery in Europe*, pp. 462 ff.

26 Tirpitz's phrase: see *Politische Dokumente*, I, p. 299. The Anglo-German talks are analysed in Fischer, *War of Illusions*, pp. 63 ff.; Geiss, *German Foreign Policy*, pp. 130 ff,; Steiner, op. cit., pp. 54 ff.

27 BD, VI, no 344 (minute); and see his other 1909 minute that 'unless we had the Entente we should be isolated, and might have everybody against us', in Lowe and Dockrill, *The Mirage of Power*, I, p. 39.

28 E. W. Edwards, 'The Franco-German agreement on Morocco, 1909', *English Historical Review*, vol. 78 (1963), p. 494. For the economic co-operation, see Poidevin's massive study; and H. Pogge von Strandmann, 'Rathenau, die Gebrüder Mannesmann und die Vorgeschichte der Zweiten Marokkokrise', in Geiss and Wendt (eds), *Deutschland in der Weltpolitik . . .*, pp. 251–70.

29 Steiner, op. cit., p. 56.

30 I. C. Barlow, *The Agadir Crisis* (Durham, NC, 1940); J. S. Mortimer, 'Commercial interests and German diplomacy in the Agadir crisis', *Historical Journal*, vol. X (1967), pp. 440–56; M. L. Dockrill, 'British policy during the Agadir crisis of 1911', in Hinsley (ed.), op. cit., pp. 271–87.

31 Cited in Fischer, *War of Illusions*, p. 91; and see the press coverage in Carroll, *Germany and the Great Powers*, ch. XII; and Wernecke, *Wille zur Weltgeltung*, pp. 26 ff.

32 Berghahn, *Germany and the Approach of War in 1914*, pp. 100–1.

33 BD, VII, no. 392.

34 For this debate, see Taylor, *The Struggle for Mastery in Europe*, pp. 469–71; R. A. Cosgrove, 'A note on Lloyd George's speech at the Mansion House 21 July 1911', *Historical Journal*, vol. XII (1969), pp. 698–701; K. Wilson, 'The Agadir crisis, the Mansion House speech, and the double-edgedness of agreements', *Historical Journal*, vol. XV (1972), pp. 513–32.

35 W. S. Churchill, *The World Crisis 1911–1914* (New York, 1930 edn), p. 44; Hammond, *C. P. Scott of the Manchester Guardian*, p. 161; T. Wilson (ed.), *The Political Diaries of C. P. Scott 1911–1928* (New York, 1970), p. 47.

36 K. Wilson, 'The War Office, Churchill, and the Belgian option, August to December 1911', *Bulletin of the Institute of Historical Research*, vol. 50 (1977), pp. 218–28; R. S. Churchill, *Winston S. Churchill*, vol. II.

37 M. L. Dockrill, 'David Lloyd George and foreign policy before 1914', in A. J. P. Taylor (ed.), *Lloyd George: Twelve Essays* (London, 1971), pp. 14 ff.; M. G. Fry, *Lloyd George and Foreign Policy*, Vol. 1, *The Education of a Statesman 1890–1916* (Montreal/London, 1977), chs 7 ff.

38 Lord Hankey, *The Supreme Command 1914–1918*, 2 vols (London, 1961), I, p. 82; but see also

K. Wilson, 'To the western front . . . ', *passim*, which shows that there remained some strategical flexibility. The works of S. R. Williamson, *The Politics of Grand Strategy*, Summerton, *The Development of British Military Planning for a War against Germany*, ch. 8 (especially full), and Marder, op. cit., pp. 383 ff., are important here. For a 'maritime school' attack upon the army's triumph, see D'Ombrain, *War Machinery and High Policy*, *passim*.

39 Williamson, op. cit., pp. 202–4. The radical agitations are covered in Robbins, *Grey*, ch. 12; K. Schröder, *Parlament und Aussenpolitik in England 1911–1914* (Göttingen, 1974), pp. 53 ff.; J. A. Murray, 'Foreign policy debated: Sir Edward Grey and his critics, 1911–1912', in L. P. Wallace and W. C. Askew (eds), *Power, Public Opinion and Diplomacy* (Durham, NC, 1959), pp. 140–71.

40 Berghahn, *Germany and the Approach of War in 1914*, ch. 6; Kelly, *The Naval Policy of Imperial Germany*, pp. 415 ff.; J. C. G. Röhl, 'Admiral von Müller and the approach of War, 1911–1914', *Historical Journal*, vol. XII (1969), pp. 654–9.

41 Steiner, op. cit., p. 96. See also, Cecil, *Ballin*, pp. 180ff.; Langhorne, 'Great Britain and Germany, 1911–1914', in Hinsley (ed.), op. cit., pp. 288–304; and the two clever articles, J. Steinberg, 'Diplomatie als Wille und Vorstellung: Die Berliner Mission Lord Haldanes im Februar 1912', and G. Schmidt, 'Rationalismus und Irrationalismus in der englischen Flottenpolitik', in Schottelius and Deist (eds), *Marine und Marinepolitik im kaiserlichen Deutschland*.

42 PRO, FO 800/61 (Grey Papers), Asquith to Grey, 10/4/1912.

43 BD, VI, no. 580.

44 There is a brief summary in Kennedy, *British Naval Mastery*, pp. 222–7; and fuller details in Marder, op. cit., pp. 287–98; Williamson, op. cit., pp. 227–99; P. G. Halpern, *The Mediterranean Naval Situation 1908–1914* (Cambridge, Mass., 1971), pp. 1–110; H. I. Lee, 'Mediterranean strategy and Anglo-French relations 1908–1912', *Mariners' Mirror*, 57 (1971), pp. 267–85.

45 Langhorne, 'The naval question in Anglo-German relations, 1912–14', p. 369.

46 See above, pp. 413–15.

47 Williamson, op. cit., chs 13–14; Steiner, op. cit., ch. 5 and pp. 121 ff. The impact of the Anglo-Russian naval talks upon Berlin is stressed in Hölzle, *Die Selbstentmachtung Europas*, pp. 241 ff., and E. Zechlin, 'Cabinet versus economic warfare in Germany . . . ', in H. W. Koch (ed.), *The Origins of the First World War* (London, 1972), pp. 151 ff. If Bethmann Hollweg and his circle were so depressed by this news, then logically it should have increased the urgency in their minds to keep the peace, rather than driven them to accept the army's gamble a month later. It also would make even more questionable the argument that Bethmann hoped for British neutrality.

48 See their evidence in Cab. 16/18A, CID sub-committee on 'Trading with the Enemy'; and pp. 303-4 above.

49 Churchill College Archives, Cambridge, Esher Papers 21/16, Esher lecture on 'Modern War and Peace', Cambridge 1912; H. Weinroth, 'Norman Angell and *The Great Illusion*', *Historical Journal*, vol. XVII (1974), pp. 559–74.

50 G. Schmidt, 'Innenpolitische Blockbildungen in Deutschland am Vorabend des Ersten Weltkrieges'; idem, 'Deutschland am Vorabend des Ersten Weltkrieges', in Stürmer (ed.), *Das kaiserliche Deutschland*; Mommsen, 'Die latente Krise . . . ', *passim*; Berghahn, *Germany and the Approach of War in 1914*, chs 8–9; Fischer, *War of Illusions*, pp. 95 ff.; Stegmann, *Die Erben Bismarcks*, pp. 257 ff.

51 Craig, *Germany 1866–1945*, p. 292.

52 H. Pogge von Strandmann, 'Staatsstreichpläne, Alldeutsche und Bethmann Hollweg', in idem and I. Geiss, *Die Erforderlichkeit des Unmöglichen* (Frankfurt a.M., 1965), pp. 7–45.

53 See again the references in note 50 above. Also extremely useful are K. Jarausch, 'The illusion of limited war: Chancellor Bethmann Hollweg's calculated risk, July 1914', *Central European History*, vol. 2 (1969), pp. 48–76, and his larger study, *The Enigmatic Chancellor*, chs 4–6; as well as F. Stern, 'Bethmann Hollweg and the war: the limits of responsibility', in L. Krieger and F. Stern (eds), *The Responsibility of Power* (Garden City, NY, 1967), pp. 252–85.

54 Two useful comparative studies of the political scene in Britain and Germany before 1914 are M. R. Gordon, 'Domestic conflict and the origins of the war' (stressing the differences), and G. Schmidt, 'Parlamentarisierung oder "Präventive Konterrevolution"?' (emphasising the

similarities). Neither, in my view, have it exactly right, although my own position is closer to Gordon's.

55 D. W. French, 'War and the fear of economic dislocation', MSS (draft). This forms part of Mr French's larger study, and I am grateful to him for allowing me to read it.

56 Apart from the references in the two preceding notes, see A. J. Mayer, 'Domestic causes of the First World War', in Krieger and Stern (eds), *The Responsibility of Power*, pp. 286–300; D. Lammers, 'Arno Mayer and the British decision for war in 1914', *Journal of British Studies*, vol. XII (1973), pp. 137–65; and Steiner, *Britain and the Origins of the First World War*, ch. 7.

57 Lee, *Europe's Crucial Years*, chs 10–12; Taylor, *The Struggle for Mastery in Europe*, ch. XXI; V. Dedijer, *The Road to Sarajevo* (London/New York, 1966); E. C. Helmreich, *The Diplomacy of the Balkan Wars, 1912–1913* (Cambridge, Mass., 1938).

58 L. C. F. Turner, 'The edge of the precipice: a comparison between November 1912 and July 1914', *RMC Historical Journal* (Canberra), vol. 3 (1974), pp. 3–20.

59 Morris, *Radicalism against War*, ch. 9; M. Ekstein, 'Some notes on Sir Edward Grey's policy in July 1914', *Historical Journal*, vol. XV (1972), pp. 321–4; H. Butterfield, 'Sir Edward Grey in July 1914', *Irish Historical Studies*, V (1965), pp. 1–25.

60 Röhl, 'Admiral von Muller and the approach of war . . . ', *passim*; idem, 'An der Schwelle zum Weltkrieg: Eine Dokumentation über den "Kriegsrat" vom 8. Dezember 1912', *Militärgeschichtliche Mitteilungen*, 1/1977, pp. 77–134; idem, 'Die Generalprobe. Zur Geschichte und Bedeutung des "Kriegsrates" vom 8. Dezember 1912' in D. Stegmann, B.-J. Wendt and P.-C. Witt (eds), *Industrielle Gesellschaft und politisches System* (Bonn, 1978), pp. 357–73; Fischer, *War of Illusions*, ch. 9; but see also the contrary opinions of Turner, 'The edge of the precipice', p. 18; and W. J. Mommsen, 'Domestic factors in German foreign policy before 1914', *Central European History*, vol. 6 (1973), pp. 12 ff.

61 Fischer, *War of Illusions*, pp. 392–403. The works of L. C. F. Turner, and U. Trumpener's article 'War premeditated? German Intelligence operations in July 1914', *Central European History*, vol. 9 (1976), p. 84, suggest that the German army was engaged in certain preparations which would not be complete until 1915 – although this is not the argument against Moltke deciding to seize the opportunity offered when Sarajevo occurred.

62 Much of the important literature on this debate has been referred to in the notes above. For general surveys, see Moses, *The Politics of Illusion*; W. Schieder (ed.), *Erster Weltkrieg* (Cologne, 1969); '1914', *Journal of Contemporary History*, vol. 1, no. 3 (1966); J. Remak, *The Origins of World War I* (New York, 1967); L. C. F. Turner, *Origins of the First World War* (London, 1970); I. Geiss (ed.), *July 1914: Selected Documents* (London, 1972); J. Joll, 'The 1914 debate continues', *Past and Present*, no. 34 (1966), pp. 100–13. The detailed coverage in Hölzle, *Die Selbstentmachtung Europas*, pp. 223 ff., is also worth reading, despite certain eccentricities.

63 Steiner, op. cit., p. 226; Robbins, *Grey*, pp. 293–4; Cecil, *Ballin*, pp. 204–13.

64 See pp. 422–3 above; and the revealing correspondence in V. R. Berghahn and W. Deist, 'Kaiserliche Marine und Kriegsausbruch 1914. Neue Dokumente zur Juli-Krise', *Militärgeschichtliche Mitteilungen*, 1/1970, pp. 37–58.

65 Berghahn, *Germany and the Approach of War in 1914*, ch. 10; Jarausch, 'The illusion of limited war', *passim*; and Mommsen, 'Die latente Krise . . . ', pp. 84–112, are best here. K. D. Erdmann (ed.), *Kurt Riezler: Tagebücher, Aufsätze, Dokumente* (Göttingen, 1972), reproduces the diary entries; see also, J. A. Moses, 'Karl Dietrich Erdmann, the Riezler Diary and the Fischer Controversy', *Journal of European Studies*, vol. 3 (1973), pp. 241–54.

66 I have discussed these points in the Introduction to my edition, *The War Plans of the Great Powers 1880–1914* (London, 1979). In theory, the conflict could also have been transferred to western Europe by French military action; in practice, the French held back their forces some miles from the frontier in early August – a noticeable difference.

67 Good surveys are in Steiner, op. cit., ch. 9; ch. 23 of Hinsley (ed.), op. cit.; Hazlehurst, *Politicians at War*, pt I; Butterfield, 'Sir Edward Grey in July 1914', *passim*; and Schröder, *Parlament und Aussenpolitik in England*, pp. 136 ff.

68 Robbins, *The Abolition of War*, ch. 2; Morris, *Radicalism against War*, pp. 376 ff.; M. Swartz, 'A study in futility: the British Radicals at the outbreak of the First World War', in Morris (ed.), *Edwardian Radicalism*, pp. 246–61; Marquand, *MacDonald*, ch. 9; C. Howard,

'MacDonald, Henderson and the Outbreak of War, 1914', *Historical Journal*, vol. xx (1977), pp. 878–82.

69 Cited in Morris, *Radicalism against War*, p. 412.

70 *History of the Times*, IV, pt I, pp. 208 ff.; Steed, *Through Thirty Years*, II, pp. 8–12. The impact of the European crisis upon the financial world is detailed in a fascinating Treasury memorandum by W. R. Fraser, 'The Emergency Financial Measures of 1914', August 1914, in PRO, T 172/163, pt 2.

71 *History of the Times*, IV, pt I, p. 208; and see also, Postgate and Vallance, *Those Foreigners*, pp. 219–20; and D. C. Watt, 'British reactions to the Assassination at Sarajevo', *European Studies Review*, vol. 1 (1971), pp. 233–47.

72 BD, XI, no. 369; and Steiner, *The Foreign Office and Foreign Policy*, pp. 153–64.

73 Callwell, *Wilson*, I, pp. 152–6.

74 ibid.; Steed, loc. cit., II, p. 7; Amery, *My Political Life*, II, pp. 15 ff.; L. J. Maxse, 'A Fateful Breakfast', *National Review*, August 1918; A. Chamberlain, *Down the Years* (London, 1935), pp. 93–105. Blake, *The Unknown Prime Minister*, pp. 219 ff., portrays Bonar Law in a more favourable light than Amery, who wrote that the Conservative leader did not wish to abandon his tennis game (!) and was 'with some difficulty' persuaded to return to London.

75 See the very important article by K. Wilson, 'The British Cabinet's decision for war, 2 August 1914', *British Journal of International Studies*, vol. 1 (1975), pp. 148–59; the superb commentary in Steiner, *Britain and the Origins of the First World War*, pp. 230–7; and also Hazlehurst, *Politicians at War*, pp. 114–16. All of this contradicts the strong claims of Lammers, 'Arno Mayer and the British decision for war . . .', that the message from the Conservatives played no role in the Cabinet's calculations.

76 Dockrill, 'David Lloyd George and foreign policy before 1914', pp. 25–31; and Fry, *Lloyd George and Foreign Policy*, ch. 9, analyse the Chancellor's position. Esher's comment is in *Journals and Letters*, III, p. 174.

77 Hinsley (ed.), *The Foreign Policy of Sir Edward Grey*, p. 407; Fry, op. cit., p. 213.

78 Williamson, *The Politics of Grand Strategy*, pp. 361–7; Wilson, 'To the western front . . .', pp. 165–6.

79 AA Bonn, *Nachlass* Eisendecher, vol. 3, pt 4, Tirpitz to Eisendecher, 20/12/1914; and see Tirpitz's many references to England in *Politische Dokumente*, Vol. 2.

80 Schröter, 'Chauvinism and its tradition: German writers at the outbreak of the First World War', esp. pp. 130–3; L. L. Snyder, *German Nationalism* (Harrisburg, Pa, 1952), p. 275; F. Stern, 'The political consequences of the unpolitical German', reproduced in his *The Failure of Illiberalism* (New York, 1972), esp. pp. 19–22; Dockhorn, *Deutscher Geist und Angelsächsische Geistesgeschichte*, pp. 9 ff.

81 Hatton, 'Harcourt and Solf', p. 130; M. Ekstein, 'Sir Edward Grey and Imperial Germany in 1914', *Journal of Contemporary History*, vol. 6, no. 3 (1971), pp. 121–31.

82 Cited in P. M. Kennedy, 'Idealists and realists: British views of Germany, 1864–1939', *Transactions of the Royal Historical Society*, 5th series, vol. 24 (1975), pp. 147–8.

## CONCLUSION

1 *Journal of the Royal Statistical Society*, vol. LXXVII (1913–14), pp. 807–8.

2 See the perceptive comments on this point in P. W. Schroeder, 'Munich and the British tradition', *Historical Journal*, vol. XIX (1976), pp. 223–43.

3 H. Nicolson, *Sir Arthur Nicolson, Bart., First Lord Carnock: A Study in the Old Diplomacy* (London, 1930), p. xvi.

4 Quoted in Marder, *Dreadnought to Scapa Flow*, I, p. 322.

5 A. J. P. Taylor, in a review of G. A. Craig's *Germany 1866–1945*, in the *Observer* (22/10/1978), p. 34.

6 Calleo, *The German Problem Reconsidered*, pp. 216–17.

7 K. P. Fischer, 'The Liberal image of German history', *Modern Age. A Quartely Review*, vol. 22. no. 4 (Fall 1978), pp. 371–83.

8 Chaudhuri, *Scholar Extraordinary*, p. 250.

9 Dehio, *Germany and World Politics in the Twentieth Century*, pp. 92–5.

10 BD, III, p. 402.

APPENDIX

1 *Statistical Abstract for the Principal and other Foreign Countries in Each Year from 1880 to 1890*, in *Accounts and Papers* (1892), LXXVII, p. 141.
2 *European Historical Statistics*, p. 526.
3 Bondi, *Deutschlands Aussenhandel 1815–1870*, p. 149.
4 *Statistical Abstract for the Principal and other Foreign Countries in Each Year from 1871 to 1880/81*, in *Accounts and Papers* (1882), LXXIII, p. 493.
5 'Statistics of the Foreign Trade of Germany' (C 5597), reproduced in *Accounts and Papers* (1888), CVII, pp. 89–120; Gastrell, *Our Trade in Relation to Foreign Countries 1885 to 1895*, pp. 10, 19.
6 B. Ellinger, 'Value and comparability of English and German foreign trade statistics', *Transactions of the Manchester Statistical Society* (1903–4), p. 143.
7 ibid., pp. 144–5.
8 ibid., pp. 150, 156.

# Bibliography

## UNPUBLISHED SOURCES

To provide a full description and listing of the archival sources used for this book would add considerably to its length. Virtually all of the official records provided me with useful material. The private collections were another matter; some were exceedingly valuable, others contained little for this topic. I have placed an asterisk alongside the names of the collections which were of particular value to me.

*Private Papers*
(a) British
 1 The British Library (formerly the British Museum), London: Arnold-Foster*; Avebury; A. J. Balfour*; Burns; Campbell-Bannerman; E. T. Cook; Cross; J. A. Crowe; Curzon-Middleton (Brodrick); Dilke; Escott; Gladstone, W. E. and H.; Halsbury; E. Hamilton; Iddesleigh; Kilbracken; Layard; Alexander and Edward Malet (microfilm); Marker; W. Morris; Northcliffe*; Paget; Ripon; Sir Charles Scott; C. P. Scott; J. A. Spender; Stanmore; Sydenham; E. Wrench.
 2 Public Record Office, London: Amthill (Odo Russell)*; Ardagh; G. W. Balfour; Bertie*; Bradbury; Bryce; Clarendon; Cromer*; E. A. Crowe; Curzon; Fergusson; Granville*; Grey*; E. Hamilton; E. Hammond; Hardinge; C. M. Kennedy; Kitchener; W. Langley; Lansdowne*; Lascelles*; G. Lowther; MacDonald; Malet*; Midleton; Nicolson*; Ponsonby; Roberts*; Sanderson; Satow; Spring-Rice; Tenterden; Villiers; W. White.
 3 House of Lords Record Office, London: Blumenfeld; Lloyd George*; Hannon; Bonar Law; Samuel; St Loe Strachey*; Wargrave; Willoughby de Broke.
 4 British Library of Political and Economic Science, London: Courtney; Disraeli (microfilm); Gardiner; Giffen; F. Harrison; LRC and Labour Party minutes; E. D. Morel; Passfield; Tariff Commission Papers*.
 5 Guildhall Library, London: Association of British Chambers of Commerce.
 6 National Maritime Museum, London: A. White*; Horton-Smith; Thursfield; Slade (microfilm).
 7 Naval Library, Ministry of Defence, London: Tweedmouth; Berlin naval attaché reports*.
 8 Imperial War Museum, London: Battenberg (microfilm); Dumas (microfilm); Henry Wilson (microfilm); Grant-Duff.
 9 National Army Museum, London: Roberts*.
10 Army Museums Ogilby Trust, London: Spenser Wilkinson.
11 King's College, London: Robertson; Aston; Edmonds.
12 Conservative Central Office, Research Dept, London: Party Files; Campaign literature*.
13 India Office Library, London: Curzon*; Hamilton*; Morley; Dufferin.
14 *The Times* archives, London: Chirol*; Saunders*; Steed*; Foreign Editor's Letter-Books*; Manager's Letter-Books; Subjects and Countries Files – 'Germany'.
15 Royal Archives, Windsor Castle: various series, especially 'Germany'*.

16 Bodleian Library, Oxford: Asquith*; Bryce*; Clarendon*; Mrs Creighton; Goschen; Grey-Newbolt letters; Gwynne; J. L. Hammond; W. V. Harcourt*; L. Harcourt; Milner*; Monk Bretton; Monson; Ponsonby; Horace Rumbold, jun.; Sandars*; Selborne*; Stuart-Wortley; Tweedmouth; Oxford University Anglo-German Society, minute book.
17 Rhodes House, Oxford: Rhodes.
18 Balliol College, Oxford: Morier*; C. P. Scott.
19 Nuffield College, Oxford: Mottistone.
20 All Souls College, Oxford: Onslow-Malcolm letters.
21 St Antony's College, Oxford: Boyle.
22 Christ Church College, Oxford: Drage.
23 Corpus Christi College, Oxford: Ensor.
24 Cambridge University Library, Cambridge: Acton; Blennerhassett; Crewe; Hardinge*; Kidd; Mackenzie Wallace.
25 Churchill College, Cambridge: R. Churchill; Croft; Drax; Esher*; Hankey; Lyttelton; McKenna; Saunders*; Spring-Rice*.
26 University Library, Birmingham: Beazley; A. Chamberlain; J. Chamberlain*; W. H. Dawson.
27 West Sussex Record Office, Chichester: Maxse*.
28 Guildford Muniment Room, Guildford: Onslow (4th and 5th Earls).
29 Gloucester Record Office, Gloucester: Hicks Beach.
30 Newcastle University Library, Newcastle-upon-Tyne: Runciman; C. P. Trevelyan*.
31 Liverpool Record Office, Liverpool: Derby (15th Earl)*.
32 National Library of Scotland, Edinburgh: Haldane*; Rosebery*; Kimberley (part).
33 Scottish Record Office, Edinburgh: Balfour of Burleigh; A. J. Balfour*; G. W. Balfour; Novar.
34 St Andrews University Library, St Andrews: Fisher (temporary deposit).
(in private hands)
35 Amery (London).
36 Cassel (Broadlands, Hampshire; and partly on microfilm at Churchill College, Cambridge).
37 Devonshire (Chatsworth, Derbyshire).
38 Fisher (Kilverstone, Norfolk).
39 Malet (Somerset).
40 Horace Rumbold, Sen. (Dorsetshire).
41 Salisbury, 3rd and 4th Marquesses (Hatfield, Herts.)*.
42 Duke University Library, North Carolina: various small collections, incl. Malet Papers (part).
(b) German
43 *Deutsches Zentralarchiv* I, Potsdam: Bassermann; Hammann*; Holstein; Kayser; Kusserow; Naumann; Puttkamer; Stulpnagel-Dargitz; Wolff-Metternich; Pan-German League archives*; German Colonial Society archives*.
44 *Geheimes Staatsarchiv (Stiftung Preussischer Kulturbesitz)*, Berlin-Dahlem: Albedyll; Caprivi; Schiemann*; Schnee.
45 *Auswärtiges Amt Archiv*, Bonn: Bülow, Sen.; Busch; Eckardstein; Eisendecher*; Eulenberg-Marschall letters; Richthofen.
46 *Bundesarchiv*, Koblenz: Junius Alter; Bismarck; Ludwig Boas; Boetticker; Brentano*; Bülow*; Delbrück; Eulenburg*; Harden; Hohenlohe*; Richthofen*; Rottenburg; Solf; *Kleine Erwerbungen* (Bethmann Hollweg; Julius Erbelding; Sidney Whitman).

47 *Bundesarchiv-Militärarchiv*, Freiburg: Büchsel; Capelle; Hollweg; Knorr; Levetzow; Müller*; Senden-Bibran; Schlieffen; Schulenburg-Tressow; Tirpitz*.
48 *Staat- und Universitatsbibliothek*, Hamburg: Kayser.
49 Foreign and Commonwealth Library, London: Holstein*.
(in private hands)
50 Bismarck, Otto* and Herbert*; Rantzau* (Friedrichsruh).
51 Hatzfeldt* (Haste, Niedersachsen).
52 Marschall von Bieberstein* (Neuershausen, Freiburg).
53 Münster* (Schloss Derneburg; occasional deposit in *Niedersächsisches Hauptstaatsarchiv*, Hanover).
54 Trotha (on deposit, *Staatsarchiv*, Bückeburg).

*Official Papers*
(a) British
  1 Public Record Office, London.
    Admiralty series 1 (Admiralty and Secretariat Papers); 116 (Secretary's Casebooks); 137 (War Histories); 167 (Board Minutes).
    Board of Trade series 6 (Miscellaneous); 11 (Commercial Department).
    Cabinet and Committee of Imperial Defence series 1 (Miscellaneous Records); 2 (CID Memoranda); 3 (Memoranda, Home Defence); 4 (Memoranda, Miscellaneous); 8 (Memoranda, Colonial Defence Sub-Committee); 16 (Ad Hoc Committees of Enquiry); 17 (Correspondence and Miscellaneous Papers); 20 (Schlieffen Papers); 37 (Cabinet Memoranda); 41 (Prime Minister's letters to the Monarch); 63 (Hankey Papers).
    Colonial Office series 225 (Pacific Islands); 234 (Queensland); 537 (Supplementary); 879 (Africa – Confidential Print); 881 (Australasia – Confidential Print).
    Foreign Office series 2 (Africa); 30 (Germany); 58 (Pacific Islands); 63 (Portugal); 64 (Prussia and Germany); 83 (Great Britain and General); 97 (Supplementary and General); 244 (British Embassy, Berlin); 368 (Commercial); 371 (Political); 425 (Western Europe – Confidential Print); 881 (Confidential Print).
    Treasury series 1 (Treasury Board papers); 171 (Budget and Finance Bill Papers); 172 (Miscellaneous).
    War Office series 32 (Registered Papers, General Series); 33 (Reports and Miscellaneous Papers); 106 (DMO and Intelligence).
(b) German
  2 *Auswärtiges Amt Archiv*, Bonn.
    *Abteilung* 1 A (Political Division) series Deutschland; Preussen; Sachsen-Coburg-Gotha; Europa Generalia; England; Frankreich; Russland; Spanien; Afrika Generalia; Aegypten; Marokko; Orientalia Generalia; China; Vereinigten Staaten von Amerika; Südsee.
    London Embassy Records (especially the *Geheim-Akten* and various colonial files).
  3 *Bundesarchiv*, Koblenz.
    Reichskolonialamt (xeroxes).
    Reichsschatzamt.
    Auswärtiges Amt Abt. II (Commercial Division).
  4 *Bundesarchiv-Militärarchiv*, Freiburg.
    Various series from the records of the Admiralität; Admiralstab; Kreuzer-Geschwader; Marine-Kabinett; Reichsmarineamt.
  5 *Badisches Generallandesarchiv*, Karlsruhe.
    Abteilung 49, Haus- und Staatsarchiv: Gesandtschaftsakten.
    Abteilung 233, Staatsministerium: Gesandtschaftsberichte from Berlin, and other series.

6 *Staatsarchiv*, Hamburg.
  Hanseatische Gesandtschaft (Berlin).
  Senatskommission für die Reichs- und Auswärtigen Angelegenheiten.
7 *Geheimes Staatsarchiv*, Munich.
  Staatsministerium.
  Gesandtschaftsakten (Berlin).
8 *Bayerisches Kriegsarchiv*, Munich.
  Reports of the Bavarian Military Plenipotentiary (Berlin).
9 *Württembergisches Hauptstaatsarchiv*, Stuttgart.
  Ministerium der Auswärtigen Angelegenheiten.
  Gesandtschaftsaken (Berlin).
10 *Geheimes Staatsarchiv* (*Stiftung Preussischer Kulturbesitz*), Berlin-Dahlem.
  Brandenburg-Preussisches Hausarchiv.
  Preussische Gesandtschaft in Dresden (xeroxes).
11 *Deutsches Zentralarchiv* I, Potsdam.
  Reichskanzlei.
  Reichskolonialamt.
  Auswärtiges Amt, Abteilung II (Commercial Division).
(c) Austro-Hungarian
12 *Haus-, Hof- und Staatsarchiv*, Vienna.
  Politisches Archiv (Foreign Ministry) series I (Allgemeines); III (Preussen); VIII (England).

## PUBLISHED SOURCES

The following is a list of the secondary works cited in the notes; it is in no way an exhaustive bibliography of Anglo-German relations in the period covered. The documentary series *British Documents on the Origins of the War*, *Die Grosse Politik* and *The Letters of Queen Victoria*, already abbreviated, are not mentioned again here; nor are such annual series as *The Statesman's Yearbook*, *Statistisches Jahrbuch des Deutschen Reiches*, and the *Statistical Abstract . . .* and *Annual Statement . . .* series from *Accounts and Papers*; nor, finally, are contemporary pamphlets and other publications by various leagues and individuals which appear in the notes.

## SECONDARY SOURCES

'1914', *Journal of Contemporary History*, vol. 1, no. 3 (1966).
Lord Acton, *Historical Essays and Studies* (London, 1926).
P. Adelman, *Gladstone, Disraeli and Later Victorian Politics* (London, 1970).
P. Adelman, 'Frederick Harrison and the 'positivist' attack on orthodox political economy', *History of Political Economy*, vol. 3 (1971).
D. Albers, *Reichstag und Aussenpolitik 1871–79* (Berlin, 1927).
L. Albertini, *The Origins of the War of 1914*, 3 vols (Oxford, 1952–7).
D. H. Aldcroft (ed.), *The Development of British Industry and Foreign Competition 1875–1914* (London, 1968).
H. C. Allen, *Great Britain and the United States . . . 1783–1952* (London, 1954).
M. J. Allison, *The National Service Issue 1899–1914* (Ph.D. thesis, London, 1975).
J. L. Altholz, 'Gladstone and the Vatican decrees', *The Historian*, vol. xxv (1963).
L. S. Amery, *My Political Life*, 3 vols (London, 1953).
E. N. Anderson, *The First Moroccan Crisis 1904–1906* (Chicago, 1930).

E. N. Anderson, *Social and Political Conflict in Prussia 1858–1864* (Lincoln, Neb., 1954).

P. R. Anderson, *The Background of Anti-English Feeling in Germany, 1890–1902* (New York, 1969 reprint).

C. Andrew, *Théodore Delcassé and the Making of the Entente Cordiale* (London, 1968).

Anon., *The History of the Times*, 5 vols (London, 1935–52).

S. W. Armstrong, 'The Social Democrats and the unification of Germany 1863–1871', *Journal of Modern History*, vol. 12 (1940).

S. W. Armstrong, 'The internationalism of the early Social Democrats in Germany', *American Historical Review*, vol. XLVII (1942).

W. H. G. Armytage, *The German Influence on English Education* (London, 1969).

T. Arnold, *Introductory Lectures on Modern History* (London, 1871).

A. Ascher, 'Professors as propagandists: the politics of the *Kathedersozialisten*', *Journal of Central European Affairs*, 23 (1963).

R. D. Attick, *The English Common Reader* (Chicago, 1957).

H. Aubin and W. Zorn (eds), *Handbuch der deutschen Wirtschafts- und Sozialgeschichte*, vol. 2 (Stuttgart, 1976).

J. W. Auld, 'The pro-Boers', *Journal of British Studies*, vol. XIV (1975).

W. O. Aydelotte, 'Wollte Bismarck Kolonien?', in W. Conze (ed.), *Deutschland und Europa* (Düsseldorf, 1951).

W. O. Aydelotte, *Bismarck and British Colonial Policy: The Problem of South West Africa 1883–1885* (Westport, Conn., 1970 reprint).

K. J. Bade, *Friedrich Fabri und der Imperialismus in der Bismarckzeit* (Freiburg, 1975).

M. L. Balfour, *The Kaiser and his Times* (New York, 1972 edn).

A. Banze, *Die deutsch-englische Wirtschaftsrivalität* (Berlin, 1935).

T. Barclay, *Thirty Years Anglo-French Reminiscences* (London, 1914).

K. D. Barkin, *The Controversy over German Industrialisation 1890–1902* (Chicago, 1970).

K. D. Barkin, 'Conflict and concord in Wilhelmian social thought', *Central European History*, vol. 5 (1972).

I. C. Barlow, *The Agadir Crisis* (Durham, NC, 1940).

C. Barnett, *The Collapse of British Power* (London/New York, 1972).

C. J. Bartlett, 'The mid-Victorian reappraisal of naval policy', in K. Bourne and D. C. Watt (eds), *Studies in International History* (London, 1967).

C. J. Bartlett (ed.), *Britain Pre-eminent. Studies of British World Influence in the Nineteenth Century* (London, 1969).

P. Bastin, *La Rivalité commerciale anglo-allemande et les origines de la première guerre mondiale 1871–1914* (dissertation, Brussels, 1959).

T. A. Bayer, *England und der neue Kurs 1890–1895* (Tübingen, 1955).

J. O. Baylen, 'The "new journalism" in late Victorian England', *Australian Journal of Politics and History*, vol. 18 (1972).

J. Becker, 'Der Krieg mit Frankreich als Problem der kleindeutschen Einigungspolitik Bismarcks 1866–1870', in M. Stürmer (ed.), *Das kaiserliche Deutschland* (Düsseldorf, 1970).

M. Beloff, 'The special relationship: an Anglo-American myth', in M. Gilbert (ed.), *A Century of Conflict 1850–1950* (London, 1966).

M. Beloff, *Imperial Sunset*, Vol. 1, *Britains Liberal Empire 1897–1921* (London, 1969).

E. A. Benians, J. R. M. Butler and C. E. Carrington (eds), *Cambridge History of the British Empire*, Vol. III (Cambridge, 1959).

R. M. Berdahl, 'Conservative politics and aristocratic landowners in Bismarckian Germany', *Journal of Modern History*, vol. 44 (1972).

R. M. Berdahl, 'New thoughts on German nationalism', *American Historical Review*, vol. 77 (1972).

V. R. Berghahn, 'Zu den Zielen des deutschen Flottenbaues unter Wilhelm II', *Historische Zeitschrift*, 210 (1970).

V. R. Berghahn, *Der Tirpitz-Plan* (Düsseldorf, 1971).

V. R. Berghahn, *Germany and the Approach of War in 1914* (London, 1973).

V. R. Berghahn, (ed.), *Militarismus* (Cologne, 1975).

V. R. Berghahn and W. Deist, 'Kaiserliche Marine und Kriegsausbruch 1914. Neue Dokumente zur Juli-Krise', *Militärgeschichtliche Mitteilungen*, 1/1970.

B. Bergonzi, 'Before 1914: writers and the threat of war', *Critical Quarterly*, vol. 6 (1964).

S. Bernstein, 'The First International and the great powers', *Science and Society*, vol. XVI (1952).

G. F. A. Best, 'Popular Protestantism in Victorian England', in R. Robson (ed.), *Ideas and Institutions of Victorian Britain* (London, 1967).

G. F. A. Best, 'Militarism and the Victorian public schools', in B. Simon and I. Bradley (eds), *The Victorian Public School* (London, 1975).

Otto von Bismarck, *Die gesammelten Werke*, ed. H. von Petersdorff *et al.*, 15 vols (Berlin, 1923–33).

D. Blackbourn, 'The political alignment of the Centre Party in Wilhelmine Germany: a study of the party's emergence in nineteenth century Württemberg', *Historical Journal*, vol. XVIII (1975).

D. Blackbourn, 'Class and politics in Wilhelmine Germany: the Centre Party and the Social Democrats in Württemberg', *Central European History*, vol. IX (1976).

D. Blackbourn, 'The problem of democratisation: German Catholics and the role of the Centre Party', in R. J. Evans (ed.), *Society and Politics in Wilhelmine Germany* (London/New York, 1978).

R. Blake, *The Unknown Prime Minister* (London, 1955).

R. Blake, *Disraeli* (London, 1966).

R. Blake, *The Conservative Party from Peel to Churchill* (London, 1972 edn).

N. Blewett, 'The franchise in the United Kingdom, 1885–1918', *Past and Present*, 32 (1965).

N. Blewett, 'Free fooders, Balfourites, whole hoggers. Factionalism within the Unionist Party, 1906–10', *Historical Journal*, vol. XI (1968).

H. Bley, *Bebel und die Strategie der Kriegsverhütung 1904–1913* (Göttingen, 1975).

S. F. Bloom, *The World of Nations* (New York, 1941).

F. Boese, *Geschichte des Vereins für Sozialpolitik 1879–1932* (Berlin, 1939).

E. Böhm, *Ueberseehandel und Flottenbau* (Düsseldorf, 1972).

H. Böhme, *Deutschlands Weg zur Grossmacht* (Cologne/Berlin, 1966).

H. Böhme, 'Big-business pressure groups and Bismarck's turn to protectionism, 1873–79', *Historical Journal*, vol. X (1967).

G. Bondi, *Deutschlands Aussenhandel 1815–1870* (Berlin, 1958).

H. Booms, *Die Deutschkonservative Partei* (Düsseldorf, 1954).

K. E. Born, 'Structural changes in German social and economic development at the end of the nineteenth century', in J. J. Sheehan (ed.), *Imperial Germany* (New York/London, 1976).

H. Bornkamm, 'Die Staatsidee im Kulturkampf', *Historische Zeitschrift*, vol. 170 (1950).

K. Bosl, 'Die Verhandlungen über den Eintritt der süddeutschen Staaten in den Norddeutschen Bund und die Entstehung der Reichverfassung', in T. Schieder and E. Deuerlein (eds), *Reichsgründung 1870/71* (Stuttgart, 1970).

K. Bourne, *The Foreign Policy of Victorian England 1830–1902* (Oxford, 1970).

D. Bowen, *The Idea of the Victorian Church* (Montreal, 1968).

R. H. Bowen, *German Theories of the Corporative State* (New York, 1947).

T. Boyle, *The Liberal Party and Foreign Affairs, 1895–1905* (M. Phil. thesis, London, 1969).

M. V. Brett and O. Esher, *The Journals and Letters of Reginald Viscount Esher*, 4 vols (London, 1934–8).

F. R. Bridge, *From Sadowa to Sarajevo: The Foreign Policy of Austria-Hungary, 1866–1914* (London, 1972).

G. Brook-Shepherd, *Uncle of Europe* (London, 1975).

B. H. Brown, *The Tariff Reform Movement in Great Britain 1881–1895* (New York, 1943).

K. D. Brown, 'The Trade Union Tariff Reform Association, 1903–1913', *Journal of British Studies*, vol. IX (1970).

K. D. Brown (ed.), *Essays in Anti-Labour History* (London, 1973).

L. Brown, 'The treatment of the news in mid-Victorian newspapers', *Transactions of the Royal Historical Society*, 5th series, vol. 27 (1977).

M. L. Brown, 'The monarchical principle in Bismarckian diplomacy after 1870', *The Historian*, vol. 15 (1952).

K. Buchheim, *Ultramontanismus und Demokratie* (Munich, 1963).

I. Buisson, 'Aussenpolitische Vorstellungen Bismarcks nach seiner Entlassung', in A. Fischer, G. Moltmann and K. Schwabe (eds), *Russland–Deutschland–Amerika* (Wiesbaden, 1978).

B. von Bülow, *Deutsche Politik* (Berlin, 1916).

B. von Bülow, *Denkwürdigkeiten*, 4 vols (Berlin, 1930).

W. L. Burn, *The Age of Equipoise* (London, 1964).

B. C. Busch, *Britain and the Persian Gulf, 1894–1914* (Berkeley, Calif., 1967).

M. Busch, *Bismarck, Some Secret Pages of his History*, 3 vols (London, 1898).

W. Bussmann, *Treitschke, sein Welt- und Geschichtsbild* (Göttingen, 1952).

W. Bussmann, 'Monarchie und Republik: Das zweite Ministerium Gladstones im Spiegel der Privatkorrespondenz Herbert Bismarcks', in W. Berges and C. Hinricks (eds), *Zur Geschichte und Problematik der Demokratie* (Berlin, 1958).

W. Bussmann, 'Zur Geschichte des deutschen Liberalismus in 19. Jahrhundert', *Historische Zeitschrift*, vol. 186 (1958).

W. Bussmann (ed.), *Staatssekretär Graf Herbert von Bismarck. Aus seiner politischen Privatkorrespondenz* (Göttingen, 1964).

D. Butler and J. Freeman, *British Political Facts 1900–1968* (London, 1969).

J. Butler, 'The German factor in Anglo-Transvaal relations', in P. Gifford and W. R. Louis (eds), *Britain and Germany in Africa* (New Haven, Conn., 1967).

J. R. M. Butler, *Lord Lothian* (London, 1960).

H. Butterfield, 'Sir Edward Grey in July 1914', *Irish Historical Studies*, V (1965).

K. Büttner, *Die Anfänge der deutschen Kolonialpolitik in Ostafrika* (East Berlin, 1959).

D. Calleo, *The German Problem Reconsidered* (Cambridge, 1978).

C. E. Callwell, *Field-Marshall Sir Henry Wilson. His Life and Diaries*, 2 vols (New York, 1927).

C. S. Campbell, *From Revolution to Rapprochement: The United States and Great Britain 1783–1900* (New York, 1974).

S. C. Carpenter, *Church and People, 1789–1889* (London, 1933).

E. M. Carroll, *Germany and the Great Powers 1866–1914* (New York, 1938).

G. Cecil, *Life of Robert . . . Marquis of Salisbury*, 4 vols (London, 1921–32).

L. Cecil, 'Coal for the fleet that had to die', *American Historical Review*, vol. LXIX (1964).

L. Cecil, *Albert Ballin* (Princeton, 1967).

L. Cecil, *The German Diplomatic Service 1871–1914* (Princeton, 1976).

O. Chadwick, *The Secularisation of the European Mind* (Cambridge, 1975).

A. Chamberlain, *Down the Years* (London, 1935).

M. E. Chamberlain, 'Clement Hill's memoranda and the British interest in East Africa', *English Historical Review*, vol. LXXXVII (1972).

J. D. Chambers, *The Workshop of the World*, 2nd edn (Oxford, 1968).

J. D. Chamier, *Fabulous Monster* (London, 1934).

V. E. Chancellor, *History for their Masters* (Bath, 1970).

M. K. Chapman, *Great Britain and the Bagdad Railway, 1870–1914* (Northampton, Mass., 1948).

S. D. Chapman, 'The international houses: the continental contribution to British commerce, 1800–1860', *Journal of European Economic History*, vol. 6 (1977).

N. C. Chaudhuri, *Scholar Extraordinary* (London/New York, 1974).

S. G. Checkland, 'The mind of the City 1870–1914', *Oxford Economic Papers*, 9 (1957).

S. G. Checkland, 'Growth and progress: the nineteenth-century view in Britain', *Economic History Review*, 2nd series, vol. XII (1959).

R. Chickering, *Imperial Germany and a World without War: The Peace Movement and German Society, 1892–1914* (Princeton, 1975).

R. Chickering, 'Problems of a German peace movement, 1890–1914', in S. Wank (ed.), *Doves and Diplomats* (London, 1978).

R. Chickering, 'Der "Deutsche Wehrverein" und die Reform der deutschen Armee 1912–1914', *Militärgeschichtliche Mitteilungen*, 1/1979.

V. Chirol, *Fifty Years in a Changing World* (London, 1927).

H. Christern, 'Einfluss und Abwehr englisher politischer Ideologie in Deutschland vom 18. bis ins 20. Jahrhundert', in C. A. Weber (ed.), *Die englische Kulturideologie* (Stuttgart/Berlin, 1943).

R. S. Churchill, *Winston S. Churchill*, Vol. II, and Companion Vol. II, pts 1–3 (London, 1967–9).

W. S. Churchill, *Randolph Churchill*, 2 vols (London, 1906).

W. S. Churchill, *The World Crisis 1911–1914* (New York, 1930 edn).

J. H. Clapham, *The Economic Development of France and Germany 1815–1914* (Cambridge, 1968 edn).

E. A. Clark, 'Adolph Wagner: from National Economist to National Socialist', *Political Science Quarterly*, vol. 55 (1940).

I. F. Clarke, 'The Battle of Dorking, 1871–1914', *Victorian Studies*, vol. VIII (1965).

I. F. Clarke, *Voices Prophesying War 1763–1984* (London, 1970 edn).

P. F. Clarke, *Lancashire and the New Liberalism* (Cambridge, 1971).

P. F. Clarke, 'The end of laissez faire and the politics of cotton', *Historical Journal*, vol. XV (1972).

P. F. Clarke, 'The electoral position of the Liberal and Labour parties 1910–1914', *English Historical Review*, vol. 90 (1975).

P. F. Clarke, *Liberals and Social Democrats* (Cambridge, 1978).

H. A. Clegg, A. Fox and A. F. Thompson, *A History of British Trade Unions since 1899*, Vol. 1 (Oxford, 1964).

G. D. H. Cole, *A Short History of the British Working-Class Movement 1789–1947* (London, 1948).

H. Collins, 'The English branches of the First International', in A. Briggs and J. Saville (eds), *Essays in Labour History* (London, 1960).

H. Collins, 'The international and the British labour movement', *Society for the Study of Labour History*, Bulletin no. 9 (autumn 1964).

H. Collins and C. Abramsky, *Karl Marx and the British Labour Movement* (London, 1965).

557

R. O. Collins, 'Origins of the Nile struggle: Anglo-German negotiations and the Mackinnon agreement of 1890', in P. Gifford and W. R. Louis (eds), *Britain and Germany in Africa* (New Haven, Conn., 1967).

W. Conze, 'Friedrich Naumann. Grundlagen und Ansatz seiner Politik in der national-sozialen Zeit (1895 bis 1903)', in W. Hubatsch (ed.), *Schicksalwege deutscher Vergangenheit* (Düsseldorf, 1950).

W. Conze and D. Groh, *Die Arbeiterbewegung in der Nationalbewegung* (Stuttgart, 1966).

V. Conzemius (ed.), *Johann Joseph Ignaz von Döllinger: Briefwechsel mit Lord Acton*, 3 vols (Munich, 1963–71).

C. Cook, 'Labour and the downfall of the Liberal Party, 1906–1914', in A. Sked and C. Cook (eds), *Crisis and Controversy* (London, 1976).

E. Cook, *Delane of The Times* (London, 1916).

J. Cornford, 'The transformation of conservatism in the late 19th century', *Victorian Studies*, vol. VII (1963).

R. A. Cosgrove, 'A note on Lloyd George's speech at the Mansion House 21 July 1911', *Historical Journal*, vol. XII (1969).

R. Coupland, *The Exploitation of East Africa 1856–1890*, 2nd edn (London, 1968).

M. Cowling, *1867: Disraeli, Gladstone and Revolution* (Cambridge, 1967).

G. A. Craig, 'Great Britain and the Belgian railways dispute of 1869', *American Historical Review*, vol. 50 (1945).

G. A. Craig, *The Politics of the Prussian Army 1640–1945* (New York, 1975 reprint).

G. A. Craig, *Germany 1866–1945* (Oxford, 1978).

E. Crammond, 'The economic relations of the British and German empires', *Journal of the Royal Historical Society*, vol. LXXVII (1914).

R. J. Crampton, 'August Bebel and the British Foreign Office', *History*, vol. 58 (1973).

S. E. Crowe, *The Berlin West African Conference 1884–1885* (Westport, Conn., 1970 reprint).

M. A. Crowther, *Church Embattled: Religious Controversy in Mid-Victorian England* (Newton Abbott, 1970).

H. Cunningham, *The Volunteers* (Hamden, Conn., 1975).

*Daily News Year Book, 1911* (London, 1911).

G. Dangerfield, *The Strange Death of Liberal England* (New York, 1935).

E. Daniels, 'Die englischen Liberalen und Fürst Bismarck', *Preussischer Jahrbücher*, 123 (1906).

A. I. Dasent, *John Thadeus Delane*, 2 vols (London, 1908).

P. Deane and W. A. Cole, *British Economic Growth 1688–1959. Trends and Structures* (Cambridge, 1967).

M. de Cecco, *Money and Empire. The International Gold Standard 1890–1914* (London, 1974).

G. Deckart, *Deutsch-englische Verständigung: Eine Darstellung der nichtoffiziellen Bemühungen um eine Wiederannäherungen der beiden Länder zwischen 1905 und 1914* (phil. Diss., Munich, 1967).

V. Dedijer, *The Road to Sarajevo* (London/New York, 1966).

L. Dehio, *Germany and World Politics in the Twentieth Century* (New York, 1959).

L. Dehio, *The Precarious Balance* (London, 1963).

W. Deist, *Flottenpolitik und Flottenpropaganda* (Stuttgart, 1976).

C. Derwent, *The Derwent Story* (New York, 1953).

K. Dockhorn, *Der deutsche Historismus in England* (Göttingen, 1950).

K. Dockhorn, *Deutsche Geist und angelsächsische Geistesgeschichte* (Göttingen, 1954).

M. L. Dockrill, 'David Lloyd George and foreign policy before 1914', in A. J. P. Taylor (ed.), *Lloyd George: Twelve Essays* (London, 1971).

M. L. Dockrill, 'British policy during the Agadir crisis of 1911', in F. H. Hinsley (ed.), *The Foreign Policy of Sir Edward Grey* (Cambridge, 1977).

J. Doerr, 'Domestic influences on Bismarck's foreign policy', in D. K. Buse (ed.), *Aspects of Imperial Germany* (vol. 5, no. 3 of *Laurentian University Review*, 1973).

P. Domann, *Sozialdemokratie und Kaisertum unter Wilhelm II* (Wiesbaden, 1974).

A. Dorpalen, 'Emperor Frederick III and the German Liberal movement', *American Historical Review*, vol. 54 (1948).

A. Dorpalen, 'The German Conservatives and the parliamentarisation of Imperial Germany', *Journal of Central European Affairs*, vol. 11 (1951).

A. Dorpalen, *Heinrich von Treitschke* (New Haven, Conn., 1957).

R. Douglas, 'Labour in decline, 1910–14', in K. D. Brown (ed.), *Essays in Anti-Labour History* (London, 1974).

A. Drue, *The Church in the Nineteenth Century: Germany 1800–1918* (London, 1963).

W. Duden, *Die Wurzeln des deutsch-englischen Gegensatzes* (phil. Diss., Hamburg, 1933).

D. Düding, *Der Nationalsozialen Verein 1896–1903* (Munich/Vienna, 1972).

E. M. Earle, *Turkey, the Great Powers and the Bagdad Railway* (New York, 1923).

G. Ebel (ed.), *Botschafter Paul Graf von Hatzfeldt Nachgelassene Papiere 1838–1901*, 2 vols (Boppard, 1976).

K. Eberhard, *Herbert von Bismarcks Sondermissionen in England 1882–1889* (phil. Diss., Erlangen, 1949).

H. von Eckardstein, *Lebenserinnerungen und Politische Denkwürdigkeiten*, 3 vols (Leipzig, 1919–21).

E. W. Edwards, 'The Franco-German agreement on Morocco, 1909', *English Historical Review*, vol. 78 (1963).

M. Ekstein, 'Sir Edward Grey and Imperial Germany in 1914', *Journal of Contemporary History*, vol. 6, no. 3 (1971).

M. Ekstein, 'Some notes on Sir Edward Grey's policy in July 1914', *Historical Journal*, vol. xv (1972).

C. C. Eldridge, *England's Mission: The Imperial Idea in the Age of Gladstone and Disraeli* (London, 1973).

G. Eley, 'Sammlungspolitik, social imperialism and the Navy Law of 1898', *Militärgeschichtliche Mitteilungen*, 1/1974.

G. Eley, 'Defining social imperialism: use and abuse of an idea', *Social History*, no. 3 (1976).

G. Eley, 'Reshaping the Right: radical nationalism and the German Navy League, 1898–1908', *Historical Journal*, vol. xxi (1978).

G. Eley, 'The Wilhelmine Right: how it changed', in R. J. Evans (ed.), *Society and Politics in Wilhelmine Germany* (London, 1978).

A. Ellegård, 'The readership of the periodical press in mid-Victorian Britain', *Göteborgs Universitets Årsskrift*, vol. lxiii (1957), pt 3.

B. Ellinger, 'Value and comparability of English and German foreign trade statistics', *Transactions of the Manchester Statistical Society* (1903–4).

L. E. Elliott-Binns, *English Thought 1860–1900. The Theological Aspect* (London, 1956).

E. W. Ellsworth, 'The Austro-Prussian War and the British press', *The Historian*, vol. xx (1958).

L. Elm, *Zwischen Fortschritt und Reaktion. Geschichte der Parteien der liberalen Bourgeoisie in Deutschland 1893–1918* (Berlin, 1968).

H. V. Emy, 'The impact of financial policy on English politics before 1914', *Historical Journal*, vol. xv (1972).

H. V. Emy, *Liberals, Radicals and Social Politics 1892–1914* (Cambridge, 1973).

E. Engelberg, 'Die Rolle von Marx und Engels bei der Herausbildung einer selbstständigen deutschen Arbeiterpartei (1864–1869)', *Zeitschrift für Geschichtswissenschaft*, vol. 2 (1954).

E. Engelberg, *Revolutionäre Politik und Rote Feldpost 1878–1890* (Berlin, 1960).

R. C. K. Ensor, *England 1870–1914* (Oxford, 1936).

K. Epstein, *Matthias Erzberger and the Dilemma of German Democracy* (Princeton, 1959).

K. D. Erdmann (ed.), *Kurt Riezler: Tagebücher, Aufsätze, Dokumente* (Göttingen, 1972).

E. M. Everett, *The Party of Humanity: The Fortnightly Review and its Contributors 1865–1874* (Chapel Hill, NC, 1939).

E. Eyck, *Das persönliche Regiment Wilhelm II . . . 1890 bis 1914* (Erlenbach-Zurich, 1948).

E. Eyck, *Bismarck and the German Empire* (London, 1950).

K. G. Faber, 'Realpolitik als Ideologie: Die Bedeutung des Jahres 1866 für das politische Denken in Deutschland', *Historische Zeitschrift*, 203 (1966).

Lord Farrar, *Free Trade versus Fair Trade*, ed. C. H. Chomley (London, 1904 edn).

L. L. Farrar, 'Importance of omnipotence: the paralysis of the European great power system, 1871–1914', *International Review of History and Political Science*, vol. IX, no. 1 (1972).

G. E. Fasnacht, *Acton's Political Philosophy. An Analysis* (London, 1952).

H. Fawcett, *Free Trade and Protection* (London, 1878).

E. J. Feuchtwanger, *Disraeli, Democracy and the Tory Party* (Oxford, 1968).

S. G. Firth, 'The New Guinea Company, 1885–1899: a case of unprofitable imperialism', *Historical Studies*, vol. 15 (1972).

S. G. Firth, 'German firms in the Pacific islands, 1857–1914', in J. Moses and P. M. Kennedy (eds), *Germany in the Pacific and Far East 1870–1914* (St Lucia, Queensland, 1977).

F. Fischer, *War of Illusions* (London, 1975).

K. P. Fischer, 'The Liberal image of German history', *Modern Age. A Quarterly Review*, vol. 22, no. 4 (fall 1978).

W. Fischer, 'Matthew Arnold und Deutschland', *Germanisch-Romanische Monatsschrift*, vol. 35 (1947).

I. Fischer-Frauendienst, *Bismarcks Pressepolitik* (Münster, 1963).

H. A. L. Fisher, 'Sir John Seeley', *Fortnightly Review* (August 1896).

E. Fitzmaurice, *Life of Lord Granville*, 2 vols (London, 1905).

M. P. Fleischer, 'Die AntiBismarckbroschüren Ludwig von Gerlachs als tagespolitischer Niederschlag einer Geschichtphilosophie', *Historische Zeitschrift*, vol. 225 (1977).

R. Fletcher, 'An English advocate in Germany: Eduard Bernstein's analysis of Anglo-German relations, 1900–1914', *Canadian Journal of History*, vol. XIII (1978).

J. E. Flint, 'Britain and the partition of West Africa', in J. E. Flint and G. Williams (eds), *Perspectives of Empire* (London, 1973).

F. R. Flournoy, 'British Liberal theories of international relations, 1848–1898', *Journal of the History of Ideas*, vol. 7 (1946).

M. R. D. Foot, 'Great Britain and Luxembourg 1867', *English Historical Review*, vol. 67 (1952).

I. L. D. Forbes, 'German informal imperialism in South America before 1914', *Economic History Review*, 2nd series, vol. XXXI (1978).

H. R. Fox Bourne, *English Newspapers. Chapters in the History of Journalism*, 2 vols (New York, 1966 reprint).

J. D. Fraley, 'Government by procrastination: Chancellor Hohenlohe and Kaiser Wilhelm II, 1894–1900', *Central European History*, vol. VII (1974).

R. M. Francis, 'The British withdrawal from the Bagdad Railway project in April 1903', *Historical Journal*, vol. XVI (1973).

B. W. Franke, 'Handelsneid und Grosse Politik in den deutsch-englischen Beziehungen 1871–1914', *Zeitschrift für Politik*, vol. XXIX (1939).

G. Franz, *Bismarcks Nationalgefühl* (Leipzig, 1926).

P. Fraser, 'The Liberal Unionist alliance: Chamberlain, Hartington and the Conservatives, 1886–1904', *English Historical Review*, vol. 77 (1962).

P. Fraser, 'Unionism and Tariff Reform: the crisis of 1906', *Historical Journal*, vol. V (1962).

P. Fraser, 'The Unionist debacle of 1911 and Balfour's retirement', *Journal of Modern History*, vol. XXXV (1963).

P. Fraser, *Lord Esher* (London, 1973).

M. Freeden, *The New Liberalism* (Oxford, 1978).

D. French, 'Spy fever in Britain, 1900–1915', *Historical Journal*, vol. XXI (1978).

D. Fricke, 'Der Reichsverband gegen die Sozialdemokratie von seiner Gründung bis zu den Reichstagwahlen von 1907', *Zeitschrift für Geschichtswissenschaft*, 7 (1959).

D. Fricke (ed.), *Die bürgerlichen Parteien in Deutschland*, 2 vols (Leipzig, 1968–70).

E. G. Friehe, *Geschichte der "National-Zeitung" 1848 bis 1878* (Leipzig, 1933).

M. G. Fry, *Lloyd George and Foreign Policy*, Vol. 1, *The Education of a Statesman 1890–1916* (Montreal/London, 1977).

R. Fulford (ed.), *Your Dear Letter. Private Correspondence of Queen Victoria and the Crown Princess of Prussia 1865–1871* (London, 1971).

R. Fulford (ed.), *Darling Child: Private Correspondence of Queen Victoria and the Crown Princess of Prussia 1871–1878* (London, 1976).

J. S. Galbraith, *Mackinnon and East Africa 1878–1895* (Cambridge, 1972).

L. Gall, 'Bismarck und England', in P. Kluke and P. Alter (eds), *Aspekte der deutsch-britischen Beziehungen im Laufe der Jahrhunderte* (Stuttgart, 1978).

L. H. Gann and P. Duignan, *The Rulers of German Africa 1884–1914* (Stanford, Calif., 1977).

A. Harding Ganz, *The Role of the Imperial German Navy in Colonial Affairs* (Ph.D. thesis, Ohio State University, 1972).

A. Harding Ganz, 'Colonial policy and the Imperial German Navy', *Militärgeschichtliche Mitteilungen*, 1/1977.

A. Harding Ganz, 'The German navy in the Far East and Pacific: the seizure of Kiautschou and after', in J. Moses and P. M. Kennedy (eds), *Germany in the Pacific and Far East 1870–1914* (St Lucia, Queensland, 1977).

A. G. Gardiner, *Life of Sir William Harcourt*, 2 vols (London, 1923).

J. L. Garvin and J. Amery, *Life of Joseph Chamberlain*, 6 vols (London, 1932–69).

W. S. H. Gastrell, *Our Trade in the World in Relation to Foreign Competition 1885–1895* (London, 1897).

A. E. Gathorne-Hardy (ed.), *Gathorne-Hardy, First Earl of Cranbrook* . . . 2 vols (London, 1910).

P. Gay, *The Dilemma of Democratic Socialism: Eduard Bernstein's Challenge to Marx* (New York, 1952).

D. Geary, 'The German labour movement 1848–1919', *European Studies Review*, vol. 6 (1976).

I. Geiss (ed.), *July 1914: Selected Documents* (London, 1972).

I. Geiss, *German Foreign Policy 1871–1914* (London, 1976).

R. Gellately, *The Politics of Economic Despair: Shopkeepers and German Politics 1890–1914* (London, 1974).

H. Gemkov, 'Dokumente des Kampfes der deutschen Sozialdemokratie gegen Bismarcks Kolonialpolitik und gegen den Rechtsopportunismus in den Jahren 1884/85', *Beiträge zur Geschichte der deutschen Arbeiterbewegung*, vol. 1 (1959).

A. Gerschrenkon, *Bread and Democracy in Germany* (New York, 1966 edn).

B. B. Gilbert, 'Health and politics: the British Physical Deterioration Report of 1904', *Bulletin of the History of Medicine*, vol. 34 (1965).

B. B. Gilbert, 'David Lloyd George: land, the budget, and social reform', *American Historical Review*, vol. 81 (1976).

M. Gilbert, *Sir Horace Rumbold* (London, 1973).

D. R. Gillard, *Lord Salisbury's Foreign Policy 1888–1892, with Special Reference to Anglo-German Relations* (Ph.D thesis, University of London, 1952).

D. R. Gillard, 'Salisbury's African policy and the Heligoland offer of 1890', *English Historical Review*, vol. 75 (1960).

D. R. Gillard, 'Salisbury's Heligoland offer: the case against the "Witu Thesis"', *English Historical Review*, vol. 80 (1965).

D. R. Gillard, 'Salisbury and the Indian defence problem, 1885–1902', in K. Bourne and D. C. Watt (eds), *Studies in International History* (London, 1967).

G. Gillessen, *Lord Palmerston und die Einigung Deutschlands* (Lübeck/Hamburg, 1961).

F. J. Glendenning, 'Attitudes to colonialism and race in British and French history schoolbooks', *History of Education*, 3 (1974).

W. Goetz (ed.), *Briefe Wilhelms II. an den Zaren 1894–1914* (Berlin, 1920).

C. S. Goldman (ed.), *The Empire and the Century* (London, 1905).

A. M. Gollin, *The Observer and J. L. Garvin* (London, 1960).

A. M. Gollin, *Proconsul in Politics* (London, 1964).

A. M. Gollin, *Balfour's Burden* (London, 1965).

J. Gooch, *The Plans of War. The General Staff and British Military Strategy, c.1900–1916* (London/New York, 1974).

J. Gooch, 'Sir George Clarke's career at the Committee of Imperial Defence, 1904–1907', *Historical Journal*, vol. XVIII (1975).

S. Gopal, *British Policy in India 1858–1905* (Cambridge, 1965).

M. R. Gordon, 'Domestic conflict and the origins of the First World War: the British and German cases', *Journal of Modern History*, vol. 46 (1974).

W. Görlitz (ed.), *Der Kaiser . . .* (Göttingen, 1965).

P. Gottfried, 'Adam Smith and German social thought', *Modern Age*, 21 (1977).

H. Gottwald, 'Der Umfall des Zentrums. Die Stellung der Zentrumspartei zur Flotten-Vorlage von 1897', in F. Klein (ed.), *Studien zum deutschen Imperialismus vor 1914* (Berlin, 1976).

J. M. Goudswaard, *Some Aspects of the End of Britain's 'Splendid Isolation', 1898–1904* (Rotterdam, 1952).

P. A. Gourevitch, 'International trade, domestic coalitions, and liberty: comparative responses to the crisis of 1873–1896', *Journal of Interdisciplinary History*, vol. VIII (1977).

G. S. Graham, 'Cobden's influence on Bismarck', *Queen's Quarterly*, vol. XXXVIII (1931).

R. L. Greaves, *Persia and the Defence of India 1884–1892* (London, 1959).

H. Grebing, *A History of the German Labour Movement* (London, 1969).

K. H. Grenner, *Wirtschaftsliberalismus und katholisches Denken* (Cologne, 1967).

J. A. S. Grenville, 'Goluchowski, Salisbury, and the Mediterranean Agreements, 1895–1897', *Slavonic and East European Review*, vol. XXXVI (1958).

J. A. S. Grenville, *Lord Salisbury and Foreign Policy* (London, 1964).

J. A. S. Grenville and G. B. Young, *Politics, Strategy and American Diplomacy: Studies in Foreign Policy 1873–1917* (London/New Haven, 1966).

Lord Grey, *Twenty-Five Years*, 2 vols (London, 1925).

D. Groh, 'The "unpatriotic" Socialists and the state', *Journal of Contemporary History*, vol. 1, no. 4 (1966).

D. Groh, *Negative Integration und revolutionäre Attentismus* (Frankfurt a.M., 1973).

E. de Groot, 'Great Britain and Germany in Zanzibar: Consul Holmwood's papers 1886–7', *Journal of Modern History*, vol. xxv (1953).

R. H. Gross, *Factors and Variations in Liberal and Radical Opinion on Foreign Policy, 1885–1899* (D.Phil. thesis, Oxford, 1950).

O. Groth, *Die Zeitung*, 4 vols (Mannheim, 1928–30).

W. D. Gruner, 'Bayern, Preussen und die süddeutschen Staaten 1866–1870', *Zeitschrift für bayerische Landesgeschichte*, vol. 37 (1974).

W. D. Gruner, 'Europäische Friede als nationales Interesse. Die Rolle des deutschen Bundes in der britischen Politik 1814–1832', *Bohemia*, vol. 18 (1977).

P. Guillen, *L'Allemagne et le Maroc de 1870 à 1905* (Paris, 1967).

S. Gwynn, *The Letters and Friendships of Sir Cecil Spring-Rice*, 2 vols (London, 1929).

S. Gwynn and G. M. Tuckwell, *The Life of the Right Hon. Sir Charles Dilke*, 2 vols (London, 1917).

M. von Hagen, *Bismarck und England* (Stuttgart/Berlin, 1941).

P. Haggie, 'The Royal Navy and war planning in the Fisher era', *Journal of Contemporary History*, vol. 8, no. 3 (1973).

George Haines IV, *German Influence upon English Education and Science 1800–1866* (New London, Conn., 1957).

George Haines IV, 'German influence upon scientific education in England, 1867–1887', *Victorian Studies*, vol. I (1958).

George Haines IV, *Essays on German Influence upon English Education and Science 1850–1919* (Hamden, Conn., 1969).

O. J. Hale, *Germany and the Diplomatic Revolution . . . 1904–1906* (Philadelphia, 1931).

O. J. Hale, *Publicity and Diplomacy with Special Reference to England and Germany 1890–1914* (Gloucester, Mass., 1964 reprint).

A. Hall, 'The war of words: anti-socialist offensives and counter-propaganda in Wilhelmine Germany 1890–1914', *Journal of Contemporary History*, vol. 11 (1976).

A. Hall, *Scandal, Sensation and Social Democracy: The SPD Press and Wilhelmine Germany 1890–1914* (Cambridge, 1977).

A. Hall, 'Youth in rebellion: the beginnings of the Socialist Youth Movement 1904–1914', in R. J. Evans (ed.), *Society and Politics in Wilhelmine Germany* (London/New York, 1978).

W. H. Haller, 'Regional and national free-trade associations in Germany 1859–79', *European Studies Review*, vol. 6 (1976).

G. W. F. Hallgarten, *Imperialismus vor 1914*, 2 vols (Munich, 1951).

G. W. F. Hallgarten, 'War Bismarck ein Imperialist?', *Geschichte in Wissenschaft und Unterricht*, vol. xxii (1971).

H. Hallmann, *Krügerdepesche und Flottenfrage* (Stuttgart, 1927).

H. Hallmann, *Der Weg zum deutschen Schlachtflottenbau* (Stuttgart, 1933).

P. G. Halpern, *The Mediterranean Naval Situation 1908–1914* (Cambridge, Mass., 1971).

I. Hamel, *Völkischer Verband und Nationale Gewerkschaft. Der Deutschnationale Handlungsgehilfen-Verband 1893–1933* (Frankfurt a.M., 1967).

D. A. Hamer, *John Morley* (Oxford, 1968).

D. A. Hamer, *Liberal Politics in the Age of Gladstone and Rosebery* (Oxford, 1972).

T. S. Hamerow, *The Social Foundations of German Unification 1858–1871*, 2 vols (Princeton, 1969–72).

Lord George Hamilton, *Parliamentary Reminiscences and Reflections 1886–1906* (London, 1922).

W. M. Hamilton, *The Nation and the Navy: Methods and Organisation of British Navalist Propaganda 1889–1914* (Ph.D thesis, London, 1977).

J. L. Hammond, *C. P. Scott of the Manchester Guardian* (London, 1934).

H. J. Hanham, *Elections and Party Management. Politics in the Time of Disraeli and Gladstone* (London, 1959).

M. Hank, *Kanzler ohne Amt* (Munich, 1977).

Lord Hankey, *The Supreme Command 1914–1918*, 2 vols (London, 1961).

K. D. Hardach, *Die Bedeutung wirtschaftlicher Faktoren bei der Wiedereinführung der Eisen- und Getreidezölle in Deutschland 1879* (Berlin, 1967).

K. W. Hardach, 'Anglomanie und Anglophobie während der industriellen Revolution in Deutschland', *Schmollers Jahrbuch*, 91 (1971).

F. Hardie, *The Political Influence of Queen Victoria 1861–1901* (London, 1965 edn).

J. D. Hargreaves, '*Entente manquée*: Anglo-French relations 1895–1896', *Cambridge Historical Journal*, vol. XI (1953).

J. D. Hargreaves, 'Lord Salisbury, British isolation and the Yangtse valley, June–September 1900', *Bulletin of the Institute of Historical Research*, vol. 30 (1957).

J. D. Hargreaves, *Prelude to the Partition of West Africa* (London, 1963).

J. D. Hargreaves, *West Africa Partitioned* (London, 1974).

D. Harris, 'Bismarck's advance to England, 1876', *Journal of Modern History*, vol. III (1931).

J. Harris and C. Hazlehurst, 'Campbell-Bannerman as Prime Minister', *History*, vol. LV (1970).

J. F. Harris, 'Eduard Lasker and compromise liberalism', *Journal of Modern History*, vol. 42 (1970).

F. Harrison, *Autobiographical Memoirs*, 2 vols (London, 1911).

R. Harrison, 'E. S. Beesly and Karl Marx', *International Review of Social History*, vol. IV (1959).

R. Harrison, *Before the Socialists: Studies in Labour and Politics* (London, 1965).

E. Hartwig, *Zur Politik und Entwicklung des Alldeutschen Verbandes . . . 1891–1914* (phil. Diss., Jena, 1966).

C. Harvie, *The Lights of Liberalism* (London, 1976).

U. von Hassell, 'Tirpitz' aussenpolitische Gedankenwelt', *Berliner Monatshefte*, 17 Jg. (1939).

E. Hasselmann, 'The impact of Owen's ideas on German social and cooperative thought during the nineteenth century', in S. Pollard and J. Salt (eds), *Robert Owen* (London, 1971).

P. H. S. Hatton, 'Harcourt and Solf: the search for an Anglo-German understanding through Africa 1912–1914', *European Studies Review*, vol. 1 (1971).

O. Hauser, *Deutschland und der englisch-russische Gegensatz 1900–1914* (Göttingen, 1958).

A. F. Havighurst, *Radical Journalist: H. W. Massingham, 1860–1924* (Cambridge, 1974).

J. R. Hay, *The Origins of the Liberal Welfare Reforms 1906–1914* (London, 1975).

D. Hayes, *Conscription Conflict* (London, 1949).

C. Hazlehurst, 'Asquith as Prime Minister, 1908–1916', *English Historical Review*, vol. LXXXV (1970).

C. Hazlehurst, *Politicians at War*, Vol. 1 (London, 1971).

B. Heckart, *From Bassermann to Bebel. The Grand Bloc's Quest for Reform in the Kaiserreich, 1900–1914* (New Haven/London, 1974).

E. C. Helmreich, *The Diplomacy of the Balkan Wars, 1912–1913* (Cambridge, Mass., 1938).

W. O. Henderson, *Studies in German Colonial History* (London, 1962).

W. O. Henderson, *Britain and Industrial Europe 1750–1870*, 2nd edn (Leicester, 1965).

W. O. Henderson, 'Mitteleuropäische Zollvereinspläne 1840–1940', in *Zeitschrift für das gesamte Staatswissenschaft*, vol. LXXII (1966).

W. O. Henderson, *The Rise of German Industrial Power 1834–1914* (London, 1975).

H. Henning, *Deutschlands Verhältnis zu England in Bethmann Hollwegs Aussenpolitik 1909–1914* (phil. Diss., Cologne, 1962).

L. Herbst, *Die erste Internationale als Problem der deutschen Politik in der Reichsgründungszeit* (Göttingen, 1975).

J. L. Herkless, 'Lord Clarendon's attempt at Franco-Prussian disarmament, January to March 1870', *Historical Journal*, vol. XV (1972).

W. Herrmann, *Dreibund, Zweibund, England 1890–1895* (Stuttgart, 1929).

H. H. Herwig, *The German Naval Officer Corps. A Social and Political History 1890–1918* (Oxford, 1973).

H. H. Herwig, *Politics of Frustration: The United States in German Naval Planning 1889–1941* (Boston, 1976).

H. H. Herwig and J. L. Helguera, *Alemania y el bloqueo internacional de Venezuela 1902–03* (Caracas, 1977).

T. Heuss, *Friedrich Naumann* (Stuttgart, 1949).

T. Heuss, *Theodor Mommsen und das 19. Jahrhundert* (Kiel, 1956).

W. A. S. Hewins, *The Apologia of an Imperialist*, 2 vols (London, 1929).

T. W. Heyck, *The Dimensions of British Radicalism: The Case of Ireland 1874–95* (London, 1974).

J. Heyderhoff (ed.), *Im Ring der Gegner Bismarcks* (Leipzig, 1943).

J. Heyderhoff and P. Wentzcke (eds), *Deutscher Liberalismus in Zeitalter Bismarcks*, 2 vols (Bonn/Leipzig, 1924–5).

L. Hilbert, *The Role of Military and Naval Attachés in the British and German Service with Particular Reference to those in Berlin and London and their Effect on Anglo-German Relations 1871–1914* (Ph.D. thesis, Cambridge, 1954).

K. Hildebrand, 'Von der Reichseinigung zur "Krieg-in-Sicht"–Krise. Preussen-Deutschland als Faktor der britischen Aussenpolitik 1865–1875', in M. Stürmer (ed.), *Das kaiserliche Deutschland* (Düsseldorf, 1970).

K. Hildebrand, 'Imperialismus, Wettrüsten und Kriegsausbruch 1914', *Neue Politische Literatur*, Jg. XX (1975).

K. Hildebrand, 'Die deutsche Reichsgründung im Urteil der britischen Politik', *Francia*, vol. 5 (1977).

A. Hillgruber, 'Die "Krieg-in-sicht"-Krise 1875', in E. Schulin (ed.), *Gedenkschrift Martin Göhring, Studien zur europäischen Geschichte* (Wiesbaden, 1968).

A. Hillgruber, *Bismarcks Aussenpolitik* (Freiburg, 1972).

G. Himmelfarb, *Lord Acton. A Study in Conscience and Politics* (London, 1952).

F. H. Hinsley, 'Bismarck, Salisbury and the Mediterranean Agreements of 1887', *Historical Journal*, vol. I (1958).

F. H. Hinsley (ed.), *The Foreign Policy of Sir Edward Grey* (Cambridge, 1977).

E. Hobsbawm, *Industry and Empire* (Harmondsworth, Middlesex, 1969).

K. H. Höfele, 'Sendungsglaube und Epochbewusstsein in Deutschland 1870–71', *Zeitschrift für Religions- und Geistesgeschichte*, 15 (1963).

R. J. S. Hoffman, *Great Britain and the German Trade Rivalry 1875–1914* (New York, 1964 reprint).

W. G. Hoffmann, *Das Wachstum der deutschen Wirtschaft seit der Mitte des 19. Jahrhunderts* (Berlin, 1965).

Hohenlohe-Schillingsfürst, Chlodwig zu, *Denkwürdigkeiten*, 2 vols, ed. F. Curtius (Stuttgart/Leipzig, 1907).

R. Höhn, *Sozialismus und Heer*, Vol. 3, *Der Kampf des Heeres gegen die Sozialdemokratie* (Bad Harzburg, 1969).

K. Holl, 'Krieg und Frieden und die liberalen Parteien', in K. Holl and G. List (eds), *Liberalismus und imperialistischer Staat* (Göttingen, 1975).

G. Hollenberg, *Englisches Interesse am Kaiserreich* (Wiesbaden, 1974).

G. Hollenberg, 'Zur Genesis des Anglo-Hegelianismus. Die Entdeckung Hegels als Ausweg aus der viktorianische Glaubenskrise', *Zeitschrift für Religions- und Geistesgeschichte*, vol. XXVI (1974).

G. Hollenberg, 'Die Englische Goethe Society und die deutsch-englischen kulturellen Beziehungen im 19. Jahrhundert', *Zeitschrift für Religions- und Geistesgeschichte*, vol. XXX (1978).

L. W. Hollingworth, *Zanzibar under the Foreign Office 1890–1913* (London, 1953).

P. Hollis (ed.), *Pressure from Without in Early Victorian England* (London, 1974).

F. B. M. Hollyday, 'Bismarck and the legend of the Gladstone ministry', in L. P. Wallace and W. C. Askew (eds), *Power, Public Opinion and Diplomacy* (Durham, NC, 1959).

F. B. M. Hollyday, *Bismarck's Rival. A Political Biography of General and Admiral Albrecht von Stosch* (Durham, NC, 1960).

F. B. M. Hollyday, '"Love Your Enemies! Otherwise Bite Them!": Bismarck, Herbert, and the Morier affair, 1888–1889', *Central European History*, vol. 1 (1968).

E. Hölzle, *Die Selbstentmachtung Europas* (Göttingen, 1975).

M. P. Hornik, 'The mission of Sir Henry Drummond Wolff to Constantinople, 1885–7', *English Historical Review*, vol. LV (1940).

M. P. Hornik, 'The Anglo-Belgian agreement of 12 May 1894', *English Historical Review*, vol. 57 (1942).

C. Howard, *Splendid Isolation* (London, 1967).

C. Howard, 'The policy of isolation', *Historical Journal*, vol. X (1967).

C. Howard, *Britain and the Casus Belli* (London, 1974).

C. Howard, 'MacDonald, Henderson and the outbreak of war, 1914', *Historical Journal*, vol. XX (1977).

M. Howard, 'William I and the reform of the Prussian army', in M. Gilbert (ed.), *A Century of Conflict 1850–1950* (London, 1966).

M. Howard, *The Continental Commitment* (Harmondsworth, Middlesex, 1974).

W. Hubatsch, *Die Aera Tirpitz* (Göttingen, 1955).

W. Hubatsch, *Kaiserliche Marine* (private print?, 1975).

E. R. Huber, *Deutsche Verfassungsgeschichte seit 1789*, Vol. IV (Stuttgart, 1969).

H. Stuart Hughes, *Consciousness and Society: The Reorientation of European Social Thought 1890–1930* (London, 1974 edn).

M. E. Humble, 'The breakdown of a consensus: British writers and Anglo-German relations 1900–1920', *Journal of European Studies*, vol. VII (1977).

J. C. Hunt, 'Peasants, grain tariffs and meat quotas: imperial German protectionism re-examined', *Central European History*, vol. 7 (1974).

J. C. Hunt, *The People's Party in Württemberg and Southern Germany 1890–1914* (Stuttgart, 1975).

J. C. Hunt, 'The bourgeois middle in German politics, 1871–1933: recent literature', *Central European History*, vol. XI (1978).

T. W. Hutchison, 'Economists and economic policy in Britain after 1870', *History of Political Economy*, vol. 1 (1969).

R. Hyam, *Britain's Imperial Century, 1815–1914* (London, 1976).

W. G. Hynes, 'British mercantile attitudes towards imperial expansion', *Historical Journal*, vol. 19 (1976).

R. Ibbeken, *Das aussenpolitische Problem, Staat und Wirtschaft in der deutschen Reichspolitik 1880–1914* (Schleswig, 1923).

G. G. Iggers, *The German Conception of History* (Middletown, Conn., 1968).

A. H. Imlah, *Economic Elements in the Pax Britannica* (Cambridge, Mass., 1958).

M. C. Jacobs, 'The Colonial Office and New Guinea', *Historical Studies: Australia and New Zealand*, vol. 5 (1952).

H.-P. Jaeck, 'Die deutsche Annexion', in H. Stoecker (ed.), *Kamerun unter deutscher Kolonialherrschaft*, 2 vols (East Berlin, 1960–8).

H. Jaeckel, *Die Nordwestgrenze in der Verteidigung Indiens 1900–1908* . . . (Cologne, 1968).

H. Jaeger, *Unternehmer in der deutschen Politik (1890–1918)* (Bonn, 1967).

K. Jagow (ed.), *Letters of the Prince Consort 1831–1861* (London, 1938).

D. James, *Lord Roberts* (London, 1954).

R. Rhodes James, *Lord Randolph Churchill* (London, 1959).

R. Rhodes James, *Rosebery, A Biography* (London, 1963).

G. Jantzen, *Ostafrika in der deutsch-englischen Politik 1884–1890* (Hamburg, 1934).

K. Jarausch, 'The illusion of limited war: Chancellor Bethmann Hollweg's calculated risk, July 1914', *Central European History*, vol. 2 (1969).

K. Jarausch, *The Enigmatic Chancellor* (New Haven/London, 1973).

M. M. Jeffries, 'Lord Salisbury and the Eastern Question 1890–1898', *Slavonic and East European Review*, vol. XXXIX (1960).

R. Jenkins, *Asquith* (London, 1964).

Nancy E. Johnson, *The Role of the Cabinet in the Making of Foreign Policy, 1885–1895* . . . (D.Phil. thesis, Oxford, 1970).

J. Joll, *The Second International 1889–1914* (London, 1955).

J. Joll, 'The 1914 debate continues', *Past and Present*, no. 34 (1966).

J. Joll, 'The English, Friedrich Nietzsche and the First World War', in I. Geiss and B.-J. Wendt (eds), *Deutschland in der Weltpolitik des 19. und 20. Jahrhunderts* (Düsseldorf, 1974).

J. Joll, 'War guilt 1914: a continuing controversy', in P. Kluke and P. Alter (eds), *Aspekte der deutsch-britischen Beziehungen in Laufe der Jahrhunderte* (Stuttgart, 1978).

A. Jones, *The Politics of Reform* (Cambridge, 1972).

Kennedy Jones, *Fleet Street and Downing Street* (London, 1920).

G. H. S. Jordan, 'Pensions not Dreadnoughts: the Radicals and naval retrenchment', in A. J. A. Morris (ed.), *Edwardian Radicalism 1900–1914* (London, 1974).

D. Judd, *Balfour and the British Empire* (London, 1968).

S. A. Kaehler, 'Bemerkungen zu einem Marginal Bismarcks von 1887', *Historische Zeitschrift*, vol. 167 (1943).

H. Kaelble, *Industrielle Interessenpolitik in der Wilhelminischen Gesellschaft* (Berlin, 1967).

F. Kahlenberg, 'Das Epochenjahr 1866 in der deutschen Geschichte', in M. Stürmer (ed.), *Das kaiserliche Deutschland* (Düsseldorf, 1970).

S. von Kardorff, *Wilhelm von Kardorff* (Berlin, 1929).

S. E. Katzenellenbogen, 'British economic activity in the German colonies 1884–1914', in B. M. Ratcliffe (ed.), *Great Britain and her World 1750–1914* (Manchester, 1975).

K. Kawaii, 'Anglo-German rivalry in the Yangtse region, 1895–1902', *Pacific Historical Review*, vol. 8 (1939).

F. Kazemzadeh, *Russia and Britain in Persia, 1864–1914* (New Haven, Conn., 1968).

E. Kehr, *Battleship Building and Party Politics in Germany, 1894–1901* (Chicago/London, 1973).

E. Kehr, *Economic Interest, Militarism, and Foreign Policy. Essays on German History*, ed. G. A. Craig (Berkeley/Los Angeles/London, 1977).

A. Keim, *Erlebtes und Erstrebtes: Lebenserinnerungen* (Hanover, 1925).

P. Kelly, *The Naval Policy of Imperial Germany 1900–1914* (Ph.D. thesis, Georgetown University, 1970).

P. Kelly, 'Tirpitz as bureaucratic thinker: episodes of the interactions among politics, technology and bureaucracy' (private paper, 1975).

P. Kemp (ed.), *The Fisher Papers*, Vol. II (Navy Records Society, vol. CVI, London, 1964).

P. M. Kennedy, 'Tirpitz, England and the second Navy Law of 1900: a strategical critique', *Militärgeschichtliche Mitteilungen*, 2/1970.

P. M. Kennedy, 'Bismarck's imperialism: the case of Samoa 1880–1890', *Historical Journal*, vol. XV (1972).

P. M. Kennedy, 'German colonial expansion: has the "manipulated Social Imperialism" been ante-dated?', *Past and Present*, 54 (1972).

P. M. Kennedy, 'Maritime Strategieprobleme der deutsch-englischen Flottenrivalität', in H. Schottelius and W. Deist (eds), *Marine und Marinepolitik im kaiserlichen Deutschland 1871–1914* (Düsseldorf, 1972).

P. M. Kennedy, 'German world policy and the alliance negotiations with England, 1897–1900', *Journal of Modern History*, vol. 45 (1973).

P. M. Kennedy, *The Samoan Tangle: A Study in Anglo-German-American Relations, 1878–1900* (Dublin/New York, 1974).

P. M. Kennedy, 'The development of German naval operations plans against England, 1896–1914', *English Historical Review*, vol. LXXXIX (1974).

P. M. Kennedy, 'Mahan versus Mackinder: two interpretations of British sea power', *Militärgeschichtliche Mitteilungen*, 2/1974.

P. M. Kennedy, 'Idealists and realists: British views of Germany, 1864–1939', *Transactions of the Royal Historical Society*, 5th series, vol. 24 (1975).

P. M. Kennedy, *The Rise and Fall of British Naval Mastery* (London/New York, 1976).

P. M. Kennedy (ed.), *The War Plans of the Great Powers 1880–1914* (London, 1979).

E. Kessel, 'Bismarck und die "Halbgötter"', *Historische Zeitschrift*, 181 (1956).

L. Kettenacker, *Lord Acton and Ignatius von Döllinger* (B.Litt. thesis, Oxford, 1971).

R. H. Keyserlingk, *Bismarck and the Press: The Example of the National Liberals 1871–84* (Ph.D. thesis, London, 1965).

C. P. Kindleberger, 'Germany's overtaking of England, 1806 to 1914', in *Economic Response. Comparative Studies in Trade, Finance, and Growth* (Cambridge, Mass., 1978).

W. T. C. King, *History of the London Discount Market* (London, 1936).

M. Kitchen, *The German Officer Corps 1890–1914* (Oxford, 1968).

M. Kitchen, *A Military History of Germany* (London, 1975).

M. Kitchen, *The Political Economy of Germany 1815–1914* (London, 1978).

P. Kluke, 'Bismarck und Salisbury: ein diplomatisches Duell', *Historische Zeitschrift*, 175 (1953).

P. Knaplund (ed.), *Letters from the Berlin Embassy, 1871–74, 1880–85*, in *Annual Report of the American Historical Association for the Year 1942* (Washington, 1944).

P. Knaplund, *Gladstone's Foreign Policy* (London, 1970 edn).

M. P. Knight, 'Britain, Germany and the Pacific, 1880–87', in J. Moses and P. M. Kennedy (eds), *Germany in the Pacific and Far East 1870–1914* (St Lucia, Queensland, 1977).

H. W. Koch, 'The Anglo-German alliance negotiations: missed opportunity or myth?', *History*, vol. LIV (1969).

H. W. Koch (ed.), *The Origins of the First World War* (London, 1972).

H. Kohn, *The Mind of Germany* (New York, 1960).

S. E. Koss, *Sir John Brunner: Radical Plutocrat* (Cambridge, 1970).

S. E. Koss, *Fleet Street Radical: A. G. Gardiner and the Daily News* (London, 1973).

S. E. Koss (ed.), *The Pro-Boers* (London, 1973).

K. Koszyk, *Deutsche Presse im 19. Jahrhundert* (Berlin, 1966).

H. Krausnick, *Holsteins Geheimpolitik in der Aera Bismarck 1886–1890* (Hamburg, 1942).

H. Krausnick, 'Botschafter Graf Hatzfeldt und die Aussenpolitik Bismarcks', *Historische Zeitschrift*, 167 (1943).

H. Krausnick, 'Holstein und das deutsch-englische Verhältnis von 1890 bis 1901', *Internationales Jahrbuch für Geschichtsunterricht*, vol. 1 (1951).

L. Krieger, *The German Idea of Freedom* (Boston, 1957).

H.-H. Krill, *Die Ranke-Renaissance* (Berlin, 1962).

U. Kröll, *Die internationale Buren-Agitation 1899–1902* (Münster, 1973).

A. Kruck, *Geschichte des Alldeutschen Verbandes 1890–1939* (Wiesbaden, 1954).

R. Kutsch, *Queen Victoria und die deutsche Einigung* (phil. Diss., Berlin, 1938).

H. Lademacher, *Die belgische Neutralität als Problem der europäischen Politik 1830–1914* (Bonn, 1971).

I. Lambi, 'The agrarian-industrial front in Bismarckian politics, 1873–1879', *Journal of Central European Affairs*, vol. xx (1961).

I. Lambi, *Free Trade and Protection in Germany 1868–1879* (Wiesbaden, 1963).

I. Lambi, 'Die Operationspläne der Kaiserlichen Marine bis zur Auflösung des Oberkommandos in europäischen Gewässern im Jahr 1899', in J. Hütter, R. Meyers and D. Papenfuss (eds), *Tradition und Neubeginn* (Cologne, 1975).

R. Lamer, *Der englische Parlamentarismus in der deutschen politischen Theorien im Zeitalter Bismarcks (1857–1890)* (Lübeck/Hamburg, 1963).

D. Lammers, 'Arno Mayer and the British decision for war in 1914', *Journal of British Studies*, vol. xii (1973).

W. L. Langer, *The Franco-Russian Alliance 1890–1894* (Cambridge, Mass., 1929).

W. L. Langer *The Diplomacy of Imperialism 1890–1902*, 2nd edn (New York, 1951).

W. L. Langer, *European Alliances and Alignments 1871–1890* (New York, 1964 edn).

R. Langhorne, 'The naval question in Anglo-German relations 1912–1914', *Historical Journal*, vol. xiv (1971).

R. Langhorne, 'Anglo-German negotiations concerning the future of the Portuguese colonies, 1911–1914', *Historical Journal*, vol. xvi (1973).

R. Langhorne, 'Great Britain and Germany, 1911–1914', in F. H. Hinsley (ed.), *The Foreign Policy of Sir Edward Grey* (Cambridge, 1977).

W. C. Langsam, 'Nationalism and history in the Prussian elementary schools under Wilhelm II', in E. E. Earle (ed.), *Nationalism and Internationalism* (New York, 1950).

K. S. Latourette, *Christianity in a Revolutionary Age*, Vol. ii, *The Nineteenth Century in Europe: The Protestant and Eastern Churches* (New York, 1959).

P. G. Lauren, *Diplomats and Bureaucrats* (Stanford, 1976).

H. Lebovics, '"Agrarians" versus "industrialisers": social conservative resistance to industrialism and capitalism in late 19th century Germany', *International Review of Social History*, vol. 12 (1967).

A. J. Lee, 'Franlin Thomasson and "The Tribune"', *Historical Journal*, vol. xvi (1973).

A. J. Lee, 'The radical press', in A. J. A. Morris (ed.), *Edwardian Radicalism 1900–1914* (London, 1974).

A. J. Lee, *The Origins of the Popular Press 1855–1914* (London, 1976).

D. E. Lee, *Europe's Crucial Years. The Diplomatic Background of World War I* (Hanover, NH, 1974).

H. I. Lee, 'Mediterranean strategy and Anglo-French relations 1908–1912', *Mariner's Mirror*, 57 (1971).

S. Lee, *King Edward VII*, 2 vols (London, 1925).

A. Lees, 'Critics of urban society in Germany', *Journal of the History of Ideas*, vol. XL (1979).

J. Lehmann, *Die Aussenpolitik und die "Kölnische Zeitung" während der Bülow-Zeit (1897–1909)* (phil. Diss., Leipzig, 1937).

F. M. Leventhal, 'H. N. Brailsford and Russia', *Albion* (summer 1973).

R. S. Levy, *The Downfall of the Anti-Semitic Political Parties in Imperial Germany* (New Haven, Conn., 1975).

G. Lichtheim, *A Short History of Socialism* (London, 1970).

R. Lill, 'Die deutschen Katholiken und Bismarcks Reichsgründung', in T. Schieder and E. Deuerlein (eds), *Reichsgründung 1870/71* (Stuttgart, 1970).

B. E. Lippincott, *Victorian Critics of Democracy* (New York, 1964 edn).

A. Loftus, *Diplomatic Reminiscences*, 2nd series, 2 vols (London, 1894).

R. H. Lord, 'Bismarck and Russia in 1863', *American Historical Review*, vol. XXIX (1923).

A. Lothholz, *Die Haltung der Sozialdemokratie in den Heeres-, Flotten- und Weltmachtfragen (1890–1914)* (phil. Diss., Freiburg, 1954).

W. R. Louis, 'Sir Percy Anderson's Grand African Strategy, 1883–1893', *English Historical Review*, vol. LXXVII (1966).

W. R. Louis, *Great Britain and Germany's Lost Colonies 1914–1919* (Oxford, 1967).

R. I. Lovell, *The Struggle for South Africa 1875–1899* (New York, 1934).

C. J. Lowe, *Salisbury and the Mediterranean 1886–1896* (London, 1965).

C. J. Lowe, *The Reluctant Imperialists: British Foreign Policy 1878–1902*, 2 vols (London, 1967).

C. J. Lowe and M. L. Dockrill, *The Mirage of Power: British Foreign Policy 1902–1922*, 3 vols (London, 1972).

H. Lutz, *Eyre Crowe, der böse Geist des Foreign Office* (Stuttgart, 1931).

C. W. Macara et al., *Why Tariff 'Reform' must be Repelled. The Case for the Cotton Industry* (Manchester, 1910).

C. E. McClelland, *The German Historians and England* (Cambridge, 1971).

C. E. McClelland, 'Berlin historians and German politics', *Journal of Contemporary History*, vol. 8, no. 3 (1973).

N. McCord, *Free Trade. Theory and Practice from Adam Smith to Keynes* (Newton Abbott, 1970).

J. McDermott, 'The revolution in British military thinking from the Boer War to the Moroccan crisis', *Canadian Journal of History*, vol. IX (1974).

J. McDermott, 'The British Foreign Office and its German consuls before 1914', *Journal of Modern History* (On-Demand Supplement), Abstract in vol. 50, no. 1 (1978).

R. B. McDowell, *British Conservatism 1832–1914* (London, 1959).

J. J. McGlashan, *German Influence on Aspects of English Educational and Social Reform, 1867–1908* (Ph.D. thesis, Hull, 1973).

G. I. T. Machin, *Politics and the Churches in Great Britain 1832 to 1868* (Oxford, 1977).

R. F. Mackay, 'The Admiralty, the German navy, and the redistribution of the British fleet, 1904–1905', *Mariner's Mirror*, vol. 56 (1970).

R. F. Mackay, *Fisher of Kilverstone* (Oxford, 1973).

K. Mackenzie, 'Some British reactions to German colonial methods, 1885–1907', *Historical Journal*, vol. XVII (1974).

H. J. Mackinder, 'The geographical pivot of history', *Geographical Journal*, vol. XXIII (1904).

D. McLean, 'Finance and "informal empire" before the First World War', *Economic History Review*, 2nd series, vol. XXIX (1976).

W. Maehl, 'The triumph of nationalism in the German Socialist Party on the eve of the First World War', *Journal of Modern History*, vol. 24 (1952).

W. H. Maehl, 'German socialist opposition to Russian imperialism, 1848–1891', *The New Review. A Journal of East European History*, vol. 12 (1972).

W. H. Maehl, 'Bebel and the revolutionary solution of the German problem 1866–1871', *Internationale wissenschaftliche Korrespondenz zur Geschichte der deutschen Arbeiterbewegung*, Jg. 10 (1974).

W. H. Maehl, 'August Bebel and the development of a responsible German socialist foreign policy 1878–96', *Journal of European Studies*, vol. VI (1976).

W. H. Maehl, 'Bebel's fight against the *Schlachtflotte*, nemesis to the primacy of foreign policy', *Proceedings of the American Philosophical Society*, vol. 121 (1977).

L. Maenner, 'Deutschlands Wirtschaft und Liberalismus in der Krise von 1879', *Archiv für Politik und Geschichte*, vol. 9 (1927).

A. T. Mahan, *Retrospect and Prospect* (London, 1902).

B. Mallet, *British Budgets 1887–1913* (London, 1913).

A. J. Marder (ed.), *Fear God and Dread Nought: The Correspondence of Admiral of the Fleet Lord Fisher of Kilverstone*, 3 vols (London, 1952–9).

A. J. Marder, *From the Dreadnought to Scapa Flow*, Vol. 1, *The Road to War, 1904–1914* (London, 1961).

A. J. Marder, *The Anatomy of British Sea Power: A History of British Naval Policy in the Pre-Dreadnought Era 1880–1905* (Hamden, Conn., 1964 reprint).

W. Marienfeld, *Wissenschaft und Schlachtflottenbau in Deutschland 1897–1906* (Frankfurt, 1957).

D. Marquand, *Ramsay MacDonald* (London, 1977).

P. Marshall, 'The imperial factor in the Liberal decline, 1880–1885', in J. E. Flint and G. Williams (eds), *Perspectives of Empire* (London, 1973).

A. von Martin, 'Weltanschauliche Motive im altkonservativen Denken', in G. A. Ritter (ed.), *Deutsche Parteien vor 1918* (Cologne, 1973).

K. Marx and F. Engels, *The Russian Menace to Europe*, ed. P. W. Blackstock and B. F. Hoselitz (London, 1953).

P. W. Massing, *Rehearsal for Destruction. A Study of Political Anti-Semitism in Imperial Germany* (New York, 1949).

N. C. Masterman, *John Malcolm Ludlow* (Cambridge, 1963).

P. Mathias, *The First Industrial Nation* (London, 1969).

P. Mathias and M. M. Postan (eds), *Cambridge Economic History of Europe*, vol. VII, pt I (Cambridge, 1978).

D. Matthew, *Lord Acton and his Times* (London, 1968).

H. C. G. Matthew, *The Liberal Imperialists* (Oxford, 1973).

H. C. G. Matthew, R. I. McKibbin and J. A. Kay, 'The franchise factor in the rise of the Labour Party', *English Historical Review*, vol. 91 (1976).

L. J. Maxse, 'A fateful breakfast', *National Review* (August 1918).

Sir H. Maxwell, *The Life and Letters of . . . the Fourth Earl of Clarendon*, 2 vols (London, 1913).

A. J. Mayer, 'Domestic causes of the First World War', in L. Krieger and F. Stern (eds), *The Responsibility of Power* (Garden City, NY, 1967).

A. J. Mayer, 'The lower middle class as historical problem', *Journal of Modern History*, vol. 47 (1975).

S. L. Mayer, 'Anglo-German rivalry at the Algeciras Conference', in P. Gifford and W. R. Louis (eds), *Britain and Germany in Africa* (New Haven, Conn., 1967).

S. Meacham, 'The sense of an impending clash: English working-class unrest before the First World War', *American Historical Review*, vol. 77 (1972).

W. N. Medlicott, 'The Mediterranean Agreements of 1887', *Slavonic Review*, vol. v (1926).

W. N. Medlicott, *The Congress of Berlin and After* (London, 1938).

W. N. Medlicott, *Bismarck, Gladstone and the Concert of Europe* (London, 1956).

W. N. Medlicott, 'Bismarck and Beaconsfield', in O. A. Sarkissian (ed.), *Studies in Diplomatic History* (London, 1961).

K. Meine, *England und Deutschland in der Zeit des Uebergangs vom Manchestertum zum Imperialismus 1871 bis 1876* (Vaduz, 1965 reprint).

F. Meinecke, *Geschichte des deutsch-englischen Bündnisproblems 1890–1901* (Munich/Berlin, 1927).

F. Meinecke, *Historism: The Rise of a New Historical Outlook* (London, 1972 trans.).

H. Mejcher, 'Die Bagdadbahn als Instrument deutscher wirtschaftlichen Einflusses im Osmanischen Reich', *Geschichte und Gesellschaft*, 1 Jg. (1975).

A. Mendel, 'The debate between Prussian Junkerdom and the forces of urban industry, 1897–1902', *Jahrbuch des Instituts für Deutsche Geschichte* (Israel), 4 (1975).

A. Mendelssohn-Bartholdy, 'Bismarck und Salisbury', *Europäische Gespräche*, vol. 1 (1923).

H. P. Meritt, 'Bismarck and the German interest in East Africa 1884–1885', *Historical Journal*, vol. xxi (1978).

M. Messerschmidt, *Deutschland in englischer Sicht* (Düsseldorf, 1955).

M. Messerschmidt, *Militär und Politik in der Bismarckzeit und im Wilhelminischen Deutschland* (Darmstadt, 1975).

I. Metz, *Die deutsche Flotte in der englischen Presse. Der Navy Scare vom Winter 1904/5* (Berlin, 1936).

G. Meyer, 'German interests and policy in the Netherlands East Indies and Malaya, 1870–1914', in J. A. Moses and P. M. Kennedy (eds), *Germany in the Pacific and Far East 1870–1914* (St Lucia, Queensland, 1977).

J. Meyer, *Die Propaganda der deutschen Flottenbewegung, 1897–1900* (phil. Diss., Berne, 1967).

G. Michalik, *Probleme des deutschen Flottenbaues* (Breslau, 1931).

C. R. Middleton, *The Administration of British Foreign Policy 1782–1846* (Durham, NC, 1977).

S. Mielke, *Der Hansa-Bund für Gewerbe, Handel und Industrie 1909–1914* (Göttingen, 1976).

S. Miers, 'The Brussels Conference of 1889–1890: the place of the slave tradè in the policies of Great Britain and Germany', in P. Gifford and W. R. Louis (eds), *Britain and Germany in Africa* (New Haven, Conn., 1967).

K. E. Miller, *Socialism and Foreign Policy* (The Hague, 1967).

R. Millman, *British Foreign Policy and the Coming of the Franco-Prussian War* (Oxford, 1965).

A. Mitchell, 'Bonapartism as a model for Bismarckian politics', *Journal of Modern History*, vol. 49 (1977).

B. R. Mitchell, *European Historical Statistics 1750–1970* (London, 1975).

W. J. Mommsen, *Max Weber und die deutsche Politik 1890–1920* (Tübingen, 1959).

W. J. Mommsen, 'Domestic factors in German foreign policy before 1914', *Central European History*, vol. 6 (1973).

W. J. Mommsen, 'Die latente Krise des Deutschen Reiches 1909–1914', in L. Just (ed.), *Handbuch der Deutschen Geschichte*, Vol. iv, pt i (Frankfurt a.M., 1973 edn).

W. J. Mommsen, 'Wandlungen der liberalen Idee im Zeitalter des Imperialismus', in K. Holl and G. List (eds), *Liberalismus und imperialistischer Staat* (Göttingen, 1975).

W. J. Mommsen, 'Europäischer Finanzimperialismus vor 1914', *Historische Zeitschrift*, vol. 224 (1977).

W. F. Moneypenny and G. E. Buckle, *The Life of Benjamin Disraeli*, 6 vols (London, 1910–20).

G. L. Monger, *The End of Isolation* (London, 1963).

J. P. Moody (ed.), *Church and Society: Catholic Social and Political Thought and Movements 1789–1950* (New York, 1953).

H. R. Moon, *The Invasion of the United Kingdom: Public Controversy and Official Planning 1888–1918*, 2 vols (Ph.D. thesis, London, 1968).

K. O. Morgan, *Keir Hardie* (London, 1975).

R. Morgan, *The German Social Democrats and the First International 1864–1872* (Cambridge, 1965).

A. Moritz, *Das Problem des Präventivkrieges in der deutschen Politik während der ersten Marokkokrise* (Frankfurt a.M., 1974).

G. R. Mork, 'Bismarck and the "capitulation" of German liberalism', *Journal of Modern History*, vol. 43 (1971).

J. Morley, *Life of Gladstone*, 3 vols (London, 1903).

W. P. Morrell, *Britain in the Pacific Islands* (Oxford, 1960).

A. J. A. Morris, 'Haldane's army reforms 1906–8: the deception of the Radicals', *History*, vol. 56 (1971).

A. J. A. Morris, *Radicalism Against War 1906–1914* (London, 1972).

R. Morsey, 'Zur Pressepolitik Bismarcks. Die Vorgeschichte des Pressedezernats im Auswärtigen Amt (1870)', *Publizistik*, vol. 1 (1956).

R. Morsey, 'Die deutschen Katholiken und der Nationalstaat zwischen Kulturkampf und dem ersten Weltkrieg', *Historisches Jahrbuch*, 90 (1970).

J. S. Mortimer, 'Commercial interests and German diplomacy in the Agadir crisis', *Historical Journal*, vol. x (1967).

J. A. Moses, 'Karl Dietrich Erdmann, the Riezler diary and the Fischer controversy', *Journal of European Studies*, vol. 3 (1973).

J. A. Moses, *The Politics of Illusion* (London, 1975).

G. L. Mosse, *The Crisis of German Ideology* (New York, 1964).

W. E. Mosse, 'The Crown and foreign policy: Queen Victoria and the Austro-Prussian conflict, March–May 1866', *Cambridge Historical Journal*, vol. x (1951).

W. E. Mosse, *The European Powers and the German Question 1848–1871* (Cambridge, 1958).

W. E. Mosse, 'Public opinion and foreign policy: the British public and the war scare of November 1870', *Historical Journal*, vol. vi (1963).

W. E. Mosse, 'Queen Victoria and her ministers in the Schleswig-Holstein crisis 1863–1864', *English Historical Review*, vol. 78 (1963).

W. E. Mosse, *Liberal Europe: The Age of Bourgeois Realism 1848–1875* (London, 1974).

M. G. Mulhall, *The Dictionary of Statistics* (London, 1903 edn).

H.-J. Müllenbrock, *Literatur und Zeitgeschichte in England zwischen dem Ende des 19. Jahrhunderts und dem Ausbruch des Ersten Weltkrieges* (Hamburg, 1967).

F. F. Müller, *Deutschland–Zanzibar–Ostafrika 1884–1890* (East Berlin,. 1959).

J. Müller, *Die Jugendbewegung als deutsche Hauptrichtung neukonservativer Reform* (Zurich, 1971).

H. Müller-Link, *Industrialisierung und Aussenpolitik: Preussen-Deutschland und das Zarenreich von 1860 bis 1890* (Göttingen, 1977).

J. A. Murray, 'Foreign policy debated: Sir Edward Grey and his critics, 1911–1912', in L. P. Wallace and W. C. Askew (eds), *Power, Public Opinion and Diplomacy* (Durham, NC, 1959).

A. E. Musson, 'The Great Depression in Britain 1873–1896: a reappraisal', *Journal of Economic History*, vol. XIX (1959).

H. Muthesius, *Das englische Haus*, 3 vols (Berlin, 1904–5).

S. Muthesius, *Das englische Vorbild* (Munich, 1974).

E. Naujoks, 'Bismarck und das Wolffsche Telegraphenbüro', *Geschichte in Wissenschaft und Unterricht*, vol. 14 (1963).

E. Naujoks, 'Bismarck und die Organisation der Regierungspresse', *Historische Zeitschrift*, vol. 205 (1967).

E. Naujoks, *Bismarcks auswärtige Pressepolitik und die Reichsgründung (1865–1871)* (Wiesbaden, 1968).

E. Naujoks, 'Rudolf Lindau und die Neuorientierung der auswärtigen Pressepolitik Bismarcks', *Historische Zeitschrift*, vol. 215 (1972).

E. Naujoks, *Die parlamentarische Entstehung des Reichspressegesetzes in der Bismarckzeit (1848–74)* (Düsseldorf, 1975).

E. Naujoks, 'Bismarck in den Wahlkampagnen von 1879 und 1881: Der Zusammenhang von innerer und auswärtiger Pressepolitik', in H. Fenske, W. Reinhard and E. Schulin (eds), *Historia Integra* (Berlin/Munich, 1978).

J. A. La Nauze, *Alfred Deakin*, 2 vols (Melbourne, 1965).

J. P. Nettl, 'The Social Democratic Party 1890–1914 as a political model', *Past and Present*, 30 (1965).

C. W. Newbury, 'The tariff factor in Anglo-French West African partition', in P. Gifford and W. R. Louis (eds), *France and Britain in Africa* (New Haven, Conn., 1971).

Lord Newton, *Lord Lyons*, 2 vols (London, 1913).

Lord Newton, *Lord Lansdowne* (London, 1929).

D. Nicholls, 'Positive liberty 1880–1914', *American Political Science Review*, vol. 56 (1962).

J. A. Nicholls, *Germany after Bismarck: The Caprivi Era 1890–1894* (New York, 1968 edn).

H. Nicolson, *Sir Arthur Nicolson, Bart., First Lord Carnock: A Study in the Old Diplomacy* (London, 1930).

R. T. Nightingale, 'The personnel of the British Foreign Office and Diplomatic Service 1851–1929', *American Political Science Review*, vol. 24 (1930).

T. Nipperdey, 'Interessenverbände und Parteien in Deutschland vor dem ersten Weltkrieg', in H.-U. Wehler (ed.), *Modern deutsche Sozialgeschichte* (Cologne/Berlin, 1966).

I. H. Nish, *The Anglo-Japanese Alliance* (London, 1966).

R. Nöll von der Nahmer, *Bismarcks Reptilienfonds* (Mainz, 1968).

E. R. Norman, *Anti-Catholicism in Victorian England* (London, 1968).

F. S. Northedge, *The Troubled Giant: Britain among the Great Powers 1916–1939* (London, 1966).

H. Nostitz, *Bismarcks unbotmässiger Botschafter, Fürst Münster von Derneburg* (Göttingen, 1968).

R. Nürnberger, 'Imperialismus, Sozialismus und Christentum bei Friedrich Naumann', *Historische Zeitschrift*, CLXX (1950).

M. Nussbaum, *Vom "Kolonialenthusiasmus" zur Kolonialpolitik der Monopole* (East Berlin, 1962).

B. I. Obichere, *West African States and European Expansion* (New Haven, Conn., 1971).

L. O'Boyle, 'Liberal political leadership in Germany 1867–84', *Journal of Modern History*, vol. 28 (1956).

A. O'Day, *The English Face of Irish Nationalism* (Dublin, 1977).

A. J. O'Donnell, *National Liberalism and the Mass Politics of the German Right, 1890–1907* (Ph.D. thesis, Princeton, 1973).

N. D'Ombrain, *War Machinery and High Politics* (Oxford, 1973).

B. F. Oppel, 'The waning of a traditional alliance: Russia and Germany after the Portsmouth peace conference', *Central European History*, vol. 5 (1972).

H. Oppel, *Englisch-deutsche Literaturbeziehungen*, 2 vols (West Berlin, 1971).

F. Oppenheimer, *Stranger Within* (London, 1960).

W. Pack, *Das parlamentarische Ringen um das Sozialistengesetz Bismarcks 1879–1890* (Düsseldorf, 1961).

P. Padfield, *The Great Naval Race* (London, 1974).

A. W. Palmer, 'Lord Salisbury's approach to Russia, 1898', *Oxford Slavonic Papers*, 6 (1955).

E. B. Parsons, 'The German-American crisis of 1902–1903', *The Historian*, vol. 33 (1971).

K. S. Pasieka, 'The British press and the Polish insurrection of 1863', *Slavonic and East European Review*, vol. 42 (1963–4).

A. T. Peacock and J. Wiseman, *The Growth of Public Expenditure in the United Kingdom*, 2nd edn (London, 1967).

H. Pelling, *The Origins of the Labour Party 1880–1900* (London, 1954).

H. Pelling, *Popular Politics and Society in Late Victorian Britain* (London, 1968).

C. D. Penner, 'Germany and the Transvaal before 1896', *Journal of Modern History*, vol. XII (1940).

C. D. Penner, 'The Bülow-Chamberlain recriminations of 1900–1901', *The Historian*, vol. 5 (1943).

L. M. Penson, 'The New Course in British foreign policy, 1892–1902', *Transactions of the Royal Historical Society*, 4th series, vol. XXV (1943).

C. Petrie, *The Life and Letters of the Right Hon. Sir Austen Chamberlain*, 2 vols (London, 1939).

J. Petrus, 'Marx and Engels on the national question', *Journal of Politics*, vol. 33 (1971).

O. Pflanze, 'Bismarck and German nationalism', *American Historical Review*, vol. LX (1955).

O. Pflanze, 'Bismarck's Realpolitik', *Review of Politics*, vol. 20 (1958).

O. Pflanze, *Bismarck and the Development of Germany*, vol. 1 (Princeton, 1971 edn).

E. H. Phelps Brown and S. J. Handfield Jones, 'The climacteric of the 1890s', *Oxford Economic Papers*, new series, vol. 4 (1952).

H. Philippi, 'Zur Geschichte des Welfenfonds', *Niedersächsisches Jahrbuch für Landesgeschichte*, vol. 31 (1959).

G. A. Philipps, 'The Triple Economic Alliance in 1914', *Economic History Review*, 2nd series, vol. 24 (1971).

G. D. Philipps, *The Diehards* (Cambridge, Mass., 1978).

R. V. Pierard, *The German Colonial Society 1882–1914* (Ph.D. thesis, Iowa State University, 1964).

M. Pinto-Duschinsky, *The Political Thought of Lord Salisbury 1854–1868* (London, 1967).

M. G. Plachetka, *Die Getreide-Autarkiepolitik Bismarcks und seiner Nachfolger im Reichskanzleramt* (Bonn, 1969).

J. B. Plass, *England zwischen Russland und Deutschland: Der Persische Gulf in der britischen Vorkriegspolitik, 1899–1907* (Hamburg, 1966).

D. C. M. Platt, *Finance, Trade and Politics in British Foreign Policy 1815–1914* (Oxford, 1968).

D. C. M. Platt, 'Economic factors in British policy during the "New Imperialism"', *Past and Present*, 39 (1968).

D. C. M. Platt, *Latin America and British Trade 1806–1914* (New York, 1972).

C. E. Playne, *The Pre-War Mind in Britain* (London, 1928).

H. Pogge von Strandmann, 'Staatsstreichpläne, Alldeutsche und Bethmann Hollweg', in Pogge von Strandmann and I. Geiss, *Die Erforderlichkeit des Unmöglichen* (Frankfurt a.M., 1965).

H. Pogge von Strandmann, 'Domestic origins of Germany's colonial expansion under Bismarck', *Past and Present*, 42 (1969).

H. Pogge von Strandmann, 'Nationale Verbände zwischen Weltpolitik und Kontinentalpolitik', in H. Schottelius and W. Deist (eds), *Marine und Marinepolitik im kaiserlichen Deutschland 1871–1914* (Düsseldorf, 1972).

H. Pogge von Strandmann, 'Rathenau, die Gebrüder Mannesmann und die Vorgeschichte der Zweiten Marokkokrise', in I. Geiss and B.-J. Wendt (eds), *Deutschland in der Weltpolitik des 19. und 20. Jahrhunderts* (Düsseldorf, 1974).

H. Pogge von Strandmann, *Unternehmenspolitik und Unternehmensführung. Der Dialog zwischen Aufsichtsrat und Vorstand bei Mannesmann 1900 bis 1919* (Düsseldorf, 1978).

R. Poidevin, *Les Relations économiques et financières entre la France et l'Allemagne de 1898 à 1914* (Paris, 1969).

S. Pollard, 'British and world shipbuilding 1890–1914', *Journal of Economic History*, vol. XVII (1957).

S. Pollard and P. Robertson, *The British Shipbuilding Industry 1870–1914* (Cambridge, Mass., 1979).

F. Ponsonby, *Letters of the Empress Frederick* (London, 1928).

B. Porter, *Critics of Empire: British Radical Attitudes to Colonialism in Africa 1895–1914* (London, 1968).

B. Porter, *The Lion's Share. A Short History of British Imperialism 1850–1970* (London, 1975).

R. Postgate and A. Vallance, *Those Foreigners. The English People's Opinion on Foreign Affairs as Reflected in their Newspapers since Waterloo* (London, 1937).

R. Pound, *Albert: A Biography of the Prince Consort* (London, 1973).

H. Preller, *Salisbury und die Turkische Frage im Jahre 1895* (Stuttgart, 1930).

G. Pretsch, 'Dietrich Schäfer – der Alldeutsche', *Wissenschaftliche Zeitschrift der Karl-Marx-Universitat Leipzig*, 9 Jg. (1959/60).

L. M. Price, *The Reception of English Literature in Germany* (Berkeley, 1932).

R. Price, *An Imperial War and the British Working Class* (London, 1972).

F. Prill, *Ireland, Britain and Germany 1870–1914* (Dublin, 1975).

H.-J. Puhle, *Agrarische Interessenpolitik und preussischer Konservatismus in Wilhelminischen Reich (1893–1914)* (Hanover, 1968).

H.-J. Puhle, 'Parlament, Parteien und Interessenverbände 1890–1914', in M. Stürmer (ed.), *Das kaiserliche Deutschland* (Düsseldorf, 1970).

P. Pulzer, *The Rise of Political Anti-Semitism in Germany and Austria* (London, 1964).

F. Rachfahl, 'Eugen Richter und der Linksliberalismus im neuen Reich', *Zeitschrift für Politik*, V (1912).

A. Ramm (ed.), *The Political Correspondence of Mr. Gladstone and Lord Granville 1868–1876*, 2 vols (Camden Society, vols LXXXI–LXXXII, London, 1952).

A. Ramm (ed.), *The Political Correspondence of Mr. Gladstone and Lord Granville 1876–1886*, 2 vols (Oxford, 1962).

A. Ramm, *Sir Robert Morier, Envoy and Ambassador in the Age of Imperialism 1876–1893* (Oxford, 1973).

A. A. W. Ramsay, *Idealism and Foreign Policy . . . 1860–1878* (London, 1925).

P. Rassow, 'Schlieffen und Holstein', *Historische Zeitschrift*, vol. 173 (1952).

L. Rathmann, 'Bismarck und der Uebergang Deutschlands zur Schutzzollpolitik', *Zeitschrift für Geschichtswissenschaft*, vol. 4 (1956).

M. Rauh, *Die Parlamentarisierung des Deutschen Reiches* (Düsseldorf, 1977).

H. Raulff, *Zwischen Machtpolitik und Imperialismus: Die deutsche Frankreichpolitik 1904–5* (Düsseldorf, 1976).

D. N. Raymond, *British Policy and Opinion during the Franco-Prussian War* (New York, 1967 reprint).

B. M. G. Reardon, *From Coleridge to Gore. A Century of Religious Thought in Britain* (London, 1971).

R. W. Reichard, *Crippled from Birth: German Social Democracy 1844–1870* (Ames, Iowa, 1969).

J. Remak, *The Origins of World War I* (New York, 1967).

J. Remak, '1914 – the Third Balkan War: origins reconsidered', *Journal of Modern History*, vol. 43 (1971).

M. Reuss, 'Bismarck's dismissal and the Holstein circle', *European Studies Review*, vol. 5 (1975).

M. Reuss and G. W. Hartwig, 'Bismarck's imperialism and the Rohlfs mission', *South Atlantic Quarterly*, vol. 74 (1975).

*Rhodes Scholarships: Record of Past Scholars elected between 1903 and 1927 Inclusive* (Oxford, 1931).

N. Rich, *Friedrich von Holstein*, 2 vols (Cambridge, 1965).

N. Rich and M. H. Fisher (eds), *The Holstein Papers*, 4 vols (Cambridge, 1955–63).

M. Richter, *The Politics of Conscience: T. H. Green and his Age* (London, 1964).

I. Rieger, *Die Wilhelminische Presse im Ueberblick 1888–1918* (Munich, 1957).

J. Riesser, *The Great German Banks and their Concentration in connection with the Economic Development of Germany* (Washington, DC, 1911).

K. Ringhoffer (ed.), *The Bernstorff Papers*, 2 vols (London, 1908).

G. Ritter, *The Schlieffen Plan* (New York, 1956).

G. Ritter, *The Sword and the Sceptre: The Problem of Militarism in Germany*, 4 vols (London, 1972–3).

G. A. Ritter, *Die Arbeiterbewegung im Wilhelminischen Reich* (Berlin–Dahlem, 1959).

J. Roach, 'Liberalism and the Victorian intelligentsia', *Cambridge Historical Journal*, vol. XIII (1957).

K. Robbins, *Sir Edward Grey* (London, 1971).

K. Robbins, *The Abolition of War. The 'Peace Movement' in Britain, 1914–1919* (Cardiff, 1976).

W. R. Robertson, *Soldiers and Statesmen 1914–1918*, 2 vols (London/New York, 1926).

R. Robinson and J. A. Gallagher, *Africa and the Victorians* (London, 1961).

H. Rogge (ed.), *Friedrich von Holstein Lebensbekenntnis* (Berlin, 1932).

J. C. G. Röhl, 'A document of 1892 on Germany, Prussia and Poland', *Historical Journal*, vol. VII (1964).

J. C. G. Röhl, 'Staatsstreichplan oder Staatsstreichbereitschaft? Bismarcks Politik in der Entlassungskrise', *Historische Zeitschrift*, vol. 203 (1966).

J. C. G. Röhl, *Germany without Bismarck: The Crisis of Government in the Second Reich, 1890–1900* (London, 1967).

J. C. G. Röhl, 'Admiral von Müller and the approach of war, 1911–1914', *Historical Journal*, vol. XII (1969).

J. C. G. Röhl, (ed.), *Philipp Eulenburgs Politische Korrespondenz*, Vol. 1 (Boppard a.R., 1976).

J. C. G. Röhl, 'An der Schwelle zum Weltkrieg: Eine Dokumentation über den "Kriegsrat" vom 8. Dezember 1912', *Militärgeschichtliche Mitteilungen*, 1/1977.

J. C. G. Röhl, 'Die Generalprobe. Zur Geschichte und Bedeuting des "Kriegsrates" vom 8. Dezember 1912', in D. Stegmann, B.-J. Wendt and P.-C. Witt (eds), *Industrielle Gesellschaft und politisches System* (Bonn, 1978).

J. Rohwer, 'Kriegsschiffbau und Flottengesetze um die Jahrhundertwende', in H. Schottelius and W. Deist (eds), *Marine und Marinepolitik im kaiserlichen Deutschland 1871–1914* (Düsseldorf, 1972).

E. Rosenbaum, 'M. M. Warburg and Co., merchant bankers of Hamburg', *Leo Baeck Institute*, bk VII (London, 1962).

E. Rosenbaum and J. Sherman, *Das Bankhaus M. M. Warburg & Co. 1798–1938* (Hamburg, 1976).

H. Rosenberg, 'Political and social consequences of the Great Depression of 1873–1896 in central Europe', *Economic History Review*, vol. 13 (1943).

H. Rosenberg, *Grosse Depression und Bismarckzeit* (Berlin, 1967).

A. Ross, *New Zealand Aspirations in the Pacific in the Nineteenth Century* (Oxford, 1964).

R. J. Ross, *Beleaguered Tower: The Dilemma of Political Catholicism in Wilhelmine Germany* (Notre Dame, Ind., 1976).

G. Roth, *The Social Democrats in Imperial Germany* (Totowa, NJ, 1963).

H. Rothfels, *Bismarcks englische Bündnispolitik* (Stuttgart, 1924).

B. A. Rowley, 'Die Entwicklung der Germanistik in Grossbritannien und Irland anhand britischer Antrittsvorlesungen', *Akten des V. Internationalen Germanisten-Kongresses Cambridge 1975* (Berne, 1976).

H. R. Rudin, *Germany in the Cameroons 1884–1914* (Hamden, Conn., 1968 reprint).

A. K. Russell, *Liberal Landslide: The General Election of 1906* (Newton Abbott, 1973).

G. N. Sanderson, 'The Anglo-German agreement of 1890 and the upper Nile', *English Historical Review*, vol. 78 (1963).

G. N. Sanderson, 'England, Italy, the Nile valley and the European balance, 1890–91', *Historical Journal*, vol. VII (1964).

G. N. Sanderson, *England, Europe and the Upper Nile 1882–1899* (Edinburgh, 1965).

G. N. Sanderson, 'The African factor in Anglo-German relations, 1892–95' (private paper delivered to the Commonwealth and Overseas Seminar, Cambridge University).

J. M. Sanderson, *The Universities and British Industry 1850–1970* (London, 1972).

K. A. P. Sandiford, *Great Britain and the Schleswig-Holstein Question 1848–1864* (Toronto, 1975).

A. Sandison, *The Wheel of Empire* (London, 1967).

K. Saul, 'Der "Deutsche Kriegerbund": Zur innenpolitischen Funktion eines "nationalen" Verbands im Kaiserlichen Deutschland', *Militärgeschichtliche Mitteilungen*, 2/1969.

K. Saul, 'Der Kampf um die Jugend zwischen Volksschule und Kaserne', *Militärgeschichtliche Mitteilungen*, 1/1971.

K. Saul, *Staat, Industrie Arbeiterbewegung im Kaiserreich* (Düsseldorf, 1973).

S. B. Saul, *Studies in British Overseas Trade 1870–1914* (Liverpool, 1960).

S. B. Saul, *The Myth of the Great Depression 1873–1896* (London, 1969).

R. S. Sayers, *The Bank of England 1891–1944*, 3 vols (Cambridge, 1976).

R. J. Scally, *The Origins of the Lloyd George Coalition. The Politics of Social-Imperialism, 1900–1918* (Princeton, 1975).

D. Schäfer, *Mein Leben* (Berlin/Leipzig, 1926).

W. Schenk, *Die deutsch-englische Rivalität vor dem Ersten Weltkrieg in der Sicht deutscher Historiker* (Aarau, 1967).

P. Scherer, 'The Benedetti draft treaty and British neutrality in the Franco-Prussian War', *International Review of History and Political Science*, vol. 9, no. 1 (1972).

W. Schieder (ed.), *Erster Weltkrieg* (Cologne, 1969).

W. Schiefel, *Bernhard Dernburg* (Zurich, 1976).

K. Schilling, *Beiträge zu einer Geschichte des radikalen Nationalismus in der Wilhelminischen Aera 1890–1909* (phil. Diss., Cologne, 1968).

W. F. Schirmer, *Der Einfluss der deutschen Literatur auf die Englische im 19. Jahrhundert* (Halle, 1947).

H. Schleier, 'Treitschke, Delbrück und die "Preussische Jahrbücher" in den 80er Jahren des 19. Jahrhunderts', *Jahrbuch für Geschichte*, vol. 1 (1967).

W. Schlote, *British Overseas Trade from 1700 to the 1930s* (Oxford, 1952).

G. Schmidt, 'Deutschland am Vorabend des Ersten Weltkrieges', in M. Stürmer (ed.), *Das kaiserliche Deutschland* (Düsseldorf, 1970).

G. Schmidt, 'Innenpolitische Blockbildungen in Deutschland am Voraben des Ersten Weltkrieges', *Aus Politik und Zeitgeschichte* (*Beilage* to *Das Parlament*), B20/72, 13 May 1972.

G. Schmidt, 'Rationalismus und Irrationalismus in der englischen Flottenpolitik', in H. Schottelius and W. Deist (eds), *Marine und Marinepolitik im kaiserlichen Deutschland 1871–1914* (Düsseldorf, 1972).

G. Schmidt, 'Parlamentarisierung oder "Präventive Konterrevolution"?', in G. A. Ritter (ed.), *Gesellschaft, Parlament und Regierung* (Düsseldorf, 1974).

G. Schmidt, 'Politischer Liberalismus, 'landed interests', und Organisierte Arbeiterschaft 1850–1880: ein deutsch-englischer Vergleich', in H.-U. Wehler (ed.), *Sozialgeschichte Heute* (Göttingen, 1974).

H. D. Schmidt, *The Characteristics of British Policy and Imperial History as Conceived by the German Historians of the Nineteenth Century, 1848–1902* (B.Litt. thesis, Oxford, 1953).

B. E. Schmitt, *England and Germany, 1740–1914* (Princeton, 1916).

B. E. Schmitt, *The Annexation of Bosnia 1908–1909* (Cambridge, Mass., 1937).

G. von Schmoller, *Zwanzig Jahre deutscher Politik 1897–1917* (Munich/Leipzig, 1920).

C. E. Schorske, *German Social Democracy 1905–1917* (New York, 1970 reprint).

E. Schraepler, 'Die politische Haltung des liberalen Bürgertums im Bismarckreich', *Geschichte in Wissenschaft und Unterricht*, vol. 5 (1954).

P. E. Schramm, *Hamburg, Deutschland und die Welt* (Munich, 1943).

P. E. Schramm, *Deutschland und Uebersee* (Brunswick, 1950).

P. E. Schramm, 'Deutschlands Verhältnis zur englischen Kultur nach der Begründung des Neuen Reiches', in W. Hubatsch (ed.), *Schicksalwege deutscher Vergangenheit* (Düsseldorf, 1950).

P. E. Schramm, 'Deutschland in englischer Auffassung am Vorabend des ersten Weltkrieges', in *Tymbos für Wilhelm Ahlmann* (Berlin, 1951).

P. E. Schramm, 'Englands Verhältnis zur deutschen Kultur zwischen der Reichsgründung und der Jahrhundertwende', in W. Conze (ed.), *Deutschland und Europa* (Düsseldorf, 1951).

D. Schreuder, 'Gladstone as "troublemaker": Liberal foreign policy and the German annexation of Alsace-Lorraine, 1870–71', *Journal of British Studies*, vol. XVII (1978).

H.-C. Schröder, *Sozialismus und Imperialismus* (Hanover, 1968).

K. Schröder, *Parlament und Aussenpolitik in England 1911–1914* (Göttingen, 1974).

P. W. Schroeder, 'Munich and the British tradition', *Historical Journal*, vol. XIX (1976).

K. Schröter, 'Chauvinism and its tradition: German writers at the outbreak of the First World War', *Germanic Review*, 43 (1968).

O.-E. Schüddekopf, *Die deutsche Innenpolitik im letzten Jahrhundert und der konservative Gedanke* (Braunschweig, 1951).

B.-F. Schulte, *Die deutsche Armee 1900–1914. Zwischen Beharren und Verändern* (Düsseldorf, 1977).

P. H. von Schwabach, *Aus meinen Akten* (Berlin, 1927).

C.-C. Schweitzer, *Die Kritik der westlich-liberalen Oppositionsgruppen an der Aussenpolitik Bismarcks von 1863 bis 1890* (phil. Diss., Freiburg, 1950).

G. R. Searle, *The Quest for National Efficiency 1899–1914* (Oxford, 1971).

G. R. Searle, *Eugenics and Politics in Britain 1900–1914* (Leyden, 1976).
G. Seeber, *Zwischen Bebel und Bismarck. Zur Geschichte des Linksliberalismus in Deutschland 1871–1893* (East Berlin, 1965).
G. Seeber (ed.), *Bismarcks Sturz* (Berlin, 1977).
J. R. Seeley, *The Life and Times of Stein*, 3 vols (Cambridge, 1878).
F.-C. Sell, *Die Tragödie des deutschen Liberalismus* (Stuttgart, 1953).
M. Sell, *Das deutsch-englische Abkommen von 1890 im Lichte der deutschen Presse* (Berlin, 1926).
B. Semmel, *Imperialism and Social Reform* (Cambridge, Mass., 1960).
L. Senelich, 'Politics as entertainment: Victorian music-hall songs', *Victorian Studies*, vol. XIX (1975).
R. W. Seton-Watson, *Britain in Europe 1789–1914* (Cambridge, 1937).
C. Seymour, *The Intimate Papers of Colonel House*, 4 vols (Boston, 1926–8).
J. Shanahan, 'Liberalism and foreign affairs: Naumann and the prewar German view', *Review of Politics*, vol. 21 (1959).
R. T. Shannon, *Gladstone and the Bulgarian Agitation 1876*, 2nd edn (London, 1975).
R. T. Shannon, *The Crisis of Imperialism 1865–1915* (London, 1976 edn).
J. J. Sheehan, *The Career of Lujo Brentano* (Chicago, 1966).
J. J. Sheehan, *German Liberalism in the Nineteenth Century* (Chicago/London, 1978).
J. S. G. Simmons, 'Slavonic studies at Oxford: the proposed Slavonic Chair at the Taylor Institution in 1844', *Oxford Slavonic Papers*, III (1952).
W. M. Simon, *European Positivism in the Nineteenth Century* (Ithaca, NY, 1963).
C. L. Smith, *The Embassy of Sir William White at Constantinople 1886–1891* (Oxford, 1957).
F. B. Smith, *The Making of the Second Reform Bill* (Cambridge, 1966).
P. Smith, *Disraelian Conservatism and Social Reform* (London, 1967).
W. D. Smith, 'The ideology of German colonialism, 1840–1906', *Journal of Modern History*, vol. 46 (1974).
W. D. Smith, *The German Colonial Empire* (Chapel Hill, NC, 1978).
J. L. Snell and H. Schmitt, *The Democratic Movement in Germany 1789–1914* (Chapel Hill, NC, 1976).
L. L. Snyder, *German Nationalism* (Harrisburg, Pa, 1952).
R. J. Sontag, 'The Cowes interview and the Kruger Telegram', *Political Science Quarterly*, vol. XL (1925).
R. J. Sontag, 'German foreign policy, 1904–1906', *American Historical Review*, vol. XXXIII (1928).
R. J. Sontag, *Germany and England. Background of Conflict 1848–1894* (New York, 1964 edn).
D. Southgate, *The Passing of the Whigs 1832–1886* (London, 1962).
H. Spellmeyer, *Deutsche Kolonialpolitik im Reichstag* (Stuttgart, 1931).
J. A. Spender, *The Life of the Right Hon. Sir Henry Campbell-Bannerman*, 2 vols (London, 1923).
J. Springhall, 'Lord Meath, Youth, and Empire', *Journal of Contemporary History*, vol. 5, no. 4 (1970).
J. Springhall, *Youth, Empire and Society. British Youth Movements, 1883–1940* (London, 1977).
R. Stadelman, 'Die Epoche der deutsch-englischen Flottenrivalität', in *Deutschland und Westeuropa* (Schloss Laupheim, 1948).
F.-C. Stahl, *Botschafter Graf Wolff Metternich und die deutsch-englischen Beziehungen* (phil. Diss., Hamburg, 1951).
P. Stansky, *Ambitions and Strategies: The Struggle for the Leadership of the Liberal Party in the 1890s* (Oxford, 1964).

H. W. Steed, *Through Thirty Years*, 2 vols (London, 1924).

H. W. Steed, 'From Frederick the Great to Hitler: the consistency of German aims', *International Affairs*, vol. XVII (1938).

L. D. Steefel, *The Schleswig-Holstein Question* (Cambridge, Mass., 1932).

W. Steglich, 'Bismarcks Englische Bündnissondierungen und Bündnisvorschläge 1887–1889', in H. Fenske, W. Reinhard and E. Schulin (eds), *Historia Integra* (Berlin/Munich, 1978).

D. Stegmann, *Die Erben Bismarcks* (Cologne/Berlin, 1970).

H.-J. Steinberg, *Sozialismus und deutsche Sozialdemokratie* (Hanover, 1967).

H.-J. Steinberg, 'Sozialismus, Internationalismus und Reichgründung', in T. Schieder and E. Deuerlein (eds), *Reichsgründung 1870–71* (Stuttgart, 1970).

J. Steinberg, *Yesterday's Deterrent* (London, 1965).

J. Steinberg, 'The Copenhagen Complex', *Journal of Contemporary History*, vol. 1, pt 3 (1966).

J. Steinberg, 'Germany and the Russo-Japanese War', *American Historical Review*, vol. LXXV (1970).

J. Steinberg, 'The Novelle of 1908: necessities and choices in the Anglo-German naval arms race', *Transactions of the Royal Historical Society*, 5th series, vol. 21 (1971).

J. Steinberg, 'Diplomatie als Wille und Vorstellung: Die Berliner Mission Lord Haldanes in Februar 1912', in H. Schottelius and W. Deist (eds), *Marine und Marinepolitik im kaiserlichen Deutschland 1871–1914* (Düsseldorf, 1972).

Z. S. Steiner, 'Great Britain and the creation of the Anglo-Japanese Alliance', *Journal of Modern History*, vol. XXXI (1959).

Z. S. Steiner, *The Foreign Office and Foreign Policy 1895–1914* (Cambridge, 1969).

Z. S. Steiner, *Britain and the Origins of the First World War* (London, 1977).

W. R. W. Stephens, *The Life and Letters of Edward A. Freeman*, 2 vols (London, 1895).

F. Stern, 'Bethmann Hollweg and the war: the limits of responsibility', in L. Krieger and F. Stern (eds), *The Responsibility of Power* (Garden City, NY, 1967).

F. Stern, *The Failure of Illiberalism* (New York, 1972).

F. Stern, *Gold and Iron: Bismarck, Bleichröder and the Building of the German Empire* (London, 1977).

S. D. Stirk, *German Universities – Through English Eyes* (London, 1946).

H. Stoecker, 'Zur Politik Bismarcks in der englisch-russischen Krise von 1885', *Zeitschrift für Geschichtswissenschaft*, vol. IV (1956).

Otto zu Stolberg-Wernigerode, *Die unentschiedene Generation* (Munich, 1968).

N. Stone, 'Moltke-Conrad: relations between the Austro-Hungarian and German General Staffs, 1909–14', *Historical Journal*, vol. IX (1966).

O. Strecker, 'Der Kampf um die Agrarzölle in Grossbritannien (Anti-Corn-Law-League) und Deutschland (1871–1902)', *Berichte über Landwirtschaft. Zeitschrift für Agrarpolitik und Landwirtschaft*, neue Folge, vol. XXXVI (1958).

W. Stribny, *Bismarck und die deutsche Politik nach seiner Entlassung (1890–1898)* (Paderborn, 1977).

R. N. Stromberg, 'The intellectuals and the coming of war in 1914', *Journal of European Studies*, vol. 3 (1973).

M. Stürmer, 'Staatsstreichgedanken im Bismarckreich', *Historische Zeitschrift*, vol. 209 (1969).

M. Stürmer, *Regierung und Reichstag im Bismarckstaat 1871–1880: Cäsarismus oder Parlamentarismus?* (Düsseldorf, 1974).

S. G. Sturmey, *British Shipping and World Competition* (London, 1962).

W. Suehlo, *Georg Herbert Graf zu Münster . . .* (Hildesheim, 1968).

A. Summers, 'Militarism in Britain before the Great War', *History Workshop Journal*, issue 2 (autumn 1976).

N. W. Summerton, *The Development of British Military Planning for a War against Germany, 1904–1914* (Ph.D. thesis, London, 1970).

N. W. Summerton, 'Dissenting attitudes to foreign relations, peace and war 1840–1890', *Journal of Ecclesiastical History*, vol. 28 (1977).

M. Swartz, 'A study in futility: the British Radicals at the outbreak of the First World War', in A. J. A. Morris (ed.), *Edwardian Radicalism 1900–1914* (London, 1974).

M. Swartz, *The Politics of British Foreign Policy 1865–1885* (forthcoming).

D. W. Sweet, 'The Bosnian crisis', in F. H. Hinsley (ed.), *The Foreign Policy of Sir Edward Grey* (Cambridge, 1977).

A. Sykes, 'The Confederacy and the purge of the Unionist Free Traders, 1906–1910', *Historical Journal*, vol. 18 (1975).

W. Taffs, 'The war scare of 1875', *Slavonic Review*, vol. XI (December 1930 and March 1931).

W. Taffs, *Ambassador to Bismarck: Lord Odo Russell* (London, 1938).

*Tariff Commission, Report of the*, Vol. 1, *The Iron and Steel Trades* (London, 1904); Vol. 4, *The Engineering Industries* (London, 1909).

A. J. P. Taylor, *Germany's First Bid for Colonies 1884–1885: A Move in Bismarck's European Policy* (London, 1938).

A. J. P. Taylor, *The Struggle for Mastery in Europe 1848–1918* (Oxford, 1952).

A. J. P. Taylor, *The Troublemakers* (London, 1969 edn).

A. J. P. Taylor, *Beaverbrook* (London, 1972).

H. Temperley and L. M. Penson, *Foundations of British Foreign Policy from Pitt to Salisbury* (Cambridge, 1938).

P. Thane (ed.), *The Origins of British Social Policy* (London, 1978).

P. F. Thiede, *Chamberlain, Irland und das Weltreich 1880–95* (Frankfurt a.M., 1977).

F. Thimme, 'Die Krüger-Depesche: Genesis und historische Bedeutung', *Europäische Gespräche*, Jg. 2 (1924).

F. Thimme, 'Der Ausklang der deutsch-englischen Bündnisverhandlungen 1901', *Berliner Monatshefte*, vol. 16 (1938).

F. M. L. Thompson, *English Landed Society in the Nineteenth Century* (London, 1963).

L. V. Thompson, *Robert Blatchford* (London, 1951).

P. Thompson, *Socialists, Liberals and Labour: The Struggle for London 1885–1914* (London, 1967).

A. P. Thornton, *The Imperial Idea and its Enemies* (London, 1966).

M. Trachtenberg, 'The social interpretation of foreign policy', *Review of Politics*, vol. 40 (1978).

A. Thorold, *The Life of Henry Labouchere* (London, 1913).

R. H. Tilly, 'Los von England: Probleme des Nationalismus in der deutschen Wirtschaftsgeschichte', *Zeitschrift für das gesamte Staatswissenschaft*, vol. 124 (1968).

F. B. Tipton, 'Farm labor and power politics: Germany 1850–1914', *Journal of Economic History*, vol. XXXIV (1974).

A. von Tirpitz, *My Memoirs*, 2 vols (London, 1919).

A. von Tirpitz, *Politische Dokumente*, 2 vols (Stuttgart/Berlin, 1924–6).

P. Towle, 'The European balance of power in 1914', *Army Quarterly and Defence Journal*, 104 (1974).

M. E. Townsend, *Origins of Modern German Colonialism 1871–1885* (New York, 1974 reprint).

C. Trebilcock, 'Legends of the British armaments industry, 1890–1914: a revision', *Journal of Contemporary History*, vol. 5, no. 4 (1970).

C. Trebilcock, *The Vickers Brothers, Armaments and Enterprise 1854–1914* (London, 1977).

H. von Treitschke, *Deutsche Geschichte im neunzehnten Jahrhundert*, vol. 5 (Leipzig, 1894).

G. M. Trevelyan, *Grey of Falloden* (London, 1937).

U. Trumpener, 'War premeditated? German Intelligence operations in July 1914', *Central European History*, vol. 9 (1976).

C. Tsuzuki, *H. M. Hyndman and British Socialism* (London, 1961).

E. L. Turk, 'The press of Imperial Germany: a new role for a traditional resource', *Central European History*, vol. 10 (1977).

H. A. Turner, 'Bismarck's imperialist venture: anti-British in origin?', in P. Gifford and W. R. Louis (eds), *Britain and Germany in Africa* (New Haven, Conn., 1967).

L. C. F. Turner, 'The significance of the Schlieffen Plan', *Australian Journal of Politics and History*, vol. XIII (1967).

L. C. F. Turner, *Origins of the First World War* (London, 1970).

L. C. F. Turner, 'The edge of the precipice: a comparison between November 1912 and July 1914', *RMC Historical Journal* (Canberra), vol. 3 (1974).

G. N. Uzoigwe, *Britain and the Conquest of Africa* (Ann Arbor, Mich., 1974).

A. Vagts, *Deutschland und die Vereinigten Staaten in der Weltpolitik*, 2 vols (New York, 1935).

A. Vagts, 'Wilhelm II and the Siam episode', *American Historical Review*, vol. LXV (1940).

A. Vagts, 'M. M. Warburg und Co. Ein Bankhaus in der deutschen Weltpolitik 1905–1933', *Vierteljahrsschrift für Sozial- und Wirtschaftsgeschichte*, vol. 45 (1958).

V. Valentin, *Bismarcks Reichsgründung im Urteil englischer Diplomaten* (Amsterdam, 1937).

V. Valentin, 'Bismarck and England in the earlier period of his career', *Transactions of the Royal Historical Society*, 4th series, vol. XX (1937).

H. J. Varain, *Interessenverbände in Deutschland* (Cologne, 1973).

T. Veblen, *Imperial Germany and the Industrial Revolution* (New York, 1966 edn).

M. Victor, 'Die Stellung der deutschen Sozialdemokratie zu den Fragen der auswärtigen Politik (1869–1914)', *Archiv für Sozialwissenschaft und Sozialpolitik*, vol. 60 (1928).

R. Vierhaus (ed.), *Das Tagebuch der Baronin Spitzemberg* (Göttingen, 1960).

J. Vincent, *The Formation of the Liberal Party 1857–1868* (London, 1966).

J. Viner, 'International finance and balance of power diplomacy 1880–1914', in *International Economics* (Glencoe, Ill., 1951).

B. Vogel, *Deutsche Russlandpolitik 1900–1906* (Düsseldorf, 1973).

W. Vogel, 'Die Organisation der amtlichen Presse und Propagandapolitik des Deutschen Reiches von den Anfängen unter Bismarck bis zum Beginn des Jahres 1933', *Zeitungswissenschaft*, vol. XVI (1941).

S. Volkov, *The Rise of Popular Antimodernism in Germany* (Princeton, 1978).

A. P. Wadsworth, 'Newspaper circulations, 1800–1954', *Transactions of the Manchester Statistical Society* (1954–5).

M. Walker, *Germany and the Emigration 1816–65* (Cambridge, Mass., 1964).

L. P. Wallace, *The Papacy and European Diplomacy 1869–1878* (Chapel Hill, NC, 1948).

B. Waller, *Bismarck at the Crossroads: The Reorientation of German Foreign Policy after the Congress of Berlin 1878–1880* (London, 1974).

M. M. Warburg, *Aus meinen Aufzeichnungen* (Glückstadt, 1952).

P. R. Warhurst, *Anglo-Portuguese Relations in South-Central Africa 1890–1900* (London, 1962).

D. C. Watt, 'British reactions to the assassination at Sarajevo', *European Studies Review*, vol. 1 (1971).

K. Wegner, *Theodor Barth und die Freisinnige Vereinigung* (Tübingen, 1968).

H.-U. Wehler, *Sozialdemokratie und Nationalstaat* (Würzburg, 1962).

H.-U. Wehler, *Bismarck und der Imperialismus* (Cologne/Berlin, 1969).

H.-U. Wehler, 'Bismarcks Imperialismus und späte Russlandpolitik unter dem Primat der Innenpolitik', in M. Stürmer (ed.), *Das kaiserliche Deutschland* (Düsseldorf, 1970).

H.-U. Wehler, *Das deutsche Kaiserreich 1871–1918* (Göttingen, 1973).

G. Weinberger, 'Die deutsche Sozialdemokratie und die Kolonialpolitik', *Zeitschrift für Geschichtswissenschaft*, vol. 15 (1967).

H. Weinroth, 'The British Radicals and the balance of power 1902–14', *Historical Journal*, vol. XIII (1970).

H. Weinroth, 'Left-wing opposition to naval armaments in Britain before 1914', *Journal of Contemporary History*, vol. 6, no. 4 (1971).

H. Weinroth, 'Norman Angell and *The Great Illusion*', *Historical Journal*, vol. XVII (1974).

F. Wellesley, *The Paris Embassy during the Second Empire: From the Papers of Earl Cowley* (London, 1928).

R. Wemyss, *Memoirs and Letters of the Right Hon. Sir Robert Morier from 1826 to 1876*, 2 vols (London, 1911).

H. Wendt, *Bismarck und die polnische Frage* (Halle, 1922).

K. Wernecke, *Der Wille zur Weltgeltung* (Düsseldorf, 1970).

M. S. Wertheimer, *The Pan-German League 1890–1914* (New York, 1924).

K. Westarp, *Konservative Politik im letzten Jarhzehnt des Kaiserreiches*, 2 vols (Berlin, 1935–6).

D. S. White, *The Splintered Party. National Liberalism in Hessen and the Reich 1867–1918* (Cambridge, Mass., 1976).

F. Whyte, *The Life of W. T. Stead*, 2 vols (London, 1925).

F. W. Wiemann, 'Lloyd George and the struggle for the navy estimates of 1914', in A. J. P. Taylor (ed.), *Lloyd George: Twelve Essays* (London, 1971).

E.-T. Wilke, 'Clipping the wings of the Hohenlohe ministry', *Studies in Modern European Culture and History*, vol. 2 (1976).

H. S. Wilkinson, *Thirty-Five Years, 1874–1909* (London, 1933).

P. Wilkinson, 'English youth movements, 1908–30', *Journal of Contemporary History*, vol. 4, no. 2 (1969).

J. Willequet, *Le Congo Belge et la Weltpolitik 1894–1914* (Brussels/Paris, 1962).

J. Willequet, 'Anglo-German rivalry in Belgian and Portuguese Africa?', in P. Gifford and W. R. Louis (eds), *Britain and Germany in Africa* (New Haven/London, 1967).

B. J. Williams, 'The strategic background to the Anglo-Russian entente of August 1907', *Historical Journal*, vol. IX (1966).

J. B. Williams, *British Commercial Policy and Trade Expansion 1750–1850* (Oxford, 1972).

J. G. Williamson, *Karl Helfferich 1872–1924* (Princeton, 1971).

S. R. Williamson, *The Politics of Grand Strategy: Britain and France Prepare for War, 1904–1914* (Cambridge, Mass., 1969).

A. Wilson, *The Strange Ride of Rudyard Kipling* (London/New York, 1977).

J. Wilson, *C-B: A Life of Sir Henry Campbell-Bannerman* (London, 1973).

K. Wilson, 'The Agadir crisis, the Mansion House speech, and the double-edgedness of agreements', *Historical Journal*, vol. XV (1972).

K. Wilson, 'The British Cabinet's decision for war, 2 August 1914', *British Journal of International Studies*, vol. 1 (1975).

K. Wilson, 'To the western front: British war plans and the "military entente" with

France before the First World War', *British Journal of International Studies*, vol. 3 (1977).

K. Wilson, 'The War Office, Churchill, and the Belgian option, August to December 1911', *Bulletin of the Institute of Historical Research*, vol. 50 (1977).

T. Wilson (ed.), *The Political Diaries of C. P. Scott 1911–1928* (New York, 1970).

H. A. Winckler, 'From social protectionism to National Socialism: German small business movement in comparative perspective', *Journal of Modern History*, vol. 48 (1976).

H. A. Winckler, 'Vom linken zum rechten Nationalismus', *Geschichte und Gesellschaft*, vol. 4, issue 1 (1978).

M. B. Winckler, *Bismarcks Bündnispolitik und die europäische Gleichgewicht* (Stuttgart, 1964).

W. Windelband, *Bismarck und die europäischen Grossmächte 1879–1885* (Essen, 1940).

G. G. Windell, *The Catholics and German Unity* (Minneapolis, 1954).

G. G. Windell, 'The Bismarckian empire as a federal state 1866–1880: a chronicle of failure', *Central European History*, vol. II (1969).

J. M. Winter (ed.), *War and Economic Development* (Cambridge, 1975).

J. M. Winter, 'Balliol's "lost generation"', *Balliol College Record* (1975).

P. Winzen, *Die Englandpolitik Friedrich von Holsteins 1895–1901* (phil. Diss., Cologne, 1975).

P. Winzen, 'Prince Bülow's *Weltmachtpolitik*', *Australian Journal of Politics and History*, vol. XXII (1976).

P. Winzen, *Bülow's Weltmachtkonzept* (Boppard a.R., 1977).

P.-C. Witt, *Die Finanzpolitik des deutschen Reiches von 1903 bis 1913* (Lübeck/Hamburg, 1970).

P.-C. Witt, 'Reichsfinanzen und Rustungspolitik 1898–1914', in H. Schottelius and W. Deist (eds), *Marine und Marinepolitik im kaiserlichen Deutschland 1871–1914* (Düsseldorf, 1972).

R. Wittram, 'Bismarcks Russlandpolitik nach der Reichsgründung', *Historische Zeitschrift*, 186 (1958).

C. Witzig, 'Bismarck et la Commune', *International Review of Social History*, vol. 17 (1972).

L. Wolf, *Life of the First Marquess of Ripon*, 2 vols (London, 1921).

J. B. Wolff, *The Diplomatic History of the Bagdad Railway* (Missouri, 1936).

M.-L. Wolff, *Botschafter Graf Hatzfeldt, seine Tätigkeit in London 1885–1901* (phil. Diss., Munich, 1935).

H. Wolter, *Alternative zu Bismarck: Die deutsche Sozialdemokratie und die Aussenpolitik des preussisch-deutschen Reichs 1878–1890* (East Berlin, 1970).

W. Woodruff, *Impact of Western Man. A Study of Europe's Role in the World Economy 1750–1960* (London/New York, 1966).

E. L. Woodward, *Great Britain and the German Navy* (London, 1935).

C. J. Wrigley, *David Lloyd George and the British Labour Movement* (New York, 1976).

H. F. Young, *Prince Lichnowsky and the Great War* (Athens, Ga, 1977).

L. K. Young, *British Policy in China 1895–1902* (Oxford, 1970).

S. H. Zebel, 'Fair trade: an English reaction to the breakdown of the Cobden treaty system', *Journal of Modern History*, vol. 12 (1940).

S. H. Zebel, *Balfour* (Cambridge, 1973).

E. Zechlin, *Staatsstreichpläne Bismarcks und Wilhelms II., 1890–1894* (Stuttgart, 1929).

E. Zechlin, 'Cabinet versus economic warfare in Germany . . .', in H. W. Koch (ed.), *The Origins of the First World War* (London, 1972).

THE RISE OF THE ANGLO-GERMAN ANTAGONISM 1860–1914

J. K. Zeender, *The German Center Party 1890–1906* (Transactions of the American Philosophical Society, vol. 66, pt 1, Philadelphia, 1976).

M. D. Zier, *Anglo-German Relations 1871–1878* (M.Sc.Econ. thesis, London, 1966).

S. Zucker, *Ludwig Bamberger* (Pittsburg/London, 1975).

# Index

591